W9-COB-114

Microsoft

Core Reference

PROGRAMMING MICROSOFT® VISUAL BASIC® .NET

Francesco Balena

Microsoft® .net

Wintellect

PUBLISHED BY
Microsoft Press
A Division of Microsoft Corporation
One Microsoft Way
Redmond, Washington 98052-6399

Library of Congress Cataloging-in-Publication Data
Balena, Francesco, 1960-
Programming Microsoft Visual Basic.NET (Core Reference) / Francesco Balena.
p. cm.
Includes index.
ISBN 0-7356-1375-3
1. Microsoft Visual BASIC. 2. BASIC (Computer program language) I. Title.

QA76.73.B3 B346 2002
005.2'762--dc21 2001059059

Printed and bound in the United States of America.

1 2 3 4 5 6 7 8 9 QWT 7 6 5 4 3 2

Distributed in Canada by Penguin Books Canada Limited.

A CIP catalogue record for this book is available from the British Library.

Microsoft Press books are available through booksellers and distributors worldwide. For further information about international editions, contact your local Microsoft Corporation office or contact Microsoft Press International directly at fax (425) 936-7329. Visit our Web site at www.microsoft.com/mspress. Send comments to *mspinput@microsoft.com*.

Acquisitions Editor: Danielle Bird
Project Editor: Kathleen Atkins
Technical Editor: Jack Beaudry

Body Part No. X08-04502

Contents

Front
Top
Left
Back

Foreword

When Microsoft has some new technology its developers want to start getting feedback about, it holds a System Design Review (SDR). In October 1999, I was fortunate enough to be invited to an SDR for what was then called COM+ 2.0. In my career, I've always been much more interested in Win32 APIs than in COM, so I normally wouldn't go to such an event. However, since I didn't have too much else going on during the days of the SDR, I decided to attend and see what new stuff Microsoft had planned for COM. Well, let me tell you—I was blown away! COM+ 2.0 wasn't just some enhancements added to COM; this new COM was a totally different way of developing software and components.

To me, it was obvious: this new COM was the future of almost all software development. When Microsoft developers realized that what they were building was so much more than a new version of COM, the company changed the name of the technology from COM+ 2.0 to the Microsoft .NET Framework—which is how this new development platform is known today. The .NET Framework allows developers to create robust applications quickly and easily. This new platform also solves a lot of the problems that have plagued Windows for years: DLL Hell, security issues, memory leaks, memory corruption, inconsistent APIs and error handling, and so on.

Immediately after the SDR, I became a consultant on the .NET Framework team and have been programming to this new platform almost exclusively for more than two years. I must say I love it! And I never want to go back to my old C and C++ ways. If you plan on having a software development career, you should definitely start learning how to use the .NET Framework today.

Currently Microsoft offers many different technologies that accomplish different tasks:

- To create dynamic Web sites, you must learn Visual Basic Scripting Edition or JScript.
- To create high-performance databases, you must learn T-SQL.
- To create scalable memory-efficient components, you must use C/C++ and optionally MFC and ATL.
- To automate personal productivity applications (such as Microsoft Word and Excel), you must learn Visual Basic for Applications.
- To rapidly build GUI applications, you must learn Visual Basic.

Today's "solutions" are built by developers using many of these technologies. For example, many dynamic Web sites use scalable components that access a database, which means that many programmers must be fluent in all these different technologies and in all the different programming languages. Obviously, this is an enormous amount of work, and very few people (if any) are able to become masters of all these technologies and programming languages.

Because the .NET Framework can be used to accomplish every one of the tasks I just listed, we'll see all the current technologies collapse into one technology—The .NET Framework. The .NET Framework enables developers to build dynamic Web sites and scalable, memory-efficient components, and it will enable them to build GUI applications rapidly. Shortly after its initial release, the .NET Framework will be used by Microsoft SQL Server to offer high-performance database access. Further down the road, we should see productivity applications such as Microsoft Word and Excel using the .NET Framework to process macros that automate these applications. Learning the .NET Framework today will give you a huge head start in knowing how to perform all these tasks. It will really be possible for someone to become fluent in all these technologies.

Francesco's book is a great first step toward understanding the .NET Framework. His book covers all the main topics that every .NET Framework developer will need to know. To explain and demonstrate these topics, Francesco has chosen the popular Visual Basic .NET programming language. Programmers already familiar with Visual Basic will find this book a big help when migrating their existing code because Francesco clearly points out where things have changed from Visual Basic 6 to Visual Basic .NET. But developers who aren't familiar with Visual Basic will still find this book to be a great way to get started learning the .NET Framework because the concepts explained apply to all programming languages that target the .NET Framework.

Francesco also presents the material in a unique bottom-up approach—that is, he starts with the basic programming language and common language runtime concepts (such as classes, delegates, events, garbage collection, and serialization). After you understand the basics, he explains how these concepts and technologies are applied to enterprise solutions (such as ADO.NET and ASP.NET Web Forms and XML Web services). Finally, after reading this book, you'll find it a valuable reference guide that you'll be able to turn to time and time again to get answers to your nagging problems as you develop your .NET Framework applications.

I have no doubt that Francesco's book will quickly become an indispensable resource for any .NET Framework developer.

Jeffrey Richter
http://www.Wintellect.com
January 2002

Acknowledgments

Thanks to all the friends who have helped me make *Programming Microsoft Visual Basic .NET*.

Let's begin with Jeffrey Richter, for writing such a friendly foreword and for helping me understand what happens behind the .NET curtain. Even though he was busy writing his own *Applied Microsoft .NET Framework Programming*—a book that all .NET developers should have on their desks—he always found the time to reply to my weirdest queries. By the way, I am currently working with Jeffrey on *Applied Microsoft .NET Framework Programming in Visual Basic .NET*, to be released in summer 2002, for the joy of the millions of developers who still prefer Visual Basic to C#.

Next comes Giuseppe Dimauro, whose deep knowledge of Windows, COM, and SQL Server programming—and the speed at which he can translate all this knowledge into fully working, bug-free applications—continues to astonish me after so many years. Giuseppe is my partner in Code Architects, an Italian .NET-focused software and consulting company, and he spends a lot of his time speaking at MSDN conferences and consulting for Microsoft Italy.

I don't have to introduce Dino Esposito, probably the most prolific writer in the developer community, as well as cofounder of the *www.vb2themax.com* site. The great thing about Dino is his attitude in going beyond the usual programming clichés that often kill creativity. If you're serious about Web Forms, don't miss Dino's *Building Web Solutions with ASP.NET and ADO.NET*, also from Microsoft Press. We had many interesting conversations in these twelve months, traces of which are silently scattered in both his book and mine.

This is the right place to thank all the other brains at Wintellect, including Jeff Prosise, John Robbins, Kenn Scribner, Peter DeBetta, Jason Clark, Doug Boling, and John Lam. Being a Wintellectual is such an enriching experience that I feel very proud to be part of this group. And thanks to Lewis Frazer and Jim Bail for letting me complete the book before throwing me again into the .NET training arena.

Finding documentation about the .NET Framework isn't a problem today, but it was as scarce as gold (and almost as precious) when the product was in early beta version. My gratitude goes to my friend Francesco Albano of Microsoft Italy, for sharing his knowledge and for helping me find great technical material when I badly needed it.

My friend Giovanni Librando is the acquisitions editor at Mondadori, the Italian publisher that translates my Microsoft Press books. But above all, he is an experienced teacher with a keen talent for finding the comic side of programming.

I had never realized how much fun speaking at a developers' conference could be until I gave my first four-hand session with him.

I am very grateful to Marco Bellinaso and Alberto Falossi for proofreading draft versions of these chapters and, above all, for keeping the VB-2-The-Max site running when I was busy with the book. Knowing that I can rely on clever guys like you is very reassuring.

Kathleen Atkins is my favorite editor from the time I wrote my first Microsoft Press book over three years ago, so I felt the luckiest writer ever when she was given this project. If only you could look at the original version of this manuscript, you'd be grateful to her as well. Not only did Kathleen spend her evenings and weekends trying to put my prose into understandable English, she also gave me great tips about a few jazz singers I wasn't familiar with.

Danielle Bird has been the acquisitions editor for this book, and she did her job in the best way possible. She always had an immediate answer to all my requests and had the CDs of all the Visual Studio .NET beta versions sent to me no later than a couple of days after their release. (Quickly enough, if you consider that I live nine time zones away.)

Speaking of beta versions, in these months I have chased the .NET Framework while it evolved from the March 2000 PDC tech preview to the definitive version. Whenever a new beta was released, I had to revise all the text and the code samples written up to that point. If it weren't for Jack Beaudry, my eagle-eyed tech editor, I would have gone mad in the process. He found more mistakes and typos than I'd like to admit, but of course I am responsible for all those that might have survived in these pages.

— Francesco

Introduction

I can hardly believe I've finished this big tome, at last. I have rather confused memories of when I started it, more than a year ago. At that time, the .NET Framework was in the early beta stages and few of the things I describe in this book were working properly. The documentation was incomplete for the majority of topics (and was completely missing in the remaining cases). Just having a piece of code compile correctly—not to mention execute correctly—often required a lot of guesswork (and pure luck).

Nevertheless, I can't help admitting that exploring the new Microsoft Visual Basic language and the .NET Framework in depth has been quite an exciting experience. The more I dug into the .NET class library, the more I was thrilled by what I was discovering. This explains why the 700 pages that were originally planned for this book grew to what you're reading now.

Why a Book This Large

Granted, I might have written two books, perhaps even three, with the material you can find in these pages. For example, I might have written a book about Visual Basic .NET, another about Win32 applications and database applications, and a third about Web Forms and XML Web services. I even suspect that it might have been a wiser decision, from a business perspective. Why didn't I do that, then?

In my opinion, the revolutionary aspect of the .NET initiative is that it lets developers adopt a unified programming paradigm, regardless of the language they're using or the type of application they're building. All the objects in the .NET class library are closely interrelated, and you can't create great applications by focusing on a small portion of the .NET Framework and ignoring the rest. For example, Win32 developers should learn not only about the Windows Forms portion of the Framework but also about multithreading and GDI+. Programmers working on Web Forms should know about .NET data types, collections, and regular expressions. XML Web services programs require familiarity with object serialization and asynchronous delegates. Finally, you must master class inheritance, interfaces, assembly binding, and low-level details of memory management and garbage collection to write any type of .NET application. I could provide other examples, but I think I've made the point clear.

For all these reasons, I believe that a single volume can cover all the many facets of .NET programming better than many smaller books, which would inevitably overlap in their explanation of .NET fundamentals. And only a book from a single author can ensure that there are neither repetitions nor glaring omissions and can provide the .NET big picture.

Who Should Read This Book

Let me make another point clear up front. This book isn't for beginner developers wishing to learn Visual Basic .NET. Rather, it's for experienced Visual Basic 6 developers who want to leverage the full potential of the new .NET platform. If you don't feel at ease with Visual Basic 6 and its forms, if you don't know how to work with classes and objects, or if you've never accessed a database using ADO, this isn't the book for you. There are no step-by-step instructions about creating projects, nor tutorials about what a variable, a class, or a database connection is.

Visual Basic .NET is a brand-new language, but fortunately you can still leverage your experience with its predecessors. For example, ADO.NET evolved from ADO, so you need to know what a connection string is and how to build it. Even if Windows Forms controls are more powerful than their Visual Basic 6 cousins, many of the techniques you've developed in recent years are still useful. For those who need to refresh their memory, I include the full electronic version of my *Programming Microsoft Visual Basic 6* on the companion CD. For example, you can have a look at it for a tutorial of object-oriented concepts (Chapters 6 and 7), the SQL language (Chapter 8), the ADO object model (Chapter 13), and IIS applications (Chapter 20). The book on the companion CD is fully searchable, so you can find what you're looking for in a matter of seconds, and I provide references to specific topics when it's useful to do so.

Because *Programming Microsoft Visual Basic .NET* is aimed at experienced developers, it contains few complete, ready-to-run applications. Instead, I chose to focus on shorter code examples that illustrate how a specific .NET feature works. Most of the listings in this book are one page or shorter and include only the relevant portions of complete examples provided on the companion CD. For example, I don't waste precious pages including the complete listings of related examples that differ only in a handful of statements or including the tons of statements that the Visual Studio designer creates when you drop a few controls on a Windows Form. Shorter code listings mean improved readability, and I can use the saved space for something more interesting.

Companion Content

The companion CD included with this book contains files to aid in your understanding of Visual Basic .NET. The companion CD includes the following:

- **Demo Applications** The project source code that demonstrates the concepts discussed in each chapter.
- ***Programming Microsoft Visual Basic 6.0* Electronic Book** The previous edition of this book is available in its electronic form to act as a reference for core concepts not explained in this book.

In addition to the companion CD, this book includes a trial version of Visual Studio .NET on DVD. The demo applications are also available for downloading at *http://www.microsoft.com/mspress/books/5199.asp.*

System Requirements

You'll need the following hardware and software to use the demo applications included on the companion CD:

- **Microsoft Visual Studio .NET** A 60-day trial version of Visual Studio .NET is included on DVD.
- **A computer capable of running Microsoft Visual Studio .NET**. The following hardware configuration is recommended by the Microsoft Visual Studio .NET Web site, at *http://msdn.microsoft.com/vstudio.*
  - **Computer/Processor**
    PC with a Pentium II-class processor, 450 megahertz (MHz)
  - **Operating System**
    Microsoft Windows NT 4 or later operating system
  - **Minimum RAM Requirements**
    Microsoft Windows XP Professional: 160 megabytes (MB) of RAM
    Windows 2000 Professional: 96 MB of RAM
    Windows 2000 Server: 192 MB of RAM
    Windows NT 4 Workstation: 64 MB of RAM
    Windows NT 4 Server: 160 MB of RAM
  - **Hard Disk**
    2.5 gigabytes (GB) on installation drive, which includes 500 MB on system drive

- **Drive**
  DVD-ROM drive
- **Display**
  Super VGA (800 x 600) or higher-resolution monitor with 256 colors
- **Input Device**
  Microsoft Mouse or compatible pointing device

Installing and Using the Demo Files

Follow these steps to install the demo application files:

1. Remove the companion CD from the package inside the back cover of this book, and insert the CD into your CD-ROM drive.
2. Double-click the My Computer icon on the Desktop.

> **Tip** On some computers, the start-up program might run when you close the CD-ROM drive. In this case, skip steps 2 through 5 and follow the instructions on screen.

3. Double-click the icon for your CD-ROM drive.
4. Double-click StartCD.exe.
5. Click Install Sample Code.

   The setup program window appears with the recommended options preselected for you. For best results in using the demo files with this book, accept the default settings.
6. When the files have been installed, remove the CD from your CD-ROM drive and replace it in the package inside the back cover of the book.

A folder named VBNET has been created on your hard disk, and the demo files have been placed in that folder.

Using the Demo Files

The demo files for the book are organized by chapter. In general, the demo files are complete projects that can be opened and run inside Visual Studio .NET. However, some projects might require specific settings or installation to operate correctly. Please review the readme.txt file in the root folder of the companion CD for more information.

Corrections, Comments, and Help

Every effort has been made to ensure the accuracy of this book and the contents of the demo files on the companion CD. Microsoft Press provides corrections and additional content for its books through the World Wide Web at

http://www.microsoft.com/mspress/support/

If you have problems, comments, or ideas regarding this book or the companion CD, please send them to Microsoft Press.

Send e-mail to

mspinput@microsoft.com

Or send postal mail to

Microsoft Press
Attn: Programming Series Editor
One Microsoft Way
Redmond, WA 98052-6399

Please note that support for the Visual Studio .NET software product itself isn't offered through the preceding address. For help using Visual Studio .NET, visit *http://www.microsoft.com/support*.

Visit the Microsoft Press World Wide Web Site

You're also invited to visit the Microsoft Press World Wide Web site at the following location:

http://mspress.microsoft.com

You'll find descriptions for the complete line of Microsoft Press books, information about ordering titles, notice of special features and events, additional content for Microsoft Press books, and much more.

You can also find out the latest in Visual Studio .NET software developments and news from Microsoft Corporation by visiting the following World Wide Web site:

http://msdn.microsoft.com/vstudio/

A Bottom-Up Approach to the .NET Framework

Although I spend most of my time consulting and writing applications, I also do a lot of teaching in public seminars and on-site workshops. I've been delivering my five-day course on .NET programming both in the U.S. and in Europe, and I've been giving sessions and full-day workshops at conferences such as VBITS and WinSummit for about a year now.

Teaching Visual Basic .NET while I was writing this book has been an enriching and useful experience because I could refine the structure and the actual contents of this book based on the feedback from attendees and students. For example, I changed the sequence of a few chapters when I realized it made the comprehension of later topics easier.

This book follows a bottom-up approach that starts from an introduction to the Microsoft .NET initiative and language basics (Part I), then progresses through inheritance and new features such as delegates and attributes (Part II), and continues with a thorough description of the base classes in the .NET Framework (Part III). At this point, readers have all the necessary means to understand what comes next, such as Windows Forms and GDI+ (Part IV), database programming with ADO.NET and XML (Part V), and ASP.NET applications (Part VI).

I suggest that you read this book without jumping back and forth from chapter to chapter because each chapter builds on those that come before it. This dependency on continuity is especially true for the chapters in Parts I, II, and III. After you've become familiar with .NET foundations, you can decide to focus on Win32 applications, on database applications, or on Internet applications, depending on your priorities.

The .NET Framework is so huge that I had to leave a few topics out because of both time and space constraints. For example, I don't cover COM interoperability, security, interaction with COM+, and remoting. I might write chapters on these topics and include them in a second edition of this book, or I might publish them on my *www.vb2themax.com* Web site. You should also subscribe to the *VB-2-The-Max* newsletter to find out when I upload errata and updates for existing chapters and to receive new tech tips on .NET every week in your mailbox.

Programming Microsoft Visual Basic .NET is my attempt to write a book that explains how you can build great real-world, robust, easily maintainable applications with Visual Basic .NET and Visual Studio .NET. I want to demonstrate what I consider the best coding practices in the .NET environment as well as provide you with a reference to the most important classes of the .NET Framework, a collection of tips for high-performance and scalable applications, and many code examples that you can reuse in your programs.

I hope I've achieved this goal and that you'll have as much fun reading this book as I had writing it—without having to stay awake until the crack of dawn, as I did so frequently during all these months.

Francesco Balena
fbalena@vb2themax.com

Part I

The Basics

Front
Top
Left
Back

1

Getting Started with Visual Basic .NET

Virtually all books about a programming language start with an introductory chapter that praises that language, offers a first working example, describes some cool feature of the language, or takes a mixture of all three approaches. As a matter of fact, this is more or less what I did in the first chapter of my *Programming Microsoft Visual Basic 6* book (which you can read in electronic format on the companion CD).

Visual Basic .NET calls for a different treatment, however. Before you can fully appreciate the features of this new, almost revolutionary version of the language, you must understand what the .NET architecture is all about.

Why .NET?

At the risk of oversimplifying, you can think of the .NET initiative as the convergence of several distinct but loosely tied goals, the most important of which are overcoming the limitations of the COM programming model and finding a common programming paradigm for Internet-related applications.

Issues with Today's Software Development

If you've been in the software industry for years, you probably agree that software development is still more like a craft than a mature industrial activity. In spite of much progress in recent years—in terms of such available programming tools as rapid application development languages, debuggers, and code generators—writing robust enterprise-level applications is still a complex job, within reach of only skilled professionals. The main reason is, of course, that writing software *is* difficult, but many other factors make producing good software harder and more complicated than it should be.

Windows Inconsistencies

The Windows platform has evolved chaotically in recent years. We have at least three different programming models for producing graphic-intensive applications (GDI, DirectX, and OpenGL), for example, with each model completely different from the others. Microsoft has also produced several programming models for accessing databases—Data Access Objects (DAO), Remote Data Objects (RDO), and ActiveX Data Objects (ADO)—which, again, are largely incompatible with one another.

On top of that, Windows itself comes in so many flavors—Windows 95, 98, Me, NT, 2000, CE, and XP, not counting variants such as Professional, Server, and Advanced Server versions. Not all versions support all features, and the net result is that developers often give up specific Windows features, aiming at making their applications available to as many users as possible. (And programmers' lives are going to become *really* hard when 64-bit Windows versions become popular.)

Security is another area of concern that's heavily affected by the Windows platform developers write for, in that they must choose to address a range of security features, from the minimal in Windows 95, 98, and ME to the more robust security scheme of Windows NT and 2000 Server Edition. To make things worse, a developer must often account for the differences between Windows security and the "classic" COM security model, which in turn is different from the COM+ security model. With all these different models to consider, it's no surprise that security is often an afterthought in most enterprise applications, which makes them vulnerable to attacks.

COM Shortcomings

Over the years, the Component Object Model (COM) has proven to be versatile enough to work as the infrastructure for many enterprise and distributed applications, but at the same time it has shown itself to be just too complex for developers who want to focus more on the business problem at hand than on the countless low-level details that all COM experts have to face daily. Worse, COM applications are inherently fragile because they depend heavily on the information stored in the system Registry, which has a reputation for becoming corrupted easily. Sometimes the only way to make a malfunctioning application work is to reinstall it; in the worst cases, even this extreme measure doesn't suffice.

COM applications suffer from another serious problem: versioning. Apparently, COM designers didn't anticipate the need to install multiple versions of the same component on a given system. As you know, each newer version of a COM component overwrites older ones, so, for example, you can't have multiple versions of ADO on the same computer. In theory, this overwriting should have no unfortunate consequences because each new version is supposed to encompass all the functionality of previous versions. In practice, however, this means that an application that uses ADO 2.0 or ADO 2.1 can suddenly stop working if the user installs ADO 2.5 or later versions because of minor incompatibilities among these versions. Versioning is a thorny problem even if you're the author of your own component. Visual Basic 6 programmers can use the Binary Compatibility feature to ensure complete or partial compatibility among different versions of their components, but this feature has several serious bugs. C++ developers have more control over versioning but at the cost of added time and effort spent writing COM interfaces and IDL files.

A third defect of COM is in deployment: as you all know, installing a COM-based application isn't a simple task because you have to install all the necessary components in system directories, register them in the Registry (taking care not to override newer versions), configure them, and so on. In short, writing installation programs has become an art of its own, with tricks and secrets. And when the installation fails on an end user's machine, you're usually left in the dark.

Object-Oriented Issues

Programming would be much easier if developers had a simple and secure way to reuse and extend code that they (or someone else) wrote, but the COM programming model offers very little in this respect. For example, you can't inherit from a COM class and extend it. Inheriting and extending Windows functions is even more difficult because the Windows API doesn't expose classes.

COM permits an object-oriented approach to programming but doesn't really encourage it. For example, the OOP theory promotes complex object hierarchies, but these complex hierarchies have a hard time in the COM world. As all experienced developers (and readers of the previous edition of this book) know, two COM objects that establish a circular reference to each other aren't automatically released when they go out of scope. Circular references are common in real-world hierarchies, such as when you have two objects in parent-child relationship or two Person objects that reference each other through their Spouse property. The COM memory manager relies on the concept of a *reference counter* and has no way to detect when the main program has no reference to a given object if the object is also pointed to by another object. As a result, the two (or more) objects continue to remain in memory until the application ends. In demo applications and other simple, short-lived programs, this situation is seldom a problem, but it becomes a serious issue with server-side components designed to run for weeks or months. Memory leakage is the main reason why the latest version of COM+, version 1.5, provides a means to periodically shut down and restart COM applications.

Visual Basic increments and decrements the internal reference counter of COM objects as necessary, so at least you don't have to worry about these details. This isn't the case if you work with other languages, such as C++, that force you to do it manually. When you're working in such languages, a missing call to the AddRef or Release method of the IUnknown interface can cause unexpected crashes or (worse) elusive memory leaks that manifest themselves only after hours or days.

Cross-Language Interoperability

The Windows platform makes it extremely difficult to integrate pieces of code written in different languages because each language has its own call conventions, limitations, and idiosyncrasies. For example, a Visual Basic programmer can call a C++ DLL but must take extra care with unsigned integers (which aren't recognized by Visual Basic). A VBScript application can use a COM component but can't take advantage of any interface other than the IDispatch interface that the component exposes. Furthermore, each language has its preferred way of dealing with errors: COM uses negative HRESULT values (and Visual Basic adopts this approach behind the scenes), Java and C++ use structured exception handling, and functions in the Windows API report errors by returning special values (in a highly inconsistent way).

Because integrating different languages is so difficult, many software shops prefer to standardize on a single language, thus missing the particular advantages that each language can offer. For example, Visual Basic is by a large margin more productive for business and database applications, yet many developers prefer to work with C++ because of its added power and flexibility. If cross-language interoperability were easier, each portion of a large application might be developed with the language that fit better, and software development would be less expensive in terms of both time and money.

The Problems of Active Server Pages

While all the preceding issues played an important role in pushing Microsoft toward a new programming model, by far their most important goal was to provide a consistent platform for delivering robust Internet applications. What's wrong with yesterday's way of coding for the Internet?

To begin with, after many attempts to provide credible Internet programming tools—a list that includes ActiveX controls, ActiveX documents, and WebClasses—Microsoft discovered that its most widely accepted platform for the Web was Internet Information Services (IIS) with Active Server Pages (ASP). ASP has one great advantage: it delivers dynamic page content that works well with any browser (because all processing occurs on the server, and not in the client's browser). This technology, in fact, is fueling many Internet applications of all sizes. Yet you shouldn't forget the many shortcomings of ASP, such as the following:

- You can use only script languages, such as VBScript or JScript, so you're subject to the many limitations of script languages: programs are interpreted and not compiled, so they execute slower; code uses late binding, and any misspelled method name raises an error at run time instead of compile time; script languages can't access advanced features in the Windows API.
- ASP code is intermixed with user-interface (UI) code—that is, the HTML sent to the browser. This makes it exceedingly difficult to separate the business logic from the UI code and makes it nearly impossible to let a graphic designer update the UI if she isn't also an expert developer. In addition, debugging an ASP application is a nightmare, and in practice it means cluttering your code with tons of Response.Write statements to help you understand what went wrong.
- Although you can fix script-code shortcomings by using compiled COM components (COM components are compiled and can access virtually any API, including Windows functions), COM components are also problematic. First of all, you can't replace a COM component with a new version without stopping and restarting the Web site (and in a few cases IIS itself), which is clearly undesirable on a production site. On top of that, COM components make the deployment of the Web application more difficult because they must be registered in the system Registry. If you use Visual Basic to author COM components for ASP, you must take other limitations into account—for example, all your components are apartment-threaded and might cause a performance bottleneck if used improperly.
- Large-scale code reuse is virtually impossible under ASP. In practice, the only way you can reuse code in ASP is either by using include files (in which case you are importing and parsing *all* the routines in the include file, including those that you don't use in a given page) or by using compiled COM components (which pose the problems outlined in the previous point).

- Most ASP Web sites store information about individual connected clients in Session variables because ASP programming (and Internet programming in general) is stateless, which means that values aren't preserved between consecutive requests to the server. Session variables offer storage for the client's state, but they have a couple of remarkable limitations: they don't work on Web farms (that is, when the site runs on multiple computers), and they don't work if users disabled cookie support in their browsers.

The Challenges of the Internet

Even if you don't worry about the problems of programming with ASP—which, after all, is just one of the many programming technologies you can use on the Internet—you probably agree that Internet programming is still in its infancy and therefore overly difficult. One of the crucial problems is the lack of standardization in how information can be shared over the Internet. HTML dictates only how information is displayed in browsers but makes it difficult to extract that information for use by a program.

Here's a very simple example that should make this concept clear. Suppose you build an e-commerce site to sell books. (You have a lot of competition in that endeavor, but at least bookselling is easily understandable.) As added services, you want to provide international customers with the ability to translate prices into their own currency and any customer the ability to track shipments. The first task can be accomplished relatively easily—in theory, at least—because many Internet sites provide timely information about exchange rates with foreign countries. The second task is also simple—again, in theory—because your favorite courier has a site at which you can check the shipment status of any parcel as long as you have its tracking ID.

If you have ever tried to implement a system like this one, you already know why this picture doesn't work easily: both the information about the currency exchange rate and the information about shipment status are buried inside an HTML page on their respective sites, and you have to dig it out after discarding the hundreds of tags that tell how the page is to be displayed in a browser. In most cases, you can extract the information you're after, but the effort is large and performance is less than optimal. Worse, nobody can guarantee that your solution will continue to work in the future because even a minor change in the page layout might break your code (unless of course you have an unbreakable agreement with the company that runs that site). In addition, you aren't always legally allowed to extract that information, especially if the other site supports itself by selling advertising on its pages.

A reasonable solution to these problems would be that sites delivering information—such as the sites that expose information on currency exchange rates or shipment status—should expose this information using a format other than HTML. Microsoft and other large software companies—including Sun and IBM—have joined with the W3C committee to produce the Simple Object Access Protocol (SOAP) standard, which is based on XML. Using SOAP, you can query a site and get a return value through TCP/IP and XML. XML has a well-defined syntax and can be parsed unambiguously, unlike HTML. You can use SOAP even without switching to .NET, for example, by using Visual Basic 6 and the Microsoft SOAP Toolkit (which you can download from the Microsoft Web site). But as you'll see in a moment, Microsoft has taken an additional step by formulating the concept of XML Web services.

> **Tip** You can download the latest SOAP specifications from the World Wide Web Consortium at *http://www.w3.org*.

The Solution According to Microsoft .NET

OK, now that you know what's wrong with today's software development tools, you might be curious to see how .NET can remedy these problems. Let's tackle one issue at a time.

Leveling Windows Platforms

Microsoft .NET offers an object-oriented view of the Windows operating system and includes hundreds of classes that encapsulate all the most important Windows kernel objects. For example, a portion of .NET named GDI+ contains all the objects that create graphic output in a window. Depending on the specific Windows version, these objects might use the plain GDI functions, DirectX, or even OpenGL (in the future), but as far as the developer is concerned there is only one programming model to code against. I describe GDI+ in greater depth in Chapter 18.

Security is built right into .NET, so you don't have to worry much about the underlying operating system's security model. .NET security goes further than Windows security, and the administrator can grant or revoke individual applications the right to access the Registry or the file system, among many other things. This security model is independent of the specific version of Windows the application is running on.

.NET components and applications are also inherently safer than COM components and "old-style" Windows applications. For example, .NET components are automatically checked to ensure that their code hasn't been altered. You can also sign a .NET application with a digital signature and use a technology such as Authenticode to let users know who the author of the application is.

.NET as a Better COM

You can look at .NET as the next generation of COM if you like, in that the two programming models let you solve more or less the same problems. Behind the scenes, however, they're completely different, and .NET is superior to COM in many respects.

First and foremost, a .NET application can consist of one or more *assemblies*. Each assembly is usually an individual EXE or DLL executable file. An assembly can also include other files, such as additional DLLs or .html, .gif, or other non-executable files. Assemblies are the unit of versioning and logical deployment in the sense that all the files in an assembly have the same version number, and you can't deploy an assembly with files marked with different version numbers. Typically an application uses several external assemblies, including those belonging to the .NET Framework itself. I'll discuss assemblies later in this chapter and in greater depth in Chapter 14.

.NET doesn't use the Registry to store any information about assemblies (even though it still uses the Registry to store information about the .NET Framework itself). In general, all the information related to an application and the components it uses is stored in configuration files held in the application's main directory. A configuration file uses XML syntax to store hierarchical data and therefore is more flexible than old .ini files. For example, an entry in this configuration file might contain the connection string to the main database used by the application so that the administrator can change it with an editor as simple as Notepad.

Let's see how .NET solves the component versioning problem. There are two kinds of .NET components: private and shared. Private components are stored in the application's main directory (or in one of its subdirectories) and aren't visible to other applications. So each application uses its own private components, and distinct applications can use different versions of these components because they're stored in different directories. Shared components, on the other hand, are visible to all the .NET applications and are typically stored in a central repository named global assembly cache (GAC) located under the C:\WinNT\Assembly directory. Each component in the GAC is kept in a separate directory, and different versions of the same shared component can coexist on a computer. Each application compiled against version X.Y of a given component continues to work correctly even if the user installs a newer (or older) version of the same component.

Versioning even extends to the .NET Framework itself. When a new version of the .NET Framework is available, you'll be able to install it on a computer without removing any previous version of the framework so that applications using previous versions will continue to work.

.NET versioning is more flexible than COM's. In fact, a developer or a system administrator can use a configuration file to redirect a request for a given component to another version of the same component. So the component author can release a new version that fixes a few bugs or that's more efficient and indirectly improve the robustness and speed of all the applications that use that component without introducing any version incompatibility problems.

.NET solves another problem I mentioned previously: deployment. Because .NET applications can use private assemblies only if they're stored in the applications' own directory trees, you can install most .NET applications by using the so-called *XCOPY deployment*, that is, simply by copying all the files to a directory on the target system. That you can use this simple installation method doesn't mean that real-world .NET applications don't need an installation procedure, however; you usually need to create shortcuts on the Start menu or let the end user select which portions of the applications should be installed. In addition, the installation routine might need to install shared components in the GAC. Even considering these ancillary tasks, however, installing a .NET application is much simpler than a similar COM application because fewer things can go wrong.

The .NET Framework Class Hierarchy

Unlike COM, the .NET Framework is designed around the concept of inheritance. All the objects in the .NET Framework form a hierarchy with a single root, the System.Object class, from which all the other classes derive. These classes provide functionality in almost any conceivable area, including the user interface, data access, Internet programming, XML processing, security, and cross-machine communication.

Most of the time, programming under .NET means extending one of these classes. For example, you can create a text box control that accepts only numbers by deriving a new class from the System.Windows.Forms.TextBox class and adding all the necessary code that rejects invalid entries. Classes that don't inherit from a specific .NET class implicitly inherit from System.Object and therefore benefit in other ways from being part of the .NET object hierarchy. Needless to say, this approach encourages code reuse.

The .NET Framework takes a novel approach to mutual object references, which gets rid of the circular reference problem that has plagued COM applications for years. This isn't the right place to discuss how the .NET approach works, but it should suffice to say that .NET classes aren't reference counted and that they aren't responsible for their own lifetime (as is the case with COM components). All .NET objects inherit from System.Object the ability to be released when the main application doesn't hold a reference to them any longer. This technique works both with direct references (the application has a variable pointing to the object) and with indirect references (when there are intermediate objects between the application and the object in question). For this reason, circular references don't cause memory leaks under .NET. And because there's no reference counter to be increased or decreased, programming against .NET components is simpler even in languages other than Visual Basic because there are no AddRef or Release calls to be made.

All .NET Languages Are Born Equal

.NET moves most of the functionality from the language to the .NET Framework itself. For example, the .NET Framework includes classes for opening, reading, and writing text and binary files, so there is no point in having this functionality embedded in programming languages. Another example: a portion of the .NET Framework named Windows Forms offers classes that can create windows and controls. (You can think of this portion as the heir of forms in Visual Basic 6.) All .NET languages can use these classes, and therefore all languages have the same capabilities in creating applications with a rich user interface, without having to resort to low-level, advanced techniques such as subclassing.

Microsoft provides several languages with .NET, including Visual Basic .NET, C# (pronounced C sharp), Managed C++, and JScript. Many C++ developers are expected to switch to C#, which they might consider the best language for .NET applications. C# is actually a great language, which takes the best ideas from many existing languages, such as C++ and Java. But the truth is that C# and Visual Basic .NET are roughly equivalent, and both of them let you tap the full power of the .NET Framework. A few developers criticize Microsoft for making this first version of Visual Basic slightly less capable than C# in matters such as pointers and operation overloading. While this is true, it should also be said that Visual Basic .NET has a few advantages over C#. For example, error handling under Visual Basic is more flexible: you can use either the old system based on the On Error statement or the newer structured exception handling. (Only the second alternative is available to C# developers.) Visual Basic provides modules, makes late binding easier, provides a more granular way to shadow methods in derived classes, and provides an easier way to resize an array.

As you see, the differences are in the details: the two languages have the same potential, and you should choose one or the other depending on which makes you more productive. Execution speed is also equivalent because the C# and Visual Basic compilers generate more or less the same code. Nobody knows how the two languages will evolve, but at this time they're just a relatively thin layer over the .NET Framework and are therefore very similar.

If you've worked with previous editions of Visual Basic, obviously my advice is that you should use Visual Basic .NET to explore the .NET Framework and become familiar with the .NET way of doing things, such as working with files, databases, the user interface, XML, HTTP, and so on until you feel comfortable. Then you might want to have a look at C#—you'll be surprised to see how easily you learn it. The C# language consists of only a handful of keywords, the majority of which have close counterparts in Visual Basic .NET. The real difficulty in learning C# directly from Visual Basic 6 is that you have to absorb complex concepts such as inheritance and structured exception handling, so making a two-step transition is surely less traumatic.

Another interesting point to consider is that both the Visual Basic and C# compilers belong to the .NET Framework, not to the Visual Studio package. In theory, you can write and compile Visual Basic .NET applications using any editor—yes, including Notepad—and compile the applications using the vbc.exe compiler provided with the .NET Framework. As a matter of fact, some portions of the framework—the XML parser, for example—actually rely on the presence of the C# compiler to dynamically create and compile code on the fly, a technique that provides stunning performance.

Because all the objects you work with belong to the .NET object hierarchy—or extend objects in that hierarchy—you can easily manipulate such objects with any .NET language. This approach offers a degree of cross-language interoperability that's simply impossible using COM. For example, you can inherit a Visual Basic .NET class from a C# class, and you can define an interface with Visual Basic and write a C# class that implements it. .NET maintains a degree of compatibility with COM-based languages thanks to a portion of the .NET Framework known as COM Interoperability.

Web Forms, the Successor to Active Server Pages

ASP.NET is arguably the most important portion of the .NET Framework, or at least the main reason why all serious Internet developers should think about migrating to the new platform. ASP.NET is a dream come true for anyone who has ever built (or attempted to build) large-size applications using ASP or any comparable server-side technology.

Broadly speaking, ASP.NET comprises two distinct but tightly related technologies: Web Forms and XML Web services. Web Forms are used for Internet applications with a user interface and are meant to replace ASP applications, although you can still run ASP and ASP.NET on the same computer. Web Services are for Internet applications without a user interface and are discussed in the next section. A partial list of the most intriguing features of Web Forms follows; I'll describe each feature more thoroughly in Chapter 23 and Chapter 24.

ASP.NET applications are written in full-featured, compiled languages such as Visual Basic .NET and C#, so you can expect ASP.NET code to run faster than the equivalent ASP script code. Even more important in my opinion is that you can now use early binding and strongly typed variables (which reduce the number of run-time errors) and have full access to components and functions in the Windows API. VBScript isn't supported any longer (because Visual Basic .NET supersedes it), but you can still use JScript to quickly migrate old ASP applications written with that language. (New applications should be written with the more capable C# or Visual Basic language.) ASP.NET version 1.0 is available for Windows 2000, Windows XP, and Windows .NET Server.

Unlike its predecessor, ASP.NET offers the gamut of debugging features, including breakpoints set inside the IDE and the ability to print tracing and profiling information about pages being browsed. Debugging an ASP.NET application isn't much different from debugging a standard Visual Basic application, and maybe it's even easier, thanks to the new trace facilities.

Another step forward from ASP is that ASP.NET truly permits and promotes separation between the user interface (that is, the HTML code) and the code that makes the application work (written in C#, Visual Basic, or any other .NET language). Thanks to the concept of *code behind* modules, you can split an ASP.NET page into two distinct files, one containing the HTML code and controls and the other containing the source code. The very first time the page is requested by a browser, the ASP.NET infrastructure passes the source code file to the proper compiler and dynamically ties the compiled code with events produced by the user interface controls. You can still intermix UI code and application logic code in the same file if you prefer, and you can precompile the code-behind file if you don't want to distribute your source code.

Speaking of events, ASP.NET is based on the familiar event-driven programming model that millions of Visual Basic developers know so well. For example, when an ASP.NET page is loaded your code receives a Page_Load event, and so forth. This does *not* mean that you can easily move code from a traditional client-side application into a server-side ASP.NET application (this wasn't a goal of the ASP.NET initiative), but you don't have to learn yet another programming model for working with Web programs.

Because ASP.NET uses compiled code, you probably won't need to write components as frequently as you did under ASP. However, you might need to write a component to gather common functionality in a single place (to improve code reuse) or to take advantage of COM+ transactional features. An important new feature of ASP.NET is that you can overwrite a component even while an application is using it. This is possible thanks to a feature known as *shadow copying*. An ASP.NET application doesn't load the component from its original file; instead, it copies the file into a temporary directory and loads the component from there. The original file isn't locked, and you can overwrite it at will. All subsequent requests to the pages that use that component will use the new instance instead of the old one. If you consider that all the configuration values of an ASP.NET application are stored in an XML file in its main directory, you see that you can upgrade an ASP.NET application by simply copying the new files over the old ones, without having to stop and restart the IIS application.

ASP.NET supports a more flexible version of the Session object. Under ASP.NET, Session variables can be held on the machine that hosts IIS (as in traditional ASP), on another machine in the same network, or inside a SQL Server database. The latter two arrangements make it possible to access those variables from any machine on the LAN, so you can distribute an application over Web farms with little effort. Just as important, you can decide to create Session objects that don't rely on client-side cookie support, so ASP.NET applications can work even with browsers whose cookie support has been disabled.

ASP.NET expands on traditional ASP in many other areas as well. For example, ASP.NET pages that don't vary frequently can be cached, a technique that delivers much better performance, especially if the page is built from data stored in a database. Another great feature of ASP.NET is its open architecture, which makes it possible to create your custom handlers associated with files with a given extension. (Accomplishing the same in pre-.NET days required mastery of the Internet Services API [ISAPI] programming model and a lot of C++ wizardry.)

XML Web Services, the Internet of the Future

Rather than just delivering a better ASP, the .NET initiative is trying to shape how the Internet works in the future. As you read earlier in the section "The Challenges of the Internet," one problem with today's Internet is that there's no integration among the millions of sites around the world because there isn't a standard way to query them and get the information they store.

Microsoft and other software companies are now trying to remedy this situation by introducing XML Web services. An *XML Web service* is nothing but an application that listens to requests coming to a TCP socket and reacts to the commands each request contains. For example, a Web Service that provides foreign currency exchange rates will presumably react to requests containing the name of the source currency, the amount of money, and the name of the target currency. The XML Web service will then do the conversion from source to target currency and return the result to the client. Both the requests and the result are sent and received using SOAP, and there will be no ambiguity about the meaning of each piece of information sent through the wire.

An important point about XML Web services is that they aren't based on any proprietary technology. Clients need only to format a SOAP request and send it through HTTP, and the server needs only to decode the request and send the result. All the protocols and technologies used by XML Web services—such as SOAP, XML, HTTP, and TCP/IP—are open standards. Microsoft doesn't own any of these standards, even though it's working with other companies and with the W3C to shape them. As a matter of fact, you can implement an XML Web service on operating systems other than Microsoft Windows.

Because XML Web services are based on off-the-shelf technologies, you see that you don't need .NET to implement them. In fact, you can create an XML Web service using Visual Basic 6 and the SOAP Toolkit. However, the more you learn about the .NET Framework, the more you realize that you can be much more productive creating and consuming XML Web services using .NET than you can using traditional technologies. For example, you can invoke an XML Web service asynchronously with just a handful of statements in Visual Basic .NET.

The Microsoft .NET Project

By now you should be convinced that the .NET initiative isn't just marketing hype and that it delivers many real benefits to developers and users alike. It's time to have a closer look at the new architecture.

Requirements

As of this writing, you can run the .NET Framework only on a Windows computer. All Windows versions are supported, with the notable exception of Windows 95: you can use Windows 98, Windows 98 SE, Windows Me, Windows NT 4, Windows 2000, and Windows XP in all their Professional, Server, or Advanced Server variants.

You can download the .NET Framework from Microsoft's Web site and install it to make the above systems .NET-compliant. However, since this book is about Visual Basic .NET, I assume that you'll install the .NET Framework from Visual Studio .NET CDs. The complete framework takes up about 20 MB on the hard disk, but you can expect that individual .NET applications have a smaller footprint than their COM counterparts because they reuse much of the code in the .NET class hierarchy. For example, Visual Basic applications don't need any extra DLLs as they did until Visual Basic 6. Future versions of Windows will include the .NET Framework, so you won't have to ask your users to install it to run your applications.

The .NET Framework comes in two versions: standard (or desktop) and compact. The standard version includes all the features described in this book—console applications, Windows Forms, Web Forms, XML Web services, and the command-line compilers and tools, for example—and runs on all Windows platforms except Windows 95. The compact .NET Framework is meant to run on PDAs and smaller devices such as mobile phones or home devices such as TVs. The initial version of the compact framework runs on Windows CE, but Microsoft is supplying a kit that OEMs and hardware producers can use to port the compact framework to other, proprietary, operating systems.

Technically speaking, you don't need any additional development tools to develop .NET applications because the framework contains the compilers and other command-line utilities to link modules together and install .NET components in the GAC. In practice, however, you need Visual Studio .NET (or a similar environment from another vendor) to do serious programming. For example, Visual Studio contains the designers for creating Windows Forms and Web Forms applications visually and a tool for exploring the methods that an XML Web service exposes using a standard object browser.

Visual Studio runs on all Windows platforms that support the .NET Framework, with the sole, notable exception of Windows NT 4. In practice, you should install Visual Studio .NET on Windows 2000 (Server Edition, preferably) or Windows XP to take advantage of all the capabilities of .NET.

.NET Architecture

The best way to understand how .NET works is to have a look at the many layers in the .NET Framework, as you see in Figure 1-1. Let me describe each individual layer, starting from the bottom.

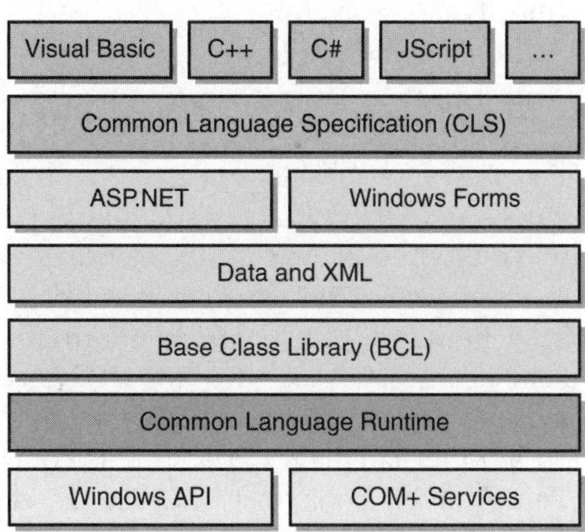

Figure 1-1. The layers in the .NET Framework.

At the bottom of the hierarchy sits the Windows API: .NET offers an object-oriented view of the operating system's functions but doesn't replace them, so you shouldn't forget that most calls into the .NET Framework are ultimately resolved as calls into one of the Windows kernel DLLs.

You might be surprised to find COM+ Services at this level of the .NET hierarchy. Microsoft believed that rewriting the COM+ kernel from scratch would have been too much for this initial release of .NET, so they decided to have the .NET Framework rely on Component Services. You can therefore create .NET components that take advantage of the transaction, synchronization, and security services offered by COM+, even though this approach adds overhead because execution must flow from .NET to COM. (Each time execution crosses this border you're going to waste some CPU cycles.) In most applications, this overhead is negligible, however. On the plus side, .NET programmers can continue to write enterprise-level applications using the programming model they've learned in past years, and they can leverage the same services they used under COM+ because all the same concepts apply (even though the syntax used to achieve those services is different).

The common language runtime is the first layer that belongs to the .NET Framework. This layer is responsible for .NET base services, such as memory management, garbage collection, structured exception handling, and multithreading. If .NET is ever ported to non-Windows architectures—as of this writing, a few projects are pursuing this goal—writing a version of the common language runtime for the new host must be the very first step to take. The runtime is contained in the MSCorEE.dll file, and all the .NET applications call a function in this DLL when they begin executing.

The Base Class Library (BCL) is the portion of the .NET Framework that defines all the basic data types, such as System.Object (the root of the .NET object hierarchy), numeric and date types, the String type, arrays, and collections. The BCL also contains classes for managing .NET core features, such as file I/O, threading, serialization, and security. The way types are implemented in the BCL follows the Common Type System (CTS) specifications. For example, these specifications dictate how a .NET type exposes fields, properties, methods, and events; it also defines how a type can inherit from another type and possibly override its members. Because all .NET languages recognize these specifications, they can exchange data, call into each other's classes, and even inherit from classes written in other languages. The BCL is contained in the MSCorLib.dll component. Part III of this book, that is, Chapters 8 through 15, is devoted to the BCL.

The Data And XML layer contains the .NET classes that work with databases and with XML. Here you can see that support for XML is built right into the .NET Framework, rather than through external components, as is the case with pre-.NET languages. In fact, XML can be considered the format that .NET uses to store virtually any kind of information. All the .NET configuration files are based on XML, and any object can be saved to XML with just a few statements. Of course, the .NET Framework comes with a powerful and fast XML parser. I cover XML features in Chapter 22.

The Data portion of this layer is what is commonly called ADO.NET and is the .NET counterpart of the ActiveX Data Objects (ADO) technology. In spite of their similar names, ADO and ADO.NET are very different. Whereas classic ADO covers virtually all the database techniques available—including server-side and client-side cursors, disconnected resultsets, and batch updates—ADO.NET is focused mainly on disconnected resultsets (called DataSets in ADO.NET terminology) and currently offers no support for server-side cursors. The DataSet object is much more powerful than the ADO Recordset object and can store data coming from multiple tables, in the same database or different databases. You can create relationships among different data tables, and you can import or export both the data and the metadata as XML. Chapter 20 and Chapter 21 cover all ADO.NET features in depth.

The next two layers are ASP.NET and Windows Forms, which are located at the same level in the diagram. These portions of the framework contain all the classes that can generate the user interface—in a browser in the former case, and using standard Win32 windows in the latter case. As I explained earlier, ASP.NET comprises both Web Forms and XML Web services. Even if these two portions appear at the same level in the diagram and in spite of their similarities, it should be clear that these technologies are very different. Web Forms run on the server and produce HTML code that's rendered in a browser on the client (which can run on virtually any operating system), whereas Windows Forms run on the client (and this client must be a Windows machine). However, you can mix them in the same application, to some extent at least. For example, you can have a .NET application that queries a remote XML Web service through the Internet and displays its result using Windows Forms. I cover Windows Forms in Part IV of this book (Chapters 16 through 19) and ASP.NET applications in Part VI (Chapters 23 through 26).

The .NET Framework class library consists of a collection of assemblies, each one comprising one or more DLLs. For example, ADO.NET is contained in the System.Data.Dll assembly, and the XML portion of the framework is contained in the System.Xml.Dll assembly. You can see all the assemblies that make up the .NET Framework class library by browsing the Assembly directory under the main Windows directory, as you can see in Figure 1-2. I'll describe the portions of the .NET Framework class library later in this chapter.

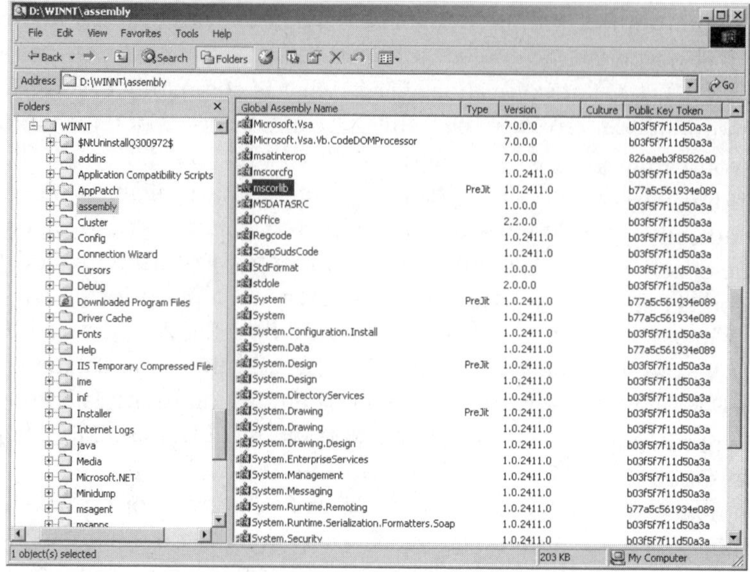

Figure 1-2. The list of assemblies installed with the .NET Framework.

.NET Languages

The Common Language Specification (CLS) is a set of specifications that Microsoft has supplied to help compiler vendors. These specifications dictate the minimum group of features that a .NET language must have, such as support for signed integers of 16, 32, or 64 bits, zero-bound arrays, and structured exception handling. A compiler vendor is free to create a language that exceeds these specifications—for example, with unsigned integers or arrays whose lowest index is nonzero—but a well-designed application should never rely on these non-CLS-compliant features when communicating with other .NET components because the other component might not recognize them. Interestingly, Visual Basic .NET matches the CLS specifications almost perfectly, so you don't have to worry about using non-CLS-compliant features in your applications. C# developers can use a Visual Studio .NET option to ensure that only CLS-compliant features are exposed to the outside.

At the top of the diagram in Figure 1-1 are the programming languages that comply with CLS. Microsoft offers the following languages: Visual Basic .NET, C#, Managed C++, and JScript. Many other language vendors are working on .NET languages, so you can expect that other popular languages will be available soon. The list of languages under development as I'm writing this book includes Perl, COBOL, Smalltalk, Eiffel, Python, Pascal, and APL, plus a few that—to be honest—I've never heard of. In part, this proliferation of programming languages can be explained by the formidable support that common language runtime and BCL offer to language authors, who don't have to worry about complex matters such as memory management and threading. Also, it's relatively simple to create a translator that converts source code written in a programming language to the corresponding C# source code and then compile it. (You can assume that C# is always available on any .NET implementation, including non-Windows ones.) For example, creating a Perl or Awk compiler that actually generates C# and then compiles it should be relatively easy, thanks to the excellent support for regular expressions that the .NET Framework offers. Of course, such a naive approach doesn't offer integrated debugging features, but it might be enough for a quick-and-dirty initial release.

All the .NET languages produce *managed code*, which is code that runs under the control of the runtime. Managed code is quite different from the native code produced by traditional compilers, which is now referred to as *unmanaged code*. Of all the new language offerings from Microsoft, only C++ can produce both managed and unmanaged code, but even C++ developers should resort to unmanaged code only if strictly necessary—for example, for doing low-level operations or for performance reasons—because only managed code gets all the benefits of the .NET platform.

Because all the .NET languages—from Microsoft or other vendors—target the CLS and use the classes and the data types in the .NET Framework, they're more similar than languages used to be in the past. For example, all .NET languages handle errors using structured exception handlers and support 16-bit, 32-bit, and 64-bit signed integers. Another example: because the common language runtime and the CTS support only single inheritance (which means that a type can inherit only from one type), all languages support single inheritance; there's no room for multiple inheritance in the .NET world. The similarity among all languages has three important consequences.

First, the execution speed of all languages tends to be the same, as I have already explained, so your choice of language should be based on other factors, such as productivity. Second, language interoperability is ensured because all the languages use the same data types and the same way to report errors, so you can write different portions of an application with different languages without worrying about their integration.

Third, and maybe most important from the perspective of us developers: learning a new .NET language is surprisingly effortless if you've already mastered another .NET language. Developers who know both Visual Basic .NET and C# (and possibly other languages as well) will undoubtedly have more job opportunities, so .NET is also a great opportunity for all professionals and consultants. I believe that all Windows developers should start working with the new version of the language they know better—Visual Basic .NET if they've worked with Visual Basic 6, or C# if they've worked with C++ or Java—and then learn the other language as soon as they feel comfortable with the .NET way of doing things.

The Visual Basic .NET Compiler

Before we continue with our exploration of the .NET world, let's create our first Visual Basic program, compile it, and run it. In the process, you'll learn several interesting things about the .NET architecture. In this first example, I use Notepad to create a simple program and the command-line vbc.exe compiler to produce an executable. In most real cases, you'll use Visual Studio .NET and its integrated editor, but I don't want you to be distracted by that environment during this first experiment.

Launch Notepad (or any other text editor), and type the following code:

```
Module Module1
    Sub Main()
        Dim x As Double, res As Double
        x = 12.5
        res = Add(x, 46.5)
        System.Console.Write("The result is ")
        System.Console.WriteLine(res)
    End Sub

    Function Add(ByVal n1 As Double, ByVal n2 As Double) As Double
        Add = n1 + n2
    End Function
End Module
```

Even though the syntax is different from Visual Basic 6, it should be clear what this program does. The only new statement is the call to the Write and WriteLine methods of the System.Console object, which send their argument to the console window. (The WriteLine method also appends a newline character.) Save this source file with the name Test.vb: the name of the file isn't important, but its extension is; all Visual Basic source files should have the .vb extension.

Next open a command window and move to the directory in which you saved the Test.vb file, and then run the VBC compiler and pass it the Test.vb file. The vbc.exe file is located in this directory:

```
C:\WindowsDir\Microsoft.NET\Framework\vx.y.zzzz
```

where *WindowsDir* is the main Windows directory and *x.y.zzzz* is the version of the runtime in use. For example, on my system this is the command I have to type:

```
C:\WINNT\Microsoft.NET\Framework\v1.0.2914\vbc Test.vb
```

Note Instead of typing the preceding command each time you run the Visual Basic compiler, you can open the command window by invoking the Visual Studio .NET Command Prompt command in the Visual Studio .NET Tools submenu under the main Visual Studio .NET menu that you reach from the Start button. Or you can add the directory in which the compiler and other .NET tools are located to the system path. The .NET installation procedure creates the corvars.bat batch file that performs this action, so you just have to run it. This file is stored at the following path:

```
C:\Program Files\Microsoft Visual Studio
.NET\FrameworkSDK\Bin\corvars.bat
```

but the actual path depends on what path you selected at installation time. You might want to copy the corvars.bat file to a directory on the system path (such as Windows' main directory) so that you can run it by simply typing its name at the command prompt and pressing Enter. Once the corvars.bat program has updated the PATH environment variable, you can launch any .NET tool from the command prompt by just typing its name.

Because the value of all environment variables is lost when you close the command window, you must run the corvars.bat program each time that you open a new command window. Or you can change the value of the PATH variable from the Windows' System Properties window. (In Windows 2000, you can reach this dialog box by right-clicking the My Computer icon and clicking Properties on the shortcut menu.)

The preceding VBC command creates an executable file named Test.exe, which you can run from the command prompt. If everything goes well, you see the result in the console window and the prompt appears again:

```
The result is 59
```

Congratulations! You have just created your first Visual Basic .NET program.

More precisely, you have created a *console application*, which can take its input from the keyboard and can output its results in the console window. Needless to say, you'll write few (if any) commercial programs as console applications. In fact, Visual Basic .NET and C# can also deliver standard Windows EXE applications and DLL components. Creating an executable from multiple source files is also very simple because you simply need to pass all the filenames on the command line. (You can even use * and ? wildcards.)

```
vbc main.vb test.vb functions.vb
```

The name of the executable files is derived from the name of the first file passed on the command line (it would be main.exe in the preceding example), but you can select a different name using the /out option, as here:

```
vbc *.vb /out:myapp.exe
```

Unlike traditional compilers—but like all other .NET languages—the Visual Basic .NET compiler doesn't produce .obj files that you later assemble into an executable file by using a linker. The .NET Framework comes with a linker, the Assembly Linker (AL) utility, but you will rarely need it. One task for which you need this linker is to produce an assembly made up of modules authored with different programming languages. You'll learn more about the VBC compiler in Chapter 14.

The C# Compiler

This is a book about Visual Basic .NET, so I'm not going to discuss C# or any other language in any detail. However, I feel this is the right place to show how you can write and compile a C# console application similar to the one you've just created with Visual Basic. Start by creating the following code using Notepad, and save it in a file named Test.cs. (The .cs extension stands for *C sharp* source files.)

```
namespace CSharpDemo
{
    class Test
    {
        static void Main(string[] args)
        {
            double x;
            double res;
            x = 12.5;
            res = Add(x, 46.5);
            System.Console.Write("The result is ");
            System.Console.WriteLine(res);
        }

        static double Add(double n1, double n2)
        {
            return n1 + n2;
        }
    }
}
```

You can compile this source code using CSC.EXE, the C# compiler:

```
csc Test.cs
```

Not surprisingly, the resulting Test.exe executable file produces the same outcome as its Visual Basic counterpart. Here are a few matters to consider after this simple example:

- The structure of the Visual Basic and C# programs is similar, the only difference being the namespace block (which you can omit in Visual Basic because a default namespace is created) and the class block in lieu of the module block (C# doesn't support modules). I describe namespaces in Chapter 2.
- C# is a terse language, which uses curly braces for marking the beginning and end of all syntactical blocks. This contrasts with Visual Basic, which uses different keywords to close different blocks, such as End Module and End Sub and the less consistent Next to close a For block and Loop to close a Do block. All C# statements that aren't followed by a block terminate with a semicolon, without exception.
- Except for the syntactical differences between the two languages, both the Visual Basic and C# versions output their result using the Write and WriteLine methods of the System.Console class.

The last point is crucial: everything you learn about the BCL and the .NET Framework when you're working with one language can be applied and reused when you're working with any other .NET language. You should start separating in your mind what belongs to the language (syntax structures) and what belongs to the .NET Framework; you'll spend most of your effort and time consolidating your knowledge about the framework, not learning the language.

Many programmers claim that C# is the language of choice under .NET and that Visual Basic 6 developers should ignore Visual Basic .NET and switch to C# instead. I don't believe that this is the best way to go: learning the intricacies of the .NET Framework is a major task, and, as I said earlier, I believe you can do it in less time if you don't have to learn a completely new language at the same time.

C# does have a few advantages over Visual Basic .NET, in the following areas:

- Data types: C# supports unsigned integers (which aren't CLS-compliant, though).
- Pointers: you can address memory using C# pointers and can implement some algorithms more easily than under Visual Basic .NET.
- Operating overloading: you can redefine how the == equality operator works for your classes; this feature permits you to write more concise code but doesn't really add anything to the language's spectrum of possibilities.

- C# code might run slightly faster in a few circumstances; for example, the C# compiler generates code that reclaims the memory used by objects more aggressively than under Visual Basic. However, most of the time the difference in performance won't be greater than 5 percent, so it's hardly an argument for selecting one language over the other.

On the other hand, C# is less flexible in a few cases, which might become an issue if you've always written code using Visual Basic exclusively:

- Visual Basic developers can handle errors using either the old-style Visual Basic 6 approach (the On Error statement) or the newer Try...Catch...Finally block that works with exceptions; C# programmers can work only with the latter and can't enjoy the flexibility of the Resume and Resume Next statements.
- By default, Visual Basic .NET doesn't enforce strict type checking, so you can assign a value to a variable of a different type without any cast operation, which is mandatory in C#. Unless you enforce type checking with the new Option Strict statement, late-bound method calls are a breeze in Visual Basic. (By comparison, they always require several statements in C#.) In this book, I suggest that you change the default mode so that strict type checking is enabled, but it's good to know that you have a choice.
- Visual Basic .NET supports optional arguments in procedures, whereas C# does not and requires that you provide overloaded variations of the same method. (I cover overloading in Chapter 4.)
- A few other programming tasks are easier in Visual Basic .NET than in C#—for example, event declarations. In addition, Visual Basic .NET is somewhat more flexible at working with arrays, which can be resized without losing their contents (if you use the ReDim-Preserve statement).
- In the first Visual Studio .NET release, support for IntelliSense under Visual Basic is better than under C#. The list of all the compilation errors and available methods is always up-to-date under Visual Basic, whereas you have to rebuild a C# project to update the task list.

The purpose of this list of differences isn't to convince you that one language is better than the other. On the contrary, I want to emphasize that most of the time the few advantages of one language over the other shouldn't be a factor in the decision about which language to adopt. Again, just choose the language that makes you more productive, and let's hope that .NET finally puts an end to the silly language wars that have flamed among programmers in recent decades.

Microsoft Intermediate Language (MSIL)

I haven't yet described one of the most important (and controversial) features of the .NET architecture. Unlike traditional programming languages, .NET compilers don't produce *native code* that can be directly fed to and executed by the CPU. Instead, they produce the so-called Microsoft Intermediate Language (MSIL or just IL) code, which is a sort of machine language for a virtual processor that doesn't correspond to any commercial CPU available today. While the IL code is lower level than most modern programming languages, it's higher level than pure Intel assembly language. IL is a stack-oriented language that doesn't directly address CPU registers and is aware of high-level concepts such as exceptions and object creation.

Disassembling a .NET Executable

Looking at the IL code is quite simple because the .NET Framework gives you a tool named ILDASM (IL Disassembler), which can display the IL code stored inside any executable produced by a .NET compiler. This utility can run both as a command-line program and as a standard Windows application with its own user interface. For now, let's use it as a command-line utility to disassemble the Test.exe file we created in the preceding section:

```
Ildasm Test.exe /Out=Test.il
```

(This command assumes that Ildasm.exe is on the system path, which is the case if you run the corvars.bat program, as suggested in a previous note.) This is the abridged content of the Test.il file produced by the disassembler:

```
.assembly extern mscorlib
{
  .publickeytoken = (B7 7A 5C 56 19 34 E0 89 )   // .z\V.4..
  .ver 1:0:2411:0
}
.assembly extern Microsoft.VisualBasic
{
  .publickeytoken = (B0 3F 5F 7F 11 D5 0A 3A )   // .?_....:
  .ver 7:0:0:0
}
```

(continued)

```
.assembly Test
{
  .hash algorithm 0x00008004
  .ver 0:0:0:0
}
.module Test.exe
// MVID: {04008867-1531-4A47-B05E-F4E1C9245472}
.imagebase 0x00400000
.subsystem 0x00000003
.file alignment 512
.corflags 0x00000001
// Image base: 0x03090000
.class private auto ansi sealed Module1
       extends [mscorlib]System.Object
{
  .custom instance void [Microsoft.VisualBasic]Microsoft.VisualBasic.Globals/
    StandardModuleAttribute::.ctor() = ( 01 00 00 00 )
  .method public static void  Main() cil managed
  {
    .entrypoint
    .custom instance void [mscorlib]System.STAThreadAttribute::.ctor()
      = ( 01 00 00 00 )
    // Code size       43 (0x2b)
    .maxstack  2
    .locals init (float64 V_0,
                  float64 V_1)
    IL_0000:  ldc.r8     12.5
    IL_0009:  stloc.1
    IL_000a:  ldloc.1
    IL_000b:  ldc.r8     46.5
    IL_0014:  call       float64 Module1::Add(float64,
                                              float64)
    IL_0019:  stloc.0
    IL_001a:  ldstr      "The result is "
    IL_001f:  call       void [mscorlib]System.Console::Write(string)
    IL_0024:  ldloc.0
    IL_0025:  call       void [mscorlib]System.Console::WriteLine(float64)
    IL_002a:  ret
  } // end of method Module1::Main

  .method public static float64  Add(float64 n1,
                                     float64 n2) cil managed
  {
    // Code size       6 (0x6)
    .maxstack  2
    .locals init (float64 V_0)
    IL_0000:  ldarg.0
    IL_0001:  ldarg.1
```

```
    IL_0002:  add
    IL_0003:  stloc.0
    IL_0004:  ldloc.0
    IL_0005:  ret
  } // end of method Module1::Add

} // end of class Module1
```

I won't comment on each line of this IL listing, but I just want to draw your attention to a few important details:

- The .assembly extern statements declare the external DLLs that this program is going to use. mscorlib is the main .NET component, in which the main types are defined. Microsoft.VisualBasic is the component that provides support for most Visual Basic statements.
- The .method public static void Main() cil managed statement marks the beginning of the IL code produced by the Sub Main procedure in the original Visual Basic code. IL has retained the name of this and the Add procedures, so these names are visible to whoever disassembles your code. In general, an IL disassembly is much more descriptive than the code that you get by running a traditional disassembler on a standard Windows executable.
- The IL sees floating-point numbers and strings as native types. The ldc.r8 statement loads a Double value onto the stack, and the ldstr statement loads a string onto the stack. This is another example of the higher-level nature of the IL when compared with native assembly code.

  Calls to methods—both to internal methods such as Add and to external methods such as System.Console::Write—store the method name because the address of those methods is evaluated at run time.

The IL Assembler

You can consider IL the true native language of the .NET architecture because every piece of source code written in any .NET language is ultimately translated into IL. The .NET Framework comes with an IL assembler named ILASM, which compiles IL source code into an executable EXE or DLL file. To see this tool in action, use Notepad to change the following statement in the IL code

```
IL_001a:  ldstr      "The result is "
```

into the following line:

```
IL_001a:  ldstr      "12.5 + 46.5 = "
```

Next save the file as Test2.il and run the following command (which, again, assumes that you run corvars.bat to include all main .NET directories in the system path):

```
Ilasm Test2.il
```

This command produces the Test2.exe executable, which you can run to see the new result in the console window:

```
12.5 + 46.5 = 59
```

The ability of ILDASM to generate IL listings that you can feed directly to ILASM is known as *round-trip compilation*. Unfortunately, a developer has no simple way to protect details of her application because anyone can disassemble her code and read class and method names as well as the values of strings and other important pieces of information. Thanks to round-trip code generation, it is possible—in theory at least—to decipher what an application does, which might be a serious issue for some applications. Here are a few considerations that should lessen your worry:

- Most .NET applications are meant to run on the server so that no casual user can disassemble them and study their IL code. This protection should prevent hackers' attacks that take advantage of weak points they might discover by looking at the source code.
- Most real-world applications are so complex that having the IL code doesn't really help in reverse-engineering them.
- Microsoft is working on a product named Obfuscator, which is able to scramble the IL code produced by ILDASM and hide the names of several program entities so that the job of reverse-engineering is even more complex.

Anyway, it can't be denied that decompiling a .NET application is a relatively easy task—at least, it's much easier than decompiling applications in the pre-.NET world—so you should keep this detail in mind when building your applications. For example, you might decide to embed sensitive portions of your application in a COM component created using a traditional compiler such as Visual Basic 6 or Visual C++. Routines that have to do with security and authentication or that implement proprietary algorithms might qualify for such treatment.

The Just-in-Time (JIT) Compiler

No currently available CPU can run IL code, so your next question probably is, "When and how is the IL code converted to native code and executed?" I can answer this question by explaining what happens when a .NET application starts its execution.

1. The first thing that all .NET executables do once launched is load the MSCorEE.dll file that's the actual .NET runtime and then call the _CorMainExe function that this DLL exposes.
2. The code in _CorMainExe looks into the metadata stored inside the executable file to retrieve the address of the application's entry point (most often, the Sub Main procedure).
3. The IL code in the entry point procedure is handed to the Just-in-Time (JIT) compiler, which is located in the .NET runtime, converted to native code, and then executed.
4. As the main procedure invokes other methods, the .NET runtime uses the JIT compiler to transform the IL code in those methods into native code and then executes the native code. This on-the-fly compilation is done only once per method in the application's lifetime because the native code is kept in memory and reused when that specific method is called again.

Here are a couple of things you can deduce from the preceding sketchy description:

- Even if there's an increase in overhead caused by the compilation of each method, .NET applications run as fast as native code. Don't confuse the JIT compiler with traditional interpreters, such as those provided with early versions of Java.
- The application is never compiled all at once, so the start-up time is usually negligible even for large applications. Only applications that make many method calls as soon as they run might suffer from a perceivable increase in overhead. (This is the case with large Windows Forms programs.)

An interesting consequence of the JIT compilation approach is that a .NET compiler doesn't need to adopt aggressive and time-consuming low-level optimization techniques—such as registry allocations—and can deliver an executable faster than a traditional compiler, also because no link step is needed. A faster compilation step means that you'll spend less time watching the monitor and waiting for the compiler to finish.

To be honest, however, Visual Basic developers have lost an important feature in the transition from Visual Basic 6 to .NET: interpreted p-code. You can't run or debug an application before you compile it to IL and then JIT-compile it to native code. This "innovation" makes Visual Basic more similar to other programming languages and is going to disappoint many long-time

Visual Basic developers. On the plus side, debugging capabilities in Visual Studio .NET are much better than those in the Visual Basic 6 debugger, and you don't have to worry about minor differences between the p-code and native code.

> **Note** Like all Visual Basic 5 and 6 developers, I used to do most of my developing and debugging inside the IDE, that is, I ran p-code instead of native code. In most cases, I can compile to native code as the last step before delivering the final executable. However, in at least a couple of large projects the native code version raised too many weird and unexplainable errors; in both cases, I couldn't afford the extra time required for additional debugging and decided to deliver the p-code version.
>
> In those specific cases, the p-code version ran adequately fast and took far less memory than the native code version, so it wasn't a real problem. But the point I'm making is that you can't simply test a large Visual Basic 6 project inside the IDE and assume it will work flawlessly when compiled. From this perspective, debugging the *real* compiled application isn't a bad idea after all, even if it means slowing down the test phase a little.

Performance Myths

Many developers are worried about the quality of the code produced by the JIT compiler and assume that it will run slower than the code produced by a traditional optimizing compiler. I was rather skeptical about the JIT compiler myself until I made some benchmark studies and examined the .NET internals more carefully. So it's time to debunk a few popular beliefs.

Most optimization techniques adopted by traditional compilers are (or can be) still used by .NET compilers: for example, loop unrolling, constant folding, and common subexpression elimination. The IL code that the JIT compiler converts to native code has already been digested by the Visual Basic compiler or whatever .NET compiler you're using.

The JIT compiler has a deeper knowledge of the executing environment than a traditional compiler. For example, the JIT compiler can emit code for a specific CPU instead of generating code for a generic Intel x86 microprocessor, so it can take advantage of the Intel P4 or Itanium, AMD Athlon, and new processors as they are released. (Of course, the runtime has to be updated with a new version of the JIT compiler to leverage new processors' features.) Because all applications are compiled when they run, even old applications benefit from the adoption of a new CPU—a benefit you don't enjoy with traditional compiled applications.

There are other runtime-only optimization techniques that traditional compilers can't use. For example, the JIT compiler can optimize method calls even across different components because it can control the entire execution environment. Another example: method calls in the COM world work through indirection and use function pointers in the vtable; methods must work this way because the compiler doesn't know where the target object is loaded at run time. On the contrary, a JIT compiler knows where the target object is in memory and can get rid of those indirections by directly calling the method with a single and faster CALL assembly opcode.

A JIT compiler can make its optimizations more effective by monitoring the main application's behavior. For example, the JIT compiler might decide to perform *method inlining* (an optimization technique that gets rid of method calls by moving the code from the called procedure into the caller routine) only for the routines that are called more frequently. The JIT compiler's current capabilities in flow-control analysis are minimal, but they will surely improve in forthcoming versions.

JIT Compiler Versions

So far, I've described the JIT compiler that you will use more frequently on Windows systems. You should be aware that there are two more variants of this piece of software.

The .NET Framework comes with a Native Image Generator (NGEN) utility that can compile an entire application at installation time instead of at run time. This approach improves the load time of a .NET application or component, so it's especially useful with shared class and function libraries. Not surprisingly, Microsoft uses this utility when it installs some key portions of the framework itself, such as MSCorLib.dll. In Windows Explorer, such precompiled .NET Framework class library components are marked with the PreJit label, as you can see in Figure 1-2. Some white papers and technical documents refer to NGEN as the *pre-JIT compiler* because this was the name used until Beta 2 was released. (You can learn more about NGEN in Chapter 14.)

Before you decide to use NGEN to precompile all your applications, you should consider that this approach reduces start-up time for only a small number of applications, most notably those that make a lot of method calls when they start. In some cases, precompiling an application can even make performance worse because NGEN has no knowledge about the run-time environment, so it can't use such optimization techniques as adaptive method inlining and cross-assembly optimization. Finally, remember that you can't use NGEN to convert IL to native code and run the executable on another system, so you can't use this tool to make the reverse engineering of your .NET applications more difficult.

The other variant of the JIT compiler, known as the *economy compiler*, has been designed for Windows CE and devices with little RAM and relatively slow processors. This JIT compiler—also known as the *econo-JIT* compiler—translates each IL statement into the corresponding native code opcode (or group of opcodes), without attempting any optimization. Thus, the compilation process is more efficient than with an interpreter, but the resulting code isn't as good as the code produced by the standard JIT compiler. To make the best use of memory, the economy compiler supports *code pitching*, a feature that enables the .NET runtime to discard the native code for methods that haven't been invoked recently and to reuse that memory block for other pieces of code.

Cross-Platform Compatibility

Because the IL isn't tied to a specific CPU, .NET applications can run on any platform for which a common language runtime has been developed. In theory, you can compile an application on your Windows 2000 computer and run it on Windows CE; you can even run it on Linux or other versions of UNIX if the .NET runtime is ever ported to those platforms. This might sound like science fiction, but there are at least a couple of current open source projects that go in that direction as I am writing this chapter. Only time will tell whether they are successful.

In practice, however, only a fairly limited number of applications will ever benefit from cross-platform portability, and most of them will be command-line utilities. In this respect, the BCL is similar to Java's virtual machine. Even though it's technically possible to write Java source code that runs well on multiple platforms, in most cases it needs to be refined (and thoroughly debugged) for each specific platform. This problem is common to all programming tools—languages, libraries, and so on—that work across different platforms: they can target only the functionality that all the platforms have in common. For that reason, the resulting applications can't take advantage of the most advanced features of each specific platform.

If cross-platform portability isn't one of the goals of the .NET project—at least, not an immediate one—why did Microsoft decide to work with IL instead of native code? The answer is code security and verification. But before discussing these concepts, I need to explain in greater detail what an assembly is.

Working with Assemblies

The .NET Framework supports the creation of several kinds of applications:

- **Windows console applications** Command-line utilities and tools
- **Windows Forms** Standard Windows GUI applications
- **Windows Services** Applications controlled by the Windows Control Manager
- **Components** Reusable code conceptually similar to COM components
- **Web Forms** Server-side Web applications with user interface
- **XML Web services** Server-side Web applications that can be queried programmatically

Regardless of its type, a .NET application is deployed in the form of one assembly. You can also decide to split an application into multiple assemblies, for example, if you want to reuse code in other applications more easily.

As I have mentioned before, an assembly can include one or more executable files, each of which is individually known as a managed module. A *managed module* contains both IL code and metadata that describes both the types that the module exposes and the types that the module references.

Single-File and Multiple-File Assemblies

Most .NET compilers, including the Visual Basic and the C# compilers, transform one or more source files into a single-module assembly:

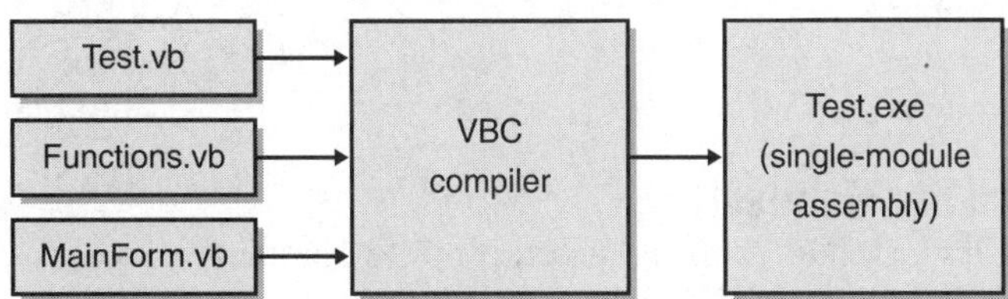

If the assembly contains managed modules written in different languages or if the assembly contains nonexecutable files, such as .html, .doc, .gif, or .jpg files, you must create a multifile assembly by using a tool named Assembly

Linker (AL.EXE). In this case, you must use the /target:module option to inform the VBC compiler that it must output a managed module that will be later passed to the AL utility:

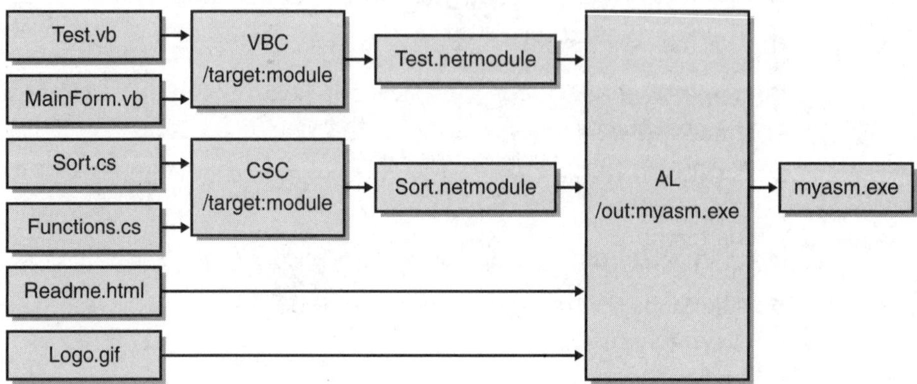

In the case depicted in the preceding diagram, the resulting assembly consists of five files: Myasm.exe, Test.netmodule, Sort.netmodule, Readme.html, and Logo.gif. When you assemble resource files, you can decide whether the resource file is included in the output file (using the /embed AL option) or just referenced by the assembly (using the /linkres AL option).

> **Note** At the present time, you can't create a multifile assembly from inside Visual Studio .NET or by using other visual tools, so you're forced to use AL from the command line to link multiple modules in one assembly.

Metadata and the Manifest

The metadata included in each managed module completely describes each type defined in the module: name, public members, and the signature of each distinct method, down to the type of its private variables. Metadata also records information about every type that this module uses, including the name of the assembly that contains that type.

In short, you can think of metadata as a superset of type libraries used under COM, with an important difference: you can't separate IL from its metadata. (By comparison, you can create stand-alone type libraries.) While you can do COM programming without using a type library, you can't invoke code inside a .NET assembly if you can't access its metadata (and therefore the assembly file itself because the metadata is always stored inside the assembly's modules).

The most important use of metadata is in ensuring that methods and fields are accessed in a correct way: you must pass the correct number of arguments of the right type and assign the return value to a variable of the proper type. When referencing a type in another assembly, the metadata makes certain that the correct version of the assembly is used. Remember that a given system can host multiple versions of the same assembly.

Another good thing about metadata is that it makes a managed module self-describing. By looking at metadata, BCL knows exactly what an assembly needs to run (such as a specific version of the .NET runtime), which external assemblies it references, and so on. No additional information is to be stored outside the assembly—for example, in the system Registry—and you can install the assembly by making a simple XCOPY of its files in a directory on the hard disk. (As you already know, this simplified scenario doesn't account for shared assemblies, which also require registration in the GAC.)

More generally, the entire .NET architecture is based on metadata. For example, the .NET memory manager uses metadata to calculate how much memory must be allocated when a .NET object is created. Metadata is also used when your code is serializing the state of an object to a file or a database field and also when your code is remoting an object (which occurs when the runtime serializes an object and sends its state to another workstation, where a perfect copy of the object can be re-created). I explain serialization in Chapter 11. IntelliSense in Visual Studio also exploits metadata to list members of a given type, as does the Object Browser tool to display all the types contained in an assembly and their members. The action of reading metadata to retrieve information about types in an assembly is known as *reflection* (which I cover in Chapter 15).

The file you specify with the /out option of AL—or the only executable file that you have when you create single-file assemblies with the VBC or CSC compiler—is special in that it contains the assembly's manifest. The *manifest* is a special metadata section that lists the names of all the files that make up the assembly and of all the types that the assembly exposes to the outside.

When a .NET application instantiates or uses a type from an assembly, the runtime loads the module that contains the manifest and determines which module contains the IL code for that specific type. If the requested type is in another module, the runtime loads it, compiles the IL code of the method being invoked (or the constructor method if the type is being instantiated), and finally runs it. Of course, execution is faster if the requested type is hosted in the module that contains the manifest (because the runtime doesn't need to load a different module), so you should arrange a multimodule assembly so that all the types used more frequently are defined in the module that contains the manifest.

Code Verification

Metadata and JIT compilation make it possible to achieve one of the most important features of the .NET platform: code security and verification. As you'll see in a moment, these features have far-reaching consequences.

Verification is the process through which the runtime checks that each method is called with the correct number and type of arguments, that all pointers point to the correct data type, and that in general the application doesn't read or modify memory that doesn't belong to it. For example, verification ensures that data and code aren't misused and that the application won't be stopped because of fatal errors caused by pointers that contain bogus values. An incorrect pointer is one of the most frequent causes for GPF errors in C/C++ applications (and even in Visual Basic 6 applications if you play low-level tricks with API functions).

Verification guarantees that .NET applications are inherently more robust than non-.NET ones, an important factor that will decrease the total cost of software production, debugging, and support. But verification has another important benefit: because the runtime can guarantee that applications won't read or modify memory they don't own, you can run multiple applications inside the same address space (that is, the same Win32 process).

As you might know already, Windows processes offer code isolation at the expense of memory and other resources. Windows NT and 2000 have a good reputation for robustness because their processes are better isolated than, say, under Windows 95 or Windows 98, which in turn are much more robust than old 16-bit Windows 3.1, whose processes share the same address space. If each process is completely isolated, it can crash without affecting any other process or the operating system as a whole.

In spite of the process isolation provided by Windows, a clever programmer working in the unmanaged world can read and modify memory belonging to another application and can even write code that runs in the context of the other application (for example, by using a technique known as *DLL injection*). This security breach opens up the door to malicious pieces of code, such as viruses and Trojan horses.

By comparison, .NET applications enjoy far more robust isolation than traditional Windows programs because there's absolutely no way for managed code to affect another program, no matter how hard it tries. A system administrator can install a managed application and be reasonably sure that it won't harm the system. (More follows on this topic in the next section.)

It should be noted that the verification process occurs during the JIT compilation step but isn't mandatory, and a system administrator can turn it off for a specific application, for example, to speed up its start-up phase. The .NET Framework SDK comes with a tool named PEVerify.exe, which allows a system administrator to verify whether a program passes the verification test and can be considered safe. Developers should run this utility to ensure that they didn't accidentally produce unsafe code, for example, by calling a function in an old-style DLL, such as a Windows API function.

AppDomains

While traditional Windows applications can be isolated by being loaded in separate address spaces (and therefore in different processes), isolation under .NET doesn't rely on virtual memory features offered by the CPU. This means that multiple .NET applications can run inside the same Windows process without compromising their robustness.

Because application and process aren't synonyms in the .NET world, a new concept has been coined: *Application Domain*, or *AppDomain*. An AppDomain is a logical managed application that runs inside a physical Windows process. (See Figure 1-3.) A Windows process can host multiple AppDomains, which can be multiple copies of the same application or different applications. In general, you load multiple AppDomains in the same physical process only if they run related applications.

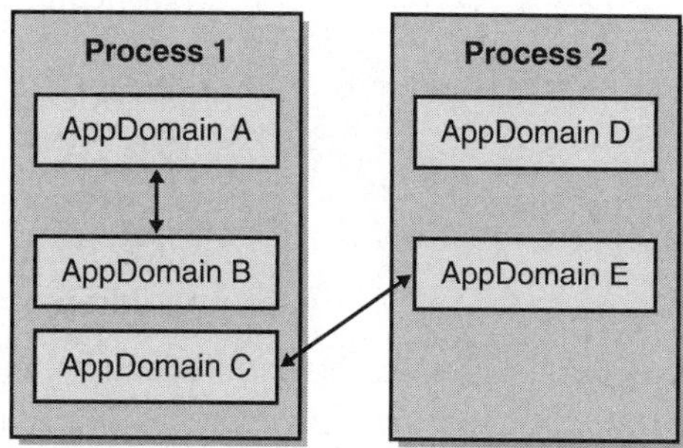

Figure 1-3. AppDomains are logical applications running in the same physical Windows process.

AppDomains have at least two major advantages:

- They use less memory and fewer resources than Windows processes, so they're launched and destroyed faster, and scale better.
- Communication between AppDomains hosted in the same process is much faster than between traditional Windows programs because the AppDomains share the same address space and can simply call into one another (after verifying the method signature and checking that the caller has the right to call the method). For example, communication between AppDomain A and AppDomain B in Figure 1-3 is much faster than communication between AppDomain C and AppDomain E.

Server-side applications are the perfect scenario for using multiple AppDomains in the same physical processes. For example, you might have distinct but related ASP.NET applications that can communicate without much overhead yet are completely isolated from one another. You don't have to trade performance for robustness, as you do when you select Medium (pooled) or High (isolated) application protection levels for ASP applications under Internet Information Services 5.

AppDomains are especially convenient when you load multiple copies of an assembly in a single physical Windows process. In this case, the code for the application is JIT-compiled and loaded only once—the first time the assembly is launched—so you save both start-up time and memory. (This optimization works only with assemblies marked as *domain neutral*.)

Security

Another great benefit of managed code is that it runs under the control of the common language runtime, which can therefore prevent applications from performing potentially dangerous actions, such as deleting a file and manipulating the Registry. Because security is built right into the .NET runtime, it's more flexible and granular than security enforced at the operating system or COM level, but at the same time it offers a more consistent, unified model that's also simpler to learn.

The key to .NET security is the permission object. When the common language runtime decides whether a piece of managed code can perform a given operation, it takes three different kinds of permissions into account:

- Code access permissions, which represent access or other operations that you perform on a protected resource. For example, PrintingPermission is the permission to access the printer, RegistryPermission is the permission to access the registry, and so on. Permission objects arbitrate access to environment variables, files, the user interface, the Windows event log, Active Directory functions, system services, OLE DB and SQL Server databases, and more.
- Identity permissions, which represent the identity of the running code and contain information such as the name of the assembly, the Web site and URL where the code was downloaded from, and the identity of the software publisher (which is authenticated using a digital signature).
- Role-based security permissions, which can be used to ascertain the identity of the user who is running the code.

I won't discuss security in detail in this book, but for now it should suffice to say that both the developer and the system administrator can use security to ensure that an application performs only legal operations.

A developer can use either declarative or imperative security in code to ensure that the program is used correctly. The main difference between these modes is that imperative security offers finer granularity in exchanges of larger amounts of code. For example, a program deleting a file might verify that the user who made the request is authorized to do so. Managed code can also check the credentials of the caller, so a .NET component can ensure that it's being called by an application that has the necessary permissions to perform a given action.

An administrator can decide precisely what an application can or can't do by adding specific items to configuration files. For example, an administrator can use identity permissions to prevent executables that were downloaded from Internet sites that don't belong to a list of trusted sites from accessing the file system or the Registry.

The .NET Framework Class Library

I've already explained that the .NET Framework class library is a collection of classes that managed applications use to access the operating system, the file system, databases, and any other resource. In this section, I'll briefly introduce the most interesting portions of the .NET class library.

To better organize the hundreds of classes in the library, the .NET Framework supports the concept of namespaces. Namespaces are similar to directories on disk: just as a directory can contain files and other directories, a namespace can contain classes and other (nested) namespaces. For example, all the classes that have to do with database programming are grouped in the System.Data namespace. The System namespace is arguably the most important namespace because all the basic types are defined there, including numeric, data, and string types.

I've summarized the most interesting namespaces in Table 1-1, sorted in alphabetical order. Note that a namespace can be split into more DLLs; in fact, the logical organization of the types in an assembly is distinct from its physical organization. For example, you can put types that are used less frequently into a separate DLL so that they aren't loaded if they aren't used.

Table 1-1 The Most Important Namespaces in the .NET Framework

Namespace	DLL Name	Sample Classes	Description
System	MSCorLib.dll	Double, String, Array, Exception, Math	The core .NET classes and all the basic data types
System.CodeDom	System.dll	CodeExpression, CodeNamespace	Types for programmatically creating code
System.Collections	MSCorLib.dll	ArrayList, Hashtable, SortedList, BitArray	Collectionlike data types
System.ComponentModel	System.dll	Component, PropertyDescriptor	Types for controlling components
System.ComponentModel.Design	System.dll and System.Design.dll	DesignerCollection, DesignerVerb	Types for implementing design-time features of components
System.Data	System.Data.dll	DataSet, DataTable, DataRow	Types for client-side processing of database data
System.Data.OleDb	System.Data.dll	OleDbConnection, OleDbCommand	Types for working with OLE DB databases
System.Data.SqlClient	System.Data.dll	SqlConnection, SqlCommand	Types for working with SQL Server databases
System.Diagnostics	MSCorLib.dll and System.dll	Debug, EventLog	Types for aiding testing and debugging
System.DirectoryServices	System.DirectoryServices.dll	DirectoryEntry, SearchResult	Types for working with Active Directories
System.Drawing	System.Drawing.dll	Brush, Pen, Font	Types for creating graphics in Windows Forms applications
System.Drawing.Drawing2D	System.Drawing.dll	HatchBrush, Matrix	Additional types for more sophisticated 2-D graphics
System.Drawing.Imaging	System.Drawing.dll	BitmapData, Metafile	Types for working with image files

Table 1-1 The Most Important Namespaces in the .NET Framework *(continued)*

Namespace	DLL Name	Sample Classes	Description
System.Drawing.Printing	System.Drawing.dll	PageSettings, PrintController	Types for outputting to a printer device
System.Drawing.Text	System.Drawing.dll	FontCollection, InstalledFontCollection	Types for enumerating and installing fonts
System.Globalization	MSCorLib.dll	CultureInfo, Calendar	Types for authoring multi-language applications
System.IO	MSCorLib.dll	Path, File, Stream, FileStream, StreamReader	Types that provide access to files' attributes and contents
System.Messaging	System.Messaging.dll	Message, MessageQueue	Types for working with Microsoft Message Queue Server (MSMQ)
System.Net	System.dll	HttpWebRequest, Dns, WebResponse	Types for sending HTTP Web requests
System.Net.Sockets	System.dll	Socket, UdpClient	Types for working with sockets
System.Reflection	MSCorLib.dll	Assembly, PropertyInfo, MethodInfo	Types for reflecting over existing assemblies and types
System.Reflection.Emit	MSCorLib.dll	AssemblyBuilder, MethodBuilder	Types for programmatically creating new assemblies
System.Resources	MSCorLib.dll	ResourceReader, ResourceWriter	Types for working with resource files
System.Runtime.InteropServices	MSCorLib.dll	Marshal, COMException	Types for working with unmanaged COM components
System.Runtime.Remoting	MSCorLib.dll	ObjHandle, SoapServices	Types for enabling remote execution

(continued)

Table 1-1 The Most Important Namespaces in the .NET Framework *(continued)*

Namespace	DLL Name	Sample Classes	Description
System.Runtime.Serialization.Formatters.Binary	MSCorLib.dll	BinaryFormatter	Type for serialization in binary format
System.Runtime.Serialization.Formatters.Soap	System.Runtime.Serialization.Formatters.Soap.dll	SoapFormatter	Type for serialization in SOAP format
System.Security	MSCorLib.dll	PermissionSet, CodeAccessPermission	Types for security support
System.Security.Cryptography	MSCorLib.dll	DES, RSA	Types for cryptographic services
System.Security.Permissions	MSCorLib.dll	FileIOPermission, RegistryPermission	Types for querying for security permissions
System.ServiceProcess	System.ServiceProcess.dll	ServiceController, ServiceBase	Types for creating and controlling Windows services
System.Text.RegularExpressions	System.dll	Regex, Match	Types for working with regular expressions
System.Threading	MSCorLib.dll and System.dll	Thread, Monitor, ThreadPool	Types for controlling multithreading capabilities
System.Timers	System.dll	Timer	Timer class for server-side applications
System.Web	System.Web.dll	HttpApplication, HttpCookie	Types for working with generic HTTP applications
System.Web.UI	System.Web.dll	Page, DataBinding	Basic types for working with ASP.NET applications
System.Web.UI.HtmlControls	System.Web.dll	HtmlButton, HtmlTable	ASP.NET controls that parallel old-style HTML controls

Table 1-1 The Most Important Namespaces in the .NET Framework *(continued)*

Namespace	DLL Name	Sample Classes	Description
System.Web.UI.WebControls	System.Web.dll	Button, CheckBox, Table	ASP.NET controls with rich user-interface capabilities
System.Web.Services	System.Web.Services.dll	WebService, WebMethodAttribute	Types for creating XML Web services
System.Web.Services.Protocols	System.Web.Services.dll	SoapHeader, SoapExtension	Types for low-level work with Web Services
System.Windows.Forms	System.Windows.Forms.dll	Form, TextBox, ListBox	Types for creating Windows Forms applications
System.Xml	System.Xml.dll	XmlDataDocument, XmlNode	Types for working with XML documents
System.Xml.Schema	System.Xml.dll	XmlSchema, XmlSchemaElement	Types for working with XML schemas
System.Xml.XPath	System.Xml.dll	XPathDocument, XPathExpression	Types for working with XML XPath queries
System.Xml.Xsl	System.Xml.dll	XslTransform, XslContent	Types for working with XSL transformations

You're already familiar with the goal of a few entries in Table 1-1—for example, System.Windows.Forms (for creating client-side Win32 applications), System.Web (for creating ASP.NET applications with a user interface), and System.Web.Services (for creating XML Web services). A glance at the other namespaces offers a quick way to learn about other intriguing features of the framework.

ADO.NET

System.Data and its nested namespaces include types for working with databases. The classes in these namespaces make up the portion of the .NET Framework known as ADO.NET (and called ADO+ in articles and papers based on early beta versions). Compared with "classic" ADO, ADO.NET is more focused on client-side data processing and doesn't offer support for server-side cursors such as keysets and dynamic cursors, at least not in its first version.

There are two basic flavors of ADO.NET, depending on whether you're connecting to a SQL Server database (version 7 or 2000) or an OLE DB source.

Unlike ADO, which attempts to promote independence from a specific database, ADO.NET recognizes that most developers work with a single database server and want to take advantage of all its features. ADO.NET is further subdivided into two namespaces, with the types in the System.Data.SqlClient namespace able to leverage specific SQL Server 2000 features, such as the ability to return XML text from a query. Even if you don't plan to take advantage of specific SQL Server features, you should use classes in this namespace if possible because they interact with SQL Server using more efficient communication channels than System.Data.OleDb classes. (The System.Data.OleDb classes use the standard OLE DB Provider for SQL Server and have to traverse more software layers to get to the data.)

GDI+

Windows programmers have used Graphics Device Interface (GDI) functions for years to create graphic shapes, bitmaps, metafiles, color palettes, and so on. Types in the System.Drawing namespace give you a way to access these functions using an object-oriented programming model, which simplifies graphic programming enormously and minimizes the risk of resource leaking (a serious problem with all graphic-intensive applications).

Typically, you'll use GDI+ classes in Windows Forms, but nothing prevents you from working with them in server-side ASP.NET applications. For example, you might create an ASP.NET application that creates a chart on the server and sends it to the client in an HTML page, or an XML Web service application that performs sophisticated graphic processing on bitmaps submitted in input. I cover GDI+ in Chapter 18.

P/Invoke and COM Interoperability

Even if Microsoft is hoping that the majority of developers will jump on the .NET bandwagon, they don't expect that the thousands of applications written in recent years should be suddenly just thrown away. More realistically, large applications will be ported to .NET gradually, for example, as developers write new components that interact with the existing code.

Another problem that developers have to face is that all the devices from third-party hardware manufacturers are provided as traditional or COM DLLs, so there must be a way to access them from managed code. This holds true also for the (relatively) few functions in Windows DLLs that haven't yet been encapsulated in .NET classes.

The .NET Framework gives you a bunch of classes and utilities that help you write code that interacts with the so-called *legacy applications*, written as traditional DLL or COM components. The portion of the runtime known as *P/Invoke* is in charge of calling functions embedded in traditional DLLs, including Windows DLLs (the P in P/Invoke stands for *Platform*). The portion of the runtime known as *COM Interoperability* is in charge of exchanging data with

COM components. COM Interoperability works in both directions: you can consume a COM component from a .NET application, but you can also expose a .NET component to a COM application, for example, an application authored with Visual Basic 6.

The .NET Framework SDK contains a few command-line utilities that let you take advantage of COM Interoperability, or you can use Visual Studio .NET to do all the work in a visual fashion. Most of the time, you can use a COM component from Visual Basic .NET by using the same code you'd use for a native .NET component. Similarly, you can use a .NET component from Visual Basic 6 as if it were a regular COM component because COM Interoperability works transparently for you behind the scenes. A few classes in the System.Runtime.InteropServices namespace can help you overcome the few problems that might arise.

.NET Remoting

In a nutshell, *remoting* is the managed code counterpart of Distributed COM (DCOM); it lets you access objects located on another machine. More precisely, remoting lets you access and code against objects located in a different AppDomain—whether the other AppDomain is running on the same or another computer.

.NET doesn't use COM, and communication with the other process or machine occurs through channels of a different nature, such as HTTP channels. The classes that help you manage remoting are located in the System.Runtime.Remoting namespace or in one of its nested namespaces. I don't cover remoting in this book.

Other Namespaces

While the bulk of managed classes are in the System namespace or one of the namespaces nested inside System, you might find yourself working with other classes that don't belong to this namespace, such as those listed in Table 1-2.

Classes in the Microsoft.Win32 namespace are specific to the Windows platform and will never be ported to other operating systems. These classes encapsulate Windows-specific objects, such as the Registry or system events. I cover a few of these classes in Chapter 19.

The Microsoft.VisualBasic namespace gathers classes that help you write Visual Basic .NET code with a syntax as close to Visual Basic 6 as possible. In most cases, classes in this namespace duplicate functionality offered by other classes in the .NET Framework, so you have a choice: you can use them to retain the good old Visual Basic flavor, or you can opt for the more generic classes in the System namespace. The former approach minimizes time spent in producing real-world .NET applications, while the latter one is preferable if you plan to learn other .NET languages, such as C#. In this book I'll use both approaches, starting with the classes in the Microsoft.VisualBasic namespace and then exploring in depth the more generic .NET classes, which are often more powerful and versatile.

I won't cover the EnvDTE namespace in this book, but you might want to have a look at it anyway, using the documentation that comes with Visual Studio .NET. The types and the interfaces in this namespace let you build Visual Studio macros and add-ins by using an object model that's similar to but much more powerful than the add-in object model provided with Visual Basic 6.

Table 1-2 Other .NET Namespaces

Namespace	DLL Name	Sample Classes	Description
Microsoft.Win32	MSCorLib.dll and System.dll	Registry, SystemEvents	Types to access the registry and control other OS features
Microsoft.VisualBasic	Microsoft. VisualBasic.dll	ControlChars, DateAndTime, FileSystem	Types to ease conversion of Visual Basic 6 applications to Visual Basic .NET
EnvDTE	envdte.dll	DTE, Addin, Debugger	Types to control Visual Studio .NET and create add-ins

Introduction to Visual Studio .NET

Microsoft has been promising for years that they would offer a single integrated development environment (IDE) for all their programming languages. Now this environment is finally available and comes with Visual Studio .NET. You can use Visual Studio .NET (or Visual Studio 7, if you prefer to think in terms of version numbers) to write Visual Basic and C# applications. Even more interesting, you can load tons of other file types and use the IDE as a resource editor, an image editor, an HTML browser, and so on.

Old and Renewed Tools

The Visual Studio .NET environment doesn't look like the Visual Basic 6 IDE, so odds are that you'll feel rather disoriented when you look at the new environment for the first time. Let's have a quick exploration of the tools you'll be using more often.

The Start Page

By default, at startup Visual Studio .NET shows its Start Page, an HTML page that lets you load one of your most recently used projects. (See Figure 1-4.) You can access areas of the Microsoft site and learn about updated tools, newsgroups, code downloads, and more by clicking on items in the leftmost column.

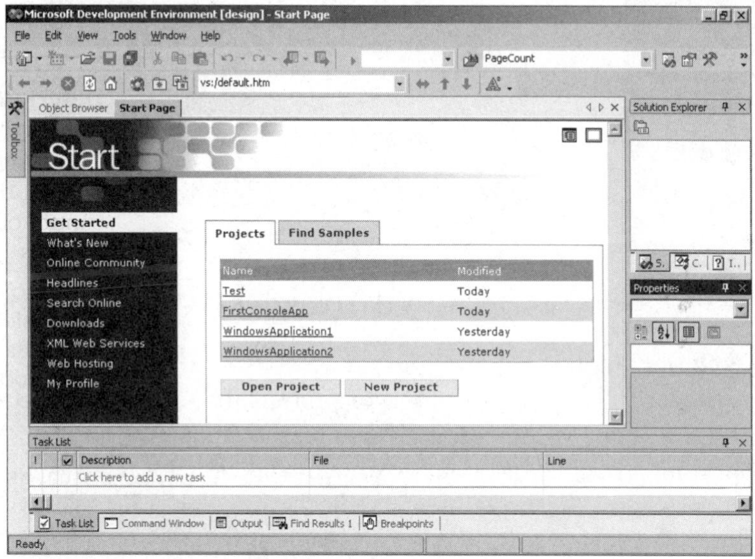

Figure 1-4. Visual Studio .NET Start Page.

The last item in this column, My Profile, lets you select a few important Visual Studio settings, as you can see in Figure 1-5. By using options on this page, you can have Visual Studio mimic behavior such as windows layout and keyboard settings of other environments, including Visual Basic 6 or Microsoft InterDev. I suggest that you attempt to become familiar with Visual Studio .NET "native" settings. It will surely take a while to abandon old habits, but this effort pays off in the long run, especially considering that you'll probably live with this new environment for years. On the other hand, you might want to preserve Visual Basic 6's settings if you continue to develop code in that language and you don't want to retrain your fingers as you switch among different environments.

Because most of the time you'll work on a single project over a long period of time, I suggest that you change the default action at startup so that Visual Studio automatically loads the most recently used solution.

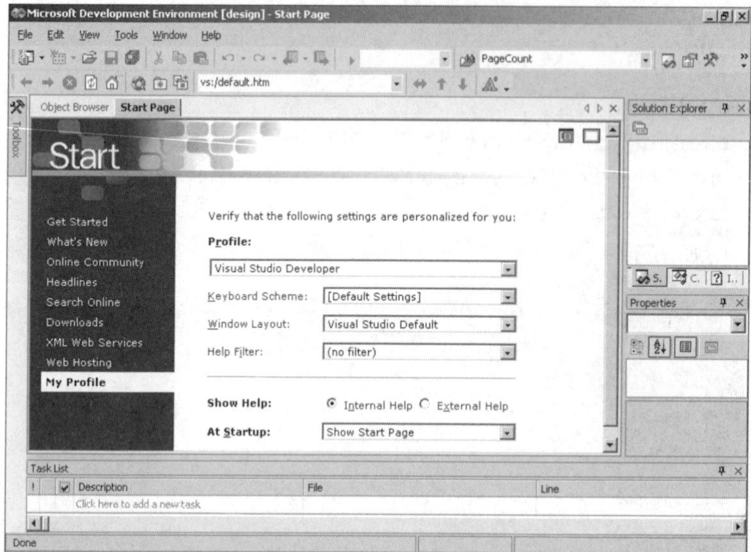

Figure 1-5. Setting a user profile from Visual Studio's Start Page.

The Solution Explorer

A Visual Studio solution is a group of projects that work together to create an application. They're conceptually similar to Visual Basic 6's project groups except that a Visual Studio solution can contain virtually any type of file, including HTML pages, XML documents and schemas, and XSLT files, bitmaps, cursors, icons, and resource and text files. Each solution corresponds to an .sln file on disk, which contains the names of the individual projects in the solution.

You create a new project by pointing to New on the File menu and clicking Project, and then selecting which type of project you want to create in the New Project dialog box. (See Figure 1-6.) Here's a list of supported project types:

- **Windows Application** Win32 applications that use the Windows Forms namespace
- **Class Library** One or more .NET components that you use from inside another application
- **Windows Control Library** One or more controls that can be used in a Windows Forms application
- **ASP.NET Web Application** A Web Form application

- **ASP.NET Web Service** An XML Web service application
- **Web Control Library** One or more controls that can be used in a Web Form application
- **Console Application** A command-line CUI (Character User Interface) Windows program
- **Windows Service** A Windows service application that can run before any user logs in to the computer

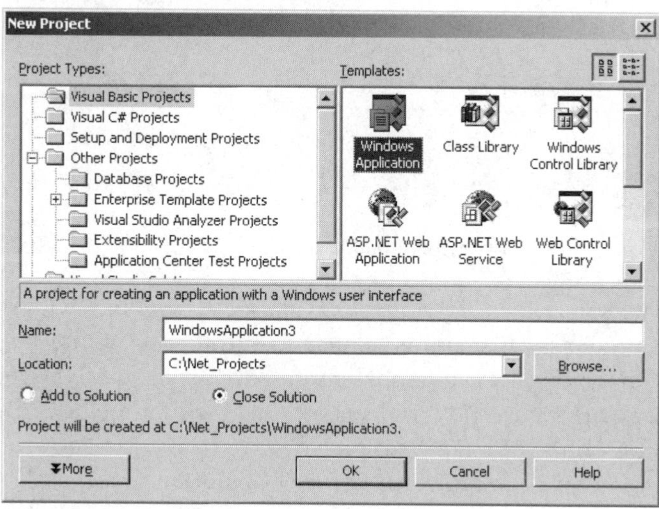

Figure 1-6. The Add New Project dialog box.

A key difference from Visual Basic 6 is that Visual Studio actually creates all the files in the project when you click the OK button and stores them in a directory named after the project, located under the directory you specify in the Location box. (For example, the options visible in Figure 1-6 would create a new project in the C:\NET_Projects\WindowsApplication3 directory.) Visual Basic projects are stored in .vbproj files, in XML syntax so that you can easily load and parse them should you need to do so.

You can add a new file to a project by clicking Add New Item on the File menu. (See Figure 1-7.) You can also add an existing file by clicking Add Existing Item on the File menu; if the file isn't in the project's main directory, it is copied there before being added to the project.

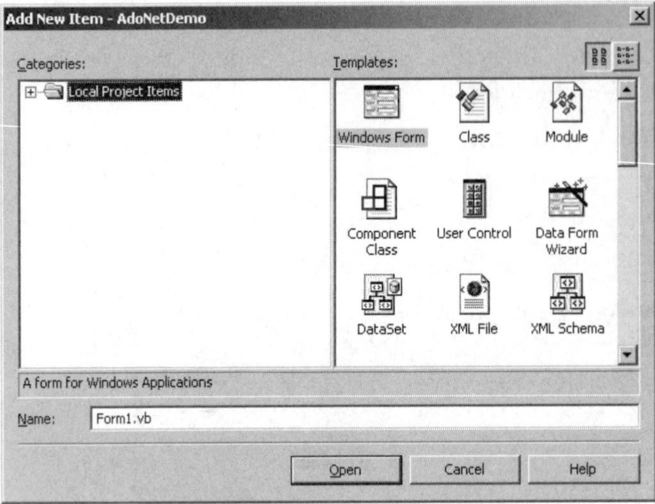

Figure 1-7. The Add New Item dialog box.

The Solution Explorer is the main tool for working with solutions and individual projects. This tool is similar to the Project window in Visual Basic 6 except that it displays additional information, such as all the references to external components used by a given project. (See Figure 1-8.) By clicking on the third icon on the Solution Explorer's toolbar, you can show or hide all the secondary files in each individual project, including executable or resource files. You can learn more about each file—and even rename it—by highlighting it in the Solution Explorer and then switching to the Properties window.

You can add a reference to a given project by right-clicking on the References folder. (This command corresponds to Add Reference on the Project menu.) The Add Reference dialog box (shown in Figure 1-9) lets you select among all installed .NET and COM components, as well as other projects under development in the IDE. Note that you select .NET components by the name of the DLL that contains them, which is information that you can derive from .NET SDK documentation. (For the majority of frequently used types, you can also use Table 1-1.) On the other hand, you select COM components by their ProgID, as you did under Visual Basic 6.

Figure 1-8. The Solution Explorer window.

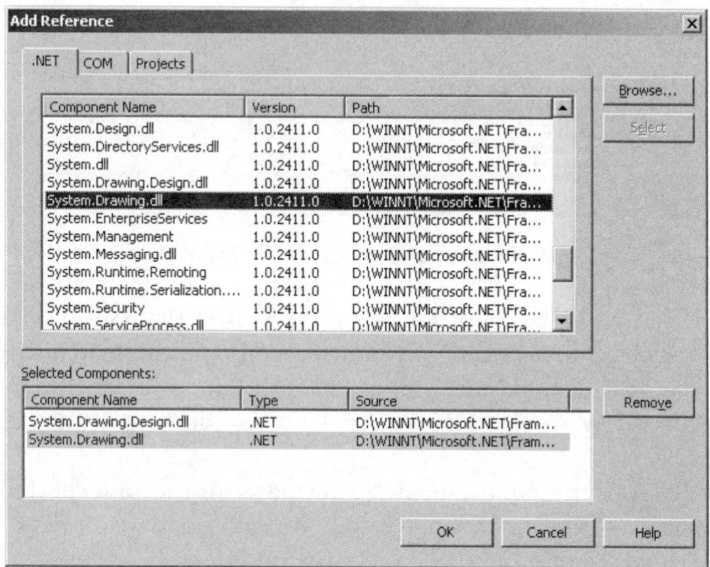

Figure 1-9. The Add Reference dialog box.

The Object Browser and the Class View Window

The Object Browser is your best friend when you start your explorations of .NET components. Given the hierarchical nature of the .NET Framework, the new Object Browser displays more information than its Visual Basic 6 version—for example, the base class from which a type derives and all the interfaces that a type implements. (See Figure 1-10.)

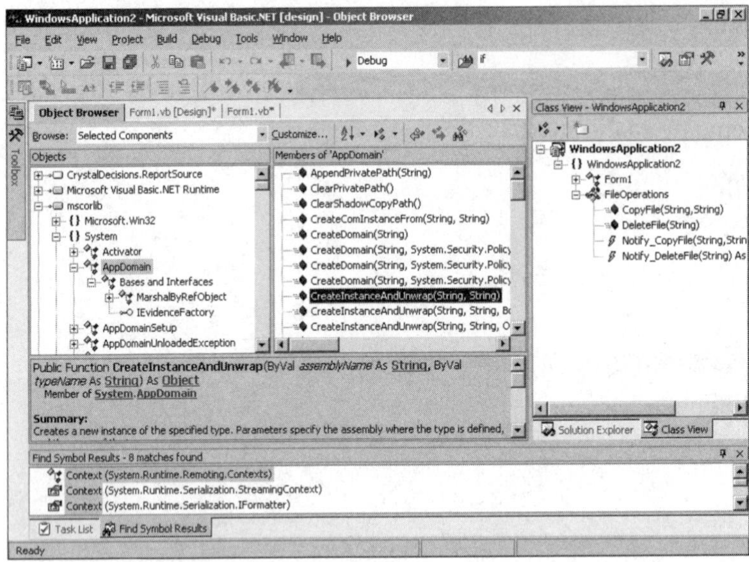

Figure 1-10. The Object Browser and the Class View window.

You can click the Find button on the Object Browser toolbar to search for all the objects that contain a character string; all the matching objects and methods appear in the Find Symbol Results window, near the bottom of the IDE main window. You can double-click on each item to display it in the class hierarchy.

By default, the Object Browser displays all the objects defined in the components referenced by any of the currently loaded projects; it also displays the types defined in the projects being edited. However, you can click the Customize button on the Object Browser toolbar to include additional .NET and COM components not referenced by any project. (You select these components using the Component Selector dialog box, which is similar to the one shown in Figure 1-9 except that it doesn't have a Projects tab.)

The Class View window—also visible in Figure 1-10—is a sort of special object browser that displays only the types in the current solution by means of a hierarchical tree that goes down to individual fields and methods. You can use the Class View window to quickly jump to a field or routine definition and arrange members by their name, type, or access (Private, Public, Friend, and so on). You can even create a new folder and drag to it the types and methods you browse more frequently so that you can jump to them in a snap without having to look for them among a collection of hundreds of items.

C# developers can use commands in the Class View's shortcut menu to quickly create new methods and properties, but this functionality hasn't been implemented in this Visual Basic .NET release.

The Code Editor

You'll probably spend more time in the code editor than in any other Visual Studio window or tool, so you should learn as much as you can about its features and capabilities.

For starters, the code window has all the features of the Visual Basic 6 code editor, including color syntax highlighting, IntelliSense, and drag-and-drop editing. Unless you opted for the Visual Basic 6 profile on the Start Page, most keyboard shortcuts are different, however. Here's a partial list of features you didn't have under Visual Basic 6:

- **Box mode selection** You can select a rectangular portion of code by pressing the Alt key while you drag the mouse or press an arrow key.
- **Smart indenting** The editor automatically sets the most logical indents for code blocks such as For loops and Select Case statements.
- **Automatic insertion of end constructs** Visual Basic 6 adds an End Sub statement when you type a Sub statement and does the same also with Function and Property procedures. The new editor extends this functionality to If, Do, Select Case, Class, and Module blocks.
- **Code navigation** You can navigate through your code as if you were using a browser, by using the buttons on the standard toolbar, or by using the Ctrl+Minus and Ctrl+Shift+Minus keyboard commands.
- **Word wrapping** You can activate this feature when browsing a piece of code with very long lines. (Point to Advanced on the Edit

menu and select Word Wrap or press Ctrl+R twice to toggle this feature on and off.)

- **Line numbers** This feature is very handy when you're locating errors or discussing a code snippet with other developers. Clicking Go To on the Edit menu lets you jump to a line given its number. (This command works even if line numbers aren't visible.)
- **Improved Find and Replace** You can now specify what you're looking for by using wildcards or regular expressions; in addition, you can use the Mark All button to create bookmarks pointing to each found occurrence so that you can later visit all of them with the Next Bookmark command.
- **Incremental search** You don't need to bring up the Find dialog box for simple searches: just press Ctrl+I and start typing what you're looking for, and the caret will move to the first word that starts with the characters you've typed. When you type Ctrl+I again, the caret moves to the next occurrence. Use the Ctrl+Shift+I shortcut to move backward in your search.
- **Outlining** You can collapse a routine or an entire class by clicking on the minus symbol to the left of its first statement. (See the BubbleSort procedure in Figure 1-11.) You can control this feature with the commands in the Outlining submenu of the Edit menu.
- **User-defined collapsible regions** You can enclose a piece of code inside #Region and #End Region statements to make it collapsible. (Figure 1-11 shows one such region.)
- **Clipboard Ring** The editor remembers the 15 pieces of text copied in the Clipboard most recently, and you can paste any one of them in a cyclic fashion by clicking Cycle Clipboard Ring on the Edit menu (or the Ctrl+Shift+V keyboard shortcut). Or you can just drag items from the Clipboard Ring section in the Toolbox.
- **Other editing commands** You can convert a string to uppercase or lowercase, for example, and you can show or hide white spaces. (Reach these features from the Advanced submenu of the Edit menu.)

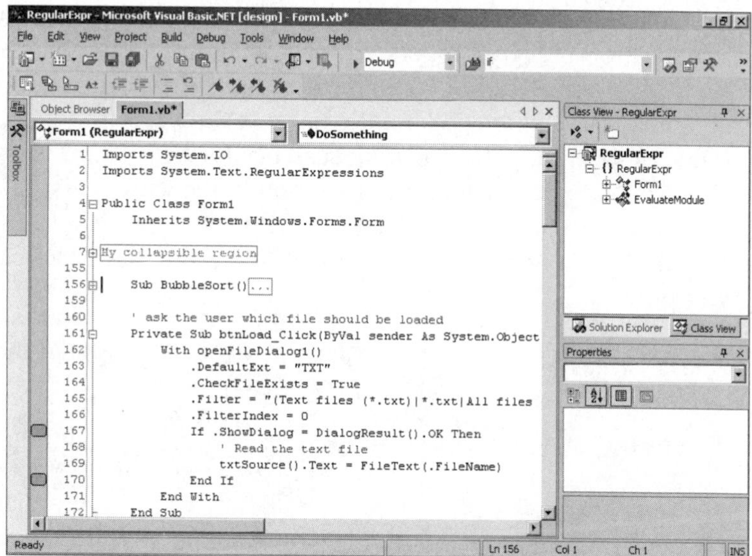

Figure 1-11. The code editor with line numbers enabled; note that line numbers account for collapsed regions of code.

The preceding descriptions should suffice to let you experiment with these new features, but user-defined collapsible regions might require an additional explanation. To see how this feature works, place the caret anywhere in the code editor, type this statement, and press Enter:

```
#Region "My collapsible region"
```

The code editor creates the #End Region statement for you:

```
#Region "My collapsible region"

#End Region
```

If you have already written the portion of code that you want to make collapsible, you just need the code in question inside the #Region block.

Another feature you might want to learn more about is regular expression searching, which you activate from inside the Find or Replace dialog box. For example, the :q regular expression searches all the quoted strings in code, :z searches for integer numbers, :n for floating point numbers, and :i for Visual Basic identifiers. You can combine these and other regular expressions for more complex searches—for example, :i = :q searches for string assignments and (Dim|Private|Public) :i As String searches for declaration of String variables.

You can get a partial list of supported regular expressions by clicking the button to the right of the Find What field. (See Figure 1-12.) One of the commands in this menu takes you to the help page that describes this feature in greater detail.

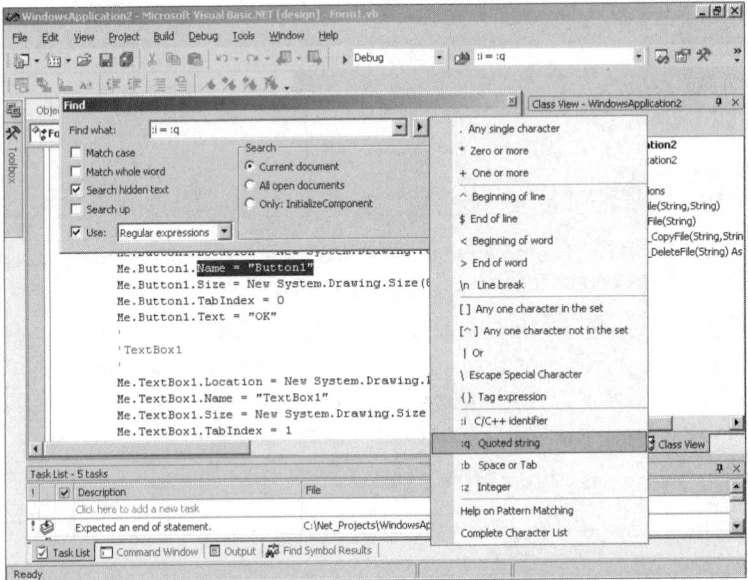

Figure 1-12. The Find dialog box with its pop-up menu to help the developer with regular expression syntax.

The Form Designer and the Toolbox

The form designer works more or less the same way it did under Visual Basic 6: you select a control from the one of the tabs in the Toolbox and drag it over the form's surface. There are only minor differences worth mentioning:

- **The designer's tray area** The Timer control and other controls invisible at run time are displayed in a special area below the form called the component tray.
- **In-place menu editor** Menus are just controls that can be edited in place, in a far more natural way than the clumsy menu editor that has accompanied Visual Basic for 10 years, virtually unchanged since version 1.

- **Individual control locking** Each control can be locked individually so that you don't move it accidentally with the mouse. (You could either lock all controls or none of them in Visual Basic 6.)
- **Visual TabIndex setting** You can set the TabIndex property in a simple, visual fashion by clicking Tab Order on the Edit menu.

The Toolbox is similar to the one in Visual Basic 6 except that it supports both ListView display (as you can see in Figure 1-13) and the traditional Icon view (as in Visual Basic 6). The commands in the Toolbox's context menu let you add or remove tabs, customize the Toolbox with additional .NET and COM components, and list items alphabetically. By default, the Toolbox runs in auto-hide mode, so it appears only when you move the mouse cursor near the left border of the IDE window. (I disabled this feature when I was capturing Figure 1-13 so that I could display the form's designer in its entirety.)

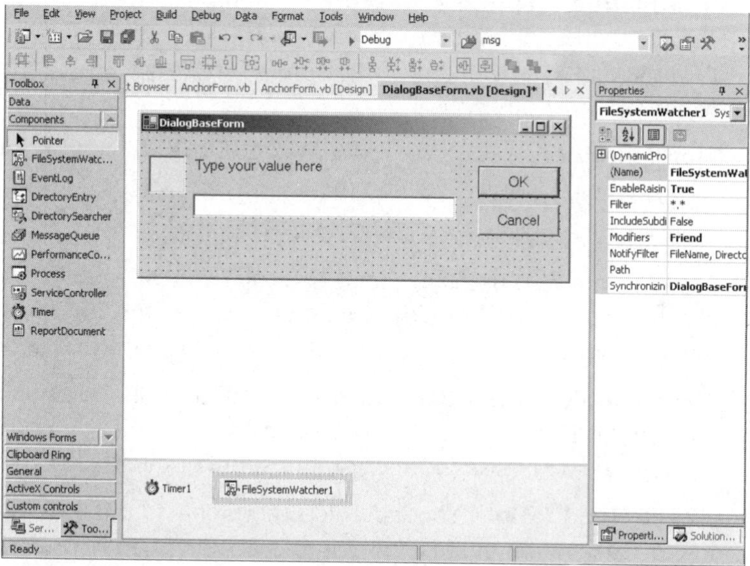

Figure 1-13. The form designer, with the Toolbox on its left and the Properties window on its right; note that controls invisible at run time are displayed in the designer's tray area.

The Components section of the toolbox contains a few .NET components that support visual editing of their properties, such as the FileSystemWatcher component. Because none of these components are visible at run time, they appear in the designer's tray area, but you can edit their properties in the Properties window as if they were controls. The Clipboard Ring section of the toolbox contains snippets of text that you can copy into the Clipboard and that you can paste into the code editor using drag-and-drop.

New Tools

Some of the new Visual Studio .NET features are used only for specific programming tasks, so I'll cover them only when necessary. However, a few new tools can make your job much easier from day one, so this is the right place to introduce them.

The Task List Window

The Task List is used for annotating pieces of information of four different kinds, as you can see in Figure 1-14. In the first three cases, you can jump to the corresponding statement in code by double-clicking the Task List item:

- **Compilation errors and warnings** Compilation errors and warnings are marked with the same icon (a stack of paper sheets with a downward blue arrow), but compilation errors also have a red exclamation mark.
- **User comments** You can add a TODO user comment in the Task List by typing the following comment anywhere in the code window:

  ```
  ' TODO: text of the comment
  ```

  You can also use other markers, such as HACK and UNDONE, and you can define your own markers or alter the priority of predefined markers in the Task List page of the Options dialog box.
- **Named bookmarks** You can add a named bookmark pointing to a statement in your code by right-clicking in the code editor and clicking Add Task List Shortcut on the shortcut menu.
- **User-defined tasks** You can add other items to the Task List window by clicking on the first entry in the Task List window and starting to type.

You must right-click the Task List, point to Show Tasks, and click All on the shortcut menu to see all types of Task List entries. Other commands on the shortcut menu let you filter the contents of this window by their type. In addition, named bookmarks and user-defined tasks have check boxes that you can select or deselect, and you can later use the commands in the Show Tasks submenu to filter items according to the state of their associated check boxes. You can click on a Task List column header to sort tasks by their description, filename, or line number.

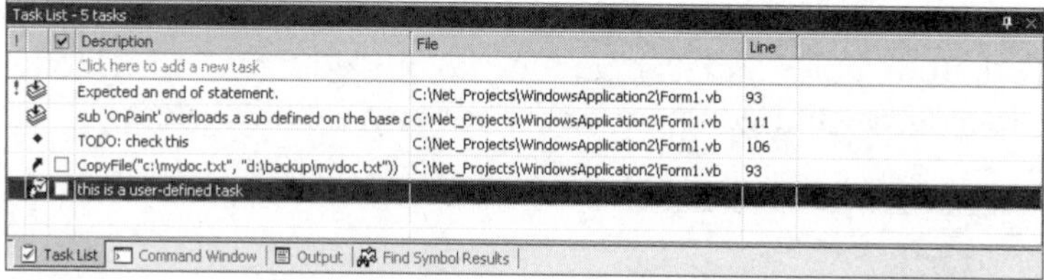

Figure 1-14. The Task List window, with a compilation error, a compilation warning, a user comment, a named bookmark, and a user-defined task (in that order).

The Server Explorer Window

The Server Explorer window displays some of the resources located on the current or a remote computer, including Event Logs, Message Queues, Windows Services, and SQL Server databases. (See Figure 1-15.) Using this tool, you can perform the following operations:

- Right-click on the Data Connection node to create a new data connection; expand existing data connection nodes to view SQL Server databases, tables, and fields and browse their properties. (Note that properties are displayed in Visual Studio's Properties window.) Data connections are very handy; with them, you can quickly create a database connection in code.
- Right-click on the Servers node to add a remote computer to the list of machines that can be administered from inside the Server Explorer.
- Expand the Event Logs categories (Application, System, and so on) to access event log entries grouped by the application or system services that created them; details of each event log entry are visible in Visual Studio's Properties window. You can also right-click on the Event Logs node to launch the Event Viewer.
- Expand the Performance Counters node to browse the properties (but not the current value) of all the performance counters defined on the selected computer.
- View the properties of all the services installed on the selected computer; you can also start, stop, pause, and resume them.
- Administer one or more instances of SQL Servers. The Solution Explorer exposes most of the commands you can execute from inside the SQL Server Enterprise Manager, so you can create new

databases, diagrams, tables, views, triggers, and indexes; retrieve data from tables and change their layout; edit, run, and debug stored procedures; and generate scripts for any database item.

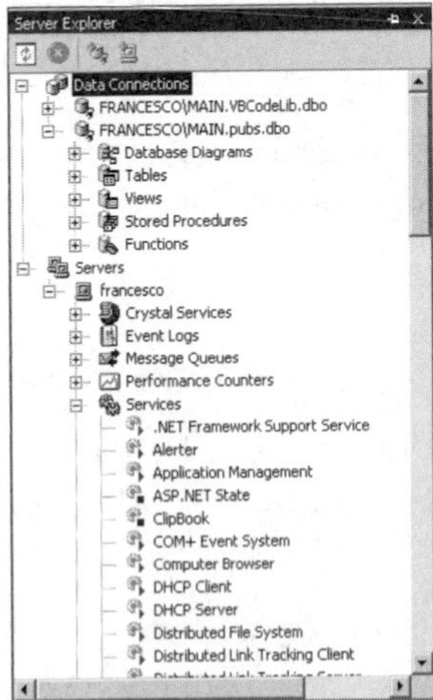

Figure 1-15. The Server Explorer window.

The Server Explorer is more than just an administration tool because it gives you a visual way to code against the components in its window. In fact, you can drag and drop the majority of the items from the Solution Explorer window onto a form designer's tray area to create an instance of the corresponding .NET component. For example, drag the Services\IIS Admin Service node to the tray area and create a component named ServiceController1, which you can then reference from inside the form's code module to start, stop, pause, and resume the Internet Information Services service, as here:

```
ServiceController1.Stop
```

The Command Window

In the default Visual Studio window layout, the Command window is located near the bottom edge of the IDE window and shares the screen area with the Task List and Search Results window. (You can switch among these windows by using tabs.) The Command window can work in two distinct modes:

- In command mode, to execute Visual Studio commands such as loading a new file or searching a string in the code module. The Command window displays a > prompt when in command mode. You display the Command window in this mode by pointing to Other Windows on the View menu and clicking Command Window.

- In immediate mode, to evaluate expressions, invoke methods, and read or write variables and properties. The Command window doesn't display a prompt when in this mode. You display the Command window in immediate mode by pointing to Windows on the Debug menu and clicking Immediate. (This mode can be activated only while you're debugging a running application.)

Most of the commands available in command mode reflect the Visual Studio menu structure: you just have to discard the spaces from menu captions and use the dot to separate submenus. For example, the following command from the Command window is equivalent to clicking Add Existing Item on the File menu:

```
>File.AddExistingItem
```

Commands that display a dialog box can take arguments that correspond to the values you would enter in the dialog box's fields. For example, the following command searches for the "End Sub" string in case-sensitive mode and follows the Up direction:

```
>Edit.Find "End Sub" /case /up
```

Most options can be shortened to one character and blended together; for example, the preceding command can be rewritten in a more concise form as follows:

```
>Edit.Find "End Sub" /cu
```

You don't have to remember the spelling of every command because the Command window supports IntelliSense (see Figure 1-16); however, IntelliSense doesn't support command arguments, and the only way to learn about them is by looking at Visual Studio documentation.

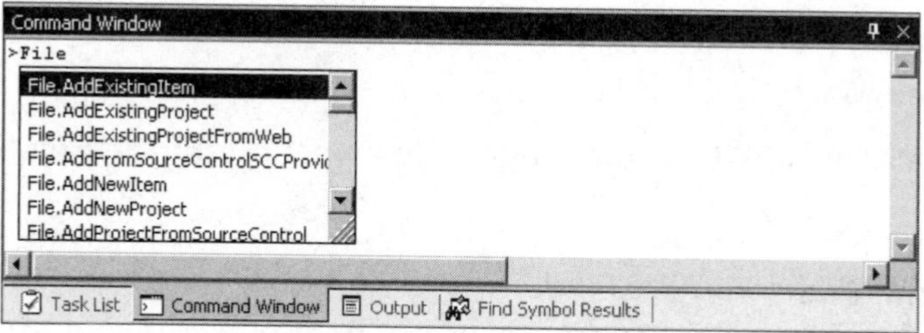

Figure 1-16. The Command window offers IntelliSense support when in command mode.

If you work often with a given command, you might want to create a shorter alias for it. You create a command alias using the alias command. For example, you can create the efuc alias for the Edit.Find /uc command as follows:

```
>alias efuc Edit.Find /uc
```

After you've created the preceding alias, you can search a string in case-sensitive mode and follow in the Up direction with the following command:

```
>efuc "End Sub"
```

Visual Studio comes with several aliases already defined; you can list them by typing the alias command without an argument. Another way to invoke a command without typing its entire name is by assigning it a keyboard shortcut. (See the "Macro Explorer" section later in this chapter.)

You can switch the Command window to immediate mode by pointing to Windows on the Debug menu and clicking Immediate or by typing the immed command while in command mode:

```
>immed
```

When in immediate mode, the Command window behaves much like the Visual Basic 6 Immediate window: you can assign variables, run procedures, and invoke methods in standard Visual Basic syntax. For example, if you break the program inside a form class, you can change the form's caption using this statement:

```
Me.Text = "my new window title"
```

As in Visual Basic 6, you display the value of a variable, property, or expression by prefixing it with a ? (question mark):

```
? Me.Text
```

You can run a Visual Studio command while in immediate mode by prefixing the command with the > symbol, as you see here:

```
>efuc "Property "
```

You can switch back from immediate mode to command mode by typing >cmd.

Debug Windows

The Visual Studio .NET debugger is much more powerful than the integrated debugger that comes with Visual Basic 6. Figure 1-17 shows the many commands available on the Debug menu and a few of the windows you can use to debug your application, including these:

- The Breakpoint window, from which you can create, view, disable, and delete breakpoints in code. Visual Studio .NET supports breakpoints that always fire, fire when a condition is true, fire when a particular expression's value changes, or fire only when they are hit a given number of times.
- Watch windows, which display the value of one or more expressions that you enter. (Visual Studio supports up to four Watch windows.)
- The Me window, which displays the value of all the properties of the object whose code is executing.
- The Autos window, which displays the value of all the variables referenced in the current statement and the three statements on either side of the current statement.
- The Locals window, which displays the value of all the properties of the running object and the local variables and arguments of the current procedure.
- The Call Stack window, which displays all the pending procedures that called the current one.
- The Threads window, which displays information about all the running threads.
- The Modules window, which lists all the DLLs used by the program being debugged. The path and the version of each DLL are displayed, so you can use this tool to detect subtle versioning problems.
- Memory windows, which display the contents of memory as bytes and ASCII strings; you can watch up to four memory regions at the same time. (If you know what you're doing, you can even modify memory with this tool.)
- The Disassembly window, in which you see the native code produced by each statement of your Visual Basic or C# program and even step through each assembly instruction.
- The Registers window, in which you see the contents of individual CPU registers. (This window is commonly used with the Disassembly window.)

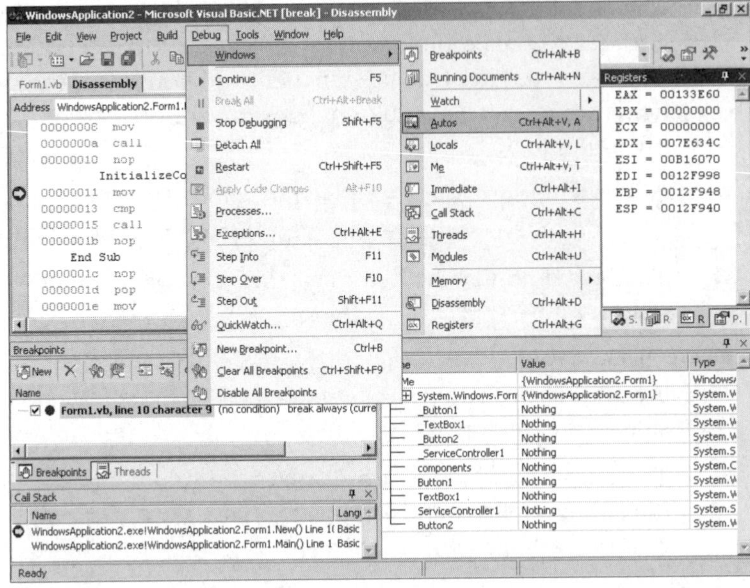

Figure 1-17. All the commands in the Windows Debug and Debug menus. You can also see a few debug windows in the background, such as Disassembly, Registers, Breakpoints, Call Stack, and Me.

Using the commands in the Debug menu, you can display two additional dialog boxes:

- The Processes dialog box, which lists all the running Windows processes and lets you select which ones you want to debug; this tool is great for debugging multiple applications at once.
- The Exceptions dialog box, which lets you decide what happens when a given exception occurs.

I'll describe a few of these debugging windows later in this book.

Macro Explorer

One of the most exciting features of the new version of Visual Studio is its ability to record and play macros to automate repetitive editing actions. Even better, you can browse the actual macro code and modify it if you want.

You record a macro by pointing to Macro on the Tools menu and clicking Record TemporaryMacro (or pressing the Ctrl+Shift+R keyboard shortcut), and then using the mouse or typing something in the code editor; the macro recorder also records menu commands, find and replace commands, window activations, and select actions in the Solution Explorer.

When you have completed your action, stop recording by pressing Ctrl+Shift+R again, or just click the Stop Recording button on the Recorder toolbar that has appeared in the meantime. You can also cancel the recording without saving by clicking the Cancel Recording button on this toolbar.

If you didn't cancel the macro recording, a new macro named TemporaryMacro will have been created. You can play all the actions in this macro by pointing to Macros on the Tools menu and clicking Run TemporaryMacro or by pressing the Ctrl+Shift+P keyboard shortcut.

Each time you record a new macro, the macro named TemporaryMacro is overwritten, so you should rename it something else if you want to save the macro you've just recorded. Do so by pointing to Macros on the Tools menu and clicking Macro Explorer to open the Macro Explorer, which you can see in Figure 1-18. Then right-click on TemporaryMacro, click Rename on the shortcut menu, and change the macro's name.

> **Note** If you're a curious developer, click Edit in the shortcut menu to open the Macro IDE and look at the code produced for you by the macro recorder. The Macro IDE is a complete environment for writing, running, and debugging macros.

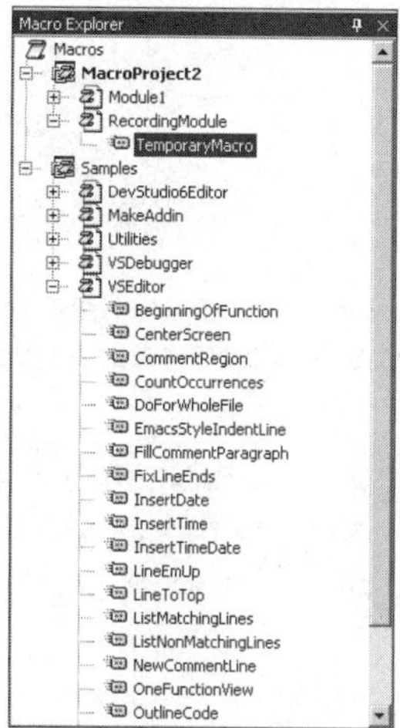

Figure 1-18. The Macro Explorer.

You can run a nontemporary macro in three ways:

- Double-click it in the Macro Explorer (or click Run on the shortcut menu).
- Type its name in the Command window in command mode. This action works because your new macro has, in effect, become a Visual Studio command.
- Assign it a keyboard shortcut. You can do this from inside the Keyboard page of the Options dialog box, as shown in Figure 1-19. (Click Options on the Tools menu to display this dialog box.) You can use this dialog box to assign keyboard shortcuts to any Visual Studio command, not just the commands you create by recording a macro.

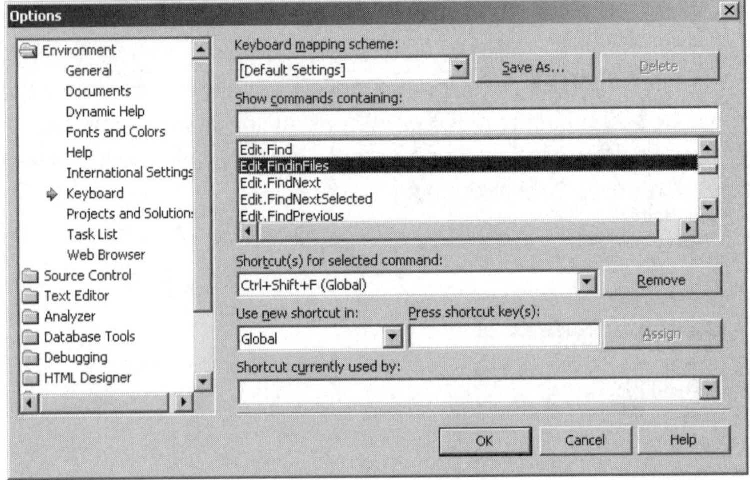

Figure 1-19. The Keyboard page in the Options dialog box lets you assign a keyboard shortcut to any Visual Studio built-in command as well as your own macros.

If you want to learn more about macros, look at the items under the Samples node in the Macro Explorer. These macros come with Visual Studio and are excellent examples of macro programming; a few of these macros are useful in themselves. For example, the VSEditor.FillCommentParagraph macro reformats a multiline comment with the specified right margin, and VSEditor.SaveBackup saves the current document with the .bak extension.

Running a Visual Basic Console Application

Earlier in this chapter, I showed you how to use the VBC compiler to create console applications with Visual Basic .NET. In this section, I'll show you how to create a console application from inside the Visual Studio IDE.

First point to New on the File menu, and click Project; select Console Application in the Templates pane on the right of the New Project dialog box. Then name the project FirstConsoleApp, and click OK. Visual Studio then creates a project with two files: Module1.vb and AssemblyInfo.vb. (All Visual Basic projects contain the latter file: its purpose will be clear only in Chapter 14, so let's ignore it for now.) Module1.vb contains the following code template:

```
Module Module1

    Sub Main()

    End Sub

End Module
```

All console applications use the System.Console object, which represents the console window. This object exposes several properties and methods, but we will use only three of them:

- The ReadLine method waits for the end user to enter a value and press the Enter key; it then returns the typed string.
- The Write method outputs a string to the console window.
- The WriteLine method is similar to the Write method but also appends a newline character.

You can embed numbered placeholders in the output string you pass to the Write and WriteLine methods; these placeholders are replaced by the value of additional arguments passed to the method. The following code shows how to use these placeholders:

```
Module Module1

    Sub Main()
        Dim username As String

        ' Ask for user name.
        Console.Write("Enter your name: ")
        username = Console.ReadLine()
        ' Say hi, and tell current time.
        Console.WriteLine("Hello, {0}. Current time is {1}", username, Now)
    End Sub

End Module
```

You can run a program from inside the Visual Studio IDE by pressing the F5 key (as in Visual Basic 6), which corresponds to the Start command on the Debug menu. The problem with this command is that the console window is closed as soon as the Main procedure is exited, so you can't see the output from the last Console.WriteLine method.

You can work around this issue by inserting a call to the Console.ReadLine method just before the End Sub statement. Or you can run the program by pressing the Ctrl+F5 key (or the Start Without Debugging command on the Debug menu); in this case, the console window is closed when the user presses a key. (See Figure 1-20.) However, as the command name implies, the program is compiled without debugging support, and you can't set breakpoints or check variable values during its execution.

Figure 1-20. Output of the sample console application when run with the Debug command from the Start Without Debugging menu.

Note I talk about Windows Forms and user-interface techniques beginning in Chapter 16, so most of the code samples in Chapters 2 through 15 are implemented as console applications. In practice, each example is a separate procedure whose name starts with Test; for example, the sample code for Chapter 2 is a project named ModulesDemo that contains the TestFactorial and TestBasicInheritance procedures.

All test procedures are invoked from the Sub Main procedure, but all call statements are remarked, as you see here:

```
Sub Main()
    ' Run one of the Textxxxx procedures by uncommenting only
    ' one statement.
    ' TestFactorial()
    ' TestBasicInheritance()
    ⋮
End Sub
```

As the remark suggests, you can run each individual test procedure by uncommenting the corresponding call statement in the Sub Main routine.

I know, it has been a long chapter—and you have read a lot of new concepts and seen very little code. Believe me, I needed this chapter to introduce the most important features of .NET and Visual Studio. You'll see *plenty* of code in the following chapters, starting with the next chapter, in which you'll learn about new syntax and data types in Visual Basic .NET.

Front
Top
Left
Back

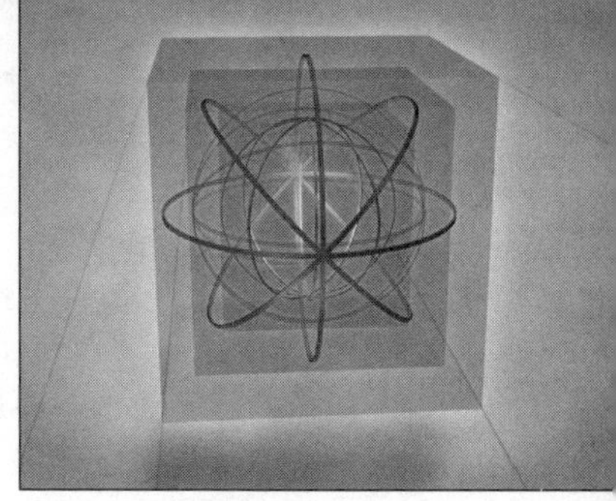

2 Modules and Variables

In my opinion, the best way to approach Visual Basic .NET is to consider it a brand-new language, whose syntax is only vaguely compatible with versions 1 through 6. On the other hand, it's unmistakably Visual Basic: even novice Visual Basic programmers will find themselves comfortable with Visual Basic .NET, although they might need some time to get familiar with the new language features and the many syntax changes. If you're a longtime Visual Basic developer, keep in mind that these changes are for the good and that they're intended to make Visual Basic more similar to other .NET programming languages. A consequence of this approach is that switching to another .NET language, such as C#, will be relatively simple because you don't have to significantly change your practices.

Modules and Namespaces

The first new important characteristic of all the Visual Basic .NET files is that they have the same extension and are basically the same type of file. In fact, Visual Studio .NET uses the file extension to determine the language that each file contains; therefore, all Visual Basic .NET files have the .vb extension, all C# files have the .cs extension, and so on.

This detail might be disorienting at first if you have a lot of experience with Visual Basic 6 and earlier versions, in which you could count at least six different file extensions, such as .frm for forms, .bas for standard modules, and .cls for class modules. Without a doubt, however, the new way to label files is more rational, and you won't take long to get accustomed to it.

The reason Visual Basic .NET uses just one file extension for all its files is that basically there aren't many differences between, say, a Module file and a Class file. More precisely, the concept of *module file* and *class file* has disappeared under

Visual Basic .NET in that a file can contain multiple modules and multiple classes, and even a combination of the two.

A file can also contain a form, but remember that Visual Basic .NET forms are nothing but classes that inherit from the System.Windows.Forms.Form class defined in the .NET Framework. From the developer's perspective, forms are classes with which a designer has been associated. A *designer* is just a tool that lets you visually design the user interface of a form (or a UserControl)—for example, by dropping controls from the Toolbox and modifying their properties at design time from within the Properties window. Visual Basic 6 and earlier versions offer designers for forms and UserControls, with an important difference: form and control properties are saved in the .frm file but are invisible in the code window. By comparison, all the Visual Basic .NET designers produce code that can be browsed in the code window; in fact, you might theoretically define the appearance of a form and its control without even using the designer.

The developer decides how modules, classes, and forms (and other types of components, such as UserControls) are distributed among the files in the current project. For example, you can use a file for a form and all the classes the form uses, which can be a good solution, especially if no other form uses those classes. Similarly, you can gather all the (nonevent) procedures that a form uses in a module and include both the form and the module in the same file.

Finally, a single file can even include two or more forms—or other classes with an associated designer. In practice, however, you rarely want to organize your forms that way because the Visual Studio .NET integrated development environment (IDE) can associate the designer with only one class in a given file, which means that you can visually edit only one of the forms in the file. All the other forms could be edited only by manually writing code, but you would forgo one of the most productive features of the environment.

Modules

The module block is delimited by the Module and End Module keywords and can contain any number of variables, Subs, and Functions. Here's an example of a module named MathFunctions that contains a constant that's visible to the entire project, a variable that's visible only to the code inside the block, and a Public function:

```
Module MathFunctions
    ' A public constant
    Public Const DoublePI As Double = 6.28318530717958

    ' A private array
    Private factValues(169) As Double
```

```
    ' Return the factorial of a number in the range 0-169.
    Public Function Factorial(ByVal n As Integer) As Double
        ' Evaluate all possible values in advance during the first call.
        If factValues(0) = 0 Then
            Dim i As Integer
            factValues (0) = 1
            For i = 1 To 169
                factValues(i) = factValues(i - 1) * CDbl(i)
            Next
        End If

        ' Check the argument.
        If n >= 0 And n <= 169 Then
            ' Return the value in the array if argument is in range.
            Factorial = factValues(n)
        Else
            ' Raise an error otherwise.
            Err.Raise(6, , "Overflow")
        End If
    End Function
End Module
```

The code in the Factorial function checks whether factValues(0) is 0, in which case it fills the factValues array with all the possible factorial values for numbers in the range 0 through 169. (The Factorial function won't work for negative numbers, and the factorial for numbers higher or equal to 170 can't be stored in a Double variable.)

Using the Public keyword allows you to access both the DoublePI constant and the Factorial function from elsewhere in the project, like this:

```
Circumference = radius * DoublePI
```

The Sub New Procedure

As you see, Module...End Module blocks are similar to modules in previous Visual Basic versions in that they work as containers for procedures and variables. They have additional features, however, such as the New constructor method. If a module contains a Sub New procedure, the runtime calls this procedure before running any code inside the module itself. You can take advantage of this detail to simplify (and slightly optimize) the code in the Factorial function by moving the initialization code for the factValues array inside the Sub New procedure:

```
Module MathFunctions
    ' A public constant
    Public Const DoublePI As Double = 6.28318530717958
```

```
    ' A private array
    Private factValues(169) As Double

    Sub New()
        ' Evaluate all possible values in advance.
        Dim i As Integer
        factValues(0) = 1
        For i = 1 To 169
            factValues(i) = factValues(i - 1) * CDbl(i)
        Next
    End Sub

    ' Return the factorial of a number in the range 0-169.
    Function Factorial(ByVal n As Integer) As Double
        ' Check the argument.
        If n >= 0 And n <= 169 Then
            ' Return the value in the array if argument is in range.
            Factorial = factValues(n)
        Else
            ' Raise an error otherwise.
            Err.Raise(6, , "Overflow")
        End If
    End Function
End Module
```

An important detail: the runtime invokes the Sub New procedure the very first time a variable or a procedure in the module is referenced by the running project. The Sub New procedure doesn't run when a constant defined in the module is accessed.

The Sub Main Procedure

As with previous Visual Basic versions, you can decide whether your application starts with a given visible object (typically a form) or by executing a Sub Main procedure defined in a module. A problem that occurs with previous language versions is that only one module in your application can contain a Sub Main procedure because otherwise, an ambiguity might result; that is, the Visual Basic compiler would be unable to decide which Sub Main procedure is the entry point for the program. With Visual Basic .NET, you can select which module contains the Sub Main procedure that runs when your program starts from inside the project Property Pages dialog box, which you bring up with the Properties command on the Project menu or by selecting the project name in the Solution Explorer window and then clicking the Properties button near the top border of the window. (See Figure 2-1.) If you select the generic Sub Main entry in the list, however, you get a compilation error if two or more modules (or no module at all) contain a Sub Main procedure. Similarly, you get a compilation error if you specify the name of a module that doesn't contain a Sub Main procedure.

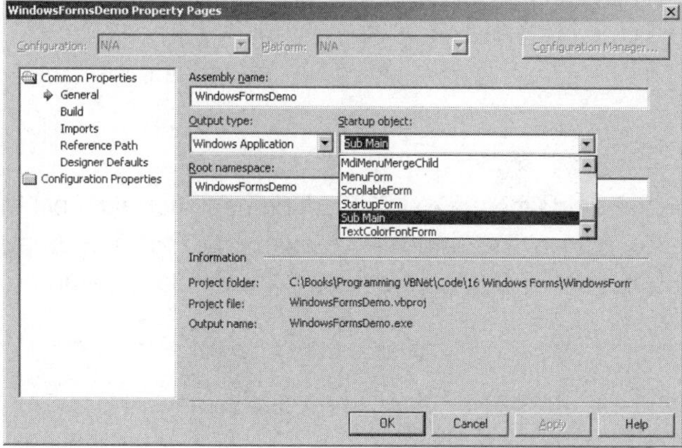

Figure 2-1. The project Property Pages dialog box.

If you're writing a Windows Forms application, the Sub Main procedure typically performs all the initialization chores required by the application and then displays a form, as in the following code snippet:

```
Module MainModule
    Sub Main()
        Dim frm As New Form1()
        ' Call a procedure that does the initialization (not shown here).
        InitializeAllVariables()
        ' Display the form modally.
        frm.ShowDialog()
    End Sub
End Module
```

Classes

I'll talk about Class modules in detail in Chapter 4, so here I'll simply outline a few basic syntactical guidelines that you need for understanding other portions of this chapter.

A Visual Basic .NET class is defined by the code inside a Class...End Class block. A class can contain Private and Public variables (or fields, in the .NET terminology) and procedures. The following code defines a simple Person class that exposes one constant, two fields, and one method:

```
Public Class Person
    Public Const Title As String = "Mr. "
```

(continued)

```
    Public FirstName As String
    Public LastName As String

    Function CompleteName() As String
        CompleteName = FirstName & " " & LastName
    End Function
End Class
```

Note Naming guidelines in the .NET documentation suggest that you use PascalCase in class names—for example, PartTimeEmployee—and that you *not* use a *C* character as a prefix in class names.

Using the Person class elsewhere in the application is straightforward:

```
Dim aPerson As New Person()
aPerson.FirstName = "Joe"
aPerson.LastName = "Doe"
Console.WriteLine(aPerson.Title & aPerson.CompleteName)    ' => Mr. Joe Doe
```

A class can expose public constants of any type, such as the Title string constant in the preceding code. This capacity makes Visual Basic .NET classes more flexible than classes in previous language versions, which can contain only private constants. (In Visual Basic 6, you can simulate public constants through read-only properties, a technique that requires more code and is less efficient.)

The most anticipated innovation in classes is the Visual Basic .NET support for class inheritance. All you need to inherit a new class from Person is an Inherits statement immediately after the Class statement:

```
Class Employee
    Inherits Person

    Public BirthDate As Date                    ' A new field

    Function ReverseName() As String            ' A new method
        ReverseName = LastName & ", " & FirstName
    End Function
End Class
```

This code demonstrates that the new class inherits all the properties in the base class and also shows how you can make your code less verbose using the With block, as you do in Visual Basic 6:

```
Dim anEmployee As New Employee()
With anEmployee
```

```
    .FirstName = "Robert"
    .LastName = "Smith"
    ' Use the new (noninherited) members.
    .BirthDate = #2/5/1960#
    Console.WriteLine(.ReverseName)         ' => Smith, Robert
End With
```

I'll describe inheritance in depth in Chapter 5, even though I make use of inheritance before that chapter. Inheritance is so central to the .NET architecture that it's impossible to explain several key concepts without referring to it.

Forms

I'll cover Windows Forms in detail in Chapter 16. In this section, I'll just acquaint you with what a Windows Form is.

Under .NET, a form is simply a class that inherits from the System.Windows.Forms.Form class in the .NET Framework. When you create a form inside the Visual Studio .NET environment, the following code is generated:

```
Public Class Form1
    Inherits System.Windows.Forms.Form

#Region " Windows Form Designer generated code "
    Public Sub New()
        MyBase.New()
        'This call is required by the Windows Form Designer.
        InitializeComponent()
        'Add any initialization after the InitializeComponent() call.
    End Sub

    'Form overrides dispose to clean up the component list.
    Protected Overloads Overrides Sub Dispose(ByVal disposing As Boolean)
        If disposing Then
            If Not (components Is Nothing) Then
                components.Dispose()
            End If
        End If
        MyBase.Dispose(disposing)
    End Sub

    'Required by the Windows Form Designer
    Private components As System.ComponentModel.Container

    'NOTE: The following procedure is required by the Windows Form Designer.
    'It can be modified using the Windows Form Designer.
    'Do not modify it using the code editor.
```

(continued)

```
    <System.Diagnostics.DebuggerStepThrough()> _
    Private Sub InitializeComponent()
        '
        'Form1
        '
        Me.AutoScaleBaseSize = New System.Drawing.Size(5, 13)
        Me.ClientSize = New System.Drawing.Size(292, 273)
        Me.Name = "Form1"
        Me.Text = "Form1"
    End Sub
#End Region

End Class
```

The Inherits keyword tells you that this Form1 class inherits from System.Windows.Forms.Form and therefore can be considered a Windows Form. As with all inherited classes, the first statement in the Sub New procedure must invoke the New method of the base class from which this Form1 class inherits. As the comments in the code clearly indicate, the code inside the InitializeComponents procedure is under the direct control of the form designer, and you shouldn't modify it directly in the code editor. Better yet, you should leave the #Region block in a collapsed state so that you don't modify its contents accidentally.

Namespaces

Modules and classes live in namespaces. The thousands of classes defined in the .NET Framework are grouped in namespaces—for instance, the System namespace that gathers the basic type classes, such as Integer, String, and Array.

Namespace Blocks

All the classes and modules in your Visual Basic .NET project belong to the default namespace defined in the Root Namespace field in the project Property Pages dialog box. (See Figure 2-1.) However, you can create explicit Namespace...End Namespace blocks anywhere in your source files. For example, you can define the HumanBeings namespace as a container for the Person class defined previously:

```
Namespace HumanBeings

    Public Class Person
        Public Const Title As String = "Mr. "
```

```
        Public FirstName As String
        Public LastName As String

        Function CompleteName() As String
            CompleteName = FirstName & " " & LastName
        End Function
    End Class

End Namespace
```

If a piece of code references a class or procedure in another namespace, it must include the complete namespace of the referenced element, as you see here:

```
' Use the Person class from another namespace.
Dim p As New HumanBeings.Person
p.FirstName = "Joe"
```

You can't define variable declarations or procedures directly inside a Namespace block. For example, the following code snippet won't compile:

```
Namespace MyNamespace
    Function MyFunction()
        ⋮
    End Function
End Namespace
```

Interestingly, you can have multiple Namespace blocks with the same name in a project, in the same or a different source file. This feature lets you keep the logical organization of your source code entities completely distinct from the physical structure. For example, you can have a file that contains multiple namespaces, or you can have all the elements of a namespace scattered in different source files. (In fact, all the source files in your project belong to the root namespace defined in the project Property Pages dialog box.)

> **More Info** A Namespace block—defined either in code or on the General page of the project Property Pages dialog box—can contain only five types of blocks: Module, Class, Structure, Interface, and Enum. I've already shown you the Module and Class blocks. Enum blocks are described in the "Constants and Enums" section, later in this chapter (and more in depth in Chapter 8). I'll talk about Structure blocks at the end of this chapter. I cover Interface blocks in Chapter 6.

Nested Namespaces

Namespaces can be nested. The System.Collections namespace, for example, contains several collectionlike classes, and the System.IO namespace includes classes that let you read from and write to files. There is no theoretical limit to nesting namespaces, and namespaces nested at three or more levels are quite common in the .NET Framework, so you can see, for example, System.Xml.Schema or System.Windows.Forms.ComponentModule.Com2Interop.

You can create nested namespaces in your Visual Basic .NET projects simply by nesting Namespace...End Namespace blocks. For example, the following code defines the Animals.Mammals.Dog, Animals.Mammals.Cat, and Animals.Reptiles.Lizard classes:

```
Namespace Animals
    Namespace Mammals
        Class Dog
            ⋮
        End Class

        Class Cat
            ⋮
        End Class
    End Namespace

    Namespace Reptiles
        Class Lizard
            ⋮
        End Class
    End Namespace
End Namespace
```

The scope rules for referencing classes and functions in other namespaces can be easily extended to nested namespaces. For example, the code inside the Dog class can directly reference the Cat class, but it needs to go through the Reptiles namespace to reach the Lizard class:

```
Class Dog
    Dim aCat As New Cat()
    Dim aLizard As New Reptiles.Lizard()
    ⋮
End Class
```

The Imports Statement

When working with nested namespaces, you can make your code remarkably less verbose by using the Imports statement. In practice, each Imports statement tells the compiler that the code in the source file can access all the classes, procedures, and structures defined in a given namespace, without your having to specify the name of the namespace itself. For example, consider the following Imports statements:

```
Imports System.Drawing
Imports System.Windows.Forms
Imports System.ComponentModel
```

These three Imports statements let you use more concise code to refer to elements in those namespaces:

```
Dim bmp As Bitmap       ' Same as System.Drawing.Bitmap
Dim ctrl As Control     ' Same as System.Windows.Forms.Control
Dim comp As Component   ' Same as System.ComponentModel.Component
```

The Visual Basic 6 concept closest to the Imports statement is the list of selected items in the Project References dialog box. However, Visual Basic 6 doesn't support nested references because classes in a type library can't be nested.

You can save some typing even if you don't have an Imports statement that matches exactly the namespace of the element you want to reference. For example, the following Imports statement for the System namespace lets you make most of your external references more concise because many important objects are in the System namespace or in a namespace nested in System:

```
Imports System

⋮
Dim bmp As Drawing.Bitmap       ' same as System.Drawing.Bitmap
```

You can run into problems if you have distinct Imports statements referring to namespaces that contain classes with the same name. For example, say that both the Animals.Mammals namespace and the Computers.Accessories namespace expose a class named Mouse. In this situation, the following code won't compile because the Mouse reference is ambiguous:

```
' *** This code doesn't compile.
Imports Animals.Mammals
Imports Computers.Accessories

Sub TestImports
    Dim m As Mouse
    ⋮
End Sub
```

Even in this case, you can use the Imports statement to reduce your labor by specifying an alias for one of the conflicting namespaces:

```
Imports Animals.Mammals
Imports Acc = Computers.Accessories

Sub TestImports
    Dim m As Mouse        ' Same as Animals.Mammals.Mouse
    Dim m2 As Acc.Mouse ' Same as Computers.Accessories.Mouse
    ⋮
End Sub
```

Although you can use the Imports statement to shorten references to namespaces inside a source file, you can't shorten namespace names inside an Imports statement itself. For example, say that you have the following two Imports statements:

```
Imports System.Runtime.Serialization
Imports System.Runtime.Serialization.Formatters
```

You might believe that you can make the second Imports statement more concise by dropping the initial portion of the namespace name because it's the argument of the first Imports statement, as you see here:

```
' *** This code doesn't compile.
Imports System.Runtime.Serialization
Imports Formatters
```

However, the preceding code snippet won't compile because the Imports statement requires a *complete* namespace reference. This detail becomes important when you want to use the Imports statement to create shortcuts to namespaces defined elsewhere in your project.

For example, consider the following namespace hierarchy defined in an application whose root namespace is ModulesDemo:

```
Namespace Animals
    Namespace Mammals
        ⋮
    End Namespace
End Namespace
```

Let's say that you want to simplify access to the Animals.Mammals namespace so that other portions of the same application can access elements inside that namespace using a more concise syntax. You might believe that this Imports statement does the trick:

```
Imports Animals.Mammals
```

Instead, it raises a compilation error, "The namespace or type 'Mammals' for the import 'Animals.Mammals' cannot be found." The problem is that all the namespaces defined inside the current project are nested inside the ModulesDemo root namespace. Here's the correct Imports statement:

```
Imports ModulesDemo.Animals.Mammals
```

Keep in mind that you can use an Imports statement only if the current application has a reference to the target namespace and so permits the namespace to appear in the Object Browser. New Visual Basic .NET projects have a reference to the most important classes in the Framework, but not all. If the namespace you're interested in isn't listed in the Solution Explorer, you must add a reference to it by right-clicking References in the Solution Explorer and clicking Add Reference on the shortcut menu. (See Figure 2-2.) Or you can use the Add Reference command on the Project menu. The Add Reference dialog box (Figure 2-3) lists all the .NET components as well as all the Component Object Model (COM) components registered in the system.

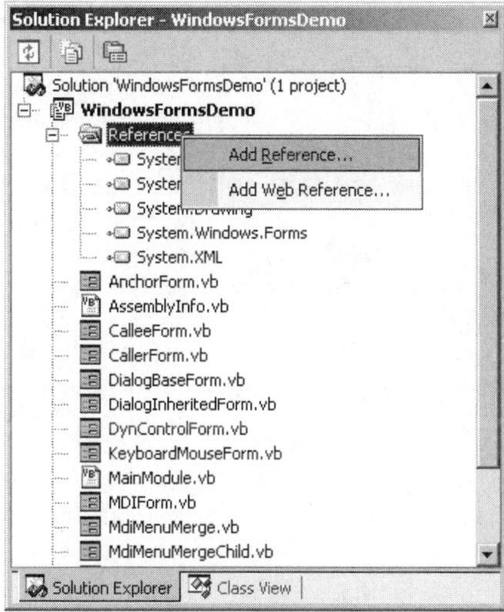

Figure 2-2. The References subtree of the Solution Explorer.

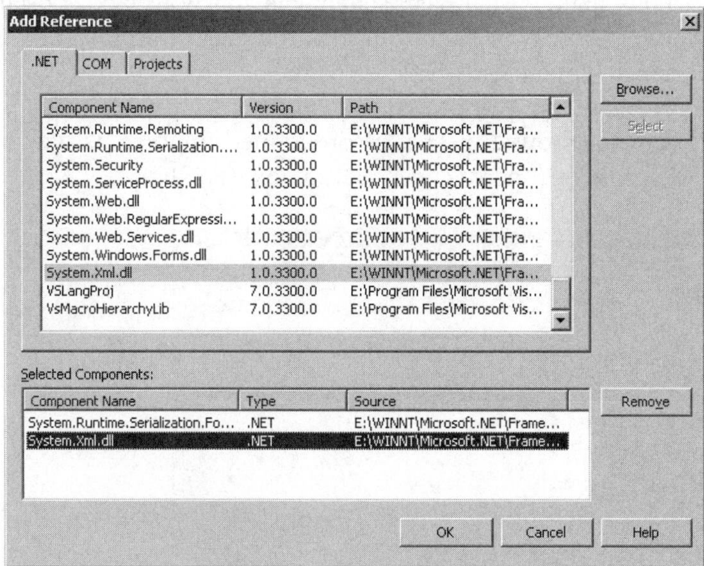

Figure 2-3. The Add Reference dialog box.

Visual Basic lets you specify the name of a class in an Imports statement, a feature that lets you access the static members of a class without prefixing them with the class name. Consider this class, defined in the ModulesDemo root namespace:

```
Class NumericConstants
    Public Const Zero As Integer = 0
    Public Const One As Integer = 1
    ⋮
End Class
```

Here's how your application can access the two constants as if they were globally defined:

```
' This statement imports a class, not a namespace.
Imports ModulesDemo.NumericConstants

Module MainModule
    Sub Main()
        Dim value As Integer = One      ' Assigns 1.
    End Sub
End Module
```

Projectwide Imports

As you can imagine, most Visual Basic .NET projects rely heavily on a few namespaces in the .NET Framework, such as the System namespace, which contains all the basic data types, and the Microsoft.VisualBasic namespace, which contains all the Visual Basic statements, functions, and constants. Repeatedly importing these namespaces into all the files of a project is surely a nuisance. Fortunately, you don't have to do that.

Visual Basic .NET applications can define a number of projectwide imports. You can browse the list of predefined imports, as well as add your own, in the project Property Pages dialog box. (See Figure 2-4.)

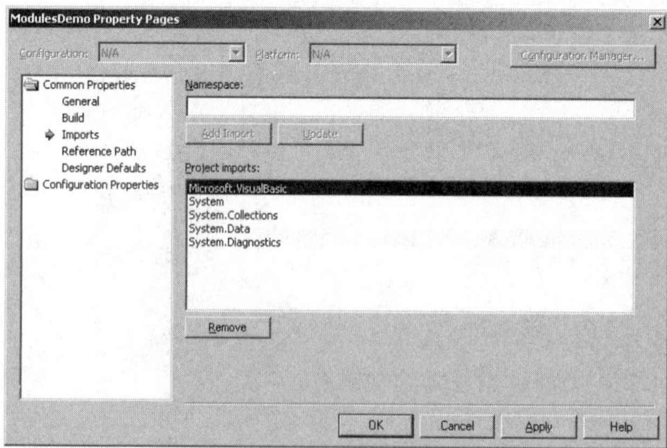

Figure 2-4. You can define projectwide imports in the project Property Pages dialog box.

Variables

Visual Basic .NET programs declare and use their variables in ways that are similar to previous language versions. Under the surface, however, there are many important differences, and you need to be aware of all of them to fully exploit the potential of .NET and not be trapped in subtle conversion issues when you're porting your code from Visual Basic 6.

Declarations

You can declare a variable using the Dim, Private, Public, or Static keyword. The scope rules are simple and are similar to Visual Basic 6 scope rules:

- You use Dim inside a procedure to declare a local (dynamic) variable, which is visible only inside that procedure.
- You use Dim or Private outside procedure blocks—but inside a Class or Module block—to create variables that can be accessed from anywhere inside that class or module but not from elsewhere in the project. (A Dim inside a Structure has a Public scope, however.)
- You use Public inside a Module block to create global variables—that is, variables that exist for the entire program's lifetime and that can be accessed from anywhere in the current project.
- You use Public inside a Class block to create a public field for that class.
- You use the Static keyword to declare static variables inside a procedure. (Note that you can't use the Static keyword in a procedure declaration to make all the variables in the procedure Static as you can in Visual Basic 6.)

The following piece of code demonstrates the five types of variables:

```
Module MyModule
    ' This global variable is visible to the entire application.
    Public myGlobalVar As String
    ' These variables are visible only inside the current module.
    Private myModuleVar As String
    Dim myModuleVar2 As String

    Sub MyProcedure()
        ' This private variable is visible only inside this procedure.
        Dim myPrivateVar As String
        ' This static variable maintains its value between
        ' consecutive calls to this procedure.
```

(continued)

```
        Static counter As Integer
        ⋮
    End Sub
End Module
```

Visual Basic .NET documentation and tools—such as the Intermediate Language Disassembler (ILDASM), which I describe in Chapter 14—make a distinction between class properties implemented as Public variables (known as fields) and properties implemented as Property procedures (the real properties). While most of the time you can ignore this difference and use fields as if they were first-class properties (as you do in previous Visual Basic versions), sometimes their different implementation explains subtle differences in their behavior. For more information about these subtleties, see Chapter 4.

Naming Guidelines

The .NET documentation comes with a set of clear rules about naming procedures, variables, arguments, and other programming entities. These are just guidelines, so you may adhere to them or ignore them. Here's a brief summary:

- Don't use so-called Hungarian notation for variables and parameters. Visual Studio .NET lets you browse the declaration of a variable by simply moving the mouse cursor over it, so you don't need a prefix to make the variable's type explicit, as in lngValue.
- Parameters are lowercase or camelCase—for example, firstName or currentValue.
- Private variables should be camelCase, whereas public fields in classes that appear as properties to clients should be PascalCase. This leads to weird situations, as in this code:

```
Public FirstName As String        ' Global variable or public field in
                                  ' a class
Dim lastName As String            ' Private variable
```

Personally, I like these guidelines because they are similar to those I've come to use in recent years, and I adopted them for the code samples in this book. For example, I have never been fond of Hungarian notation, which I think makes your code *less* readable than usual. (Incidentally, my dislike for prefixes in variable names allowed me to move my Visual Basic 6 code to .NET without having to change prefixes from Integer, Long, and Variant variables.) I use Hungarian notation sparingly in this book, however, when I want to draw your attention to the type of a variable.

The Option Explicit and Option Compare Statements

Visual Basic .NET supports the Option Explicit statement, but its syntax is different from that in previous language versions because it can be followed by an On or Off qualifier:

```
' These statements force explicit declaration of all the
' variables in the module.
Option Explicit On
Option Explicit       ' The On clause can be omitted.

' This statement makes variable declarations optional in the current module.
Option Explicit Off
```

Visual Basic .NET continues to support the Option Compare statement, whose syntax hasn't changed from previous language versions:

```
' Make string comparisons in the module work in a case-sensitive way.
Option Compare Binary

' Make string comparisons in the module work in a case-insensitive way.
Option Compare Text
```

In a difference from Visual Basic 6, you can select the default setting in the project Property Pages dialog box for all the modules of the project that don't contain an Option Explicit or Option Compare statement. (See Figure 2-5.)

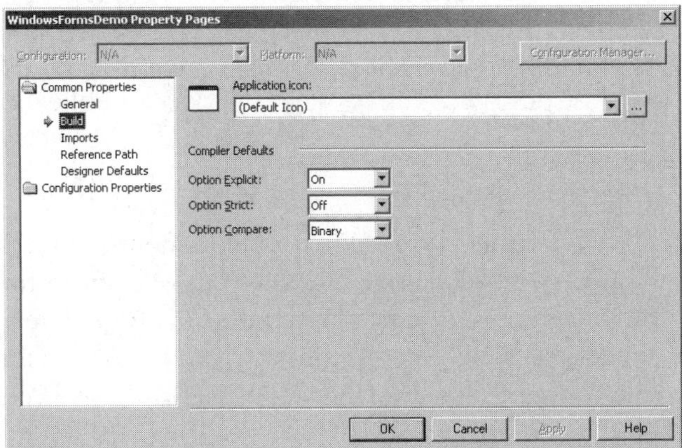

Figure 2-5. Projectwide settings for Option Explicit, Option Strict, and Option Compare.

Finally, you can set the default Option Explicit setting when you're compiling from the command prompt by using the /OPTIONEXPLICIT+ switch to enforce variable declarations and /OPTIONEXPLICIT- to make them optional:

```
vbc /optionexplicit+ source.vb
```

Similarly, you can set the default Option Compare setting when compiling from the command prompt by using either the /OPTIONCOMPARE:BINARY or the /OPTIONCOMPARE:TEXT switch. (Note that the case of switches on the command line isn't significant.)

Multiple Declarations

As in previous language versions, you can declare multiple variables in the same Dim, Private, or Public statement. However, the syntax is different because you can use one single As clause for multiple variables of the same type:

```
' Declare three Long variables.
Dim x, y, z As Long
```

The semantics are different from previous Visual Basic versions as well in that all the variables in the statement are of the same type (Long, in the preceding code snippet). By comparison, under Visual Basic 6 the same statement declares one Long variable and two Variant variables (or whatever was the default type established by a Defxxx statement). This behavior is going to disorient many developers, but it makes Visual Basic resemble other languages, such as C# and C++. As in Visual Basic 6, you can have multiple As clauses in the same statement:

```
' Declare three variables of different types.
Dim i As Long, k As Integer, s As String
```

Visual Basic .NET doesn't support Defxxx statements—that is, DefInt A-Z—which is good news. Those statements were left over from the GW-Basic days about 20 years ago. Among their many unfortunate qualities, they make code reuse problematic because you can't move a code block to another module without also worrying about the Defxxx in use in the source and target modules.

Block-Scoped Variables

Visual Basic .NET also supports the so-called block variables, a special type of dynamic variables that you declare using Dim inside a For...Next, Do...Loop, or While...End While block of code:

```
Dim x As Integer
For x = 1 To 10
    Dim y As Integer    ' A block variable
    ⋮
Next
```

These variables can be used only inside the block in which they're defined:

```
' *** This code doesn't compile.
For x = 1 To 10
    Dim y As Integer    ' A block variable
    ⋮
Next
x = y    ' y isn't accessible from outside the For block.
```

Block variables improve the readability of your code because they make clear where a variable is used. But Visual Basic .NET raises a compilation error if the same variable is declared at the procedure level, as in this code:

```
' *** This code doesn't compile.
Dim y As Integer        ' Procedure variable with the same name
For x = 1 To 10
    Dim y As Integer  ' Block variable
    ⋮
Next
```

It's OK to have a block variable with the same name as a variable declared outside the procedure at the class level or globally in the application. If you have two distinct non-nested blocks in the same procedure, you can declare the same variable in both blocks and even use a different type for the two instances:

```
For x = 1 To 10
    Dim y As Integer       ' A block variable
    ⋮
Next
Do
    Dim y As Long       ' Another block variable
    ⋮
Loop
```

One more detail about block variables: although their scope is the block in which they are declared, their lifetime coincides with the procedure's lifetime. In other words, if you reenter the same block, the variable isn't initialized again and contains the value it had the last time the block was exited. For example, consider this code:

```
For z = 1 To 2
    ⋮
    For x = 1 To 2
        Dim y As Long
        y = y + 1
        Console.WriteLine(y)
    Next
Next
```

After you run the preceding code, the console window contains the values 1 2 3 4. If this behavior isn't exactly what you meant to achieve, you must reinitialize the variable inside the block by using an explicit assignment or by using an initializer, which I explain later in this chapter.

Data Types

Visual Basic .NET supports most of the data types available under previous versions of Visual Basic, including Single, Double, and String. Things aren't smooth at all in this area, though, because many important under-the-covers changes have been made and will affect you, especially if you're porting legacy applications to Visual Basic .NET.

The Object Data Type

First and foremost, the Variant type isn't supported any longer. The .NET data type closest to Variant is the System.Object type. The Object type has become the one-size-fits-all data type under Visual Basic .NET in that it can contain *any* type and therefore is significantly different from the Object data type that you find in previous language versions. Object variables can be assigned any type because, in the .NET Framework, *everything* is an object, including Integer and String values. More precisely, all the basic data types are defined in the System namespace and directly inherit from the System.Object. As you will see in greater detail in Chapter 5, a variable can always be assigned a value whose type inherits from the variable's class. Therefore, the following statements are legal under Visual Basic .NET:

```
Dim o As Object
Dim s As String
s = "ABCDE"
o = 123            ' Assign an integer to an Object variable.
o = s              ' Assign a string to an Object variable.
```

You might argue that using an object to hold a scalar value such as a string or an integer sounds like a waste of memory and that the practice can slow down your application considerably. This is partly true, but you should consider that Visual Basic .NET objects take fewer resources and are inherently more efficient than Visual Basic 6 objects. There's more to learn about this topic, as you'll see in the "Value Types and Reference Types" section later in this chapter.

Integer Data Types

Visual Basic .NET Long variables hold 64-bit integer values—and are therefore ready for future CPUs and operating systems—while Integer variables hold 32-bit values and therefore should replace Long variables when you're porting Visual Basic 6 applications. The new Short data value can accommodate 16-bit values, while the Byte data type still works with unsigned 8-bit values. For example, let's see how you can convert a group of variable declarations from Visual Basic 6 to Visual Basic .NET:

```
' A Visual Basic 6 group of variable declarations
Dim b As Byte
Dim i As Integer
Dim l As Long

' The corresponding Visual Basic .NET code fragment
Dim b As Byte
Dim i As Short
Dim l As Integer
```

Most of the time, you can keep the Integer and Long data types when you're converting a legacy application to Visual Basic .NET, and the resulting code will work as it used to. However, 64-bit integer operations map to multiple assembly opcodes on 32-bit processors, so unnecessarily using Long can hurt performance.

The Boolean Data Type

The Boolean data type has survived the transition from Visual Basic 6 to Visual Basic .NET, but there are two points to be considered. First, the new Boolean type takes 4 bytes instead of 2, so large Boolean arrays take more memory and tax your application's performance. Second, whereas in the .NET runtime the True value is rendered as 1, Visual Basic .NET uses the value -1 for better compatibility with previous versions of the language.

In earlier Visual Basic .NET beta versions, the True value was rendered as 1 for the sake of uniformity with other .NET languages. Starting at Beta 2, however,

Microsoft decided that improving backward compatibility was a more pressing goal than language interoperability, so the product team restored the Visual Basic 6 behavior. The good news is that the True value is automatically converted to 1 when passed from Visual Basic to other languages, so language interoperability shouldn't be seriously affected by this decision.

Most Visual Basic programs don't depend on how True values are rendered because you typically use Boolean values from comparison operators in If and Do expressions, as in this code:

```
' The expression (x < 100) creates a temporary Boolean value.
If x < 100 Then x = x + 1
```

The internal value of True becomes important when you use comparison operators inside assignment statements. For example, a Visual Basic 6 developer can replace the preceding statement with the following one, which is more concise even though not necessarily faster:

```
' Increment x if it is less than 100.
x = x - (x < 100)
```

The preceding expression works correctly under Visual Basic .NET as well. However, you must convert the Boolean expression to an Integer explicitly if Option Strict is on. (I cover the Option Strict statement later in this chapter.)

```
' Increment x if it is less than 100.
' (This works also when Option Strict is on.)
x = x - CInt(x < 100)
```

The Decimal Data Type

The Currency data type isn't supported in the .NET Framework and has been replaced by the Decimal type, which offers wider range and better precision. Indirect evidence that the Decimal type is meant to replace the Currency type shows up in the trailing @ symbol (once reserved for Currency values) that you now use to tell the compiler that you're actually working with a Decimal value:

```
Dim d As Decimal
⋮
' Make it clear that you're adding a Decimal constant.
d = d + 123.45@
```

The Decimal data type is different from the Decimal subtype available under Visual Basic 6, which allows you to store Decimal values only in Variant variables. The Decimal type holds a number in fixed-point format and is useful for preventing rounding and truncating problems; it can hold values in the range + or −79,228,162,514,264,337,593,543,950,335 with no decimal point, or + through −7.9228162514264337593543950335 with 28 places to the right of the decimal. The smallest nonzero number that you can represent with this data type is + or −0.0000000000000000000000000001.

The Char Data Type

The Char data type is a new entry in the list of data types that Visual Basic supports. A Char variable can hold a single Unicode character and therefore takes 2 bytes. When assigning a literal character to a Char variable, you should use a trailing *c* to let Visual Basic .NET know that the literal character must be converted to a Char before the assignment:

```
Dim ch As Char
ch = "A"c          ' Note the trailing "c" character.

' *** The following line raises a compilation error.
ch = "ABC"c        ' More than one character
```

You can't assign a string expression to a Char variable; instead, you must explicitly ask for a conversion from String to Char data type using the new CChar function:

```
ch = CChar(Mid("Francesco", 3, 1))
```

You can use the Chr function to convert a Unicode code to a character, as in this code snippet:

```
ch = Chr(65)     ' This is the "A" character.
```

In case you're wondering why you should use the more limited Char variable instead of a full-featured String value, the answer is simple: better performance. The reasons for this, however, will be clear only when I discuss garbage collection later in this chapter.

Mapping .NET Data Types

Visual Basic .NET supports a subset of all the data types defined in the .NET Framework, as summarized in Table 2-1 (taken from the .NET Framework Developers Guide). The correspondence is perfect, and you can even declare your variables using the .NET data type if you prefer:

```
' Declare a String and a Date the .NET way.
Dim s As System.String          ' Equivalent to As String
Dim d As System.DateTime        ' Equivalent to As Date
```

Table 2-1 Data Types Supported Under Visual Basic .NET and Their Corresponding .NET Framework Types

Visual Basic Type	.NET Runtime Type	Storage Size	Value Range
Boolean	System.Boolean	4 bytes	True or False
Byte	System.Byte	1 byte	0 to 255 (unsigned)
Char	System. Char	2 bytes	0 to 65535 (unsigned)
Date	System. DateTime	8 bytes	January 1, 1 CE to December 31, 9999
Decimal	System.Decimal	12 bytes	+/-79,228,162,514,264,337,593,543,950,335 with no decimal point; +/-7.9228162514264337593543950335 with 28 places to the right of the decimal; smallest nonzero number is +/-0.0000000000000000000000000001
Double	System.Double	8 bytes	-1.79769313486231E308 to -4.94065645841247E-324 for negative values; 4.94065645841247E-324 to 1.79769313486232E308 for positive values
Integer	System.Int32	4 bytes	-2,147,483,648 to 2,147,483,647
Long (long integer)	System.Int64	8 bytes	-9,223,372,036,854,775,808 to 9,223,372,036,854,775,807
Object	System.Object (class)	4 bytes	Any type can be stored in a variable of type Object.
Short	System.Int16	2 bytes	-32,768 to 32,767
Single	System.Single	4 bytes	-3.402823E38 to -1.401298E-45 for negative values; 1.401298E-45 to 3.402823E38 for positive values
String	System.String (class)	10 bytes + (2 * string length)	0 to approximately 2 billion Unicode characters
User-Defined Type (Structure block)	(Inherits from System.ValueType)	Sum of the size of its members	Each member of the structure has a range determined by its data type and is independent of the ranges of the other members.

Fixed-Length Strings

You might have noticed that I haven't raised the subject of fixed-length strings yet. I haven't mentioned them because fixed-length strings aren't supported in

Visual Basic .NET. Fixed-length strings should be considered leftovers from the old QuickBasic days; in fact, they've had a difficult life since Microsoft released Visual Basic 4, the first version that embraces the COM paradigm. Because of the many limitations that fixed-length strings endured under Visual Basic—for one, they couldn't be used as arguments and return values—most Visual Basic developers haven't used them in recent projects. So the lack of support for fixed-length strings under .NET shouldn't have a serious impact on how new applications are developed.

To help you port Visual Basic 6 code that uses fixed-length strings, Microsoft has provided the FixedLengthString class in the Microsoft.VisualBasic.Compatibility.VB6 namespace.

> **Note** The .NET library that contains this DLL isn't added to the list of references when you create a new project. If you get a compiler error when running any code sample in this section, you should use the Add Reference command on the Project menu to manually add a reference to the Microsoft Visual Basic .NET Compatibility Runtime library.

The FixedLengthString class has a New constructor method that takes a numeric value (the size of the fixed-length string) and the Value property, so the syntax for using this data type is different from that of previous language versions:

```
' This statement declares a fixed-length string of 10 characters
' and is therefore equivalent to the Visual Basic 6 statement:
'     Dim s As String * 10
Dim s As New Microsoft.VisualBasic.Compatibility.VB6.FixedLengthString(10)
```

In real-world applications, you might want to use an Imports statement to shorten the class name:

```
Imports Microsoft.VisualBasic.Compatibility.VB6
:
Dim s As New FixedLengthString(10)
```

Because Visual Basic .NET doesn't support default properties, you must explicitly refer to the Value property whenever you want to assign or read the value of a FixedLengthString object:

```
' ...(Continuing previous example)...
s.Value = "123456789012345"           ' 15 characters
' The characters in excess have been truncated.
Console.WriteLine(s.Value)            ' => 1234567890
```

Initializers

Under Visual Basic .NET, you can declare and initialize a variable in the same statement. This long-awaited feature lets you simplify your code and improve its readability:

```
' Two examples of variable initializers
Dim width As Single = 1000
Dim firstName As String = "Francesco"
```

The preceding lines are therefore functionally equivalent to the following Visual Basic 6 code:

```
Dim width As Single: width = 1000
Dim firstName As String: firstName = "Francesco"
```

Note that you can initialize a variable only if it's the sole variable declared in the Dim, Public, or Private statement:

```
' *** This line doesn't compile.
Dim x, y, z As Long = 1
```

One feature of initializers is that the value being assigned doesn't need to be a constant:

```
Dim startDate As Date = Now()
```

More Concise Code with Initializers

Initializers are especially useful for class-level variables and global variables. For example, consider the following Visual Basic class, which contains a Public property that is initialized in the Class_Initialize event:

```
' *** This is VB6 code - doesn't run under VB .NET.
' The Person class module
Public Country As String

Private Sub Class_Initialize()
    ' Provide a default for the Country property.
    Country = "USA"
End Sub
```

You can achieve the same result under Visual Basic .NET with a single statement:

```
Class Person
    Public Country As String = "USA"
End Class
```

Similarly, consider the code that you need under Visual Basic 6 to correctly initialize a global variable defined in a module:

```
' *** This is VB6 code - doesn't run under VB .NET.
Public StartDate As Date

Sub Main()
    ' Provide initial value for the StartDate variable.
    StartDate = Now()
End Sub
```

Visual Basic .NET initializers let you merge the declaration and the assignment in one statement:

```
Module MainModule
    Public StartDate As Date = Now()
End Module
```

Finally, initializers are especially useful with block variables to ensure that the variable is correctly reinitialized to a given value whenever the block is reentered. This is the only case in which it makes sense to use initializers to assign a variable its default value (0 for numbers, empty string for String variables, and so on):

```
For z = 1 To 2
    ⋮
    For x = 1 To 2
        ' Ensure that the y variable always starts at 0.
        Dim y As Long = 0
        ⋮
    Next
Next
```

Initializers and Object Variables

Initializers also work with variables holding object references. For example, the following statements declare and create an ADO.NET DataSet object:

```
Dim ds As System.Data.DataSet
ds = New System.Data.DataSet
```

You can make your code more concise as follows:

```
Dim ds As System.Data.DataSet = New System.Data.DataSet
```

Even better, Visual Basic .NET supports a special syntax that lets you get rid of the repeated class name:

```
Dim ds As New System.Data.DataSet
```

The preceding statement looks like a Visual Basic 6 declaration, but don't let the resemblance confuse you. Under previous language versions, the As New syntax creates a so-called *auto-instancing* object variable: the compiler generates code that checks such a variable before each reference to it and automatically creates an object of the corresponding type if the variable is found to be Nothing. As a result, no object is ever created if the variable is never referenced during the execution path.

Under Visual Basic .NET, the preceding statement is simply a special form of a variable initializer, and an object is always created when the Dim statement is executed. Visual Basic .NET doesn't support any syntax form that corresponds to the Visual Basic 6 auto-instancing variables.

Initializers also support object constructors that take parameters. (I cover constructors in Chapter 4.) For example, the constructor for the DataSet object supports a string argument to which you pass the name of the DataSet object itself:

```
Dim ds As New System.Data.DataSet("Publishers")
```

Assignments

Most of the time, you assign values to variables as you do under Visual Basic 6 or earlier versions. However, the way you deal with conversions between different types and the way you assign object variables have changed dramatically under Visual Basic .NET.

The Option Strict Statement

One defect of Visual Basic that many detractors have mentioned was the lack of control over conversions between different types. For example, in Visual Basic 6 the following code is perfectly legal:

```
Dim s As Single, d As Double
d = 1 / 3
s = d
```

The problem with the preceding code is that when you assign a Double variable or expression to a Single variable, you're going to lose precision and might even incur an overflow error. This type of conversion is also known as *narrowing conversion*. Other examples of narrowing conversions are from Long to Integer or to Byte, or from Double to Long. A conversion in the opposite direction—for example, from Single to Double—is known as *widening conversion* and should always be allowed because you can't lose precision or cause overflow errors.

Visual Basic .NET supports the new Option Strict compiler directive, which you can set to On to disable implicit narrowing conversions. For example, the following code doesn't compile:

```
Option Strict      ' Same as Option Strict On

Module MyModule
    Sub Main
        Dim d As Double = 1.123
        Dim s As Single
        s = d      ' Narrowing conversion raises compilation error.
    End Sub
End Module
```

Note that you can omit the On keyword because Option Strict is sufficient to activate this feature. You don't need to include this directive in all your modules because you can set a projectwide setting in the project Properties Page dialog box. (See Figure 2-5.)

By default, Option Strict is set to Off at the project level, presumably in order to facilitate importing of Visual Basic 6 projects. However, I strongly suggest that you turn it on—at least for all new projects—so that you can take advantage of this new feature. You'll spend more time writing code because you have to manually convert values to the target type, but this extra effort pays off nicely at debug time because you don't have to worry about subtle conversion bugs.

If Option Strict is on for the entire project, you can turn it off locally by inserting the following statement at the top of individual source files:

```
Option Strict Off
```

When Option Strict is off, you can implicitly convert between strings and dates, string and Boolean values, and string and numeric values, as you did in Visual Basic 6. If Option Strict is on, you must explicitly state your intention by using a conversion function, such as CInt, CLng, or CSng:

```
' This code works regardless of the current Option Strict setting.
Dim d As Double = 1.123
Dim s As Single = CSng(d)
```

The Option Strict On statement implicitly forces you to declare all your variables, so you can omit an Option Explicit On statement in the same module because Option Strict On implies Option Explicit On. If Option Strict is on, any undeclared variable raises a compilation error. Another side effect of the Option Strict option is to disallow late binding operations:

```
' If Option Strict is on, the following code doesn't compile.
Dim o As Object
o = New Form1
o.Show               ' Late binding method call
```

You must disable Option Strict to assign a Boolean value to a Short, an Integer, or a Long variable. This behavior is a bit disconcerting at first because a Boolean variable can hold only the values 0 and –1, so an assignment of this kind is never a narrowing conversion, and you might not see the need for setting Option Strict to Off:

```
Dim s As Short
Dim b As Boolean
' The following line doesn't compile if Option Strict is on.
s = b
' The following line always compiles.
' (Note the new CShort conversion function.)
s = CShort(b)
```

Similarly, you must use the CChar conversion function when you're converting a string to a Char variable because such an assignment is correctly considered a narrowing conversion. The Option Strict On statement has other effects on what your code can do:

- You can't use the integer division operator \ with floating-point numbers because this operator silently converts its operands to Long (a narrowing conversion).
- The ^ operator always returns a Double value, so you can't assign its result to anything other than a Double variable.
- Because conversions from integer types to Boolean are forbidden, you can't use an integer variable by itself in an If expression as a concise way to determine whether it's equal to 0:

```
' This statement doesn't work if Option Strict is on.
If intValue Then Console.WriteLine("intValue is <> 0")
' The correct way to translate the above statement for
' Visual Basic .NET
If intValue <> 0 Then Console.WriteLine("intValue is <> 0")
```

Finally, you can set the default Option Strict setting when you're compiling from the command prompt. And you can use the /OPTIONSTRICT+ switch to enforce it and /OPTIONSTRICT– to disable it:

```
vbc /optionstrict+ source.vb
```

Assigning Object Values

One of the major syntax changes in Visual Basic .NET is that the Set keyword is no longer needed to assign an object reference to an object variable, and in fact the Set keyword isn't valid in variable assignments. To understand the reason for this change, you must consider why the Set keyword was necessary under previous versions of the language.

All Visual Basic versions have supported the notion of default object members. Most Visual Basic 6 controls expose a default property (the Text property for TextBox controls, for example), the Collection object exposes the Item default method, and so on. The default property makes the following statement possible:

```
' Copy the contents of Text1 into Text2.
Text2 = Text1
```

which is actually a shorthand for the more verbose

```
Text2.Text = Text1.Text
```

Default properties and methods also work with classes you define in your application. For example, the following code uses a Person class that exposes Name as its default property:

```
Dim p1 As New Person
' Assign a name to this person.
p1 = "Francesco Balena"
' Copy the name into another object.
Dim p2 As New Person
p2 = p1
```

Note that the preceding code copies a string property from one object to another. But what happens if you want to store a reference to *p1* in the *p2* variable? The answer under Visual Basic 6 and earlier versions is the Set keyword:

```
' Correctly assign p2 a reference to p1 in Visual Basic 6.
Dim p2 As Person              ' New isn't required.
Set p2 = p1
```

The Set keyword is one of those Visual Basic anomalies that you can't find in other languages and that tends to confuse many novices. Worse, many developers—including expert ones—often mistakenly omit the Set keyword when assigning object references. Unfortunately, a missing Set keyword isn't flagged as a compiler error if the source object exposes a default member. In that event, the Visual Basic 6 compiler assumes that you're just assigning the default property or the result from the default method, rather than the object reference itself:

```
' Assign p2 a reference to p1 in Visual Basic 6.
Dim p2 As Person
'*** This statement doesn't work because Set is missing,
'*** but the compiler doesn't flag it as an error.
p2 = p1
```

Visual Basic .NET solves this ambiguity in a completely different, more radical way: default members are not supported under .NET, period. In other words, neither .NET classes nor classes that you define in your code can expose a default property or method. So you don't need a special keyword to deal with those default values in assignments, and you assign scalar values and object references in the same way:

```
' Assign p2 a reference to p1 in Visual Basic .NET.
Dim p1 As New Person
Dim p2 As New Person
p1.Name = "Francesco Balena"
' Copy the Name property from p1 to p2.
p2.Name = p1.Name
' Copy a reference to p1 into p3.
Dim p3 As Person
p3 = p1
```

You can even assign object references through initializers. For example, you can substitute the last two statements of the previous code snippet with this:

```
Dim p3 As Person = p1
```

Whereas the equal sign works for object assignments, you must still use the Is operator to test whether two object variables point to the same object in memory. This restriction has been added so that, if and when Visual Basic ever supports operator overloading, existing code based on the = comparison operator won't break because the code called an overloaded version rather than merely comparing the object instances.

Here's the one exception to the rule that states that classes can't have a default member: a property or method can be the default member for its class if it accepts one or more arguments. Take the Collection object as an example:

```
Sub TestCollections()
    ' The .NET version of the Collection object
    Dim col As New Microsoft.VisualBasic.Collection()
    ' Add two elements.
    col.Add("Francesco", "FirstName")
    col.Add("Balena", "LastName")
    ' The following statements are equivalent. (Item is the default member.)
    Console.WriteLine(col.Item(1))              ' => Francesco
    Console.WriteLine(col(1))                   ' => Francesco
    ' The following statements are equivalent. (Item is the default member.)
    Console.WriteLine(col.Item("LastName"))     ' => Balena
    Console.WriteLine(col("LastName"))          ' => Balena
End Sub
```

The reason for this exception to the general rule is that the presence of arguments makes the syntax unambiguous. For example, the following statement:

```
Dim o As Object
o = col(1)
```

can only mean that you're accessing the default Item method, whereas

```
o = col
```

means that you're assigning a reference to the Collection object.

Shorthand for Common Operations

Visual Basic .NET supports a variation of the standard assignment operation, which you can use when you're performing a math or string operation on a variable and are going to store the result in the variable itself. This shorthand is especially useful when you're incrementing or decrementing a variable:

```
Dim x As Long = 9
Dim y As Double = 6.8

' Increment x by one (same as x = x + 1).
x += 1
' Decrement y by two (same as y = y - 2).
y -= 2
' Double x (same as x = x * 2).
x *= 2
' Divide x by ten (same as x = x \ 10).
x \= 10
' Divide y by four (same as y = y / 4).
y /= 4
' Raise y to the 3rd power (same as y = y ^ 3).
y ^= 3
```

Finally, you can use either the &= operator or the += operator to append a value to a string variable:

```
Dim s As String
' Append a constant to a string (same as s = s & "ABC").
s &= "ABC"
```

If Option Strict is on, you can use neither the \= operator with floating-point variables (because the \ operator converts its operands to Long) nor the ^= operator with anything but a Double variable (because the ^ operator returns a Double value).

Value Types and Reference Types

You can group all the data types that the .NET Framework supports—both the native types and the types you create—in two broad categories: reference types and value types. In a nutshell, reference types behave like objects, whereas value types behave like scalar types (Integer or Single). You need to understand the differences between the two, or you might introduce subtle bugs into your code.

In the .NET Framework, everything is an object, and most data types are reference types. When you declare a variable of a reference type, you're allocating a pointer variable (a 32-bit integer value on current Windows platforms) that points to the actual object. The object itself is stored in a memory area called the *managed heap* and is under the supervision of the .NET Framework runtime, whereas the pointer variable can be stored elsewhere (for example, on the stack if it's a dynamic variable declared inside a procedure). After all the pointer variables that point to a given object go out of scope or are explicitly set to Nothing, the object undergoes a process known as *garbage collection*, and the memory it takes in the heap is freed. Unlike Visual Basic 6 and COM objects, the memory allocated for .NET objects isn't released immediately after all the pointer variables are destroyed because garbage collection occurs only when the .NET runtime runs out of memory in the managed heap. This phenomenon is also known as *nondeterministic finalization*, and I'll talk about it in greater detail in Chapter 4.

Value types inherit from System.ValueType. This class inherits from System.Object (as do all the classes defined in the .NET Framework, either directly or indirectly) but redefines its methods. Value types aren't allocated in the managed heap, and the corresponding variable *holds* the value rather than *points* to it. The actual location in which a value type is stored depends on its scope: for example, local value type variables are allocated on the stack. All .NET numeric types are value types, as are Enums and the types you define with a Structure...End Structure block; .NET strings and arrays are reference types, as are all the objects you define with a Class...End Class block. If you're in doubt as to whether a .NET type is a class or a structure, just read the documentation or view it in the object browser (which displays different icons for classes and structures).

You'll learn more about value types in Chapter 8, but you need at least these basics to understand a few topics in this and the next chapter.

In general, value types are faster than similar reference types, for two reasons: you don't need to dereference a pointer to get to the actual data, and, more important, you don't need to allocate and then release memory in the managed heap. If a value type variable is held on the stack (as you see in the following illustration), the variable is automatically destroyed and no time-consuming cleanup operation is needed when you exit the procedure.

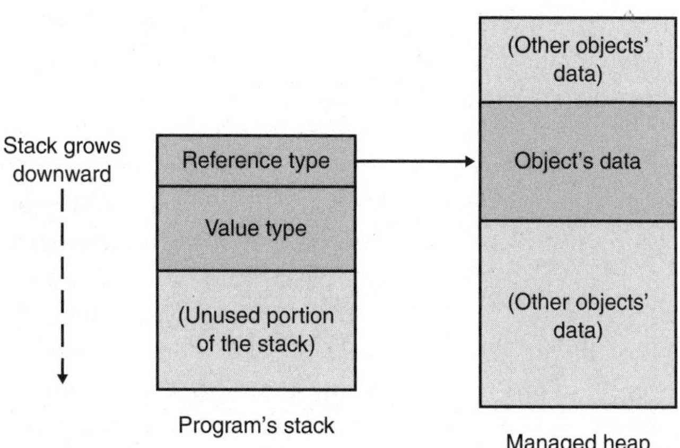

You must pay attention to whether you're dealing with a reference or a value type for two reasons. First and foremost, the assignment operation works differently in the two cases. When you assign a reference type to a variable, you're actually assigning the pointer so that the target variable will now point to the original value. No data is duplicated, and you can modify the original data through both the original and the new variable. This is typical object behavior, and includes objects that you instantiate from classes defined in your application:

```
' Person is a class defined in the current application.
Dim p1 As New Person
p1.FirstName = "Francesco"
' Assign to another Person variable.
Dim p2 As Person
p2 = p1
' You can modify the original object through the new variable.
p2.FirstName = "Joe"
Console.WriteLine(p1.FirstName)    ' => Joe
```

Conversely, when you assign a value type—such as a numeric data type—to a variable of the same type, a *copy* of the original data is assigned, and therefore the original data and the new variable are completely unrelated.

An important detail: the .NET String class is a reference type, as the following code snippet demonstrates:

```
Dim s1 As String = "Francesco"
Dim s2 As String = s1
' Prove that the two variables point to the same String object.
Console.WriteLine(s2 Is s1)             ' => True
```

The second reason you must pay attention to the nature of the data you process—reference type or value type—concerns performance. As I've explained, value types are usually faster. In addition, sometimes a value type is converted to a reference type and back without your being aware of this internal conversion that silently slows down your code.

To refine this explanation, whenever you pass a value type to a method that takes an object argument, the value is converted to a reference type: the .NET runtime allocates a block of memory in the managed heap, copies the value in that area, and passes the method a pointer to that memory location. This operation is known as *boxing*. For example, you have a hidden boxing operation when you pass a number to the Debug.Write method because that method can take only an Object or a String argument.

The simplest example of a boxing operation occurs when you assign a value type—an integer, for example—to an Object variable:

```
Dim i As Integer = 1234
' The next statement causes the following sequence of operations:
' (1) a block of memory is allocated in the heap;
' (2) the original integer value is copied in that memory block;
' (3) the address of the block is assigned to the Object variable.
Dim o As Object = i
```

As you might guess, boxing a value is a time-consuming activity. Likewise, you waste CPU time when you reassign a boxed value back to a variable of a value type—an operation known as *unboxing*:

```
' ...(Continuing the previous example)...
' The next statement causes the following sequence of operations:
' (1) the pointer in the o variable is used to locate the data;
' (2) the integer is copied into the target variable;
' (3) the heap memory used by the o variable is garbage collected
'     (eventually, some time after the o variable is set to Nothing).
' (Next statement doesn't compile if Option Strict is on.)
Dim i2 As Integer = o
```

Note that the previous code snippet works only if Option Strict is disabled; if Option Strict is on, you must rewrite the last statement this way:

```
Dim i2 As Integer = CInt(o)
```

Here's the bottom line: always use value types rather than reference types if you have a choice. For example, use Char variables instead of String variables if you're working with one-character strings. And enable Option Strict at the application level so that an unboxing operation can't go unnoticed.

There's more to reference types, value types, boxing, and unboxing, as you'll learn in Chapter 8.

The CType Operator

As you know, the Option Strict On statement prevents the programmer from inserting code that might fail at run time because of a failed conversion. For this reason, when you're unboxing a value from an Object variable to a value type variable, you need an explicit conversion function (CInt in the following statement):

```
' obj is an Object variable.
Dim i As Integer = CInt(obj)
```

Whereas you can always assign a Person object to an Object variable without any particular precaution—because this assignment can never fail at run time—the opposite assignment might fail if the object isn't compatible with the type of the target variable. Because this assignment is a narrowing conversion, you must tell the compiler that you know what you're doing if Option Strict is on. You do this by manually converting (or *coercing*, or *casting*) the object to the target type, using the CType operator:

```
' obj is an Object variable.
Dim pers As Person = CType(obj, Person)
```

Note that the second argument of the CType operator is the name of the target class and isn't enclosed in quotes.

If the argument can't be directly cast to the target type, CType attempts to convert it. For example, the following statement successfully converts the string to the integer, even if it means dropping the fractional portion of the original number embedded in the string:

```
Dim res As Integer = CType("123.45", Integer)
Console.WriteLine(res)                    ' => 123
```

If the argument cannot be converted to the target type, CType throws an InvalidCastException object.

In case you're wondering why I classify CType as an operator instead of as a function, the reason is that the Visual Basic .NET compiler translates CType directly to MSIL language in most cases, as it does for operators such as + and *.

The DirectCast Operator

The DirectCast keyword offers yet another way to convert between types. This keyword has the same syntax as CType but differs from the latter in a few important details. First, DirectCast works only with arguments of reference types and attempts to pass value types are flagged as compilation errors. (CType works with both reference and value types.)

Second, CType always attempts to convert the argument to the target type and is therefore able to convert a string into a numeric type (if the string actually contains a number, of course); DirectCast works only if the source argument can be cast to the target type and throws an InvalidCastException object otherwise. (DirectCast is unable of performing even widening conversions from Short to Integer or Single to Double.)

Third, DirectCast is slightly faster than CType, so you should use the former when you want to cast rather than convert a value. In practice you can (and should) use the DirectCast keyword on three occasions:

- When unboxing a value type that was previously boxed in an Object variable
- When casting a variable of a base class to a variable of a derived class—for example, a Person variable to an Employee variable or an Object variable to another reference type
- When casting an object variable to an interface variable

Constants and Enums

In a difference from previous language versions, Visual Basic .NET classes can expose public constants, which are seen from outside the class as read-only fields. Except for this detail, their syntax is similar to that in Visual Basic 6:

```
' This works only if Option Explicit is off.
Public Const DefaultPassword = "mypwd"
```

If Option Explicit is enabled, constants require an explicit type declaration:

```
' This works always and is the recommended syntax.
Public Const DefaultPassword As String = "mypwd"
```

Enum blocks can appear anywhere in a source file, an inside module, a class, or structure blocks or directly at the namespace level.

```
Enum Shape
    Triangle        ' This takes a zero value.
    Square          ' 1
    Rectangle       ' 2
    Circle          ' 3
    Unknown = -999  ' (Values don't need to be sorted.)
End Enum

' A variable that can be assigned an Enum type
Dim aShape As Shape = Shape.Square
```

In another difference from Visual Basic 6, which implicitly used 32-bit integers for Enum values, you can choose among the Byte, Short, Integer, and Long data types, where Integer is the default type if omitted. (SDK documentation suggests that you use Integer unless you have a good reason to do otherwise.) You can't omit the name of the Enum when you're using an enumerated constant:

```
' 16 bits are enough for this Enum, so we can use Short.
Enum Shape As Short
```

```
    Triangle        ' This takes a zero value.
    ⋮
End Enum

' *** The following line doesn't compile because you
'     must use the complete name Shape.Square.
Dim aShape As Shape = Square
```

If no explicit value is provided, the first member inside the Enum block is assigned the value 0, the second member is assigned the value 1, and so on. Even though Enum values are internally stored as integers, by default you aren't allowed to assign a number to an Enum variable if Option Strict is on, and you must convert the number to the proper Enum type before assigning it an Enum variable:

```
aShape = CType(1, Shape)
```

Arrays

Arrays have undergone many changes in the migration to Visual Basic .NET. First of all, arrays are always zero-based:

```
' This statement always declares an array of 11 elements.
Dim arr(10) As Integer
```

Because the first element of all arrays has a zero index, the To keyword inside a Dim statement is forbidden, and the Option Base statement isn't supported any longer.

The ReDim Statement

As in Visual Basic 6 and previous versions, you can declare an array with the Dim statement and actually allocate memory for it with a subsequent ReDim statement. Under Visual Basic .NET, however, the ReDim statement can't be used to declare an array—in other words, you can't have a ReDim statement without a Dim statement for a given array. Because ReDim can never declare the type of an array, it doesn't support the As clause:

```
' Declare the array.
Dim arr() As Integer
⋮
' Create the array.
ReDim arr(100)          ' Note that no As clause is used here.
```

One problem that the Visual Basic 6 compiler copes with is that the ReDim statement can change the number of dimensions in the array; this feature keeps the compiler from producing the most efficient code possible because it must always check how many dimensions an array has before accessing its elements. For example, the following code is legal under previous versions of Visual Basic:

```
' *** This code works under VB6 but not under Visual Basic .NET.
' You must declare the array with a separate Dim statement.
Dim arr() As Integer
' Create a one-dimensional array, and use it.
ReDim arr(10) As Integer
arr(1) = 123
' Re-create the array as bidimensional, and use it.
ReDim arr(10, 10) As Integer
arr(1, 1) = 199
```

To let the compiler produce more efficient code, Visual Basic .NET introduces the concept of *rank*, that is, the number of dimensions in an array. New syntax rules dictate that ReDim can change the number of elements in an array but can't change the rank of the array itself. You indicate the rank of an array in a Dim statement by inserting the appropriate number of commas inside the parentheses:

```
' Declare a two-dimensional array.
Dim arr2(,) As String
' Declare a three-dimensional array.
Dim arr3(,,) As String
⋮
' Create the arrays.
ReDim arr2(10, 10)
ReDim arr3(10, 10, 10)
```

You can re-create the array as many times as you need, provided you don't change the rank of the array. You can also use ReDim Preserve if you want to keep values already in the array. As in Visual Basic 6 and previous versions, ReDim Preserve lets you change only the number of elements in the last dimension:

```
' ...(Continuing the previous code snippet)...
ReDim Preserve arr2(10, 20)
ReDim Preserve arr3(10, 10, 20)

'*** The following statements raise an
'    ArrayTypeMismatchException exception at run time.
ReDim Preserve arr2(20, 10)
ReDim Preserve arr3(10, 20, 20)
```

Array Initializers

Initializers also work with arrays, and you can initialize the values in an array by using a comma-delimited list of values enclosed by curly braces:

```
' Declare and create an array of 5 integers.
Dim arr() As Integer = {0, 1, 2, 3, 4}
```

You must omit the number of elements in the Dim statement if you use an initializer. When creating multidimensional arrays, however, you must indicate the rank of the array, and you use nested blocks of curly braces:

```
' Declare and create a two-dimensional array of strings
' with two rows and four columns.
Dim arr2(,) As String = { {"00", "01", "02", "03"}, _
                          {"10", "11", "12", "13"} }
```

Copying Arrays

Starting with Visual Basic 6, you can assign one array to another:

```
' *** Visual Basic 6 code
Dim arr1(3) As Integer
Dim arr2() As Integer
' Initialize the array with some data.
arr1(1) = 111: arr1(2) = 222: arr1(3) = 333
' Copy the array into another array.
arr2() = arr1()
```

Visual Basic .NET also supports array assignment, but the result is different from what you might expect because the Visual Basic .NET array is a *reference type*—in other words, it's more akin to an object than to an old-style array. See what a difference the reference nature of an array can make:

```
' *** Visual Basic .NET code
Dim arr1() As Integer = {0, 111, 222, 333}
Dim arr2() As Integer
' Create another reference to the array.
arr2 = arr1
' Modify the array through the second variable.
arr2(1) = 9999
' Check that the original array has been modified.
Console.WriteLine(arr1(1))      ' => 9999
```

Does this mean that Visual Basic .NET isn't able to copy arrays? Of course not, but you have to use a different syntax. Being objects, arrays expose several methods. One of these methods is Clone, which creates a *copy* of the original array and returns a reference to that copy. Let's rewrite the previous example to use the Clone method:

```
Dim arr3() As Integer = {0, 111, 222, 333}
' Create a copy (clone) of the array.
' (This code assumes that Option Strict is off.)
Dim arr4() As Integer
```

(continued)

```
arr4 = arr3.Clone
' Modify an element in the new array.
arr4(1) = 9999
' Check that the original array hasn't been affected.
Console.WriteLine(arr3(1))      ' => 111
```

If Option Strict is on, the preceding code fragment fails because the Clone method returns an Object value and the assignment results in a narrowing conversion. Note the empty pair of parentheses that you must use in the second argument of the CType or DirectCast operator when converting to an array of types:

```
' (This code works regardless of current Option Strict setting.)
arr4 = DirectCast(arr3.Clone, Integer())
' Modify an element in the new array.
```

In general, if you're converting a value to an array, the second argument of the CType or DirectCast operator must specify the rank of the target array, which you can do by using zero or more commas inside the pair of parentheses:

```
Dim arr5(,) As Integer = {{0, 1, 2, 3}, {0, 10, 20, 30}}
Dim arr6(,) As Integer
' Create a copy of the 2-dimensional array.
arr6 = CType(arr5.Clone, Integer(,))
```

If Option Strict is off, you can also assign an array to an Object variable and access the array's element through late binding:

```
' ...(Continuing the preceding code fragment)...
' (This code assumes that Option Strict is off.)
Dim o As Object = arr5
Console.WriteLine(o(1, 1))          ' => 10
```

Surprisingly, if you have an array of object elements (as opposed to value types, such as numbers and structures), you can even assign the array to an Object array. For example, because the Visual Basic .NET String type is an object type, the following code runs flawlessly:

```
Dim strArr() As String = {"00", "11", "22", "33", "44"}
Dim objArr() As Object = strArr
Console.WriteLine(objArr(2))        ' => 22
```

This is a particular case of a more general rule, which states that you can assign an array of type X to an array of type Y if the X type derives from Y. Because all classes inherit from Object, you can always assign an array of object types to an Object array. (You don't need Option Strict to be off for this assignment to succeed.) However, this kind of assignment works only if X is a reference type. For example, it works with strings and with classes you define but fails with numeric arrays and arrays of user-defined Structure types. (Read on to learn about Structure types.)

The Array object exposes many other intriguing methods, as you will learn in Chapter 9.

Arrays as Public Members of a Class

An interesting new feature of arrays is that you can expose them as public members of a class. This means that the following code—which would raise a compiler error under previous versions of the language—is legal under Visual Basic .NET:

```
Class Person
    ' Provide up to 4 lines for address.
    Public Address(4) As String
    ⋮
End Class
```

Under Visual Basic 6, you must create a Property Let and Property Get pair of procedures that take a numeric index argument and set or return the corresponding element of a private array. The Visual Basic .NET solution is more concise and efficient.

Structures

The Type...End Type block isn't supported in Visual Basic .NET and has been replaced by the Structure...End Structure block, which offers many additional features and is actually more similar to classes than to the old user-defined types (or UDTs) allowed in previous language versions. You can have a structure at the namespace level, inside a Class or Module block, or even inside another structure.

Members inside a structure must be prefixed with an accessibility (visibility) qualifier, as in this code:

```
Structure PersonStruct
    Dim FirstName As String        ' Dim means Public here.
    Dim LastName As String
    Public Address As String
    Private SSN As String
End Structure
```

The declaration of the structure's data members can neither include initializers nor use the As New declaration syntax. As comments in the preceding example suggest, the default accessibility level for structures—that is, the visibility level implied by a Dim keyword—is Public (unlike classes, where the default level is Private). Visual Basic .NET unifies the syntax of classes and structures, and structures support most of the functionality of classes, including methods:

```
Structure PersonStruct
    Dim FirstName As String
    Dim LastName As String
    Public Address As String
    Private SSN As String

    Function CompleteName() As String
        CompleteName = FirstName & " " & LastName
    End Function
End Structure
```

Like classes, structures can also embed properties. (For more information, read the "Properties" section of Chapter 4.) Unlike classes, however, structures are value types rather than reference types. Among other things, this means that Visual Basic .NET automatically initializes a structure when you declare a variable of that type; in other words, this line:

```
Dim p As PersonStruct
```

is equivalent to one of the following statements:

```
Dim p As PersonStruct = New PersonStruct()      ' Verbose initializer
Dim p As New PersonStruct                       ' Shortened syntax
```

Each structure implicitly defines a parameterless constructor, which initializes each member of the structure to its default value (0 for numeric members, null string for String members, and Nothing for object members). It's illegal to define an explicit parameterless constructor or a destructor for the structure. But you can define a New constructor method with arguments, as follows:

```
Structure PersonStruct
    Dim FirstName As String
    Dim LastName As String
    Public Address As String
    Private SSN As String

    ' A constructor for this structure
    Sub New(ByVal FirstName As String, ByVal LastName As String)
        ' Note how you can use the Me keyword.
        Me.FirstName = FirstName
        Me.LastName = LastName
    End Function
    ⋮
End Structure
```

(See Chapter 4 for more information about constructor methods.) The constructor method is especially important because it lets you initialize the structure's members correctly. That you manage this task is vital, for example, when the structure contains fixed-length strings or, more precisely, their closest approximation under the .NET Framework:

```
' A structure with a fixed-length string

Structure PersonStruct
    Dim FirstName As String
    Dim LastName As String
    ' Simulate a fixed-length string.
    Dim ZipCode As Microsoft.VisualBasic.Compatibility.VB6.FixedLengthString

    Sub New(ByVal firstName As String, ByVal lastName As String)
        Me.FirstName = firstName
        Me.LastName = lastName
        ' Initialize the fixed-length string.
        ZipCode = New _
            Microsoft.VisualBasic.Compatibility.VB6.FixedLengthString(10)
    End Sub

    ' ...(The remainder of the code as in preceding code snippet)...
    ⋮
End Structure
```

That said, consider fixed-length strings your last resort because it's far preferable to convert them to regular strings when you're porting an application from previous versions of the language.

A consequence of the value type nature of Structure variables is that the actual data is copied when you assign a structure variable to another variable, whereas only a pointer to data is copied when you assign a reference value to a variable. Also note that the equality operator isn't supported for structures. This code summarizes the differences between classes and structures:

```
' This code assumes you have a PersonClass class, with the same structure
' as the PersonStruct structure.

Sub TestCompareStructuresAndClasses()
    ' Creation is similar, but structures don't require New.
    Dim aPersonObject As New Person()
    Dim aPersonStruct As PersonStruct         ' New is optional.

    ' Assignment to members is identical.
    aPersonObject.FirstName = "Joe"
```

(continued)

```
    aPersonObject.LastName = "Doe"
    aPersonStruct.FirstName = "Joe"
    aPersonStruct.LastName = "Doe"

    ' Method and property invocation is also identical.
    Console.WriteLine(aPersonObject.CompleteName())         ' => Joe Doe
    Console.WriteLine(aPersonStruct.CompleteName())         ' => Joe Doe

    ' Assignment to a variable of the same type has different effects.

    Dim aPersonObject2 As Person = aPersonObject
    ' Classes are reference types; hence, the new variable receives
    ' a pointer to the original object.
    aPersonObject2.FirstName = "Ann"
    ' The original object has been affected.
    Console.WriteLine(aPersonObject.FirstName)    ' => Ann
    '
    Dim aPersonStruct2 As PersonStruct = aPersonStruct
    ' Structures are value types; hence, the new variable receives
    ' a copy of the original structure.
    aPersonStruct2.FirstName = "Ann"
    ' The original structure hasn't been affected.
    Console.WriteLine(aPersonStruct.FirstName)    ' => Joe
End Sub
```

A few other features of classes aren't supported by structures in Visual Basic .NET. For example, structures implicitly inherit all the methods of the Object class, but they can't explicitly inherit from another structure, nor can they be inherited from.

After this first exposure to the most important syntax changes in how modules, classes, and variables are declared and used, you're ready to see what has changed in the language and how you can control execution flow under Visual Basic .NET.

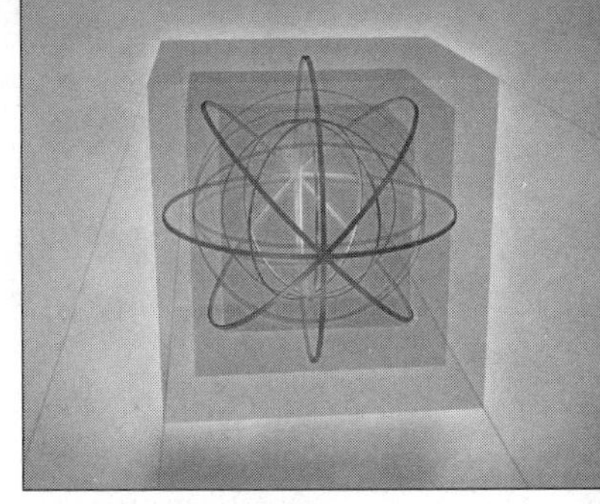

3

Control Flow and Error Handling

Even with the many changes in the core language syntax, Visual Basic .NET code continues to look like Visual Basic. Most of the differences are in the details, which means sometimes you must dig far into the language specifications to find what's new in Visual Basic.

That you must look carefully is especially true of statements that have to do with flow control, such as procedure definitions and execution flow statements, which I cover in the first part of this chapter. Later in this chapter, I show you which Visual Basic commands have been preserved in the transition to Visual Basic .NET and which have been replaced by something else. Finally, the last portion of this chapter explains what exceptions are and the .NET way of handling errors.

Execution Flow Control

Visual Basic .NET has inherited the syntax of most execution flow statements, such as the If, For, and Do loops, but a few old-style instructions have been dropped, such as GoSub. Most syntax changes are related to how procedures are defined and invoked.

Procedures

As in previous versions, Visual Basic .NET supports Sub and Function procedures, which can be Private, Public, or Friend. A procedure's definition can include ByVal and ByRef parameters, Optional parameters, and ParamArray arguments. However, there are a few important differences that you must take into account when porting a legacy application to avoid subtle bugs, and when building an application from scratch to avoid unnecessary performance hits.

Calling Procedures

A major syntax change under Visual Basic .NET is that the list of arguments being passed to a procedure must be always enclosed in brackets, whether you're calling a Sub or a Function procedure:

```
' A call to a Sub procedure
MySubProc(first, second)
```

Conveniently, the Visual Studio .NET editor puts a pair of parentheses around the argument list if you forget to add them yourself. If you consistently used the Call statement to invoke a procedure in your Visual Basic 6 applications, you don't have to alter the code in any way because the Call statement is still supported:

```
Call MySubProc(first, second)
```

If Option Strict is on, you can't rely on implicit narrowing conversions when you're passing arguments to a procedure. For example, when passing a Double variable to a Single argument you must make the conversion explicit by using the CSng function:

```
Dim d As Double = 1.23
MyProc(CSng(d))

Sub MyProc(ByVal s As Single)
    ⋮
End Sub
```

However, if Option Strict is off, Visual Basic .NET is even more permissive than previous versions of the language. For example, the following piece of code raises a "ByRef argument type mismatch" compiler error under Visual Basic 6:

```
Sub TestCallByRef()
    Dim intValue As Integer
    ' Pass an Integer argument to a ByRef Long parameter.
    Call MyProc(intValue)
End Sub

Sub MyProc(ByRef lngArg As Long)
    lngArg = 9999
End Sub
```

The same code compiles and runs correctly under Visual Basic .NET (again, if Option Strict is off). If the value assigned to the parameter inside the procedure (lngArg in the preceding example) is too large for the actual type of the original variable (intValue in the example), an overflow error is raised when the called procedure exits.

> **Note** The rule that requires enclosing arguments in parentheses doesn't apply to a small group of Visual Basic .NET commands, which includes Throw, AddHandler, and RemoveHandler. The key difference here is that these commands are language keywords rather than method calls.

ByVal and ByRef Arguments

By default, Visual Basic .NET passes arguments using ByVal, not ByRef as was the case with previous language versions, up to and including Visual Basic 6. If you're manually porting a legacy application, you must carefully add the ByRef keyword for all those arguments that don't have the explicit ByVal keyword. For example, the following Visual Basic procedure:

```
Sub MyProc(x As Integer, ByVal y As Long)
    ⋮
End Sub
```

must be translated as follows. (Note the change in data type as well.)

```
Sub MyProc(ByRef x As Short, ByVal y As Integer)
    ⋮
End Sub
```

As I explained previously, the ByVal keyword is optional, but it's a good practice to specify it, especially if the code will be used by developers who aren't familiar with new Visual Basic .NET conventions. Even better, while porting code from an older language version, you should reconsider whether the variable should be actually passed by reference: Visual Basic 6 developers often mindlessly omit the ByVal keyword but don't really mean to pass all the arguments by reference.

The point is that an argument that should be passed by value can also be passed by reference without causing any apparent problems, in most cases. (The opposite isn't true, of course: you immediately see when you're mistakenly passing by value an argument that should be passed by reference because the caller receives an unmodified value.) However, when you use an implicit ByRef where ByVal should be explicitly used in Visual Basic 6, you're creating a potential source for subtle bugs, and you're also preventing the compiler from doing the best job optimizing the resulting code. If you then migrate the code in Visual Basic .NET—for example, by importing the project in Visual Studio .NET—the inefficiency and the possibility of introducing bugs persists.

Passing Arrays

In a difference from previous Visual Basic versions, you can use the ByVal keyword for array parameters as well. However, Visual Basic .NET array variables are reference types—in other words, they point to the actual memory area in the managed heap where array items are stored. So you're passing a 4-byte pointer whether you're passing the array by value or by reference. In all cases, all changes to array elements inside the called procedure are reflected in the original array:

```
Sub TestArrayByVal()
    Dim anArray() As Integer = {0, 1, 2, 3, 4}
    ' Pass the array by value to a procedure.
    Call ArrayProcByVal(anArray)
    ' Prove that the array element has been modified.
    Console.WriteLine(anArray(3))     ' => 300
End Sub

' A procedure that modifies its array argument's elements
Sub ArrayProcByVal(ByVal arr() As Integer)
    Dim i As Integer
    For i = 0 To UBound(arr)
        arr(i) = arr(i) * 100
    Next
End Sub
```

Passing an array using ByRef or ByVal makes a difference if you use a ReDim statement inside the called procedure. In this case, the original array is affected if you pass it to a ByRef argument, but it isn't if you pass it to a ByVal argument. To show how this works, let's build a procedure that takes two array arguments with different passing mechanisms:

```
Sub TestArrayByRef()
    Dim byvalArray(10) As Integer
    Dim byrefArray(10) As Integer
    ' Pass both arrays to the procedure.
    Call ArrayProcByRef(byvalArray, byrefArray)
    ' Check which array has been affected by the ReDim.
    Console.WriteLine(UBound(byvalArray))   ' => 10 (not modified)
    Console.WriteLine(UBound(byrefArray))   ' => 100 (modified)
End Sub

Sub ArrayProcByRef (ByVal arr() As Integer, ByRef arr2() As Integer)
    ' Change the size of both arrays.
    Redim arr(100)
    Redim arr2(100)
End Sub
```

Array parameters must specify the rank of the incoming array. For example, the following procedure takes a two-dimensional Long array and a three-dimensional String array:

```
Sub MyProc(ByVal arr(,) As Long, ByVal arr2(, ,) As String)
    ⋮
End Sub
```

Optional Arguments

You can define optional arguments by using the Optional keywords, as you did with Visual Basic 6 procedures. However, you must always provide an explicit default value for each optional argument, even though the default value is 0 or an empty string:

```
Sub MyProc(Optional ByVal x As Integer = 0, _
    Optional ByVal y As String = "")
    ⋮
End Sub
```

The IsMissing function isn't supported under Visual Basic .NET for this simple reason: the IsMissing function can return True only when a Variant argument has been omitted, but the Variant type isn't supported under the current version of Visual Basic. Instead, you provide a special default value for an argument and test it inside the procedure if you want to determine whether it was omitted:

```
Sub MyProc(Optional ByVal x As Short = -1)
    If x = -1 Then
        ' The x argument has been omitted (presumably).
    End If
    ⋮
End Sub
```

You normally use –1 as a special value if the argument shouldn't take negative values; or you can use the largest negative or positive number for that numeric type. In this case, you might use the MinValue and MaxValue properties that all numeric classes expose:

```
Sub MyProc(Optional ByVal x As Long = Long.MinValue)
    If x = Long.MinValue Then
        ' The x argument has been omitted (presumably).
        Console.WriteLine(x)   ' => -9223372036854775808
    End If
    ⋮
End Sub
```

If the optional argument is a Single or a Double, you can also use the special NaN (Not-a-Number) value for its default:

```
Sub MyProc(Optional ByVal x As Double = Double.NaN)
    If Double.IsNaN(x) Then
        ' The x argument has been omitted.
    End If
End Sub
```

The NaN value is assigned to a floating-point number when you perform operations that don't return a real number, as when you pass a negative argument to the Log or Sqrt function. So there's a (very small) chance that you could mistakenly pass it to a procedure, as in the following code:

```
' This statement passes a NaN value to MyProc,
' which is mistakenly taken as a missing argument.
MyProc(Math.Sqrt(-1))
```

ParamArray Arguments

You can create procedures that take any number of optional arguments by using the ParamArray keyword. In a welcome improvement on previous language versions, you can define arrays of arguments of any type. (Visual Basic 6 and previous versions support only Variant arrays for ParamArray arguments.)

```
Function Sum(ParamArray ByVal args() As Integer) As Integer
    Dim sumResult As Integer
    Dim index As Integer
    For index = 0 To UBound(args)
        sumResult += args(index)
    Next
    Sum = sumResult
End Function
```

In two other differences from previous language versions, notice first that ParamArray arguments are always passed by value so that any change inside the procedure itself doesn't affect the caller. Second, you can never omit a parameter to a procedure that expects a ParamArray:

```
' *** If Sum takes a ParamArray, this statement compiles
'     in Visual Basic 6 but not under Visual Basic .NET.
Result = Sum(1, , 3)
```

Interestingly, the ParamArray parameter is an array in all aspects, and you can apply to it all the methods defined for arrays in the .NET Framework. Consider the following function, which returns the minimum value among all the arguments passed to it:

```
Function MinValue(ParamArray ByVal args() As Object) As Object
    Dim i As Short
    ' Note: this routine raises an error
    '       if no argument is passed to it.
    Dim result As Object = args(0)
    For i = 1 To UBound(args)
        If args(i) < result then result = args(i)
    Next
    MinValue = result
End Function
```

The .NET Framework offers a Sort method that can sort an array of any type, so you can rewrite the MinValue function in a more concise (though not necessarily faster) way:

```
Function MinValue(ParamArray ByVal args() As Object) As Object
    ' Sort the array, and then return its first element.
    System.Array.Sort(args)
    MinValue = args(0)
End Function
```

Returning a Value

Functions can return a value by assigning it to the function's name (as you do in Visual Basic 6) or by using the new Return statement:

```
Function DoubleIt(ByVal x As Long) As Long
    Return x * 2
End Function
```

The Return statement is especially handy when a function has multiple exit points because it saves your having to write an explicit Exit Function statement. You can also use the Return statement to return arrays, as you can see in this code:

```
' Return an array initialized with Integer values
' in the range 0 to n-1.
Function InitializeArray(ByVal n As Integer) As Integer()
    Dim res(n), i As Integer
    For i = 0 To n - 1
        res(i) = i
    Next
    Return res
End Function
```

Even when you don't have multiple exit points—as in the previous examples—you might prefer the new Return statement to the old syntax because you can then change the function name without also having to modify all the occurrences of the function name inside the procedure. It's a little detail that can save you some time during the refining phase.

Visual Basic .NET (like previous versions) allows you to use a function's name as a local variable inside the procedure. In many cases, this tactic spares you the trouble of using a local variable declaration and allows you to write more concise code. For example, the following alternative version of the Sum function doesn't use the result variable and doesn't require a final assignment to the Sum return value:

```
Function Sum2(ParamArray ByVal args() As Integer) As Integer
    Dim index As Integer
    For index = 0 To UBound(args)
```

(continued)

```
        Sum2 += args(index)
    Next
End Function
```

Microsoft documentation, however, states that the Return statement can improve performance because the local variable named after the function can prevent the Just-in-Time (JIT) compiler from optimizing your code. I have never observed a substantial difference in performance between the two approaches, at least in small routines used for my benchmarks, but this is yet another reason for using the new Return statement when possible.

Conditional and Loop Statements

Visual Basic .NET supports all of the conditional and loop statements supported by its predecessors—that is, the If and Select conditional blocks and the For, Do, and While loop statements. Nevertheless, the .NET Framework offers some new features in this area as well.

Short-Circuit Evaluation with AndAlso and OrElse Operators

Short-circuit evaluation allows you to avoid the unnecessary evaluation of Boolean subexpressions if they wouldn't affect the value of the main expression. Let's see a simple example:

```
If n1 > 0 And Sqr(n2) < n1 ^ 2 Then ok = True
```

If the *n1* variable is 0 or negative, the entire expression can only be False, whether the subexpression following the And operator evaluates to True or False. Previous Visual Basic versions always evaluate the entire If expression, so they incur an unnecessary performance hit.

Visual Basic .NET lets you produce smarter code using the new AndAlso and OrElse operators, which enforce short-circuit evaluation:

```
If n1 > 0 AndAlso Sqr(n2) < n1 ^ 2 Then ok = True
```

This expression is equivalent to the following, more verbose, code:

```
' "Manual" short-circuit evaluation
If n1 > 0 Then
    If Sqr(n2) < n1 ^ 2 Then ok = True
End If
```

You can have short-circuit evaluation in situations in which you use the Or operator:

```
If n1 > 0 Or Log(n2) > 2 Then ok = True
```

In this case, if the *n1* variable is greater than 0 the entire expression is surely True, so evaluating the second subexpression Log(n2) can be sidestepped. You can enforce this smarter behavior with the new OrElse operator:

```
If n1 > 0 OrElse Log(n2) > 2 Then ok = True
```

These new operators work also inside complex Boolean expressions:

```
Dim n1, n2, n3 As Integer          ' All variables are 0.
' The expression following the OrElse operator isn't evaluated
' because the test on n1 and n2 is sufficient.
If n1 = 0 AndAlso (n2 = 0 OrElse n3 = 0) Then ok = True
```

Short-circuit evaluation helps you avoid many run-time errors without writing much code. For example, you can use the following approach to read an array element only if the index is in the valid range:

```
' This line might raise an error under Visual Basic 6
' but always works fine under Visual Basic .NET.
If i >= 0 AndAlso i <= UBound(arr) AndAlso arr(i) > 0 Then
    ' arr(i) exists and is positive.
End If
```

Here's another example:

```
' You can avoid a division by zero error.
If n1 <> 0 AndAlso n2 \ n1 = n3 Then ok = True
```

The AndAlso operator lets you avoid errors when you check the property of an object variable that might be Nothing, or array elements that might not exist:

```
' Set ok to True if obj.Value is defined and non-negative.
If Not (obj Is Nothing) AndAlso obj.Value >= 0 Then ok = True

' Set ok to True if arr(n) is defined and equal to -1.
If n <= Ubound(arr) AndAlso arr(n) = -1 Then ok = True
```

Short-circuit evaluation can speed up your applications, but you must account for subtle bugs that might slip into your code. This is especially true when the subexpression contains user-defined functions that can alter the program's behavior. Consider this code:

```
' Is n2 incremented or not?
If n1 = 0 AndAlso Increment(n2) > 10 Then ok = True

Function Increment(ByRef value As Integer) As Integer
    value += 1
    Increment = value
End Function
```

Unless you're familiar with short-circuit evaluation—which might be the case if you're a C/C++ or Java developer—you might not immediately realize that the *n2* variable is incremented only if the *n1* variable is 0. You can make your code more readable by using nested If statements—in other words, by writing what you might call *manual* short-circuiting code:

```
' Is n2 incremented or not?
If n1 = 0 Then
    If Increment(n2) > 10 Then ok = True
End If
```

The And and Or operators work as they do in Visual Basic 6 and perform bitwise operations rather than truly Boolean operations. You can use them for bit-manipulation code as you've always done:

```
' Check whether bit 1 is set.
' (You need the CBool function if Option Strict is On.)
If CBool(n1 And 2) Then ...
```

> **Note** Microsoft introduced the new AndAlso and OrElse operators in Beta 2 of Visual Basic .NET; in Beta 1, the And and Or operators performed short-circuit evaluation automatically. Microsoft restored their Visual Basic 6 semantics because the porting of Visual Basic 6 code would have been too complicated—automatic short-circuit evaluation could have introduced bugs. (Curiously, the long-lived Visual Basic for MS-DOS supported short-circuit evaluation about 10 years ago, but I don't remember anyone complaining about backward compatibility with the then-popular QuickBasic language.)

The While...End While Loop

Visual Basic .NET supports For and Do loops, and they follow exactly the same syntax as under previous versions of the language. Visual Basic .NET supports the While keyword as well, but this kind of loop must be closed by an End While keyword (instead of the discontinued Wend keyword). You can exit a While loop with an Exit While statement:

```
While x = 0
    ⋮
    If y = 0 Then Exit While
    ⋮
End While
```

While blocks can have their test condition only at the beginning of the loop, unlike Do loops, which let you test the exit condition at either the beginning or the end of the loop. Consequently, you have no reason for preferring While...End While to Do...Loop, and, in fact, in this book you won't see any other While...End While example.

GoTo and Its Variants

Visual Basic 6 and previous versions support four flavors of intraprocedure jump instructions: GoTo, GoSub, On...GoTo, and On...GoSub. The last three instructions aren't supported any longer, and only Goto has survived the transition to Visual Basic .NET, although with a slightly different casing ("Goto" instead of "GoTo"). The Return keyword—once used to return from GoSub subroutines—is still supported but has a different syntax and semantics. (See the section "Returning a Value" earlier in this chapter.)

Even though Goto is still available, you shouldn't abuse it. A good rule of thumb is to use Goto only when exceptional conditions occur, such as when you want to exit a deeply nested loop or If structure:

```
    If x = 0 Then
        ⋮
        If y = 0 Then
            ⋮
            If z = 0 Then
                ⋮
                If k = 0 Then Goto SkipOverIfs
                ⋮
            End If
            ⋮
        Else
            ⋮
            If k = 0 Then Goto SkipOverIfs
            ⋮
        End If
    Else
        ⋮
    End If
SkipOverIfs:
```

The Goto statements in the preceding example are probably the cleanest way to implement the required flow control (short of moving the entire If block into a separate procedure), and they make your code clear. Just don't take this as an excuse to create old-style spaghetti code!

Speaking of labels, you should take notice of a weird behavior of the Visual Basic .NET language. As you know, you can insert multiple statements on the same line, using the colon as a separator:

```
x = 1: y = 2
```

When the first statement is a call to a procedure without parameters, the compiler is confused into thinking that you're actually using a label:

```
' This code doesn't work as expected.
WriteHello: Console.WriteLine("World")        ' => World

Sub WriteHello()
    Console.Write("Hello ")
End Sub
```

This behavior is common to all Visual Basic versions. You can solve the ambiguity in Visual Basic .NET by adding a pair of parentheses after the procedure name:

```
' This code works correctly.
WriteHello(): Console.WriteLine("World")      ' => Hello World
```

The Declare Statement

Visual Basic .NET supports the Declare statement to enable you to call procedures and functions in external DLLs. In a difference from previous language versions, you can use a public Declare statement anywhere in your application, including module, form, and class blocks.

In Visual Basic .NET, you can add a modifier that tells whether strings should be converted to ANSI or Unicode. This modifier must immediately follow the Declare keyword and can be one of the following values:

- **Ansi** All strings are converted to ANSI. (This is the default behavior.)
- **Unicode** All strings are converted to Unicode.
- **Auto** Strings are converted to ANSI on Windows 98 and Windows Me systems and to Unicode on Windows NT, Windows 2000, and Windows XP systems; moreover, if no alias name is provided, the actual entry point is derived by appending *A* to the function name on Windows 98 and Windows Me systems and *W* on Windows NT, Windows 2000, and Windows XP systems.

When you're converting your Declare statements from Visual Basic 6, you must carefully convert all Integer arguments to Short and all Long arguments to Integer. Take, for example, the following piece of Visual Basic 6 code, which retrieves the handle of a window titled Untitled - Notepad, resizes it, and moves it to the upper left corner of the string:

```
Private Declare Function FindWindow Lib "user32" Alias "FindWindowA" _
    (ByVal lpClassName As String, ByVal lpWindowName As String) As Long
Private Declare Function MoveWindow Lib "user32" _
    (ByVal hWnd As Long, ByVal x As Long, ByVal y As Long, _
    ByVal nWidth As Long, ByVal nHeight As Long, _
    ByVal bRepaint As Long) As Long

' NOTE: launch Notepad on an empty document before running this code.
Sub TestFindWindow()
    Dim hWnd As Long
    ' We pass vbNullString because we don't know the window class.
    hWnd = FindWindow(vbNullString, "Untitled - Notepad")
    ' Resize the window, and move to upper left corner of the screen.
    If hWnd <> 0 Then MoveWindow hWnd, 0, 0, 600, 300, True
End Sub
```

The preceding code should be translated to Visual Basic .NET as follows:

```
' (The Ansi qualifier is optional.)
Private Declare Ansi Function FindWindow Lib "user32" _
    Alias "FindWindowA" (ByVal lpClassName As String, _
    ByVal lpWindowName As String) As Integer
Private Declare Function MoveWindow Lib "user32" Alias "MoveWindow" _
    (ByVal hWnd As Integer, ByVal x As Integer, ByVal y As Integer, _
```

```
    ByVal nWidth As Integer, ByVal nHeight As Integer, _
    ByVal bRepaint As Integer) As Integer

' NOTE: launch Notepad on an empty document before running this code.
Sub TestFindWindow()
    Dim hWnd As Integer = FindWindow(Nothing, "Untitled - Notepad")
    If hWnd <> 0 Then MoveWindow(hWnd, 0, 0, 600, 300, 1)
End Sub
```

An important detail: Visual Basic .NET doesn't support the vbNullString constant any longer, and you have to replace it with Nothing when calling a function defined in a DLL.

There's a lot more to learn about calling external procedures, as you'll see in the section "The DllImport Attribute" in Chapter 7.

Commands, Functions, and Constants

As I explained in the section "The Imports Statement" in Chapter 2, new projects typically import a few important namespaces that are vital to the correct working of most Visual Basic .NET projects. One such namespace is Microsoft.VisualBasic, which exposes most of the language commands, functions, and constants. Another is Microsoft.VisualBasic.Compatibility.VB6, which contains classes that help you port applications to Visual Basic .NET from older versions using the Visual Basic Upgrade Wizard.

Most commands in these namespaces have retained their original syntax, and I assume that you already know how to use them. In this section, I'll focus only on the differences and a few problems you might have in the porting process.

String Constants

Visual Basic 6 string constants, such as vbCrLf and vbTab, are still supported as fields of the Microsoft.VisualBasic.Constants class (together with all the other Visual Basic 6 constants). This class is marked as a global class by using the StandardModule attribute, so you don't have to include the name of the class in your code, as you'd do if it were a regular class:

```
' vbCrLf is a field of the Microsoft.VisualBasic.Constants class.
Dim separator As String = vbCrLf
```

Alternatively, you can use the fields exposed by the Microsoft.VisualBasic.ControlChars class. Because this class isn't declared globally, you must include the name of the class itself (unless you use an Imports statement to import the entire class). The names of constants are the same as in Visual Basic 6 except that they don't include the *vb* prefix:

```
' A more .NET-oriented syntax
Dim separator As String = ControlChars.CrLf
```

The ControlChars class contains the following constants: Back, Cr, CrLf, FormFeed, NewLine, NullChar, Quote, Tab, and VerticalTab. Note that the vbNullString constant isn't supported any longer; as I explain in the section "The Declare Statement" earlier in this chapter, you can pass a null string to an API function by using the Nothing constant.

String Functions

The Microsoft.VisualBasic.Strings class exposes most of the Visual Basic string functions, including Asc, Chr, ChrW, Filter, Format, FormatCurrency, FormatDateTime, FormatNumber, FormatPercent, InStr, InStrRev, Join, LCase, Left, Len, LTrim, Mid, Replace, Right, RTrim, Space, Split, StrComp, StrReverse, Trim, and UCase. Functions that support multiple syntax forms—such as InStr and Mid—have been conveniently overloaded, and all the usual forms are supported. (Read Chapter 4 for more details about overloading.) These methods are globally defined, so you don't have to include the complete class name to invoke them, even though you do need to specify the complete names of the constants that are related to them:

```
' Compare two strings in case-insensitive mode.
If StrComp(s1, s2, CompareMethod.Text) = 0 Then res = "Equal"
```

The new StrDup function replaces the String function, which can't be used any longer because String is a reserved word:

```
' These statements print a line of 50 dashes.
Console.WriteLine(StrDup(50, "-"))
```

GetChar is a new function that returns a single character at a given position in a string:

```
Console.WriteLine(GetChar("ABCDE", 2))      ' => B
```

As you might suspect, Visual Basic .NET doesn't support *$* functions, such as Left$ or Space$.

Math Functions

Visual Basic .NET math functions are implemented in the System.Math class, defined in the Microsoft.VisualBasic namespace. You can classify the math functions in these groups:

- **Arithmetic functions** Abs, Ceiling, Floor, Min, Max, Sqrt, Exp, Log, Log10, Round, Pow, Sign, IEEERemainder
- **Trig and inverse trig functions** Sin, Cos, Tan, Asin, Acos, Atan, Atan2

- **Hyperbolic trig functions** Sinh, Cosh, Tanh
- **Constants** E, PI

The calling syntax of functions that were supported under Visual Basic 6—possibly under a different name, such as Sqrt, Sign, and Atan—hasn't changed. The Log function supports one argument (natural logarithms) or two arguments (logarithms in any base):

```
' The natural logarithm of 10
Console.WriteLine(Math.Log(10))              ' => 2.30258509299405
' Two ways to evaluate the decimal logarithm of 1000
Console.WriteLine(Math.Log(1000, 10))        ' => 3
Console.WriteLine(Math.Log10(1000))          ' => 3
```

The Min and Max methods do what their name suggests and are conveniently overloaded to work with any type of value:

```
Console.WriteLine(Math.Min(1.5, 0.7))        ' => 0.7
Console.WriteLine(Math.Max(99, 87))          ' => 99
```

The Floor function returns the integer less than or equal to the argument, whereas Ceiling returns the integer greater than or equal to the argument:

```
Console.WriteLine(Math.Floor(-1.5))          ' => -2
Console.WriteLine(Math.Ceiling(2.5))         ' => 3
```

Atan2 returns the angle formed by an object of a given height y at a given distance x; it's similar to Atan, but it returns an unambiguous value for all the four quadrants. The IEEERemainder function returns the remainder of a division; it's therefore similar to the Mod operator but works correctly also with floating-point numbers:

```
Console.WriteLine(Math.IEEERemainder(2, 1.5))      ' => 0.5
```

Date and Time Functions

The DateAndTime class includes several date and time functions, among which are DateAdd, DateDiff, DatePart, DateSerial, DateValue, Year, Month, Day, Hour, Minute, Second, MonthName, Weekday, WeekdayName, TimeSerial, and TimeValue. This class also exposes two read-only properties, Now and Timer. In general, the syntax hasn't changed from Visual Basic 6 except for the DateAdd, DateDiff, and DatePart functions, which now take an enumerated constant instead of a string constant:

```
' Get the date two weeks from now.
newDate = DateAdd(DateInterval.WeekOfYear, 2, Now())
```

You have two new properties to retrieve and set the current date and time:

```
' Reset system time to midnight.
TimeOfDay = #12:00:00 PM#
' Evaluate days left until December 31 of current year.
days = DateDiff(DateInterval.Day, Today, _
    DateSerial(Year(Today), 12, 31))
```

These properties replace Time and Date respectively. The MonthName and WeekdayName functions support an extra Boolean argument, to retrieve the abbreviated month or day name:

```
Console.WriteLine(MonthName(1, True))        ' => Jan
```

Interaction Commands and Functions

The Microsoft.VisualBasic.Interaction class exposes many useful commands and methods that were available in Visual Basic 6, including AppActivate, Beep, CallByName, Choose, Command, Environ, IIf, InputBox, MsgBox, Partition, Shell, and Switch; and the registry-related DeleteSetting, GetSetting, GetAllSettings, and SaveSetting methods. These methods are globally defined, so you don't have to include the class name when you use them. However, the constants related to these methods are in a different class, and their complete names must be specified:

```
MsgBox("Goodbye", Microsoft.VisualBasic.MsgBoxStyle.Information)
```

When you use these functions, it's a good idea to import the Microsoft.VisualBasic namespace at the project level so that you can shorten constant names. (Depending on which project you have created, Visual Studio might have added an Imports statement pointing to this namespace at the project level.)

```
Dim userChoice As MsgBoxResult
userChoice = MsgBox("Goodbye", _
    MsgBoxStyle.Question Or MsgBoxStyle.YesNo)
```

Notice that the constant name is similar to the corresponding Visual Basic 6 constant but without the *vb* prefix.

The Shell function expands on the original version and supports an additional argument that enables you to specify whether to wait until the shelled program terminates, with an optional timeout. This solves an old problem known to many Visual Basic developers without your having to resort to Windows API functions:

```
' Run Notepad.exe, and wait until the user terminates it.
Shell("notepad", AppWinStyle.NormalFocus, True)

' Run Notepad, and then wait max 10 seconds.
Dim taskID As Long
```

```
taskId = Shell("notepad", AppWinStyle.NormalFocus, True, 10000)
If taskID = 0 Then
    Console.WriteLine("Notepad has been closed within 10 seconds.")
Else
    Console.WriteLine("Notepad is still running after 10 seconds.")
End If
```

Other Commands, Functions, and Objects

The FileSystem class includes all the usual Visual Basic file commands and functions, including ChDir, ChDrive, CurDir, Dir, FileCopy, FileDateTime, FileLen, GetAttr, Kill, MkDir, RmDir, and SetAttr. There are no relevant differences from their counterparts under previous versions of the language except that the new FileOpen, FileClose, FileGet, FilePut, PrintLine, InputLine, and InputString commands have superseded the Open#, Close#, Get#, Put#, Print#, LineInput#, and Input statements (whose nonstandard syntax isn't supported in Visual Basic .NET):

```
' Read a text file.
Dim handle As Integer = FreeFile()
' Open a file for input.
FileOpen(handle, "C:\autoexec.bat", OpenMode.Input, OpenAccess.Read)
' Read the entire file in one operation.
Dim fileText As String = InputString(handle, CInt(LOF(handle)))
' Close the file.
FileClose(handle)
```

In most cases, however, you should avoid these file-related functions in the Microsoft.VisualBasic namespace and use other objects offered by the .NET Framework because you'll write more flexible code that way. (See Chapter 10 for more details about .NET file and directory classes.)

The Conversion class provides support for functions such as Fix, Hex, Int, Oct, Str, and Val, which have the same syntax and meaning as under Visual Basic 6. This class also includes the ErrorToString function, which converts an error code to a description. The ErrorToString function is similar to Err.Description, but you don't need to have an actual error to retrieve the description associated with an error code:

```
' Display the description associated with error code 9.
Console.WriteLine(ErrorToString(9))    ' => Subscript out of range.
```

The Information class gathers miscellaneous functions, such as Erl, Err, IsArray, IsDate, IsError, IsNothing, IsNumeric, LBound, UBound, and TypeName. Note that you can't use the Len function to determine the length in bytes of a variable, as you do in Visual Basic 6. Instead, you must use the SizeOf method of the System.Runtime.InteropServices.Marshal class:

```
Dim x As Integer
Console.WriteLine(Runtime.InteropServices.Marshal.SizeOf(x))    ' => 4
```

The SystemTypeName function converts a Visual Basic data type to the corresponding .NET name, while the VbTypeName function does the opposite conversion. These functions might be useful when developing code generators and utilities that convert code from Visual Basic to another .NET language:

```
Console.WriteLine(SystemTypeName("Long"))          ' => System.Int64
Console.WriteLine(VbTypeName("System.Int16"))      ' => Short
```

The new IsReference function returns True if the argument is a reference type, or False if it's a value type:

```
Dim n As Integer = 1
Dim s As String = "ABC"
Console.WriteLine(IsReference(n))     ' => False
Console.WriteLine(IsReference(s))     ' => True
```

The IsEmpty and IsNull functions aren't supported because they made sense only with Variant arguments, which in turn aren't supported. However, the .NET Framework supports the DBNull data type (which represents a null value coming from a database field), and Visual Basic .NET conveniently exposes an IsDBNull function, which has therefore more or less the same meaning as IsNull.

Finally, the Financial class implements all the usual Visual Basic financial functions, including DDB, FV, IPmt, IRR, MIRR, NPer, NPV, PMT, PPMT, PV, Rate, Sln, and Syd.

The Environment Class

The System.Environment class exposes several properties and methods that were formerly part of the language and that give you access to information related to the operating system—for example, the current directory:

```
' Display the current directory.
Console.WriteLine(Environment.CurrentDirectory)
' Change it.
Environment.CurrentDirectory = "c:\"
```

You can read environment variables (but not modify them) in three ways:

```
' Get the value of a single variable.
Console.WriteLine("Username=" & _
    Environment.GetEnvironmentVariable("USERNAME"))

' Expand a string that contains %variables%.
Dim msg As String = "CPU is %PROCESSOR_LEVEL%, " _
    & "revision is %PROCESSOR_REVISION%"
Console.WriteLine(environment.ExpandEnvironmentVariables(msg))

' Get a list of all environment variables and their values.
Dim de As DictionaryEntry
For Each de In Environment.GetEnvironmentVariables
```

```
    Console.WriteLine("{0} = {1}", de.Key, de.Value)
Next
```

You can retrieve the program command line (which includes the executable file name) as a string, or get an array of strings, where each element is an item on the command string:

```
' The command line passed to this program (includes EXE name).
Console.WriteLine(Environment.CommandLine)

' The list of all the command line arguments.
' (First element is the executable name.)
Dim arg As String
For Each arg In Environment.GetCommandLineArgs
    Console.WriteLine(arg)
Next
```

Conveniently, multiple words enclosed in double quotes are considered a single command line argument. For example, only two arguments are retrieved when you call the application using this command from the prompt:

```
MyApp "first argument" "second argument"
```

You can debug a Visual Basic .NET application that takes command-line arguments from inside the IDE, by entering the command line in the Debugging page of the project Property Pages dialog box, which you display by clicking Properties on the Project menu.

There are also several properties that weren't available in Visual Basic 6, short of calling one or more Windows API functions, such as the system directory and the amount of memory allocated to the current process:

```
' Windows system directory
Console.WriteLine(Environment.SystemDirectory)
' Physical memory allocated to the current process
Console.WriteLine(Environment.WorkingSet)
```

The OSVersion property returns an OperatingSystem object, which in turn exposes properties such as Platform and Version:

```
Console.WriteLine(Environment.OSVersion.Platform)     ' => 2
    ' Platform = 2 means Windows NT/2000.
Console.WriteLine(Environment.OSVersion.Version)      ' => 5.0.2195.0
    ' Major version number = 5 means Windows 2000.
```

The Version property returns the version of the common language runtime under which the application is running:

```
' I run this code in Release Candidate 3 (RC3) beta version.
Console.WriteLine("common language runtime version = {0}", Environment.Version)
    ' => 1.0.3512.0
```

Other properties return the name of the user who started the current thread, the network domain name associated with the current user, and the NETBios name of the current computer:

```
' Display information about the current user.
Console.WriteLine("UserName = {0}", Environment.UserName)
Console.WriteLine("UserDomain = {0}", Environment.UserDomainName)
Console.WriteLine("MachineName = {0}", Environment.MachineName)
```

Finally, the Exit method lets you exit the current application and return an error code to the operating system. This method is especially useful in console programs that are meant to be invoked from the command line and from batch files:

```
' Return error code 1 to the operating system.
Environment.Exit(1)
```

Error Handling

For years, Visual Basic programmers have trapped errors by using the time-honored but admittedly limited On Error statement in its two variants: On Error GoTo and On Error Resume Next. Visual Basic .NET supports both of them, even though their use is discouraged in favor of the newer Try...Catch...Finally statement.

Throwing Exceptions

The main problem with the traditional way of dealing with errors under Windows is that there's no approach with which everyone agrees. For example, functions in most DLLs (including Windows system DLLs) report errors through a return value and do that in a very confusing way. In some cases, 0 means success and 1 means error, while in other cases the meaning is reversed. COM components return an error code by means of a 32-bit HRESULT value, and Visual Basic applications raise errors using a COM-compliant mechanism behind the scenes. Other languages, such as C++ and Java, can use an error handling mechanism based on *exceptions*.

To allow cross-language interoperability, the .NET Framework has standardized on a single method of raising and trapping errors based on *exceptions*. You can think of exceptions as unexpected conditions that occur during execution of your application or while code is running inside the .NET Framework itself. When this situation occurs, the code is said to *throw an exception* that some other code is expected to *catch*.

An exception can be caught by code in the same procedure in which the error occurs. If it isn't, the exception is thrown to the caller, and it's up to the caller to remedy the error and possibly retry the operation that caused the malfunction. If the caller doesn't catch the exception, the exception is automatically thrown to the caller's caller. The exception "bubbles up" the call chain until it finds a calling procedure that's willing to catch it. (You'll see in a moment what catching an exception means in practice.)

By default, if no procedure in the call chain catches the exception, the end user is notified by means of an error dialog box, such as the one in Figure 3-1. You can change how the common language runtime behaves when an uncaught exception is thrown by modifying the DbgJITDebugLaunchSetting value under the HKEY_LOCAL_MACHINE\Software\Microsoft\.NETFramework Registry key. By default this value is 0, which makes the error dialog appear; setting it to 1 always terminates the application, whereas setting it to 2 always runs the debugger.

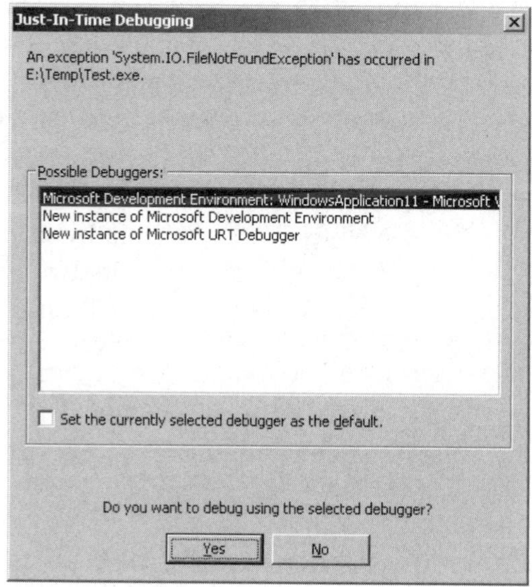

Figure 3-1. The error dialog box that appears when one or more .NET debuggers are installed on the computer.

The phrase *throwing an exception* is appropriate because an Exception object is actually passed back to the caller when an exception occurs. The code that catches the exception can examine the Exception object's properties, invoke its methods, and take any step it deems necessary—such as informing the user or silently canceling the operation that caused the problem. Alternatively, the code can throw the Exception object again—possibly after adjusting one or more of its properties—or it can throw a completely different Exception object to its own caller.

The Exception object being thrown back and forth exposes properties, such as Message (the error's description), Source (a string that tells where the error occurred), and HelpLink (the position of a help page that describes how to recover from the error). The next section describes these properties in greater detail.

If you're thinking that all this sounds familiar, you're right. Even though the inner details are different, .NET exceptions work and behave in much the same way Visual Basic's own error handling mechanism does. The Exception object resembles the Err object (with different names for its properties); *throwing an exception* works surprisingly like *raising an error*; the "bubbling up" behavior is the one Visual Basic 6 uses when notifying procedures of errors if those procedures don't have an active error handler. This is known ground for us Visual Basic developers.

The Exception Object

The Exception object is defined in the .NET Framework, and its complete name is System.Exception. Both .NET classes and your own applications don't usually throw this raw exception object, though. The framework defines two other generic classes, System.SystemException and System.ApplicationException: nearly all the exception objects defined in the .NET Framework inherit from SystemException, whereas custom and application-specific exception objects should inherit from ApplicationException. These two classes don't add any properties or methods to the base Exception class, but they offer an effective way to categorize exceptions.

Table 3-1 lists a few of the most common system exception objects. For example, math operations can throw an ArithmeticException or a DivideByZeroException object, while functions can throw an ArgumentOutOfRangeException object. For a complete list of exception objects, just use the search command in the object browser and look for the Exception substring.

Table 3-1 Some of the Exception Classes in the Most Important .NET Framework Namespaces

Namespace	Exception Classes
System	ArgumentNullException, ArgumentOutOfRangeException, DivideByZeroException, IndexOutOfRangeException, NullReferenceException, OverflowException, StackOverflowException
System.IO	DirectoryNotFoundException, EndOfStreamException, FileNotFoundException, PathTooLongException
System.Data	DuplicateNameException, InvalidConstraintException, InvalidExpressionException, MissingPrimaryKeyException, NoNullAllowedException, ReadOnlyException
System.Runtime.InteropServices	InvalidComObjectException, InvalidOleVariantTypeException, SEHException

Let's have a look at the most important properties and methods that all these exception objects have in common. (Note that all properties are read-only except Source and HelpLink.)

The Message property is the descriptive text for the exception and is therefore similar to the Err.Description property. For example, the Message property of a DivideByZeroException returns the string "Attempted to divide by zero."

The Exception object inherits the ToString property from System.Object, and it returns the same error message that would be displayed to the end user in a dialog box. This is similar to the Message property, but it includes also the name of the module. If debug information has been embedded in the executable, this property also returns the name of the procedure and the exact line number where the error occurred:

```
System.DivideByZeroException: Attempted to divide by zero.
at MyApplication.Form1.TestProc in C:\MyApplication\Form1.vb:line 70
```

The TargetSite property returns the name and signature of the procedure in which the exception was first thrown, expressed in C# syntax:

```
Int32 DivideNumber(Int32 x, Int32 y)
```

The StackTrace property returns a string that describes the stack path from the place the exception was originally thrown—that is, where the error occurred—to the place the error was caught. For example, say that your TestProc procedure calls the EvalResult procedure, which in turns calls the DivideNumber function, and assume that the latter two procedures don't catch exceptions. If the innermost DivideNumber function throws a DivideByZeroException, the value of the StackTrace property as read in the TestProc procedure looks like the following code:

```
at MyApplication.Form1.DivideNumber(Int32 x, Int32 y)
    in C:\MyApplication\Form1.vb:line 91
at MyApplication.Form1.EvalResult() in
    C:\MyApplication\Form1.vb:line 87
at MyApplication.Form1.TestProc() in C:\MyApplication\Form1.vb:line 77
```

You get this detailed information only if the executable embeds debug information; if you compiled the program in Release mode, you don't see the name of the source file and the line number. Needless to say, the StackTrace property is your best friend when you're trying to figure out what actually happens when your code throws an exception.

The Source property sets or returns the name of the component in which the exception was thrown and is therefore similar to the Err.Source property. For exceptions thrown in the current application, this property returns a null string.

The HelpLink property sets or returns a Uniform Resource Name (URN) or Uniform Resource Locator (URL) to the help file associated with the Exception object, as you see here:

```
file://C:/MyApplication/manual.html#ErrorNum42
```

The Try...Catch...Finally Statement

So far, you've seen how the exception throwing mechanism works and what information an exception object carries. Now you're ready to fully appreciate the power and flexibility of the new Try...Catch...Finally block.

The Catch Keyword

Whenever you execute code that might throw an exception, you should enclose it in a Try...End Try block. The portion of code between the Try keyword and the first Catch keyword is guarded against exceptions, and if an exception is thrown Visual Basic passes the control to the first Catch block, which is also called an exception filter. In the Catch code block, you can examine the properties of the exception object and decide how to react to the error. Here's a simple example:

```
Dim x, y As Integer
Try
    x = x \ y
    ' If y is 0, the following statement is never executed.
    y = CInt(10 ^ x)
Catch ex As Exception
    If ex.Message = "Attempted to divide by zero." Then
        ' Deal with division by zero errors here.
    Else
        ' Deal here with other types of exceptions.
    End If
End Try
```

As soon as an error occurs—or an exception is thrown, to comply with the new terminology—the program jumps to the Catch block, executes that code block, and then jumps to the first statement after the End Try keyword.

Testing the Message string isn't the correct way to deal with exceptions, however. Instead, you should have multiple Catch blocks, each one testing a different exception object:

```
Try
    x = x \ y
    y = CInt(10 ^ x)
Catch ex As DivideByZeroException
    ' Deal here with divide by zero exceptions.
    ⋮
```

```
Catch ex As OverflowException
    ' Deal here with overflow exceptions.
    ⋮
Catch ex As Exception
    ' Deal here with all other exceptions.
    ⋮
End Try
```

Visual Basic compares the type of the exception object being thrown with the expressions in Catch clauses in the order in which they appear, and it executes the first one that matches. It's a good idea to have a final Catch expression that matches the System.Exception object because this code is guaranteed to execute if no previous Catch expression matches the exception. A Catch clause for the System.Exception object always matches any exception because all exception objects inherit from System.Exception. (This last Catch clause is conceptually similar to the Else clause in a Select Case block.)

Because all Catch expressions are evaluated in the order in which they appear, you should test for most specific exceptions first, followed by less specific ones. The test for the System.Exception object should be in the very last Catch block because it matches any exception; consequently, no Catch block after it can ever execute. When sorting Catch blocks, though, you should have a look at the exception hierarchy depicted in Figure 3-2, and check that you never catch an exception object after catching its parent exception. For example, the Catch block for a DivideByZeroException object should never follow the Catch block for a less specific ArithmeticException object.

If no matching Catch expression is found, Visual Basic deals with the exception as if no Try...End Try block were there and bubbles the exception up the call stack (after running the Finally block if there is a matching Catch expression, as I'll explain in a moment). The As expression in the Catch block is optional, and you can omit it if you don't need to examine the exception object's properties to make a decision.

```
Try
    ⋮
Catch ex As DivideByZeroException
    ⋮
Catch ex As OverflowException
    ⋮
Catch ex As ArithmeticException
    ' Catch less specific arithmetic exceptions here.
    ⋮
Catch
    Console.WriteLine("An error has occurred.")
End Try
```

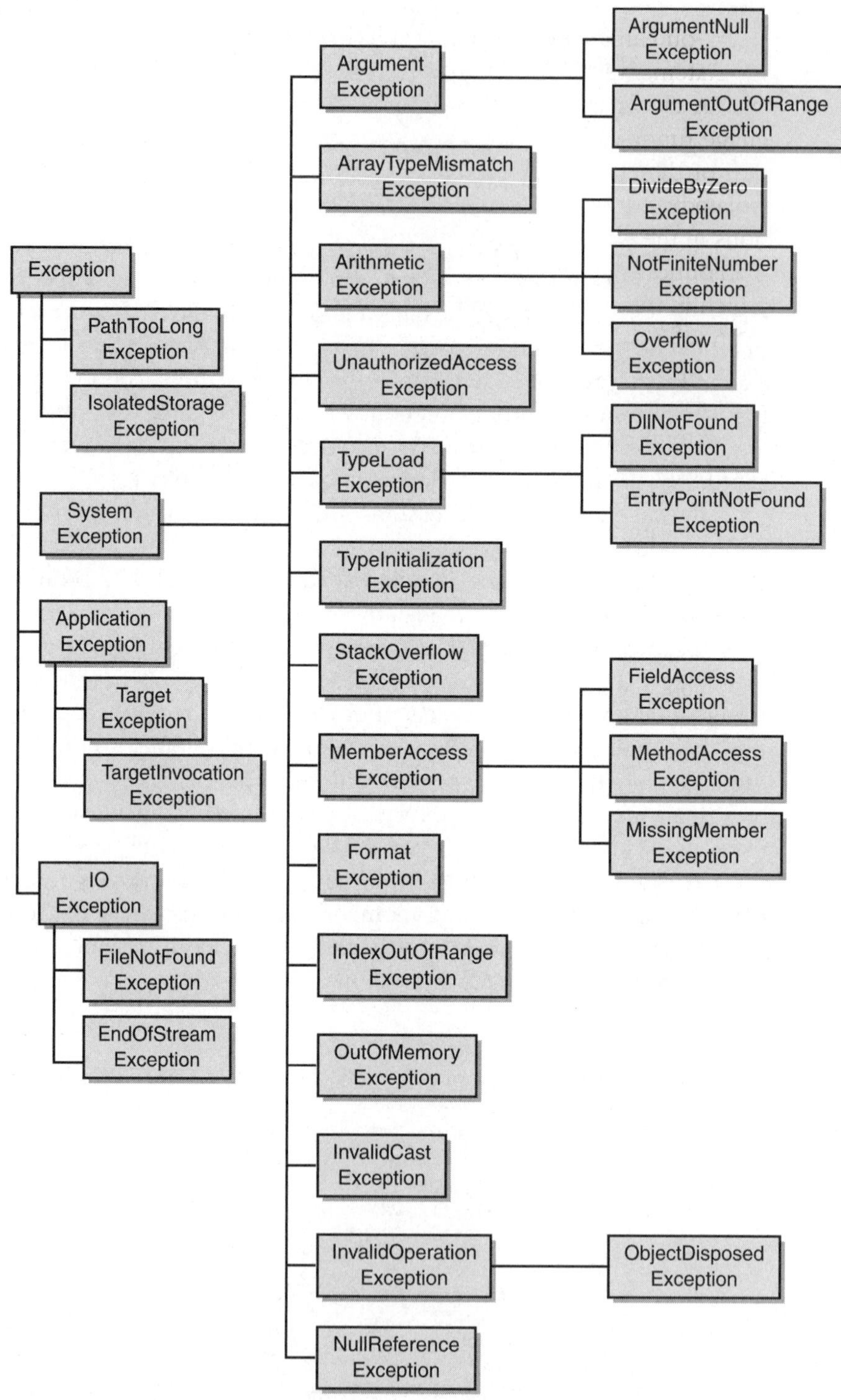

Figure 3-2. The hierarchy of the most important exception objects in the System namespace.

You can exit from a Try...End Try structure at any time by calling the Exit Try statement, which can appear inside the Try block or any Catch block.

A closer look at the exception hierarchy reveals that the common language runtime can throw a few exceptions that inherit from ApplicationException or directly from Exception. For example, the PathTooLongException and IsolatedStorageException classes derive directly from Exception; a few exceptions in the System.IO namespace—namely DirectoryNotFoundException, FileNotFoundException, and EndOfStreamException—inherit from IOException, which in turn derives directly from Exception (and not from SystemException). Even worse, some exception classes in the System.Reflection namespace inherit from ApplicationException instead of SystemException. This means that you can't assume that you can trap *all* system-related exceptions using a Catch filter on SystemException, and you can't assume that a Catch clause on ApplicationException will filter only application-related exceptions.

> **Note** The .NET runtime defines a few exceptions that occur in really exceptional (and catastrophic) circumstances, namely StackOverflowException, OutOfMemoryException, and ExecutionEngineException. A common trait among these exceptions is that they can occur at any time because they aren't really caused by your application. Although you can catch them, in practice you should never do anything else but terminate the application with a suitable error message because after these exceptions the application might be in an unstable state. (By comparison, Visual Basic 6 doesn't even let you trap the "Out of Stack Space" error, so at least with Visual Basic .NET you have the opportunity to inform the end user of what exactly went wrong.)

The When Keyword

The Catch clause supports an optional When expression, which lets you specify an additional condition that must evaluate to True for the Catch block to be selected. This feature lets you define more specific exception filters. Look at this code, for example:

```
Dim x, y, z, res As Integer        ' All variables are 0.
Try
    ' You can see different behaviors by commenting out or changing
    ' the order of the following statements.
    ' ...
    res = y \ x
    ' ...
```

(continued)

```
    res = x \ y
    ' ...
    res = x \ z
Catch ex As DivideByZeroException When (x = 0)
    Console.WriteLine("Division error: x is 0.")
Catch ex As DivideByZeroException When (y = 0)
    Console.WriteLine("Division error: y is 0.")
Catch ex As DivideByZeroException
    Console.WriteLine("Division error: no information on variables")
Catch ex As Exception
    Console.WriteLine("An error has occurred.")
End Try
```

In general, you can achieve the same behavior using an If...ElseIf block inside a Catch block, but the When clause makes for a better organization of your error handling code. For example, if no combination of Catch and When clauses matches the current exception, execution flow will go to the last Catch block, and you don't have to duplicate any code whatsoever.

The When clause can also reference the exception object's properties, so you can partition your exceptions in subcategories and have a distinct Catch block for each one of them. For example, the following code parses the Message property to extract the name of the file that hasn't been found:

```
Try
    ' Comment out next statement to see the behavior
    ' when another file is missing.
    FileOpen(1, "c:\myapp.ini", OpenMode.Input)
    FileOpen(2, "c:\xxxxx.dat", OpenMode.Input)

Catch ex As System.IO.FileNotFoundException _
    When InStr(ex.Message, """c:\myapp.ini""") > 0
    ' The ini file is missing.
    Console.WriteLine("Can't initialize: MyApp.Ini file not found")
Catch ex As System.IO.FileNotFoundException
    ' Another file is missing.
    ' Extract the filename from the Message property.
    Dim filename As String = Split(ex.Message, """")(1)
    Console.WriteLine("The following file is missing: " & filename)
End Try
```

An explanation is in order: The Message property of the FileNotFoundException object returns a string in the following format:

```
Could not find file "<filename>".
```

Therefore, you can use the InStr function to test whether a file you're looking for is embedded in this string. (Just remember to enclose the searched-for filename in double quotes.) Or you can parse the string to extract the name of the file. The easiest way to do so is by using the Split function and specifying the double quote character as a separator: this function returns an array of three elements, the second of which is the filename.

```
Dim tmpArr() As String = Split(ex.Message, """")
Dim filename As String = tmpArr(1)      ' Take the second element.
```

Because you don't need to process the other elements of the array returned by Split, you can make your code more concise by getting rid of the *tmpArr* variable:

```
Dim filename As String = Split(ex.Message, """")(1)
```

You can take advantage of the When keyword in other ways as well. For example, you might have a local variable that tracks the progress status of the procedure so that you can take different actions depending on where the error occurred. The following code should render the idea:

```
Dim currentStep As Integer    ' You can also use an Enum value.
Try
    CurrentStep = 1           ' Initialize the program.
    ⋮
    currentStep = 2           ' Open the data file.
    ⋮
    currentStep = 3           ' Process the file's contents.
    ⋮
    currentStep = 4           ' ...And so on ...
    ⋮
Catch ex As Exception When currentStep = 1
    Console.WriteLine("An error occurred in the initialization step.")
Catch ex As System.IO.FileNotFoundException When currentStep = 2
    Console.WriteLine("The data file wasn't found.")
Catch ex As Exception When currentStep = 2
    Console.WriteLine("An error occurred while opening the data file.")
Catch ex As Exception When currentStep = 3
    Console.WriteLine("An error occurred while processing data.")
' Add here other Catch blocks.
⋮
End Try
```

Note that it's acceptable to have the first block catch the generic Exception object because the When condition makes the test succeed only if the error occurred in the first (initialization) step of the procedure. When sorting Catch blocks related to the same step, you should catch more specific exception objects first (as when *currentStep* is 2 in the preceding code).

You can use this technique when you're translating Visual Basic 6 old-style error handlers that use numeric labels and the Erl function to determine where the error has occurred. (The Erl function is still available in Visual Basic .NET, both as a stand-alone function and as a property of the Err object.)

The Finally Keyword

In most real-world applications, you often need to execute a cleanup code when an exception is thrown. For example, you want to close a file if an error occurred while the code was processing that file, and you want to release a lock on a database table if an error occurred while the application was processing records in that table. In cases like these, you need a Finally clause. The code between the Finally keyword and the End Try keyword is guaranteed to run whether or not the code in the Try block threw an exception. The Finally block runs even if the code in a Catch block throws an exception or the Try...End Try block is exited because of an Exit Try statement.

Here's an example of a block of code that changes the current directory and ensures that the original directory is restored before exiting the Try...End Try structure:

```
Dim cdir As String
Try
    ' Remember the current directory.
    cdir = FileSystem.CurDir()
    ' Change to another directory.
    FileSystem.ChDir("c:\xxx")
    ⋮
Catch ex As Exception
    ' Deal here with errors.
    ⋮
Finally
    ' In all cases, restore the current directory.
    FileSystem.ChDir(cdir)
End Try
```

It's legal to have a Try...Finally...End Try block without any Catch block. Such code might be appropriate when you want the caller to catch and process all the errors in the current procedure, but at the same time you have some cleanup code that must be executed no matter what. Such a block might be useful also to provide a common block of cleanup code for a procedure that has multiple Exit Sub, Exit Function, or Return statements scattered in code:

```
Function TestMultipleExitPointFunction() As Integer
    Dim x, y, z As Integer
    Try
        ⋮
        If x > 0 Then Return 1
        ⋮
        If y = 0 Then Return 2
        ⋮
        If z > 0 Then Return 3
        ⋮
        Return 4
    Finally
```

```
        ' This code runs whatever exit path the code takes.
        ⋮
        Console.Write ("This function is returning the value ")
        Console.WriteLine(TestMultipleExitPointFunction)
    End Try
End Function
```

As the preceding code snippet demonstrates, the code in the Finally block is even able to inspect (and modify) the value being returned by the function to the caller. This technique works also if the return value was assigned using a Return statement (as opposed to being assigned to the local variable named after the function).

Finally, note that if the code in the Finally block throws an exception, the Finally block is immediately exited and the exception is thrown to the caller. Therefore you should always check that no error can occur while the Finally code is being processed; if you can't guarantee this, you might use a nested Try...End Try structure inside the Finally block.

The Throw Statement

Under Visual Basic 6 and previous versions, you can raise an error using the Err.Raise method, which takes the error numeric code, the Source, the Description, the HelpFile, and the HelpContext of the error. (All arguments after the first one are optional.) The Err object is still supported under Visual Basic .NET, so any code based on its Raise method will continue to work as before. However, you should throw your exceptions using the new Throw command to comply with the exception mechanism and make your code compatible with components written in other .NET languages.

Throwing an Exception

Unlike Err.Raise, the Throw command takes only one argument, the exception object being thrown. You must create such an object and set its properties as required. In most cases, you can create an exception object and throw it in one statement:

```
' This statement broadly corresponds to
'     Err.Raise 53, , "File not found" .
Throw New System.IO.FileNotFoundException()
```

When you're creating the exception object, you can specify a more precise message by passing an argument to the exception object's constructor:

```
Dim msg As String = "Initialization File Not Found"
Throw New System.IO.FileNotFoundException(msg)
```

The Throw statement is especially useful for catching a subset of all the possible exceptions and delegating the remaining ones to the caller. This is quite a common programming pattern: each portion of the code deals with the errors it knows how to fix and leaves the others to the calling code. As I have explained previously, if no Catch expression matches the current exception, the exception is automatically thrown to the caller. But it's a good practice to do the throwing explicitly so that you make it clear that you aren't just a lazy or distracted programmer:

```
Try
    ' Do some math operations here.
    ⋮
Catch ex As DivideByZeroException
    ⋮
Catch ex As OverflowException
    ⋮
Catch ex As Exception
    ' Explicitly throw this unhandled exception to the caller.
    Throw
Finally
    ' This code runs in all cases.
    ⋮
End Try
```

The Throw statement without an argument rethrows the current exception object and must appear in a Catch clause to be valid. The only other significant difference from the version that takes an argument is that the latter also resets the StackTrace property of the exception object (as if a brand-new exception were created), so the version without an argument is preferable for rethrowing the same exception because it lets the caller routine determine exactly where the exception occurred.

Here are some additional rules about throwing exceptions:

- Throw an InvalidOperationException if a property or method call occurs when the object is in a state that can't handle the method call.
- Throw an ArgumentException (or a class that inherits from ArgumentException) if a bad argument was passed.
- Stick to predefined exceptions, and don't define custom exceptions unless strictly required. (See "Custom Exception Objects" later in this chapter.)
- Don't throw exceptions for relatively common errors, such as end-of-file or timeout; instead, return a special value to the caller. For example, the Math.Sqrt function returns NaN (Not-a-Number) when it receives a negative argument instead of raising an error as the Sqr function in Visual Basic 6 does.

Coexisting with Old-Style Error Handlers

The Visual Basic .NET Err.Raise method and the Throw command are partially compatible. For example, you can use a Try...End Try block to catch an error raised with the Err.Raise method, and you can use an On Error Resume Next statement and the Err object to neutralize and inspect an exception object created by the Throw command. The old and the new error trapping mechanisms don't coexist well, though, and there are a few limitations. For example, you can't have an On Error Resume Next statement and a Try...End Try block in the same procedure.

To assist you in porting existing applications to Visual Basic .NET, the Err object has been extended with the new GetException method, which returns the Exception object that corresponds to the current error. This feature lets you preserve old-style error handlers in those procedures that don't lend themselves to easy porting to the new syntax. This new method enables such procedures to correctly throw an exception object to their caller, where the exception can be processed using a Try block as usual:

```
Sub TestGetExceptionMethod()
    Try
        Call OldStyleErrorHandlerProc()
    Catch ex As DivideByZeroException
        Console.WriteLine("A DivideByZeroException has been caught.")
    End Try
End Sub

' This procedure traps an error using an old-style On Error Goto
' and returns it to the caller as an exception.

Sub OldStyleErrorHandlerProc()
    On Error Goto ErrorHandler

    ' Cause a division by zero error.
    Dim x, y As Integer
    y = 1 \ x
    Exit Sub

ErrorHandler:
    ' Add cleanup code here as necessary.
    ⋮
    ' Then report the error to the caller as an Exception object.
    Throw Err.GetException
End Sub
```

The ability to mix old-style error trapping and the structured exception handling mechanism is important. Whereas the latter approach makes for a more streamlined way of dealing with errors, you shouldn't automatically assume that it is also the best way to deal with errors in all circumstances. As a matter of fact, you might argue that structured exception handling is *less* flexible than the mechanism based on the time-honored On Error Goto statement because there is no simple way to duplicate the functionality of Resume and Resume Next statements using the Try...Catch...Finally block. If you need to reexecute the statement that caused the problem or just ignore it and skip to the statement that follows, using On Error might simplify your coding noticeably. The bottom line: use the technique that suits the problem at hand, and take advantage of what the Visual Basic language offers you. (C# programmers don't have this choice, by the way.) You should keep in mind, however, that backward compatibility with the Visual Basic 6 way of dealing with errors doesn't come free. If you use either On Error Goto or On Error Resume Next, the compiler generates additional IL code after each statement. This additional code can make the procedure run up to five times slower than a procedure without error trapping. By comparison, the Try…Catch…Finally statement adds a fixed overhead (the code that sets up the exception handler), which tends to be negligible for procedures of several statements.

Custom Exception Objects

The old Err.Raise method has one advantage over the Throw command and the more modern exception-based mechanism: it makes it easy to define custom error codes, as in this line of code:

```
Err.Raise 1001, , "Initialization File Not Found"
```

As you saw in the preceding section, by means of the Throw command you can create a new System.Exception object (or an object that inherits from System.Exception) and set its Message property, but you can't do more than that. Sometimes you need to be able to create entirely new exception objects, which, according to .NET guidelines, should inherit from System.Application-Exception (as opposed to .NET runtime exceptions, which derive from System.SystemException).

I'll cover inheritance in Chapter 5, but for now let me show how easy it is to create a class that inherits from System.ApplicationException and that overrides the Message property with a custom string:

```
' By convention, the name of all classes that inherit
' from System.Exception must end with "Exception".

Class UnableToLoadIniFileException
    Inherits System.ApplicationException

    Overrides ReadOnly Property Message() As String
        Get
            Return "Unable to load initialization file"
        End Get
```

```
    End Property
End Class
```

It's that easy! Because this class inherits from System.Exception, you can use it in a Throw command and in a Catch block:

```
' The caller code
Sub TestCustomException()
    Try
        LoadIniFile
    Catch ex As UnableToLoadIniFileException
        ' Deal with the most specific error here.
        ' Next statement displays custom message "Unable to load..."
        Console.WriteLine(ex.Message)
    Catch ex As Exception
        ' Deal with other errors here.
    End Try
End Sub

' The routine that opens the ini file
Sub LoadIniFile()
    Try
        ' Try to open the ini file. (Cause an error in this demo.)
        ⋮
        FileOpen(1, "c:\missingfile.ini", OpenMode.Input)
    Catch ex As Exception
        ' Whatever caused the error, throw a more specific exception.
        Throw New UnableToLoadIniFileException()
    End Try
End Sub
```

Custom exception objects have many uses other than reporting a custom error message. For example, they can include custom methods that resolve the error condition or at least attempt to do so. For instance, you might devise a DriveNotReadyException class with a method named ShowMessage that displays an error message and asks the user to insert a disk in the drive and retry the operation. Putting this code inside the exception class makes its reuse much easier.

> **Note** If your custom exception object can be thrown across different assemblies, possibly in different processes, you should make the exception class serializable. Read Chapter 11 for more details about serialization.

Nested Exception Objects

Whether or not you use custom exception objects, hiding the original exception from the caller is a good practice if you can throw a more descriptive exception. Say that you have a routine that takes one or more arguments, which you process with a sequence of math operations. If you get an overflow or a division by zero, throwing the corresponding exception to the caller isn't advisable because the specific exception has to do with the inner implementation of your routine and is of no use to the caller. In this case, a more generic ArgumentException object is more appropriate:

```
Sub MathIntensiveProc(Byval x As Integer, ByVal y As Integer)
    Try
        ' Process arguments here.
        ⋮
        x = x \ y
    Catch ex As Exception
        ' Map any exception to the ArgumentException object.
        Throw New ArgumentException("Wrong arguments")
    End Try
End Sub
```

On the other hand, if your code maps all the possible errors to the ArgumentException object, the caller misses an opportunity to understand what *really* went wrong. (This information might be more important to your tech support than to the end user.)

To cope with this issue, the System.Exception object supports the InnerException property, which is expected to return an inner exception object (or Nothing if no inner exception has been defined). The InnerException property is read-only, and you can set it only when you create the exception object, using an overloaded version of the constructor method:

```
    ' ...(Inside the MathIntensiveProc procedure)...
    Catch ex As Exception
        ' Map any exception to the ArgumentException object,
        ' but remember the inner (actual) exception object.
        Throw New ArgumentException("Wrong arguments", ex)
```

Now the caller has the opportunity to check what the actual exception is by querying the InnerException property of the exception object thrown to it:

```
' The caller code
Sub TestInnerException()
    Dim x, y As Integer

    Try
        MathIntensiveProc(x, y)     ' This causes a division by zero.
    Catch ex As ArgumentException
```

```
        Console.WriteLine("An argument exception has occurred.")
        ' Display a detailed message about the cause of the error.
        Console.WriteLine(ex.InnerException.Message)
    Catch ex As Exception
        ' Deal with other errors.
        Console.WriteLine(ex.Message)
    End Try
End Sub
```

When an error occurs in a deeply nested procedure, you might end up with a series of exception objects, in which each object but the innermost one encapsulates another exception object. The System.Exception object (and all the objects that inherit from it) exposes the GetBaseException method, which returns a reference to the innermost exception:

```
Catch ex As ArgumentException
    Console.WriteLine("An argument exception has occurred.")
    ' Print a description of the innermost exception.
    Console.WriteLine(ex.GetBaseException.Message())
```

Custom classes that inherit from System.ApplicationException don't derive the capability to work with nested exceptions automatically, and you need some extra code to implement a custom constructor method that supports the second argument in the Throw command. The following code is a modified version of the UnableToLoadIniFileException class with this new capability:

```
Class InitializationFailedException
    Inherits System.ApplicationException

    ' We need this to support a parameterless constructor as well.
    Sub New()
        ' No executable statements here
    End Sub

    ' Custom constructor method
    Sub New(ByVal inner As System.Exception)
        MyBase.New("Unable to load initialization file", inner)
    End Sub

    ' We don't need to override the Message property in this new
    ' version because it is initialized in the base class constructor.
End Class
```

Here's a routine that uses the new exception object:

```
Sub InitializeApplication()
    Try
        ' Try to open the ini file. (Just cause an error in this demo.)
```

(continued)

```
        FileOpen(1, "c:\missingfile.ini", OpenMode.Input)
    Catch ex As Exception
        ' Whatever caused the error, throw a more specific exception,
        ' but remember the current exception object.
        Throw New InitializationFailedException(ex)
    End Try
End Sub
```

Performance Tips

Throwing and catching exceptions adds overhead to your applications, so you should use exceptions as sparingly as possible. For example, design your classes in such a way that exceptions are managed internally and not thrown to the caller, and return Nothing or another special value for error conditions that occur frequently. I've prepared a simple procedure that lets you benchmark these two different approaches:

```
Dim rand As New Random()          ' A random number generator

Sub TestExceptionOverhead()
    ' This is the probability that the called method raises an error.
    Const Probability As Double = 0.001
    Const Repetitions As Integer = 1000000

    Dim i As Integer
    Dim startTime As Date
    Dim errorCount As Integer

    ' Test the method that notifies an error by throwing an exception.
    startTime = Now
    errorCount = 0
    For i = 1 To Repetitions
        Try
            CanThrowException(Probability)
        Catch
            errorCount += 1
        End Try
    Next
    Console.WriteLine("Exceptions: {0} secs.", Now.Subtract(startTime))

    ' Test the method that notifies an error by returning False.
    startTime = Now
    errorCount = 0
    For i = 1 To Repetitions
        If CanReturnFalse(Probability) = False Then
            errorCount += 1
        End If
    Next
    Console.WriteLine("Return value: {0} secs.", Now.Subtract(startTime))
```

```
End Sub

' This method can throw an exception with a given probability.
Sub CanThrowException(ByVal probability As Double)
    If rand.NextDouble <= probability Then
        Throw New System.Exception()
    End If
End Sub

' This method can signal an error condition by returning False.
Function CanReturnFalse(ByVal probability As Double) As Boolean
    If rand.NextDouble < probability Then
        ' This means an error occurred.
        Return False
    Else
        ' This means a successful operation.
        Return True
    End If
End Function
```

Here's the result of the preceding benchmark on my 900-MHz system when the test application is compiled in Debug mode:

```
Exceptions: 00:00:01.4621024 secs.
Return value:  00:00:00.1201728 secs.
```

In other words, even if the called procedure throws an exception only once every 1000 iterations of the loop (probability = 0.1 percent), those exceptions make the code run slower by a factor of about 12 times. That's a *lot* of overhead! When your application is running in Release mode, the overhead is less evident, but it can still slow your application remarkably.

By now you should be convinced that you should never use exceptions as a mechanism to return special values from a method and that you should reserve them for truly rare cases. Most methods in the .NET runtime adhere to this practice, and they throw an exception less frequently than methods in Visual Basic 6. For example, the Math.Log and Math.Sqrt methods return the special NaN (Not-a-Number) value when you pass them a negative number.

When authoring your own classes, you can provide clients with a read-only property that lets them understand whether a call to a method would result in an exception being thrown. For example, expose an EOF property that returns True when you're at the end of a data file or a bit-coded State property that tells what operations are allowed on the object. (This is the pattern used by the ADO and ADO.NET connection objects.)

Another performance tip that has to do with exceptions: by default, Visual Basic checks the overflow flag after each operation on integers so that it can throw an exception if the result is outside the valid range. If you're sure that this can't happen in your application, you can improve its performance by selecting the Remove Integer Overflow Checks check box (on the Optimizations page of the project Property Pages dialog box). In my informal benchmarks, I saw that operations on Integer variables run about 20 percent faster and operations on Long variables up to 40 percent faster when this option is enabled.

Debugging .NET Applications

Debugging is a topic that can be considered related to control flow and exception handling, and for this reason I'm covering it in this chapter. In this section, you'll learn a few things about debugging techniques in Visual Studio .NET as well as about diagnostic techniques that can work even after you release your application.

Project and Solution Configurations

The first thing to know about debugging in Visual Studio is that you can create many specific project configurations, wherein each configuration specifies its own optimization settings, compilation constants, command line arguments, and debugging options. If you're working with a multiproject solution, you can even define a configuration setting that defines which specific project configuration must be applied when you compile each project in the solution.

Project Configuration Properties

When Visual Studio .NET creates a new project, it also creates two project configurations: Debug and Release. As its name suggests, the former is designed for debugging the application: it defines the DEBUG compilation constants and disables optimizations. By contrast, the Release configuration doesn't produce any .pdb files containing information for symbolic debugging.

To change these configuration settings, select the project in the Solution Explorer and click on the Properties icon (or select Properties on the Project menu) to open the project Property Pages dialog box. The Configuration Properties section of this window contains four pages—Debugging, Optimizations, Build, and Deployment—inside which you define compilation constants, required optimization settings, and so on. (I'll discuss most of these options later in this chapter or in following chapters.) All the options you select apply to the configuration visible in the Configuration combo box. (See Figure 3-3.) Items in the combo box let you apply your choices to all existing settings or to just a well-defined subset of them, so you don't have to select similar settings individually for multiple configurations. (In theory, you might also choose the target platform, but a Visual Basic .NET program can target only the .NET platform, at least in this release.)

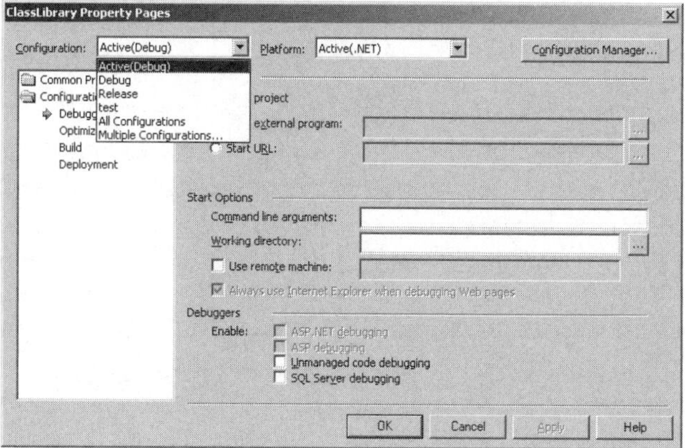

Figure 3-3. The Debugging page in the project Property Pages dialog box.

Solution Configurations

A Visual Studio .NET solution can contain multiple projects. In general, when you debug the application, you want to compile each project in Debug mode, whereas all projects should be compiled in Release mode before you deploy the application. However, during the debugging and refining phase of the application, you might need to compile constituent projects with different configurations: some in Debug mode, others in Release mode, and yet others in some custom configuration that you've defined for them. Solution configurations let you define how each project is compiled when the solution is rebuilt.

The tool that lets you define new solution configurations is the Configuration Manager, which you can activate from the Build menu or by clicking Configuration Manager in one of the Configuration Properties pages in the project Property Pages dialog box. In the Configuration Manager, you select a configuration in the Active Solution Configuration combo box and then decide the project configuration to be used for each constituent project—you can even create a new one. By clearing the check box in the Build column, you can exclude a project from the compilation step in a particular solution configuration. (This feature lets you save a lot of time if you've thoroughly tested one of the projects in the solution.) Other options in the Active Solution Configuration combo box let you rename or remove a solution configuration, or create a new one. (See Figure 3-4.)

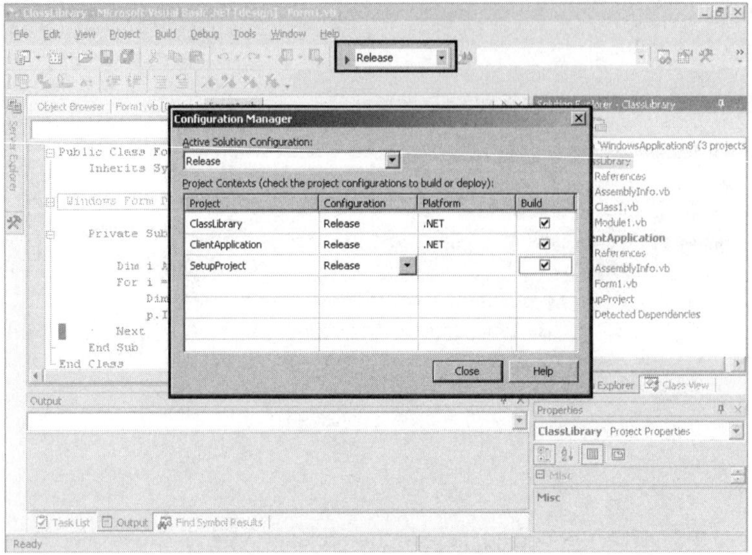

Figure 3-4. The Configuration Manager dialog box lets you define multiple build configurations. The highlighted combo box on the standard toolbar lets you activate a different solution configuration without displaying this window.

You can select the active solution configuration also by using the combo box on the standard toolbar. (See the highlighted portion of Figure 3-4.) You can then rebuild the solution using the configuration that's currently active by selecting the Build Solution command on the Build menu or by pressing the F5 key to run the application. You can also rebuild an individual project by activating the Solution Explorer window, right-clicking the selected project, and clicking Build on the shortcut menu.

Debugging Tools

Visual Studio .NET debugging capabilities are a superset of those available in Visual Studio 6, so you're already familiar with most of them. For example, you can still step into, over, and out of a procedure; you can set a breakpoint by clicking in the gray area to the left of the code editor; and you can display the value of a variable just by hovering the mouse cursor over its name. However, the menu commands and the keyboard shortcuts associated with these operations have changed, at least in the default Visual Studio keyboard configuration. If you don't want to retrain your fingers, you can opt for the Visual Basic 6–compatible keyboard layout from the Options dialog box, which you can reach from the Tools menu. Here's a quick survey of a few new debugging tools you might want to learn about.

The Breakpoints Window

The Breakpoints window lets you manage all your breakpoints from a central location. (See Figure 3-5.) You can disable all or some breakpoints without removing them, which is a handy feature. This window also displays how many times an enabled breakpoint has been hit. You can display the Breakpoints window from the Windows submenu of the Debug menu.

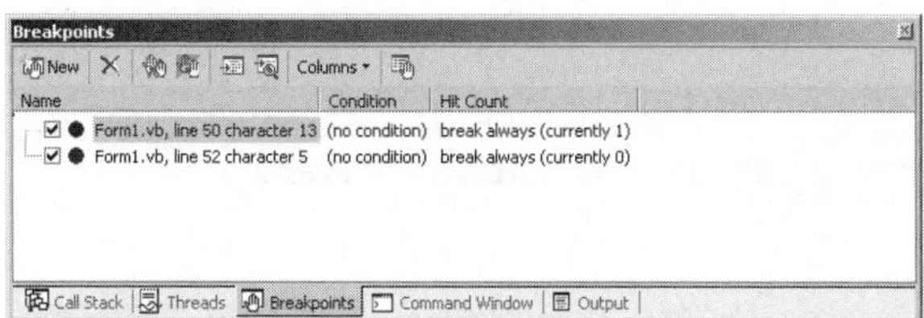

Figure 3-5. The Breakpoints window.

The Properties button in the Breakpoints window's toolbar opens a Properties dialog box, which lets you define more precisely how the breakpoint behaves. (See Figure 3-6.) For example, you can break into the running program when a given expression changes or becomes True. A great new feature allows you to break into the application when the breakpoint has been hit a given number of times. (See Figure 3-6.) It's hard to overestimate the value of such tools when debugging a loop.

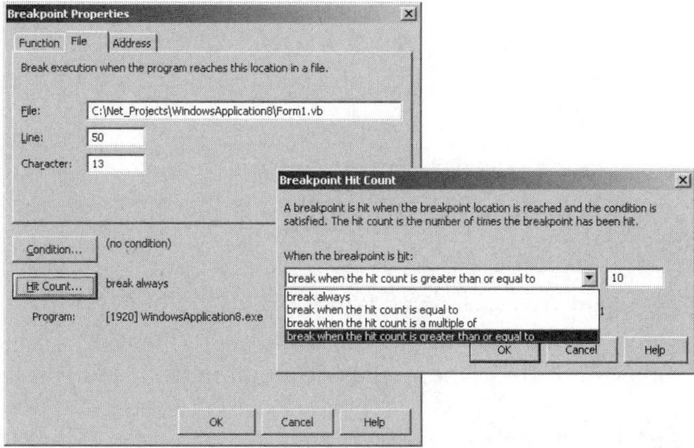

Figure 3-6. The Breakpoint Properties dialog box and the Breakpoint Hit Count dialog box, which lets you select whether the breakpoint should be activated only after a specified number of hits.

The Call Stack Window

The Call Stack window, which was a modal dialog box in Visual Basic 6, has become a dockable window in Visual Studio .NET. In another difference from previous Visual Studio versions, it displays both the pending procedures in your application and the pending procedures in the .NET runtime. (See Figure 3-7.) Another great feature is the ability to read the values of all parameters passed to each pending routine.

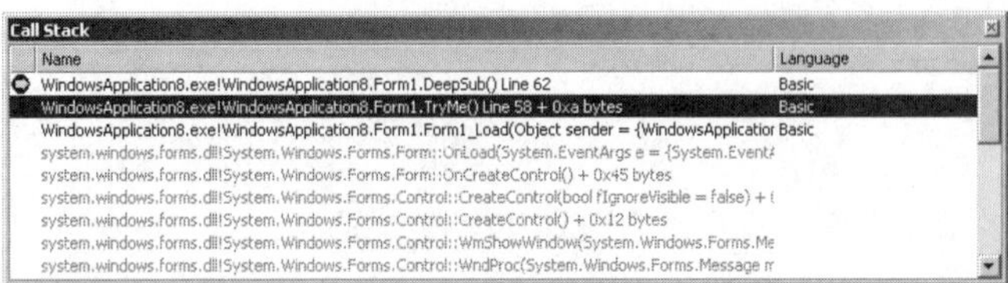

Figure 3-7. The Call Stack window.

The Locals, Me, and Autos Windows

Three windows in the Visual Studio IDE let you browse the names of variables after hitting a breakpoint while debugging an application (see Figure 3-8); you display these windows by selecting the appropriate commands from the Debug menu's Windows submenu:

- The Locals window displays local variables and variables accessible from the current context.
- The Me window displays member variables of the current object. (In general, this is a subset of the information displayed in the Locals window.)
- The Autos window displays member variables accessible from the current statement and the three statements that precede and follow the current statement.

When any value changes, these windows highlight it in red. You can modify any scalar value by clicking on it and beginning to type. (A warning: you might incur rounding errors when entering floating-point numbers.)

The Exceptions Dialog Box

The Visual Studio debugger offers complete control of what happens when an application throws an exception or calls a .NET method that throws an exception. You set all the relevant options from inside the Exceptions dialog box (see Figure 3-9), which you open by selecting Exceptions on the Debug menu. This dialog box shows all the exception types defined in the .NET runtime, grouped by their namespace. Depending on which node you select, you can decide the behavior of all the .NET exceptions, only the exceptions in a given namespace, or individual exceptions. The Add button lets you add other exceptions to the list, such as your own custom exception objects.

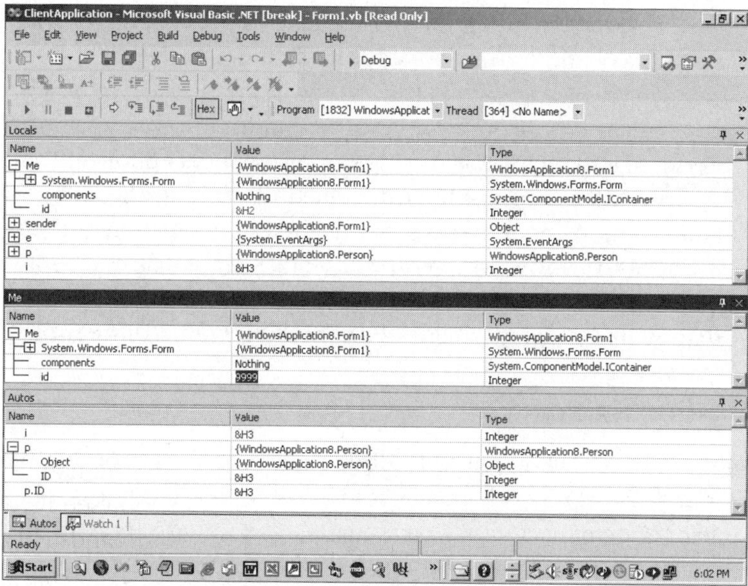

Figure 3-8. The Locals, Me, and Autos windows.

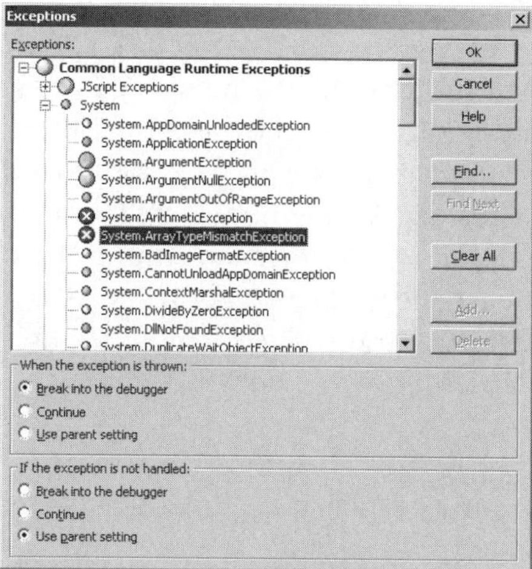

Figure 3-9. The Exceptions dialog box. A larger circular icon marks exceptions that are ignored (the Continue option); a red cross icon marks exceptions that bring up the debugger as soon as they are thrown.

For each selected exception or group of exceptions, you can decide what happens as soon as the exception is thrown—that is, before the application has a chance to deal with it—and what happens if the exception isn't handled somewhere in the application. (By default, the debugger comes into play only in the latter case.) Activating the debugger also for exceptions that the application is going to handle can be useful in debugging the error handlers in your code or in catching exceptions that would go unnoticed otherwise. For example, you can activate this option if a procedure performs much too slowly and you suspect that the reason is the high number of exceptions it has to deal with.

In most cases, you apply your selections only to the Common Language Runtime Exceptions node because by default all nodes inherit their parent's setting. If necessary, however, you can establish a distinct behavior of each namespace or individual exception type. Exceptions that are handled in a way other than with the default method are marked with a different icon.

Tracing Application Behavior

Visual Studio .NET's integrated debugging features are powerful enough for finding and fixing most bugs and logic errors, but in some cases you need to add tracing statements to your code that let you understand why the application is misbehaving. This is especially useful when the problems occur only in compiled applications already deployed at your customer's site. Fortunately, the .NET Framework offers several classes that simplify this task.

The Debug and Trace Classes

The primary classes for adding tracing statements to your code are the Debug and Trace classes, both of which reside in the System.Diagnostics namespace. (This namespace is imported at the project level by all Visual Basic projects, so you never need to specify the complete class names in your code.)

The Debug and Trace classes expose methods for sending a message to the Output window in Visual Studio or to another output device. All these methods are shared methods, which means that you don't need to instantiate an instance of these classes to use them. (You will learn more about shared methods in Chapter 4.) For example, both these statements display a string in the Output window in Visual Studio:

```
Debug.WriteLine("Program has started")
Trace.WriteLine("Program has started")
```

The Write method works similarly except that it doesn't append a newline character:

```
Debug.Write("These two strings ")
Debug.WriteLine("appear on the same line.")
```

The Debug and Trace classes are identical and expose the same methods. The only difference between them is that calls to methods of the Debug class are included in the compiled application only if the DEBUG compilation constant is defined, whereas calls to methods of the Trace class are included only if the TRACE compilation constant is defined. By default, the Debug project configuration defines both these compilation constants, while the Release project configuration defines only the TRACE constant. Thus, output from the Trace class is included in all compiled applications, whereas output from the Debug class is discarded in applications compiled in Release mode. Of course, you can change this default behavior by defining or undefining the two compilation constants on the Build page of the project Property Pages dialog box. (See Figure 3-10.)

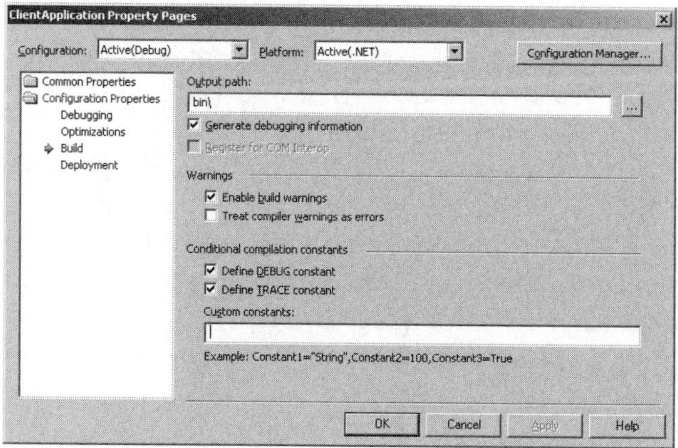

Figure 3-10. The Build page of the project Property Pages dialog box.

Unlike the Visual Basic 6 Debug object, which has rather limited functionality, the .NET Debug and Trace classes offer many ways to control how trace messages are sent to the Output window. For example, the WriteIf and WriteLineIf methods emit the trace string only if the expression passed to the first argument is True:

```
Debug.WriteLineIf(x < 0, "Warning: x is negative")
```

The Fail method stops the application and displays a message box that lets the user abort the program, debug it, or just ignore the error. (See Figure 3-11.)

```
' You can specify a message and a detailed message.
Trace.Fail("An error has occurred", "File app.ini not found")
```

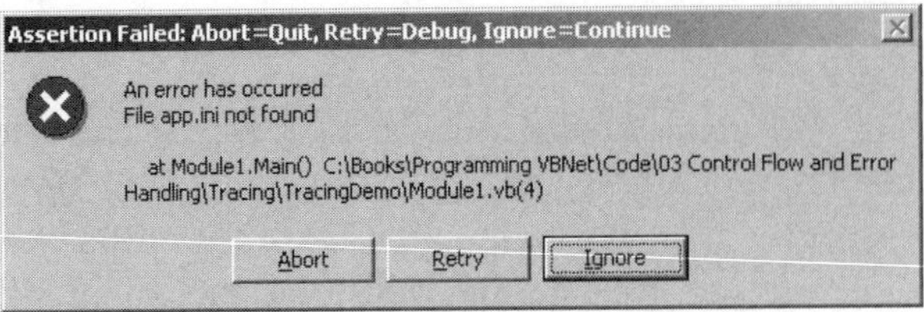

Figure 3-11. The effect of a Trace.Fail method.

The Assert method is similar to Fail, with a few key differences. First, it displays the message box only if its first argument is False:

```
' You can omit the detailed message or both messages.
Trace.Assert(obj Is Nothing, "Unable to continue", "Object is Nothing")
```

Second, and more important, you can use a configuration file to control whether the message box is displayed and even specify a text log file that must receive all error messages. I will explain .NET configuration files in detail in Chapter 14, but for now let's see how you can disable message boxes coming from Assert methods and redirect them to a text file.

Run Notepad, and prepare the following XML file; then save it with a name obtained by appending the .config suffix to the name of your application's executable file in the same directory as the EXE file. For example, if your application's executable file is named c:\progs\myapp.exe, the configuration file must be named c:\progs\myapp.exe.config:

```
<configuration>
   <system.diagnostics>
      <trace autoflush="false" indentsize="4"/>
      <assert assertuienabled="false" logfilename=".\ErrorLog.txt"/>
   </system.diagnostics>
</configuration>
```

You can now run the application, and you'll see no message boxes on the screen. The autoflush attribute should be false when the application is outputting to a file, so the output isn't flushed to the file at each Assert method. (You can control this feature also with the AutoFlush property of the Debug or Trace class.)

The Debug and Trace classes also expose the Indent and Unindent methods for controlling the indentation level of the output. These methods help you make clear how your routines are nested:

```
Sub MyProc()
    Debug.WriteLine("Entering MyProc")
    Debug.Indent()
    ⋮
    Debug.WriteLine("Inside MyProc")
    Debug.Unindent()
```

```
    Debug.WriteLine("Exiting MyProc")
End Sub
```

The preceding debugging code produces this output:

```
Entering MyProc
    Inside MyProc
Exiting MyProc
```

You can control the number of spaces in the indentation by means of the IndentSize property or with the indentsize attribute in the configuration file.

Trace Listeners

The feature of the Debug and Trace classes that makes them superior to a typical custom trace technique is their ability to add trace listeners to their output. The mechanism is simple and powerful: the Listeners property holds a collection of listener objects that are notified whenever the application emits a trace message. By adding new elements to the Listeners collection, you can send the trace output virtually anywhere. For example, you might define a custom listener class that sends your tech support an e-mail when something catastrophic occurs. The .NET Framework ships with three listener classes:

- DefaultTraceListener, which sends output to the Output window or any debugger able to trap strings sent via the OutputDebugString API function. This listener is added by default to the Listeners collection, so you don't have to do anything special to use it. (You can use the Listeners.Clear method to remove it.)
- TextWriterTraceListener, which can send its output to the console window, a file, or a .NET stream. (Streams are described in Chapter 10.)
- EventLogTraceListener, which sends its output to the system log. (Event logs are described in Chapter 19.)

The following example shows how you can add one or more elements to the Listeners collection to achieve a variety of results:

```
' Send trace output to the console window.
Trace.Listeners.Add(New TextWriterTraceListener(Console.Out))

' Send trace output to a text file.
Dim sw As New System.IO.StreamWriter("trace.txt")
Trace.Listeners.Add(New TextWriterTraceListener(sw))
:
' Close the stream before exiting the program.
sw.Close()
```

(continued)

```
' Send trace output to the Application log on the local machine,
' using a source named TracingDemo.
Dim ev As New EventLog("Application", ".", "TracingDemo")
Trace.Listeners.Add(New EventLogTraceListener("TracingDemo"))
⋮
' Close the event log before exiting the program.
ev.Close()
```

(You might want to have a second look at the preceding code when you know more about stream and event logs, which I explain later in this book.)

The great thing about trace listeners is that you don't have to initialize them and add them to the Listeners collection in code because you can achieve the same effect by means of the application's configuration file. Here's an example that shows how you can send trace output to a text file. (Note that you must set the autoflush attribute to True.)

```
<configuration>
   <system.diagnostics>
      <trace autoflush="true" indentsize="4">
        <listeners>
           <add name="FileListener"
                type="System.Diagnostics.TextWriterTraceListener,System"
                initializeData=".\trace.txt" />
        </listeners>
      </trace>
   </system.diagnostics>
</configuration>
```

The .NET Framework even supports custom trace listeners, which you define by writing a class that inherits from the TraceListener abstract class and redefines its Write and WriteLine methods. I haven't explained exactly how inheritance works, but for now you can see how easy this mechanism is. I have prepared a new listener class that sends all trace messages to a file and prefixes them with the current time (including milliseconds in the output):

```
Class ProfileTraceListener
    Inherits TraceListener

    ' Create a log file named PROFILE.LOG.
    Dim sw As New System.IO.StreamWriter("PROFILE.LOG")

    Public Overloads Overrides Sub Write(ByVal message As String)
        ' Display indentation and time only at beginning of line.
        If Me.NeedIndent Then
            sw.Write("[" & Now.ToString & " " & Now.Millisecond & "] ")
            Me.WriteIndent()
        End If
        sw.Write(message)
        sw.Flush()       ' Ensure data is written to file.
    End Sub
```

```
    Public Overloads Overrides Sub WriteLine(ByVal message As String)
        ' Use the Write method to display an entire line.
        Me.Write(message & ControlChars.CrLf)
        ' Next line must be indented,
        ' and current time must be displayed.
        Me.NeedIndent = True
    End Sub
End Class
```

You add this class to the Listeners collection in the usual way, either by adding an element to the configuration file or via code:

```
Trace.Listeners.Add(New ProfileTraceListener())
```

Here is a sample of the output this custom listener produces in the PROFILE.LOG file:

```
[11/24/2001 12:58:53 PM 453] Entering MyProc
[11/24/2001 12:58:54 PM 263] Exiting MyProc
[11/24/2001 12:58:54 PM 283] Entering MyProc2
[11/24/2001 12:58:54 PM 813] Exiting MyProc2
```

The companion CD contains an improved version of this class that keeps track of procedures being entered and exited and displays the total time spent inside a procedure.

Trace Switches

The .NET Framework also offers a couple of classes that help you in limiting the number of messages sent to the trace device. The BooleanSwitch class can be used when the trace message should be either sent or not sent, in a yes-or-no fashion. The TraceSwitch class allows more granular control of how messages are output by defining the five tracing levels listed in Table 3-2.

Table 3-2 Tracing Levels for the TraceSwitch Class

Enumerated Value	Numeric Value	Trace Messages Displayed
Off	0	None
Error	1	Only serious error messages
Warning	2	Warnings and error messages
Info	3	Informational messages, warnings, and error messages
Verbose	4	All messages

You usually create trace switches near the beginning of your application. Their constructor takes a display name and a description string:

```
' Create the trace switches used by your application.
Dim bsProfile As New BooleanSwitch("bsProfile", _
    "Define whether profile information is displayed")
Dim tsDiagnostic As New TraceSwitch("tsDiagnostic", _
    "Set the threshold level for visible diagnostic messages")
```

You can set the state of a BooleanSwitch by setting its Enabled Boolean property, and the threshold level of a TraceSwitch by assigning an enumerated value to its Level property:

```
' Enable profile messages.
bsProfile.Enabled = True
' Display both warning and error diagnostic messages.
tsDiagnostic.Level = TraceLevel.Warning
```

In most cases, however, you want to set these values in the application's configuration file so that the user (possibly guided by your technical support team) can modify them before restarting the program, without your having to recompile the application. To set the values, you just have to add one or more entries in the <switches> section, as the following example illustrates:

```
<configuration>
  <system.diagnostics>
    <switches>
      <!   Enable/disable profiling messages(0=disable, 1=enable)   >
       <add name="bsProfile" value="1"/>
       <!   Set threadshold for diagnostic messages
           (0=none, 1=errors, 2=warnings, 3=info, 4=verbose)    >
       <add name="tsDiagnostic" value="4" />
     </switches>
    <trace autoflush="false" indentsize="4"/>
    <assert assertuienabled="false" logfilename=".\TraceLog.txt"/>
  </system.diagnostics>
</configuration>
```

The comments before each <add> section are optional, but they can be very useful for letting users know how to achieve the desired behavior. The values in the configuration file are read when the trace switch object is created, and it is mandatory that the first argument in the constructor match the name attribute in the configuration file. When using a configuration file, you should refrain from assigning the Enabled and Level properties via code because you would overwrite the settings found in the file.

Once you've successfully initialized a trace switch, you can use it to make decisions related to tracing. Typically, you will use a BooleanSwitch's Enabled property in the first argument of a WriteIf or WriteLineIf method of the Debug or Trace class:

```
' Display profiling information only if requested.
Trace.WriteLineIf(bsProfile.Enabled, "Starting the application at " _
    & Now.ToString)
```

When working with a TraceSwitch object, you can use its TraceError, TraceWarning, TraceInfo, and TraceVerbose properties to decide whether a message should be displayed. For example, the TraceWarning property returns True only if the current trace level is 2 or higher. Here's a piece of code that gives you some hints at how you might use trace switches in a real application:

```
' Create the trace switches used by your application.
Dim bsProfile As New BooleanSwitch("bsProfile", _
    "Define whether profile information is displayed")
Dim tsDiagnostic As New TraceSwitch("tsDiagnostic", _
    "Set the threshold level for visible diagnostic messages")

Sub Main()
    MyProc2("")
End Sub

Sub MyProc2(ByVal arg1 As String)
    ' Display profiling information only if requested.
    Trace.WriteLineIf(bsProfile.Enabled, _
        "Entering MyProc2 at " & Now.ToString)
    Trace.Indent()
    ' Display argument values only if in verbose mode.
    Trace.WriteLineIf(tsDiagnostic.TraceVerbose, "arg1 = " & arg1)
    ' Display a warning if argument is a null string.
    Trace.WriteLineIf(arg1 = "" AndAlso tsDiagnostic.TraceWarning, _
        "Arg1 is a null string!")

    Try
        ' Do some operations.
        Throw New DivideByZeroException()
    Catch ex As DivideByZeroException
        ' Display a warning for errors that can be remedied.
        Trace.WriteLineIf(tsDiagnostic.TraceWarning, _
            "DivideByZero exception in MyProc2")
    Catch ex As Exception
        ' Display an error message for unhandled exceptions.
        Trace.WriteLineIf(tsDiagnostic.TraceError, _
            "Unhandled exception in MyProc2: " & ex.message)
    End Try
    Trace.Unindent()
    Trace.WriteLineIf(bsProfile.Enabled, _
        "Exiting MyProc2 at " & Now.ToString)
End Sub
```

This chapter introduced a large number of new language features, although the list is far from complete. In fact, I left out all the object-oriented additions to Visual Basic, which deserve two long chapters of their own. So take a deep breath and start reading about them in the next chapter.

Part II

Object-Oriented Programming

Front
Top
Left
Back

4

Class Fundamentals

Microsoft Visual Basic has always been the Cinderella of object-oriented programming languages (OOPLs), to the point that some purists of object-oriented programming didn't even consider Visual Basic an OOPL at all. And to tell the truth, they were at least partly right because too many features were missing—most notably, constructors and inheritance. Creating truly object-oriented applications with Visual Basic 6 was so difficult that many developers thought it wasn't worth the effort. Just think of the tons of lines you had to write to implement an inheritance-like mechanism based on delegation. (For more information about this and other object-oriented techniques available under Visual Basic 6, see my book *Programming Microsoft Visual Basic 6*, available on the companion CD.)

Well, all these issues are going to vanish because all .NET languages are born equal, and Visual Basic finally offers all the features that you look for in a mature object-oriented language. (Well, you might argue that inheritance from multiple classes isn't supported, but this limitation is common to all other .NET languages because it's imposed by the .NET runtime itself.)

Because of the many new object-oriented features, getting familiar with classes and interfaces under Visual Basic .NET might take longer than with changes in other areas. At any rate, the new syntax is far more rational than under Visual Basic 6, and there are fewer restrictions and exceptions to account for.

Fields

As I explain in Chapter 2, Visual Basic .NET classes are blocks of code enclosed between the Class and End Class statements. You can use these statements in any source file, even if the file contains a Form class. You can also have multiple classes in the same file, which isn't permitted under Visual Basic 6.

```
Class Person
    ' The class implementation goes here.
    ⋮
End Class
```

Classes are visible only from inside the same project if you don't specify a scope qualifier, so their default scope is Friend and you must explicitly add the Public keyword to make them visible to other applications. This is a major change from Visual Basic 6, whose classes have a default public scope. (You can read more about exposing objects to other applications in Chapter 14.)

Microsoft guidelines dictate that class names should use names or name combinations and not include a prefix (such as *C*) or an underscore character. If the class name includes multiple words, you should use Pascal casing (as in PartTimeEmployee).

A class can contain both public and private fields, which are nothing but variables declared directly inside the Class block:

```
Class Person
    ' Fields visible from outside the class
    Public FirstName As String
    Public LastName As String
    ' Fields that can be used only from inside the class
    Dim m_BirthDate As Date
    Dim m_LoginDate As Date
    Private EmailUserName As String
    Private EmailEnabled As Boolean = True

    ' The class's properties and methods
    ⋮
End Class
```

Microsoft guidelines dictate that field names use PascalCase when they contain multiple words (for example, FirstName) and never use a prefix to indicate the field's data type. In other words, the Hungarian naming convention is discouraged, also because Visual Studio offers better ways to quickly see the type of a field. You can view the declaration of a variable simply by placing the mouse cursor on it.

You can use all the syntax variations that you would use with plain variables, including initializers and multiple declarations on the same line (even though the latter practice is discouraged because it degrades code readability). Note that the Dim statement defines a Private field inside a Class block, whereas it declares a Public field when it appears in a Structure block. A significant improvement over Visual Basic 6 is that now variables can be declared with a Friend scope, which means that the field is visible from other modules of the same project but not from outside the project:

```
' Inside the Person class
Friend EmailPassword As String
```

You have to implement a pair of Friend Property procedures to get the same effect under Visual Basic 6. From outside the class, Public and Friend fields appear as plain properties and can be used as such:

```
' A block of code that uses the Person class
Dim aPerson As New Person
aPerson.FirstName = "Francesco"
aPerson.LastName = "Balena"
```

Visual Basic .NET is more flexible than its predecessors in that you can also declare an array as a Public field:

```
' You can define up to four addresses for this person,
' from Address(0) to Address(3).
Public Address(4) As String
```

You can access this element as you would access any property with an index:

```
aPerson.Address(0) = "1234 North Street"
```

In another difference from Visual Basic 6, you can declare fields and variables anywhere in a class, not just at its beginning. For example, you can declare a private variable immediately before (or after) the property that encapsulates it or move all your variables just before the End Class statement.

Another minor but significant difference from previous versions is how a field behaves when passed by reference to a procedure that modifies it. I can illustrate this concept using an example:

```
' Raise to the 4th power.
Function Power4(ByRef x As Double) As Double
    ' This is faster than x^4.
    x = x * x
    Power4 = x * x
End Sub

' Here's a VB6 code procedure that passes the Power4 function
' a Public variable defined in a class.
Sub TestByRefPassing()
    Dim obj As New SampleClass
    obj.Number = 3
    Debug.Print Power4(obj.Number)    ' => 81
    ' Prove that the property hasn't changed.
    Debug.Print obj.Number            ' => 3
End Sub
```

The preceding code contains a logic error because the Power4 function unnecessarily modifies an argument passed to it, but you aren't going to see this error if Visual Basic 6 never passes a variable (as opposed to a class field) to the Power4 function. The Number field isn't affected because Visual Basic 6 wraps a pair of hidden Property Get and Property Let procedures around the Number variable, and the Power4 functions can't alter the inner variable.

Visual Basic .NET doesn't wrap any hidden procedure around class fields; therefore, a literal translation of the preceding code makes the bug appear:

```
' A Visual Basic .NET code snippet that passes the Power4 function
' a Public variable defined in a class
Sub TestByRefPassing()
    Dim obj As New SampleClass
    obj.Number = 3
    Console.WriteLine(Power4(obj.Number))  ' => 81
    ' The Number property has changed as well.
    Console.WriteLine(obj.Number)          ' => 9
End Sub
```

Oddly, you can regard this behavior as a return to the past because Visual Basic 4 worked in the same way as Visual Basic .NET. The behavior of Public class fields changed in Visual Basic 5 and broke existing Visual Basic 4 code. You can expect to encounter a similar problem when you're porting Visual Basic 5 or 6 code to Visual Basic .NET. Incidentally, because there are no hidden wrappers, accessing a field is usually remarkably faster than accessing an equivalent property.

Visual Basic .NET doesn't support ByVal in a method invocation:

```
' This statement works in Visual Basic 6
' but raises a compilation error in Visual Basic .NET.
Dim n As Integer: n = 3
res = Power4(ByVal n)
```

The only way to pass a number by value to a procedure that expects a ByRef argument is by enclosing the argument in parentheses:

```
obj.Number = 3
' This statement passes the obj.Number property by value.
Console.WriteLine(Power4((obj.Number))    ' => 81
' Prove that the Number property hasn't changed.
Console.WriteLine(obj.Number)             ' => 3
```

In a difference from previous language versions, Visual Basic .NET classes can expose Public constants, which are seen outside the class as read-only properties:

```
Public Const DefaultPassword As String = "mypwd"
```

When using a numeric constant in an expression, you can explicitly define its type by appending one of the following characters to the value: I (Integer), L (Long), D (Double), S (Short), or @ (Decimal):

```
Average = sum / 10D     ' Divide by a Double.
```

The old type suffix characters %, &, !, and # are still supported.

Methods

You can implement class methods as Sub and Function procedures, exactly as you do under Visual Basic 6. You must account for the syntax changes already described in Chapter 3—for example, those affecting Optional arguments and argument passing:

```
Function CompleteName(Optional ByVal title As String = "") As String
    ' Use the title if provided.
    If title <> "" Then CompleteName = title & " "
    ' Append first and last name.
    CompleteName &= FirstName & " " & LastName
End Function
```

Microsoft guidelines dictate that you use PascalCase for the names of methods (for example, ClearAll). Parameters should use camelCase (for example, mainAddress) and never use a prefix that indicates their data type (the so-called Hungarian notation). Note that, unlike the Visual Basic 6 code editor, Visual Studio .NET can distinguish parameters from variables and doesn't automatically change the casing of a parameter to match the casing of a variable with the same name.

Another interesting suggestion from Microsoft is that you never define a parameter that has as its only purpose "reserved for future use" because newer versions of the class can overload a method (see next section) to support additional arguments without breaking backward compatibility with existing code.

Overloading

Visual Basic .NET lets you *overload* a method. Method overloading means that you can provide multiple methods with the same name but different parameter signatures—that is, with a different number of parameters or with parameters of a different type. Before explaining how you implement overloaded methods, I think it makes sense to illustrate why overloading can be useful. Suppose you're creating a collection-like class and include an Item method that provides access to the collection's elements though either a numeric or a string argument. This is the code that you write under Visual Basic 6 to implement such a method:

```
Function Item(index As Variant) As String
    If VarType(index) = vbLong Or VarType(index) = vbInteger Then
        ' Access an element through its numeric index.
        ⋮
    ElseIf VarType(index) = vbString Then
        ' Access an element through its string key.
        ⋮
```

```
    Else
        ' Raise a run-time error otherwise.
        Err.Raise 999, , "Invalid index type"
    End If
End Function
```

The Visual Basic .NET solution is cleaner: you define multiple procedures with the same name and different syntax. You can explicitly state that you're overloading the Item method by prefixing it with the Overloads keyword:

```
' The Visual Basic .NET solution
Overloads Function Item(ByVal index As Integer) As String
    ' Access an element through its numeric index.
    :
End Function

Overloads Function Item(ByVal key As String) As String
    ' Access an element through its string key.
    :
End Function
```

Note that the Overloads keyword is optional, but if you use it for one overloaded method you must use it for all of them. Not only is the code less cluttered, it's also more efficient: the compiler decides which version of the Item function is called, and no test is necessary at run time:

```
' This statement calls the first overloaded version.
result = myObj.Item(1)
' This statement calls the second overloaded version.
result = myObj.Item("foo")
```

Just as important, the compiler can flag invalid arguments, so you don't have to trap arguments of invalid type:

```
' *** The following code doesn't compile (if Option Strict is On).
Dim value As Double = 1.23
result = myObj.Item(value)
```

Method overloading lets you solve cases that are almost unmanageable under Visual Basic 6. For example, say that you're implementing an InstrWord function, which searches whole words and exposes a syntax similar to that of the standard InStr function. The problem with InStr is that it comes with two different syntax forms:

```
result = InStr(text, search)
result = InStr(index, text, search, Optional compareMethod)
```

If you want your InstrWord function to closely mimic the InStr function, your only option under Visual Basic 6 is to declare a function that takes variants and resolves all the possible cases at run time:

```
Function InstrWord(arg1 As Variant, arg2 As Variant, _
    Optional arg3 As Variant, Optional arg4 As Variant) As Long
    If VarType(arg1) = vbString Then
        ' First case - but check that you don't have too many arguments.
        If Not IsMissing(arg3) Then
            Err.Raise 997, , "Too many arguments"
        End If
        ⋮
    ElseIf VarType(arg1) = vbLong or VarType(arg1) = vbInteger Then
        ' Second case - but check that the Search argument is there.
        If IsMissing(arg3) Then
            Err.Raise 998, , "Too few arguments"
        End If
        ⋮
    Else
        ' Raise an error.
        Err.Raise 999, , "Invalid arguments"
    End If
End Function
```

Here's the Visual Basic .NET solution. (Notice that I have omitted the optional Overloads keyword.)

```
Function InstrWord(ByVal source As String, _
    ByVal search As String) As Long
    ' First case is just a special case of the more general case.
    Return InstrWholeWord(1, source, search, CompareMethod.Binary)
End Function

Function InstrWord(ByVal index As Long, _
    ByVal text As String, ByVal search As String, _
    ByVal Optional cmpMethod As CompareMethod = CompareMethod.Binary) As Long
    ' Second case is the more general case.
    ⋮
End Function
```

Again, not only is the code cleaner and easier to maintain, it is also more efficient (because the compiler makes its decisions at compile time) and robust (because invalid calls don't even compile). IntelliSense correctly recognizes overloaded methods and displays a list of all the supported syntax forms, and you can visit all of them using the up and down arrow keys:

```
result = InstrWholeWord(
    2 of 2  InstrWholeWord (Index As Long, Source As String, Search As String, [CmpMethod As Microsoft.VisualBasic.CompareMethod = 0]) As Long
```

Another argument against optional arguments: a few .NET languages—most notably, C#—don't recognize optional arguments. Therefore, C# developers calling a Visual Basic .NET method must pass all the arguments whether they're required or optional. You should implement overloaded methods rather than methods with optional arguments if you plan to expose those methods to languages other than Visual Basic.

Keep in mind that optional arguments are resolved when you compile the client code, not the method that defines them. If the client code omits one or more optional arguments, the compiler adds the necessary (hidden) statements that push their default values onto the stack. This can lead to versioning problems when the client code and the target method belong to different assemblies and therefore are compiled separately. If you then recompile the method and change the default value of the optional argument, you should recompile all its clients as well; otherwise, they'll pass the wrong value. You don't have this problem if you stay clear of optional arguments and replace them with overloaded methods.

Overloading and Coercion

When the argument types don't match exactly the parameter signature of any available method, the compiler attempts to match them through widening coercion exclusively. (Review the section "The Option Strict Statement" in Chapter 2 for the difference between widening and narrowing coercion.) For example, assume that you have two overloaded Sum functions that contain Console.WriteLine statements to help you understand which version is invoked:

```
Function Sum(ByVal n1 As Long, ByVal n2 As Long) As Long
    Sum = n1 + n2
    Console.WriteLine("The integer version has been invoked.")
End Function
Function Sum(ByVal n1 As Single, ByVal n2 As Single) As Single
    Sum = n1 + n2
    Console.WriteLine("The floating-point version has been invoked.")
End Function
```

Now consider what happens when you invoke the Sum function with Integer arguments:

```
Dim intValue As Short = 1234
' This statement invokes the integer version.
Console.WriteLine(Sum(intValue, 1))     ' => 1235
```

In this case, both arguments are 16-bit Integer, but Visual Basic correctly promotes them to Long and calls the first version of the Sum function. Here's another example:

```
' This statement invokes the floating-point version.
' Note that you must specify that the 2nd argument is a Single.
Console.WriteLine(Sum(intValue, 1.25!))     ' => 1235.25
```

In this case, Visual Basic realizes that only the second version can be invoked without losing precision. Finally, consider this third example:

```
Dim dblValue As Double = 1234
' *** The next statement raises a compiler error if Option Strict is On.
Console.WriteLine(Sum(dblValue, 1.25))
```

In this last case, you can't call either Sum function without the risk of losing precision or throwing an out-of-range exception at run time, so Visual Basic refuses to compile this piece of code.

Ambiguous Cases

Visual Basic must be able to resolve a method call at compile time. Therefore, two overloaded procedures of the same method must differ in more respects than in an optional argument. For example, the following third variant of the Sum function can't compile because it differs from the second form only in an optional argument:

```
Function Sum(ByVal n1 As Single, _
    Optional ByVal n2 As Single = 1) As Single
    Sum = n1 + n2
End Function
```

The compiler shows what's wrong with the following message:

```
'Function Sum(n1 As Single, n2 As Single) As Single' and 'Function
Sum(n1 As Single, [n2 As Single = 1]) As Single' differ only by optional
parameters. They cannot override each other.
```

A corollary of this concept is that you can't create overloaded variations of a function that differ only in the type of the returned value. For example, you can't overload a ClearValue function that returns either a null string or a null integer:

```
' *** This code doesn't compile.
Function ClearValue() As String
    ClearValue = ""
End Function
Function ClearValue() As Long
    ClearValue = 0
End Function
```

You can work around this limitation by using Sub procedures instead of functions, with the type of the argument passed to it by reference determining which version of the procedure is actually called:

```
' This code compiles correctly.
Sub ClearValue(ByRef arg As String)
    arg = ""
End Sub
Sub ClearValue(ByRef arg As Long)
    arg = 0
End Sub
' You should add versions for other numeric types.
⋮
```

Finally, remember that you can also overload class properties and that overloading isn't limited to classes; you can overload Sub and Function defined in Module and Structure blocks too.

Properties

Implementing properties under Visual Basic .NET is more straightforward than under Visual Basic 6 once you get accustomed to the new syntax. Instead of having distinct Property Get, Property Let, and Property Set procedures, now you have a single Property...End Property block, which defines the property's name, its type, and its argument signature:

```
Property BirthDate() As Date
    ' Implementation of BirthDate property goes here.
    :
End Property
```

Inside the Property block, you write a Get...End Get block, which defines what value the property returns, and a Set...End Set block, which defines how values are assigned to the property. In most cases, a property simply maps to a Private field, so the code for these two blocks often looks like this:

```
' You can define variables anywhere in a class or module.
Dim m_BirthDate As Date

Property BirthDate() As Date
    Get
        Return m_BirthDate
    End Get
    Set(ByVal Value As Date)
        m_BirthDate = Value
    End Set
End Property
```

At least two points are worth noticing here. First, Let...End Let blocks aren't supported because Visual Basic .NET doesn't support parameterless default properties and there's no need to differentiate between a Let and a Set block. (You might argue that a Let...End Let block would be more appropriate than a Set...End Set block, but this argument is groundless because everything is ultimately an object in the .NET Framework.) Second, the Get...End Get block can return a value either through the new Return keyword or by assigning the value to the property name (as you would do under Visual Basic 6):

```
Property BirthDate() As Date
    Get
        ' Another way to return a value
```

```
        BirthDate = m_BirthDate
    End Get
    ⋮
End Property
```

The Set...End Set block always receives a Value argument that stands for the value being assigned to the property itself. This argument must be of the same type as the type defined in the Property statement and must be declared using ByVal. If you happen to have a field named Value, you can distinguish between the field and the Value keyword by prefixing the field with the Me keyword or, more simply, by changing the parameter name to something else:

```
' A class that has a Value field
Class ValueClass
    Private Value As Double

    ' A property that uses the Value field
    Property DoubleValue() As Double
        Get
            Return Me.Value * 2
        End Get
        Set(ByVal newValue As Double)
            Me.Value = newValue / 2
        End Set
    End Property
End Class
```

Note that Me.Value is a legal syntax, even if the Value field is private. Under Visual Basic 6, only public variables could be accessed through the Me keyword, but this restriction doesn't apply to Visual Basic .NET.

Interestingly, you can pass a property to a ByRef parameter of a procedure, and any change to the argument is reflected in the property. The same happens when you increment or decrement a property using the += and -= operators, as this code shows:

```
Sub TestByRefProperty
    Dim vc As New ValueClass
    vc.DoubleValue = 100
    ClearValue(vc.DoubleValue)
    ' Show that the method actually changed the property.
    Console.WriteLine(vc.DoubleValue)            ' => 0

    vc.DoubleValue += 10
    ' Show that the property was actually incremented.
    Console.WriteLine(vc.DoubleValue)            ' => 10
End Sub
```

(continued)

```
Sub ClearValue(ByRef Value As Double)
    Value = 0
End Sub
```

This behavior differs from that of Visual Basic 6, in which a property—implemented as either a Public field or a pair of property procedures—is never modified if passed to a ByRef argument.

Visual Basic .NET property syntax is the same whether the property returns a simple value or an object: after all, everything is an object in the .NET Framework. Therefore, you don't have to worry about the many syntax variations that exist under Visual Basic 6, for which a Variant property can map to three distinct Property procedures. For example, the following Spouse property can return a Person object that represents the wife or husband of the current Person object:

```
Private m_Spouse As Person

Property Spouse() As Person
    Get
        Return m_Spouse
    End Get
    Set(ByVal Value As Person)
        m_Spouse = Value
    End Set
End Property
```

As you see, this syntax is no different from that of a regular property that returns a string or a numeric value.

Read-Only and Write-Only Properties

You define read-only properties by omitting the Set...End Set block, as you do under Visual Basic 6. However, you must use the ReadOnly keyword to explicitly state that you mean to create a read-only property:

```
' The Age property is read-only.
ReadOnly Property Age() As Integer
    Get
        Return Year(Now) - Year(m_BirthDate) ' Simplistic age calculation
    End Get
End Property
```

Similarly, you can create a write-only property by omitting the Get...End Get block and using the WriteOnly keyword in the Property block:

```
' LoginDate is a write-only property.
WriteOnly Property LoginDate() As Date
    Set(ByVal Value As Date)
        m_LoginDate = Value
    End Set
End Property
```

Attempts to write read-only properties, as well as attempts to read write-only properties, are trapped at compile time. Note that the ReadOnly keyword is also allowed for fields, as you see here:

```
Public ReadOnly ID As Long
```

Read-only fields can be written to only from inside constructor methods. (Read "Constructors" later in this chapter.) You can determine whether a property of a .NET class is read/write or read-only by looking at it in the Object Browser. (See Figure 4-1.)

The only limitation of the Visual Basic .NET way of declaring properties is that you can't use different scope qualifiers for the Get and Set blocks. Thus, you can't create a property that's read/write from inside the current project and read-only from outside it. You must create instead two separate properties with different names: one Public read-only property that delegates to another Friend read/write property.

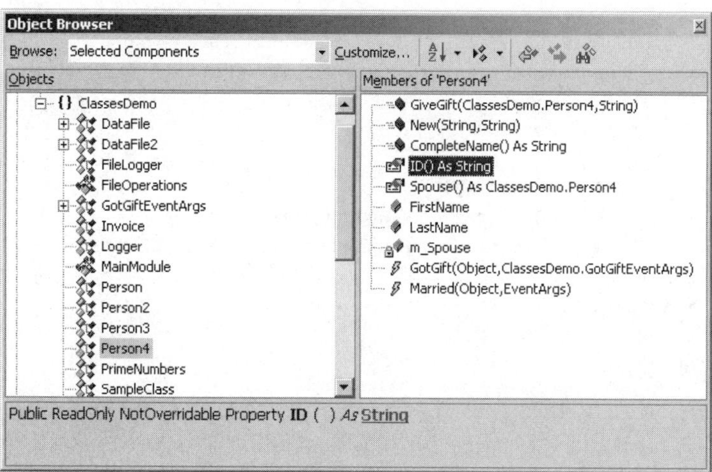

Figure 4-1. The Object Browser uses the same icon for fields and methods, but with different colors (cyan for fields and fuchsia for methods). Those icons are combined with other, smaller icons (an envelope, a padlock, and so on) that indicate the member's scope.

Properties with Arguments

You can define properties that take one or more arguments in a straightforward way:

```
' ...(Add to the Person class)...

Dim m_Notes(10) As String

' The Attachment property takes an Integer argument.
Property Notes(ByVal index As Integer) As String
    Get
        Return m_Notes(index)
    End Get
    Set(ByVal Value As String)
        m_Notes(index) = Value
    End Set
End Property
```

As you would expect, you get an IndexOutOfRangeException run-time error if the Index argument is less than 0 or greater than the last valid index of the array. You can provide a more descriptive description by trapping invalid index values and throwing the exception yourself:

```
Property Notes(ByVal index As Integer) As String
    Get
        If index < 0 Or index > UBound(m_Notes) Then
            Throw New IndexOutOfRangeException("Invalid note index.")
        End If
        Return m_Notes(index)
    End Get
    Set(ByVal Value As String)
        If index < 0 Or index > UBound(m_Notes) Then
            Throw New IndexOutOfRangeException("Invalid note index.")
        End If
        m_Notes(index) = Value
    End Set
End Property
```

Properties with arguments are somewhat less important than they are under Visual Basic 6 because Visual Basic .NET lets you expose an array as a Public field directly. Typically, you'll use properties with arguments when you want to arbitrate access to a more complex structure or when your arguments aren't just indexes into an array. For example, you can build a property that returns a person's age expressed in any time units, not just years:

```
' This code assumes that the following statement is used:
'    Imports Microsoft.VisualBasic

ReadOnly Property Age(Optional ByVal unit As DateInterval _
    = DateInterval.Year) As Integer
    Get
        Return CInt(DateDiff(unit, m_BirthDate, Now))
    End Get
End Property
```

Note that you can overload properties, with or without arguments, as you would overload methods.

Default Properties

As I explained in the "Assigning Object Values" section in Chapter 2, Visual Basic .NET supports default properties only if the property takes one or more arguments because assignments aren't ambiguous in this case. Declaring a property with arguments that also works as the default property requires that you use the Default keyword:

```
' Define an Attachment property in an e-mail class.
Default Property Notes(ByVal index As Integer) As String
    Get
        Return m_Notes(index)
    End Get
    Set(ByVal Value As String)
        m_Notes(index) = Value
    End Set
End Property
```

Now you can omit the property's name when using it:

```
Sub TestDefaultProperty()
    ' Set a note for a person.
    Dim aPerson As New Person
    aPerson.FirstName = "Joe"
    ' Prove that Notes is the default property.
    aPerson(0) = "Remind Joe to review the proposal"
    aPerson(2) = "Joe's birthday is on June 5"

    ' Display all the notes.
    Dim i As Integer
    For i = 0 To 9
        Console.WriteLine(aPerson(i))
    Next
End Sub
```

Constructors

Support for constructors is an important addition to the Visual Basic language. Briefly, a *constructor* is a method that runs when a new instance of the class is created. In Visual Basic .NET, the constructor method is always named Sub New:

```
Class Person
    Dim CreateTime As Date

    Sub New()
        ' Display a diagnostic message.
        Console.WriteLine("A new instance of Person is being created.")
        ' Remember when this instance was created.
        CreateTime = Now()
        ' Perform other initialization chores.
        ⋮
    End Sub
End Class
```

The New name is appropriate because the client code uses the New keyword to create an instance of the class:

```
Dim aPerson As Person
aPerson = New Person
```

When the constructor runs, all the fields with initializers have been already initialized, so if you access such fields from within the constructor you will find the value assigned to them by the initializer:

```
Class Person
    Public Citizenship As String = "American"

    Sub New
        ' Prove that the field has already been initialized.
        Console.WriteLine(Citizenship)        ' => American
    End Sub
End Class
```

Constructors with Arguments

As an experienced Visual Basic developer, you might associate the constructor concept with the Class_Initialize event, and you would be right—to an extent, at least. The point to grasp is that the constructor method can take arguments and therefore you can define which values the calling code *must* pass in order to correctly create an object. For example, you can force the calling code to pass the first and last name when the caller creates a Person2 object:

```
Class Person2
    Public FirstName As String
    Public LastName As String
```

```
    Sub New(ByVal firstName As String, ByVal lastName As String)
        ' Note that you can resolve the argument vs. field
        ' ambiguity using the Me keyword.
        Me.FirstName = firstName
        Me.LastName = lastName
    End Sub
End Class
```

This new version of the Person2 class must be instantiated in this way:

```
Dim aPerson As Person2
aPerson = New Person2("Joe", "Doe")
```

You can also use a shortened syntax:

```
Dim aPerson As New Person2("Joe", "Doe")
```

The ability to define parameters for the New method takes Visual Basic .NET constructors far ahead of the old Class_Initialize event—which isn't supported any longer—and can make your classes more robust because you can be altogether sure that objects are created in a valid state. To achieve this goal, however, you have to ensure that only valid arguments are passed to the constructor:

```
'...(A new version of the Person2 constructor)...
Sub New(ByVal firstName As String, ByVal lastName As String)
    If firstName = "" Or lastName = "" Then
        Throw New ArgumentException()
    End If
    Me.FirstName = firstName
    Me.LastName = lastName
End Sub
```

For a cleaner and more robust design, you should morph all your fields into properties and validate their values in Set...End Set blocks. Once you have this code in place, the constructor method can simply assign the received argument to the corresponding property. If an exception is thrown, it will be reported to the caller as if it were thrown from inside the New procedure.

```
'...(A more robust version of Person2)...
Sub New(ByVal firstName As String, ByVal lastName As String)
    ' Delegate validation to Property procedures.
    Me.FirstName = firstName
    Me.LastName = lastName
End Sub

Private m_FirstName As String
Private m_LastName As String
```

(continued)

```
Property FirstName() As String
    Get
        Return m_FirstName
    End Get
    Set(ByVal Value As String)
        If Value = "" Then
            Throw New ArgumentException("Invalid FirstName property")
        End If
        m_FirstName = Value
    End Set
End Property

Property LastName() As String
    Get
        Return m_LastName
    End Get
    Set(ByVal Value As String)
        If Value = "" Then
            Throw New ArgumentException("Invalid LastName property")
        End If
        m_LastName = Value
    End Set
End Property
```

This coding pattern ensures the best results in terms of robustness and code maintenance because all the validation code is inside the Property Set block: this is the only portion of the class that has to be updated when new validation requirements arise.

Well-designed constructors can improve the usability of your class. For example, you can define optional arguments that let the client code initialize other properties that aren't mandatory:

```
'...(A new version of the constructor that takes an optional argument)...
Sub New(ByVal firstName As String, ByVal lastName As String, _
    Optional ByVal birthDate As Date = #1/1/1800#)
    ' Delegate validation to Property procedures.
    Me.FirstName = firstName
    Me.LastName = lastName
    ' Delegate to the actual Property procedure only if an
    ' argument has been passed.
    If birthDate <> #1/1/1800# Then
        Me.BirthDate = birthDate
    End If
End Sub
```

Overloaded Constructors

Like all methods, the Sub New method can be overloaded. In practice, this means that you can provide users with many ways to instantiate objects, which improves the usability of your class. For example, you might have a Product class that can be instantiated by passing the product name or the product numeric code:

```
Class Product
    Dim m_Id As Integer
    Dim m_Name As String

    Sub New(ByVal id As Integer)
        m_Id = id
    End Sub

    Sub New(ByVal name As String)
        m_Name = name
    End Sub
End Class
```

Note that you can't use the Overloads keyword with constructors. In another example, see how you can improve the Person2 class with the capability of being initialized with a complete name rather than with separate first and last names:

```
' A read-only field that can be assigned only from inside the constructor
Public ReadOnly CreateTime As Date

' First version takes first and last name.
Sub New(ByVal firstName As String, ByVal lastName As String)
    Me.FirstName = firstName
    Me.LastName = lastName
    ' Remember when this instance was created.
    CreateTime = Now()
End Sub

' Second version takes complete name (for example, "Joe Doe").
Sub New(ByVal completeName As String)
    Dim i As Integer
    i = Instr(completeName, " ")
    ' Throw an exception if there are fewer than two words.
    If i = 0 Then Throw New ArgumentException("Invalid Name")
    ' Initialize main properties.
    Me.FirstName = RTrim(Left(completeName, i - 1))
    Me.LastName = LTrim(Mid(completeName, i + 1))
    ' Remember when this instance was created.
    CreateTime = Now()
End Sub
```

The preceding code might be simplified remarkably if you could call the first constructor from inside the second one. However, this action seems to be illegal in Visual Basic, and in fact, the following code snippet doesn't compile:

```
' *** Simplified second version - but doesn't work!
Sub New(ByVal completeName As String)
    Dim i As Integer
    i = Instr(completeName, " ")
    ' Throw an exception if there are fewer than two words.
    If i = 0 Then Throw New ArgumentException("Invalid Name")
    ' Manually invoke the first constructor.
    ' *** Expected type error
    Call New(RTrim(Left(completeName, i - 1)), _
        LTrim(Mid(completeName, i + 1)))
End Sub
```

It seems that the Visual Basic parser incorrectly interprets the call to New as an attempt to create an instance of the class itself, but this isn't the case because an instance has been already created at this point. Dropping the Call keyword prompts a different error message ("Syntax error") but doesn't help either. Prefixing the New keyword with the Me keyword still doesn't work, but that action at least raises a different error: "A direct call to a constructor is allowed only as the first statement in a constructor." Armed with this new knowledge, you can define two auxiliary functions that do the trick:

```
' (This version works.)
Sub New(ByVal completeName As String)
    Me.New(GetFirstName(completeName), GetLastName(completeName))
End Sub

' Auxiliary functions
Private Function GetFirstName(ByVal name As String) As String
    GetFirstName = RTrim(Left(name), InStr(name, " ") - 1)
End Function
Private Function GetLastName(ByVal name As String) As String
    GetLastName = LTrim(Mid(name), InStr(name, " ") + 1)
End Function
```

In this particular case, a more concise (but slightly less efficient) solution is to arrange for the first constructor to call the second one:

```
' First version takes first and last name.
Sub New(ByVal firstName As String, ByVal lastName As String)
    Me.New(firstName & " " & lastName")
End Sub
```

```
' Second version takes complete name (for example, "Joe Doe").
Sub New(ByVal completeName As String)
    Dim i As Integer
    i = Instr(completeName, " ")
    ' Throw an exception if there are fewer than two words.
    If i = 0 Then Throw New ArgumentException("Invalid Name")
    ' Initialize main properties.
    Me.FirstName = RTrim(Left(completeName, i - 1))
    Me.LastName = LTrim(Mid(completeName, i + 1))
    ' Remember when this instance was created.
    CreateTime = Now()
End Sub
```

The advantage of this approach is that all the initialization code is held in a single procedure—for example, the initialization of the *CreateTime* variable—so you don't have to worry about subtle bugs caused by multiple constructors performing slightly different initialization chores.

Constructors and Read-Only Fields

A constructor procedure is the only place from inside a class where you can assign a value to read-only fields (not counting assignments made through initializers). For example, the CreateTime field is logically a read-only field and should be declared as such:

```
' This read-only field can be assigned
' only from inside a constructor method.
Private ReadOnly CreateTime As Date

' This is also equivalent except that the field is Public.
Public ReadOnly CreateTime As Date
```

You can also omit the Private or Public scope qualifier and use just the ReadOnly keyword. In this situation, the Dim keyword is implicit and the field is private:

```
' A private read-only field
ReadOnly CreateTime As Date
```

Most of the time, read-only fields have a public scope: you declare a read-only private field only to protect unwanted modifications from code inside the class itself, an infrequent requirement. Private read-only fields can be a good choice with larger classes, especially when different programmers develop distinct portions of the class, but in many cases they are overkill.

Object Lifetime

Visual Basic .NET classes don't have a destructor method. In other words, no method or event in the class fires when the instance is destroyed. This major difference from Visual Basic 6 classes stems from the different approach that the .NET Framework uses to reclaim allocated memory. This is arguably one of the most controversial features of the framework and was discussed for months in forums and newsgroups while the .NET Framework was in beta version.

COM and the Reference Counter

Before exploring the .NET way to deal with object destruction, let's see how Visual Basic 6 objects (and COM objects in general) behave in this respect. All COM objects maintain a memory location known as the *reference counter*. An object's reference counter is set to 1 when the object is created and its reference is assigned to a variable; the object's reference counter is incremented by 1 when a reference to the object is assigned to another variable. Finally, the object's reference counter is decremented when a variable that points to the object is set to Nothing. This mechanism is hidden from Visual Basic developers and is implemented behind the scenes through the AddRef and Release methods of the IUnknown interface, an interface that all COM objects must expose.

At any given moment, a COM object's reference counter contains the number of variables that are pointing to that specific object. When the Release method is called, the object checks whether the reference counter is going to be decreased from 1 to 0, in which case the object knows it isn't required any longer and can destroy itself. (If the object is written in Visual Basic 6, a Class_Terminate event fires at this point.) In a sense, a COM object is responsible for its own life, and an erroneous implementation of the AddNew or Release method, or an unbalanced number of calls to these methods, can be responsible for memory and resource leakage, a serious potential shortcoming in COM applications. Besides, managing the reference counter itself and frequently calling the AddRef and Release methods can be a time-consuming process, which has a negative impact on the application's performance.

Even more important, it frequently happens that two objects keep themselves alive, such as when you have two Person objects that point to each other through their Spouse property. Unless you take some special steps to account for this situation, these objects will be released only when the application terminates, even if the application cleared all the variables pointing to them. This is the notorious *circular reference problem* and is the most frequent cause of memory leakage, even in relatively simple COM applications.

When Microsoft designed the .NET Framework, the designers decided to get rid of reference counting overhead and all the problems associated with it:

.NET objects have no reference counter, and there is no counterpart for the AddRef and Release methods. Creating an object requires that a block of memory be allocated from the *managed heap*, an area in memory that holds all objects. (I introduced the heap in the "Value Types and Reference Types" section of Chapter 2.) Assigning an object reference requires storing a 32-bit address in a variable (under 32-bit Windows platforms, at least), and clearing an object variable requires storing 0 in it. These operations are extremely fast because they involve no method calls. However, this approach raises an issue that doesn't exist under COM: how can the .NET Framework determine when an object isn't used by the application and can be safely destroyed to make available the memory that that object uses in the heap?

Garbage Collection

The .NET Framework memory management relies on a sophisticated process known as *garbage collection*, or GC. When an application tries to allocate memory for a new object and the heap has no sufficient free memory, the .NET Framework starts the garbage collection process. The garbage collector visits all the objects in the heap and marks those objects that are pointed to by any variable in the application. (These variables are known as *roots* because they're at the top of an object graph.) This process is quite sophisticated in that it also recognizes objects referenced indirectly from other objects, such as when you have a Person object that references another Person object through its Spouse property. After marking all the objects that can be reached from the application's code, the garbage collector can safely release the remaining (unmarked) objects because they're guaranteed to be unreachable by the application. Next the garbage collector compacts the heap and makes the resulting block of free memory available to new objects. Interestingly, this mechanism indirectly resolves the circular reference problem because the garbage collector doesn't mark unreachable objects and therefore correctly releases memory associated with objects pointed to by other objects but not used by the main program.

In most real-world applications, the .NET way to deal with object lifetime is remarkably faster than the COM way—and this is an all-important advantage because everything is an object in the .NET architecture. On the other hand, the garbage collection mechanism introduces a new problem that COM developers don't have: *nondeterministic finalization*. A COM object always knows when its reference counter goes from 1 to 0, so it knows when the main application doesn't need the object any longer. When that time arrives, the Class_Terminate event fires and the code inside the event handler can execute the necessary cleanup chores, such as closing any open file and releasing Win32 resources (brushes, device contexts, and kernel objects). Conversely, a .NET object is actually released *some time* after the last variable pointing to it was set to Nothing.

If the application doesn't create many objects, a .NET object is collected only when the program terminates. Because of the way .NET garbage collection works, there's no way to provide a .NET class with a Class_Terminate event, regardless of the language used to implement the class.

If memory is the only resource an object uses, deferred destruction is seldom a problem: after all, if the application requires more memory, a garbage collection eventually fires and a block of new memory is made available. However, if the object allocates other types of resources—files, database connections, serial or parallel ports, internal Windows objects—you want to make such releases as soon as possible so that other applications can use these resources. In some cases, the problem isn't just a shortage of resources: for example, if the object opens a window to display the value of its properties, you surely want that window to be closed as soon as the object is destroyed so that a user doesn't have to look at outdated information. So the problem is, how can you run some code when your .NET object is *logically* destroyed?

This question has no definitive and complete answer. A partial solution comes in the form of two special methods: Finalize and Dispose.

The Finalize Method

The Finalize method is a special method that the garbage collector calls before releasing the memory allocated to the object. It works more or less the same way the Class_Terminate event under Visual Basic 6 works except that it can be called several seconds (or even minutes or hours) after the application has *logically* killed the object by setting the last variable pointing to the object to Nothing (or by letting the variable go out of scope, which has the same effect). Because all .NET objects inherit the Finalize method from the System.Object class, this method must be declared using the Overrides and Protected keywords (for reasons I'll explain in Chapter 5):

```
' ...(Add this to the Person2 class.)...
Protected Overrides Sub Finalize()
    Debug.WriteLine("Person " & Me.FirstName() _
        " " & Me.LastName & " is being destroyed.")
End Sub
```

The following application shows that the Finalize method isn't called immediately when all variables pointing to the object are set to Nothing:

```
Module MainModule
    ' This is the main entry point for the application.
    Sub Main()
        TestFinalize()
        Debug.WriteLine("About to terminate the application.")
    End Sub
```

```
    Sub TestFinalize()
        Debug.WriteLine("About to create a Person object.")
        Dim aPerson As New Person2("Joe", "Doe")
        Debug.WriteLine("Exiting the TestFinalize procedure.")
    End Sub
End Module
```

These are the messages that you'll see in the Debug window:

```
About to create a Person object.
Exiting the TestFinalize procedure.
About to terminate the application.
Person Joe Doe is being destroyed.
```

The sequence of messages makes it apparent that the Person2 object isn't destroyed when the TestFinalize procedure exits—as would happen in Visual Basic 6—but only some time later, when the application itself terminates.

Caution The code in the Finalize method uses the Debug.WriteLine method to display a diagnostic message instead of the Console.WriteLine method used elsewhere in this chapter. I recommend this other method because when the last garbage collection invokes the Finalize method, the Console object has already been destroyed. If you used the Console.WriteLine method, you'd get an exception. This detail highlights one important .NET programming guideline: *never access any external object from a Finalize procedure* because that object might have been destroyed already.

This rule is valid even if your object is being finalized before the application ends. In this case, in fact, the object is being collected because it can't be reached from the main application, so a reference to another object isn't going to keep that object alive. The garbage collector can reclaim unreachable objects in any order, so the other object might be finalized before the current one.

The Debug object is one of the few objects that are guaranteed to be active while your code is still running. Another object that can be safely accessed from a Finalize method is the base object of the current object. (

See the section "The MyBase Keyword" in Chapter 5.)

You can force a garbage collection during the lifetime of an application by creating a sufficiently large number of objects. For example, try this code:

```
Sub Main()
    TestFinalize2
End Sub
```

(continued)

```
Sub TestFinalize2()
    Dim i As Integer
    ' NOTE: If no Finalize method is invoked on your system,
    ' increment the loop upper limit.
    For i = 1 To 10000
        TestFinalize_Create()
    Next
    Debug.WriteLine("About to terminate the application.")
End Sub

Sub TestFinalize_Create()
    Dim aPerson As New Person2("Joe", "Doe")
End Sub
```

Here's a much simpler way to force a garbage collection: you just ask the garbage collector to do it. The garbage collector is just one .NET object defined in the Framework, and it conveniently exposes a Collect method, which fires a garbage collection. You can see how this works by calling this procedure:

```
Sub TestFinalize3()
    Debug.WriteLine("About to create a Person object.")
    Dim aPerson As New Person2("Joe", "Doe")
    aPerson = Nothing
    Debug.WriteLine("About to fire a garbage collection.")
    GC.Collect()
    GC.WaitForPendingFinalizers()
End Sub
```

The WaitForPendingFinalizers method stops the current thread until all objects are correctly finalized; this action is necessary because the garbage collection process might run on a different thread. The sequence of messages in the Debug window is now different:

```
About to create a Person object.
About to fire a garbage collection.
Person object named Joe Doe is being destroyed.
About to create a Person object.
:
```

However, calling the GC.Collect method manually is usually a bad idea. The preceding code example, which uses the GC.Collect method only to fire the object's Finalize method, illustrates what you should *never* do in a real .NET application. If you run a garbage collection frequently, you're missing one of the most promising performance optimizations that the new .NET Framework offers. You should invoke the GC.Collect method only when the application is idle—for example, while it waits for user input—and only if you see that unexpected (that is, not explicitly requested) garbage collections are slowing the program noticeably during time-critical operations. For example, unrequested

GCs might be an issue when your application is in charge of controlling hardware devices that require a short response time.

Here's another reason for staying clear of the Finalize method: objects that expose such a method aren't immediately reclaimed and usually require at least another garbage collection before they are swept out of the heap. The reason for this behavior is that the code in the Finalize method might assign the current object (using the Me keyword) to a global variable, a technique known as *resurrection*, which I talk about later in this chapter. If the object would be garbage collected at this point, the reference in the global variable would become invalid; the runtime can't detect this special case until the subsequent garbage collection and must wait until then to definitively release the object's memory.

The Dispose Method

Because .NET objects don't have real destructors, well-designed classes should expose a method to let well-behaved clients manually release any resource such as files, database connections, and system objects as soon as they don't need the object any longer—that is, just before setting the reference to Nothing—rather than waiting for the subsequent garbage collection.

Classes that want to provide this feature should implement IDisposable, an interface defined in the .NET Framework. This interface exposes only the Dispose method:

```
Class Widget
    Implements IDisposable

    Sub Dispose() Implements IDisposable.Dispose
        ' Close files and release other resources here.
        ⋮
    End Sub
End Class
```

(The Implements keyword is described in Chapter 6.) Even if the Dispose method belongs to the IDisposable interface, it's marked as Public and therefore appears in the class interface as well. Thus, you don't need to cast the object to an IDisposable variable to call this special method (as you'd do in Visual Basic 6):

```
' Using an object that exposes a Dispose method
Sub TestDispose()
    ' Create the object.
    Dim obj As New Widget()
    ' Use the object.
    ⋮
    ' Clean up code.
    obj.Dispose
End Sub
```

.NET programming guidelines dictate that the Dispose method of an object should invoke the Dispose method of all the inner objects that the current object owns and that are hidden from the client code. For example, if the Widget object has created a System.Timers.Timer object, the Widget class's Dispose method should call the timer's Dispose method. This suggestion and the fact that an object can be shared by multiple clients might cause a Dispose method to be called multiple times, and in fact a Dispose method shouldn't raise any errors when called more than once, even though all calls after the first one should be ignored. You can easily avoid releasing resources multiple times by using a Static local variable:

```
Sub Dispose() Implements IDisposable.Dispose
    Static disposed As Boolean
    If Not disposed Then
        ' Close files and release other resources here.
        ⋮
        ' Ensure that further calls are ignored.
        disposed = True
    End If
End Sub
```

The IDisposable interface gives you the ability to test whether an object exposes the Dispose method and to write generic cleanup routines, such as the following:

```
' Set an object to Nothing and clear its Dispose method if possible.
Sub ClearObject(ByRef obj As Object)
    If TypeOf obj Is IDisposable Then
        ' You need an explicit cast if Option Explicit is On.
        DirectCast(obj, IDisposable).Dispose
    End If
    ' This works because the object is passed by reference.
    obj = Nothing
End Sub
```

If you use an object that implements IDisposable, you should bracket critical statements in a Try...End Try block so that you're sure that the Dispose method is called in the Finally clause:

```
Dim obj As New Widget
Try
    ' Use the object.
    ⋮
Catch ex As Exception
    ⋮
Finally
    ' Ensure that the Dispose method is always invoked.
    obj.Dispose
End Try
```

Interestingly, C# offers a *using* statement that simplifies this kind of code and that automatically invokes the Dispose method of any object exposing the IDisposable interface. No similar statement is present in the current version of Visual Basic .NET.

Combining the Dispose and Finalize Methods

Once again, note that the Dispose method doesn't recover allocated memory because only the system's garbage collectors can do that. You need to implement the IDisposable interface only if your object allocates resources other than memory: in other words, only if your object allocates *unmanaged* resources. Here's an example of a DataFile object that can open a file and close it in the Dispose method:

```
Class DataFile
    Implements IDisposable

    ' The file handle
    Private handle As Integer

    ' Open a file, and store its handle.
    Sub Open(ByVal inputFile As String)
        handle = FreeFile
        FileOpen(handle, inputFile, OpenMode.Input)
    End Sub

    ' Close the file, and don't throw an exception if already closed.
    Sub Close()
        If handle <> 0 Then
            FileClose(handle)
            handle = 0
        End If
    End Sub

    ' This private variable is True if the object has been disposed.
    Dim disposed As Boolean

    Sub Dispose() Implements IDisposable.Dispose
        Debug.WriteLine("Dispose method")
        ' Exit if we've already cleaned up this object.
        If disposed Then Exit Sub

        ' Close the file.
        Close()
        ' Perform other cleanup chores.
        ⋮
        ' Remember that we've executed this code.
        disposed = True
    End Sub
```

```
    Protected Overrides Sub Finalize()
        Debug.WriteLine("Finalize method")
        ' Let Dispose run the cleanup code, only if not done already.
        Dispose()
    End Sub
End Class
```

As the preceding code shows, it's a good practice to call the Dispose method from inside the Finalize method because the cleanup code is usually the same. You can use a class-level variable (disposed, in the preceding code) to ensure that cleanup code doesn't run twice, once when the client invokes Dispose and once when the garbage collector calls the Finalize method; the same variable also ensures that nothing happens if clients call the Dispose method multiple times.

A Better Dispose-Finalize Pattern

A problem with the technique just illustrated is that the garbage collector calls the Finalize method even if the client has already called the Dispose method. As I explained previously, the Finalize method affects performance negatively because an additional garbage collection is required to completely destroy the object. Fortunately, you can control whether the Finalize method is invoked via the GC.SuppressFinalize method. Using this method is straightforward: you typically call it from inside the Dispose method so that the garbage collector knows that it shouldn't call the Finalize method during the subsequent garbage collection.

Another problem that you have to solve is that the code in the Finalize method shouldn't be allowed to access other objects pointed to by the current object because the other objects might have already been finalized, in which case the results would be unpredictable. You can solve this issue by moving the actual cleanup code to an overloaded version of the Dispose method: this method takes a Boolean argument that specifies whether the object is being disposed or finalized and avoids accessing external objects in the latter case.

A third problem that the preceding code example doesn't address is that public methods other than Dispose should throw an exception if they are called after the object has been disposed because this would be a symptom of a programming mistake. The common language runtime defines the special ObjectDisposedException object for this type of error. Here's a new version of the DataFile class that solves these issues:

```
Class DataFile2
    Implements IDisposable
```

```
' The file handle
Private handle As Integer

' Open a file, and store its handle.
Sub Open(ByVal inputFile As String)
    ' Throw an exception if the object has already been disposed.
    If disposed Then Throw New ObjectDisposedException("DataFile2")
    ' Continue with regular operations.
    handle = FreeFile
    FileOpen(handle, inputFile, OpenMode.Input)
End Sub

' Close the file; don't throw an exception if already closed.
Sub Close()
    ' Throw an exception if the object has already been disposed.
    If disposed Then Throw New ObjectDisposedException("DataFile2")
    ' Continue with regular operations.
    If handle <> 0 Then
        FileClose(handle)
        handle = 0
    End If
End Sub

' This private variable is True if the object has been disposed.
Dim disposed As Boolean

Sub Dispose() Implements IDisposable.Dispose
    Debug.WriteLine("Dispose method")
    ' Execute the code that does the cleanup.
    Dispose(True)
    ' Let the common language runtime
    ' know that Finalize doesn't have to be called.
    GC.SuppressFinalize(Me)
End Sub

Protected Overrides Sub Finalize()
    Debug.WriteLine("Finalize method")
    ' Execute the code that does the cleanup.
    Dispose(False)
End Sub

' This procedure is where the actual cleanup occurs.
Protected Sub Dispose(ByVal disposing As Boolean)
    ' Exit now if the object has already been disposed.
    If disposed Then Exit Sub
```

(continued)

```
        If disposing Then
            ' The object is being disposed, not finalized.
            ' It is safe to access other objects (other than the base
            ' object) only from inside this block.
            ⋮
        End If

        ' Perform cleanup chores that have to be executed in either case.
        Close()
        ⋮

        ' Remember that the object has been disposed.
        disposed = True
    End Sub
End Class
```

Finalization issues can become even more problematic if you consider that the Finalize method runs even if the object threw an exception in its constructor method. This means that the code in the Finalize method might access members that haven't been initialized correctly; thus, your finalization code should always avoid accessing class members if there is any chance that an error occurred in the constructor. Even better, the constructor method might use a Try...Catch block to trap errors, release any allocated resource, and then call GC.SuppressFinalize(Me) to prevent the standard finalization code from running on uninitialized members.

Object Resurrection

Earlier in this chapter, I briefly described the technique known as *object resurrection*, through which an object being finalized can store a reference to itself in a variable defined outside the class so that this new reference keeps the object alive. A minor problem with this technique is that by default, the garbage collector calls the Finalize method exactly once. The object being resurrected will eventually be set to Nothing or go out of scope again, but its Finalize method isn't going to be invoked again unless you call the GC.ReRegisterForFinalize method to ask the garbage collector to do so.

Object resurrection is an advanced technique that's likely to be useful only in unusual scenarios, such as when you're implementing a pool of objects whose creation and destruction is time-consuming. The companion CD includes an application named ObjectPool, an example that demonstrates how resurrection can be used to implement an object pool. (See Figure 4-2.) In these pages, I'll merely sketch how the application works.

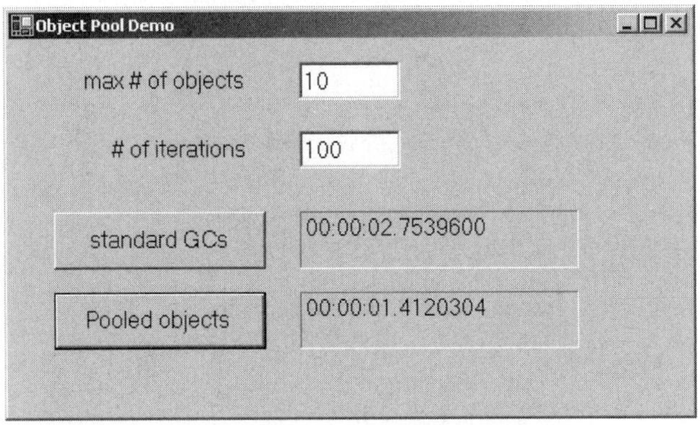

Figure 4-2. The ObjectPool demo application.

The ObjectPool demo application shows that an object pool manager can improve performance when many objects are frequently created and destroyed. Assume that you have a RandomArray class, which encapsulates an array of random numbers. The main program creates and destroys thousands of RandomArray objects, even though only a few objects are alive in a given moment. Because the class creates the random array in its constructor method (a time-consuming operation), this situation is ideal for a pooling technique:

```
Class RandomArray
    Public ReadOnly ArrRand(100000) As Double

    ' The constructor creates the random array.
    Sub New()
        Dim i As Integer
        Dim rand As New Random()

        ' A time-consuming operation
        For i = 0 To UBound(ArrRand)
            ArrRand(i) = rand.NextDouble
        Next
    End Sub

    ' The PoolManager that owns this instance
    Public OwnerPoolManager As PoolManager

    ⋮
End Class
```

The program also contains a class named PoolManager, whose purpose is to provide the main program with a function that returns an initialized RandomArray object. This method takes a RandomArray object from an internal stack if possible; otherwise, it creates it using a New operator in the usual way.

```
Class PoolManager
    Implements IDisposable

    ' This stack contains all the objects in the pool.
    Public PooledObjects As New System.Collections.Stack()

    ' Return a new instance of the RandomArray class.
    Function NewRandomArray() As RandomArray
        If PooledObjects.Count > 1 Then
            ' If there is an object in the pool, use it.
            Return PooledObjects.Pop
        Else
            ' Otherwise, create a new object.
            NewRandomArray = New RandomArray()
            ' Let it know that it's owned by this PoolManager object.
            NewRandomArray.OwnerPoolManager = Me
        End If
    End Function

    ⋮
End Class
```

(I describe the System.Collections.Stack object in the section "The Stack Class" in Chapter 9.) The main program creates a new instance of the RandomArray class using this syntax:

```
Dim PoolMan As New PoolManager
Dim ra As RandomArray = PoolMan.NewRandomArray()
```

The crucial point in the pooling technique is that the PoolManager class contains a reference to unused objects in the pool (in the PooledObjects Stack object) but not to objects that are being used by the main program. In fact, the latter objects are kept alive only by references in the main program. When the main program sets a RandomArray object to Nothing (or lets it go out of scope) and a garbage collection occurs, the garbage collector invokes the object's Finalize method. The code inside the RandomArray's Finalize method has therefore an occasion to resurrect itself by storing a reference to itself in the PoolManager's PooledObjects structure. So when the NewRandomArray function is called again, the PoolManager object can return a pooled object to the client without going through the time-consuming process of creating a new one:

```
' ... (Inside the RandomArray class) ...

Protected Overrides Sub Finalize()
    If OwnerPoolManager Is Nothing Then
        ' This instance isn't owned by a pool manager.
```

```
        ElseIf OwnerPoolManager.PooledObjects Is Nothing Then
            ' This instance had an owner that was already finalized.
        Else
            ' Put this object back in the PooledObjects structure.
            OwnerPoolManager.PooledObjects.Push(Me)
            ' Reregister current object for the Finalize method.
            GC.ReRegisterForFinalize(Me)
        End If
    End Sub
```

The most important statement in the preceding Finalize method is the GC.ReRegisterForFinalize call. Remember that by default, the garbage collector doesn't call the Finalize method again when an object resurrects itself; therefore, the object will be pooled only once. The call to ReRegisterForFinalize ensures that RandomArray objects go in and out of the pool as many times as necessary. (Just ensure that you don't call ReRegisterForFinalize more than once because that would cause the Finalize method to be called multiple times.)

The only missing part in the pooling schema is the Dispose method in the PoolManager class. The code in this method frees all the objects in the pool and sets the PooledObjects stack structure to Nothing so that the objects currently referenced by the main application can determine that they shouldn't resurrect themselves:

```
' ...(Inside the PoolManager class)...

Sub Dispose() Implements IDisposable.Dispose
    ' Suppress Finalize for all objects still in the pool.
    Dim ra As RandomArray
    For Each ra In PooledObjects
        ra.OwnerPoolManager = Nothing
        GC.SuppressFinalize(ra)
    Next
    ' Let unpooled objects (that is, objects owned by the main program)
    ' know that they shouldn't put themselves back in the pool.
    PooledObjects = Nothing
End Sub
```

The ObjectPool demo application lets you test and benchmark two similar pieces of code that create thousands of RandomArray objects, with or without the support of the PoolManager class. Depending on how many objects you create and on the speed of your CPU, the pooled version runs from 1.5 to 2 times faster than the nonpooled version. Of course, this ratio heavily depends on the nature of the application that uses the PoolManager, so I suggest that you perform similar benchmarks before applying this technique in a real-world Visual Basic .NET program.

Generations

If the garbage collector had to visit all the objects referenced by an application, the GC process might impose a severe overhead. Fortunately, some recurring patterns in object creation make it possible for the garbage collector to use heuristics that often trim the total execution time.

It has been observed that, from a statistical point of view, objects created early in the program's lifetime tend to stay alive longer than objects created later in a program. Here's how you can intuitively justify this theory: objects created early are usually assigned to global variables and will be set to Nothing only when the application ends, whereas objects created inside a class constructor method are usually released when the object is set to Nothing. Finally, objects created inside a procedure are destroyed when the procedure exits (unless they have been assigned to a variable defined outside the procedure, for example, an array or a collection).

The garbage collector has a simple way to determine how "old" an object is. Each object maintains a counter telling how many garbage collections that object has survived. The value of this counter is the object's *generation*. The higher this number is, the smaller the chances are that the object is collected during the next garbage collection.

The current version of the runtime supports only three distinct generation values. The generation value of an object that never underwent a garbage collection is 0; if the object survives a garbage collection, its generation becomes 1; if it survives a second garbage collection, its generation becomes 2. Any subsequent garbage collection leaves the generation counter at 2 (or destroys the object).

The runtime can use this information to optimize the garbage collection process—for example, by moving the generation-2 objects toward the beginning of the heap, where they are likely to stay until the program terminates; they are followed by generation-1 objects and finally by generation-0 objects. This algorithm has proven to speed up the garbage collection process because it dramatically reduces the fragmentation of the managed heap.

You can learn the current generation of any object by passing it to the GC.GetGeneration method. The following code should give you a taste of how this method works:

```
Sub TestGeneration()
    Dim s As String = "dummy string"

    ' This is a generation-0 object.
    Console.WriteLine(GC.GetGeneration(s))    ' => 0
```

```
    ' Make it survive a first garbage collection.
    GC.Collect()
    Console.WriteLine(GC.GetGeneration(s))    ' => 1
    ' Make it survive a second garbage collection.
    GC.Collect()
    Console.WriteLine(GC.GetGeneration(s))    ' => 2
    ' Subsequent garbage collections don't increment the generation counter.
    GC.Collect()
    Console.WriteLine(GC.GetGeneration(s))    ' => 2
End Sub
```

The GC.Collect method is overloaded to take a generation value as an argument, which results in the garbage collection of all the objects whose generation is lower than or equal to that value:

```
' Reclaim memory for unused generation-0 objects.
GC.Collect(0)
```

In general, the preceding statement is faster than running a complete garbage collection. To understand exactly why, let's examine the three steps the garbage collection process consists of:

1. The garbage collector marks root objects and in general all the objects directly or indirectly reachable from the application.
2. The heap is compacted, and all the marked (reachable) objects are moved toward the beginning of the managed heap to create a block of free memory near the end of the heap. Objects are sorted in the heap depending on their generation, with generation-2 objects near the beginning of the heap and generation-0 objects near the end of the heap, just before the free memory block. (To avoid time-consuming memory move operations, objects larger than about 85 KB are allocated in a separate heap that's never compacted.)
3. Root object variables in the main application are updated to point to the new positions of objects in the managed heap.

You speed up the second step (fewer objects must be moved in the heap) as well as the third step (because only a subset of all variables are updated) when you collect only generation-0 objects. Under certain conditions, even the first step is completed in less time, but this optimization technique might seem counterintuitive and requires an additional explanation.

For example, let's say that the garbage collector reaches a generation-1 object while traversing the object graph. Let's call this object A. In general, the collector can't simply ignore the portion of the object graph that has object A as its root because this object might point to one or more generation-0 objects that need to be marked. (For example, this might happen if object A is an array that contains objects created later in the program's lifetime.) However, the runtime can detect whether fields of object A have been modified since the previous garbage collection. If it turns out that object A hasn't been written to in the meantime, it means that it can point only to generation-1 and generation-2 objects, so there is no reason for the collector to analyze that portion of the object graph because it was analyzed during the previous garbage collection and can't point to any generation-0 object. (Of course, a similar reasoning applies when you use the GC.Collect(1) statement to collect only generation-0 and generation-1 objects.)

The common language runtime often attempts to collect only generation-0 objects to improve overall performance; if the garbage collection is successful in freeing enough memory, no further steps are taken. Otherwise, the common language runtime attempts to collect only generation-0 and generation-1 objects and collects all three generations only if strictly necessary. This means that older-generation objects might live undisturbed in the heap a long time after the application logically killed them. The exact details of the type of garbage collection the common language runtime performs each time are vastly undocumented, and above all, they might—and likely will—change over time.

In general, as a developer you shouldn't be interested in these low-level details. However, if for some reason you think that garbage collection is hurting your application's performance, or if you're just curious, you can visualize how often garbage collections fire, how large the managed heap is, and other information about memory usage by running the Performance tool and monitoring a few key performance counters exposed by the .NET CLR Memory object. The most interesting ones are # Gen 0 Collections, # Gen 1 Collections, # Gen 2 Collections, Gen 0 heap size, Gen 1 Heap Size, Gen 2 Heap Size, Large Object Heap Size, and % Time In GC. (See Figure 4-3.)

> **Note** Future versions of the .NET runtime might support a different number of generations. You can determine the number of generations supported by querying the GC.MaxGeneration field.

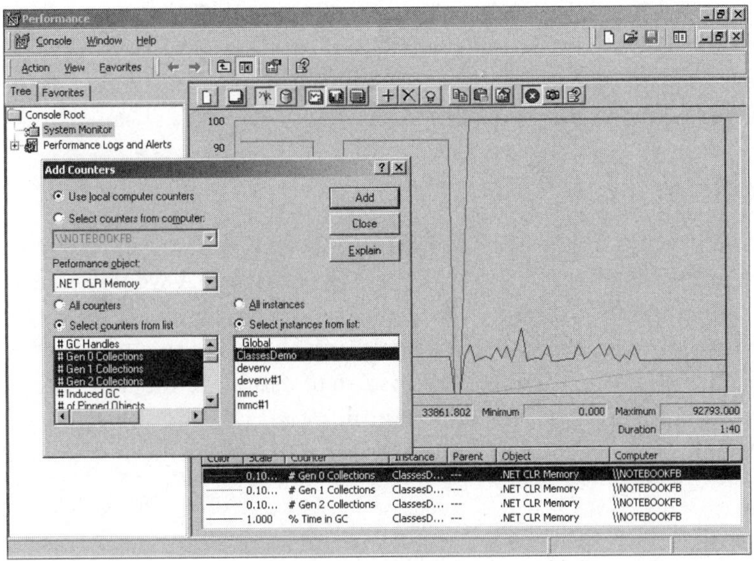

Figure 4-3. You can use the System Monitor in the Performance tool to investigate memory usage and garbage collections.

Garbage Collection and Threading

When the .NET runtime is executing on a workstation, it's important that the user interface work as smoothly as possible, even at the cost of some loss of overall performance. On the other hand, performance becomes the top priority when an enterprise-level .NET application runs on a server machine. To account for these differences, the .NET Framework comes with two types of garbage collectors, implemented in two different DLLs: the workstation version (mscorwks.dll) and the multi-CPU server version (mscorsvr.dll).

When running on a single-CPU machine, the collector always works in workstation mode. In this mode, the collector runs on a concurrent thread to minimize pauses, but the additional thread switching activity can slow down the application as a whole. When the server version runs on a multi-CPU system, objects are allocated from multiple heaps; the program freezes during a garbage collection, and each CPU works concurrently to compact one of the heaps. This technique improves overall performance and scales well when you install additional CPUs. Read the .NET SDK documentation for details about how to enforce either version.

Regardless of which garbage collector you're using, you can decide whether it runs concurrently with your application by using a setting in the application's configuration file. For more information, see the "Garbage Collection Behavior" section in Chapter 14.

Weak Object References

The .NET Framework provides a special type of object reference that doesn't keep an object alive: the so-called *weak reference*. A weakly referenced object can be reclaimed during a garbage collection and must be re-created afterward if you want to use it again. Typical candidates for this technique are objects that take a lot of memory but whose state can be re-created with relatively little effort in a short time. For example, consider the following class, whose main purpose is to expose a Boolean array that tells whether a number is prime or not:

```
Class PrimeNumbers
    ' IsPrime(n) contains True if n is prime, False otherwise.
    Public IsPrime() As Boolean

    ' The constructor evaluates "primeness" for the first N integers.
    Sub New(ByVal maxPrimeNumber As Integer)
        ReDim IsPrime(maxPrimeNumber)
        Dim i, j As Integer

        ' For debugging purposes
        Console.WriteLine("Initializing PrimeNumbers")

        ' A rather inefficient algorithm (hey, it's just a demo).
        ' Start assuming that all numbers are prime.
        For i = 1 To maxPrimeNumber
            IsPrime(i) = True
        Next

        ' Next visit all items, starting at IsPrime(2).
        For i = 2 To maxPrimeNumber
            ' If this number is prime, then all its multiples aren't prime.
            If IsPrime(i) Then
                For j = i * 2 To maxPrimeNumber Step i
                    IsPrime(j) = False
                Next
            End If
        Next
    End Sub
End Class
```

Using this class is easy:

```
' Evaluate prime numbers in the range 1-1000.
Dim pn As New PrimeNumbers(1000)
' Check that 11 is prime.
Console.WriteLine(pn.IsPrime(11))     ' => True
```

The PrimeNumbers class has a defect, however: it takes a good amount of memory for its IsPrime array, and your application might run faster if this block of memory were available to other objects. (You might argue that you can save memory by using a BitArray, a class that I describe in Chapter 9, but let's keep this example as simple as possible.) Because you can re-create the internal state of a PrimeNumber class quite easily, it appears to be a perfect candidate for being weakly referenced. As a result, the object will take memory only until other objects in the application ask for it.

You create a weak reference by passing your object to the constructor of a System.WeakReference object; usually, you complete this first step by setting the original (strong) reference to Nothing:

```
Dim pn As New PrimeNumbers(1000)
Dim pnWR As New WeakReference(pn)
pn = Nothing
```

Should a garbage collection occur now, the PrimeNumbers object will be reclaimed because the weak reference to it doesn't keep it alive. When you later need to get a reference to the PrimeNumbers object, you query the WeakReference object's Target property. If it returns Nothing, the PrimeNumbers object has been collected and you must re-create the PrimeNumbers object from scratch:

```
Sub TestWeakReferences()
    ' Evaluate all prime numbers in the range 1-1000.
    Dim pn As New PrimeNumbers(1000)
    ' Check whether 11 is a prime number.
    Console.WriteLine(pn.IsPrime(11))     '  => True

    ' We aren't going to use the object for a while, so let's make it
    ' weakly referenced and eligible for a garbage collection.
    Dim pnWR As New WeakReference(pn)
    pn = Nothing

    ' Uncomment these two statements to simulate a garbage collection.
    ' GC.Collect()
    ' GC.WaitForPendingFinalizers()

    ' Get a strong reference again.
    pn = DirectCast(pnWR.Target, PrimeNumbers)
    If pn Is Nothing Then
        ' We must re-create the object from scratch.
        pn = New PrimeNumbers(1000)
    End If
```

(continued)

```
    ' Check whether 71 is prime.
    Console.WriteLine(pn.IsPrime(71))     ' => True
End Sub
```

Try running this code as is and then after uncommenting the call to GC.Collect. You'll see that the PrimeNumbers object is re-created because the reference in the WeakReference object didn't prevent it from being reclaimed during the garbage collection.

One last note: if you plan to resurrect your object, you should pass True as the second argument of the WeakReference object's constructor:

```
Dim pn As New PrimeNumbers(1000)
' If you plan to resurrect the PrimeNumbers object, use this
' syntax when creating a weak reference to it.
Dim pnWR As New WeakReference(pn, True)
```

Events

The internal implementations of .NET and COM events are completely different, yet Visual Basic .NET has preserved more or less the same syntax you use in Visual Basic 6, and the changes you have to make are minimal.

Declaring and Raising an Event

The Event keyword declares that a class can raise a given event and defines the list of arguments passed to the event. The syntax for this statement is exactly the same that Visual Basic 6 supports:

```
Class Logger
    Event LogAction(ByVal actionName As String)
    ⋮
End Class
```

You can raise the event using the RaiseEvent command, again as you do under Visual Basic 6:

```
Class Logger
    Event LogAction(ByVal actionName As String)

    Sub OpenFile()
        RaiseEvent LogAction("OpenFile")
    End Sub

    Sub ReadData()
        RaiseEvent LogAction("ReadData")
    End Sub
```

```
    Sub CloseFile()
        RaiseEvent LogAction("CloseFile")
    End Sub
End Class
```

Trapping Events with WithEvents

As in Visual Basic 6, you can trap events using a variable declared with the WithEvents keyword, with two significant improvements. First, the variable can appear inside classes and (unlike previous versions) also inside Modules and Structure blocks; second, you can use the New keyword and the WithEvents keyword in the same statement:

```
Module MainModule
    ' A WithEvents variable declared in a module block with the New keyword
    Dim WithEvents Log As New Logger

    ' This procedure causes some events to be fired.
    Sub TestWithEvents()
        Log.OpenFile()
        Log.ReadData()
        Log.CloseFile()
    End Sub
End Module
```

Trapping events is where Visual Basic .NET differs most from previous versions. In the current version, the name of the event procedure is meaningless, and you tell the compiler which procedure is going to trap the event by using the Handles keyword, as you see in this code:

```
    ' Add inside MainModule.
    Sub LogActionEvent(ByVal actionName As String) Handles Log.LogAction
        Console.WriteLine("LogAction event: " & actionName)
    End Sub
```

Visual Studio .NET can create the syntax for you: just select the object in the leftmost combo box near the upper border of the code editor, and select the specific event in the rightmost combo box—exactly as you do in Visual Basic 6. However, you can then rename the procedure as you prefer because its name doesn't have to abide by the object_eventname name format.

Although the new syntax is slightly more verbose than in previous language versions, it's more versatile because the Handles keyword supports multiple events. For example, you can write one procedure trapping the same event from two different variables, as in the following code:

```
Dim WithEvents Log1 As New Logger
Dim WithEvents Log2 As New Logger
```

(continued)

```
Sub LogActionEvent(ByVal actionName As String) _
    Handles Log1.LogAction, Log2.LogAction
    Console.WriteLine("LogAction event: " & actionName)
End Sub
```

You can also write a procedure that traps events with different names, from the same or distinct variables, provided that the events in question have the same argument signature. It's evident, though, that mapping multiple events to the same procedure makes sense only if you have other means to discern which object is raising the event.

Trapping Events with AddHandler

Visual Basic .NET allows you to decide at run time which routine should serve a given event. The key to this feature is the AddHandler command, which takes two arguments: the event that you want to redirect to a procedure in your application (in the format object.eventname) and the address of the routine that handles the event (in the format AddressOf routinename). To show how this works in practice, let's rewrite the previous code snippet to use AddHandler instead of two WithEvents variables:

```
Dim Log1 As New Logger
Dim Log2 As New Logger

Sub TestAddHandler()
    AddHandler Log1.LogAction, AddressOf LogActionEvent2
    AddHandler Log2.LogAction, AddressOf LogActionEvent2

    ' Cause some events to be fired.
    Log.OpenFile()
    Log.ReadData()
    Log.CloseFile()
End Sub

' Note that no Handles clause is used here.
Sub LogActionEvent2(ByVal actionName As String)
    Console.WriteLine("LogAction event: " & actionName)
End Sub
```

AddHandler is a rather peculiar command: it doesn't follow the usual syntax rules and doesn't require a pair of parentheses around the argument list.

The counterpart of AddHandler is the RemoveHandler command, which you use to stop a routine from handling a specific event from a given object:

```
RemoveHandler Log1.LogAction, AddressOf LogActionEvent2
RemoveHandler Log2.LogAction, AddressOf LogActionEvent2
```

Note that you don't need to manually remove event handlers before setting an object to Nothing because the runtime performs this sort of cleanup code automatically when the object is finalized. (Read on for one exception to this rule.)

You should be aware that using WithEvents or AddHandler could make a difference when the object is referenced by two or more variables. In fact, the WithEvents keyword ties an event handler to a specific *variable*, whereas the AddHandler command ties an event handler to a specific *object*. It seems a minor detail, but it can affect your code significantly. Consider this code, which traps events from a Logger object declared with WithEvents:

```
Dim WithEvents Log As New Logger

Sub TestWithEvents2()
    ' Create another variable that points to the same object.
    Dim logobj As Logger = Log

    ' These statements raise three events, even though we access
    ' the object through the new variable.
    logobj.OpenFile
    logobj.ReadData
    logobj.CloseFile

    ' Clear the WithEvents variable.
    Log = Nothing
    ' These statements don't raise any event because the event handler
    ' is tied to the WithEvents variable, not the object.
    logobj.OpenFile
    logobj.ReadData
    logobj.CloseFile
End Sub

Sub LogActionEvent(ByVal actionName As String) Handles Log.LogAction
    Console.WriteLine("LogAction event: " & actionName)
End Sub
```

The next code sample follows the same pattern except that it creates the event handler using AddHandler instead of WithEvents. As you see, the behavior is different:

```
Dim Log2 As New Logger

Sub TestAddHandler2()
    ' Enable the event handler.
    AddHandler Log2.LogAction, AddressOf LogActionEvent2
    ' Create another variable that points to the same object.
    Dim logobj As Logger = Log2
```

(continued)

```
        ' These statements raise three events, even though we access
        ' the object using the new variable.
        logobj.OpenFile
        logobj.ReadData
        logobj.CloseFile

        ' Clear the WithEvents variable.
        Log2 = Nothing
        ' These statements raise three events as well because handlers created
        ' with AddHandler are tied to the object, not a specific variable.
        logobj.OpenFile
        logobj.ReadData
        logobj.CloseFile
    End Sub

    Sub LogActionEvent2(ByVal actionName As String)
        Console.WriteLine("LogAction event: " & actionName)
    End Sub
```

A corollary of this rule is that you might continue to receive events from an object even after all the variables in your class pointing to it are cleared if the object is kept alive by variables defined elsewhere in the current application and you defined its event handlers using the AddHandler command.

In a few special cases, you might receive extra events from an object even after all its clients have set all their variables to Nothing and the object is about to be garbage collected. For example, this situation occurs when the object raises an event from its Finalize method. Another case occurs when the object uses a timer to poll a system resource (CPU usage or free space on disk) and raises an event when that resource goes below a given threshold: such a timer would continue to run even after the object has been logically destroyed, until the next garbage collection.

To see what happens in practice, let's modify the Logger class to raise an event from inside its Finalize method:

```
Class Logger
    Protected Overrides Sub Finalize()
        RaiseEvent LogAction("Finalize")
    End Sub

    ' ...(The remainder of the class is unchanged)...
    ⋮
End Sub
```

Now consider this client code, which traps events from an object using the WithEvents keyword:

```
Dim WithEvents Log As New Logger
```

```
Sub TestWithEvents3()
    ' This raises an event.
    Log.OpenFile

    ' Clear the WithEvents variable (and logically destroy the object).
    Log = Nothing
    ' Force the Finalize method - we get no event because the
    ' event handler is tied to the variable, not the object.
    GC.Collect
End Sub

Sub LogActionEvent(ByVal actionName As String) Handles Log.LogAction
    Console.WriteLine("LogAction event: " & actionName)
End Sub
```

Here's a slightly different version of the same code, which traps events using the AddHandler command. As you see, in this case the main application traps the event even after setting the object variable to Nothing:

```
Dim Log2 As New Logger

Sub TestAddHandler3()
    ' Create the event handler dynamically with AddHandler.
    AddHandler Log2.LogAction, AddressOf LogActionEvent2
    ' This raises an event.
    Log2.OpenFile

    ' Clear the variable (and logically destroy the object).
    Log2 = Nothing
    ' Force the Finalize method - we do get one additional event because
    ' the event handler is tied to the object, not the variable.
    GC.Collect
End Sub

Sub LogActionEvent2(ByVal actionName As String)
    Console.WriteLine("LogAction event: " & actionName)
End Sub
```

The bottom line: if you use AddHandler to dynamically create event handlers and you share the object with another client or your class is able to raise events even after the object has been destroyed, you must use the RemoveHandler command to detach all the event handlers in your code before destroying the object:

```
    ' Destroy the object only after removing all event handlers.
    RemoveHandler Log2.LogAction, AddressOf LogActionEvent2
    Log = Nothing
```

Module Events

The AddHandler command is useful for taking advantage of a new feature of Visual Basic .NET: the capability to raise an event from inside a Module block. Consider the following module, which exposes a couple of procedures that process a file and raise an event when the operation has completed:

```
Module FileOperations
    Event Notify_CopyFile(ByVal source As String, ByVal destination As String)
    Event Notify_DeleteFile(ByVal filename As String)

    Sub CopyFile(ByVal source As String, ByVal destination As String)
        ' Perform the file copy.
        System.IO.File.Copy(source, destination)
        ' Notify that a copy occurred.
        RaiseEvent Notify_CopyFile(source, destination)
    End Sub

    Sub DeleteFile(ByVal filename As String)
        ' Perform the file deletion.
        System.IO.File.Delete(filename)
        ' Notify that a deletion occurred.
        RaiseEvent Notify_DeleteFile(filename)
    End Sub
End Module
```

A client procedure might use the event mechanism to keep a log of all the file operations that have occurred. You can't use the WithEvents keyword to take advantage of these events because you can't assign a module to a variable. However, the AddHandler command fits the bill nicely:

```
Private Sub TestModuleEvents()
    ' Install the event handlers.
    AddHandler FileOperations.Notify_CopyFile, AddressOf NotifyCopy
    AddHandler FileOperations.Notify_DeleteFile, AddressOf NotifyDelete

    ' Create a copy of Autoexec.bat, and then delete it.
    CopyFile("c:\autoexec.bat", "c:\autoexec.$$$")
    DeleteFile("c:\autoexec.$$$")

    ' Remove the event handlers.
    RemoveHandler FileOperations.Notify_CopyFile, AddressOf NotifyCopy
    RemoveHandler FileOperations.Notify_DeleteFile, AddressOf NotifyDelete
End Sub

' These procedures log the file operation to the console window.
Sub NotifyCopy(ByVal source As String, ByVal destination As String)
    Console.WriteLine(source & " copied to " & destination)
End Sub
```

```
Sub NotifyDelete(ByVal filename As String)
    Console.WriteLine(filename & " deleted")
End Sub
```

Trapping Events from Arrays

The AddHandler command lets you overcome one of the most serious limitations of the WithEvents keyword: the inability to trap events from an array or a collection of objects. Solving this problem under Visual Basic 6 isn't easy because it requires a pair of auxiliary classes. (See the "Dynamic Control Creation" section of Chapter 9 in my *Programming Microsoft Visual Basic 6* book on the companion CD for an example of this technique.) The AddHandler command makes the solution straightforward under Visual Basic .NET.

To support event trapping from an array of objects, the event should pass the client code a reference pointing to the object that's raising the event. For example, let's create a Person3 class that exposes a GotEmail event:

```
Class Person3
    Event GotEmail(ByVal p As Person3, ByVal msgText As String)

    Public FirstName As String
    Public LastName As String

    Sub New(ByVal firstName As String, ByVal lastName As String)
        Me.FirstName = firstName
        Me.LastName = lastName
    End Sub

    Function CompleteName() As String
        Return FirstName & " " & LastName
    End Function

    ' Send an e-mail message to this person.
    ' (In this demo, it just raises a GotEmail event.)
    Sub SendEmail(ByVal msgText As String)
        ' Let the client know which object raised the event.
        RaiseEvent GotEmail(Me, msgText)
    End Sub
End Class
```

Here's a client program that declares an array of Person3 objects and traps events from each of its elements:

```
Dim Persons() As Person3 = {New Person3("Joe", "Doe"), _
    New Person3("Robert", "Smith"), _
    New Person3("Ann", "Ross")}
```

```
Sub TestArrayEvents()
    ' Have the GotEmail procedure serve all the objects in Persons.
    Dim p As Person3
    For Each p In Persons
        AddHandler p.GotEmail, AddressOf GotEmailEvent
    Next

    ' Send two e-mail messages, and check that two events are raised.
    Persons(0).SendEmail("Sample e-mail message #1")
    Persons(2).SendEmail("Sample e-mail message #2")
End Sub

Private Sub GotEmailEvent(ByVal p As Person3, ByVal msgText As String)
    Console.WriteLine(p.CompleteName & " got this message: " & msgText)
End Sub
```

After you run this code, the console window contains the following text, which proves that the client is actually trapping events from all the elements in the Persons array:

```
Joe Doe got this message: Sample e-mail message #1
Ann Ross got this message: Sample e-mail message #2
```

Guidelines for Event Syntax

The .NET documentation contains the guidelines for naming fields, methods, properties, and events—among other things. For example, these guidelines dictate that you should *not* use prefixes for variable and parameter names to indicate their type because Visual Studio .NET lets you browse the definition of a variable by simply bringing the mouse cursor to hover over its name. (Personally, I have always hated Hungarian notation, so I warmly welcome this suggestion.) Other naming guidelines state that you should use PascalCasing for fields, properties, and methods and that you should use camelCasing for procedure arguments.

Naming guidelines are exactly that: guidelines, so you can follow them or you can ignore them if you prefer. In most cases, naming is a matter of coding style and personal preference because these rules don't usually have an impact on code functionality. The important point is that you define a set of rules for naming programming entities on which all the members of your team agree so that they have little problem reading one another's code.

Microsoft naming guidelines are simply one more set of rules, which nevertheless are likely to be followed by a relatively large number of developers. Because I find that all the guidelines make sense, I tried to follow those guidelines throughout this book. But again, the coding style you choose usually has an impact only on your code's readability, not on its functionality.

However, Microsoft rules about event parameters can have a far-reaching effect on how versatile your code is. According to these guidelines, events should have only two arguments: an Object argument named sender, which represents the object that's raising the event; and an argument named e, which exposes the event's arguments through its fields or properties. This second argument should be a System.EventArgs object or an object whose class inherits from System.EventArgs. (The name of such a class should end with EventArgs.)

Why is this naming convention so important? Well, you've already seen that Visual Basic .NET lets you have a single procedure handle events from multiple objects, or even arrays or collections of objects. If an event procedure can handle events from multiple objects, the sender argument is the only way for a client to learn which specific object raised the event. So it makes sense to define all your events with the sender argument, whether or not you plan to work with arrays of objects in the near future. This naming convention requires only a little extra code today, but it might simplify your job a great deal tomorrow.

The rule stating that all events should expose a second argument named e isn't as important as the one related to the sender argument because it doesn't have an impact on your code's functionality. However, all the events in the .NET Framework follow this pattern, and adhering to this rule means that other developers will find it easier to use your objects.

Let's create a Person4 class to expose two events that follow Microsoft's guidelines: Married and GotGift. The Married event fires when the Spouse property is assigned a new value. Because the client can check the Spouse property to learn the spouse's name, there's no point in passing additional arguments in the event, and the e argument can be of type System.EventArgs:

```
Class Person4
    Event Married(ByVal sender As Object, ByVal e As System.EventArgs)

    Dim m_Spouse As Person4

    Property Spouse() As Person4
        Get
            Return m_Spouse
        End Get
        Set(ByVal Value As Person4)
            ' Raise an event only if this is a different object.
            If Not (m_Spouse Is Value) Then
                m_Spouse = Value
                ' Create an empty EventArgs object on the fly.
                RaiseEvent Married(Me, New System.EventArgs())
            End If
        End Set
    End Property
```

(continued)

```
    ' ...(Plus all the usual properties, methods, and constructors)...
    ⋮
End Class
```

The GotGift event must pass two pieces of information to the caller: the Person who gave the gift and a string that describes the gift itself. To comply with Microsoft guidelines, you must define a new class named GotGiftEventArgs that inherits from System.EventArgs and that defines two new fields. I will explain inheritance in depth later in Chapter 5, but the following code should be rather self-explanatory.

```
Class GotGiftEventArgs
    Inherits System.EventArgs

    ' The additional fields exposed by this class
    Public Giver As Person4
    Public GiftDescription As String

    ' A convenient constructor
    Sub New(ByVal giver As Person4, ByVal giftDescription As String)
        Me.Giver = giver
        Me.GiftDescription = giftDescription
    End Sub
End Class
```

Now you can extend the Person4 class with the support for the GotGift event:

```
' ...(Add anywhere in the Person4 class)...

Event GotGift(ByVal sender As Object, ByVal e As GotGiftEventArgs)

' Client code calls this method to give a gift to this person.
Sub GiveGift(ByVal giver As Person4, ByVal description As String)
    ' (In this demo, we just raise an event.)
    ' Create a GotGiftEventArgs object on the fly.
    RaiseEvent GotGift(Me, New GotGiftEventArgs(giver, description))
End Sub
```

In the procedure that handles the GotGift event, you extract the Giver and GiftDescription fields of the GotGiftEventArgs object you receive in the second argument:

```
Dim WithEvents joe As New Person4("Joe", "Doe")

Sub TestNewEventSyntax()
    ' Create another Person4 object (Joe's wife).
    Dim ann As New Person4("Ann", "Smith")

    ' Test the Married event.
    joe.Spouse = ann
```

```
    ' Let Ann give Joe a gift, and test the GotGift event.
    joe.GiveGift(ann, "a book")
End Sub

Sub Married(ByVal sender As Object, ByVal e As System.EventArgs) _
    Handles joe.Married
    ' Get a strongly typed reference to the object that raised the event.
    Dim p As Person4 = DirectCast(sender, Person4)
    Console.WriteLine(p.CompleteName() & " married " & _
        p.Spouse.CompleteName())
End Sub

Sub GotGift(ByVal sender As Object, ByVal e As GotGiftEventArgs) _
    Handles joe.GotGift
    ' Get a strongly typed reference to the object that raised the event
    ' (that is, the Person4 object that got the gift).
    Dim p As Person4 = DirectCast(sender, Person4)
    Console.WriteLine(e.Giver.CompleteName() & " gave " & p.CompleteName() _
        & " the following gift: " & e.GiftDescription)
End Sub
```

Shared Members

Visual Basic .NET classes support *shared* fields, properties, and methods, a feature missing in Visual Basic 6. Shared members are also known as *static* or *class members* in other object-oriented languages.

Shared Fields

Shared fields are variables that can be accessed (that is, shared) by all the instances of a given class. You declare a shared field as you would define any regular field except that you prefix the variable name with the Shared keyword:

```
Class DataFile
    ' This variable holds the number of instances created so far.
    Shared InstanceCount As Integer

    Sub New()
        ' Increment the number of created instances.
        InstanceCount += 1
        ⋮
    End Sub
End Class
```

The default scope for shared fields is Private, but you can create shared members that are visible from outside the class by using the Public or Friend keyword:

```
' This shared variable is visible from inside the current assembly.
Friend Shared InstanceCount As Integer
```

Shared members are useful for many occasions. For example, you can use the InstanceCount shared variable to implement a read-only ID property that returns a unique number for each instance of this particular class during the application's lifetime:

```
Class Invoice
    ' This variable holds the number of instances created so far.
    Shared InstanceCount As Integer

    ' A unique ID for this instance
    ReadOnly Public Id As Long

    Sub New()
        ' Increment number of created instances.
        InstanceCount += 1
        ' Use the current count as the ID for this instance.
        Id = InstanceCount
        :
    End Sub
End Class
```

Shared fields are useful also when all the instances of a class compete for a limited amount of resources. For example, say that you have a SerialPort class, whose instances are meant to operate on the serial ports installed on the machine. Whenever you instantiate the SerialPort class, the new object should allocate the first available serial port for itself, and therefore it needs to know which ports aren't taken by other objects. Under Visual Basic 6, you can solve this problem only by using a Public array defined in a BAS module. Visual Basic .NET offers a more elegant and better-encapsulated solution:

```
Class SerialPort
    Implements IDisposable

    ' This array is shared by all instances of the class.
    ' (This example assumes that 4 ports are available.)
    Public Shared AllocatedPorts(3) As Boolean

    ' The serial port used by this instance (in the range 0-3)
    ReadOnly Public Port As Short

    Sub New()
        ' Search the first available port.
        Dim i As Short
        For i = 0 To 3
            If AllocatedPorts(i) = False Then
                ' This port is still available.
                Port = i
                ' Mark the port as unavailable.
```

```
                AllocatedPorts(i) = True
                Exit Sub
            End If
        Next        ' Throw an exception if all ports are used.
        Throw New Exception()
    End Sub

    ' Mark the port as available when this instance is destroyed.
    Sub Dispose() Implements IDisposable.Dispose
        AllocatedPorts(Port) = False
    End Sub
End Class
```

You can even have ReadOnly shared fields, which are logically equivalent to class-level Const statements, with an important difference. Constants are assigned at compile time, whereas a ReadOnly shared field is assigned at run time either by means of an initializer or from inside the shared constructor. (Read on to learn more about shared constructors.)

```
Public Shared ReadOnly StartExecutionTime As Date = Now()
```

Shared Methods

You can use the Shared keyword to mark a method as static, which makes the method callable without your needing to instantiate an object of that class. For example, assume that an application wants to determine which serial port an instance of the SerialPort class is going to use, before actually creating the instance. This information logically belongs to the SerialPort class (as opposed to individual SerialPort instances) and should be exposed through a shared GetAvailablePort function. The code in this method can be reused in the class constructor, so the new version of the class is this code:

```
Class SerialPort
    Implements IDisposable

    ' This array is shared by all instances of the class.
    ' (This examples assumes that 4 ports are available.)
    Public Shared AllocatedPorts(3) As Boolean

    ' Return the number of the first available serial port.
    Shared Function GetAvailablePort() As Short
        Dim i As Short
        For i = 0 To 3
            If AllocatedPorts(i) = False Then
                ' This port is still available.
                GetAvailablePort = i
                Exit For
            End If
```

(continued)

```
        Next
        ' Return -1 if no port is available.
        GetAvailablePort = -1
    End Function

    ' The serial port used by this instance (in the range 0-3)
    Public ReadOnly Port As Short

    Sub New()
        Port = GetAvailablePort
        ' Throw a (generic) exception if no available port.
        If Port < 0 Then Throw New Exception()
        ' Mark the port as unavailable.
        AllocatedPorts(Port) = True
    End Sub

    ' Mark the port as available when this instance is destroyed.
    Sub Dispose() Implements IDisposable.Dispose
        AllocatedPorts(Port) = False
    End Sub
End Class
```

You can access a shared method from outside the class in two ways: through an instance variable (as for all methods) and through the name of the class, as you see here:

```
port = SerialPort.GetAvailablePort
```

When you type the name of a class and press the dot key, IntelliSense correctly omits instance members and displays only the list of all the shared fields, properties, and methods:

```
port = SerialPort.
```

AllocatedPorts
GetAvailablePort

Code inside a shared method must abide by special scoping rules: it can access shared members but can't access instance fields, properties, and methods. This is a reasonable limitation in that the code in the shared method wouldn't know which specific object should provide the instance data. (Because shared methods can be invoked before you create an instance of a given class, there might be no running object at all.)

When you're creating a class that works as a library of functions, you can use shared functions if you don't want to force the user to create an object just to access those functions (as you have to do under Visual Basic 6). For example, consider the following Triangle class, which exposes functions for evaluating the perimeter and the area of a triangle given its three sides:

```
Class Triangle
    Shared Function GetPerimeter(ByVal side1 As Double, _
        ByVal side2 As Double, ByVal side3 As Double) As Double
        Return side1 + side2 + side3
    End Function

    Shared Function GetArea(ByVal side1 As Double, _
        ByVal side2 As Double, ByVal side3 As Double) As Double
        ' First evaluate half of the perimeter.
        Dim halfP As Double = (side1 + side2 + side3) / 2
        ' Then apply the Heron formula.
        Return (halfP * (halfP - side1) * (halfP - side2) * _
            (halfP - side3)) ^ 0.5
    End Function
End Class
```

Using this class is straightforward because you don't need to instantiate a Triangle object:

```
Console.WriteLine(Triangle.GetPerimeter(3, 4, 5))     ' => 12
Console.WriteLine(Triangle.GetArea(3, 4, 5))          ' => 6
```

You don't even need to prefix method names with the class name if you use a proper Imports statement, such as this one:

```
' This statement assumes that Triangle is defined in
' the MyProject namespace.
Imports MyProject.Triangle
' Invoke the GetArea shared method without specifying the class name.
Console.WriteLine(GetArea(3, 4, 5))                    ' => 6
```

Note that this Imports statement works correctly even if the Triangle class is defined in the current project.

The closest approximation of this feature under Visual Basic 6 is GlobalMultiUse classes, with three important differences:

- Visual Basic instantiates a hidden instance of a global multiuse class, and this instance is released only when the application ends.
- You can access methods of a GlobalMultiUse class without having to go through an object variable only if the class is defined in a compiled DLL; a GlobalMultiUse class is considered a regular class when it's accessed from inside the project where it's defined.
- Only Visual Basic clients can use GlobalMultiUse classes as such: clients written in any other language can use them only as regular COM components, and you can access their methods only after explicitly instancing an object.

If a class contains only shared methods, there's no point in instantiating it. You can make a class noncreatable simply by adding a Private constructor, whose only purpose is to suppress the automatic generation of the Public constructor that the Visual Basic compiler would perform if no constructor were provided:

```
' A class that contains only shared members
Class LibraryFunctions
    :
    Private Sub New()
        ' This private constructor contains no code. Its only purpose
        ' is to prevent clients from instantiating this class.
    End Sub
End Class
```

> **Note** A class can contain a special shared method named Shared Sub Main. This procedure can be used as the entry point of the entire application: simply select the class name in the Startup Object combo box on the General page of the project Property Pages dialog box.

Shared Constructors

If you define a parameterless Shared Sub New method in a class, this procedure is called automatically just before the first instance of that class is instantiated. Typically, you use such a shared constructor to correctly initialize Shared fields. For example, let's say that all the instances of a class should write to a log file. This file must be opened when the very first object of this class is created, and it must be kept open until the application terminates. One solution to this problem is to check whether the log file is opened in the standard constructor:

```
Class FileLogger
    Shared FileHandle As Integer

    Sub New()
        ' Open the log file if not done already.
        If FileHandle = 0 Then
            FileHandle = FreeFile
            FileOpen(FileHandle, "C:\data.log", OpenMode.Output)
        End If
    End Sub
End Class
```

Here's a more structured solution, which is also slightly faster because it doesn't check whether the log file has to be created whenever a new object is instantiated:

```
Class FileLogger
    Shared FileHandle As Integer

    ' The shared constructor
    Shared Sub New()
        ' Open the log file before the first object from
        ' this class is instantiated.
        FileHandle = FreeFile
        FileOpen(FileHandle, "C:\data.log", OpenMode.Output)
    End Sub

    Sub New()
        ' Here goes the initialization code for a specific instance.
        ⋮
    End Sub
End Class
```

The Shared Sub New procedure runs before the Sub New procedure for the first object instantiated for the class. Shared constructors are implicitly Private (unlike other shared procedures, which are Public by default) and can't be declared with the Public or Friend scope qualifier. Shared constructors are the only places where you can assign a Shared ReadOnly field:

```
Public Shared ReadOnly InitialDir As String

Shared Sub New()
    ' Assign the directory that's current when the first
    ' instance of this type is created.
    InitialDir = System.IO.Directory.GetCurrentDirectory()
End Sub
```

Note that there isn't such a thing as a shared destructor method. If you want to perform an operation when the last instance of a class is destroyed—typically to clean up resources shared by all instances of that class—you must forgo the shared constructor and handle a counter yourself, which you increment in the instance constructor and decrement in the Finalize method:

```
Class MyDataType
    ' This shared variable holds the number of running instances.
    Shared InstanceCount As Integer

    Sub New()
        If InstanceCount = 0 Then
            ' Allocate shared resources, open shared files, etc.
            ⋮
        End If
        InstanceCount += 1
        ' Continue with the regular constructor code.
        ⋮
    End Sub
```

(continued)

```
    Protected Overrides Sub Finalize()
        ' Clean up resource used by this specific instance.
        ⋮
        InstanceCount -= 1
        If InstanceCount = 0 Then
            ' Clean up shared resources, close shared files, etc.
            ⋮
        End If
    End Sub
End Class
```

Shared Events

You can define shared events in much the same way that you define shared fields, methods, and properties:

```
Class Triangle
    Shared Event InvalidTriangle(ByVal t As Triangle)
    ⋮
End Class
```

You can raise shared events from both shared methods and instance methods. (Conversely, you can't raise a regular event from a shared method.) For example, consider this version of the Triangle class, where both the shared GetPerimeter function and the instance Perimeter property raise the shared event InvalidTriangle if the three sides can't make a valid triangle:

```
Class Triangle
    Shared Event InvalidTriangle(ByVal side1 As Double, _
        ByVal side2 As Double, ByVal side3 As Double)
    ' You need at least an unshared event to be able to create
    ' a WithEvents variable of type Triangle.
    Event DummyEvent()

    Shared Function GetPerimeter(ByVal side1 As Double, _
        ByVal side2 As Double, ByVal side3 As Double) As Double
        If side1 < side2 + side3 And side1 > Math.Abs(side2 - side3) Then
            Return side1 + side2 + side3
        Else
            RaiseEvent InvalidTriangle(side1, side2, side3)
        End If
    End Function

    ' The three sides
    Public Side1 As Double
    Public Side2 As Double
    Public Side3 As Double
```

```
    ReadOnly Property Perimeter() As Double
        Get
            If Side1 < Side2 + Side3 And Side1 > Math.Abs(Side2 - Side3) Then
                Return Side1 + Side2 + Side3
            Else
                RaiseEvent InvalidTriangle(Side1, Side2, Side3)
            End If
        End Get
    End Property
End Class
```

The great thing about static events is that you can define one WithEvents variable and have it trap events coming from *all* the instances of that class—as well as all shared events. The following code should clarify this concept:

```
' Declare a triangle variable - this variable is used only to
' trap shared events from all the instances of the Triangle class.
Dim WithEvents AnyTriangle As New Triangle

Sub TestSharedEvents()
    Dim p As Double
    ' Create *another* triangle instance with invalid sides.
    With New Triangle()
        .Side1 = 10
        .Side2 = 2
        .Side3 = 3
        ' This action will cause an InvalidTriangle event.
        p = .Perimeter
    End With

    ' Calling the shared method with invalid sides also fires
    ' the InvalidTriangle event.
    p = Triangle.GetPerimeter(12, 3, 5)
End Sub

' The event procedure
Sub InvalidTriangle(ByVal side1 As Double, ByVal side2 As Double, _
        ByVal side3 As Double) Handles AnyTriangle.InvalidTriangle
    Console.Write("These sides don't form a valid triangle: ")
    Console.WriteLine(CStr(side1) & ", " & CStr(side2) & ", " & CStr(side3))
End Sub
```

The InvalidTriangle event is called twice: once when reading the Perimeter standard property and once when invoking the GetPerimeter shared method. But the key point here is that the AnyTriangle variable is trapping events raised from another instance of that class, and this happens because InvalidTriangle is a shared event.

A minor flaw of shared events is that the class must expose at least one instance event in order to declare a WithEvents variable of that type. For example, I had to add an instance event named DummyEvent in the Triangle class for the client code to declare the AnyTriangle variable with the WithEvents class. However, you can overcome this limitation by getting rid of the AnyTriangle variable and defining an event handler with the AddHandler command:

```
Sub TestSharedEvents2()
    ' Create a handler for the InvalidTriangle shared event.
    AddHandler Triangle.InvalidTriangle, AddressOf InvalidTriangle2

    ' ...(Remainder of the class is as TestSharedEvents)...
End Sub

' The event procedure doesn't require the Handles keyword.
Sub InvalidTriangle2(ByVal side1 As Double, ByVal side2 As Double, _
        ByVal side3 As Double)
    Console.Write("These sides don't form a valid triangle: ")
    Console.WriteLine(CStr(side1) & ", " & CStr(side2) & ", " & CStr(side3))
End Sub
```

In this long chapter, you've seen many new object-oriented features in Visual Basic .NET, such as constructors and shared members. They prepare the ground for the next chapter, in which I'll describe what undoubtedly is the most important innovation in the Visual Basic language: inheritance.

5

Inheritance

To the majority of developers, the most important new feature of Visual Basic is implementation inheritance. In a nutshell, inheritance is the ability to derive a new class (the *derived* or *inherited* class) from a simpler class (the *base* class). The derived class inherits all the fields, properties, and methods of the base class and can modify the behavior of any of those properties and methods by *overriding* them. And you can also add new fields, properties, and methods to the inherited class.

Inheritance is especially effective for rendering an *is-a* relationship between two classes. For example, you can create a Bird class from the Animal class because a bird is an animal and therefore inherits the characteristics and behaviors of the generic animal, such as the ability to move, sleep, feed itself, and so on. You can then extend the new Bird class with new properties and methods, such as the Fly and LayEgg methods. Once the Bird class is in place, you can use it as the base class for a new Falcon class, and so on. A more business-oriented example of inheritance is an Employee class that derives from the Person class, an example that we will use often in the following sections.

A few programming languages, such as Microsoft Visual C++, support multiple-class inheritance, by which a class can derive from more than one base class. All .NET languages, however, support at most single-class inheritance.

Inheritance in Previous Visual Basic Versions

Inheritance is an effective way to reuse code in a class. Visual Basic 6 and previous versions offered no native support for inheritance, but you could simulate it, to an extent at least, by writing a good amount of code. It's interesting to revisit this technique because in some cases you'll find it useful in Visual Basic .NET as well.

Inheritance by Delegation

Say you have a Person class that exposes properties such as FirstName, LastName, Address, and BirthDate, and you want to create a new Employee class that exposes these properties and a few additional ones, such as BaseSalary and HourlySalary. Under Visual Basic 6, you have only two choices: you can copy the Person source code into the Employee class—an approach some developers ironically call *cut-and-paste inheritance*—or you can use a coding technique called *inheritance by delegation.* In the latter case, the derived class delegates all the inherited properties and methods to an instance of the base class, which is conveniently instantiated in the Class_Initialize event (or through an auto-instancing variable, as in the following code snippet).

```
' A Visual Basic 6 version of the Employee class
'
' The inner object of the base class
Private Person As New Person

' A FirstName property that delegates to the inner object
Property Get FirstName() As String
    FirstName = Person.FirstName
End Property
Property Let FirstName(ByVal newValue As String)
    Person.FirstName = newValue
End Property
' Add here other delegated properties and methods.
⋮
```

Inheritance and Late-Bound Polymorphic Code

Another benefit of inheritance—including simulated inheritance achieved through delegation——is that you can create polymorphic code that can operate on both the base class and the derived class. In Visual Basic 6, such polymorphic code must use a variable of type Variant or Object, and therefore, you can refer to the actual object's methods and properties only through late binding. Thus, the downside is that you have polymorphism at the expense of performance and robustness:

```
' This procedure works with both Person and Employee objects.
Sub DisplayName(obj As object)
    ' This code uses late binding.
    Print obj.FirstName & " " obj.LastName
End Sub
```

The delegation technique works well and is flexible enough to handle all cases, but it has two severe shortcomings: it requires that you manually write a lot of code, and it requires that you modify the derived class whenever you add or delete a member in the base class. Moreover, all the delegation code tends to slow down your applications, so you can't use it in time-critical cases. (You can learn more about inheritance by delegation in Chapter 7 of my book *Programming Microsoft Visual Basic 6*, provided on the companion CD.)

Early-Bound Polymorphic Code

Visual Basic 6 developers can implement yet another variant of inheritance, the so-called *interface inheritance*, a fancy name for a very common way to use the Implements keyword. In this case, you "inherit" only the methods' signature from the base class, not their implementation. Again, it's up to you to write all the code that performs the actual operation:

```
' A Visual Basic 6 class that inherits Person's interface
Implements Person
' Private members
Private m_FirstName As String
Private m_LastName As String
⋮

Private Property Get Person_FirstName() As String
    Person_FirstName = m_FirstName
End Property
Private Property Let Person_FirstName(ByVal RHS As String)
    m_FirstName = RHS
End Property
' Add here other properties and methods.
⋮
```

This coding technique lets you write more efficient polymorphic code that uses early binding:

```
' You can pass either a Person or an Employee object
' to this procedure.
Sub DisplayName(p As Person)
    ' This code uses early binding.
    Print p.FirstName & " " p.LastName
End Sub
```

Finally, you can mix the two techniques—inheritance by delegation and the interface implementation—and have the methods in the Person interface delegate their action to an inner Person object. This latter approach offers the best in terms of code reuse but requires that you write a large amount of code. (For more details, see Chapter 7 of *Programming Microsoft Visual Basic 6*, on the companion CD.) Or you can switch to Visual Basic .NET.

Inheritance in Visual Basic .NET

To see how inheritance works in Visual Basic .NET, let's start by defining a simple Person base class:

```
Class Person
    ' Fields visible from outside the class
    Public FirstName As String
    Public LastName As String
End Class
```

You don't have to write any delegation code to implement inheritance in Visual Basic .NET because all you need is an Inherits clause immediately after the Class statement:

```
' The Employee class inherits from Person
Class Employee
    Inherits Person
    ⋮
End Class
```

Or you can use the following syntax to convince your C# colleagues that Visual Basic. NET is a first-class language:

```
' A more C++-like syntax
Class Employee: Inherits Person
    ⋮
End Class
```

The great thing about inheritance in Visual Basic .NET is that you can inherit from *any* object, including objects for which you don't have the source code, because all the plumbing code is provided by the .NET Framework. The only exception to this rule occurs when the author of the class you want to derive from has marked the class *sealed*, which means that no other class can inherit from it. (You'll find more information later in this chapter about sealed classes.)

The derived class inherits all the Public and Friend fields, properties, and methods of the base class. Note that inheriting a field could be a problem because a derived class becomes dependent on that field, and the author of the base class can't change the implementation of that field—for example, to make it a calculated value—without breaking the derived class. For this reason, it's usually preferable that classes meant to work as base classes should include only Private fields. You should always use a property instead of a field to make a piece of data visible outside the class because you can always change the internal implementation of a property without any impact on derived classes. (To save space and code, some of the examples in this section use fields instead of properties: in other words, do as I say, not as I do.)

Extending the Derived Class

You can extend the derived class with new fields, properties, and methods simply by adding these new members anywhere in the class block:

```
Class Employee
    Inherits Person

    ' Two new public fields
    Public BaseSalary As Single
    Public HoursWorked As Integer
    ' A new private field
    Private m_HourlySalary As Single

    ' A new property
    Property HourlySalary() As Single
        Get
            Return m_HourlySalary
        End Get
        Set(ByVal Value As Single)
            m_HourlySalary = Value
        End Set
    End Property

    ' A new method
    Function Salary() As Single
        Return BaseSalary + m_HourlySalary * HoursWorked
    End Function
End Class
```

Using the Derived Class

You can use the new class without even knowing that it derives from another class. However, being aware of the inheritance relationship between two classes helps you write more flexible code. For example, inheritance rules state that you can always assign a derived object to a base class variable. In this case, the rule guarantees that you can always assign an Employee object to a Person variable:

```
Sub TestInheritance()
    Dim e As New Employee
    e.FirstName = "Joe"
    e.LastName = "Doe"
    ' This assignment always works.
    Dim p As Person = e
    ' This proves that p points to the Employee object.
    Console.WriteLine(p.CompleteName)    '=> Joe Doe
End Sub
```

The compiler knows that Person is the base class for Employee, and it therefore knows that all the properties and methods that you can invoke through the p variable are exposed by the Employee object as well. As a result, these calls can never fail. This sort of assignment is always successful also when the derived class inherits from the base class indirectly. *Indirect inheritance* means that there are intermediate classes along the inheritance path, such as when you have a PartTimeEmployee class that derives from Employee, which in turn derives from Person.

A consequence of this rule is that you can assign any object reference to an Object variable because all .NET classes derive from System.Object either directly or indirectly:

```
' This assignment *always* works, regardless of
' the type of sourceObj.
Dim o As Object = sourceObj
```

Assignments in the opposite direction don't always succeed, though. Consider this code:

```
' This code assumes that Option Strict is Off.

Dim p As Person
If Math.Rnd < .5 Then
    ' Sometimes P points to an Employee object.
    p = New Employee()
Else
    ' Sometimes P points to a Person object.
    p = New Person()
End If
' This assignment fails with an InvalidCastException
' error if Math.Rnd was >= .5.
Dim e As Employee = p
```

The compiler can't determine whether the reference assigned to the e variable points to an Employee or a Person object, and the assignment fails in the latter case. For this reason, this assignment is rejected if Option Strict is on. (As you remember from Chapter 2, you should set Option Strict On for all the files in the project or from inside the Build page of the project Property Pages dialog box.) An assignment that is accepted by the compiler regardless of the Option Strict setting requires that you perform an explicit cast to the destination type, using the CType or the DirectCast operator:

```
' This statement works also when Option Strict is On.
Dim e As Employee = DirectCast(p, Employee)
```

Inheriting Events

A derived class inherits also the events defined in the base class. Let's make a concrete example and assume that the base class exposes a GotMail event:

```
Class Person
    ⋮
    Event GotMail(ByVal msgText As String)

    Sub NotifyNewMail(ByVal msgText As String)
        ' Let all listeners know that we got mail.
        RaiseEvent GotMail(msgText)
    End Sub

End Class
```

If Employee inherits from Person, you can use an Employee object in the following way:

```
Dim WithEvents anEmployee As Employee

Sub TestInheritance2()
    ' Create the event sink.
    anEmployee = New Employee()
    anEmployee.FirstName = "Joe"
    anEmployee.LastName = "Doe"

    ' Notify this employee that he got new mail.
    ' (This indirectly raises the event.)
    anEmployee.NotifyNewMail("Message from VB2TheMax")
End Sub

' The event procedure
Sub Employee_NewMail(ByVal msgText As String) Handles anEmployee.GotMail
    Console.WriteLine("NEW MAIL: " & msgText)
End Sub
```

Inheriting Shared Members

A derived class inherits all the shared methods of the base class. For example, let's enhance the Person class with a shared method that returns True when two persons are brothers (where brotherhood is defined as having at least one parent in common). To implement this shared function, we have to add two fields to the Person base class:

```
Class Person
    ⋮
    ' Public fields
    Public Father As Person
    Public Mother As Person
```

(continued)

```
    Shared Function AreBrothers(ByVal p1 As Person, ByVal p2 As Person) _
        As Boolean
        Return (p1.Father Is p2.Father) Or (p1.Mother Is p2.Mother)
    End Function
End Class
```

Because the Employee class inherits from Person, you can check whether two employees are brothers using this code:

```
Sub TestInheritance3()
    Dim e1 As New Employee()
    e1.FirstName = "Joe"
    e1.LastName = "Doe"

    Dim e2 As New Employee()
    e2.FirstName = "Robert"
    e2.LastName = "Doe"

    Dim e3 As New Employee()
    e3.FirstName = "Ann"
    e3.LastName = "Doe"

    ' Joe is Robert and Ann's father.
    e2.Father = e1
    e3.Father = e1
    ' Call the inherited shared method in the Employee class.
    Console.WriteLine(Employee.AreBrothers(e2, e3))    ' => True
End Sub
```

Polymorphic Behavior

As I mentioned previously, inheriting from a base class implicitly adds a degree of polymorphism to your code. Under Visual Basic 6, you achieve efficient early-bound polymorphism by having the derived class expose the base class as a secondary interface. (See "Early-Bound Polymorphic Code" earlier in this section.) Visual Basic .NET doesn't require any interface gimmick to get the same behavior:

```
Dim p As Person
If Math.Rnd < .5 Then
    ' Sometimes P points to an Employee object.
    p = New Employee()
Else
    ' Sometimes P points to a Person object.
    p = New Person()
End If
' In either case, this polymorphic code uses early binding.
Console.WriteLine(p.FirstName & " " & p.LastName)
```

Notice that a base class variable can't access methods defined only in the derived class. For example, the following code doesn't compile:

```
' *** This code doesn't compile because you're trying to access
'     a method defined in the Employee class through a Person variable.
p.BaseSalary = 10000
```

As an exception to this rule, you can access—more precisely, you can try to access—any member in any class via an Object variable and late binding as long as Option Strict is Off:

```
' *** This code requires that Option Strict be Off.
⋮
Dim o As Object = New Employee()
' The following statement uses late binding.
o.BaseSalary = 10000
```

Overriding Members in the Base Class

The derived class can modify the behavior of one or more properties and methods in the base class. Visual Basic .NET requires that you slightly modify your code in both the base class and the derived class to implement this new behavior. For example, say that you have a CompleteName method in the Person class. You must prefix it with the Overridable keyword to tell the compiler that this method can be overridden:

```
' ...(In the Person (base) class)...
Overridable Function CompleteName() As String
    Return FirstName & " " & LastName
End Function
```

You must use the Overrides keyword to redefine the behavior of this method in the derived class:

```
' ...(In the Employee (derived) class)...
Overrides Function CompleteName() As String
    Return LastName & ", " & FirstName
End Function
```

Another common term for such a method is *virtual* method. Your code won't compile if you omit either the Overridable keyword in the base class or the Overrides keyword in the derived class. This behavior is a nuisance when you're creating large classes meant to work as base classes because you must remember to use the Overridable keyword for each and every member.

Visual Studio offers a simple and effective way to create the template code for an overridden method: click the down arrow for the Class Name drop-down list, scroll until you find the name of the derived class, and click the (Overrides) element immediately below it. (See Figure 5-1.) Then click the down arrow for the Method Name drop-down list, and click the method you want to override. You can use this technique also to generate the template for event handlers and for procedures that implement methods of a secondary interface. (I explain interfaces in the next chapter.)

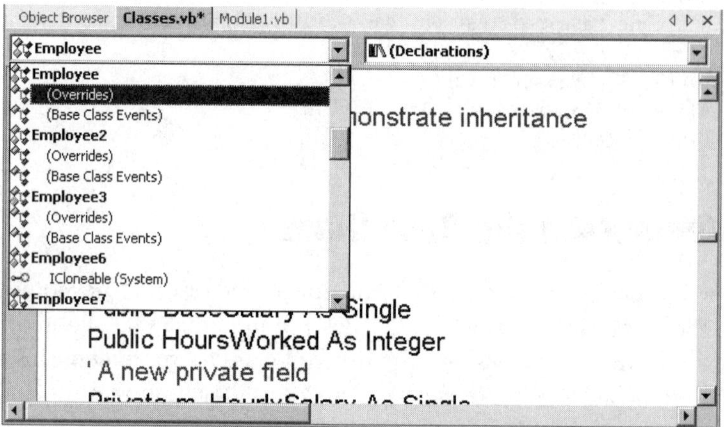

Figure 5-1. Generating the template code for an overridden method in Visual Studio.

Visual Basic .NET also supports the NotOverridable keyword, which explicitly states that a method can't be overridden; however, this is the default behavior, and in fact you can use this keyword only in conjunction with the Overrides keyword, as I explain in the following section.

When you override a property in the base class, you can redefine its internal implementation, but you can't alter the read or write attribute. For example, if the base class exposes a ReadOnly property, you can't make it writable by overriding it in the derived class. Similarly, you can't define a read-write property that overrides a WriteOnly property in the base class. Along the same lines, if you're overriding a default member in the base class, the method in the derived class must be the default member in the derived class and requires the Default keyword.

Note that you can't override fields, constants, or shared members defined in the base class.

Override Variations

By default, a method marked with the Overrides keyword is itself overridable, so you never need both the Overrides and Overridable keywords in the same procedure definition, even though using both is legal. You need the NotOverridable keyword to explicitly tell the compiler that an overridden method isn't overridable in derived classes:

```
' This procedure overrides a procedure in the base class, but this
    ' procedure can't be overridden in any class that inherits from the current
    ' class.
NotOverridable Overrides Sub MyProc()
    ⋮
End Sub
```

You need neither the Overrides keyword in the derived class nor the Overridable keyword in the base class if you're adding a member with the same name but a different signature. For example, if the Employee class contains a CompleteName method with one argument, it doesn't override the parameterless method with the same name in the Person class, and therefore no special keyword is necessary in either class. Oddly enough, however, the method in the derived class does require the Overloads keyword:

```
' ...(In the Person (base) class)...
' Note: no Overridable keyword
Function CompleteName() As String
    Return FirstName & " " & LastName
End Function

' ...(In the Employee (derived) class)...
' Note: no Overrides keyword, but Overloads is required.
Overloads Function CompleteName(ByVal title As String) As String
    Return title & " " & LastName & ", " & FirstName
End Function
```

The general rule is therefore as follows: you don't need the Overloads keyword when a class defines multiple members with identical names, but you need the Overloads keyword in the derived class when the derived class exposes multiple members with the same name, regardless of whether they're inherited from the base classes or added in the derived class. However, you must use Overrides in the derived class (and Overridable in the base class) only if the derived class is redefining an overloaded method that already exists in the base class with the same argument signature.

> **Note** The compiler can generate more efficient code when calling nonoverridable methods instead of overridable methods (also known as virtual methods), so you might want to avoid using the Overridable keyword if you can. For example, the JIT compiler can inline regular methods but not virtual methods (*Inlining* is an optimization technique through which the compiler moves code from the called method into the caller's procedure.) In addition, allocating an object that contains virtual methods takes slightly longer than the allocation of an object that has no virtual methods.
>
> However, benchmarks prove that invoking a nonoverridable method is less than 15 percent faster than invoking an empty method marked with the Overridable keyword, and in practice the difference is hardly noticeable with actual nonempty methods in real-world applications. In absolute terms, the difference in timing is so small that you can disregard it unless you're performing millions of method calls.
>
> While we're talking performance, remember that calling a virtual method on a value type forces the compiler to consider it a reference type, which causes the object to be boxed in the heap and therefore degrades the overall execution speed. For example, this happens when you call the ToString method on a value type such as a Structure, as you can easily see by looking at the IL code produced by such a call.

The MyBase Keyword

The MyBase keyword is useful when you want to reference a field, property, or method of the base object. If a member hasn't been overridden in the derived class, the expressions *Me.membername* and *MyBase.membername* refer to the same member and execute the same code. However, when *membername* has been redefined in the inherited class, you need the MyBase keyword to access the member as defined in the base class. Consider the following method:

```
' ...(In the Person (base) class)...
Overridable Function CompleteName() As String
    Return FirstName & " " & LastName
End Function
```

Now, let's assume that the Employee class overrides this method to prefix the complete name with the employee's title. Here's a not-so-smart implementation of this method:

```
' ...(In the Employee (derived) class)...
Public Title As String

Overrides Function CompleteName() As String
    If Title <> "" Then CompleteName = Title & " "
    CompleteName &= FirstName & " " & LastName
End Function
```

The preceding solution isn't optimal because it doesn't reuse any code in the base class. In this particular case, the code in the base class is just a string concatenation operation, but in a real class it might be dozens or hundreds of statements. Worse, if you later change or improve the implementation of the CompleteName function in the base class, you must dutifully apply these changes to all the classes that inherit from Person. The MyBase keyword lets you implement a better solution:

```
Overrides Function CompleteName() As String
    If Title <> "" Then CompleteName = Title & " "
    CompleteName &= MyBase.CompleteName
End Function
```

If you worked with simulated inheritance under Visual Basic 6, you see that the coding pattern is the same as the one you used with inheritance by delegation, for which MyBase corresponds to the private instance of the base class managed by the inherited class.

.NET programming guidelines dictate that an inherited class that overrides the IDisposable.Dispose method of its base class should manually invoke its base class's Dispose method:

```
Overrides Sub Dispose()
    ' Put your cleanup code here.
    ⋮
    ' Call the base class's Dispose method.
    MyBase.Dispose
End Sub
```

Constructors in Derived Classes

Even though you declare constructor procedures with the Sub keyword, they aren't ordinary methods and aren't inherited from the base class in the way all other methods are. It's up to you to provide the derived class with one or more constructors if you want the derived class to be creatable using the same syntax as the base class.

If the base class has no constructor method or has a Sub New procedure that takes no arguments, you don't strictly need to define an explicit constructor for the derived class. As a matter of fact, all the preceding examples show that you can create an instance of the Employee class without defining a constructor for it:

```
Dim e As Employee = New Employee()
```

Things are different when the base class doesn't include a parameterless constructor method either implicitly or explicitly. In this case, the derived class has to contain a constructor method, and the very first executable line of this method must be a call to the base class's constructor. Say that the Person2 class has the following constructor method:

```
Class Person2
    Sub New(ByVal firstName As String, ByVal lastName As String)
        Me.FirstName = firstName
        Me.LastName = lastName
    End Sub
    ' ...(other properties and methods as in Person class) ...
    ⋮
End Class
```

The derived Employee2 class must therefore contain the following code:

```
Class Employee2
    Inherits Person2

    Sub New(ByVal firstName As String, ByVal lastName As String)
        ' The first executable statement *must* be a call
        ' to the constructor in the base class.
        MyBase.New(firstName, lastName)
        ' You can continue with the initialization step here.
        ⋮
    End Sub
    ' ...(other properties and methods) ...
    ⋮
End Class
```

The constructor in the derived class can have a different argument signature from the constructor in the base class, but also in this case the first executable statement must be a call to the base class's constructor:

```
Public Title As String                   ' A new field

Sub New(ByVal firstName As String, ByVal lastName As String, _
    ByVal title As String)
    MyBase.New(firstName, lastName)
    Me.Title = title
End Sub
```

Sometimes you're forced to create auxiliary functions whose only purpose is to comply with the requirement that the first executable statement be a call to the base class's constructor. (For an example of this technique, see the "Overloaded Constructors" section in Chapter 4.)

Finalizers in Derived Classes

As you know from Chapter 4, a well-written class that uses unmanaged resources (files, database connections, Windows objects, and so on) should implement both a Finalize method and the IDisposable.IDispose method. If you're inheriting from a class that uses unmanaged resources, you should check whether your inherited class uses any additional unmanaged resources. If not, you don't have to write any extra code because the derived class will inherit the base class's implementation of both the Finalize and the Dispose methods. However, if the inherited class does use additional unmanaged resources, you should override the implementation of these methods, correctly release the unmanaged resources that the inherited class uses, and then call the base class's corresponding method. For example, the Finalize method should always call the base class's Finalize procedure:

```
Protected Overrides Sub Finalize()
    ' Release unmanaged resources created by the inherited class.
    ⋮
    ' Ask the base class to release its own unmanaged resources.
    MyBase.Finalize()
End Sub
```

In section "A Better Dispose-Finalize Pattern" of Chapter 4, I illustrated a generic technique for correctly implementing these methods in a class, based on an overloaded Dispose method that contains the code for both the IDisposable.Dispose and the Finalize methods. As it happens, this overloaded Dispose method has a Protected scope, so in practice you can correctly implement the Dispose-Finalize pattern in derived classes by simply overriding one method:

```
Class BetterDataFile2
    Inherits DataFile2

    ' Insert here regular methods, some of which may allocate additional
    ' unmanaged resources.
    ⋮

    ' The only method we need to override to implement the Dispose-Finalize
    ' pattern for this class.
    Protected Overloads Overrides Sub Dispose(ByVal disposing As Boolean)
        ' Exit now if the object has been already disposed.
        ' (The disposed variable is declared as Protected in the base class.)
```

(continued)

```
        If disposed Then Exit Sub

        If disposing Then
            ' The object is being disposed, not finalized.
            ' It is safe to access other objects (other than the base
            ' object) only from inside this block.
            :
        End If

        ' Perform clean up chores that have to be executed in either case.
        :

        ' Call the base class's Dispose method.
        MyBase.Dispose(disposing)
    End Sub
End Class
```

The MyClass Keyword

You can easily miss a subtle but important detail of inheritance: when a client calls a nonoverridden method of an inherited class, the code runs in the base class (as you would expect) but in the context of the derived class.

The simplest way to explain this concept is through an example, once again based on the Person-Employee pair. Let's define a Person3 base class exposing a TitledName method that returns the complete name of the person, prefixed with his or her title if one has been specified:

```
Enum Gender
    NotSpecified
    Male
    Female
End Enum

Class Person3
    ' (In a real-world class, these would be properties.)
    Public FirstName As String
    Public LastName As String
    Public Gender As Gender = Gender.NotSpecified
    ' ...(other members omitted for brevity) ...
    :

    Dim m_Title As String
    Overridable Property Title() As String
        Get
            Return m_Title
        End Get
```

```
        Set(ByVal Value As String)
            m_Title = Value
        End Set
    End Property

    ' Prefix the name with a title if one has been specified.
    Function TitledName() As String
        If Title <> "" Then
            Return Title & " " & FirstName & " " & LastName
        Else
            Return FirstName & " " & LastName
        End If
    End Function
End Class
```

The derived Employee3 class doesn't override the TitledName method, but it does override the Title property, so it's never an empty string:

```
Class Employee3
    Inherits Person3

    ' Always provide a title if one hasn't been assigned.
    Overrides Property Title() As String
        Get
            If MyBase.Title <> "" Then
                Return MyBase.Title
            ElseIf Gender = Gender.Male Then
                Return "Mr."
            ElseIf Gender = Gender.Female Then
                Return "Mrs."
            End If
        End Get
        Set(ByVal Value As String)
            MyBase.Title = Value
        End Set
    End Property
End Class
```

Because the derived class doesn't override the TitledName property, the version in the base class is used. However, that code runs in the context of the derived class, and therefore, it uses the overridden version of the Title property, the one defined in Employee3 instead of the one defined in Person3:

```
Dim e As New Employee3("Joe", "Doe")
e.Gender = Gender.Male
' The TitledName method defined in Person3 uses the overridden
' version of Title property defined in Employee3.
Console.WriteLine(e.TitledName)     ' => Mr. Joe Doe
```

A better way to anticipate the effect of inheritance is to pretend that all the nonoverridden routines in the base class have been pasted inside the derived class. So if they reference another property or method, they call the version of that member that's defined in the derived class—not the original one defined in the base class.

However, sometimes you want a piece of code in the base class to use the nonoverridden version of the properties and methods it references. Let's use another example to clarify this concept. Let's say that a person can vote only if he or she is 18 years old, so the Person3 class contains this code:

```
' This code assumes that the following Imports statement has been used.
Imports Microsoft.VisualBasic

Class Person3
    :
    Public BirthDate As Date

    ' Age is defined as the number of whole years passed from BirthDate.
    Overridable ReadOnly Property Age() As Integer
        Get
            Age = CInt(DateDiff(DateInterval.Year, BirthDate, Now()))
            If Month(Now) < Month(Birthdate) Or _
                (Month(Now) = Month(BirthDate) And _
                Day(Now) < Day(BirthDate)) Then
                ' Correct if this year's birthday hasn't occurred yet.
                Age = Age - 1
            End If
        End Get
    End Property

    ReadOnly Property CanVote() As Boolean
        Get
            Return (Age >= 18)
        End Get
    End Property
End Class
```

The Employee3 class uses a looser definition of the age concept and overrides the Age property with a simpler version that returns the difference between the current year and the year when the employee was born:

```
Class Employee3
    :

    ' Age is defined as difference between the current year
    ' and the year the employee was born.
    Overrides ReadOnly Property Age() As Integer
```

```
        Get
            Age = CInt(DateDiff(DateInterval.Year, BirthDate, Now()))
        End Get
    End Property
End Class
```

Do you see the problem? The CanVote property incorrectly uses the Age property defined in the Employee3 class rather than the original version in the Person3 class. To see what kind of bogus result this logical error can cause, run this code:

```
Sub TestMyClassKeyword()
    ' Create a person and an employee.
    Dim p As New Person3("Joe", "Doe")
    Dim e As New Employee3("Robert", "Smith")
    ' They are born on the same day.
    p.BirthDate = #12/31/1984#
    e.BirthDate = #12/31/1984#
    ' (Assuming that you run this code in the year 2002...)
    ' The person can't vote yet (correct).
    Console.WriteLine(p.CanVote)          ' => False
    ' The employee appears to be allowed to vote (incorrect).
    Console.WriteLine(e.CanVote)          ' => True
End Sub
```

Once you understand where the problem is, its solution is simple: you must use the MyClass keyword to be sure that a method in a base class always uses the properties and methods in that base class (as opposed to their overridden version in the inherited class). Here's how to fix the problem in our example:

```
    ' ...(In the Person3 class)...
    ReadOnly Property CanVote() As Boolean
        Get
            ' Ensure that it always uses the nonoverridden
            ' version of the Age property.
            Return (MyClass.Age >= 18)
        End Get
    End Property
```

Member Shadowing

.NET lets you inherit from a class in a compiled DLL for which you neither have nor control the source code. This raises an interesting question: what happens if you extend the base class with a method or a property and then the author of the base class releases a new version that exposes a member with the same name?

Visual Basic copes with this situation in such a way that the application that uses the derived class isn't broken by changes in the base class. If the derived class has a member with the same name as a member in the base class, you get a compilation warning, but you are still able to compile the two classes. In this case, the member in the derived class is said to be *shadowing* the member with the same name in the base class. Visual Basic offers three different syntax forms of shadowing:

- A member in the derived class shadows all the members in the base class with the same name, regardless of their parameter signatures; as I've explained, you get a compilation warning that doesn't prevent successful compilation (unless you select the Treat Compiler Warnings As Errors check box on the Build page of the project Property Pages dialog box).
- A member in the derived class marked with the Shadows keyword hides all the members in the base class with the same name, regardless of their signatures; the effect is exactly the same as in the preceding case. In addition, you don't get any compilation warning, so you should use the Shadows keyword to make it clear that you are intentionally shadowing one or more members in the base class.
- A member in the derived class marked with the Overloads keyword shadows only the member in the base class that has the same name and argument signature. (Note that you can apply the Shadows and Overloads keywords to the same member.)

Shadowing can be quite confusing, so it's best to look at a concrete example:

```
Class AAA
    Sub DoSomething()
        Console.WriteLine("AAA.DoSomething")
    End Sub
    Sub DoSomething(ByVal msg As String)
        Console.WriteLine("AAA.DoSomething({0})", msg)
    End Sub

    Sub DoSomething2()
        Console.WriteLine("AAA.DoSomething2")
    End Sub
    Sub DoSomething2(ByVal msg As String)
        Console.WriteLine("AAA.DoSomething2({0})", msg)
    End Sub
End Class
```

```
Class BBB
    Inherits AAA

    Overloads Sub DoSomething()
        Console.WriteLine("BBB.DoSomething")
    End Sub
    Shadows Sub DoSomething2()
        Console.WriteLine("BBB.DoSomething2")
    End Sub
End Class
```

The following routine calls the methods in the two classes:

```
Sub TestMemberShadowing()
    Dim b As New BBB()
    b.DoSomething()          ' => BBB.DoSomething
    b.DoSomething("abc")     ' => AAA.DoSomething(abc)
    b.DoSomething2()         ' => BBB.DoSomething2
End Sub
```

As you see, the DoSomething procedure in class BBB shadows the procedure DoSomething with zero arguments in class AAA, but the procedure that takes one argument isn't shadowed and can be accessed as usual. This behavior contrasts with the DoSomething2 procedure in class BBB, which is declared with the Shadows keyword and therefore hides both procedures with the same name in class AAA; for this reason, the following statement raises a compilation error:

```
' *** This statement doesn't compile.
b.DoSomething2("abc")
```

If you drop the Shadows keyword in class BBB, the overall effect is the same, the only difference being that the call to DoSomething2 causes a compilation warning.

You've just seen that you can shadow a property or a method even if the procedure isn't marked with Overridable (or is marked with NotOverridable Overrides) in the base class. This raises an interesting question: what is the point of omitting the Overridable keyword, then?

In practice, member shadowing makes it impossible for a developer to prevent a method from being overridden, at least from a logical point of view. In fact, let's say that by omitting the Overridable keyword, the author of the Person3 class makes the Address property not overridable:

```
Class Person3
    ⋮
    Dim m_Address As String
```

(continued)

```
    Property Address() As String
        Get
            Return m_Address
        End Get
        Set(ByVal Value As String)
            m_Address = Value
        End Set
    End Property
End Class
```

The author of the Employee3 class can still override the Address property—for example, to reject null string assignments—by using the Shadows keyword (to suppress compilation warnings) and manually delegating to the base class using the MyBase.Address expression:

```
Class Employee3
    Inherits Person3

    ⋮

    Shadows Property Address() As String
        Get
            Return MyBase.Address
        End Get
        Set(ByVal Value As String)
            If Value = "" Then Throw New ArgumentException()
            MyBase.Address = Value
        End Set
    End Property
End Class
```

Here's the client code that uses the Address property:

```
Sub TestShadows()
     ' Create a Person3 object.
     Dim p As New Person3("Joe", "Doe")
     ' You can assign a null string to its Address property
     ' without raising any error.
     p.Address = ""

     ' Create an Employee3 object.
     Dim e As New Employee3("Ann", "Doe")
     ' Show that Employee overrides the (nonoverridable) Address property.
     ' NOTE: Next statement throws an exception because the code in
     '       Employee3 trapped the invalid assignment.
     e.Address = ""
End Sub
```

As you see, you can't prevent a class member from being overridden. However, you see a different behavior when you access the member through a base class variable, depending on whether you override the member in the standard way or you shadow it implicitly or explicitly using the Shadows keyword. When a member has been overridden with Overrides, you always access the member in the derived class, even if you're referencing it through a base class variable. When a member has been shadowed (with or without the Shadows keyword), no inheritance relationship exists between the two members and therefore you access the member in the base class. An example can make this concept clearer:

```
Sub TestShadows2()
    Dim e As New Employee3("Joe", "Doe")
    ' This statement correctly raises an ArgumentException
    ' because of the code in the Employee class.
    e.Address = ""

    ' Access the same object through a base class variable.
    Dim p As Person3 = e
    ' This raises no run-time error because the Address property procedure
    ' in the base class is actually executed.
    p.Address = ""
End Sub
```

If the Address property had been redefined using the Overrides keyword, the last statement would invoke the Address property procedure in the derived class, not in the base class.

Because the redefined method in the derived class has nothing to do with the original method in the base class, the two members can have different scope qualifiers, which isn't allowed if the method in the derived class overrides the method in the base class. For example, you can have a Public method in the derived class that shadows (and possibly delegates to) a Protected method in the base class. However, keep in mind that a Private member in the derived class does not shadow a member in the base class: in other words, the Shadows keyword has no effect on Private members.

One last detail on shadowing: you can't shadow a method that is defined as MustOverridable in the base class; in this case, the compiler expects a method marked with the Overrides keyword and flags the derived class as incomplete.

Redefining Shared Members

You can use neither the Overridable nor the Overrides keyword with shared members because shared members can't be overridden. Either they're inherited as they are or they must be shadowed and redefined from scratch in the derived class.

You *cannot* use the *MyBase* variable to invoke shared methods defined in the base class if you're redefining them in the derived class because *MyBase* is forbidden in shared methods. For example, say that you have a Person class with the following shared method:

```
' ...(In the Person (base) class)...
Shared Function AreBrothers(ByVal p1 As Person, ByVal p2 As Person) As Boolean
    Return (p1.Father Is p2.Father) Or (p1.Mother Is p2.Mother)
End Function
```

In addition, you have an Employee class that inherits from Person and that redefines the AreBrothers shared method so that two Employee objects can be considered brothers if they have one parent in common and the same family name. The following code builds on the AreBrother shared method in the Person class so that if you later change the definition in the Person class, the Employee class automatically uses the new definition:

```
' In the Employee (derived) class
Shared Shadows Function AreBrothers(ByVal e1 As Employee, _
    ByVal e2 As Employee) As Boolean
    Return Person.AreBrothers(e1, e2) And (e1.LastName = e2.LastName)
End Function
```

Unfortunately, no keyword lets you reference the base class in a generic way, so you have to hard-code the name of the base class inside the source code of the derived class when calling a shared method of the base class.

Sealed and Virtual Classes

Visual Basic .NET provides a few additional keywords that let you decide whether other developers can or must inherit from your class and whether they have to override some of its members.

The NotInheritable Keyword

For security (or other) reasons, you might want to ensure that no one extends a class you created. You can achieve this by simply marking the class with the NotInheritable keyword:

```
' Ensure that no one can inherit from the Employee class.
NotInheritable Class Employee
    ⋮
End Class
```

Classes that can't be inherited from are also called *sealed classes*. In general, you rarely need to seal a class, but good candidates for the NotInheritable keyword are utility classes that expose functions as shared members. As you might expect, the Overridable keyword can't be used inside a sealed class.

The MustInherit Keyword

A situation that arises more frequently is that you want to prevent users from using your class as is and instead force them to inherit from it. In this case, the class is called a *virtual* or *abstract class* because you can use it only to derive new classes and can't instantiate it directly. The closest concept in Visual Basic 6 is the idea of abstract classes that you create to define an interface, with an important difference: you can reuse code inside Visual Basic .NET abstract classes, whereas you can't when you use a Visual Basic 6 class to define an interface.

To prevent direct usage of a class, you must flag it with the MustInherit keyword. You typically use this keyword when a class is meant to define a behavior or an archetypal object that never concretely exists. A typical example is the Animal class, which should be defined as virtual because you never instantiate a generic animal; rather, you create a specific animal—a cat, a dog, and so on, which derives some of its properties from the abstract Animal class.

Here's a more business-oriented example: your application deals with different types of documents—invoices, orders, payrolls, and so on—and all of them have some behaviors in common in that they can be stored, printed, displayed, or attached to an e-mail message. It makes sense to gather this common behavior in a Document class, but at the same time you want to be sure that no one mistakenly creates a generic Document object because your application doesn't know how to deal with it.

```
MustInherit Class Document
    ' Contents in RTF format
    Private m_RTFText As String

    Overridable Property RTFText() As String
        Get
            Return m_RTFText
        End Get
        Set(ByVal Value As String)
            m_RTFText = Value
        End Set
    End Property
```

(continued)

```
    ' Save RTF contents to file.
    Overridable Sub SaveToFile(ByVal fileName As String)
        ⋮
    End Sub

    ' Load RTF contents from file.
    Overridable Sub LoadFromFile(ByVal fileName As String)
        ⋮
    End Sub

    ' Print the RTF contents.
    Overridable Sub Print()
        ⋮
    End Sub

    ⋮
End Class
```

Now you can define other classes that inherit their behavior from the Document virtual class:

```
Class PurchaseOrder
    Inherits Document

    ' Redefines how a PO is printed.
    Overrides Sub Print()
        ⋮
    End Sub
End Class
```

Note that you must explicitly use the Overridable keyword in the base class and the Overrides keyword in the inherited class, even if the base class is marked with MustInherit.

The MustOverride Keyword

In general, users of a virtual class aren't forced to override its properties and methods. After all, the main benefit in defining a virtual class is that derived classes can reuse the code in the base class. Sometimes, however, you want to force inherited classes to provide a custom version of a given method.

For example, consider this Shape virtual class, which defines a few properties and methods that all geometrical shapes have in common:

```
MustInherit Class Shape
    ' Position on the X-Y plane
    Public X, Y As Single
```

```
    ' Move the object on the X-Y plane.
    Sub Offset(ByVal deltaX As Single, ByVal deltaY As Single)
        X = X + deltaX
        Y = Y + deltaY
        ' Redraw the shape at the new position.
        Display
    End Sub

    Sub Display()
        ' No implementation here
    End Sub
End Class
```

The Shape virtual class must include the Display method—otherwise, the code in the Offset procedure won't compile—even though that method can't have any implementation because actual drawing statements depend on the specific class that will be inherited from Shape. Alas, the author of the derived class might forget to override the Display method, and no shape will be ever displayed.

In cases like this, you should use the MustOverride keyword to make it clear that the method is virtual and must be overridden in derived classes. When using the MustOverride keyword, you specify only the method's signature and must omit the End Property, End Sub, or End Function keyword:

```
MustInherit Class Shape
    ' ... (Other members as in previous code snippet) ...
    ⋮
    MustOverride Sub Display()
End Class
```

If a class has one or more virtual methods, the class itself is virtual and must be marked with the MustInherit keyword. The following Square class inherits from Shape and overrides the Display method:

```
Class Square
    Inherits Shape

    Public Side As Single

    Overrides Sub Display()
        ' Add here the statements that draw the square.
        ⋮
    End Sub
End Class
```

Scope

Visual Basic .NET accepts five different scope qualifiers: the three qualifiers available to Visual Basic 6 developers (Public, Friend, and Private) plus two new ones, Protected and Protected Friend. These two new qualifiers are related to inheritance, which explains why I have deferred their description until now. Before diving into a thorough discussion of scope, though, you must learn about one more Visual Basic .NET feature: nested classes.

Nested Classes

Unlike previous versions of the language, Visual Basic .NET lets you nest class definitions:

```
Class Outer
    ⋮
    Class Inner
        ⋮
    End Class
End Class
```

The code inside the Outer class can always create and use instances of the Inner class, regardless of the scope qualifier used for the Inner class. If the nested class is declared using a scope qualifier other than Private, the nested class is also visible to the outside of the Outer class, using the dot syntax:

```
Dim obj As New Outer.Inner
```

Nested classes serve a variety of purposes. First, they're useful for organizing all your classes in groups of related classes and for creating namespaces that help resolve name ambiguity. For example, you might have a Mouse class nested in an Animal class and another Mouse class nested inside a Peripheral class:

```
Class Animal
    ⋮
    ' This class can be referred to as Animal.Mouse.
    Class Mouse
        ⋮
    End Class
End Class

Class Peripheral
    ⋮
    ' This class can be referred to as Peripheral.Mouse.
    Class Mouse
        ⋮
    End Class
End Class
```

(You saw a similar example in "The Imports Statement" section of Chapter 2, but on that occasion we used classes nested in namespaces instead of other classes.) Code in the Animal class can refer to the inner Mouse class without using the dot syntax, and it can refer to the other mouse class using the Peripheral.Mouse syntax. Things become more complex when you have multiple nesting levels, as in the following code:

```
Class Peripheral
    Dim m As Mouse
    Dim kb As Keyboard
    Dim k As Keyboard.Key

    ⋮
    ' This class can be referred to as Peripheral.Mouse.
    Class Mouse
        Dim kb As Keyboard
        Dim k As Keyboard.Key
        ⋮
    End Class

    ' This class can be referred to as Peripheral.Keyboard.
    Class Keyboard
        Dim m As Mouse
        Dim k As Key
        ⋮

        ' This class can be referred to as Peripheral.Keyboard.Key.
        Class Key
            Dim m As Mouse
            Dim kb As Keyboard
            ⋮
        End Class
    End Class
End Class
```

Only classes nested immediately inside the outer class can be referenced without the dot syntax from inside the outer class (or its nested classes). For example, you need the dot syntax to refer to the Key class from any class other than Keyboard. However, the rule isn't symmetrical: you can refer to the Mouse class without the dot syntax from inside the Key class.

Another common use for nested classes is to encapsulate one or more auxiliary classes inside the class that uses them and to avoid making them visible to other parts of the application. In this case, the inner class should be marked with the Private scope qualifier. For example, you might create an XMLParser class that parses an XML text and internally uses the Tag and Attribute classes to do the parsing. These classes aren't meant to be visible from the outside, so they're marked as private:

```
Class XMLParser
    ⋮
    ' These classes aren't visible from outside the XMLParser class.
    Private Class Tag
        ⋮
    End Class
    Private Class Attribute
        ⋮
    End Class
End Class
```

Inner classes have one peculiar feature: they can access private members in their container class if they're provided with a reference to an object of that container class. Consider these two classes:

```
Class Keyboard
    Dim m_Brand As String          ' A private member

    ReadOnly Property Brand() As String
        Get
            ' Code inside the outer class can access a private
            ' member without any reference. (Me is implicit.)
            Return m_Brand
        End Get
    End Property

    Class Key
        ' This public field is meant to be assigned when you're creating
        ' an instance of the Key class.
        Public ParentKeyboard As Keyboard

        ReadOnly Property Brand() As String
            Get
                ' Code inside the inner class can access a private member
                ' in the outer class but requires an object reference.
                Return ParentKeyboard.m_Brand
            End Get
        End Property
    End Class
End Class
```

You don't need an object reference to access a shared member in the outer class:

```
Class Keyboard
    ' This shared member is True if this class supports
    ' non-Latin keyboards.
```

```
    Public Shared SupportsNonLatinKeyboards As Boolean

    Class Key
        ReadOnly Property SupportsNonLatin() As Boolean
            Get
                ' You can access a shared member in the outer class
                ' without an object reference.
                Return SupportsNonLatinKeyboards
            End Get
        End Property
    End Class
End Class
```

Note that the outer class can't expose a public field, property, or function that returns an instance of a private nested class:

```
Class Outer
    ' This public field is legal because it returns a Public inner class.
    Public Field1 As InnerPublic

    ' *** This public field isn't legal because you can't return
    '     a private inner class - you get a compilation error!
    Public Field2 As InnerPrivate

    ' This field is legal because it refers to a private nested class
    ' but the field is private.
    Dim Field3 As InnerPrivate

    Private Class InnerPrivate
        ⋮
    End Class
    Public Class InnerPublic
        ⋮
    End Class
End Class
```

Public, Private, and Friend Scope Qualifiers

As a Visual Basic 6 developer, you're already familiar with three of the five scope keywords in Visual Basic .NET.

The Public scope qualifier makes a class or one of its members visible outside the current assembly if the project is a library project. The meaning of Public scope is therefore the same as in Visual Basic 6.

The Private scope makes a class private and usable only inside its container. This container is usually the current application except in the case of nested classes. (As we've seen in the preceding section, a private nested class is usable only inside its container class.) A private member is usable only inside the class in which it's defined, and this includes any nested class defined in the same container. Leaving aside nested classes, the Private keyword has the same meaning as it does in Visual Basic 6.

The Friend scope qualifier makes a class or one of its members visible to the current assembly. So this keyword has almost the same meaning as under Visual Basic 6 if you replace the word *assembly* with *project*. Because most assemblies are made of just one project, for most practical purposes this keyword has retained its meaning in the transition to Visual Basic .NET. You can use the Friend keyword to make a nested class visible from outside its container without making it Public and visible also from outside the project. Note that Friend is the default scope for classes, unlike Visual Basic 6 classes, whose default scope is Public. To make a Visual Basic .NET class visible outside the assembly that contains it, you must explicitly flag the class with the Public keyword.

In general, no restriction applies to using and mixing these attributes unless the result would make no sense. For example, you can have a Private class that exposes a Public method, but a Public method in a Public class can't expose a Protected or Private member because Visual Basic .NET wouldn't know how to marshal it outside the current assembly. Similarly, you can't inherit a Friend class from a Private class, nor you can have a Public class that inherits from a Friend or Private class. The reason is that all the members in the base class should be visible to clients of the inherited class, so the scope of members in the base class can't be more limited than the scope of members in the derived class.

You can't use scope qualifiers to alter the scope of an overridden method. If a base class contains a Public method, for example, you can't override it with a Private or Friend method in the derived class. This rule ensures that if you assign a reference to a derived object to a base class variable, it's guaranteed that you can call all the overridden methods:

```
' If DerivedClass inherits from BaseClass,
' inheritance rules ensure that this assignment works.
Dim obj As BaseClass = New DerivedClass
' Because overridden methods can't have a narrower scope,
' the following statement is guaranteed to compile correctly.
obj.DoSomething
```

The Protected Scope Qualifier

Protected is a new scope qualifier that makes a member or a nested class visible inside the current class as well to all classes derived by the current class. Put another way, Protected members are private members that are also inherited by derived classes. Consider the following class, which has three Protected members and one Public method:

```
Class Customer
    ' This member is visible to this class and
    ' classes derived from this class.
    Protected AlwaysPaysOnTime As Boolean

    ' Compute the discount percentage on products.
    Protected Overridable Function ProductDiscount() As Single
        ' Offer an additional discount if the customer always pays on time.
        If AlwaysPaysOnTime Then
            ProductDiscount = 15
        Else
            ProductDiscount = 10
        End If
    End Function

    ' By default make no discount on shipment.
    Protected Overridable Function ShipmentDiscount() As Single
        Return 0
    End Function

    ' Compute the actual discount on an order, given the
    ' amount of products purchased and the amount of shipment.
    Function TotalOrderAmount(ByVal ProductAmount As Single, _
        ByVal ShipmentAmount As Single) As Single
        Return ProductAmount * (1 - ProductDiscount / 100) _
            + ShipmentAmount * (1 - ShipmentDiscount / 100)
    End Function
End Class
```

Unless you provide a way to modify the value of the AlwaysPaysOnTime field, the TotalOrderAmount method always evaluates the amount for an order by discounting it by 10 percent. You can implement a public method or property that lets clients modify the AlwaysPaysOnTime field, or you can create a new class that sets that field to True:

```
Class GoodCustomer
    Inherits Customer

    Sub New()
        ' Note that no MyBase.New is needed because the base
        ' class has no constructor with parameters.
        AlwaysPaysOnTime = True
    End Sub
End Class
```

The GoodCustomer class can access the AlwaysPaysOnTime protected field because the GoodCustomer class inherits from Customer. You can easily show that setting this field to True changes the way discounts are evaluated:

```
Sub TestProtectedScope()
    Dim c1 As New Customer()
    Dim c2 As New GoodCustomer()
    Console.WriteLine(c1.TotalOrderAmount(10000, 100))    ' => 9100
    Console.WriteLine(c2.TotalOrderAmount(10000, 100))    ' => 8600
End Sub
```

At the same time, you can verify that the AlwaysPaysOnTime field is private and can't be seen by regular clients:

```
' *** This statement doesn't compile.
c1.AlwaysPaysOnTime = True
```

Code inside the GoodCustomer class can invoke Protected methods defined in the Customer class, and a Protected property or method can be overridden to provide custom versions. For example, let's define a ForeignCustomer class that doesn't charge shipping fees to well-behaved foreign customers:

```
Class ForeignCustomer
    Inherits Customer

    ' A convenient constructor that lets us test well- and
    ' ill-behaved foreign customers
    Sub New(ByVal alwaysPaysOnTime As Boolean)
        Me.AlwaysPaysOnTime = alwaysPaysOnTime
    End Sub

    ' We don't charge shipping to well-behaved foreign customers.
    Protected Overrides Function ShipmentDiscount() As Single
        If AlwaysPaysOnTime Then ShipmentDiscount = 100
    End Function
End Class
```

The ShipmentDiscount function in the ForeignCustomer class redefines how shipping is charged and overrides the function defined in the base class (where it was conveniently marked with the Overridable keyword). Let's prove that this works as expected:

```
Sub TestProtectedScope2()
    Dim c3 As New ForeignCustomer(False)     ' Ill-behaved
    Dim c4 As New ForeignCustomer(True)      ' Well-behaved

    Console.WriteLine(c3.TotalOrderAmount(10000, 400))    ' => 9400
    Console.WriteLine(c4.TotalOrderAmount(10000, 400))    ' => 8500
End Sub
```

You can apply the Protected keyword to nested classes as well. You can use a nested Protected class only from inside the containing class and from inside derived classes, but not from elsewhere in the application. Here is an example:

```
Class Customer
    :
    Protected Class OrderHistory
        Public Count As Integer
        Public TotalAmount As Single
        :
    End Class
End Class

Class GoodCustomer
    Inherits Customer

    ' A derived class sees protected nested classes.
    Dim oh As Customer.OrderHistory
    ' Note that you don't even need the dot syntax.
    Dim oh2 As OrderHistory
    :
End Class

' This class doesn't inherit from Customer.
Class AnotherClass
    ' *** This statement doesn't compile.
    Dim oh As Customer.OrderHistory
    :
End Class
```

The Protected Friend Scope Qualifier

The fifth scope qualifier available in Visual Basic .NET is Protected Friend, which combines the features of the Friend and Protected keywords and therefore defines a member or a nested class that's visible to the entire assembly and to all inherited classes. This keyword seems to be redundant—you might think that Friend also comprises inherited classes—until you consider that Visual Basic .NET allows you to inherit classes from other assemblies. Let's rewrite the previous example, this time using the Protected Friend qualifier:

```
Class Customer
    :
    Protected Friend Class OrderHistory
        Public Count As Integer
        Public TotalAmount As Single
        :
    End Class
End Class
```

In this new version, the nested OrderHistory class is now fully visible to the assembly that hosts the Customer class *and* to all the classes inherited from Customer, regardless of whether they're defined inside or outside the current assembly.

Using Scope Qualifiers with Constructors

You might find it interesting to see what happens when you apply a scope qualifier other than Public to a constructor procedure. Using a Friend constructor makes the class creatable from inside the assembly but not from outside it: this is the closest equivalent of PublicNotCreatable classes in Visual Basic 6.

```
Public Class Widget
    ' This class can be created only from inside the current assembly.
    Friend Sub New()
        ⋮
    End Sub
End Class
```

You can define a Private Sub New method if you want to prevent clients—inside and outside the assembly—from instancing the class. This approach can be useful if the class contains only shared members, so there's no point in creating an instance of it:

```
Class Triangle
    ' This private constructor prevents clients from
    ' instancing this class.
    Private Sub New()
        ' No implementation code here.
    End Sub

    ' Add here all the shared members for this class.
    Shared Function GetArea( ... ) As Double
        ⋮
    End Function
    ⋮
End Class
```

Another use for Private constructors arises when you want clients to create instances through a shared member rather than with the usual New keyword, as in the following example:

```
Class Square
    Public Side As Double

    ' This private constructor prevents clients from
    ' instancing this class directly.
```

```
    Private Sub New(ByVal side As Double)
        Me.Side = side
    End Sub

    ' Clients can create a square only through this shared method.
    Shared Function CreateSquare(ByVal side As Double) As Square
        Return New Square(side)
    End Function
End Class
```

Clients can create a new Square object using this syntax:

```
Dim sq As Square = Square.CreateSquare(2.5)
```

Some classes in the .NET Framework expose this sort of constructor method, but in general you should stick to standard constructor methods because this alternative technique doesn't offer any clear advantage, except for the ability to run custom code before actually creating the instance.

The scope of the constructor has a far-reaching and somewhat surprising effect on the inheritance mechanism. To begin with, a class that has only Private constructors can't be used as a base class, even if it isn't flagged with the NotInheritable keyword. In fact, the derived class should have its own constructor (because the base class doesn't have a Public parameterless default constructor), but any attempt to call MyBase.New will fail because the Sub New procedure isn't visible outside the base class.

Along the same lines, a Public class that has one or more Friend Sub New methods can be used as a base class, but only if the derived class is defined in the same assembly. Any attempt to inherit that class from outside the assembly would fail because the inherited class can't call a constructor with a Friend scope. If clients outside the current assembly should be able to instantiate the base class, you can add a shared function that returns a new instance of the class:

```
' This class is visible from outside the assembly but can't
' be used as a base class for classes outside the assembly.
Public Class Widget
    ' This constructor can be called only from inside
    ' the current assembly.
    Friend Sub New()
        ⋮
    End Sub

    ' A pseudoconstructor method for clients located
    ' outside the current assembly.
    Public Shared Function CreateWidget() As Widget
        Return New Widget()
    End Function
End Class
```

Even if clients outside the current assembly shouldn't use the Widget class, you still have to mark it as Public (rather than Friend or Private) if you use Widget as the base class for other Public classes, as I explained in the preceding section.

If the constructor has Protected scope, the class can be used as a base class because the constructor of the derived class can always access this constructor, but the class can't be instantiated from inside or outside the current assembly. Finally, if the constructor has Protected Friend scope, the class can be used as a base class but can be instantiated only from inside the assembly it resides in and from inside derived classes.

Understanding from where you can instantiate a class and from where you can use it as a base class is made more complicated by the fact that nested classes can always access Private and Protected constructors. Table 5-1 can help you determine the effect of the scope of the constructor and the class itself.

Table 5-1 The Effect of Class Scope and Constructor Scope on a Class's Ability to Be Instantiated or Used as a Base Class

Class Scope*	Constructor Scope	Types That Can Instantiate This Class	Classes That Can Inherit from This Class
Private	Private	Nested types	Nested classes
	Protected	Nested types and inherited classes	Private classes defined in the same container
	Friend, Protected Friend, Public	Types defined in the same container	Private classes defined in the same container
Protected	Private	Nested types	Nested classes
	Protected	Nested types and inherited classes	Private/Protected classes defined in the same container
	Friend, Protected Friend, Public	Types defined in the same container and inherited classes	Private/Protected classes defined in the same container
Friend, Protected Friend	Private	Nested types	Nested classes
	Protected	Types defined in the same container and inherited classes	Classes defined in current assembly

Table 5-1 The Effect of Class Scope and Constructor Scope on a Class's Ability to Be Instantiated or Used as a Base Class *(continued)*

Class Scope*	Constructor Scope	Types That Can Instantiate This Class	Classes That Can Inherit from This Class
	Friend, Protected Friend, Public	Types defined in current assembly	Classes defined in current assembly
Public	Private	Nested types	Nested classes
	Protected	Nested types and inherited classes	All classes, inside or outside current assembly
	Friend	Types defined in current assembly	Classes defined in current assembly
	Protected Friend	Types defined in current assembly and inherited classes	All classes, inside or outside current assembly
	Public	All types, inside or outside current assembly	All classes, inside or outside current assembly

* Note that you can have Private, Protected, and Protected Friend classes only inside a container type.

Redefining Events

You can't override events in the same way you override properties and methods, and in fact, you can't use the Overrides keyword on events. (However, you can use the Shadows keyword on events.)

Occasionally, you might want to redefine what happens when the base class raises an event. For example, the inherited class might need to perform some additional processing when an event is fired from inside the base class, or it might need to suppress some or all of the events that the base class raises. These two tasks require two different approaches.

If the derived class just needs to get a notification that an event is being raised from inside the base class, the simplest solution is to set up a WithEvents variable and assign it the Me reference. In other words, the derived class becomes a listener for its own events. Let's say that you have the following base class:

```
Class DataReader
    Event DataAvailable()
```

(continued)

```
    Sub GetNewData()
        RaiseEvent DataAvailable()
    End Sub
End Class
```

Next you create a derived FileDataReader class that inherits from DataReader but needs to get a notification whenever the DataAvailable event is fired to accomplish a noncritical task, such as incrementing a counter. The following implementation does the trick:

```
Class FileDataReader
    Inherits DataReader

    ' This variable will point to the object itself (Me).
    Dim WithEvents EventSink As FileDataReader
    ' This counter must be incremented after each event.
    Public EventCounter As Integer

    Sub New()
        MyBase.New()
        EventSink = Me
    End Sub

    Private Sub NotifyDataAvailable() Handles EventSink.DataAvailable
        ' Increment the counter.
        EventCounter += 1
    End Sub
End Class
```

This programming technique doesn't require that you change the base class in any way, but it has two serious shortcomings. First, the derived class has no control over the event itself, and it can't modify its arguments or prevent it from firing. Second, you aren't guaranteed that the event in the derived class fires before (or after) the event in clients, so different clients might see different values for the public EventCounter field during the event notification chain.

To solve both these problems, you must change the way the base class fires events—in other words, you must build the base class with inheritance in mind. Instead of using the RaiseEvent statement whenever you want to raise an event in the base class, you call an overridable method, which by convention is named OnEventName:

```
Class DataReader2
    Event DataAvailable()

    Sub GetNewData()
        OnDataAvailable()
    End Sub
```

```
    ' This procedure contains only the RaiseEvent statement.
    Protected Overridable Sub OnDataAvailable()
        RaiseEvent DataAvailable()
    End Sub
End Class
```

After this edit, the derived class can easily take control of how events are dispatched to clients and whether they are dispatched at all. For example, this new version raises no more than 10 events in clients:

```
Class FileDataReader2
    Inherits DataReader2

    ' This counter must be incremented after each event.
    Public EventCounter As Integer

    Protected Overrides Sub OnDataAvailable()
        ' Increment the counter.
        EventCounter += 1
        ' Raise only up to 10 events.
        If EventCounter <= 10 Then MyBase.OnDataAvailable()
    End Sub
End Class
```

Note that the derived class can't directly use the RaiseEvent statement to raise one of its own events if the event is defined in the base class. The only way to indirectly raise the event is by calling the OnDataAvailable method in the base class, as shown in the preceding code.

Inheritance is so central to Visual Basic .NET programming that you'll probably come back to this chapter to revisit these concepts more than once. But for now, you're ready to see how you can implement interfaces and take advantage of a completely new feature of the language—delegates, one of the topics of the next chapter.

Front
Top
Left
Back

6

Interfaces and Delegates

This chapter covers two topics that are central to .NET programming. In the first part, you'll learn how to implement an interface and, above all, how to use a few all-important .NET interfaces. In the second half of this chapter, you'll read about delegates and how you can put them to good use in your applications.

Interfaces

As you might remember, an interface is a set of properties and methods that a class exposes. An interface defines only the *signature* of such properties and methods (member name, number and type of each parameter, and type of return value), while a class can implement that interface by providing actual code for those properties and methods as necessary. The code in each property or method can differ from class to class, provided the semantics of each method are preserved. The fact that each class can implement the same property or method in a different way is the basis for polymorphic behavior.

Visual Basic .NET supports the definition of interfaces in a much more streamlined way than its predecessors. Under Visual Basic 6, you can define an interface only indirectly, by using a class module that contains property and method signatures but no implementation code. This lame approach has been replaced in Visual Basic .NET by the Interface...End Interface block:

```
Interface IPluggableAddin
    Readonly Property Id() As Long

    Property State() As Boolean

    Function OnConnection(ByVal environment As String) As Boolean

    Sub OnDisconnection()

End Interface
```

Visual Basic .NET interfaces blocks can't contain executable code, and you can include only method and property signatures. The ReadOnly and WriteOnly keywords let you define whether a property can be read from and written to without your having to omit the Get and Set procedures, as you would have to do in Visual Basic 6. An interface can't include variables, and properties and methods can't take scope qualifiers because all of them are implicitly Public. The structure and meaning of the interface is clear, and you can't accidentally write executable statements that are never actually executed or Private members that don't actually appear in the interface. In a difference from Visual Basic 6, a Visual Basic .NET interface can contain an event definition:

```
Interface IPluggableAddin
    Event Connected()

    ' ...(Other method definitions as before)...
    ⋮
End Interface
```

Interfaces have a scope, whether or not you declare it explicitly. The default scope for interfaces is Friend, so a Public class can't expose a Public member that returns an interface whose declaration doesn't include a scope:

```
Public Class MyComponent
    ' *** Next statement raises a compilation error because a Public
    '     class can't expose a Friend type as a Public member.
    Public addin As IPluggableAddin
End Class
```

The preceding code snippet works only if the IPluggableAddin interface is explicitly declared as Public:

```
Public Interface IPluggableAddin
    ' ...(all members as in the original definition)...
End Interface
```

Interfaces with a scope other than Public or Friend can be declared only inside another type, as in

```
Class MyComponent
    ⋮
    Private Interface IPluggableAddin
        ' ...(all members as in the original definition)...
    End Interface
End Class
```

Surprisingly, you can also do the opposite and define a type—a class, a structure, an Enum, or another interface—inside an Interface...End Interface block. However, the nested type doesn't really belong to the interface and its being placed inside the interface means only that you need an additional dot to reach it. For example, consider this interface:

```
Interface IGetRange
    Function GetRange() As Range

    Class Range
        Public StartValue, EndValue As Double
    End Class
End Interface
```

In this case, having the Range class defined inside the interface might make sense, so that you ensure that there is no name conflict with any other class with the same name. Here's a routine that receives an interface argument and retrieves a Range object:

```
Sub UseTheRangeClass(ByVal igr As IGetRange)
    Dim r As IGetRange.Range
    r = igr.GetRange
    ⋮
End Sub
```

Microsoft guidelines dictate that all interface names start with the *I* character, that they not include the underscore character, and that they use Pascal casing when the name contains multiple words.

Implementing the Interface

You tell Visual Basic that a class exposes an additional interface by means of the Implements keyword, as you do in Visual Basic 6:

```
Class MyAddin
    Implements IPluggableAddin
    ⋮
End Class
```

(Visual Basic .NET supports the Implements keyword inside Structure blocks as well.) The syntax for implementing individual properties and methods differs from the one you use in Visual Basic 6, resembling instead what you do when you're writing event procedures. In fact, you reuse the Implements keyword to tell the compiler which procedure in your class implements what member in the interface:

```
Class MyAddin
    Implements IPluggableAddin
    Event Connected() Implements IpluggableAddin.Connected

    Private ReadOnly Property Id() As Long Implements IPluggableAddin.ID
        Get
            ⋮
        End Get
    End Property
```

(continued)

```
    Private Property State() As Boolean Implements IPluggableAddin.State
        Get
            ⋮
        End Get
        Set(ByVal Value As Boolean)
            ⋮
        End Set
    End Property

    Private Function OnConnection(ByVal environment As String) As Boolean _
        Implements IPluggableAddin.OnConnection
        ⋮
    End Function

    Private Sub OnDisconnection() Implements IPluggableAddin.OnDisconnection
        ⋮
    End Sub
End Class
```

Note that the preceding code uses Private scope for all the procedures so that those procedures can't be invoked directly from clients of the MyAddin class, but working this way isn't a requirement. As a matter of fact, you can omit the Private keyword and make the procedures implicitly Public, specify an explicit scope qualifier, and even use other keywords, such as Overridable:

```
Class MyAddin
    Implements IPluggableAddin

    Protected Overridable Function OnConnection( _
        ByVal Environment As String) As Boolean _
           Implements IPluggableAddin.OnConnection
        ⋮
    End Function

    ⋮
End Class
```

Visual Studio .NET gives you an effective way to create templates for these procedures: just drop-down the Class Name list in the code editor and click one of the interfaces implemented by the current class, and then click a specific method in the Method Name list. You follow a similar procedure in Visual Basic 6. A Visual Basic .NET file can contain multiple classes, however, so you have to select the right one. (See Figure 6-1.)

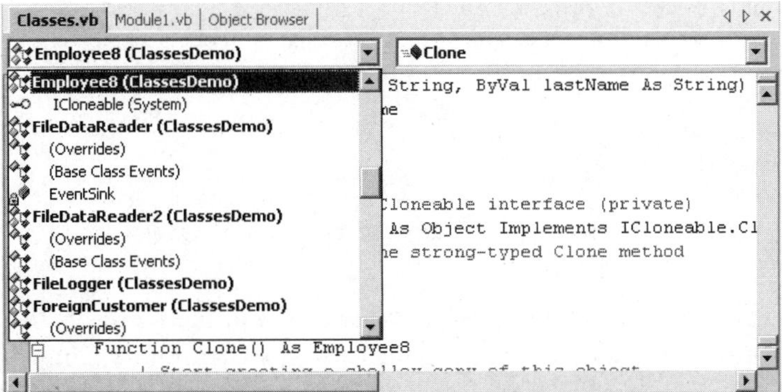

Figure 6-1. Letting Visual Studio .NET create a template for a procedure in a secondary interface.

Speaking of scope, notice that Visual Basic enforces no constraint related to the scope of the interface that a class can implement. For example, you can have a Public class that implements a Private interface, a Private class that implements a Public interface, or any other combination of the supported scope qualifiers. However, only clients that have access to the interface's definition can access that interface's members though an interface variable. For example, if a class exposes an interface declared with Friend scope, only clients inside the same assembly can access that interface through an interface variable. Unless the individual procedures that implement the interface's members are declared with Public scope, there is no way for a client outside the current assembly to access the code inside those procedures.

The Implements keyword supports multiple arguments, so you can have methods from multiple interfaces that map to the same procedure. The following example shows that methods in the interfaces and methods in the class that implements the interface can have different names:

```
' Another interface with just one property
Interface IHostEnvironment
    ReadOnly Property HashCode() As Long
End Interface

' This new version of the class implements two interfaces.
Class MyAddin
    ' You can have two distinct Implements statements if you prefer.
    Implements IPluggableAddin, IhostEnvironment

    Event Connected() Implements IpluggableAddin.Connected

    ' The following procedure implements two read-only properties
    ' from distinct interfaces.
```

(continued)

```
    ReadOnly Property Id() As Long _
        Implements IPluggableAddin.ID, IHostEnvironment.HashCode
        Get
            ⋮
        End Get
    End Property

    ' ...(Other implemented methods have been omitted)...
End Class
```

A variant of this technique lets you map multiple methods from one interface to the same procedure in the class. It goes without saying that mapping multiple methods to the same procedures works only if all the methods have the same argument signature and the same data type for the return value.

Accessing the Interface

You access the interface that a class implements exactly as you do in Visual Basic 6, which is by assigning the object to a variable typed after the interface:

```
Sub TestInterface()
    ' An instance of the class
    Dim addin As New MyAddin()
    ' Cast to an interface variable.
    Dim iplug As IPluggableAddin = addin
    ' Now you can access all the methods and properties in the interface.
    iplug.State = True
End Sub
```

If you're calling just one or two methods in the interface, you might find it convenient to do the cast operation on the fly with a CType or a DirectCast operator:

```
' Cast to the interface type and invoke a method in one operation.
' (These two statements are equivalent.)
CType(addin, IPluggableAddin).OnConnection("MyHost")
DirectCast(addin, IPluggableAddin).OnConnection("MyHost")
```

You can also use a With...End With block:

```
' Create a hidden, temporary interface variable.
With CType(addin, IPluggableAddin)
    .OnConnection("MyHost")
    .State = True
End With
```

If a member of an interface is implemented through a Public procedure, you don't need to cast the object to a different type, and you can access the interface's member through a standard variable pointing to the object. For example, classes that implement the IDisposable interface usually expose a Public Sub Dispose method, which can therefore be accessed through the main object variable. (See "The Dispose Method" section in Chapter 4).

As I mentioned in the previous section, even a Structure can implement an interface. However, keep two points in mind when you access an interface implemented in a value type. First, you can't use the DirectCast operator, because it requires that its first argument is a reference type. Second, and more important, the value type needs to be boxed before one of its interface members can be accessed, so you pay a performance penalty each time you access an interface method through an interface variable.

Interfaces and Inheritance

An interface can inherit from another interface. An inherited interface contains all the members that it defines, plus all members in the base interface. This feature is especially useful when you're creating a new, extended version of an interface:

```
Public Interface IPluggableAddin2
    Inherits IPluggableAddin
    Property Description() As String
End Interface
```

A derived interface can't redefine any member in the base interface, so you can't use the Overridable or Overrides keyword inside an interface's definition. If the derived interface contains a member with the same name as a member in the base interface, the member in the derived interface shadows the member in the base class; in this case, you get a compilation warning that you can suppress using the Shadows keyword in the derived interface. In all cases, however, the class that implements the interface must implement both the member in the base class and the member in the derived class with the same name, which can become quite confusing. For this reason, you should refrain from defining a derived interface that contains a member with the same name as a member in its base interface, even though Visual Basic .NET allows you to do so.

A derived class automatically inherits all the interfaces (and their implementation) defined in the base class, whether they're implemented through public or private methods. You must not include any Implements statement in the derived class.

```
' This class inherits all the interfaces defined in the MyAddin class.
Class AnotherAddin
    Inherits MyAddin
```

(continued)

```
End Class

' Client code
Dim addin2 As New AnotherAddin
' Prove that the inherited class exposes the IPluggableAddin interface.
CType(addin2, IPluggableAddin).State = True
```

The derived class can even override the implementation of interface methods defined in the base class as long as methods in the base class aren't Private and have been defined using the Overridable keyword. The code in the derived class must not use the Implements keyword in the method declaration.

```
' This class inherits all the interfaces defined in the MyAddin class.
Class AnotherAddin
    Inherits MyAddin

    Protected Overrides Function OnConnection(ByVal Environment As String) _
        As Boolean
        ⋮
    End Function
End Class
```

As I showed in the "Finalizers in Derived Classes" section of Chapter 5, if the base class implements the IDisposable interface, .NET programming guidelines dictate that you override the Dispose method, perform your cleanup chores, and finally call the Dispose method in the base class:

```
' Assuming that the MyAddin base class implements IDisposable...

Class AnotherAddin
    Inherits MyAddin

    Overrides Sub Dispose()
        ' Clean up code for the AnotherAddin class.
        ' ...(omitted)...

        ' Complete the cleanup step by calling the base class's
        ' Dispose method.
        MyBase.Dispose
    End Function
End Class
```

Using .NET Interfaces

The .NET Framework defines and consumes dozens of different interfaces, and expert Visual Basic .NET developers should learn how to take advantage of them. In this section, you'll see how such systemwide interfaces can make your life simpler.

The IComparable Interface

In the "ParamArray Arguments" section of Chapter 3, you saw that the System.Array class exposes the Sort shared method, which lets you sort an array of simple data types, such as numbers or strings. However, the Sort method can't directly sort more complex objects, such as Person, because it doesn't know how two Person objects compare with one another.

Implementing the IComparable interface makes your objects sortable by means of the Array.Sort method; you'll need to write very little code. This interface exposes only one method, CompareTo, which receives an object and is expected to return –1 , 0, or 1, depending on whether the current object is less than, equal to, or greater than the object passed as an argument. Let's see how you can define a Person class that's sortable on its ReverseName property:

```
Class Person
    Implements IComparable

    ' Public fields
    Public FirstName As String
    Public LastName As String

    ' A simple constructor
    Sub New(ByVal firstName As String, ByVal lastName As String)
        Me.FirstName = firstName
        Me.LastName = lastName
    End Sub

    ' A property that returns the name in the format "Doe, Joe"
    ReadOnly Property ReverseName() As String
        Get
            Return LastName & ", " & FirstName
        End Get
    End Property

    ' This procedure adds sorting capabilities to the class.
    Private Function CompareTo(ByVal obj As Object) As Integer _
        Implements IComparable.CompareTo
        ' Any non-Nothing object is greater than Nothing.
        If obj Is Nothing Then Return 1
        ' Cast to a specific Person object to avoid late binding.
        Dim other As Person = CType(obj, Person)
        ' Use StrComp to simplify case-insensitive comparisons.
        Return StrComp(ReverseName, other.ReverseName, CompareMethod.Text)
    End Function
End Class
```

Here's the client code that demonstrates how the IComparable interface works:

```
Sub TestIComparable()
    Dim Persons() As Person = { New Person("John", "Smith"), _
        New Person("Robert", "Doe"), New Person("Joe", "Doe") }
    Array.Sort(Persons)

    ' Print all the elements in sorted order.
    Dim p As Person
    For Each p In Persons
        Console.WriteLine(p.ReverseName)
    Next
End Sub
```

The IComparer Interface

The IComparable interface is all you need when your objects can be compared in one way only. Most real-world objects, however, can be compared and sorted on different fields or field combinations; in this case, you can use a variation of the Array.Sort method that takes an IComparer interface as its second argument. The IComparer interface exposes only one method, Compare, which receives two object references and returns –1, 0, or 1 depending on whether the first object is less than, equal to, or greater than the second object.

A class that can be sorted on different field combinations might expose two or more nested classes that implement the IComparer interface, one class for each possible sort method. For example, you might want to sort the Person class on either the (LastName, FirstName) or (FirstName, LastName) field combination; these combinations correspond to the ReverseName and CompleteName read-only properties in the code that follows. Here's a new version of the class that supports these features:

```
Class Person2
    ' Public fields
    Public FirstName As String
    Public LastName As String

    ' A simple constructor
    Sub New(ByVal firstName As String, ByVal lastName As String)
        Me.FirstName = firstName
        Me.LastName = lastName
    End Sub

    ' A property that returns a name in the format "Joe Doe"
    ReadOnly Property CompleteName() As String
        Get
            Return FirstName & " " & LastName
        End Get
    End Property
```

```
    ' A property that returns a name in the format "Doe, Joe"
    ReadOnly Property ReverseName() As String
        Get
            Return LastName & ", " & FirstName
        End Get
    End Property

    ' First auxiliary class, to sort on CompleteName
    Class ComparerByName
        Implements IComparer

        Function Compare(ByVal o1 As Object, ByVal o2 As Object) _
            As Integer Implements IComparer.Compare
            ' Two null objects are equal.
            If (o1 Is Nothing) And (o2 Is Nothing) Then Return 0
            ' AnyAny non-null object is greater than a null object.
            If (o1 Is Nothing) Then Return 1
            If (o2 Is Nothing) Then Return -1
            ' Cast both objects to Person, and do the comparison.
            ' (Throws an exception if arguments aren't Person objects.)
            Dim p1 As Person2 = CType(o1, Person2)
            Dim p2 As Person2 = CType(o2, Person2)
            Return StrComp(p1.CompleteName, p2.CompleteName, _
                CompareMethod.Text)
        End Function
    End Class

    ' Second auxiliary class, to sort on ReverseName
    Class ComparerByReverseName
        Implements IComparer

        Function Compare(ByVal o1 As Object, ByVal o2 As Object) _
            As Integer Implements IComparer.Compare
            ' Two null objects are equal.
            If (o1 Is Nothing) And (o2 Is Nothing) Then Return 0
            ' AnyAny non-null object is greater than a null object.
            If (o1 Is Nothing) Then Return 1
            If (o2 Is Nothing) Then Return -1
            ' Save code by casting to Person objects on the fly.
            Return StrComp(CType(o1, Person2).ReverseName, _
                CType(o2, Person2).ReverseName, CompareMethod.Text)
        End Function
    End Class
End Class
```

Using the two auxiliary classes is straightforward:

```
Sub TestIComparer()
    Dim Persons() As Person2 = { New Person2("John", "Smith"), _
        New Person2("Robert", "Doe"), New Person2("Joe", "Doe") }
```

(continued)

```
    ' Sort the array on name.
    Array.Sort(Persons, New Person2.ComparerByName)
    ' Sort the array on reversed name.
    Array.Sort(Persons, New Person2.ComparerByReverseName)
End Sub
```

You can also provide two shared functions in the Person class that instantiate the CompareBy*xxxx* classes and return the IComparer interface:

```
Class Person
    ⋮
    ' First part of implementation as in previous example
    ⋮

    ' Shared methods that return an auxiliary object
    Shared Function CompareByName() As IComparer
        Return New ComparerByName()
    End Function

    Shared Function CompareByReverseName() As IComparer
        Return New ComparerByReverseName()
    End Function
End Class
```

The client code becomes

```
' Sort the array on name.
Array.Sort(Persons, Person.CompareByName())
' Sort the array on reversed name.
Array.Sort(Persons, Person.CompareByReverseName())
```

The Array.Sort method works in case-sensitive mode by default, but the System.Collections namespace contains a class, a CaseInsensitiveComparer, which implements the IComparer interface and lets you compare strings in case-insensitive mode:

```
' Sort a string using case-insensitive comparisons:
Array.Sort(arr, System.Collections.CaseInsensitivComparer.Default)
```

String comparisons are based on the current locale, or more precisely on the value of Thread.CurrentCulture. Case-insensitive comparisons are different from what Visual Basic 6 developers might expect, however, because they are never based on ASCII values of individual characters. For example, under Visual Basic .NET, all the variations of the character A (uppercase, lowercase, or accented) come before the character B. If you're migrating Visual Basic code that relies on ASCII code sorting for case-insensitive string comparisons, you should define a custom class that works as a custom comparer, as follows:

```
Class CaseInsensitiveComparerVB6
    Implements IComparer

    Function Compare(ByVal o1 As Object, ByVal o2 As Object) As Integer _
       Implements IComparer.Compare
       ' Let the StrComp function do the work for us.
       Return StrComp(o1.ToString, o2.ToString, CompareMethod.Binary)
    End Function
End Class
```

The ICloneable Interface

Everything is an object under Visual Basic .NET. One consequence of this arrangement is that when you assign a variable to another variable, you get two variables pointing to the same object rather than two distinct copies of the data (unless you're working with value types instead of reference types, of course). Typically, you can get a copy of the data by invoking a special method that the class exposes. In the .NET world, a class should implement the ICloneable interface and expose its only method, Clone, to let the outside world know that it can create a copy of its instances. Several objects in the framework implement this interface, including Array, ArrayList, BitArray, Font, Icon, Queue, and Stack.

Most of the time, implementing the ICloneable interface is straightforward:

```
Class Employee
    Implements ICloneable

    Public FirstName As String
    Public LastName As String
    Public Boss As Employee

    Sub New(ByVal firstName As String, ByVal lastName As String)
        Me.FirstName = firstName
        Me.LastName = lastName
    End Sub

    ' The only method of the ICloneable interface
    Public Function Clone() As Object Implements ICloneable.Clone
        ' Create a new Employee with same property values.
        Dim e As New Employee(FirstName, LastName)
        ' Properties not accepted in the constructors
        ' must be copied manually.
        e.Boss = Me.Boss
        Return e
    End Function
End Class
```

The System.Object class, from which all other classes derive, defines the MemberwiseClone method, which helps you clone an object without your having to manually copy every property. See how we can use this method to simplify the implementation of the Clone method in the Employee class:

```
Public Function Clone() As Object Implements ICloneable.Clone
    Return Me.MemberwiseClone
End Function
```

The ICloneable interface is never called by the .NET runtime, and its only purpose is to provide a standardized way to let other developers know that your class supports cloning by means of a well-established syntax:

```
Sub TestICloneable()
    ' Define an employee and his boss.
    Dim joe As New Employee("Joe", "Doe")
    Dim robert As New Employee("Robert", "Smith")
    joe.Boss = robert

    ' Clone it--The Clone method returns an object,
    ' so you need CType if Option Strict is On.
    Dim joe2 As Employee = CType(joe.Clone, Employee)
    ' Prove that all properties were copied.
    Console.WriteLine(joe2.FirstName & " " & joe2.LastName _
        & ", whose boss is " & joe2.Boss.FirstName & " " & joe2.Boss.LastName)
        ' => Joe Doe, whose boss is Robert Smith
End Sub
```

Shallow Copies and Deep Copies

The Clone method can create either a *shallow copy* or a *deep copy* of the object. A *shallow copy* creates only a copy of the object in question; it doesn't make copies of secondary objects referenced by it. In contrast, a *deep copy* operation clones all secondary objects as well. The following code snippet makes this difference clear:

```
Sub TestICloneable2()
    ' Define an employee and its boss.
    Dim joe As New Employee("Joe", "Doe")
    Dim robert As New Employee("Robert", "Smith")
    joe.Boss = robert
    ' Clone it.
    Dim joe2 As Employee = CType(joe.Clone, Employee)
    ' Prove that the Employee object was cloned but his boss wasn't.
    Console.WriteLine(joe Is joe2)                    ' => False
    Console.WriteLine(joe.Boss Is joe2.Boss)          ' => True
End Sub
```

When shallow copying isn't enough and you really need to create a clone of the entire *object graph* that has the object at its root, you can't rely on the MemberwiseClone method alone; you must manually copy properties of each object. Here's a new Employee2 class that correctly clones the entire object graph:

```
Class Employee2
    Implements ICloneable

    Public Boss As Employee2
    ' ... (other fields and constructor as in Employee) ...

    Public Function Clone() As Object Implements ICloneable.Clone
        ' Start creating a shallow copy of this object.
        ' (This copies all nonobject properties in one operation.)
        Dim e As Employee2 = CType(Me.MemberwiseClone, Employee2)
        ' Manually copy the Boss property, reusing its Clone method.
        If Not (e.Boss Is Nothing) Then
            e.Boss = CType(Me.Boss.Clone, Employee2)
        End If
        Return e
    End Function
End Class
```

This new version of the Clone method is still rather concise because it uses the MemberwiseClone method to copy all nonobject values, and it builds on the Clone method for the secondary objects (only Boss, in this case). This approach also works correctly if the employee's boss has her own boss.

However, most real-world object graphs are more complex than this example, and exposing a Clone method that works correctly isn't a trivial task. For example, if the Employee2 class had a Colleagues property (a collection holding other Employee2 objects), the circular references that would ensue would cause the Clone method to enter a recursion that would end with a stack overflow error. Fortunately, the .NET Framework offers a clean solution to this problem, but you won't learn it until Chapter 11, "Serialization."

A Strongly Typed Clone Method

The ICloneable interface is highly generic, so its Clone method returns an Object value. As you've seen in previous examples, this involves a hidden boxing and unboxing sequence and forces you to use a CType function to assign the cloned object to a strongly typed variable. Is there a way to avoid this overhead?

The answer is yes, and the technique is surprisingly simple. You define a public, strongly typed Clone method in the main class interface of your object and have a private ICloneable.Clone method point to it. Here's a new Employee3 class that uses this technique:

```
Class Employee3
    Implements ICloneable
    Public Boss As Employee3
    ' ... (other fields and constructor as in Employee) ...

    ' The only method of the ICloneable interface (private)
    Private Function CloneMe() As Object Implements ICloneable.Clone
        ' Reuses the code in the strongly typed Clone method.
        Return Clone
    End Function

    ' The strongly typed Clone method (public)
    Function Clone() As Employee3
        ' Start creating a shallow copy of this object.
        ' (This copies all nonobject properties in one operation.)
        Clone = CType(Me.MemberwiseClone, Employee3)
        ' Manually copy the Boss property, reusing its Clone method.
        If Not (Clone.Boss Is Nothing) Then
            Clone.Boss = Me.Boss.Clone
        End If
    End Function
End Class
```

The client code isn't cluttered with CType functions or slowed down by hidden unboxing operations:

```
Dim joe2 As Employee3 = joe.Clone
```

Using a strongly typed Clone method makes your code faster and more robust at the same time because the compiler can flag incorrect assignments that would otherwise throw an exception at run time. Note that you can still access the original, weakly typed, Clone method by means of an ICloneable variable or by using a CType operator, as in this line of code:

```
Dim c As Object = CType(joe, ICloneable).Clone
```

The IEnumerable and IEnumerator Interfaces

I'll conclude this discussion about .NET system interfaces with the IEnumerable and IEnumerator interfaces. These interfaces work together to provide For Each support so that the class looks like a collection class to its clients. (You can also create collection classes by inheriting from classes defined in the .NET Framework, as you'll learn in Chapter 9.)

When Visual Basic .NET compiles a For Each statement, it checks that the object following the In keyword supports the IEnumerable interface. (In the same circumstances, Visual Basic 6 checks for the IEnumVARIANT interface only at run time.) When the For Each statement is actually executed, Visual Basic invokes the only method in this interface, GetEnumerator. This function must return an object that supports the IEnumerator interface, which in turn exposes the following three methods:

- **MoveNext function** This method is called at each For Each iteration and should return True if a new value is available or False if there are no more elements.
- **Current read-only property** It should return the current value.
- **Reset procedure** This method resets the internal pointer so that the next returned value is the first one in a new series.

Implementing the Interface

To illustrate these interfaces in action with a nontrivial example, I created a WordParser class that lets you iterate over all the words in a sentence using a For Each loop. The simplest way to build such a class is to inherit it from a collection, fill the inner collection with the data, and then rely on inheritance to do all the work. (Read Chapter 9 for more details about this technique.) The approach based on inheritance works, but it isn't very efficient and takes a lot of extra memory when you're parsing long strings because you need an array to store all the parsed words. Instead, the following solution uses no additional memory because words are parsed and extracted one at a time:

```
Class WordParser
    ' This Implements statement means that this class supports For Each.
    Implements IEnumerable

    ' The sentence being parsed
    Public Source As String

    ' A simple constructor
    Sub New(ByVal source As String)
        Me.Source = source
    End Sub

    ' This function is called when a For Each is encountered.
    ' It must return an object that supports the IEnumerator interface.
    Function GetEnumerator() As IEnumerator _
        Implements IEnumerable.GetEnumerator
        ' Return an instance of the nested class.
        Return New WordParserEnumerator(Source)
    End Function

    ' The nested class that supports IEnumerator
    Class WordParserEnumerator
        ' This Implements statement ensures that this class can be used
```

(continued)

```
' to enumerate items in a For Each.
Implements IEnumerator

' The sentence being parsed (passed in the constructor)
Dim Source As String
' This index is used to visit all the characters in the sentence.
Dim CharIndex As Integer
' The current word
Dim CurrentWord As String

' The outer class passes the Source string through this constructor.
Sub New(ByVal Source As String)
    Me.Source = Source
    ' Reset CharIndex.
    Reset()
End Sub

' Reset the counter.
' Note that Visual Basic .NET does *not* call this method when a For
' Each loop starts, so you must call it in this class's constructor.
Private Sub Reset() Implements IEnumerator.Reset
    CharIndex = 0
End Sub

' This property returns the current element.
Private ReadOnly Property Current() As Object _
    Implements IEnumerator.Current
    Get
        ' When Visual Basic .NET calls this property, the MoveNext method
        ' has already found the current word.
        Return CurrentWord
    End Get
End Property

' This function advances the pointer and returns True if a new word
' has been found, False otherwise.
Private Function MoveNext() As Boolean Implements IEnumerator.MoveNext
    ' Advance CharIndex if it is currently pointing to a separator.
    ' (Note that CharIndex is zero-based, so we need to add one.)
    Do While CharIndex < Len(source) And _
        IsSeparator(Mid(Source, CharIndex + 1, 1))
        CharIndex += 1
    Loop
    ' Return False if there are no more characters.
    If CharIndex >= Len(Source) Then Return False

    ' Remember current position of index.
    Dim StartIndex As Integer = CharIndex
```

```
            ' Continue to loop until we find another separator.
            Do While CharIndex < Len(Source) And _
                Not IsSeparator(Mid(Source, CharIndex + 1, 1))
                CharIndex += 1
            Loop

            ' We found a new word.
            CurrentWord = Mid(Source, StartIndex + 1, CharIndex - StartIndex)
            ' Return True to signal success.
            Return True
        End Function

        ' Auxiliary function that determines whether a char is a separator.
        Private Function IsSeparator(ByVal c As String) As Boolean
            Return Instr(" ,.:;?!", c) > 0
        End Function
    End Class
End Class
```

Using the WordParser class is a breeze:

```
Sub TestIEnumerable()
    Dim msg As String = "Please, split this into individual words!"
    Dim o As Object
    For Each o In New WordParser(msg)
        Console.WriteLine(o)
    Next
End Sub
```

Note that you might make the code a bit more concise by having WordParser implement both the IEnumerable and the IEnumerator interface. In general, however, keeping the enumerator in a distinct class makes for a better design and helps make your code reusable.

The WordParseEnumerator class uses a parsing technique that is similar to the one you'd implement in Visual Basic 6, and it works pretty efficiently. However, you can make your code fly—and keep it more concise at the same time—by using regular expression classes found in the System.Text.RegularExpressions namespace. Here's a new version of the MoveNext method that uses this alternate technique and doesn't require the auxiliary IsSeparator function:

```
' This regular expression searches for individual words.
Dim re As New System.Text.RegularExpressions("\w+")

Private Function MoveNext() As Boolean Implements IEnumerator.MoveNext
    ' Find the next word.
    Dim ma As System.Text.RegularExpressions.Match
    ma = re.Match(Source, CharIndex)
    ' Return False if not found.
    If Not ma.Success Then Return False
```

(continued)

```
        ' We found a new word.
        CurrentWord = ma.Value
        ' Remember current position of index.
        CharIndex = ma.Index + ma.Length
        ' Return True to signal success.
        Return True
    End Function
```

I explain regular expressions in Chapter 12.

Calling IEnumerator Members

Most of the .NET classes that implement the IEnumerable interface expose a Public GetEnumerator method so that you can call it explicitly (instead of implicitly through a For Each loop). But most of the time, you don't need to call the IEnumerable interface explicitly because you can deliver more elegant code simply by using the class in a For Each loop.

However, calling GetEnumerator to get the IEnumerator object and then invoking the enumerator's methods directly sometimes makes sense. When you want to retrieve all the elements from an enumerator but can't do that inside a loop would be such an occasion.

The following FileTree class is a nontrivial example of this concept. This class lets you iterate over all the files in a directory tree and internally uses the System.IO.Directory class to enumerate the files and the subdirectory in a given path.

```
Class FileTree
    Implements IEnumerable

    ' The search path
    Public ReadOnly DirPath As String

    ' The constructor
    Sub New(ByVal DirPath As String)
        Me.DirPath = DirPath
    End Sub

    ' Return an Enumerable object (an instance of the inner class).
    Function GetEnumerator() As IEnumerator _
        Implements IEnumerable.GetEnumerator
        Return New FileTreeEnumerator(DirPath)
    End Function

    ' The IEnumerator private object
    Class FileTreeEnumerator
        Implements IEnumerator

        Dim DirPath As String
```

```
' This variable contains the Enumerator object for the file list
' in the directory being scanned.
Dim FileEnumerator As IEnumerator
' This variableis contains the stack of the Enumerator objects
' for subdirectories of all pending directories.
Dim DirEnumerators As New System.Collections.Stack()

' A simple constructor
Sub New(ByVal DirPath As String)
    ' Save the directory path.
    Me.DirPath = DirPath
    ' Manually call the Reset method.
    Reset()
End Sub

Sub Reset() Implements IEnumerator.Reset
    ' The DirectoryInfo object that represents the root object
    Dim di As New System.IO.DirectoryInfo(DirPath)

    ' Get the Enumerator object for the file list, and reset it.
    FileEnumerator = di.GetFiles.GetEnumerator
    FileEnumerator.Reset()

    ' Get the Enumerator object for the subdirectory list,
    ' and reset it.
    Dim dirEnum As IEnumerator = di.GetDirectories.GetEnumerator
    dirEnum.Reset()
    ' Push it onto the stack.
    DirEnumerators.Push(dirEnum)
End Sub

Function MoveNext() As Boolean Implements IEnumerator.MoveNext
    ' Simply delegate to the File Enumerator object.
    If FileEnumerator.MoveNext Then
        ' It returned True, so we can exit.
        Return True
    End If

    ' If there are no files in the current directory, check
    ' for another subdirectory in the current directory.

    ' First get the current directory enumerator.
    Dim dirEnum As IEnumerator = _
        CType(DirEnumerators.Peek, IEnumerator)
    ' Check whether current subdirectory enumerator has more items.
    Do Until dirEnum.MoveNext
        ' There are no more subdirectories at this level,
        ' so we must pop another element of the stack.
        DirEnumerators.Pop()
```

(continued)

```
                If DirEnumerators.Count = 0 Then
                    ' Return False if no more subdirectories to scan.
                    Return False
                End If
                ' Get the current enumerator.
                dirEnum = CType(DirEnumerators.Peek, IEnumerator)
            Loop

            ' We can create a DirectoryInfo.
            Dim di As System.IO.DirectoryInfo = _
                CType(dirEnum.Current, System.IO.DirectoryInfo)

            ' Store the file enumerator, and reset it.
            FileEnumerator = di.GetFiles.GetEnumerator
            FileEnumerator.Reset()
            ' Get the Enumerator object for the subdirectory list,
            ' and reset it.
            dirEnum = di.GetDirectories.GetEnumerator
            dirEnum.Reset()
            ' Push it onto the stack.
            DirEnumerators.Push(dirEnum)

            ' Recursive call, to process the file enumerator
            Return Me.MoveNext
        End Function

        ' The Current property simply delegates to FileEnumerator.Current.
        ReadOnly Property Current() As Object Implements IEnumerator.Current
            Get
                Return FileEnumerator.Current
            End Get
        End Property
    End Class

End Class
```

Let's analyze the preceding code. The FileTree class implements IEnumerable and exposes a GetEnumerator method, which does nothing but return an instance of the inner, private, FileTreeEnumerator class, which implements IEnumerator.

Each time the client code invokes the MoveNext method in FileTreeEnumerator, the code in the class must return True and be ready to return a filename through the Current property or return False to stop enumeration when there are no more files to scan in the directory tree.

The FileTreeEnumerator class delegates its job to two different types of enumerator objects, one for iterating over all the files in a given directory and the other for enumerating all the subdirectories in a given directory. There is only one file enumerator object in any given moment, and it's stored in the FileEnumerator variable. However, you need to store several directory enumerator objects because you're traversing a directory tree, and you need to save the enumerator for all the directories above the one you're parsing currently. For this reason, instead of a single variable, you maintain directory enumerators in a System.Collections.Stack structure named DirEnumerators. (Read Chapter 9 for a detailed description of the Stack class.)

When the client calls the MoveNext method—either explicitly or implicitly through a For Each loop—the FileTreeEnumerator class attempts to delegate its job to the FileEnumerator.MoveNext method. If this method returns True, there's nothing more to do, and you can exit:

```
Function MoveNext() As Boolean Implements IEnumerator.MoveNext
    ' Simply delegate to the File Enumerator object.
    f FileEnumerator.MoveNext Then
        ' It returned True, so we can exit.
        Return True
    End If
```

If the FileEnumerator.MoveNext method returns False, no more files in the directory are being scanned, so you must retrieve the directory enumerator from the DirEnumerators stack and invoke its MoveNext method. If this method returns False, it means that you've already scanned all the subdirectories in the current directory, so you can pop one element off the DirEnumerators stack and try again:

```
        ' First get the current directory enumerator.
        Dim dirEnum As IEnumerator = _
            CType(DirEnumerators.Peek, IEnumerator)
        ' Check whether current subdirectory enumerator has more items.
        Do Until dirEnum.MoveNext
            ' There are no more subdirectories at this level,
            ' so we must pop another element off the stack.
            DirEnumerators.Pop()

            If DirEnumerators.Count = 0 Then
                ' Return False if no more subdirectories to scan.
                Return False
            End If
            ' Get the current enumerator.
            dirEnum = CType(DirEnumerators.Peek, IEnumerator)
        Loop
```

You can exit the preceding loop for only two reasons: there are no more items in DirEnumerators (in which case you've visited all the directories in the tree and can return False to the client program), or you've found a directory enumerator whose MoveNext method returned True, which means that you've found a directory that hasn't been scanned yet. In the latter case, you can reinitialize FileEnumerator with the enumerator returned by the GetFiles method and then get the enumerator returned by the GetDirectories method to push onto the DirEnumerators stack:

```
        ' Store the file enumerator, and reset it.
        FileEnumerator = di.GetFiles.GetEnumerator
        FileEnumerator.Reset()
        ' Get the Enumerator object for the subdirectory list,
        ' and reset it.
        dirEnum = di.GetDirectories.GetEnumerator
        dirEnum.Reset()
        ' Push it onto the stack.
        DirEnumerators.Push(dirEnum)
```

The last thing to do is recursively call the MoveNext method to correctly process the enumerator, which is now contained in the FileEnumerator variable:

```
    ' Recursive call, to process the file enumerator
    Return Me.MoveNext
End Function
```

By comparison, the code in the Current property is really simple because it only has to delegate to the FileEnumerator.Current property:

```
ReadOnly Property Current() As Object Implements IEnumerator.Current
    Get
        Return FileEnumerator.Current
    End Get
End Property
```

The FileTree class uses a few objects that I haven't described so far, such as the Stack class (in the System.Collections namespace, described in Chapter 9) and the Directory and DirectoryInfo classes (in the System.IO namespace, described in Chapter 10), so you might not understand every single detail of its inner workings. Using the FileTree class, on the other hand, couldn't be simpler:

```
Sub TestGetEnumerator()
    Dim f As System.IO.FileInfo
    ' Enumerate all files in the C:\DOCS directory tree.
    For Each f In New FileTree("C:\DOCS")
        Console.WriteLine(f.FullName)
    Next
End Sub
```

Delegates

The use of delegates is new to Visual Basic developers. Broadly speaking, a delegate is similar to a C function pointer in that it lets you call a procedure through a pointer to the procedure itself. However, there are a few important differences between function pointers and delegates:

- Each delegate can invoke only procedures with a given argument signature, which you specify in the delegate declaration; for example, a given delegate can point only to a sub that takes an Integer argument by value. This constraint makes delegates inherently safer than C function pointers because the compiler can check that a delegate doesn't point to an arbitrary procedure or region in memory.
- Unlike function pointers, a delegate can point to either a static procedure (such as a procedure declared in a module or a Shared method in a class) or an instance procedure. By comparison, a C function pointer can call only a static procedure. When you call an instance procedure, it's as if you're calling a particular method or property of an object. So in this respect, a delegate behaves more like the Visual Basic 6 CallByName function, with the difference that it's faster (being early bound), more robust (you can't pass an arbitrary method name at run time), and safer (you can't pass arguments that don't match the called procedure's parameters).

Delegates play a central role in the .NET architecture. For example, .NET events are internally implemented through delegates, as are asynchronous operations and many other features of the .NET base classes. Even if you aren't going to use these .NET Framework features in your applications, delegates can be useful in themselves because they let you implement programming techniques that would be otherwise impossible.

Invoking Static Methods

You must define a delegate before you can use it. The following line declares a delegate named OneArgSub, which points to a procedure that takes a string argument:

```
' In the declaration section of a module or a class
Delegate Sub OneArgSub(ByVal msg As String)
```

The preceding line doesn't declare a single delegate. Rather, it defines a *class* of delegates. Behind the scenes, in fact, Visual Basic creates a new class named OneArgSub that inherits from the System.Delegate class. (More precisely, it inherits from System.MulticastDelegate, which in turns inherits from System.Delegate.) Once you have defined the OneArgSub delegate class, you can declare a variable of the new class:

```
Dim deleg As OneArgSub
```

Now you're ready to create an instance of the OneArgSub delegate class:

```
deleg = New OneArgSub(AddressOf DisplayMsg)
```

where DisplayMsg is a procedure that has the same argument signature as the OneArgSub delegate:

```
' Display a string in the Output window.
Sub DisplayMsg(ByVal msgText As String)
    Debug.WriteLine(msgText)
End Sub
```

Finally, you're ready to call the DisplayMsg procedure through the deleg variable, using its Invoke method. (The OneArgSub class has inherited this method from the System.Delegate class.)

```
' This statement displays the "FooBar" string in the Output window.
deleg.Invoke("FooBar")
```

It's a long trip to just display a message, so you might wonder why delegates are so important in the .NET architecture and why you should use them. Alas, Visual Basic developers aren't accustomed to function pointers and the degree of flexibility they can introduce in a program. To give you an example, let's define another procedure that follows the OneArgSub syntax:

```
' Display a string in a pop-up message box.
Sub PopupMsg(ByVal msgText As String)
    Microsoft.VisualBasic.MsgBox(msgText)
End Sub
```

Now you can decide that all the messages in your program should be displayed in message boxes instead of in the Output window, and you need only to replace the statement that creates the delegate variable to do so:

```
deleg = New OneArgSub(AddressOf PopupMsg)
```

All the existing deleg.Invoke statements scattered in the source code will work flawlessly but will send their output to the window instead.

You might have noticed the use of the AddressOf operator. This operator has the same syntax that it had in previous language versions, but in general, it can't be applied to the same situations you used it for in Visual Basic 6. The Visual Basic .NET keyword creates a Delegate object pointing to a given procedure, and in fact, you can usually assign the result of AddressOf to a Delegate variable without having to explicitly create a Delegate object of the proper type:

```
deleg = AddressOf PopupMsg
```

When you use this shortened syntax, the compiler checks that the target procedure has an argument signature compatible with the Delegate variable being assigned. In this chapter, I will use the more verbose syntax based on the New operator when I want to emphasize the class of the Delegate object being created, but you should be aware that both syntax forms are legal and that they are equally fast and robust.

Delegates work as described for any static methods, that is, Sub and Function procedures in Module and shared procedures in classes. For example, here's a complete example that uses a delegate to invoke a shared Function method in a class:

```
Imports Microsoft.VisualBasic

Module MainModule
    ' Declare a delegate class.
    Delegate Function AskYesNoQuestion(ByVal msg As String) As Boolean

    Sub Main()
        ' Declare a delegate variable.
        Dim question As AskYesNoQuestion
        ' Have the delegate point to a class Shared function.
        question = New AskYesNoQuestion(AddressOf MessageDisplayer.AskYesNo)

        ' Call the shared method. (Note that Invoke is omitted.)
        If question("Do you want to save?") Then
            ' ... (save whatever needs to be saved here)...
        End If
    End Sub
End Module

Class MessageDisplayer
    ' Show a message box; return True if user clicked Yes.
    Shared Function AskYesNo(ByVal msgText As String) As Boolean
        Dim answer As MsgBoxResult
        ' Display the message.
        answer = MsgBox(msgText, MsgBoxStyle.YesNo Or MsgBoxStyle.Question)
        ' Return True if the user answered yes.
        Return (answer = Microsoft.VisualBasic.MsgBoxResult.Yes)
    End Function
End Class
```

When working with delegates, you must pay attention to optional arguments. The procedure pointed to by the delegate can include Optional and ParamArray arguments, and the delegate will correctly pass the expected number of arguments. This holds true even if the target procedure is overloaded, in which case the delegate will correctly invoke the correct overloaded version of that procedure. However, the delegate definition itself cannot include Optional or ParamArray arguments.

Invoke is the default member for the System.Delegate class and all the classes that derive from it; thus, you can omit it when calling it. In the end, invoking a procedure through a delegate variable looks like a call to a method:

```
If question("Do you want to save?") Then
```

Surprisingly, omitting the Invoke method works even if the delegate is pointing to a procedure that takes no arguments, and this seems to be a sort of exception to the general rule that states that only methods and properties with arguments can become the default member of a class.

Invoking Instance Methods

Using delegates with instance methods and properties is also straightforward: the only remarkable difference is in the argument to the AddressOf operator, which must include a reference to an instance of the class. Here's a complete example that invokes an instance method of the MessageDisplayer class through a delegate:

```
Imports Microsoft.VisualBasic

Module MainModule
    Delegate Function AskQuestion(ByVal DefaultAnswer As Boolean) As Boolean

    Sub Main()
        ' Create an instance of the class, and initialize its properties.
        Dim msgdisp As New MessageDisplayer()
        msgdisp.MsgText = "Do you want to save?"
        msgdisp.MsgTitle = "File has been modified"

        ' Create the delegate to the instance method.
        ' (Note the object reference in the AddressOf clause.)
        Dim question As AskQuestion = _
            New AskQuestion(AddressOf msgdisp.YesOrNo)

        ' Call the instance method through the delegate.
        If question(False) Then
            ' ... (save whatever needs to be saved here)...
        End If
    End Sub
End Module

Class MessageDisplayer
    Public MsgText As String
    Public MsgTitle As String
```

```
    ' Display a message box, and return True if the user selects Yes.
    Function YesOrNo(ByVal DefaultAnswer As Boolean) As Boolean
        Dim style As MsgBoxStyle

        ' Select the default button for this msgbox.
        If DefaultAnswer Then
            style = MsgBoxStyle.DefaultButton1      ' Yes button
        Else
            style = MsgBoxStyle.DefaultButton2      ' No button
        End If
        ' This is a yesy/no question.
        style = style Or MsgBoxStyle.YesNo Or MsgBoxStyle.Question
        ' Display the msgbox, and return True if the user replied Yes.
        Return (MsgBox(MsgText, style, MsgTitle) = MsgBoxResult.Yes)
    End Function
End Class
```

Other Properties

All delegate classes derive from System.Delegate, and therefore they inherit all the properties and methods defined in this base class. The two properties you're're likely to find useful are Target and Method.

The Target property simply returns a reference to the object that is the target of the delegate. In the previous example, you might access a property of the MessageDisplayer object with the following code:

```
' The Target method returns an Object, so you need an explicit
' cast if Option Strict is On.
Console.WriteLine(CType(log.Target, MessageDisplayer).MessageDisplayerMsgText)
```

If the delegate is pointing to a shared method, the Target method returns a reference to the System.Type object that represents the class. In this case, you need to use reflection methods to extract information about the class itself.

The other useful delegate property is Method, which returns a System.Reflection.MethodInfo object that describes the method being called, its attributes, and so on. For example, you can learn the name of the target method as follows:

```
Console.WriteLine(log.Method.Name)
```

For more information about reflection, see Chapter 15.

Defining Polymorphic Behavior

By now you should have realized that delegates give you an unparalleled flexibility in how you call procedures in your application. For example, the bulk of your code can invoke procedures through a delegate, and you decide which specific procedure is actually called only at run time. The sole requirement is that all the involved procedures have the same argument signature. For example, consider the following:

- You can use a delegate to call one method from a group of static methods; these can be either methods in modules or static methods in classes.
- You can use a delegate to call different methods of the same object instance.
- You can use a delegate to call different methods of different objects of the same class.
- You can use a delegate to call different methods of objects belonging to different classes.

Some of these behaviors could be achieved with late binding or with the CallByName function under Visual Basic 6. Delegates, however, deliver more robust and efficient code because once the delegate object has been created and associated with a given method, it behaves in early binding mode from that point on.

To illustrate the kind of flexibility delegates give you, let's say that you want to display log messages from your application, either to the Console window or to a file, based on an argument on the command line. Of course, you can resolve this simple task without delegates, for example by using the tracing techniques outlined in the "Tracing Application Behavior" section of Chapter 3. However, this task offers a great occasion to show delegates in action:

```
Delegate Sub LogWriter(ByVal Msg As String)

Dim log As LogWriter                ' A delegate variable
Dim fw As System.IO.StreamWriter    ' A stream writer

Sub TestLogDelegate()
    ' Get command-line arguments.
    Dim args() As String = Environment.GetCommandLineArgs

    If args.Length > 1 Then
        ' If the command line contains a filename, open that file.
        fw = New System.IO.StreamWriter(args(1))
        ' Have the delegate point to the stream's WriteLine method.
        log = New LogWriter(AddressOf fw.WriteLine)
    Else
        ' If no argument has been specified, send to the console.
        log = New LogWriter(AddressOf Console.WriteLine)
```

```
        End If

        Call DoTheRealJob()

        ' This is necessary to flush the output buffer.
        If Not (fw Is Nothing) Then fw.Close()
    End Sub

    Sub DoTheRealJob()
        log("Start of program")
        :
        log("In the middle of the program.")
        ::
        log("End of program")
    End Sub
```

Delegates and Windows API Callbacks

Delegates can be effectively used to receive callback notifications from the Windows API. A *callback procedure* is a procedure in your program that another routine calls when it has something to notify. The callback mechanism is used by several Windows API functions, such as EnumWindows and EnumFonts, so you might be already familiar with it. For example, the EnumWindows API function enumerates all the upper top-level windows in the system and calls the caller back for each window found. The program can then use the callback routine to do something useful with that piece of information. This approach promotes code reuse in that one single API function (EnumWindows, in this case) can be called for several tasks, such as displaying the list of windows in a ListBox control, filling a TreeView control with the window tree, or just checking that a given window is open. TheThe actual action depends on the callback procedure you specify when you call the EnumWindows function.

The callback mechanism is useful because it helps saving memory. If the EnumWindows function didn't rely on callback procedures, it would have to return its results in a large array, whereas the callback routine can consume the incoming data immediately without having to store it if the application's logic doesn't require it. In addition, a callback implementation often provides a way for the callback routine to stop the enumeration once the value searched for has been found, so the callback mechanism can also save CPU time.

Visual Basic 6 applications can call EnumWindows, EnumFonts, and other Enum*xxxx* functions in the Windows API by passing them the address of a local callback function (using the AddressOf operator). This technique is unsafe because the application crashes if your callback routine doesn't adopt the expected syntax for arguments and return values. (You can learn about the expected syntax of Enum*xxxx* procedures from the Windows SDK documentation.)

Visual Basic .NET lets you call any Windows API function that works with callback procedures, but you must adopt a different syntax based on—you guessed it—delegates. First you must specify a delegate that defines the syntax of the callback routine:

```
' This is the syntax that the EnumWindows callback procedure
' must adhere to.
Delegate Function EnumWindows_Callback(ByVal hWnd As Integer, _
    ByVal lParam As Integer) As Integer
```

Next you must write a Declare statement for the API function. This statement defines the callback procedure in terms of the preceding delegate (instead of a 32-bit routine address, as is the case under Visual Basic 6):

```
Declare Function EnumWindows Lib "user32" ( _
    ByVal lpEnumFunc As EnumWindows_Callback, _
    ByVal lParam As Integer) As Integer
```

Finally, you can write the actual callback function and pass its address to the first argument of EnumWindows. The delegate definition forces you to pass the address of a procedure that adheres to the delegate's syntax; hence, the Visual Basic .NET approach is inherently safer than that of Visual Basic 6's, even though the call syntax is exactly the same:

```
Sub TestAPICallback()
    EnumWindows(AddressOf EnumWindows_CBK, 0)
End Sub

' The second argument to the callback function is ignored in
' this demo--in a real application, it helps discern the
' reason why this procedure has been called.
Function EnumWindows_CBK(ByVal hWnd As Integer, _
    ByVal lParam As Integer) As Integer
    ' Display the handle of this top-level window.
    Console.WriteLine(hWnd))
    ' Return 1 to continue enumeration.
    Return 1
End Function
```

The preceding piece of code displays the 32-bit handle of all the top-level windows in the system. The complete demo on the companion CD shows how you can use delegates with the EnumWindows and EnumChildWindows API functions in a recursive fashion to display the handle and other pieces of information about all the open windows in the system.

Implementing Callback Procedures

As I mentioned in the preceding section, Visual Basic 6 lets you *pass* the address of a routine in your application to an API function that works with a callback procedure. However, you can't write a procedure that *receives* the address of a routine and uses it to invoke the corresponding routine in plain Visual Basic 6 (that is, without resorting to some sort of hack). In other words, you can't create a reusable procedure in Visual Basic 6 that calls back its caller. The closest approximation in Visual Basic 6 to the callback technique is based on events and secondary interfaces or on the CallByName command. (And you can't use any of these techniques if the callback procedure is in a standard BAS module.)

Delegates offer a clean, efficient, and safe solution to this problem in Visual Basic .NET. In fact, you can write a routine that takes a delegate as an argument, and the routine can call the caller through the delegate when there's something to report. You decide whether the caller can return a special value to the routine—through a ByRef argument or the delegate's return value—to stop whatever the routine is doing.

The following code shows a TraverseDirectoryTree procedure that scans an entire directory tree and calls back the caller for each new directory found. The structure of this procedure is slightly complicated by its recursive nature and the need to preserve the value of the Canceled static variable but reset it before returning to the caller:

```
' This is a delegate that defines the syntax of the function whose address
' can be passed to TraverseDirectoryTree.
' If this function returns True, the enumeration should be stopped.
Delegate Function TraverseDirectoryTree_CBK(ByVal dirName As String) _
    As Boolean

' The following is a reusable procedure that traverses a directory tree
' and calls back the caller for each new directory.
Sub TraverseDirectoryTree(ByVal path As String, _
    ByVal callback As TraverseDirectoryTree_CBK)
    Dim dirName As String
    Static nestLevel As Integer      ' Nesting level
    Static isCanceled As Boolean     ' True if client canceled the enumeration.

    nestLevel += 1                   ' Entering this nesting level.

    For Each dirName In System.IO.Directory.GetDirectories(path)
        ' Call back the program to notify this directory.
        isCanceled = callback.Invoke(dirName)
        ' Exit the loop if the client canceled the enumeration.
        If isCanceled Then Exit For
        ' Otherwise, call this routine recursively.
        TraverseDirectoryTree(dirName, callback)
```

(continued)

```
    Next

    nestLevel -= 1                 ' Exiting this nesting level.
    ' Reset isCanceled if we are about to return to the user.
    ' (Otherwise the nextx call won't work correctly.)
    If nestLevel = 0 Then isCanceled = False
End Sub
```

Using this procedure is straightforward:

```
Sub TestCallbacks()
    ' Print the name of all the directories under c:\DOCS, but stop
    ' as soon as the C:\DOCS\PROGRAMMINGVB6 directory is found.
    TraverseDirectoryTree("C:\DOCS", AddressOf DisplayDirectoryName)
End Sub

' A function that complies with the TraverseDirectoryTree_CBK syntax
Function DisplayDirectoryName(ByVal path As String) As Boolean
    Console.WriteLine(path)
    ' Stop when the C:\DOCS\PROGRAMMINGVB6 directory has been reached.
    If path = "C:\DOCS\PROGRAMMINGVB6" Then Return True
End Function
```

Multicast Delegates

You can get extra flexibility using multicast delegates, which can dispatch a call to more than just one procedure. You can do this by taking two delegates of the same type and combining them to create a new delegate that invokes both the procedures pointed to by the original delegate objects. You can have a multicast delegate point to either a Sub or a Function, but it should be clear that when a delegate performs a chain of calls to functions, only the return value from the last function in the series is returned to the caller.

> **Note** Early beta versions of .NET made a distinction between single-cast delegates and multicast delegates, where the latter ones could point only to Sub procedures, on the grounds that the return value from all called procedures except the last one would be lost. In the release version, this limitation has been lifted, and now all delegates are actually multicast delegates (and in fact inherit from System.MulticastDelegate).

You combine two delegates into a multicast delegate by using the Combine shared method of the System.Delegate class and then assigning the result to a delegate variable of the same type. This target variable can be one of the two original delegate variables or a third delegate variable of the proper type:

```
' Define two distinct delegates.
Dim log As LogWriter = New LogWriter(AddressOf Console.WriteLine)
Dim log2 As LogWriter = New LogWriter(AddressOf fw.WriteLine)
' Combine them into a multicast delegate.
log = System.Delegate.Combine(log, log2)
```

Because shared methods are exposed by object instances, you can also combine two delegates as follows:

```
log = log.Combine(log, log2)
```

You can make your code more concise if you create the second delegate on the fly:

```
log = log.Combine(log, New LogWriter(AddressOf fw.WriteLine))
```

There's one problem, however: if the Option Strict option is On, Visual Basic prevents you from assigning the result of the Combine method (which returns a generic Delegate) to a variable of a different type. So you must cast explicitly, using the CType or DirectCast function:

```
' We need this statement if Option Strict is On.n
log = DirectCast(log.Combine(log, New LogWriter(AddressOf fw.WriteLine)), _
    LogWriter)
```

The following is a variant of the procedure you saw previously. In this case, the code always logs to the console, and it also writes log messages to a file if an argument is specified on the command line:

```
Sub TestMultiCastDelegate()
    ' Always log to the console.
    log = New LogWriter(AddressOf Console.WriteLine)
    ' Prepare another delegate.
    Dim log2 As LogWriter

    ' Get command-line arguments.
    Dim args() As String = Environment.GetCommandLineArgs

    If args.Length > 1 Then
        ' The command line contains a filename.
        fw = New System.IO.StreamWriter(args(1))
        ' Create another delegate pointing to the stream's WriteLine method.
        log2 = New LogWriter(AddressOf fw.WriteLine)
        ' Combine it on the fly with the existing delegate.
        log = DirectCast(log.Combine(log, log2), LogWriter)
    End If

    Call DoTheRealJob()
```

(continued)

```
    ' This is necessary to flush the output buffer.
    If Not (fw Is Nothing) Then fw.Close()
End Sub
```

The preceding code creates two distinct delegate objects and then combines them. Keeping the two delegates in separate variables makes it easier to remove them (using the Remove shared method) from the list that the multicast delegate maintains internally. Because Remove is a shared method, you can invoke it from any instance or by specifying the System.Delegate prefix name. The Remove method returns a multicast delegate that points to all the procedures originally in the delegate, minus the one being removed:

```
' Change the log delegate so that it doesn't log to the file any longer.
log = DirectCast(log.Remove(log, log2), LogWriter)
' This method only displays a log message on the console.
log("Application ended")
```

Multicast delegates have many traits in common with events. For example, the code that raises an event or invokes a delegate never knows how many calls will be actually performed. So it shouldn't surprise you that .NET events are internally implemented through multicast delegates. The two concepts are so close that you can define the syntax of an event in terms of a delegate:

```
' These two event declarations are equivalent.
Event LogToFile(ByVal msg As String)
Event LogToFile As LogWriter
```

As with events, if any called method throws an exception, any subsequent delegate in the chain won't be invoked and the exception is immediately reported to the code that called the delegate's Invoke method.

A relevant difference between the two mechanisms is that you can raise an event even if no listeners have been registered for that event, but you can't use a multicast delegate that doesn't contain at least one valid reference to a method. Also note that you can't use a delegate of Function type in the definition of an event, because event handlers can't have a return value.

A perfectly reasonable limitation of multicast delegates is that all the individual delegates you combine must have the same argument signature. However, nothing prevents you from combining variables from different delegate classes as long as these delegates have the same argument signature.

You can list all the individual delegate objects in a multicast delegate using the GetInvocationList method, which returns an array of System.Delegate objects. For example, the following code prints the name of the target for each delegate that has been combined in a multicast delegate:

```
' Note that Delegate is a reserved word and
' must be enclosed in square brackets.
```

```
' (Alternatively, you can use System.Delegate.)
Dim delegs() As [Delegate]
' Get the list of individual delegates in a multicast delegate.
delegs = log.GetInvocationList()

' List the names of all the target methods.
Dim d As [Delegate]
For Each d In delegs
    Console.WriteLine(d.Method.Name)
Next
```

You can make the preceding code more concise by using the GetInvocationList method directly in the For loop, as follows:

```
Dim d As [Delegate]
For Each d In log.GetInvocationList()
    Console.WriteLine(d.Method.Name)
Next
```

The GetInvocationList method is also useful when you don't maintain references to the individual delegates and you want to remove one of them:

```
' Remove the first delegate in the Log multicast delegate
log = DirectCast(log.Remove(log, log.GetInvocationList(0)), LogWriter)
```

Now you know all you need to know to work with delegates in your programs, but this isn't the last time that you'll see code based on delegates in this book.

In the preceding three chapters, you've seen all the Visual Basic .NET object-oriented features in action and examined the many traps you must guard against when porting your code from Visual Basic 6. Before you can get your hands dirty with the .NET Framework and the objects it offers you, you have to learn about attributes, the topic of the next chapter.

Front
Top
Left
Back

7

Attributes

The *attribute* is a new concept in programming and is used virtually everywhere in the .NET Framework. The underlying idea is that—regardless of the language you're using—some aspects of your application can't be expressed with plain executable statements. For example, consider these:

- In Visual Basic 6, the description of a class or a UserControl module and other pieces of information, such as the value for HelpContextID associated with individual properties or methods, are entered in the Member Attributes window. These values are saved in the .cls or .ctl file but don't appear in the code window.
- Instancing, transactional, and databinding behaviors for Visual Basic 6 classes are defined in the Properties window. These values are saved in the .cls file and don't appear in the code window.
- Projectwide properties, such as the project's description and companion help file, are defined in the Project Properties window and are stored in the VBP file.
- Other attributes for COM components and interfaces, such as their GUIDs, can be defined in a separate IDL file that you then feed to the type-library compiler. (Most Visual Basic developers don't go that far; they let the language create GUIDs transparently. But C++ programmers have to worry about this detail.)
- C/C++ developers use pragma directives to fine-tune the compiler behavior—for example, to turn on and off specific optimization or to control the kinds of warnings the compiler emits.

As you see, there isn't any consistency in how these attributes are associated with code; each language has its own way of associating information with code, and different types of information often require different techniques, even within the same language. Worse, you can't extend these techniques and create custom attributes for your own purposes. For example, say you want to create a new attribute that states who authored or revised a component or one of its methods so that you can query the component to retrieve this information. Unfortunately, I can't think of any traditional, mainstream language in which you can do that.

.NET attributes can solve all these problems and offer a streamlined, standardized way to associate additional information with specific pieces of code. Different languages use a slightly different syntax for attributes, but there's a unified mechanism for querying a data type for all the attributes associated with it. Even better, attributes are themselves a data type, and you can create your own custom attribute by simply creating a new class that inherits from System.Attribute.

Attribute Syntax

You can consider attributes annotations that you intersperse throughout your code. You can apply attributes to nearly every programming entity that Visual Basic .NET supports, including classes, modules, structures, properties, methods, and enumeration blocks. Not all attributes can be applied to all entities, but the general syntax you use for inserting an attribute is consistent within each .NET language. For example, all Visual Basic .NET attributes require an identical syntax, which differs from C# syntax.

Under Visual Basic .NET, you enclose an attribute in angle brackets (<>) and insert it immediately before the item to which it refers. For example, you can apply System.ComponentModel.DescriptionAttribute to a class as follows:

```
<System.ComponentModel.DescriptionAttribute("Person")> Class Person
    ⋮
End Class
```

You can simplify attribute syntax in many ways. First, because attributes are .NET classes, you can shorten an attribute name by using a suitable Imports statement. Second, .NET guidelines dictate that the names of all attribute classes end with *Attribute*, but most .NET compilers, including Visual Basic and C#, let you drop *Attribute* from the name. Finally, you can break long lines using the underscore character to make code more readable. After applying these three rules, our initial example becomes

```
Imports System.ComponentModel
```

```
<Description("Person")> _
Class Person
    ⋮
End Class
```

Attributes are rather peculiar .NET classes: they support properties and methods, but you can't reference them in code as you would do with regular classes. In fact, most of the time you set one or more properties only when you create the attribute, and those properties don't change during the application's lifetime.

The syntax seen in the preceding code snippet is actually a call to the Description attribute's constructor method, which takes the value of the Description property as an argument. Once this property has been set, it isn't changed or queried, at least not by the application that uses the attribute. The properties of specific attributes can be queried, however, by the compiler or the .NET Framework, by using reflection, as you'll see in Chapter 15. Because of their nature, few attribute classes, if any, have methods other than the constructor method.

An attribute's constructor method takes zero or more arguments; it can also take optional *named* arguments. Named arguments allow you to set additional properties not required in the constructor. The following section shows you an example of this syntax.

Attributes for Visual Basic .NET

In this section, I focus on a few attributes that are related to language entities that I described in earlier chapters.

The StructLayout Attribute

Visual Basic .NET defines a couple of attributes that let you control how the elements of a Structure block are arranged in memory and how the runtime should marshal them when they're passed to a function in an external DLL (typically, a Windows DLL).

Members of Visual Basic structures are arranged in memory in the order they appear in source code, even though the compiler is free to insert padding bytes to arrange members so that 16-bit values are aligned with word boundaries, 32-bit values are aligned with double-word boundaries, and so on. This arrangement—known as *unpacked* layout—delivers the best performance because Intel processors work faster with aligned data.

Visual Basic 6 user-defined structures are unpacked, and you can't change this default setting. Visual Basic .NET lets you change this setting, and you can finely control where each structure member is located by means of the System.Runtime.InteropServices.StructLayout attribute. The allowed values for this attribute are StructLayout.Auto (the compiler can reorder elements for best performance, for example by grouping value types together), StructLayout.Sequential (elements are laid out and properly aligned sequentially in memory), and StructLayout.Explicit:

```
' A convenient Imports statement to make the code more concise
Imports System.Runtime.InteropServices

<StructLayout(LayoutKind.Explicit)> _
Structure ARGBColor
    ⋮
End Structure
```

The StructLayout attribute supports three additional fields: CharSet, Pack, and Size. CharSet defines how string members in the structure are marshaled when the structure is passed to a DLL and can be Unicode, Ansi, or Auto. The default value is Auto, which means that strings are marshaled as Unicode strings under Windows NT, Windows 2000, or Windows XP and as ANSI strings on Windows 95, Windows 98, and Windows Me.

The Pack field defines the packing size for the structure, and can be 1, 2, 4, 8, 16, 32, 64, 128, or the special value 0 that uses the default packing size for the current platform; the default is 8 bytes. A structure whose LayoutKind is Sequential always aligns elements to this number of bytes. The Size field is significant only for compiler writers, so I won't cover it.

You won't often change these default settings in your applications, but it's interesting to see the syntax for setting these optional values in the attribute's constructor, which mimics the way you pass named optional arguments to procedures:

```
<StructLayout(LayoutKind.Sequential, CharSet:=CharSet.Unicode, Pack:=4)> _
Structure ARGBColor
    ⋮
End Structure
```

> **Note** The StructLayout attribute—as well as the FieldOffset and MarshalAs attributes, which are described in the following sections—are usually applied when you're passing a structure to unmanaged code in a DLL. These attributes can be applied to class and class elements too, even though this latter usage is far less frequent.

The FieldOffset Attribute

When you opt for an explicit layout, the definition of all the variables in a structure must include a FieldOffset attribute, whose argument specifies the distance in bytes from the beginning of the structure:

```
<StructLayout(LayoutKind.Explicit)> _
Structure ARGBColor
    <FieldOffset(0)> Dim Red As Byte
    <FieldOffset(1)> Dim Green As Byte
    <FieldOffset(2)> Dim Blue As Byte
    <FieldOffset(3)> Dim Alpha As Byte
End Structure
```

The StructLayout and the FieldOffset attributes let you implement a *union*, a language feature that many languages, such as C and C++, have had for years but that has always been out of reach for Visual Basic developers. A union is a structure in which two or more elements overlap in memory. Or, if you prefer, a union permits you to refer to the same memory location using different names. The key to unions in .NET is the support for explicit structure layout. Consider the following example:

```
<StructLayout(LayoutKind.Explicit)> _
Structure RGBColor
    <FieldOffset(0)> Dim Red As Byte
    <FieldOffset(1)> Dim Green As Byte
    <FieldOffset(2)> Dim Blue As Byte
    <FieldOffset(3)> Dim Alpha As Byte
    <FieldOffset(0)> Dim Value As Integer
End Structure
```

The following figure makes it clear how these elements are located in memory:

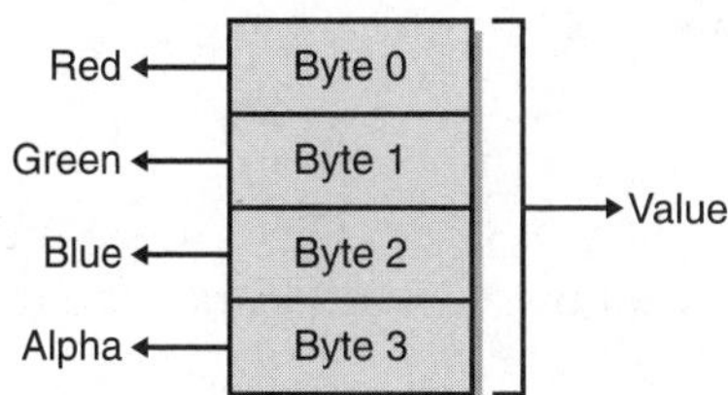

In other words, you can access the 4 bytes as a whole through the Value field, or individually through the Red, Green, Blue, and Alpha fields. The following code shows how useful this feature can be:

```
' Split a color into its components.
Dim rgb As RGBColor
rgb.Value = &H112233          ' This is equal to 1122867.
```

(continued)

```
Console.WriteLine("Red={0}, Green={1}, Blue={2}", _
    rgb.Red, rgb.Green, rgb.Blue)
    ' => Red=51, Green=34, Blue=17
```

Of course, you can also combine the three RGB components into a single color:

```
rgb.Red = 51
rgb.Green = 34
rgb.Blue = 17
Console.WriteLine("RGB color = {0}", rgb.Value)    ' => 1122867
```

Unions make it possible to implement some tricky conversion routines far more efficiently than using standard math operators. Consider the following structure:

```
<StructLayout(LayoutKind.Explicit)> _
Structure IntegerTypes
    ' A 64-bit integer
    <FieldOffset(0)> Dim Long0 As Long
    ' Two 32-bit integers
    <FieldOffset(0)> Dim Integer0 As Integer
    <FieldOffset(4)> Dim Integer1 As Integer
    ' Four 16-bit integers
    <FieldOffset(0)> Dim Short0 As Short
    <FieldOffset(2)> Dim Short1 As Short
    <FieldOffset(4)> Dim Short2 As Short
    <FieldOffset(6)> Dim Short3 As Short
    ' Eight 8-bit integers
    <FieldOffset(0)> Dim Byte0 As Byte
    <FieldOffset(1)> Dim Byte1 As Byte
    <FieldOffset(2)> Dim Byte2 As Byte
    <FieldOffset(3)> Dim Byte3 As Byte
    <FieldOffset(4)> Dim Byte4 As Byte
    <FieldOffset(5)> Dim Byte5 As Byte
    <FieldOffset(6)> Dim Byte6 As Byte
    <FieldOffset(7)> Dim Byte7 As Byte
End Structure
```

This structure takes exactly 8 bytes, but you can refer to those memory locations in multiple ways. For example, see how you can extract the low and high bytes of a 16-bit integer:

```
Dim it As IntegerTypes
it.Short0 = 517                    ' Hex 0205
Console.WriteLine(it.Byte0)        ' => 5
Console.WriteLine(it.Byte1)        ' => 2
```

Even better, you can extend the IntegerTypes structure with custom methods:

```
<StructLayout(LayoutKind.Explicit)> _
Structure IntegerTypes
    ' ...(Member declarations as before)...
    ⋮
    ' Low byte of a word
    Function LowByte(ByVal Value As Long) As Byte
        Long0 = Value
        Return Byte0
    End Function

    ' High byte of a word
    Function HighByte(ByVal Value As Long) As Byte
        Long0 = Value
        Return Byte1
    End Function

    ' Low word of a double word
    Function LowWord(ByVal Value As Long) As Short
        Long0 = Value
        Return Short0
    End Function

    ' High word of a double word
    Function HighWord(ByVal Value As Long) As Short
        Long0 = Value
        Return Short1
    End Function
End Structure
```

Using these methods is straightforward:

```
Console.WriteLine(it.LowByte(517))          ' => 5
Console.WriteLine(it.HighByte(517))         ' => 2
Console.WriteLine(it.LowWord(&HFFFF1000))   ' => 4096
Console.WriteLine(it.HighWord(&HFFFF1000))  ' => -1
```

This technique works also if the structure members are declared as Private. However, you should use it only with integer member types, such as Byte, Short, Integer, and Long; trying to interpret locations as Single or Double values often returns the special NaN (Not-a-Number) value. Trying to map a reference type (such as a string) throws an exception because the Visual Basic .NET compiler rejects structures where reference types overlap with other members or aren't aligned properly.

The DllImport Attribute

In Chapter 3, I explained that you can use the Declare statement to call a procedure in an external DLL. However, Visual Basic .NET provides another, more modern construct based on the DllImport attribute. In this case, you provide a method signature without any implementation code and qualify it with a DllImport attribute to let the compiler know that the actual implementation can be found in the specified DLL.

The following code rewrites the example you saw in Chapter 3, this time using the DllImport attribute applied to standard methods rather than using Declare statements:

```
' Note that this code works even though the actual procedure
' is named FindWindowA because the compiler tracks it automatically.
<DllImport("user32")> Function FindWindow(ByVal lpClassName As String, _
    ByVal lpWindowName As String) As Integer
    ' No implementation code
End Function

<DllImport("user32")> Function MoveWindow _
    (ByVal hWnd As Integer, ByVal x As Integer, ByVal y As Integer, _
    ByVal nWidth As Integer, ByVal nHeight As Integer, _
    ByVal bRepaint As Integer) As Integer
    ' No implementation code
End Function

Sub TestDllImport()
    ' NOTE: open Notepad with an empty document before running this code.
    ' (This code assumes you're running English or U.S.
    ' version of Windows.)
    Dim hWnd As Integer = FindWindow(Nothing, "Untitled - Notepad")
    ' If found, resize it and move it to upper left corner.
    If hWnd<>0 then MoveWindow(hWnd, 0, 0, 600, 300, 1)
End Sub
```

The DllImport attribute supports several optional named arguments that let you precisely define how the external procedure should be called and how it returns a value to the caller:

- The CharSet argument tells how strings are passed to the external routine; it can be CharSet.Ansi (the default), CharSet.Unicode, or CharSet.Auto. This argument has the same meaning as the Ansi, Unicode, or Auto qualifier in the Declare statement. (See Chapter 3 for more details.) The Ansi setting appends the letter *A* to the function name; the Unicode setting appends the letter *W* to the function name (unless ExactSpelling is True; see next point).

- The ExactSpelling argument is a Boolean value that determines whether the method name must match exactly the name in the DLL; if True (the default setting), the CharSet setting has no effect on the name of the function being searched.
- The EntryPoint argument specifies the actual function name in the DLL and is therefore equivalent to the Alias clause in a Declare statement. As the preceding example demonstrates, you don't need to use this argument when the entry point name differs from the method name only in a trailing *A* if CharSet.Ansi is implicitly or explicitly used. In practice, you use this argument only when the entry point name is an invalid or reserved name in Visual Basic (such as Friend), when it duplicates a name already defined in the application, or when it's an ordinal entry point (such as *#123*).
- The CallingConvention argument specifies the calling convention for the entry point. Available values are WinApi (the default), CDecl, FastCall, StdCall, and ThisCall.
- The SetLastError argument tells whether the called function sets the Win32 last error code (if True), which you can later read using the Err.LastDllError method or the Marshal.GetLastWin32Error method. If the value is True (the default in Visual Basic .NET), the compiler has to emit additional code that saves the last error code, so you should set the value to False if possible and let the compiler produce more efficient code. (Using this argument is one of the reasons why you might prefer the DllImport attribute to the Declare statement, which is slightly less efficient because it saves the error code in all cases.)
- The PreserveSig argument is a Boolean value that, if True, tells the compiler that the method shouldn't be transformed into a function that returns an HRESULT value.

The following example shows how you can use the DllImport attribute to call a method named Friend in a DLL named myfunctions.dll, which takes Unicode strings and affects the Win32 last error code:

```
' We must use an aliased name because Compare is a reserved keyword.
<DllImport("myfunctions.dll", EntryPoint:="Friend", _
    CharSet:=CharSet.Unicode, SetLastError:=True)> _
Function MakeFriends(ByVal s1 As String, ByVal s2 As String) As Integer
    ' No implementation code
End Function
```

The Conditional Attribute

Visual Basic has always offered a way to include or exclude pieces of code in the compiled code, using #If directives. All the techniques based on compiler directives have a weak point, which is apparent in the following piece of code:

```
#If LOG Then
    Sub LogMsg(ByVal MsgText As String)
        Console.WriteLine(MsgText)
    End Sub
#End If

    Sub Main()
        LogMsg("Program is starting")
        ⋮
        LogMsg("Program is ending")
    End Sub
```

Clearly you can exclude the LogMsg procedure from the compiled code by simply setting the LOG constant to a zero value, but you would get many compile errors if you did so because all the calls to that procedure would be unresolved. The only way to deal with this problem (short of adding one #If statement for each call to LogMsg) is to exclude just the body of the procedure itself:

```
    Sub LogMsg(ByVal MsgText As String)
#If LOG Then
        Console.WriteLine(MsgText)
#End If
    End Sub
```

This solution is clearly unsatisfactory, however, because it doesn't avoid the overhead of all the calls to the empty LogMsg procedure. Visual Basic .NET (and other .NET languages, such as C#) offers a much cleaner solution, based on the Conditional attribute:

```
<Conditional("LOG")> _
Sub LogMsg(ByVal MsgText As String)
    Console.WriteLine(MsgText)
End Sub

Sub TestConditionalAttribute()
    LogMsg("Program is starting")
    ⋮
    LogMsg("Program is ending")
End Sub
```

The procedure marked with the Conditional attribute is always included in the compiled application; however, calls to it are included only if the specified compilation constant has been defined and has a nonzero value. Otherwise, these calls are discarded. This practice produces the most efficient code without forcing you to add too many directives to your listing.

You define application-wide compilation constants in the Build page of the project Property Pages dialog box, as shown in Figure 7-1. This dialog box lets you define a couple of often-used compilation constants, named DEBUG and TRACE, with a click of the mouse, as you might remember from the section "Tracing Application Behavior" in Chapter 3. For the task at hand, you might have used the TRACE constant instead of your custom LOG constant.

Because the compiler can drop all the calls to the target method—LogMsg, in the preceding example—the Conditional attribute works only with procedures that don't return a value and is ignored when applied to Function procedures. If you want to use the Conditional attribute with a procedure that should return a value to the caller, you must use a Sub procedure with ByRef arguments.

One more thing about the Conditional attribute: it allows multiple definitions, which means that you can specify a number of Conditional attributes for the same method. In this case, calls to the method are included in the compiled application if *any* of the mentioned compilation constants have a nonzero value:

```
<Conditional("LOG"), Conditional("TRACE")> _
Sub LogMsg(ByVal MsgText As String)
    Console.WriteLine(MsgText)
End Sub
```

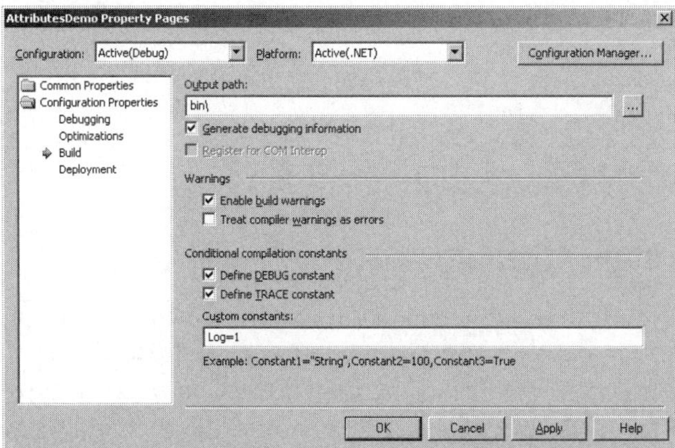

Figure 7-1. The Build page of the project Property Pages dialog box lets you define application-wide compilation constants.

The Obsolete Attribute

Let's say that you inherited a nontrivial project and your job is to improve its performance by rewriting some portions of it. Consider the following procedure:

```
Sub BubbleSort(arr() As String)
    ⋮
End Sub
```

BubbleSort isn't very efficient, so you create a new sort routine based on a more efficient sort algorithm (or just use the Array.Sort method) and start replacing all calls to BubbleSort. You don't want to perform a straight find-and-replace operation, however, because you want to double-check each call. In the end, the BubbleSort routine will be deleted, but you can't do it right now because some portions of the application won't compile. The framework offers a simple solution to this recurring situation in the form of the Obsolete attribute. The constructor method for this attribute can take no arguments, one argument (the warning message), or two arguments (the message and a Boolean value that indicates whether the message is to be considered a compilation error):

```
' Mark BubbleSort as obsolete.
<Obsolete("Replace BubbleSort with ShellSort")> _
Sub BubbleSort(arr() As String)
    ⋮
End Sub
```

The following variant also causes the BubbleSort routine to appear as a compilation error:

```
' Mark BubbleSort as obsolete.
<Obsolete("Replace BubbleSort with ShellSort", True)> _
Sub BubbleSort(arr() As String)
    ⋮
End Sub
```

The DebuggerStepThrough Attribute

You can use the System.Diagnostics.DebuggerStepThrough attribute to mark a routine that should be skipped over by the Visual Studio .NET debugger because it must run as a whole or just because it has been already tested and debugged. The form designer uses this attribute for the InitializeComponent procedure:

```
<System.Diagnostics.DebuggerStepThrough()> _
Private Sub InitializeComponent()
    ⋮
End Sub
```

Custom Attributes

Most of the time, you'll use only predefined attributes that are defined in the .NET Framework and documented in the .NET SDK documentation. Occasionally, however, you might want to define your own custom attributes, and this section tells you how to do it.

Building a Custom Attribute Class

A custom attribute is nothing but a class that satisfies the following requirements:

- Its name ends with *Attribute.*
- It inherits from System.Attribute.
- It contains an AttributeUsage attribute that tells the compiler what program entities this attribute class can be applied to (classes, modules, methods, and so on).
- It contains a constructor method that specifies the mandatory arguments to be passed to the attribute and any field or property whose value can be passed as an optional named argument when an instance of the attribute is created. (An attribute class can also contain multiple overloaded constructors.)
- It contains fields, properties, and methods that accept and return values only of the following types: Boolean, Byte, Short, Integer, Long, Char, Single, Double, String, Object, System.Type, and public Enum. (It can also receive and return one-dimensional arrays of one of the preceding types.)

The following example shows a custom attribute class that lets you annotate any class or class member with the name of the author, the source code version when the member was completed, and an optional property that specifies whether the code has been reviewed:

```
' The AttributeTargets.All value means that this attribute
' can be used with any program entity.
<AttributeUsage(AttributeTargets.All)> _
Class VersioningAttribute
    ' All attribute classes inherit from System.Attribute.
    Inherits System.Attribute

    ' These should be Property procedures in a real application,
    ' but fields are OK in this demo.
    Public Author As String
    Public Version As Single
    Public Tested As Boolean
```

(continued)

```
    ' The Attribute constructor takes two required values.
    Sub New(ByVal Author As String, ByVal Version As Single)
        Me.Author = Author
        Me.Version = Version
    End Sub
End Class
```

The argument passed to the AttributeUsage attribute specifies that the VersioningAttribute attribute—or just Versioning because the trailing Attribute portion of the name can always be omitted—can be used with any program entity. The argument you pass to the AttributeUsage's constructor is a bit-coded value formed by adding one or more elements listed in Table 7-1. (This value corresponds to the ValidOn property of the AttributeUsageAttribute class defined in the .NET Framework.)

Table 7-1 All Possible Values for the AttributeTarget Argument in the AttributeUsage Constructor Method

Enumerated Value	Numeric Value (Hex)	Applies To
Assembly	1	Current program assembly
Module	2	Current program file
Class	4	Classes
Struct	8	Structures
Enum	10	Enum blocks
Constructor	20	Constructor methods
Method	40	Methods (member functions)
Property	80	Properties
Field	100	Fields
Event	200	Events
Interface	400	Interfaces
Parameter	800	Method parameters
Delegate	1000	Delegates
ReturnValue	2000	Method return values
All	3FFF	Everything

The AttributeUsage attribute supports two additional properties, which can be passed as named arguments in the constructor method. The AllowMultiple property specifies whether the attribute being defined—VersioningAttribute, in our case—can be used multiple times inside angle brackets. The Inherited attribute tells whether a derived class inherits the attribute. The default value for both properties is False.

The Conditional attribute, which I described earlier in this chapter, is an example of an attribute that supports multiple instances and is also an example of an attribute that's inherited by derived classes. If the Conditional attribute class were implemented in Visual Basic, its source code would be more or less as follows:

```
<AttributeUsage(AttributeTargets.Method, _
    AllowMultiple:=True, Inherited:=True)> _
Class ConditionalAttribute
    ' All attribute classes inherit from System.Attribute.
    Inherits System.Attribute

    Private m_ConditionString As String

    ' The constructor method
    Sub New(ByVal ConditionString As String)
        Me.ConditionString = ConditionString
    End Sub

    ' The only property of this attribute class
    Property ConditionString() As String
        Get
            Return m_ConditionString
        End Get
        Set(ByVal Value As String)
            m_ConditionString = Value
        End Set
    End Property
End Class
```

Discovering Attributes at Run Time

Creating a custom attribute class would hardly be useful if you couldn't list the custom attributes that you added to your source code. The classes in the System.Reflection namespace help you keep track of your custom attributes. Reflection plays an important role in the .NET Framework and does a lot more than offer support for custom attributes. I explain reflection in detail in Chapter 15, but for now I'll give you an example of code that uses reflection classes to find and list all the custom attributes inserted in your code.

Here's a class that contains some Versioning attributes:

```
<Versioning("John", 1.01)> _
Class TestClass
    <Versioning("Robert", 1.01, Tested:=True)> _
    Sub MyProc()
        ⋮
    End Sub
```

(continued)

```
    <Versioning("Ann", 1.02)> _
    Function MyFunction() As Long
        ⋮
    End Function
End Class
```

The following procedure shows how you can use reflection to list the Versioning attributes for the class and its methods:

```
Sub TestListVersioningAttributes()
    Dim attributes() As Object
    Dim att As VersioningAttribute
    Dim method As System.Reflection.MethodInfo
    ' Get the System.Type for the attribute and the explored class.
    Dim attType As Type = GetType(VersioningAttribute)
    Dim classType As Type = GetType(TestClass)

    ' Retrieve all the custom attributes of type VersioningAttribute.
    attributes = Attribute.GetCustomAttributes(classType, attType)

    ' Check whether the array contains an element.
    ' (It should contain one.)
    If attributes.Length > 0 Then
        ' Move to a specific type so that we can use early binding.
        att = DirectCast(attributes(0), VersioningAttribute)
        ' Display versioning information on the TestClass itself.
        Console.WriteLine("Class TestClass")
        Console.WriteLine("  Author = " & att.Author)
        Console.WriteLine("  Version = " & att.Version.ToString)
        Console.WriteLine("  Tested = " & att.Tested.ToString)
    End If

    ' Iterate over all the methods in TestClass.
    For Each method In classType.GetMethods
        ' Get Versioning attributes for this method.
        attributes = Attribute.GetCustomAttributes(method, attType)
        ' If there are custom Versioning attributes
        If attributes.Length > 0 Then
            ' Get a Versioning object to use early binding.
            att = DirectCast(attributes(0), VersioningAttribute)
            ' Display the name of this method.
            Console.WriteLine("Method " & method.Name)
            ' Display versioning information on this method.
            Console.WriteLine("  Author = " & att.Author)
            Console.WriteLine("  Version = " & att.Version.ToString)
            Console.WriteLine("  Tested = " & att.Tested.ToString)
        End If
    Next
End Sub
```

Here's the result displayed in the Output window:

```
Class TestClass
  Author = John
  Version = 1.01
  Tested = False
Method MyProc
  Author = Robert
  Version = 1.01
  Tested = True
Method MyFunction
  Author = Ann
  Version = 1.02
  Tested = False
```

The GetCustomAttributes method isn't the only way of discovering attributes in a .NET assembly, and for sure it isn't the most efficient one. For example, it returns an array of attributes because it must be able to work with attributes that allow multiple instances for each code element—that is, attributes for which AllowMultiple is True, as is the case of our custom VersioningAttribute class. When you deal with attributes that allow only one instance at a time, you can use the simpler and more efficient GetCustomAttribute method, which returns either the found attribute or Nothing. If the VersioningAttribute class were defined with AllowMultiple equal to False, you could simplify the body of the TestListVersioningAttributes procedure as follows:

```
' Retrieve the only custom attribute of type VersioningAttribute.
att = DirectCast(Attribute.GetCustomAttribute(classType, attType) _
    , VersioningAttribute)
    ' Check whether we found an attribute.
If Not (att Is Nothing) Then
    ' Display versioning information on the TestClass itself.
    ⋮
End If

For Each method In classType.GetMethods
    ' Get the Versioning attribute for this method.
    att = DirectCast(Attribute.GetCustomAttribute( _
        method, attType), VersioningAttribute)
    ' If there are custom Versioning attributes
    If Not (att Is Nothing) Then
        ' Display name and versioning information of this method.
        ⋮
    End If
Next
```

Both the GetCustomAttributes and GetCustomAttribute methods work by actually instantiating the attribute object—as you can verify by inserting a Debug.WriteLine statement in the attribute's constructor method—so they perform relatively slowly. If you just have to check whether an attribute is present, you can use the IsDefined shared method, which doesn't instantiate the attribute and is therefore slightly faster:

```
' Check whether VersioningAttribute is defined for the TestClass.
' (Assumes that classType and attType are defined as in preceding
'  code snippets.)
If Attribute.IsDefined(classType, attType) Then
    ⋮
End If
```

One last word about these three shared methods of the Attribute class: you can use them to check both custom attributes and attributes defined in the .NET Framework, such as the Conditional and the DebuggerStepThrough attributes. However, to optimize memory usage, the .NET runtime stores the information about a few common attributes—such as the DllImport, StructLayout, and FieldOffset attributes—in the assembly's metadata using a different format, and therefore you can't retrieve them by using the technique seen in this section. (But you can usually access these special attributes by means of other reflection properties, such as the IsSerializable and the IsLayoutSequential properties, as you'll learn in Chapter 15.)

This chapter concludes our long journey across the Visual Basic .NET language and the new object-oriented extensions. Now you have all the tools you need to start your explorations of the .NET Framework, to see how you can write powerful applications easily with the many classes that it gives to developers.

Part III

Programming the .NET Framework

Front
Top
Left
Back

8

.NET Framework Basic Types

The .NET Framework exposes hundreds of different classes to accomplish such jobs as opening files, parsing XML, and updating databases. As a Visual Basic developer, you're accustomed to working with libraries of objects that perform tasks whose implementation in plain Visual Basic would be impractical: just think of the Data Access Objects (DAO), Remote Data Objects (RDO), ActiveX Data Objects (ADO), and FileSystemObject libraries you've used in these years to work with databases and files.

The .NET Framework is more than just a collection of useful objects: it's a well-structured object tree that also provides objects to *store* values such as numbers, dates, and strings. Everything in the .NET Framework is a class, and at the top of the object hierarchy sits the System.Object class.

The System.Object Type

All classes inherit—directly or indirectly—from System.Object, which means that you can always assign any object to a System.Object variable and never get a compilation or run-time error when you do so:

```
' Most .NET programs import the System namespace; therefore,
' you can drop the System prefix from the Object class name.
Dim o As Object = New AnyOtherClass()
```

Incidentally, note that the only thing in the .NET Framework that does *not* derive from System.Object is interfaces.

Public and Protected Methods

Because .NET classes inherit from System.Object (see Figure 8-1), all of them expose the five methods that System.Object exposes, namely:

- **Equals** An overridable method that checks whether the current object has the same value as the object passed as an argument. It returns True when two object references point to the same object instance, but many classes override this method to implement a different type of equality. For example, numeric classes override this method so that it returns True if the objects being compared have the same numeric value.
- **GetHashCode** An overridable method that returns a hash code for the object. This method is used when you use the object as a key for collections and hash tables. Ideally, the hash code should be unique for any given object instance so that you can check that two objects are "equal" by comparing their hash code, but this is seldom possible, and different objects might return the same hash code; a class can override this method to implement a different hash algorithm to improve performance when its objects are used as keys in collections. A class that overrides the Equals method should always override the GetHashCode method as well so that two equal objects also return the same hash code.
- **GetType** A method that returns a value that identifies the type of the object. The returned value is typically used in reflection operations. (See Chapter 15.)
- **ToString** An overridable method that returns the complete name of the class, for example, MyNamespace.MyClass. However, most classes redefine this method so that it returns a string that describes the value of the object. For example, basic types such as Integer, Double, and String override this method to return the object's numeric or string value. The ToString method is implicitly called when you pass an object to the Console.Write and Debug.Write methods. Interestingly, ToString is culture aware: for example, it uses a comma as the decimal separator if the current culture requires it.
- **ReferenceEquals** A shared method that takes two object arguments and returns True if they reference the same instance; thus, it corresponds to the Is operator in Visual Basic. This method is similar to the Equals method except that derived classes can't override it.

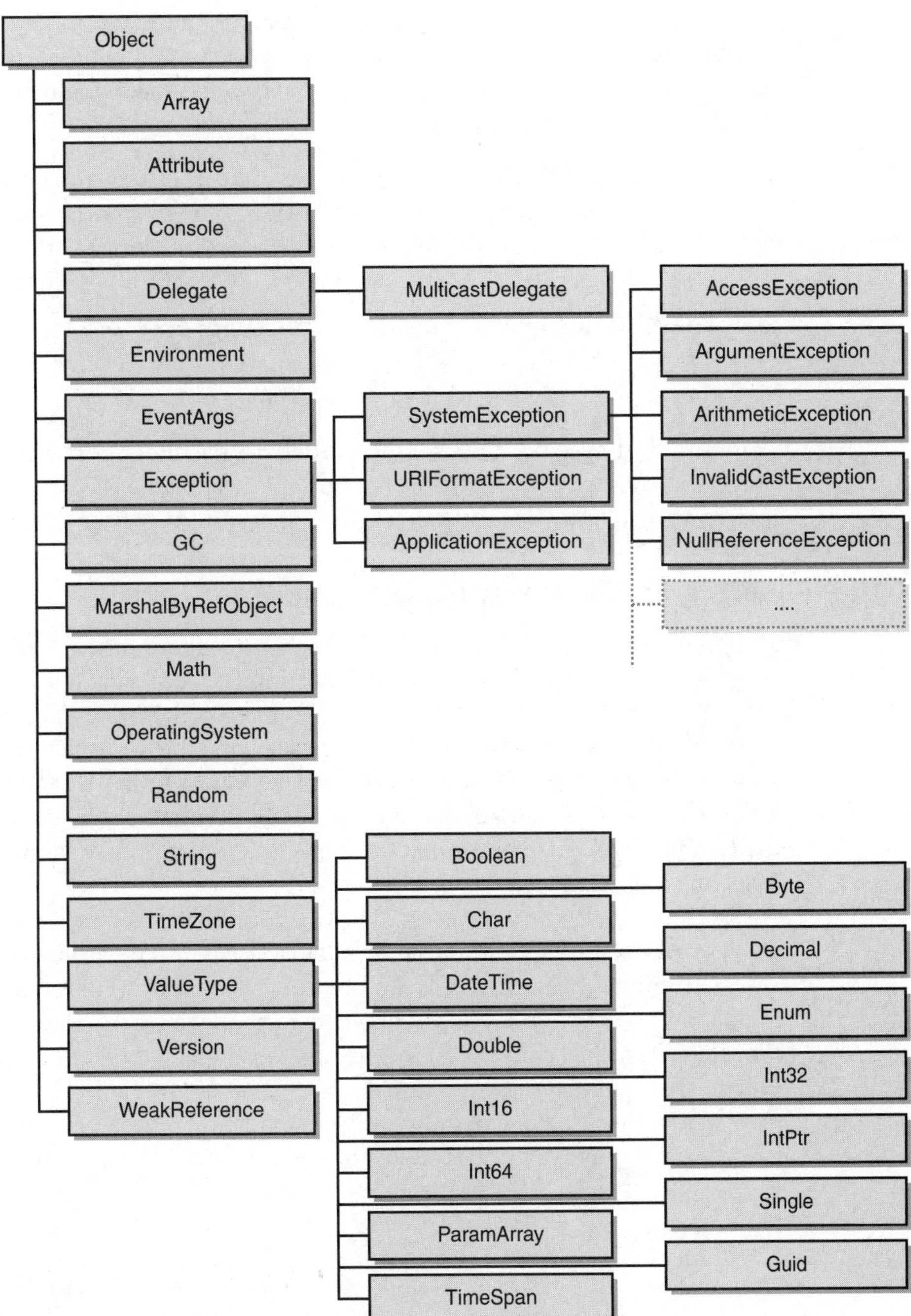

Figure 8-1. The most important classes in the System hierarchy.

The System.Object class also exposes two protected methods. Because everything in the .NET Framework derives directly or indirectly from System.Object, all the classes you write can invoke the following methods in their base class and can override them:

- **MemberwiseClone** A method that returns a new object of the same type and initializes the new object's fields and properties so that the new object can be considered a copy (a clone) of the current object.
- **Finalize** An overridable method that the .NET Framework calls when the object is garbage collected. (For more information about this method, see the section "Object Lifetime" in Chapter 4.)

The System class hierarchy includes all the most common and useful objects in the .NET Framework, including all the basic data types. The most important classes are depicted in Figure 8-1.

Value Types and Reference Types (Revisited)

Most basic data types (numbers, dates, and so on) in the .NET hierarchy inherit from System.ValueType and so have a common behavior. For example, System.ValueType overrides the Equals method and redefines equality so that two object references are considered equal if they have the same value (which is the way we usually compare numbers and dates) rather than if they point to the same instance. In addition, all classes deriving from System.ValueType override the GetHashCode method so that the hash code is created by taking the object's fields into account.

Classes that inherit from System.ValueType are commonly referred to as *value types*, to distinguish them from other classes, which are named *reference types*. All numeric and Enum types are value types. Note that the .NET documentation uses the term *type* to encompass the meaning of value and reference types. I follow that convention in this book and reserve the word *class* for reference types only.

Visual Basic .NET prevents you from explicitly inheriting from System.ValueType. The only way to create a value type is by creating a Structure block:

```
Structure PositionXY
    Dim X As Integer
    Dim Y As Integer
    ' Add here other fields, properties, methods, and interfaces.
    :
End Structure
```

Broadly speaking, value types are more efficient than reference types because their data isn't allocated in the managed heap and therefore isn't subject to garbage collection. For example, a value type declared in a procedure is allocated on the stack; when the procedure is exited, the value is simply discarded without making any extra work for the garbage collector. (The Finalize method is ignored in structures.) This description isn't strictly accurate if the Structure includes a member of reference type, though. Consider this new version of the PositionXY type:

```
Structure PositionXY
    Dim X As Integer
    Dim Y As Integer
    Dim Description As String     ' A reference type
    ⋮
End Structure
```

The garbage collector has to reclaim the memory used for the Description string member when such a structure is destroyed. In other words, value types are significantly faster than reference types only if they don't expose any members of a reference type.

Other factors might affect your choice of a value type or a reference type. You should use a Structure if your object acts like a primitive type and doesn't need to inherit special behaviors from other classes, and other classes don't need to derive from it. (Value classes are implicitly sealed and marked as NotInheritable.) Also, Structures can't be abstract and can't contain virtual methods.

A detail that might confuse many Visual Basic veterans is that the String class is a reference type, not a value type. (See Figure 8-1.) You can easily demonstrate this by assigning a String variable to another variable and then testing whether both variables point to the same object:

```
Sub TestStringsAreObjects()
    Dim s1 As String = "ABCD"
    Dim s2 As String = s1
    ' Prove that both variables point to the same object.
    Console.WriteLine(s1 Is s2)     ' => True
End Sub
```

.NET arrays are reference types too, and assigning an array to an Array variable copies only the object's reference, not the array contents. The Array class exposes the Clone method to let you make a (shallow) copy of its elements. (See the section "The ICloneable Interface" in Chapter 6 for a discussion of shallow and deep copy operations.)

Boxing and Unboxing

Even if performance is your primary concern, you shouldn't opt for value types in every situation because sometimes reference types are faster. For example, an assignment between value types involves the copy of every field in the object, whereas assigning a reference value to a variable requires only the copy of the object's address (4 bytes in 32-bit versions of Windows).

A different kind of performance hit occurs when you pass a value type to a method that expects an Object argument, because the value must be boxed in this case. As you might remember from the section "Value Types and Reference Types" in Chapter 2, *boxing a value* means that the compiler creates a copy of it in the managed heap and then assigns the address of this copy to an Object variable or argument so that the type can now be used as a reference type. A boxed value doesn't maintain a link to the original value, so you can modify either one without affecting the other.

If this boxed value is later assigned to a variable of the original (value) type, the object is said to be *unboxed* and data is copied from the managed heap into the memory allocated to the variable (for example, on the stack if it's a local variable). Not surprisingly, boxing and unboxing takes CPU time and eventually requires some memory to be reclaimed during a garbage collection. The bottom line: if you carry out many assignments or frequently perform operations that would result in a boxing and unboxing sequence, implementing a reference type might be a wiser choice.

Boxing occurs transparently in most cases, whereas you require an explicit CType function to convert back from an Object to a value type if Option Strict is On. You can determine whether a call causes a boxing operation by looking at the method's declaration in the object browser or in the class's documentation. If the method takes an argument of the type you're passing, no boxing occurs; if it takes a generic Object argument, your argument will be boxed. When creating your own methods, you might consider including overloaded variations that take arguments of different types as well as a catchall procedure that takes an Object argument.

In general, it doesn't make sense to compare the performance of a method that uses boxing with a similar method that doesn't. However, I prepared a simple benchmark that gives you a broad idea of what kind of overhead boxing and unboxing is going to add to your applications:

```
Sub TestBoxing()
    Dim i As Integer
    Dim start As Date
    Dim res As Integer

    ' Benchmark the version that does NOT use boxing.
    start = Now
    For i = 1 To 10000000
        res = GetInteger(i)
    Next
    Console.WriteLine("Without boxing: {0}", Now.Subtract(start))
```

```
    ' Benchmark the version that uses boxing and unboxing.
    start = Now
    For i = 1 To 10000000
        res = CInt(GetObject(i))
    Next
    Console.WriteLine("With boxing: {0}", Now.Subtract(start))
End Sub

Function GetInteger(ByVal n As Integer) As Integer
    Return n
End Function

Function GetObject(ByVal o As Object) As Object
    Return o
End Function
```

On my Pentium III 900-MHz machine, the first loop runs six times faster than the second loop (0.2 vs. 1.2 seconds), which makes it evident that boxing and unboxing should be avoided if possible. However, note that I had to repeat the loop 10 million times to get significant values, from which you can infer that a boxing and unboxing sequence takes approximately 100 nanoseconds on my machine, or in more general terms, 90 CPU cycles. (This time includes the time spent on intervening garbage collections.) Of course, results vary in accordance with the system on which you run the benchmark, but boxing and unboxing clearly won't significantly slow down most applications.

Sometimes you can change your code to help the compiler produce more efficient code. For example, if you repeatedly pass a value type to a method that takes an object (or a compatible reference type), you can speed things up by caching the value type in a reference variable and passing that reference variable instead.

The String Type

You saw in Chapter 2 that Visual Basic .NET supports the String data type, which maps to the System.String class. In earlier chapters, we used this class as a storage medium for string data exclusively and operated on them through string functions, such as Trim and Left, as we've done for years under previous versions of the language. However, the System.String class is much more powerful than what we've seen so far because it exposes methods that let you adopt a more object-oriented syntax and—in some cases—achieve better performance than old-style string functions.

To begin with, the String class exposes many overloaded constructor methods, so you can create a string in a variety of ways—for example, as a sequence of N same characters. (This technique duplicates the functionality of

Visual Basic 6's String function, which has been dropped because String is now a reserved keyword.)

```
' A sequence of <N> characters - similar to the VB6 String function
'    (Note the c suffix to make "A" a Char rather than a String.)
Dim s As New String("A"c, 10)                ' => AAAAAAAAAA

'  Another way to get the same result
s = New String(CChar("A"), 10)               ' => AAAAAAAAAA
```

Properties and Methods

The only properties of the String class are Length and Chars. The former returns the numbers of characters in the string and therefore corresponds to the Len function; the latter returns the character at a given index and is therefore similar to the Mid function when it extracts one character only:

```
Dim s As String = "ABCDEFGHIJ"
Console.WriteLine(s.Length)          ' => 10
' Note that index is always zero-based.
Console.WriteLine(s.Chars(3))        ' => D
```

Sometimes the reference nature of the String type causes behaviors you might not anticipate. For example, consider this simple code:

```
Dim s As String
Console.WriteLine(s.Length)
```

You probably expect that the second statement displays the value zero, but what actually happens is that this statement throws a NullReferenceException because the string object hasn't been initialized. A simple way to avoid this problem is to get into the habit of initializing all String variables explicitly, as in this code:

```
Dim s As String = ""
```

You can tap the power of the String class by invoking one of its many methods. I have listed its main methods in Table 8-1, with a brief description and the corresponding Visual Basic 6 function that returns the same result. I won't provide a code example for every method, but you can easily see that Visual Basic .NET strings are richer in functionality and let you adopt a more object-oriented, concise syntax in your applications. For example, see how much simpler and more readable the operation of inserting a substring is:

```
Dim s As String = "ABCDEFGHIJ"
' The VB6 way of inserting a substring after the third character
s = Left(s, 3) & "1234" & Mid(s, 4)

' The VB.NET object-oriented way to perform the same operation
s = s.Insert(3, "1234")      ' => ABC1234DEFGHIJ
```

Here's another example of the compactness that you can get by using the String methods. Let's say that you want to trim all the space and tab characters from the beginning of a string. This is the Visual Basic 6 solution:

```
s = "  A sentence to be trimmed  "
For i = 1 To Len(s)
    If InStr(" " & vbTab, Mid(s, i, 1)) = 0 Then
        ' Found a nonspace character: discard leading chars and exit.
        If i > 1 Then s = Mid(s, i)
        Exit For
    End If
Next
```

The Visual Basic .NET solution is simpler because you just have to load all the characters to be trimmed in an array of Chars and pass the array to the TrimStart function. (And you can use the same pattern with the TrimEnd and Trim functions.)

```
Dim cArr() As Char = { " "c, Chr(9) }
s = s.TrimStart(cArr)
```

In many cases, the new methods can deliver better performance because you can state more precisely what you're after. For example, you can determine whether a string begins with a given sequence of characters by a variety of means under Visual Basic 6, but none of the available techniques is very efficient:

```
' Check whether string S starts with the "abc" sequence.
' First approach: using the Left function
'   (Inefficient because it creates a temporary string)
If Left(s, 3) = "abc" Then ok = True
' Second approach: using the InStr function
'   (Inefficient if the search fails and S is a long string)
If InStr(s, "abc") = 1 Then ok = True
```

Visual Basic .NET strings solve this problem elegantly with the StartsWith method:

```
' The Visual Basic .NET solution
If s.StartsWith("abc") Then ok = True
```

The next example shows how to pad a string to the right with zeros so that the resulting length is 10 characters. This is the Visual Basic 6 solution:

```
' Append zeros if length is less than 10 (Visual Basic 6 code).
If Len(s) < 10 Then s = s & String(10 - Len(s), "0")
```

Here's the Visual Basic .NET solution, more concise and faster at the same time:

```
s = s.PadRight(10, "0"c)
```

Although most of the time you can use the newer methods to replace the old-style functions, you should pay attention to the subtle differences that can break your code:

- String indexes are always zero-based in Visual Basic .NET.
- PadLeft and PadRight are similar to the RSet and LSet commands, respectively, but they never trim the current string if it's longer than the requested number of characters.
- CompareTo is similar to the StrComp function but doesn't support case-insensitive comparisons; it considers empty strings greater than null references (Nothing).
- IndexOf and LastIndexOf are similar to the InStr and InStrRev functions, respectively, but don't support case-insensitive searches.

The String class also exposes a GetEnumerator method, which means that it supports enumeration of its own characters in a For Each loop:

```
Dim s As String = "ABCDE"
Dim c As Char
For Each c In s
    Console.Write(c & ".")          ' => A.B.C.D.E.
Next
```

However, iterating over individual characters of a long string in this way is significantly slower (in the range of two to five times) than extracting individual characters using the Chars property in a standard For loop. Microsoft has said that the speed of a For Each loop on a String will improve in future versions of the compiler.

Table 8-1 Instance Methods of the System.String Class

Syntax	Description
Clone	Returns a copy of the current string.
TrimStart ([chars])	Trims all the leading spaces from the string. If an array of characters is passed, it trims all the leading characters that are specified in the array. (Similar to the LTrim function.)
TrimEnd ([chars])	Trims all the trailing spaces from the string. If an array of characters is passed, it trims all the trailing characters that are specified in the array. (Similar to the RTrim function.)
Trim ([chars])	Trims all the leading and trailing spaces from the string. If an array of characters is passed, it trims all the leading and trailing characters that are specified in the array. (Similar to the Trim function.)

Table 8-1 Instance Methods of the System.String Class *(continued)*

Syntax	Description
StartsWith (prefix)	Returns True if the string passed as an argument is a prefix for the current string. Comparison is case sensitive; passing a null string returns True. (Same as using InStr and comparing the result with 1.)
EndsWith (postfix)	Returns True if the current string ends with the characters in the argument. Comparison is case sensitive. (Similar to using InStrRev and testing the result.)
IndexOf (search[, start[, end]])	Searches a substring inside the current string and returns the index of the first match, or -1 if the substring isn't found. The search can start and end at given indexes. The first argument can be a String, a Char, or an array of Chars. (Similar to InStr but more powerful because it also supports an end index.)
LastIndexOf (search[, start[, end]])	Same as IndexOf but returns the index of the last occurrence of a substring. (Similar to InStrRev but more powerful because it supports both start and end indexes.)
IndexOfAny (chars[, start[, end]])	Searches for any of the characters specified by the Char array passed as the first argument and returns the index of the first occurrence, or -1 if the search failed.
LastIndexOfAny (chars[, start[, end]])	Same as IndexOfAny but returns the index of the last occurrence of any character among those specified in the Char array, or -1 if the search failed.
ToUpper	Converts the current string to uppercase. (Same as UCase.)
ToLower	Converts the current string to lowercase. (Same as LCase.)
Substring (start[, length])	Extracts a substring of the current string, starting at a given index and continuing for the specified number of characters, or to the end of the string if the length is omitted. (Same as Mid function.)
Replace (search, replace)	Replaces all the occurrences of a substring with another substring.
Insert (index, substring)	Inserts a substring into the current string at the given index. (Same as using a combination of the & operator and the Left and Mid functions.)
Remove (index, length)	Removes the specified number of characters, starting at the specified index. (Same as concatenating the return value from the Left and Mid functions.)

(continued)

Table 8-1 Instance Methods of the System.String Class *(continued)*

Syntax	Description
PadLeft (totallength[, char])	Pads the current string by adding a number of spaces to the left to reach the specified length. If a second argument is passed, it uses that character to do the padding. If the current string is longer than the total length requested, no characters are added and the string isn't trimmed. (Similar to using the RSet command for aligning a value to the right but is more flexible because you can select the padding character.)
PadRight (totallength[, char])	Same as PadLeft but appends characters to the right. (Similar to using the LSet command but more flexible.)
CompareTo (string)	Compares the current string with another string (or any object that can be converted to a string) in a case-sensitive way and returns -1, 0, or 1, depending on whether the current string is less than, equal to, or greater than the argument. (Similar to StrComp but lacks the ability to compare in a case-insensitive way.)
CopyTo (index, chars, destIndex, length)	Copies a substring of the current string into the Char array passed as the second argument. The first argument is the position of the substring, the third argument is the index in the destination Char array, and the last argument is the number of characters to be copied.
Split (chars[, maxcount])	Splits a string into words and returns them as an array of strings. The first argument is a Char array holding all the valid separators. The second argument indicates the maximum number of words; if there are more words than this value, the last item in the result array contains all the unsplit words. (Similar to the Split function, plus it can take multiple single-character separators; however, it can't take a separator longer than one character.)
ToCharArray ([start, length])	Converts the current string (or a portion of it) to a Char array.

String Optimizations

An important detail to keep in mind is that a String object is *immutable*: once you create a string, its contents can never change. In fact, all the methods seen so far don't modify the original String; rather, they return *another* String object that you can assign to the same String variable. If you make that assignment, the original String becomes unreachable from the application (unless there are other variables pointing to it) and will eventually be garbage collected. If you think that this is a waste of memory and CPU resources, just remember that this train of events is similar to what happens with a regular string in Visual Basic 6: any time the string changes its length, a new block of memory is allocated and the old memory is marked as free and will be reclaimed when a garbage collection starts. (Visual Basic 6 can reduce the number of garbage collections and optimize string operations by allocating a buffer that is larger than the initial length of the string.)

Because String values are immutable, the compiler can optimize the resulting code in ways that wouldn't be possible otherwise. For example, consider this code fragment:

```
Dim s1 As String = "1234" & "5678"
Dim s2 As String = "12345678"
Console.WriteLine(s1 Is s2)                         ' => True
```

The compiler computes the & operator at compile time and realizes that both variables contain the same characters, so it can allocate only one block of memory for the string and have the two variables pointing to it. Because the string is immutable, a new object is created behind the scenes as soon as you attempt to modify the characters in that string:

```
' ...(Continuing the previous code fragment)...
' Attempt to modify the S1 string using the Mid statement.
Mid(s1, 2, 1) = "x"
' Prove that a new string was created behind the scenes.
Console.WriteLine(s1 Is s2)                         ' => False
```

Because of this behavior, you rarely need to invoke the Clone method to explicitly create a copy of the String: simply use the string as you would normally, and the compiler creates a copy for you if and when necessary. Also note that the Mid statement isn't as fast as it is in Visual Basic because it doesn't prevent the memory manager from allocating a new block of memory for the new string value.

A .NET application can optimize string management by maintaining an internal pool of string values known as an *intern pool*. If the value being assigned to a string variable coincides with one of the strings already in the intern pool, no additional memory is created and the variable receives the address of the string value in the pool. As you saw at the beginning of the current section, the compiler is capable of using the intern pool to optimize string initialization and have two string variables pointing to the same String object in memory. This optimization step isn't performed at run time, though, because the search in the pool takes time and in most cases it would fail, adding overhead to the application without bringing any benefit.

```
' Prove that no optimization is performed at run time.
s1 = "1234"
s1 &= "5678"
s2 = "12345678"
' These two variables point to different String objects.
Console.WriteLine(s1 Is s2)                         ' => False
```

You can optimize string management by using the Intern shared method. This method searches a string value in the intern pool and returns a reference to the pool element that contains the value if the value is already in the pool. If the search fails, the string is added to the pool and a reference to it is returned. See how you can "manually" optimize the preceding code snippet by using the String.Intern method:

```
s1 = "ABCD"
s1 &= "EFGH"
' Move S1 to the intern pool.
s1 = String.Intern(s1)
' Assign S2 a string constant (that we know is in the pool).
s2 = String.Intern("ABCDEFGH")
' These two variables point to the same String object.
Console.WriteLine(s1 Is s2)                         ' => True
```

This optimization technique makes sense only if you're working with long strings that appear in multiple portions of the applications. Another good time to use this technique is when you have many instances of a server-side component that contain similar string variables, such as a database connection string. Even if these strings don't change during the program's lifetime, they're usually read from a file, and therefore, the compiler can't optimize their memory allocation automatically. Using the Intern method, you can help your application produce a smaller memory footprint.

Here's another simple performance tip: try to gather multiple & operators in the same statement instead of spreading them across separate lines. The Visual Basic compiler can optimize multiple concatenation operations only if they're in the same statement.

Shared Methods

The String class exposes additional shared (static) methods that you can call without first instancing a String object. For example, the Concat method supports an arbitrary number of String arguments (or Object arguments that can be converted to strings) and returns the string that results from the concatenation of all the arguments:

```
Console.Write(String.Concat("ABC ", "DEF ", "GHI"))   ' => ABC DEF GHI
```

In some cases, these methods are more flexible than the corresponding instance methods in Table 8-1. For example, the Compare method compares two strings and is overloaded to support case-insensitive comparisons:

```
' Compare two strings in case-insensitive mode.
Select Case String.Compare(s1, s2, True)
    Case 0: Console.WriteLine("s1 = s2")
```

```
    Case 1: Console.WriteLine("s1 > s2")
    Case -1: Console.WriteLine("s1 < s2")
End Select
```

Two overloaded variations of this method let you compare a portion of two strings in a case-sensitive or case-insensitive way:

```
' Compare the first four characters in s1 and s2 in a case-sensitive way.
' Second and fourth arguments are the index in the two strings;
' the last argument is the length of the substrings to compare.
If String.Compare(s1, 1, s2, 1, 4) = 0 Then Console.Write("Equal")

' Same as above, but in a case-insensitive way
If String.Compare(s1, 1, s2, 1, 4, True) = 0 Then Console.Write("Equal")
```

All the overloaded versions of the Compare method make the comparison by considering the local national language or culture. Another shared method, CompareOrdinal, compares two strings (or substrings) without considering the local national language:

```
' Compare two strings.
If String.CompareOrdinal(s1, s2) = 0 Then Console.Write("Equal")
' Compare two substrings.
If String.CompareOrdinal(s1, 1, s2, 1, 4) = 0 Then Console.Write("Equal")
```

On average, CompareOrdinal is three to four times faster than Compare because it works with the numeric code of individual characters. Also, you can get better performance if you use Option Compare Binary so that regular comparison operations such as = and >= work in the same way as CompareOrdinal. Note that Option Compare Binary is the default projectwide setting, but you can change it in the Build page of the Project Properties dialog box or via the Option Compare Text statement at the top of a specific source code module.

Visual Basic .NET also lets you compare strings using any language, not just the end user's language: you just have to pass the proper CultureInfo object to the Compare method.

The CultureInfo Auxiliary Class

The System.Globalization.CultureInfo class defines an object that you can inspect to determine some key properties of any installed languages. The class exposes a shared property that returns the CultureInfo object for the current language:

```
' The following code assumes that the module contains this Imports statement.
Imports System.Globalization

' Get information about the current locale.
Dim ci As CultureInfo = CultureInfo.CurrentCulture
```

(continued)

```
' Assuming that the current language is Italian, we get:
Console.WriteLine(ci.Name)                              ' => it
Console.WriteLine(ci.EnglishName)                       ' => Italian
Console.WriteLine(ci.NativeName)                        ' => italiano
Console.WriteLine(ci.LCID)                              ' => 16
Console.WriteLine(ci.TwoLetterISOLanguageName)          ' => it
Console.WriteLine(ci.ThreeLetterISOLanguageName)        ' => ita
Console.WriteLine(ci.ThreeLetterWindowsLanguageName)    ' => ITA
```

You can get additional information about the locale through the TextInfo object, exposed by the property with the same name:

```
Dim ti As TextInfo = ci.TextInfo
Console.WriteLine(ti.ANSICodePage)                      ' => 1252
Console.WriteLine(ti.EBCDICCodePage)                    ' => 20280
Console.WriteLine(ti.OEMCodePage)                       ' => 850
Console.WriteLine(ti.ListSeparator)                     ' => ;
```

The CultureInfo object exposes two properties, NumberFormat and DateTimeFormat, which return information about how numbers and dates are formatted according to a given locale. For example, consider this code:

```
' How do you spell "Sunday" in German?
' First create a CultureInfo object for German/Germany.
' (Note that you must pass a string in the form "locale-COUNTRY" if
' a given language is spoken in multiple countries.)
Dim ciDe As New CultureInfo("de-DE")
' Next get the corresponding DateTimeFormatInfo object.
Dim dtfi As DateTimeFormatInfo = ciDe.DateTimeFormat
' Here's the answer:
Console.WriteLine(dtfi.GetDayName(DayOfWeek.Sunday))    ' => Sonntag
```

The GetCultures shared method returns an array of all the installed cultures, so you can inspect all the languages that your operating system supports:

```
' Get info on all the installed cultures.
Dim ciArr() As CultureInfo = CultureInfo.GetCultures(CultureTypes.AllCultures)

' Print abbreviation and English name of each culture.
Dim c As CultureInfo
For Each c In ciArr
    Console.WriteLine(c.Name & " (" & c.EnglishName & ")")
Next
```

The auxiliary TextInfo object permits you to convert a string to uppercase, lowercase, or title case (for example, "These Are Four Words") for a given language:

```
' Create a CultureInfo object for Canadian French.
Dim ciFr As CultureInfo = New CultureInfo("fr-CA")
```

```
' Convert a string to title case using Canadian French rules.
s = ciFr.TextInfo.ToTitleCase(s)
```

Now that you know how you can use the CultureInfo object to retrieve information about installed languages, let's see how you can pass it to the String.Compare shared method so that you can compare strings according to the collation rules defined by a given language. One overloaded version of the Compare method takes four arguments: the two strings to be compared, a Boolean value that indicates whether the comparison is case insensitive, and a CultureInfo object that specifies the language to be used:

```
' Compare these two strings in case-insensitive mode
' according to rules of Italian language.
Dim s1 As String = "cioè"
Dim s2 As String = "CIOÈ"
' You can create a CultureInfo object on the fly.
If String.Compare(s1, s2, True, New CultureInfo("it")) = 0 Then
    Console.WriteLine("s1 = s2")
End If
```

Here also is an overloaded version that compares two substrings:

```
If String.Compare(s1, 1, s2, 1, 4, True, New CultureInfo("it")) = 1 Then
    Console.WriteLine("s1's first four chars are greater than s2's")
End If
```

The CultureInfo object exposes another property of interest, Calendar, which returns a Calendar object. See the .NET Framework SDK for additional information about this object.

Formatting Numeric Values

The Format shared method of the String class allows you to format a string and include one or more numeric or date values in it, in a way similar to the C language's printf function or the Console.Write method. The string being formatted can contain placeholders for arguments, in the format {N} where N is an index that starts at 0:

```
' Print the value of a string variable.
Dim xyz As String = "foobar"
Dim msg As String
msg = String.Format("The value of {0} variable is {1}", "XYZ", xyz)
    ' => The value of XYZ variable is foobar
```

> **Note** The Console.Write and Console.WriteLine methods support the same formatting characters as the String.Format method, so in the preceding example and all the examples that follow, I could have displayed the result of the formatting operation by passing the same arguments to the Console.WriteLine method, as in this code:
>
> ```
> Console.WriteLine("The value of {0} variable is {1}", "XYZ", xyz)
> ```

If the argument is numeric, you can add a colon after the argument index and then a character that indicates what kind of formatting you're requesting. The available characters are G (General), N (Number), C (Currency), D (Decimal), E (Scientific), F (Fixed-point), P (Percent), R (Round-trip), and X (Hexadecimal):

```
' Format a Currency according to current locale.
msg = String.Format("Total is {0:C}, balance is {1:C}", 123.45, -67)
    ' => Total is $123.45, balance is ($67.00)
```

The number format uses commas—or to put it more precisely, the thousands separator defined by the current locale—to group digits:

```
msg = String.Format("Total is {0:N}", 123456.78)
    ' => Total is 123,456.78
```

You can append an integer after the N character to round or extend the number of digits after the decimal point:

```
msg = String.Format("Total is {0:N4}", 123456.785555)
    ' => Total is 123,456.7856
```

The decimal format works with integer values only and throws a FormatException if you pass a noninteger argument; you can specify a length that, if longer than the result, causes one or more leading zeros to be added:

```
msg = String.Format("Total is {0:D8}", 123456)
    ' => Total is 00123456
```

The fixed-point format is useful with decimal values, and you can indicate how many decimal digits should be displayed (two if you omit the length):

```
msg = String.Format("Total is {0:F3}", 123.45678)
    ' => Total is 123.457
```

The scientific (or exponential) format displays numbers as n.nnnnE+eeee, and you can control how many decimal digits are used in the mantissa portion:

```
msg = String.Format("Total is {0:E}", 123456.789)
    ' => Total is 1.234568E+005
msg = String.Format("Total is {0:E3}", 123456.789)
    ' => Total is 1.235E+005
```

The general format converts to either fixed-point or exponential format, depending on which format delivers the most compact result:

```
msg = String.Format("Total is {0:G}", 123456)
    ' => Total is 123456
msg = String.Format("Total is {0:G4}", 123456)
    ' => Total is 1235E5
```

The percent format converts a number to a percentage with two decimal digits by default, using the format specified for the current culture:

```
msg = String.Format("Percentage is {0:P}", 0.123)
    ' => Total is 12.30%
```

The round-trip format converts a number to a string containing all significant digits so that the string can later be converted back to a number without any loss of precision:

```
' The number of digits you pass after the "R" character is ignored.
msg = String.Format("Value of PI is {0:R}", Math.PI)
    ' => Value of PI is 3.1415926535897931
```

Finally, the hexadecimal format converts numbers to hexadecimal strings. If you specify a length, the number is padded with leading zeros if necessary:

```
msg = String.Format("Total is {0:X8}", 65535)
    ' => Total is 0000FFFF
```

You can also build custom format strings by using a few special characters, whose meaning is summarized in Table 8-2. Here are a few examples:

```
msg = String.Format("Total is {0:##,###.00}", 1234.567)
    ' => Total is 1,234.57
msg = String.Format("Percentage is {0:##.000%}", .3456)
    ' => Percentage is 34.560%

' An example of prescaler
msg = String.Format("Length in {0:###,.00 }", 12344)
    ' => Total is 12.34

' Two examples of exponential format
msg = String.Format("Total is {0:#.#####E+00}", 1234567)
    ' => Total is 1.23457E+06
msg = String.Format("Total is {0:#.#####E0}", 1234567)
    ' => Total is 1.23457E6
```

(continued)

```
' Two examples with separate sections
msg = String.Format("Total is {0:##;<##>}", -123)
    ' => Total is <123>
msg = String.Format("Total is {0:#;(#);zero}", 1234567)
    ' => Total is 1234567
```

You can also use two or three sections in some cases to avoid If or Select Case logic. For example, you can replace the following code:

```
If n1 > n2 Then
    msg = "n1 is greater than n2"
ElseIf n1 < n2 Then
    msg = "n1 is less than n2"
Else
    msg = "n1 is equal to n2"
End If
```

with the more concise but somewhat more cryptic code:

```
msg = String.Format("n1 is {0:greater than;less than;equal to} n2", n1 - n2)
```

Table 8-2 Special Formatting Characters in Custom Formatting Strings

Format	Description
#	Placeholder for a digit or a space.
0	Placeholder for a digit or a zero.
.	Decimal separator.
,	Thousands separator; if used immediately before the decimal separator, it works as a prescaler. (For each comma in this position, the value is divided by 1,000 before formatting.)
%	Displays the number as a percentage value.
E+000	Displays the number in exponential format, that is, with an E followed by the sign of the exponent, and then a number of exponent digits equal to the number of zeros after the plus sign.
E-000	Like the previous exponent symbol, but the exponent sign is displayed only if negative.
;	Section separator. The format string can contain one, two, or three sections. If there are two sections, the first applies to positive and zero values, and the second applies to negative values. If there are three sections, they are used for positive, negative, and zero values, respectively.
\	Escape character, to insert characters that would be otherwise taken as special characters (for example, \; to insert a semicolon and \\ to insert a backslash).
'...' "..."	A group of literal characters. You can add a sequence of literal characters by enclosing them in single or double quotes.

Formatting Date Values

The String.Format method also supports date and time values with both standard and custom formats. Table 8-3 summarizes all the standard date and time formats and makes it easy to find the format you're looking for at a glance.

```
msg = String.Format("Current Date Time is {0:f}", Now())
    ' => Current Date Time is Sunday, January 06, 2002 3:54 PM
```

If you can't find a standard date and time format that suits your needs, you can create a custom format by putting together the special characters listed in Table 8-4:

```
msg = String.Format("Current year is {0:yyyy}", Now())
    ' => Current year is 2002
```

The / and : formatting characters are particularly elusive because they're replaced by the default date and time separator defined for the current locale. In some cases—most notably when formatting dates for an SQL SELECT or INSERT command—you want to be sure that a given separator is used on all occasions. In this case, you must use the backslash escape character to force a specific separator yourself:

```
' Format a date in the format mm/dd/yyyy, regardless of current locale.
msg = String.Format("{0:MM\/dd\/yyyy}", Now())
    ' => 01/06/2002
```

Table 8-3 Standard Formats for Date and Time Values*

Format	Description	Pattern	Example
d	ShortDatePattern	MM/dd/yyyy	1/6/2002
D	LongDatePattern	dddd, MMMM dd, yyyy	Sunday, January 06, 2002
f	full date and time (long date and short time)	dddd, MMMM dd, yyyy HH:mm	Sunday, January 06, 2002 3:54 PM
F	FullDateTimePattern (long date and long time)	dddd, MMMM dd, yyyy HH:mm:ss	Sunday, January 06, 2002 3:54:20 PM
g	general (short date and short time)	MM/dd/yyyy HH:mm	1/6/2002 3:54 PM
G	General (short date and long time)	MM/dd/yyyy HH:mm:ss	1/6/2002 3:54:20 PM
M,m	MonthDayPattern	MMMM dd	January 06
Y,y	YearMonthPattern	MMMM, yyyy	January, 2002

(continued)

Table 8-3 Standard Formats for Date and Time Values* *(continued)*

Format	Description	Pattern	Example
t	ShortTimePattern	HH:mm	3:54 PM
T	LongTimePattern	HH:mm:ss	3:54:20 PM
s	SortableDateTime-Pattern (conforms to ISO 8601) using local time	yyyy-MM-dd HH:mm:ss	2002-01-06T15:54:20
u	UniversalSortable-DateTimePattern (conforms to ISO 8601) using universal time	yyyy-MM-dd HH:mm:ss	2002-01-06 20:54:20Z
U	UniversalSortable-DateTimePattern	dddd, MMMM dd, yyyy HH:mm:ss	Sunday, January 06, 2002 5:54:20 PM
R,r	RFC1123Pattern	ddd, dd MMM yyyy HH':'mm':'ss 'GMT'	Sun, 06 Jan 2002 15:54:20 GMT

* Notice that formats U, u, R, and r use Universal (Greenwich) Time, so they are 5 hours ahead of the regular time (which is assumed to be U.S. eastern time). The Pattern column specifies the corresponding custom format string made up of the characters listed in Table 8-4.

Table 8-4 Character Sequences That Can Be Used in Custom Date and Time Formats

Format	Description
d	Day of month (one or two digits as required)
dd	Day of month (always two digits, with a leading zero if required)
ddd	Day of week (three-character abbreviation)
dddd	Day of week (full name)
M	Month number (one or two digits as required)
MM	Month number (always two digits, with a leading zero if required)
MMM	Month name (three-character abbreviation)
MMMM	Month name (full name)
y	Year (last one or two digits, no leading zero)
yy	Year (last two digits)
yyyy	Year (four digits)
H	Hour in 24-hour format (one or two digits as required)
HH	Hour in 24-hour format (always two digits, with a leading zero if required)

Table 8-4 Character Sequences That Can Be Used in Custom Date and Time Formats *(continued)*

Format	Description
h	Hour in 12-hour format (one or two digits as required)
hh	Hour in 12-hour format
m	Minutes (one or two digits as required)
mm	Minutes (always two digits, with a leading zero if required)
s	Seconds (one or two digits as required)
ss	Seconds
t	The first character in the AM/PM designator
tt	The AM/PM designator
z	Time zone offset, hour only (one or two digits as required)
zz	Time zone offset, hour only (always two digits, with a leading zero if required)
zzz	Time zone offset, hour and minute (hour and minute values always have two digits, with a leading zero if required)
/	Default date separator
:	Default time separator
\	Escape characters, to include literal characters that would be otherwise considered special characters

The IFormattable Interface

So far, I've shown you how you can use special characters to format simple data types, such as numbers and dates. But what happens with more complex objects? Can you pass your own objects as arguments to the String.Format function? If so, what value is actually printed?

Several .NET methods—most notably String.Format, Console.WriteLine, Debug.WriteLine, and a few others—take any object you pass them and automatically call that object's ToString method. This call is guaranteed to succeed because all objects inherit the ToString method from System.Object object. So you can make your objects behave well with String.Format simply by overriding the ToString method. Here's a complete example:

```
Class PointXY
    Public X, Y As Double

    Sub New(ByVal X As Double, ByVal Y As Double)
        Me.X = X
        Me.Y = Y
    End Sub
```

(continued)

```
    ' Return the X-Y coordinates in the "(X,Y)" format.
    Overrides Function ToString() As String
        Return "(" & X.ToString & "," & Y.ToString & ")"
    End Function
End Class
```

Now that you have overridden the ToString method, you can successfully pass a PointXY object to the String.Format function:

```
Dim msg As String
msg = String.Format("First point is {0}.", New PointXY(10, 15))
Console.WriteLine(msg)          ' => First point is (10,15).
```

Your class can even support custom format strings. To receive a notification when the client code specifies a custom format string for an instance of a class you authored, your class must implement the IFormattable interface. This interface exposes only one method, Format, whose first parameter receives the custom string passed after the colon character (for example, "G8" in the custom string "{0:G8}"), or an empty string for the default format. Here's a new version of the PointXY class that supports a template string in which the *X* and *Y* characters are replaced by the actual coordinate values:

```
Class PointXY2
    Implements IFormattable

    Public X, Y As Double

    Sub New(ByVal X As Double, ByVal Y As Double)
        Me.X = X
        Me.Y = Y
    End Sub

    Overrides Function ToString() As String
        Return "(" & X.ToString & "," & Y.ToString & ")"
    End Function

    Private Function Format(ByVal FormatStr As String, _
        ByVal fp As IFormatProvider) As String _
        Implements IFormattable.ToString
        If FormatStr = "" Then
            ' If no formatting is passed, use default formatting.
            Return Me.ToString
        Else
            ' Otherwise, replace X and Y characters with actual coordinates.
            Return Replace(Replace(formatstr, "X", X.ToString), _
                "Y", Y.ToString)
        End If
    End Function
End Class
```

The following code takes advantage of the new ability to change the format of the result:

```
msg = String.Format("First point is {0:[X-Y]}", New PointXY2(1, 5))
Console.WriteLine(msg)         ' => First point is [1-5]
```

Note that you can insert literal curly braces in the format string by doubling the characters, that is, by using {{ and }}. Your class should throw a FormatException object if the specified format isn't valid.

The IFormatProvider and ICustomFormatter Interfaces

Clearly, you can't rely on the IFormattable interface to supply a new format for an object that you didn't author, but the .NET Framework lets you achieve a good degree of flexibility in this situation. The String.Format method—as well as similar methods such as Console.Write—is overloaded to provide a version that takes an array of values and an IFormatProvider interface:

```
String.Format(fp As IFormatProvider, _
    format As String, _
    args() As Object)
```

The first argument is an object that you define and that implements the IFormatProvider interface. This generic interface is implemented by classes that provide formatting services to other classes. The .NET Framework queries the object through the IFormatProvider.GetFormat method; this method receives a Type object that states which particular service is requested and must return an object that implements the requested functionality (which can be the same object that implements IFormatProvider) or Nothing if the requested functionality isn't supported. When the IFormatProvider interface is called from within String.Format, the GetFormat method must return an object that implements the ICustomFormatter interface, whose Format method will be called later for each argument in the format string.

The following MetricConverter class exhibits a simple but not trivial example of how you can put this functionality to good use. The MetricConverter class implements both the IFormatProvider interface and the ICustomFormatter interface. The IFormatProvider.GetFormat method therefore queries the requested functionality and returns Me if the interface is ICustomFormatter. The ICustomFormatter.Format method converts the value from inches to meters or from feet to meters if the format specification is *in* or *fe*, respectively.

```
Class MetricConverter
    Implements IFormatProvider
    Implements ICustomFormatter

    ' The only method of the IFormatProvider interface
    Private Function GetFormat(ByVal Service As System.Type) _
        As Object Implements IFormatProvider.GetFormat

        If Service.Name = "ICustomFormatter" Then
            ' Return this instance if called from the String.Format method.
            Return Me
        Else
            ' Return Nothing in all other cases.
            Return Nothing
        End If
    End Function

    ' The only method of the ICustomFormatter interface
    Function Format(ByVal formatStr As String, ByVal arg As Object, _
        ByVal fp As IFormatProvider) As String _
        Implements ICustomFormatter.Format

        If formatStr = "" Then
            ' No format string; return the argument.
            Return arg.ToString
        ElseIf formatStr = "in" Then
            ' Convert inches to meters.
            Return (CDbl(arg) * 0.0254).ToString
        ElseIf formatStr = "fe" Then
            ' Convert feet to meters.
            Return (CDbl(arg) * 0.33).ToString
        End If
    End Function
End Class
```

Here's a code snippet that tests the MetricConverter class:

```
Sub TestIFormatProvider()
    ' Prepare an array of arguments (25 inches and 5.2 feet).
    Dim args() As Object = {25, 5.1}
    ' Note that we create an instance of MetricConverter on the fly.
    Console.WriteLine(String.Format(New MetricConverter(), _
        "Width is {0:in}, Height is {1:fe} meters", args))
        ' => Width is 0.635, Height is 1.683 meters
End Sub
```

Interestingly, three classes in the .NET runtime—CultureInfo, NumberFormatInfo, and DateTimeFormatInfo—implement the IFormatProvider interface and therefore can be used directly whenever an IFormatProvider object is expected. For example, this code prints a Canadian currency value:

```
Sub TestIFormatProvider2()
    ' Create a CultureInfo object for French-Canadian.
    Dim ci As New System.Globalization.CultureInfo("fr-CA")
    ' This is the amount to be formatted as Canadian money (dollars).
    Dim amount As Double = 12345.6
    Dim msg As String = String.Format(ci, "{0:C}", amount)
    Console.WriteLine(msg)        ' => 12 345,60 $
End Sub
```

The Char Type

The Char class represents a single character. There isn't much to say about this data type, other than that it exposes a number of useful shared methods that let you test a single character according to several criteria. All these methods are overloaded and take either a single Char or a String plus an index in the string. For example, you check whether a character is a digit as follows:

```
' Check an individual Char value.
Console.WriteLine(Char.IsDigit("1"c))          ' => True
' Check the nth character in a string.
Console.WriteLine(Char.IsDigit("A123", 0))     ' => False
```

This is the list of the most useful static methods that test single characters: IsControl, IsDigit, IsLetter, IsLetterOrDigit, IsLower, IsNumber, IsPunctuation, IsSymbol, IsUpper, and IsWhiteSpace.

The StringBuilder Type

As you might remember, a String object is immutable, and its value never changes after the string has been created. This means that anytime you apply a method that changes its value, you're actually creating a new String object. For example, the following statement:

```
S = S.Insert(3, "1234")
```

doesn't modify the original string in memory. Instead, the Insert method creates a new String object, which is then assigned to the S object variable. The original string object in memory is eventually reclaimed during the next garbage collection unless another variable points to it, as is often the case with strings in the intern pool. The superior memory allocation scheme of .NET ensures that this mechanism adds a relatively low overhead, but too many allocate and release operations can degrade your application's performance. The System.Text.StringBuilder object offers a solution to this problem.

You can think of a StringBuilder object as a buffer that can contain a string with the ability to grow from zero characters to the buffer's current capacity. Until you exceed that capacity, the string is assembled in the buffer and no memory is allocated or released. If the string becomes longer than the current capacity, the StringBuilder object transparently creates a larger buffer. The default buffer initially contains 16 characters, but you can change this by assigning a different capacity in the StringBuilder's constructor or by assigning a value to the Capacity property:

```
' Create a StringBuilder object with initial capacity of 1000 characters.
Dim sb As New System.Text.StringBuilder(1000)
```

You can process the string held in the StringBuilder object with several methods, most of which have the same name as and work similarly to methods exposed by the String class—for example, the Insert, Remove, and Replace methods. The most common way to build a string inside a StringBuilder object is by means of its Append method, which takes an argument of any type and appends it to the current internal string:

```
' Create a comma-delimited list of the first 100 integers.
Dim n As Integer
For n = 1 To 100
    ' Note that two Append methods are faster than a single Append,
    ' whose argument is the concatenation of N and ",".
    sb.Append(n)
    sb.Append(",")
Next
' Insert a string at the beginning of the buffer.
sb.Insert(0, "List of numbers: ")
Console.WriteLine(sb)    ' => List of numbers: 1,2,3,4,5,6,...
```

There's also an AppendFormat method, which lets you specify a format string and even an IFormatProvider interface, much like the String.Format method. The Length property returns the current length of the internal string:

```
' Continuing previous example...
Console.WriteLine("Length is " & sb.Length.ToString)    ' => 309
```

The following procedure compares how quickly the String and StringBuilder classes perform a large number of string concatenations:

```
Sub TestStringBuilderVsStrings()
    Dim i As Integer
    Dim s As String
    Dim dt As DateTime
```

```
    Const TIMES As Integer = 10000

    Console.Write("Appending to a regular string: ")
    dt = Date.Now
    For i = 1 To TIMES
        s &= CStr(i) & ","
    Next
    Console.WriteLine(Now.Subtract(dt).ToString & " secs.")

    Console.Write("Appending to a StringBuilder: ")
    dt = Date.Now
    Dim sb As New System.Text.StringBuilder(TIMES * 4)
    For i = 1 To TIMES
        sb.Append(CStr(i))
        sb.Append(",")
    Next
    Console.WriteLine(Now.Subtract(dt).ToString & " secs.")
End Sub
```

This is the result that appears in the console window:

```
Appending to a regular string: 00:00:02.2231968 secs.
Appending to a StringBuilder: 00:00:00.0200288 secs.
```

from which it's apparent that the StringBuilder object can be more than 100 times faster than the regular String class.

The StringBuilder object is also useful when you're passing an argument to a method in a DLL that returns a string value in a string buffer; using a StringBuilder in this case is necessary because you can't use a regular String (which is immutable). This code shows how to retrieve the path of the temporary directory associated with the current user:

```
' This Declare is taken from Visual Basic 6's API Viewer utility, but I changed
' Long into Integer and String into StringBuilder.
Private Declare Function GetTempPath Lib "Kernel32" Alias "GetTempPathA" _
    (ByVal nBufferLength As Integer, _
    ByVal lpBuffer As System.Text.StringBuilder) As Integer
:
' Prepare the receiving buffer.
Dim tmpPath As New System.Text.StringBuilder(256)
' GetTempPath returns the number of characters in the result.
Dim length As Integer = GetTempPath(tmpPath.Capacity, tmpPath)
' Trim the StringBuilder to the new length and display it.
tmpPath.Length = length
Console.WriteLine(tmpPath.ToString)     ' => C:\DOCUME~1\ADMINI~\LOCALS~1\Temp\
```

Numeric Types

I illustrated most of the useful operations you can perform on numbers and dates in Chapter 3. In this section, I'll complete the discussion showing you a few methods exposed by the basic numeric and date classes, particularly those related to parsing and formatting.

As you know, Short, Integer, and Long types are nothing but .NET Int16, Int32, and Int64 classes with Visual Basicish names. By recognizing their class nature, you can exploit these types better, for example, by using their methods and properties. This section applies to all the numeric classes in the .NET Framework, such as Boolean, Byte, Short (Int16), Integer (Int32), Long (Int64), Single, Double, and Decimal.

Properties and Methods

All numeric types—and all .NET classes, for that matter—expose the ToString method, which converts their numeric value to a string. This method is especially useful when you're appending the number value to another string:

```
Dim myValue As Double = 123.45
Console.Write("The final value is " & myValue.ToString)
```

The ToString method is culture aware. For example, it uses a comma as a decimal separator if the current culture is Italian or German. Numeric types overload the ToString method to take either a format string or a custom formatter object. (For more detail, refer to the sections "Formatting Numeric Values" and "The IFormatProvider and ICustomFormatter Interfaces" earlier in this chapter.)

```
' Convert an integer to hexadecimal.
Console.WriteLine(1234.ToString("X"))       ' => 4D2

' Display PI with 6 digits (in all).
Dim d As Double = Math.PI
Console.WriteLine(d.ToString("G6"))         ' => 3.14159
```

As a rule, the ToString method is more efficient than the Format method and should be preferred if its formatting features are sufficient for your purposes.

You can use the CompareTo method to compare a number with another numeric value of the same type. This method returns 1, 0, or -1, depending on whether the current instance is greater than, equal to, or less than the value passed as an argument:

```
Dim sngValue As Single = 1.23
' Compare the Single variable sngValue with 1.
```

```
' Note that you must force the argument to Single.
Select Case sngValue.CompareTo(CSng(1))
    Case 1
        Console.WriteLine("sngValue is > 1")
    Case 0
        Console.WriteLine("sngValue is = 1")
    Case -1
        Console.WriteLine("sngValue is < 1")
End Select
```

Note that the argument must be the same type as the value you're applying the CompareTo method to, so you must convert it if necessary. You can use a conversion function, such as the CSng function in the preceding code, or append a conversion character, such as ! for Single, I for Integer, and so on:

```
' ...(Another way to write the previous code snippet)...
Select Case sngValue.CompareTo(1!)
⋮
```

All the numeric classes expose the MinValue and MaxValue shared properties, which return the smallest and greatest value that you can express with the corresponding type:

```
' Display the greatest value you can store in a Double variable.
Console.WriteLine(Double.MaxValue)      ' => 1.79769313486232E+308
```

The numeric classes that support floating-point values—namely Single and Double classes—expose a few additional shared read-only properties. The Epsilon property returns the smallest positive (nonzero) number that can be stored in a variable of that type:

```
Console.WriteLine(Single.Epsilon)       ' => 1.401298E-45
Console.WriteLine(Double.Epsilon)       ' => 4.94065645841247E-324
```

The NegativeInfinity and PositiveInfinity properties return a constant that represents an infinite value, whereas the NaN property returns a constant that represents the not-a-number value. In some cases, you can use infinite values in expressions:

```
' Any number divided by infinity gives 0.
Console.WriteLine(1 / Double.PositiveInfinity)     ' => 0
```

The Single and Double classes also expose some instance methods that let you test whether they contain some special values: IsInfinity, IsNegativeInfinity, IsPositiveInfinity, and IsNaN.

Formatting Numbers

All the numeric classes support an overloaded form of the ToString method that lets you apply a format string:

```
Dim intValue As Integer = 12345
Console.WriteLine(intValue.ToString("##,##0.00", Nothing))  ' => 12,345.00
```

The method uses the current locale to interpret the formatting string. For example, in the preceding code it uses the comma as the thousands separator and the period as the decimal separator.

Another overloaded ToString method takes an IFormatProvider object to format the current value. You already saw how to author a class that implements this interface earlier in this chapter (see the section "The IFormatProvider and ICustomFormatter Interfaces"), so in this section I'll show you how you can take advantage of one of the several .NET objects that implement this interface, the NumberFormatInfo object.

The NumberFormatInfo class exposes many properties that determine how a numeric value is formatted, such as NumberDecimalSeparator (the decimal separator character), NumberGroupSeparator (the thousands separator character), NumberDecimalDigits (number of decimal digits), CurrencySymbol (the character used for currency), and many others. The simplest way to create a valid NumberFormatInfo object is by means of the CurrentInfo shared method of the NumberFormatInfo class; the returned value is a read-only NumberFormatInfo object based on the current locale:

```
' All the code samples in this section assume this Imports statement.
Imports System.Globalization
:
Dim nfi As NumberFormatInfo = NumberFormatInfo.CurrentInfo
```

(You can also use the InvariantInfo property, which returns a default read-only NumberFormatInfo object that is culture independent.) The problem with the preceding code is that the returned NumberFormatInfo object is read-only, so you can't modify any of its properties: this object is therefore virtually useless because the ToString method implicitly uses the current locale anyway when formatting a value. The solution is to create a clone of the default NumberFormatInfo object and then modify its properties, as in the following snippet:

```
' Format a number with current locale formatting options, but
' use a comma for the decimal separator and a space for the thousands
' separator. (You need DirectCast because the Clone method returns an Object.)
Dim nfi As NumberFormatInfo = _
    DirectCast(NumberFormatInfo.CurrentInfo.Clone, NumberFormatInfo)
' The nfi object is a read-write object, so you can change its properties.
nfi.NumberDecimalSeparator = ","
nfi.NumberGroupSeparator = " "
```

```
' You can now format a value with the custom NumberFormatInfo object.
Dim sngValue As Single = 12345.5
Console.WriteLine(sngValue.ToString("##,##0.00", nfi)) ' => 12 345,50
```

For the complete list of NumberFormatInfo properties and methods, see the .NET Framework SDK documentation.

Parsing Strings into Numbers

All numeric types support the Parse shared method, which parses the string passed as an argument and returns the corresponding numeric value. The simplest form of the Parse method takes one string argument:

```
' Next line assigns 1234 to the variable.
Dim shoValue As Short = Short.Parse("1234")
```

The second overloaded form of the Parse method takes a NumberStyle enumerated value as its second argument. NumberStyle is a bit-coded value that specifies which portions of the number are allowed in the string being parsed. Valid NumberStyle values are AllowLeadingWhite (1), AllowTrailingWhite (2), AllowLeadingSign (4), AllowTrailingSign (8), AllowParentheses (16), AllowDecimalPoint (32), AllowThousand (64), AllowExponent (128), AllowCurrencySymbol (256), and AllowHexSpecifier (512). You can specify which portions of the strings are valid by using the OR operator on these values, or you can use some other predefined compound values, such as Any (511, allows everything), Integer (7, allows trailing sign and leading/trailing white), Number (111, like Integer but allows thousands separator and decimal point as well), Float (167, like Integer but allows also decimal separator and exponent), and Currency (383, allows everything except exponent).

The following example extracts a Double from a string and recognizes white spaces and all the supported formats:

```
Dim dblValue As Double = Double.Parse(" 1,234.56E6  ", NumberStyles.Any)
    ' dblValue is assigned the value 1234560000.
```

You can be more specific about what is valid and what isn't:

```
Dim style As NumberStyles = NumberStyles.AllowDecimalPoint _
    Or NumberStyles.AllowLeadingSign
' This works and assigns -123.45 to sngValue.
Dim sngValue As Single = Single.Parse("-123.45", style)
' This throws a FormatException because of the thousands separator.
sngValue = Single.Parse("12,345.67", style)
```

The Convert Class

The System.Convert class exposes several shared methods that help you in converting to and from the many data types available in .NET. In their simplest form, these methods can convert any base type to another type and are therefore equivalent to the conversion functions that Visual Basic offers:

```
' Convert the string "123.45" to a Double (same as CDbl function).
Dim dblValue As Double = Convert.ToDouble("123.45")
```

The Convert class exposes many Toxxxx methods, one for each base type: ToBoolean, ToByte, ToChar, ToDateTime, ToDecimal, ToDouble, ToInt16, ToInt32, ToInt64, ToSingle, and ToString (plus a few non-CLS compliant methods: ToSByte, ToUInt16, ToUInt32, and ToUInt64).

You see the added flexibility of the Convert class when you pass an IFormatProvider object as a second argument to a Toxxxx method to describe how the value being converted is formatted. You can author a class that works as a formatter, or you can use a .NET object that implements IFormatProvider, such as a NumberFormatInfo or a DateTimeFormatInfo object:

```
Sub TestConvertClass()
    Dim nfi As NumberFormatInfo = _
        CType(NumberFormatInfo.CurrentInfo.Clone, NumberFormatInfo)
    ' Use a period to group digits, and a comma as a decimal separator.
    nfi.NumberGroupSeparator = "."
    nfi.NumberDecimalSeparator = ","

    ' Parse a string using the specified separators.
    Dim dblValue As Double = Convert.ToDouble("12.345,56", nfi)
    Console.WriteLine(dblValue)      ' => 12345.56
End Sub
```

The Convert class exposes two methods that make conversions to and from Base64-encoded strings a breeze. (This is the format used for MIME e-mail attachments.) The ToBase64String method takes an array of bytes and encodes it as a Base64 string. The FromBase64String method does the conversion in the opposite direction:

```
Sub TestBase64Conversions()
    ' An array of 16 bytes (two identical sequences of 8 bytes)
    Dim b() As Byte = {12, 45, 213, 88, 11, 220, 34, 0, _
        12, 45, 213, 88, 11, 220, 34, 0}
    ' Convert it to a Base64 string.
    Dim s64 As String = Convert.ToBase64String(b)
    Console.WriteLine(s64)

    ' Convert it back to an array of bytes, and display it.
    Dim b2() As Byte = Convert.FromBase64String(s64)
```

```
    Dim i As Integer
    For i = 0 To b.GetUpperBound(0)
        Console.Write(b2(i).ToString & " ")
    Next
End Sub
```

In addition, the Convert class exposes the ToBase64CharArray and FromBase64CharArray methods, which convert a Byte array to and from a Char array instead of a String.

Random Number Generators

Visual Basic .NET still supports the time-honored Randomize statement and Rnd function for backward compatibility, but serious .NET developers should use the System.Random class instead. You can set the seed for random number generation in this class's constructor method:

```
' The argument must be a 32-bit integer.
Dim rand As New Random(12345)
```

When you pass a given seed number, you always get the same random sequence. To get different sequences each time you run the application, you can have the seed depend on the current time. In Visual Basic 6, you used the following statement:

```
Randomize Timer
```

This is the closest Visual Basic .NET statement that delivers the same result:

```
' You need these conversions because the Ticks property
' returns a 64-bit value that must be truncated to a 32-bit integer.
Dim rand As New Random(CInt(Date.Now.Ticks And Integer.MaxValue))
```

Once you have an initialized Random object, you can extract random positive 32-bit integer values each time you query its Next method:

```
Dim i As Short
For i = 1 To 10
    Console.WriteLine(rand.Next)
Next
```

You can also pass one or two arguments to keep the return value in the desired range:

```
' Get a value in the range 0 to 1000.
Dim intValue As Integer = rand.Next(1000)
' Get a value in the range 100 to 1000.
intValue = rand.Next(100, 1000)
```

The NextDouble method is similar to the old Rnd function in that it returns a random floating-point number between 0 and 1:

```
Dim dblValue As Double = rand.NextDouble
```

Finally, you can fill a Byte array with random values with the NextBytes method:

```
' Get an array of 100 random byte values.
Dim buffer(100) As Byte
rand.NextBytes(buffer)
```

The DateTime Type

System.DateTime is the main .NET class for working with date and time values. Not only does it offer a place to store data values, it also exposes many useful methods that virtually replace all the Visual Basic 6 date and time functions. For backward compatibility's sake, Visual Basic .NET lets you use the Date type as a synonym for the System.DateTime type. In this section, I'll use the Date class name, but keep in mind that you can always replace it with System.DateTime or just DateTime (because of the projectwide Imports System statement).

You can initialize a Date value in a number of ways:

```
' Create a Date value by providing year, month, and day values.
Dim dt1 As Date = New Date(2002, 1, 6)              ' January 6, 2002

' Provide also hour, minute, and second values.
Dim dt2 As Date = New Date(2002, 1, 6, 18, 30, 20) ' January 6, 2002 6:30:20 PM

' Add millisecond value (half a second in this example).
Dim dt3 As Date = New Date(2002, 1, 6, 18, 30, 20, 500)

' Create a time value from ticks (10 million ticks = 1 second).
Dim ticks As Long = 20000000                        ' 2 seconds
' This is considered the time elapsed from Jan. 1, 2001.
Dim dt4 As Date = New Date(ticks)                   ' 1/1/0001 12:00:02 AM
```

Because Date and System.DateTime are perfect synonyms, the first Dim statement in the preceding code could have been written in one of the following ways:

```
Dim dt1 As Date = New DateTime(2002, 1, 6)
Dim dt2 As DateTime = New Date(2002, 1, 6)
Dim dt3 As DateTime = New DateTime(2002, 1, 6)
```

You can use the Now and Today shared properties:

```
' The Now property returns the system date and time.
Dim dt5 As Date = Date.Now        ' For example, January 06, 2002 3:54:20 PM
' The Today property returns the system date only.
Dim dt6 As Date = Date.Today      ' For example, January 06, 2002 12:00:00 AM
```

Once you have an initialized Date value, you can retrieve individual portions by using one of its read-only properties, namely Date (the date portion), TimeOfDay (the time portion), Year, Month, Day, DayOfYear, DayOfWeek, Hour, Minute, Second, Millisecond, and Ticks:

```
' Is today the first day of the current month?
If Date.Today.Day = 1 Then Console.WriteLine("First day of month")
' How many days have passed since January 1?
Console.WriteLine(Date.Today.DayOfYear)
' Get current time - note that ticks are included.
Console.WriteLine(Date.Now.TimeOfDay)     ' => 10:39:28.3063680
```

The TimeOfDay property is peculiar in that it returns a TimeSpan object, which represents a difference between dates. While this class is distinct from the Date class, it shares many of its properties and methods and nearly always works together with Date values, as you'll see shortly.

Adding and Subtracting Dates

The Date class exposes several instance methods that let you add and subtract a number of years, months, days, hours, minutes, or seconds to or from a Date value. The names of these methods leave no doubt about their function: AddYears, AddMonths, AddDays, AddHours, AddMinutes, AddSeconds, AddMilliseconds, AddTicks. You can add an integer value when you're using AddYears and AddMonths and a decimal value in all other cases. In all cases, you can pass a negative argument to subtract rather than add a value:

```
' Tomorrow's date
Console.WriteLine(Date.Today.AddDays(1))
' Yesterday's date
Console.WriteLine(Date.Today.AddDays(-1))
' What time will it be 2 hours and 30 minutes from now?
Console.WriteLine(Date.Now.AddHours(2.5))

' A CPU-intensive way to pause for 5 seconds.
Dim endTime As Date = Date.Now.AddSeconds(5)
Do: Loop Until Date.Now > endTime
```

A generic Add method takes a TimeSpan object as an argument. Before you can use it, you must learn to create a TimeSpan object, choosing one of its overloaded constructor methods:

```
' One Long value is interpreted as a Ticks value.
Dim ts1 As TimeSpan = New TimeSpan(13500000)          ' 1.35 seconds
' Three Integer values are interpreted as hours, minutes, seconds.
Dim ts2 As TimeSpan = New TimeSpan(0, 32, 20)         ' 32 minutes, 20 seconds
' Four Integer values are interpreted as days, hours, minutes, seconds.
Dim ts3 As TimeSpan = New TimeSpan(1, 12, 0, 0)       ' 1 day and a half
' (Note that arguments aren't checked for out-of-range errors; therefore,
'  the next statement delivers the same result as the previous one.)
Dim ts4 As TimeSpan = New TimeSpan(0, 36, 0, 0)       ' 1 day and a half
' A fifth argument is interpreted as a millisecond value.
Dim ts5 As TimeSpan = New TimeSpan(0, 0, 1, 30, 500) ' 90 seconds and a half
```

Now you're ready to add an arbitrary date or time interval to a Date value:

```
' What will be the time 2 days, 10 hours, and 30 minutes from now?
Console.WriteLine(Date.Now.Add(New TimeSpan(2, 10, 30, 0)))
```

The Date class also exposes a Subtract instance method that works in a similar way:

```
' What was the time 1 day, 12 hours, and 20 minutes ago?
Console.WriteLine(Date.Now.Subtract(New TimeSpan(1, 12, 20, 0)))
```

The Subtract method is overloaded to take another Date object as an argument, in which case it returns the TimeSpan object that represents the difference between the two dates:

```
' How many days, hours, minutes, and seconds have elapsed
' since the beginning of the third millennium?
Dim startDate As New Date(2001, 1, 1)
Dim ts As TimeSpan = Date.Now.Subtract(startDate)
' (I am running this code on July 26, 2001, late morning.)
Console.WriteLine(ts)                   ' => 206.11:11:35.4627792
```

The Subtract method offers a simple way to benchmark a piece of code, and I have used this technique elsewhere in this book:

```
Dim startTime As Date = Now()
:
' ...(Place here the code to be benchmarked)...
:
Console.WriteLine("{0} seconds.", Now.Subtract(startTime))
```

Once you have a TimeSpan object, you can extract the information buried in it by using one of its many properties, whose names are self-explanatory: Days, Hours, Minutes, Seconds, Milliseconds, Ticks, TotalDays, TotalHours, TotalMinutes, TotalSeconds, and TotalMilliseconds. The TimeSpan class also exposes methods such as Add, Subtract, Negate, and CompareTo.

You don't need the Subtract method if you simply have to determine whether a Date value is greater or less than another Date value because the CompareTo method is more appropriate for this job:

```
' Is current date later than October 30, 2001?
Select Case Date.Today.CompareTo(New Date(2001, 10, 30))
    Case 1    ' Later than Oct. 30, 2001
    Case -1   ' Earlier than Oct. 30, 2001
    Case 0    ' Today is Oct. 30, 2001.
End Select
```

Of course you can also use comparison operators if you don't need three-state logic:

```
If Date.Today > New Date(2001, 10, 30) Then ...
```

Finally, the Date class exposes two shared methods that can be handy in many applications:

```
' Test for a leap year.
Console.WriteLine(Date.IsLeapYear(2000))          ' => True
' Retrieve the number of days in a given month.
Console.WriteLine(Date.DaysInMonth(2000, 2))      ' => 29
```

Formatting Dates

The Date type overrides the ToString method to provide a compact representation of the date and time value it contains. (This is the format implicitly used by Console.Write and similar methods.) You can format a Date value in other ways by using some peculiar methods that only this type exposes:

```
' This is January 6, 2002 6:30:20.500 PM - U.S. Eastern Time.
Dim dt As Date = New Date(2002, 1, 6, 18, 30, 20, 500)

Console.WriteLine(dt.ToShortDateString)   ' => 01/06/2002
Console.WriteLine(dt.ToLongDateString)    ' => Sunday, January 06, 2002
Console.WriteLine(dt.ToShortTimeString)   ' => 6:30 PM
Console.WriteLine(dt.ToLongTimeString)    ' => 6:30:20 PM
Console.WriteLine(dt.ToFileTime)          ' => 126548334205000000
Console.WriteLine(dt.ToOADate)            ' => 37262.7710706019
Console.WriteLine(dt.ToUniversalTime)     ' => 1/6/2002 11:30:20 PM
Console.WriteLine(dt.ToLocalTime)         ' => 1/6/2002 1:30:20 PM
```

A few of these formats might require additional explanation:

- The ToFileTime method returns an unsigned 8-byte value representing the date and time as the number of 100-nanosecond intervals that have elapsed since 1/1/1601 12:00 AM.

- The ToOADate method converts to an OLE Automation–compatible value. (This is a Double value similar to the Date values used in Visual Basic 6.)
- The ToUniversalTime method considers the Date value a local time and converts it to Coordinated Universal Time (UTC).
- The ToLocalTime method considers the Date value a UTC value and converts it to a local time.

Parsing Dates

The operation complementary to date formatting is date parsing. The Date class provides a Format shared method for parsing jobs of any degree of complexity:

```
Dim dt As Date = Date.Parse("2002/1/6 12:30:20")
```

The flexibility of this method becomes apparent when you pass an IFormatProvider object as a second argument to it—for example, the DateTimeFormatInfo object. This object is conceptually similar to the NumberFormatInfo object described earlier in this chapter. (See the "Formatting Numbers" section.) This object, however, holds information about separators and formats allowed in date and time values:

```
' Get a writable copy of the current locale's DateTimeFormatInfo object.
Dim dtfi As DateTimeFormatInfo
dtfi = CType(DateTimeFormatInfo.CurrentInfo.Clone, DateTimeFormatInfo)
' Change date and time separators.
dtfi.DateSeparator = "-"
dtfi.TimeSeparator = "."
' Now we're ready to parse a date formatted in a nonstandard way.
Dim dt2 As Date = Date.Parse("2002-1-6 12.30.20", dtfi)
```

Many non-U.S. developers will appreciate the ability to parse dates in formats other than month/day/year. In this case, you have to assign a correctly formatted pattern to the DateTimeFormatInfo object's ShortDatePattern, LongDatePattern, ShortTimePattern, LongTimePattern, or FullDateTimePattern property before doing the parse:

```
' Prepare to parse (dd/mm/yy) dates, in short or long format.
dtfi.ShortDatePattern = "d/M/yyyy"
dtfi.LongDatePattern = "dddd, dd MMMM, yyyy"

' Both dt3 and dt4 are assigned the date "January 6, 2002".
Dim dt3 As Date = Date.Parse("6-1-2002 12.30.44", dtfi)
Dim dt4 As Date = Date.Parse("Sunday, 6 January, 2002", dtfi)
```

You can use the DateTimeFormatInfo object to retrieve standard or abbreviated names for weekdays and months, according to the current locale or any locale:

```
' Print the abbreviated names of months.
Dim s As String
For Each s In DateTimeFormatInfo.CurrentInfo.AbbreviatedMonthNames
    Console.WriteLine(s)
Next
```

Even more interesting, you can set weekday and month names with arbitrary strings if you have a writable DateTimeFormatInfo object, and then you can use the object to parse a date written in any language, including invented ones. (Yes, including Klingon!)

Another way to parse strings in formats other than month/day/year is to use the ParseExact shared method. In this case, you pass the format string as the second argument, and you can pass Nothing to the third argument if you don't need a DateTimeFormatInfo object to further qualify the string being parsed:

```
' dt5 is assigned the date "January 6, 2002".
Dim dt5 As Date = Date.ParseExact("6-1-2002", "d-M-yyyy", Nothing)
```

Finally, the Date class exposes two shared methods, FromFileTime and FromOADate, for the less common operations of parsing from a date, formatted as a file time, or from an OLE Automation date value.

Working with Time Zones

The .NET Framework supports time-zone information via the System.TimeZone object, which you can use to retrieve information about the time zone set in Windows regional settings:

```
' Get the TimeZone object for the current time zone.
Dim tz As TimeZone = TimeZone.CurrentTimeZone
' Display name of time zone, without and with daylight saving time.
' (I got these results by running this code in Italy.)
Console.WriteLine(tz.StandardName)   ' => W. Europe Standard Time
Console.WriteLine(tz.DaylightName)   ' => W. Europe Daylight Time
```

The most interesting piece of information here is the offset from Universal time (UTC), which you retrieve by means of the GetUTCOffset method. You must pass a date argument to this method because the offset depends on whether daylight saving time is in effect. The returned value is in ticks:

```
' Display the time offset of W. Europe time zone in March 2001,
' when no daylight saving time is active.
Console.WriteLine(tz.GetUTCOffset(New Date(2001, 3, 1)))   ' => 01:00:00
```

(continued)

```
' Display the time offset of W. Europe time zone in July,
' when daylight saving time is active.
Console.WriteLine(tz.GetUTCOffset(New Date(2001, 7, 1)))  ' => 02:00:00
```

The IsDaylightSavingTime method returns True if daylight saving time is in effect:

```
' No daylight saving time in March
Console.WriteLine(tz.IsDaylightSavingTime(New Date(2001, 3, 1)))
' => False
```

Finally, you can determine when daylight saving time starts and ends in a given year by retrieving an array of DaylightTime objects with the TimeZone's GetDaylightChanges method:

```
' Retrieve the DaylightTime object for year 2001.
Dim dlc As System.Globalization.DaylightTime = _
    tz.GetDaylightChanges(2001)
' Note that you might get different start and end dates if you
' run this code in a country other than the United States.
Console.WriteLine("Starts at " & dlc.Start)
    ' => Starts at 4/1/2001 2:00:00 AM
Console.WriteLine("Ends at " & dlc.End)
    ' => Ends at 10/28/2001 3:00:00 AM
' Delta returns a TimeSpan object.
Console.WriteLine("Delta is {0} minutes", dlc.Delta.TotalMinutes)
    ' => Delta is 60 minutes.
```

The Guid Type

The System.Guid type exposes several shared and instance methods that can help you work with GUIDs, that is, those 128-bit numbers that serve to uniquely identify elements and that are ubiquitous in Windows programming. The NewGuid shared method is useful for generating a new unique identifier:

```
' Create a new GUID.
Dim guid1 As Guid = Guid.NewGuid
' By definition, you'll surely get a different output here.
Console.WriteLine(guid1.ToString)
    '=> 3f5f1d42-2d92-474d-a2a4-1e707c7e2a37
```

If you already have a GUID—for example, a GUID you have read from a database field—you can initialize a Guid variable by passing the GUID representation as a string or as an array of bytes to the type's constructor:

```
' Initialize from a string.
Dim guid2 As New Guid("45FA3B49-3D66-AB33-BB21-1E3B447A6621")
```

There are only two more things you can do with a Guid object: you can convert it to a Byte array with the ToByteArray method, and you can compare two Guid values for equality using the Equals method (inherited from System.Object):

```
' Convert to an array of bytes.
Dim bytes() As Byte = guid1.ToByteArray
Dim b As Byte
For Each b In bytes
    Console.Write(b.ToString & " ")
        ' => 239 1 161 57 143 200 172 70 185 64 222 29 59 15 190 205
Next

' Compare two GUIDs.
If Not guid1.Equals(guid2) Then
    Console.WriteLine("GUIDs are different.")
End If
```

Enums

I briefly covered enumerated values in Chapter 2. Now I complete the description of Enum blocks by mentioning all the methods you can apply to them.

Any Enum you define in your application derives from System.Enum, which in turn inherits from System.ValueType. Ultimately, therefore, user-defined Enums are value types, but they are special in that you can't define additional properties, methods, or events. All the methods they expose are inherited from System.Enum. (Note that it's illegal to explicitly inherit a class from System.Enum in Visual Basic.)

All the examples in this section refer to the following Enum block:

```
' This Enum defines the data type accepted for a
' value entered by the end user.
Enum DataEntry As Integer             ' As Integer is optional.
    IntegerNumber
    FloatingNumber
    CharString
    DateTime
End Enum
```

By default, the first enumerated type is assigned the value 0. You can change this initial value if you want, but you aren't encouraged to do so. In fact, it is advisable that 0 be a valid value for any Enum blocks you define; otherwise, a noninitialized Enum variable will contain an invalid value.

The .NET SDK defines a few guidelines for Enum values:

- Use names without the *Enum* suffix; use singular names for regular Enum types and plural for bit-coded Enum types.
- Use PascalCase for the name of both the Enum and its member. (An exception is constants from the Windows API, which are usually all uppercase.)
- Use Integer unless you need a larger range, which normally happens only if you have a bit-coded Enum with more than 32 possible values.
- Don't use Enums for open sets, that is, sets that you might need to expand in the future (for example, operating system versions).

Displaying and Parsing Enum Values

The Enum class overrides the ToString method to return the value as a readable string format. This method is useful when you want to expose a (nonlocalized) string to the end user:

```
Dim de As DataEntry = DataEntry.DateTime
' Display the numeric value.
Console.WriteLine(de)                   ' => 3
' Display the symbolic value.
Console.WriteLine(de.ToString)          ' => DateTime
```

Or you can use the capability to pass a format character to an overloaded version of the ToString method—for example, using the "X" formatting option to display the value in hexadecimal format:

```
' Show the value in hexadecimal format, with 4 digits.
Console.WriteLine(de.ToString("X"))    ' => 0003
```

Other overloaded versions of the ToString method accept an IFormatProvider object, so you can easily create your custom formatter objects—for example, to convert an Enum value to a localized string.

The opposite of ToString is the Parse shared method, which takes a string and converts it to the corresponding enumerated value:

```
de = DataEntry.Parse(GetType(DataEntry), "CharString"))
Console.WriteLine(de)                   ' => CharString
```

There are two things worth noticing in the preceding code. First, the Parse method takes a Type argument, so you must convert DataEntry to a type with the GetType function. Second, Parse is a shared method and can be invoked through any Enum object, including DataEntry itself. In some cases, however, you don't have a specific variable to use as a prefix for the Parse method, and you are forced to use the generic Enum class. Enum is a reserved Visual Basic word, so you must either use its complete System.Enum name or enclose its name between square brackets:

```
' These statements are equivalent to the one in the previous fragment.
Console.WriteLine([Enum].Parse(GetType(DataEntry), "CharString"))
Console.WriteLine(System.Enum.Parse(GetType(DataEntry), "CharString"))
```

Being inherited from the generic Enum class, the Parse method returns a generic object, so you have to set Option Strict to Off or use an explicit cast to assign it to a specific enumerated variable:

```
' You can use the GetType method (inherited from System.Object)
' to get the Type object required by the Parse method.
de = CType([Enum].Parse(de.GetType, "CharString"), DataEntry)
```

The Parse method throws an ArgumentException if the name doesn't correspond to a defined enumerated value. Names are compared in a case-sensitive way, but you can pass a True optional argument if you don't want to take the string case into account:

```
' *** This statement throws an exception.
Console.WriteLine([Enum].Parse(de.GetType, "charstring"))
' This works well because case-insensitive comparison is used.
Console.WriteLine([Enum].Parse(de.GetType, "charstring", True))
```

Other Enum Methods

The GetUnderlyingType shared method returns the base type for an enumerated class:

```
Console.WriteLine([Enum].GetUnderlyingType(de.GetType))    ' => System.Int16
```

The IsDefined method lets you check whether a numeric value is acceptable as an enumerated value of a given class:

```
' NOTE: the IsDefined method requires that the value being checked be
'       the same underlying value as the Enum (Short in this case).
If [Enum].IsDefined(GetType(DataEntry), 3S) Then
    ' 3 is a valid value for the DataEntry class.
    de = CType(3, DataEntry)
End If
```

The IsDefined method is useful because the CType operator doesn't check whether the value being converted is in the valid range for the target enumerated type. In other words, the following statement doesn't throw any exception:

```
' This code produces an invalid result, yet it doesn't throw an exception.
de = CType(123, DataEntry)
```

Another way to check whether a numeric value is acceptable for an Enum object is the GetName method, which returns the name of the enumerated value, or Nothing if the value is invalid:

```
' GetName doesn't require that the value being converted be
' the same type as the Enum.
If [Enum].GetName(GetType(DataEntry), 3) <> "" Then
    de = CType(3, DataEntry)
End If
```

You can quickly list all the values of an enumerated type with the GetNames and GetValues methods: the former returns a String array holding the individual names (sorted by the corresponding values); the latter returns an Object array that holds the numeric values:

```
' List all the values in DataEntry.
Dim names() As String = [Enum].GetNames(GetType(DataEntry))
Dim values As Array = [Enum].GetValues(GetType(DataEntry))
Dim i As Integer

For i = 0 To names.Length - 1
    Console.WriteLine("{0} = {1}", names(i), CInt(values.GetValue(i)))
Next
```

Here's the output of the preceding code snippet:

```
IntegerNumber = 0
FloatingNumber = 1
CharString = 2
DateTime = 3
```

Bit-Coded Values

The .NET Framework supports a special Flags attribute that you can use to specify that an Enum object represents a bit-coded value. For example, let's create a new class named ValidDataEntry class, which lets the developer specify two or more valid data types for values entered by an end user:

```
<Flags()> Enum ValidDataEntry As Short
    None = 0              ' Always define an enum value = 0.
    IntegerNumber = 1
    FloatingNumber = 2
    CharString = 4
    DateTime = 8
End Enum
```

The FlagAttribute class doesn't expose a property, and its constructor takes no arguments: the presence of this attribute is sufficient to label this Enum type as bit coded.

Bit-coded enumerated types behave exactly like regular Enum values except that their ToString method recognizes the Flags attribute. When an enumerated type is composed of two or more flag values, this method returns the list of all the corresponding values, separated by commas:

```
Dim vde As ValidDataEntry
vde = ValidDataEntry.IntegerNumber Or ValidDataEntry.DateTime
Console.WriteLine(vde.ToString)        ' => IntegerNumber, DateTime
```

If no bit is set, the ToString method returns the name of the enumerated value corresponding to the zero value:

```
Dim vde2 As ValidDataEntry
Console.WriteLine(vde2.ToString)     ' => None
```

If the value doesn't correspond to a valid combination of bits, the Format method returns the number unchanged:

```
vde = CType(123, ValidDataEntry)
Console.WriteLine(vde.ToString)      ' => 123
```

The Parse method is affected by the Flags attribute too:

```
vde = CType([Enum].Parse( _
    vde.GetType, "IntegerNumber, FloatingNumber"), ValidDataEntry)
Console.WriteLine(CInt(vde))         ' => 3
```

This chapter concludes the description of .NET basic data types; in the next chapter, you'll read about more complex data structures, such as arrays, collections, and hash tables, and you'll learn how to create your own collection and dictionary classes.

Front
Top
Left
Back

9

Arrays, Lists, and Collections

The .NET Framework doesn't merely include classes for managing system objects, such as files, directories, processes, and threads. It also exposes objects, such as complex data structures (queues, stacks, and hash tables), that help developers solve recurring problems.

Many real-world applications use arrays and collections, and the .NET Framework support for arrays and collection-like objects is really outstanding. It can take a while for you to get familiar with the many possibilities that the .NET runtime offers, but this effort pays off nicely at coding time.

The Array Class

The Array class has no public constructor because its New procedure has a Protected scope. In practice, this is no problem because you create an array using the standard Visual Basic syntax, and, as you saw in Chapter 2, you can even use initializers:

```
' An array initialized with the powers of 2
Dim intArr() As Integer = {1, 2, 4, 8, 16, 32, 64, 128, 256, 512}
' Noninitialized two-dimensional array
Dim lngArr(10, 20) As Long
' An empty array
Dim dblArr() As Double
```

A variation of this syntax lets you create an array and initialize it on the fly, which is sometimes useful for passing an argument or assigning a property that takes an array without having to create a temporary array. Consider the code at the top of the next page.

```
' Create a temporary array.
Dim tmp() As Integer = {2, 5, 9, 13}
' The obj.ValueArray property takes an array of Integer.
obj.ValueArray = tmp
' Clear the temporary variable.
tmp = Nothing
```

The ability to create and initialize an array in a single statement makes the code more concise, even though the syntax you need isn't exactly intuitive:

```
obj.ValueArray = New Long() {2, 5, 9, 13}
```

As in Visual Basic 6, you get an error if you access an empty array, which is an array that has no elements. Because the array is an object, you can test it using a plain Is operator and use ReDim on the array if necessary:

```
If dblArr Is Nothing Then
    ReDim dblArr(100)              ' Note: no As clause in ReDims
End If
```

You can query an array for its rank (that is, the number of dimensions) by using its Rank property, and you can query the total number of its elements by means of its Length property:

```
' ...(Continuing preceding example)...
Console.WriteLine(lngArr.Rank)     ' => 2
' lngArr has 11*21 elements.
Console.WriteLine(lngArr.Length)   ' => 231
```

The GetLength method returns the number of elements along a given dimension, whereas GetLowerBound and GetUpperBound return the lowest and highest index along the specified dimension. Unlike values returned by the LBound and UBound functions, the dimension number is 0-based, not 1-based:

```
' ...(Continuing previous example)...
Console.WriteLine(lngArr.GetLength(0))        ' => 11
Console.WriteLine(lngArr.GetLowerBound(1))    ' => 0
Console.WriteLine(lngArr.GetUpperBound(1))    ' => 20
```

You can visit all the elements of an array using a single For Each loop and a strongly-typed variable; this is an improvement on Visual Basic 6, which forces you to use a Variant (and therefore late binding) when working with numeric or string arrays. This technique also works with multidimensional arrays, so you can process all the elements in a two-dimensional array with just one loop:

```
Dim strArr(,) As String = {{"00", "01", "02"}, {"10", "11", "12"}}
Dim s As String
For Each s In strArr
    Console.Write(s & ",")      ' => 00,01,02,10,11,12
Next
```

For-Each loops on multidimensional arrays work in previous language versions as well, with an important difference: Visual Basic 6 visits array elements in a column-wise order (all the elements in the first column, then all the elements in the second column, and so on), whereas Visual Basic .NET follows the more natural row-wise order.

Creating Nonzero-Based Arrays

The GetLowerBound method might look unnecessary because all Visual Basic arrays have indexes beginning with 0. However, it turns out that you can create arrays with arbitrary starting indexes by means of the shared Array.CreateInstance method, even though the required syntax isn't exactly straightforward:

```
Sub TestArraysWithNonZeroLBound()
    ' Create a bidimensional array that is equivalent
    ' to the following Visual Basic 6 declaration:
    '     Dim(1 To 5, -10 To 10) As Integer

    ' Prepare an auxiliary array with the length along each direction.
    Dim lengths() As Integer = {5, 21}
    ' An auxiliary array with the starting index along each direction
    Dim lbounds() As Integer = {1, -10}
    ' Create a generic Array object from the shared CreateInstance method.
    Dim arrObj As Array = _
        Array.CreateInstance(GetType(Integer), lengths, lbounds)
    ' Assign it to an array with the right rank.
    Dim arr(,) As Integer = CType(arrObj, Integer(,))

    ' Prove that it worked.
    Console.WriteLine(arr.GetLowerBound(0))        ' => 1
    Console.WriteLine(arr.GetUpperBound(0))        ' => 5
    Console.WriteLine(arr.GetLowerBound(1))        ' => -10
    Console.WriteLine(arr.GetUpperBound(1))        ' => 10
    ' Assign an element, and read it back.
    arr(1, -1) = 1234
    Console.WriteLine(arr(1, -1))                  ' => 1234
End Sub
```

Now that I have shown you how to create arrays with nonzero lower bounds, I ask you not to use them for anything other than impressing your friends at the local VB user group. The main problem with this technique is that it works well only with multidimensional arrays: when you use it with one-dimensional arrays it forces you to read and write array elements by calling the GetValue and SetValue methods, a rather clumsy practice. (This difference is caused by the fact that one-dimensional arrays, also known as vectors in .NET, are implemented differently from other arrays.) In addition, arrays with a lower index other than 0 aren't Common Language Specification (CLS) compliant, so you might have problems sharing them with other .NET languages.

Finally, a nonzero lower index changes the way some methods of the Array class work. For example, the IndexOf method (see later in the "Searching Values" section) is expected to return –1 if an element isn't found, which apparently makes it unusable with arrays whose lowest index is a negative number. The truth is, IndexOf returns the lowest index minus 1 when an element isn't found and therefore does work correctly even with these arrays, but this detail makes working with them even more confusing.

Copying Arrays

The Array class supports the ICloneable interface, so you can create a shallow copy of an array using the Clone instance method. (See the section "The ICloneable Interface" in Chapter 6 for a discussion about shallow and deep copy operations.)

```
' This works if Option Strict is Off.
Dim anotherArray(,) As Integer = arr.Clone

' This is the required syntax if Option Strict is On.
' (You can also use CType instead of DirectCast.)
Dim anotherArray(,) As Integer = DirectCast(arr.Clone, Integer())
```

You can copy a one-dimensional array to another, and you decide the starting index in the destination array:

```
' Create and initialize an array (10 elements).
Dim sourceArr() As Integer = {1, 2, 3, 5, 7, 11, 13, 17, 19, 23}
' Create the destination array (must be same size or larger).
Dim destArr(20) As Integer
' Copy the source array into the second half of the destination array.
sourceArr.CopyTo(destArr, 10)
```

Pay attention to an important detail: the index in the target array is actually the offset from the array starting index. If the target array is 0-based (as are all the arrays created with the Dim statement), you can safely pass the index of the first element that will be overwritten in the target array. However, if you used Array.CreateInstance to create an array whose lowest index is a number other than 0, you must modify the second argument of the CopyTo method accordingly. For example, if the array is 1-based, pass the value 9 so that destArr(10) is the first overwritten element.

Sorting Elements

The Array class offers several shared methods for processing arrays quickly and easily. In Chapter 3, you read about the Array.Sort method, and in Chapter 6, you learned that you can sort arrays of objects using an arbitrary group of keys by means of the IComparable and IComparer interfaces. The Sort method is even more flexible than anything you've seen so far. For example, you can sort just a portion of an array:

```
' Sort only elements [10,100] of the targetArray.
' Second argument is starting index; last argument is length of the subarray.
Array.Sort(targetArray, 10, 91)
```

You can also sort an array of values using another array that holds the sorting keys, which lets you sort arrays of structures or objects. To see how this overloaded version of the Sort method works, let's start defining a structure:

```
Structure Employee
    Public FirstName As String
    Public LastName As String
    Public HireDate As Date

    Sub New(ByVal firstName As String, ByVal lastName As String, _
        ByVal hireDate As Date)
        Me.FirstName = firstName
        Me.LastName = lastName
        Me.HireDate = hireDate
    End Sub

    ' A function to display an element's properties easily
    Function Description() As String
        Return FirstName & " " & LastName & _
            " (hired on " & HireDate.ToShortDateString & ")"
    End Function
End Structure
```

The following code creates a main array of Employee structures, then creates an auxiliary key array that holds the hiring date of each employee, and finally sorts the main array using the auxiliary array:

```
' Create a test array.
Dim employees() As Employee = { _
    New Employee("Joe", "Doe", #3/1/2001#), _
    New Employee("Robert", "Smith", #8/12/2000#), _
    New Employee("Ann", "Douglas", #11/1/1999#)}

' Create a parallel array of hiring dates.
Dim hireDates(UBound(employees)) As Date
Dim j As Integer
```

(continued)

```
For j = 0 To employees.Length - 1
    hireDates(j) = employees(j).HireDate
Next
' Sort the array of Employees using HireDates to provide the keys.
Array.Sort(hireDates, employees)
' Prove that the array is sorted on the HireDate field.
For j = 0 To employees.Length - 1
    Console.WriteLine(employees(j).Description)
Next
```

Interestingly, the key array is sorted as well, so you don't need to initialize it again when you add another element to the main array:

```
' Add a fourth employee.
ReDim Preserve employees(3)
employees(3) = New Employee("Chris", "Doe", #5/9/2000#)
' Extend the key array as well - no need to reinitialize it.
ReDim Preserve hireDates(3)
hireDates(3) = employees(3).HireDate
' Re-sort the new, larger array.
Array.Sort(hireDates, employees)
```

An overloaded version of the Sort method lets you sort a portion of an array of values for which you provide an array of keys. This is especially useful when you start with a large array that you fill only partially:

```
' Create a test array with a lot of room.
Dim employees(1000) As Employee
' Initialize only its first four elements.
⋮
' Sort only the portion actually used.
Array.Sort(hireDates, employees, 0, 4)
```

All the versions of the Array.Sort method that you've seen so far can take an additional IComparer object, which dictates how the array elements or keys are to be compared with one another. For more information, see the section "The IComparer Interface" in Chapter 6.

The Array.Reverse method reverses the order of elements in an array or in a portion of an array, so you can apply it immediately after a Sort method to get descending sorting:

```
' Sort an array of Integers in reverse order.
Array.Sort(intArray)
Array.Reverse(intArray)
```

You pass the initial index and number of elements to reverse only a portion of an array:

```
' Reverse only the first 10 elements in intArray.
Array.Reverse(intArray, 0, 10)
```

You have a special case when you reverse only two elements, which is the same as swapping two consecutive elements, a frequent operation when you're working with arrays:

```
' Swap elements at indexes 5 and 6.
Array.Reverse(intArray, 5, 2)
```

Clearing, Copying, and Moving Elements

You can clear a portion of an array with the Clear method, without a For loop:

```
' Clear elements [10,100] of an array.
Array.Clear(arr, 10, 91)
```

The Array.Copy method lets you copy elements from a one-dimensional array to another. There are two overloaded versions for this method. The first version copies a given number of elements from the source array to the destination array:

```
Dim intArr() As Integer = {1, 2, 3, 4, 5, 6, 7, 8, 9, 10}
Dim intArr2(20) As Integer
' Copy the entire source array into the first half of the target array.
Array.Copy(intArr, intArr2, 10)
Dim i As Integer
For i = 0 To 20
    Console.Write(CStr(intArr2(i)) & " ")
        ' => 1 2 3 4 5 6 7 8 9 10 0 0 0 0 0 0 0 0 0 0 0
Next
```

The second version lets you decide the starting index in the source array, the starting index in the destination array (that is, the index of the first element that will be overwritten), and the number of elements to copy:

```
' Copy elements at indexes 5-9 to the end of destArr.
Array.Copy(intArr, 5, intArr2, 15, 5)
' This is the first element that has been copied.
Console.WriteLine(intArr2(15))                ' => 6
```

You get an exception of type ArgumentOutOfRangeException if you provide wrong values for the indexes or the destination array isn't large enough, and you get an exception of type RankException if either array has two or more dimensions.

The Copy method works correctly even when source and destination arrays have a different type, in which case it attempts to cast each individual source element to the corresponding element in the destination array. The actual behavior depends on many factors, though, such as whether the source or the destination is a value type or a reference type. For example, you can always copy from any array to an Object array, from an Integer array to a Long array, and from a Single array to a Double array because they are widening conversions and can't fail. Copy throws an exception of type TypeMismatchException when you attempt a narrowing conversion between arrays of value types, even though individual elements in the source array might be successfully converted to the destination type:

```
' This Copy operation succeeds even if array types are different.
Dim intArr3() As Integer = {1, 2, 3, 4, 5, 6, 7, 8, 9, 10}
Dim lngArr3(20) As Long
Array.Copy(intArr3, lngArr3, 10)

' This Copy operation fails with TypeMismatchException.
'   (But you can carry it out with an explicit For loop.)
Dim lngArr4() As Long = {1, 2, 3, 4, 5, 6, 7, 8, 9, 10}
Dim intArr4(20) As Integer
Array.Copy(lngArr4, intArr4, 10)
```

Conversely, if you copy from and to an array of reference type, the Array.Copy method attempts the copy operation for each element; if an InvalidCastException object is thrown for an element, the method copies neither that element nor any of the values after the one that raised the error. For more details about the Array.Copy method, see the .NET Framework SDK documentation.

The SDK documentation doesn't mention one of the most important features of the Array.Copy method: the ability to copy a portion of an array over itself. In this case, the Copy method performs a "smart copy," in the sense that elements are copied correctly, in ascending order when you're copying to a lower index and in reverse order when you're copying to a higher index. So you can use the Copy method to delete one or more elements and fill the hole that would result by shifting all subsequent elements one or more positions toward lower indexes:

```
Dim lngArr5() As Long = {1, 2, 3, 4, 5, 6, 7, 8, 9, 10}
' Delete element at index 4.
Array.Copy(lngArr5, 5, lngArr5, 4, 5)
' Complete the delete operation by clearing the last element.
Array.Clear(lngArr5, lngArr5.GetUpperBound(0), 1)
' Now the array contains: {1, 2, 3, 4, 6, 7, 8, 9, 10, 0}
```

You can use this code as the basis for a reusable routine that works with any type of array:

```
Sub ArrayDeleteElement(ByVal arr As Array, ByVal index As Integer)
    ' Shift elements from arr(index+1) to arr(index).
    Array.Copy(arr, index + 1, arr, index, UBound(arr) - Index)
    ' Clear the last element.
    arr.Clear(arr, arr.GetUpperBound(0), 1)
End Sub
```

Inserting an element is also easy, and again you can create a generic routine that works with arrays of any type:

```
Sub ArrayInsertElement(ByVal arr As Array, ByVal index As Integer, _
    Optional ByVal newValue As Object = Nothing)
    ' Shift elements from arr(index) to arr(index+1) to make room.
    Array.Copy(arr, index, arr, index + 1, arr.Length - index - 1)
    ' Assign the element using the SetValue method.
    arr.SetValue(newValue, index)
End Sub
```

The Array class exposes the SetValue and GetValue methods to assign and read elements; you don't normally use these methods in regular programming, but they turn out to be useful in generic routines (such as the two preceding routines) that work with any type of array. SetValue and GetValue are also useful for working with elements of non-CLS-compliant arrays with a nonzero lowest index. (See "Creating Nonzero-Based Arrays" earlier in this chapter.)

You can also use Copy with multidimensional arrays, in which case the array is treated as if it were a one-dimensional array with all the rows laid down in memory one after the other.

Searching Values

The IndexOf method searches an array for a value and returns the index of the first element that matches or –1 if the search fails:

```
Dim strArray() As String = {"Robert", "Joe", "Ann", "Chris", "Joe"}
Console.WriteLine(Array.IndexOf(strArray, "Ann"))    ' => 2
' Note that string searches are case sensitive.
Console.WriteLine(Array.IndexOf(strArray, "ANN"))    ' => -1
```

More precisely, IndexOf returns the lowest index value minus 1 when the search fails; this difference is important only when the array isn't 0-based. You can also specify a starting index and an optional ending index; if an ending index is omitted, the search continues until the end of the array.

You can use this overloaded form to find all the values in the array with a given value:

```
' Search for all the occurrences of the "Joe" string.
Dim index As Integer = -1
Do
    ' Search next occurrence.
    index = Array.IndexOf(strArray, "Joe", index + 1)
    ' Exit the loop if not found.
    If index = -1 Then Exit Do
    Console.WriteLine("Found at index {0}", index)
Loop
```

(continued)

The preceding loop displays the following messages in the console window:

```
Found at index 1
Found at index 4
```

The LastIndexOf method is similar to IndexOf except that it returns the index of the last occurrence of the value. Because the search is backward, you must pass a start index higher than the end index:

```
' A revised version of the search loop, which searches
' from higher indexes toward the beginning of the array.
index = strArr.Length
Do
    index = Array.LastIndexOf(strArr, "Joe", index - 1)
    If index = -1 Then Exit Do
    Console.WriteLine("Found at index {0}", index)
Loop
```

The IndexOf and LastIndexOf methods perform a linear search, so their performance degrades linearly with larger arrays. You deliver much faster code if the array is sorted and you use the BinarySearch method:

```
' Binary search on a sorted array
Dim strArr2() As String = {"Ann", "Chris", "Joe", "Robert", "Sam"}
Console.WriteLine(Array.BinarySearch(strArr2, "Chris"))      ' => 1
```

If the binary search fails, the method returns a negative value that's the bitwise complement of the index of the first element that's larger than the value being searched. This feature lets you determine where the value should be inserted in the sorted array:

```
index = Array.BinarySearch(strArr2, "David")
If index >= 0 Then
    Console.WriteLine("Found at index {0}", index)
Else
    ' Negate the result to get the index for the insertion point.
    index = Not index
    Console.WriteLine("Not Found. Insert at index {0}", index)
        ' => Not found. Insert at index 2
End If
```

You can pass a start index and the length of the portion of the array to the point at which you want to perform the search, which is useful when you're working with an array that's only partially filled:

```
Console.Write(Array.BinarySearch(strArr2, 0, 3, "Chris"))   ' => 1
```

Finally, both syntax forms for the BinarySearch method support an IComparer object at the end of the argument list, which lets you determine how array elements are to be compared. In practice, you can use the same IComparer object that you passed to the Sort method to have the array sorted.

Arrays of Arrays

Visual Basic .NET also supports arrays of arrays, that is, arrays whose elements are arrays. This is a familiar concept to most C++ programmers, but it might be new to many Visual Basic programmers. In my book *Programming Microsoft Visual Basic 6*, I showed how you can create such structures in previous versions of the language by using the ability to store arrays in Variants. The good news is that Visual Basic .NET supports arrays of arrays natively, so you don't have to resort to any hack.

Arrays of arrays—also known as *jagged arrays*—are especially useful when you have a two-dimensional matrix whose rows don't have the same length. You can render this structure by using a standard two-dimensional array, but you'd have to size it to accommodate the row with the highest number of elements, which would result in a waste of space. The arrays of arrays concept isn't limited to two dimensions only, and you might need three-dimensional or four-dimensional jagged arrays. Here is an example of a "triangular" matrix of strings:

```
"a00"
"a10"  "a11"
"a20"  "a21"  "a22"
"a30"  "a31"  "a32"  "a33"
```

Even though Visual Basic .NET supports arrays of arrays natively, I can't consider their syntax to be intuitive. The next code snippet shows how you can initialize the preceding structure and then process it by expanding its rows:

```
Sub TestJaggedArray()
    ' Initialize an array of arrays.
    Dim arr()() As String = {New String() {"a00"}, _
        New String() {"a10", "a11"}, _
        New String() {"a20", "a21", "a22"}, _
        New String() {"a30", "a31", "a32", "a33"}}

    ' Show how you can reference an element.
    Console.WriteLine(arr(3)(1))                       ' => a31

    ' Assign an entire row.
    arr(0) = New String() {"a00", "a01", "a02"}
```

(continued)

```
    ' Read an element just added.
    Console.WriteLine(arr(0)(2))                            ' => a02

    ' Expand one of the rows.
    ReDim Preserve arr(1)(3)
    ' Assign the new elements. (Currently they are Nothing.)
    arr(1)(2) = "a12"
    arr(1)(3) = "a13"
    ' Read back one of them.
    Console.WriteLine(arr(1)(2))                            ' => a12
End Sub
```

The System.Collections Namespace

The System.Collections namespace exposes many classes that can work as generic data containers, such as collections and dictionaries. You can learn the features of all these objects individually, but a smarter approach is to learn about the underlying interfaces that these classes might implement.

The ICollection, IList, and IDictionary Interfaces

All the collection classes in the .NET Framework implement the ICollection interface, which inherits from IEnumerable and defines an object that supports enumeration through a For Each loop. The ICollection interface exposes a read-only Count property and a CopyTo method, which copies the elements from the collection object to an array.

The ICollection interface defines the minimum features that a collection-like object should have. The .NET Framework exposes two more interfaces whose methods add power and flexibility to the object: IList and IDictionary.

Many classes in the framework implement the IList interface. This interface inherits from ICollection, and therefore from IEnumerable, and represents a collection of objects that can be individually indexed. All the implementations of the IList interface fall into three categories:

- **Read-only** The collection's elements can't be modified or deleted, nor can new elements be inserted.
- **Fixed-size** Existing items can be modified, but elements can't be added or removed.
- **Variable-size** Items can be modified, added, and removed.

Table 9-1 summarizes the main properties and methods of the IList interface. You should already be familiar with most of them because they're implemented in many other collection-like objects that you've worked with in the past, most notably Collection and Dictionary objects in Visual Basic 6.

Table 9-1 Members of the IList Interface

Syntax	Description
Count	Returns the number of elements in the collection (inherited from ICollection).
CopyTo(array, index)	Copies elements from the collection to an array, starting at the specified index in the array (inherited from ICollection).
Item(index)	Gets or sets the element at the specified 0-based index. This is the default member.
Clear	Removes all items from the collection.
Add(object)	Appends an element after the last element in the collection and returns the index where it was inserted.
Insert(index, object)	Inserts an element at a given index.
Remove(object)	Removes an object from the collection.
RemoveAt(index)	Removes an element at the specified index.
Contains(object)	Returns True if an object is in the collection.
IndexOf(object)	Returns the index of the object in the collection, or –1 if not found.
IsFixedSize	Returns True if no item can be added to the collection.
IsReadOnly	Returns True if items can't be written to.

The IDictionary interface defines a collection-like object that contains one or more (key, value) pairs for which the key can be any object (not just a string in Visual Basic 6 collections). The IDictionary interface inherits from ICollection and extends it using the methods defined in Table 9-2. As for the IList interface, implementations of the IDictionary interface can be read-only, fixed-size, or variable-size.

Table 9-2 Members of the IDictionary Interface

Syntax	Description
Count	Returns the number of elements in the dictionary (inherited from ICollection).
CopyTo(array, index)	Copies elements from the dictionary to an array, starting at the specified index in the array (inherited from ICollection).
Item(key)	Gets or sets the element associated with the specified key. This is the default member.

(continued)

Table 9-2 Members of the IDictionary Interface *(continued)*

Syntax	Description
Clear	Removes all items from the dictionary.
Add(key, value)	Inserts a (key, value) pair into the dictionary; key must not be Nothing.
Remove(key)	Removes the dictionary element associated with a given key.
Contains(key)	Returns True if an element with the specified key is in the dictionary.
Keys	Returns an ICollection object that contains all the keys in the dictionary.
Values	Returns an ICollection object that contains all the values in the dictionary.
IsFixedSize	Returns True if no item can be added to the dictionary.
IsReadOnly	Returns True if items can't be written to.

A class that implements the ICollection, IList, or IDictionary interface isn't required to expose all the interface's properties and methods as Public members. For example, the Array class implements IList, but the Add, Insert, and Remove members don't appear in the Array class interface because the array has a fixed size. (You get an exception if you try to access these methods by casting an array to an IList variable.)

A trait that all the classes in System.Collections except the BitArray class have in common is that they can store Object values. (As its name implies, the BitArray class stores Boolean values.) This means that you can store any type of value inside them and even mix data types inside the same structure. In this sense, they're similar to the Collection object in Visual Basic 6, which used Variants internally and could therefore store numbers, strings, dates, and objects.

The BitArray Class

The BitArray object can hold a large number of Boolean values in a compact format, using a single bit for each element. This class implements IEnumerable (and thus supports For Each), ICollection (and thus supports indexing of individual elements), and ICloneable (and thus supports the Clone method). You can create a BitArray object in many ways:

```
' Provide the number of elements (all initialized to False).
Dim ba As New BitArray(1024)
' Provide the number of elements, and initialize them to a value.
Dim ba2 As New BitArray(1024, True)

' Initialize the BitArray from an array of Boolean, Byte, or Integer.
Dim boolArr(1023) As Boolean
```

```
' ...(Initialize the boolArr array)...
Dim ba3 As New BitArray(boolArr)

' Initialize the BitArray from another BitArray object.
Dim ba4 As New BitArray(ba)
```

You can retrieve the number of elements in a BitArray by using either the Count property or the Length property. The Get method reads and the Set method modifies the element at the specified index:

```
' Set element at index 9, and read it back.
ba.Set(9, True)
Console.WriteLine(ba.Get(9))     ' => True
```

The CopyTo method can move all elements back to an array of Booleans, or it can perform a bitwise copy of the BitArray to a 0-based Byte or Integer array:

```
' Bitwise copy to an array of Integers
Dim intArr(31) As Integer        ' 32 elements * 32 bits each = 1024 bits
' Second argument is the index in which the copy begins in target array.
ba.CopyTo(intArr, 0)
' Check that bit 9 of first element in intArr is set.
Console.WriteLine(intArr(0))     ' => 512
```

The Not method complements all the bits in the BitArray object:

```
ba.Not()                            ' No arguments
```

The And, Or, and Xor methods let you perform the corresponding operation on pairs of Boolean values stored in two BitArray objects:

```
' Perform an AND operation of all the bits in the first BitArray
' with the complement of all the bits in the second BitArray.
ba.And(ba2.Not)
```

Finally, you can set or reset all the bits in a BitArray class using the SetAll method:

```
' Set all the bits to True.
ba.SetAll(True)
```

The BitArray class doesn't expose any methods that let you quickly determine how many True (or False) elements are in the array. You can take advantage of the IEnumerator support of this class and use a For Each loop:

```
Dim b As Boolean
Dim TrueCount As Integer
For Each b In ba
    If b Then TrueCount += 1
Next
Console.Write("Found {0} True values.", TrueCount)
```

The Stack Class

In Visual Basic 6, you can simulate a last-in-first-out (LIFO) structure by using an array and an Integer variable that works as the pointer to the current element. Under Visual Basic .NET, you can build a stack structure by simply instantiating a System.Collections.Stack object:

```
' Define a stack with initial capacity of 50 elements.
Dim st As New Stack(50)
```

The three basic methods of a Stack object are Push, Pop, and Peek; the Count property returns the number of elements currently in the stack:

```
' Create a stack that can contain 100 elements.
Dim st As New Stack(100)
' Push three values onto the stack.
st.Push(10)
st.Push(20)
st.Push(30)
' Pop the value on top of the stack, and display its value.
Console.WriteLine(st.Pop)        ' => 30
' Read the value on top of the stack without popping it.
Console.WriteLine(st.Peek)       ' => 20
' Now pop it.
Console.WriteLine(st.Pop)        ' => 20
' Determine how many elements are now in the stack.
Console.WriteLine(st.Count)      ' => 1
' Pop the only value still on the stack.
Console.WriteLine(st.Pop)        ' => 10
' Check that the stack is now empty.
Console.WriteLine(st.Count)      ' => 0
```

The only other method that can prove useful is Contains, which returns True if a given value is currently in the stack:

```
' Is the value 10 somewhere in the stack?
If st.Contains(10) Then Console.Write("Found")
```

The Queue Class

A first-in-first-out (FIFO) structure, also known as a *queue* or *circular buffer*, is often used to solve recurring programming problems. You need a queue structure when a portion of an application inserts elements at one end of a buffer and another piece of code extracts the first available element at the other end. This situation occurs whenever you have a series of elements that you must process sequentially but you can't process immediately.

In Visual Basic 6, you typically implement queues by using an array for holding elements; a pointer to the element added, or *enqueued*, more recently;

and another pointer to the element about to be extracted, or *dequeued*, from the queue. When you're creating a circular buffer, you must anticipate several potential error conditions, such as the attempt to extract an element from an empty queue, and decide what to do when the array is full. (Should you refuse the insertion, or should you extend the buffer?)

You don't need to write any code to render a queue in Visual Basic .NET because you can leverage the System.Collections.Queue object. Queue objects have an initial capacity, but the internal buffer is automatically extended if the need arises. You create a Queue object by specifying its initial capacity and an optional growth factor:

```
' A queue with initial capacity of 200 elements; a growth factor equal to 1.5
' (When new room is needed, the capacity will become 300, then 450, 675, etc.)
Dim qu As New Queue(200, 1.5)
' A queue with 100 elements and a default growth factor of 2
Dim qu As New Queue(100)
' A queue with 32 initial elements and a default growth factor of 2
Dim qu As New Queue()
```

The key methods of a Queue object are Enqueue, Peek, and Dequeue. Check the output of the following code snippet, and compare it with the behavior of the Stack object:

```
Dim qu As New Queue(100)
' Insert three values in the queue.
qu.Enqueue(10)
qu.Enqueue(20)
qu.Enqueue(30)
' Extract the first value, and display it.
Console.WriteLine(qu.Dequeue)     ' => 10
' Read the next value, but don't extract it.
Console.WriteLine(qu.Peek)        ' => 20
' Extract it.
Console.WriteLine(qu.Dequeue)     ' => 20
' Check how many items are still in the queue.
Console.WriteLine(qu.Count)       ' => 1
' Extract the last element, and check that the queue is now empty.
Console.WriteLine(qu.Dequeue)     ' => 30
Console.WriteLine(qu.Count)       ' => 0
```

The Queue object also supports the Contains method, which checks whether an element is in the queue, and the Clear method, which clears the queue's contents.

The ArrayList Class

You can think of the ArrayList class as a hybrid of the Array and Collection objects, in that it lets you work with a set of values as if it were an array and a collection at the same time. For example, you can address elements by their indexes, sort and reverse them, and search a value sequentially or by means of a binary search as you do with an array; you can append elements, insert them in a given position, or remove them as you do with a collection.

The ArrayList object has an initial capacity—in practice, the number of slots in the internal structure that holds the actual values—but you don't need to worry about that because an ArrayList is automatically expanded as needed, as all collections are. However, you can optimize your code by choosing an initial capability that offers a good compromise between used memory and the overhead that occurs whenever the ArrayList object has to expand:

```
' Create an ArrayList with default initial capacity of 16 elements.
Dim al As New ArrayList
' Create an ArrayList with initial capacity of 1000 elements.
Dim al2 As New ArrayList(1000)
```

You can modifiy the capacity at any moment to enlarge the internal array or shrink it, by assigning a value to the Capacity property. However, you can't make it smaller than the current number of elements actually stored in the array (which corresponds to the value returned by the Count property):

```
' Have the ArrayList take just the memory that it strictly needs.
al.Capacity = al.Count
' Another way to achieve the same result
al.TrimToSize
```

When the current capacity is exceeded, the ArrayList object doubles its capacity automatically. You can't control an ArrayList's growth factor as you can a Queue object's, so it's critical that you set the Capacity property to a suitable value in order to avoid time-consuming memory allocations.

Another way to create an ArrayList object is by means of its shared Repeat method, which lets you determine an initial value for the specified number of elements:

```
' Create an ArrayList with 100 elements equal to a null string.
Dim al As ArrayList = ArrayList.Repeat("", 100)
```

The ArrayList class fully implements the IList interface, so you're already familiar with its basic methods. You add elements to an ArrayList object by using the Add method (which appends the new element after the last item) or the Insert method (which inserts at the specified index). You remove a specific object by using the Remove method, remove the element at a given index by using the RemoveAt method, or remove all elements by using the Clear method:

```
' Be sure that you start with an empty ArrayList.
al.Clear
' Append the elements "Joe" and "Ann" at the end of the ArrayList.
al.Add("Joe")
al.Add("Ann")
' Insert "Robert" item at the beginning of the list. (Index is 0-based.)
al.Insert(0, "Robert")
' Remove "Joe" from the list.
al.Remove("Joe")
' Remove the first element of the list ("Robert" in this case).
al.RemoveAt(0)
```

The Remove method removes only the first occurrence of a given object, so you need a loop to remove all the elements with a given value. You can't simply iterate through the loop until you get an error, however, because the Remove method doesn't throw an exception if the element isn't found. Therefore, you must use one of these two approaches:

```
' Using the IndexOf method is concise but not very efficient.
' (You can use also the Contains method.)
Do While al.IndexOf("element to remove") >= 0
    al.Remove("element to remove")
Loop

' A more efficient technique: loop until the Count property becomes constant.
Dim saveCount As Integer
Do
    saveCount = al.Count
    al.Remove("element to remove")
Loop While al.Count < saveCount
```

You can read and write any ArrayList element using the Item property. This property is the default property, so you can omit it and deal with this object as if it were a standard 0-based array. The main difference between a real array and an ArrayList object is that an element in an ArrayList object is created only when you invoke the Add method, so you can't reference an element whose index is equal to or higher than the ArrayList's Count property:

```
al(0) = "first element"
```

As with collections, the preferred way to iterate over all elements is through the For Each loop:

```
Dim o As Object
For Each o In al
    Console.WriteLine(o)
Next
```

The ArrayList class exposes methods that allow you to manipulate ranges of elements in one operation. The AddRange method appends to the current

ArrayList object all the elements contained in another object that implements the ICollection interface. Many .NET classes other than those described in this chapter implement ICollection, such as the collection of all the items in a ListBox control and the collection of nodes in a TreeView control. The following routine takes two ArrayList objects and returns a third ArrayList that contains all the items from both arguments:

```
Function ArrayListJoin(ByVal al1 As ArrayList, ByVal al2 As ArrayList) _
    As ArrayList
    ' Note how we avoid time-consuming reallocations.
    ArrayListJoin = New ArrayList(al1.Count + al2.count)
    ' Append the items in the two ArrayList arguments.
    ArrayListJoin.AddRange(al1)
    ArrayListJoin.AddRange(al2)
End Function
```

The InsertRange method works in a similar way but lets you insert multiple elements at any index in the current ArrayList object:

```
' Insert all the items of al2 at the beginning of the current ArrayList.
al.InsertRange(0, al2)
```

RemoveRange deletes multiple elements in the current ArrayList object:

```
' Delete the last four elements (assumes there are at least four elements).
al.RemoveRange(al.Count - 4, 4)
```

You can quickly extract all the items in the ArrayList object by using the ToArray method or the CopyTo method. Both of them support one-dimensional target arrays of any compatible type, but the latter also allows you to extract a subset of ArrayList:

```
' Extract elements to an Object array (never raises an error).
Dim objArr() As Object = al.ToArray()
' Extract elements to a String array (might throw an exception
' of type InvalidCastException).
' (Requires CType or DirectCast if Option Strict is On.)
Dim strArr() As String = CType(al.ToArray(GetType(String)), String())

' Same as above but uses the CopyTo method.
' (Note that the target array must be large enough.)
Dim strArr2(al.Count) As String
al.CopyTo(strArr2)
' Copy only items [1,2], starting at element 4 in the target array.
Dim strArr3() As String = {"0", "1", "2", "3", "4", "5", "6", "7", "8", "9"}
' Syntax is: sourceIndex, target, destIndex, count.
al.CopyTo(0, strArr3, 4, 2)
```

The ArrayList class supports other useful methods, such as Sort, SortRange, BinarySearch, IndexOf, LastIndexOf, and Reverse. I've already described most of these methods in depth in the section devoted to arrays, so I won't repeat their description here.

The last feature of the ArrayList class that's worth mentioning is its Adapter shared method. This method takes an IList-derived object as its only argument and creates an ArrayList wrapper around that object. In other words, instead of creating a copy of the argument, the Adapter method creates an ArrayList object that "contains" the original collection: all the changes you make on the outer ArrayList object are duplicated in the inner collection. The reason you might want to use the Adapter method is that the ArrayList class implements several methods—Reverse, Sort, BinarySearch, ToArray, IndexOf, and LastIndexOf, just to name a few—that are missing in the inner IList object. The following code sample demonstrates how you can use this technique to reverse (or sort, and so on) all the items in a ListBox control:

```
' Create a wrapper around the Listbox.Items IList collection.
Dim lbAdapter As ArrayList = ArrayList.Adapter(ListBox1.Items)
' Reverse their order.
lbAdapter.Reverse()
```

If you don't plan to reuse the ArrayList wrapper further, you can make this code even more concise:

```
ArrayList.Adapter(ListBox1.Items).Reverse()
```

The Hashtable Class

The Hashtable class implements the IDictionary interface, and it behaves much like the Scripting.Dictionary object you might have used from Visual Basic 6 days. (The Dictionary object can be found in the Microsoft Scripting Runtime library; see Chapter 4 in my *Programming Microsoft Visual Basic 6* book included on the companion CD for additional details.) All objects based on IDictionary manage two internal series of data, values and keys, and you can use a key to retrieve the corresponding value. The actual implementation of the methods in this interface depends on the specific object; for example, the Hashtable class uses an internal hash table, a well-known data structure that has been studied for decades by computer scientists and has been thoroughly described in countless books on algorithms.

When a (key, value) pair is added to a Hashtable object, the position of an element in the internal array is based on the numeric hash code of the key. When you later search for that key, the key's hash code is used again to locate the associated value as quickly as possible, without sequentially visiting all the elements in the hash table. Collection objects in Visual Basic 6 use a similar mechanism except that the key's hash code is derived from the characters in the key and the key must necessarily be a string. Conversely, the .NET Hashtable class lets you use *any* object as a key as long as its hash code can't change during the application's lifetime. Behind the scenes, the Hashtable object uses the key object's GetHashCode, a method that all objects inherit from System.Object, so you can even affect the way in which hash codes are used by overriding the GetHashCode method of the objects you're going to store in the Hashtable.

Depending on how the hash code is evaluated, it frequently happens that multiple keys map to the same slot (or *bucket*) in the hash table: in this case, you have a *collision*. The Hashtable object uses double hashing to minimize collisions, but it can't avoid collisions completely. To get optimal performance you must select an adequate initial capacity for the hash table: a larger table doesn't speed up searches remarkably, but it makes insertions faster.

You can also get better performance by selecting a correct *load factor* when you create a Hashtable object. This number determines the maximum ratio between values and buckets before the hash table is automatically expanded: the smaller this value is, the more memory is allocated to the internal table and the fewer collisions occur when you're inserting or searching for a value. The default load factor is 1.0, which in most cases delivers a good-enough performance, but you can set a smaller load factor when you create the Hashtable if you're willing to trade memory for better performance. You can initialize a Hashtable object in many ways:

```
' Default load factor and initial capacity
Dim ht As New Hashtable
' Default load factor and specified initial capacity
Dim ht2 As New Hashtable(1000)
' Specified initial capability and custom load factor
Dim ht3 As New Hashtable(1000, 0.8)
```

You can also initialize the Hashtable by loading it with the elements contained in any other object that implements the IDictionary interface (such as another Hashtable or a SortedList object). This technique is especially useful when you want to change the load factor of an existing hash table:

```
' Decrease the load factor of the current Hashtable.
ht = New HashTable(ht, 0.5)
```

Other, more sophisticated, variants of the constructor let you pass an IComparer object to compare keys in a customized fashion or an IHashCodeProvider object to supply a custom algorithm for calculating hash codes of keys.

The Hashtable object is very similar to the Scripting.Dictionary object in that you can add a key and value pair, read or modify the value associated with a given key through the Item property, and remove an item with the Remove method:

```
' Syntax for Add method is Add(key, value).
ht.Add("Joe", 12000)
ht.Add("Ann", 13000)
' Referencing a new key creates an element.
ht.Item("Robert") = 15000
' Item is the default member, so you can omit its name.
ht("Chris") = 11000
Console.Write(ht("Joe"))      ' => 12000
' The Item property lets you overwrite an existing element.
' (You need CInt or CType if Option Strict is On.)
ht("Ann") = CInt(ht("Ann")) + 1000
' Note that keys are compared in case-insensitive mode,
' so the following statement creates a *new* element.
ht("ann") = 15000
' Reading a nonexistent element doesn't create it.
Console.WriteLine(ht("Lee"))        ' Doesn't display anything.

' Remove an element given its key.
ht.Remove("Chris")
' How many elements are now in the hashtable?
Console.WriteLine(ht.Count)         ' => 4

' Adding an element that already exists throws an exception.
ht.Add("Joe", 11500)                ' Throws ArgumentException.
```

As I explained earlier, you can use virtually anything as a key, including a numeric value. When you're using numbers as keys, a Hashtable looks deceptively similar to an array:

```
ht(1) = 123
ht(2) = 345
```

But never forget that the expression between parentheses is just a key and not an index; thus, the ht(2) element isn't necessarily stored "after" the ht(1) element. As a matter of fact, the elements in a Hashtable object aren't stored in a particular order, and you should never write code that assumes that they are. This is the main difference between the Hashtable object and the SortedList object (which is described next).

The Hashtable object implements the IEnumerable interface, so you can iterate over all its elements with a For Each loop. Each element of a Hashtable is a DictionaryEntry object, which exposes a Key and a Value property:

```
Dim de As DictionaryEntry
For Each de In ht
    Console.WriteLine("ht('{0}') = {1}", de.Key, de.Value)
Next
```

The Hashtable's Keys and Values properties return an ICollection-based object that contains all the keys and all the values, respectively, so you can assign them to any object that implements the ICollection interface. Or you can use these properties directly in a For Each loop:

```
' Display all the keys in the Hashtable.
Dim o As Object
For Each o In ht.Keys          ' Or use ht.Values for all the values.
    Console.WriteLine(o)
Next
```

One last note: by default, keys are compared in a case-sensitive way, so *Joe*, *JOE*, and *joe* are considered distinct keys. You can create case-insensitive instances of the Hashtable class through one of its many constructors, or you can use the CreateCaseInsensitiveHashtable shared method of the System.Collections.Specialized.CollectionsUtil, as follows:

```
Dim ht2 As Hashtable = _
    Specialized.CollectionsUtil.CreateCaseInsensitiveHashtable()
```

The SortedList Class

The SortedList object is arguably the most versatile collection-like object in the .NET Framework. It implements the IDictionary interface, like the Hashtable object, and also keeps its elements sorted. Alas, you pay for all this power in terms of performance, so you should use the SortedList object only when your programming logic requires an object with all this flexibility.

The SortedList object manages two internal arrays, one for the values and one for the companion keys. These arrays have an initial capacity, but they automatically grow when the need arises. Entries are kept sorted by their key, and you can even provide an IComparer object to affect how complex values (an object, for example) are compared and sorted. The SortedList class provides several constructor methods:

```
' A SortedList with default capacity (16 entries)
Dim sl As New SortedList()
' A SortedList with specified initial capacity
Dim sl2 As New SortedList(1000)

' A SortedList can be initialized with all the elements in an IDictionary.
Dim ht As New Hashtable()
ht.Add("Robert", 100)
ht.Add("Ann", 200)
ht.Add("Joe", 300)
Dim sl3 As New SortedList(ht)
```

As soon as you add new elements to the SortedList, they're immediately sorted by their key:

```
' Iterate over all the DictionaryEntry items in a SortedList.
Dim de As DictionaryEntry
For Each de In sl3
    Console.WriteLine("sl3('{0}') = {1}", de.Key, de.Value)
Next
```

Here's the result that appears in the console window:

```
sl3('Ann') = 200
sl3('Joe') = 300
sl3('Robert') = 100
```

Keys are sorted according to the order implied by their IComparable interface, so numbers and strings are always sorted in ascending order. If you want a different order, you must create an object that implements the IComparer interface. For example, you can use the following class to invert the natural string ordering:

```
Class ReverseStringComparer
    Implements IComparer

    Function CompareValues(ByVal x As Object, ByVal y As Object) As Integer _
        Implements IComparer.Compare
        ' Just change the sign of the StrComp function's result.
        Return -StrComp(x.ToString, y.ToString)
    End Function
End Class
```

You can pass an instance of this object to one of the two overloaded constructors that take an IComparer object:

```
' A SortedList that sorts elements through a custom IComparer
Dim sl4 As New SortedList(New ReverseStringComparer)

' Here's a SortedList that loads all the elements in a Hashtable and
' sorts them with a custom IComparer object.
Dim sl5 As New SortedList(ht, New ReverseStringComparer)
```

Here are the elements of the resulting SortedList object:

```
sl5('Robert') = 100
sl5('Joe') = 300
sl5('Ann') = 200
```

Table 9-3 summarizes the most important properties and methods of the SortedList class. You have already met most of them, and the ones you never met before are almost self-explanatory, so I won't describe them in detail.

The SortedList class compares keys in case-sensitive mode, with lowercase characters coming before their uppercase versions (for example with *Ann* coming before *ANN*, which in turn comes before *Bob*). If you want to compare keys without taking case into account, you can create a case-insensitive SortedList object using the auxiliary CollectionsUtil object in the System.Collections.Specialized namespace:

```
Dim sl6 As SortedList = _
    Specialized.CollectionsUtil.CreateCaseInsensitiveSortedList()
```

In this case, trying to add two elements whose keys differ only in case throws an ArgumentException object.

> **Note** As I said before, the SortedList class is the most powerful collection-like object, but it's also the most demanding in terms of resources and CPU time. To see what kind of overhead you can expect when using a SortedList object, I created a routine that adds 100,000 elements to an ArrayList object, a Hashtable object, and a SortedList object. The results were pretty interesting: The ArrayList object was about 4 times faster than the Hashtable object, which in turn was from 8 to 100 times faster than the SortedList object. Even though you can't take these ratios as reliable in all circumstances, you clearly should never use a more powerful data structure if you don't really need its features.

Table 9-3 Properties and Methods of the SortedList Class

Syntax	Description
Capacity	Sets or returns the capacity of the SortedList object.
Count	Returns the number of elements currently in the SortedList object.
Item(key)	Sets or returns a value given its key (default member).
Keys	Returns all the keys in the SortedList object as an ICollection object.
Values	Returns all the values in SortedList as an ICollection object.
Add(key, value)	Adds a (key, value) pair to SortedList.
Clear	Removes all the elements from SortedList.
Clone	Creates a shallow copy of the SortedList object.
Contains(key)	Returns True if a given key exists.

(continued)

Table 9-3 Properties and Methods of the SortedList Class *(continued)*

Syntax	Description
ContainsKey(key)	Returns True if a given key exists (same as Contains).
ContainsValue(value)	Returns True if a given value exists.
CopyTo(array, index)	Copies all the DictionaryEntries elements to a one-dimensional array, starting at a specified index in the target array.
GetByIndex(index)	Retrieves a value by its index. (Similar to the Item property but works with the index instead of the key.)
GetKey(index)	Retrieves the key associated with the element at the given index.
GetKeyList	Returns all the keys as an IList object; all the changes in SortedList are reflected in this IList object. (Similar to the Keys property but returns an IList object instead of an ICollection object, and the result continues to be linked to the list of keys.)
GetValueList	Returns all the values as an IList object; all the changes in the SortedList are reflected in this IList object. (Similar to Values property but returns an IList object instead of an ICollection object, and the result continues to be linked to the list of values.)
IndexOfKey(key)	Returns the 0-based index of an element with a given key, or –1 if the key isn't in the SortedList object.
IndexOfValue(value)	Returns the 0-based index of the first occurrence of the specified value, or –1 if the value isn't in the SortedList object.
Remove(key)	Removes the element associated with a given key.
RemoveAt(index)	Removes the element at the given index.
SetByIndex(index, value)	Assigns a new value to the element at the specified index. (Similar to the Item property but works with the index instead of the key.)
TrimToSize	Sets the capacity to the current number of elements in the SortedList object.

The StringCollection and StringDictionary Classes

The StringCollection class (contained in the System.Collections.Specialized namespace) is a low-overhead class that manages a small collection of strings in a very efficient way. It exposes most of the properties and methods of the ArrayList class: Item, Count, Clear, Add, AddRange, Insert, Remove, RemoveAt, IndexOf, Contains, and CopyTo. The Capacity property is missing, however, and the constructor takes no arguments:

```
' Create a StringCollection (no support for initial capability).
Dim sc As New System.Collections.Specialized.StringCollection

' Fill it with month names in current language, in one operation.
' (We leverage the DateFormatInfo object's MonthNames method, which
```

(continued)

```
'   returns an array of strings, which in turn implements the IList interface.)
sc.AddRange(System.Globalization.DateTimeFormatInfo.CurrentInfo.MonthNames())

' Display the elements in the StringCollection.
Dim s As String
For Each s In sc
    Console.WriteLine(s)
Next
```

In general, you should prefer StringCollection objects to more resource-intensive objects, such as the ArrayList object, when you're working with small sets of elements (say, 100 elements or fewer). If a StringCollection object resolves the majority (but not all) of your programming tasks, consider using a temporary ArrayList object for implementing missing functionality. For example, say that a StringCollection satisfies your needs except that you need to sort its elements once in a while during the application's lifetime. Because the StringCollection object implements the IList interface, you can pass it to the shared ArrayList.Adapter method to create a temporary ArrayList that does what you need:

```
' A temporary ArrayList that wraps around the StringCollection object
Dim al As ArrayList = ArrayList.Adapter(sc)
' Sort the inner StringCollection in reverse order through the wrapper.
al.Sort
al.Reverse
' Destroy the wrapper object, which isn't necessary any longer.
al = Nothing
```

The temporary ArrayList object works as a wrapper for the inner StringCollection object, so all the operations you perform on the ArrayList are actually carried out in the StringCollection object instead.

The StringDictionary class, a lightweight version of the Hashtable object, takes only string keys and values. It exposes only the IEnumerable interface (to support For Each loops) and the following properties and methods: Item, Count, Add, Remove, Clear, ContainsKey, ContainsValue, Keys, and Values. The StringDictionary object compares keys in case-insensitive mode and throws an exception if you add two elements whose keys differ only in case:

```
Dim sd As New System.Collections.Specialized.StringDictionary
sd.Add("Ann", "Marketing")
sd.Add("Joe", "Sales")
sd.Add("Robert", "Administration")

Dim de As DictionaryEntry
For Each de In sd
    Console.WriteLine("{0} = {1}", de.Key, de.Value)
Next
```

The System.Collections.Specialized namespace offers two more lightweight classes: ListDictionary and NameValueCollection. The ListDictionary class is a lightweight implementation of the IDictionary interface. It offers a subset of the properties and methods of the Hashtable object but should be used only for very small sets of elements because its performance degrades with more than 10 elements. This object can take both object keys and object values.

The NameValueCollection class is a lightweight sorted collection of strings that can be retrieved by their key or index. Its peculiarity is the capability to store multiple string values under the same key.

Custom Collection and Dictionary Classes

In the section "The IEnumerable and IEnumerator Interfaces" in Chapter 6, I showed how you can create your own collection classes by implementing the IEnumerable interface for adding support for the For Each statement. In most cases, however, creating a collection class is as simple as inheriting from one of the special abstract classes that the .NET Framework kindly provides. These classes provide much of the functionality you need in a collection-like object, and you simply have to add the missing pieces. In this section, I'll describe three such objects: the CollectionBase class, for implementing full-featured collection classes; the ReadOnlyCollectionBase class, which is more convenient for collection classes with fixed membership (that is, collections you can't add items to or remove items from); and the DictionaryBase class, for implementing dictionary-like objects.

The ReadOnlyCollectionBase Abstract Class

Let's start with a simple collection with fixed membership that contains all the powers of 2, up to a given maximum exponent whose value is passed in the collection's constructor. This class inherits from the ReadOnlyCollectionBase abstract class, and its code for this class couldn't be simpler:

```
Class PowersOfTwoCollection
    Inherits System.Collections.ReadOnlyCollectionBase

    Sub New(ByVal MaxExponent As Integer)
        MyBase.New()

        ' Fill the inner ArrayList object.
        Dim index As Integer
        For Index = 0 To MaxExponent
            ' InnerList is a protected member of the base class.
            InnerList.Add(2 ^ Index)
```

(continued)

```
        Next
    End Sub

    ' Add support for the Item element (read-only).
    Default ReadOnly Property Item(ByVal Exponent As Integer) As Long
        Get
            Return CLng(InnerList.Item(Exponent))
        End Get
    End Property
End Class
```

InnerList is a protected property through which the derived class can access the internal ArrayList object that actually contains the values. You reference this internal ArrayList both when you're loading values in the constructor method and when you're returning them in the Item property.

In this specific example, the Item property is marked ReadOnly because a client isn't supposed to change the powers of 2 once the collection has been initialized. But don't confuse this ReadOnly attribute with the fact that the collection inherits from ReadOnlyCollectionBase: when applied to a collection, read-only means that the collection has a fixed size, not that individual elements aren't writable. Note that the Item property returns a Long data type, rather than the Object data type, as all default collections do: in fact, one of the main reasons for implementing a custom collection class is to make it strongly typed. The following code snippet uses the collection just created:

```
' Display powers of 2 up to 2^20.
Dim powers As New PowersOfTwoCollection(20)
' The Count property is provided by the base class.
Console.WriteLine(powers.Count)     ' => 21

' For Each support is also provided by the base class.
Dim n As Long
For Each n In powers
    Console.WriteLine(n)
Next

' Assign the value of 2^15 to a variable.
' (No casting is required because the collection is strongly typed.)
Dim lngValue As Long = powers(15)
```

The CollectionBase Abstract Class

You can create a regular read/write, strongly typed collection by inheriting a class from CollectionBase: you just need to implement an Add method that takes an argument of the expected type, and an Item property that sets or returns an element. The following code defines a simple Square class and a SquareCollection collection class:

```
Class Square
    Public Side As Single

    ' A simple constructor
    Sub New(ByVal side As Single)
        Me.Side = side
    End Sub
End Class

' A collection object that can store only Square objects
Class SquareCollection
    Inherits System.Collections.CollectionBase

    ' The Item property sets or returns a Square object.
    Default Property Item(ByVal index As Integer) As Square
        Get
            Return CType(InnerList.Item(index), Square)
        End Get
        Set(ByVal Value As Square)
            InnerList.Item(index) = Value
        End Set
    End Property

    ' You can add only Square objects to this collection.
    Sub Add(ByVal value As Square)
        InnerList.Add(value)
    End Sub
End Class
```

The SquareCollection class doesn't need to override the RemoveAt method because this method doesn't take or return a typed object, and therefore the base class can implement it:

```
Dim squares As New SquareCollection()
squares.Add(New Square(10))
squares.Add(New Square(20))
squares.Add(New Square(30))

' The RemoveAt method is provided by the base class.
Squares.RemoveAt(0)
```

You aren't limited to the members that a generic collection exposes. For example, you might add a Create method that works as a constructor for a Square object that's then added to the collection. (Methods like this are also called *factory methods*.)

```
' ...(Add this method to the SquareCollection class.)...
Function Create(ByVal Side As Single) As Square
    Dim sq As New Square(Side)
    Add(sq)
    Return sq
End Function
```

With this factory method, adding new elements to the collections is even simpler:

```
squares.Create(40)
squares.Create(50)
```

The CollectionBase abstract class exposes several protected methods that let the derived class take control when an operation is performed on the collection. For example, say that the SquareCollection class exposes the TotalArea read-only property, which contains the sum of the area of all the squares in the collection. You must modify the Add method to implement this new property:

```
' Keep track of the total area of squares.
Dim m_TotalArea As Single

Sub Add(ByVal value As Square)
    InnerList.Add(value)
    ' Keep the total area updated.
    m_TotalArea += (value.Side * value.Side)
End Sub

ReadOnly Property TotalArea() As Single
    Get
        Return m_TotalArea
    End Get
End Property
```

The next problem to solve is that the m_TotalArea variable must be updated when an element is removed from the collection. You achieve this behavior by overriding the OnRemoveComplete protected method, which runs after an item has been removed from the collection:

```
Protected Overrides Sub OnRemoveComplete(ByVal index As Integer, _
    ByVal value As Object)
    ' Get a reference to the square being removed.
    Dim sq As Square = CType(value, Square)
    ' Keep the total area updated.
    m_TotalArea -= (sq.Side * sq.Side)
End Sub
```

These are the protected methods you can override in classes that derive from CollectionBase: OnInsert, OnInsertComplete, OnClear, OnClearComplete, OnRemove, OnRemoveComplete, OnSet, OnSetComplete, and OnValidate.

The DictionaryBase Abstract Class

Now that you know the mechanism, you should have no problem grasping how you can use the DictionaryBase class to implement a strongly typed, custom dictionary-like object. Again, all you have to do is provide your custom Add and Item procedures, and reference the protected Dictionary object that you inherit from DictionaryBase. The following example creates a SquareDictionary object that can manage Square objects and associate them with a string key:

```
Class SquareDictionary
    Inherits System.Collections.DictionaryBase

    Sub Add(ByVal key As String, ByVal value As Square)
        Dictionary.Add(key, value)
    End Sub

    Function Create(ByVal key As String, ByVal side As Single) As Square
        Create = New Square(side)
        ' Use the function name as a local variable.
        Dictionary.Add(key, Create)
    End Function

    Default Property Item(ByVal key As String) As Square
        Get
            Return CType(Dictionary.Item(key), Square)
        End Get
        Set(ByVal Value As Square)
            Dictionary.Item(key) = Value
        End Set
    End Property
End Class
```

Here's a sample of client code:

```
Dim sq As New SquareDictionary()
sq.Create("First", 10)
sq.Create("Second", 20)
sq.Create("Third", 30)

Console.WriteLine(sq("Second").Side)     ' => 20
```

The custom SquareDictionary class should be completed with properties such as Values and Keys, and a few other methods that aren't implemented in the DictionaryBase class. As with the CollectionBase class, you can intervene when an operation is performed on the inner dictionary object through several protected methods, such as OnClear, OnClearComplete, OnGet, OnInsert, OnInsertComplete, OnRemove, OnRemoveComplete, OnSet, and OnSetComplete.

At this point, you have added many new classes to your data structure arsenal and you should have become more familiar with how things work in the .NET world, such as how you use inheritance to derive new and more powerful data classes. It's now time to start working with other classes in the .NET Framework, such as files and directories.

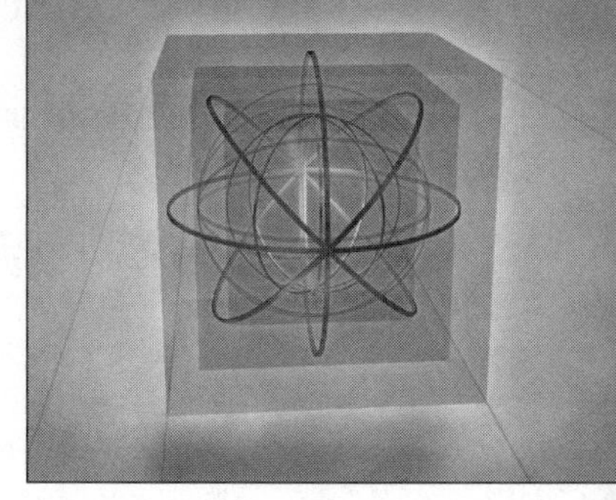

10

Files, Directories, and Streams

The .NET Framework offers excellent support for working with files and directories via the classes in the System.IO namespace. These are the five classes of interest:

- **Directory** Contains shared methods that let you enumerate and manipulate directories.
- **File** Contains shared methods that let you enumerate and manipulate files.
- **Path** Contains shared methods to manipulate path information.
- **DirectoryInfo** Represents an individual directory and exposes the methods to query its attributes and manipulate them.
- **FileInfo** Represents an individual file and exposes the methods to query its attributes and manipulate them.

> **Note** To avoid long lines, all the code samples in this section assume that the following Imports statement is used at the file or project level:
>
> ```
> Imports System.IO
> ```

The Directory and File Classes

The Directory and File classes contain only shared methods that set or return information about entries in the file system. Both classes will look familiar to developers who have worked with the FileSystemObject object hierarchy in the Microsoft Scripting Runtime library; even though property and method names are different in some cases, the underlying principles are the same. Table 10-1 recaps all the methods in these classes, so in the paragraphs following the table I'll draw your attention to the most interesting ones.

Table 10-1 Shared Methods of the Directory and File Classes

Class	Syntax	Description
Directory and File	Delete(path)	Deletes a file or directory.
	Move(source, dest)	Moves a file or directory.
	Exists(path)	Returns True if a file or directory exists.
	GetCreation-Time(path)	Returns the creation time of a file or directory.
	SetCreationTime (path, datetime)	Sets the creation time of a file or directory.
	GetLastAccess-Time(path)	Returns the last access time of a file or directory.
	SetLastAccess-Time(path, datetime)	Sets the last access time of a file or directory.
	GetLast-WriteTime(path)	Returns the last write time of a file or directory.
	SetLast-WriteTime(path, datetime)	Sets the last write time of a file or directory.
Directory only	GetCurrentDirectory	Returns the current directory (string).
	GetParent(path)	Returns the parent directory, as a DirectoryInfo object.
	GetDirectoryRoot (path)	Returns the root directory for the specified path (string).
	CreateDirectory (path)	Creates the specified directory and all the directories on its path if necessary.

Table 10-1 Shared Methods of the Directory and File Classes *(continued)*

Class	Syntax	Description
	GetLogicalDrives	Returns a String array with all the logical drives in the system.
	GetDirectories (path[, filespec])	Returns a String array with all the subdirectories in a directory, optionally filtered by the specified criteria.
	GetFiles (path[, filespec])	Returns a String array with all the files in a directory, optionally filtered by the specified criteria.
	GetFileSystemEntries(path[, filespec])	Returns a String array with all the files and subdirectories in a directory, optionally filtered by the specified criteria.
	Delete(path[, recursive])	Deletes a directory and all its subdirectories if the second argument is True.
File only	GetAttributes(file)	Returns the attributes of a file (but works with directories as well).
	SetAttributes(file, attributes)	Sets the attributes of a file.
	Copy(source, dest[, overwrite])	Copies a file to a new destination, also in different drives, and optionally overwrites the destination file if necessary.
	Create(file [,buffersize])	Creates and opens the specified file and returns a FileStream object; the optional argument specifies the buffer size.
	Open(file [,mode [,access [,share]]])	Opens a file with specified mode, access, and share; returns a FileStream.
	CreateText(file)	Creates a text file and returns a StreamWriter.
	AppendText(file)	Opens a text file in append mode and returns a StreamWriter.
	OpenRead(file)	Opens a file in read mode and returns a FileStream.
	OpenWrite(file)	Opens a file in write mode and returns a FileStream.
	OpenText(file)	Opens a text file for reading and returns a StreamReader.

The SetCurrentDirectory and GetCurrentDirectory methods of the Directory class set and return the current directory and therefore are equivalent to the ChDrive and ChDir commands and the CurDir function in Visual Basic 6:

```
' Save the current directory.
Dim currDir As String = Directory.GetCurrentDirectory
' Change the current directory to something else.
Directory.SetCurrentDirectory("C:\Temp")
⋮
' Restore the current directory.
Directory.SetCurrentDirectory(currDir)
```

The following code uses the GetLogicalDrives shared method to display the root path for all the drives in the system:

```
' Retrieve all the root paths.
Dim strRoots() As String = Directory.GetLogicalDrives
Dim s As String
For Each s In strRoots
    Console.WriteLine(s)          ' => C:\  D:\
Next
```

Thanks to the GetDirectories and GetFiles methods, you need very little code to iterate over all the directories and files of a directory tree. For example, the following code snippet prints the structure of a directory tree and (optionally) the names of files in each directory:

```
Sub PrintDirTree(ByVal dir As String, ByVal showFiles As Boolean, _
    Optional ByVal level As Integer = 0)
    Dim subdir As String
    Dim fname As String

    ' Display the name of this directory with correct indentation.
    Console.WriteLine(New String("-"c, level * 2) & dir)

    Try
        ' Display all files in this directory with correct indentation.
        If showFiles Then
            For Each fname In Directory.GetFiles(dir)
                Console.WriteLine(New String(" "c, level * 2 + 2) & fname)
            Next
        End If
        ' A recursive call for all the subdirectories in this directory
        For Each subdir In Directory.GetDirectories(dir)
            PrintDirTree(subdir, showFiles, level + 1)
        Next
    Catch
        ' Do nothing if any error (presumably "Drive not ready").
    End Try
End Sub
```

> **Note** As an exercise, you can modify the PrintDirTree procedure into a more generic procedure that takes a delegate and calls back the caller when a new file or directory has been found. See the section "Implementing CallBack Procedures" in Chapter 6. You might also want to review the section "Calling IEnumerator Members" in the same chapter, to see how you can work directly with the IEnumerator objects returned by the GetDirectories and GetFiles methods.

You can pass a directory name to the PrintDirTree procedure or print the directory tree of all the drives in your system by using this code:

```
Dim rootDir As String
For Each rootDir In Directory.GetLogicalDrives
    PrintDirTree(rootDir, True)
Next
```

The GetFiles and GetDirectories methods can take a second argument containing wildcards to filter the result:

```
' Display all the *.txt files in C:\DOCS.
Dim fname As String
For Each fname In Directory.GetFiles("c:\docs", "*.txt")
    Console.WriteLine(fname)
Next
```

You can use the GetCreationTime, GetLastAccessTime, GetLastWriteTime, and GetAttributes shared methods to display information about a file or a directory or to filter files according to their attributes:

```
For Each fname In Directory.GetFiles("c:\docs", "*.txt")
    ' Display only read-only files.
    ' (You need CBool if Option Strict is On.)
    If CBool(File.GetAttributes(fname) And FileAttributes.ReadOnly) Then
        Console.WriteLine(fname)
    End If
Next
```

The Directory class doesn't expose a GetAttributes method, so it seems that you can't retrieve the attributes for a directory. However, the File.GetAttributes method works also for directories, so this limitation isn't a problem. You can also use the Attributes property of a DirectoryInfo object that points to the directory of interest, as you'll see shortly.

The SetAttributes and GetAttributes methods set or return a bit-coded FileAttributes value, which is a combination of Normal (no attributes), Archive, ReadOnly, Hidden, System, Directory, Compressed, Encrypted, Temporary, NotContentIndexed, and a few other values.

```
' Display system and hidden files in C:\.
For Each fname In Directory.GetFiles("C:\")
    Dim attr As FileAttributes = File.GetAttributes(fname)
    ' Display the file if marked as hidden or system (or both).
    If CBool(attr And FileAttributes.Hidden) Or _
        CBool(attr And FileAttributes.System) Then
        Console.WriteLine(fname)
    End If
Next
```

With a little bit-tweaking, you can make the If expression more concise, as follows:

```
If CBool(attr And (FileAttributes.Hidden Or FileAttributes.System)) Then
```

The Directory.CreateDirectory method creates a directory and all the intermediate directories in the path if necessary:

```
' Next line works even if the C:\MyApp directory doesn't exist yet.
Directory.CreateDirectory("C:\MyApp\Data")
```

The SetCreationTime, SetLastWriteTime, and SetLastAccessTime methods let you modify the date attributes of a file or directory:

```
' Change the access date and time of all files in C:\DOCS.
For Each fname In Directory.GetFiles("c:\docs")
    File.SetLastAccessTime(fname, Date.Now)
Next
```

The SetCreationTime method can easily create a "touch" utility that modifies the last write time of all the files specified on its command line:

```
' Change the access date and time of all files whose names are
' passed on the command line.
Dim args() As String = Environment.GetCommandLineArgs
' The first item in args is the EXE name, and it must be skipped.
Dim i As Integer
For i = 1 To Ubound(args)
    File.SetCreationTime(args(i), Date.Now)
Next
```

The File object serves primarily two purposes. First, you can use it to process *closed* files—for example, to delete, copy, or move them or to retrieve information such as creation date and attributes. Second, you can use it to open a file and create a FileStream object, which you then use to actually read from and write to the open file. You set three values when you call the Open method:

- FileMode can be Append, Create, CreateNew, Open, OpenOrCreate, or Truncate. Open and Append modes fail if the file doesn't exist; Create and CreateNew fail if the file exists already. Use OpenOrCreate to open a file and to create one if it doesn't exist yet.

- FileAccess can be Read, Write, or ReadWrite.
- FileShare tells which operations other FileStreams can perform on the open file. It can be None (all operations are prohibited), ReadWrite (all operations are allowed), Read, Write, or Inheritable. (Inheritable isn't supported directly by Win32.)

The File class exposes three variants of the Open method: Create, OpenRead, and OpenWrite. Both the generic Open method and these variants return a FileStream object, and I'll illustrate all of them later in this chapter. There are also three specific methods for working with text files (CreateText, OpenText, and AppendText) that return a StreamReader or StreamWriter object.

The DirectoryInfo and FileInfo Classes

The DirectoryInfo and FileInfo classes represent individual directories and files. Both classes inherit from the FileSystemInfo virtual class and therefore have several properties and methods in common, such as Name, FullName, and Attributes. (See Table 10-2 for the complete list.) You can get a reference to a DirectoryInfo or FileInfo object by using its constructor method, which takes the path of a specific directory or file:

```
' Create a DirectoryInfo object that points to C:\.
Dim rootDi As New DirectoryInfo("C:\")
' Create a FileInfo object that points to C:\Autoexec.bat.
Dim batFi As New FileInfo("C:\Autoexec.bat")
```

Once you have a reference to a DirectoryInfo object, you can use its methods to enumerate its contents and get other DirectoryInfo or FileInfo objects. (You can apply filter criteria.)

```
' List the directories in C:\.
Dim di As DirectoryInfo
For Each di In rootDi.GetDirectories
    Console.WriteLine(di.Name)
Next

' List all the *.txt files in C:\.
Dim fi As FileInfo
For Each fi In rootDi.GetFiles("*.txt")
    Console.WriteLine(fi.Name)
Next
```

The DirectoryInfo.GetFileSystemInfos method returns an array of FileSystemInfo objects. Both the DirectoryInfo and FileInfo classes inherit from the FileSystemInfo class, so you can have a single loop that processes both files and subdirectories in a directory, as you can see in the next code snippet.

```
Dim fsi As FileSystemInfo

' Note that we can create the DirectoryInfo object on the fly.
For Each fsi In (New DirectoryInfo("C:\")).GetFileSystemInfos
    ' Use the [dir] or [file] prefix.
    If CBool(fsi.Attributes And FileAttributes.Directory) Then
        Console.Write("[dir] ")
    Else
        Console.Write("[file] ")
    End If
    ' Print name and creation date.
    Console.WriteLine(fsi.Name & " - " & fsi.CreationTime)
Next
```

Table 10-2 Properties and Methods of the DirectoryInfo and FileInfo Classes

Class	Syntax	Description
DirectoryInfo and FileInfo (inherited from FileSystemInfo)	Name	Returns the name of the file or directory.
	FullName	Returns the full name of the file or directory (including its path).
	Extension	Returns the extension of the file or directory.
	Exists	Returns True if the file or directory exists.
	Attributes	Sets or returns the attributes of the file or directory as a bit-coded FileAttributes value.
	CreationTime	Sets or returns the creation time of the file or directory (Date value).
	LastWriteTime	Sets or returns the last write time of the file or directory (Date value).
	LastAccessTime	Sets or returns the last access time of the file or directory (Date value).
	Refresh	Refreshes the properties of this FileInfo or DirectoryInfo object.
	Delete	Deletes the file or directory.
DirectoryInfo only	Parent	Returns the DirectoryInfo object for the parent directory.
	Root	Returns the DirectoryInfo object for the root directory.
	Create	Creates the directory.
	MoveTo(destpath)	Moves the current directory to another path.

Table 10-2 Properties and Methods of the DirectoryInfo and FileInfo Classes

Class	Syntax	Description
	Delete ([recursive])	Deletes the current directory. The Boolean argument specifies whether all the subdirectories should be deleted as well.
	CreateSubdirectory (path)	Creates a subdirectory of the current directory and returns the corresponding DirectoryInfo object.
	GetDirectories ([filespec])	Returns information about the subdirectories in the current directory as an array of DirectoryInfo objects; can take an optional search criterion, such as "A*".
	GetFiles([filespec])	Returns information about the files in the current directory as an array of FileInfo objects; can take an optional search criterion, such as "*.txt".
	GetFileSystemInfos([filespec])	Returns information about the files and subdirectories in the current directory as an array of FileSystemInfo objects; can take an optional search criterion, such as "*.txt".
FileInfo only	Length	Returns the length of the file.
	Directory	Returns the DirectoryInfo object for the parent directory.
	DirectoryName	Returns the name of the parent directory.
	Create	Creates the file.
	MoveTo(destpath)	Moves the current file to another path.
	CopyTo(destfile [,overwrite])	Copies the current file to another path and optionally overwrites an existing file.
	Open (mode [,access [,share]])	Opens the current file with specified mode, access, and share; returns a FileStream object.
	OpenRead	Opens the current file in read mode and returns a FileStream object.
	OpenWrite	Opens the current file in write mode and returns a FileStream object.
	OpenText	Opens the current file in read mode and returns a StreamReader object.
	CreateText	Creates a text file and returns a StreamWriter object.
	AppendText	Opens the current text file in append mode and returns a StreamWriter object.

The Path Class

The Path class exposes shared fields and methods that can help you process file and directory paths. The five static fields return information about valid drive and filename separators. You might want to query them only to prepare your programs to run on other operating systems if and when the .NET Framework is ported to platforms other than Windows:

```
Console.WriteLine(Path.AltDirectorySeparatorChar)  ' => /
Console.WriteLine(Path.DirectorySeparatorChar)     ' => \
Console.WriteLine(Path.InvalidPathChars)           ' => "<>|
Console.WriteLine(Path.PathSeparator)              ' => ;
Console.WriteLine(Path.VolumeSeparatorChar)        ' => :
```

The GetTempPath and GetTempFileName methods take no arguments and return the location of the temporary directory in Windows and the name of a temporary file, respectively:

```
' Note that paths are in 8.3 MS-DOS format.
Console.WriteLine(Path.GetTempPath)
    ' => C:\DOCUME~1\ADMINI~1\LOCALS~1\Temp\
Console.WriteLine(Path.GetTempFileName)
    ' => C:\DOCUME~1\ADMINI~1\LOCALS~1\Temp\tmp1B2.tmp
```

A number of other methods let you extract information from a file path, without your having to worry about whether the file or the directory exists:

```
Dim fil As String = "C:\MyApp\Bin\MyApp.exe"
Console.WriteLine(Path.GetDirectoryName(fil))             ' => C:\MyApp\Bin
Console.WriteLine(Path.GetFileName(fil))                  ' => MyApp.exe
Console.WriteLine(Path.GetExtension(fil))                 ' => .exe
Console.WriteLine(Path.GetFileNameWithoutExtension(fil)) ' => MyApp
Console.WriteLine(Path.GetPathRoot(fil))                  ' => C:\
Console.WriteLine(Path.HasExtension(fil))                 ' => True
Console.WriteLine(Path.IsPathRooted(fil))                 ' => True
```

The GetFullPath method expands a relative path to an absolute path, taking the current directory into account:

```
' Next line assumes that current directory is C:\MyApp.
Console.WriteLine(Path.GetFullPath("MyApp.Exe"))      ' => C:\MyApp\MyApp.Exe
```

The ChangeExtension method returns a filename with a different extension:

```
Console.WriteLine(Path.ChangeExtension("MyApp.Exe", "Dat"))  ' => MyApp.Dat
```

Finally, the Combine method takes a pathname and a filename and combines them into a valid filename, adding or discarding backslash characters:

```
Console.WriteLine(Path.Combine("C:\MyApp\", "MyApp.Dat"))
    ' => C:\MyApp\MyApp.Dat
```

The Stream Class

The Stream abstract class represents a sequence of bytes going to or coming from a storage medium (such as a file) or a physical or virtual device (such as a parallel port, an interprocess communication pipe, or a TCP/IP socket). Streams allow you to read from and write to a backing *store*, which can correspond to one of several storage mediums. For example, you can have file streams, memory streams, network streams, and tape streams.

Because it's an abstract class, you don't create a Stream object directly, and you rarely use a Stream variable in your code. Rather, you typically work with classes that inherit from it, such as the FileStream class.

Stream Operations

The fundamental operations you can perform on streams are read, write, and seek. Not all types of streams support all these operations—for example, the NetworkStream object doesn't support seeking. You can check which operations are allowed by using the stream's CanRead, CanWrite, and CanSeek properties.

Most stream objects perform data buffering in a transparent way. For example, data isn't immediately written to disk when you write to a file stream; instead, bytes are buffered and are eventually flushed when the stream is closed or when you issue an explicit Flush method. Needless to say, buffering can improve performance remarkably. File streams are buffered, whereas memory streams aren't because there's no point in buffering a stream that maps to memory. You can use a BufferedStream object to add buffering capability to a stream object that doesn't offer it natively—for example, a NetworkBuffer. (See the SDK documentation for details about the BufferedStream object.)

Most of the properties of the Stream class—and of classes that inherit from Stream—work as you would intuitively expect them to work:

- The Length property returns the total size of the Stream, whereas the Position property determines the current position in the Stream (that is, the offset of the next byte that will be read or written). You can change the stream's length using the SetLength method and change the position using the Seek method.
- The Read method reads a number of bytes from the specified position into a Byte array, then advances the stream pointer, and finally returns the number of bytes read. The ReadByte method reads and returns a single byte.

- The Write method writes a number of bytes from an array into the stream and then advances the stream pointer. The WriteByte method writes a single byte to the stream.
- The Close method closes the stream and releases all the associated resources. The Flush method empties a buffered stream and ensures that all its contents are written to the underlying store. (It has no effect on nonbuffered streams.)
- The BeginRead and BeginWrite methods start an asynchronous operation on the stream; when a read operation ends, you can call EndRead to learn how many bytes were actually read.

Specific streams can implement additional methods and properties, such as the following:

- The FileStream class exposes the Handle property (which returns the operating system file handle) and the Lock and Unlock methods (which lock or unlock a portion of the file). When you're working with FileStream objects, the SetLength method actually trims or extends the underlying file.
- The MemoryStream class exposes the Capacity property (which returns the number of bytes allocated to the stream), the WriteTo method (which copies the entire contents to another stream), and the GetBuffer method (which returns the array of unsigned bytes from which the stream was created).
- The NetworkStream class exposes the DataAvailable property (which returns True when data is available on the stream for reading).

Stream Readers and Writers

Because the generic Stream object can read and write only individual bytes or groups of bytes, most of the time you use auxiliary *stream reader* and *stream writer* objects that let you work with more structured data, such as a line of text or a Double value. The .NET Framework offers several stream reader and writer pairs:

- The BinaryReader and BinaryWriter classes can work with primitive data in binary format, such as a Single value or an encoded string.
- The StreamReader and StreamWriter classes can work with strings of text in ANSI format, such as the text you read from or write to a text file. These classes can work in conjunction with an Encoder object, which determines how characters are encoded in the stream.

- TextReader and TextWriter are abstract classes that define how to work with strings of text in Unicode format. The StringReader and StringWriter classes inherit from TextReader and TextWriter and can read and write characters from a Unicode string in memory.
- The XmlTextReader and XmlTextWriter classes work with XML text. (For more information about these classes, see Chapter 22.)
- The ResourceReader and ResourceWriter classes work with resource files.

Reading and Writing Text Files

You typically use a StreamReader object to read from a text file. You can obtain a reference to such an object in many ways:

```
' With the File.OpenText shared method
Dim sr As StreamReader = File.OpenText("c:\autoexec.bat")

' With the OpenText instance method of a FileInfo object
Dim fi2 As New FileInfo("c:\autoexec.bat")
Dim sr2 As StreamReader = fi2.OpenText

' By passing a FileStream from the Open method of the File class to
' the StreamReader's constructor method
' (This technique lets you specify mode, access, and share mode.)
Dim st3 As Stream = File.Open("C:\autoexec.bat", _
    FileMode.Open, FileAccess.ReadWrite, FileShare.ReadWrite)
Dim sr3 As New StreamReader(st3)

' By opening a FileStream on the file and then passing it
' to the StreamReader's constructor method
Dim fs4 As New FileStream("C:\autoexec.bat", FileMode.Open)
Dim sr4 As New StreamReader(fs4)

' By getting a FileStream from the OpenRead method of the File class
' and passing it to the StreamReader's constructor
Dim sr5 As New StreamReader(File.OpenRead("c:\autoexec.bat"))

' By passing the filename to the StreamReader's constructor
Dim sr6 As New StreamReader("c:\autoexec.bat")

' By passing the filename and encoding
Dim sr7 As New StreamReader("c:\autoexec.bat", System.Text.Encoding.Unicode)
Dim sr8 As New StreamReader("c:\autoexec.bat", System.Text.Encoding.ASCII)
' As before, but we let the system decide the best encoding.
Dim sr9 As New StreamReader("c:\autoexec.bat", True)
```

After you get a reference to a StreamReader object, you can use one of its many methods to read one or more characters or whole text lines. The Peek method returns the code of the next character in the stream without actually extracting it, or it returns the special –1 value if there are no more characters. In practice, this method is used to test an end-of-file condition:

```
' Display all the text lines in the file.
Do Until sr.Peek = -1
    ' The ReadLine method reads whole lines.
    Console.WriteLine(sr.ReadLine)
Loop
' Always close a StreamReader when you're done with it.
sr.Close()
```

You can also read one character at a time using the Read method, or you can read all the remaining characters using the ReadToEnd method:

```
' Read the entire contents of C:\Autoexec.bat in one shot.
sr = New StreamReader("c:\autoexec.bat")
Dim fileContents As String = sr.ReadToEnd()
```

If you opened the StreamReader through a Stream object, you can use the Stream object's Seek method to move the pointer or even just read its current position. If you did *not* open the StreamReader through a Stream object, you can still access the inner Stream object that the .NET runtime creates anyway, through the StreamReader's BaseStream property:

```
' ...(Continuing previous code example)...
' If the file is longer than 100 chars, process it again, one character at a
' time (admittedly a silly thing to do, but it's just a demo).
If fileContents.Length >= 100 Then
    ' Reset the stream's pointer to the beginning.
    sr.BaseStream.Seek(0, SeekOrigin.Begin)
    ' Read individual characters until EOF is reached.
    Do Until sr.Peek() = -1
        ' Read method returns an integer, so convert it to Char.
        Console.Write(sr.Read.ToString)
    Loop
End If
sr.Close
```

You use a StreamWriter object to write to a text file. As with the StreamReader object, you can create a StreamWriter object in many ways:

```
Dim sw1 As StreamWriter = File.CreateText("c:\temp.dat")

' By passing a FileStream from the Open method of the File class to
' the StreamWriter's constructor method
Dim st2 As Stream = File.Open("C:\temp.dat", _
    FileMode.Create, FileAccess.ReadWrite, FileShare.None)
```

```
Dim sw2 As New StreamWriter(st2)

' By opening a FileStream on the file and then passing it
' to the StreamWriter's constructor method
Dim fs3 As New FileStream("C:\autoexec.bat", FileMode.Open)
Dim sw3 As New StreamWriter(fs3)

' By getting a FileStream from the OpenWrite method of the File class
' and passing it to the StreamWriter's constructor
Dim sw4 As New StreamWriter(File.OpenWrite("C:\temp.dat"))

' By passing the filename to the StreamWriter's constructor
Dim sw5 As New StreamWriter("C:\temp.dat")
```

The StreamWriter class exposes the Write and WriteLine methods: the Write method can write the textual representation of any basic data type (Integer, Double, and so on); the WriteLine method works only with strings and automatically appends a newline character. Leave the AutoFlush property set to False (the default value) if you want the StreamWriter to adopt a limited form of caching; you'll probably need to issue a Flush method periodically in this case. Set this property to True for those streams or devices, such as the console window, from which the user expects immediate feedback.

The following code uses a StreamReader object to read from a file and a StreamWriter object to copy the text to another file, after converting the text to uppercase:

```
Dim sr As New StreamReader("C:\Autoexec.bat")
Dim sw As New StreamWriter("C:\Autoexec.new")

Do Until sr.Peek = -1
    ' The ReadLine method returns a string, so we can
    ' convert it to uppercase on the fly.
    sw.WriteLine(sr.ReadLine.ToUpper)
Loop
sr.Close()
sw.Close()      ' This actually writes data to the file and closes it.
```

If you're working with smaller text files—say, 50 KB or less—you can also trade some memory for speed and do without a loop:

```
sr = New StreamReader("C:\Autoexec.bat")
sw = New StreamWriter("C:\Autoexec.new")
sw.Write(sr.ReadToEnd.ToUpper)
sr.Close()
sw.Close()
```

Caution You should always close the Stream object after using it. Otherwise, the stream keeps the file open until the next garbage collection calls the Stream's Finalize method. There are at least two reasons why you'd rather close the stream manually. First, if the file is kept open longer than strictly necessary, you can't delete or move it, nor can another application open it for reading and/or writing (depending on the access mode you specified when opening the file). The second reason is performance: the code in the Stream's Close method calls the GC.SuppressFinalize method, so the stream isn't finalized and therefore the resources it uses are released earlier.

Reading and Writing Binary Files

The BinaryReader and BinaryWriter classes are suitable for working with binary streams; one such stream might be associated with a file containing data in native format. In this context, *native format* means the actual bits used to store the value in memory. You can't create a BinaryReader or BinaryWriter object directly from a filename as you can with the StreamReader and StreamWriter objects. Instead, you must create a Stream object explicitly and pass it to the constructor method of either the BinaryReader or the BinaryWriter class:

```
' Associate a stream with a new file opened with write access.
Dim st As Stream = File.Open("c:\values.dat", FileMode.Create, _
    FileAccess.Write)
' Create a BinaryWriter associated with the output stream.
Dim bw As New BinaryWriter(st)
```

Working with the BinaryWriter object is especially simple because its Write method is overloaded to accept all the primitive .NET types, including signed and unsigned integers; Single, Double, and String values; and so on. The following code snippet writes 10 random Double values to a binary file:

```
' ...(Continuing previous example)...
' Save 10 Double values to the file.
Dim i As Integer, rand As New Random
For i = 1 To 10
    bw.Write(rand.NextDouble)
Next
' Flush the output data to the file.
bw.Close()
st.Close()
```

The BinaryReader class exposes many Read*xxxx* methods, one for each possible native data type, and a PeekChar method that returns –1 when you reach the end of the stream:

```
' Read back values written in previous example.

' Associate a stream with an existing file, opened with read access.
Dim st2 As Stream = File.Open("c:\values.dat", FileMode.Open, FileAccess.Read)
' Create a BinaryReader associated with the input stream.
Dim br2 As New BinaryReader(st2)

' Loop until data is available.
Do Until br2.PeekChar = -1
    ' Read the next element. (We know it's a Double.)
    Console.WriteLine(br2.ReadDouble)
Loop
br2.Close()
st2.Close()
```

Outputting strings with a BinaryWriter requires some additional care, however. Passing a string to the Write method outputs a length-prefixed string to the stream. If you want to write only the actual characters (as happens when you're working with fixed-length strings), you must pass the Write method an array of Chars; the Write method is overloaded to take additional arguments that specify which portion of the array should be written.

Reading back strings requires different techniques as well, depending on how the string was written. You use the ReadString method for length-prefixed strings and the ReadChars method for fixed-length strings. You can see an example of these methods in action in the next section.

File streams can be opened for asynchronous read and write operations, which can speed up your code's performance significantly. You'll learn about asynchronous file operations in Chapter 13.

Reading and Writing Memory Streams

Stream readers and writers aren't just for files. For example, you can use them in conjunction with a MemoryStream object to deal with memory as if it were a temporary file (which usually delivers better performance than using an actual file). The following code snippet performs the same operation seen in the preceding section; this time, the code uses a memory stream instead of a file stream:

```
' Create a memory stream with initial capacity of 1 KB.
Dim st As New MemoryStream(1024)
Dim bw As New BinaryWriter(st)
Dim i As Integer, rand As New Random()
' Write 10 random Double values to the stream.
```

(continued)

```
For i = 1 To 10
    bw.Write(rand.NextDouble)
Next

' Rewind the stream to the beginning.
st.Seek(0, SeekOrigin.Begin)
Dim br As New BinaryReader(st)

Do Until br.PeekChar = -1
    Console.WriteLine(br.ReadDouble)
Loop
br.Close()
st.Close()
```

Of course, in this particular example you might have used an array to store random values and read them back. However, the approach based on streams lets you move from a memory stream to a file-based stream by changing only one statement (the stream constructor). In a real application, you might test how much memory is available on the computer and decide whether to use memory or a temporary file for your intermediate results. This example writes two strings to a MemoryStream and then reads them back:

```
' Write two strings to a MemoryStream.
Dim st As New MemoryStream(1000)
Dim bw As New BinaryWriter(st)
bw.Write("length-prefixed string")

' We'll use this 1-KB buffer for both reading and writing.
Dim buffer(1024) As Char

Dim s As String = "13 Characters"           ' A fixed-length string
s.CopyTo(0, buffer, 0, 13)                  ' Copy into the buffer.
bw.Write(buffer, 0, 13)                     ' Output first 13 chars in buffer.
bw.Write(buffer, 0, 13)                     ' Do it a second time.

' Rewind the stream, and prepare to read from it.
st.Seek(0, SeekOrigin.Begin)
Dim br As New BinaryReader(st)
' Reading the length-prefixed string is simple.
Console.WriteLine(br.ReadString)            ' => length-prefixed string

' Read the fixed-length string (13 characters) into the buffer.
br.Read(buffer, 0, 13)
s = New String(buffer, 0, 13)               ' Convert to a string.
Console.WriteLine(s)                        ' => 13 Characters

' Another way to read a fixed-length string (13 characters)
' (ReadChars returns a Char array that we can pass to the string constructor.)
s = New String(br.ReadChars(13))
Console.WriteLine(s)                        ' => 13 Characters
```

Reading and Writing Strings in Memory

If the data you want to read is already contained in a string variable, you might want to use a StringReader object to retrieve it. For example, you can load the entire contents of a text file or a multiline textbox control into a string and then extract the individual lines by using the StringReader.ReadLine method:

```
' The veryLongString variable contains the text to parse.
Dim strReader As New StringReader(veryLongString)
' Display individual lines of text.
Do Until strReader.Peek = -1
    Console.WriteLine(strReader.ReadLine)
Loop
```

Of course, you can solve this problem in other, equivalent, ways—for example, by using the Split function to get an array with all the individual lines of code—but the solution based on the StringReader object is more resource-friendly because it doesn't duplicate the data in memory. As a matter of fact, the StringReader and StringWriter classes don't even create an internal stream object because they use the string itself as the stream. (This fact explains why these two classes don't expose the BaseStream property.)

You use a StringWriter object to output values to a string. However, you can't associate it with a String object because String objects are immutable. Instead, you have to create a StringBuilder and then associate it with a StringWriter object:

```
' This code assumes that you added the following Imports:
'    Imports System.Globalization
' Create a string with the space-separated abbreviated names of weekdays.
' A StringBuilder of 7*4 characters is enough.
Dim sb As New System.Text.StringBuilder(28)
' The StringWriter associated with the StringBuilder
Dim strWriter As New StringWriter(sb)

' Output day names to the string.
Dim d As String
For Each d In DateTimeFormatInfo.CurrentInfo.AbbreviatedDayNames
    strWriter.Write(d)
    strWriter.Write(" ")          ' Append a space.
Next
Console.WriteLine(sb)             ' => Sun Mon Tue Wed Thu Fri Sat
```

Custom Stream Readers and Writers

Thanks to inheritance, you can easily create custom stream readers and writers that work with custom objects. The following listing is an example of this technique: it defines two new classes, BinaryWriterEx and BinaryReaderEx, which can work with all the usual data types plus our ubiquitous Person class.

```
Class Person
    Public FirstName As String
    Public LastName As String

    Sub New(ByVal firstName As String, ByVal lastName As String)
        Me.FirstName = firstName
        Me.LastName = lastName
    End Sub
End Class

Class BinaryWriterEx
    Inherits System.IO.BinaryWriter

    Sub New(ByVal st As System.IO.Stream)
        MyBase.New(st)
    End Sub

    ' Add to the series of Write methods.
    Overloads Sub Write(ByVal p As Person)
        MyBase.Write(p.FirstName)
        MyBase.Write(p.LastName)
    End Sub
End Class

Class BinaryReaderEx
    Inherits System.IO.BinaryReader

    Sub New(ByVal st As System.IO.Stream)
        MyBase.New(st)
    End Sub

    ' A custom function that reads a Person object
    Function ReadPerson() As Person
        Dim FirstName As String = MyBase.ReadString()
        Dim LastName As String = MyBase.ReadString()
        ReadPerson = New Person(FirstName, LastName)
    End Function
End Class
```

The following sample code proves that our new classes can work with all the usual data types and Person objects as well:

```
Dim st As New MemoryStream(1000)
Dim bw As New BinaryWriterEx(st)

' Write a Person object and then a -1 value (short).
Dim p As New Person("Joe", "Doe")
bw.Write(p)
bw.Write(-1S)
```

```
' Rewind the stream, and prepare to read from it.
st.Seek(0, SeekOrigin.Begin)
Dim br As New BinaryReaderEx(st)

' Read a Person object, and prove that properties have been preserved.
Dim p2 As Person = br.ReadPerson()
Console.WriteLine(p.FirstName & " " & p.LastName)  ' => Joe Doe
' Read the Short value.
Console.WriteLine(br.ReadInt16)                     ' => -1
' Clean everything up.
bw.Close
br.Close
st.Close
```

> **Note** These classes write or read the contents of a Person object one property at a time, so they must be updated when you add a new property to the Person class. In the next chapter, you'll learn how you can make a class serializable so that it knows how to write and read its own properties.

You might need to retrieve the actual bytes that make up a data type when building custom reader and writer classes. You can do this by using the System.BitConverter auxiliary class. (See the .NET Framework SDK documentation for more information about this class.)

Now you know all you need to know about directories, files, and stream objects, and you'll probably agree that—once you get accustomed to the new syntax—working with these .NET objects can provide extra flexibility and power. The next chapter covers an important topic in the .NET Framework: object serialization, which builds on the concepts described in this chapter.

Front
Top
Left
Back

11

Object Serialization

Serialization is the term for the act of saving (or *serializing*) an object onto a storage medium—a file, a database field, a buffer in memory—and later deserializing it from the storage medium to re-create an object instance that can be considered identical to the original one. Serialization is a key feature in the .NET Framework and is transparently used by the runtime for tasks other than simply saving an object to a file—for example, for marshaling an object by value to another application. You should make an object serializable if you're planning to send it to another application or save it on disk, in a database field, or in an ASP.NET session object. For example, even exception objects should be made serializable if they can be thrown from another AppDomain. (Because the System.Exception class is serializable, your custom exception objects inherit this behavior automatically.)

Serialization and *persistence* are often used as synonyms, so you can also say that an object is *persisted* and *depersisted*. The SDK documentation makes a distinction, however, and uses *persistence* to mean that the data is stored in a durable medium, such as a file or a database field, while *serialization* can be applied to objects stored in nondurable media, such as memory buffers.

Basic Serialization

The Framework knows how to serialize all basic data types, including numbers, strings, and arrays of numbers and strings, so you can save and reload these types to and from a file stream (or any other type of stream) with minimal effort. All you need to serialize and deserialize a basic object is a proper *formatter* object.

Formally speaking, a formatter is an object that implements the IFormatter interface (defined in the System.Runtime.Serialization namespace). You can create your own formatter by defining a class that implements this interface, but most of the time you can use one of the formatter objects provided by the .NET Framework:

- The BinaryFormatter object, defined in the System.Runtime.Serialization.Formatters.Binary namespace, provides an efficient way to persist an object in a compact binary format. In practice, the actual bits in memory are persisted, so the serialization and deserialization processes are very fast.
- The SoapFormatter object, defined in the System.Runtime.Serialization.Formatters.Soap namespace, persists data in human-readable XML format, following the Simple Object Access Protocol (SOAP) specifications. The serialization and deserialization processes are somewhat slower than with the BinaryFormatter object. On the other hand, data can be sent easily to another application through HTTP.

Binary Serialization

The key methods that all formatter objects support are Serialize and Deserialize, whose purpose is rather evident. The Serialize method takes a Stream object as its first argument and the object to be serialized as its second argument:

```
Imports System.IO
Imports System.Runtime.Serialization
Imports System.Runtime.Serialization.Formatters.Binary

Sub TestSaveArray()
    ' Create an array of integers.
    Dim arr() As Integer = {1, 2, 4, 8, 16, 32, 64, 128, 256}

    ' Open a file stream for output.
    Dim fs As FileStream = New FileStream("c:\powers.dat", FileMode.Create)
    ' Create a binary formatter for this stream.
    Dim bf As New BinaryFormatter()

    ' Serialize the array to the file stream, and flush the stream.
    bf.Serialize(fs, arr)
    fs.Close()
End Sub
```

Reading back the file data and deserializing it into an object require the Deserialize function, which takes the input Stream as its only argument and returns an Object value, which must be cast to a properly typed variable:

```
Sub TestLoadArray()
    ' Open a file stream for input.
    Dim fs As FileStream = New FileStream("c:\powers.dat", FileMode.Open)
    ' Create a binary formatter for this stream.
    Dim bf As New BinaryFormatter()

    ' Deserialize the contents of the file stream into an Integer array.
    Dim arr() As Integer
    ' Deserialize returns an object that must be coerced.
    arr = CType(bf.Deserialize(fs), Integer())

    ' Display the result.
    Dim n As Integer
    For Each n In arr
        Console.Write(n.ToString & " ")
    Next
End Sub
```

You can indicate the reason you're creating a formatter by passing a StreamingContext object to the second argument of its constructor. The streaming context object contains information about the serialization and deserialization process and can be used by the object being serialized. For example, an object might opt for a compression algorithm if it's being serialized to a file. Even if you don't know whether the object you're serializing takes advantage of this additional information, specifying it is a good programming rule. Here's how you define a formatter that's used to serialize an object to a file:

```
Dim sc As New StreamingContext(StreamingContextStates.File)
    Dim bf As New BinaryFormatter(Nothing, sc)
```

I'll discuss the other values you can pass to the StreamingContext's constructor in the section "The StreamingContext Structure" later in this chapter, where I'll also show how you can use serializable classes that leverage this information to optimize the serialization process.

SOAP Serialization

You can change the serialization format to SOAP by simply using another formatter object, the SoapFormatter in the System.Runtime.Serialization.Formatters.Soap namespace. This namespace isn't available in the default Visual Basic console project, so you have to click Add Reference on the Project menu in Visual Studio to add the System.Runtime.Serialization.Formatters.Soap.dll library to the list of libraries that appear in the Object Browser. When you're working with SOAP serialization, it's a good idea to add these Imports statements to the top of your source file:

```
Imports System.IO
Imports System.Runtime.Serialization
Imports System.Runtime.Serialization.Formatters.Soap
```

The following listing contains two reusable routines that let you save and restore any object to a file in SOAP format. Note that the formatter's constructor receives a StreamingContext object that specifies where the serialization data is stored:

```
' Serialize an object to a file in SOAP format.
Sub SaveSoapData(ByVal path As String, ByVal o As Object)
    ' Open a file stream for output.
    Dim fs As FileStream = New FileStream(path, FileMode.Create)
    ' Create a SOAP formatter for this file stream.
    Dim sf As New SoapFormatter(Nothing, _
        New StreamingContext(StreamingContextStates.File))
    ' Serialize the array to the file stream, and close the stream.
    sf.Serialize(fs, o)
    fs.Close()
End Sub

' Deserialize an object from a file in SOAP format.
Function LoadSoapData(ByVal path As String) As Object
    ' Open a file stream for input.
    Dim fs As FileStream = New FileStream(path, FileMode.Open)
    ' Create a SOAP formatter for this file stream.
    Dim sf As New SoapFormatter(Nothing, _
        New StreamingContext(StreamingContextStates.File))
    ' Deserialize the contents of the file stream into an object.
    LoadSoapData = sf.Deserialize(fs)
    ' Close the stream.
    fs.Close()
End Function
```

Here's a test routine that saves and reloads a Hashtable object, using the routine just defined:

```
' An example that uses the preceding routines
Sub TestSoapSerialization()
    ' Create a Hashtable object, and fill it with some data.
    Dim ht As New Hashtable()
    ht.Add("One", 1)
    ht.Add("Two", 2)
    ht.Add("Three", 3)
```

```
    ' Save the Hashtable to disk in SOAP format.
    SaveSoapData("c:\hashtbl.xml", ht)

    ' Reload the file contents into another Hashtable object.
    Dim ht2 As Hashtable
    ht2 = CType(LoadSoapData("c:\hashtbl.xml"), Hashtable)

    ' Display values.
    Dim de As DictionaryEntry
    For Each de In ht2

        Console.WriteLine("Key={0}  Value={1}", de.Key, de.Value)
    Next
End Sub
```

The following text is the XML file created by the SaveSoapData routine. (I have indented elements to emphasize the relationship between them.)


```
<SOAP-ENV:Envelope xmlns:xsi="http://www.w3.org/2001/XMLSchema-instance"
  xmlns:xsd="http://www.w3.org/2001/XMLSchema"
  xmlns:SOAP-ENC="http://schemas.xmlsoap.org/soap/encoding/"
  xmlns:SOAP-ENV="http://schemas.xmlsoap.org/soap/envelope/"
  xmlns:clr="http://schemas.microsoft.com/soap/encoding/clr/1.0"
  SOAP-ENV:encodingStyle="http://schemas.xmlsoap.org/soap/encoding/">
  <SOAP-ENV:Body>
    <a1:Hashtable id="ref-1"
      xmlns:a1="http://schemas.microsoft.com/clr/ns/System.Collections">
      <LoadFactor>0.72</LoadFactor>
      <Version>3</Version>
      <Comparer xsi:null="1"/>
      <HashCodeProvider xsi:null="1"/>
      <HashSize>11</HashSize>
      <Keys href="#ref-2"/>
      <Values href="#ref-3"/>
    </a1:Hashtable>
    <SOAP-ENC:Array id="ref-2" SOAP-ENC:arrayType="xsd:anyType[3]">
      <item id="ref-4" xsi:type="SOAP-ENC:string">One</item>
      <item id="ref-5" xsi:type="SOAP-ENC:string">Three</item>
      <item id="ref-6" xsi:type="SOAP-ENC:string">Two</item>
    </SOAP-ENC:Array>
    <SOAP-ENC:Array id="ref-3" SOAP-ENC:arrayType="xsd:anyType[3]">
      <item xsi:type="xsd:int">1</item>
      <item xsi:type="xsd:int">3</item>
      <item xsi:type="xsd:int">2</item>
    </SOAP-ENC:Array>
  </SOAP-ENV:Body>
</SOAP-ENV:Envelope>
```

The Serializable and NonSerialized Attributes

The .NET Framework can inspect any object at run time to discover, read, and assign all the object's fields and properties. This mechanism is made possible by a portion of the .NET Framework called reflection (which is explored in Chapter 15) and is the basis for automatic persistence of any class you write with a minimum of effort on your part.

In practice, the only thing you do to make a class serializable is to flag it with the Serializable attribute, whose constructor takes no arguments:

```
<Serializable()> Class Person
    ⋮
End Class
```

The only other attribute you must learn about is NonSerialized, which you use for those fields or properties that you don't want to be persisted when the object is serialized. As a rule, you don't persist variables that cache values that you can easily derive from other properties or properties that aren't going to be valid when the object is being deserialized. Among such variables would be pointers, file handles, and references to transient, nonserialized objects. Here's a version of the Person class, which serializes all of its fields except m_Age:

```
<Serializable()> _
Class Person
    Public FirstName As String
    Public LastName As String
    Private BirthDate As Date
    <NonSerialized()> Private m_Age As Integer

    ' Note that BirthDate can be set only by means of the constructor method.
    Sub New(ByVal FirstName As String, ByVal LastName As String, _
        ByVal BirthDate As Date)
        Me.FirstName = FirstName
        Me.LastName = LastName
        Me.BirthDate = BirthDate
    End Sub

    ' The Age property caches its value in the m_Age private variable.
    ReadOnly Property Age() As Integer
        Get
            ' Evaluate the Age if not cached already. Note that this is an
            ' approximate way to evaluate age; in a real application, you
            ' should subtract 1 if this year's birthday hasn't occurred yet.
            If m_Age = 0 Then m_Age = Year(Now) - Year(BirthDate)
            Return m_Age
        End Get
    End Property
End Class
```

The presence of the Serializable attribute is all that the Framework needs to make the class persistable. For example, the following piece of code builds on the SaveSoapData and LoadSoapData routines described in the preceding section and shows how you can serialize and deserialize an ArrayList object containing three Person objects:

```
Sub TestSerializableClass()
    Dim al As New ArrayList()
    al.Add(New Person("Joe", "Doe", #1/12/1960#))
    al.Add(New Person("John", "Smith", #3/6/1962#))
    al.Add(New Person("Ann", "Doe", #10/4/1965#))

    ' Save the ArrayList to disk in SOAP format.
    SaveSoapData("c:\hashtbl.xml", al)

    ' Reload the file contents into another ArrayList object.
    Dim al2 As ArrayList
    al2 = CType(LoadSoapData("c:\hashtbl.xml"), ArrayList)

    ' Display values.
    Dim p As Person
    For Each p In al2
        Console.WriteLine("{0} {1} ({2})", p.FirstName, p.LastName, p.Age)
    Next
End Sub
```

This result appears in the console window:

```
Joe Doe (41)
John Smith (39)
Ann Doe (36)
```

The noteworthy detail here is that although the BirthDate field is private, the deserialization mechanism is able to correctly restore it from the input stream. (The evidence is the fact the Age property is evaluated correctly.) In other words, the deserialization mechanism is capable of ignoring scope rules.

Object Graphs

Before I illustrate the more complex job of custom serialization, I need to draw your attention to a few important details of the serialization infrastructure. Serialization in the .NET Framework uses several classes, either explicitly or under the covers:

- The Formatter converts atomic data to the output stream, interprets the bits in the stream, and converts the bits back to data for the object being deserialized. As you saw earlier, the runtime provides a couple of such Formatter objects for outputting to binary or SOAP format.

- The ObjectIDGenerator generates unique IDs for the objects being serialized. You need this component because an object might be referenced by multiple elements in the array or ArrayList object being persisted, and the object must be serialized only once. The ObjectIDGenerator keeps a list of all the objects being serialized. When an object is submitted for serialization, the ObjectIDGenerator knows whether it's a new object (in which case a new ID must be generated) or an object already serialized (in which case it returns an existing ID). This object is active only during the serialization process.
- The ObjectManager keeps track of objects being deserialized and in a sense is the counterpart of the ObjectIDGenerator. The deserialization infrastructure queries the ObjectManager to learn whether an object reference found in the input stream refers to an object already deserialized (a backward reference) or to an object that hasn't been deserialized yet (a forward reference). This object is active only during the deserialization process.

The beauty of the serialization mechanism is that an object provided by the programmer can replace each of these three objects. For example, you can create your own formatter class that correctly implements the IFormatter interface. In most cases, however, you can get along with the default ObjectIDGenerator and ObjectManager objects.

The importance of the ObjectIDGenerator and ObjectManager objects becomes apparent when you're persisting object graphs, not individual objects. An *object graph* is a set of multiple objects with references to one another. The previous code examples show a simple form of object graph in that an ArrayList holds references to individual Person objects. As a result, serializing an ArrayList object indirectly causes the serialization of all the referenced Person objects. In general, the serialization infrastructure persists all the objects that are directly or indirectly reachable from the root object (the one passed to the Formatter.Serialize method).

In the simplest cases, when there are no circular references between objects, each object is met exactly once during both the serialization and deserialization processes and no ObjectIDGenerator is required. Real-world object hierarchies are usually more complex than that, but the serialization infrastructure is capable of dealing with these cases too. To demonstrate this, you can add the following field to the Person class:

```
' In the Person class
Public Spouse As Person
```

Then you can serialize and deserialize an entire object graph with this code:

```
Sub TestSerializableGraph()
    ' Create three Person objects.
    Dim p1 As New Person("Joe", "Doe", #1/12/1960#)
    Dim p2 As New Person("John", "Smith", #3/6/1962#)
    Dim p3 As New Person("Ann", "Doe", #10/4/1965#)
    ' Define the relationship between two of them.
    p2.Spouse = p3
    p3.Spouse = p2

    ' Load them into an ArrayList object.
    Dim al As New ArrayList()
    al.Add(p1)
    al.Add(p2)
    al.Add(p3)

    ' Save the Hashtable to disk in XML format.
    SaveSoapData("c:\hashtbl.xml", al)

    ' Reload the file contents into another Hashtable object.
    Dim al2 As ArrayList
    al2 = CType(LoadSoapData("c:\hashtbl.xml"), ArrayList)

    ' Display values.
    Dim p As Person
    For Each p In al2

        Console.WriteLine("{0} {1} ({2})", p.FirstName, p.LastName, p.Age)
        If Not (p.Spouse Is Nothing) Then
            ' Show the spouse's name if there is one.
            Console.WriteLine("   Spouse of " & p.Spouse.FirstName)
        End If
    Next
End Sub
```

This new version contains a circular reference between p2 and p3 objects, so p3 can be reached from both the root object (the ArrayList) and the p2.Spouse property. This might cause an endless loop, but the serialization mechanism is smart enough to understand that both references point to the same object, which is therefore persisted only once. A look at the Output window can easily prove this point:

```
Joe Doe (42)
John Smith (40)
   Spouse of Ann
Ann Doe (37)
   Spouse of John
```

It's interesting to see how object references are stored in the XML file produced by the SOAP formatter:

```
<a3:Form1_x002B_Person id="ref-4"
xmlns:a3="http://schemas.microsoft.com/clr/nsassem/...
  <FirstName id="ref-9">John</FirstName>
  <LastName id="ref-10">Smith</LastName>
  <BirthDate>1962-03-06T00:00:00.0000000-06:00</BirthDate>
  <Spouse href="#ref-5"/>
</a3:Form1_x002B_Person>
<a3:Form1_x002B_Person id="ref-5"
xmlns:a3="http://schemas.microsoft.com/clr/nsassem/...
  <FirstName id="ref-11">Ann</FirstName>
  <LastName href="#ref-8"/>
  <BirthDate>1965-10-04T00:00:00.0000000-05:00</BirthDate>
  <Spouse href="#ref-4"/>
</a3:Form1_x002B_Person>
```

As you see, value types (such as BirthDate) aren't assigned an ID, whereas Strings and other object references are. The Spouse object property has no textual value; rather, it has an href attribute equal to the ID of the referenced object. Object properties equal to Nothing aren't included in the XML stream.

Deep Object Cloning

As you might remember from the "Shallow Copies and Deep Copies" section in Chapter 6, you can use the protected MemberwiseClone member (inherited from System.Object) to easily implement the ICloneable interface and its Clone method in any class you define:

```
Class Person
    Implements ICloneable

    ' ...(Variables and methods as in previous example)...

    Public Function Clone() As Object Implements ICloneable.Clone
        Return Me.MemberwiseClone
    End Function
End Class
```

This approach to object cloning has two limitations. First, you can clone an object only if you can modify its source code because the MemberwiseClone method is protected and accessible only from inside the class itself. Second, and more important in many circumstances, the MemberwiseClone method performs a shallow copy of the object—that is, it creates a copy of the object but not of any object referenced by the object. For example, the Clone method of the preceding Person class would not clone also the Person object pointed to by the Spouse property. In other words

```
' Define husband and wife.
Dim p1 As New Person("Joe", "Doe", #1/12/1960#)
Dim p2 As New Person("Ann", "Doe", #10/4/1965#)
p1.Spouse = p2
p2.Spouse = p1
' Clone the husband.
Dim q1 As Person = DirectCast(p1.Clone, Person)
' The Spouse person hasn't been cloned, because it's a shallow copy.
Console.WriteLine(q1.Spouse Is p1.Spouse)            ' => True
```

Using the ability of object serialization to work with complex object graphs lets you solve both the problems I mentioned previously. In fact, you can create a generic routine that performs a deep copy of any object passed to it. For the best performance, it uses a memory stream and a binary formatter, and specifies that the object is being serialized for cloning:

```
Function CloneObject(ByVal obj As Object) As Object
    ' Create a memory stream and a formatter.
    Dim ms As New MemoryStream(1000)
    Dim bf As New BinaryFormatter(Nothing, _
        New StreamingContext(StreamingContextStates.Clone))
    ' Serialize the object into the stream.
    bf.Serialize(ms, obj)
    ' Position stream pointer back to first byte.
    ms.Seek(0, SeekOrigin.Begin)
    ' Deserialize into another object.
    CloneObject = bf.Deserialize(ms)
    ' Release memory.
    ms.Close()
End Function
```

Here's the code that drives the CloneObject routine:

```
' ...(p1 and p2 are initialized as in preceding example)...

' Clone the husband.
Dim q1 As Person = DirectCast(CloneObject(p1), Person)
Dim q2 As Person = q1.Spouse
' Prove that properties were copied correctly.
Console.WriteLine(q1.FirstName & " " & q1.LastName)  ' => Joe Doe
Console.WriteLine(q2.FirstName & " " & q2.LastName)  ' => Ann Smith
' Prove that both objects were cloned, because it's a deep copy.
Console.WriteLine("p1 is q1 = {0}", p1 Is q1)        ' => False
Console.WriteLine("p2 is q2 = {0}", p2 Is q2)        ' => False
```

Custom Serialization

The .NET Framework provides developers with all the means they need to implement custom serialization through the ISerializable interface. You should resort to custom serialization only when the standard mechanism based on the Serializable attribute isn't flexible enough for your needs. You can have trouble, for example, when you want to dynamically decide which information should be persisted or when you need to execute code when the object is deserialized, possibly to recalculate values that aren't valid any longer.

A few Framework objects support the ISerializable interface, including Delegate, Hashtable, Icon, Font, Image, Regex, Assembly, Module, and Thread. You can get the complete list from the .NET SDK documentation, but you generally don't need to know whether an object supports ISerializable because these objects can be persisted and depersisted in the same manner as any other object.

The ISerializable Interface

You can implement the ISerializable interface in your own classes to enhance them with a custom persistence scheme. The ISerializable interface exposes only one method, GetObjectData, which has the following syntax:

```
Sub GetObjectData(ByVal info As SerializationInfo, _
    ByVal context As StreamingContext)
    ⋮
End Sub
```

The GetObjectData method is invoked when the object is passed to the Formatter.Serialize method, and its purpose is to fill the SerializationInfo object with all the information about the Me object (that is, the object being serialized). The code inside this method can examine the StreamingContext structure to retrieve additional details about the serialization process. (See the section "The StreamingContext Structure" later in this chapter.)

The presence of the ISerializable interface implies the existence of a special constructor method with the following syntax:

```
Private Sub New(ByVal info As SerializationInfo, _
    ByVal context As StreamingContext)
    ⋮
End Sub
```

This special constructor is called by the runtime when the object is deserialized. You should use a Private scope for this constructor so that regular clients can't call it. You won't get a compilation error if you omit this constructor, but you get a run-time error when you try to deserialize the object if this constructor is missing. Note that a serializable class must have at least another constructor with Public scope; otherwise, you won't be able to instantiate it from your code.

The SerializationInfo object acts like a dictionary object, to which you add one or more values using the AddValue method:

```
' Save the FirstName value.
info.AddValue("FirstName", FirstName)
```

You can later retrieve values with the GetValue method, which requires the value name and type, as you see here:

```
' Retrieve the FirstName value.
' (The conversion is necessary if Option Strict is On.)
FirstName = CStr(info.GetValue("FirstValue", GetType(String)))
```

Conveniently, the SerializationInfo object exposes many other Get*xxxx* methods, such as GetString and GetInt32, that return data in a specific format:

```
' A more concise way to retrieve the FirstName value
FirstName = info.GetString("FirstValue")
```

In all cases, values in the stream are converted to the requested type, or an InvalidCastException is thrown if the conversion isn't possible.

A Custom Serialization Example

The following example explains how to build the CompactDoubleArray class, which behaves like an array object that contains Double values except that it can serialize itself in a more compact format by discarding all the elements equal to its DefaultValue property. The CompactDoubleArray class inherits most of its functionality from ArrayList, and it implements the ISerializable interface for dealing with the custom serialization and deserialization process. Here's the complete listing of the CompactDoubleArray class:

```
<Serializable()> _
Class CompactDoubleArray
    Inherits ArrayList
    Implements ISerializable

    ' Elements that have this value aren't persisted.
    Public DefaultValue As Double

    ' We need this default constructor; otherwise, the class
    ' can't be instantiated from regular clients.
    Sub New()
        MyBase.New()
```

(continued)

```
    End Sub

    ' The special constructor implied by ISerializable
    Private Sub New(ByVal info As SerializationInfo, _
        ByVal context As StreamingContext)

        ' Create the base ArrayList object.
        MyBase.New()
        ' Retrieve DefaultValue.
        DefaultValue = info.GetDouble("DefaultValue")
        ' Retrieve number of elements.
        Dim elCount As Integer = info.GetInt32("Count")

        Dim index As Integer, Value As Double
        For index = 0 To elCount - 1
            Try
                ' Try to assign the value in the SerializationInfo object.
                Value = info.GetDouble(Index.ToString)
            Catch
                ' If SerializationInfo doesn't contain that value,
                ' use the default value.
                Value = DefaultValue
            End Try
            ' Add the value to the inner ArrayList.
            MyBase.Add(Value)
        Next
    End Sub

    ' Serialize this object.
    Sub GetObjectData(ByVal info As SerializationInfo, _
        ByVal context As StreamingContext) _
        Implements ISerializable.GetObjectData

        ' Remember DefaultValue.
        info.AddValue("DefaultValue", DefaultValue)
        ' Remember the total number of elements.
        info.AddValue("Count", MyBase.Count)

        ' Serialize only elements whose value is different from DefaultValue.
        Dim index As Integer, Value As Double
        For index = 0 To MyBase.Count - 1
            ' The AddValue method requires a specific type.
            Value = CType(MyBase.Item(index), Double)
            If Value <> DefaultValue Then
                ' Store only if different from default value.
                info.AddValue(Index.ToString, Value)
            End If
        Next
    End Sub
End Class
```

The following code is the test program that uses the SaveSoapData and LoadSoapData routines, defined earlier in this chapter:

```
Sub TestCustomSerialization()
    ' Create a compact array of Double, whose DefaultValue is 1.
    Dim ca As New CompactDoubleArray()
    ca.DefaultValue = 1
    ' Add some elements (including some default values).
    ca.Add(1)
    ca.Add(2)
    ca.Add(3)
    ca.Add(1)
    ca.Add(4)
    ca.Add(5)
    ca.Add(1)
    ' Serialize the array.
    SaveSoapData("c:\compact.xml", ca)

    ' Read it back.
    Dim ca2 As CompactDoubleArray
    ca2 = CType(LoadSoapData("c:\compact.xml"), CompactDoubleArray)

    ' Print its contents.
    Dim o As Object
    For Each o In ca2
        Console.Write(o.ToString & " ")     ' => 1 2 3 1 4 5 1
    Next
End Sub
```

The StreamingContext Structure

Both the ISerialization.GetObjectData method and the special constructor implied by the ISerialization interface receive a StreamingContext structure, which allows you to learn additional details about the serialization and deserialization process. This StreamingContext is the value that is (optionally) passed as the second argument of the formatter's constructor.

In practice, the only property of this structure that can prove helpful is State, which returns a bit-coded enumeration value whose values are summarized in Table 11-1. For example, if an object contains the handle of a window, you shouldn't persist it if the CrossMachine or Remoting flag is set because that handle isn't going to be valid on another machine. Similarly, you shouldn't save a window handle if either the File or Persistence bit is set because that window might be closed when the object is depersisted. If no argument was passed to the formatter's constructor, a default StreamingContext structure with the State property set to All is used.

Table 11-1 StreamingContextStates Bits

Name	Value	Description
All	127	The serialized data might be transmitted to or received from any of the other contexts. This is the value used if you don't explicitly pass a StreamingContext object to the formatter's constructor.
Clone	64	The object graph is being cloned. Users can assume that the cloned graph will continue to exist within the same process and that it will be safe to access handles or references to unmanaged resources.
CrossMachine	2	The source or destination context is on a different machine.
CrossProcess	1	The source or destination context is a different process on the same machine.
CrossAppDomain	128	The source or destination context is a different AppDomain.
File	4	The source or destination context is a file. Developers should serialize objects in such a way that deserialization won't need to access any data from the current process because the current process will probably be gone in the meantime.
Other	32	The serialization context is unknown.
Persistence	8	The source or destination context is a persisted store (a database or a file). Developers should serialize objects in such a way that deserialization won't need to access any data from the current process because the current process will probably be gone in the meantime.
Remoting	16	The source or destination context is remoting to an unknown location. Developers can't make any assumptions as to whether it's on the same machine.

You can improve the persistence scheme of the CompactDoubleArray class by compacting its serialized image when you're persisting to a file (to save disk space) or to a remote machine (to reduce network traffic). This job is particularly simple because you can rely on the ArrayList base class for the standard, noncompact, format. You have to modify the CompactDoubleArray class only at two points to implement this new feature. (Additions are in boldface.)

```
Private Sub New(ByVal info As SerializationInfo, _
    ByVal context As StreamingContext)

    ' Create an ArrayList object of a given number of elements.
    MyBase.New()

    ' Attempt to get the serialized ArrayList.
    Try
        ' Try to read an element named ArrayList.
        Dim al As ArrayList
        al = CType(info.GetValue("ArrayList", GetType(ArrayList)), ArrayList)
        ' If all went well, add to inner ArrayList and exit.
        MyBase.AddRange(al)
        Exit Sub
    Catch
        ' If failed, continue to extract elements.
    End Try

    ' ...(The remainder of the procedure is unchanged)...
    ⋮
End Sub

Sub GetObjectData(ByVal info As SerializationInfo, _
    ByVal context As StreamingContext) Implements ISerializable.GetObjectData

    ' If not serializing to a file or a remote machine,
    ' use standard, noncompact, format.
    If context.State <> StreamingContextStates.File _
        And context.State <> StreamingContextStates.CrossMachine Then
        ' Serialize the inner ArrayList, and exit.
        info.AddValue("ArrayList", MyBase.Clone)
        Exit Sub
    End If

    ' ...(The remainder of the procedure is unchanged)...
End Sub
```

The IDeserializationCallback Interface

The approach we've followed so far has one defect, which can also be a source of subtle bugs: when the serialization infrastructure calls the object's constructor, the object graph might not have been completely deserialized yet. For example, the root object might have been read and deserialized completely, but its child objects might not have been. This situation arises when one or more forward reference fix-ups haven't been resolved yet—that is, when the ObjectManager finds a reference to an object that hasn't been deserialized yet.

The CompactDoubleArray class doesn't suffer from this problem because it doesn't have any child objects. (It contains Double elements only, which are a value type.) The problem can manifest itself when you're creating a class that holds object references rather than plain values. In this case, your serializable object should implement the IDeserializationCallback interface. This interface has only one method, OnDeserialization, which is called when the object graph (whose root is your object) has been completely deserialized and all forward references have been fixed up.

The following code sample is similar to the previous snippet but uses a serializable Point value and a CompactPointArray class that implements both the ISerialization and IDeserializationCallback interfaces. The logic behind this code is simple: the statements in the special constructor method store a reference to the SerializationInfo object in a private variable; when the runtime eventually calls OnDeserialization, information is extracted from that private variable. The comments in the code should help you follow the execution flow:

```
' A very simple serializable class
<Serializable()> Class Point
    Public X As Single
    Public Y As Single

    Sub New(ByVal X As Single, ByVal Y As Single)
        Me.X = X
        Me.Y = Y
    End Sub

    Overrides Function ToString() As String
        Return "(" & X.ToString & "," & Y.ToString & ")"
    End Function
End Class

<Serializable()> Class CompactPointArray
    Inherits ArrayList
    Implements ISerializable, IDeserializationCallback

    ' This variable caches the object passed to the constructor.
    Dim m_info As SerializationInfo

    ' We need this constructor.
    Sub New()
        MyBase.New()
    End Sub

    ' The special constructor implied by ISerializable
    Private Sub New(ByVal info As SerializationInfo, _
        ByVal context As StreamingContext)
        ' Create an ArrayList object.
```

```
        MyBase.New()
        ' Cache the SerializationInfo object.
        m_info = info
    End Sub

    ' This method is called when the object graph has been
    ' completely deserialized.
    Sub OnDeserialization(ByVal sender As Object) _
        Implements IDeserializationCallback.OnDeserialization
        ' Retrieve number of elements.
        Dim elCount As Integer = m_info.GetInt32("Count")

        Dim index As Integer, p As Point
        For index = 0 To elCount - 1
            Try
                ' Try to assign the value in the SerializationInfo object.
                p = CType(m_info.GetValue(Index.ToString, _
                    GetType(Point)), Point)
            Catch
                p = New Point(0, 0)
            End Try
            ' Add to the inner ArrayList.
            MyBase.Add(p)
        Next
        ' We don't need this object any longer.
        m_Info = Nothing
    End Sub

    ' Serialize only points that aren't equal to (0,0).
    Sub GetObjectData(ByVal info As SerializationInfo, ByVal _
        context As StreamingContext) Implements ISerializable.GetObjectData

        ' Remember the total number of elements.
        info.AddValue("Count", MyBase.Count)

        ' Serialize only elements whose value is different from (0,0).
        Dim index As Integer, p As Point
        For index = 0 To MyBase.Count - 1
            ' The AddValue method requires a specific type.
            p = CType(MyBase.Item(index), Point)
            If p.X <> 0 Or p.Y <> 0 Then
                ' Add to SerializationInfo only if <> (0,0).
                info.AddValue(Index.ToString, p)
            End If
        Next
    End Sub
End Class
```

Here's the program that test drives the CompactPointArray class:

```
Sub TestIDeserializationCallback()
    ' Create a compact array of Point objects.
    Dim ca As New CompactPointArray()
    ' Add some elements (including some (0,0) points).
    ca.Add(New Point(1, 3))
    ca.Add(New Point(0, 0))
    ca.Add(New Point(3, 5))
    ca.Add(New Point(1, 6))
    ca.Add(New Point(0, 0))
    ca.Add(New Point(4, 8))
    ca.Add(New Point(0, 0))
    ' Serialize it.
    SaveSoapData("c:\points.xml", ca)

    ' Read it back.
    Dim ca2 As CompactPointArray
    ca2 = CType(LoadSoapData("c:\Points.xml"), CompactPointArray)

    ' Print its contents.
    Dim o As Object
    For Each o In ca2
        Console.Write(o.ToString & " ")
    Next
End Sub
```

XML Serialization

The .NET Framework supports yet another form of object serialization known as XML serialization (not to be confused with SOAP serialization). In a nutshell, XML serialization allows you to persist an object's state in an XML stream while maintaining control over the XML elements used to persist data. For example, you can decide the XML namespace to use, whether a property should be serialized as an XML element or attribute, and the name of that element or attribute. (You don't have such control when you're persisting to SOAP format.)

While XML serialization sounds more flexible than SOAP serialization, it has a few shortcomings as well:

- It works only with public classes.
- Only public fields and properties can be serialized.
- An object graph can't be serialized if it contains circular references.
- Data in the class is serialized, but object identity is lost, as is information about the assembly.

What's XML serialization good for? Most often you'll use this technique to quickly serialize your objects in an XML stream whose syntax is understood by another application. The opposite operation is also quite common—that is, reading XML data coming from another application into your objects. This technique opens up many interesting possibilities, as you'll see in the remainder of this chapter.

The XmlSerializer Class

The workhorse of XML serialization is the System.Xml.Serialization.XmlSerializer object, which works pretty much like the SoapFormatter object you saw earlier in this chapter. The main difference is that each XmlSerializer object is good only for serializing the class specified in its constructor. To see how XML serialization works, let's start with a simple class:

```
Public Class Customer
    Public ID As Integer
    Public Name As String
    Public Address As String
    Public City As String

    ' All XML-serializable classes must support a parameterless constructor.
    Sub New()
        ' There's nothing to do in this example.
    End Sub

    Sub New(ByVal id As Integer, ByVal name As String, _
        ByVal address As String, ByVal city As String)
        Me.ID = id
        Me.Name = name
        Me.Address = address
        Me.City = city
    End Sub
End Class
```

Let's see how you can create an XmlSerializer object that saves an instance of the Customer class to a file and then reloads it:

```
' This code assumes that the following Imports are used:
'     Imports System.Xml.Serialization
'     Imports System.IO

Sub TestXmlSerializer()
    ' Create an XmlSerializer object for the Publisher class.
    Dim ser As New XmlSerializer(GetType(Customer))
```

(continued)

```
    ' Create a Customer object.
    Dim cust As New Customer(1, "Joe Doe", Nothing, "New York")

    ' Open the destination file.
    Dim fs As New FileStream("c:\customer.xml", FileMode.Create)
    ' Serialize the object to the stream, and close it.
    ser.Serialize(fs, cust)
    fs.Close()

    ' Reopen the stream.
    Dim fs2 As New FileStream("c:\customer.xml", FileMode.Open)
    ' Deserialize the file into another Customer object, and close the stream.
    Dim cust2 As Customer = CType(ser.Deserialize(fs2), Customer)
    fs2.Close()
    ' Check object properties.
    Console.WriteLine(cust2.Name & ", " & cust2.City)    ' => Joe Doe, New York
End Sub
```

Here's the XML text in the c:\customer.xml file, after I indented some lines to make the XML structure more evident:

```
<?xml version="1.0"?>
<Customer xmlns:xsd="http://www.w3.org/2001/XMLSchema"
  xmlns:xsi="http://www.w3.org/2001/XMLSchema-instance">
  <ID>1</ID>
  <Name>Joe Doe</Name>
  <City>New York</City>
</Customer>
```

As you see, the name of the class is used for the outermost XML root element (Customer), and all fields are rendered as nested XML elements. Interestingly, if a property is Nothing (as is the case with the Address property), it's rendered with an explicit xsi:nil XML attribute. Note that the XmlSerializer object deals correctly with characters inside String fields or properties that have a special meaning in XML by converting them to their escaped forms (for example, < for the < character and > for the > character).

Serialization Attributes

You have precise control over the XML serialization process, thanks to a group of attributes that let you modify how individual fields of the class are persisted. Among such attributes are these:

- The XmlRoot attribute lets you set the name used for the outermost XML root element, the namespace for the element, and whether the xsi:null attribute appears if the object being persisted is Nothing.

- The XmlElement attribute lets you specify a different name for the XML element corresponding to a given field or property. It also lets you decide whether the element should appear at all if it's Nothing.
- The XmlAttributeAttribute attribute lets you flag fields and properties that should be serialized as attributes rather than elements, decide which name should be used for the attribute, and decide whether it should be omitted if the field's value is Nothing. (Note that you can't shorten this attribute's name in code to XmlAttribute.)
- The XmlText attribute lets you specify that a field or a property should be rendered as XML text without being enclosed in XML tags.
- The XmlIgnore attribute lets you flag a field or a property that shouldn't be serialized at all.

(See Table 11-2 for the complete list of supported attributes.) Let's create a new Customer2 class that exploits some of these attributes:

```
<XmlRootAttribute("Customer", _
    Namespace:="http://www.vb2themax.com", IsNullable:=False)> _
Public Class Customer2
    <XmlAttributeAttribute("CustId")> _
    Public ID As Integer
    <XmlElement("name")> _
    Public Name As String
    <XmlIgnore()> _
    Public Address As String
    <XmlElement("city", IsNullable:=False)> _
    Public City As String
    <XmlText()> _
    Public Notes As String

    ' ...(Constructors as in Customer class)...
End Class
```

The XmlElement attribute can take optional values. The IsNullable value specifies the behavior when the field or property is Nothing: if True, the XML element is preserved and an xsi:nil XML attribute is appended; if False or omitted, the XML element is discarded when the field's value is Nothing.

Serializing the Customer2 class delivers this XML text. (Differences are in boldface.)

```
<?xml version="1.0" ?>
<Customer xmlns:xsi="http://www.w3.org/2001/XMLSchema-instance"
    xmlns:xsd="http://www.w3.org/2001/XMLSchema"
```

(continued)

```
    CustId="1" xmlns="http://www.vb2themax.com">
  <name>Joe Doe</name>
  <city>New York</city>
</Customer>
```

As you see, the ID field was rendered into the CustId attribute, the Address field wasn't serialized at all (because it's Nothing), the root element is qualified with the http://www.vb2themax.com namespace, and remaining XML elements are lowercase. The root XML element is still Customer, even if the class name has changed to Customer2, thanks to the XmlRoot attribute. (We might have used an XmlType attribute as well.)

The constructor of both the XmlAttributeAttribute and XmlElement attributes can also take a Namespace value, which specifies the namespace for the generated attribute or element. To see how the Namespace value affects the result, modify the Customer2 class as follows:

```
Public Class Customer3
    <XmlAttributeAttribute("CustId", Namespace:="www.abc.com")> _
    Public ID As Integer
    <XmlElement("name", Namespace:="www.abc.com")> _

    ' ...(The remainder of the class as before)...
End Class
```

The new version of the class produces this XML text. (Differences are in boldface.)

```
<?xml version="1.0" ?>
<Customer xmlns:xsi="http://www.w3.org/2001/XMLSchema-instance"
    xmlns:xsd="http://www.w3.org/2001/XMLSchema"
    n1:CustId="1" xmlns:n1="www.abc.com"
    xmlns="http://www.vb2themax.com">
  <n1:name>Joe Doe</n1:name>
  <city>New York</city>
</Customer>
```

The XmlArray and XmlArrayItem attributes are usually applied together to fields and properties that return an array of complex objects that are rendered as nested XML elements. The XmlArray attribute defines the name of the outer element, whereas the XmlArrayItem attribute defines the name of the inner element. For example, let's define a Customer4 class that contains an array of Order objects:

```
Public Class Customer4
    <XmlArray("CustOrders"), XmlArrayItem("CustOrder", IsNullable:=True)> _
    Public Orders(3) As Order

    ' ...(All other members as before)...
End Class
```

```
Public Class Order
    <XmlAttributeAttribute("OrderId")> _
    Public ID As Integer
    Public [Date] As Date          ' Note how we deal with a VB reserved word.
    Public Total As Decimal

    ' All XML serializable classes must have a default constructor.
    Sub New()
        ' There's nothing to do in this example.
    End Sub

    Sub New(ByVal id As Integer, ByVal [date] As Date, ByVal total As Decimal)
        Me.ID = id
        Me.Date = [date]
        Me.Total = total
    End Sub
End Class
```

This is the XML text produced by a Customer4 object that has two child Order objects:

```
<?xml version="1.0" ?>
<Customer4 xmlns:xsi="http://www.w3.org/2001/XMLSchema-instance"
    xmlns:xsd="http://www.w3.org/2001/XMLSchema"
    n1:CustId="1" xmlns:n1="www.abc.com">
  <n1:name>Joe Doe</n1:name>
  <city>New York</city>
  <CustOrders>
    <CustOrder OrderId="1">
      <Date>2001-01-02T00:00:00.0000000+01:00</Date>
      <Total>123.5</Total>
    </CustOrder>
    <CustOrder OrderId="2">
      <Date>2001-04-08T00:00:00.0000000+02:00</Date>
      <Total>450.8</Total>
    </CustOrder>
    <CustOrder xsi:nil="true" />
    <CustOrder xsi:nil="true" />
  </CustOrders>
</Customer4>
```

The XmlArrayItem element can take an IsNullable property. If this property is set to True, the XML text contains xsi:nil attributes for each child object set to Nothing (as you see in the last two elements of the CustOrders array in the preceding code, shown in boldface). If the IsNullable property is set to False or omitted, null child objects don't appear in the XML result.

Table 11-2 Attributes to Control XML Serialization (Taken from .NET Documentation)

Attribute	Applies To	Description
XmlAnyAttribute-Attribute	Public fields that return an array of XmlAttribute objects.	During deserialization, the array will be filled with XmlAttribute objects that represent all XML attributes unknown to the schema.
XmlAnyElement-Attribute	Public fields that return an array of XmlElement objects.	During deserialization, the array will be filled with XmlElement objects that represent all XML elements unknown to the schema.
XmlArrayAttribute	Public properties and fields that return arrays of complex objects.	The members of the array will be generated as members of an XML array.
XmlArrayItem-Attribute	Public properties and fields that return arrays of complex objects.	Derived types that can be inserted into an array.
XmlAttribute-Attribute	Public properties and fields.	The class will be serialized as an XML attribute.
XmlElementAttribute	Public properties and fields.	The field or property will be serialized as an XML element.
XmlEnumAttribute	Enumeration identifiers.	The element name of an enumeration member.
XmlIgnoreAttribute	Public properties and fields.	The property or field should be ignored when the containing class is serialized.
XmlIncludeAttribute	Public derived class declarations, and public methods. (For WSDL documents, see Chapter 26.)	The class should be included when generating schemas (and will thus be recognized when serialized).
XmlRootAttribute	Public class declarations.	The class represents the root element of the XML document. (Use the attribute to further specify the namespace and the element name.)
XmlTextAttribute	Public properties and fields.	The property or field should be serialized as XML text.
XmlTypeAttribute	Public class declarations.	The class should be serialized as an XML type; is ignored if used together with XmlRootAttribute. (Use the attribute to further specify the namespace and the element name.)

The XmlSerializerNamespaces Object

In the preceding section, you saw that the XmlAttributeAttribute and XmlElement attributes support a Namespace value, which gives you some control over the XML namespace of the serialized value. You can use another method for changing the default namespace of elements that is based on the XmlSerializerNamespaces auxiliary object and that doesn't require you to embed an attribute in the class code.

Using the XmlSerializerNamespaces object is quite simple: you use its Add method to associate a namespace with a given XML element, and then you pass the object as the last argument of the XmlSerializer.Serialize method:

```
Dim ns As New XmlSerializerNamespaces()
' Change the namespace of the Customer4 element.
s.Add("Customer4", "http://www.vb2themax.com")
' Change the namespace of the Order element.
s.Add("Order", "http://www.wintellect.com")

' Open the destination file.
Dim fs As New FileStream("c:\customer.xml", FileMode.Create)
' Serialize the object to the stream, enforcing the specified namespaces.
ser.Serialize(fs, cust, ns)
```

This is the XML text produced by the previous code:

```
<?xml version="1.0" ?>
<Customer4 xmlns:Customer4="http://www.vb2themax.com"
     xmlns:Order="http://www.wintellect.com"
     n1:CustId="1" xmlns:n1="www.abc.com">
  <CustOrders>
    <CustOrder OrderId="1">
      <Date>2001-01-02T00:00:00.0000000+01:00</Date>
      <Total>123.5</Total>
    </CustOrder>
    <CustOrder OrderId="2">
    <Date>2001-04-08T00:00:00.0000000+02:00</Date>
    <Total>450.8</Total>
    </CustOrder>
    <CustOrder n1:nil="true"
       xmlns:n1="http://www.w3.org/2001/XMLSchema-instance" />
    <CustOrder n1:nil="true"
       xmlns:n1="http://www.w3.org/2001/XMLSchema-instance" />
  </CustOrders>
  <n1:name>Joe Doe</n1:name>
  <city>New York</city>
</Customer4>
```

Deserialization Events

The XmlSerializer object can raise four different events during the deserialization process if it encounters any XML entity it doesn't recognize. Two of these events are particularly interesting for our purposes: the UnknownElement and UnknownAttribute events, which fire when the XmlSerializer object reads an unrecognized XML element and attribute. If you don't write any code for these events, the XmlSerializer object simply ignores elements that it doesn't recognize.

You can use deserialization events for a variety of purposes—for example, to keep a log of elements that failed to convert correctly. A better use for these events, however, is to provide a way to import XML data that doesn't exactly match the structure of your class. For example, say that you want to import this XML file into a Customer class:

```
<?xml version="1.0" ?>
<Customer xmlns:xsi="http://www.w3.org/2001/XMLSchema-instance"
    xmlns:xsd="http://www.w3.org/2001/XMLSchema">
  <ID>1</ID>
  <FirstName>Joe</FirstName>
  <LastName>Doe</LastName>
  <Address xsi:nil="true" />
  <City>New York</City>
</Customer>
```

The boldface portion highlights the problem: instead of having one Name element, this file contains two distinct elements, FirstName and LastName. Unless you take additional steps, the XmlSerializer object ignores these two pieces of information, and the Customer.Name property remains unassigned. Thanks to the UnknownElement event, however, you can trap these elements and combine them into a value that you later assign to the Name property. Here's the code that does the trick:

```
Sub TestDeserializationEvents()
    ' Create an XmlSerializer object for the Publisher class.
    Dim ser As New XmlSerializer(GetType(Customer))
    ' Dynamically create the event.
    AddHandler ser.UnknownElement, AddressOf Deserialization_UnknownElement

    ' Reopen the stream.
    Dim fs2 As New FileStream("c:\customer2.xml", FileMode.Open)
    ' Deserialize the file into another Customer object, and close the stream.
    Dim cust2 As Customer = CType(ser.Deserialize(fs2), Customer)
    fs2.Close()
    ' Check that the name was read correctly.
    Console.WriteLine(cust2.Name & ", " & cust2.City)    ' => Joe Doe, New York
End Sub
```

```
' This event is raised when the XmlSerializer finds an unknown XML element.
Sub Deserialization_UnknownElement(ByVal sender As Object, _
    ByVal e As XmlElementEventArgs)
    ' Cast the element to a Customer object.
    Dim cust As Customer = CType(e.ObjectBeingDeserialized, Customer)
    ' There are two cases: we've found either a FirstName or a LastName
    ' XML element.
    If e.Element.Name = "FirstName" Then
        ' If it is a FirstName element, assign to Name property.
        cust.Name = e.Element.InnerXml
    ElseIf e.Element.Name = "LastName" Then
        ' If it is a LastName element, append to Name property.
        cust.Name &= " " & e.Element.InnerXml
    End If
End Sub
```

The XmlElementEventArgs object exposes four interesting properties:

- **ObjectBeingDeserialized** Its name says it all: this is the object currently deserialized. You can test its type to learn which object is failing to be deserialized correctly, or you can assign its fields and properties (as the preceding event procedure does).
- **LineNumber and LinePosition** These properties return the line and the column number where the unrecognized element has been encountered. They're useful for reporting errors in the incoming XML data.
- **Element** This XmlElement object represents the unrecognized XML element; it exposes several properties, the most important of which are Name (the name of the element) and InnerXml (its contents).

The UnknownAttribute event receives an XmlAttributeEventArgs object, which exposes the following properties: ObjectBeingDeserialized, LineNumber, LinePosition, and Attr. You already know about the first three properties. Attr is an XmlAttribute object that represents the unrecognized XML attribute; this object exposes several properties, the most important of which are Name (the name of the attribute) and Value (its contents).

Overriding Behavior

The XML serialization mechanism seen so far has two major drawbacks. First, it assumes that you have the source code of the class being serialized, so it doesn't work with classes in a compiled DLL or with classes that you inherit from a class in a DLL. Second, the serialization format is fixed for each given class, so you can't serialize a class in two or more different ways (which might be necessary if you're importing data from one application, processing it, and exporting to a different application). Overriding the default behavior of the XmlSerializer class can solve both these issues.

Assume that you have the AddressBook class, which contains an array of Person objects:

```
Class AddressBook
    Public Name As String
    Public Contacts() As Person
End Class

Class Person
    Public ID As Integer
    Public Name As String
    Public PhoneNumber As String
End Class
```

You can serialize these classes using an XmlSerializer object, as I have shown you previously. For example, this is the XML that you get when you serialize an AddressBook object that contains two Person objects in its Contacts array:

```
<?xml version="1.0" ?>
<AddressBook xmlns:xsi="http://www.w3.org/2001/XMLSchema-instance"
    xmlns:xsd="http://www.w3.org/2001/XMLSchema">
  <Name>My Address Book</Name>
  <Contacts>
    <Person>
      <ID>1</ID>
      <Name>Joe Doe</Name>
      <PhoneNumber>234-555-6789</PhoneNumber>
    </Person>
    <Person>
      <ID>2</ID>
      <Name>Robert Smith</Name>
      <PhoneNumber>234-555-6543</PhoneNumber>
    </Person>
  </Contacts>
</AddressBook>
```

Let's suppose that you want to modify this XML output because you must pass it to an application that recognizes XML input in a slightly different format. For example, say that you want to change the output as follows. (Changes are in boldface.)

```
<?xml version="1.0" ?>
<EmployeeList xmlns:xsi="http://www.w3.org/2001/XMLSchema-instance"
      xmlns:xsd="http://www.w3.org/2001/XMLSchema">
  <Name>My Employee Book</Name>
  <Employees>
    <Employee ID="1">
      <Name>Joe Doe</Name>
      <Phone>234-555-6789</Phone>
    </Employee>
    <Employee ID="2">
     <Name>Robert Smith</Name>
     <Phone>234-555-6543</Phone>
    </Employee>
  </Employees>
</EmployeeList>
```

If you can modify the source code of the AddressBook and Person classes, getting this new format requires only a few appropriate Xml*xxxx* attributes:

```
<XmlRootAttribute("EmployeeList")> _
Public Class AddressBook
    Public Name As String
    <XmlArray("Employees"), XmlArrayItem("Employee")> _
    Public Contacts() As Person
End Class

Public Class Person
    <XmlAttributeAttribute("ID")> _
    Public ID As Integer
    Public Name As String
    <XmlElement("Phone")> _
    Public PhoneNumber As String
End Class
```

Here's the problem: what if you can't modify the source code of these classes (for example, because you must read or write XML also in the default format) or you don't even have their source code (because these classes are defined in a compiled DLL)? In these circumstances, your only option is to override the default behavior of the XmlSerializer object.

In practice, you use an XmlAttributeOverrides object to specify which attributes you would add to source code if you were allowed to do so. Here's the complete sequence of actions you must perform:

1. Create an XmlAttributeOverrides object.
2. Create an XmlAttributes object. (Note the plural.) This object will contain one or more Xml*xxxx*Attribute objects, one for each attribute that you want to apply to a field or property that must be overridden.

3. Create an Xml*xxxx*Attribute object, which represents an attribute that you want to apply to a given field or property. For example, you can create an XmlElementAttribute object to render a field or property as an XML element or an XmlAttributeAttribute object to render a field or property as an XML attribute. This object is the same Xml*xxxx*Attribute attribute that you would insert in the source code of the class being serialized; and in fact, you can use the attribute's constructor as you do when inserting the attribute between < and > brackets. Or you can assign individual properties, such as ElementName (the name of the XML element or attribute that will be rendered) and Type (the class that renders that specific element or attribute).

4. Assign the Xml*xxxx*Attribute that you have created at a previous point to the appropriate property of the XmlAttributes object you created in step 2. For example, you assign an XmlTextAttribute to the XmlAttributes.XmlText property. If an attribute can be specified multiple times, you'll have to add it to a suitable collection that the XmlAttributes object exposes. (For example, you add an XmlElementAttribute object to the XmlAttributes.XmlElements collection.)

   Repeat steps 3 and 4 for each attribute that you want to assign to a given element.

5. Use the Add method of the XmlAttributeOverrides object to add the XmlAttributes object you created in step 2. The XmlAttributeOverrides.Add method takes both a System.Type object corresponding to the class that contains the overridden member and the name of the XML element or attribute being overridden.

   Repeat steps 2 through 5 for each XML syntax entity that you want to override.

6. Finally, create the XmlSerializer object, passing the XmlAttributeOverrides object to the second argument of its constructor.

As you see, it's a long and winding road, so an actual code example is in order. The following procedure produces the modified XML text seen previously by "virtually inserting" new attributes in the AddressBook and Person classes. The comments in the following code refer to the steps mentioned in the preceding list, so you should have no problem following the execution flow:

```
Sub TestSerializationOverriding()
    ' Step 1: create an XmlAttributeOverrides object.
    Dim xmlAttrOver As New XmlAttributeOverrides()

    ' (A) Add the XmlRootAttribute("EmployeeList") attribute.

    ' Step A2: create the XmlAttributes object.
```

```
Dim xmlAttrs As New XmlAttributes()
' Step A3: create and initialize the XmlRootAttribute object.
Dim attr1 As New XmlRootAttribute("EmployeeList")
' Step A4: assign it to the correct property of the XmlAttributes object.
xmlAttrs.XmlRoot = attr1
' Step A5: pass XmlAttributes to the Add method of XmlAttributeOverrides.
' When adding an XmlRootAttribute, you specify only two arguments:
'   first argument is the class that contains the overridden member;
'   second argument is the XmlAttributes object that defines the
'   new attributes.
xmlAttrOver.Add(GetType(AddressBook), xmlAttrs)

' (B) Add XmlArray("Employees") and XmlArrayItem("Employee") attributes.

' Step B2: create a new XmlAttributes object.
xmlAttrs = New XmlAttributes()
' Step B3: create and initialize the XmlArrayAttribute object.
Dim attr2 As New XmlArrayAttribute("Employees")
' Step B4: assign it to the correct property of the XmlAttributes object.
xmlAttrs.XmlArray = attr2
' Repeat steps B3/B4, this time for the XmlArrayItemAttribute object.
' (Note how you can do both creation and assignment in one step.)
xmlAttrs.XmlArrayItems.Add(New XmlArrayItemAttribute("Employee"))
' Step B5: pass XmlAttributes to the Add method of XmlAttributeOverrides:
'   first argument is the class that contains the overridden member;
'   second argument is the member being overridden;
'   third argument is the XmlAttributes object that defines the new
'   attributes.
xmlAttrOver.Add(GetType(AddressBook), "Contacts", xmlAttrs)

' (C) Add the XmlAttributeAttribute("ID") attribute.

' Step C2: create a new XmlAttributes object.
xmlAttrs = New XmlAttributes()
' Steps C3/C4: create and initialize the XmlArrayAttribute object,
' and assign it to the proper property of the XmlAttributes object.
xmlAttrs.XmlAttribute = New XmlAttributeAttribute("id")
' Step C5: pass XmlAttributes to the Add method of XmlAttributeOverrides.
' (Arguments are as in step B5.)
xmlAttrOver.Add(GetType(Person), "ID", xmlAttrs)

' (D) Add the XmlElement("Phone") attribute.

' Step D2: create a new XmlAttributes object.
xmlAttrs = New XmlAttributes()
' Steps D3/D4: create and initialize the XmlElementAttribute object,
' and add it to XmlAttributes' XmlElements collection.
```

(continued)

```
    xmlAttrs.XmlElements.Add(New XmlElementAttribute("Phone"))
    ' Step D5: pass XmlAttributes to the Add method of XmlAttributeOverrides.
    ' (Arguments are as in step B5.)
    xmlAttrOver.Add(GetType(Person), "PhoneNumber", xmlAttrs)

    ' Step 6: create the XmlSerializer that uses XmlAttributeOverrides.
    Dim ser As New XmlSerializer(GetType(AddressBook), xmlAttrOver)

    ' Serialize an AddressBook object using XmlSerializer.
    ' ...(omitted)...
End Sub
```

Unfortunately, what we've done so far doesn't suffice in many real-world applications. For example, let's say that you have two classes that inherit from Person—Employee and CandidateEmployee:

```
Class Employee
    Inherits Person
    Public SSN As String
    Public HireDate As String
End Class

Class CandidateEmployee
    Inherits Person
    Public InterviewDate As Date
End Class
```

You might want to store both the Employee and CandidateEmployee objects in the AddressBook.Contacts array, but you want to render custom XML text for these classes. For example, let's say you want to suppress the HireDate property and render the SSN property as an XML attribute. This is a sample of the XML text you want to achieve:

```
<?xml version="1.0" ?>
<EmployeeList xmlns:xsi="http://www.w3.org/2001/XMLSchema-instance"
      xmlns:xsd="http://www.w3.org/2001/XMLSchema">
  <Name>My Employee Book</Name>
  <Employees>
    <Employee id="1"SSN="111-222-3333">
      <Name>Joe Doe</Name>
      <Phone>234-555-6789</Phone>
    </Employee>
    <CandidateEmployee id="2">
     <Name>Robert Smith</Name>
     <Phone>234-555-6543</Phone>
     <InterviewDate>2001-02-08</InterviewDate>
    </CandidateEmployee>
  </Employees>
</EmployeeList>
```

The preceding XML text corresponds to the application of the following attributes to the AddressBook and Employee classes. (Additions are in boldface.)

```
<XmlRootAttribute("EmployeeList")> _
Public Class AddressBook
    Public Name As String
    <XmlArray("Employees"), XmlArrayItem("Employee", GetType(Employee)), _
        XmlArrayItem("CandidateEmployee", GetType(CandidateEmployee)) > _
    Public Contacts() As Person
End Class

Class Employee
    Inherits Person
    <XmlAttributeAttribute("SSN")> _
    Public SSN As String
    <XmlIgnore()> _
    Public HireDate As String
End Class
```

Note that you need two XmlArrayItem attributes, each one describing the XML element that must be used for a different object that can be contained in the Contacts array.

Here's a revised routine that creates an XmlSerializer object capable of serializing and deserializing the AddressBook object tree using the custom XML format. To save space, I'm showing only code changes and additions (specific differences in boldface), but you can get the complete source code on the companion CD.

```
Sub TestSerializationOverriding2()
    ' Step 1: create an XmlAttributeOverrides object.
    Dim xmlAttrOver As New XmlAttributeOverrides()

    ' ...(Section A as before)...

    ' (B) Add XmlArray("Employees") and XmlArrayItem("Employee") attributes.

    ' Step B2: create a new XmlAttributes object.
    xmlAttrs = New XmlAttributes()

    ' Steps B3/B4: create and initialize the XmlArrayAttribute object,
    '  and assign it to the correct property of the XmlAttributes object.
    xmlAttrs.XmlArray = New XmlArrayAttribute("Employees")
    ' Repeat steps B3/B4, this time for the two XmlArrayItemAttribute objects.
    xmlAttrs.XmlArrayItems.Add(New XmlArrayItemAttribute( _
        "Employee", GetType(Employee)))
    xmlAttrs.XmlArrayItems.Add(New XmlArrayItemAttribute( _
        "CandidateEmployee", GetType(CandidateEmployee)))
```

(continued)

```
    ' Step B5: pass XmlAttributes to the Add method of XmlAttributeOverrides:
    '   first argument is the class that contains the overridden member;
    '   second argument is the member being overridden;
    '   third argument is the XmlAttributes object that defines the new
    '   attributes.
    xmlAttrOver.Add(GetType(AddressBook), "Contacts", xmlAttrs)

    ' ...(Sections C-D as before)...

    ' (E) Add the XmlAttribute() attribute to SSN element in Employee class.

    ' Step E2: create a new XmlAttributes object.
    xmlAttrs = New XmlAttributes()
    ' Steps E3/E4: create and initialize the XmlAttribute object,
    ' and assign it to the correct property of XmlAttributes object.
    xmlAttrs.XmlAttribute = New XmlAttributeAttribute("SSN")
    ' Step E5: pass XmlAttributes to the Add method of XmlAttributeOverrides.
    xmlAttrOver.Add(GetType(Employee), "SSN", xmlAttrs)

    ' (F) Add the XmlIgnore() attribute to HireDate element in Employee class.

    ' Step F2: create a new XmlAttributes object.
    xmlAttrs = New XmlAttributes()
    ' Steps F3/F4: note that you don't actually create an XmlIgnoreAttribute
    ' object; for all those attributes whose presence is enough to affect the
    ' serialization behavior, you just set the corresponding property to True.
    xmlAttrs.XmlIgnore = True
    ' Step F5: pass XmlAttributes to the Add method of XmlAttributeOverrides.
    xmlAttrOver.Add(GetType(Employee), "HireDate", xmlAttrs)

    ' Step 6: create the XmlSerializer that uses XmlAttributeOverrides.
    Dim ser As New XmlSerializer(GetType(AddressBook), xmlAttrOver)

    ' Serialize an AddressBook object using the XmlSerializer.
    ' ...(omitted)...
End Sub
```

Working with XSD Schemas

The .NET Framework comes with a great tool named xsd.exe. This is a command-line utility that can perform several useful tasks related to XML Schema Definition (XSD) files. For example, you can feed it an assembly file (a DLL or an EXE file) and have it create one or more XSD files that describe all the public types in that assembly:

```
xsd myasm.exe
```

By default, XSD files are created in the current directory and are named schema0.xsd, schema1.xsd, and so on. You can redirect the output to another directory with the /out option. (All the options of this utility can be shortened to their first character.)

```
xsd myasm.exe /o:anotherdir
```

You can also generate the schema for just one of the types defined in the assembly by using the /type option (beware: type name is case sensitive):

```
xsd myasm.exe /t:Customer
```

For example, this is the XSD produced for the Person class used in the preceding section:

```
<?xml version="1.0" encoding="utf-8"?>
<schema attributeFormDefault="qualified" elementFormDefault="qualified"
      targetNamespace="" xmlns="http://www.w3.org/2001/XMLSchema">
  <element name="Person" nillable="true" type="Person" />
  <complexType name="Person">
    <sequence>
      <element minOccurs="1" maxOccurs="1" name="ID" type="int" />
      <element minOccurs="1" maxOccurs="1" name="Name" nillable="true"
          type="string" />
      <element minOccurs="1" maxOccurs="1" name="PhoneNumber" nillable="true"
          type="string" />
    </sequence>
  </complexType>
</schema>
```

Even if you aren't an XSD wizard, you can clearly see that the XSD file embeds detailed information about the class and its fields. If the class contains Xml*xxxx* attributes that redefine the names of elements in the XML output, these names appear in the XSD file as well. In other words, this XSD defines the serialization structure of the type, not necessarily its source code definition.

You can affect the contents of the XSD schema by embedding XmlType attributes in your source code. You can apply this attribute to a Visual Basic class and decide the name of the corresponding XML element in the XSD schema, its namespace, and whether it should appear at all in the schema. In the following example, the AddressBook class isn't exported to the XSD and the Person class appears in the schema as the Contact element:

```
<XmlType(IncludeInSchema:=False)> _
Public Class AddressBook
    Public Name As String
    Public Contacts() As Person
End Class
```

(continued)

```
<XmlType("Contact", Namespace:="www.vb2themax.com")> _
Public Class Person
    Public ID As Integer
    Public Name As String
    Public PhoneNumber As String
End Class
```

The beauty of XSD files is that they thoroughly and unambiguously define the structure of your classes, so you can hand these files to other programmers without giving the classes' source code. In this sense, an XSD file is a bit like the type library that accompanies COM components.

The xsd.exe utility can perform the transformation in the opposite direction as well, and it can convert an XSD file to a set of classes written in either C# or Visual Basic .NET. This operation requires that you use the /classes option to specify that you want to generate one or more classes, and you use the /language option to indicate which language is to be generated. (The language identifier can be C#, VB, or JS for JavaScript.) These two options can be shortened to /c and /l, respectively:

```
xsd schema1.xsd /c /l:vb
```

You can specify the element or elements in the schema for which you want to generate code by using one or more /element options. (If the /element options are omitted, the utility generates code for all classes.) You can also specify the namespace for the generated types by using the /namespace option. See the .NET SDK documentation for more details about the xsd.exe utility and all its command-line options.

Here's a scenario in which the xsd.exe utility can be useful. Say that you have an application that serializes its types to XML and you want to give other developers the ability to read this XML output (and maybe resubmit another XML stream with their changes). Understandably, you feel uncomfortable with the idea of giving them your source code, and fortunately you don't have to. In fact, you can use xsd.exe to generate an XSD file that accurately describes the XML coming out of your application. Other developers can feed xsd.exe with this XSD file and create one or more classes that are isomorphic with your original classes by using the /classes option. (Interestingly, they can use the /language option to generate the source code for these classes in a programming language that's different from the language you used to create the original classes.)

After developers create a set of classes that mirror the original classes in your application, they can use an XmlSerializer object to read your XML data into their objects and write any changes back to the same or another XML file so that you can read back their changes. (In practice, you might not use files at all and work with data sent through HTTP or SOAP.) This approach clearly gives you an unparalleled degree of flexibility interoperating with other applications (not necessarily running on the same machine).

Did you think there was so much to say about object serialization? I surely didn't—before I began studying the intricacies of this topic. But it's time to move on to the next chapter, in which I'll illustrate another great (and often underrated) feature of the .NET Framework: regular expressions.

Front
Top
Left
Back

12

Regular Expressions

Regular expressions are a well-established and standard way to parse text files as well as to search and optionally replace occurrences of substrings and text patterns. If you aren't familiar with regular expressions, just think about the wildcard characters you use in MS-DOS to indicate a group of files (as in **.txt*) or the special characters you can use with the LIKE statement in SQL queries:

```
SELECT name, city FROM customers WHERE name LIKE "A%"
```

Many computer scientists have thoroughly researched regular expressions, and a few programming languages—most notably Perl and Awk—are heavily based on regular expressions. In spite of their usefulness in virtually every text-oriented task (including parsing log files and extracting information from HTML files), regular expressions are relatively rarely used among Windows programmers for at least a couple of reasons:

- Many developers believe that regular expressions are associated closely with Perl and Awk and can't be accessed from other languages.
- Regular expressions are based on a rather obscure syntax, which has gained them a reputation for complexity—this reputation keeps many developers from learning more about them.

The first point is only partially true. Starting with version 5.0, the VBScript language comes with a good implementation of a regular expression engine, and you can access it even from Visual Basic 6 by adding a reference to the Microsoft VBScript Regular Expressions type library. (Incidentally, the VBScript regular expression engine supports a large subset of the features of the .NET engine, so you can apply many of the techniques I describe in this chapter to your VBScript and Visual Basic 6 applications.)

The second point has some merit: you can regard regular expressions as a highly specific programming language, and you know that all languages take time to learn and have their idiosyncrasies. But when you see how much time regular expressions can save you—and I am talking about both coding time and CPU time—you'll probably agree that the effort you spend learning their contorted syntax is well spent.

Regular Expression Overview

The .NET Framework comes with a very powerful regular expression engine that's accessible from any .NET language, so you can leverage the parsing power of languages such as Perl without having to switch from your favorite language.

The powerful .NET Framework regular expression engine allowed Microsoft to clean up the Visual Basic language by getting rid of regular expression–like (but far less versatile) features, such as the LIKE operator or the Replace string function. (The Replace function in the Microsoft.VisualBasic namespace is for backward compatibility only, and the String.Replace method supports only the replacement of single characters.)

> **Note** All the classes you need to work with regular expressions belong to the System.Text.RegularExpressions namespace, so all the code in this section assumes that you added the following Imports statement at the top of your module:
>
> ```
> Imports System.Text.RegularExpressions
> ```

The Fundamentals

Regex is the most important class in this group, and any regular expression code instantiates at least an object of this class (or uses the class's shared methods). This object represents an immutable, compiled regular expression: you instantiate this object by passing to it the search pattern, written using the special regular expression language, which I'll describe later:

```
' This regular expression defines any group of 2 characters
' consisting of a vowel followed by a digit (\d).
Dim re As New Regex("[aeiou]\d")
```

The Matches method of the Regex object applies the regular expression to the string passed as an argument; it returns a MatchCollection object, a read-only collection that represents all the nonoverlapping matches:

```
Dim re As New Regex("[aeiou]\d")
' This source string contains 3 groups that match the Regex.
Dim source As String = "a1 = a1 & e2"
' Get the collection of matches.
Dim mc As MatchCollection = re.Matches(source)
' How many occurrences did we find?
Console.WriteLine("Found {0} occurrences", mc.Count)
    ' => Found 3 occurrences
```

You can also pass to the Matches method a second argument, which is interpreted as the index where the search begins.

The MatchCollection object contains individual Match objects, which expose properties such as Index (the position in the source string at which the matching string was found) and Length (the length of the matching string, which is useful when the regular expression can match strings of different lengths):

```
' ...(Continuing the previous example)...
Dim m As Match
For Each m In mc
    ' Display text and position of this match.
    Console.WriteLine("'{0}' at position {1}" , m.ToString, m.Index)
Next
```

The preceding code displays these lines in the console window:

```
'a1' at position 0
'a1' at position 5
'e2' at position 10
```

The Regex object is also capable of modifying a source string by searching for a given regular expression and replacing it with something else:

```
Dim source As String = "a1 = a1 & e2"
' Search for the "a" character followed by a digit.
Dim re As New Regex("a\d")
' Drop the digit that follows the "a" character.
Console.WriteLine(re.Replace(source, "a"))    ' => a = a & e2
```

The Regex class also exposes shared versions of the Match, Matches, and Replace methods. You can use these shared methods when you don't want to explicitly instantiate a Regex object:

```
' This code snippet is equivalent to the previous one, but it doesn't
' instantiate a Regex object.
Console.WriteLine(Regex.Replace("a1 = a1 & e2", "a\d", "a"))
```

As you would find for any programming language new to you, the best way to learn regular expressions is, not surprisingly, through practice. To help you in this process, I have created a RegexTester application, which lets you test any regular expression against any source string or text file. (See Figure 12-1.) This application has been a precious tool for me in exploring regular expression intricacies, and I routinely use it whenever I have a doubt about how a construct works.

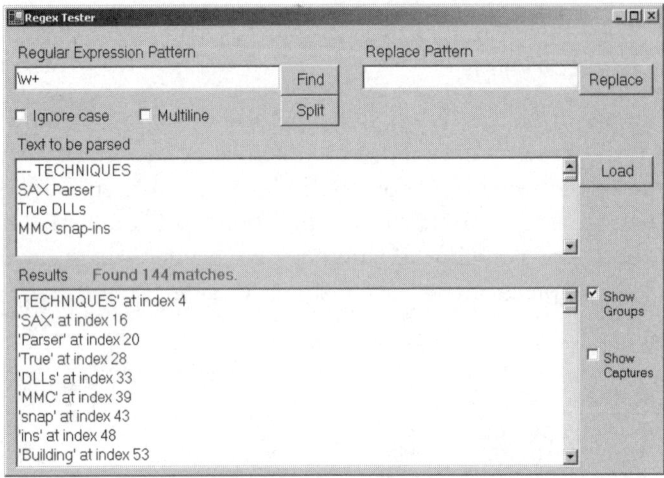

Figure 12-1. The RegexTester application lets you experiment with all the most important methods and options of the Regex object.

The Regular Expression Language

Table 12-1 lists all the constructs that are legal as regular expression patterns, grouped in the following categories:

- **Character escapes** are used to match single characters. You need them to deal with nonprintable characters (such as the newline and the tab character) and to provide escaped versions for the characters *.$^{[(|)*+?* which have a special meaning inside regular expression patterns.

- **Character classes** offer a means to match one character from a group that you specify between square brackets as in *[aeiou]*. Note that you don't need to escape special characters when they appear in square brackets except in the cases of the dash and the closing square bracket because they're the only characters that have special meaning inside square brackets. For example, *[()[\]{}]* matches opening and closing parentheses, square brackets, and curly brackets.

- **Atomic zero-width assertions** don't cause the engine to advance through the source string and don't consume characters. For example, the *abc$* regular expression matches any *abc* word immediately before the end of a line without also matching the end of the line.
- **Quantifiers** add optional quantity data to regular expressions. A particular quantifier applies to the character, character class, or group that immediately precedes it. For example, *\w+* matches all the words with one or more characters, whereas *\w{3,}* matches all the words with at least three characters.
- **Grouping constructors** can capture and name groups of subexpressions as well as increase the efficiency of regular expressions with noncapturing look-ahead and look-behind modifiers. For example, *(abc)+* matches repeated sequences of the "abc" string; *(?<total>\d+)* matches a group of one or more consecutive digits and assigns it the name *total*, which can be used later inside the same regular expression pattern or for substitution purposes.
- **Substitutions** can be used only inside a replacement pattern and, together with character escapes, are the only constructs that can be used inside replacement patterns. For example, when the sequence *(${total})* appears in a replacement pattern, it inserts the value of the group named *total*, after enclosing it in parentheses. Note that parentheses have no special meanings in replacement patterns, so you don't need to escape them.
- **Backreference constructs** let you reference a previous group of characters in the regular expression pattern via its group number or name. You can use these constructs as a simple way to say "match the same thing again." For example, *(?<value>\d+)=\k<value>* matches identical numbers separated by an = symbol, as in the "123=123" sequence.
- **Alternating constructs** provide a way to specify alternatives; for example, the sequence *I (am|have)* can match both the "I am" and "I have" strings.

- **Miscellaneous constructs** include constructs that allow you to modify one or more regular expression options in the middle of the pattern. For example, *A(?i)BC* matches all the variants of the "ABC" word that begin with uppercase "A" (such as "Abc", "ABc", "AbC", and "ABC"). See Table 12-2 for a description of all the regular expression options.

Table 12-1 The Regular Expression Language*

Category	Sequence	Description
Character escapes	any character	Characters other than .$^{[(|)*+?\ are matched to themselves.
	\a	The bell alarm character (same as \x07).
	\b	The backspace (same as \x08), but only when used between square brackets or in a replacement pattern. Otherwise, it matches a word boundary.
	\t	The tab character (same as \x09).
	\r	The carriage return (same as \x0A).
	\v	The vertical tab character (same as \x0B).
	\f	The form-feed character (same as \x0C).
	\n	The newline character (same as \x0D).
	\e	The escape character (same as \x1B).
	\040	An ASCII character expressed in octal notation (must have exactly three octal digits). For example, \040 is a space.
	\x20	An ASCII character expressed in hexadecimal notation (must have exactly two digits). For example, \x20 is a space.
	\cC	An ASCII control character. For example, \cC is control+C.
	\u0020	A Unicode character in hexadecimal notation (must have exactly four digits). For example, \u0020 is a space.
	*	When the backslash is followed by a character in a way that doesn't form an escape sequence, it matches the character. For example, * matches the * character.
Character classes	.	The dot character matches any character except the newline character. It matches any character, including newline, if you're using the Singleline option.
	[aeiou]	Any character in the list between the square brackets; [aeiou] matches any vowel.
	[^aeiou]	Any character except those in the list between the square brackets; [^aeiou] matches any nonvowel.

Table 12-1 The Regular Expression Language* *(continued)*

Category	Sequence	Description
	[a-zA-Z]	The - (dash) character lets you specify ranges of characters: [a-zA-Z] matches any lowercase or upper-case character; [^0-9] matches any nondigit character.
	\w	A word character, which is an alphanumeric character or the underscore character; same as [a-zA-Z_0-9].
	\W	A nonword character; same as [^a-zA-Z_0-9].
	\s	A white-space character, which is a space, a tab, a form-feed, a newline, a carriage return, or a vertical-feed character; same as [\f\n\r\t\v].
	\S	A character other than a white-space character; same as [^ \f\n\r\t\v].
	\d	A decimal digit; same as [0-9].
	\D	A nondigit character; same as [^0-9].
Atomic zero-width assertions	^	The beginning of the string (or the beginning of the line if you're using the Multiline option).
	$	The end of the string (or the end of the line if you're using the Multiline option).
	\A	The beginning of a string (like ^ but ignores the Multiline option).
	\Z	The end of the string or before the newline character at the end of the line (like $ but ignores the Multiline option).
	\z	Exactly the end of the string, whether or not there's a newline character (ignores the Multiline option).
	\G	The position at which the current search started—usually one character after the point at which the previous search ended.
	\b	The word boundary between \w (alphanumeric) and \W (nonalphanumeric) characters. It indicates the first and last characters of a word delimited by spaces or other punctuation symbols.
	\B	Not on a word boundary.
Quantifiers	*	Zero or more matches; for example, \bA\w* matches a word that begins with "A" and is followed by zero or more alphanumeric characters; same as {0,}.
	+	One or more matches; for example, \b[aeiou]+\b matches a word composed only of vowels; same as {1,}.

(continued)

Table 12-1 The Regular Expression Language* *(continued)*

Category	Sequence	Description
	?	Zero or one match; for example, *\b[aeiou]\d?\b* matches a word that starts with a vowel and is followed by zero or one digits; same as *{0,1}*.
	{N}	Exactly *N* matches; for example, *[aeiou]{4}* matches four consecutive vowels.
	{N,}	At least *N* matches; for example, *\d{3,}* matches groups of three or more digits.
	{N,M}	Between *N* and *M* matches; for example, *\d{3,5}* matches groups of three, four, or five digits.
	**?*	Lazy ***: the first match that consumes as few repeats as possible.
	+?	Lazy +: the first match that consumes as few repeats as possible, but at least one.
	??	Lazy *?*: zero repeats if possible, or one.
	{N}?	Lazy *{N}*: equivalent to *{N}*.
	{N,}?	Lazy *{N,}*: as few repeats as possible, but at least N.
	{N,M}?	Lazy *{N,M}*: as few repeats as possible, but between N and M.
Grouping constructs	*(substr)*	Captures the matched substring. These captures are numbered automatically, based on the order of the left parenthesis, starting at 1. The zeroth capturing group is the text matched by the whole regular expression pattern.
	(?<name>substr) *(?'name'substr)*	Captures the substring and assigns it a name. The name must not contain any punctuation symbols.
	(?:substr)	Noncapturing group.
	(imnsx-imnsx: subexpr)	Enables or disables the options specified in the subexpression. For example, *(?i-s)* uses case-insensitive searches and disables single-line mode. (See Table 12-2 for information about regular expression options.)
	(?=subexpr)	Zero-width positive look-ahead assertion: continues match only if the subexpression matches at this position on the right. For example, *\w+(?=,)* matches a word followed by a comma, without matching the comma.
	(?!subexpr)	Zero-width negative look-ahead assertion: continues match only if the subexpression doesn't match at this position on the right. For example, *\w+\b(?![,:;])* matches a word that isn't followed by a comma, a colon, or a semicolon.

Table 12-1 The Regular Expression Language* (continued)

Category	Sequence	Description
	(?<=subexpr)	Zero-width positive look-behind assertion: continues match only if the subexpression matches at this position on the left. For example, (?<=\d+[EeDd])\d+ matches the exponent part of a number in exponential notation (the 45 in 123E45). This construct doesn't backtrack.
	(?<!subexpr>	Zero-width negative look-behind assertion: continues match only if the subexpression doesn't match at this position on the left. For example, (?<!,)\b\w+ matches a word that doesn't follow a comma.
	(?>subexpr)	Nonbacktracking subexpression. The subexpression is fully matched once, and it doesn't participate in backtracking. (The subexpression matches only strings that would be matched by the subexpression alone.)
Substitutions	$N	Substitutes the last substring matched by group number N.
	${name}	Substitutes the last substring matched by a (?<name>) group.
Back reference constructs	\N \NN	Back reference to a previous group. For example, (\w)\1 finds doubled word characters, such as ss in expression. A backslash followed by a single digit is always considered a back reference (and throws a parsing exception if such a numbered reference is missing); a backslash followed by two digits is considered a numbered back reference if there's a corresponding numbered reference; otherwise, it's considered an octal code. In case of ambiguity, use the \k<name> construct.
	\k<name> \k'name'	Named back reference. (?<char>\w)\d\k<char> matches a word character followed by a digit and then by the same word character, as in the "B2B" string.
Alternating constructs	|	Either/or. For example, vb | c# | java. Leftmost successful match wins.
	(?(expr)yes | no)	Matches the yes part if the expression matches at this point; otherwise, matches the no part. The expression is turned into a zero-width assertion. If the expression is the name of a named group or a capturing group number, the alternation is interpreted as a capture test. (See next case.)
	(?(name)yes | no)	Matches the yes part if the named capture string has a match; otherwise, matches the no part. The no part can be omitted. If the given name doesn't correspond to the name or number of a capturing group used in this expression, the alternation is interpreted as an expression test. (See previous case.)

(continued)

Table 12-1 The Regular Expression Language* *(continued)*

Category	Sequence	Description
Miscellaneous constructs	*(?imnsx-imnsx)*	Enables or disables one or more regular expression options. For example, it allows case sensitivity to be turned on or off in the middle of a pattern. Option changes are effective until the closing parenthesis. (See also the corresponding grouping construct, which is a cleaner form.)
	(?#)	Inline comment inserted within a regular expression. The text that follows the # sign and continues until the first closing) character is ignored.
	#	X-mode comment: the text that follows an unescaped # until the end of line is ignored. This construct requires that the *x* option or the *RegexOptions.IgnorePatternWhiteSpace* enumerated option be activated. (X-mode comments are currently experimental.)

* The regular expression language; only the constructs in the character escapes and substitutions categories can be used in replacement patterns.

Regular Expression Options

The Match, Matches, and Replace shared methods of the Regex object support an optional argument, which lets you specify one or more options to be applied to the regular expression search. (See Table 12-2.) For example, the following code searches for all the occurrences of the "abc" word, regardless of its case:

```
Dim source As String = "ABC Abc abc"
Dim mc As MatchCollection = Regex.Matches(source, "abc")
Console.WriteLine(mc.Count)              ' => 1
mc = Regex.Matches(source, "abc", RegexOptions.IgnoreCase)
Console.WriteLine(mc.Count)              ' => 3
```

By default, the Regex class transforms the regular expression into a sequence of opcodes, which are then interpreted when the pattern is applied to a specific source string. If you specify the RegexOptions.Compiler option, however, the regular expression is compiled into explicit Microsoft Intermediate Language (MSIL) rather than regular expression opcodes. This feature enables the Microsoft .NET Framework Just-in-Time (JIT) compiler to convert the expression to native CPU instructions, which clearly deliver better performance. This extra compilation step adds some overhead, so you should use this option only if you plan to use the regular expression multiple times.

Another factor that you should take into account when using the RegexOptions.Compiler option is that the compiled MSIL code isn't unloaded when the Regex object is released and garbage collected—it continues to take memory until the application terminates. So you should preferably limit the number of compiled regular expressions, especially on systems with scarce memory.

Also, consider that the Regex class caches all regular expression opcodes in memory, so a regular expression isn't generally reparsed each time it's used. (The caching mechanism also works when you use shared methods and don't create Regex instances.) The *Regex* class also exposes a *CompileToAssembly* shared method for explicitly compiling a regular expression into an assembly. (See the .NET Framework SDK for more details about this method.)

The RegexOptions.Multiline option enables multiline mode, which is especially useful when you're parsing text files instead of plain strings. This option modifies the meaning and the behavior of the ^ and *$* assertions so that they match the start and end of each line of text, respectively, rather than the start or end of the whole string. The following example parses a .vb file looking for all the lines that contain a variable assignment. Notice that you can combine multiple Regex options by using the Or operator:

```
Sub TestRegexOptions()
    ' Read a .vb file into a string.
    Dim source As String = FileText("Module1.vb")
    Dim pattern As String = "^\s*[A-Z]\w* ?=.+(?=\r\n)"
    ' Get the collection of all matches, in multiline mode.
    Dim mc As MatchCollection = Regex.Matches(source, pattern, _
        RegexOptions.IgnoreCase Or RegexOptions.Multiline)
    ' Display all variable assignments and their offset in source file.
    Dim m As Match
    For Each m In mc
        Console.WriteLine("[{0}]  {1}", m.Index, m.ToString)
    Next
End Sub

' Read the contents of a text file.
Function FileText(ByVal path As String) As String
    ' Open a file stream and define a stream reader.
    Dim fs As New System.IO.FileStream(path, System.IO.FileMode.Open)
    Dim sr As New System.IO.StreamReader(fs)
    ' Read the entire contents of this file.
    FileText = sr.ReadToEnd
    ' Clean up code.
    sr.Close()
    fs.Close()
End Function
```

Let's analyze the regular expression pattern *^\s*[A-Z]\w* ?=.+(?=\r\n)* used in the preceding example, one subexpression at a time:

1. The ^ character means that the matching string should be at the beginning of each line (and not just at the beginning of the string because of the RegexOptions.Multiline option).

2. The *\s** subexpression means there can be zero or more white spaces at the beginning of the line.

3. The [A-Z]\w* subexpression means that there must be an alphabetic character followed by zero or more alphanumeric characters. (This portion of the regular expression represents a variable name in Visual Basic syntax.) The leading character can be uppercase or lowercase because of the RegexOptions.IgnoreCase option.

4. The space followed by a *?* character means there can be zero or one space after the variable name.

5. The = character matches itself, so there must be an equal sign after the space (or directly after the variable name if the optional space is missing).

6. The *.+(?=\r\n)* subexpression means that we're matching any character up to the end of the current line, that is, up to the CR-LF pair of characters, but without including the CR-LF pair in the match. (Note that we might use the simpler *.+$* subexpression, but in that case the CR character would be included in the match.)

Another way to specify a regular expression option is by means of the *(?imnsx-imnsx)* construct, which lets you enable or disable one or more options from the current position to the end of the pattern string. The following code snippet is similar to the preceding one except that it matches all the Dim, Private, and Public variable declarations. Note that the regular expression options are specified inside the pattern string instead of as an argument of the Regex.Matches method:

```
Dim source As String = FileText("Module1.vb")
Dim pattern As String = "(?im)^\s+(dim|public|private) [A-Z]\w* As .+(?=\r\n)"
Dim mc As MatchCollection = Regex.Matches(source, pattern)
```

Table 12-2 Regular Expression Options*

RegexOptions enum Value	Option	Description
None		No option.
IgnoreCase	*i*	Case insensitivity match.
Multiline	*m*	Multiline mode: changes the behavior of ^ and $ so that they match the beginning and end of any line, respectively, instead of the whole string.
ExplicitCapture	*n*	Captures only explicitly named or numbered groups of the form *(?<name>)* so that naked parentheses act as noncapturing groups without your having to use the *(?:)* construct.

Table 12-2 Regular Expression Options* *(continued)*

RegexOptions enum Value	Option	Description
Compiled	*c*	Compiles the regular expression and generates MSIL code; this option generates faster code at the expense of longer start-up time.
Singleline	*s*	Single-line mode: changes the behavior of the . (dot) character so that it matches any character (instead of any character except newline).
IgnorePattern-Whitespace	*x*	Eliminates unescaped white space from the pattern and enables X-mode comments.
RightToLeft	*r*	Searches from right to left. The regular expression will move to the left of the starting position, so the starting position should be specified at the end of the string instead of its beginning. This option can't be specified in the middle of the pattern. (This restriction avoids endless loops.) The *(?<)* look-behind construct provides something similar, and it can be used as a subexpression.
ECMAScript		Enables ECMAScript-compliant behavior. This option can be used only in conjunction with the Ignore-Case, Multiline, and Compiled flags; in all other cases, the method throws an exception.

* These regular expression options can be specified when you create the Regex object or from inside a *(?)* construct. All these options are turned off by default.

Regular Expression Classes

Now that I have illustrated the fundamentals of regular expressions, it's time to dissect all the classes in the System.Text.RegularExpressions namespace.

The Regex Class

As you've seen in the preceding section, the Regex class provides two overloaded constructors—one that takes only the pattern and another that also takes a bit-coded value that specifies the required regular expression options:

```
' This Regex object can search the word "dim" in a case-insensitive way.
Dim re As New Regex("\bdim\b", RegexOptions.IgnoreCase)
```

The Regex class exposes only two properties, both of which are read-only. The Options property returns the second argument passed to the object constructor, while the RightToLeft property returns True if you specified the RightToLeft option. (The regular expression matches from right to left.) No property returns the regular expression pattern, but you can use the ToString method for this purpose.

Searching for Substrings

The Matches method searches the regular expression inside the string provided as an argument and returns a MatchCollection object that contains zero or more Match objects, one for each nonintersecting match. The Matches method is overloaded to take an optional starting index:

```
' Get the collection that contains all the matches.
Dim mc As MatchCollection = re.Matches(source)

' Print all the matches after the 100th character in the source string.
Dim m As Match
For Each m In re.Matches(source, 100)
    Console.WriteLine(m.ToString)
Next
```

You can change the behavior of the Matches method (as well as the Match method, described later) by using a *\G* assertion to disable scanning. In this case, the match must be found exactly where the scan begins: this point is either at the index specified as an argument (or the first character if this argument is omitted) or immediately after the point where the previous match terminates. In other words, the *\G* assertion finds only *consecutive* matches:

```
' Finds consecutive groups of space-delimited numbers.
Dim re As New Regex("\G\s*\d+")
' Note that search stops at the first non-numeric group.
Console.WriteLine(re.Matches("12 34 56 ab 78").Count)     ' => 3
```

Sometimes, you don't really want to list all the occurrences of the pattern, and determining whether the pattern is contained in the source string would suffice. If that's your interest, the IsMatch method is more efficient than the Matches method because it stops the scan as soon as the first match is found. You pass to this method the input string and an optional start index:

```
' Check whether the input string is a date in the format mm-dd-yy or
' mm-dd-yyyy. (The source string can use slashes as date separators and
' can contain leading or trailing white spaces.)
Dim re As New Regex("^\s*\d{1,2}(/|-)\d{1,2}\1(\d{4}|\d{2})\s*$")
If re.IsMatch(" 12/10/2001  ") Then
    Console.WriteLine("The date is formatted correctly.")
    ' (We don't check whether month and day values are in valid range.)
End If
```

The regular expression pattern in the preceding code requires an explanation:

1. The ^ and *$* characters mean that the source string must contain one date value and nothing else.
2. The *\s** subexpression at the beginning and end of the string means that we accept leading and trailing white spaces.
3. The *\d{1,2}* subexpression means that the month and day numbers can have one or two digits, whereas the *(\d{4}|\d{2})* subexpression means that the year number can have four or two digits. Note that the four-digit case must be tested first; otherwise, only the first two digits are matched.
4. The *(/|-)* subexpression means that we take either the slash or the dash as the date separator between the month and day numbers. (Note that you don't need to escape the slash character inside a pair of parentheses.)
5. The *\1* subexpression means that the separator between day and year numbers must be the same separator used between month and day numbers.

The Matches method is rarely used for parsing very long strings because it returns the control to the caller only when the entire string has been parsed. When parsing long strings, you should use the Match method instead; this method returns only the first Match object and lets you iterate over the remaining matches using the Match.NextMatch method, as this example demonstrates:

```
' Search all the dates in a source string.
Dim source As String = " 12-2-1999  10/23/2001 4/5/2001 "
Dim re As New Regex("\s*\d{1,2}(/|-)\d{1,2}\1(\d{4}|\d{2})")

' Find the first match.
Dim m As Match = re.Match(source)
' Enter the following loop only if the search was successful.
Do While m.Success
    ' Display the match, but discard leading and trailing spaces.
    Console.WriteLine(m.ToString.Trim)
    ' Find the next match; exit if not successful.
    m = m.NextMatch
Loop
```

The Split method is similar to the String.Split method except that it defines the delimiter by using a regular expression rather than a single character. For example, the following code prints all the elements in a comma-delimited list of numbers, ignoring leading and trailing white-space characters:

```
Dim source As String = "123, 456,,789"
```

```
Dim re As New Regex("\s*,\s*")

Dim s As String
For Each s In re.Split(source)
    ' Note that the third element is a null string.
    Console.Write(s & "-")     ' => 123-456--789-
Next
```

(You can modify the pattern to *\s*[,]+\s** to discard empty elements.) The Split method supports several overloaded variations, which let you define the maximum count of elements to be extracted and a starting index. (If there are more elements than the given limit, the last element contains the remainder of the string.)

```
' Split max 5 items.
Dim arr() As String = re.Split(source, 5)
' Split max 5 items, starting at the 100th character.
Dim arr2() As String = re.Split(source, 5, 100)
```

The Replace Method

As I explained earlier in this chapter, the Regex.Replace method lets you selectively replace portions of the source string. The Replace method requires that you create numbered or named groups of characters in the pattern and then use those groups in the replacement pattern. The following code example takes a string that contains one or more dates in the mm-dd-yy format (including their variations with / separator and four-digit year number) and converts them to the dd-mm-yy format, while preserving the original date separator:

```
Dim source As String = "12-2-1999  10/23/2001  4/5/2001 "
Dim pattern As String = _
    "\b(?<mm>\d{1,2})(?<sep>(/|-))(?<dd>\d{1,2})\k<sep>(?<yy>(\d{4}|\d{2}))\b"
Dim re As New Regex(pattern)
Console.WriteLine(re.Replace(source, "${dd}${sep}${mm}${sep}${yy}"))
    ' => 2-12-1999  23/10/2001  5/4/2001
```

The pattern string is similar to the one seen previously, with an important difference: it defines four groups—named *mm*, *dd*, *yy*, and *sep*—that are later rearranged in the replacement string. The *\b* assertion at the beginning and end of the pattern ensures that the date is a word of its own.

The Replace method supports other overloaded variants. For example, you can pass two additional numeric arguments, which are interpreted as the maximum number of substitutions and the starting index:

```
' Expand all "ms" abbreviations to "Microsoft," regardless of their case.
Dim source As String = "Welcome to MS Ms ms MS"
```

```
Dim re As New Regex("\bMS\b", RegexOptions.IgnoreCase)
' Replace up to three occurrences, starting at the tenth character.
Console.WriteLine(re.Replace(source, "Microsoft", 3, 10))
    ' => Welcome to Microsoft Microsoft Microsoft MS
```

If the replacement operation does something more sophisticated than simply delete or change the order of named groups, you can use another overloaded version of the Replace function, which uses a delegate to call a function that you define in your application. This feature gives you tremendous flexibility, as the following code demonstrates:

```
Sub TestReplaceWithCallback()
    ' This pattern defines two integers separated by a plus sign.
    Dim re As New Regex("\d+\s*\+\s*\d+")
    Dim source As String = "a = 100 + 234: b = 200+345"
    ' Replace all sum operations with their results.
    Console.WriteLine(re.Replace(source, AddressOf DoSum))
        ' => a = 334: b = 545
End Sub

Function DoSum(ByVal m As Match) As String
    ' Find the position of the plus sign.
    Dim i As Integer = m.ToString.IndexOf("+"c)
    ' Parse the two operands.
    Dim n1 As Long = Long.Parse(m.ToString.Substring(0, i))
    Dim n2 As Long = Long.Parse(m.ToString.Substring(i + 1))
    ' Return their sum, as a string.
    Return (n1 + n2).ToString
End Function
```

The delegate must point to a function that takes a Match object and returns a String object. The code inside this function can query the Match object's properties to learn more about the match. For example, you can use the Index property to peek at what immediately precedes or follows in the source string so that you can make a more informed decision.

Shared Methods

All the methods seen so far are also available as shared methods, so most of the time you don't even need to explicitly create a Regex object. You generally pass the regular expression pattern to the shared methods as a second argument, after the source string. For example, you can split a string into individual words as follows:

```
' \W means "any nonalphanumeric character."
Dim words() As String = Regex.Split("Split these words", "\W+")
```

The Regex class exposes two shared methods that have no instance method counterpart. The Escape method takes a string and converts the special characters *.$^{[(|)*+?* to their equivalent escaped sequence. This method is especially useful when you let the end user enter the search pattern:

```
Console.Write(Regex.Escape("(x)"))      ' => \(x\)

' Check whether the character sequence the end user entered in
' the txtChars TextBox control is contained in the source string.
If Regex.IsMatch(source, Regex.Escape(txtChars.Text))
```

The Unescape shared method converts a string that contains escaped sequences back into its unescaped equivalent.

Working with Groups

The Regex class exposes four instance methods that let you quickly access the groups (both numbered or named) defined in the pattern string. For example, let's start by assuming that you have a Regex object defined as follows:

```
' The Regex object used for all the examples that follow.
' (Note that there are two named and two unnamed groups.)
Dim re As New Regex("(\s*)(?<name>\w+)\s*=\s*(?<value>\d+)(.*)")
```

The GetGroupNames method returns an array of strings that contains the names of all the groups in the pattern string. Groups without an explicit name are assigned names such as 1, 2, and so on. Group 0 always exists and corresponds to the entire pattern. The array returned by GetGroupNames contains all the numbered groups followed by all the named groups, so they aren't necessarily in the same order in which they appear in the pattern string:

```
Dim s As String
For Each s In re.GetGroupNames
    Console.Write(s & " ")      ' => 0 1 2 name value
Next
```

The GetGroupNumbers method works in a similar way but returns an Integer array, whose elements correspond to all the named or unnamed groups in the pattern string (which is not really useful information, admittedly):

```
Dim n As Integer
For Each n In re.GetGroupNumbers
    Console.Write(n.ToString & " ")      ' => 0 1 2 3 4
Next
```

The GroupNameFromNumber method returns the group name corresponding to the given group number. If the group has no name, its number is returned; if the number is higher than the number of existing groups, an IndexOutOfRange exception is thrown:

```
Console.WriteLine(re.GroupNameFromNumber(2))      ' => 2
```

```
Console.WriteLine(re.GroupNameFromNumber(3))      ' => name
```

The GroupNumberFromName method returns the group number if a group with that name exists or –1 if no group with that name exists:

```
Console.WriteLine(re.GroupNumberFromName("name"))  ' => 3
Console.WriteLine(re.GroupNumberFromName("foo"))   ' => -1
```

The MatchCollection and Match Classes

The MatchCollection class represents a set of matches. It has no constructor because you can create a MatchCollection object only by using the Regex.Matches method. This class supports the ICollection and IEnumerable interfaces, and therefore it exposes all the properties and methods that collections make available, including Count, Item, CopyTo, and GetEnumerator.

The Match class represents a single match. You can obtain an instance of this class either by iterating on a MatchCollection object or directly by means of the Match method of the Regex class. The Match object is immutable and has no public constructor.

The Match class's main properties are Value, Length, and Index, which return the matched string, its length, and the index at which it appears in the source string. (The ToString method returns the same string as the Value property does.) I already showed you how to use the Match class's IsSuccess property and its NextMatch method to iterate over all the matches in a string:

```
' Find the first match.
Dim m As Match = re.Match(source)
' Enter the following loop only if the search was successful.
Do While m.Success
    Console.WriteLine("{0} (found at {1})", m.Value, m.Index)
    ' Find the next match; exit if not successful.
    m = m.NextMatch
Loop
```

You must pay special attention when the search pattern matches an empty string, for example, *\d** (which matches zero or more digits). When you apply such a pattern to a string, you typically get one or more empty matches, as you can see here:

```
Dim re As New Regex("\d*")
Dim m As Match
For Each m In re.Matches("1a23bc456de789")
    ' The output from this loop shows that some matches are empty.
    Console.Write(m.Value & ",")  ' => 1,,23,,456,,,789,,
Next
```

As I explained earlier, a search generally starts where the previous search ends. However, the rule is different when the engine finds an empty match because it advances by one character before repeating the search. You would get trapped in an endless loop if the engine didn't behave this way.

If the pattern contains one or more groups, you can access the corresponding Group object by means of the Match object's Groups collection, which you can index by the group number or group name. I'll discuss the Group object in a moment, but you can already see how you can use the Groups collection to extract the variable names and values in a series of assignments:

```
Dim source As String = "a = 123: b=456"
Dim re As New Regex("(\s*)(?<name>\w+)\s*=\s*(?<value>\d+)")

Dim m As Match
For Each m In re.Matches(source)
    Console.WriteLine("Variable: {0}  Value: {1}", _
       m.Groups("name").Value, m.Groups("value").Value)
Next
```

This is the result displayed in the console window:

```
Variable: a  Value: 123
Variable: b  Value: 456
```

The Result method takes a replace pattern and returns the string that would result if the match were replaced by that pattern:

```
' This code produces exactly the same result as the preceding snippet.
For Each m In re.Matches(source)
    Console.WriteLine(m.Result("Variable: ${name}  Value: ${value}"))
Next
```

The only Match member left to be discussed is the Captures property, which I'll cover in the "CaptureCollection and Capture Classes" section later in this chapter.

The Group Class

The Group class represents a single group in a Match object and exposes a few properties whose meaning should be evident: Value (which produces the same result as the ToString method—the text associated with the group), Index (its position in the source string), Length (the group's length), and Success (True if the group has been matched). This code sample is similar to the preceding example, but it also displays information concerning where each variable appears in the source string:

```
Dim source As String = "a = 123: b=456"
Dim re As New Regex("(\s*)(?<name>\w+)\s*=\s*(?<value>\d+)")

Dim m As Match, g As Group
' Iterate over all the matches.
For Each m In re.Matches(source)
    ' Get information on variable name.
    g = m.Groups("name")
    Console.Write("Variable '{0}' found at index {1}", g.Value, g.Index)
    ' Get information on variable value.
    Console.WriteLine(", value is {0}", m.Groups("value").Value)
Next
```

This is the result displayed in the console window:

```
Variable 'a' found at index 0, value is 123
Variable 'b' found at index 9, value is 456
```

The following example is more complex but also more useful: it shows how you can parse <A> tags in an HTML file and display the anchor text (that is, the text that appears underlined in an HTML page) and the URL it points to. As you see, it's just a matter of a few lines of code:

```
Sub TestSearchHyperlinks()
    Dim re As New Regex("<A\s+HREF\s*=\s*""?([^"" >]+)""?>(.+)</A>", _
        RegexOptions.IgnoreCase)
    ' Load the contents of an HTML file.
    Dim source As String = FileText("test.htm")
    ' Display all occurrences.
    Dim m As Match = re.Match(source)
    Do While m.Success
        Console.WriteLine("{0} => {1}", m.Groups(2).Value, _
            m.Groups(1).Value)
        m = m.NextMatch()
    Loop
End Sub
```

To understand how the preceding code works, you must keep in mind that the <A> tag is followed by one or more spaces and then by an HREF attribute, which is followed by an equal sign and then the URL, optionally enclosed between double quotation marks. All the text that follows the closing angle bracket and up to the ending tag </A> is the anchor text. The regular expression defined in the preceding code defines two unnamed groups—the

URL and the anchor text—so displaying details for all the <A> tags in the HTML file is just a matter of looping over all the matches. The regular expression syntax is complicated by the fact that double quotation mark characters must be doubled when they appear in a string constant. Also, note that the URL group is defined by the repetition of any character other than the double quotation marks, spaces, and closing angle brackets.

The CaptureCollection and Capture Classes

The search pattern can include one or more *capturing groups*, which are named or unnamed subexpressions enclosed in parentheses. Capturing groups can be nested and can capture multiple substrings of the source strings because of quantifiers. For example, when you apply the *(\w)+* pattern to the "abc" string, you get one match for the entire string and three captured substrings, one for each character.

You can access the collection of capture substrings through the Captures method of either the Match or the Group object. This method returns a CaptureCollection object that in turn contains one or more Capture objects. Individual Capture objects let you determine where individual captured substrings appear in the source string. The following code displays all the captured strings in the "abc def" string:

```
Dim source As String = "abc def"
Dim re As New Regex("(\w)+")
Dim m As Match, s As String, c As Capture

' Get the name or numbers of all the groups.
Dim groups() As String = re.GetGroupNames

' Iterate over all matches.
For Each m In re.Matches(source)
    ' Display information on this match.
    Console.WriteLine("Match '{0}' at index {1}", m.Value, m.Index)
    ' Iterate over the groups in each match.
    For Each s In groups
        ' Get a reference to the corresponding group.
        Dim g As Group = m.Groups(s)
        ' Get the capture collection for this group.
        Dim cc As CaptureCollection = g.Captures
        ' Display the number of captures.
        Console.WriteLine("  Found {0} capture(s) for group {1}", cc.Count, s)
        ' Display information on each capture.
        For Each c In cc
            Console.WriteLine("    '{0}' at index {1}", c.Value, c.Index)
        Next
    Next
Next
```

The code that follows is the result produced in the console window. (Notice that group 0 always refers to the match expression itself.)

```
Match 'abc' at index 0
  Found 1 capture(s) for group 0
    'abc' at index 0
  Found 3 capture(s) for group 1
    'a' at index 0
    'b' at index 1
    'c' at index 2
Match 'def' at index 4
  Found 1 capture(s) for group 0
    'def' at index 4
  Found 3 capture(s) for group 1
    'd' at index 4
    'e' at index 5
    'f' at index 6
```

The following example is somewhat more useful in that it defines a pattern that lets you parse a number in exponential format and shows how to locate individual portions of the mantissa and the exponent:

```
Dim source As String = "11.22E33  4.55E6 "
Dim re As New Regex("((\d+).?(\d*))E(\d+)")
' ... (The remainder of code as in previous snippet)...
```

Note that the previous regular expression defines as many as five groups: the entire number, the entire mantissa, the integer portion of the mantissa, the decimal portion of the mantissa, and the exponent. This is the result displayed in the console window:

```
Match '11.22E33' at index 0
  Found 1 capture(s) for group 0
    '11.22E33' at index 0
  Found 1 capture(s) for group 1
    '11.22' at index 0
  Found 1 capture(s) for group 2
    '11' at index 0
  Found 1 capture(s) for group 3
    '22' at index 3
  Found 1 capture(s) for group 4
    '33' at index 6
Match '4.55E6' at index 10
  Found 1 capture(s) for group 0
    '4.55E6' at index 10
  Found 1 capture(s) for group 1
    '4.55' at index 10
  Found 1 capture(s) for group 2
    '4' at index 10
  Found 1 capture(s) for group 3
```

(continued)

```
  '55' at index 12
Found 1 capture(s) for group 4
  '6' at index 15
```

Regular Expressions at Work

By now it should be evident that regular expressions are a powerful tool in the hands of expert developers. Admittedly, the regular expression sublanguage has a steep learning curve, but the effort pays off nicely. In this section, I show you how you can use regular expressions to implement a full-featured expression evaluator—that is, a routine that takes a string containing a math expression and returns its result. (See Figure 12-2.)

```
Console.Write(Evaluate("10 + (8 - 3) * 4"))     ' => 30
```

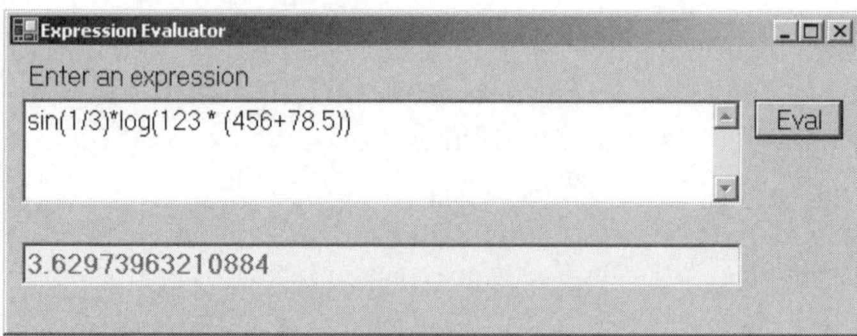

Figure 12-2. The ExprEvaluator application on the companion CD offers a simple front end for the Evaluate function.

If you have ever tried to build an expression evaluator, you know that it isn't for the faint of heart. I once wrote an expression evaluator in Visual Basic 5 that took me a few days and more than 1000 lines of code, so I decided to see whether the task could have been solved in a simpler way with regular expressions. To my surprise, I was able to come up with a complete solution with a little more than 100 lines of executable code (not counting remarks). The result is even more sophisticated than my original expression evaluator and even supports niceties such as functions with variable numbers of arguments. Here is its complete source code:

```
Function Evaluate(ByVal expr As String) As Double
    ' A number is a sequence of digits optionally followed by a dot and
    ' another sequence of digits. The number is in parentheses in order to
    ' define an unnamed group.
    Const Num As String = "(\-?\d+\.?\d*)"
    ' List of 1-operand functions
```

```
Const Func1 As String = _
    "(exp|log|log10|abs|sqr|sqrt|sin|cos|tan|asin|acos|atan)"
' List of 2-operand functions
Const Func2 As String = "(atan2)"
' List of N-operand functions
Const FuncN As String = "(min|max)"
' List of predefined constants
Const Constants As String = "(e|pi)"

' Define one Regex object for each supported operation. These DIMs
' are outside the loop, so they are compiled only once.
' Binary operations are defined as two numbers with a symbol between
' them and optional spaces in between.
Dim rePower As New Regex(Num & "\s*(\^)\s*" & Num)
Dim reAddSub As New Regex(Num & "\s*([-+])\s*" & Num)
Dim reMulDiv As New Regex(Num & "\s*([*/])\s*" & Num)
' These Regex objects resolve calls to functions (case insensitivity).
Dim reFunc1 As New Regex(Func1 & "\(\s*" & Num & "\s*\)", _
    RegexOptions.IgnoreCase)
Dim reFunc2 As New Regex(Func2 & "\(\s*" & Num & "\s*,\s*" & Num _
    & "\s*\)", RegexOptions.IgnoreCase)
Dim reFuncN As New Regex(FuncN & "\((\s*" & Num & "\s*,)+\s*" & Num _
    & "\s*\)", RegexOptions.IgnoreCase)
' This Regex object drops a + when it follows an operator.
Dim reSign1 As New Regex("([-+/*^])\s*\+")
' This Regex object converts a double minus into a plus.
Dim reSign2 As New Regex("\-\s*\-")
' This Regex object drops parentheses around a number. (It must not
' be preceded by an alphanum char because it might be a function name.)
Dim rePar As New Regex("(?<![A-Za-z0-9])\(\s*([-+]?\d+.?\d*)\s*\)")
' This Regex tells when the expression has been reduced to a number.
Dim reNum As New Regex("^\s*[-+]?\d+\.?\d*\s*$")

' The Regex object deals with constants. (Requires case insensitivity.)
Dim reConst As New Regex("\s*" & Constants & "\s*", _
    RegexOptions.IgnoreCase)
' This statement resolves constants. (Can be kept out of the loop.)
expr = reConst.Replace(expr, AddressOf DoConstants)

' Loop until the entire expression becomes just a number.
Do Until reNum.IsMatch(expr)
    ' Remember current expression.
    Dim saveExpr As String = expr

    ' Perform all the math operations in the source string,
    ' starting with operands with higher operands.
    ' Note that we continue to perform each operation until there are
    ' no matches because we must account for expressions such as
    ' (12*34*56).
```

(continued)

```
            ' Perform all power operations.
            Do While rePower.IsMatch(expr)
                expr = rePower.Replace(expr, AddressOf DoPower)
            Loop

            ' Perform all divisions and multiplications.
            Do While reMulDiv.IsMatch(expr)
                expr = reMulDiv.Replace(expr, AddressOf DoMulDiv)
            Loop

            ' Perform functions with variable numbers of arguments.
            Do While reFuncN.IsMatch(expr)
                expr = reFuncN.Replace(expr, AddressOf DoFuncN)
            Loop

            ' Perform functions with 2 arguments.
            Do While reFunc2.IsMatch(expr)
                expr = reFunc2.Replace(expr, AddressOf DoFunc2)
            Loop

            ' One-operand functions must be processed last to deal correctly with
            ' expressions such as SIN(ATAN(1)).
            Do While reFunc1.IsMatch(expr)
                expr = reFunc1.Replace(expr, AddressOf DoFunc1)
            Loop

            ' Discard plus signs (unary pluses) that follow another operator.
            expr = reSign1.Replace(expr, "$1")
            ' Simplify two consecutive minus signs into a plus sign.
            expr = reSign2.Replace(expr, "+")

            ' Perform all additions and subtractions.
            Do While reAddSub.IsMatch(expr)
                expr = reAddSub.Replace(expr, AddressOf DoAddSub)
            Loop

            ' Attempt to discard parentheses around numbers.
            expr = rePar.Replace(expr, "$1")

            ' If the expression didn't change, we have a syntax error.
            ' (This serves to avoid endless loops.)
            If expr = saveExpr Then Throw New SyntaxErrorException()
        Loop

        ' Return the expression, which is now a number.
        Return CDbl(expr)
    End Function

    ' These functions perform the actual math operations.
```

```
' In all cases, the incoming Match object has groups that identify
' the two operands and the operator.

Function DoConstants(ByVal m As Match) As String
    Select Case m.Groups(1).Value.ToUpper
        Case "PI"
            Return Math.PI.ToString
        Case "E"
            Return Math.E.ToString
    End Select
End Function

Function DoPower(ByVal m As Match) As String
    Dim n1 As Double = CDbl(m.Groups(1).Value)
    Dim n2 As Double = CDbl(m.Groups(3).Value)
    ' Group(2) is always the ^ character in this version.
    Return (n1 ^ n2).ToString
End Function

Function DoMulDiv(ByVal m As Match) As String
    Dim n1 As Double = CDbl(m.Groups(1).Value)
    Dim n2 As Double = CDbl(m.Groups(3).Value)
    Select Case m.Groups(2).Value
        Case "/"
            Return (n1 / n2).ToString
        Case "*"
            Return (n1 * n2).ToString
    End Select
End Function

Function DoAddSub(ByVal m As Match) As String
    Dim n1 As Double = CDbl(m.Groups(1).Value)
    Dim n2 As Double = CDbl(m.Groups(3).Value)
    Select Case m.Groups(2).Value
        Case "+"
            Return (n1 + n2).ToString
        Case "-"
            Return (n1 - n2).ToString
    End Select
End Function

Function DoFunc1(ByVal m As Match) As String
    ' Function argument is second group.
    Dim n1 As Double = CDbl(m.Groups(2).Value)
    ' Function name is first group.
    Select Case m.Groups(1).Value.ToUpper
        Case "EXP"
            Return Math.Exp(n1).ToString
        Case "LOG"
```

(continued)

```
            Return Math.Log(n1).ToString
        Case "LOG10"
            Return Math.Log10(n1).ToString
        Case "ABS"
            Return Math.Abs(n1).ToString
        Case "SQR", "SQRT"
            Return Math.Sqrt(n1).ToString
        Case "SIN"
            Return Math.Sin(n1).ToString
        Case "COS"
            Return Math.Cos(n1).ToString
        Case "TAN"
            Return Math.Tan(n1).ToString
        Case "ASIN"
            Return Math.Asin(n1).ToString
        Case "ACOS"
            Return Math.Acos(n1).ToString
        Case "ATAN"
            Return Math.Atan(n1).ToString
    End Select
End Function

Function DoFunc2(ByVal m As Match) As String
    ' Function arguments are second and third groups.
    Dim n1 As Double = CDbl(m.Groups(2).Value)
    Dim n2 As Double = CDbl(m.Groups(3).Value)
    ' Function name is first group.
    Select Case m.Groups(1).Value.ToUpper
        Case "ATAN2"
            Return Math.Atan2(n1, n2).ToString
    End Select
End Function

Function DoFuncN(ByVal m As Match) As String
    ' Function arguments are from group 2 onward.
    Dim args As New ArrayList()
    Dim i As Integer = 2
    ' Load all the arguments into the array.
    Do While m.Groups(i).Value <> ""
        ' Get the argument, replace any comma with a space,
        ' and convert to double.
        args.Add(CDbl(m.Groups(i).Value.Replace(","c, " "c)))
        i += 1
    Loop

    ' Function name is 1st group.
    Select Case m.Groups(1).Value.ToUpper
        Case "MIN"
            args.Sort()
```

```
            Return args(0).ToString
        Case "MAX"
            args.Sort()
            Return args(args.Count - 1).ToString
    End Select
End Function
```

I won't explain every single line of code in the preceding listing because you can follow the many comments in the code. The code exclusively uses the regular expression features I've described earlier in this chapter, so you shouldn't have problems understanding how it works. But here are just a few hints:

- The feature on which this expression evaluator is built is the ability to provide a delegate function as an argument of the Replace method. The program uses several delegate functions, one for each class of operators and functions. The delegate function receives a Match object whose groups reference the operator or the function name and all the operands.
- The Evaluate function receives a string, which is then passed to the Replace method of the several Regex objects defined internally, where each Regex object is in charge of parsing a given set of operations or of simplifying the expression—for example, by dropping a pair of parentheses around a number.
- A single Regex object processes operators with the same priority—for example, + and -, or * and /. All the Regex objects are instantiated outside the main loop so that they compile to byte codes only once. Inside the main loop, Regex objects related to operators with higher priority are given a chance to process the string before those related to operations with lower priority.
- Thanks to subsequent replacements, the expression string becomes simpler at each iteration of the main loop. The loop is repeated until the string becomes a number in a valid format for the CDbl function.

It's easy to extend the expression evaluator with new functions because you simply need to extend the Func1, Func2, or FuncN constant and add a Case block in the corresponding callback function (DoFunc1, DoFunc2, or DoFuncN). It takes a little more effort to improve the function even further with the ability to define your own variables—but I gladly leave it to you as an exercise.

Multithreading has always been the Achilles' heel of Visual Basic, and in fact you've had to resort to coding in another language to achieve free-threaded applications. Well, this problem will soon become a thing of the past, thanks to the multithreading support offered by the .NET Framework, as you'll learn in the next chapter.

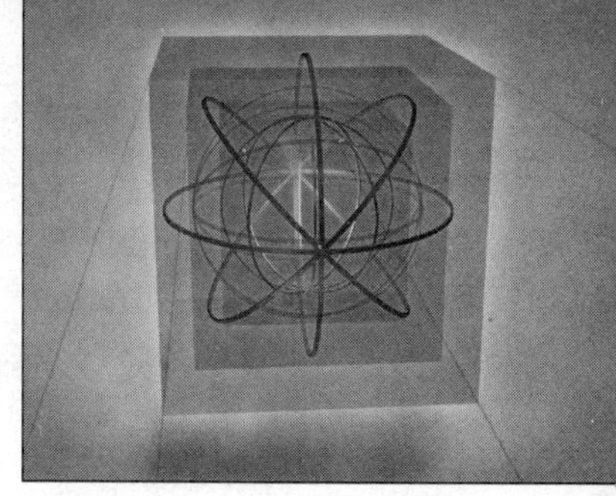

13

Threading

If you weren't looking closely at the Windows architecture, you might think that the operating system allocates CPU time to processes so that they can execute at the same time, even on single-CPU systems. The truth is that CPU time is allocated to threads, not processes. You can think of threads as independent execution paths, which can access resources such as memory. Processes, on the other hand, are passive containers for running threads, even though they have many other interesting features, such as the ability to allocate resources and provide a linear address space where you can store your variables and arrays.

The .NET Framework fully supports multithreaded applications, thanks to a rich set of classes in the base library. To ensure safe multithreaded applications, the language must offer a special synchronization construct, as you'll learn later in this chapter.

> **Note** The majority of the classes I discuss in this chapter belong to the System.Threading namespace. To make the code more concise, all the samples assume that you have the following Imports statement at the top of their module:
>
> ```
> Imports System.Threading
> ```

Threading Fundamentals

Microsoft Windows allows *preemptive multitasking*, a fancy term that means that a thread can be suspended at almost any time and another thread can be given CPU time. This contrasts with *cooperative multitasking*, allowed by versions of

Windows through 3.1, in which each thread had to explicitly ask for suspension. (As you might imagine, cooperative multitasking makes the operating system more fragile because a thread crash affects the entire system.)

When to Use Threads

Each thread maintains a private set of structures that the operating system uses to save information (the *thread context*) when the thread isn't running, including the values of CPU registers at the time when the thread was suspended and the processor was allocated to another thread. A thread also maintains its own exception handlers and a priority level. For example, you can assign higher priority to threads that manage the user interface (so that they're more responsive) and lower priority to threads for less urgent tasks, such as background printing. In all cases, the time slice allocated to each thread is relatively short, so the end user has the perception that all the threads (and all the applications) run concurrently.

Alas, the thread scheduler—that is, the portion of the operating system that schedules existing threads and preempts the running thread when its time slice expires—takes some CPU time for its own chores. Moreover, the operating system consumes some memory to keep the context of each thread, be it active or temporarily suspended. For this reason, if too many threads are active at the same time, this scheduling activity can take a non-negligible amount of time and can degrade the overall performance, leaving less spare time to *worker threads* (the threads that do something useful). So you should never create more threads than strictly necessary, or you should use threads taken from the thread pool, as I explain at the end of this chapter.

You might want to create additional threads to perform operations such as asynchronous file or database I/O, communication with a remote machine or a Web server, or low-priority background jobs. You make the most of multithreading when you allocate distinct threads to tasks that have different priority or that take a lot of time to complete. Before opting for a multithreading application, you should consider available alternatives, such as using timers for scheduling recurring tasks, as I'll explain later in this chapter.

The main problem with threads is that they can compete for shared resources, where a resource can be as simple as a variable or as complex as a database connection or a hardware device. You must synchronize access to such resources—otherwise, you can get into trouble, for reasons that will be clear shortly. Visual Basic .NET provides the SyncLock construct to help you deal with these problems, and the runtime offers several synchronization objects. The key to effective multithreading is learning how to use these features properly.

Creating Threads

The System.Threading.Thread class offers all the methods and properties you need to create and manage threads. To create a new thread, you simply instantiate a new Thread object and then invoke its Start method. The Thread object's constructor requires one argument, a ThreadStart delegate object that points to the routine that runs when the thread starts. Such a routine must be a Sub without any arguments.

The following Visual Basic application spawns a second thread that prints some messages to the console window:

```
Sub TestThread()
    ' Create a new thread, and define its starting point.
    Dim t As New Thread(New ThreadStart(AddressOf DoTheTask))
    ' Run the new thread.
    t.Start()

    ' Print some messages to the Console window.
    Dim i As Integer
    For i = 1 to 10
        Console.WriteLine("Msg #" & i.ToString & " from main thread")
        ' Wait for 0.2 second.
        Thread.CurrentThread.Sleep(200)
    Next
End Sub

Sub DoTheTask()
    Dim i As Integer
    For i = 1 To 10
        Console.WriteLine("Msg #" & i.ToString & " from secondary thread")
        ' Wait for 0.2 second.
        Thread.CurrentThread.Sleep(200)
    Next
End Sub
```

The console window will contain intermixed messages from both the main and the secondary thread, evidence that both of them are running at the same time. Note that the Start method is asynchronous, in the sense that it might return before the spawned thread has actually started its execution. A thread terminates when its main routine (DoTheTask, in this case) exits or when the thread is programmatically killed by a Thread.Abort method. The application as a whole terminates only when all its threads terminate. You can check how many threads an application has created by using the Process Viewer utility. (See Figure 13-1.) This utility also displays the CPU time consumed by each thread, its priority, the number of context switches it underwent, and so on. (Interestingly, this utility shows that .NET applications might have additional threads—for example, the thread that manages garbage collections and finalizers—over which you apparently have no control.)

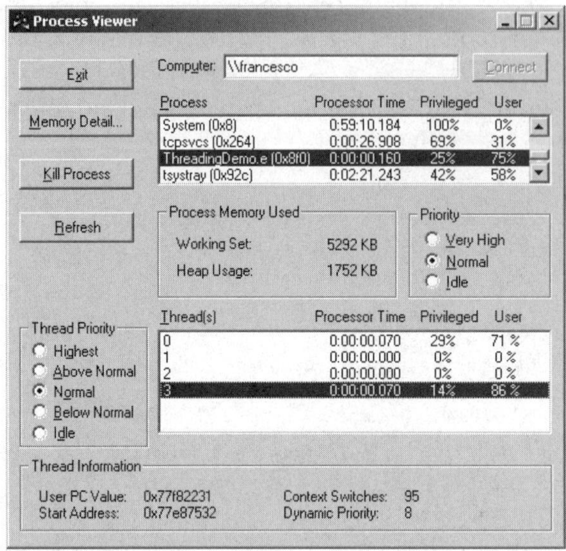

Figure 13-1. The Process Viewer utility displays diagnostic information about processes and their threads.

Working with Threads

To manipulate a Windows thread, you need a reference to the corresponding Thread object. This can be a reference to a new thread or a reference to the current thread—that is, the thread that is running the code—which you get by using the Thread.CurrentThread shared method. Once you have a reference to a Thread object, you can start, suspend, resume, or abort it using methods of the Thread class.

As I explained earlier, a thread naturally terminates when it reaches the Exit Sub or End Sub statement of its main procedure, but it can also be suspended or aborted by another thread (or by itself) by means of a Suspend or Abort method. Like the Start method, the Suspend and Abort methods are asynchronous, in the sense that they don't suspend or abort the thread immediately. In fact, threads can be suspended or aborted only when they reach a safe point. In general, a *safe point* is a point in time when it's safe to perform a garbage collection—for example, when a method call returns.

The runtime has several ways to take control when a thread reaches a safe point for a garbage collection. It can, for example, *hijack* the thread: when the thread is making a call to a class in the framework, the runtime pushes an extra return address (which points to a location in the runtime itself) onto the call stack. Then, when the method call completes, the runtime can take control and decide whether it's time to perform a garbage collection, to suspend the thread, or to abort it if there's a pending Abort method.

The Abort method doesn't immediately halt a thread for another reason as well. Instead of killing the thread immediately—as is the case with the ExitThread and TerminateThread Windows API functions—the Abort method causes a ThreadAbortException to be thrown in the target thread. This exception is special in that managed code can't catch it. However, if the target thread is executing inside a Try...End Try block, the code in the Finally clause is guaranteed to be executed and the thread is aborted only at the completion of the Finally clause. A thread might even detect that it's being aborted (by means of the ThreadState property, described in the next section) and might continue to run code in the Finally clause to postpone its death. (Trusted code can also cancel an Abort method using the ResetAbort method—see the SDK documentation for additional details.)

The Suspend and Resume instance methods let you temporarily suspend and then resume a thread. (A thread can suspend itself, but obviously it can't resume itself from a suspended state.) As for Abort, a thread is actually suspended only when it can be suspended safely, even though the Suspend method never blocks the caller (unless the calling thread is suspending itself, of course). The Suspend method has no effect on threads that are already suspended, and the Resume method doesn't have any effect on threads that are running. However, calls to the Suspend and Resume methods must be balanced. In addition, both methods throw a ThreadStateException if the target thread hasn't started yet or is already dead, or they throw a SecurityException if the caller doesn't have the necessary security permissions:

```
' Define and start a new thread.
' (Note that you don't strictly need a New ThreadStart object explicitly
'  because the AddressOf operator returns a delegate.)
Dim t As New Thread(AddressOf DoTheTask)
t.Start
⋮
' Suspend the thread.
t.Suspend
⋮
' Resume the thread.
t.Resume
⋮
' Abort the thread.
t.Abort
```

A thread can suspend itself temporarily by using the Thread.Sleep shared method, which takes a timeout in milliseconds:

```
' Pause for half a second.
Thread.Sleep(500)
```

The Sleep method works only on the current thread. (Using this method is similar to calling the Sleep Windows API function.) You can use the special 0 timeout value to terminate the current time slice and relinquish control to the thread scheduler, or you can use the Timeout.Infinite value (–1) to suspend the current thread indefinitely until another thread wakes it up. You can also pass a TimeSpan object to specify the length of the timeout.

It's quite common to wait for a thread to terminate; for example, the main thread can start a worker thread and then continue to execute to the point at which it must ensure that the worker thread has completed its task. You can use the Join method to easily achieve this behavior, as you can see in the following snippet:

```
Dim t As New Thread(AddressOf DoTheTask)
t.Start
' ...(Do something else.)...
⋮
' Wait for the other thread to die.
t.Join
```

The Join method can take an optional timeout, expressed in milliseconds or as a TimeSpan object. The method returns True if the thread died within the specified timeout; it returns False if the method returned because the timeout elapsed:

```
' Wait for the other thread to die, but print a message every second.
Do Until t.Join(1000)
    Console.WriteLine("Waiting for the other thread to die...")
Loop
```

When a thread calls Sleep on itself or Join on another thread, the calling thread enters the WaitSleepJoin state. (See Table 13-1.) A thread exits this state when the timeout expires or when another thread invokes the Interrupt method on it. When the Interrupt method is called, the target thread receives a ThreadInterruptedException, which must be caught or the thread will be killed. So the following is the typical code that you should write for threads that go to sleep and are waiting for another thread to wake them up:

```
Sub DoTheTask2()
    Dim interrupted As Boolean
    Try
        ' Go to sleep for 10 seconds or until another thread
        ' calls the Interrupt method on this thread.
        Thread.Sleep(10000)
        ' We get here if the timeout elapsed and no exception is thrown.
        ' (Not really necessary because the variable is already False.)
        interrupted = False
    Catch e As ThreadInterruptedException
        ' We get here if the thread has been interrupted.
        interrupted = True
    End Try
    If interrupted Then
        ' The thread was restarted by an Interrupt method.
    End If
End Sub
```

Speaking of thread termination, a thread is also terminated when an exception occurs. However, an exception on a secondary thread—for example, a thread used by the garbage collector to call the Finalize method, a thread created with the Thread class, or a thread taken from the thread pool—isn't fatal for the application (even if it might cause error messages to appear). Only uncaught exceptions thrown by the main thread or an unmanaged thread—that is, a thread that's running in COM objects called by a .NET assembly—terminate the application.

Thread Properties

You can test whether a thread is active—that is, it has started and isn't dead yet—using the IsAlive read-only property. When it's applied to the current thread, this property always returns True, for obvious reasons.

You can also check the state of any thread—including the current one—by using the ThreadState enumerated property, whose values are summarized in Table 13-1. This is a bit-coded value because a thread can be in more than one state at any given time, so you should test individual bits with the And operator:

```
If Thread.CurrentThread.ThreadState And ThreadState.StopRequested Then
    ' The current thread is stopping.
End If
```

The IsBackground property tells whether a thread is a low-priority background thread. Interestingly, you can change the background state of a thread by assigning True or False to this property before the thread starts:

```
' Make a thread a background thread before starting it.
t.IsBackground = True
t.Start
```

An important detail: background threads don't keep an application alive, so if your application has created one or more background threads, it should check the IsAlive property of all of them before exiting the main thread. Otherwise, those threads are mercilessly killed, regardless of what they're doing that moment.

The Priority property offers a different way to affect a thread's priority without making it a background thread. This property sets or returns one of the following ThreadPriority enumerated values: Normal, AboveNormal, BelowNormal, Highest, or Lowest:

```
' Supercharge the current thread.
Thread.CurrentThread.Priority = ThreadPriority.Highest
```

Windows can decide to adjust the priority of threads automatically—for example, when an application becomes the foreground application. Remember that changing the priority of a thread isn't recommended, so you should do it only for a good reason.

Finally, all threads have a Name property. This property is usually a null string, but you can assign it a value for the threads you create. The Name property doesn't change the behavior of a thread, but it turns useful during the debugging phase, as you'll read in the next section. For example, the thread name is reported in the message that the Visual Studio .NET debugger displays when a thread terminates.

Oddly, the Thread class doesn't expose any property that returns the ID of the underlying Windows physical thread. Under Windows you can retrieve the physical thread ID with a call to the GetCurrentThreadId Windows API function or, even better, by calling the AppDomain.GetCurrentThreadId static property:

```
Dim currThreadId As Integer = AppDomain.GetCurrentThreadId()
```

Table 13-1 The Possible Values for the ThreadState Property

State	Description
Aborted	The thread has been aborted.
AbortRequested	The thread is responding to an Abort request.
Background	The thread is running in the background (same as the IsBackground property).
Running	The thread is running. (Another thread has called the Start method.)
Stopped	The thread has been stopped. (A thread can never leave this state.)
StopRequested	The thread is about to stop.
Suspended	The thread has been suspended.
SuspendRequested	The thread is responding to a Suspend request.
Unstarted	The thread has been created, but the Start method hasn't been called yet.
WaitSleepJoin	The thread has called Monitor.Wait or Thread.Join on another thread.

Debugging Threads

You can see the name of the running thread—as well as other information such as the application name and the stack frame—by activating the Debug Location toolbar inside Visual Studio .NET. This data is especially useful when you want to determine where a thread is executing when you hit a breakpoint. You can display this toolbar by right-clicking on any toolbar and clicking Debug Location on the shortcut menu. (See Figure 13-2.)

The Thread window in Visual Studio .NET lets you list all the running threads, their status, and their priority. You activate this window by pointing to Windows on the Debug menu and clicking Threads. (The current program must be in break mode for you to see this menu command.) The yellow arrow on the left identifies the current thread, and you can switch to another thread by right-clicking on it. (See Figure 13-3.) You can also freeze a thread, which is then displayed with two vertical blue bars, and restart (thaw) it.

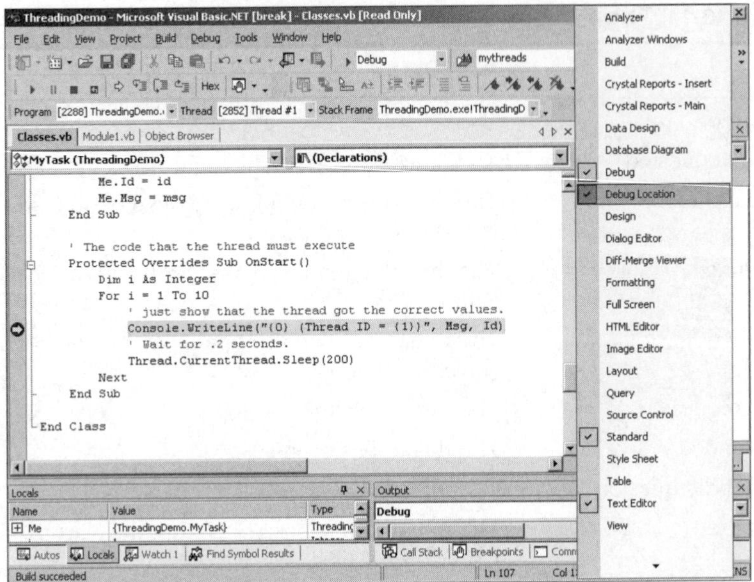

Figure 13-2. The Debug Location toolbar displays the thread name and other information about the running process.

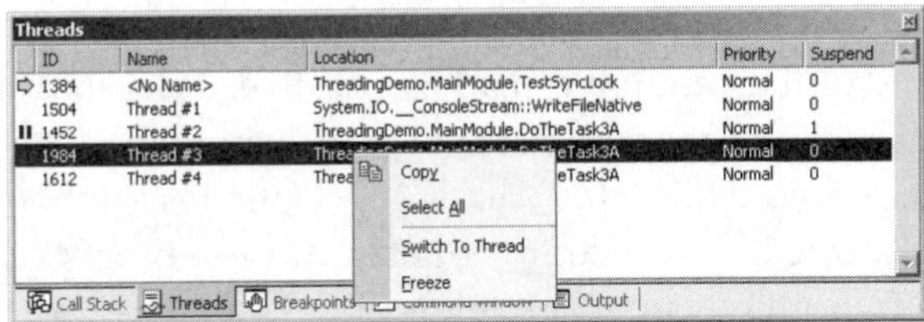

Figure 13-3. The Threads window lists all threads and lets you freeze and restart them.

The Performance utility offers a way to monitor threads and the performance bottlenecks they might create. (See Figure 13-4.) The .NET Framework has a performance object named .NET CLR LocksAndThreads that exposes several counters, the most important of which are

- **# of current logical threads** The current number of threads in the application known to the common language runtime.
- **# of current physical threads** The number of native Windows threads created and owned by the common language runtime.

- **# of current recognized threads** The number of threads that were created outside the common language runtime (for example, in a COM component) that the runtime has recognized.
- **Contention Rate/sec** Rate at which threads in the runtime fail to acquire a managed lock—for example, when reaching a SyncLock block. A high number for this counter is a symptom that the application isn't well designed for multithread operations.
- **Total # of Contentions** The total number of times threads in the common language runtime have failed to acquire a managed lock.
- **Current Queue/sec** The average number of threads waiting to acquire a lock; a high value means that most threads spend most of their time waiting for a lock to become available.

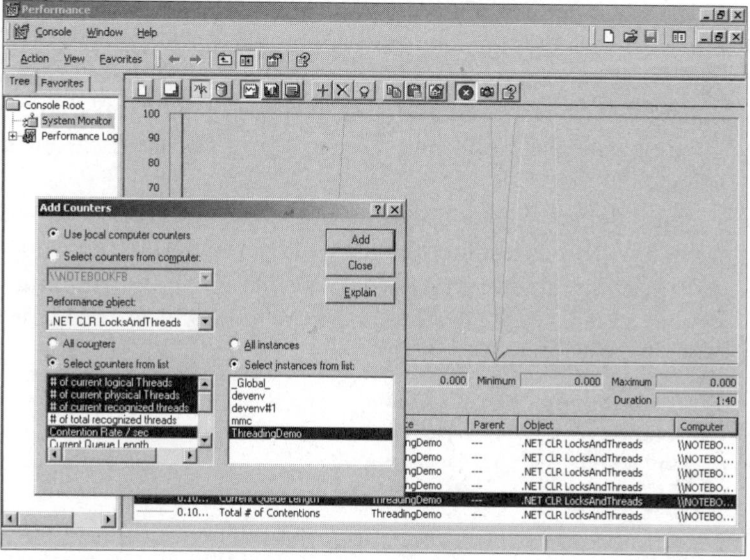

Figure 13-4. The Performance utility lets you visualize several statistics regarding common language runtime threads.

The meaning of some of these counters—most notably, those related to contention and locks—will become evident later in this chapter.

Storing and Sharing Data

If you ever wrote multithreaded COM components in Visual Basic 6, you might recall that each thread sees a different set of variables. In fact, sharing data among threads in Visual Basic 6 isn't a trivial task. (You can use a single-threaded

DLL that works as a bridge among the different threads, but it's a rather inefficient solution.) The game is completely different under the .NET Framework, so be prepared to forget what you learned with Visual Basic so far.

Before I dive into details, you should realize that whenever you have multiple threads that share data you also need a way to synchronize access to that data. If two threads can access the same (shared) variables, you might ensure that they don't change them at the same time because the result isn't a pleasant one. Data sharing and synchronization are always two facets of the same issue.

Local, Class, and Static Variables

The scope of a variable determines whether multiple threads can share it. Threads never share local dynamic variables—that is, variables defined inside a procedure and not marked by the Static keyword—even if the threads happen to be executing inside that procedure in the same moment. The reason is simple: local variables are allocated on the stack. Each thread maintains its own private stack and keeps its own copy of all local dynamic variables, which means that you can't share data among threads using local dynamic variables. The good news is that you don't have to worry about synchronizing access to such variables.

By default, threads share all other types of variables—that is, class-level fields and properties, module-level variables, and local Static variables. You can use these variables to make data visible to all the running threads; unfortunately, you also have to provide a way to synchronize access to this data. Consider this simple code:

```
If globalVar = 0 Then
    Console.WriteLine("About to change globalVar")
    globalVar = globalVar + 1
End If
```

If access to the globalVar variable isn't arbitrated and synchronized in some way, a thread might execute, test the value of globalVar, find that it's 0, and enter the Then code block. The first statement in this block is a call into the runtime, which gives the thread manager a chance to perform a thread switch and activate another thread. What happens if the other thread enters the same block of code? As you might expect, it finds that the globalVar variable is still 0, and the other thread (incorrectly) enters the block. As a result, the variable is incremented twice, which you probably don't want and which might cause an error later in the application. Logic errors of this kind are problematic because they occur in random fashion and are rarely reproducible, and therefore are very difficult to debug.

This code summarizes which variables are shared among threads:

```
Class SampleClass
    Dim Field As Integer            ' Field (shared)

    Sub SampleSub()
        Dim dynamicVar As Integer   ' Dynamic variable (nonshared)
        Static staticVar As Integer ' Static variable (shared)
        ⋮
    End Sub
End Class
```

The ThreadStatic Attribute

To understand the kinds of problems you have to watch out for when you're working with multithreaded applications, consider this very simple Property procedure:

```
Dim m_ThreadId As String

Property ThreadId() As String
    Get
        Return m_ThreadId
    End Get
    Set(ByVal Value As String)
        m_ThreadId = Value
    End Set
End Property
```

Suppose that an individual instance of this class can be used by multiple threads but that each thread wants to store and retrieve a distinct value for the ThreadId property. Unfortunately, the m_ThreadId variable is shared among all the threads, so each thread is likely to override the current value with its own ThreadId.

To obviate this problem, the .NET runtime supports the concept of *Thread-Relative Static* fields, which are class or module variables that aren't shared among threads. You create a Thread-Relative Static variable by marking a variable declaration with the ThreadStatic attribute:

```
' The m_ThreadId variable isn't shared among threads.
<ThreadStatic()> Dim m_ThreadId As String
```

Note that you can't use the ThreadStatic attribute for Static local variables: if you need a thread static variable that retains its value between consecutive calls to a procedure, you must use a class-level or module-level variable marked by the ThreadStatic attribute.

> **Caution** Even if you decide not to explicitly create new threads in your applications, you might have to worry about arbitrating access to shared variables anyway. In fact, by default the Finalize method of your objects might run on a different thread than your application's main thread; therefore, you should ensure that either you don't access any shared variables from Finalize methods or you protect these variables by using synchronization blocks (which I explain later).

Thread Local Storage

Thread local storage (TLS) provides an additional way for threads to maintain specific information that shouldn't be shared with other threads. You can think of TLS as a set of *data slots* that are unique for each thread. A thread can store any object in a given data slot and be assured that this data will survive calls to other components or DLLs. In a sense, a TLS data slot is a variable associated with the thread, and the thread can access that variable at any moment, even if the thread isn't running inside a given module or class.

The two types of TLS data slots are *allocated data store slots* and *named slots*. You create an allocated (unnamed) data store slot by using the Thread.AllocateDataSlot shared method, which takes no arguments:

```
' Allocate a new unnamed TLS slot.
Dim slot As LocalDataStoreSlot = Thread.AllocateDataSlot()
```

If you create a named slot, that slot is visible to all the threads in the application, but each thread receives its own distinct copy of the slot. You can choose from two ways to allocate a named data slot, depending on whether you want the operation to fail if there's already a slot with that name (created by either the current thread or another thread). Both statements in the following code create a slot named *id*:

```
' The AllocateNamedDataSlot method fails if the slot exists already.
Dim namedSlot As LocalDataStoreSlot = Thread.AllocateNamedDataSlot("id")

' The GetNamedDataSlot method returns a reference to an existing named slot
' or creates a new slot if necessary.
Dim namedSlot2 As LocalDataStoreSlot = Thread.GetNamedDataSlot("id")
```

Regardless of how the slot was created, you can use the SetData shared method to store an object in it and the GetData shared method to retrieve a value:

```
' Store a value in the slot created previously.
Thread.SetData(slot, 123)
:
' Read the value back.
Console.Write(Thread.GetData(slot))      ' => 123
```

The only other difference between named and unnamed slots is that you should explicitly destroy the named slots when they aren't needed any longer:

```
' Destroys the slot named ID in all the threads in the current application
Thread.FreeNamedDataSlot("id")
```

Note that a thread can read and write only to its own TLS data slots and can't access slots belonging to another thread. In other words, you can't use TLS to share data among threads.

> **Note** Thread local storage is used by the common language runtime itself to store the Thread logical object that corresponds to each physical thread. Threads are known to the runtime because they have been created by managed code or because they entered the runtime by means of PInvoke or COM Interop (which can happen when you expose .NET objects to the outside world as COM components). Whenever a foreign thread calls the managed code, the runtime checks whether its TLS contains a specific Threading.Thread object. If not, this call marks the first time that the thread enters the runtime, so a new Thread object is created for it and the thread is added to the list of threads the runtime knows about.

Passing Data to and from a Thread

More often than not, you must pass data to a thread before starting its execution. This isn't a trivial task because you can't pass data as an argument. (The ThreadStart delegate doesn't take arguments.) Nor can you store data in a global variable and let the code in the other thread read it. (Other threads might override this value in the meantime.) You often need to solve the opposite problem as well, which is to retrieve data from a thread that has produced a result.

A general solution, which doesn't pose any limit to the amount of data that can be passed in both directions, is to create a class for the sole purpose of sharing data between the main application and the thread and have this class expose the instance method that works as the entry point for the thread. Here's an example that shows how you can pass data in both directions:

```
Class ThreadData
    Public Id As Integer
    Public Msg As String
    Public Done As Boolean

    ' The entry point for the thread
    Sub DoTheTask()
        Dim i As Integer
        For i = 1 To 10
            ' Show that the thread received the correct values.
            Console.WriteLine("{0} (Thread ID = {1})", msg, id)
            ' Wait for 0.2 second.
            Thread.CurrentThread.Sleep(200)
        Next
        ' Let the main thread know that this thread has completed.
        Done = True
    End Sub
End Class
```

Here's a routine that uses the ThreadData class:

```
Sub TestThreadData ()
    Dim i As Integer
    Dim dc(9) As ThreadData
    Dim t As Thread
    Dim allDone As Boolean

    ' Create multiple threads.
    For i = 0 To 9
        ' Create a new data object, and initialize its property.
        dc(i) = New ThreadData
        dc(i).Id = i + 1
        dc(i).Msg = "A message"
        ' Create a new thread, and define its starting point.
        t = New Thread(AddressOf dc(i).DoTheTask)
```

```
        t.Start()
    Next

    ' Poll until all threads have completed.
    ' (Just an example that retrieves values from threads.)
    Do Until allDone
        Console.WriteLine("Waiting...")
        Thread.CurrentThread.Sleep(200)
        ' Check that all threads have set Done = True.
        allDone = True
        For i = 0 To 9
            allDone = allDone And dc(i).Done
        Next
    Loop
End Sub
```

In the preceding example, the main thread polls the Done property in every data object to learn when all the threads have completed their jobs. A much cleaner approach is to have the data class raising an event when it wants to notify that something has happened, or that new data is available, or that the thread has completed its job. Here's a new ThreadData2 class that notifies the thread termination through an event:

```
Class ThreadData2
    Event TaskCompleted(ByVal sender As Object, ByVal endTime As Date)

    Public Id As Integer
    Public Msg As String
    Public Done As Boolean

    ' The entry point for the thread
    Sub DoTheTask()
        ' ...(Code this procedure as in original ThreadData class)...
        ⋮
        ' Raise an event before this thread terminates
        RaiseEvent TaskCompleted(Me, Date.Now)
    End Sub
End Class
```

Of course, you must modify the caller's code to take advantage of the new TaskCompleted event:

```
Dim runningThreads As Integer

Sub TestEventNotifications()
```

(continued)

```
    Dim i As Integer
    Dim dc(9) As ThreadData2
    Dim t As Thread
    ' Set a name for the main thread.
    Thread.CurrentThread.Name = "Main thread"

    ' Create multiple threads.
    For i = 0 To 9
        ' Create a new data object, and initialize its property.
        dc(i) = New ThreadData2()
        dc(i).Id = i + 1
        dc(i).Msg = "A message"
        ' Have this object's event point to the local event procedure.
        AddHandler dc(i).TaskCompleted, AddressOf TaskCompleted
        ' Create a new thread, and define its starting point.
        t = New Thread(AddressOf dc(i).DoTheTask)
        ' Name this thread, to recognize it later.
        t.Name = "Thread #" & dc(i).Id.ToString
        t.Start()
        ' Increment number of running threads.
        ' *** NOTE: this and other statements that access runningThreads
        ' ***    aren't safe (read text for explanation).
        runningThreads += 1
    Next

    ' Loop until all threads have completed.
    Do Until runningThreads = 0
        Console.WriteLine("Waiting...")
        Thread.CurrentThread.Sleep(200)
    Loop
End Sub

' An event procedure that runs when a thread terminates

Sub TaskCompleted(ByVal Sender As Object, ByVal endTime As Date)
    ' Get the ID of the thread that is about to terminate.
    Dim id As Integer = DirectCast(Sender, ThreadData2).Id
    ' Display a message; append name of thread running this code.
    Console.WriteLine("Thread {0} terminated (Running on {2})", _
       id, endTime, Thread.CurrentThread.Name)
    ' Decrement counter of running threads.
    runningThreads -= 1
End Sub
```

The application works as expected: each time the TaskCompleted event fires, the runningThreads variable is decremented until it reaches 0. However, the output in the console window is somewhat surprising. Following are the last few lines. (Their order can vary from execution to execution.)

```
Thread 1 terminated (Running on Thread #1)
Waiting...
Thread 2 terminated (Running on Thread #2)
Thread 4 terminated (Running on Thread #4)
Thread 3 terminated (Running on Thread #3)
Thread 5 terminated (Running on Thread #5)
⋮
```

These messages bring up a very important point: *code in event procedures raised by an object runs in the same thread on which the object runs.* This can be surprising if you're accustomed to COM-based events in previous Visual Basic versions. A Visual Basic 6 application can have a WithEvents variable pointing to an object that runs in another COM apartment, but the code in the event procedure always runs in the caller's apartment. This arrangement is necessary because only the code running in the application's apartment can access its variables. (In fact, each apartment receives a distinct set of variables.) To ensure that the code runs in the correct thread, the COM infrastructure creates a pair of proxy-stub objects that perform the thread switching and take care of marshaling data between the two apartments. Visual Basic .NET events are radically different because they're based on delegates, which ultimately are nothing but function pointers. The .NET Framework doesn't create a proxy-stub pair between the application and the object. The result is that .NET events always run in the same thread as the object that calls the RaiseEvent statement, and no thread switching occurs. This means that the runningThreads variable is actually shared among all threads, and therefore, you should arbitrate accesses to it using a synchronization primitive (such as a SyncLock block, as I'll describe shortly).

Using a Wrapper Class

The more multithreaded applications you write, the more often you'll find yourself writing the same code for creating the thread, starting it, and waiting for its completion. Thanks to inheritance, you can encapsulate much of this code in a wrapper class with minimal effort on your part. The following

ThreadWrapperBase abstract class contains all the logic that creates and starts the thread, and it sets the Done flag to True when the thread completes its task:

```
MustInherit Class ThreadWrapperBase
    ' This public member exposes the Thread object.
    Public ReadOnly Thread As System.Threading.Thread

    ' The constructor creates the thread object and runs the code.
    Sub New()
        Me.Thread = New System.Threading.Thread(AddressOf Me.RunThread)
    End Sub

    ' This method starts the thread.
    Overridable Sub Start()
        Me.Thread.Start()
    End Sub

    ' This private procedure is where the thread starts its execution;
    ' when the thread terminates, the Done flag is set to True.
    Private Sub RunThread()
        m_Done = False
        OnStart()
        m_Done = True
    End Sub

    Dim m_Done As Boolean

    ' This property returns True if the thread has completed its task.
    ReadOnly Property Done() As Boolean
        Get
            Return m_Done
        End Get
    End Property

    ' Derived classes must override this procedure
    ' to provide the actual code for the thread.
    Protected MustOverride Sub OnStart()
End Class
```

The following MyTask class inherits from ThreadWrapperBase, to which it adds the instance data and an implementation of the OnStart method containing the actual code that the thread must execute. Because the base class has a parameterless constructor, the constructor in the derived class is optional and serves only to initialize instance data with a single statement:

```
Class MyTask
    Inherits ThreadWrapperBase

    ' Instance data - might be marked as ReadOnly.
    Public Id As Integer
    Public Msg As String

    Sub New(ByVal id As Integer, ByVal msg As String)
        Me.Id = id
        Me.Msg = msg
    End Sub

    ' The code that the thread must execute
    Protected Overrides Sub OnStart()
        Dim i As Integer
        For i = 1 To 10
            Console.WriteLine("{0} (Thread ID = {1})", Msg, Id)
            Thread.CurrentThread.Sleep(200)
        Next
    End Sub
End Class
```

Using the MyTask class is simple:

```
Sub TestWrapperClass()
    Dim i As Integer
    Dim mytasks(9) As MyTask

    For i = 0 To 9
        ' Initialize thread data, and then start the thread.
        mytasks(i) = New MyTask(i, "Message from thread")
        mytasks(i).Start()
    Next

    ' Wait until all threads have completed.
    For i = 0 To 9
        Do Until mytasks(i).Done
            Console.WriteLine("Waiting...(Main thread)")
            Thread.Sleep(200)
        Loop
    Next
End Sub
```

The inherited MyTask class exposes the Thread object by means of the property with the same name, so you can invoke any of the properties or methods of the Thread object, such as those described in the sections that follow.

Thread Synchronization

Now that you know how a thread can share data or prevent data from being shared, you're ready to tackle synchronization issues related to concurrent access to variables and objects accessible by multiple threads at the same time.

The SyncLock Statement

As you know, a thread can be preempted at any time, usually at the completion of a call to an object's method. The following example demonstrates what can happen when a piece of code isn't guaranteed to execute atomically:

```
Sub TestSynchronizationProblem()
    ' Create five auxiliary threads.
    Dim i As Integer
    For i = 1 To 5
        Dim t As New Thread(AddressOf DoTheTask3)
        ' Assign a name to this thread so that we can track its output.
        t.Name = "Thread # " & i.ToString
        t.Start()
    Next
End Sub

Sub DoTheTask3()
    ' Print a lot of information to the console window.
    Dim i As Integer
    For i = 1 To 100
        ' Split the output line in pieces.
        Console.Write("Message ")
        Console.Write("from ")
        Console.WriteLine(Thread.CurrentThread.Name)
    Next
End Sub
```

A glance at the console window shows some interruptions of a thread between the Console.Write*xxxx* statements, which results in scrambled output.

The runtime offers no means for ensuring that a group of statements behaves as an atomic, uninterruptible operation. This would be too stiff a requirement in an operating system that must guarantee multitasking to all applications. However, you don't really need atomicity most of the time. In the preceding code, for example, it would be enough to ensure that only one thread can execute that specific block of statements at a time. You can achieve this by enclosing those statements in a SyncLock...End SyncLock block, a language construct that was obviously missing in Visual Basic 6 (which didn't support free threading at all). The SyncLock block requires a variable as an argument, and this variable must satisfy the following requirements:

- It must be a variable shared by all the threads (typically, a class-level or module-level variable without the ThreadStatic attribute).
- It must be a reference type, for example, a String or an Object variable. (Using a value type causes a compilation error.)
- It must not have a Nothing value. (Using a Nothing value causes a run-time error.)

Here's the code seen before, revised to leverage the SyncLock block. (Additions are in boldface.)

```
' The lock object. (Any non-Nothing reference value will do.)
Dim consoleLock As String = "lock me"

Sub DoTheTask3()
    ' Print a lot of information to the console window.
    Dim i As Integer
    For i = 1 To 100
        SyncLock consoleLock
            ' Split the output line in pieces.
            Console.Write("Message ")
            Console.Write("from ")
            Console.WriteLine(Thread.CurrentThread.Name)
        End SyncLock
    Next
End Sub
```

The preceding code uses the consoleLock variable to arbitrate access to the Console object, which is the only resource that all threads share in this trivial example and is therefore the only resource for which you need to provide synchronization. Real-world applications might contain many SyncLock blocks; such blocks can share the same object variable or use different variables for finer granularity. As a rule of thumb, you should have a distinct object variable for each shared resource that must be synchronized or for each group of statements that must be executed by one thread at a time.

Each SyncLock block implicitly uses a hidden Try...End Try block because Visual Basic must ensure that the lock is correctly released if an exception is thrown. (A lock release requires a Monitor.Exit method.) For this reason, jumping into a SyncLock block by using a Goto statement is illegal.

One final tip: if the SyncLock block is placed inside an instance method of a class and all threads are running inside a method of that instance, you can pass Me to the SyncLock statement because this object surely satisfies all the requirements. It's accessible by all threads, it's a reference value, and it surely is non-Nothing.

```
Class TestClass
    Sub DoTheTask()
        SyncLock Me
            ' Only one thread at a time can access this code.
            ⋮
        End SyncLock
    End Sub
End Class
```

You can use Me in this fashion only for one SyncLock block in the class. If you have multiple synchronization blocks, you'll typically use different variables as the argument of the SyncLock block.

Synchronized Objects

Another problem related to threading is that not every .NET object can be safely shared among threads: in other words, not all .NET objects are *thread-safe*. When you're writing a multithreaded application, you should always check the documentation to determine whether the objects and the methods you're using are thread-safe. For example, all the shared methods of the Regex, Match, and Group classes are thread-safe, but their instance methods aren't and shouldn't be invoked by different threads at the same time. Some .NET objects—most notably, Windows forms and controls—pose even more severe limitations, in that only the thread that created them can call their methods. (You'll learn how to access Windows forms and controls from other threads in the "Multithreaded Controls" section of Chapter 17.)

Synchronized .NET Classes

Several objects that aren't thread-safe natively—including ArrayList, Hashtable, Queue, SortedList, Stack, TextReader, TextWriter, and regular expressions' Match and Group classes—expose a Synchronized shared method, which returns a thread-safe object that's equivalent to the one you pass as an argument. Most of these classes also expose the IsSynchronized property, which returns True if you're dealing with a thread-safe instance:

```
' Create an ArrayList object, and add some values to it.
Dim al As New ArrayList()
al.Add(1)
al.Add(2)
al.Add(3)
' Create a synchronized, thread-safe version of this ArrayList.
Dim syncAl As ArrayList = ArrayList.Synchronized(al)
```

```
' Prove that the new object is thread-safe.
Console.WriteLine(al.IsSynchronized)        ' => False
Console.WriteLine(syncAl.IsSynchronized)    ' => True
```

Now that you're thread-safe, you can share the syncAl object among different threads.

The Synchronization Attribute

Using the System.Runtime.Remoting.Contexts.Synchronization attribute is the simplest way to provide synchronized access to an entire object so that only one thread can access its instance fields and methods. That is, any thread can use that instance of the class, but only one thread at a time. If a thread is executing code inside the class, any other thread that attempts to use the fields or methods of that class has to wait. In other words, it's as if there were SyncLock blocks enclosing every method of that class.

The following code shows how you can synchronize a class using the Synchronization attribute. Note also that the class must inherit from ContextBoundObject to be marked as a context-bound object:

```
<System.Runtime.Remoting.Contexts.Synchronization()> _
Class Display
    ' Synchronized classes must inherit from ContextBoundObject.
    Inherits ContextBoundObject

    Sub DisplayData()
        Console.Write("Message ")
        Console.Write("from ")
        Console.WriteLine(Thread.CurrentThread.Name)
    End Sub
End Class
```

The Synchronization attribute automatically synchronizes access to all instance fields, properties, and methods, but it doesn't provide synchronization for shared members.

The MethodImpl Attribute

In most cases, making an entire class synchronized is overkill, and you can often be satisfied just protecting a few of its methods from concurrent accesses. You can do this by wrapping the body of such methods in a SyncLock block (using a different variable for each block). On the other hand, here's a simpler technique, based on the System.Runtime.CompilerServices.MethodImpl attribute:

```
' This code assumes that the following Imports statement has been used:
'   Imports System.Runtime.CompilerServices

Class MethodImplDemoClass
```

(continued)

```
    ' This method can be executed by one thread at a time.
    <MethodImpl(MethodImplOptions.Synchronized)> _
    Sub SynchronizedMethod()
        Dim i As Integer
        For i = 1 To 16
            Console.Write(Thread.CurrentThread.Name)
        Next
    End Sub
End Class
```

Here's an example that uses the preceding class:

```
Sub TestMethodImpl()
    Dim i As Integer
    For i = 0 To 9
        Dim t As New Thread(AddressOf DoTheTask4)
        t.Name = i.ToString                    ' Assign a unique name.
        t.Start()
    Next
End Sub

Sub DoTheTask4()
    ' All threads see the same instance.
    Static obj As New MethodImplDemoClass()

    Dim i As Integer
    For i = 1 To 10
        obj.SynchronizedMethod()
    Next
End Sub
```

The Monitor Class

The SyncLock block provides an easy-to-use method for dealing with synchronization issues, but it can be inadequate in many situations. For example, a thread can't just *test* a SyncLock code block and avoid being blocked if another thread is already executing that SyncLock block or another SyncLock block is associated with the same object.

SyncLock blocks are internally implemented via Monitor objects. Interestingly, you can use a Monitor object directly and get more flexibility, although it's at the expense of somewhat more complex code. (In fact, you might claim that the SyncLock statement is just a way to write code in a concise fashion.)

You never instantiate individual Monitor objects, and in fact, all the methods I'm going to illustrate are shared methods of the Monitor class. The most important method is Enter, which takes an object as an argument. This object works exactly like the argument you pass to a SyncLock block and undergoes the same constraints: it must be a non-Nothing reference variable that's shared by all the threads. If no other thread owns the lock on that object, the current thread acquires the lock and sets its internal lock counter to 1. If another thread currently owns the lock, the calling thread must wait until the other thread releases the lock and the lock becomes available. If the calling thread already owns the lock, each call to Monitor.Enter increments the internal lock counter.

The Monitor.Exit method takes the lock object as an argument and decrements its internal lock counter. If the counter reaches 0, the lock is released so that other threads can acquire it. Calls to Monitor.Enter and Monitor.Exit clearly must be balanced, or the lock will never be released:

```
' A non-Nothing module-level object variable
Dim objLock As New Object

' Attempt to enter the critical section;
' wait if the lock is currently owned by another thread.
Monitor.Enter(objLock)
⋮
' ...(Do something.)...
⋮
' Release the lock.
Monitor.Exit(objLock)
```

If a thread calls the Interrupt method on another thread currently waiting inside a Monitor.Enter method, the thread receives a ThreadInterruptedException, so you should consider whether the call to Monitor.Enter should be enclosed in a Try...End Try block. In general, if the statements between Monitor.Enter and Monitor.Exit are likely to raise an exception, you should consider putting all the code in a Try…End Try block because it's imperative that you always release the lock:

```
Try
    Monitor.Enter(objLock)
    ⋮
    ' ...(Do something here.)...
    ⋮
Finally
    ' Always release the lock, even if an error occurred.
    Monitor.Exit(objLock)
End Try
```

The Enter and Exit methods of a Monitor object let you replace a SyncLock block but don't bring you any additional advantages. You see the extra flexibility of the Monitor class when you apply its TryEnter method. This method is similar to Enter, but the method exits and returns False if the lock can't be acquired in the specified timeout. For example, you can attempt to get the monitor lock for 10 milliseconds and then give up, without blocking the current thread indefinitely. The following code rewrites a previous example based on SyncLock, this time using the Monitor object, and also displays the failed attempts to acquire the lock:

```
Sub DoTheTask5()
    ' Print a lot of information to the console window.
    Dim i As Integer
    For i = 1 To 100
        Do Until Monitor.TryEnter(consoleLock, 10)
            Console.WriteLine("{0} failed to acquire the lock", _
                Thread.CurrentThread.Name)
        Loop

        ' Split the output line in pieces.
        Console.Write("Message ")
        Console.Write("from ")
        Console.WriteLine(Thread.CurrentThread.Name)
        ' Release the lock.
        Monitor.Exit(consoleLock)
    Next
End Sub
```

The Monitor.Wait method can be called only from inside a synchronized region—that is, a region delimited by a call to the Monitor.Enter and Monitor.Exit methods. A thread should call Monitor.Wait when it doesn't want to leave the synchronized region but is willing to give up some of its CPU time, perhaps waiting for another thread to complete a chunk of its task.

The Wait method always works together with the Monitor.Pulse (or PulseAll) method. A thread that calls Monitor.Wait releases the lock and immediately reenters the waiting queue for the same lock, so it stays blocked until it eventually acquires the lock again. (The Wait method takes an optional timeout, which ensures that the calling thread is the first thread to acquire the lock again after that timeout elapses.) While the first thread is blocked by the Wait method, another thread can gain control of the lock and do a chunk of its task. When the second thread wants to temporarily stop—perhaps because it has no more data to process—it calls Monitor.Pulse and enters a wait status. This Pulse method causes one of the waiting threads to get the control of the monitor lock.

The Wait and Pulse methods are often used in producer-consumer situations, when a thread produces some data and another thread consumes it. The producer thread produces data and calls a Monitor.Wait method so that the consumer thread has a chance to consume the data. When the consumer completes its task, it can call Monitor.Pulse, which wakes up the producer thread, which has now another opportunity to generate data, and so on. You can learn more about these two methods from the .NET Framework SDK documentation.

The Interlocked Class

The Interlocked class provides a way to perform the simple atomic operations of incrementing and decrementing a shared memory variable. This class exposes only shared methods (not counting members inherited from Object). Consider the following code:

```
' Increment and Decrement methods work with 32-bit integers.
Dim lockCounter As Integer

' The procedure that contains the critical section
Sub DoTheTask6()
    ' Increment the lock counter, and return the new value.
    If Interlocked.Increment(lockCounter) = 1 Then
        ' Enter the critical section only if lockCounter was 0.
        ⋮
        ' ... (The critical section) ...
        ⋮
    End If
    ' Allow other threads to enter the critical section.
    Interlocked.Decrement(lockCounter)
End Sub
```

You can see that only one thread at a time can enter the critical section, so in practice, you get the same effect you'd get with the Monitor.TryEnter method. However, the Interlocked class permits something that the Monitor class doesn't allow: you can set a threshold (higher than 1) for the number of threads that run inside the critical section. To see what I mean, just replace one line in the preceding code:

```
' Up to four threads are allowed to run in the critical section.
    If Interlocked.Increment(lockCounter) <= 4 Then
```

The Interlocked class exposes two additional shared methods. The Exchange method lets you assign a value of your choosing to an Integer, a Single, or an Object variable and return its previous value, as an atomic operation. The CompareExchange method works similarly, but it does the swap only if the memory location is currently equal to a specific value that you provide as an argument.

The Mutex Class

The Mutex class provides yet another synchronization primitive. The Mutex object is a Windows kernel object that can be owned by one thread at a time and is said to be in a *signaled* state if no thread currently owns it.

A thread requests ownership of a Mutex object by means of the Mutex.WaitOne method (which doesn't return until the ownership has been successfully achieved) and releases it by means of the Mutex.ReleaseMutex method. A thread can request ownership of a Mutex object that it owns already without blocking itself, but in that case, it must call ReleaseMutex an equal number of times. This is how you can implement a synchronized section using a Mutex object:

```
' This Mutex object must be accessible to all threads.
Dim m As New Mutex

Sub DoTheTask7()
    m.WaitOne()
    ' Enter the synchronized section.
    ⋮
    ' Exit the synchronized section.
    m.ReleaseMutex()
End Sub
```

If you pass WaitOne an optional timeout argument, the method returns the control to the thread when the ownership is successfully achieved or the timeout expires. You can tell the difference between the two results by looking at the return value: True means that ownership was acquired, False that the timeout expired.

```
Sub DoTheTask8()
    ' Attempt to enter the critical section, but give up after 0.1 second.
    If m.WaitOne(100, False) Then
        ' Enter the critical section.
        ⋮
        ' Exit the critical section, and release the Mutex.
        m.ReleaseMutex()
    End If
End Sub
```

When used in this way, the Mutex object provides you with a mechanism equivalent to the Monitor.TryEnter method, without offering any additional features. You see the added flexibility of the Mutex object when you consider its WaitAny or WaitAll shared method. The WaitAny method takes an array of

Mutex objects and returns when it manages to acquire the ownership of a Mutex object in the list (in which case, that Mutex becomes signaled) or when the optional timeout expires. The return value is the array index of the Mutex object that became signaled or the special value 258 if the timeout expired.

You typically use an array of Mutex objects when you have a limited number of resources, such as communication ports, and you want to allocate each one to a thread as soon as the resource becomes available. In this situation, a signaled Mutex object means that the corresponding resource is available, so you can use the Mutex.WaitAny method for blocking the current thread until *any* of the Mutex objects become signaled. Here's the skeleton of an application that uses this approach:

```
' An array of three Mutex objects
Dim mutexes() As Mutex = { New Mutex(), New Mutex(), New Mutex() }

Sub DoTheTask9()
    Dim mutexNdx As Integer
    ' Wait until a resource becomes available.
    ' (Returns the index of the available resource)
    mutexNdx = Mutex.WaitAny(mutexes)
    ' Enter the critical section.
    ' (This code should use only the resource corresponding to mutexNdx.)
    ' ...
    ' Exit the critical section, and release the resource.
    mutexes(mutexNdx).ReleaseMutex()
End Sub
```

The WaitAll shared method takes an array of Mutex objects and returns the control to the application only when *all* of them have become signaled. This method is especially useful when you can't proceed until all the other threads have completed their jobs:

```
' Wait until all resources have been released.
Mutex.WaitAll(resources)
```

The ReaderWriterLock Class

Many resources in the real world can be either read from or written to. Often these resources allow either multiple read operations or a single write operation running in a given moment. For example, multiple clients can read a data file or a database table, but if the file or the table is being written to, no other read or write operation can occur on that resource. You can create a lock that implements single-writer, multiple-reader semantics by using a ReaderWriter-Lock object.

Using this object is straightforward: all the threads intending to use the resource should share the same instance of the ReaderWriterLock class. Before attempting an operation on the resource, a thread should call either the AcquireReaderLock or the AcquireWriterLock method, depending on the operation to be performed. These methods block the current thread until the lock of the requested type can be acquired. (For example, until no other thread is holding the lock if you requested a writer lock.) Finally, you should call the ReleaseReaderLock or ReleaseWriterLock method when you've completed the read or write operation on the resource.

The following code example creates 10 threads that perform either a read or a write operation on a shared resource (relevant statements are in boldface):

```
Dim rwl As New ReaderWriterLock()
Dim rnd As New Random()

Sub TestReaderWriterLock()
    Dim i As Integer
    For i = 1 To 10
        Dim t As New Thread(AddressOf DoTheTask10)
        t.Name = i.ToString
        t.Start()
    Next
    Thread.Sleep(20000)
End Sub

Sub DoTheTask10()
    Dim i As Integer
    Dim tname As String = Thread.CurrentThread.Name()
    ' Perform 10 read or write operations. (Reads are more frequent.)
    For i = 1 To 10
        If rnd.NextDouble < 0.8 Then
            ' Attempt a read operation.
            rwl.AcquireReaderLock(Timeout.Infinite)
            Console.WriteLine("Thread {0} is reading", tname)
            Thread.Sleep(300)
            Console.WriteLine("Thread {0} completed the read operation", _
                tname)
            rwl.ReleaseReaderLock()
        Else
            ' Attempt a write operation.
            rwl.AcquireWriterLock(Timeout.Infinite)
            Console.WriteLine("Thread {0} is writing", tname)
            Thread.Sleep(300)
            Console.WriteLine("Thread {0} completed the write operation", _
                tname)
```

```
            rwl.ReleaseWriterLock()
        End If
    Next
End Sub
```

If you run this application, you'll see that multiple threads can be reading at the same time and that a writing thread blocks all the other threads.

The AcquireReaderLock and AcquireWriterLock methods can take a timeout argument, expressed as a number of milliseconds or a TimeSpan value. You should test whether the lock was acquired successfully by means of the IsReaderLockHeld or IsWriterLockHeld read-only property if you passed a value other than Timeout.Infinite:

```
' Attempt to acquire a reader lock for no longer than 1 second.
rwl.AcquireWriterLock(1000)
If rwl.IsWriterLockHeld Then
    ' The thread has a writer lock on the resource.
    ⋮
End If
```

A thread that owns a reader lock can also attempt to upgrade to a writer lock by calling the UpgradeToWriterLock method and later go back to the reader lock by calling DowngradeFromWriterLock.

The great thing about ReaderWriterLock objects is that they are lightweight objects and can be used in large numbers without affecting performance significantly. Additionally, they don't really privilege either writers or readers in any special way, so each thread eventually has a chance to run. And since the method takes a timeout, a well-designed application should never suffer from deadlocks. (A deadlock occurs when two threads are waiting for a resource that the other thread won't release until the operation completes.)

The ManualResetEvent and AutoResetEvent Classes

The last synchronization objects I'll illustrate in this chapter are a pair of classes that work in a similar way, ManualResetEvent and AutoResetEvent. They're most useful when you want to temporarily stop one or more threads until another thread says it's OK to proceed. You use these objects to wake up a thread much like an event handler can execute code in an idle thread, but don't be fooled by the "event" in their names: you don't use regular event handlers with these objects.

An instance of these classes can be in either a signaled or an unsignaled state. These terms don't really have any special meaning; just think of them as on or off states. You pass the initial state to their constructor, and any thread that can access the object can change the state to signaled (using the Set method) or unsignaled (using the Reset method). Other threads can use the WaitOne method to wait until the state becomes signaled or until the specified timeout expires.

The only difference between ManualResetEvent and AutoResetEvent objects is that the latter automatically reset themselves (that is, become unsignaled) immediately after a thread blocked on a WaitOne method has been restarted. In practice, AutoResetEvent objects wake up only one of the waiting threads when the object becomes signaled, whereas ManualResetEvent objects wake up all the waiting threads (and must be manually reset to unsignaled, as their name suggests).

Like many other synchronization objects, AutoResetEvent and ManualResetEvent objects are especially useful in producer-consumer situations. You might have a single producer thread that evaluates some data—or reads it from disk, a serial port, the Internet, and so on—and then calls the Set method on a shared synchronization object so that one or more consumer threads can be restarted and process the new data. You should use an AutoResetEvent object if only one consumer thread should process such data or a ManualResetEvent object if the same data should be processed by all consumers.

The following example shows how you can have multiple threads (the producer threads) performing file searches on different directories at the same time but a single thread (the consumer thread) collecting their results. This example uses a shared AutoResetEvent object to wake up the consumer thread when new filenames have been added to an ArrayList object, and it also uses the Increment and Decrement methods of the Interlocked class to manage the counter of running threads so that the main thread knows when there's no more data to consume.

```
' The shared AutoResetEvent object
Public are As New AutoResetEvent(False)
' The ArrayList where matching filenames should be added
Public filesAl As New ArrayList()
' The number of running threads
Public searchingThreads As Integer

Sub TestAutoResetEvent()
    ' Search the file in all the subdirectories of C:
    Dim dirname As String
    For Each dirname In System.IO.Directory.GetDirectories("C:\")
        Interlocked.Increment(searchingThreads)
        ' Create a new wrapper class, pointing to a subdirectory.
        Dim sf As New FileFinder(dirname, "*.zip")
        ' Create a new thread for that subdirectory only, and run it.
```

```
        Dim t As New Thread(AddressOf sf.StartSearch)
        t.Start()
    Next

    ' Remember how many results we have so far.
    Dim resCount As Integer = 0
    Do While searchingThreads > 0
        ' Wait until there are new results.
        are.WaitOne()

        ' Note that you should always use the SyncRoot property when using
        ' an ArrayList and other collection-like objects as lock objects.
        SyncLock filesAl.SyncRoot
            ' Display names of all new results.
            Dim i As Integer
            For i = resCount To filesAl.Count - 1
                Console.WriteLine(filesAl(i))
            Next
            ' Remember that you've displayed these filenames.
            resCount = filesAl.Count
        End SyncLock
    Loop
    Console.WriteLine("")
    Console.WriteLine("Found {0} files", resCount)
End Sub
```

Each producer thread runs inside a different FileFinder object, which must be able to access the public variables defined in the preceding code.

```
Class FileFinder
    Dim StartPath As String       ' The starting search path
    Dim SearchedPattern As String ' The search pattern (can contain wildcards)

    Sub New(ByVal path As String, ByVal search As String)
        Me.StartPath = path
        Me.SearchedPattern = search
    End Sub

    ' This is the method with which thread execution starts.
    Sub StartSearch()
        Search(Me.StartPath)
        ' Decrease the number of running threads before exiting.
        Interlocked.Decrement(searchingThreads)
        are.Set()
    End Sub
```

(continued)

```
    ' This recursive procedure does the actual job.
    Sub Search(ByVal path As String)
        Dim files() As String
        ' Get all the files that match the search pattern.
        files = System.IO.Directory.GetFiles(path, SearchedPattern)
        ' If there is at least one file, let the main thread know about it.
        If Not files Is Nothing Then
            ' Get a lock on the ArrayList that holds the result.
            SyncLock filesAl.SyncRoot
                ' Add all found files.
                filesAl.AddRange(files)
                ' Let the consumer thread know about the new filenames.
                are.Set()
            End SyncLock
        End If

        ' Repeat the search on all subdirectories.
        Dim dirname As String
        For Each dirname In System.IO.Directory.GetDirectories(path)
            Search(dirname)
        Next
    End Sub
End Class
```

The ThreadPool Class

As you know, creating too many threads can easily degrade your system's performance, especially when the additional threads spend most of their time in a sleeping state and are restarted periodically only to poll a resource or to update the display. You can often improve the performance of your code significantly by resorting to a thread pool, which permits the most efficient use of thread resources. Some objects in the System.Threading namespaces, such as Timers, transparently use the thread pool. (See the following sections for more details about timers.)

The thread pool is created the first time you invoke the ThreadPool.QueueUserWorkItem method or when a timer or a registered wait operation queues a callback operation. The pool has a default limit of 25 active threads; each thread uses the default stack size and runs at the default priority. The thread pool is available in all Windows versions.

You can borrow a thread from the pool by using the ThreadPool.QueueUserWorkItem method, which requires a WaitCallback delegate and an optional object that holds the data you want to pass to the thread. The WaitCallback delegate must point to a Sub procedure that receives one Object argument (whose value is either the optional object passed to the delegate or Nothing). The following code shows how you can use a large number of threads to call an instance method of a class:

```
Sub TestThreadPool()
    Dim i As Integer
    For i = 1 To 20
        ' Create a new object for the next lightweight task.
        Dim task As New LightweightTask()
        ' Pass additional information to that object.
        ' (Not used in this demo)
        task.SomeData = "other data"
        ' Run the task with a thread from the pool.
        ' (Pass the counter as an argument.)
        ThreadPool.QueueUserWorkItem( _
            New WaitCallback(AddressOf task.DoTheTask), i)
    Next

    ' Give all lightweight threads a chance to complete.
    Thread.Sleep(4000)
End Sub
```

This next block is the LightweightTask class, which contains the code that actually runs in the thread taken from the pool:

```
Class LightweightTask
    Public SomeData As String

    ' The method that contains the interesting code
    ' (Not really interesting in this example)
    Sub DoTheTask(ByVal state As Object)
        Console.WriteLine("Message from thread #{0}", state)
    End Sub
End Class
```

The preceding code stops the main thread for four seconds, which gives all the other threads a chance to complete. In a real application, you should use a more robust mechanism, based on events or shared counters.

The running thread can determine whether it has been taken from the thread pool by querying the Thread.CurrentThread.IsThreadPoolThread property. You can retrieve the highest number of threads in the pool by invoking the ThreadPool.GetMaxThreads shared method, and the number of the threads that are currently available by invoking the ThreadPool.GetAvailableThreads shared method.

You might sometimes be puzzled about whether you should create a thread yourself or borrow a thread from the pool. A good heuristic rule: use the Thread class if you want to run the associated task as soon as possible or if you perform a time-consuming task that doesn't run often. In the majority of cases, you should use the thread pool for more scalable server-side tasks.

For more information about the thread pool, see the sample application provided with the .NET Framework SDK, in the Program Files\Microsoft Visual Studio .Net\FrameworkSDK\Samples\Technologies\Threading\Pools\vb folder.

Timers

The .NET Framework offers three different types of timers, each one with its strengths and limitations. This section describes the System.Timers.Timer and System.Threading.Timer objects. A third type of timer is the System.Windows.Forms.Timer control, which I'll talk about in Chapter 17. If your application doesn't have a user interface, you should use one of the first two types of timers.

The System.Timers.Timer Class

The System.Timers.Timer class lets you schedule simple tasks, and you can define whether its Elapsed event fires only once or repeatedly. This class represents a server-based timer and has been designed to work efficiently in a multithreaded environment.

This Timer class has a very simple interface, with a handful of properties and methods whose purpose should be self-explanatory. The following example is a complete program that uses a Timer object to display the system time every second. (I'm sure you will promptly think of more interesting uses for this object.)

```
Dim WithEvents Timer As System.Timers.Timer
Dim eventCount As Integer

Sub TestServerTimer()
    ' Initialize the time to fire every second.
    ' (You can change it later through the Interval property.)
    Timer = New System.Timers.Timer(1000)
    ' True means it fires repeatedly; False means it fires only once.
    Timer.AutoReset = True
    ' Ensure that the timer is enabled. (Same as Start method)
    Timer.Enabled = True
```

```
    ' Pause here until five events fire.
    Do
        Console.WriteLine("Message from main thread")
        Thread.Sleep(100)
    Loop Until eventCount = 5

    ' Stop the timer (not really necessary in this example).
    Timer.Stop()                        ' Same as Timer.Enabled = False.
    ' Release all resources.
    Timer.Close()
End Sub

' The Elapsed event
Public Sub Timer_Elapsed(ByVal sender As Object, _
    ByVal e As System.Timers.ElapsedEventArgs) Handles Timer.Elapsed

    ' Display current system time in console window.
    Console.WriteLine("Event raised at {0}", e.SignalTime)
    ' Remember how many events fired so far.
    eventCount += 1
End Sub
```

If you set the AutoReset property to False, the Elapsed event fires only once; you must set it to True to have the timer behave like Visual Basic 6 timers. The default value for Interval is 100 milliseconds. Note that each time you set the Interval or the Enabled property, the count is restarted.

For the greatest accuracy, the Timer's Elapsed event can be served by any thread, so you shouldn't make any assumptions about the thread on which it runs. For example, you shouldn't access variables marked by the ThreadStatic attribute from inside this event. This implementation detail can have an undesirable consequence: in some cases, the Elapsed event can fire one more time *after* the main thread invokes the Stop method. If it's important that this doesn't happen, you should store the time that you issue the Stop command in a class-level or global variable and compare it with the SignalTime property of the ElapsedEventArgs object, which records the time that the event was raised.

The System.Threading.Timer Class

The Timer class in the System.Threading namespace offers yet another way to create a timer. For example, you can use the Timer class to schedule an action in the future, and this action can be performed with whatever frequency you decide, including once only. Unlike the System.Timers.Timer class, the System.Threading.Timer class works with callbacks instead of events.

The Timer's constructor takes four arguments:

- A TimerCallback delegate that points to the procedure that's called when the timer's timeout elapses. The callback procedure must be a Sub that takes a single Object as an argument.
- An object that will be passed to the callback procedure. This object can be an instance of a class that contains additional data for the timer event, or it can be just a string or an integer that lets the callback routine determine which action should be performed. (This might be necessary because one callback procedure can serve multiple timers.) Use Nothing if you don't need to pass additional data to the callback procedure.
- A TimeSpan value that specifies the *due time*—that is, when the timer must invoke the callback routine for the first time. This argument can be specified as a Long value, in which case the elapsed time is measured in ticks (1 second = 10 million ticks).
- A TimeSpan value that specifies the timer's period—that is, how often the timer must invoke the callback routine after the first time. If you pass Nothing, the callback routine is invoked only once. This argument can be specified as a Long value, in which case the elapsed time is measured in ticks.

The values that you pass to the Timer's constructor aren't exposed as properties. After the timer is running, you can change these values only by means of a Change method, which takes only two arguments, the due time and the period. The Timer object has no Stop method: you stop the timer by calling its Dispose method. The following example shows how to use the timer with a callback procedure:

```
Sub TestThreadingTimer()
    ' Get the first callback after one second.
    Dim dueTime As New TimeSpan(0, 0, 1)
    ' Get additional callbacks every half second.
    Dim period As New TimeSpan(0, 0, 0, 0, 500)
    ' Create the timer.
    Dim t As New System.Threading.Timer( _
        New TimerCallback(AddressOf TimerProc), Nothing, dueTime, period)
    ' Wait for five seconds in this demo.
    Thread.Sleep(5000)
    ' Destroy the timer.
    t.Dispose()
End Sub
```

```
' The callback procedure
Sub TimerProc(ByVal state As Object)
    ' Display current system time in console window.
    Console.WriteLine("Callback proc called at {0}", Date.Now)
End Sub
```

The callback procedure runs on a thread taken from the thread pool, so you should arbitrate access to variables and other resources used by the main thread by using one of the synchronization features that I described in this chapter.

> **Note** Although the System.Timers.Timer and System.Threading.Timer objects require different syntax and might have different internal implementations, they offer substantially the same features, so you might wonder why the .NET Framework duplicates the same functionality in two different classes. My honest answer is, I don't know, and I doubt whether anyone outside Microsoft does. So feel free to use the one you like most.

Asynchronous Operations

By now, you should be familiar with the Thread class and all the synchronization issues that you have to address when you're creating multithreading applications. At times, however, you'd like simply to execute a method call without blocking the main thread. For example, you might want to perform a long math calculation on a secondary thread while the application's main thread takes care of the user interface. In this case, what you really want to do is make a single *asynchronous method call*, which runs on another thread while the caller thread continues its normal execution. This programming model is so common that the .NET Framework offers special support for it so that *all methods can be called asynchronously*, without your having to specifically design the target method to support asynchronous calls.

This generic mechanism is based on asynchronous delegates. In addition, the framework offers more asynchronous support in many specific areas, including file I/O, XML Web services, and messages sent over Microsoft Message Queuing (MSMQ). Thanks to this unified approach, you need to learn the asynchronous programming pattern only once, and you can apply it to all these areas.

Asynchronous Delegates

I described how delegates work in Chapter 6, but I intentionally left out a few details that are related to asynchronous use of delegates. In this section, I'll show how you can use advanced features of delegates to call a method asynchronously. Let's start by defining a method that could take a significant amount of time to complete and therefore is a good candidate for an asynchronous call:

```
' This procedure scans a directory tree for a file.
' It takes a path and a file specification and returns an array of
' filenames; it returns the number of directories that have been
' parsed in the third argument.

' This variable keeps track of nesting level for each running thread.
<ThreadStatic()> Dim nestLevel As Integer

Function FindFiles(ByVal path As String, ByVal fileSpec As String, _
    ByRef parsedDirs As Integer) As ArrayList
    Dim subdir As String

    ' If this is the first call, reset number of parsed directories.
    If nestLevel = 0 Then parsedDirs = 0
    nestLevel += 1

    ' Prepare the result ArrayList.
    FindFiles = New ArrayList()

    ' Put everything in Try...End Try, to be sure that
    ' nestLevel is correctly decremented if an error occurs.
    Try
        ' Get all files in this directory that match the file spec.
        ' (This statement is valid because GetFiles returns a String array,
        '  which implements ICollection.)
        FindFiles.AddRange(System.IO.Directory.GetFiles(path, fileSpec))
        ' Remember that a directory has been parsed.
        parsedDirs += 1

        ' Scan subdirectories.
        For Each subdir In System.IO.Directory.GetDirectories(path)
            ' Add all the matching files in subdirectories.
            FindFiles.AddRange(FindFiles(subdir, fileSpec, parsedDirs))
        Next
```

```
    Finally
        nestLevel -= 1
    End Try
End Function
```

You call the FindFiles routine by passing a starting path, a file specification (which can be a filename or contain wildcards), and an Integer variable. On returning from the function, the Integer variable holds the number of directories that have been parsed, whereas the function itself returns an ArrayList object that contains the names of the files that match the specification:

```
Sub TestSynchronousCall()
    Dim parsedDirs As Integer

    ' Find *.txt files in the C:\DOCS directory tree.
    Dim files As ArrayList = FindFiles("c:\docs", "*.txt", parsedDirs)
    Dim file As String
    For Each file In files
        Console.WriteLine(file)
    Next
    ' Use the output argument.
    Console.WriteLine("  {0} directories have been parsed.", parsedDirs)
End Sub
```

Asynchronous Calls

The first step in implementing an asynchronous call to the FindFiles function is defining a delegate class that points to it:

```
Delegate Function FindFilesDelegate(ByVal path As String, _
    ByVal fileSpec As String, ByRef parsedDirs As Integer) As ArrayList
```

To call the FindFiles procedure asynchronously, you create a delegate that points to the routine and use the delegate's BeginInvoke method to call the routine as you would use the delegate's Invoke method. The BeginInvoke method—which has been created for you by the Visual Basic .NET compiler—takes the same arguments as the procedure the delegate points to, plus two additional arguments that I'll describe later. Unlike the Invoke method, though, BeginInvoke returns an IAsyncResult object. You can then query the IsCompleted read-only property of this IAsyncResult object to determine when the called routine has completed its execution. If this property returns True, you call the delegate's EndInvoke method to retrieve both the return value and the value of any argument that was passed by using ByRef (parsedDirs in the following procedure):

```
Sub TestAsynchronousCall()
    Dim parsedDirs As Integer

    ' Create a delegate that points to the target procedure.
    Dim findFilesDeleg As New FindFilesDelegate(AddressOf FindFiles)

    ' Start the asynchronous call; get an IAsyncResult object.
    Dim ar As IAsyncResult = findFilesDeleg.BeginInvoke( _
        "c:\docs", "*.txt", parsedDirs, Nothing, Nothing)

    ' Wait until the method completes its execution.
    Do Until ar.IsCompleted
        Console.WriteLine("The main thread is waiting for FindFiles results.")
        Thread.Sleep(500)
    Loop

    ' Now you can get the results.
    Dim files As ArrayList = findFilesDeleg.EndInvoke(parsedDirs, ar)

    Dim file As String
    For Each file In files
        Console.WriteLine(file)
    Next
    Console.WriteLine("  {0} directories have been parsed.", parsedDirs)
End Sub
```

Note that you should call EndInvoke only after IAsyncResult.IsCompleted returns True; otherwise, the EndInvoke method blocks the calling thread until the called procedure completes. (And you would lose the advantage of making an asynchronous call.)

The code in the preceding procedure polls the IsCompleted property to determine when the asynchronous call has completed. A less CPU-intensive means that achieves the same result uses the IAsyncResult.AsyncWaitHandle property, which returns a WaitHandle synchronization object. You can then use the WaitOne method of this object to make the main thread wait until the asynchronous call completes:

```
ar.AsyncWaitHandle.WaitOne()
```

The WaitHandle class exposes two other shared methods, WaitAny and WaitAll, which are especially useful when you run multiple asynchronous operations in parallel. Both methods take an array of WaitHandle objects: the Wait-

Any method blocks the calling thread until any of the asynchronous operations complete, whereas the WaitAll method blocks the calling thread until all the asynchronous operations complete. Unfortunately, you can't call these two methods from a thread running in a single-thread apartment (STA), thus you must create a separate thread using the Thread class, and run the asynchronous operations from this new thread (unless you're already running in a thread outside an STA). See the sample code on the companion CD for an example of this technique.

Asynchronous Callback Procedures

As I've already explained, the BeginInvoke method takes all the arguments in the original method's signature, plus two additional arguments. The second-to-last argument is a delegate pointing to a callback procedure that's called when the asynchronous method completes its execution. This callback procedure offers a viable alternative to your making the main thread use the IsCompleted or AsyncWaitHandle property of the IAsyncResult object to determine when it's safe to gather the return value and any ByRef arguments.

The callback procedure must follow the syntax of the AsyncCallback delegate (defined in the System namespace), which defines a Sub procedure that takes an IAsyncResult object as its only argument. The code inside the callback procedure should call the delegate's EndInvoke method to retrieve the return value and the value of any ByRef arguments. Here's a possible implementation of the callback procedure for the example seen previously:

```
Sub MethodCompleted(ByVal ar As IAsyncResult)
    Dim parsedDirs As Integer
    Dim files As ArrayList = findFilesDeleg.EndInvoke(parsedDirs, ar)
    ' Display found files.
    ' ...(Omitted, same as in TestAsynchronousCall routine)...
End Sub
```

This approach poses two minor problems. First, the callback routine doesn't have any way to know why it has been called, so it's difficult to reuse the same callback routine for multiple asynchronous calls. Second, the delegate variable (findFilesDeleg in this particular example) must be visible to both the routine that makes the asynchronous call and the callback routine; this isn't a serious problem when both routines belong to the same class or module (you can just declare it as a private class-level variable), but it makes the approach rather clumsy when the callback routine is in another class, possibly located in a different assembly.

Both problems can be solved if you take advantage of the last argument of the BeginInvoke method. This argument can be any object, so you can pass a number or a string that helps the callback routine understand which asynchronous method has just completed. More interestingly, you can define a class that holds both an identification string and the original delegate object that you used to make the asynchronous call. This approach helps you solve the second problem as well. For example, you can define a simple class that holds both pieces of information:

```
Class Cookie
    Public Id As String
    Public AsyncDelegate As [Delegate]

    Sub New(ByVal id As String, ByVal asyncDelegate As [Delegate])
        Me.Id = id
        Me.AsyncDelegate = asyncDelegate
    End Sub
End Class
```

Now you can rewrite our example to use a callback procedure to determine when the asynchronous method call has completed:

```
Sub TestAsynchronousCallback()
    Dim parsedDirs As Integer

    ' Create a delegate that points to the target procedure.
    Dim findFilesDeleg As New FindFilesDelegate(AddressOf FindFiles)

    ' Create a cookie object, and initialize it with an ID and the delegate.
    Dim cookieObj As New Cookie("TXT files in C:\DOCS", findFilesDeleg)

    ' Start the async call, pass a delegate to the MethodCompleted proc,
    ' and get an IAsyncResult object.
    Dim ar As IAsyncResult
    ar = findFilesDeleg.BeginInvoke("c:\docs", "*.txt", parsedDirs, _
        New AsyncCallback(AddressOf MethodCompleted), cookieObj)

    ' ...(Perform other operations on the main thread)...
    ⋮
End Sub

' This is the callback method.

Sub MethodCompleted(ByVal ar As IAsyncResult)
    ' Get the cookie, and display its ID (just to show it's the right object).
    Dim cookieObj As Cookie = DirectCast(ar.AsyncState, Cookie)
```

```
    Console.WriteLine("Cookie ID = {0}", cookieObj.Id)
    Console.WriteLine("")

    ' Get a reference to the original delegate.
    Dim deleg As FindFilesDelegate = _
        DirectCast(cookieObj.AsyncDelegate, FindFilesDelegate)
    ' Call the EndInvoke method, and get the return value.
    Dim parsedDirs As Integer
    Dim files As ArrayList = deleg.EndInvoke(parsedDirs, ar)

    ' Display found files.
    Dim file As String
    For Each file In files
        Console.WriteLine(file)
    Next
    Console.WriteLine("  {0} directories have been parsed.", parsedDirs)
End Sub
```

If you don't need to pass an ID value to the callback routine, you can simplify the code even further, by omitting the Cookie class and by passing the asynchronous delegate object to the last argument of its own BeginInvoke method:

```
ar = findFilesDeleg.BeginInvoke("c:\docs", "*.txt", parsedDirs, _
    New AsyncCallback(AddressOf MethodCompleted), findFilesDeleg)
```

In this case, the code inside the MethodCompleted procedure can extract a reference to the delegate as follows:

```
Dim deleg As FindFilesDelegate = DirectCast(ar.AsyncState, FindFilesDelegate)
```

More on Asynchronous Method Invocation

The only relevant detail I haven't covered yet is how the asynchronous architecture deals with exceptions. It turns out that both the BeginInvoke and EndInvoke methods can throw an exception.

If BeginInvoke throws an exception, you know that the asynchronous call hasn't been queued and you shouldn't call the EndInvoke method. These exceptions might be thrown by the .NET asynchronous infrastructure—for example, when the target of the asynchronous call is a remote object that can't be reached.

EndInvoke can throw an exception too; this happens either when the asynchronous method throws an exception or when the .NET asynchronous infrastructure throws an exception—for example, when the remote object can't be reached any longer.

I don't cover remote objects in this book, so let's focus on regular exceptions that the called method throws and that you receive when attempting an EndInvoke method. The obvious suggestion is that you should bracket EndInvoke calls inside a Try…End Try block, as you would do for any regular method call that can throw an exception.

Sometimes, however, you don't really care whether the called method actually throws an exception. This might be the case, for example, if the procedure doesn't return a value and doesn't take ByRef arguments. You can inform the .NET runtime that you aren't interested in the outcome of the method, including any exceptions it might throw, by marking the method with the System.Runtime.Remoting.Messaging.OneWay attribute:

```
<System.Runtime.Remoting.Messaging.OneWay()> _
Sub MethodThatMayThrow(ByVal anArgument As Object)
    ⋮
End Sub
```

(You get no error if this attribute is applied to a method that includes a ByRef argument or a return value, but such argument or return value isn't returned to the calling application.) Here are a few more tips about asynchronous calls:

- The effect of calling EndInvoke twice on the same IAsyncResult object is indefinite, so you should avoid performing this operation.
- Even if BeginInvoke takes a ByRef argument, the .NET asynchronous infrastructure doesn't record the address of this argument anywhere, and therefore, it can't automatically update the variable when the method completes. The only way to retrieve the value of an output argument is by passing it to the EndInvoke method.
- If the called method takes a reference to an object (passed with either ByVal or ByRef), it can assign new values to that object's properties. The caller can see those new values even before the asynchronous method completes. If both the caller and the called method access the same object, however, you might want to provide some form of synchronization of its property procedures.
- The .NET asynchronous infrastructure provides no generic means to cancel an asynchronous method once the BeginInvoke method has been called because in many cases there's no reliable way to cancel a running operation. In general, it's up to the class's author to implement a method that cancels an asynchronous method call.

Asynchronous File Operations

The great thing about asynchronous support in .NET is that once you become familiar with its programming pattern, you can apply it to several classes that expose asynchronous operations natively—that is, without the need of an explicit asynchronous delegate to the method. In this section, I'll show you how to use the BeginRead, EndRead, BeginWrite, and EndWrite methods of the Stream class to perform asynchronous file I/O. All the stream-based classes, including FileStream, inherit these methods.

The BeginWrite method takes a Byte array that contains the data to be written to the stream, the index of the first element to write, and the number of bytes to write: these are the same arguments that the regular, synchronous Write method accepts. You also pass an AsyncCallback delegate and a state object, as you do with all the asynchronous method invocations that you've seen in earlier sections. The callback routine must conclude the write operation by invoking the EndWrite method and then close the stream.

The BeginRead method has the same argument signature as BeginWrite, with the first three values defining the location at which data read from the stream will be stored. The callback routine must conclude the asynchronous read operation by invoking an EndRead method and then close the stream. The EndRead method returns the total number of bytes read; a 0 value means that there were no more bytes to read.

The following code shows an example of asynchronous write and read operations on the same file. A single callback routine serves both the write and the read operation: the type of operation is passed as a string in the last argument to BeginWrite and BeginRead. To keep the code simple, both the caller routine and the callback routine share the variable pointing to the Byte array buffer and the FileStream object. In a real-world application, you might want to pack this data into an object and pass it as the last argument to BeginWrite and BeginRead:

```
' The file being read from or written to
Const FileName As String = "C:\TESTDATA.TMP"
' The FileStream object used for both reading and writing
Dim fs As System.IO.FileStream
' The buffer for file I/O
Dim buffer() As Byte

' This procedure tests asynchronous file read.

Sub TestAsyncFileOperations()
    Dim i As Integer
    Dim ar As IAsyncResult
```

(continued)

```
        ' Fill the buffer with 20 KB of random data.
        ReDim buffer(1048575)
        For i = 0 To UBound(buffer)
            buffer(i) = CByte(i Mod 256)
        Next

        ' Create the target file in asynchronous mode (open in asynchronous mode).
        fs = New System.IO.FileStream(FileName, IO.FileMode.Create, _
            IO.FileAccess.Write, IO.FileShare.None, 65536, True)
        ' Start the async write operation.
        Console.WriteLine("Starting the async write operation")
        ar = fs.BeginWrite(buffer, 0, UBound(buffer) + 1, _
            AddressOf AsyncFileCallback, "write")

        ' Wait a few seconds until the operation completes.
        Thread.Sleep(4000)

        ' Now read the file back.
        fs = New System.IO.FileStream(FileName, IO.FileMode.Open, _
            IO.FileAccess.Read, IO.FileShare.None, 65536, True)
        ' Size the receiving buffer.
        ReDim buffer(CInt(fs.Length) - 1)
        ' Start the async read operation.
        Console.WriteLine("Starting the async read operation")
        ar = fs.BeginRead(buffer, 0, UBound(buffer) + 1, _
            AddressOf AsyncFileCallback, "read")
    End Sub

    ' This is the callback procedure for both async read and write.

    Sub AsyncFileCallback(ByVal ar As IAsyncResult)
        ' Get the state object (the "write" or "read" string).
        Dim opName As String = ar.AsyncState.ToString

        ' The behavior is quite different in the two cases.
        Select Case opName
            Case "write"
                Console.WriteLine("Async write operation completed")
                ' Complete the write, and close the stream.
                fs.EndWrite(ar)
                fs.Close()
            Case "read"
                Console.WriteLine("Async read operation completed")
                ' Complete the read, and close the stream.
                Dim bytes As Integer = fs.EndRead(ar)
                Console.WriteLine("Read {0} bytes", bytes)
                fs.Close()
        End Select
    End Sub
```

You get the best benefits from asynchronous file I/O if you also open the FileStream for asynchronous operations by passing True in the last argument of the object's constructor:

```
fs = New FileStream(path, mode, access, share, bufferSize, useAsync)
```

When you open a FileStream in this way, synchronous operations are slowed down, but asynchronous operations are completed faster. Keep in mind that read and write operations of less then 64 KB are usually performed synchronously anyway, even if you use BeginWrite or BeginRead, and that the useAsync argument might be ignored on Windows platforms that don't support asynchronous file operations. You can test whether the FileStream was actually opened for asynchronous operation by testing its IsAsync property.

This concludes my explanation of multithreading. As you know by now, creating multithreaded applications isn't simple, and you have to face and solve many issues. Even if you decide not to create additional threads, you have to account for matters such as synchronization and access to shared variables if your objects expose a Finalize method that, as you've learned, can run on virtually any thread. Let's put threads aside and focus on .NET assemblies, the topic of the next chapter.

Front
Top
Left
Back

14

Assemblies and AppDomains

You deploy Windows .NET applications in the form of *assemblies*, which in turn include *executables* and *components*. Assemblies correspond to the time-honored concept of standard EXE programs and their ancillary DLLs, but you'll soon discover that things are different in the .NET world. Not more complex, just different.

Modules

When you compile your Visual Basic .NET application—or any application written in a .NET language, for that matter—what you get is a *managed module*. It can be an EXE or a DLL, depending on whether you were creating a stand-alone application or a .NET component. A managed module can be self-sufficient or depend on other modules for its execution: a group of one or more related modules makes up an *assembly*.

A managed module consists of the following four parts:

- **Windows PE file header** This is the standard Windows Portable Executable (PE) header that all Windows applications have.
- **.NET Framework file header** This portion contains information about the entry point for the current executable and the run-time version that this module was compiled against, plus pointers to other sections, such as the module's metadata. (See next point.)

- **Metadata** This portion describes the types (that is, the Module, Class, Enum, Interface, and Structure blocks) that the particular managed module contains, as well as the types defined in other modules to which this module refers.
- **Microsoft Intermediate Language (MSIL, or simply IL) code** This is the managed code produced by the compiler.

I'll now describe the parts of a managed module in greater detail.

Headers

All Windows executable files must have a PE header, and managed modules are no exception. One of the key fields in a PE header is the code location to jump to when the operating system loads the application. A managed module doesn't really contain directly executable assembly code. Rather, it contains MSIL code that must be transformed into native instructions that are understood by the target CPU. For this reason, the entry point for all the managed modules is a JMP instruction into the .NET runtime, more precisely to the _CorExeMain entry point in the MsCorEE.dll file (or the _CorDllMain entry point in the case of a DLL), which is therefore loaded if it isn't already in memory. This routine receives the location of MSIL code and can immediately compile and then execute it on the fly, using the appropriate Just-In-Time (JIT) compiler.

The mechanism has been slightly improved in Microsoft Windows XP and Windows .NET Servers; these newer versions understand when they're about to run a managed module, so they can load the .NET runtime directly and start the JIT compilation step. While this innovation makes the overall design cleaner, it doesn't speed up the startup phase noticeably.

Metadata

Broadly speaking, you can think of metadata as the .NET counterpart of type libraries in the COM world, in that metadata describes all the public classes, methods, and interfaces that an executable exposes to the outside world. Beyond this superficial comparison, however, the parallel is misleading because .NET metadata is much more complete than COM type libraries. For one thing, metadata describes the types that the current module *references*, not just the types it *defines* internally; it also includes information about attributes associated with modules, types, and individual methods. In a difference from type libraries, metadata is always embedded in the file of the module it refers to, and there's no way to deliver a module without its metadata or metadata without its module.

While you can do COM programming without using type libraries—as expert C++ developers can attest—metadata is absolutely essential to .NET programming, and that's the reason you can't separate a module from its metadata. The runtime uses metadata to ensure that a caller is passing the right number and type of arguments to a routine, which makes managed code inherently safer and more robust than COM-based code. Metadata is also necessary to marshal objects between applications or even different computers, as well as to save objects' state to a file or in a database field.

Managed code can read metadata by means of a set of .NET classes defined in the System.Reflection namespace. For example, you can use reflection classes to write a utility that lists all the classes in a module and all the methods in a class, including their argument signatures and return types. Something similar is possible even in the COM world if you have a component's type library, but it isn't simple. Doing this with reflection techniques is a breeze, as you'll see in Chapter 15.

Microsoft Intermediate Language (MSIL)

All the compilers for .NET languages—including C# and Visual Basic .NET—produce code known as Microsoft Intermediate Language (MSIL, or just IL). As you saw in Chapter 1, IL has two major benefits:

- It provides an intermediate assembly language that can be easily translated to the opcode set of most modern CPUs. For example, the MSIL instruction set includes an ldfld opcode that pushes a field's value onto the stack and an add opcode that sums two operands on the stack. A JIT compiler can easily and quickly convert these IL opcodes to actual CPU opcodes because in many cases there is a one-to-one correspondence between the two instruction sets.

- It provides all the means to check that a piece of code can't harm other pieces of code running in the same address space, either intentionally or accidentally. This makes managed code more robust and, above all, makes it possible for two components (or even full-fledged applications) to share the same address space without any risk. Having two distinct but related applications share the same address space—and therefore the same Windows process—can significantly improve overall performance because the communication is in-process and data doesn't need to be marshaled from one address space to the other.

The simplest way to see a sample of MSIL is to run the ILDASM (IL Disassembler) tool that comes with the .NET SDK. (The standard setup program stores it in the \Program Files\Microsoft Visual Studio .NET\FrameworkSDK\Bin directory.) To see this tool in action, add the following class to a Visual Basic project, and compile it to an EXE or a DLL:

```
Class Operation
    Public n1 As Double
    Public n2 As Double
    Function Add() As Double
        Return n1 + n2
    End Function
End Class
```

Run ILDASM, and drag the EXE file you have created from Windows Explorer to the ILDASM main window so that ILDASM can display the structure of the executable, in all its classes and methods. (See Figure 14-1.) Next ensure that the Show Source Lines command in the View menu is checked, and double-click the icon for the corresponding Add method. The source code for that method and the corresponding MSIL code will appear in a new window. (See Figure 14-2.)

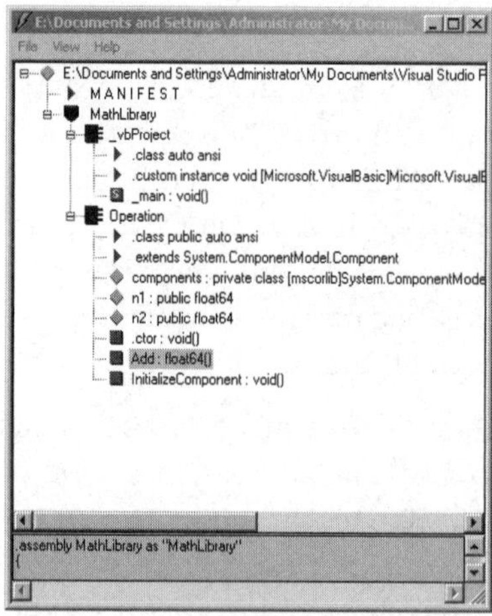

Figure 14-1. The ILDASM tool main window shows all the types and the methods defined in a .NET component.

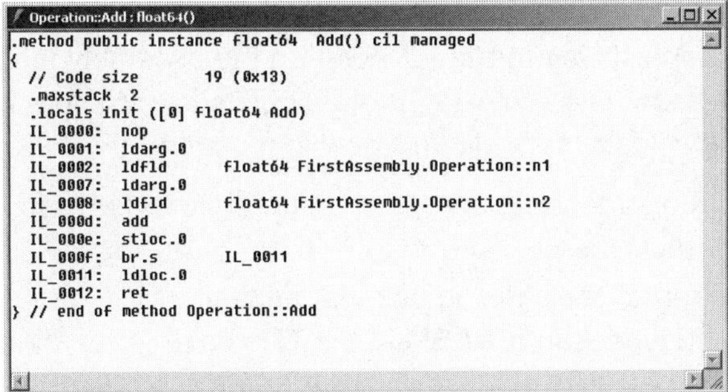

Operation::Add : float64()
.method public instance float64 Add() cil managed
{
// Code size 19 (0x13)
.maxstack 2
.locals init ([0] float64 Add)
IL_0000: nop
IL_0001: ldarg.0
IL_0002: ldfld float64 FirstAssembly.Operation::n1
IL_0007: ldarg.0
IL_0008: ldfld float64 FirstAssembly.Operation::n2
IL_000d: add
IL_000e: stloc.0
IL_000f: br.s IL_0011
IL_0011: ldloc.0
IL_0012: ret
} // end of method Operation::Add

Figure 14-2. Double-clicking the Add method in ILDASM opens this window, which shows the MSIL source code.

ILDASM shows even the code for methods that you haven't written explicitly and that the Visual Basic compiler adds on your behalf, such as the ctor:void method, which corresponds to the parameterless default constructor method that all classes implicitly have if you don't specify a custom constructor in code. Figure 14-3 shows the page of the ILDASM Help file that explains the meaning of each symbol that can appear in the main window. You can include or exclude specific items by checking or unchecking the corresponding command on the View menu.

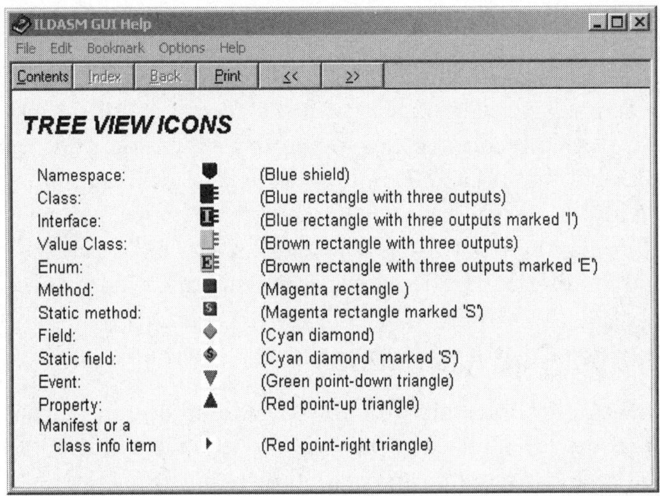

Figure 14-3. The Help page that explains the meaning of all the symbols used in ILDASM's tree-view pane.

Note The simplest way to run ILDASM on the assembly that you're working with from inside Visual Studio .NET is by adding a custom command to the Tools menu. Here's how to proceed:

1. On the Tools menu, choose the External Tools command from the Tools menu.
2. In the External Tools dialog box that appears, click the Add button and type **Run ILDASM** in the Title box.
3. Type the complete path of Ildasm.exe in the Command box; in a default installation, this is C:\Program Files\Microsoft Visual Studio .NET\FrameworkSDK\Bin\ILDASM.exe.
4. Type **$(TargetPath)** in the Arguments box, select the Use Output Window check box, and then click OK to close the dialog box.

Now you can compile an executable and then load it into ILDASM by choosing Run ILDASM on the Tools menu.

Assemblies

.NET compilers produce modules, but the .NET runtime itself works with assemblies. The assembly has no analogous concept in the pre-.NET programming world, so it might be confusing at first. From a physical point of view, an *assembly* is just a collection of one or more executable and nonexecutable modules. (Examples of nonexecutable modules are resource, image, and html files.) From a logical perspective, an assembly is the smallest unit of reuse, versioning, and deployment for .NET applications. For example, you can't assign different version numbers to the various files that make up an assembly.

Single-File and Multiple-File Assemblies

Your first .NET applications will probably be assemblies that consist of a single module. This is the case, for example, when you have a single module and no resource files. In this case, you can create the assembly using the .NET compiler of choice, such as the Visual Basic command-line compiler (vbc.exe) and, of course, Visual Studio .NET. If you're gathering multiple files in one assembly, you must use different tools that come with the .NET Framework SDK, such as AL (the Assembly Generation tool, also known as Assembly Linker).

Even if the assembly consists of multiple files, you can think of it as a single, *logical* DLL or EXE executable. The advantage of having it split into multiple files becomes apparent when you have some classes or resources that are infrequently used: keeping them in a separate file means that a DLL is loaded in memory only if strictly necessary. Another occasion for using multiple-file assemblies is when you're putting together modules created from different languages.

When you're deciding which files should go in the same assembly, consider the following points:

- **Code reuse** The assembly is the smallest unit of reuse, so you should keep together modules that contain types that are normally used together.
- **Versioning** The assembly is also the smallest unit of versioning, and all the modules in an assembly have the same versioning information.
- **Security** The types in an assembly have the same security permissions, so you might be forced to split a group of types into different assemblies if they require different permission settings.
- **Scoping** The assembly scope (enforced by the Friend keyword) lets you define which types are visible from outside the module in which they're defined, but not from the outside world.

Depending on how they're created, the .NET runtime supports two types of assemblies: static and dynamic. Most .NET compilers (including C# and Visual Basic) produce static assemblies, which are by far the most common type of assemblies; they correspond to one or more physical files, as we'll see in a moment. Dynamic assemblies are created on the fly in RAM and don't correspond to any physical files (even though you might save a dynamic assembly to disk if necessary). Dynamic assemblies are typically created by script code, but you can create them in any .NET language, thanks to the classes in the System.Reflection.Emit namespace.

In the remainder of this chapter, I'll discuss static assemblies exclusively.

The Manifest

Even though an assembly can include multiple files, not all the files have equal importance. One of the files in the assembly is special in that its metadata section contains the assembly's *manifest*. The manifest holds information about the assembly's name, version, and culture and the public key of the company that produced it, as well as the list of operating systems and CPUs that the assembly supports. The manifest also contains a collection of tables with the list of the files that make up the assembly, the list of all the types that the modules in the assembly expose, and the list of the resources embedded in the assembly's files.

The manifest provides the runtime with a single place in which to check the types and resources a given assembly exposes, without having to search the individual files in the assembly. However, some information is available only in the metadata section of the file that actually exposes the type or the resource—for example, the name and signature of individual methods. The manifest does *not* include information about types exposed by the file that holds the manifest itself because this data is already available in that file's metadata section: this omission serves as an optimization technique to reduce the manifest's size.

The manifest can also host custom assembly attributes, which are added by the developer for informational purposes and are never used by the runtime. These attributes include the assembly's title (a friendly name that can include spaces), a description, configuration data, and product information, such as trademark, copyright, company name, and informational version.

In theory, you can create a Windows PE file that holds the manifest and no executable code, but in practice such an arrangement is never convenient. In fact, the manifest defines the entry point for the assembly's code—that is, the method of a given class that must execute when the assembly is started. If the manifest contains only metadata, the runtime must load a second file to actually start the execution, which adds unnecessary overhead.

> **Note** The .NET Framework comes with an intriguing sample utility named ADepends, which displays the list of all the assemblies referenced by a given assembly in a TreeView control, as well as the assemblies referenced by the referenced assemblies, and so on in a recursive fashion. You can find the C# source code for this utility in the C:\Program Files\Microsoft Visual Studio .NET\FrameworkSDK\Tool Developers Guide\Samples\adepends directory; before you can use ADepends, you must build it, using the directions found in the companion Readme.htm file in the same directory.

Private and Shared Assemblies

The .NET Framework supports two different types of assemblies: private and shared.

A private assembly can be stored only in the main application's directory (or one of its subdirectories) and therefore can be used only by that application or another application installed in the same directory. Private assemblies are simpler to build and administer than shared assemblies; they support *XCOPY deployment*, a fancy term that means that you can install a complete application by simply copying all its files and directories to the target computer's hard disk without having to register anything. (Of course, you still have to create shortcuts from the Start menu and other, similar amenities, but the concept should be clear.) In most circumstances, private assemblies are the best choice to make, even though you might end up with multiple identical copies of the same assembly in different directories. Private assemblies can help put an end to so-called DLL Hell, and any developer or system administrator should be glad to trade some inexpensive disk space for more robust code.

A shared assembly is usually installed in a well-defined location of the hard disk, under the \Windows\Assembly directory. This location is known as the global assembly cache (GAC). The .NET Framework installs a special shell extension (contained in shfusion.dll) that lets you browse this directory with Windows Explorer and display information about all the shared assemblies installed on the computer, as you can see in Figure 14-4, including their version and culture. You can also browse the public key token, which is a sort of reduced public key of the software company that published the assembly. The public key token is a 64-bit hash value derived from the publisher's public key (which is 1024 bits long, or 128 bytes); it isn't guaranteed to be universally unique like the public key, but it can be considered unique for most practical purposes.

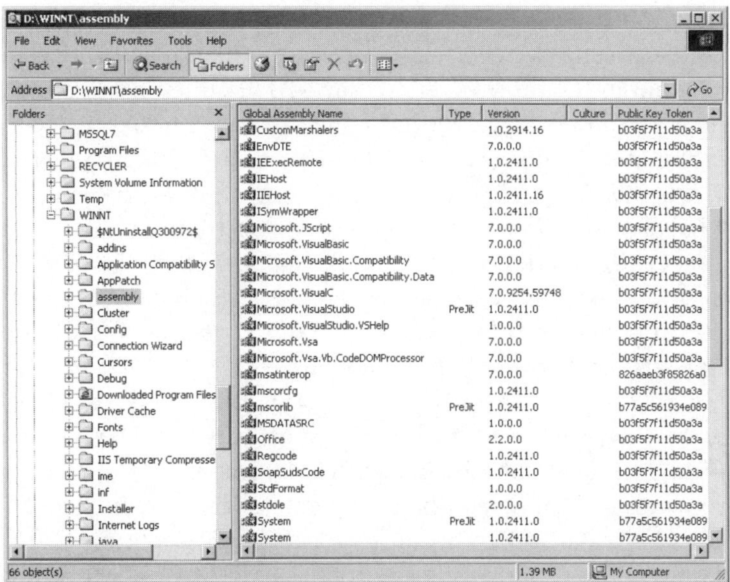

Figure 14-4. The global assembly cache viewer.

You can also display more extensive version information by right-clicking an item and clicking Properties on the shortcut menu, an action that brings up the Properties dialog box for that shared assembly. (See Figure 14-5.)

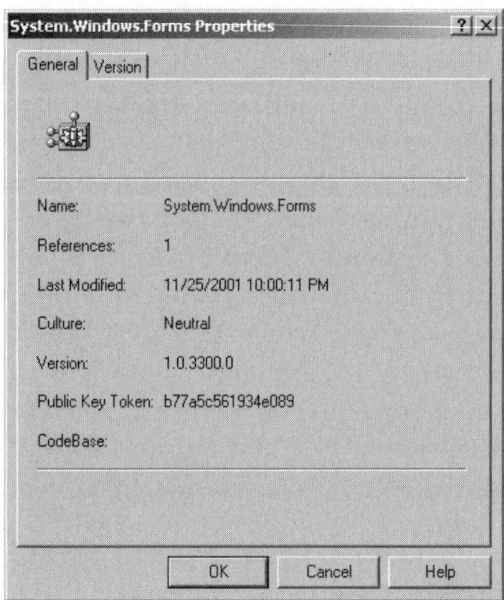

Figure 14-5. The Properties dialog box for the System.Windows.Forms shared assembly.

The codebase property is the location from which the assembly was copied. For the assemblies that make up the framework, this value points to a directory under \Windows\Microsoft.NET\Framework\v*x.y.zzzz* (where *x.y.zzzz* is the framework's version number—for example, 1.0.3705). Note that several assemblies belonging to the framework have been pre-JIT-compiled, so they start up faster.

What you see in Windows Explorer doesn't match the actual physical structure of the \Windows\Assembly directory. In fact, the GAC contains several directories—one for each shared assembly; each directory in turn contains individual subdirectories for each version of the assembly. This directory structure allows you to store different versions of the same assembly without any filename conflicts. You can bypass the Windows shell extension and freely explore the real structure of the GAC by opening an MS-DOS command prompt window and navigating to the C:\WinNT\Assembly\GAC directory.

You can add and delete shared assemblies only if you have administrative rights on the system, which obviously makes .NET applications that work with shared assemblies inherently more robust than those that work with private assemblies. You can add or remove assemblies to or from the GAC using a utility named GACUTIL, and you can delete an existing shared assembly also by right-clicking it and clicking Delete on the shortcut menu. (Read the section "The Global Assembly Cache Utility [GACUTIL]" later in this chapter for more about this utility.)

There are several key differences between a private and a shared assembly:

- A shared assembly supports version information, and the GAC can keep different versions of the same assembly without conflict so that each application can continue to work with the version it was compiled against (unless the administrator opts for a different binding policy, a topic that I take up later in this chapter). Private assemblies can be versioned, but version information is for your reference only, and the runtime doesn't use it. A private assembly is supposed to be deployed with the application itself, so the runtime doesn't enforce any special versioning policy.
- A shared assembly in the GAC makes your applications more robust in two ways: First, when the assembly is added to the cache, an integrity check is performed over all the files in the assembly to ensure that they haven't been altered. Second, only the system administrator can delete an assembly from the GAC.
- A shared assembly in the GAC is more efficient than a private assembly because the runtime can locate it faster and it doesn't need to be verified. Moreover, if multiple applications reference the same shared assembly, the runtime loads only one instance in memory in most circumstances (which saves resources and improves load time even more).
- Two (or more) different versions of a shared assembly can run in the same process. For example, an application might use version 1.0 of the AAA assembly and a BBB assembly that uses version 1.1 of the AAA assembly. This important feature is called *side-by-side execution*, and it ensures that you can't have any compatibility problem when you mix components together.
- A shared assembly can be signed with a public key. The signing mechanism uses a public key encryption schema, which guarantees that a particular assembly was created by a given manufacturer and that no one tampered with it.

Note that shared assemblies are usually stored in the GAC, but this isn't a strict requirement. For example, you might deploy a shared assembly in a known directory on the hard disk, where two or more applications from your company can find it. However, the advantages in the preceding list apply only to shared assemblies in the GAC. (Shared assemblies deployed in other directories do support side-by-side execution and public key signing, though.)

As a rule, you write code for private and shared assemblies in the same way because you build a shared assembly by adding an attribute to your code. However, the main goal in building shared assemblies is to share them among different applications, so you must take this constraint into account. For example, a shared assembly shouldn't create temporary files with fixed names and paths because calls from different clients might overwrite such files. Moreover, the .NET Framework supports side-by-side execution of shared assemblies in the same process (not just the same machine), so a shared assembly shouldn't depend on processwide resources.

Strong Names

The .NET runtime looks for private assemblies only inside the caller application's directory tree, so the developer is in charge of avoiding naming conflicts for the private assemblies the application references. On the other hand, shared assemblies are typically deployed in the GAC, so it's vital for the runtime to distinguish shared assemblies that have the same name but that come from different publishers.

The .NET Framework ensures that a shared assembly's name is unique at the system level by assigning the assembly a *strong name*. You can think of a strong name as the combination of a textual name, a version number, a culture, and a public key. The security mechanism is based on a public key encryption method, but you don't have to be a cryptography wizard to create assemblies with strong names.

You generate strong name assemblies in a two-step process: first you run the Strong Name (SN) command-line utility to create an .snk file that contains a random-generated public and private key pair; second you tell the compiler that the public key in that .snk file must be burned into the executable file.

You generate a random public and private key pair by using the –k option of the SN utility, which is located in the \Program Files\Microsoft Visual Studio .NET\FrameworkSDK\Bin directory:

```
sn -k mykey.snk
```

This command creates the mykey.snk file, which contains the two keys. Store this file in a safe place (and make copies of it if necessary) because from now on you should use it to sign all the shared assemblies produced by you or your company.

After creating an .snk file, you can choose from several ways to produce an assembly with a strong name. If you're compiling from the command prompt, you use the VBC program with the /keyfile option for single-file assemblies, or you use the Assembly Linker utility (AL) with the /keyfile option for assemblies made of multiple files. For example, the following command compiles the Class1.vb and Module1.vb source files into an assembly named myasm.dll and signs the assembly with the key found in the mykey.snk file we produced previously:

```
vbc class1.vb module1.vb /out:myasm.dll /keyfile:mykey.snk
```

This command uses a hash algorithm to produce a signature of the assembly and stores the signature in a reserved portion of the PE file together with the publisher's public key. This reserved portion of the assembly isn't included in the hash. (See the section about the Assembly Linker utility later in this chapter to learn how you can sign multiple-file assemblies.)

Another method for creating a signed assembly—which, by the way, is the only one that you can use from inside Visual Studio .NET and therefore the one that is going to be used most frequently—is that of inserting an AssemblyKeyFile attribute in the application's source code (typically in the AssemblyInfo.vb file):

```
<Assembly: AssemblyKeyFile("c:\myapp\mykey.snk")>
```

The filename should be an absolute path so that it can reference the only .snk file that you use for all the strong assemblies you produce. This attribute is ignored if you compile from the command line to create a module that you later combine into a multimodule assembly.

Any other assembly that references the shared assembly you've just signed will include the shared assembly's public key in the reference section of its manifest. When the caller assembly invokes one of the types in the shared assembly, the runtime compares the public key token in the caller's manifest with the public key token of the shared assembly so that the caller can be completely sure that the shared assembly hasn't been tampered with. (The runtime uses this 8-byte token instead of the entire public key to save space in the caller assembly's manifest.)

Remember that this mechanism can ensure that the shared assembly hasn't been modified, but it doesn't ensure that the shared assembly actually comes from a specific software manufacturer. This latter issue is solved through full Authenticode signatures that can be applied to shared assemblies. These Authenticode signatures add a certificate that establishes trust. You can apply this Authenticode signature to an existing assembly by running the Signcode.exe utility.

Because strong names are a combination of a text name and a public key, they guarantee name uniqueness. If two companies accidentally use the same name for their (distinct) assemblies, their public keys are different and therefore the strong names are different as well. Name uniqueness extends to all versions of the same assembly, and the runtime ensures that—when it's opting for a more recent version of an assembly requested by a managed class—only assemblies coming from the same software company will be taken into account.

Partial Signing and Key Containers

As I suggested in the preceding section, you should store the private key in a safe place. In large software shops, only a few trusted individuals can access the private key, for obvious reasons. This poses a problem for programmers working on an assembly: they must be able to sign the assembly in order to assign it a strong name during the development stage (which is necessary to deploy the assembly in the GAC), but they might not have access to the private key. The solution to the problem is *partial* or *delayed signing*, a process that lets you develop a shared assembly without a private key. Here's how it works.

First you extract the company's public key into a file, using the –p option of the SN utility, for example:

```
sn -p mykey.snk public.key
```

Next you pass the public.key filename to the tool you use to create the assembly. If you're signing the assembly using the VBC or the AL utility, you pass this file using its /keyfile option (as when you're working with a regular shared assembly), but you also add a /delaysign+ option to inform the utility that you're going to sign the assembly with the actual private and public key pair later:

```
vbc class1.vb module1.vb /out:myasm.dll
    /keyfile:public.key /delaysign+
```

When working in Visual Studio. NET, you use the AssemblyKeyFile and AssemblyDelaySign attributes in source code:

```
<Assembly: AssemblyKeyFile("public.key")>
<Assembly: AssemblyDelaySign(True)>
```

Regardless of the method you used, the public key is stored in the assembly manifest, and all the other assemblies that reference this one can correctly enter this public key in their manifests.

In the last step in delayed signing, you "sign" the assembly with the SN tool, but using the –Vr option. This step forces the runtime to skip verification and to accept the assembly, even if it doesn't have a valid signature yet:

```
SN -Vr myasm.dll
```

When the assembly has been completely built and debugged, you finally sign it properly to create a "real" shared assembly that would pass the verification step. You do so by running SN again, this time with the –R option and the name of the file that contains the private key:

```
SN -R myasm.dll mykey.snk
```

You can verify a shared assembly using the –v option:

```
SN -v myasm.dll
```

Keep in mind that all SN options are case sensitive. For more information about the –Vr and –R options, read the section "The Strong Name Utility (SN)" later in this chapter.

To make the private key even safer, some software companies can store the private key in a hardware device, such as a smart card, and never store it to disk (where it might be retrieved even after the file has been deleted). To cope with this situation, Cryptographic Service Providers (CSPs) support the notion of *key containers* that, when accessed, retrieve the key from the hardware device. When using a key container, you use the /keyname switch instead of /keyfile when working with AL or VBC or the AssemblyKeyName attribute instead of AssemblyKeyFile when using attributes embedded in the source code.

The Binding Process

When the running application references a different assembly, the runtime must resolve this reference—that is, it must *bind* the assembly of your choice to the caller application; this portion of the runtime is known as the *assembly resolver*. The reference stored in the calling assembly contains the name, version, culture, and public key token of the requested assembly if the assembly is shared; the version is ignored and the public key is missing if the assembly is private. The process that the runtime follows to locate the correct assembly consists of several heuristic steps:

1. Checks version policy in configuration files
2. Uses the assembly if it has been loaded previously
3. Searches the assembly in the global assembly cache (GAC)
4. Searches the assembly using codebase hints if there are any
5. Probes the application's main directory tree

These five steps apply to a shared assembly. When you're binding a private assembly, the runtime skips step 1 because the runtime ignores version information in private assemblies. Similarly, the runtime skips steps 3 and 4 when binding private assemblies because they can't be stored in the GAC and can't be associated with codebase hints. The following sections describe each step in detail.

Version Policy in Application Configuration Files

You can change the behavior of .NET applications and assemblies by means of configuration files. This mechanism gives both developers and system administrators great flexibility in deciding how managed applications search for the assemblies they must bind to. For example, the many settings in these files let you decide whether requests for version 1.0 of a given assembly should be redirected to version 2.0 of the same assembly. There are three types of configuration files: the application configuration file, the publisher configuration file, and the machine configuration file.

The application configuration file affects the behavior of a single .NET application. This file must reside in the application's directory and have the same name as the application's main executable and the .config extension. For example, the application C:\bins\sampleapp.exe can have a configuration file named C:\bins\sampleapp.exe.config. When an application runs inside the browser as a script in an HTML page, the HTML code can include the explicit URL to the configuration file, as follows:

```
<LINK rel="Configuration" href=myapp.exe.config"
```

The publisher configuration file is tied to a shared assembly and affects all the managed applications that use that assembly. Typically, publishers of .NET components provide a configuration file when they release a new version of the component that fixes a few known bugs: the statements in the publisher's configuration file will therefore redirect all requests for the old version to the new one. A component vendor should provide a publisher configuration file only if the new version is perfectly backward compatible with the assembly being redirected. Each *major.minor* version of an assembly can have its own publisher configuration file. An application can decide to disable this feature for some or all the assemblies that it uses.

Finally, the machine configuration file (also known as the administrator configuration file) affects the behavior of all the managed applications running under a given version of the .NET runtime. This file is named machine.config and is located in the \Windows\Microsoft.NET\Framework\v*x.y.zzzz*\Config directory (where *x.y.zzzz* is the .NET Framework version). The settings in this file override the settings in both the application and publisher configuration files and can't themselves be overridden.

All three types of configuration files are standard XML files that can contain several sections. The outermost section is marked by the <configuration> tag and might contain the <runtime> section (among others), which finally contains the information about the assemblies you want to redirect. Here's an example of an application configuration file:

```
<?xml version="1.0" encoding="UTF-8" ?>

<configuration>
   <runtime>
      <assemblyBinding xmlns="urn:schemas-microsoft-com:asm.v1">
         <dependentAssembly>
            <assemblyIdentity name="myAsm"
                              publicKeyToken="378b4bc89e0bb9a3"
                              culture="en-us" />
            <bindingRedirect oldVersion="1.0.0.0"
                             newVersion="2.0.0.0"/>
            <publisherPolicy apply="no"/>
         </dependentAssembly>
      </assemblyBinding>
   </runtime>
</configuration>
```

Important XML tags and attributes are case sensitive, so you must type the tags exactly as reported in the preceding example. Visual Basic developers are accustomed to case-insensitive identifiers and can easily overlook this important detail.

Each <assemblyBinding> section is related to an assembly for which you want to establish a new version policy. This section *must* contain an <assemblyIdentity> subsection that identifies the assembly itself, with the name, culture, and public key token attributes. You can determine the public key token of a shared assembly by browsing the GAC from Windows Explorer (see Figure 14-4) or by using the SN command-line utility, as follows:

```
sn -T myasm.dll
```

After the mandatory <assemblyIdentity> subsection, the <assemblyBinding> section can contain the following subsections:

- The <bindingRedirect> section redirects one version of the assembly to another. For example, the preceding configuration file redirects all requests for version 1.0.0.0 of the assembly to version 2.0.0.0. The four numbers specified in the oldVersion and newVersion attributes are in the form *major.minor.revision.build*. The oldVersion attribute can specify a range of versions; for example, the following setting specifies that any version from 1.0 to 1.2 should be redirected to version 1.3, regardless of revision and build numbers:

```
<bindingRedirect oldVersion="1.0.0.0-1.2.65535.65535"
                 newVersion="1.3.0.0"/>
```

- The <publisherPolicy> section determines whether the publisher configuration file should be applied to this assembly. If you specify a "no" value for the apply attribute, as in the preceding example, the publisher configuration file is ignored and the application is said to work in *safe mode*.
- The <codeBase> section specifies where the assembly is located. This information is especially useful for assemblies downloaded from the Internet. (For more information, read the "Codebase Hints" section coming up shortly.)

By default, the publisher's policy is enabled for all assemblies. You can disable it for a specific assembly by using a <publisherPolicy> tag inside a <dependentAssembly> section (as seen in the preceding example), or you can disable it for all the assemblies that an application uses by inserting a <publisherPolicy> tag directly inside the <assemblyBinding> section:

```
<configuration>
  <runtime>
    <assemblyBinding xmlns="urn:schemas-microsoft-com:asm.v1">
      <publisherPolicy apply="no"/>
    </assemblyBinding>
  </runtime>
</configuration>
```

If you disable the publisher's policy for the entire application, you can't reenable it for individual assemblies. For this reason, the only reasonable setting for the apply attribute is the "no" value, both at the global level and at the individual assembly level.

Previously Loaded Assemblies and GAC Searches

In the second step in the binding process, the runtime checks whether that specific assembly had been requested in previous calls. If this is the case, the runtime redirects the call to the assembly already loaded, and the binding process stops here.

The runtime uses the assembly's strong name to decide whether the assembly is already in memory; this can happen even if the application never requested the assembly previously but another assembly in the same process did so and the requested assembly can be safely shared between multiple clients. As I've already explained, the strong name is a combination of the assembly's name, version, culture, and publisher's public key. The filename isn't part of the identity of the assembly, so you should never assign the same identity to different files.

If the assembly hasn't already been loaded, the binding process continues by searching the GAC for an assembly with that identity. This step applies only to assemblies with strong names because private assemblies can't be stored in the GAC. If the assembly is found in the GAC, the binding process stops here.

Codebase Hints

Once the version of the assembly is known and the assembly isn't in the GAC, the runtime has to locate the assembly file. The runtime usually accomplishes this task by means of a search process known as *probing* (described in the next section), but the developer, the publisher of the component, or the system administrator can disable probing by adding a codebase hint to one of the three configuration files. A codebase hint is a <codeBase> tag that appears in a <dependentAssembly> section.

Codebase hints are especially useful and common in browser-based scenarios for informing the browser of the location from which a given assembly can be downloaded. For example, the following portion of the configuration file tells the runtime that versions from 1.0 through 1.4 of the MathFns assembly can be downloaded from *http://www.vb2themax.com/asms/mathfns.dll.* (This is just an example—there is no such assembly at this URL.)

```
<configuration>
   <runtime>
      <assemblyBinding xmlns="urn:schemas-microsoft-com:asm.v1">
         <dependentAssembly>
            <assemblyIdentity name="mathfns"
                              publicKeyToken="378b4bc89e0bb9a3"
                              culture="en-us" />
```

(continued)

```
            <bindingRedirect oldVersion="1.0.0.0"
                             newVersion="2.0.0.0"/>
            <publisherPolicy apply="no"/>
            <codeBase version="1.0.0.0-1.4.65535.65535"
              href="http://www.vb2themax.com/ams/mathfns.dll"/>
          </dependentAssembly>
        </assemblyBinding>
      </runtime>
    </configuration>
```

In some cases, you don't even need a codebase hint for every assembly used by an application. For example, if the MathFns assembly references the TrigFns assembly, the runtime automatically reuses the hint for MathFns and assumes that TrigFns can be downloaded from *http://www.vb2themax.com/assemblies/trigfns.dll.*

You can use codebase hints to reference assemblies outside the application's main directory, provided the assembly has a strong name. Either using a codebase hint or installing the assembly in the GAC is the only valid way to reference an assembly located outside the application's main directory, and both methods work only with assemblies with strong names. For example, you might decide to install an assembly in a separate directory if it is going to be used by multiple applications from your company (and you don't want to deploy all these applications in the same directory). In general, however, strong name assemblies deployed to a location other than the GAC don't offer any advantages other than a simpler installation; on the con side, they load more slowly than assemblies in the GAC and aren't protected from accidental deletions.

If a codebase hint is provided but no assembly is found at the specified address, or the assembly is found but its identity doesn't match the identity of the assembly the runtime is looking for, the binding process stops with an error.

Probing

Probing is the process by which the runtime can locate an assembly inside the application's directory or one of its subdirectories. As I explained in the preceding section, the runtime begins probing only if no codebase hint has been provided for the assembly. Probing is a set of heuristic rules based on the following criteria:

- The application's base directory
- The assembly's name
- The assembly's culture
- The application's private binpath

The *binpath* is a list of directories, expressed as relative names that implicitly refer to subdirectories under the application's main directory. (Absolute paths are invalid.) The binpath is specified as a semicolon-delimited list of directories and is assigned to the privatePath attribute of the <probing> tag, inside the <assemblyBinding> section of an application configuration file:

```
<configuration>
   <runtime>
      <assemblyBinding xmlns="urn:schemas-microsoft-com:asm.v1">
         <probing privatePath="bin;bin2\subbin;utils"/>
      </assemblyBinding>
   </runtime>
</configuration>
```

The sequence of directories searched for during the probing process depends on whether the assembly in question has a culture or not. For assemblies without a culture, the search is performed in each location in the order listed:

1. The application's base directory
2. The subdirectory named after the assembly
3. Each directory in the binpath list
4. The subdirectory named after the assembly under each directory in the binpath list

The runtime scans these directories first looking for a DLL named after the assembly (for example, myasm.dll). If the search fails, the runtime performs the search again in all these directories, this time looking for an EXE named after the assembly (myasm.exe). However, you can't add a reference to an EXE file from inside Visual Studio .NET.

For example, let's assume that the runtime is searching for an assembly named myasm.dll and the binpath is the one defined in the previous configuration file. Here are the files that the runtime searches for (assuming that the main application directory is C:\myapp):

```
C:\myapp\myasm.dll
C:\myapp\myasm\myasm.dll
C:\myapp\bin\myasm.dll
C:\myapp\bin\subbin\myasm.dll
C:\myapp\utils\myasm.dll
C:\myapp\bin\myasm\myasm.dll
C:\myapp\bin\subbin\myasm\myasm.dll
C:\myapp\utils\myasm\myasm.dll
```

(continued)

```
C:\myapp\myasm.exe
C:\myapp\myasm\myasm.exe
C:\myapp\bin\myasm.exe
C:\myapp\bin\subbin\myasm.exe
C:\myapp\utils\myasm.exe
C:\myapp\bin\myasm\myasm.exe
C:\myapp\bin\subbin\myasm\myasm.exe
C:\myapp\utils\myasm\myasm.exe
```

For assemblies with a culture, the sequence is slightly different:

1. The application's base subdirectory named after the culture
2. The subdirectory named after the assembly under the directory defined in point 1
3. The subdirectory named after the culture under each subdirectory defined in the binpath
4. The subdirectory named after the assembly under each directory defined in point 3

Again, the runtime searches these directories for a DLL named after the assembly and then for an EXE named after the assembly.

For example, let's assume that an application using the preceding configuration file is requesting an assembly named myasm and marked as Italian culture ("it"). These are the places where the runtime would search for this assembly:

```
C:\myapp\it\myasm.dll
C:\myapp\it\myasm\myasm.dll
C:\myapp\bin\it\myasm.dll
C:\myapp\bin\subbin\it\myasm.dll
C:\myapp\utils\it\myasm.dll
C:\myapp\bin\it\myasm\myasm.dll
C:\myapp\bin\subbin\it\myasm\myasm.dll
C:\myapp\utils\it\myasm\myasm.dll

C:\myapp\it\myasm.exe
C:\myapp\it\myasm\myasm.exe
C:\myapp\bin\it\myasm.exe
C:\myapp\bin\subbin\it\myasm.exe
C:\myapp\utils\it\myasm.exe
C:\myapp\bin\it\myasm\myasm.exe
C:\myapp\bin\subbin\it\myasm\myasm.exe
C:\myapp\utils\it\myasm\myasm.exe
```

If even this last step fails, the runtime checks whether the assembly was part of a Windows Installer package; if this is the case, the runtime asks the Windows Installer to install the assembly. (This feature is known as *on-demand installation.*) The Windows Installer 2.0 program has other important features, such as the ability to advertise the application's availability, use the Add/Remove Program option in Control Panel, and easily repair the application if necessary.

The Assembly Binding Log Viewer Utility (FUSLOGVW)

You now know everything you need to know about assembly binding, although in practice you're in the dark when the runtime can't locate one or more assemblies at run time. In such a situation, the Assembly Binding Log Viewer can be a real lifesaver. You can run the FUSLOGVW utility from the command line or add it to the Start menu. (See Figure 14-6.)

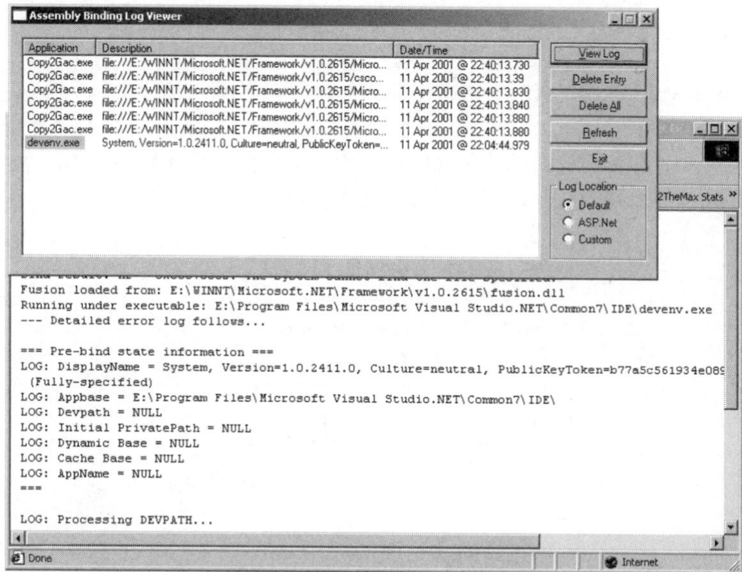

Figure 14-6. The FUSLOGVW utility in action; the window in the background displays the detailed information about a specific entry in the log file.

The .NET runtime maintains three log files: the default log, the ASP.NET log, and a custom log. You select which one to display by clicking one of the three radio buttons near the lower right corner of the FUSLOGVW window. The default log is used for all the failed binding operations of the current user: in other words, each user sees a different log in this window. The ASP.NET log is used for all binding operations related to ASP.NET because ASP.NET runs under a system identity, and failed operations can't be registered in any default user log. The Custom log shows only failed binding operations in a directory that you specify in the following registry key:

```
HKEY_LOCAL_MACHINE\Software\Microsoft\Fusion\LogPath
```

You can fine-tune the behavior of FUSLOGVW by setting a couple of other registry keys; as with the preceding key, you must manually add these keys to the registry if necessary. By setting the HKEY_LOCAL_MACHINE\Software\Microsoft\Fusion\ForceLog registry value to 1, you log all the binding operations, not just the unsuccessful ones. As a result, you can exactly detect the location from which an assembly is loaded, which can be useful when you're trying to spot elusive bugs caused by the wrong version of an assembly being bound successfully.

Finally, by setting the HKEY_LOCAL_MACHINE\Software\Microsoft\Fusion\LogResourceBind registry value to 1, you get a log also of the failed bind operations related to satellite assemblies (which aren't recorded in the log by default).

A Real Example

The best way to fully understand how the binding process works is by looking at a real example. Let's create a class library project named TestAssembly, containing only the VersionInfo class, which exposes a read-only property that returns information about the assembly itself:

```
Public Class VersionInfo
    ReadOnly Property Description() As String
        Get
            ' Get a reference to the current assembly.
            Dim asm As System.Reflection.Assembly
            asm = System.Reflection.Assembly.GetExecutingAssembly
            ' Return its version, culture, and public key token.
            Return "FULLNAME = " & asm.FullName
        End Get
    End Property
End Class
```

The Description property uses .NET reflection to return information about the running assembly, including name, version, culture, and public key token. (Reflection is described in Chapter 15.) For simplicity's sake, I'll assume that the TestAssembly project has been created in the C:\TestAssembly directory and that therefore it produces a TestAssembly.dll executable file in the C:\TestAssembly\bin directory.

Creating a Sample Client Application

Next create a Visual Basic console application named AssemblyDemo in the C:\AssemblyDemo directory. You can create this new project in a separate instance of Visual Studio, or you can use the Add Project command in the File menu to add the project to the current solution. In a real application, you would probably use the latter approach because Visual Studio can track references between projects in the same solution even if the referenced project changes significantly, which is usually a good thing. In this specific case, however, this tracking feature would effectively prevent us from seeing what happens when one compiled assembly references another compiled assembly; for this reason, it's preferable to load the new project in another instance of Visual Studio.

The AssemblyDemo project contains only a few lines of code that instantiate a TestAssembly.VersionInfo object and display its version information:

```
Module Module1
    Sub Main()
        Dim vi As New TestAssembly.VersionInfo()
        Console.WriteLine(vi.Description)
    End Sub
End Module
```

To make this code work, however, you must do two things. First you must copy the TestAssembly.dll file into the C:\AssemblyDemo\Bin directory so that the executable file can find it through probing. You must follow this procedure because the TestAssembly.dll doesn't have a strong name. The runtime can find the file during the probing process only if it's located under the main application's directory tree.

Your second action is to add a reference to the DLL from inside the AssemblyDemo project, which you accomplish by clicking Add Reference on the Project menu and by setting the reference in the Add Reference dialog box. (See Figure 14-7.)

> **Note** Visual Studio .NET has an interesting feature: if you add a reference to a DLL outside the current project's directory, Visual Studio automatically copies the DLL in the bin subdirectory of the current project, regardless of whether the referenced assembly has a strong name. Even more interesting, the DLL is automatically copied again before you run the current project if the DLL has changed in the meantime. This feature is very handy when you work with multiple assemblies, regardless of whether they're included in the same solution, but it prevents us from understanding what is actually going on. For this reason, it's preferable to copy the DLL in the bin directory manually and then add a reference to the copy.

Run the program now from inside the environment to verify that the DLL is bound correctly; in the console window, you will read a message similar to this:

```
FULLNAME = TestAssembly, Version=1.0.586.29345, Culture=neutral,
PublicKeyToken=null
```

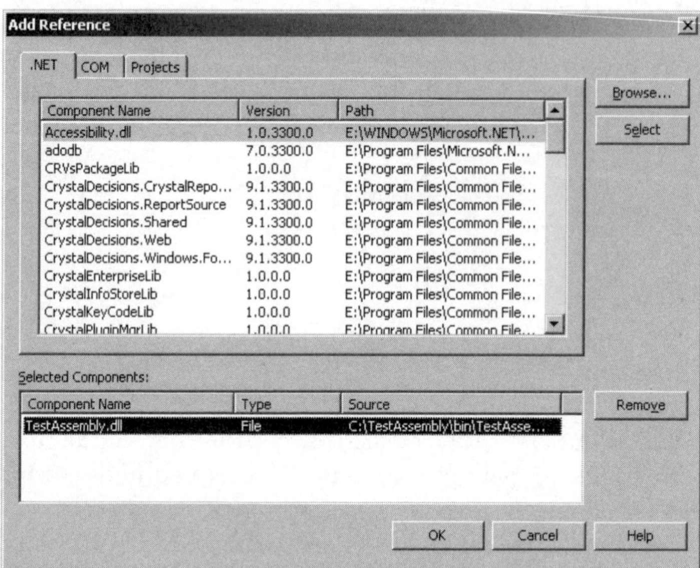

Figure 14-7. The Add Reference dialog box lets you add a reference to a .NET component, a COM component, or another project in Visual Studio.

The version number consists of four portions: major version, minor version, revision, and build. The version assigned to a compiled assembly depends on the AssemblyVersion attribute that Visual Studio created for you in the AssemblyInfo.vb file:

```
<Assembly: AssemblyVersion("1.0.*")>
```

When an asterisk is used after the minor version number, the compiler generates the revision and build numbers automatically, as follows: the version number is set equal to the number of days since January 1, 2000, and the build number is the number of seconds since midnight, divided by 2.

Let's now see whether the AssemblyDemo application is able to find the assembly even though its version number changes. To do this, you just have to recompile TestAssembly.dll and move it again to the AssemblyDemo\Bin directory. This time, however, open a console window and run the Assembly-

Demo.Exe program from there. Even though the message is slightly different, your evidence that binding succeeded shows up in the larger version number:

```
FULLNAME = TestAssembly, Version=1.0.586.30245, Culture=neutral,
PublicKeyToken=null
```

The binding has succeeded because the version number is ignored when you're binding to assemblies without a strong name.

Probing Subdirectories

Our next experiment is about probing private assemblies located in subdirectories of the application's main directory. You don't have to recompile the client application or the DLL in this case. From Windows Explorer or from the command prompt, create a TestAssembly directory under C:\AssemblyDemo\bin, and move the DLL there. Run the AssemblyDemo.Exe application once again, and you'll see that the assembly is bound correctly because the probing process always searches a subdirectory named after the assembly itself.

Let's show that the probing process is unable to locate assemblies in other subdirectories, at least without some help from us. From Windows Explorer or the command prompt, rename the TestAssembly subdirectory Assemblies, and rerun the application. This time the binding process fails, and the runtime displays the window shown in Figure 14-8, which offers you the assistance of a debugger. Click the No button, and the following error message appears in the console window:

```
Unhandled Exception: System.IO.FileNotFoundException: File or assembly name
TestAssembly, or one of its dependencies, was not found.
File name: "TestAssembly"
   at AssemblyDemo.Module1.Main()

Fusion log follows:
LOG: Post policy reference: TestAssembly, Version=1.0.586.30245,
Culture=neutral, PublicKeyToken=null
LOG: Attempting download of new URL file:///C:/AssemblyDemo/bin/
TestAssembly.DLL.
LOG: Attempting download of new URL file:///C:/AssemblyDemo/bin/
TestAssembly/TestAssembly.DLL.
LOG: Attempting download of new URL file:///C:/AssemblyDemo/bin/
TestAssembly.EXE.
LOG: Attempting download of new URL file:///C:/AssemblyDemo/bin/
TestAssembly/TestAssembly.EXE.
```

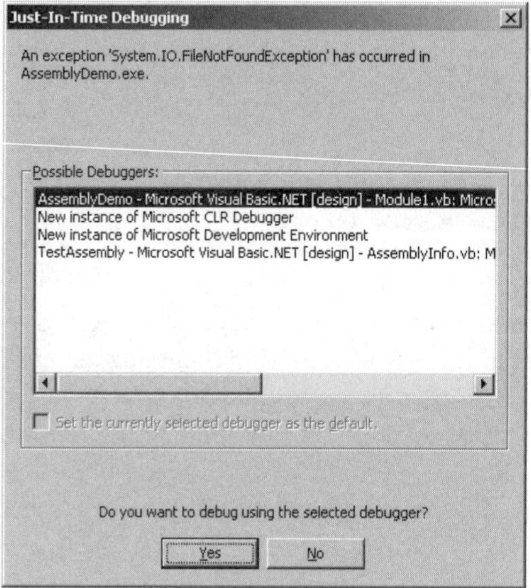

Figure 14-8. The dialog box that appears when an assembly is about to terminate with an error.

As you see, the .NET runtime attempted to locate an assembly named TestAssembly.dll in the application's main directory and then in a subdirectory named after the assembly itself, corresponding to steps 1 and 2 of the probing process I described previously. Next it made another attempt with a file named TestAssembly.exe, again in those two directories. You might want to run the FUSLOGVW utility to see a new entry in the list of failed binding operations and request more details about what happened.

Using the Binpath

It's time to create a configuration file for the application. Run Notepad, type the following text, and save it in a file named AssemblyDemo.exe.config in C:\AssemblyDemo\bin:

```
<?xml version="1.0" encoding="UTF-8" ?>
<configuration>
   <runtime>
      <assemblyBinding xmlns="urn:schemas-microsoft-com:asm.v1">
         <probing privatePath="assemblies;components"/>
      </assemblyBinding>
   </runtime>
</configuration>
```

(Note that the <?xml> directive in the first line is optional.) Run the application once again, and you'll see that the assembly is correctly bound because it's located in one of the subdirectories listed in the <probing> section of the configuration file.

To see the probing sequence that the runtime uses when the <probing> tag contains one or more subdirectories, delete the DLL and run the application once again. Both the error message in the console window and the log in the FUSLOGVW utility show the list of files searched for before the exception occurred:

```
C:\AssemblyDemo\bin\TestAssembly.DLL
C:\AssemblyDemo\bin\TestAssembly\TestAssembly.DLL
C:\AssemblyDemo\bin\assemblies\TestAssembly.DLL
C:\AssemblyDemo\bin\assemblies\TestAssembly\TestAssembly.DLL
C:\AssemblyDemo\bin\components\TestAssembly.DLL
C:\AssemblyDemo\bin\components\TestAssembly\TestAssembly.DLL
C:\AssemblyDemo\bin\TestAssembly.EXE
C:\AssemblyDemo\bin\TestAssembly\TestAssembly.EXE
C:\AssemblyDemo\bin\assemblies\TestAssembly.EXE
C:\AssemblyDemo\bin\assemblies\TestAssembly\TestAssembly.EXE
C:\AssemblyDemo\bin\components\TestAssembly.EXE
C:\AssemblyDemo\bin\components\TestAssembly\TestAssembly.EXE
```

Creating Assemblies with Culture

Let's continue the experiment by embedding a culture qualifier in the assembly. You can do so by adding the following statement somewhere in the AssemblyInfo.vb module of the TestAssembly project:

```
' Mark the assembly with the Italian culture identifier.
<Assembly: AssemblyCulture("it")>
```

Recompile the DLL, copy it once again in the C:\AssemblyDemo\bin directory, and run the AssemblyDemo.exe application. The result is an error message that, as usual, lists all the directories that were scanned during the failed search. The last text line in the message explains why the binding failed:

```
LOG: Post policy reference: TestAssembly, Version=1.0.586.30245,
Culture=neutral, PublicKeyToken=null
LOG: Attempting download of new URL file:///C:/AssemblyDemo/bin/
TestAssembly.DLL.
WRN: Assembly name comparison mismatch: CULTURE
```

This is an interesting result: if the runtime finds an assembly with the right name but a different culture qualifier during the binding process, the binding is immediately aborted and the runtime doesn't even attempt to search subdirectories.

Run Visual Studio again, and delete the reference to the old DLL by selecting the reference in the Solution Explorer and pressing the Delete key. This operation also deletes the physical DLL pointed to by the reference, without even asking for confirmation! So if you followed these directions closely, this action has deleted the new DLL, and you'll have to copy the DLL again into the C:\AssemblyDemo\bin directory. Next add a reference to the new, localized version of the DLL.

If you run AssemblyDemo.exe again, you still get an error message. You should expect this result because the runtime ignores the main application's directory when it's probing culture-aware assemblies. In fact, this is the sequence of files in which the runtime expects to find this specific assembly:

```
C:\AssemblyDemo\bin\it\TestAssembly.DLL
C:\AssemblyDemo\bin\it\TestAssembly\TestAssembly.DLL
C:\AssemblyDemo\bin\assemblies\it\TestAssembly.DLL
C:\AssemblyDemo\bin\assemblies\it\TestAssembly\TestAssembly.DLL
C:\AssemblyDemo\bin\components\it\TestAssembly.DLL
C:\AssemblyDemo\bin\components\it\TestAssembly\TestAssembly.DLL
C:\AssemblyDemo\bin\it\TestAssembly.EXE
C:\AssemblyDemo\bin\it\TestAssembly\TestAssembly.EXE
C:\AssemblyDemo\bin\assemblies\it\TestAssembly.EXE
C:\AssemblyDemo\bin\assemblies\it\TestAssembly\TestAssembly.EXE
C:\AssemblyDemo\bin\components\it\TestAssembly.EXE
C:\AssemblyDemo\bin\components\it\TestAssembly\TestAssembly.EXE
```

To avoid the binding error, create a directory named "it" under the C:\AssemblyDemo\bin directory, move the TestAssembly.dll file there, and then run the application again. This time, the AssemblyDemo application will run smoothly.

Signing the Assembly with a Strong Name

The final steps in our experiment require that you sign the assembly with a strong name. Earlier in this chapter, I showed how to generate a public/private key pair by using the SN utility:

```
SN -k keyfile.snk
```

You then copy the .snk file to the directory where the TestAssembly source files are (not the bin subdirectory) and create an AssemblyKeyFile attribute in the source code that points to the .snk file:

```
<Assembly: AssemblyKeyFile("keyfile.snk")>
```

Next load the AssemblyDemo project, delete a reference to the previous version of the assembly (the one without a strong name), copy the new DLL into the AssemblyDemo\bin\it directory, add a reference to this DLL by clicking Add Reference on the Project menu and using the Add Reference dialog box, compile the main application, and run it from inside Visual Studio or from the command prompt. If you have followed these directions correctly, the following message appears (but of course with a different version number and public key token) and confirms that everything worked correctly:

```
FULLNAME = TestAssembly, Version=1.0.586.33241, Culture=it,
PublicKeyToken=c45847cebed47e36
```

Now change the version number of TestAssembly.dll, and attempt a new binding. To create a newer version, you can make a small edit in the assembly source code, such as typing a space, and recompiling. (If you don't edit the source files, Visual Studio doesn't generate new revision and build numbers.) In this example, however, we'll promote the assembly to version 1.1 by editing the AssemblyVersion attribute in AssemblyInfo.vb:

```
<Assembly: AssemblyVersion("1.1.0.0")>
```

Recompile, and copy the new DLL over the old one in C:\AssemblyDemo\bin\it. Run the main application from the console window, and you'll see that the binding fails with this error log:

```
LOG: Post policy reference: TestAssembly, Version=1.0.586.33241, Culture=it,
PublicKeyToken=c45847cebed47e36
LOG: Attempting download of new URL file:///C:/AssemblyDemo/bin/it/
TestAssembly.DLL.
WRN: Assembly name comparison mismatch: Minor Version
```

Important When the runtime binds an application to a shared assembly, the runtime always checks the version number, even if the assembly is located in the main application's directory tree. What makes an assembly private or shared isn't where the assembly is located on the hard disk; rather, it's the fact that it has a strong name.

If an assembly has a strong name, you can redirect the original request to a different version of the assembly. You can do this by adding a <dependentAssembly> section to the application configuration file. For example, the following configuration file redirects all requests for version 1.0 assemblies (regardless of their revision and build numbers) to version 1.1:

```
<?xml version="1.0" encoding="UTF-8" ?>
<configuration>
   <runtime>
      <assemblyBinding xmlns="urn:schemas-microsoft-com:asm.v1">
         <dependentAssembly>
           <assemblyIdentity name="TestAssembly"
                             publicKeyToken="c45847cebed47e36"
                             culture="it" />
           <bindingRedirect oldVersion="1.0.0.0-1.0.65535.65535"
                            newVersion="1.1.0.0"/>
         </dependentAssembly>
```

(continued)

```
            <probing privatePath="assemblies;components"/>
        </assemblyBinding>
    </runtime>
</configuration>
```

Store this new configuration file in the application main directory, and run the AssemblyDemo.exe application again. The message that appears in the console window confirms that the original request has been redirected:

```
FULLNAME = TestAssembly, Version=1.1.0.0, Culture=it,
PublicKeyToken=c45847cebed47e36
```

Adding Codebase Hints

Even if the configuration file redirects a request to a different version of a shared assembly, the probing rules are still valid and the DLL must be located within the application's directory tree, in one of the subdirectories that the probing process scans.

A clear advantage of shared assemblies is that you don't need to copy them inside the client application's directory. You can choose from two ways to inform the runtime that a given (shared) assembly is outside the application's directory tree: you can use a codebase hint in the configuration file, or you can register the assembly in the GAC. Let's see how the first method works.

If you used the same paths I have so far, the original assembly DLL should be stored in the C:\TestAssembly\bin directory; you need a codebase hint that points to the DLL in that directory:

```
<?xml version="1.0" encoding="UTF-8" ?>
<configuration>
    <runtime>
        <assemblyBinding xmlns="urn:schemas-microsoft-com:asm.v1">
            <dependentAssembly>
                <assemblyIdentity name="TestAssembly"
                                  publicKeyToken="c45847cebed47e36"
                                  culture="it" />
                <bindingRedirect oldVersion="1.0.0.0-1.0.65535.65535"
                                 newVersion="1.1.0.0"/>
                <codeBase version="1.1.0.0"
                    href="file://c:/TestAssembly/bin/TestAssembly.dll"/>
            </dependentAssembly>
            <probing privatePath="assemblies;components"/>
        </assemblyBinding>
    </runtime>
</configuration>
```

To ensure that you aren't mistakenly binding to an assembly in the application directory tree, delete all occurrences of TestAssembly.dll under C:\AssemblyDemo\bin and its subdirectories. Now run the application to see that Test-

Assembly.dll is indeed bound correctly. To double-check the mechanism, delete the <codeBase> tag and save the configuration file, and you'll see that the binding fails.

Installing in the GAC

The preferred way to install shared assemblies is to register them in the GAC. You can use drag-and-drop or the GACUTIL command-line utility.

Using drag-and-drop is very simple: use Windows Explorer to navigate to the \Windows\Assembly directory, and drop the DLL on the right-hand pane. (See Figure 14-4.) Running the GACUTIL utility is also straightforward:

```
gacutil /i testassembly.dll
```

The advantage of using the latter method is that you can automate the registration process—for example, by running a batch or a script program. Even better, you can add a command to the Tools menu in Visual Studio .NET by using a sequence of operations similar to the one I explained for the ILDASM program earlier in this chapter. For running GACUTIL, you must enter the complete path of the utility in the Command box (**C:\Program Files\Microsoft Visual Studio .NET\FrameworkSDK\Bin\gacutil.exe** for a default installation) and type **–i $(TargetPath)** in the Arguments box.

Registering an assembly in the GAC doesn't automatically unregister any previous version of the same assembly. (One of the goals of the GAC is to store multiple versions of the same assembly.) Each new version that you register is added to the GAC, so you should periodically clear intermediate versions of the assembly from the GAC or run GACUTIL using the /u option to unregister an outdated version of the assembly before registering a more recent one.

Configuration Files

You've already seen that you can affect the behavior of a specific application or the whole system by means of configuration files. In this section, I'll describe them more in depth, even though I leave out some major topics, such as ASP.NET settings, which I cover in later chapters.

Unless otherwise noted, everything I describe in this section applies to both application.config files and the machine.config file located in \Windows\Microsoft.NET\Framework\v*x.y.zzzz*\Config (where *x.y.zzzz* is the runtime version). When it decides which setting should be applied, the runtime examines the machine.config file and then the application.config file; the latter has a higher priority. The exception to this rule is assembly redirection, in which case machine-level settings are examined last and have a higher priority.

Runtime Version

You can run multiple versions of the .NET runtime on the same machine, and each application can use any installed version. When an application starts, the .NET loader decides which runtime version should be used. Three factors affect this choice:

1. The version of the runtime under which the application was compiled.
2. The value of the <requiredRuntime> setting in the application's configuration file. (If present, this value overrides the runtime version number embedded in the application's executable file.)
3. If the runtime version that the application would use (as deduced from previous points) is redirected to another version; this information is stored in the registry but can be ignored if the safemode attribute is set to true.

If none of the installed runtime versions can serve the request, the application isn't loaded and an error message is displayed instead. You can change the runtime version that an application requires by using the <requiredRuntime> setting in the <startup> subsection under the <configuration> section, as in this code:

```
<configuration>
   <startup>
      <requiredRuntime version="v1.0.3705" safemode="true"/>
   </startup>
</configuration>
```

The preceding application's configuration file states that the application requires the runtime version 1.0.3705 and that any redirection policy specified in the registry should be ignored.

Garbage Collection Behavior

By default, the garbage collector executes concurrently on a separate thread. This setting is adequate for single-threaded Windows Forms applications in that it minimizes the pauses and makes the user interface work smoothly but doesn't maximize the overall performance. You can optimize multithreaded applications that run on the server by disabling concurrent garbage collection, which you do by adding the following boldface line to the application's configuration file:

```
<configuration>
   <runtime>
      <gcConcurrent enabled="false"/>
   </runtime>
</configuration>
```

Dynamic Properties

All real-world applications need to store configuration values somewhere outside their own executable code so that their behavior can be modified without your having to recompile them. Database connection strings are a typical example of such configuration values. Over the years, developers have used many different approaches to this problem, including .ini files and the system registry.

In an attempt to put some order in this area, Microsoft has proposed a standardized, simple, and flexible way to store values in the application's configuration file. All configuration values, which are formally known as *dynamic properties*, are stored as key/value pairs inside the <appSettings> section, as you see here:

```
<configuration>
    <appSettings>
        <add key="Default User" value="Francesco" />
        <add key="Connection String"
             value="Data Source=P4;User ID=sa;Initial Catalog=pubs" />
        <add key="Timeout" value="50" />
    </appSettings>
</configuration>
```

A Visual Basic program can retrieve all the dynamic properties by using the AppSettings method of the System.Configuration.ConfigurationSettings object and assigning the returned value to a NameValueCollection variable, which you can then use to access each individual value:

```
Sub TestApplicationSettings()
    ' Retrieve all values in a NameValueCollection.
    Dim colValues As System.Collections.Specialized.NameValueCollection
    colValues = Configuration.ConfigurationSettings.AppSettings()

    ' Print all key/value pairs.
    Dim key As String
    For Each key In colValues.AllKeys
        Console.WriteLine("Key=""{0}""  Value=""{1}""", key, _
            colValues.Get(key))
    Next
End Sub
```

Keep in mind that the Get method returns a string, so you might need to convert it to a property data type, such as an Integer, before assigning it to a variable or an object's property:

```
Dim timeout As Integer = CInt(colValues("Timeout"))
```

Once your code invokes the AppSettings method of the Configuration.ConfigurationSettings object, dynamic properties are read from the application's file and cached in the NameValueCollection object. If you modify the .config file, the contents of this object aren't updated automatically, so in most cases you have to restart the application.

The support for dynamic properties in the .NET Framework is far more powerful than anything you've seen in this area. In fact, you can define other sections in the configuration file and indicate which class should deal with each section. The <appSettings> section is only a default section defined for you inside machine.config by these XML instructions:

```
<configuration>
  <configSections>
    ⋮
    <section name="appSettings"
        type="System.Configuration.NameValueFileSectionHandler, System,
            Version=1.0.2411.0, Culture=neutral,
            PublicKeyToken=b77a5c561934e089" />
    ⋮
  </configSections>
</configuration>
```

Each <section> element under <configSections> defines one of the sections that can appear in the <configuration> region. The type attribute defines the class that can deal with values in that specific section. By default, this class is in the runtime, but you can create such a class yourself and therefore have the greatest freedom in deciding how values can be stored in the section. For example, you can use hierarchies of XML tags to represent treelike structures or save the state of a complex object by using XML serialization. (See Chapter 11.) Read the .NET platform SDK documentation for more information about user-defined dynamic properties in configuration files.

The .NET Framework Configuration Tool

Although you should be familiar with the syntax of machine.config and applications' configuration files, most of the time you can perform your administration chores by using a Microsoft Management Console snap-in that offers a simple user interface; it lets you browse and modify those files using a visual approach. (See Figure 14-9.) Because this tool is an MMC snap-in, you can use it only with Microsoft Windows NT, Microsoft Windows 2000, and Windows XP. You can launch the Microsoft .NET Framework Configuration from the Administrative Tools submenu of the Start menu.

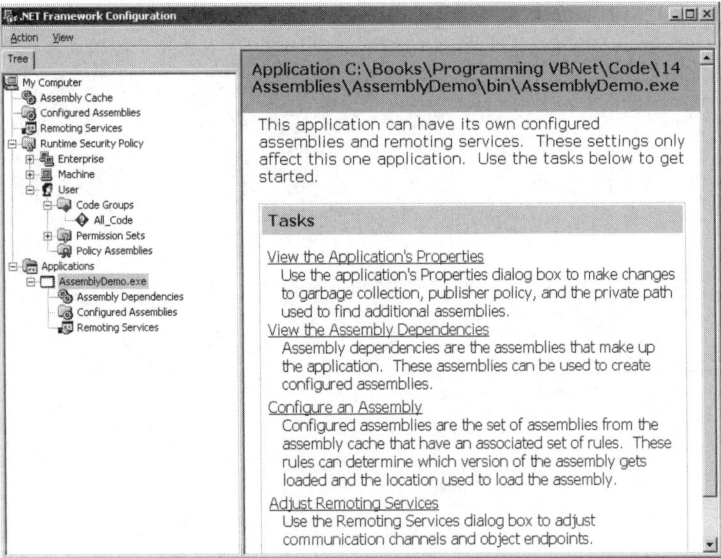

Figure 14-9. The .NET Framework Administration tool.

You can right-click the My Computer node to bring up the dialog box shown in Figure 14-10, in which you can decide whether the garbage collector runs in the background. You can indirectly affect other entries in machine.config by right-clicking the Remoting Services and Runtime Security Policy nodes.

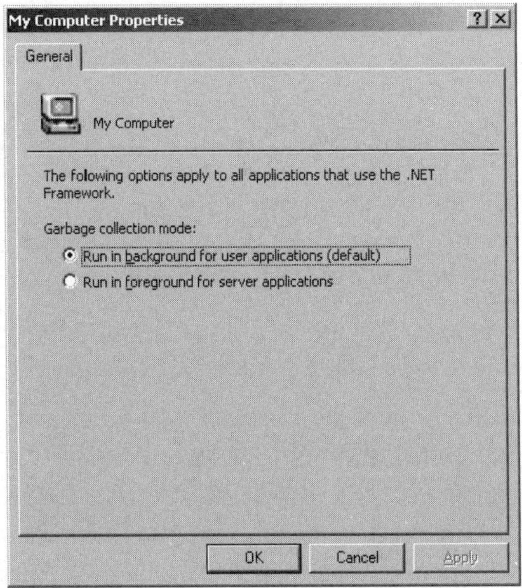

Figure 14-10. The properties of the My Computer node.

You can change the behavior of a shared assembly by right-clicking the Configured Assemblies node. After selecting the assembly from those deployed in the GAC, a dialog box like the one visible in Figure 14-11 appears. Here you specify how versions are redirected and the codebase corresponding to each version of the assembly in question. (These settings correspond to entries in the .config file for the specific assembly.) A shared assembly that appears in this list is called a *configured assembly*.

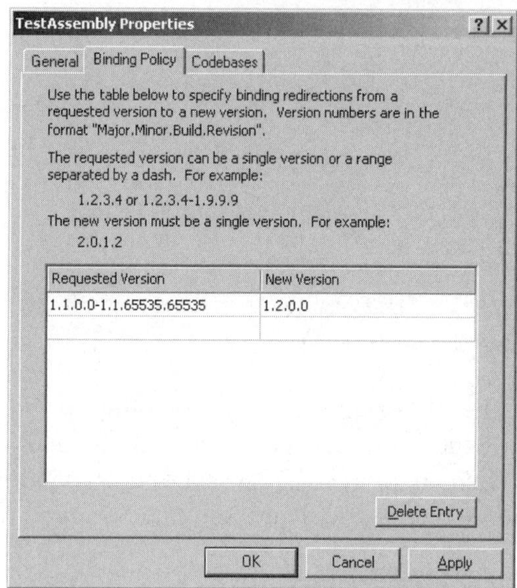

Figure 14-11. The Properties dialog box for a configured assembly.

You can add the .NET applications you want to configure under the Applications node by using the Add command in the node's shortcut menu. In contrast with the Configured Assemblies node, this list can include private assemblies. By clicking one of the three nodes under a specific application node (as shown in Figure 14-9), you can perform the following tasks:

- **Assembly Dependencies** View the list of assemblies this application needs to run correctly. (This list contains .NET runtime DLLs.)
- **Configured Assemblies** View the list of all the configured assemblies among the assemblies that this application needs to run. You can configure an assembly by right-clicking in the left pane and selecting the Add command.
- **Remoting Services** Specify communication channels and endpoints for remote objects used by this application.

One of the most intriguing features of the .NET Framework Configuration tool is the ability to *automatically* remember the five most recent configurations used by any .NET application. This feature works as follows: each time an application unloads, the .NET runtime checks the version of each of the assemblies the application has loaded. If this configuration is the same as the one used during the preceding execution, nothing happens; if the configuration is different, the runtime stores the details of the new configuration in an .ini file stored in a subdirectory in the C:\Documents and Settings directory tree.

If you later run the application and find that it isn't working properly, you can restore any of the five most recent configurations stored by the runtime. You access this feature by right-clicking the Applications node and clicking Fix An Application on the shortcut menu. (You can also access this feature from the Microsoft .NET Framework Wizards command in the Administrative Tools submenu of the Start menu.) This action brings up a list of all known .NET applications (not just those under the Applications node), so you can select the one you're interested in. The next dialog box (shown in Figure 14-12) lists each stored configuration, identified by the date interval in which it was used. The last entry is always Application SafeMode, which you can use to troubleshoot the application. When you click Apply, the .NET Framework Configuration tool generates the corresponding .config file for the specific application, using remarks to surround the portions that it added or modified.

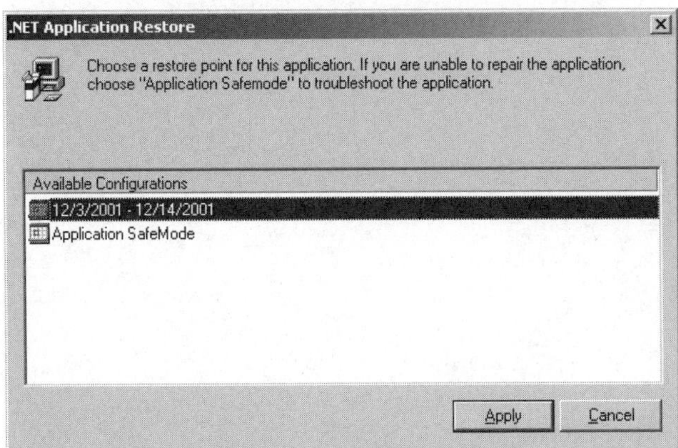

Figure 14-12. The dialog box that lets you restore a known configuration.

Command-Line Tools

This section reviews the syntax of the command-line utilities that come with the .NET Framework and that are related to creating and managing assemblies. In most situations, you can perform many of these tasks from inside Visual Studio's dialog boxes or by adding the proper attribute to your source code. However, several jobs require you to run command-line tools because they offer more options or because you might need to automate a task by means of a script or a batch file.

The simplest way to run all the command-line tools mentioned in this section is to open a command window using the Visual Studio .NET Command Prompt command on the Start menu. Or you can open a regular prompt window and then launch the corvars.bat program to correctly initialize the PATH environment variable so that you don't have to specify the complete path of these commands. (You can find the corvars.bat program in the C:\Program Files\Microsoft Visual Studio .NET\FrameworkSDK\Bin directory.) For example, I keep a copy of corvars.bat in the C:\ directory so that I can run it easily from both the command prompt and a batch program.

The Visual Basic Compiler (VBC)

VBC.exe is more than a plain compiler, in that by default it creates single-file assemblies without the aid of a linker. It can compile one or more source code files, and it produces an executable that's a self-sufficient assembly containing its own manifest. By specifying the /t:module option, you create a single module that you later add to a multifile assembly by using the AL utility, as I explain in the next section.

The simplest operation that you can perform with the VBC command-line compiler is the production of a Windows console application. To see how to proceed, create the following Module.vb and Teller.vb files (using Notepad or from inside the IDE):

```
' The Module.vb module
Module MainModule
    Sub Main
        Dim t As New Teller
        t.Say("Hello world")
    End Sub
End Module

' The Teller.vb file
Imports System

Class Teller
    Sub Say(ByVal msg As String)
        Console.WriteLine(msg)
    End Sub
End Class
```

Compiling these modules is easy:

```
vbc module.vb teller.vb
```

The preceding statement produces the executable module.exe file that, when run, displays the "Hello world" string in the console window. The name of the executable file is derived from the name of the first source file in the list, but you can specify another name by using the /out option. This option is especially useful when you use wildcards to compile all the source files in a directory, as in this line of code:

```
vbc /out:myprog *.vb
```

You can use the /recurse option to compile all the source files in the current directory and all its directories:

```
vbc /out:myprog /recurse:*.vb
```

Another useful option is /imports, which lets you specify projectwide Imports. (You can import multiple namespaces by separating each with a comma.) For example, you might delete the Imports statement in Teller.vb and be able to recompile the project anyway using this command:

```
vbc /out:myprog /imports:system *.vb
```

The /main option is necessary when two or more classes contain a Sub Main procedure so that the compiler can understand which procedure is the entry point for the application:

```
vbc /out:myprog /main:startclass *.vb
```

All the applications created so far were console applications. You can create other types of applications using the /target option, which can be shortened to /t. For example, you can create a standard Windows application with this code:

```
vbc /t:winexe /out:myprog *.vb
```

and a class library in a DLL with

```
vbc /t:library /out:mylib *.vb
```

Table 14-1 summarizes all the options that the VBC compiler supports. The rightmost column describes the corresponding option offered by Visual Studio .NET when applicable. In most cases, these options can be found in the project Property Pages dialog box. The most important option that can't be activated from inside Visual Studio .NET is /t:module, which creates a module that you can later add to an assembly by using the AL.exe utility:

```
vbc /t:module /out:mymodule *.vb
```

Note that if the program being compiled uses types defined in another module that was compiled using /target:module, you must use the /addmodule option to specify the referenced module:

```
vbc myapp /addmodule:other.netmodule
```

The other module becomes part of the application's assembly, and both executable files must be in the same directory when the application runs.

Table 14-1 Available Command-Line Options for the VBC Compiler and the Corresponding Options Inside Visual Basic .NET

Category	Option	Description	Visual Studio .NET Command
Output file	/out:*outfile*	Specifies the output filename.	Assembly Name (General page) and Output Path (Configuration Properties, Build page)
	/t[arget]:exe	Creates a console application (default if omitted).	Output Type (General page)
	/t[arget]:winexe	Creates a Windows application.	Output Type (General page)
	/t[arget]:library	Creates a library assembly.	Output Type (General page)
	/t[arget]:module	Creates a .netmodule module that can be added to an assembly.	Not available
	/main:*class*	Specifies the class that contains Sub Main.	Startup Object (General page)
	/baseaddress:*addr*	Specifies the default base address for the DLL, in hexadecimal.	DLL Base Address (Configuration Properties, Optimizations page)
Source files	*filespec* ...	Specifies one or more source files to compile; the file specification can include wildcards.	The list of files loaded in the project (as shown in Solution Explorer)
	/recurse:*filespec*	Searches subdirectories for all files to compile; the file specification can include wildcards.	Not available
References	/r[eference]:*assembly*	References an external assembly.	The Add Reference dialog box
	/libpath:*dir*	Specifies the path for external assemblies referenced with /r.	Not available
	/imports:*namespace,...*	Imports a namespace from one or more referenced assemblies.	Project Imports (Imports page)
	/addmodule:*filename*	Makes all the type information from a file compiled with /t:module available to the program being compiled.	Not available

Table 14-1 Available Command-Line Options for the VBC Compiler and the Corresponding Options Inside Visual Basic .NET *(continued)*

Category	Option	Description	Visual Studio .NET Command
Language settings	/rootnamespace:*name*	Defines the root namespace for this project.	Root Namespace (General page)
	/removeintchecks[+/-]	Removes integer checks.	Remove Integer Overflow Checks (Configuration Properties, Optimizations page)
	/d[efine]:*name=value,...*	Defines one or more compilation constants.	Custom Constants (Configuration Properties, Build page)
	/debug[+/-]	Generates debug information.	Generate Debugging Information (Configuration Properties, Build page)
	/nowarn	Suppresses the compiler's ability to generate warnings.	Enable Build Warnings (Configuration Properties, Build page)
	/warnaserror	Promotes warnings to errors.	Treat Compiler Warnings As Errors (Configuration Properties, Build page)
	/optionexplicit[+/-]	Requires explicit variable declarations.	Option Explicit (Common Properties, Build page)
	/optionstrict[+/-]	Enforces strict language semantics.	Option Strict (Common Properties, Build page)
	/optioncompare:text	Specifies text-style (case-insensitive) string comparisons.	Option Compare (Common Properties, Build page)
	/optioncompare:binary	Specifies binary-style (case sensitive) string comparisons.	Option Compare (Common Properties, Build page)
	/optimize[+/-]	Enables optimizations.	Enable Optimizations (Configuration Properties, Optimizations page)
Resources	/res[ource]:*filename*	Adds a file internally to the assembly. See SDK documentation for additional information on complete syntax.	Loaded resource files (Solution Explorer)

Table 14-1 Available Command-Line Options for the VBC Compiler and the Corresponding Options Inside Visual Basic .NET *(continued)*

Category	Option	Description	Visual Studio .NET Command
	/linkres[ource]:*file-name*	Links a file externally to the assembly. See SDK documentation for additional information on complete syntax.	Not available
	/win32icon:*iconfile*	Specifies an icon .ico file.	Application Icon (Common Properties, Build page)
	/win32resource:*resfile*	Specifies a Win32 resource file.	Not available
Assembly settings	/keyfile:*filename*	Specifies key file for the assembly.	Not available
	/keycontainer:*string*	Specifies key container name for the assembly.	Not available
	/version:*ma.mi.re.bu*	Specifies a version in the format *major.minor. revision.build*.	Not available
Miscellaneous	/nologo	Suppresses the display of the compiler copyright banner.	n/a
	/? or /help	Displays this list of available options.	n/a
	@*responsefile*	Retrieves command-line settings from a response file.	n/a
	/bugreport:*filename*	Creates a bug report file.	n/a
	/utf8output	Displays compiler output using UTF-8 encoding.	n/a
	/quiet	Suppresses display of source code lines for syntax errors.	n/a

The Assembly Linker (AL)

The Assembly Linker can take one or more managed modules (and zero or more resource files) and combine them to deliver an assembly—or more precisely, another module that contains an assembly manifest. For example, the following commands produce an assembly from the Teller.vb module:

```
vbc /t:module teller.vb
al teller.mcm /t:lib /out:mylib.dll /version:1.2.3.4
```

The /version switch supports several variants, other than the canonical major.minor.revision.build format. You can

- Specify only the major number—the minor, revision, and build numbers will be 0.
- Specify only the major and minor numbers—the revision and build numbers will be 0.
- Specify the major and minor numbers followed by an asterisk (1.2.*)—the revision number will be set equal to the number of days since January 1, 2000, and the build number will be set equal to the number of seconds since midnight, divided by 2.
- Specify the major, minor, and revision numbers followed by an asterisk (1.2.3.*)—the build number will be set equal to the number of seconds since midnight, divided by 2.

For example, I ran the following command around noon on March 31, 2000:

```
al teller.mcm /t:lib /out:mylib.dll /version:1.2.* /comp:VB2THEMAX
    /trade:"(C) 2000 Francesco Balena"
```

Then I right-clicked the teller.dll file from Windows Explorer and verified that the file version was 1.2.424.18558. (See Figure 14-13.) Also, note that you can set many other version-related properties, such as the company name and the legal trademark strings, by means of appropriate switches on the command line. See Table 14-2 for a complete list of supported switches.

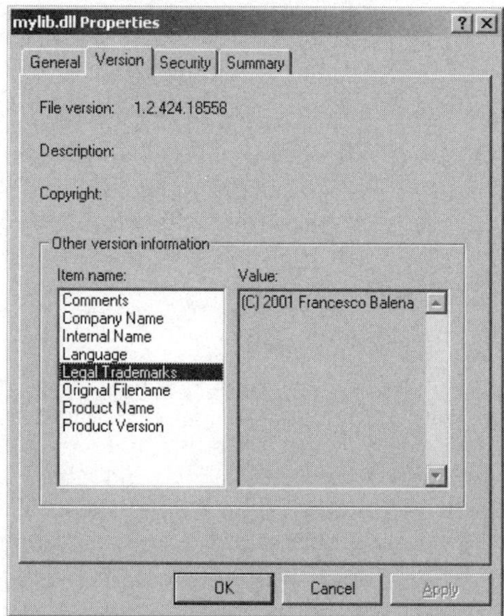

Figure 14-13. The Version tab of the Properties window for the mylib.dll file shows the revision and build generated by the AL.

I've already discussed a few other options in the "Partial Signing and Key Containers" section, such as /delaysign for partial (delayed) signing and /keyfile and /keyname for signing the assembly with a public key.

Table 14-2 Available Command-Line Options for the AL Assembly Linker Tool

Category	AL Option	Description
Source	*filename* [,*targetfile*]	A managed module that doesn't contain a manifest; if *targetfile* is provided, AL copies the file there and then begins the compilation.
	/embed[resource]: *file*	A resource file to be embedded into the PE file being created.
	/link[resource]: *file*	A resource file to be linked from the PE file being created.
Output file	/out:*filename*	The name of the file that will contain the assembly manifest.
	/t[arget]:lib | exe | win	The type of the output file: a DLL library, a console application, a Windows GUI application.
	/main: *class.method*	The method that works as the entry point to the assembly.
	/base[address]: *hexaddr*	The base address where the DLL will be loaded (hexadecimal).
Resources	/win32res:*file*	Embeds a Win32 resource file (.res) in the output file.
	/win32icon:*file*	Inserts a Win32 icon file (.ico) in the output file.
Version	/version: *ma.mi.rev.build*	The assembly version number. You can omit any version portion to the right of *major*; you can use an asterisk for *rev.build* or *build*, in which case *rev* will be the number of days since 1/1/2000 and *build* the number of seconds since midnight divided by 2.
	/fileversion:*version*	A value for the File Version string in the assembly.
	/c[ulture]: *culture*	The supported culture.
	/productv[ersion]: "*text*"	Informational version: a string version to be used in product and marketing literature. You need to enclose the string in double quotation marks if it contains spaces and other punctuation characters. (This rule applies to all of the following options in the Version category.)

Table 14-2 Available Command-Line Options for the AL Assembly Linker Tool

Category	AL Option	Description
	/product:"*text*"	The name of the product.
	/comp[any]:"*text*"	The company name.
	/copy[right]:"*text*"	The copyright string.
	/trade[mark]:"*text*"	The trademark string.
	/descr[iption]:"*text*"	The product description string.
	/config[uration]:"*text*"	The configuration string.
	/title:"*text*"	The title for the assembly.
	/template:*filename*	Specifies another assembly from which to inherit all the metadata except the culture field; this is especially useful when building satellite assemblies.
Assembly settings	/algid:*id*	The algorithm to use to hash files in a multifile assembly; *id* is a hexadecimal value equal to CALG_SHA1 (default) or CALG_MD5.
	/delay[sign][+/–]	Marks the assembly for partial or delayed signing (requires /keyfile or /keyname).
	/keyf[ile]:*file*	Specifies a file that contains the public/private key to make a shared assembly (or only the public key if partial signing).
	/keyn[ame]:*file*	Specifies a key container for the public/private key pair.
	/e[vidence]:*file*	Embeds a file in the assembly with the resource name Security.Evidence.
	/flags:*hexvalue*	A value for the Flag field in the assembly; hexvalue can be 0 (side-by-side compatible), 10 (incompatible with other versions in the same AppDomain), 20 (incompatible with other versions in the same process), or 30 (incompatible with other versions in the same system).
Miscellaneous	/nologo	Suppresses the display of the compiler copyright banner.
	/? or /help	Displays this list of available options.
	@*responsefile*	Retrieves command-line settings from a response file.
	/bugreport:*filename*	Creates a bug report file.
	/fullpaths	Displays complete filenames in error messages.

The Strong Name Utility (SN)

The SN utility helps you create assemblies with strong names and is therefore necessary to create shared assemblies. It has several options, only one of which can be specified at a given time.

The most useful command is –k, which creates a random public/private key pair and stores it in a file of your choice:

```
sn -k mykey.snk
```

This command produces the mykey.snk file, which contains the key pair.

The –p command extracts the public key from an .snk file and stores it in another file, ready to be referenced by the /keyfile option of the VBC compiler or AL linker when you're doing delayed signing:

```
sn -p mykey.snk public.key
```

The file produced by the –p command contains the public key in a binary, non-readable format. You can use the –o command to get it in a textual CSV (comma-separated value) format, which can be useful for initializing an array in source code:

```
sn -o mykey.snk public.csv
```

(The result is copied into the Clipboard if you omit the filename.) You can also extract the public key from an existing assembly by using the –e command:

```
sn -e mylib.dll public.key
```

The –T and –t commands display the token of the public key contained in an assembly file or an .snk file, respectively. As I explained in the "Private and Shared Assemblies" section, the token is an 8-byte hash value of the public key; the runtime uses this token instead of the full public key when referencing the assembly from another assembly. You can use –Tp or –tp to display the public key together with the token:

```
sn -tp mykey.snk
```

The –v option simply verifies the shared name in a given assembly—that is, it checks that the hash value is correct:

```
sn -v mylib.dll
```

I've already hinted at the –Vr and –R commands in the section "Partial Signing and Key Containers" earlier in this chapter. The –Vr option registers the assembly for verification skipping (so that you can install it in the GAC without an actual private key), and the –R command re-signs a previously signed or a partially signed assembly using the key pair in the specified file:

```
sn -R mylib.dll mykey.snk
```

For additional information about the SN utility, see the .NET Framework SDK documentation.

The Global Assembly Cache Utility (GACUTIL)

The GACUTIL tool lets you manage the global assembly cache from the command line, scripts, or make files. It provides the same functionality as the shfusion.dll GAC viewer, which you transparently use when you're browsing the GAC with Windows Explorer.

The GACUTIL tool supports only a handful of commands, which I summarize in Table 14-3. For example, the following command installs the mylib.dll assembly in the global assembly cache:

```
gacutil /i mylib.dll
```

You can remove this assembly from the GAC with the following command:

```
gacutil /u mylib
```

(Note that you pass the assembly name, not the filename.) A potential problem with the /u command is that it removes every instance of the mylib assembly, regardless of its version number, culture, and public key. To avoid undesirable deletions, you should specify precisely what you want to delete, as follows:

```
gacutil -u mylib,ver=1.2.00,loc=it,PublicKeyToken=44cd4ab12f0a88a1
```

Finally, you can list all the shared assemblies in the GAC using this command:

```
gacutil /l
```

Table 14-3 Available Command-Line Options for the GACUTIL Tool

Option	Description
/i *filename*	Installs an assembly in the GAC.
/if *filename*	Installs an assembly in the GAC and forces an overwrite if the assembly exists already.
/ir *filename refscheme id descr*	Installs an assembly in the GAC with a traced reference; the argument must include the filename, the reference scheme (typically FILEPATH), the ID (typically the path of the assembly), and a description. Example: gacutil /ir myasm.dll FILEPATH c:\myprog\myasm.dll MyAssembly.
/u *asmname*	Removes an assembly from the GAC. The name of the assembly can include version, public key token, and locale (MyAsm,Version=1.2.0.0,Culture=en, PublicKeyToken= 874e23ab874e23ab).
/ur *asmname refscheme id descr*	Removes an assembly reference from the GAC. The name of the assembly can include version, public key token, and locale; other arguments are the same as for /ir.
/uf *asmname*	Removes an assembly reference from the GAC. The name of the assembly can include version, public key token, and locale. The assembly will be removed only if not referenced by Windows Installer.
/ungen *asmname*	Removes an assembly from the cache of pre-JITted files. (For additional information, read the section on the NGEN utility later in this chapter.)
/l	Lists all the assemblies in the GAC and the assemblies in the cache of pre-JITted files.
/lr	Lists all the assemblies in the GAC with traced reference information.
/ldl	Lists the contents of the downloaded files cache.
/cdl	Deletes the contents of the download cache.
/nologo	Suppresses display of logo.
/silent	Suppresses display of all output.
/? or /help	Displays a help page.

The MSIL Disassembler (ILDASM)

I've already covered the ILDASM tool in the "Microsoft Intermediate Language (MSIL)" section earlier in this chapter. I'll just focus here on the options you can specify from the command line.

A great feature of the ILDASM tool is its ability to generate text files that can be fed to the MSIL Assembler tool (ILASM), which is a compiler that accepts MSIL code directly. This feature enables you to perform a *code round-trip*—that is, first create an executable using a more traditional, higher-level, language and then produce the MSIL code, edit it (for example, to add attributes not supported by the high-level language), and pass the edited source code to the ILASM tool. You've seen an example of round-trip code in Chapter 1.

ILDASM supports a group of advanced command-line settings, which you must explicitly enable using the /adv switch. This option works also when you're working with a graphical user interface and extends the View menu with additional commands. (See Figure 14-14.)

```
ildasm /adv mylib.dll
```

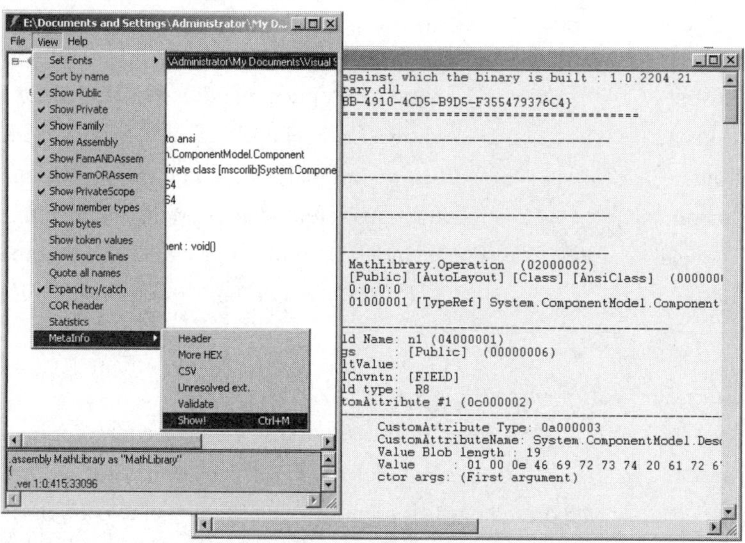

Figure 14-14. The menu commands added by the /adv option. The background window shows a sample of the output produced by clicking Show! on the MetaInfo submenu.

The following command outputs complete metadata information in a file to the console window:

```
ildasm /adv /text /all mylib.dll
```

See Table 14-4 for the complete list of all ILDASM command-line options. Note that all options are case insensitive and can be shortened to three characters (/BYT instead of /bytes). You can use the = separator instead of the colon character.

Table 14-4 Available Command-Line Options for the ILDASM Tool

Category	Option	Description
Output destination	/output:*filename*	Sends output to a file instead of a window.
	/text	Sends output to a console window.
Scope	/visibility:*vis* [+vis...]	Disassembles only types with specified visibility; vis can be PUB, PRI, FAM, ASM, FAA, FOA, or PSC.
	/pubonly	Disassembles only public types (same as /visibility:PUB).
Output contents	/all	Combines the /header, /bytes, and /tokens options.
	/bytes	Shows actual bytes as instruction comments (in hex).
	/raweh	Shows exception handler clauses in raw form.
	/tokens	Shows metadata tokens of classes and members.
	/source	Shows original source lines as comments.
	/linenum	Includes references to original source lines.
	/quoteallnames	Includes all names in single quotation marks.
Options for file/console output only	/utf8	Uses UTF-8 encoding for output (default is ANSI).
	/unicode	Uses Unicode for output.
	/noil	Suppresses MSIL assembly code output.
	/header	Includes file header information.
	/item:*class* [::*method sig*]	Disassembles only the specific class or method (.exe, .dll, .obj, .lib files; console output only if /OUT is specified).
	/objectfile: *filename*	Shows metadata of a specific object file in a library (.lib files; console output only if /OUT is specified).
Advanced options	/adv	Enables advanced command-line options and menu items. This option must precede other options in this group.
	/stats	Includes statistics on the image.
	/classlist	Includes a list of the classes defined in the module.
	/all	Combines /header, /bytes, /stats, /classlist, and /tokens options.

Table 14-4 Available Command-Line Options for the ILDASM Tool *(continued)*

Category	Option	Description
	/metadata: *specifier*	Shows metadata information; *specifier* can be MDHEADER (metadata header information and sizes), HEX (more things in hex as well as text), CSV (header sizes in CSV format), UNREX (unresolved externals), VALIDATE (validate the metadata for consistency).
Miscellaneous	/? or /help	Shows a summary of command-line switches.
	/adv /?	Shows a summary of standard and advanced command-line switches.
	/nobar	Suppresses disassembly progress bar popup.

The Native Image Generator Utility (NGEN)

The NGEN utility is what many articles and books written about beta versions of the .NET Framework refer to as the *pre-JIT compiler*. This little but useful utility works a bit like a traditional compiler in that it transforms the MSIL language in an assembly into native code that can be fed directly to the CPU. However, it differs in several important ways from a traditional compiler:

- The native code version of an assembly is stored in a special native code cache that you can't access directly. For example, you can't ship this native compiled version to your customers as you would do with the EXE files produced by Visual Basic 6.
- The .NET runtime uses the native compiled code only if the binding process would pick up the original MSIL assembly. In other words, if you use NGEN to compile version 1.0.0.0 of a given DLL, the native code version is used only when a .NET application requests that specific version of the DLL. In all other cases, the binding mechanism looks for the specific version requested by the application, and the native code version will be ignored. (But of course, you can use the application's configuration file to redirect all requests to version 1.0.0.0.) You must use NGEN for all the subsequent versions of the assembly to ensure that the native code version is always used, regardless of the requested version.

- The native code that NGEN generates is affected by the current application configuration, including binding policy, security policy, and development environment settings (such as debugging and profiling). If the configuration changes—for example, because you provide a custom configuration file that specifies a different binding policy—the runtime can't reuse the native compiled code and will load and JIT-compile the original assembly.
- Whenever you recompile the original source code and generate a new MSIL assembly with the same versions and similar attributes as one in the native-code cache, the new version becomes the active assembly and the one in the native-code cache is discarded. Hence, you need to rerun NGEN whenever you recompile an assembly to ensure that the native code version is used.
- Files in the native image cache depend on the runtime version. If you install a new version of the .NET runtime—for example, a Service Pack—you must rerun NGEN for all the assemblies you mean to precompile as native code.

As you might remember from Chapter 1, the JIT compiler transforms IL code into native code when your application invokes a method for the first time and then always uses the native code. The NGEN utility performs this transforming step before execution and can therefore reduce the start-up time of applications that perform a lot of method calls when they run. (Windows Forms applications can greatly benefit from this utility, for example.) However, the NGEN utility can't apply a few advanced optimization techniques that are possible with the JIT compiler—for example, cross-assembly optimization or code inlining based on how frequently a method is invoked—so you might even end up with code that's *slower* than standard JIT-compiled code.

Using NGEN is really easy because you just pass the list of assemblies to be compiled on its command line:

```
ngen MyApp.exe FirstLib.dll SecondLib.dll
```

You can also specify an assembly by its name (and optionally version, culture, and public key token), which makes sense for shared assemblies already installed in the GAC:

```
ngen MyApp,Ver=1.0.0.0,Culture="us",PublicKeyToken=23a123bef89123ca
```

You can use the /delete option to delete a specific assembly and the /show option to display all the assemblies in the native image cache. (If you've never run NGEN on your assemblies, the latter command displays the names of a few precompiled assemblies in the .NET runtime.)

Three options let you create native code images that can be debugged or profiled. (By default, compiled assemblies generated by NGEN don't work with debuggers or profilers.) The /debug option generates an image that works with a debugger, /debugopt generates an image that works with a debugger in optimized debugged mode, and /prof generates an image that works with a profiler that requires instrumented code. (Check your profiler's documentation to see whether it requires this option.) In practice, you will rarely use these options because it's easier to debug and profile assemblies in plain MSIL code.

Assembly Custom Attributes

You can set many assembly properties directly from inside your source code, via the many attribute classes in the System.Reflection namespace. As a matter of fact, new Visual Basic .NET projects include a file named AssemblyInfo.vb, which contains template code for all the attributes described in the next section.

The AssemblyInfo.vb File

A peculiarity of assembly attributes is that you must explicitly tell the compiler that the custom attribute refers to the assembly by prefixing the attribute name with *Assembly:*. For example, the following source code defines a few attributes for the assembly under development:

```
Imports System.Reflection
Imports System.Runtime.InteropServices

<Assembly: AssemblyVersion("1.5.*")>
<Assembly: AssemblyInformationalVersion("1.5")>
<Assembly: AssemblyCopyright("(C) 2001 VB2TheMax")>

' ... (And so on)
```

Table 14-5 lists all the assembly custom attributes that the runtime supports, together with the corresponding AL command-line switches. For more information about the AssemblyVersion attribute, read the "Creating a Sample Client Application" section earlier in this chapter.

Table 14-5 The Custom Attributes for Setting Assembly Options in Source Code, and the Corresponding AL Command-Line Switches

Attribute	AL Switch	Description
AssemblyVersion	/version	The assembly version number; can use * for the revision + build or just the build number to let the runtime generate version numbers using a time-based algorithm.
AssemblyFileVersion	/fileversion	The Win32 version number, which doesn't have to be equal to the assembly version.
AssemblyCulture	/culture	The supported culture. Note that passing a nonempty string marks the assembly as a satellite assembly, which is an assembly that contains only resources for a given culture. You shouldn't use a nonempty string for a regular assembly.
AssemblyAlgorithmId	/algid	The algorithm used to hash files in a multifile assembly.
AssemblyDelaySign	/delaysign	Marks the assembly for partial or delayed signing. (Takes True or False; requires either AssemblyKeyFile or AssemblyKeyName.)
AssemblyKeyFile	/keyfile	The file that contains the public/private key to make a shared assembly (or only the public key if partial signing).
AssemblyKeyName	/keyname	The key container that holds the public/private key pair.
AssemblyFlags	/flags	Assembly flags, which tell which degree of side-by-side support the assembly offers.
AssemblyInformational-Version	/productversion	Informational version: a string version to be used in product and marketing literature.
AssemblyProduct	/product	The name of the product.
AssemblyCompany	/company	The company name.
AssemblyCopyright	/copyright	The copyright string.
AssemblyTrademark	/trademark	The trademark string.
AssemblyDescription	/description	The product description string.
AssemblyConfiguration	/configuration	The configuration string.
AssemblyTitle	/title	The title for the assembly.
AssemblyDefaultAlias	(n/a)	A friendly default alias for the assembly manifest.

The AppDomain Class

You might remember from Chapter 1 that .NET applications are hosted in AppDomains and that a single Windows process can host more than one AppDomain. In this section, you'll learn more about AppDomains and the System.AppDomain class.

Properties, Methods, and Events

Let's start by having a look at the most important and useful properties, methods, and events of the AppDomain class. (See Table 14-6.) The easiest thing you can do with these properties is to list some information about the running application domain:

```
Sub TestAppDomainProperties()
    ' Get a reference to the running AppDomain.
    Dim ad As AppDomain = AppDomain.CurrentDomain

    ' Print main properties.
    Console.WriteLine("BaseDirectory = {0}", ad.BaseDirectory)
    Console.WriteLine("FriendlyName = {0}", ad.FriendlyName)
    Console.WriteLine("RelativeSearchPath = {0}", _
        ad.RelativeSearchPath)
    Console.WriteLine("ShadowCopyFiles = {0}", _
        ad.ShadowCopyFiles)
    Console.WriteLine("CurrentThreadId = {0}", _
        AppDomain.GetCurrentThreadId)

    ' Display more information from the AppDomainSetup object.
    Dim ads As AppDomainSetup = ad.SetupInformation

    Console.WriteLine("ApplicationName = {0}", _
        ads.ApplicationName)
    Console.WriteLine("CachePath = {0}", ads.CachePath)
    Console.WriteLine("ConfigurationFile = {0}", _
        ads.ConfigurationFile)
    Console.WriteLine("DisallowPublisherPolicy = {0}", _
        ads.DisallowPublisherPolicy)
    Console.WriteLine("LoaderOptimization = {0}", _
        ads.LoaderOptimization)
    Console.WriteLine("PrivateBinPath = {0}", ads.PrivateBinPath)
    Console.WriteLine("ShadowCopyFiles = {0}", _
        ads.ShadowCopyFiles)
```

Note that all the properties are read-only; more precisely, properties of the AppDomainSetup object are writable, but only before the application domain is actually loaded in memory. Listing all the assemblies loaded in an application domain is also easy:

```
' ...(Continuing the TestAppDomainProperties procedure)...
    ' Display the list of loaded assemblies.
    Dim asm As Reflection.Assembly
    Console.WriteLine("Assemblies loaded in current domain:")
    For Each asm In ad.GetAssemblies
        Console.WriteLine("    " & asm.FullName)
    Next
End Sub
```

Table 14-6 Main Instance and Shared Members of the AppDomain Class

Category	Syntax	Description
Properties	CurrentDomain	Returns the AppDomain object for the current thread (shared property).
	FriendlyName	Gets the friendly name for the AppDomain, formed by the name + extension of the executable file (without the path).
	BaseDirectory	Gets the main directory used for probing assemblies.
	RelativeSearchPath	Gets the path, relative to the base directory, where the runtime can probe for private assemblies.
	ShadowCopyFiles	Returns True if all assemblies loaded in the application domain are shadow copied—that is, their executable files are first copied in another directory and then loaded in memory from there. Shadow copying is an important feature of .NET in that it allows the developer to replace assemblies while the main application is running.
	SetupInformation	Returns an AppDomainSetup object that contains additional information about the application domain. (See Table 14-7.)
Methods	CreateDomain(name, evidence, setup)	Creates a new application domain with specified name, evidence, and setup information (shared method).

Table 14-6 Main Instance and Shared Members of the AppDomain Class *(continued)*

Category	Syntax	Description
	Unload(appdomain)	Unloads the specified application domain (shared method).
	GetCurrentThreadId	Returns the current thread identifier (shared method).
	ClearPrivatePath	Resets the path used when probing for private assemblies.
	AppendPrivatePath(path)	Adds a path to the list of paths used when probing for private assemblies.
	SetShadowCopyFiles	Turns on shadow copying of loaded assemblies.
	SetCachePath(path)	Sets the directory used for shadow copying loaded assemblies.
	GetAssemblies	Returns an array of Assembly objects, corresponding to all the assemblies loaded in a given application domain.
	IsFinalizingForUnload	Returns True if the application domain is unloading and the runtime is finalizing all the objects still in the managed heap.
	ExecuteAssembly(filename)	Executes the specified assembly from within a given application domain.
	CreateInstance(asmname, typename)	Creates an instance of the specified type from the specified assembly (returns an ObjectHandle).
	CreateInstanceAndUnwrap(asmname, typename)	Creates an instance of the specified type from the specified assembly and unwraps the ObjectHandle into an Object value.
	CreateInstanceFrom(asmfile, typename)	Creates an instance of the specified type from the specified assembly file (returns an ObjectHandle).
	CreateInstanceFromAndUnwrap(asmfile, typename)	Creates an instance of the specified type from the specified assembly file and unwraps the ObjectHandle into an Object value.

Table 14-6 Main Instance and Shared Members of the AppDomain Class *(continued)*

Category	Syntax	Description
	DoCallback(delegate)	Executes the delegate from a given application domain.
Events	AssemblyLoad	Fires when an assembly is loaded; the second argument exposes a LoadedAssembly property that specifies which assembly is being loaded (as a System.Reflection.Assembly object).
	AssemblyResolve	Fires when the binding to an assembly fails; the argument exposes a Name property equal to the name of the assembly in question.
	ResourceResolve	Fires when the resolution of a resource fails; the argument exposes a Name property equal to the name of the resource in question.
	TypeResolve	Fires when the resolution of a type fails; the argument exposes a Name property equal to the name of the type in question. (You get this event when the runtime can't determine the name of the assembly hosting the requested type.)
	DomainUnload	Fires when an application domain is about to terminate (but not when the process hosting the application domain is also terminating).
	ProcessExit	Fires on the main AppDomain object of a process when the process is terminating.
	UnhandledException	Fires when an exception is not caught by any exception handler; the received argument exposed the ExceptionObject property and the IsTerminating property (True if the runtime is terminating).

Table 14-7 Main Properties of the AppDomainSetup Class

Syntax	Description
ApplicationBase	The name of the directory containing the application.
ApplicationName	The name of the application.
CachePath	The name of the directory used for assemblies being shadow copied.
ConfigurationFile	The name of the configuration file.
DisallowPublisherPolicy	True if publisher policy should be disabled for this application domain.
LicenseFile	The location of the license file associated with this application domain.
LoaderOptimization	The optimization policy used to load an executable. (See the section "The LoaderOptimization Attribute" later in this chapter.)
PrivateBinPath	The list of directories used when probing for private assemblies. (The semicolon is used as a separator.)
ShadowCopyFiles	A string equal to "true" if assemblies should be shadow copied.

Creating AppDomains

Creating a new application domain is relatively simple: you create a new AppDomainSetup object and use it in the AppDomain.CreateDomain shared method:

```
' Prepare setup info.
Dim ads As New AppDomainSetup()
ads.ApplicationName = "NewApplication"
ads.ApplicationBase = "c:\windows\temp"
ads.PrivateBinPath = "bins;assemblies"
' Create the new application domain.
Dim ad As AppDomain = _
    AppDomain.CreateDomain("NewAppDomain", Nothing, ads)
' Check that setup properties were initialized correctly.
Console.WriteLine(ad.FriendlyName)      ' => NewAppDomain
Console.WriteLine(ad.BaseDirectory)     ' => c:\windows\temp
Console.WriteLine(ads.PrivateBinPath)   ' => bins;assemblies
```

Of course, after creating an application domain you should find a way to have some code running inside it; otherwise, the operation doesn't make much sense. If you have an assembly in an .exe file, you can run it inside the freshly created application domain by using the ExecuteAssembly method. For example, the demo application on the companion CD contains an executable named

ShowAppDomainData.exe, which runs the TestAppDomainProperties procedure seen in the preceding section. The following code shows how you can run this assembly in the application domain that you've just created:

```
ad.ExecuteAssembly("ShowAppDomainData.exe")
```

If the assembly is contained in a DLL, you can still run code inside it by instantiating one of the types that it defines, through the CreateInstance and CreateInstanceFrom methods. To see how this works, create a TestAppDomain.dll file containing the following class:

```
<Serializable()> _
Public Class AppDomainData
    Public ReadOnly ThreadID As Integer = _
        AppDomain.GetCurrentThreadId
    Public ReadOnly AppName As String = _
        AppDomain.CurrentDomain.FriendlyName
End Class
```

Next copy the DLL into the same directory as the current application's executable, and run this code:

```
' Create the new application domain.
Dim ad As AppDomain = _
    AppDomain.CreateDomain("NewAppDomain", Nothing, ads)
Dim oh As System.Runtime.Remoting.ObjectHandle
Dim o As Object

' Create an instance of AppDomainData; get an object handle.
oh = ad.CreateInstanceFrom("TestAppDomain.Dll", _
    "TestAppDomain.AppDomainData")
' Unwrap the object handle into an Object variable.
o = oh.Unwrap
' This code assumes that Option Strict is off.
Console.WriteLine("ThreadID = {0}", o.ThreadID)
Console.WriteLine("AppName = {0}", o.AppName)     ' => NewAppDomain
```

Note that a class must be marked as serializable to be passed by value across a different application domain: a copy of the object is sent to the calling assembly in the form of an ObjectHandle object, which must be unwrapped into a regular variable; alternatively, you can use the CreateInstanceAndUnwrap or CreateInstanceFromAndUnwrap method, which does the unwrapping automatically. If the calling assembly has a reference to the returned type, you can store the object reference in a specific variable; otherwise, you must use a generic Object variable and use late binding, as the preceding code does.

Using serializable classes isn't the only way you have to access an object from another application domain. If you create a class that inherits from System.

MarshalByRefObject, its instances will stay in the application domain that defines it and they will be passed to the other application domain by reference. This is similar to what you do in Visual Basic 6 with DCOM objects:

```
Public Class RemotableType
    Inherits MarshalByRefObject
    ⋮
End Class
```

You can use the AppDomain.Unload shared method to unload a specific application domain and all the assemblies currently loaded in it:

```
' The ad variable contains a reference to an AppDomain object.
AppDomain.Unload(ad)
```

Because the common language runtime doesn't provide a method for unloading individual assemblies, the ability to unload an application domain gives you a little granularity in how you can release memory allocated to assemblies. The Unload method aborts all the threads in the target application domain. Note that the default application domain—that is, the application domain loaded when the process starts—is unloaded only when the process terminates.

Speaking of threads, remember that there isn't a one-to-one correspondence among application domains and threads: one thread can jump from one application domain to another (in the same process), and of course, one application domain can host multiple threads.

Catching Unhandled Exceptions

Table 14-6 lists all the events exposed by the AppDomain class. Three of these events—namely, AssemblyResolve, ResourceResolve, and TypeResolve—fire when the common language runtime fails to load an assembly, a resource, or a type. They might be useful for diagnostic purposes, or when you want to provide a way to supply alternative locations for the target data, but most applications won't need to trap these events. Also, the AssemblyLoad event is useful mostly for diagnostic purposes and little more.

The DomainUnload and ProcessExit events are more interesting. For example, you might use the ProcessExit event to ensure that all resources are correctly released when the application ends. Even more interesting, this event might set a global flag that code inside Finalize methods can test to determine why the object is being finalized. Consider the following example:

```
Module MainModule
    Dim WithEvents CurrAppDomain As AppDomain
    ' This is True when the application is exiting.
```

(continued)

```
    Public AppIsExiting As Boolean

    Sub Main()
        ' Prepare to trap AppDomain events.
        CurrAppDomain = AppDomain.CurrentDomain
        ' Create a DataClass instance, and collect it.
        Dim dc As New DataClass()
        dc = Nothing
        GC.Collect()
        ' Create an instance of DataClass that is collected
        ' only when the application exits.
        Dim dc2 As New DataClass()
    End Sub

    ' This event fires when the application exits.
    Sub CurrAppDomain_ProcessExit(ByVal sender As Object, _
        ByVal e As System.EventArgs) _
        Handles CurrAppDomain.ProcessExit
        Console.WriteLine("Exiting...")
        ' Set the global flag.
        AppIsExiting = True
    End Sub
End Module

Class DataClass
    Public ID As Integer

    Protected Overrides Sub Finalize()
        Console.Write("Finalizing DataClass - ")
        Console.WriteLine("AppIsExiting is {0}", AppIsExiting)
    End Sub
End Class
```

This is what appears in the Console window:

```
Finalizing DataClass (AppIsExiting is False)
Exiting...
Finalizing DataClass (AppIsExiting is True)
```

The UnhandledException event fires whenever an unhandled exception occurs in your application. Its second argument receives an UnhandledException-EventArgs object, which exposes two properties, ExceptionObject and IsTerminating. The former is of course the exception being thrown, but it returns an Object value, and you must cast it to an Exception variable before you can read the usual properties such as Message and StackTrace. The second property is True if the exception is fatal and will terminate the application: this is the case when the exception is thrown on the main thread (the thread that was created when the application began its execution) or on an unmanaged thread created outside the .NET runtime. The IsTerminating property is False when the exception is thrown on a thread that you have created yourself, a thread borrowed from the thread pool (for example, the thread that serves a timer), or the special thread that executes all Finalize methods. The following example shows how you can trap the UnhandledException event:

```
Dim WithEvents CurrAppDomain As AppDomain

Sub Main()
    ' Prepare to trap AppDomain events.
    CurrAppDomain = AppDomain.CurrentDomain

    ' Cause an exception on a secondary thread.
    ' (It will show a message with IsTerminating = False.)
    Dim t As New Threading.Thread(AddressOf ThrowException)
    t.Start()
    Threading.Thread.Sleep(500)

    ' Cause a fatal exception on the main thread.
    ' (It will show a message with IsTerminating = True.)
    Throw New IndexOutOfRangeException()
End Sub

Sub ThrowException()
    Throw New DivideByZeroException()
End Sub

Sub CurrAppDomain_UnhandledException(ByVal sender As Object, _
    ByVal e As System.UnhandledExceptionEventArgs) _
    Handles CurrAppDomain.UnhandledException
    ' Get a reference to the exception.
    Dim ex As Exception = CType(e.ExceptionObject, Exception)
    ' Show information about the current exception.
    Console.WriteLine("{0}  (IsTerminating={1})", ex.Message, _
        e.IsTerminating)
End Sub
```

One important thing about this event: you can trap it correctly only when the application isn't running under the Visual Studio debugger, so you must start the program by choosing Start Without Debugging from the Debug menu or by pressing the Ctrl+F5 key combination. This is the output that the preceding code sends to the Console window:

```
Attempted to divide by zero.  (IsTerminating=False)
Index was outside the bounds of the array.  (IsTerminating=True)
```

All fatal exceptions cause the dialog shown in Figure 14-15 to appear, so you'll have to click No before you can see the second line in the preceding output.

Although the UnhandledException event can be useful, keep in mind that you can't catch and solve every unhandled exception using this technique. In practice, you can save only any unsaved data, log the exception somewhere (for example, in the system event log), and display a dialog box to inform the user that the application is closing. This dialog box might offer the option of sending a bug report to the producer of the application (you) and maybe restart the application on the same data file. (This is exactly what Visual Studio .NET itself does when an unhandled exception occurs.)

> **Note** In the "Global Error Handlers" section of Chapter 16, you'll learn about the ThreadException event of the Application object, which provides the ability to trap *and recover from* unhandled exceptions in Windows Forms applications.

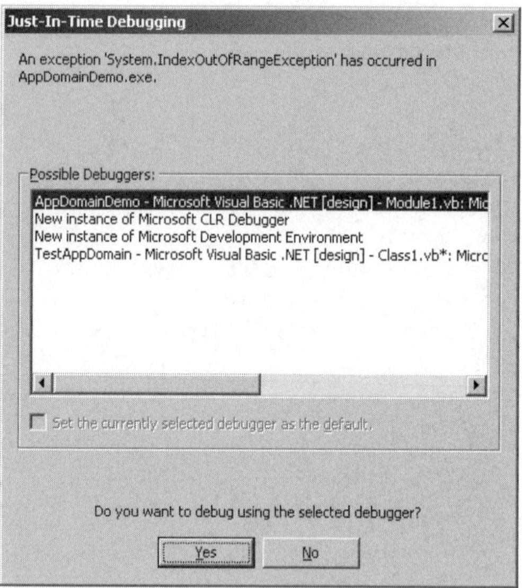

Figure 14-15. The dialog box that .NET applications display by default when an unhandled exception occurs.

The LoaderOptimization Attribute

Because all the application domains in a process share the same address space, they can share assemblies as well. For example, two ASP.NET applications running in two application domains inside the same process might load the same DLL only once. Loading an assembly only once in a process and sharing it among multiple application domains has a couple of advantages:

- Less memory is used because only one copy of the assembly code is loaded; the assembly will remain in memory until there is at least one application domain that uses it.
- The assembly is JIT-compiled only once, and therefore the start-up step is faster.

You must explicitly tell the JIT compiler that you want to share the assembly among multiple application domains in the same process; in this case, the assembly is said to be domain-neutral. The JIT compiler must ensure isolation among application domains, which it does by using an extra level of indirection to access fields and variables other than dynamic variables. This extra level of indirection causes domain-neutral assemblies to run slightly slower than regular ones; thus, you should use this setting only for large assemblies, for which saved memory makes this technique convenient.

You specify the type of optimization you want for your assembly by applying the LoaderOptimization attribute to the Sub Main procedure, as you see in the following code:

```
<LoaderOptimization(LoaderOptimization.MultiDomain)> _
Sub Main()
    ⋮
End Sub
```

(This attribute is ignored when applied to any method other than Sub Main.) You have three possible values for this attribute:

- **LoaderOptimization.SingleDomain** The assembly is optimized to work with single AppDomains, and it won't be shared among multiple application domains. (This is the default setting.)
- **LoaderOptimization.MultiDomain** The assembly is optimized to be shared among multiple application domains, all of which run the same application.
- **LoaderOptimization.MultiDomainHost** The assembly is optimized to be shared among multiple application domains, which don't necessarily run the same application.

Remember that this attribute is just a hint to the assembly loader; depending on specific circumstances, the runtime can ignore the optimization you requested and load the assembly using the default mode.

Now that you know how to create an assembly and bind it at run time, you have a more complete picture of what an assembly contains. So you're ready to master the Reflection namespace, which is what the next chapter is all about.

15

Reflection

Reflection is a set of classes that allow you to access and manipulate assemblies and modules and the types and the metadata that they contain. For example, you can use reflection to enumerate loaded assemblies, modules, and classes and the methods, properties, fields, and events that each class exposes. Reflection plays a fundamental role in the .NET Framework and works as a building block for other important portions of the runtime. For example, Visual Basic .NET implicitly uses reflection whenever you access an object's method through late binding, as in this code:

```
Dim o As Object = New Person
o.FirstName = "Francesco"                ' Late binding, uses reflection
```

The runtime uses reflection in many other circumstances, such as to enumerate fields when a type is being serialized or is being marshaled to another process or another machine.

Reflection code typically uses the classes in the System.Reflection namespace; the only class used by reflection outside this namespace is System.Type, which represents a type in a managed module. (Note that the concept of type is more generic than class, in that the former comprises classes, interfaces, value types, and enumeration types.) To keep code concise, samples in this chapter assume you have these statements at the top of your source code or as projectwide Imports:

```
Imports System
Imports System.Reflection
```

The .NET Framework also contains the System.Reflection.Emit namespace, whose classes let you create an assembly dynamically in memory. The Framework uses the classes in this namespace in many circumstances—for example, to compile a regular expression into IL code when the RegexOptions.Compiled option is specified. Because of its narrow scope, I won't cover the System.Reflection.Emit namespace in this book.

Working with Assemblies and Modules

The objects in the System.Reflection namespace form a logical hierarchy, at the top of which you find the Assembly class, as you can see in Figure 15-1. In this section, I describe the Assembly, AssemblyName, and Module classes.

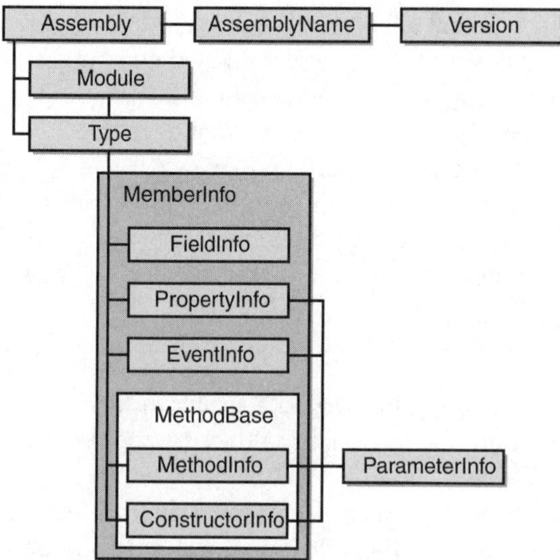

Figure 15-1. The Reflection logical hierarchy. All these classes belong to the System.Reflection namespace, except System.Type.FieldInfo, PropertyInfo, and EventInfo inherit from the MemberInfo abstract class, whereas MethodInfo and ConstructorInfo inherit from the MethodBase abstract class (which in turn derives from MemberInfo).

The Assembly Class

As its name implies, the Reflection.Assembly class represents a .NET assembly. A minor annoyance is that Assembly is also a reserved word for Visual Basic

.NET, so you must either use its complete class name or enclose its name in square brackets:

```
' These three statements are equivalent.
Dim asm As System.Reflection.Assembly
Dim asm As Reflection.Assembly       ' Assumes Imports System.
Dim asm As [Assembly]                ' Assumes Imports System.Reflection.
```

The Assembly class offers no constructor method because you never actually create an assembly, but simply get a reference to an existing assembly. Instead, the Assembly class exposes several shared methods that return a reference to an assembly, either running or not (that is, stored on disk but currently not running):

```
' Get a reference to the assembly this code is running in.
asm = Reflection.Assembly.GetExecutingAssembly()

' Get a reference to an assembly given its filename.
asm = Reflection.Assembly.LoadFrom("c:\myapp\mylib.dll")

' Get a reference to an assembly given its display name.
' (The argument can be the assembly's full name, which includes
'  version, culture, and public key.)
asm = Reflection.Assembly.Load("mscorlib")

' You can use this method when you don't have the full name.
asm = Reflection.Assembly.LoadWithPartialName("System.Xml")
' Get a reference to the assembly that contains a given Type.
' (The argument must be a System.Type value, so we need GetType.)
asm = Reflection.Assembly.GetAssembly(GetType(String))
```

Once you have a valid reference to an Assembly object, you can query its properties to learn additional information about it. For example, the FullName property returns a string that holds information about the version and the public key token. (This data is the same as the value the ToString method returns.)

```
' This is the main .NET Framework assembly.
asm = Reflection.Assembly.Load("mscorlib")
Console.Write(asm.FullName)
    ' => mscorlib, Version=1.0.3300.0, Culture=neutral,
    '     PublicKeyToken=b77a5c561934e089
```

The Location and CodeBase read-only properties both return the actual location of the assembly's file, so you can learn where assemblies in the global assembly cache are actually stored (information hidden by the shfusion.dll GAC viewer). When you're not working with assemblies downloaded from the Internet, the information these properties return differs only in format:

```
' ...(Continuing previous example)...
Console.WriteLine(asm.Location)
  ' => C:\WINNT\Microsoft.NET\Framework\v1.0.3512\mscorlib.dll
Console.WriteLine(asm.CodeBase)
  ' => file://C:/WINNT/Microsoft.NET/Framework/v1.0.3512/mscorlib.dll
' (The actual location can of course be different on your system.)
```

Note The version number of the framework and of some assemblies reported in this chapter are related to the beta RC3 version of the .NET Framework. Of course, you're going to see different values when you run this code on the release version.

The GlobalAssemblyCache property returns a Boolean value that tells whether the assembly was loaded from the GAC. The EntryPoint property returns a MethodInfo object that describes the entry point method for the assembly, or it returns Nothing if the assembly has no entry point (for example, if it's a DLL class library). MethodInfo objects are described in the "Retrieving Member Information" section later in this chapter.

The Assembly class exposes many instance methods, the majority of which allow you to enumerate all the modules, files, and types in the assembly. The GetModules method returns an array of references to all the contained Module objects, whereas the GetFiles method returns an array of FileStream objects that point to the physical files:

```
' Enumerate all the modules in an assembly.
Dim mo As [Module]
For Each mo In asm.GetModules
    Console.WriteLine(mo.FullyQualifiedName)
Next
```

(You can get a reference to a module or a file directly, via the GetModule and GetFile methods, respectively.) The GetTypes method returns an array with all the types (classes, interfaces, and so on) defined in an assembly:

```
' Enumerate all the types defined in an assembly.
Dim ty As Type
For Each ty In asm.GetTypes
    Console.WriteLine(ty.FullName)
Next
```

You can also list only the public types that an assembly exports by using the GetExportedTypes method.

The Assembly class overloads the GetType method inherited from System.Object so that it can take a class name and returns the specified Type object.

```
' Next statement assumes asm is pointing to MSCORLIB.
Dim ty As Type = asm.GetType("System.Int32")
```

If the assembly doesn't contain the specified type, the GetType method returns Nothing. You can have this method throw a TypeLoadException if the specified type isn't found by passing True as its second argument, and you can have the type name compared in a case-insensitive way by passing True as a third argument:

```
' This doesn't raise any exception because type name
' is compared in a case-insensitive way.
Dim ty As Type = asm.GetType("system.int32", True, True)
```

The CreateInstance method creates an instance of the specified type, which must be defined inside the assembly on which you invoke the method. This broadly matches the ability you have under Visual Basic 6 to create a COM component given its ProgID with the CreateObject function:

```
' A long-winded way to create an Integer
Dim o As Object = asm.CreateInstance("System.Int32")
' Prove that we created an Integer.
Console.Write(o.GetType.FullName)      ' => System.Int32
```

Two instance methods deal with custom attributes. GetCustomAttributes gets an array of all the custom attributes defined at the assembly level for this assembly, whereas IsDefined returns True if a given custom attribute is defined for this assembly. I already introduced these methods in the "Discovering Attributes at Run Time" section of Chapter 7, so I won't go into more detail concerning them here.

Finally, two methods of the Assembly class return an AssemblyName object, which is described in the next section.

The AssemblyName Class

The AssemblyName class represents the objects that .NET uses to hold the identity and to retrieve information about a shared assembly. A fully specified AssemblyName object has a name, a culture, and a version number, but the runtime can also use partially filled AssemblyName objects when searching for an assembly to be bound to a caller code.

Most often, you get a reference to an existing AssemblyName object by using the GetName property of the Assembly object:

```
' Get a reference to an assembly and its AssemblyName.
Dim asm As [Assembly] = Reflection.Assembly.Load("mscorlib")
Dim an As AssemblyName = asm.GetName
```

You can also get an array of AssemblyName objects using the GetReferencedAssemblies method:

```
' Get information on all the assemblies the current assembly references.
Dim anArr() As AssemblyName
anArr = [Assembly].GetExecutingAssembly.GetReferencedAssemblies()
```

Most of the properties of the AssemblyName object are self-explanatory, and some of them are also properties of the Assembly class (as is the case of FullName and CodeBase properties):

```
' (Of course you can get different output on your system, depending
'  on the runtime versions you've installed and system paths.)
Console.WriteLine(an.CodeBase)
    ' => file://C:/WINNT/Microsoft.NET/Framework/v1.0.3512/mscorlib.dll
' (Note that the version of mscorlib doesn't have to match the version
' of the .NET Framework.)
Console.WriteLine(an.FullName)
    ' => mscorlib, Version=1.0.3300.0, Culture=neutral,
    '     PublicKeyToken=b77a5c561934e089

' These properties come from the version object.
Console.WriteLine(an.Version.Major)         ' => 1
Console.WriteLine(an.Version.Minor)         ' => 0
Console.WriteLine(an.Version.Build)         ' => 3300
Console.WriteLine(an.Version.Revision)      ' => 0
' You can also get the version as a single number.
Console.WriteLine(an.Version.ToString)      ' => 1.0.3300.0
```

A few methods of the AssemblyName object return information about the assembly, in the form of Byte arrays. For example, you can get the public key and the public key token by using the GetPublicKey and GetPublicKeyToken methods:

```
' Display the public key token of the assembly
' as a comma-delimited list of bytes.
Dim b As Byte
For Each b In an.GetPublicKeyToken()
    Console.Write(b.ToString & ",")
Next
```

The SetPublicKey and SetPublicKeyToken methods let you modify the public key information stored in the assembly. The CultureInfo property gets or sets the culture supported by the assembly, or returns Nothing if the assembly is culture-neutral. The VersionCompatibility property gets or sets a value that tells the degree of the compatibility of the assembly with other versions of the same assembly running side by side in the same process, application domain, or machine. The result is a bit-coded AssemblyVersionCompatibility value that belongs to the System.Configuration.Assemblies enumerated type, so you have to test its bits using the And operator:

```
Dim avc As System.Configuration.Assemblies.AssemblyVersionCompatibility
avc = an.VersionCompatibility
If (avc And Configuration.Assemblies.AssemblyVersionCompatibility. _
    SameMachine) <> 0 Then
    Console.WriteLine("The assembly can run side by side with other" _
        & " versions of this assembly running on the same machine")
End If
```

The Module Class

The Module class represents one of the modules in an assembly; don't confuse it with a Visual Basic .NET program's Module block, which corresponds to a Type object instead. I already demonstrated that you can enumerate all the elements in an assembly by using the Assembly.GetModules method:

```
' Get a reference to the mscorlib assembly.
Dim asm As [Assembly] = Reflection.Assembly.Load("mscorlib")
' Enumerate all the modules in an assembly.
' (Note that Module is a reserved word in Visual Basic.)
Dim mo As [Module]
For Each mo In asm.GetModules
    Console.WriteLine(mo.Name & " - " & mo.ScopeName)
Next
```

The preceding code produces only one output line:

```
mscorlib.dll - CommonLanguageRuntimeLibrary
```

The Name property returns the name of the actual DLL or EXE, whereas the ScopeName property is a readable string that represents the module. The Assembly.GetModule method lets you retrieve a reference to a specific module if you know its ScopeName:

```
' Get a reference to the only module in mscorlib.dll.
mo = asm.GetModule("CommonLanguageRuntimeLibrary")
```

The FullyQualifiedName property returns the module filename and its path:

```
' ...(Continuing previous code snippet)...
Console.WriteLine(mo.FullyQualifiedName)
    ' => c:\winnt\microsoft.net\framework\v1.0.3512\mscorlib.dll
```

As for the Assembly object, the Module object exposes the GetType and GetTypes methods to retrieve a reference to a specific type or all the types contained in a Module. The Module object exposes two additional enumeration methods: GetFields returns an array of FieldInfo objects holding information about all the module's fields, and GetMethods returns an array of MethodInfo objects holding information about all the module's methods. I'll describe the FieldInfo and MethodInfo global objects in the "Retrieving Member Information" section later in this chapter.

Working with Types

The System.Type class is central to all reflection actions. It represents a managed type, which comprises classes, structures, interfaces, Enums, and Module blocks. The class provides all the means to enumerate a type's fields, properties, methods, and events, as well as set properties and fields and invoke methods dynamically. In addition, its InvokeMember method works as an improved version of the CallByName function in Visual Basic 6 (which is still supported in the Microsoft.VisualBasic namespace, by the way).

An interesting detail: a Type object that represents a managed type is unique in a given AppDomain. This means that when you retrieve the Type object corresponding to a given type (for example, System.String) you always get the same instance, regardless of how you retrieve the object. This feature allows for the automatic synchronization of multiple shared method invocations, among other benefits.

Getting a Type Object

The Type class itself doesn't expose any constructors because you never really create a Type object; rather, you get a reference to an existing one. You can choose from many ways to retrieve a reference to a Type object. In previous sections, you saw that you can enumerate all the types in an Assembly or a Module:

```
' Enumerate all the types defined in an assembly.
Dim ty As Type
For Each ty In asm.GetTypes
    Console.WriteLine(ty.FullName)
Next
```

More often, you get a Type object using Visual Basic's GetType function, which takes the unquoted name of a class:

```
ty = GetType(String)
Console.WriteLine(ty.FullName)       ' => System.String
```

If you already have an instance of the class in question, you can use the GetType method that all objects inherit from System.Object:

```
Dim d As Double = 123.45
ty = d.GetType
Console.WriteLine(ty.FullName)        ' => System.Double
```

The Type.GetType shared method takes a quoted class name, so you can build the name of the class dynamically (something you can't do with the GetType function):

```
' Note that you can't pass Type.GetType of a Visual Basic synonym,
' such as Short, Integer, Long, or Date.
ty = Type.GetType("System.Int64")
Console.WriteLine(ty.FullName)        ' => System.Int64
```

The GetType method looks for the specified type in the current assembly and then in the system assembly (mscorlib.dll). Like the Assembly's GetType instance method, the Type.GetType shared method returns Nothing if the specified type doesn't exist, but you can also pass True as its second argument to force a TypeLoadException in this case, and you can pass True as its third argument if you want the type name to be compared in a case-insensitive way. If the type you want to reference is neither in the caller's assembly nor in mscorlib.dll, you must append a comma and the assembly name in which the type resides. For example, here's how you get a reference to the System.Data.DataSet class, which resides in the assembly named System.Data; because the GAC might contain many assemblies with this friendly name, you must pass the complete identity of the assembly after the first comma:

```
ty = Type.GetType("System.Data.DataSet, System.Data, " _
    & "Version=1.0.3300.0, Culture=neutral, PublicKeyToken=b77a5c561934e089")
```

The GetTypeArray shared method takes an array of objects as an argument and returns an array of Type objects, one for each element in the argument array:

```
Dim anArray() As Object = {"a string", 123%, #1/2/2001#}
Dim types() As Type = Type.GetTypeArray(anArray)
Console.WriteLine(types(0).FullName)        ' => System.String
Console.WriteLine(types(1).FullName)        ' => System.Int32
Console.WriteLine(types(2).FullName)        ' => System.DateTime
```

The Type class exposes a couple of methods that are useful only to retrieve the Type object corresponding to a COM component. You can use the Type.GetTypeFromCLSID to retrieve the type corresponding to the COM component with a given CLSID, and the Type.GetTypeFromProgID to retrieve the type corresponding to the COM component with a given ProgID:

```
' Get the .NET object that wraps the Word.Application component.
Dim wordtype As Type = Type.GetTypeFromProgID("Word.Application")
' Display information on the wrapping object.
Console.WriteLine(wordtype.Name)        ' => __ComObject
' This is the CLSID value stored in the registry.
Console.WriteLine(wordtype.GUID)
    ' => 000209ff-0000-0000-c000-000000000046
' Get a reference through the CLSID.
Dim type2 As Type = Type.GetTypeFromCLSID(wordtype.Guid)
' Prove that this is the same object.
Console.WriteLine(wordtype Is type2)    ' => True
```

Retrieving Type Attributes

All the properties of the Type object are read-only, for one obvious reason: you can't change an attribute (such as name or scope) of a type defined elsewhere in code. These properties are summarized (grouped by function) in Table 15-1, and in most cases their meaning and usage are quite evident. For example, the following code lists all the types in mscorlib.dll, specifying whether each is a class, an enum, a value type, or an interface:

```
Sub TestTypeEnumeration()
    Dim asm As [Assembly] = Reflection.Assembly.Load("mscorlib")
    Dim t As Type

    For Each t In asm.GetExportedTypes()
        If t.IsClass Then
            Console.WriteLine(t.Name & " (Class)")
        ElseIf t.IsEnum Then
            ' Note that an enum is also a value type, so we must
            ' test for IsEnum before IsValueType.
            Console.WriteLine(t.Name & " (Enum)")
        ElseIf t.IsValueType Then
            Console.WriteLine(t.Name & " (Structure)")
        ElseIf t.IsInterface Then
            Console.WriteLine(t.Name & " (Interface)")
        Else
            ' This statement is never reached because a type
            ' can't be something other than one of the above.
        End If
    Next
End Sub
```

Table 15-1 Instance Properties of the Type Object

Category	Name	Description
Identity	Name	The unqualified name of the type ("String").
	AssemblyQualifiedName	The fully qualified name followed by the name of the assembly it belongs to ("System.String, mscorlib, Version= 1.0.3300.0, Culture=neutral, PublicKey-Token=b77a5c561934e089").
	FullName	The fully qualified name ("System.String").
	GUID	The GUID assigned to this type.
	Assembly	The assembly in which this type is defined.
	Module	The module where this type is defined.
	Namespace	The namespace where this type is defined.
	TypeHandle	The RuntimeTypeHandle for this type. This is an object whose Value property is a number that uniquely identifies the type in the runtime.
Classification	IsClass	True if the type is a class (not a value type nor an interface).
	IsInterface	True if the type is an interface (not a class nor a value type).
	IsEnum	True if the type is an Enum.
	IsValueType	True if the type is a value type (not a class nor an interface).
Scope	IsNestedAssembly	True if the type is nested and visible only from its assembly.
	IsNestedFamily	True if type is nested and visible only from its inherited (family) classes (same as Protected).
	IsNestedFamORAssembly	True if the type is nested and visible only from its assembly and from inherited (family) classes (same as Protected Friend).

(continued)

Table 15-1 Instance Properties of the Type Object *(continued)*

Category	Name	Description
	IsNestedFamANDAssembly	True if the type is nested and visible only from inherited (family) classes defined in its assembly. (You can't create such types in Visual Basic .NET.)
	IsNestedPrivate	True if the type is nested and declared private.
	IsNestedPublic	True if the type is nested and declared public.
	IsNotPublic	True if the type is not declared public.
	IsPublic	True if the type is declared public.
	DeclaringType	The Type object corresponding to the class that declares this class. If this is a nested class, it returns the enclosing type.
Encoding	IsAnsiClass	True if the string format attribute AnsiClass is selected for this type.
	IsUnicodeClass	True if the string format attribute UnicodeClass is selected for this type.
	IsAutoClass	True if the string format attribute AutoClass is selected for this type.
Field layout	IsAutoLayout	True if the runtime engine decides how to lay out fields of this type in memory.
	IsLayoutSequential	True if this type's fields are laid out sequentially in memory.
	IsExplicitLayout	True if the developer decides the position of this type's fields.
References to other types	HasElementType	True if the Type object encompasses or refers to other types—that is, it's an array, a pointer, or a parameter passed by reference.
	IsArray	True if the type is an array.
	IsByRef	True if this type is an argument passed by reference.
	IsPointer	True if the type is a pointer.
Inheritance	IsAbstract	True if the type is abstract and must be overridden.
	IsSealed	True if the type is declared sealed (NotInheritable).

Table 15-1 Instance Properties of the Type Object *(continued)*

Category	Name	Description
	IsPrimitive	True if the type is a primitive type (Int32).
	BaseType	The base type the current type inherits from.
Other attributes	Attributes	A bit-coded value that specifies the type's attributes. The same information is available through other Is*xxxx* properties.
	MemberType	A MemberTypes bit-coded enumerated value that tells the type of the member represented by the current type. It can be one or more of the following: Constructor, Event, Field, Method, Property, TypeInfo, or NestedType.
	IsCOMObject	True if the type is a .NET wrapper for a COM component.
	IsContextful	True if the type can be hosted in a context.
	IsImport	True if the type was imported from another class.
	IsMarshalByRef	True if this type is marshaled by reference.
	IsSerializable	True if the type is serializable.
	IsSpecialName	True if the type has a name that requires special handling.
Miscellaneous	ReflectedType	The class that was used to obtain this member; for example, the ReflectedType property of GetType(clsB).GetMethod("method") returns clsB even if the method is inherited by another class.
	TypeInitializer	The ConstructorInfo object that represents the type's constructor method.
	UnderlyingSystemType	The Type object that represents the underlying system type for the current type.

Enumerating Members

The Type class exposes an intimidating large number of methods, so I decided to gather them in related groups. (See Table 15-2.) Once methods are classified, you see some common patterns and behavior, and learning them is much simpler.

Table 15-2 Instance Methods of the Type Object

Category	Name	Description
Enumeration	GetMembers	Returns a MemberInfo array with information about all the members of this type, which is all the properties, fields, methods, events, and so on. (Can take an optional BindingFlags argument, which tells whether instance or shared items should be returned, and whether public or nonpublic items should be returned.)
	GetInterfaces	Returns a Type array with information about all the interfaces this type exposes. (Can take an optional BindingFlags argument.)
	GetFields	Returns a FieldInfo array with information about all the fields in this type. (Can take an optional BindingFlags argument.)
	GetProperties	Returns a PropertyInfo array with information about all the properties of this type. (Can take an optional BindingFlags argument.)
	GetMethods	Returns a MethodInfo array with information about all the methods of this type. (Can take an optional BindingFlags argument.)
	GetEvents	Returns an EventInfo array with information about all the events of this type. (Can take an optional BindingFlags argument.)
	GetConstructors	Returns a ConstructorInfo array with information about all the constructor methods of this type. (Can take an optional BindingFlags argument.)
	GetNestedTypes	Returns a Type array with information about all the nested types of this type. (Can take an optional BindingFlags argument.)
	GetDefaultMembers	Returns a MemberInfo array with information about all the members of this type whose DefaultMemberAttribute is set.
Get members by name	GetMember(name)	Returns a MemberInfo array with information about all the members (properties, fields, methods, etc.) of this type with specified name. (Can take an optional BindingFlags argument, which tells whether case is case sensitive, whether instance or shared items should be returned, and whether public or nonpublic items should be returned.)
	GetInterface(name)	Returns a Type array with information about all the interfaces with specified name this type exposes. (Can take an optional Boolean argument that tells whether search is case-insensitive.)

Table 15-2 Instance Methods of the Type Object *(continued)*

Category	Name	Description
	GetField(name)	Returns a FieldInfo array with information about all the fields with specified name in this type. (Can take an optional BindingFlags argument.)
	GetProperty(name)	Returns a PropertyInfo array with information about all the properties with specified name of this type. (Can take an optional BindingFlags argument.)
	GetMethod(name)	Returns a MethodInfo array with information about all the methods with specified name of this type. (Can take an optional BindingFlags argument.)
	GetEvent(name)	Returns an EventInfo array with information about all the events with specified name of this type. (Can take an optional BindingFlags argument.)
	GetConstructor (typeArr)	Returns a ConstructorInfo element with information about the constructor method of this type with the specified argument signature. (Can take an optional BindingFlags argument.)
	GetNested-Type(name)	Returns a Type array with information about the nested type with specified name of this type. (Can take an optional BindingFlags argument.)
Filtered enumeration	FindMembers(memberType, bindingAttrs, filter-Delegate, criteria)	Returns a MemberInfo array containing all the members of this type, as defined by memberType and bindingAttrs arguments, filtered by the function pointed to by filterDelegate.
	FindInterfaces(filterDelegate, criteria)	Returns a Type array containing all the interfaces of this type, filtered by the function pointed to by filterDelegate.
Custom attributes	GetCustomAttributes	Returns an Object array containing all the custom attributes defined for this type.
	IsDefined(attrType)	Returns True if the specified attribute is specified for this type.
Relationships to other types	IsSubclassOf-Type(type)	Returns True if this type is a subclass of the specified type. (Returns False if the two types are the same.)
	IsAssignable-From(type)	Returns True if the specified type can be assigned to this type.
	IsInstanceOf(object)	Returns True if the specified object is an instance of this type.
Miscellaneous	GetArrayRank	Returns the number of dimensions in an array type.

(continued)

Table 15-2 Instance Methods of the Type Object *(continued)*

Category	Name	Description
	GetElementType	Returns the Type object representing the object encompassed or referred to by this array, pointer, or ByRef type.
	InvokeMember (name, bindingFlags, binder, object, argArray)	Invokes a given member (method, property, etc.) for this type, on the specified object, and passing the given arguments.
	GetInterfaceMap (interface)	Returns an InterfaceMapping object that describes how methods of the interface type passed as an argument map the actual methods of the current type.

All the Get*xxxxs* methods (note the plural name) return an array of elements that describe the members of the type represented by the current Type object. The most generic method in this group is GetMembers, which returns an array with all the fields, properties, methods, and events that the type exposes. For example, the following code lists all the members of the System.String type:

```
' Get a reference to the System.String type.
Dim stringType As Type = Type.GetType("System.String")
Dim minfos() As MemberInfo
Dim mi As MemberInfo

' List all its members.
minfos = stringType.GetMembers()
For Each mi In minfos
    Console.WriteLine(mi.Name)
Next
```

The GetMembers function returns an array of MemberInfo elements, a type that represents a field, a property, a method, a constructor, an event, or a delegate. MemberInfo is an abstract type from which more specific types derive—for example, FieldInfo for field members and MethodInfo for method members.

The GetMembers method returns one element for each distinct version of overloaded properties and methods. So, for example, the output from the preceding code snippet includes multiple occurrences of the Format and Concat methods. You also find multiple occurrences of the constructor method, which is always named .ctor. In the next section, I'll show how you can explore the argument signature of these overloaded members. Also note that the GetMembers method returns private and shared members, as well as methods inherited by other objects, such as the ToString method inherited from System.Object.

The GetMembers method supports an optional BindingFlags enumerated argument. This bit-coded value lets you narrow the enumeration—for example, by listing only public or nonshared members. The BindingFlags type is used in many reflection methods and includes many enumerated values, but in this case only a few are useful:

- The Public and NonPublic enumerated values restrict the enumeration according to the scope of the elements.
- The Instance and Static enumerated values restrict the enumeration to instance members and shared members, respectively. (You must specify one of these flags to get a nonempty result.)
- The DeclaredOnly enumerated value restricts the enumeration to members declared in the current type (as opposed to members inherited from its base class).
- The FlattenHierarchy enumerated value is used to include static members up the hierarchy.

This code lists only the public, nonshared, and noninherited members of the String class:

```
' Get all public, nonshared, noninherited members of StringType.
minfos = stringType.GetMembers(BindingFlags.Public _
    Or BindingFlags.Instance Or BindingFlags.DeclaredOnly)
```

The preceding code snippet produces an array that includes the ToString method, which at first glance shouldn't be in the result because it's inherited from System.Object. It's included because the String class adds an overloaded version of this method, and this overloaded method is the only one that appears in the result array.

To narrow the enumeration to a given member type, you can use a more specific Get*xxxxs* method. For example, this code lists only the methods of the System.String type:

```
' Get all the methods of the String type.
' (We reuse the stringType Type variable assigned previously.)
For Each mi In stringType.GetMethods()
    Console.WriteLine(mi.Name)
Next
```

The GetInterfaces or GetNestedTypes methods return an array of Type elements, rather than a MemberInfo array, so the code in the loop is slightly different:

```
Dim ty As Type
For Each ty In stringType.GetInterfaces()
    Console.WriteLine(ty.Name)
Next
```

All the Get*xxxxs* methods—with the exception of GetDefaultMembers and GetInterfaces—can take an optional BindingFlags argument to restrict the enumeration to public or nonpublic, shared or nonshared, and declared or inherited members.

When you're using a Get*xxxxs* method other than GetMembers, you can assign the result to either a generic MemberInfo array or to an array of a more specific type. For example, when you enumerate properties, you can assign the result to an array of PropertyInfo objects:

```
' Get all the properties of the String type.
Dim pinfos() As PropertyInfo = stringType.GetProperties
```

PropertyInfo, MethodInfo, FieldInfo, and EventInfo all derive from MemberInfo, so you can always use an array of MemberInfo when you're assigning the result from the GetProperties, GetMethods, GetFields, and GetEvents methods, respectively, even though using the more specific type is usually a better idea because it circumvents the need to cast the result to a specific object to access properties not in the base class.

You can perform more sophisticated searches by using the FindMembers method. This method takes four arguments: a MemberType bit-coded value that tells the kind of members you're interested in (see the MemberType property in Table 15-1); a BindingFlags value that specifies the scope of the requested members; a MemberFilter delegate that points to a function you provide; and a generic Object passed as an argument to the delegate function. The following code is an example of what you can accomplish with the FindMembers method:

```
Sub TestFindMembers()
    ' Get a reference to the System.String type.
    Dim stringType As Type = Type.GetType("System.String")
    ' Get only public, instance methods and properties
    ' whose name begins with the "C" character.
    Dim minfos() As MemberInfo = stringType.FindMembers( _
        MemberTypes.Method Or MemberTypes.Property, _
        BindingFlags.Public Or BindingFlags.Instance, _
        AddressOf FilterByName, "C")
```

```
    ' List the results.
    Dim mi As MemberInfo
    For Each mi In minfos
        Console.WriteLine(mi.Name)
    Next
End Sub

' This filtering function returns True if the member name
' begins with the character passed as its second argument.
Function FilterByName(ByVal m As MemberInfo, _
    ByVal filterCriteria As Object) As Boolean
    If m.Name.StartsWith(filterCriteria.ToString) Then
        Return True
    End If
End Function
```

Because the filtering function receives a MemberInfo object, it can perform sophisticated tests about the member's attributes. For example, the following filtering function returns True only for properties and methods whose return type is the one specified by the second argument. Note that this code casts the incoming MemberInfo value to a more specific PropertyInfo or MethodInfo variable to access the ReturnValue property:

```
' Accept only properties and methods whose return value matches
' the Type passed as the second argument.
Function FilterByType(ByVal m As MemberInfo, _
    ByVal filterCriteria As Object) As Boolean

    If m.MemberType = MemberTypes.Property Then
        ' If it's a property, cast MemberInfo to PropertyInfo.
        Dim pi As PropertyInfo = CType(m, PropertyInfo)
        ' Return True if the property type is the one we're looking for.
        Return (pi.PropertyType Is filterCriteria)
    ElseIf m.MemberType = MemberTypes.Method Then
        ' If it's a method, cast MemberInfo to MethodInfo.
        Dim mi As MethodInfo = CType(m, MethodInfo)
        ' Return True if the return type is the one we're looking for.
        Return (mi.ReturnType Is filterCriteria)
    End If
End Function
```

Here's how you use the preceding function:

```
' We're looking for properties and functions that return a 32-bit integer.
Dim returnType As Type = Type.GetType("System.Int32")
' We're searching only public, non-shared methods and properties.
Dim minfos() As MemberInfo = stringType.FindMembers( _
    MemberTypes.Method Or MemberTypes.Property, _
    BindingFlags.Public Or BindingFlags.Instance, _
    AddressOf FilterByType, returnType)
```

In many cases, you don't need to enumerate a type's members because you have other ways to find out the name of the field, property, methods, or event you want to get information about. You can use the GetMember or other Get*xxxx* methods (where *xxxx* is a singular word) of the Type class to get the corresponding MemberInfo (or a more specific object):

```
' Get information about the String.Chars property.
Dim mi As MemberInfo = GetType(String).GetProperty("Chars")

' You can also cast the result to a more specific variable.
Dim pi As PropertyInfo = GetType(String).GetProperty("Chars")
```

If you're querying for an overloaded property or method, you actually get an array of MemberInfo elements. In such a case, you can ask for a specific version of the member by using GetProperty or GetMethod and specifying the exact argument signature by passing an array of Type objects as its second argument:

```
' Get the MethodInfo object for the IndexOf string method with the
' following signature: IndexOf(char, startIndex, endIndex).

' Prepare the signature as an array of Type objects.
' Note that you can define the type of arguments using either
' the GetType function or the Type.GetType method.
Dim argTypes() As Type = {GetType(Char), _
    Type.GetType("System.Int32"), Type.GetType("System.Int32")}
' Ask for the method with given name and signature.
Dim mi As MethodInfo = stringType.GetMethod("IndexOf", argTypes)
```

Retrieving Member Information

After you get a reference to a MemberInfo object—or a more specific object, such as FieldInfo or PropertyInfo—you can retrieve information about the corresponding member.

Working with specific objects that derive from MemberInfo can be confusing because they have methods in common (those inherited from MemberInfo) and methods with similar functionality but different name and syntax. The best way to learn how to use these objects is to compare them and see which object supports which property or method, as shown in Tables 15-3 and 15-4. Notice that MethodInfo and ConstructorInfo types differ only for two properties (ReturnType and ReturnTypeCustomAttributes) and one method (GetBaseDefinition) because all the others are inherited from the MethodBase abstract class.

The following loop displays the name of all the members exposed by the System.String type, together with a description of the member type. To make things more interesting, we're suppressing constructor methods as well as multiple definitions for overloaded methods:

```
' Get a reference to the System.String type.
Dim stringType As Type = Type.GetType("System.String")
' We use this ArrayList to keep track of items already displayed.
Dim al As New ArrayList()

Dim mi As MemberInfo
For Each mi In stringType.GetMembers()
    If (mi.MemberType And MemberTypes.Constructor) <> 0 Then
        ' Ignore constructor methods.
    ElseIf Not al.Contains(mi.Name) Then
        ' If this element hasn't been listed yet, do it now.
        ' (The MemberType property returns an enumerated value, thus we can
        ' transform it into its textual description with the ToString method.)
        Console.WriteLine("{0}  ({1})", mi.Name, mi.MemberType.ToString)
        ' Add this element to the list of processed items.
        al.Add(mi.Name)
    End If
Next
```

Table 15-3 All the Properties of MemberInfo and Its Derived Types†

Category	Name	MemberInfo	FieldInfo	PropertyInfo	MethodInfo	ConstructorInfo	EventInfo	Description
Identity	Name	D	I	I	I	I	I	Name of this member.
	MemberType	D	I	I	I	I	I	The type of this member (field, property, and so on).
	FieldHandle		D					The unique RuntimeField-Handle of this field.
	MethodHandle				I*	I*		The handle of this method.
Visibility	IsAssembly		D		I*	I*		True if this member has assembly visibility.
	IsFamily		D		I*	I*		True if this member has family visibility. (Same as Protected scope.)
	IsFamily-AndAssembly		D		I*	I*		True if this member has family and assembly visibility and can be called only by derived classes inside the same assembly.
	IsFamily-OrAssembly		D		I*	I*		True if this member has family or assembly visibility. (Same as Protected Friend.)

(continued)

Table 15-3 All the Properties of MemberInfo and Its Derived Types† *(continued)*

Category	Name	MemberInfo	FieldInfo	PropertyInfo	MethodInfo	ConstructorInfo	EventInfo	Description
	IsPrivate		D		I*	I*		True if this member is private.
	IsPublic		D		I*	I*		True if this member is public.
	IsStatic		D		I*	I*		True if this member is shared.
Inheritance	DeclaringType	D	I	I	I	I	I	The class where this member is declared. It's different from the ReflectedType class if this member is inherited.
	ReflectedType	D	I	I	I	I	I	The class that was used to retrieve this instance of MemberInfo.
	IsAbstract				I*	I*		True if this is an abstract method. (Same as MustOverride.)
	IsVirtual				I*	I*		True if this method is virtual. (Same as Overridable.)
	IsFinal				I*	I*		True if this method is final. (Same as NotOverridable.)
	IsHideBySig				I*	I*		True if a member of the same kind with exactly the same signature is hidden in the derived class.
Value type	FieldType		D					The Type object representing the type of this field.
	PropertyType			D				The Type object representing the type of this property.
	ReturnType				D			The Type object that describes the return value for this method.
Access	IsLiteral		D					True if the value is written at compile time and can't be changed (that is, it's a constant).
	IsInitOnly		D					True if this field can be set only from inside a constructor.
	CanRead			D				True if the property can be read.
	CanWrite			D				True if the property can be written to.
Attributes	Attributes		D	D	I*	I*	D	The attributes associated with this member.
	ReturnType-CustomAttributes				D			The custom attributes defined for the return value.

Table 15-3 All the Properties of MemberInfo and Its Derived Types† *(continued)*

Category	Name	MemberInfo	FieldInfo	PropertyInfo	MethodInfo	ConstructorInfo	EventInfo	Description
	IsNotSerialized		D					True if the field has the NotSerialized attribute.
	IsPinvokeImpl		D					True if the PinvokeImpl attribute is set for this member.
	IsSpecialName		D	D	I*	I*	D	True if the SpecialName attribute is set for this member.
Miscellaneous	CallingConvention				I*	I*		Returns the calling convention for this method. (See the CallingConventions enumerated type.)
	IsConstructor				I*	I*		True if this method is a constructor.
	EventHandlerType						D	The Type describing the underlying delegate for this event.
	IsMulticast						D	True if this event is multicast (that is, is based on a multicast delegate).

† D means declared in that type, I means inherited from MemberInfo, and I* means inherited from MethodBase (a base class of both MethodInfo and ConstructorInfo).

Table 15-4 Main Methods of MemberInfo and Its Derived Types†

Category	Name	MemberInfo	FieldInfo	PropertyInfo	MethodInfo	ConstructorInfo	EventInfo	Description
Invocation	GetValue		D	D				Returns the value of this member.
	SetValue		D	D				Sets the value of this member.
	GetIndexParameters			D				Returns a ParameterInfo array describing the arguments passed to this property.
	GetParameters				I*	I*		Returns a ParameterInfo array describing the arguments passed to this method.

(continued)

Table 15-4 Main Methods of MemberInfo and Its Derived Types† *(continued)*

Category	Name	MemberInfo	FieldInfo	PropertyInfo	MethodInfo	ConstructorInfo	EventInfo	Description
	Invoke				I*	I*		Invokes this method with the specified arguments.
Accessor methods	GetAccessors			D				Returns a MethodInfo array representing the accessor methods for this property.
	GetGetMethod			D				Returns the MethodInfo representing the Get accessor method.
	GetSetMethod			D				Returns the MethodInfo representing the Set accessor method.
	GetAddMethod						D	Returns the MethodInfo representing the method that adds an event handler delegate to the event source (similar to AddHandler).
	GetRemoveMethod						D	Returns the MethodInfo representing the method that removes an event handler delegate to the event source (similar to RemoveHandler).
	GetRaiseMethod						D	Returns the MethodInfo representing the method that is called when the event is raised.
	EventHandlerType						D	Returns the Type that represents the underlying delegate for this event.
Custom attributes	GetCustomAttributes	D	I	I	I	I	I	Returns all the custom attributes defined for this member.
	IsDefined	D	I	I	I	I	I	Returns True if the specified attribute is defined for this member.
	GetMethodImplementationFlags				I*	I*		Returns the MethodImplAttributes flags for this method; these flags specify whether the method is managed or unmanaged, is synchronized, and so on.
Type retrieval	GetFieldFromHandler		D					Returns the FieldInfo object corresponding to a given field handle (shared method).

Table 15-4 Main Methods of MemberInfo and Its Derived Types† (continued)

Category	Name	MemberInfo	FieldInfo	PropertyInfo	MethodInfo	ConstructorInfo	EventInfo	Description
	GetMethodFrom-Handle				I*	I*		Returns the MethodBase object corresponding to a given method handle (shared method).
	GetCurrent-Method				I*	I*		Returns the MethodBase object corresponding to the method currently executing (shared method).
Miscellaneous	GetBase-Definition				D			Returns the MethodInfo object for the method in the base class (direct or indirect) where this method was first defined.
	AddEventHandler						D	Adds an event handler to the event source.
	RemoveEvent-Handler						D	Removes an event handler from the event source.

† D means declared in that type, I means inherited from MemberInfo, and I* means inherited from MethodBase (a superclass of both MethodInfo and ConstructorInfo).

Enumerating Parameters

The one thing left to do is enumerate the parameters that a property or a method expects. Both the GetIndexParameters and GetParameters methods return an array of ParameterInfo objects, where each element describes the attributes of the arguments passed to and from the member. Table 15-5 summarizes the properties of the ParameterInfo object.

The following code shows how to print the calling syntax for a given method:

```
Sub TestCallingSyntax()
    ' Get a reference to the System.String type.
    Dim stringType As Type = Type.GetType("System.String")
    ' Get the MethodInfo for the CopyTo method.
    Dim mi As MethodInfo = stringType.GetMethod("CopyTo")
    ' Get the ParameterInfo array for this method.
    Dim pinfos() As ParameterInfo = mi.GetParameters
    Dim i As Integer

    ' Display the calling syntax for this method.
    Console.Write(mi.Name & "(")
```

(continued)

```
    For i = 0 To pinfos.GetUpperBound(0)
        ' Display the parameter name.
        Console.Write(pinfos(i).Name)
        ' If not the last parameter, append a comma.
        If i < pinfos.GetUpperBound(0) Then Console.Write(",")
    Next
    ' Display the closing parenthesis.
    Console.WriteLine(")")
End Sub
```

In the section "A Command-Line Type Browser" later in this chapter, I build on this code to create a more flexible routine that displays the complete calling syntax, including ByVal or ByRef, optional arguments, and arrays.

Table 15-5 All the Properties of the ParameterInfo Class

Category	Name	Description
Identity	Name	The name of this parameter
	Position	An integer that describes the position of this parameter in the method signature
	Member	The MemberInfo object that represents the method or property this parameter appears in
	ParameterType	The Type object that describes the type of this parameter
Direction	IsIn	True if this is an input parameter
	IsOut	True if this is an output parameter
	IsRetVal	True if this is a return value
Optional parameters	IsOptional	True if this is an optional parameter
	DefaultValue	The default value of the parameter or DBNull.Value if the parameter has no default value
Miscellaneous	Attributes	The attributes for this parameter
	IsLcid	True if this parameter is a locale identifier

Invoking Members

All the reflection operations that you've seen so far work on types but not on objects. For example, you saw how you can enumerate the types in an assembly or retrieve information about a type's member. In this section, you'll see how to actually execute a type's method that you discovered through reflection. Clearly, unless you're calling a shared method, this operation makes sense only if you have an object on which that method should be invoked. For all the tests in this section I'll use the following class:

```
Class Person
    ' Some public and private fields
    Public FirstName As String
    Public LastName As String

    Dim m_Age As Short
    Dim m_EmailAddress(4) As String

    Sub New()
        MyBase.New
    End Sub

    ' A constructor with parameters
    Sub New(ByVal FirstName As String, ByVal LastName As String)
        MyBase.New
        Me.FirstName = FirstName
        Me.LastName = LastName
    End Sub

    ' A read-write property
    Property Age() As Short
        Get
            Return m_Age
        End Get
        Set(ByVal Value As Short)
            m_Age = Value
        End Set
    End Property

    ' A property with arguments
    Property EmailAddress(ByVal Index As Short) As String
        Get
            Return m_EmailAddress(Index)
        End Get
        Set(ByVal Value As String)
            m_EmailAddress(index) = Value
        End Set
    End Property

    ' A method with optional arguments
    Sub SendEmail(ByVal msg As String, Optional ByVal Priority As Integer = 1)
        ' ... (No real code in this demo)...
        Console.WriteLine("Message to " & FirstName & " " & LastName)
        Console.WriteLine("Priority = " & Priority.ToString)
        Console.WriteLine(msg)
    End Sub
End Class
```

The easiest operation you can perform is reading or writing a field by means of the GetValue and SetValue methods:

```
Sub TestReadWriteFields()
    ' Create a Person object.
    Dim p As New Person("Joe", "Doe")
    ' Reflect on it.
    Dim ty As Type = p.GetType
    ' Get a reference to its FirstName field.
    Dim fi As FieldInfo = ty.GetField("FirstName")
    ' Display its current value.
    Console.WriteLine(fi.GetValue(p))    ' => Joe
    ' Change it.
    fi.SetValue(p, "Robert")
    ' Prove that it changed.
    Console.WriteLine(p.FirstName)       ' => Robert
End Sub
```

The syntax for GetValue and SetValue for parameterless properties requires an extra Nothing argument:

```
Sub TestReadWriteProperties()
    ' Get a Person object and reflect on it.
    Dim p As New Person("Joe", "Doe")
    Dim ty As Type = p.GetType
    ' Get a reference to the PropertyInfo object.
    Dim pi As PropertyInfo = ty.GetProperty("Age")
    ' Note that the type of value must match exactly.
    ' (Integer constants must be converted to Short, in this case.)
    pi.SetValue(p, 35S, Nothing)
    ' Read it back.
    Console.WriteLine(pi.GetValue(p, Nothing))   ' => 35
End Sub
```

If the property takes one or more parameters, you must pass an Object array containing one element for each parameter:

```
Sub TestReadWritePropertiesWithArgs()
    ' Get a Person object and reflect on it.
    Dim p As New Person("Joe", "Doe")
    Dim ty As Type = p.GetType
    ' Get a reference to the PropertyInfo object.
    Dim pi As PropertyInfo = ty.GetProperty("EmailAddress")
    ' Prepare the array of parameters.
    Dim params() As Object = {1S}
    ' Set the property.
    pi.SetValue(p, "321 North Street", params)
    ' Read it back.
    Console.WriteLine(pi.GetValue(p, params))   ' => 321 North Street
End Sub
```

A similar thing happens when you're invoking methods, except that you use Invoke instead of GetValue or SetValue:

```
Sub TestInvokeMethod()
    ' Get a Person object and reflect on it.
    Dim p As New Person("Joe", "Doe")
    Dim ty As Type = p.GetType
    ' Get the MethodInfo for this method.
    Dim mi As MethodInfo = ty.GetMethod("SendEmail")
    ' Prepare an array for expected arguments.
    Dim params(mi.GetParameters.Length - 1) As Object
    ' Set parameters values.
    params(0) = "This is a message"
    params(1) = 3
    ' Invoke the method.
    mi.Invoke(p, params)
End Sub
```

Things are more interesting when optional arguments are involved. In this case, you pass the Type.Missing special value, as in this code:

```
' ...(Initial code as above)...
' Don't pass the second argument.
params(1) = Type.Missing
mi.Invoke(p, params)
```

Alternatively, you can query the DefaultValue property of corresponding ParameterInfo to learn the default value for that specific argument:

```
' ...(Initial code as above)...
' Retrieve the DefaultValue from the ParameterInfo object.
params(1) = mi.GetParameters(1).DefaultValue
mi.Invoke(p, params)
```

The Invoke method traps all the exceptions thrown in the called method and converts them into TargetInvocationException; you must check the InnerException property of the caught exception to retrieve the real exception:

```
Try
    mi.Invoke(p, params)
Catch ex As Exception
    Console.WriteLine(ex.InnerException.Message)
End Try
```

In some cases, you might find it easier to dynamically set properties and invoke methods by means of the Type object's InvokeMember method. This method very closely resembles the CallByName function in Visual Basic 6, in that it takes the name of the member, a flag that says whether it's a field, property, or method, the object for which the member should be invoked, and an array of Objects for the arguments, if there are any. Here are a few examples:

```
Sub TestInvokeMember()
    ' Create a Person object and get its corresponding Type object.
    Dim p As New Person
    Dim ty As Type = p.GetType

    ' Set the FirstName field.
    Dim args() As Object = {"Francesco"}         ' One argument
    ty.InvokeMember("FirstName", BindingFlags.SetField, Nothing, p, args)

    ' Read the FirstName field.
    ' (Note that we're passing Nothing for the argument array.)
    Dim value As Object = ty.InvokeMember("FirstName", _
        BindingFlags.GetField, Nothing, p, Nothing)

    ' Set the Age property.
    Dim args2() As Object = {35S}                ' One argument
    ty.InvokeMember("Age", BindingFlags.SetProperty, Nothing, p, args2)

    ' Call the SendEMail method.
    Dim args3() As Object = {"This is a message", 2}
    ty.InvokeMember("SendEmail", BindingFlags.InvokeMethod, Nothing, p, args3)
End Sub
```

Creating an Object Dynamically

The last reflection feature left to be examined lets you dynamically create an object on the fly if you have its class name. This is the Visual Basic .NET counterpart of the CreateObject function. You can choose from two ways to create a .NET object in this fashion: by using the CreateInstance method of the System.Activator class or by invoking one of the type's constructor methods.

If the type has a parameterless constructor, creating an instance is trivial:

```
Sub TestObjectCreation()
    ' Next statement assumes that the Person class is defined in
    ' an assembly named "ReflectionDemo".
    Dim ty As Type = Type.GetType("ReflectionDemo.Person")
    Dim o As Object = Activator.CreateInstance(ty)
    ' Prove that we created a Person.
    Console.WriteLine("A {0} object has been created", o.GetType.Name)
End Sub
```

If you want to call a constructor that takes one or more parameters, you must prepare an array of values:

```
Sub TestObjectCreation2()
    Dim ty As Type = Type.GetType("ReflectionDemo.Person")
    ' Use the constructor that takes two arguments.
    Dim params() As Object = {"Joe", "Doe"}
    ' Call the constructor that matches the parameter signature.
    Dim o As Object = System.Activator.CreateInstance(ty, params)
End Sub
```

Creating an object through its constructor method is a bit more convoluted, but I'm reporting this technique here for the sake of completeness:

```
Sub TestObjectCreation3()
    Dim ty As Type = Type.GetType("ReflectionDemo.Person")
    ' Prepare the argument signature as an array of types (2 strings).
    Dim types() As Type = {GetType(System.String), GetType(System.String)}
    ' Get a reference to the correct constructor.
    Dim ci As ConstructorInfo = ty.GetConstructor(types)
    ' Prepare the parameters.
    Dim params() As Object = {"Joe", "Doe"}
    ' Invoke the constructor and assign the result to a variable.
    Dim o As Object = ci.Invoke(params)
End Sub
```

Security Issues

When I teach reflection in my seminars, I see students divided in their response between enthusiasm for the power that reflection gives to you, the developer, and worry about what damage it might do in the hands of malicious hackers. You surely don't want all the information about your code and types, including private types and members, to be so easily accessible.

The good news is that you have nothing to worry about: the .NET runtime enforces rules that specify how much reflection someone else can use to discover types, read their properties, and invoke their methods. More precisely, the following are the only reflection operations that a piece of code without any special permission can perform:

- Enumerate assemblies and modules.
- Enumerate public types, and obtain information about them and their public members.
- Set public fields and properties and invoke public members.
- Access and enumerate family (Protected) members of a base class of the calling code.
- Access and enumerate assembly (Friend) members from inside the assembly the calling code runs in.

You see that code can access through reflection only those types and members that it could access directly anyway. For example, a piece of code can't access a private field in another type or invoke a private member in another type, even if that type is inside the same assembly as the calling code. In other words, reflection doesn't give code more power than it already has; it just adds flexibility because of the additional level of indirection that it provides.

To access or enumerate nonpublic types, code must be granted ReflectionPermission. For example, the code in the runtime that serializes and deserializes other types is granted this permission because it has to read and reassign values to both public and private fields. For more information about code permissions, see the .NET SDK documentation.

Reflection Examples

It's time to put things together and see how we can apply the features I have described so far. In this section, I'll show how you can create a command-line type browser and how to leverage reflection to display detailed information about the running program.

A Command-Line Type Browser

The code that follows is the complete listing of a command-line type browser, which takes the name of a .NET type on the command line and an optional member name and displays the Visual Basic syntax for that member. For example, the command

```
>typebrow system.string replace
```

displays the following result:

```
Function Replace(ByVal oldChar As Char, ByVal newChar As Char) As String
Function Replace(ByVal oldValue As String, ByVal newValue As String) As String
```

You can also pass a partial member name (using a trailing *) or omit the second argument to display information about all the fields, properties, methods, events, and constructors of that type:

```
>typebrow system.string get*

Function GetTypeCode() As TypeCode
Function GetHashCode() As Integer
Function GetEnumerator() As CharEnumerator
Function GetType() As Type
```

Remember to append a comma followed by the assembly fully qualified name where the type resides, if the type isn't in mscorlib.dll. (For more information, see the description of Type.GetType, earlier in this chapter.)

```
>typebrow system.xml.xmldocument,system.xml
```

To create the typebrow utility, create a new Console Application project and paste the following code into its main Module block. Then compile and test the utility from the system prompt.

```
Imports System.Reflection

Module Module1
    Sub Main()
        ' Get command-line arguments.
        Dim args() As String = Environment.GetCommandLineArgs()
        Dim ty As Type
        Dim mbrTypes As MemberTypes = MemberTypes.All
        Dim mbrName As String = ""
        Dim mi As MemberInfo

        ' If no arguments, /? or /help
        If args.Length <= 1 OrElse args(1) = "/?" OrElse _
            String.Compare(args(1), "/help", True) = 0 Then
            ' Show command-line syntax and exit.
            Console.WriteLine("Command-line Type Browser")
            Console.WriteLine("   Syntax:  typebrow typename [membername[*]]")
            Exit Sub
        End If

        Dim i As Integer = args(1).IndexOf(","c)
        If i < 0 Then
            ' Create the type as specified by the first argument.
            ty = Type.GetType(args(1), False, True)
        Else
            ' Create the assembly specified in the 2nd part of the argument.
            Dim asmname As String = args(1).SubString(i + 1)
            Dim asm As [Assembly] = [Assembly].LoadWithPartialName(asmname)
            ' Get the type in the specified assembly.
            ty = asm.GetType(args(1).SubString(0, i), False, True)
        End If

        If ty Is Nothing Then
            ' Exit if error.
            Console.WriteLine("Unable to create type ""{0}""", args(1))
            Exit Sub
        End If

        ' If the user asked for a particular name, retrieve the name.
        If args.Length > 2 Then mbrName = args(2)

        ' Get the list of member info to be displayed.
        Dim minfos() As MemberInfo = ty.FindMembers(mbrTypes, _
            BindingFlags.Public Or BindingFlags.Instance Or _
            BindingFlags.Static, _
            New MemberFilter(AddressOf CustomMemberFilter), mbrName)

        ' Display information on all these members.
        For Each mi In minfos
```

(continued)

```
            Console.WriteLine(MemberDescription(mi))
        Next
    End Sub

    ' This is the custom filter for members.
    ' On entry filterCriteria holds the name of the member we're looking for.
    ' (Supports partial names with a trailing asterisk, as in "Repl*".)
    Function CustomMemberFilter(ByVal m As MemberInfo, _
        ByVal filterCriteria As Object) As Boolean

        ' Discard accessor methods for properties.
        If m.Name.StartsWith("get_") Or m.Name.StartsWith("set_") Then
            Return False
        End If
        ' Get the search filter in uppercase.
        Dim search As String = filterCriteria.ToString.ToUpper
        If search = "" Then Return True

        If search.EndsWith("*") Then
            ' If there is a trailing asterisk, checks for partial match.
            If m.Name.ToUpper.StartsWith(search.Substring(0, _
                search.Length - 1)) Then Return True
        Else
            ' Otherwise search for exact match.
            If m.Name.ToUpper = search Then Return True
        End If
    End Function

    ' Return the syntax for a member (field, property, methods, event).
    Function MemberDescription(ByVal mi As MemberInfo) As String
        Dim res As String

        ' Different treatment for different types
        Select Case mi.MemberType
            Case MemberTypes.Field
                ' Fields: append As clause.
                Dim fdi As FieldInfo = CType(mi, FieldInfo)
                res &= NameDescription(mi, fdi.IsStatic) & _
                    VBTypeDescription(fdi.FieldType)

            Case MemberTypes.Property
                ' Properties: append parameter list and return type.
                Dim pri As PropertyInfo = CType(mi, PropertyInfo)
                res &= NameDescription(mi, False) & _
                    ParamListDescription(pri.GetIndexParameters)
                res &= VBTypeDescription(pri.PropertyType)

            Case MemberTypes.Method
                ' Methods: append parameter list and return type.
```

```
            Dim mti As MethodInfo = CType(mi, MethodInfo)
            res &= NameDescription(mi, mti.IsStatic) & _
                ParamListDescription(mti.GetParameters)
            If Not (mti.ReturnType Is Nothing) Then
                res &= VBTypeDescription(mti.ReturnType, True)
            End If

        Case MemberTypes.Constructor
            ' Constructor
            Dim cti As ConstructorInfo = CType(mi, ConstructorInfo)
            res &= NameDescription(mi, False) & _
                ParamListDescription(cti.GetParameters)

        Case MemberTypes.Event
            ' Events: append parameter list.
            Dim evi As EventInfo = CType(mi, EventInfo)
            ' Get the type that corresponds to the underlying delegate.
            Dim delType As Type = evi.EventHandlerType
            Dim mi2 As MethodInfo = delType.GetMethod("Invoke")
            res &= NameDescription(mi, False) & _
                ParamListDescription(mi2.GetParameters)
    End Select

    Return res
End Function

' Return a description for name
' (including Shared and member type description).
Function NameDescription(ByVal mi As MemberInfo, _
    ByVal IsStatic As Boolean) As String
    Dim res As String

    ' Prefix with Shared if necessary.
    If IsStatic Then res = "Shared "

    ' Append member type, but distinguish between Sub and Function.
    If mi.MemberType <> MemberTypes.Method Then
        ' If not a method, simply use the Enum.Format method.
        res &= [Enum].Format(mi.MemberType.GetType, _
            mi.MemberType, "G") & " "
    Else
        Dim meth As MethodInfo = CType(mi, MethodInfo)
        If meth.ReturnType.Name = "Void" Then
            res &= "Sub "
        Else
            res &= "Function "
        End If
    End If
```

(continued)

```
        ' Append name and return to caller.
        If mi.MemberType = MemberTypes.Constructor Then
            ' Visual Basic constructors are named "new".
            res &= "New"
        Else
            ' A nonconstructor element
            res &= mi.Name
        End If

        Return res
    End Function

    ' Return the description for a list of parameters.
    Function ParamListDescription(ByVal pinfos() As ParameterInfo) As String
        Dim res As String = "("
        Dim i As Integer

        ' Iterate over all parameters.
        For i = 0 To pinfos.GetUpperBound(0)
            ' Append description for this parameter.
            res &= ParamDescription(pinfos(i))
            ' Append a comma if this isn't the last argument.
            If i < pinfos.GetUpperBound(0) Then res &= ", "
        Next
        ' Close the parenthesis and return to caller.
        Return res & ")"
    End Function

    ' Return a description for a single parameter.
    Function ParamDescription(ByVal pi As ParameterInfo) As String
        Dim res As String
        Dim pt As Type = pi.ParameterType

        ' Start with Optional if necessary.
        If pi.IsOptional Then res = "Optional "

        ' Append ByVal or ByRef.
        If pt.IsByRef Then
            res &= "ByRef "
        Else
            res &= "ByVal "
        End If

        ' Append the parameter name.
        res &= pi.Name
        ' Append the type, but convert it to Visual Basic syntax.
        res &= VBTypeDescription(pt)
```

```
        ' Append the default value, if there is one.
        If pi.IsOptional Then
            ' Enclose the default value within quotes if it is a string.
            If pt Is GetType(System.String) Then
                res &= " = """ & pi.DefaultValue.ToString & """"
            Else
                res &= " = " & pi.DefaultValue.ToString
            End If
        End If

        ' Return to the caller.
        Return res
    End Function

    ' Return a parameter type in Visual Basic-friendly format.
    Function VBTypeDescription(ByVal ty As Type, _
        Optional ByVal PostfixArrayMarks As Boolean = False) As String
        Dim res As String

        ' Get the return type as a string.
        res &= ty.Name
        ' Drop trailing "[]" pair, if there is one.
        If res.EndsWith("[]") Then
            res = res.Substring(0, res.Length - 2)
        End If
        ' Drop trailing *, if there is one.
        If res.EndsWith("*") Then
            res = res.Substring(0, res.Length - 1)
        End If

        ' Adjust for Visual Basic-friendly names.
        Select Case res
            Case "Int16"
                res = "Short"
            Case "Int32"
                res = "Integer"
            Case "Int64"
                res = "Long"
            Case "Void"
                ' This is the type "returned" by Sub.
                Return ""
        End Select

        ' Append "AS" and "()" if this is an array.
        If Not ty.IsArray Then
            res = " As " & res
        ElseIf PostfixArrayMarks Then
            ' Append trailing () pair.
            res = " As " & res & "()"
```

(continued)

```
        Else
            ' Prefix leading () pair.
            res = "() As " & res
        End If

        ' Return to the caller.
        Return res
    End Function
End Module
```

I won't describe each individual line of code, both because I've included many remarks in the code and because I have already explained most of these techniques in previous sections. Part of the code in this project serves to remedy the C#-oriented nature of the runtime (and of the reflection methods in particular). For example, you have to account for the fact that a data type can include a trailing asterisk (if the type is a pointer) or pair of square brackets (if the type is an array). Also, for Visual Basic–friendly output, we need to change the name of some data types (Int32 to Integer) and account for optional values and their default values.

Tracing the Stack Frame

A common question among Visual Basic 6 developers is whether a routine can identify its caller, and the caller of its caller, and so on. This feature might be valuable in case of errors (so that the error handler can display the path that led you to the problem), for debugging or profiling reasons, and more. As you probably know, you can achieve this capability in Visual Basic 6 only by augmenting your code with calls to a logging routine or by resorting to very advanced techniques that analyze the symbolic information produced by the compiler.

Finding a routine's caller is almost trivial under Visual Basic .NET, thanks to a special object named StackTrace, found in the System.Diagnostics namespace even though it's closely related to reflection. As its name implies, the StackTrace object keeps track of all the procedures that are pending, waiting for the current one to complete. For example, the StackTrace object is implicitly used by the StackTrace property of the Exception object (and all the exception objects that derive from it) to return a string that represents the entire contents of the call stack when the exception was thrown.

You can create the StackTrace object in many ways. In its simplest form, you pass no arguments to its constructor and you get the complete stack image as a collection of StackFrame objects, which you can enumerate by their index:

```
' This code assumes that the following Imports are in effect:
'    System.Reflection
'    System.Diagnostics
```

```
Dim i As Integer
Dim st As New StackTrace()
' Enumerate all the stack frame objects.
' (The frame at index 0 corresponds to the current routine.)
For i = 0 To st.FrameCount - 1
    ' Get the ith stack frame and print the method name.
    Dim sf As StackFrame = st.GetFrame(i)
    Console.WriteLine(sf.GetMethod.Name)
Next
```

Another occasion for creating a StackTrace object is when an exception is caught. In this case, you should pass the exception object to the first argument of the StackTrace constructor so that the StackTrace object contains the stack state at the time the exception was thrown, rather than when you create the StackTrace object itself. The following code creates a chain of calling procedures, with the innermost procedure causing an exception that's trapped in the outermost one:

```
Sub TestStackFrameFromException()
    Try
        ' This causes an exception.
        TestStackFrameFromException_1(1)
    Catch e As Exception
        DisplayExceptionInfo(e)
    End Try
End Sub

Sub TestStackFrameFromException_1(ByVal x As Integer)
    TestStackFrameFromException_2("abc")
End Sub

Function TestStackFrameFromException_2(ByVal x As String) As String
    TestStackFrameFromException_3()
End Function

Sub TestStackFrameFromException_3()
    ' Cause an exception (null reference).
    Dim o As Object
    Console.Write(o.ToString)
End Sub

' A reusable routine that displays error information
Sub DisplayExceptionInfo(ByVal e As Exception)
    ' Display the error message.
    Console.WriteLine(e.Message)

    Dim st As New StackTrace(e, True)
    Dim i As Integer
```

(continued)

```
        For i = 0 To st.FrameCount - 1
            ' Get the ith stack frame.
            Dim sf As StackFrame = st.GetFrame(i)
            ' Get the corresponding method for that stack frame.
            Dim mi As MemberInfo = sf.GetMethod
            ' Get the namespace where that method is defined.
            Dim res As String = mi.DeclaringType.Namespace & "."
            ' Append the type name.
            res &= mi.DeclaringType.Name & "."
            ' Append the name of the method.
            res &= mi.Name
            ' Append information about the position in the source file
            ' (but only if Debug information is available).
            If sf.GetFileName <> "" Then
                res &= " (" & sf.GetFileName & ", Line " & sf.GetFileLineNumber _
                    & ", Col " & sf.GetFileColumnNumber
            End If
            ' Append information about offset in MSIL code, if available.
            If sf.GetILOffset <> StackFrame.OFFSET_UNKNOWN Then
                res &= ", IL offset " & sf.GetILOffset.ToString
            End If
            ' Append information about offset in native code.
            res &= ", native offset " & sf.GetNativeOffset & ")"

            Console.WriteLine(res)
        Next
    End Sub
```

The code inside the DisplayExceptionInfo procedure shows how you can use other methods of the StackFrame object, such as GetFileName (the name of the source file), GetFileLineNumber and GetFileColumnNumber (the position in the source file), GetILOffset (offset in MSIL code from the top of the module), and GetNativeOffset (offset in JIT-compiled native code). By using all these pieces of information, the DisplayExceptionInfo routine can provide a more informative error report than you usually get inside the IDE. As a result you might launch ILDASM, for example, and see the individual MSIL opcode that threw the exception. Note that the source code's filename, line, and column are available only if the program was compiled with debugging information. If you compiled the executable for Release configuration, these properties return a null string or 0.

Because the GetMethod method of the StackFrame object returns a MethodInfo object, you can leverage reflection to learn more about that procedure, including its argument signature, which is useful when there are overloaded versions of the same procedure, or any custom attribute associated with it.

One last note about visiting the stack with the StackTrace object: some methods might not appear in the list because they've been inlined by the JIT compiler. In other words, the JIT compiler has eliminated the call to the method by moving its code in the calling routines. This kind of optimization can occur only when the project is compiled in Release mode, so it's never a problem in the debugging phase. If your program depends on the contents of the StackTrace object, you should disable inlining optimization by marking the method in question with the MethodImpl(MethodImplOptions.NoInlining) attribute.

This chapter on reflection completes the overview of the most important lower-level classes of the .NET runtime, which provide the building blocks you're likely to use in any application, whether it's client-side or server-side, database- or Internet-oriented. In the remainder of the book, you'll see this knowledge put to use. The first topic I'll cover in the next part of this book is Windows Forms, the heir of the Visual Basic 6 form engine that you've learned to use and love (and hate, at times) in recent years.

Front
Top
Left
Back

Part IV

Win32 Applications

Front
Top
Left
Back

16

Windows Forms Applications

Most books about earlier Visual Basic versions, say, up to version 3, were almost completely devoted to form and control programming. The first edition of *Programming Microsoft Visual Basic 6* introduces forms in the first chapter but postpones an in-depth discussion until Chapter 9. In this book about Visual Basic .NET, I talk about forms in Chapter 16. If nothing else, this is clear evidence that Visual Basic has evolved from a simple tool for creating front-end applications into something more complex and powerful—it's being used for much more than pretty user interfaces.

In spite of the potential that Visual Basic has now in areas such as component and Internet programming, I expect that many developers will continue to use the language to create standard Win32 applications. The .NET Framework offers a lot in this area and lets you create applications with a rich user interface without the annoyances and limitations of previous language versions. To qualify as a Visual Basic 6 user-interface wiz, you had to learn a lot of tricks and advanced techniques, such as tons of Windows API calls and subclassing. Now you need only to use correctly the classes and methods defined in the System.Windows.Forms namespace.

Form Basics

As I explained in Chapter 2, a Visual Basic .NET form is nothing but a class that inherits from the System.Windows.Forms.Form class; it isn't special in comparison with other .NET classes. For example, there's no global variable named after the form class (as happens in Visual Basic 6), so you can't display an instance of a form named Form1 by simply executing Form1.Show. Instead, you have to correctly create an instance of the proper form class, as in this code:

```
Dim frm As New Form1
frm.Show
```

The Form Designer

Visual Studio .NET comes with a designer similar to the one provided with earlier versions of Visual Basic. Behind the scenes, however, things work very differently. The Visual Studio .NET designer is a sophisticated code generator: when you set a control's property in the Properties window, you're just creating one or more Visual Basic statements that assign a value to that property after the form has been created.

Code Generation

For example, the code that follows is generated for a form named Form1 that contains a Label, a TextBox, and a Button control. (See Figure 16-1.) The designer encloses the generated code in a collapsed #Region so that you can't modify it accidentally:

```
Public Class Form1
    Inherits System.Windows.Forms.Form

#Region " Windows Form Designer generated code "

    Public Sub New()
        MyBase.New()

        'This call is required by the Windows Form Designer.
        InitializeComponent()

        'Add any initialization after the InitializeComponent() call.

    End Sub

    'Form overrides dispose to clean up the component list.
    Protected Overloads Overrides Sub Dispose(ByVal disposing As Boolean)
        If disposing Then
            If Not (components Is Nothing) Then
                components.Dispose()
            End If
        End If
        MyBase.Dispose(disposing)
    End Sub
    Friend WithEvents btnOK As System.Windows.Forms.Button
    Friend WithEvents txtValue As System.Windows.Forms.TextBox
    Friend WithEvents lblMessage As System.Windows.Forms.Label
```

```
    'Required by the Windows Form Designer
    Private components As System.ComponentModel.Container

    'NOTE: The following procedure is required by the Windows Form Designer.
    'It can be modified using the Windows Form Designer.
    'Do not modify it using the code editor.
    <System.Diagnostics.DebuggerStepThrough()> _
    Private Sub InitializeComponent()
        Me.btnOK = New System.Windows.Forms.Button()
        Me.txtValue = New System.Windows.Forms.TextBox()
        Me.lblMessage = New System.Windows.Forms.Label()
        Me.SuspendLayout()
        '
        'lblMessage
        '
        Me.lblMessage.Location = New System.Drawing.Point(16, 16)
        Me.lblMessage.Name = "lblMessage"
        Me.lblMessage.Size = New System.Drawing.Size(352, 40)
        Me.lblMessage.TabIndex = 0
        Me.lblMessage.Text = "Type your value here"
        '
        'txtValue
        '
        Me.txtValue.Location = New System.Drawing.Point(16, 64)
        Me.txtValue.Name = "txtValue"
        Me.txtValue.Size = New System.Drawing.Size(352, 20)
        Me.txtValue.TabIndex = 1
        Me.txtValue.Text = ""
        '
        'btnOK
        '
        Me.btnOK.Location = New System.Drawing.Point(400, 16)
        Me.btnOK.Name = "btnOK"
        Me.btnOK.Size = New System.Drawing.Size(88, 32)
        Me.btnOK.TabIndex = 2
        Me.btnOK.Text = "OK"
        '
        'Form1
        '
        Me.AcceptButton = Me.btnOK
        Me.AutoScaleBaseSize = New System.Drawing.Size(5, 13)
        Me.ClientSize = New System.Drawing.Size(496, 141)
        Me.Controls.AddRange(New System.Windows.Forms.Control() _
            {Me.lblMessage, Me.txtValue, Me.btnOK})
        Me.Name = "Form1"
        Me.Text = "First Windows Forms example"
        Me.ResumeLayout(False)
    End Sub
#End Region

End Class
```

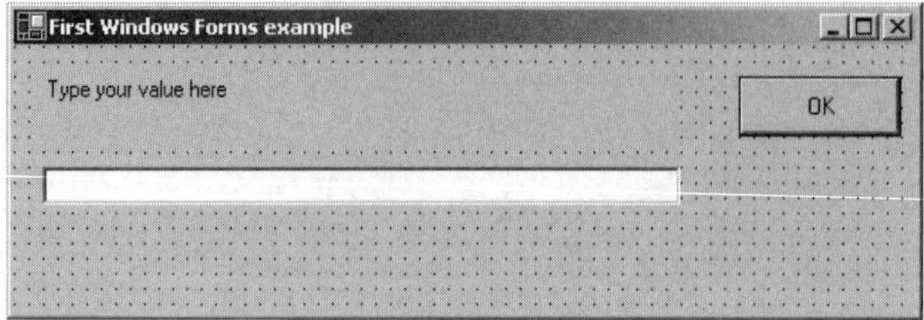

Figure 16-1. A simple form in the Visual Studio form designer.

The listing shows a few interesting features of the Form class:

- The Sub New procedure is where you can put initialization code; it broadly corresponds to the Form_Initialize event in Visual Basic 6.
- The Sub Dispose procedure is where you put cleanup code; it corresponds to the Visual Basic 6 Form_Terminate event.
- A control on the form is just an object of the proper control class, which the form instantiates in the InitializeComponent procedure and assigns to a WithEvents variable named after the control itself. By default, control variables are Friend members of the form class, but you can change this by assigning a different scope to the control's Modifiers property in the Properties window.
- Property values are set through regular assignments in code; Visual Basic .NET source code modules don't contain hidden sections that you can't load in Visual Studio's editor.
- After assigning property values, the code produced by the designer inserts individual control objects into the form's Controls collection, using a single AddRange method for best performance.

I'll talk about other interesting new properties—for example, the Size and Location properties—later in this chapter.

New Designer Features

The Visual Studio .NET form designer is virtually identical to the designer in Visual Basic 6, with a few interesting new features. For example, as I explained in Chapter 1, controls that are invisible at run time are displayed on the component tray, near the bottom border of the designer. This area isn't normally visible until you drop an invisible control, such as a Timer control, on the designer.

You can save some time by arranging the TabIndex property in a visual manner, using the Tab Order command on the View menu. This command displays little numbered labels over each control, and you can create the correct TabIndex sequence by simply clicking on each control in the order you want it to appear in relation to the others. As you see in Figure 16-2, controls that are themselves a container have a TabIndex subsequence. You terminate the Tab Order command by pressing the Esc key.

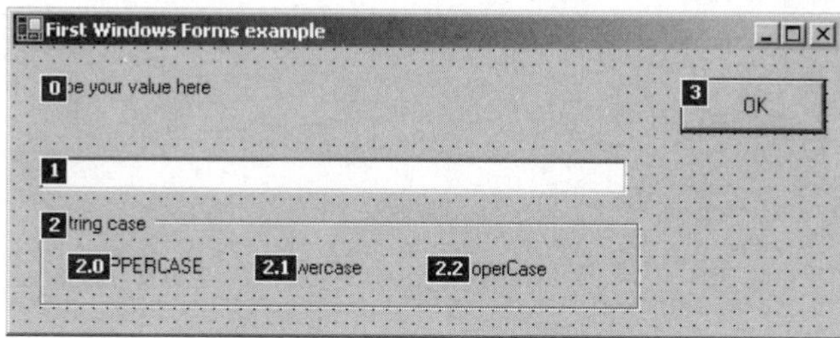

Figure 16-2. Arrange the TabIndex property using the Tab Order command.

Another timesaving feature is the ability to resize multiple controls by using the mouse. Just select multiple controls—by clicking on each one while pressing the Ctrl or the Shift key, or by pressing the Ctrl+A key combination to select all the controls on the form—and then use the mouse to resize one of them: all the selected controls will be sized accordingly. (You can't do this in Visual Basic 6.)

Finally, note that you can lock each individual control (so as not to accidentally move or resize it with the mouse) by setting its Locked property to True in the Properties window. Visual Basic 6 allows you to lock only all controls or none. (You can still lock controls Visual Basic 6–style in Visual Basic .NET by using the Lock Controls command on the Format menu.)

The Windows Forms Class Hierarchy

The classes in the System.Windows.Forms namespace make up a fairly complex hierarchy, at the root of which is the System.Windows.Forms.Control class. (See Figure 16-3.) The Control class inherits from the System.ComponentModel.Component class, which represents an object that can be placed on a container.

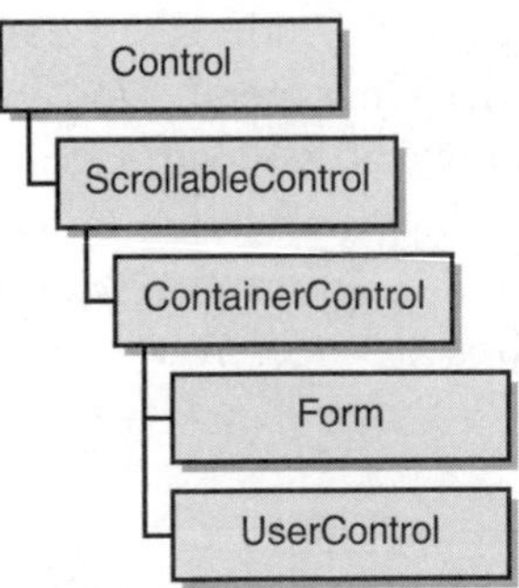

Figure 16-3. A partial view of the Windows Forms class hierarchy.

You might be surprised to see that the Form object is a descendant of the Control object; you might have expected a relationship in the opposite direction. Keep in mind that this is an inheritance diagram, not a containment diagram. The Control, ScrollableControl, and ContainerControl classes are generic objects that expose properties that are inherited by more specific controls. These classes aren't abstract classes, and you can actually create an instance of each class, even though there's no point in doing so. (You must do this from code, however, because these classes don't appear in the Toolbox.)

Even if you don't work with these classes in code directly, it's interesting to see the functionality of each class because it's inherited by other classes further down the hierarchy.

The Control class defines a generic Windows Forms control, which is an object that can be hosted in Visual Studio's Toolbox and placed on the form designer's surface. It has methods such as BringToFront and SendToBack (for controlling Z-ordering), properties such as Location and Size (for defining position and dimension), and many others. Many actual controls that don't require advanced functionality—for example, the Label and PictureBox controls—inherit directly from the System.Windows.Forms.Control class. (Note that the Visual Basic .NET PictureBox control can't work as a container for other controls.) But even a few sophisticated controls inherit directly from Control, including the DataGrid control.

The ScrollableControl class inherits all the members of the Control class, to which it adds the ability to scroll its own contents. It exposes properties such as AutoScrollPosition and methods such as ScrollControlIntoView. The Panel control—which replaces the Visual Basic 6 Frame control—inherits directly from the ScrollableControl class.

The ContainerControl class represents an object that can contain other controls. It exposes properties such as ActiveControl and BindingContext, and the Validate method. The Form class inherits directly from the ContainerControl class.

Windows Forms Controls

The System.Windows.Forms.dll library includes 46 controls, most of which are similar to their Visual Basic counterparts and most of which have retained the same names. (See Figure 16-4.)

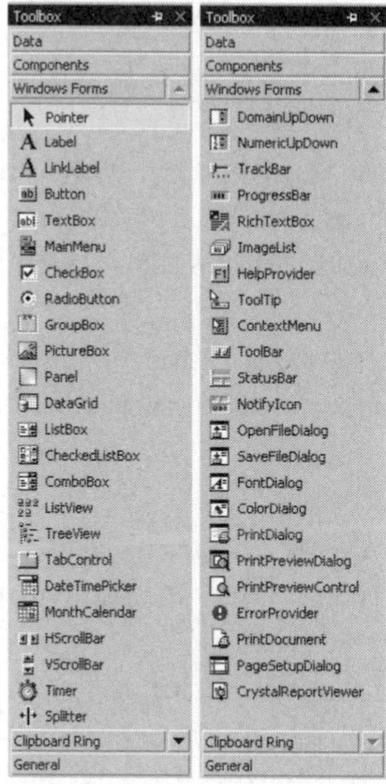

Figure 16-4. All the Windows Forms controls as they appear in the Visual Studio Toolbox.

The Label, Button, TextBox, CheckBox, RadioButton, PictureBox, ListBox, ComboBox, HScrollBar, VScrollBar, and Timer controls are virtually identical to the intrinsic controls in Visual Basic 6, but they often have additional features and different method syntax. CheckedListBox controls replace ListBox controls with the Style property set to 1-CheckBox. The old Frame control is gone and has been replaced by two new controls, GroupBox and Panel. Both these controls work as containers for other controls, but the Panel control is also scrollable. In a difference from previous Visual Basic versions, you now have two explicit menu controls, MainMenu and ContextMenu.

The majority of Windows Common Controls are available in the default Toolbox, so you don't have to reference another library. This group includes the following controls: ImageList, ListView, TreeView, ProgressBar, TrackBar (SlideBar), RichTextBox, TabControl (TabStrip), ToolBar, StatusBar, DateTimePicker, and MonthCalendar (MonthView). (The names in parentheses are the old Visual Basic 6 versions.)

The new NumericUpDown control replaces the combination of a TextBox control and an UpDown control. The new DomainUpDown is like a single-row list box. The DataGrid control has more or less the same functionality as the old control of the same name. The old CommonDialog control has been replaced by six more-specific controls: OpenFileDialog, SaveFileDialog, FontDialog, ColorDialog, PrintDialog, and PageSetupDialog.

There are also a few brand-new controls. The LinkLabel control is an enhanced label control that can be used to implement Web-like hyperlinks to other portions of the application or to URLs on the Internet. The Splitter control lets you create resizeable regions on your form. The NotifyIcon control enables your program to create those little icons in the Windows taskbar and to react to mouse actions on them.

The PrintPreviewDialog control works together with the PrintPreviewControl object to provide a WYSIWYG preview of printed documents. You can simplify actual printing operations by using the PrintControl object, and you can create complex reports using the CrystalReportViewer control.

Finally, there are three controls known as *extender provider controls* because they augment the functionality of other controls on the form. The ToolTip control displays a tooltip message when the mouse hovers over any other control. The HelpProvider control provides help functionality (and therefore replaces the help functionality previously in the CommonDialog control). The ErrorProvider control can display a red icon beside controls that don't pass input validation.

A few Visual Basic 6 controls aren't available any longer: DriveList, DirListBox, FileListBox, OLE container, UpDown, Animation, the two flat scroll bars, MSFlexGrid, and a bunch of others. Windows Forms don't support windowless controls, which explains why the Line and Shape controls aren't supported any longer. The Image control is also gone, but its lightweight capabilities have been embedded in the new PictureBox control. All the Data, RDO Data, and ADO Data controls have been dumped (even though Windows Forms still support data binding, as you'll see in Chapter 17).

Common Properties

Because all controls inherit most of their functionality from System.Windows.Forms.Control, they expose a similar set of properties. I gathered in Table 16-1 the properties that the majority of controls have in common. The third column lists the corresponding Visual Basic 6 properties, if there are any, to help you in understanding what each property does and to speed up porting of applications from previous language versions.

Table 16-1 Properties Common to Most Controls

Category	Name	VB6 Property	Description
Size and position	Location	Left and Top	The location of the object, expressed as a Point object that exposes the X and Y properties.
	Size	Width and Height	The dimension of the object. The Size object exposes the Width and Height properties.
	Left, Top, Width, Height	Left, Top, Width, Height	Individual coordinates and dimensions of the control.
	Right	Left+Width	The X coordinate of the right border.
	Bottom	Top+Height	The Y coordinate of the bottom border.
	Bounds		The rectangle that defines position and size of the control in its container's coordinate system.
	ClientRectangle		The client rectangle of the control.
	ClientSize		A Size object that defines the dimension of the client rectangle.
	Anchor		From which edges of the container this control maintains a fixed distance (bit-coded).
	Dock		Which borders of this control are docked to its container (bit-coded).
	Parent	Container	The parent for this control.
Text	Text	Caption or Text	The text string displayed in the control.
	Font	Font	The font used to display text in the control. Font properties are Name, Size, Bold, Italic, Strikeout, Underline, and Unit. (Unit can be Point, Pixel, Inch, Millimeter, Document, or World.)
	RightToLeft	RightToLeft	True if the control should draw text right-to-left for right-to-left (RTL) languages.

Table 16-1 Properties Common to Most Controls *(continued)*

Category	Name	VB6 Property	Description
	IMEMode		The Input Method Editor status of the object when selected. (Used for alphabets such as Japanese, Chinese, and Korean.)
Color and graphic	ForeColor	ForeColor	The foreground color.
	BackColor	BackColor	The background color.
Focus	TabIndex	TabIndex	The index in tab order for this control.
	TabStop	TabStop	True if the user can use the Tab key to give focus to the control.
	Visible	Visible	True if the control is visible or hidden.
	Enabled	Enabled	True if the control is enabled.
	Cursor		The Cursor object that represents the mouse state, position, and size.
	ShowFocusCues		True if the user interface is in a state to show focus rectangles (read-only).
	ShowKeyboard Cues		True if the user interface is in a state to show keyboard accelerators (read-only).
	CausesValidation	CausesValidation	True if the control causes a validation event.
Keyboard and mouse	ModifierKeys		The current state of Shift, Ctrl, and Alt keys (bit-coded).
	MouseButtons		The current state of mouse buttons (bit-coded).
	MousePosition		The current mouse position in screen coordinates (returns a Point object).
Accessibility	AccessibleName		The name reported to accessibility clients.
	Accessible Description		The description reported to accessibility clients.
	AccessibleRole		The role reported to accessibility clients (Default, Alert, Text, Graphic, Sound, and so on).

Table 16-1 Properties Common to Most Controls *(continued)*

Category	Name	VB6 Property	Description
	AccessibleDefault-ActionDescription		The description of the default action of the control.
	IsAccessible		True if this control should be accessible to accessibility applications.
Creation	Created		True if the control has been created.
	Disposing		True if the control is being disposed of (destroyed).
	Disposed		True if the control has been disposed of (destroyed).
Miscella-neous	Name	Name	The name of the control.
	AllowDrop	OLEDropMode	True if the control receives drag-and-drop notifications.
	ContextMenu		The pop-up menu to display when the user right-clicks on the control.
	ProductName		The name of this specific component.
	ProductVersion		The version of this specific component.
	CompanyName		The company name of this specific component.
Design only	Modifiers		The visibility level of the control (Public, Protected, Friend, or Private).
	Locked		True if the control can't be resized or moved on its container.
Run time only	Focused	ActiveControl (of parent form)	True if the control has the input focus.
	Handle	hWnd	The handle of the Windows control.
	CanFocus		True if the control can receive the focus.
	CanSelect		True if the control can be selected.
	Capture		True if the control has captured the mouse and receives all mouse events (read/write).

Common Methods

Table 16-2 lists the most important methods in common among controls. Once again, I indicated the corresponding Visual Basic 6 method if possible.

Table 16-2 Methods Common to Most Controls

Category	Name	VB6 Method	Description
Size and position	BringToFront	ZOrder	Brings the control to the front of the Z-order.
	SendToBack	ZOrder 1	Sends the control to the back of the Z-order.
	FindForm	Parent	Returns the form this control is on.
	GetContainer	Container	Returns the container for the control.
	GetContainerControl	Container	Returns the closest ContainerControl in the control's chain of parent controls and forms.
	PointToClient(point)		Converts a point from screen coordinates to client coordinates.
	PointToScreen(point)		Converts a point from client coordinates to screen coordinates.
	RectangleToClient(rect)		Converts a rectangle from screen coordinates to client coordinates.
	RectangleToScreen(rect)		Converts a rectangle from client coordinates to screen coordinates.
	SetBounds(left,top,width, height)	Move	Sets the bounding rectangle (same as assigning the Bounds property).
	SetSize(width,height)	Move	Sets the size of the control (same as assigning the Size property).
	SetClientSizeCore (width,height)		Sets the client size of the control.

Table 16-2 Methods Common to Most Controls *(continued)*

Category	Name	VB6 Method	Description
Child controls	Scale(horiz [,vert])		Resizes the control and its children according to the specified ratio values. (If only one value is provided, it's used as both vertical and horizontal ratio.)
	SetNewControls(ctrlarray)		Sets the array of child controls contained in this control.
	GetChildAtPoint(point)		Returns the child control at the specified client coordinates.
	Contains(ctrl)		Checks whether this control contains another control.
	ActivateControl(ctrl)		Activates a child control.
Appearance	Invalidate	Refresh	Invalidates the control and forces a repaint.
	Refresh	Refresh	Forces the control to invalidate and immediately repaint itself and its children.
	Update	Refresh	Forces the control to repaint any currently invalid areas.
	Show		Shows the control; same as setting Visible property to True.
	Hide		Hides the control; same as setting Visible property to False.
	ResetForeColor		Resets the ForeColor property to reflect the parent's foreground color.
	ResetBackColor		Resets the BackColor property to reflect the parent's background color.

Table 16-2 Methods Common to Most Controls *(continued)*

Category	Name	VB6 Method	Description
	ResetCursor		Resets Cursor property to its default value.
	ResetText		Resets the Text property to its default value.
Focus	Focus	SetFocus	Attempts to give input focus to this control.
	ContainsFocus		Returns True if the control or one of its child controls has the focus.
	GetNextControl		Returns the next control in tab order.
	Select		Selects this control.
	SelectNextControl		Gives input focus to next control in tab order.
Miscellaneous	CallWndProc(msg,wParam, lParam)		Dispatches a message to the control's window procedure directly.
	CreateControl		Forces the creation of the control, including its child controls.
	CreateGraphics		Returns the Graphics object that can be used to draw on the control's surface.
	Dispose		Destroys the control.
	DoDragDrop (allowedEffects)	OLEDrag	Begins a drag operation; the argument determines which drag operation can occur.

Common Events

Table 16-3 lists all the events common to the majority of controls, together with the corresponding Visual Basic 6 event if there is one. Keep in mind that all events receive exactly two arguments—sender and *xxxx*EventArgs—where the former is a reference to the control raising the event and the latter is an object that might contain additional information about the event. The descriptions of individual events explain which values are passed in this second argument, if any. Notice that you can create an event template in Visual Studio by selecting the (Base Class Events) element in the leftmost combo box on the right.

Table 16-3 Events Common to Most Controls

Category	Name	VB6 Event	Description
Focus	GotFocus	GotFocus	The control receives the focus.
	LostFocus	LostFocus	The control loses the focus; this event occurs after the Validated event.
	Enter		The control is entered; this event occurs before the GotFocus event.
	Leave		The control is left; this event occurs before the Validating event.
	Validating	Validate	The control is being validated.
	Validated		The control has completed validation.
	ChangeUICues		Focus cue, keyboard cue, or both cues have changed (useful only when creating custom controls).
Keyboard and Mouse	Click	Click	The control is clicked.
	DoubleClick	DblClick	The control is double-clicked.
	MouseDown	MouseDown	A mouse button has been pressed; it receives Button, Clicks, Delta, X, and Y values.
	MouseUp	MouseUp	A mouse button has been released; it receives the same values as MouseDown.
	MouseMove	MouseMove	The mouse is moved over the control; it receives the same values as MouseDown.
	MouseWheel		The mouse wheel has been rotated while the control has the focus; it receives the same values as MouseDown.
	MouseEnter		The mouse enters the control.
	MouseLeave		The mouse leaves the control.
	MouseHover		The mouse hovers over the control.

Table 16-3 Events Common to Most Controls *(continued)*

Category	Name	VB6 Event	Description
	KeyDown	KeyDown	A key is pressed while the control has the focus; it receives Alt, Control, Shift, Modifiers, KeyCode, KeyData, and Handled values.
	KeyUp	KeyUp	A key is released while the control has the focus; it receives the same values as KeyDown.
	KeyPress	KeyPress	A printable key is pressed while the control has the focus; it receives KeyChar and Handled values.
	HelpRequested		The user requests help for the control.
Drag and drop	DragDrop	OLEDragDrop	A drag-and-drop operation is complete; it receives AllowedEffect, Data, Effect, KeyState, X, and Y values.
	DragEnter	OLEDragOver, with state = vbEnter	An object is dragged into the control's border; it receives the same values as DragDrop.
	DragLeave	OLEDragOver, with state = vbLeave	An object is dragged out of the control's border; it receives the same values as DragDrop.
	DragOver	OLEDragOver, with state = vbOver	An object is being dragged over the control's border; it receives the same values as DragDrop.
	GiveFeedback	OLEGive Feedback	Occurs during a drag operation; it gives the source control a chance to change the cursor's appearance.
	QueryContinue-Drag		Occurs during a drag operation; it gives the source control a chance to cancel the operation.
Appearance	Paint	Paint	The control is being repainted; it receives ClipRectangle and Graphics values.

Table 16-3 Events Common to Most Controls *(continued)*

Category	Name	VB6 Event	Description
	Invalidated		The control has been invalidated; it receives an InvalidRect value.
	Move		The control has been moved.
	Resize	Resize	The control is resized.
	Layout		Occurs when a control has to lay out its child controls.
Container controls	ControlAdded		A new control is added; it receives a Control value.
	ControlRemoved		A control is removed; it receives a Control argument.
Miscellaneous	HandleCreated		A handle is created for the control.
	HandleDestroyed		The control's handle is destroyed.
	PropertyChanged		A control's property has been changed; it receives a PropertyName value.

Common Tasks for Forms and Controls

Before I discuss the Form object in detail, it makes sense to illustrate how you can use many of the properties, methods, and events listed in the preceding sections. Once you're familiar with the philosophy that underlies Windows Forms, learning more advanced features specific to form and control objects is considerably easier.

Working with Text and Colors

Visual Basic 6 makes a distinction between the text that a control displays and the text that the end user can edit in the control; it uses the Caption property for the former type of text and the Text property for the latter. Visual Basic .NET gets rid of this distinction, and all the controls that display a string of characters expose just one property, Text. For example, the following statement (inside a form class) changes the caption of the form itself:

```
Me.Text = "A new caption for this form"
```

The same change applies to other .NET controls that have a Caption property in previous versions of Visual Basic, such as Button, CheckBox, and RadioButton.

Some controls—most notably Label, TextBox, Button, CheckBox, RadioButton, NumericUpDown, and DomainUpDown—support the TextAlign property, which specifies where the string is displayed in the control. You can set the alignment in a visual way by using the Properties window, or by means of code, as in this snippet:

```
' Center the string in the Label control.
Label1.TextAlign = ContentAlignment.MiddleCenter
```

Only the Label, Button, CheckBox, and RadioButton controls support all the nine variations offered by the ContentAlignment enumerated type. The remaining controls support only horizontal text alignment and use the HorizontalAlignment enumeration:

```
' Align the TextBox contents to the right.
TextBox1.TextAlign = HorizontalAlignment.Right
```

All visible controls expose the ForeColor and BackColor properties. As in Visual Basic 6, you can assign a value to these properties from the Properties window, selecting the new color from the Custom palette, the System palette, or the new Web palette. (See Figure 16-5.) What has changed from previous versions is how you can define a new color in code by using shared methods of the System.Drawing.Color class. First, you can use the FromArgb method if you know the red, green, and blue components of the value you're assigning:

```
' This is the color orange.
TextBox1.BackColor = Color.FromArgb(255, 16, 0)
```

The Color class has several shared properties that return common colors, so you can rewrite the preceding statement as follows:

```
' This is the color orange.
TextBox1.BackColor = Color.Orange
```

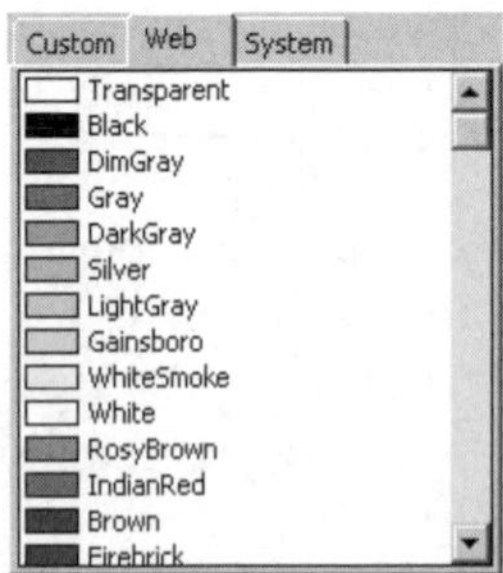

Figure 16-5. The new Web color palette.

The System.Drawing.KnownColor enumerated type exposes all the color values listed in the color palettes mentioned previously, and you can pass one of these values to the FromKnownColor method:

```
' This is the color orange too.
TextBox1.BackColor = Color.FromKnownColor(KnownColor.Orange)
```

Because all the known colors are gathered in an enumerated type, you can easily create a list from which the end user can pick a color—for example, by using a ComboBox control:

```
Dim colorName As String
For Each colorName In [Enum].GetNames(GetType(KnownColor))
    cboColors.Items.Add(colorName)
Next
```

When the user selects a color, you can update your user interface element (such as the background color of a TextBox control) by using the Color.FromName shared method:

```
Private Sub cboColors_SelectedIndexChanged(ByVal sender As Object, _
    ByVal e As System.EventArgs) Handles cboColors.SelectedIndexChanged
    TextBox1.BackColor = Color.FromName(cboColors.Text))
End Sub
```

(This is the approach used in the demo program shown in Figure 16-6.) Once you have a Color value, you can extract its red, green, and blue components by using the R, G, and B methods:

```
' Display the three components' values in a label.
Dim c As Color = TextBox1.BackColor
lblColors.Text = String.Format("Red={0}, Green={1}, Blue={2}", c.R, c.G, c.B)
```

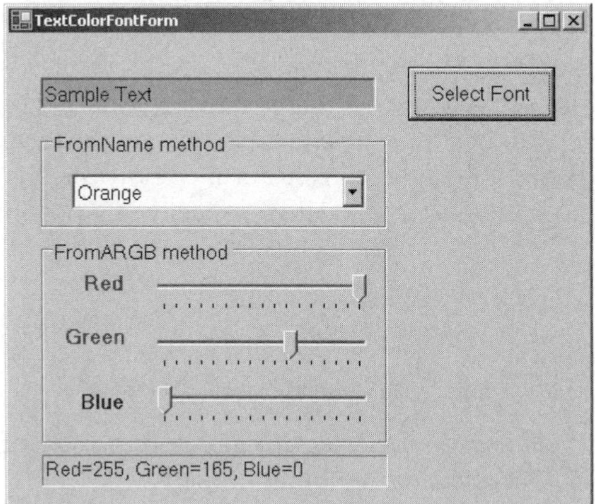

Figure 16-6. The TextColorFontForm dialog box in the demo program.

Working with Fonts

Old-style Font*xxxx* properties, such as FontName and FontSize, aren't available any longer. All Visual Basic .NET controls that can display text expose a Font property, to which you assign a System.Drawing.Font object. You can assign individual font properties at design time after expanding the Font node in the Properties window. (See Figure 16-7.)

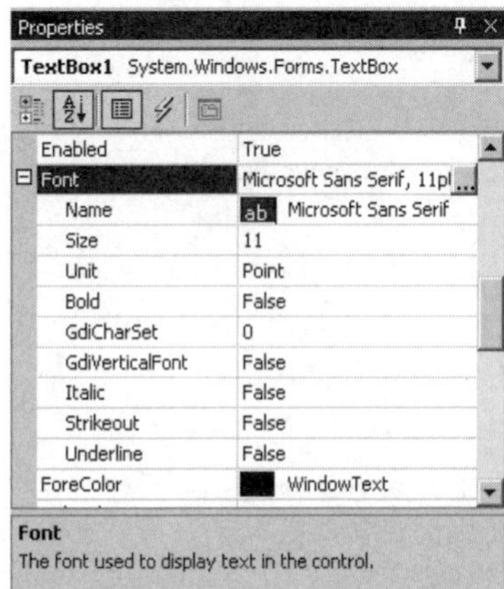

Figure 16-7. Setting Font properties in the Properties window at design time.

The Font class exposes all the properties that you would expect, plus a few new ones. The Unit property indicates the unit of measure used for the Size property and can be one of the following GraphicsUnit enumerated values: Point, Pixel, Inch, Millimeter, Display, Document, and World. (See the "Transformations" section in Chapter 18 for additional information about each unit of measure.)

In an important difference from the way you used fonts in Visual Basic 6, you can't modify a font attribute after you create a new font. In fact, properties such as Size, Height, Bold, Italic, Underline, Strikeout, and Style are read-only, and you can assign them only in the constructor method, which is overloaded to provide 13 different syntax forms that let you specify any possible combination of attributes:

```
' Font name, size, and style
TextBox1.Font = New Font("Arial", 12, FontStyle.Bold Or FontStyle.Italic)
' Font name, size, and unit
TextBox1.Font = New Font("Tahoma", 20, GraphicsUnit.Millimeter)
```

The following code shows how you can increase the size of a control's font by 30 percent without affecting any other property:

```
With TextBox1
    .Font = New Font(.Font.Name, .Font.Size * 1.3, .Font.Style, .Font.Unit)
End With
```

You can also use an existing font as a prototype and change only the style:

```
' Change the font to set Bold attribute.
TextBox1.Font = New Font(TextBox1.Font, TextBox1.Font.Style Or FontStyle.Bold)
' Toggle the italic attribute.
TextBox1.Font = New Font(TextBox1.Font, _
    TextBox1.Font.Style Xor FontStyle.Italic)
```

Another important difference from the Visual Basic 6 way of doing things is that all controls point to their parent form's font unless you set a different font for the control. This change means that if you change the form's font—either at design time or through code—all the controls will inherit the new font except the controls for which you set a custom font. If you want to assign a control the same form as its parent form but you want to change either font without affecting the other, you must use the Clone method:

```
TextBox1.Font = Me.Font.Clone()
```

The easiest way to let the user select a font at run time is by means of the FontDialog control. For example, this code lets the user dynamically change the Font property of the TextBox1 control. As you see, it couldn't be simpler:

```
With FontDialog1
    ' Ensure that current font attributes are displayed.
    .Font = TextBox1.Font
    ' Display the Font dialog.
    If .ShowDialog() = DialogResult.OK Then
        ' If the user didn't cancel the dialog, assign the Font.
        TextBox1.Font = .Font
    End If
End With
```

Other properties of the FontDialog control let you define exactly what appears in the Font dialog, the minimum and maximum font size, whether styles can be modified, and so on. Read Chapter 17 for more information about the FontDialog control.

Working with Size and Position

You specify the size and position of both forms and controls by using objects such as Size and Point instead of scalar properties such as Left, Top, Width, and Height. The old-style properties are still supported for compatibility reasons, but their use is discouraged. Controls also expose the new Bottom and Right properties, which are handy if you want to avoid simple but annoying calculations. By default, size and position are measured in pixels, not twips.

The size of all visible controls corresponds to a System.Drawing.Size object, so you can resize a control by making a single assignment:

```
' Make PictureBox1 300 pixels wide and 200 pixels high.
PictureBox1.Size = New Size(300, 200)
' Make PictureBox2 as large as PictureBox1.
PictureBox2.Size = PictureBox1.Size
```

Note that you can't change Width, Height, and other properties of the Size object because they're read-only. The only way to change a control's size is to assign it a brand-new Size object. (You can also assign a value to the control's Width or Height property, but, because these are old-style properties, this practice is discouraged and doesn't deliver better performance anyway.)

You assign a position to a control by assigning a System.Drawing.Point object to the control's Location property. The Point object exposes the X and Y properties, which correspond to the old-style Left and Top properties, respectively. From a syntactical point of view, you work with the Location property as you do with the Size property:

```
' Move PictureBox1 at coordinates (450, 230).
PictureBox1.Location = New Point(450, 230)
' Move TextBox1 over PictureBox1 so that their upper left corners coincide.
TextBox1.Location = PictureBox1.Location
```

Windows Forms controls (and the Form object itself) expose a SetBounds method, which lets you set both position and size in one operation. This method is virtually identical to the Visual Basic 6 Move method:

```
' Move PictureBox1 to the form's upper left corner, and resize it.
PictureBox1.SetBounds(0, 0, 300, 200)
```

Several other properties relate to size and position. For example, Bounds is a System.Drawing.Rectangle object that represents the external border of the control; ClientRectangle is the Rectangle object that represents the internal area; ClientSize is the Size object that represents the dimension of the internal area. These properties let you perform quite sophisticated operations with surprisingly little code, as you see here:

```
' Expand PictureBox1 to cover the form's client area.
PictureBox1.Bounds = Me.ClientRectangle

' As before, but leave a 10-pixel margin near the left and right
' edges of the PictureBox control, and an 8-pixel margin near the
' top and bottom edges.
Dim rect As Rectangle = Me.ClientRectangle
' Arguments are negative because we are deflating the rectangle.
rect.Inflate(-10, -8)
PictureBox1.Bounds = rect
```

ClientSize is read-only, so you can't assign it a value to resize. However, you can reach the same result with the SetClientSizeCore method, as follows:

```
' Resize the current form so that its client area
' is 500 pixels wide and 300 pixels high.
Me.SetClientSizeCore(500, 300)
```

Working with Docked and Anchored Controls

A frequent difficulty in creating a good user interface is moving and resizing correctly all the controls on a form when the end user resizes the form itself. As a matter of fact, several third-party vendors have proposed smart resizer controls that do this job with minimal code on your part. Windows Forms controls offer a nice solution to this problem in the Dock and Anchor properties that all of them expose.

The Dock property lets you dock a control at its container's border, so it's virtually identical to the Visual Basic 6 Align property, with this important difference: all Windows Forms controls expose the Dock property, so all controls are dockable. At design time, you can select the border at which the control is docked in the Properties window, as shown in Figure 16-8. You can also click the square in the middle to dock the control to all four borders. (In this case, the control always covers the entire client area of its container.)

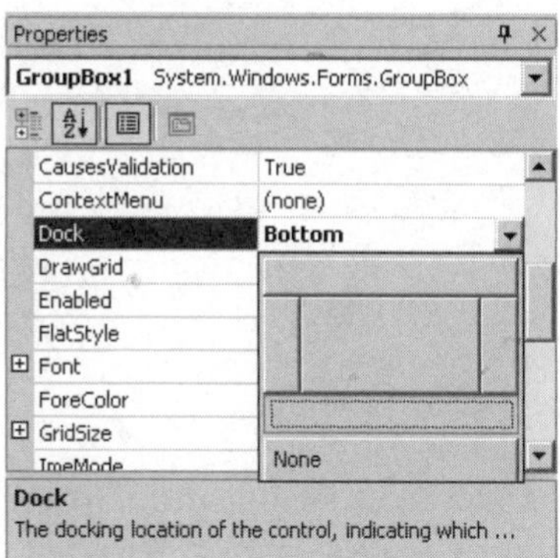

Figure 16-8. Setting the Dock property at design time.

Setting the Dock property via code is also very simple:

```
' Have the PictureBox1 control be resized to cover the entire form.
PictureBox1.Dock = DockStyle.Fill
```

Remember that a control is docked to its container's internal border, and this container isn't necessarily the parent form.

The parent form's DockPadding property affects the distance between a docked control and the form's borders. You can assign this property at design time, or at run time via code. This property returns a DockPaddingEdges structure, and you can assign a value to its fields to set the same distance from all borders or a different distance from each border:

```
' All docked controls are 6 pixels from the form's edges.
Me.DockPadding.All = 6

' Controls docked at the bottom edge use a 4-pixel docking border.
Me.DockPadding.Bottom = 4
```

The DockPadding property is exposed also by the Panel control but not by the GroupBox control. So you can dock a control in a GroupBox, even though you can't specify the distance from the contained control and the GroupBox's border.

The Anchor property is the key to automatic control resizing. You set this property at design time by using the special selector shown in Figure 16-9 to select the container's edge to which this control is anchored. You can also choose to anchor a control to all of its container's edges or to none. When the parent form is resized, the distance between the control and the specified edges will remain constant.

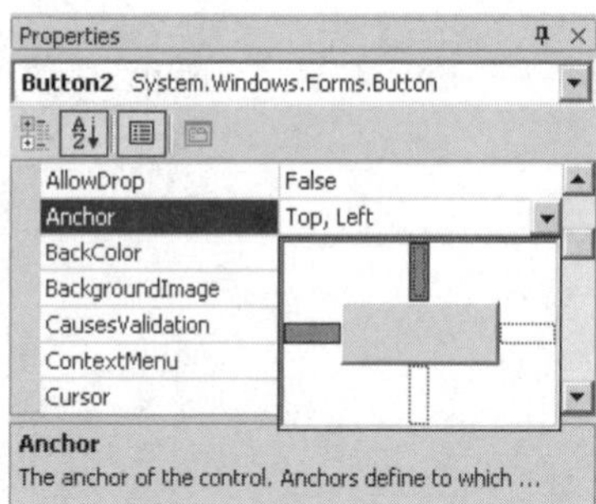

Figure 16-9. Setting the Anchor property at design time.

By default, all controls are anchored to the left and top edges of their containers, which means that a control doesn't move or get resized when the container is resized. However, interesting things happen when you select a different combination of the anchored sides:

- If you anchor a control to the top and right edges (like the Save button in Figure 16-10), the control sticks to the right border of the form and moves horizontally when the form becomes wider or narrower.
- If you anchor a control to the right and bottom edges (like the Cancel and OK buttons in Figure 16-10), the control moves to maintain a fixed distance from the lower right corner when the form is resized.

- If you anchor a control to the top, left, and right edges (as is the case with the single-line TextBox control in Figure 16-10), the control changes its width when the form is resized horizontally.
- If you anchor a control to all four edges (as is the case with the multiline TextBox control in Figure 16-10), the control is resized when the form is resized.
- If the control is anchored to neither the left nor the right edge, the control is resized and moved horizontally so that the ratio between its width and its container's width is constant. (A similar thing happens if the control is anchored to neither the top nor the bottom edge.)

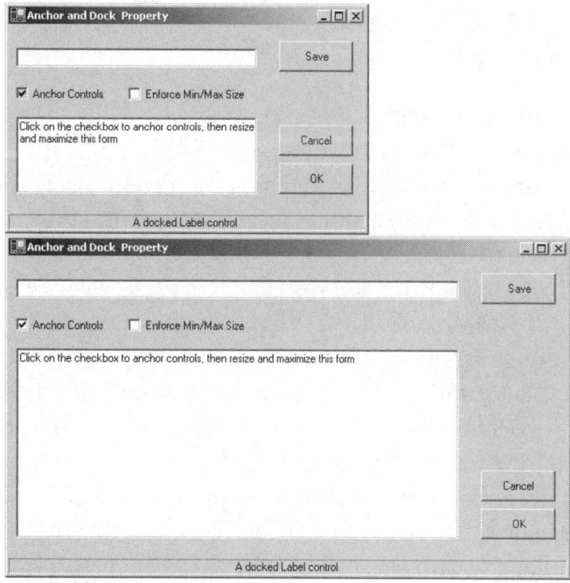

Figure 16-10. Automatic control resizing using the Anchor property.

Of course, you can set the Anchor property by using code. For example, this is the code that resizes the form shown in Figure 16-10:

```
TextBox1.Anchor = AnchorStyles.Top Or AnchorStyles.Left Or AnchorStyles.Right
TextBox2.Anchor = AnchorStyles.Left Or AnchorStyles.Right Or _
    AnchorStyles.Top Or AnchorStyles.Bottom
Button1.Anchor = AnchorStyles.Top Or AnchorStyles.Right
Button2.Anchor = AnchorStyles.Bottom Or AnchorStyles.Right
Button3.Anchor = AnchorStyles.Bottom Or AnchorStyles.Right
```

Interestingly, if you set the Dock property in the Properties window, the control is correctly moved or resized at design time as well, which makes it simple to adjust the form layout when you're adding new controls.

When you're working with resizeable dialog boxes, you often need to set a minimum and maximum size for the form itself to prevent controls from overlapping one another when the form becomes too small. The only way to implement this feature under Visual Basic 6 requires subclassing wizardry (or the purchase of a third-party control). In Visual Basic .NET, you merely have to assign a proper Size object to the form's MinimumSize and MaximumSize properties:

```
Me.MinimumSize = New Size(300, 240)
Me.MaximumSize = New Size(700, 460)
```

Setting these properties at design time is also very simple. Resize the form to its smallest acceptable size, and then switch to the Properties window and copy the current value of the Size property into the MinimumSize property. Next resize the form to its largest acceptable size, and copy the Size property into the MaximumSize property.

Working with the Keyboard

At first glance, it seems that you deal with the keyboard under Visual Basic .NET as you did under Visual Basic 6, using the three events KeyDown, KeyUp, and KeyPress. But as you'll see in a moment, you have to account for a few important differences.

Like all Windows Forms events, the KeyPress event receives two arguments. The sender argument is a reference to the object that raised the event; for this event, the e argument is a KeyPressEventArgs object that exposes only two properties: Handled and KeyChar. (You might want to read again the "Guidelines for Event Syntax" section in Chapter 4 to remind yourself why all Windows Forms events have a similar syntax.) As you might guess, KeyChar is the character corresponding to the key pressed, and Handled is a Boolean value that you can set to True to tell the form engine that you've processed the event and that the engine should take no further action regarding the key being pressed.

Let's say that you have a numeric field and you want to discard all keys except digits and control keys. This task is simple, thanks to the Handled property and a couple of shared methods of the Char class:

```
Private Sub txtNumber_KeyPress(ByVal sender As Object, _
    ByVal e As KeyPressEventArgs) Handles txtNumber.KeyPress

    If Not (Char.IsDigit(e.KeyChar) Or Char.IsControl(e.KeyChar)) Then
        ' If the character is neither a digit nor a control character,
        ' tell the form engine to ignore it.
        e.Handled = True
    End If
End Sub
```

In other cases, you use the KeyPress event to change the character being typed by the user. A typical example is when you want to convert all keys to uppercase. In a difference from Visual Basic 6, however, the character code is read-only, so you can't simply assign it a new value. A solution to this problem, which works with TextBox and ComboBox controls, consists of inserting the (modified) character yourself rather than having the form engine do it. The following code shows an example of a TextBox control that converts all keys to uppercase:

```
Private Sub txtUpperCase_KeyPress(ByVal sender As Object, _
    ByVal e As KeyPressEventArgs) Handles txtUpperCase.KeyPress

    ' Replace the selected text with an uppercase character.
    ' (Inserts at caret position if no text is selected.)
    txtUpperCase.SelectedText = e.KeyChar.ToString.ToUpper
    ' Cancel standard processing.
    e.Handled = True
End Sub
```

The KeyDown and KeyUp events fire when a key is pressed and released. (KeyDown can fire repeatedly if the key is being pressed, but only one KeyUp event fires in this case.) The second argument passed to this event is a KeyEventArgs object, which exposes the following properties: Alt, Shift, Control (the state of shift keys), Modifiers (the state of shift keys as a bit-coded value), KeyCode (the key being pressed or released, as a Keys-enumerated value), and KeyValue (the numeric code of the key). As in other events, the Handled property is a Boolean value to which you should assign True if you handle the event yourself. This example shows how you can detect a function key:

```
' Insert the current date into a TextBox control
' when the user presses Shift+F2.
Private Sub txtDate_KeyDown(ByVal sender As Object, ByVal e As KeyEventArgs) _
    Handles txtDate.KeyDown

    If e.Shift And (e.KeyCode = Keys.F2) Then
        txtDate.SelectedText = Today.Date.ToString
        e.Handled = True
    End If
End Sub
```

You might find it interesting to know that setting the Handled property to True inside a KeyDown event handler discards arrow keys and function keys but not printable keys (such as letters and digits). You don't need to be inside a keyboard event procedure to determine the current state of shift keys because you can use the Control.ModifierKeys shared method anywhere in a form module.

The HelpRequested event fires when the end user types the F1 key inside the control:

```
' Display a message box when the user presses the F1 key.
Private Sub txtDate_HelpRequested(ByVal sender As Object, _
    ByVal hlpevent As HelpEventArgs) Handles txtDate.HelpRequested

    MessageBox.Show("Insert a date", "Help Requested", _
        MessageBoxButtons.OK, MessageBoxIcon.Information)
End Sub
```

A bug in the initial release of the .NET Framework causes this event to fire twice for the form if the KeyPreview property is True.

Working with the Mouse

Visual Basic .NET offers far better support for mouse handling than Visual Basic 6. The three standard events MouseDown, MouseMove, and MouseUp are complemented by the new MouseWheel event, which fires when the mouse wheel is rotated. All these events receive rich information about the mouse status in a MouseEventArgs object:

- The Button property is a bit-coded value that tells which mouse buttons are pressed; the MouseButtons enumerated type supports the five-button Microsoft IntelliMouse Explorer mouse under Windows 2000 and Windows XP. (You can get the same information from anywhere in the form module by using the Control.MouseButtons shared property.)
- X and Y are the current mouse coordinates, in pixels and relative to the current control's upper left corner. (You can get the same information from anywhere in the form module with the Control.MousePosition shared property.)
- Clicks is the number of clicks since the last event.
- Delta is the number of detents the mouse wheel has been rotated since the last event; a positive value means the wheel was rotated forward, whereas a negative value means the wheel was rotated backward. (In the current version, this value is always a multiple of 120.)

No information about shift keys is provided directly to mouse events, but you can retrieve this piece of information by using the Control.ModifierKeys shared property. The following code shows how a single routine can serve all the main mouse events for a form, and it displays the mouse state in a Label control:

```
Private Sub Form_MouseEvent(ByVal sender As Object, _
    ByVal e As MouseEventArgs) Handles MyBase.MouseDown, _
    MyBase.MouseUp, MyBase.MouseMove, MyBase.MouseWheel

    lblInfo.Text = _
        String.Format("Mouse: Buttons={0} X={1} Y={2} Clicks={3} Delta={4}", _
        e.Button, e.X, e.Y, e.Clicks, e.Delta)
End Sub
```

All controls support the Click and DoubleClick mouse events, which behave much like the corresponding events under Visual Basic 6. They don't receive any additional information, but you can retrieve mouse position and button state using the MousePosition and MouseButtons shared properties of the Control object. Note that the Click event isn't fired when the user selects an element of a ListBox or ComboBox control with the keyboard. (In this case, a SelectedIndexChanged event is fired instead.)

All Windows Forms controls inherit three more mouse events from the Control class: MouseHover, MouseEnter, and MouseExit. The first event fires when the mouse pointer hovers over a control and is therefore similar to the MouseMove event. The other two events fire when the mouse cursor enters and exits a control's border and are especially useful for making a control react to the mouse hovering over it (as commonly happens with hyperlinks on Web pages) or for displaying a help message related to the control under the mouse:

```
' These two routines change the background color of a TextBox control
' to yellow when the mouse enters the control's area and restore it to
' white when the mouse leaves the control.

Private Sub MouseEnterEvent(ByVal sender As Object, ByVal e As EventArgs) _
    Handles txtNumber.MouseEnter, txtName.MouseEnter, txtDate.MouseEnter
    ' Convert the argument to a Control, and set its BackColor property.
    CType(sender, Control).BackColor = Color.Yellow
End Sub

Private Sub MouseLeaveEvent(ByVal sender As Object, ByVal e As EventArgs) _
    Handles txtNumber.MouseLeave, txtName.MouseLeave, txtDate.MouseLeave
    ' Convert the argument to a Control, and set its BackColor property.
    CType(sender, Control).BackColor = Color.White
End Sub
```

Thanks to the fact that you can link an event to a control at run time by using the AddHandler command, you can create a generic procedure that allows the MouseEnterEvent and MouseLeaveEvent procedures to serve all the controls on the current form or just all the controls of a given type:

```
' Initialize mouse events so that the background color of a TextBox or ComboBox
' control on the form changes when the mouse enters and leaves a control.
Private Sub InitializeMouseEvents()
    Dim ctrl As Control
    For Each ctrl In Me.Controls
        If (TypeOf ctrl Is TextBox) Or (TypeOf ctrl Is ComboBox) Then
            AddHandler ctrl.MouseEnter, AddressOf MouseEnterEvent
            AddHandler ctrl.MouseLeave, AddressOf MouseLeaveEvent
        End If
    Next
End Sub
```

The Control class exposes the Capture property, which is therefore inherited by the Form object and all the controls. When you assign True to this property, the control is said to *capture* the mouse. From this point on, the control receives all the mouse notifications and events—including MouseMove, MouseDown, MouseUp, and MouseWheel—even if the cursor moves outside the control's client area. For example, a screen-capture application might take advantage of this feature to draw a border around the window whose content is going to be grabbed. The mouse capture is released when you reset the Capture property to False or when the user clicks one of the mouse buttons.

Working with Input Focus

Very little has changed in the way you deal with input focus in controls. For example, the Enabled, TabStop, and TabIndex properties are still supported. In a minor difference from Visual Basic 6, the form engine doesn't require that all controls have different values for their TabIndex property. In fact, this happens regularly if two controls are hosted in different container controls. If two controls in the same container have the same TabIndex value, the one with the higher Z-order—the one "closer" to the user if you prefer—gets the input focus before the other.

You can use the new CanFocus property to determine whether a given control can get the input focus (which happens if its Visible and Enabled properties are both True), and you can use the new Focused property to determine whether the control actually has the focus. (In Visual Basic 6, you had to compare the control with the ActiveControl property of the parent form.)

The SetFocus method isn't supported any longer; you move the focus on a control by using the Focus method. You can use it together with another new method, GetNextControl, which returns the control visited immediately before or after another control in a given container when the user presses the Tab key. For example, the following routine handles the Down and Up arrow keys at the form level so that the end user can use these keys to move among fields in addition to Tab and Shift+Tab key combinations:

```
' This code assumes that Me.KeyPreview = True so that the form
' captures all keys before the currently active control.

Private Sub KeyboardMouseForm_KeyDown(ByVal sender As Object, _
    ByVal e As KeyEventArgs) Handles MyBase.KeyDown

    ' Move focus among controls with the Up/Down arrow keys.
    If Me.Controls.Count = 0 Then
        ' Ignore forms without any control.
    ElseIf e.KeyCode = Keys.Up Or e.KeyCode = Keys.Down Then
        ' Start at the currently selected control.
        Dim ctrl As Control = Me.ActiveControl
        ' Are we moving forward or backward?
        Dim moveForward As Boolean = (e.KeyCode = Keys.Down)

        Do
            ' Get the next control in that direction.
            ctrl = Me.GetNextControl(ctrl, moveForward)
            ' GetNextControl(ctrl,False) can return Nothing if first control.
            If Not (ctrl Is Nothing) AndAlso ctrl.CanFocus _
                AndAlso ctrl.TabStop Then
                ' If the control can receive the focus, give it.
                ctrl.Focus()
                Exit Do
            End If
        Loop
    End If
End Sub
```

Visual Basic 6 supports only three events related to input focus: GotFocus, LostFocus, and Validate. The first two events are still supported in Visual Basic .NET, but you should use the new Enter and Leave events instead. The Validate event isn't supported any longer and has been replaced by an event pair, Validating and Validated. These are the events that fire whenever the user gives the focus to another control: Enter, GotFocus, Leave, Validating, Validated, and LostFocus.

The Validating and Validated events fire only if the CausesValidation property is set to True in both the control that has the focus and the control that's trying to get the focus. Because this validation mechanism is inherited from Visual Basic 6, I won't discuss it in greater detail. (You can read about it in the previous edition of this book, provided on the companion CD.)

In general, you use the Validating event to trap invalid values in a field. If the control's value doesn't pass your validation routine, you simply set the Cancel property of the e argument to True, as in the following code:

```
Private Sub txtNumber_Validating(ByVal sender As Object, _
    ByVal e As System.ComponentModel.CancelEventArgs) _
    Handles txtNumber.Validating
    ' This is a required field, so reject null strings.
    If txtNumber.Text = "" Then e.Cancel = True
End Sub
```

If the validation fails, the focus is returned to the control that had it previously, and the Validated event and the final LostFocus event don't fire.

The new input focus management has resolved a few quirks in the previous version. For example, a Visual Basic 6 control's LostFocus and Validate events don't fire if the user activates the default pushbutton on the form by pressing the Enter key. As a matter of fact, you had to manually call the form's ValidateControls method from inside the button's Click event procedure to fire any pending Validate event. This problem has been fixed in Visual Basic .NET: both the LostFocus and Validating events fire for the active control when the end user activates the default button with the Enter key (or the Cancel button with the Esc key). The ValidateControls method isn't supported any longer because it's now unnecessary.

> **More Info** Not all the oddities in Visual Basic 6 have been purged. You can easily prove this by creating three TextBox controls named TextBox1, TextBox2, and TextBox3. Set the TextBox2.CausesValidation property to False so that when you press the Tab key on the first box, the TextBox1_Validating event doesn't fire. If you press the Tab key a second time, the focus should move to TextBox3. Because this control's CausesValidation property is True, Visual Basic .NET fires the pending TextBox1_Validating event. If this event cancels the focus shift, the focus will return to TextBox1—a rather disorienting behavior for your end user. You can test this behavior with the demo application, shown in Figure 16-11.

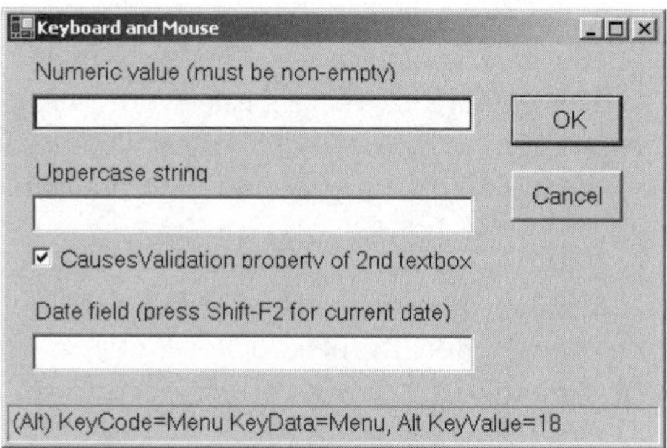

Figure 16-11. The sample application lets you test several keyboard, mouse, and validation features.

Working with Container Controls

A few objects in the Windows Forms portion of the Framework—most notably, the Form object, the Panel control, and the GroupBox control—inherit from the ContainerControl class and can therefore work as containers for other objects. The most relevant difference between the Panel control and the GroupBox control is that the former is also scrollable, whereas the latter has a border and a caption. (Note that the PictureBox control isn't a container any longer; you should use a Panel control instead.) Containers have a few specific properties and methods, which I'll describe in this section.

All container controls (and the Form object itself) have a Controls collection that you can parse to enumerate contained objects. This collection contains only the top-level objects, not objects owned by the contained objects. Let's make an example to clarify this point. Suppose you have a form with two GroupBox controls on it, which in turn contain some RadioButton objects, as in the following hierarchy:

```
Form (Me)
    GroupBox1
        RadioButton1
        RadioButton2
    GroupBox2
        RadioButton3
        RadioButton4
        RadioButton5
```

In this case, the form's Controls collection contains only the two GroupBox controls:

```
Debug.WriteLine(Me.Controls.Count)            ' => 2
Debug.WriteLine(GroupBox1.Controls.Count)     ' => 2
Debug.WriteLine(GroupBox2.Controls.Count)     ' => 3
```

Having separate Controls collections means that you don't have to test all the controls on the form to determine which ones are inside a given container, as you have to do under earlier versions of Visual Basic. You don't even have to scan the Controls collection of a container to determine whether it contains a specific control because you can take advantage of the Contains method:

```
Debug.WriteLine(GroupBox1.Contains(RadioButton1))    ' => True
```

The Visual Basic 6 Container property has been renamed Parent (it returns a reference to the container), whereas the old Parent property has been replaced by the FindForm method (it returns a reference to the containing form):

```
Debug.WriteLine(RadioButton1.Parent.Name)       ' => GroupBox1
Debug.WriteLine(RadioButton1.FindForm Is Me)   ' => True
```

You can also retrieve a reference to a child control located at given coordinates inside the container, using the GetChildAtPoint method:

```
' Determine the child control at coordinates (30, 50) inside GroupBox1.
Dim ctrl As Control = GroupBox1.GetChildAtPoint(New Point(30, 50))
If ctrl Is Nothing Then
    Debug.WriteLine("No child control at this position")
Else
    Debug.WriteLine("Child control is " & ctrl.Name)
End If
```

Finally, you can use the Scale method to move and resize one or more controls in a container. This method is inherited from Control and is therefore exposed by all controls, but I discuss it here because it's usually applied to containers. Its effect is to change the size and dimensions of a control by a scaling factor that you specify. You can specify two distinct factors for the X and Y axes, as in this code:

```
' Double both coordinates and size of a control.
RadioButton1.Scale(2, 2)
```

The great feature of this method is that it applies the transformation to all contained controls if there are any. Even better, if one of the contained controls is a container, the scaling applies to the contained control's children, and so on in a recursive fashion. This means that you can resize a form *and* all its controls using just one statement:

```
' Stretch a form by 30 percent horizontally and 20 percent vertically.
Me.Scale(1.3, 1.2)
```

Fortunately, the Scale method resizes a form but doesn't move it. (If an enlarged form also moved, it might fall outside the visible portion of the desktop.)

Working with ActiveX Controls

You aren't limited to using Windows Forms controls in your .NET applications; in fact, you can reuse ActiveX controls as well, even though their performance isn't optimal and their use is discouraged. To import an ActiveX control, select the Toolbox tab where you want to place the control, right-click the Toolbox and click Customize Toolbox, and then select which COM components you want to import.

For example, you might want to import the Microsoft WebBrowser control to let users browse the Internet from inside your .NET applications, or you might want to display an HTML file on disk. Importing an ActiveX control creates a wrapper control named Ax*controlname*. For example, the WebBrowser control is imported as AxWebBrowser. All the properties are accessible from inside the Properties window, even though a few properties are unavailable because they can't be modified at run time: these are the properties that don't appear in the Visual Basic 6 Properties window. When a property has the same name as a property or a method that the .NET default designer adds to all .NET controls—such as Visible or Refresh—it's prefixed by *Ctl* to avoid name clashing. (So you have the CtlVisible property and the CtlRefresh method.) Except for these minor details, you code against an imported ActiveX control as you would do with a regular .NET control.

You can also create an assembly for any ActiveX control from outside Visual Studio by using the Windows Forms ActiveX Control Importer tool (Aximp.exe). This tool generates a set of assemblies for all the ActiveX controls and all the COM components contained in the specified library. For example, you can run Aximp against the DLL that contains the WebBrowser control:

```
aximp c:\winnt\system32\shdocvw.dll
```

> **Important** Don't run Aximp in the same directory as the source DLL because you might accidentally overwrite it. Or use the /out option to select a different output file.

The preceding command generates two assemblies: SHDocVw.dll for the component and AxSHDocVw.dll for the ActiveX control.

ActiveX controls can be used in .NET because Visual Studio or Aximp automatically creates a wrapper class for them. Such a wrapper class is a class that inherits from System.Windows.Forms.AxHost. You can use the /source option of Aximp to generate the C# source code for the wrapper class:

```
aximp c:\winnt\system32\shdocvw.dll /source
```

Should the need arise, you can edit this source code and recompile it. You might need to edit and recompile, for example, if you want to change the control name, add new properties, or hide a few items in the Properties window.

Unfortunately, you can't successfully import any type of ActiveX control. For example, the Windows Forms portion of the Framework doesn't support windowless controls, so you can't use the Windowless Control Library (WinLess.ocx) and the Microsoft Forms 2.0 control library (FM20.Dll). Some ActiveX controls can be imported but don't always work correctly on a Visual Basic .NET form—for example, SSTab.

The Form Object

The Form object derives from the ContainerControl object, which in turn derives from ScrollableControl and ultimately from Control, so working with forms is similar to working with a control. For example, you can count on properties such as Text, Size, and Location, and you can apply most of the concepts I illustrated earlier in this chapter. Of course, forms are more complicated and richer in functionality than controls and deserve a thorough discussion in a section of their own.

Properties, Methods, and Events

I've grouped all the most important properties, methods, and events of the Form object in categories, with a brief description of each member and the corresponding member under Visual Basic 6 if there is one. In later sections, I describe in greater detail those properties that are new in Visual Basic .NET or that behave differently from Visual Basic 6.

Properties

Table 16-4 summarizes the most important properties of the Form object. This table doesn't include properties inherited from the Control object. (See Table 16-1.)

Table 16-4 Properties of the Form Object

Category	Name	VB6 Property	Description
Appearance	FormBorderStyle	BorderStyle	The style of the form's border. (Can be Sizable, None, Fixed-Single, Fixed3D, FixedDialog, Fixed-Toolwindow, or SizableToolwindow.)
	Icon	Icon	The icon for this form.
	Background-Image	Picture	The background image of the form.
	ControlBox	ControlBox	If True (default), the form displays a control box button.
	MaximizeBox	MaximizeBox	If True (default), the form displays a maximize button.
	MinimizeBox	MinimizeBox	If True (default), the form displays a minimize button.
	HelpButton	WhatsThis-Button	If True, a Help button is displayed for this form. (Requires that MaximizeBox and MinimizeBox both be False.)
	SizeGripStyles		Determines when the size grip will be displayed for this form. (Can be Auto, Show, or Hide.)
	Opacity		The degree of opacity of the form (in the range 0–1).
	TransparencyKey		The color that represents transparent areas on the form.

Table 16-4 Properties of the Form Object *(continued)*

Category	Name	VB6 Property	Description
Size and position	AutoScale		If True (the default), the form automatically scales itself and its controls based on the font assigned to the form.
	DesktopBounds		A Rectangle object that represents the size and position of the form on the desktop (without any visible taskbar).
	DesktopLocation		A Point object that represents the position of the form on the desktop (without any visible taskbar).
	StartPosition	StartPosition	Determines the position of this form when it first appears. (Can be WindowsDefaultLocation, WindowsDefaultBounds, CenterScreen, CenterParent, or Manual.)
	WindowState	WindowState	The state of the window. (Can be Normal, Minimized, or Maximized.)
	MinimumSize		A Size object that represents the smallest size for this form.
	MaximumSize		A Size object that represents the largest size for this form.
	TopLevel		If True (default), this form is displayed as a top-level form.

Table 16-4 Properties of the Form Object *(continued)*

Category	Name	VB6 Property	Description
	TopMost		If True, this form is the topmost form for the current application.
Modal forms	Modal		Returns True if this form is modal.
	AcceptButton	Default (on the Command-Button)	The Button control that's activated when the user presses the Enter key.
	CancelButton	Cancel (on the Command-Button)	The Button control that's activated when the user presses the Esc key.
	DialogResult		The result returned to the caller of this modal form. (Can be OK, Cancel, Abort, Retry, Ignore, Yes, No, or None.)
Scrolling	AutoScroll		If True, scroll bars are displayed on the form if any controls are located outside the form's client region and the client area of the form automatically scrolls to make the active control visible.
	AutoScroll-Margins		A Size object that represents the width and height in pixels of the auto-scroll area. This margin is applied to all contained controls. If any adjusted border isn't completely visible, scroll bars appear.

Table 16-4 Properties of the Form Object *(continued)*

Category	Name	VB6 Property	Description
	AutoScroll-MinSize		A Size object that represents the width and height of the scroll bars in pixels. This property is used internally to manage the screen size allocated to the automatic scroll bars.
	AutoScroll-Position		A Point object that represents the current scrolling position. This property is used internally to adjust the position of controls that are placed on the Form via the form designer.
	HScroll		Returns True if horizontal scroll bar is visible.
	VScroll		Returns True if vertical scroll bar is visible.
	DockPadding		A Scrollable-Control.DockPadding-Edges object that determines the distance from all or individual borders for docked controls.
Menus	Menu		The MainMenu control for this form. Menu is a read/write property.
	MergeMenu		Returns the merge menu for this form.
MDI forms	ActiveMDIChild	ActiveForm	Returns the active MDI child form (read-only).

Table 16-4 Properties of the Form Object *(continued)*

Category	Name	VB6 Property	Description
	IsMDIChild		If True, this form is an MDI child form.
	IsMDIContainer		If set to True, this form works as an MDI container form.
	MDIParent		Sets or returns the MDI parent for this form.
	MDIChildren		Returns an array of forms that contains all the MDI children of this form.
Ownership	OwnedForms		Returns an array of all the forms owned by this form.
	Owner		Gets or sets the form that owns this form.
	ParentForm		Returns the parent form of this form.
Miscellaneous	KeyPreview	KeyPreview	If True, the form receives keyboard events before the control that has the focus.
	ShowInTaskbar	ShowInTaskbar	If True, this form is shown in the Windows task bar.
Design-time only	Localizable		If True, all text properties are read from a resource file.
	Language		Specifies which language is currently used for text properties.

Methods

Table 16-5 lists the most important methods of the Form object. This table doesn't include methods inherited from the Control object. (See Table 16-2.)

Table 16-5 Methods of the Form Object

Category	Name	VB6 Method	Description
State	Activate	Show	Activates the form and gives it the focus.
	Close	Unload	Closes this form.
	Show	Show	Displays this form by setting its Visible property to True.
	ShowDialog ([owner])		Shows the form as modal and returns DialogResult to the caller. (Optionally passes the owner form.)
	Hide	Hide	Hides this form by setting its Visible property to False.
Size and position	SetDesktop-Bounds(x,y, width,height)	Move	Changes size and position of this form (same as setting the DesktopBounds property).
	SetDesktop-Location(x,y)	Move	Changes the location of this form.
Owned forms	AddOwned-Form(form)		Adds a form to the list of forms owned by this form. Owned forms are minimized and closed when their owner form is minimized or closed.
	Remove-OwnedForm (form)		Removes a form from the collection of owned forms.
MDI forms	Layout-MDI(value)	Arrange	Arranges the MDI children of this form. The argument can be Cascade, TileHorizontal, Tile-Vertical, or ArrangeIcons.
Scrollable forms	SetAutoScroll-Margins(x,y)		Same as setting the Auto-ScrollMargins property.
	ScrollControl-IntoView(ctrl)		Ensures that a control is visible, and scrolls the form if necessary.

Events

Table 16-6 lists the most important events of the Form object. This table doesn't include events inherited from the Control object. (See Table 16-3.) Note that New and Dispose aren't events in the usual sense of the words, but the developer can consider them as such because they're called by the form engine when the form is created and destroyed and therefore correspond to the Visual Basic 6 Initialize and Terminate events.

It's interesting to see the life cycle of a form in terms of the events it fires:

1. **New** The form object is created.
2. **Load** The form is being loaded but is still invisible.
3. **Paint** The form is being painted. (This event can fire several times in the form's lifetime.)
4. **Activated** The form is receiving the focus. (This event replaces the Enter event exposed by the Control object.)
5. **Deactivate** The form is losing the input focus. (This event replaces the Leave event exposed by the Control object.)
6. **Closing** The form is being closed. (This event corresponds to the Visual Basic 6 Unload event.)
7. **Closed** The form has been closed and is now invisible.
8. **Dispose** The form object is being destroyed.

Common Form Tasks

Let's see how to put all the properties, methods, and events I've already shown you to good use.

Moving and Resizing the Form

You can move and resize a form as you do a control—that is, by assigning a Point object to the Location property, a Size object to the Size property, or a Rectangle object to the Bounds property. (You might want to review the "Working with Size and Position" section earlier in this chapter.) The Form object, however, offers a few additional capabilities in this area.

The DesktopBounds and DesktopLocation properties are similar to the Bounds and Location properties except that they refer to the working area of the screen, which is the screen area not occupied by an always-visible task bar:

```
' Move the form to the upper left corner of the screen's working area.
Me.DesktopLocation = New Point(0, 0)
```

Table 16-6 Events of the Form Object

Category	Name	VB6 Event	Description
Size and location	Minimum-SizeChanged		The MinimumSize property has changed.
	Maximum-SizeChanged		The MaximumSize property has changed.
	MaximizedBounds Changed		The MaximizedBounds property has changed.
State	Load	Load	The form is being loaded.
	Activated	Activate	The form is being activated programmatically or by the user.
	Deactivated	Deactivate	The form is losing the focus and isn't the active form any longer.
	Closing	Unload	The form is closing; it receives a Cancel argument.
	Closed		The form has been closed.
	MDIChildActivate		An MDI child form is activated or closed within an MDI application.
	New (method)	Initialize	The form object is being created.
	Dispose (method)	Terminate	The form object is being destroyed.
Menus	MenuStart		A menu in the form gets the focus.
	MenuComplete		A menu in the form loses the focus.
Miscellaneous	InputLangChange-Request		The user attempts to change the input language for this form. This event receives the InputLanguage, Culture, SysCharSet, and Accept-Request arguments.
	InputLangChange		The input language for this form has changed. This event receives Input-Language, Culture, and SysCharSet.

The Windows.Forms.Screen object represents one of the screens that a Windows system can support, and its Screen.PrimaryScreen shared method returns a reference to the main screen object:

```
' Expand the form to cover the entire screen's working area.
Me.DesktopBounds = Screen.PrimaryScreen.WorkingArea
```

You can get the same results using the SetDesktopLocation and SetDesktop-Bounds methods, which take multiple individual coordinates and size values:

```
' Move the form to the upper left corner of the screen's working area.
Me.SetDesktopLocation(0, 0)

' Move and resize the form so that it takes the upper right
' quadrant of the screen's working area.
With Screen.PrimaryScreen.WorkingArea
    Me.SetDesktopBounds(.Width \ 2, 0, .Width \ 2, .Height \ 2)
End With
```

Centering a form doesn't require that you do any math: just use the CenterToScreen or CenterToParent method in code. Or you can set the StartupPosition property to the appropriate value, using the Properties window.

Creating a topmost form—that is, a form that's always in front of other forms belonging to the same application—is a breeze under Visual Basic .NET, thanks to the TopMost property. (This simple task required you to call the API and sometimes work with subclassing under Visual Basic 6.) Like most properties in the Windows Forms namespace, the TopMost property can be assigned in the Properties window or by means of code:

```
' Load another form, and make it the topmost form for the application.
Dim frm As New frmPalette
frm.TopMost = True
frm.Show
```

As I explained in the "Working with Docked and Anchored Controls" section earlier in this chapter, you can limit how small or large a form can be by using the MinimumSize and MaximumSize properties. To make it clear to the end user that a form can be resized, you can make sure that the form's sizing grip in the lower right corner is always visible by using the SizeGripStyle property:

```
' This property can take three values: Auto (default), Show, and Hide.
Me.SizeGripStyle = SizeGripStyle.Show
```

Creating Scrollable Forms

If a form contains many controls, you can choose from a couple of ways to make your user interface less cluttered: you can use tabbed dialog boxes or scrollable forms. Tabbed dialogs have always been a popular way to concentrate a lot of controls in a reduced screen area, but scrollable forms are probably a better choice in several situations, especially now that users have a habit of scrolling Chapter 3 of my long HTML pages in their browsers.

Creating a tabbed dialog was a simple task under Visual Basic 6, thanks to the SSTab and TabStrip controls (which have been replaced by the TabControl object in Visual Basic .NET). Implementing a scrollable form, on the other hand, required a lot of additional code (which I described in *Programming Microsoft Visual Basic 6*, on the companion CD).

Creating a scrollable form has become an easy task in Visual Basic .NET: all you have to do is set the form's AutoScroll property to True, either at design time or at run time. When the user (or the code) resizes the form in a way that would make one of its controls partly invisible, the form displays a horizontal or vertical scroll bar, as appropriate. (See Figure 16-12.)

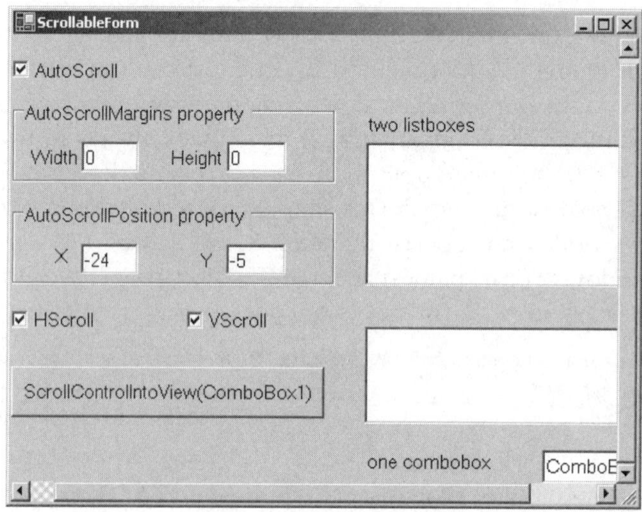

Figure 16-12. Fields and buttons in the ScrollableForm application let you test the properties and methods related to scrollable forms.

A few other properties and methods are useful when you're working with scrollable forms:

- The AutoScrollMargin property is a Size object that determines the width and the height of the invisible border drawn around each control on the form. When this border is covered by the form's edges because of a resize operation, the form displays one or both scroll bars. By default, this invisible border is 0 pixels wide and tall, but you can select a different value for this property if you want.

- The AutoScrollPosition property is a Point object that tells you whether the form has been scrolled and in which direction. The X and Y properties of this Point object always take negative values. For example, if Me.AutoScrollPosition.X is equal to –20, it means that the user scrolled the form 20 pixels to the right. You can also assign a new Point object to this property to scroll the form programmatically, as in this code:

```
' Scroll the form so that the pixel at (100, 40)
' appears at the upper left corner.
Me.AutoScrollPosition = New Point(-100, -40)
```

- You can read the HScroll and VScroll Boolean properties to determine whether either scroll bar is currently visible.
- The only method that has to do with scrolling is ScrollControlIntoView, which ensures that a given control is in the visible area of the form and scrolls the form accordingly:

```
' Ensure that ComboBox1 is visible.
Me.ScrollControlIntoView(ComboBox1)
```

No specific event fires when the end user scrolls the form. If you want to perform an action when this happens, you can use the Paint event. The demo application in Figure 16-12 uses this event to update the fields labeled X and Y inside the AutoScrollPosition Property GroupBox control.

Showing Forms

You select the start-up form of the application in the General page of the project Property Pages dialog box, much as you do with Visual Basic 6. In a difference from previous versions, however, the .NET start-up form has a peculiar feature: when you close the start-up form, all other forms are automatically closed and the application terminates. You don't have to select the start-up form at design time; instead, you can opt for the Sub Main procedure as the starting object and then use the Application.Run method to run the start-up form:

```
Dim frm As New StartupForm
Application.Run(frm)
```

You must bring up all the other forms in your program by using the Show or ShowDialog method after you create an instance of the form itself. Visual Basic .NET doesn't support the default form variable that Visual Basic 6 uses, so you must create a variable of the appropriate type:

```
' Show the form as a modeless window.
Dim frm As New CalleeForm
frm.Show
```

The Show method is inherited from the Control class and doesn't take any arguments, so you can use it only to display modeless forms. The new form doesn't stop the execution flow of the caller code, and the end user can freely switch between the new form and any other form in the application. This arrangement raises a couple of interesting questions. First, how can the caller code determine when the callee form is closed? Second, how can the caller code retrieve values currently held in the callee's controls?

The answer to the first question is quite simple: all forms raise a Closing event when they're about to be closed, so the caller code can trap this event by declaring a WithEvents variable pointing to the form or by using the AddHandler command to bind a procedure to the Closing event. Here's an example of the latter technique:

```
Sub ShowTheModelessForm()
    ' Declare the Form object.
    Dim frm As New CalleeForm()
    ' Create a handler for the Closing event.
    AddHandler frm.Closing, AddressOf CalleeForm_Closing
    ' Show the form.
    frm.Show()
End Sub

' This procedure handles the other form's Closing event.
' (It assumes the CalleeForm has two fields, txtUserName and txtAliasName.)
Sub CalleeForm_Closing(ByVal sender As Object, _
    ByVal e As System.ComponentModel.CancelEventArgs)
    ' Cast the first argument to a specific object.
    Dim frm As CalleeForm = DirectCast(sender, CalleeForm)
    ' Use a label control to display the value of two fields in CalleeForm.
    lblMessage.Text = "Name = " & frm.txtUserName.Text & ControlChars.CrLf _
        & "Alias = " & frm.txtAliasName.Text
End Sub
```

An advantage of using AddHandler instead of a WithEvents variable is that you can reuse the event handler for any number of forms. In this case, you'll need to figure out which form is being closed in the CalleeForm_Closing routine, which you can do quite easily by testing properties of the closing form, such as Text, or by using the TypeOf operator to test the class of the form being closed.

So that you can read the contents of controls placed on the callee form's surface, the controls in the callee form must be non-Private. You decide the scope of a control by setting the Modifiers property in the Properties window; this property can be Public, Protected, Friend, or Private. Because the default value for this property is Friend, most of the time you don't have to worry about this detail.

However, for a cleaner object-oriented design and better data encapsulation, you might decide to use a narrower scope for your controls—for example,

Private. (Or you might use Protected if you plan to use the form as a base class for inherited forms, as I'll explain in the section "Form Inheritance.") Using a narrower scope is usually a wiser decision because you don't expose details of your form class to the outside and you can later change its internal implementation (for example, by replacing a TextBox control with a ComboBox control), without any impact on code that creates and uses instances of the form. Another benefit of not exposing controls to the outside world is that caller code can't accidentally enter invalid values in the controls.

If you use private controls, you must provide the caller code with a way to read their contents. You can do this easily by wrapping the controls in a property procedure, as in this code:

```
' ...(In the CalleeForm code module)...
Property UserName() As String
    Get
        Return txtUserName.Text
    End Get
    Set(ByVal Value As String)
        txtUserName.Text = Value
    End Set
End Property

Property AliasName() As String
    Get
        Return txtAliasName.Text
    End Get
    Set(ByVal Value As String)
        txtAliasName.Text = Value
    End Set
End Property
```

Of course, you can use read-only properties if you want to prevent the caller form from assigning a value to these controls. The code in the caller form becomes

```
Sub CalleeForm_Closing(ByVal sender As Object, ByVal e As CancelEventArgs)
    ' Cast the first argument to a specific object.
    Dim frm As CalleeForm = CType(sender, CalleeForm)
    ' Use a label control to display the value of two fields in CalleeForm.
    lblMessage.Text = "Name = " & frm.UserName & ControlChars.CrLf _
        & "Alias = " & frm.AliasName
End Sub
```

Working with Owned Forms

The Windows operating system supports the concept of *owned forms*. If a form owns another form, the owned form will be displayed always in front of its owner form, no matter which is the active form. (See Figure 16-13.) This arrangement makes owned forms ideal for implementing tool and palette windows. In another feature of owned forms, all the owned forms are also closed or minimized when the user closes or minimizes the owner form. When minimized, the owner form and all its owned forms count as one icon in the Windows task bar.

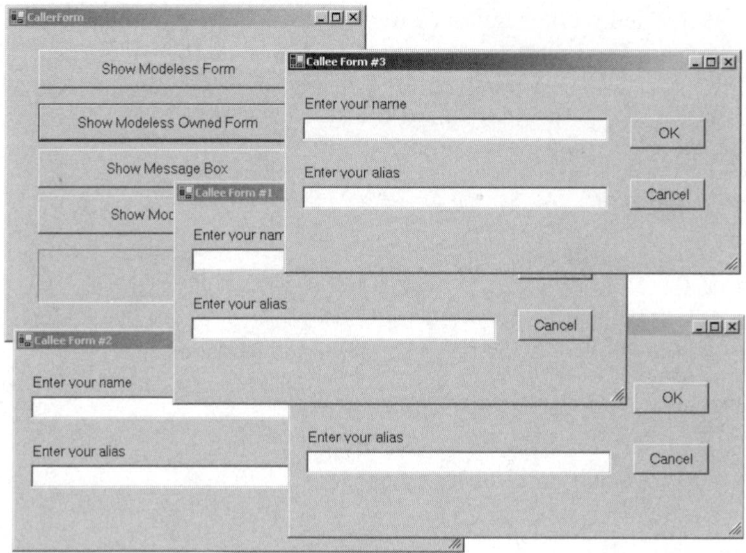

Figure 16-13. A group of owned forms; note that all forms are in front of their owner form (upper left corner), even if the owner form is the active form.

In Visual Basic 6, you can display a form as an owned form by passing Me as the second argument of the Show method:

```
' The Visual Basic 6 way for creating an owned form
Dim frm As New CalleeForm
frm.Show , Me
```

You can't pass an argument to the Show method under Visual Basic .NET, and you declare that the callee form is owned by the caller form by invoking the AddOwnedForm method:

```
' The Visual Basic .NET way for creating an owned form
Dim frm As New CalleeForm()
' Add this form to the list of owned forms.
Me.AddOwnedForm(frm)
frm.Show()
```

The Owner property allows a form to detect whether it's owned by another form. A form can enumerate its owned forms by iterating over the collection returned by the OwnedForms property:

```
If Me.Owner Is Nothing Then
    Debug.WriteLine ("No owner form for this form")
Else
    Debug.WriteLine("Owned by form " & Me.Owner.Text)
End If

Debug.WriteLine("List of owned forms:")
Dim frm As Form
For Each frm in Me.OwnedForms
    Debug.WriteLine(frm.Text)
Next
```

You can change the ownership status of an owned form by removing it from its owner's OwnedForms collection by using the RemoveOwnedForm method:

```
' Change the ownership status for all owned forms.
Dim frm As Form
For Each frm in Me.OwnedForms
    Me.RemoveOwnedForm(frm)
Next
```

Displaying Message Boxes and Dialog Boxes

Visual Basic .NET still supports the old-style MsgBox command (defined in the Microsoft.VisualBasic namespace), but you might want to use the newer MessageBox object and its Show method:

```
Sub ShowTheMessageBox()
    Dim res As DialogResult
    res = MessageBox.Show("File not found", "A MessageBox example", _
        MessageBoxButtons.AbortRetryIgnore, MessageBoxIcon.Error, _
        MessageBoxDefaultButton.Button1, _
        MessageBoxOptions.DefaultDesktopOnly)
    lblMessage.Text = "The user clicked " & res.ToString
End Sub
```

As you can see, the MessageBox.Show method doesn't require that you stuff multiple options in a bit-coded argument, as the original MsgBox command does. This approach makes for a cleaner and more readable (yet more verbose) syntax. All arguments after the first one are optional. The DialogResult enumerated type defines the seven possible return values from a message box. (This enumerated type corresponds to VbMsgBoxResult in Visual Basic 6.)

If a predefined message box isn't enough for your needs, you must create a custom form with precisely the buttons and fields you need, and you must display it modally using the ShowDialog method instead of the Show method. You can pass values to the modal form and retrieve values from it, using the technique I demonstrated in the preceding section. You don't have to set up an event handler to detect when the form is closed because the ShowDialog method doesn't return until the modal form is closed:

```
Sub ShowTheModalForm()
    ' Declare the Form object.
    Dim frm As New CalleeForm()
    ' Show the form modally.
    frm.ShowDialog()
    ' Display the value of two fields in CalleeForm.
    lblMessage.Text = "Name = " & frm.UserName & ControlChars.CrLf _
        & "Alias = " & frm.AliasName
End Sub
```

Most dialog forms, however, have multiple push buttons. Typically they have the OK and Cancel buttons, but you might also need Retry and Cancel buttons and many other combinations. In cases like this, you have to determine which action the end user selected.

To make your job easier, the Form class defines a DialogResult public enumerated property, which can take the same values that a message box can return. You typically assign this property from inside the Click event procedure in the callee form:

```
Private Sub btnOK_Click(ByVal sender As Object, ByVal e As EventArgs) _
    Handles btnOK.Click
    Me.DialogResult = DialogResult.OK
    Me.Close
End Sub

Private Sub btnCancel_Click(ByVal sender As Object, ByVal e As EventArgs) _
    Handles btnCancel.Click
    Me.DialogResult = DialogResult.Cancel
    Me.Close
End Sub
```

An interesting detail: if your form is always used as a modal form, you don't need to explicitly close the form with a Me.Close method inside the Click event procedures because assigning a value to the DialogResult property suffices. Even better, if a button's Click procedure does nothing but set the DialogResult property, you don't even need to write the event procedure because you can assign this property to each Button control at design time, in the Property window. If the end user clicks a Button control whose DialogResult property has a value other than DialogResult.None, the form is always closed automatically and the DialogResult value is sent to the caller as the return value of the ShowDialog method.

So the typical code in the caller form becomes

```
Sub ShowTheModalForm()
    ' Declare the Form object.
    Dim frm As New CalleeForm()
    ' Show the form modally, and test the result.
    If frm.ShowDialog() = DialogResult.OK Then
        ' The user clicked the OK button.
        lblMessage.Text = "Name = " & frm.UserName & ControlChars.CrLf _
            & "Alias = " & frm.AliasName
    Else
        ' The user canceled the dialog.
        lblMessage.Text = "The end user canceled the action"
    End If
End Sub
```

You can design a form so that it can be invoked in either modal or nonmodal mode. Achieving this in Visual Basic 6 was difficult because a form had no simple way to understand whether it was called modally and because most style properties of the form object—including the border style—were read-only at run time. Visual Basic .NET forms expose a Modal property, which you can test to find out whether a form was displayed using a ShowDialog method.

Say that you want to make a form nonresizeable if it's modal. All you need are the statements in boldface near the end of the Sub New procedure:

```
Public Sub New()
    MyBase.New()

    ' This call is required by the Windows Form Designer.
    InitializeComponent()

    ' Add any initialization after the InitializeComponent() call.

    ' Different style and behavior, depending on whether the form is modal
    If Me.Modal Then
        Me.FormBorderStyle = FormBorderStyle.FixedDialog
    Else
        Me.FormBorderStyle = FormBorderStyle.Sizable
        Me.SizeGripStyle = SizeGripStyle.Show
    End If
End Sub
```

Two more form properties, AcceptButton and CancelButton, affect dialog boxes. Under previous versions of Visual Basic, you decide which are the default button and the cancel button—that is, the buttons that are activated by pressing the Enter and Esc keys, respectively—by assigning True to the Default or Cancel property of the button in question. The Default and Cancel properties are gone in Visual Basic .NET, and you achieve the same result by assigning to the form's AcceptButton and CancelButton properties a reference to the proper Button control. As usual, you can set these properties in the Properties window at design time or by means of code:

```
Me.AcceptButton = btnOk
Me.CancelButton = btnCancel
```

Adding Controls Dynamically

Visual Basic .NET doesn't support control arrays, but this isn't a serious problem because the Windows Forms portion of the Framework offers everything control arrays offer, and a lot more. Under previous language versions, you typically use control arrays for dynamically creating new controls at run time or for simplifying the code by creating event routines that serve multiple controls. You have already seen that you can create the latter kind of event procedures with Visual Basic .NET by using multiple Handles clauses or by using the AddHandler command. In this section, you'll see how you can create dynamic controls in Visual Basic .NET.

As you already know, the form designer is nothing but a sophisticated code generator, and controls are actually created and placed on the form's surface at run time. So you can see how dynamic control creation works simply by looking at the code that the form designer generates for any control you place on the form.

By doing so, you can see that you create controls as you would create any other kind of objects—that is, by using the New keyword. You later assign all the necessary properties to the control—most notably, its Name, Location, Size, and TabIndex—and finally you add it to the Controls collection of the parent form. For example, the following code generates a Button control:

```
Private Sub CreateButton()
    Dim btnOK As System.Windows.Forms.Button
    ' Create the control.
    btnOK = New System.Windows.Forms.Button()
    ' Assign it a name, and set other properties.
    btnOK.Name = "Button-OK"
    btnOK.Location = New System.Drawing.Point(328, 32)
    btnOK.Size = New System.Drawing.Size(72, 32)
    btnOK.TabIndex = 10
    btnOK.Text = "OK"
```

```
    ' Add it to the parent form's Controls collection.
    Me.Controls.Add(btnOK)
End Sub
```

You should note that the Name property doesn't have the same role it had under Visual Basic 6. What we usually consider the name of the control is now the name of the variable that points to the control (btnOK in the preceding example), whereas the Name property is a string value that you can use to identify the control itself. (You can use spaces and other symbols in this property.) You can even use the same Name value used for another control on the form if you create the control in code. In this respect, the Name property is similar to the Tag property (which is still supported, mostly to help you port code from previous versions of the language).

Another thing worth noting in the preceding code snippet is that the btnOK variable is local to the procedure, so it goes out of scope when the End Sub statement is reached. The control isn't destroyed at this time, however, because the form's Controls collection keeps it alive.

In general, you might not know in advance how many controls you're going to create dynamically when you write the code portion of the application. For example, you might want to create all the controls on a form to match the structure of a database table or an SQL query typed by the end user. For this reason, most of the time you can't create the appropriate number of WithEvents variables to trap events from the controls you add dynamically, and you must use the AddHandler command instead.

I've prepared a demo form that asks the user for a number of TextBox controls, creates them dynamically, and traps a few key events from them. (See Figure 16-14.) This is the code behind the Button control:

```
Private Sub btnCreateControls_Click(ByVal sender As Object, _
    ByVal e As EventArgs) Handles btnCreateControls.Click

    Dim answer As String
    Dim index As Integer

    answer = InputBox("How many controls?", "Dynamic Control Creation", "5")
    If answer = "" Then Exit Sub

    For index = 1 To CInt(answer)
        ' Create the Nth text box.
        Dim tb As New TextBox()
        tb.Size = New System.Drawing.Size(400, 30)
        tb.Location = New System.Drawing.Point(50, 40 + index * 40)
        ' We need this to identify the control.
        tb.Name = "TextBox #" & CStr(index)
```

(continued)

```
        ' Add to the Controls collection.
        Me.Controls.Add(tb)

        ' Create event handlers.
        AddHandler tb.KeyPress, AddressOf TextBox_KeyPress
        AddHandler tb.TextChanged, AddressOf TextBox_TextChanged
        AddHandler tb.MouseEnter, AddressOf TextBox_MouseEnter
        AddHandler tb.MouseLeave, AddressOf TextBox_MouseLeave
    Next
End Sub

Private Sub TextBox_TextChanged(ByVal sender As Object, ByVal e As EventArgs)
    ' Show that an event fires by updating a Label control.
    lblStatus.Text = "TextChanged in " & CStr(CType(sender, TextBox).Name)
End Sub

' ...(Code for other event procedures omitted)...
```

As you see in the TextBox_TextChanged procedure, assigning a value to the Name property makes it easier to detect which specific control raised the event.

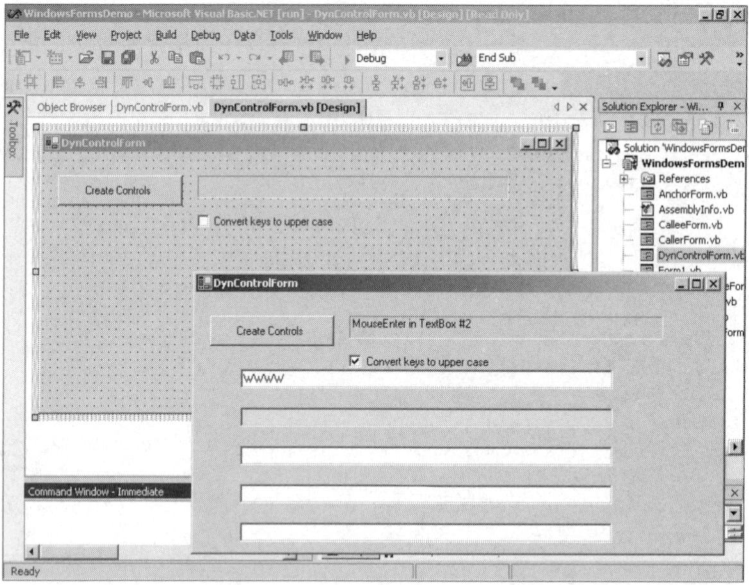

Figure 16-14. A form that creates a group of TextBox controls at run time and traps events from them.

One last note about control creation: you can destroy any control on a form by using the Remove method of the form's Controls collection. This method can remove any control, not just those that you've added after the form became visible:

```
Me.Controls.Remove(btnOk)
```

Menus

Personally, I have always disliked the Visual Basic menu editor, and above all I was bothered by the fact that this designer hasn't evolved at all in six language versions. (And I'm in good company if the comments I've heard for years at conferences and user group meetings are any indication.) The good news is that the Windows Form designer now lets you create the menu structure of your applications using a more streamlined approach, in a WYSIWYG editor. You can even move elements and entire submenus using drag-and-drop.

Creating a Menu Structure

The first step in creating a menu structure is to drag a MainMenu object from the Toolbox to the form designer. Because this object is invisible at run time, a new element named MainMenu1 appears in the designer's component tray area. You can change the name of this control if you want, but usually there's no point in doing so because most forms have only one menu structure and you don't need multiple MainMenu objects on a given form.

You can now click the menu bar and type the captions of menu items. (See Figure 16-15.) Depending on where you start typing, you can create new items on the menu bar, new submenus, or new menu items. Each item you create is automatically assigned a name—such as MenuItem1, MenuItem2, and so on—but you can edit these names as well by right-clicking the menu structure and selecting Edit Names on the shortcut menu. (See Figure 16-16.) When in Edit Names mode, you can edit the item names but can't modify their captions. The pop-up menu also lets you insert new items and delete existing ones. (You can delete items also by pressing the Delete key.) Regardless of whether you're in Edit Names mode, you can see and modify all the attributes of the current menu item in the Properties window.

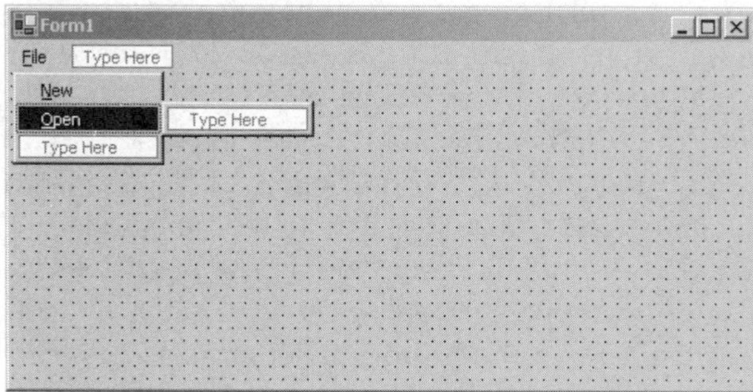

Figure 16-15. The menu designer in normal mode.

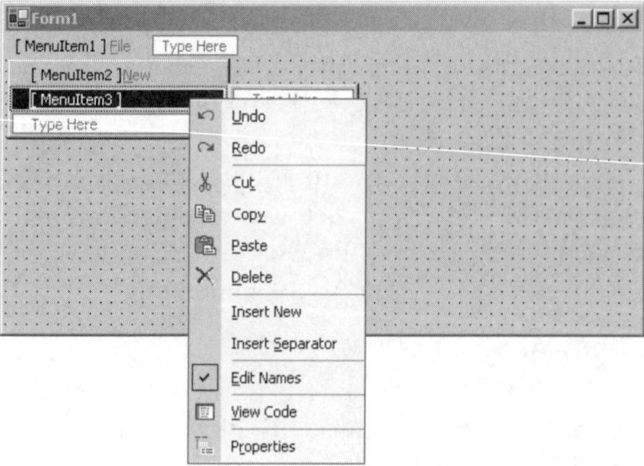

Figure 16-16. The menu designer in Edit Names mode and with the pop-up menu displayed.

As in previous versions, menu separators are just MenuItem elements whose Text property is - (hyphen). All other properties of such elements are ignored.

I've already pointed out the fact that the menu editor supports drag-and-drop to move submenus around the menu structure. You can achieve the same result also by cutting a top-level menu or a submenu and pasting it elsewhere in the menu hierarchy.

Properties, Methods, and Events

The Windows Forms namespace exposes three objects that affect menus: MainMenu, ContextMenu, and MenuItem. I'll talk about the ContextMenu object in a later section, but for now it's important to note that the MainMenu and ContextMenu objects expose a similar programming interface, and both of them work as containers for MenuItem objects. For this reason, it makes sense to describe their properties, methods, and events in one place.

I've prepared three tables that include the members that these three objects expose. Table 16-7 lists all the properties of the MainMenu, ContextMenu, and MenuItem objects; Table 16-8 lists all their methods; and Table 16-9 summarizes their events. (Note that the MainMenu object doesn't expose any events.) As you see, these objects don't expose exactly the same interface, even though they have many members in common (inherited from the generic Menu class).

For all members, I've indicated the corresponding Visual Basic 6 properties, methods, or events if there are any. You should be already familiar with most properties of the MenuItem object, and the meaning of many new properties—such as RadioCheck, Mnemonic, and Index—is quite evident.

Table 16-7 Properties of the MainMenu, ContextMenu, and MenuItem Objects

Category	Name	VB6 Property	Description
Common properties (inherited from Menu object)	Handle		The Windows handle for the menu (read-only).
	IsParent		True if this menu contains menu items.
	MenuItems		The collection of child menu items (read-only).
	MDIListItem		The MenuItem object that is used to display a list of MDI child forms (read-only).
ContextMenu only	SourceControl		The most recent control to display the context menu.
MenuItem only	Text	Caption	The text displayed on the menu item.
	Enabled	Enabled	True if the menu item is enabled.
	Visible	Visible	True if the menu item is visible.
	Checked	Checked	If True, a check mark appears next to the text of the menu item.
	RadioCheck		If True, a radio button instead of a check is displayed when the Checked property is True.
	Shortcut	Shortcut (design-time only)	The shortcut key associated with this menu item.
	ShowShortcut		If True, the shortcut is displayed to the right of the menu text.
	Mnemonic		The mnemonic character associated with this menu item (read-only).
	MDIList	WindowList	If True, the menu will be populated with the list of all MDI child windows displayed within the associated form.

Table 16-7 Properties of the MainMenu, ContextMenu, and MenuItem Objects *(continued)*

Category	Name	VB6 Property	Description
	Parent	Container	The parent menu for this menu item (read-only).
	Index		The position of the item in its menu; can be assigned to reposition the item.
	DefaultItem		True if this is the default item for its menu; is valid only if this item belongs to a context menu.
	Break		True if this item is placed on a new line (for items in a MainMenu) or in a new column (for items in a submenu or ContextMenu). You can use this property to create menus with items that extend horizontally or with multiple rows of elements.
	BarBreak		Similar to the Break property except that a bar is displayed on the left edge of each menu item that isn't top level and has the Break property set to True.
	MergeType	NegotiatePosition	The behavior of this menu item when its menu is merged with another menu. (Can be Add, Replace, Remove, or MergeItems.)
	MergeOrder		The 0-based relative position of this menu item when its menu is merged with another menu.
	OwnerDraw		If True, this menu item is drawn by code.

Table 16-8 Methods of the MainMenu, ContextMenu, and MenuItem Objects

Category	Name	VB6 Method	Description
Common methods (inherited from Menu object)	GetMainMenu		Returns the MainMenu object that contains this menu.
	GetContext-Menu		Returns the ContextMenu object that contains this menu.
	MergeMenu (sourcemenu)		Merges the items of another menu with the items of the current menu. Items are merged according to the value of their MergeType and MergeOrder properties.
	CloneMenu		Returns an object that's a clone of the current item.
MainMenu only	GetForm		Returns the Form object that contains this menu.
ContextMenu only	Show(control,point)		Displays the context menu at the specified position.
MenuItem only	MergeMenu (menuitem)		Merges this menu item with another MenuItem object.
	PerformClick		Generates a Click event for this menu item.
	PerformSelect		Generates a Select event for this menu item.

Table 16-9 Events of the ContextMenu and MenuItem Objects

Category	Name	VB6 Event	Description
Context-Menu only	Popup		The context menu is displayed.
MenuItem only	Click	Click	The menu item is clicked or selected by means of a shortcut key or an accelerator key.
	Select		The user places the cursor over the menu item.
	Popup		A menu's list of items is about to be displayed.
	Measure-Item		An owner-draw menu needs to know the size of a menu item before drawing it. (Receives Index, Graphics, ItemWidth, and ItemWeight.)
	DrawItem		An owner-draw menu is about to draw one of its menu items. (Receives Index, State, Bounds, Graphics, ForeColor, BackColor, and Font.)

Reacting to Menu Events

Windows Forms menu items raise a Click event when the user selects them, so you react to menu choices exactly as you do in Visual Basic 6.

```
Private Sub mnuFileNew_Click(ByVal sender As Object, _
    ByVal e As EventArgs) Handles mnuFilenew.Click
    ' Put the code for the File | New command here.
    ⋮
End Sub
```

Note that the second argument is a plain EventArgs object that doesn't carry any additional information with it.

The MenuItem class exposes also the Select event, which fires when the user highlights the corresponding menu command with the mouse or the keyboard without selecting it. This event is useful for displaying a short description of the menu command in a Label or a Status bar control, as shown in Figure 16-17.

```
Private Sub mnuFileNew_Select(ByVal sender As Object, _
    ByVal e As EventArgs) Handles mnuFileNew.Select
    lblStatus.Text = "Create a new file"
End Sub
```

(You have to resort to subclassing to achieve the same result under Visual Basic 6.)

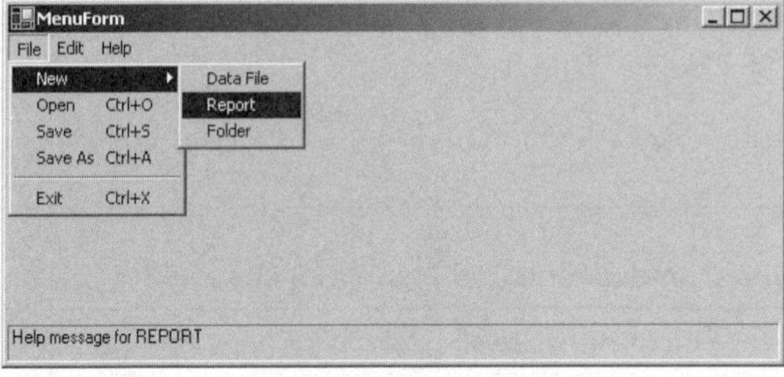

Figure 16-17. The Select event lets you display a short description of the menu command currently selected.

The Form object raises two events that are related to menus: MenuStart and MenuComplete. As their names suggest, MenuStart is raised as soon as the user activates the menu system, whereas MenuComplete fires when the user has closed the menu. (This event fires before the Click event if a menu item has been selected.) For example, you can use MenuStart to show the Label control used to display the description of each menu item and MenuComplete to make the Label control invisible again:

```
Private Sub MenuForm_MenuStart(ByVal sender As Object, _
    ByVal e As EventArgs) Handles MyBase.MenuStart
```

```
    lblStatus.Visible = True
End Sub

Private Sub MenuForm_MenuComplete(ByVal sender As Object, _
    ByVal e As EventArgs) Handles MyBase.MenuComplete
    lblStatus.Visible = False
End Sub
```

Creating Menus Using Code

The MainMenu object exposes a MenuItems collection, so creating a menu bar via code is just a matter of creating the necessary number of MenuItem objects, setting their properties as needed, and then adding them to the MainMenu.MenuItems collection. You can add each MenuItem individually, or you can add all of them in one operation by using the collection's AddRange method:

```
' Variables for the main menu and top-level menu items
Friend WithEvents MainMenu1 As System.Windows.Forms.MainMenu
Friend WithEvents mnuFile As System.Windows.Forms.MenuItem
Friend WithEvents mnuEdit As System.Windows.Forms.MenuItem
Friend WithEvents mnuHelp As System.Windows.Forms.MenuItem

Private Sub CreateMenuTree()
    ' Create all the menu objects.
    Me.MainMenu1 = New System.Windows.Forms.MainMenu()
    Me.mnuFile = New System.Windows.Forms.MenuItem()
    Me.mnuEdit = New System.Windows.Forms.MenuItem()
    Me.mnuHelp = New System.Windows.Forms.MenuItem()
    ' Set menu items' properties.
    Me.mnuFile.Index = 0
    Me.mnuFile.Text = "&File"
    Me.mnuEdit.Index = 1
    Me.mnuEdit.Text = "&Edit"
    Me.mnuHelp.Index = 2
    Me.mnuHelp.Text = "&Help"
    ' Add to the main menu's MenuItems collection.
    ' (Note how you can create a MenuItem array on the fly and pass it
    '  to the AddRange method in a single statement.)
    Me.MainMenu1.MenuItems.AddRange(New MenuItem() _
       {Me.mnuFile, Me.mnuEdit, Me.mnuHelp})

    ' Assign the MainMenu object to the form's Menu property.
    Me.Menu = Me.MainMenu1
End Sub
```

Adding menu items to the MainMenu1 object doesn't create the menu automatically because this object isn't automatically placed on the form. (This operation is called *siting*.) The statement that associates the menu structure you've created with the specific form is the last one in the preceding code, where you assign the MainMenu object to the Me.Menu property. This fact opens up very interesting possibilities: for example, a form can display another form and have that other form expose the same menu structure. The code that implements this solution is trivial:

```
Dim frm As New frmOtherForm
frm.Menu = Me.MainMenu1
frm.Show
```

Because both the caller and the callee share the same menu objects, you can place all the event procedures in one form, thus saving a lot of code.

As you see in Table 16-7, the MenuItem class also exposes the MenuItems collection, so creating items for each submenu follows the same pattern:

```
Friend WithEvents mnuFileNew As System.Windows.Forms.MenuItem
Friend WithEvents mnuFileOpen As System.Windows.Forms.MenuItem
Friend WithEvents mnuFileSave As System.Windows.Forms.MenuItem
Friend WithEvents mnuFileSaveAs As System.Windows.Forms.MenuItem
Friend WithEvents mnuFileSep As System.Windows.Forms.MenuItem
Friend WithEvents mnuFileExit As System.Windows.Forms.MenuItem

Private Sub CreateFileSubmenu()
    ' --- Create all the menu objects.
    Me.mnuFileNew = New System.Windows.Forms.MenuItem()
    Me.mnuFileOpen = New System.Windows.Forms.MenuItem()
    Me.mnuFileSave = New System.Windows.Forms.MenuItem()
    Me.mnuFileSaveAs = New System.Windows.Forms.MenuItem()
    Me.mnuFileSep = New System.Windows.Forms.MenuItem()
    Me.mnuFileExit = New System.Windows.Forms.MenuItem()

    ' Add them to the File submenu.
    Me.mnuFile.MenuItems.AddRange(New MenuItem() _
        {Me.mnuFileNew, Me.mnuFileOpen, Me.mnuFileSave, _
        Me.mnuFileSaveAs, Me.mnuFileSep, Me.mnuFileExit})

    ' Set properties of individual menu items.
    Me.mnuFileNew.Index = 0
    Me.mnuFileNew.Shortcut = System.Windows.Forms.Shortcut.CtrlN
    Me.mnuFileNew.Text = "&New"

    Me.mnuFileOpen.Index = 1
    Me.mnuFileOpen.Shortcut = System.Windows.Forms.Shortcut.CtrlO
    Me.mnuFileOpen.Text = "&Open"

    Me.mnuFileSave.Index = 2
```

```
    Me.mnuFileSave.Shortcut = System.Windows.Forms.Shortcut.CtrlS
    Me.mnuFileSave.Text = "&Save"

    Me.mnuFileSaveAs.Index = 3
    Me.mnuFileSaveAs.Shortcut = System.Windows.Forms.Shortcut.CtrlA
    Me.mnuFileSaveAs.Text = "Save &As"

    Me.mnuFileSep.Index = 4
    Me.mnuFileSep.Text = "-"          ' A menu separator

    Me.mnuFileExit.Index = 5
    Me.mnuFileExit.Shortcut = System.Windows.Forms.Shortcut.CtrlX
    Me.mnuFileExit.Text = "E&xit"
End Sub
```

Of course, you can apply this technique recursively. For example, you can create a New submenu under the File menu by adding one or more MenuItem objects to the mnuFileNew.MenuItems collection.

The code I've shown you so far is similar to what the menu designer creates. Each menu item corresponds to a MenuItem class-level variable, and each variable is declared with the WithEvents keyword, so you can easily trap events raised from the corresponding MenuItem object. However, you can also adopt other techniques that offer more flexibility.

For example, you might want to offer your customers the ability to redefine the entire menu structure on a user-by-user basis, by storing the menu tree for each user in an XML file that you parse when the application starts. In this case, you can't create an individual MenuItem variable for each menu item (because you don't know how many menu items you're going to create), and you have to add each menu item to its parent submenu's MenuItems collection as you read the XML element that describes that menu item.

Regardless of how you create the menu structure, the hierarchical nature of the menu tree suggests a simple way to create a centralized routine that handles the Click or the Select event for all the menu commands in your application. In some cases, such a centralized routine can be a superior approach. I've prepared a reusable routine that visits all the items in a menu structure to have their Click and Select events point to the specified procedures:

```
' Make the Click and Select event handlers of all the menu items
' in a form point to the same procedures.
' The main application should call this routine with m = Me.Menu.

Sub InitializeMenuEvents(ByVal m As Menu, _
    ByVal ClickEvent As EventHandler, ByVal SelectEvent As EventHandler)

    Dim mi As MenuItem
```

(continued)

```
    If TypeOf m Is MenuItem Then
        ' Cast the argument to a MenuItem object.
        mi = DirectCast(m, MenuItem)
        ' Initialize the Select event for this menu item.
        AddHandler mi.Select, SelectEvent
        ' Initialize the Click event if this isn't a submenu.
        If m.MenuItems.Count = 0 Then
            AddHandler mi.Click, ClickEvent
        End If
    End If

    ' Call recursively for all items in the MenuItems collection.
    For Each mi In m.MenuItems
        InitializeMenuEvents(mi, ClickEvent, SelectEvent)
    Next
End Sub
```

You can call this routine from the Load event procedure of a form or just before exiting the Sub New procedure, passing the Me.Menu property as the first argument and the delegates that point to the Click and Select event procedures in the remaining arguments, as in this code:

```
Private Sub MenuForm_Load(ByVal sender As Object, _
    ByVal e As System.EventArgs) Handles MyBase.Load
    ' Make the Click and Select events of all menu items in this form
    ' point to the MenuItem_Click and MenuItem_Select procedures.
    InitializeMenuEvents(Me.Menu, AddressOf MenuItem_Click, _
        AddressOf MenuItem_Select)
End Sub

' Select common routine for all menu items.
Private Sub MenuItem_Select(ByVal sender As Object, ByVal e As EventArgs)
    Dim mi As MenuItem = DirectCast(sender, MenuItem)
    ' Display a generic message in this demo.
    lblStatus.Text = "Help message for " & mi.Text.ToUpper
End Sub

' Click common routine for all menu items.
Private Sub MenuItem_Click(ByVal sender As Object, ByVal e As EventArgs)
    Dim mi As MenuItem = DirectCast(sender, MenuItem)
    ' Display a generic message in this demo.
    lblStatus.Text = mi.Text.ToUpper & " has been selected."
End Sub
```

In this example, the event procedures common to all menu items display a generic message in a status bar. In a real application, the MenuItem_Select procedure might read its messages from a database, an XML file, a resource file, and so on. A Click event procedure common to all menu items lets you group similar menu commands by using a Select Case statement, as in this code:

```
Private Sub MenuItem_Click(ByVal sender As Object, ByVal e As EventArgs)
    Dim mi As MenuItem = DirectCast(sender, MenuItem)

    Select mi.Text.ToUpper
        Case "NEW"       ' Create a new file.
            ⋮
        Case "OPEN"      ' Open an existing file.
            ⋮
    End Select
End Sub
```

The two approaches—WithEvents variables tied to standard event procedures and dynamic events created for all menu items with the AddHandler keyword—can coexist in the same form. In this case, a menu item raises two Click or Select events, and the only limitation is that their order is unpredictable.

Multiple-Column Menus

The new Break and BarBreak properties of the MenuItem object let you create menus with multiple columns. All you have to do is set either property to True for the MenuItem object that must become the first item of a new menu column. The only difference between these two properties is that BarBreak displays a vertical line between adjacent columns, whereas Break does not. (See Figure 16-18.)

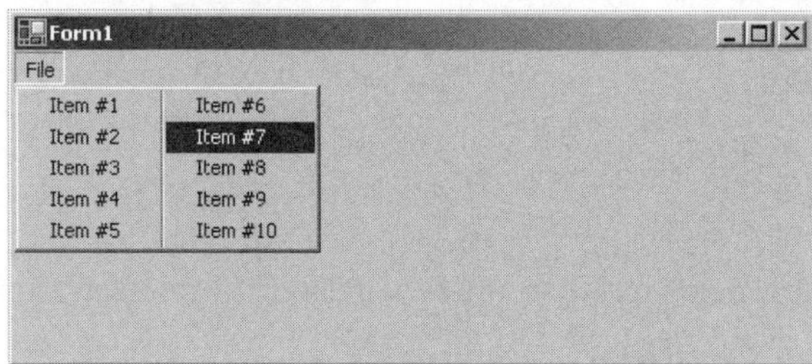

Figure 16-18. A multiple-column menu, obtained by setting the BarBreak property of item 6 to True.

A minor annoyance attached to these properties is that they don't appear in the Properties window, so you have to set them via code, as you see here:

```
mnuFileItem6.BarBreak = True
```

You can place this statement in the InitializeComponent procedure (the one generated by the form designer), at the end of the New method, or in the Form_Load event procedure. Using the latter two locations ensures that your code isn't overwritten by the form designer when you change another property of the same MenuItem object.

Displaying Context Menus

Creating and displaying a context menu isn't very different from working with a regular menu: you drag a ContextMenu object from the Toolbox to the form designer's component tray area, and then you visually create the structure of the context menu. (See Figure 16-19.) For the design of a context menu, the root of the menu tree is the fictitious node named ContextMenu, and you can create nodes only under this one. Except for this detail, the menu designer works as I've described previously.

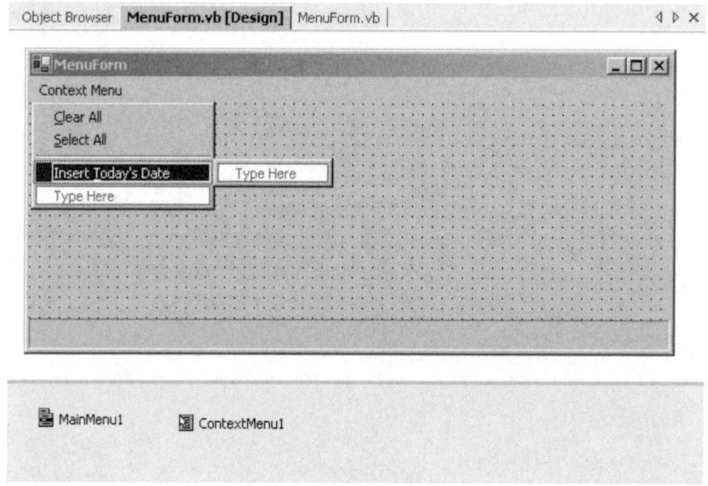

Figure 16-19. The menu designer when you're working on a ContextMenu object.

After designing the structure of the context menu object, you must associate it with one or more controls on the form's surface or with the Form object itself. You do this by assigning the ContextMenu1 object to the ContextMenu property of the form or the control, from inside the Properties window or by means of code:

```
TextBox1.ContextMenu = ContextMenu1
```

You can associate a ContextMenu object with multiple controls (which will therefore share the same context menu), or you can associate different Context-

Menu objects with different controls. It usually makes sense to create multiple ContextMenu objects on the same form, so it might be convenient to assign each object a name that suggests its function, such as ctxConvertCmds.

A ContextMenu object exposes a MenuItems collection that contains MenuItem objects, so you can create this object in code as you'd create a regular menu. The following code snippet shows how to perform this task in a concise way, without creating distinct WithEvents class-level variables and by using a variant of the MenuItem's constructor that takes the Text property and a delegate to the Click event procedure:

```
Sub CreateContextMenu()
    ' Create the ContextMenu object.
    Dim ctxConvertCmds As New ContextMenu()
    ' Create all MenuItem objects, and add them to the MenuItems collection.
    With ctxConvertCmds.MenuItems
        .Add(New MenuItem("Clear", AddressOf ContextMenu_Click))
        .Add(New MenuItem("Upper Case", AddressOf ContextMenu_Click))
        .Add(New MenuItem("Lower Case", AddressOf ContextMenu_Click))
    End With
    ' Assign the control's ContextMenu property.
    TextBox2.ContextMenu = ctxConvertCmds
End Sub

Private Sub ContextMenu_Click(ByVal sender As Object, ByVal e As EventArgs)
    ' Cast to a MenuItem object.
    Dim mi As MenuItem = DirectCast(sender, MenuItem)
    ' Select the action depending on the menu's caption.
    Select Case mi.Text
        Case "Clear"
            TextBox2.Text = ""
        Case "Upper Case"
            TextBox2.Text = TextBox2.Text.ToUpper
        Case "Lower Case"
            TextBox2.Text = TextBox2.Text.ToLower
    End Select
End Sub
```

Items in a ContextMenu object support the Select event as well.

The only other detail about context menus that I haven't discussed yet is that the ContextMenu object raises a Popup event when the menu becomes visible. You can use this event to display further information in a status bar. Unfortunately, there's no menu event that fires when a pop-up menu is being closed unless the user makes a selection (which of course fires a Click event). However, you can use the Idle event of the Application object for this purpose. (See the section "The Application Object" later in this chapter.)

MDI Forms

The Windows Forms namespace doesn't expose a separate class for MDI forms: an MDI form is nothing but a regular Form object whose IsMdiContainer property is set to True. You usually assign this property at design time, but you can also do it using code. (The demo program provided on the companion CD does exactly that.)

Here's an important difference from Visual Basic 6: an MDI form can contain any type of control, and these controls appear in front of any child form. (By comparison, the Visual Basic 6 MDI forms can host only alignable controls, such as a status bar, a toolbar, or a PictureBox control.)

The only noteworthy limitation of MDI containers is that they can't also be scrollable. If you attempt to set the IsMdiContainer property to True, the AutoScroll property resets to False, and vice versa.

Showing MDI Child Forms

An MDI child form is a regular form whose MdiParent property points to its MDI container form, so the code that creates and displays a child window is simple:

```
Sub ShowMdiChildWindow()
    ' Display the MenuForm form as a child of this form.
    Dim frm As New MenuForm()
    ' Make it a child of this MDI form before showing it.
    frm.MdiParent = Me
    frm.Show()
End Sub
```

A form that can be used as either a regular form or an MDI child form might need to determine how it's being used. It can do that by testing its MdiParent property or its read-only IsMdiChild property.

You can list all the child forms of an MDI parent by using the Form array returned by its MdiChildren property:

```
Dim frm As Form
For Each frm In Me.MdiChildren
    Debug.Write(frm.Text)
Next
```

The MDI parent form can activate one of its child forms by using the ActivateMdiChild method:

```
' Activate the first MDI child form.
If Me.MdiChildren.Length > 0 Then
    ActivateMdiChild(Me.MdiChildren(0))
End If
```

The ActiveMdiChild property returns a reference to the active child form or Nothing if there are no active child forms. Such a situation can occur when all child forms have been closed. This property is often used inside the MdiChild-Activate event, which fires when a new child form becomes active:

```
' Change the title of the MDI parent form to match the caption
' of the active child form.
Private Sub MDIForm_MdiChildActivate(ByVal sender As Object, _
    ByVal e As EventArgs) Handles MyBase.MdiChildActivate

    If Me.ActiveMdiChild Is Nothing Then
        Me.Text = "MDI Demo Program"
    Else
        Me.Text = Me.ActiveMdiChild.Text & " - MDI Demo Program"
    End If
End Sub
```

MDI forms often contain a Window menu that exposes commands to cascade, tile, arrange, or close all child forms, as shown in Figure 16-20. You can implement these commands quite easily (as you can see in the following code) by using the LayoutMdi method, which replaces the Visual Basic 6 Arrange method.

```
Private Sub mnuWindowCascade_Click(ByVal sender As Object, _
    ByVal e As EventArgs) Handles mnuWindowCascade.Click
    Me.LayoutMdi(MdiLayout.Cascade)
End Sub

Private Sub mnuWindowTileHor_Click(ByVal sender As Object, _
    ByVal e As EventArgs) Handles mnuWindowTileHor.Click
    Me.LayoutMdi(MdiLayout.TileHorizontal)
End Sub

Private Sub mnuWindowTileVer_Click(ByVal sender As Object, _
    ByVal e As EventArgs) Handles mnuWindowTileVer.Click
    Me.LayoutMdi(MdiLayout.TileVertical)
End Sub

Private Sub mnuWindowArrange_Click(ByVal sender As Object, _
    ByVal e As System.EventArgs) Handles mnuWindowArrange.Click
    Me.LayoutMdi(MdiLayout.ArrangeIcons)
End Sub

Private Sub mnuWindowCloseAll_Click(ByVal sender As System.Object, _
    ByVal e As System.EventArgs) Handles mnuWindowCloseAll.Click
    Dim frm As Form
    For Each frm In Me.MdiChildren
        frm.Close()
    Next
End Sub
```

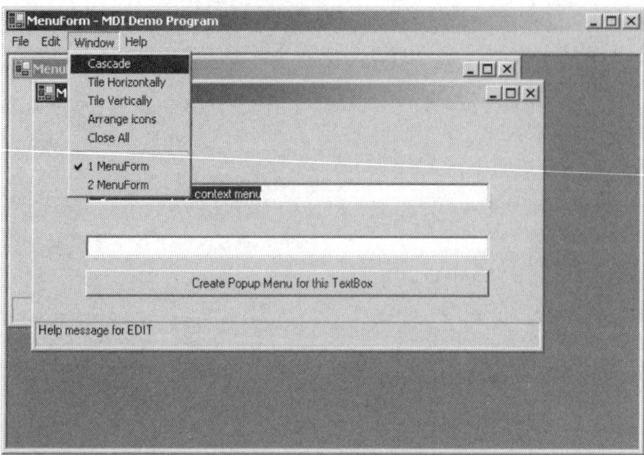

Figure 16-20. A typical MDI application with its Window menu.

As you can see in Figure 16-20, the Window menu contains a list of all visible MDI child windows, with a check mark near the one that is currently selected. The end user can use the elements in this menu to activate another child form. You can create this list simply by setting the MdiList property of the Windows MenuItem object to True. (This property replaces the Visual Basic 6 WindowList property.)

Menu Merging

If the currently active MDI child form has a menu, this menu is merged with the MDI container's menu. You can finely control how each submenu, and even each individual menu item in the child form, is merged with a menu in the MDI container form. You exert this control by using two related properties. MergeType is an enumerated value that specifies what happens to menu items (in the parent MDI form and in the MDI child form) when they are merged; the MergeOrder property specifies the relative order of items that are merged in the same submenu. The MergeType property can take four different values:

- **Add** This menu item is added to the menu in the MDI parent form; this is the default value, so the standard behavior is that all menus in the child form are added to the menu in the parent form. The position at which the item is inserted depends on the MergeOrder property.
- **Remove** This menu item never appears in the parent form's menu.
- **Replace** This menu item replaces the menu item with the same MergeOrder value in the other form.

- **MergeItems** This menu item is merged and appears in the resulting menu at the position indicated by the MergeOrder property. If this item is actually a submenu, items of this submenu are merged with items in the submenu with the same MergeOrder value in the other form; in this case, the menu merge mechanism takes into account the MergeType and MergeOrder properties of each individual menu item.

Implementing a correct menu merging is more complicated than you might think, so a practical example is in order. First create an MDI parent form with this menu structure:

```
File                    (MergeOrder = 0, MergeType = MergeItems)
    New File            (MergeOrder = 0, MergeType = MergeItems)
    Open File           (MergeOrder = 1, MergeType = Remove)
    Save File           (MergeOrder = 2, MergeType = Remove)
    Exit                (MergeOrder = 9, MergeType = MergeItems)
Window                  (MergeOrder = 5, MergeType = Add)
    Close All           (MergeOrder = 0, MergeType = Add)
Help                    (MergeOrder = 9, MergeType = MergeItems)
    Contents            (MergeOrder = 0, MergeType = MergeItems)
    About               (MergeOrder = 2, MergeType = MergeItems)
```

Next create a child form with this menu hierarchy:

```
File                    (MergeOrder = 0, MergeType = MergeItems)
    New                 (MergeOrder = 0, MergeType = Remove)
    Open                (MergeOrder = 1, MergeType = Replace)
    Save                (MergeOrder = 2, MergeType = Replace)
    Close               (MergeOrder = 3, MergeType = Add)
Edit                    (MergeOrder = 1, MergeType = Add)
    Undo                (MergeOrder = 0, MergeType = Add)
Help                    (MergeOrder = 9, MergeType = MergeItems)
    Index               (MergeOrder = 1, MergeType = Add)
```

This is the resultant menu tree when the child form becomes the active MDI form:

```
File                    (merge from both forms)
    New File            (from parent form)
    Open                (from child form)
    Save                (from child form)
    Close               (from child form)
    Exit                (from parent form)
Edit                    (from child form)
    Undo                (from child form)
Window                  (from parent form)
    Close All           (from parent form)
Help                    (merge from both forms)
```

(continued)

```
Contents            (from parent form)
Index               (from child form)
About               (from parent form)
```

Form Inheritance

Because a form is just an object, you shouldn't be surprised to learn that you can inherit a form from another form. Form inheritance isn't different from regular inheritance, and all you learned in Chapter 5 holds true in this case as well. However, the form is a peculiar object in that it exposes a user interface, and this detail has some interesting implications. Before diving into technical details, let's see what form inheritance is good for.

Advantages of Form Inheritance

Inheriting a new form from a base form means reusing the user interface, the code, and the functionality in the base form. In Visual Basic 6, the only feature you can count on for (limited) code reuse is form templates: you can save a form in the Template\Forms directory under the main Visual Basic directory, and then you can use it as a template for a new form. For example, you can create a template for a dialog box form, which has a fixed border; the OK and Cancel buttons; and some code in the buttons' Click event procedures. In practice, form templates are just a variant of the copy-and-paste approach that programmers have used for decades. Just to mention one limitation of templates, if you modify the code in the template, existing forms based on that template aren't affected.

Visual Basic .NET offers a far better approach to reusing code and user interface elements in forms. For example, you can create a DialogBaseForm that contains a Label, the OK and Cancel buttons, and some code for the buttons' Click events. If you then inherit a new form from DialogBaseForm, you inherit both the user interface and the behavior of the base form: in this case, this means that you can redefine the text of the Label and the behavior of the two buttons. You can resize the form and move the buttons accordingly (if you assigned their Anchor property correctly), and of course you can add new controls. Then you can go back to the DialogBaseForm form and add, say, a Help button and the logo of your company. When you recompile the inherited form, the new button and the logo will be part of the new form.

An Example of Form Inheritance

To see in practice how form inheritance works, let's create a dialog box that can work as a base class for other forms. (See Figure 16-21.) The DialogBaseForm

form contains three Button controls that are anchored to the top and right borders so that they move correctly when the form is resized. The TextBox and Label controls are anchored to the left, top, and right borders so that they expand and shrink when the form is resized. You'll also see a PictureBox control with an icon in it: add a little imagination, and it could be the logo of your company.

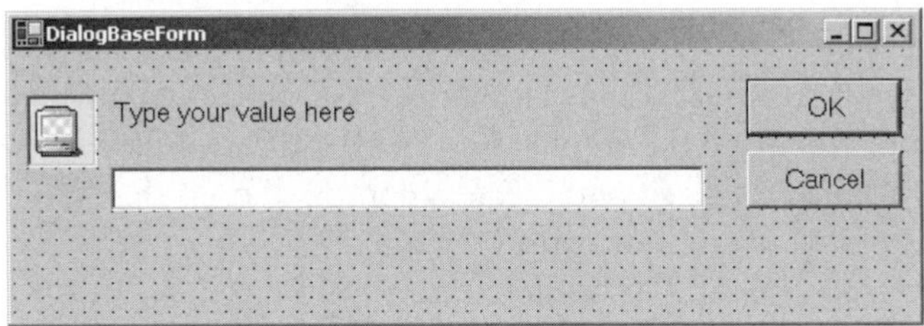

Figure 16-21. The DialogBaseForm form.

The OK and Cancel buttons have their DialogResult property set to OK and Cancel so that the dialog closes when the end user clicks on them. The Label control has a generic Text property because it's bound to be overwritten in the inherited form.

As you know, you get a better encapsulation if you use private controls only. However, when creating a base form class, you should use a Protected scope for your controls. Bear in mind that the Modifiers property of your controls corresponds to the scope of the variable that the form designer creates in the code module. If you use a Private scope for this variable, it isn't visible to the inherited form and you can't modify its properties from inside the derived form (even though the control will appear on the inherited form's surface). Therefore, you should set the Modifiers property to Protected for all controls that you want to manipulate in the inherited form but that you don't want the base or the inherited form to expose to the regular client code. Not all controls must have a Friend scope, however. Because you don't want to change your company logo any time soon, use a Private scope for the PictureBox control.

Because a Protected control isn't visible to the outside, the base class must expose the TextBox control's contents as a property, as in this code:

```
Property InputValue() As String
    Get
        Return txtValue.Text
    End Get
    Set(ByVal Value As String)
        txtValue.Text = Value
    End Set
End Property
```

You can create an inherited form by simply defining a class that inherits from an existing form class instead of the generic System.Windows.Forms.Form class:

```
Class DialogInheritedForm
    Inherits DialogBaseForm
    ⋮
End Class
```

In practice, however, you don't have to write this code manually because Visual Studio .NET lets you do it in a visual manner. For this mechanism to work correctly, you must compile the application by using the Build command on the Build menu. You need this step to create a compiled class that Visual Studio can use as a base class for the new form.

Next choose the Add Inherited Form command on the Project menu. This command displays the familiar Add New Item dialog box. Give the new form a name (use DialogInheritedForm to match the code that follows), and click the Open button. This action brings up the Inheritance Picker dialog box, which lets you select the base form among all the form classes defined in the current project. (You can use the Browse button to view forms in other assemblies.) Pick the DialogBaseForm class, as shown in Figure 16-22, and click OK.

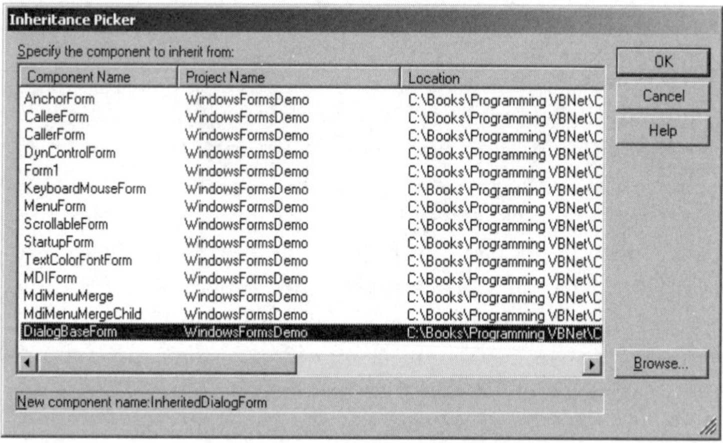

Figure 16-22. The Inheritance Picker dialog box.

Visual Studio creates a new form that inherits all the controls that are in the DialogBaseForm class, and you can add new controls and modify the properties of all controls that aren't private to the base class. Figure 16-23 shows the new DialogInheritedForm after I modified the text in the form and the Label control and added a new CheckBox control.

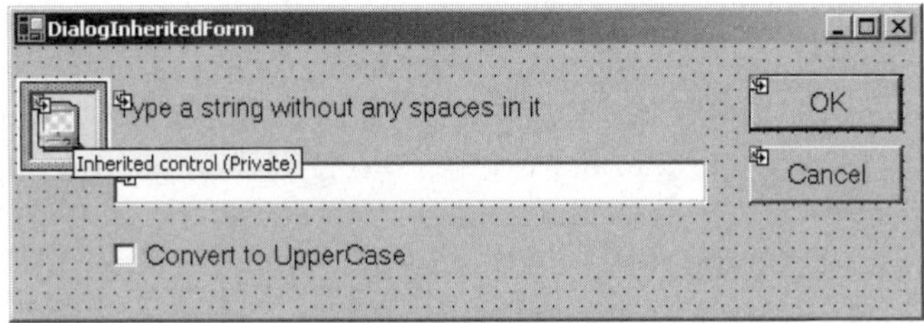

Figure 16-23. The DialogInheritedForm after changing a few properties and adding a CheckBox control.

You can select controls that were private in the base form, such as the PictureBox control that holds the computer icon, and you can browse their properties, but you can't modify them. (In fact, they're grayed in the Properties window.) However, you can browse *and* change all the properties of all other controls except the Name and Modifiers properties. This limitation is quite understandable: a derived class can't change the name or the scope of an inherited variable. You can quickly see the scope of each control in the inherited form by hovering the mouse over it to make a tooltip appear, as you can see in Figure 16-23.

Trapping and Overriding Events

Because an inherited class can access all the Protected elements in the base class, the DialogInheritedForm form can trap events raised by controls defined in the DialogBaseForm class by using standard syntax. For example, the following code in the derived class enables the OK button only if a non-null string has been typed in the txtValue control, and it converts typed characters to uppercase if the chkUpperCase control is checked:

```
' Enable the OK button only after the user enters a string.
Private Sub txtValue_TextChanged(ByVal sender As Object, _
    ByVal e As EventArgs) Handles txtValue.TextChanged
    Me.btnOK.Enabled = (txtValue.Text <> "")
End Sub

' Convert to uppercase if so requested.
Private Sub txtValue_KeyPress(ByVal sender As Object, _
    ByVal e As KeyPressEventArgs) Handles txtValue.KeyPress
    If chkUpperCase.Checked AndAlso Char.IsLower(e.KeyChar) Then
        txtValue.SelectedText = Char.ToUpper(e.KeyChar)
        e.Handled = True
    End If
End Sub
```

Just trapping an event from a control in the base form isn't enough in some cases. For example, let's say that you want to close the dialog and accept the value typed by end users only if the string doesn't contain any spaces. Creating a btnOk_Click event handler doesn't work in this case because the form engines would execute both Click events—in the base class and in the derived class—and the code in the derived class couldn't prevent the code in the Click event in DialogBaseForm from closing the form. It's obvious that in this case you need to *override* the default behavior in the base class, but it isn't immediately apparent how you can do that because you can't directly override events.

In the "Redefining Events" section inChapter 5, I describe a technique that you can use to override events. That technique applies in this situation as well. All events in the base class should delegate their job to an On*xxxx* procedure with Protected scope. For example, the btnOk_Click event procedure should call the OnOkClick procedure, the btnCancel_Click event procedure should likewise call the OnCancelClick procedure, and so on:

```
' ...(In the DialogBaseForm class)...

Private Sub btnOK_Click(ByVal sender As Object, _
    ByVal e As EventArgs) Handles btnOK.Click
    OnOkClick()
End Sub

Private Sub btnCancel_Click(ByVal sender As Object, _
    ByVal e As EventArgs) Handles btnCancel.Click
    OnCancelClick()
End Sub

' Since this form has been designed for being inherited from,
' you put the actual Button code in two Protected procedures.
Protected Overridable Sub OnOkClick()
    ' Close this form; return OK.
    Me.DialogResult = DialogResult.OK
End Sub

Protected Overridable Sub OnCancelClick()
    ' Close this form; return Cancel.
    Me.DialogResult = DialogResult.Cancel
End Sub
```

Because these procedures are marked with Overridable, the inherited form can redefine the default behavior by simply overriding them. A well-written derived class should delegate actions to the procedure in the base class if possible so that you can later improve the code in the base class and have the derived classes automatically inherit the improved code:

```
' In this inherited form, you reject strings that contain a space.
Protected Overrides Sub OnOkClick()
```

```
    If InStr(txtValue.Text, " ") = 0 Then
        ' Call the base procedure only if the string doesn't contain a space.
        MyBase.OnOkClick()
    Else
        ' Display an error message, and don't close the form.
        MessageBox.Show("Please remove all spaces from this string", _
            "Error", MessageBoxButtons.OK, MessageBoxIcon.Error)
    End If
End Sub
```

Advanced Form Techniques

In this section, I'll describe a few advanced form techniques, such as form subclassing, localization, and customization.

Window Subclassing

If you read the first edition of this book, you might remember that I devote many pages to subclassing, a technique that lets you intercept and process messages going from Windows to your form or controls. Subclassing plays an important role in Visual Basic 6 programming because it helps you overcome many limitations of the language. For example, you need subclassing to enforce a limit on form size and position, to get a notification when the form is moved or when a menu item is highlighted, to create custom menus and controls, and so on.

Windows Forms classes are so powerful that you'll rarely need to resort to subclassing anymore. For example, you can limit the size of a form with the MinimumSize and MaximumSize properties, determine when the form moves with the Move event, and get notified when a menu is highlighted with a Select event. Menus and many other controls expose the DrawMode property, which lets you customize their appearance (as I explain in Chapter 17), and there are many other features that make subclassing less important than it was in previous versions of Visual Basic.

Subclassing Principles

However, sometimes you need to implement subclassing, and it's a pleasant surprise to see that the Form object lets you do it in a simple, safe, and reliable way. (The following discussion assumes that you're familiar with subclassing; if you aren't, please read the Appendix of *Programming Microsoft Visual Basic 6*, on the companion CD.)

Subclassing a Form object relies heavily on inheritance. The System.Windows.Forms.Form class exposes the WndProc method, which is invoked for each message sent from Windows to the form. The code for this method in the base Form class processes the incoming message in the standard way: for example, a click on the form's surface activates the form, a click in the lower right corner of a form starts a resize operation, and so on.

The WndProc method is marked as Protected and Overridable, so a derived class can override it. Because all forms derive from the System.Windows.Forms.Form class, you can always redefine the behavior of your forms by overriding this method. This method receives a Message object, whose properties expose the four values that Windows sends to a form's window procedure: Msg (the number of the message), HWnd (the handle of the window), and WParam and LParam (arguments passed to the window procedure, whose meaning depends on the specific message). A fifth property, Result, is the value that will be returned to the operating system.

Subclassing Example

When you override the WndProc procedure, your primary concern should be delegating to the default procedure in the base class so that the usual message processing can take place (except in those rare cases in which you're subclassing the form to suppress the default action). Then you can check the value of the message's Msg property to see whether you want to deal with this specific message. If you're subclassing a form just to get a notification that something has happened, usually these actions are all you need to perform. For example, the following code traps the WM_DISPLAYCHANGE message to learn when the screen resolution changes, and the WM_COMPACTING message to be informed when the system is low on memory:

```
Protected Overrides Sub WndProc(ByRef m As Message)
    ' Let the base form process this message.
    MyBase.WndProc(m)

    ' Display an informative message on a Label control
    ' if this is one of the messages we want to subclass.
    Select Case m.Msg
        Case WM_DISPLAYCHANGE
            lblStatus.Text = "Screen resolution has changed"
        Case WM_COMPACTING
            lblStatus.Text = "The system is low on memory"
    End Select
End Sub
```

In some cases, you might need to check the value of WParam or LParam properties to obtain additional information about the message. For example, the WM_APPACTIVATE message comes with a 0 value in WParam if the current application is being deactivated and a nonzero value if it's being activated:

```
' ...(Insert this code in the preceding Select Case block.)...
        Case WM_ACTIVATEAPP
            ' Application has been activated or deactivated.
```

```
If m.WParam.ToInt32 <> 0 Then
    lblStatus.Text = "Application has been activated"
Else
    lblStatus.Text = "Application has been deactivated"
End If
```

You can subclass several Windows messages to obtain information about what has happened, including WM_SYSCOLORCHANGE (one or more system colors have been redefined), WM_PALETTEISCHANGING and WM_PALETTE-CHANGED (the color palette has changed), WM_FONTCHANGE (one or more fonts have changed), WM_DEVICECHANGE and WM_DEVMODECHANGE (settings of a device have changed), WM_ENDSESSION (the Windows session is closing), WM_SPOOLERSTATUS (a print job has been added to or removed from the spooler queue), and many others. For example, you can subclass WM_ENDSESSION to understand whether the form is closing because the user has closed it or because Windows is shutting down; this information can be useful in some cases, and unfortunately, you can't use the QueryUnload event to obtain it because this event isn't supported any longer.

Returning a Value to Windows

In some situations, you need to return a specific value to Windows. You can do this by setting the Result property of the Message argument, but this operation isn't as straightforward as you might think. In fact, this property doesn't directly contain the value being returned to the operating system: instead, it contains a System.IntPtr structure, which is defined as a 32-bit pointer (or a 64-bit pointer on 64-bit versions of Windows). Languages that don't support pointers natively, such as Visual Basic .NET, can use this type to get limited functionality with pointers. Many methods in .NET use this type also to store a handle whose size is platform-specific—for example, file handles.

In practice, the only operations you can execute on an IntPtr type are the creation of a pointer equal to the Integer value that you pass to its constructor, and the ToInt32 method, which reads the 32-bit value stored in the pointer. You can't create an IntPtr object that points to an arbitrary location in memory, a limitation that is necessary to guarantee complete isolation among managed applications.

Let's see how to use the IntPtr type to read and modify the value being returned to the operating system. This example subclasses the WM_NCHITTEST message that Windows sends to a form when the mouse cursor hovers on the form. The form is supposed to reply to this message by returning an integer that represents the area on the form hit by the mouse. For example, the HTCLIENT value means that the cursor is on the client area, and HTCAPTION means that the mouse is on the form's title bar.

The following example cheats a little by intercepting this message and returning HTCAPTION if the mouse is on the client area. Remember that this code executes after the base Form class has processed the WM_NCHITTEST message, so the Result property already contains the information about the actual position of the mouse:

```
Case WM_NCHITTEST
    ' If on client area, make Windows believe it's on title bar.
    If m.Result.ToInt32 = HTCLIENT Then
    ' The only way to assign an IntPtr is by creating a new object.
    m.Result = New IntPtr(HTCAPTION)
    End If
```

The effect of this code is that users can grab and move the form by clicking on its client area as if they had clicked on the title bar. (See Figure 16-24.) If the form is resizeable, it can be maximized with a double click anywhere on the client area.

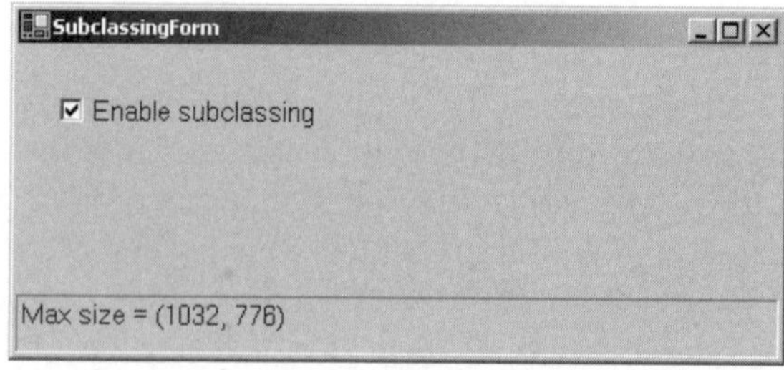

Figure 16-24. The subclassing demo contains a form that you can drag by clicking anywhere on the client area.

Sometimes the data passed together with a message is a structure pointed to by the LParam value. In this case, you can use the GetLParam method to read values in that structure. For example, when the user starts a resize operation on the form, Windows sends a WM_GETMINMAXINFO message whose LParam value points to a MINMAXINFO structure defined as follows:

```
Structure POINTAPI
    Dim X As Integer
    Dim Y As Integer
End Structure

Structure MINMAXINFO
    Dim ptReserved As POINTAPI
    Dim ptMaxSize As POINTAPI
    Dim ptMaxPosition As POINTAPI
    Dim ptMinTrackSize As POINTAPI
    Dim ptMaxTrackSize As POINTAPI
End Structure
```

The ptMinTrackSize and ptMaxTrackSize elements define the smallest and largest size that the form can assume. For example, on a 1024-by-768 screen, a form can be usually resized as large as 1032 by 776 pixels. (See Figure 16-24.) Here's the code in the demo application that reads this information:

```
Case WM_GETMINMAXINFO
    Dim mmi As MINMAXINFO
    mmi = CType(m.GetLParam(mmi.GetType), MINMAXINFO)
    lblStatus.Text = String.Format("Max size = ({0}, {1})", _
    mmi.ptMaxSize.X, mmi.ptMaxSize.Y)
```

Unfortunately, you can't modify the values in a memory block pointed to by LParam. (If this were possible, malicious code might corrupt memory belonging to the same or another AppDomain, and the code wouldn't be safe any longer.) For example, you can't modify the values in the MINMAXINFO structure to enforce a different minimum or maximum track size.

Transparency Effects

The Form object exposes a pair of properties that can add some graphical pizzazz to your applications with minimum effort.

The TransparencyKey Property

If you assign a color value to the TransparencyKey property, all the pixels of that color are considered transparent and won't be drawn. If the user clicks on one such point, the underlying window is activated instead. You can create oddly shaped forms by simply painting the area that doesn't belong to the form with the color that you assign to the TransparencyKey property.

You get the best effect if you work with a form whose FormBorderStyle is set to None so that you don't have to worry about the title bar. Then you have to select a color to be used as a transparent color, and of course you must be sure that no graphic element in the form contains any pixel of this color. If the form has a rather regular shape, such as the elliptical form in Figure 16-25, you can draw such pixels using graphic methods of the Graphics object passed to the Paint event. For example, this is the code the demo application uses to create an elliptical form:

```
Private Sub TransparentForm_Paint(ByVal sender As Object, _
    ByVal e As System.Windows.Forms.PaintEventArgs) Handles MyBase.Paint

    ' Make blue the transparent color so that only the ellipse is visible.
    Me.TransparencyKey = Color.Blue
    ' Create a brush of the same color as the form's background color.
    Dim b As New SolidBrush(Me.BackColor)
    ' Draw a blue rectangle over the entire form.
```

(continued)

```
        e.Graphics.FillRectangle(Brushes.Blue, Me.ClientRectangle)
        ' Draw a filled ellipse of the original background color.
        e.Graphics.FillEllipse(b, Me.ClientRectangle)
        ' Create a black border for the ellipse.
        e.Graphics.DrawEllipse(Pens.Black, Me.ClientRectangle)
        ' Destroy the brush.
        b.Dispose()
    End Sub
```

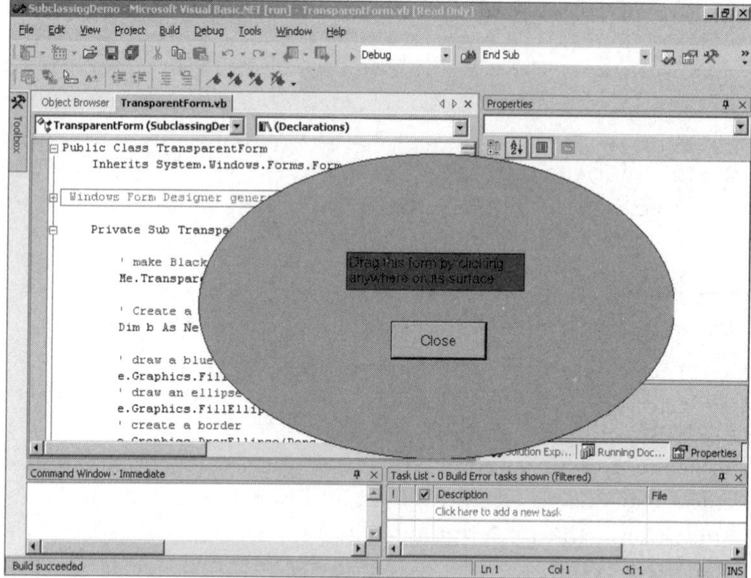

Figure 16-25. An elliptical form.

Even if you aren't familiar yet with the graphical possibilities of GDI+, the sense of the preceding code should be quite clear. If the shape of your form can't be created easily with graphic methods, you might create a bitmap with any graphic application, including Microsoft Paint, and load the image into the form's BackgroundImage property. If the form is resizeable, you should use a DrawImage method to resize the bitmap so that it always covers the entire form's surface.

Regardless of how you define the form's shape, remember that you should provide end users with the ability to move and close the form. The form in the demo application uses the subclassing technique described earlier to let the user move the form by clicking anywhere on its client area.

The Opacity Property

The Opacity property lets you apply a level of transparency to the entire form, including its title bar and borders. It's a Double value in the range 0 to 1, so you can change the opacity level with fine granularity. You can use it for special effects such as fade-ins and fade-outs. You can mix it with the TransparencyKey property, as the sample application on the companion CD demonstrates. (See Figure 16-26.)

> **Tip** Oddly, both the TransparencyKey and Opacity properties make the form completely transparent to most screen capture programs, and in fact I was in trouble when I had to shoot Figures 16-25 and 16-26. I was so desperate that I almost gave up, but I tried the nearly forgotten PrintScreen key, which of course worked perfectly and copied the screen image to the Clipboard.

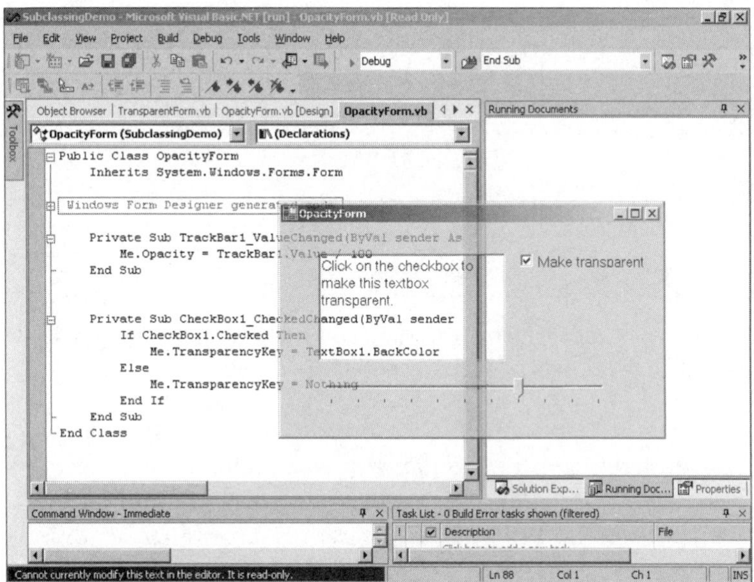

Figure 16-26. Mixing the TransparencyKey and Opacity properties on one form.

Localized Forms

Windows developers have traditionally used resource files to create multilanguage applications. The problem with resource files is that they don't lend themselves well to the Rapid Application Development (RAD) approach. For example, with all previous versions of Visual Basic you can use only one language in the form designer. To support additional languages, you have to author a resource file yourself, and you have to write the code that extracts each string or image and moves the strings or images into controls. This problem has been solved in the Visual Studio .NET form designer in a simple, elegant, and effective way.

A Simple Localization Example

Let's take the simple form shown in Figure 16-27 as an example. This form contains three strings and one image that should be localized. In general, however, the localization process can involve more than just changing the visible strings in the user interface or strings used from code. For example, you might need to move a control to a different location or make it invisible under some localized versions. At any rate, you should test your form thoroughly before you make it localizable because any change you make to its user interface afterward will require more coding and efforts.

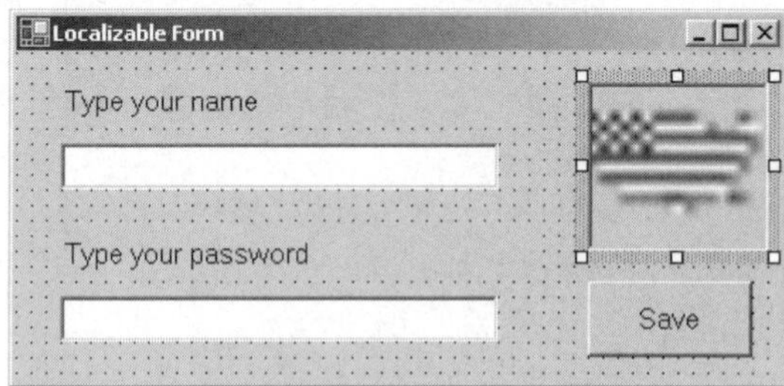

Figure 16-27. A localizable form with captions and one image, as it appears when the Language property is set to (Default).

The first step in localizing a form is to set its Localizable property to True. This is a design-time property that you won't find in the Object Browser. It tells the designer's code generator that the values of the properties of the form and its controls are to be loaded from a .resx resource file instead of hard-coded in the source code.

Next you should set the form's Language property to the alternative locale that you want to support. This is another design-time-only property, which can be assigned any of the locales that .NET supports. (See Figure 16-28.) The form designer continues to display the same interface as before, but you can now change all the properties of the form and its controls (including their position, size, visibility, and so on). All the values that you set from now on will be associated with the alternative locale just selected. Figure 16-29 shows how the form might look to an Italian end user. Of course, you can repeat this procedure with any language that you want to support.

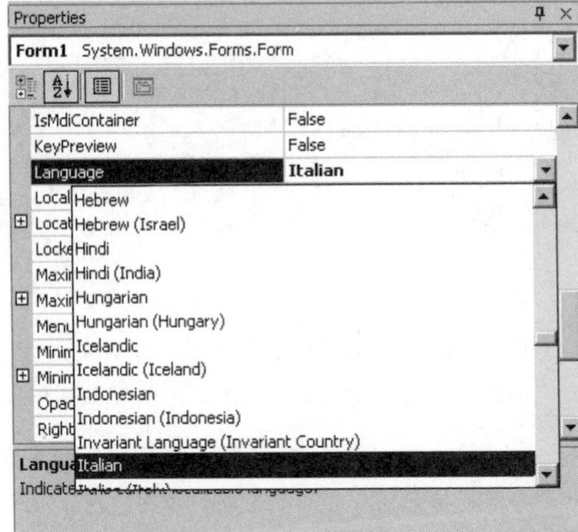

Figure 16-28. Setting the Language property to Italian.

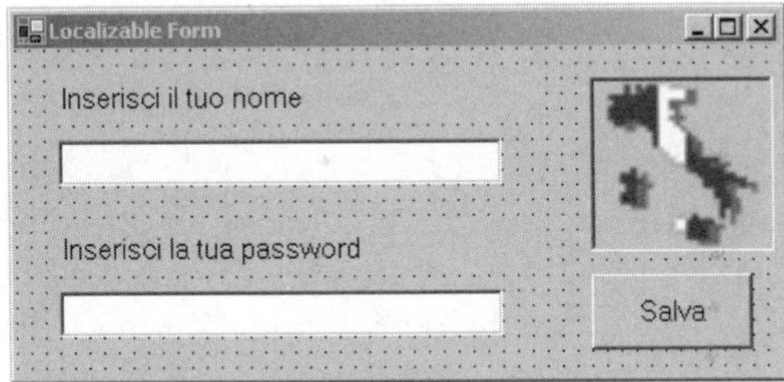

Figure 16-29. The Italian version of the original form.

Running and Testing the Localized Application

The great thing about localized forms is that in most cases, you can simply forget about them. You run an application containing localized forms as you'd run a regular application. If the culture of the current user matches one of the languages you have defined, the form and its controls will use the properties you've set for that language; otherwise, the default language will be used.

A minor problem with localized forms is that they require additional testing and debugging. The easiest way to test a localized form is to modify the culture of the UI thread, which you do by assigning a suitable CultureInfo object to the CurrentUICulture property of the Thread.CurrentThread object. This is the property tested by the form engine when it's deciding which set of localized properties should be used. You should put the following routine in a separate module so that you can call it from all the forms in your application:

```
Sub SetUICulture(ByVal culture As String)
    Try
        ' Create a new CultureInfo object and assign it to the current thread.
        System.Threading.Thread.CurrentThread.CurrentUICulture = _
            New System.Globalization.CultureInfo(culture)
    Catch
        MessageBox.Show("Locale '" & culture & "' isn't supported", _
            "Error", MessageBoxButtons.OK, MessageBoxIcon.Error)
    End Try
End Sub
```

It's essential that you call SetUICulture in the form's Sub New procedure before calling InitializeComponent, the routine where form and control properties are assigned:

```
Public Sub New()
    MyBase.New()
    ' Set Italian as the culture for the interactive user.
    SetUICulture("IT")
    ' This call is required by the Windows Form Designer.
    InitializeComponent()
    ' Add any initialization after the InitializeComponent() call.
End Sub
```

Working with Resource Files

As usual, you can leverage a feature better if you know what's going on behind the scenes. When you make a form localizable, Visual Studio creates a .resx file for each specified language, including the default one. You must click the Show All Files button in the Solution Explorer's toolbar to see these .resx files inside the Visual Studio window. (See Figure 16-30.) Each file is named after the locale to which it's bound.

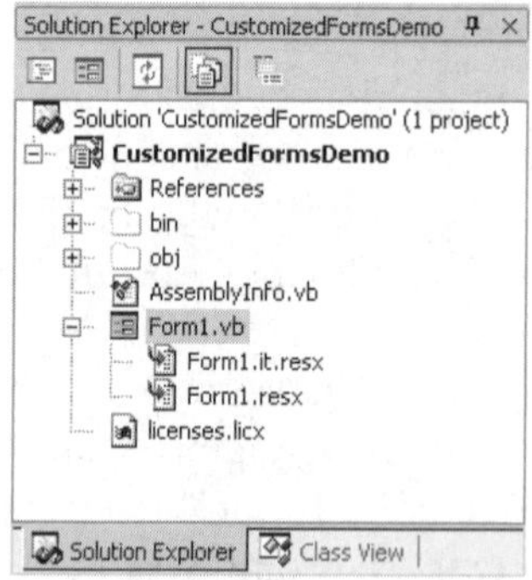

Figure 16-30. The .resx resource files as they appear in the Solution Explorer window after you click the Show All Files button.

If you double-click a .resx file in the Solution Explorer, a resource editor window appears. You can edit a resource file as XML or by using a grid, such as the one shown in Figure 16-31. The four columns in the grid are the value of the resource, its key, the corresponding .NET type (such as System.Int32 or System.String), and its MIME type. The last column holds a non-null value only for binary data, such as images.

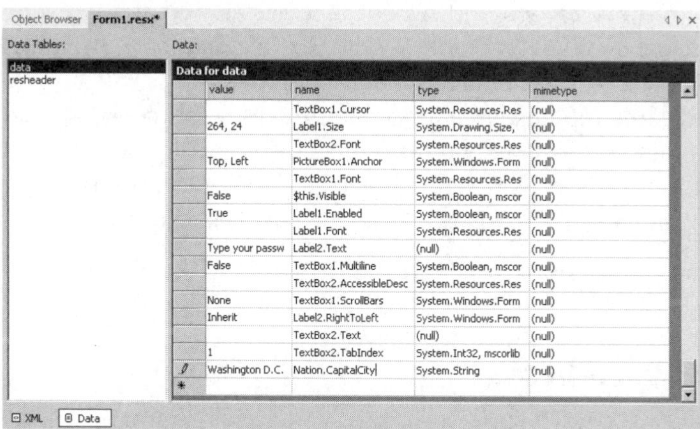

Figure 16-31. You can edit a .resx file using a grid or the XML editor; you can switch between the two approaches by clicking on the tabs near the bottom edge of the editor.

Most of the time, the key associated with each value is the *controlname.propertyname* pair that identifies which property of which control that value will be assigned to. This makes it easy to quickly revise and check the spelling of all the properties without visiting every control. Even more interesting, you can add items to the resource file by typing in the last row of the grid. To test this feature, you can add a new value whose key is Nation.CapitalCity and whose type is System.String and associate two different strings with this element in the two .resx resource files.

The new string you've added to the resource file isn't used by a specific UI element, so you must retrieve it through code. You can do this by using a piece of code similar to the one that the form designer generates for the InitializeComponent procedure. For example, the demo application uses this code to display the name of the capital city when the end user clicks on the country icon:

```
Private Sub PictureBox1_Click(ByVal sender As Object, ByVal e As EventArgs) _
    Handles PictureBox1.Click

    ' Create a ResourceManager object for the default culture.
    Dim resources As New System.Resources.ResourceManager(GetType(Form1))
```

(continued)

```
    ' Read the name of the capital city.
    Dim capital As String = CStr(resources.GetObject("Nation.CapitalCity"))
    ' Display it in a message box.
    MessageBox.Show("The capital city is " & capital, "Demo", _
        MessageBoxButtons.OK, MessageBoxIcon.Information)
End Sub
```

In a real-world application, you should instantiate the ResourceManager object when the form is created and store it in a class-level variable so that you don't have to re-create it anytime you need to extract data from the resource file. An ideal place to do this is in the Sub New procedure.

By default, the ResourceManager retrieves resources related to the current UI locale, but you can change this behavior by passing a CultureInfo object to its GetObject method. For example, let's say that you want to display the name of the Italian capital regardless of the current UI locale:

```
Dim ciIt As New System.Globalization.CultureInfo("it")
capitalCity = Str(resources.GetObject("Nation.CapitalCity", ciIt))
```

Dynamic Control Properties

Let's consider the form shown in Figure 16-32, a login dialog box for connecting to Microsoft SQL Server. To help the test phase, I've already placed the name of my SQL Server and my user name in the first two fields so that I just have to enter my password. It would be great if the end user had the ability to define these two preset values, but clearly I can't hard code them in the listing because I'd have to recompile the application for each different end user. The obvious solution is to store these values in a file so that each user can customize them. In pre-.NET days, you might have used an .ini file for this purpose, but .NET offers a more structured and standard solution in the form of dynamic properties in configuration files.

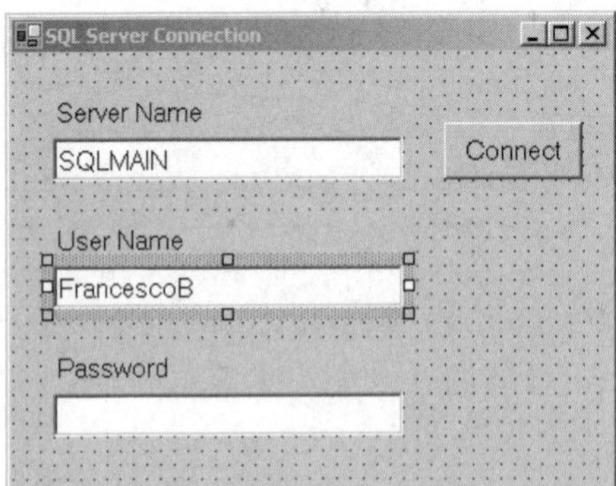

Figure 16-32. A simple form that demonstrates dynamic properties.

In the section "Dynamic Properties" of Chapter 14, I explained how you can retrieve strings stored in the <appSettings> section of the application's configuration file. The good news is that you can bind one or more properties of the form or its controls to such dynamic properties and you don't even have to write a single line of code because the form designer's code generator does it automatically for you.

To bind a property in the form designer to a value in the configuration file, you must select the control in question (or the form itself), expand the (DynamicProperties) element in the Properties window, and click the ellipses button for the Advanced item. This action brings up the dialog box visible in Figure 16-33.

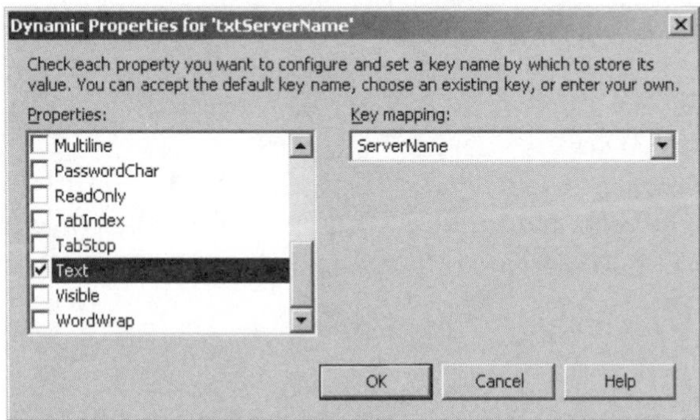

Figure 16-33. The dialog box in which you associate the properties of one or more controls with the corresponding entry in the configuration file.

Scroll down the list box until you reach the property you want to make dynamic, select the corresponding check box, and enter in the text box on the right the name of the key in the <appSettings> section that will contain the value of this property. The demo application provided on the companion CD binds the Text properties of the txtServer and txtUserName controls to the ServerName and UserName dynamic properties, but you can use the same technique for other properties, including ForeColor and BackColor. An apparent limit of this feature is that you can't bind object properties in this way—for example, Font, Size, and Location. If a property of a control has been bound to a value in the configuration file, a small green icon appears beside its name in the Properties window.

When you create one or more dynamic properties, Visual Studio creates the application's .config file if you hadn't created it already for other reasons. You can see this file if you click the Show All Files button in the Solution Explorer. If you double-click the file, you can edit it, as you can see in Figure 16-34. (Note that you'll be asked to save and close all open forms to ensure that the .config file contains up-to-date values.) You can edit all the dynamic properties in this

XML editor if you want, instead of selecting every control that exposes a bound dynamic property.

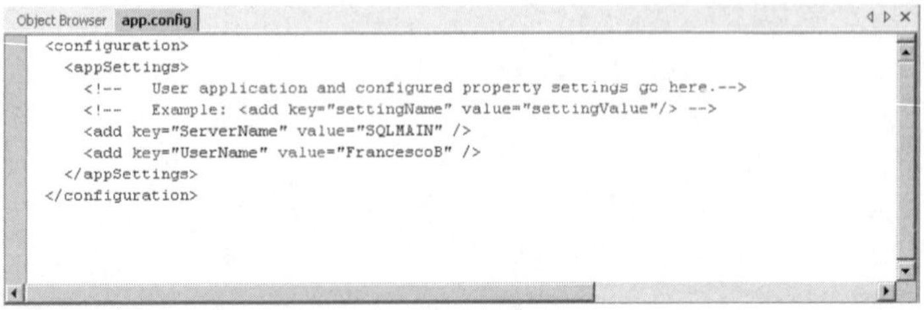

```
<configuration>
  <appSettings>
    <!--   User application and configured property settings go here.-->
    <!--   Example: <add key="settingName" value="settingValue"/> -->
    <add key="ServerName" value="SQLMAIN" />
    <add key="UserName" value="FrancescoB" />
  </appSettings>
</configuration>
```

Figure 16-34. The application configuration file, with the dynamic properties you've created in the Properties window.

Other Useful Objects

The System.Windows.Forms namespace contains many other objects that you'll surely need to know about for creating full-featured Win32 applications.

The Clipboard Object

As you can easily guess, the Clipboard object gives you the ability to copy data into the Windows Clipboard and then paste it somewhere else. If you're familiar with the Visual Basic 6 Clipboard object, you'll quickly grasp the essential concepts of this new version.

Copying Data into the Clipboard

Copying a piece of information into the Clipboard is as easy as calling Clipboard.SetDataObject: you can pass this method a string, an image, and so on. If you pass it a string that contains text in Rich Text Format (RTF), the Clipboard object detects this format automatically. For example, the following procedure copies the selected portion of a TextBox control (or the entire control's contents if no text is selected) into the Clipboard:

```
Sub CopyFromTextBox(ByVal tb As TextBox)
    ' Copy the TextBox's selected text to the Clipboard.
    Dim t As String = tb.SelectedText
    ' Copy the entire text if no text is selected.
    If t.Length = 0 Then t = tb.Text
    ' Proceed only if there is something to be copied.
    If t.Length > 0 Then
        Clipboard.SetDataObject(t)
    End If
End Sub
```

The SetDataObject method can take a second argument, which you should set to True if you want to make the copied object available after the current program terminates:

```
' Make the copied text available after the application ends.
        Clipboard.SetDataObject(t, True)
```

Remember that you can put any object in the Clipboard, including objects that are private to your application and that shouldn't be accessed by other programs.

The Clipboard object supports several formats, each identified by a string constant exposed by the DataFormats class. The list includes common formats, such as Text, Rtf, Html, Bitmap, MetafilePict, EnhancedMetafile, Tiff, and Palette. There is also a CommaSeparatedValue format that lets you import data in CSV format from spreadsheets and many other applications. If a control can export data in multiple formats, it should call the SetDataObject method once for each format. For example, a RichTextBox control should copy the value of both the SelectedRtf and SelectedText properties so that its contents can be pasted in either a TextBox or a RichTextBox control.

While the SetDataObject method can understand a few formats automatically, it doesn't give you full control over the format used to store the data in the Clipboard. For a higher degree of control, you must create a new instance of DataObject, a class that works as a storage medium for data in different formats. Next you should call DataObject's SetData method once for every format you want to support, and you should use the Clipboard.SetDataObject method to store the DataObject object in the Clipboard:

```
Sub CopyFromRichTextBox(ByVal rtf As RichTextBox)
    ' Copy the RichTextBox's selected text to the Clipboard.
    Dim data As New DataObject()

    ' Get the selected RTF text if there is a selection
    ' or the entire text if no text is selected.
    Dim t As String = rtf.SelectedRtf
    If t.Length = 0 Then t = rtf.Rtf
    ' Do the copy only if there is something to be copied.
    If t.Length > 0 Then data.SetData(DataFormats.Rtf, t)

    ' Do it again with the plaintext.
    t = rtf.SelectedText
    If t.Length = 0 Then t = rtf.Text
    ' Proceed only if there is something to be copied.
    If t.Length > 0 Then
        data.SetData(DataFormats.Text, t)
    End If
```

(continued)

```
    ' Move the DataObject into the Clipboard.
    ' (Pass True to make the data available to other applications.)
    Clipboard.SetDataObject(data, True)
End Sub
```

The first argument to the SetData method can be any string, including a user-defined string that defines a custom format. This lets you create private Clipboard formats that only your application can understand. (This technique is similar to the one I describe in the "Using Custom Formats" section of Chapter 9 of *Programming Microsoft Visual Basic 6*, provided on the companion CD.)

The DataObject class is usually used in conjunction with the Clipboard, but it doesn't have to be so. For example, you can use it as a temporary repository for your data in multiple formats. It's like having as many private Clipboards as you need.

Pasting Data from the Clipboard

Pasting data from the Clipboard requires more code because you must ascertain whether the Clipboard contains data in one of the formats you're willing to process. First use the Clipboard.GetDataObject method to retrieve an IDataObject object. Next use the GetDataPresent method of this IDataObject object to determine whether the Clipboard contains data in the format specified by the first argument. If the second argument is True or omitted, the method attempts to force the conversion to the specified format. (For example, it might try to force the conversion from RTF text to plaintext.) If the GetDataPresent method returns True, you can extract the actual value with the GetData method. The following routine attempts to paste the current contents of the Clipboard into a TextBox control:

```
Sub PasteIntoTextBox(ByVal tb As TextBox)
    ' Get the data currently in the Clipboard.
    Dim data As IDataObject = Clipboard.GetDataObject
    ' Check whether there is any data in text format,
    ' converting it if necessary.
    If data.GetDataPresent(DataFormats.Text, True) Then
        ' If yes, paste into the selection.
        tb.SelectedText = data.GetData(DataFormats.Text, True).ToString
    End If
End Sub
```

Depending on the type of the target controls, you might need to make multiple attempts before you find a matching format. For example, this procedure attempts a paste operation into a RichTextBox control. Note that you need to start by testing the richest format (RTF, in this case) without attempting a conversion and then continue with less rich formats (plaintext, in this case):

```
Sub PasteIntoRichTextBox(ByVal rtf As RichTextBox)
```

```
    ' Get the data currently in the Clipboard.
    Dim data As IDataObject = Clipboard.GetDataObject

    ' Check whether there is any data in RTF format,
    ' WITHOUT attempting a conversion.
    If data.GetDataPresent(DataFormats.Rtf, False) Then
        ' If available, paste into the RTF selection.
        rtf.SelectedRtf = data.GetData(DataFormats.Rtf).ToString
    ElseIf data.GetDataPresent(DataFormats.Text, True) Then
        ' Else, attempt to get data in plaintext format.
        rtf.SelectedText = data.GetData(DataFormats.Text, True).ToString
    End If
End Sub
```

The GetDataPresent and GetData methods are overloaded to take a System.Type argument; you can use this form to test whether the Clipboard contains an object in any class other than the standard Clipboard formats:

```
Dim data As IDataObject = Clipboard.GetDataObject
If data.GetDataPresent(GetType(Person)) Then
    ' The Clipboard contains a Person object.
    Dim p As Person = CType(data.GetData(GetType(Person)), Person)
End If
```

The IDataObject interface exposes the GetFormats method, which returns the formats of all the pieces of data currently stored in the Clipboard:

```
Sub EnumClipboardFormats()
    Dim t As String
    Dim msg As String

    ' Prepare the list of formats currently in the Clipboard.
    ' (You can pass True to include formats obtained by converting data.)
    For Each t In Clipboard.GetDataObject.GetFormats(False)
        msg &= t & ControlChars.CrLf
    Next
    ' Show the list.
    MessageBox.Show(msg, "Current Clipboard formats")
End Sub
```

Once you extract an IDataObject object from the Clipboard, this object has an independent life and doesn't necessarily reflect the *current* contents of the Clipboard.

Implementing Drag-and-Drop

Once you know how to store and retrieve data from the Clipboard, understanding drag-and-drop is a breeze. You can also leverage much of your knowledge about drag-and-drop in Visual Basic 6 because the conceptual differences are minor.

For starters, Visual Basic .NET doesn't support automatic drag-and-drop as Visual Basic 6 does. You must write code that initiates a drag-and-drop operation in the source control, and you must write code for events in the target control. In fact, the only property that is related to drag-and-drop is AllowDrop, which you must set to True to have a control raise events when it works as a drag-and-drop target.

How you initiate a drag-and-drop operation depends on which control is the target. Typically, you detect the user's intention to start a drag-and-drop operation when the mouse leaves the control while one of its buttons is being pressed. If this is the case, you should create a new DataObject instance and fill it with the data in the source control that might be dropped elsewhere. (This step is identical to what you do when copying data in the Clipboard and includes your having the ability to store data in multiple formats.) Here's the first part of a MouseMove event handler that works equally well with a TextBox control and a RichTextBox control:

```
Private Sub TextBox_MouseMove(ByVal sender As Object, _
    ByVal e As System.Windows.Forms.MouseEventArgs) _
    Handles TextBox1.MouseMove, RichTextBox1.MouseMove
    ' Exit if no button is pressed.
    If e.Button = 0 Then Exit Sub

    ' Get a reference to the control. We leverage the fact that both
    ' the TextBox and the RichTextBox control inherit from TextBoxBase.
    Dim tbase As TextBoxBase = DirectCast(sender, TextBoxBase)
    ' Exit if there is no data to be dragged.
    If tbase.TextLength = 0 Then Exit Sub
    ' Exit if the cursor is inside the control's borders.
    If e.X >= 0 And e.X < tbase.Width And e.Y >= 0 And e.Y < tbase.Height Then
        Exit Sub
    End If
    ' The mouse is being dragged outside the control's client area,
    ' so we can start a drag-and-drop operation.

    ' Create a stand-alone DataObject.
    Dim data As New DataObject()
    ' Store the selected text, or all the text if no selection.
    If tbase.SelectionLength > 0 Then
        data.SetData(DataFormats.Text, tbase.SelectedText)
    Else
        data.SetData(DataFormats.Text, tbase.Text)
    End If

    ' If the control is a RichTextBox, store also the selected Rtftext
    ' or its entire contents if no selection.
    If TypeOf sender Is RichTextBox Then
```

```
        Dim rtfbox As RichTextBox = DirectCast(sender, RichTextBox)
        If rtfbox.SelectionLength > 0 Then
            data.SetData(DataFormats.Rtf, rtfbox.SelectedRtf)
        Else
            data.SetData(DataFormats.Rtf, rtfbox.Rtf)
        End If
    End If
```

In the next step, you define which drag-and-drop effects you want to support, using a DragDropEffects bit-coded value (supported effects are Copy, Move, Scroll, Link, and All), and you pass this value and the DataObject object to the control's DoDragDrop method, which actually initiates the drag-and-drop operation. This is the point where drag-and-drop in Visual Basic .NET differs most from Visual Basic 6: the DoDragDrop method is synchronous and doesn't return until the drag-and-drop operation has been completed (or canceled). The return value from the method is another DragDropEffect value that tells which effect was chosen by the user (copy, move, or scroll), or is None if the operation was canceled; if the selected effect is Move, you must delete the selected data in the source control. Here's the second part of the MouseMove event handler that implements the entire process:

```
' Start the drag operation - wait until it's completed.
    Dim effect As DragDropEffects = _
        DragDropEffects.Copy Or DragDropEffects.Move
    effect = tbase.DoDragDrop(data, effect)

    ' Delete the text if it was a move operation.
    If effect = DragDropEffects.Move Then
        If tbase.SelectionLength > 0 Then
            tbase.SelectedText = ""
        Else
            tbase.Text = ""
        End If
    End If
End Sub
```

Let's see now what code you must write to have a control act as a drag-and-drop target. A control that works as a drag-and-drop target can receive four events: DragEnter (the mouse is entering the control's client area), DragOver (the mouse is moving inside the control), DragLeave (the mouse is exiting the control), and DragDrop (the mouse button is being released while over the control). Remember that you must set the target control's AllowDrop property to True; otherwise, none of these events will ever fire.

The DragEnter, DragOver, and DragDrop events receive a DragEventArgs object in their second argument. You can learn more about the drag-and-drop operation being performed by querying its read-only properties: AllowedEffect (a bit-coded value that specifies which actions are available), Data (the DataObject instance that contains the data), KeyState (the state of Shift, Ctrl, and Alt keys and mouse buttons), and X and Y (the position of the cursor in client coordinates). The KeyState bit-coded property doesn't correspond to any enumerated value, so you must use numeric constants: 1 (left button), 2 (right button), 4 (Shift key), 8 (Ctrl key), 16 (middle button), and 32 (Alt key).

The only writable property is Effect, to which you assign a value that reflects which operations the target control is willing to accept. In the DragEnter event, you check the format of the data being dragged, the available effects, and the state of keys and mouse buttons. If you want to accept the drag-and-drop, you assign a value other than None to the Effect property. The following procedure shows how to implement a DragEnter event handler that works equally well with a TextBox control and a RichTextBox control:

```
Private Sub TextBox_DragEnter(ByVal sender As Object, _
    ByVal e As System.Windows.Forms.DragEventArgs) _
    Handles TextBox1.DragEnter, RichTextBox1.DragEnter
    ' Check that the user is dragging some text.
    If e.Data.GetDataPresent(DataFormats.Text, True) Then
        If CBool(e.KeyState And 8) Then
            ' If Ctrl key is pressed, this is a copy operation.
            e.Effect = e.AllowedEffect And DragDropEffects.Copy
        Else
            ' Otherwise, it is a move operation.
            e.Effect = e.AllowedEffect And DragDropEffects.Move
        End If
    Else
        ' Reject any other type.
        e.Effect = DragDropEffects.None
    End If
End Sub
```

You can also use the DragEnter event to change the appearance of the target control—for example, by drawing a special border around it or changing its background color. If you do this, you should restore the original appearance in the DragLeave event handler as well as in the DragDrop event handler. When the mouse is moving inside the target control's client area, you receive DragOver events, but you need to trap this event only if you want to provide different drag-and-drop effects (or disable drag-and-drop completely) for different areas of the control.

This leaves us with the DragDrop event, which is where you write the code that manages the actual data processing. As you see in the following example, getting the data being dropped is similar to a paste operation:

```
Private Sub TextBox_DragDrop(ByVal sender As Object, _
    ByVal e As System.Windows.Forms.DragEventArgs) _
    Handles TextBox1.DragDrop, RichTextBox1.DragDrop
```

```
    ' Exit if data isn't in text format.
    If Not e.Data.GetDataPresent(DataFormats.Text, True) Then Exit Sub

    ' Decide whether this is a copy or a move operation.
    If CBool(e.KeyState And 8) Then
        e.Effect = DragDropEffects.Copy
    Else
        e.Effect = DragDropEffects.Move
    End If

    If (TypeOf sender Is RichTextBox) AndAlso _
        e.Data.GetDataPresent(DataFormats.Rtf) Then
        ' If control is a RichTextBox and data is in RTF format, get it.
        Dim rtf As RichTextBox = DirectCast(sender, RichTextBox)
        rtf.SelectedRtf = e.Data.GetData(DataFormats.Rtf).ToString
    Else
        ' Otherwise, paste plaintext.
        Dim tbase As TextBoxBase = DirectCast(sender, TextBoxBase)
        tbase.SelectedText = e.Data.GetData(DataFormats.Text).ToString
    End If
End Sub
```

The only other event that I haven't covered yet is QueryContinueDrag, which is received by the source control while the drag-and-drop operation is in progress. This event receives a QueryContinueDragEventArgs object, which exposes the KeyState, EscapePressed, and Action properties. Your code should check the pressed keys and whether the user pressed the Esc key, and assign one of the following DragAction enumerated values to the Action property: Continue (the default), Drop, or Cancel. Here's the typical implementation of this event:

```
Private Sub TextBox1_QueryContinueDrag(ByVal sender As Object, _
    ByVal e As System.Windows.Forms.QueryContinueDragEventArgs) _
    Handles TextBox1.QueryContinueDrag, RichTextBox1.QueryContinueDrag
    If e.EscapePressed Then e.Action = DragAction.Cancel
End Sub
```

The Application Object

The System.Windows.Forms.Application object exposes a few interesting properties, methods, and events. All the members of this class are shared, and you can't create an instance of the Application object. By and large, this object replaces the App object you have under Visual Basic 6 but is more powerful.

Properties, Methods, and Events

Table 16-10 lists some of the properties, methods, and events of this object, with the corresponding Visual Basic 6 member if there is one. All listed properties are read-only.

I won't give you an example of the value returned by each property because you can see them for yourself with the demo application, which lets you test the most useful features of this object. (See Figure 16-35.) Note that the demo application displays the company name, product name, and product version that I have set by using attributes in the AssemblyInfo.vb module:

```
<Assembly: AssemblyCompany("VB2TheMax Software")>
<Assembly: AssemblyProduct("WinForm Objects Demo")>
<Assembly: AssemblyVersion("1.0.2.*")>
```

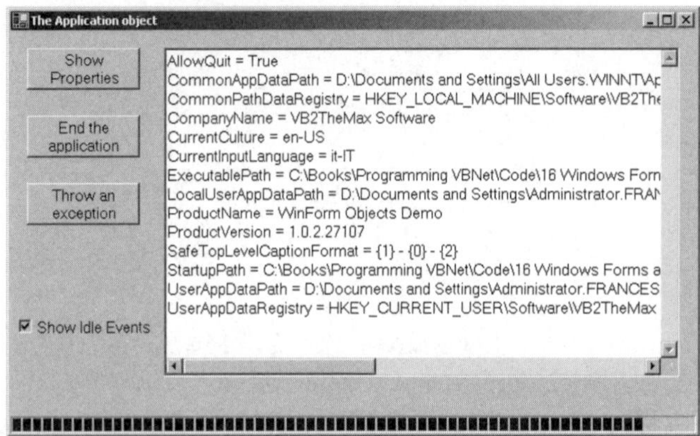

Figure 16-35. The demo program to test the Application object.

You can reach this information by using reflection methods, but the properties of the Application object are surely a handy shortcut. (You must use reflection methods for other attributes, such as AssemblyTitle and AssemblyDescription, but you rarely need to read them from inside the application.)

The Idle event can be useful for performing actions when the UI is idle. This event doesn't fire periodically, but only when the form engine has completed the processing of one or more messages in the message loop. This event is useful if you want to update variables or UI elements after every action performed by the end user. (See the next section, "The Cursor Object," for an example of this technique.)

The ApplicationExit event fires just before the application ends, so you can use it for cleanup chores. The event fires even if the application is ending because of a fatal error. Keep in mind that all windows have already been destroyed when this event fires, so you can display a message to the user only by using a message box, or you can store a message in the system log. Remember that all the Application object's events are shared events, so you must use the AddHandler command to set up an event handler for them.

Table 16-10 Members of the Application Object

Category	Name	VB6 Member	Description
Properties	CommonDataPath		The path of the application data that is shared among all users.
	CommonAppData-Registry		The Registry key of the application data that's shared among all users.
	CompanyName		The company name.
	CurrentCulture		The culture information about the current thread.
	CurrentInputLanguage		The current input language for the current thread.
	ExecutablePath	App.Path + EXEName	The complete path and filename of the executable.
	LocalUserAppDataPath		The path of the application data for a local (nonroaming) user.
	ProductName	App.Product-Name	The product name of the running application.
	ProductVersion	App.Major + Minor + Revision + Build	The version of the running application.
	StartupPath	App.Path	The path of the executable file that started the application.
	UserAppDataPath		The path of the application data of a roaming user.
	UserAppDataRegistry		The Registry key of the application data of a roaming user.
Methods	DoEvents	DoEvents	Processes all Windows messages in the queue.
	Exit	End	Closes all windows and terminates the application.
	ExitThread		Closes all windows running on the current thread.
	Run		Starts a message loop on the standard thread.
Events	ApplicationExit		Fires when the application is about to shut down, after all forms have been closed.
	Idle		Fires after the application has processed all the messages in the input queue and is entering the idle state.

Table 16-10 Members of the Application Object *(continued)*

Category	Name	VB6 Member	Description
	ThreadException		Fires when an unhandled thread exception occurs, and permits to continue or abort the application.
	ThreadExit		Fires when a thread is about to terminate. (If this is the one thread, this event fires before ApplicationExit.)

Global Error Handlers

The ThreadException event lets you leverage a powerful feature of Windows Forms, so it deserves a section of its own. To understand why this feature is so important, let's review what happens when an unhandled error occurs inside an event handler. In normal circumstances, the exception would be passed to the caller code, but an event procedure has no caller, so errors of this kind terminate the application. Visual Basic 6 developers are well aware of this issue and in fact are inclined to liberally furnish all event procedures with On Error statements. This technique is ugly and tends to decrease performance, but it's the only one that ensures a sufficient level of robustness.

The Application.ThreadException event fires whenever an unhandled exception is thrown on the current thread, so you can easily write a global error handler that protects all your forms from any unhandled errors. Your global handler can ignore the error, log it to a file, display a message box that asks the end user whether she wants to abort the application, send an e-mail message to the tech support group, and perform any other action you deem desirable. (See Figure 16-36.)

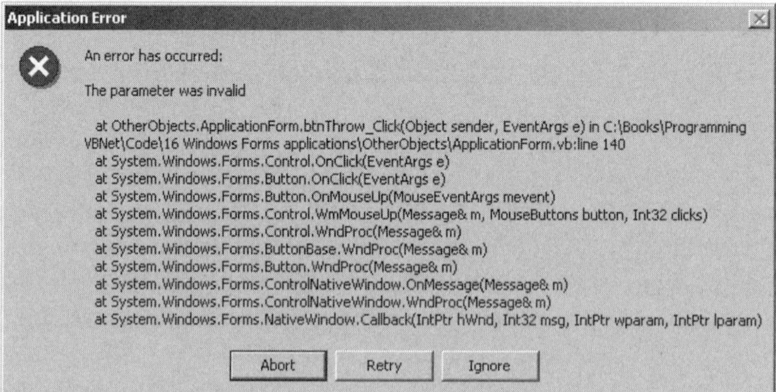

Figure 16-36. The message box shown by the global error handler in the demo application.

To implement this feature correctly, you must use a Sub Main procedure as the start-up object of your application and you must mark it with the STAThread attribute to set the threading model of the application to Single Thread Apartment (STA) mode. After you set up the ThreadException event, you can start the main form by using an Application.Run method, as shown in the following code:

```
Module MainModule
    <STAThread()> _
    Sub Main()
        ' Install the event handler.
        AddHandler Application.ThreadException, _
            AddressOf Application_ThreadException
        ' Run the start-up form.
        Application.Run(New ApplicationForm())
    End Sub

    ' This is the global error handler.
    Sub Application_ThreadException(ByVal sender As Object, _
        ByVal e As System.Threading.ThreadExceptionEventArgs)

        Try
            ' Prepare an informative message.
            Dim msg As String = _
                String.Format("An error has occurred:{0}{0}{1}{0}{0}{2}", _
                ControlChars.Cr, e.Exception.Message, e.Exception.StackTrace)
            ' Display it, asking whether the application should terminate.
            Dim result As DialogResult = _
                MessageBox.Show(msg, "Application Error", _
                MessageBoxButtons.AbortRetryIgnore, MessageBoxIcon.Error)
            ' End the application if the end user said so.
            If result = DialogResult.Abort Then
                Application.Exit()
            End If
        Catch
            ' If the message box couldn't be displayed (presumably because
            ' the Exception object wasn't available), try with a simpler
            ' message, and then close the application anyway.
            Try
                MessageBox.Show("The application will be terminated", _
                    "Fatal Error", MessageBoxButtons.OK, MessageBoxIcon.Error)
            Finally
                Application.Exit()
            End Try
        End Try
    End Sub
End Module
```

The global error handler serves all the unhandled exceptions of your application, including the most critical ones. For this reason, the code inside the handler should account for exceptional conditions—for example, the case when the e.Exception object isn't available or when it isn't possible to display a message box. (In the latter case, you might want to log the error to the system log or to a bug report file.)

> **Important** This feature clashes with the Visual Studio debugger, and global error handlers don't work well when the application runs inside Visual Studio. To see this feature in action, you should run the program using the Start Without Debugging command on the Debug menu (which corresponds to the Ctrl+F5 key combination) or run it from Windows Explorer or the command prompt.

The Cursor Object

The Cursor class has a dual purpose. Its static properties and methods allow you to control several features of the mouse cursor. Its constructor method lets you create a new mouse cursor, which you can later assign to the Mouse.Current static property or to the Cursor property of any control.

Static Properties and Methods

The Position property is the Point object that represents the position of the cursor. This property is similar to the form's MousePosition property, but it's expressed in screen coordinates, and more important, it can be written to. For example, the following code moves the mouse cursor to the center of the current form:

```
With Me.ClientRectangle
    ' The PointToScreen method converts from client to screen coordinates.
    Cursor.Position = Me.PointToScreen( _
        New Point(CInt(.Width / 2), CInt(.Height / 2)))
End With
```

The demo application takes advantage of the Application.Idle event to display the current mouse position in client coordinates. (See Figure 16-37.) This approach is extremely efficient because this event fires immediately after the form has processed a mouse move message:

```
Private Sub Application_Idle(ByVal sender As Object, ByVal e As EventArgs)
    lblStatus.Text = Me.PointToClient(Cursor.Position).ToString
End Sub
```

(By comparison, you had to set up a Timer control or trap the MouseMove event for all the controls on the form to achieve the same effect in Visual Basic 6.)

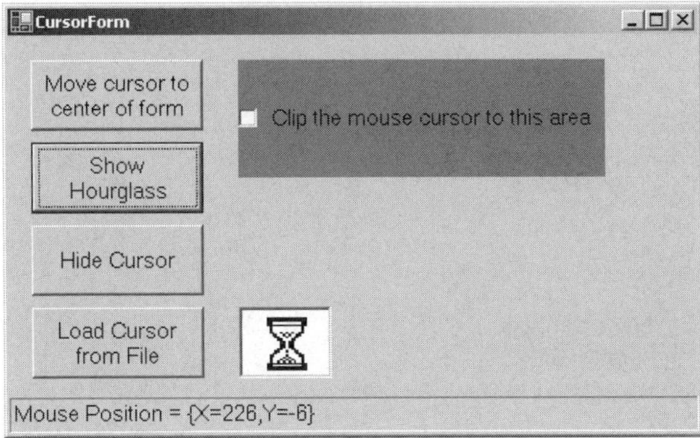

Figure 16-37. The demo application lets you test a few features of the Cursor class.

The Clip property is the rectangle within which the mouse cursor is confined, or its value is Nothing if the mouse can move over the entire screen. This rectangle is in screen coordinates, so you must do some conversions if you want to confine the mouse to an object on the form:

```
' Clip the mouse to the TextBox1 control's client area.
Cursor.Clip = TextBox1.RectangleToScreen(TextBox1.ClientRectangle)
⋮
' Free the mouse cursor.
Cursor.Clip = Nothing
```

The Current static property is the current cursor used for the mouse at the screen level, and therefore it broadly corresponds to the Screen.MouseCursor property in Visual Basic 6. You can set this property by using one of the standard cursors exposed by the Cursors type, as in this code:

```
' Show an hourglass cursor during a lengthy operation.
Cursor.Current = Cursors.WaitCursor
```

A problem with the preceding code is that the form restores its default cursor whenever the user moves or clicks the mouse, so setting the Cursor.Current property is rarely a good idea. A better approach is to set the Cursor property of the form or the individual control:

```
Me.Cursor = Cursors.WaitCursor
⋮
' Restore the default pointer.
Me.Cursor = Cursors.Default
```

The Cursors type exposes 28 different mouse cursors. You can see all of them by selecting any control and then clicking the down arrow beside the Cursor property in the Properties window. (See Figure 16-38.)

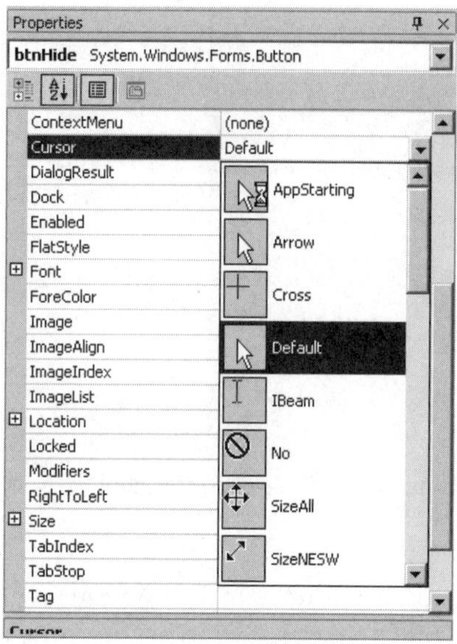

Figure 16-38. The settings for a control Cursor property.

The Hide and Show shared methods of the Cursor class let you control the visibility of the mouse cursor. You must call the Show method a number of times equal to the number of calls to the Hide method to make the mouse cursor appear again.

Creating New Cursors

You can also instantiate new Cursor objects—for example, by loading a cursor from a .cur file. (The Cursor class doesn't support animated cursors in .ani files.) You just have to pass the name of the file to the class constructor, as in this line of code:

```
Dim c As New Cursor("c:\winnt\cursors\3dsmove.cur")
```

You can also use an overloaded variation of the constructor to load the cursor from a stream, which is useful if a file contains multiple cursors.

After you create a cursor, you can assign it to the Cursor.Current property or to the Cursor property of a control. It's important, however, that you destroy the cursor in an orderly fashion when you don't use it any longer—for example, when you restore the default cursor shape for the control:

```
' Create a new cursor from the file.
Dim c As New Cursor("c:\winnt\cursors\3dsmove.cur")
```

```
' Assign it to the form.
Me.Cursor = c
' Perform a lengthy operation.
:
' Restore the default cursor.
Me.Cursor = Cursors.Default
' Destroy the cursor loaded from the file.
c.Dispose
```

Finally, you can draw the cursor on a Graphics object by using the Draw or DrawStretched method. For example, the demo application uses this code to display a cursor loaded from disk:

```
' Get the device context from the target PictureBox control.
Dim gr As Graphics = PictureBox1.CreateGraphics
' Clear the background using white color.
gr.Clear(Color.White)
' Draw the cursor, stretching it to cover the entire client area.
c.DrawStretched(gr, PictureBox1.ClientRectangle)
' Release allocated resources.
gr.Dispose()
```

The SendKeys Class

This class replaces the command of the same name that you use under Visual Basic 6. With its Send shared method, you can send one or more keystrokes to the active application—for example:

```
' Send the V and B keystrokes, followed by the Enter key.
SendKeys.Send("VB~")
' Send the HOME, Shift+END, and DEL keys.
' (If sent to a text field, this sequence deletes the current line.)
SendKeys.Send("{HOME}+{END}{DEL}")
' Insert 40 asterisks, and then move the caret to the first asterisk.
SendKeys.SendWait("{* 40}{LEFT 40}")
```

The SendWait method works in the same fashion except that it waits until the application processes all the keystrokes:

```
' Send the Ctrl+HOME, Ctrl+Shift+END, and DEL keys.
' (Clears the contents of the current text box window.)
SendKeys.SendWait("^{HOME}^+{END}{DEL}")
```

See the .NET Framework SDK documentation for more details about the syntax you can use to specify the keystroke sequence.

The third and last method, Flush, forces the processing of all the Windows messages (keystrokes and mouse actions) currently in the message queue:

```
SendKeys.Flush()
```

An interesting detail is that managed code isn't allowed to activate other applications, so you can't use the SendKeys class to send keystrokes to another program using .NET methods exclusively. A solution to this problem is to use the FindWindow and SetForegroundWindow API calls to activate the other application before sending it the keystroke, as in the following reusable routine:

```
Private Declare Function FindWindow Lib "user32" Alias "FindWindowA" _
    (ByVal lpClassName As String, ByVal lpWindowName As String) As Integer
Private Declare Function SetForegroundWindow Lib "user32" _
    Alias "SetForegroundWindow" (ByVal hwnd As Integer) As Integer

Sub SendKeysToApplication(ByVal appTitle As String, ByVal keys As String)
    ' Find the other application.
    Dim hWnd As Integer = FindWindow(Nothing, appTitle)
    ' Exit if not found.
    If hWnd <= 0 Then
        MessageBox.Show("Application not found", "Error", _
            MessageBoxButtons.OK, MessageBoxIcon.Error)
        Exit Sub
    End If
    ' Make it the active application.
    SetForegroundWindow(hWnd)
    ' Send the keys and wait.
    SendKeys.SendWait(keys)
End Sub
```

For example, you can send keys to an instance of Notepad that hasn't loaded any text file yet with this line of code:

```
SendKeysToApplication("Untitled - Notepad", "VB~")
```

The Help Class

This class encapsulates the HTML Help 1.0 engine and lets you display the index, the search page, or a specific topic in an HTML file in HTML Help format, in a compiled help file (.chm) authored with the HTML Help Workshop, or in some third-party tool.

This class exposes two shared methods, and you can't create an instance of this class. The ShowHelpIndex method displays the index of the specified help file, as in this code:

```
' The first argument is a Control object that works as the
' parent for the help dialog box.
Help.ShowHelpIndex(Me, "c:\myhelpfile.chm")
```

(You can also use a URL that uses forward slashes as separators.) The other method, ShowHelp, is overloaded to provide access to different portions of the help document:

```
' Display the contents of the help file.
Help.ShowHelp(Me, "c:\myhelpfile.chm")
' Display the index page of the help file.
Help.ShowHelp(Me, "c:\myhelpfile.chm", HelpNavigator.Index)
' Display the search page of the help file.
Help.ShowHelp(Me, "c:\myhelpfile.chm", HelpNavigator.Find)
' Display the help page for a specific keyword.
Help.ShowHelp(Me, "c:\myhelpfile.chm", "mykeyword")
' Display the help page for the specific topic #123.
Help.ShowHelp(Me, "c:\myhelpfile.chm", HelpNavigator.Topic, 123)
```

The Help class replaces the Help Common Dialog, which isn't supported any longer. In Chapter 17, you'll learn about the HelpProvider control, which encapsulates the Help object to automatically display help when the F1 key is pressed at a time that a control has the input focus.

At the end of this long chapter, you know enough to build great and highly functional Windows Forms applications. However, I haven't discussed yet all the controls you can use and how you can create eye-catching graphic effects with the classes in the GDI+ portion of the Framework. These are the topics of the next two chapters.

Front
Top
Left
Back

17

Controls

To create great Windows Forms applications, you need to be familiar with several areas of the .NET Framework, not just the Form object. For example, you have to learn more about the controls in the System.Windows.Forms namespace and know how to create new custom controls, should the provided controls be insufficient for your needs.

Windows Forms Controls

Unfortunately, I don't have space in this book to dissect all the controls in the Windows Forms package because they expose just too many properties, methods, and events. On the other hand, most of these controls are just improved versions of the controls you've worked with for years, so I decided to provide only a brief description of what has changed or has been added.

The TextBox Control

The TextBox control supports many new properties and methods, and several of the old properties have been renamed:

- The TextChanged event replaces the Change event.
- The ReadOnly property replaces the Locked property. (The Locked property now has a different meaning: it prevents controls from being accidentally moved at design time.)
- You can set the new CharacterCasing property to Upper or Lower to automatically convert characters typed by the end user, pasted from the Clipboard, or assigned from code.

- The SelectedText, SelectionStart, and SelectionLength properties replace SelText, SelStart, and SelLength. You can also select part or all of the contents by using the Select(start, length) and SelectAll methods.
- You can perform copy and paste operations by using the new Clear, Copy, Cut, and Paste methods.
- You can append text to a TextBox by using the new AppendText method, which is much faster than using the & operator with the Text property.
- The new Modified property returns True if the TextBox contents have been modified. If the CanUndo property is True, you can revert to the previous value with the Undo method or clear undo data by using the ClearUndo method.
- The TextAlign property replaces the Alignment property and can be used to align text left (the default), right, or center.
- You can set the AutoSize property to True to have the size of the control automatically reflect the current font size.
- You can decide whether Enter and Tab keys inside a multiline TextBox should insert a character instead of performing their usual actions of pushing the default button or moving to the next field, by assigning True to the AcceptReturns and AcceptTabs properties.
- By default, multiline TextBox controls work in word processing mode—that is, with word wrapping enabled, even if the ScrollBars property is set to Both; you must explicitly set the new WordWrap property to False to make the horizontal scroll bar appear and have the control work like an editor.
- You can use the Lines property to arrange for the contents of multiline TextBox controls to be read and assigned as an array of individual strings.
- The ScrollToCaret method ensures that the insertion point or selected text is in the visible portion of a TextBox control.

The Label Control

The Label control can now display an image and has a more flexible way of positioning the caption (which now corresponds to the Text property, as for all other controls):

- The TextAlignment property replaces Alignment and can be one of nine possible values, such as TopLeft, MiddleCenter, and so on.
- The FlatStyle property replaces Appearance and provides a flat or 3-D appearance.
- The PreferredWidth and PreferredHeight properties return the optimal size for the control, given its current text and font.
- The new Image property can be assigned the image to be displayed in the Label control. Or you can assign an ImageList control to the ImageList property and the index of the image to the ImageIndex property. You control the position of the image in the control by using the ImageAlign property (nine possible values).

You can set all the image properties from the Properties window. To delete an image assigned at design time, right-click on the property name and select the Reset menu command.

The LinkLabel Control

This new control is a Label control that can contain one or more hyperlink areas. You can choose from two ways to define a hyperlink inside a LinkLabel control. In the simplest case, you assign a LinkArea object to the property with the same name and define its underline behavior by using the LinkBehavior property:

```
LinkLabel1.Text = "Visit the www.vb2themax.com site"
' Make the URL a hyperlink. (Arguments are start, length.)
LinkLabel1.LinkArea = New LinkArea(10, 17)
' Underline the URL only when the mouse is over it.
LinkLabel1.LinkBehavior = LinkBehavior.HoverUnderline
```

If you have multiple links, you have to add each of them to the Links collection programmatically because you can't do it from the Properties window. After you build the collection, you can further read or modify properties of individual LinkLabel.Link objects by means of their Enabled and Visited Boolean properties:

```
LinkLabel1.Text = "Visit our Home Page, or jump to the document"
' Make "Home Page" a link.
LinkLabel1.Links.Add(10, 9, "home")
' Make "document" a link.
LinkLabel1.Links.Add(36, 8, "doc")
' Mark the Home Page document as visited.
LinkLabel1.Links(0).Visited = True
```

The third argument of the Add method can be any string or object that identifies that specific link. This value is then exposed to the LinkClicked event as a property of the LinkLabel.Link object:

```
Private Sub LinkLabel1_LinkClicked(ByVal sender As Object, _
    ByVal e As LinkLabelLinkClickedEventArgs) Handles LinkLabel1.LinkClicked

    Select Case e.Link.LinkData
        Case "home"
            MessageBox.Show("Jumping to home page")
        Case "doc"
            MessageBox.Show("Jumping to document")
    End Select

    ' Mark the link as visited, and disable it.
    e.Link.Visited = True
    e.Link.Enabled = False
End Sub
```

You can control the colors used for hyperlinks with the ActiveLinkColor, VisitedLinkColor, and DisabledLinkColor properties. The LinkLabel control (see Figure 17-1) inherits all the remaining properties from the Label control, including the ability to align text and display images.

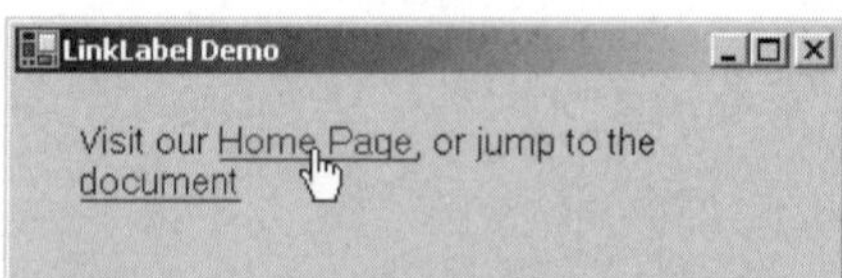

Figure 17-1. The LinkLabel control, with two link areas in it.

The CheckBox, RadioButton, and Button Controls

These three controls inherit from the same ButtonBase class, so they have several properties and features in common:

- The Text property replaces Caption. As I mentioned before, you can align the text in nine different ways by using the TextAlign property.
- The FlatStyle property replaces Appearance and provides a flat or 3-D appearance.
- You have full control of ForeColor and BackColor properties, even for Button controls.

- You can display icons by using the Image property, align them with the ImageAlign property, or load them from an ImageList control with the ImageList and ImageIndex properties. You can also assign an image to the BackgroundImage property to create a textured button. (See Figure 17-2.)
- The Appearance property replaces Style and determines whether a CheckBox or a RadioButton control is displayed as a button.

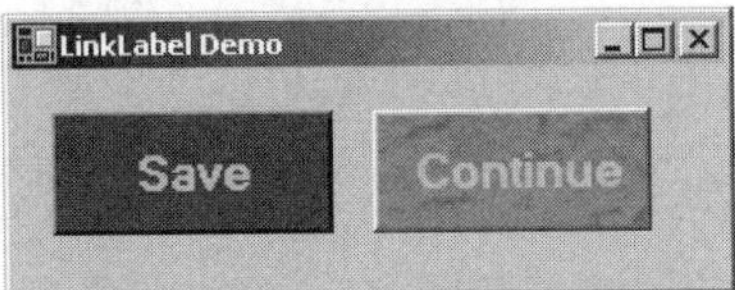

Figure 17-2. You can create a colored or textured background for all controls inherited from the ButtonBase class.

The CheckBox Control

The new CheckBox control works much like it does under Visual Basic 6, with only a few noteworthy differences:

- The AutoCheck property is True (the default) if the control automatically toggles its state when clicked. You can set it to False to get more control over when the end user can change the state of the control.
- The CheckAlign property lets you select among nine possible positions of the check box. You can combine this property with the TextAlign property to create many different visual variations. (Note that if the Style property is set to System, you can move the check box only to the MiddleLeft or MiddleRight position.)
- The ThreeState property determines whether the control should have two or three states. If the property is False, you should set or read the state of the control with the Checked property; if True, you should use the CheckState property instead. By default, the control has only two states. (The Value property isn't supported any longer.)

Depending on the value of the ThreeState property, you use three different events to react to user actions: the CheckedChanged, CheckStateChanged, and Click events. (They fire in this order.) The only case in which only the latter two events fire occurs when AutoCheck and ThreeState are both True and user clicks bring the CheckState property from Checked to Indeterminate without changing the Checked property.

Not all combinations of the new properties make sense. For example, when setting the Appearance property to Button, you should set ThreeState to False and ensure that the FlatStyle property is set to System; otherwise, the button won't appear to rise when it's clicked a second time.

The RadioButton Control

Not counting the properties inherited from ButtonBase, the only relevant new properties of this control are the Checked, CheckAlign, and AutoCheck properties, which have the same meaning that they have for the CheckBox control.

You can detect a change in state by using the CheckedChanged event or the Click event. The only new method is PerformClick, which simulates a click. (Under Visual Basic 6, you have to programmatically set the now-unsupported Value property to True to achieve this effect.)

The Button Control

Except for the new properties inherited from ButtonBase, the Button control is virtually identical to the old CommandButton control. As I explained in Chapter 16, the Default and Cancel properties have been replaced by the AcceptButton and CancelButton properties of the parent form. The Value property is gone as well.

The only new method for this control is PerformClick, which indirectly fires the Click event.

The ListBox Control

The ListBox control has been completely redesigned in its programmatic interface and has become much more powerful.

Adding Elements

For starters, the new Items property, which gathers all the elements in the control, is an ICollection object, so you can manipulate its elements using the familiar Add, AddRange, Insert, Remove, and Clear methods. (See Chapter 9 for more information about the ICollection interface.)

```
With ListBox1.Items
    .Clear()                    ' Start with a clean collection.
    .Add("One")                 ' Add two items.
    .Add("Two")
    .Insert(0, "Zero")          ' Insert before element at index 0.
End With

Dim o As Object
For Each o In ListBox1.Items
    Debug.Write(o & " ")       ' => Zero One Two
Next
```

You can add any object to this collection, not just strings. Let's make an example using our usual Person class:

```
Class Person
    Public ID As Integer
    Public FirstName As String
    Public LastName As String

    Sub New(ByVal first As String, ByVal last As String, ByVal id As Integer)
        Me.FirstName = first
        Me.LastName = last
        Me.ID = id
    End Sub

    Overrides Function ToString() As String
        Return FirstName & " " & LastName
    End Function

    ReadOnly Property ReverseName() As String
        Get
            Return LastName & ", " & FirstName
        End Get
    End Property
End Class
```

The following code loads three Person objects in the control, which will display their names by calling the ToString method:

```
ListBox1.Items.Add(New Person("Joe", "Doe", 2))
ListBox1.Items.Add(New Person("Robert", "Smith", 1))
ListBox1.Items.Add(New Person("Ann", "Doe", 3))
```

You can change this default behavior by assigning the name of any property to DisplayMember. (You must make this assignment *before* loading values into the ListBox, however.)

```
' Display names in "LastName, FirstName" format.
ListBox1.DisplayMember = "ReverseName"
```

The ItemData property isn't supported, but you see that the ability to store objects makes it superfluous. In fact, you just have to convert the items in the control to their native type and then extract any property you need:

```
' Get the ID of the first Person element in the list.
Dim id As Integer = DirectCast(ListBox1.Items(0), Person).ID
```

Working with Selected Items

The way you test whether an item is selected has changed as well. For a single-selection ListBox, you can retrieve the index of the selection by using the new

SelectedIndex property, which replaces the ListIndex property. Or you can use the new SelectedItem property, which returns the selected item or Nothing if no element is selected:

```
' Get the ID of the selected Person element.
Dim id As Integer = DirectCast(ListBox1.SelectedItem, Person).ID
```

You create a multiple-selection ListBox by setting its SelectionMode property to MultiSimple or MultiExtended. (This property replaces the MultiSelect property in Visual Basic 6.) You can choose from three ways to detect which items are selected. If you want the actual objects that are selected in the control, you use the SelectedItems collection:

```
' Print the ID of selected Person elements.
Dim p As Person
For Each p In ListBox1.SelectedItems
    Debug.WriteLine(p.ID)
Next
```

If you're interested in just the index of selected items, you can iterate over the SelectedIndices collection. For example, you can remedy the lack of the Sel-Count property as follows:

```
Dim selectedCount As Integer = ListBox1.SelectedIndices.Count
```

You can also retrieve the selection state of an item by using the GetSelected method, which works like the now-unsupported Selected property:

```
' Check whether the last element in the ListBox is selected.
Dim state As Boolean = ListBox1.GetSelected(ListBox1.Items.Count - 1)
```

You can change the selection state of an element by using the SetSelected method, which is the only way to programmatically select or deselect an element because you can't add or remove elements from the SelectedItems and SelectedIndices collections:

```
ListBox1.SetSelected(0, True)      ' Select the first element.
ListBox1.SetSelected(1, False)     ' Deselect the second element.
```

When the SelectedIndex property changes, the control raises a SelectedIndex-Changed event. You should react to user action using this event because the Click event now doesn't fire if the user is moving the selection by means of arrow keys.

Other Properties and Methods

A ListBox control can display multiple columns, but you don't use the Columns property as you do in Visual Basic 6. Instead, you must set the MultiColumn property to True and then assign a value (in pixels) to the ColumnWidth property. Or you can use the default 0 value for the latter property and let the control find out the most appropriate value. (You can then read ColumnWidth to find out which column width is being used.)

The ScrollAlwaysVisible property determines whether a vertical scroll bar is always visible. If the property is True, the scroll bar will be visible but disabled if all the elements in the control are visible. You can also display a horizontal scroll bar so that the user can read elements wider than the control's client area. The horizontal scroll bar becomes visible only if there is at least one element wider than the visible area.

The UseTabStops property can be set to True to let the control expand tab characters embedded in the elements.

The BeginUpdate and EndUpdate methods suspend and reactivate repainting of the control; they can reduce flickering and speed execution. These methods were missing under Visual Basic 6, and developers could remedy the problems these methods address only by using the LockWindowUpdate API function:

```
ListBox1.BeginUpdate
' Add many elements here.
⋮
ListBox1.EndUpdate
```

The FindString and FindStringExact methods let you quickly find an item in the list:

```
' Find the first element that begins with "Ba".
Dim index As Integer = ListBox1.FindString("Ba")
If index = -1 Then
    Debug.WriteLine("Not found")
Else
    ' Find the "Smith" element (exact search) that follows the previous one.
    index = ListBox1.FindStringExact("Smith", index)
End If
```

You can also perform searches directly on the Items collection by using its Contains and IndexOf methods.

Finally, two methods help you understand which element is under the mouse cursor: IndexFromPoint returns the index of the element under a given point specified in the control's client coordinates, whereas GetItemRectangle returns the rectangle that corresponds to an element with a given index.

Owner-Draw ListBox Controls

The most exciting new feature of the ListBox control—as well as the ComboBox control and the MenuItem object—is the complete control it gives developers over how individual elements are rendered. Exercising that control isn't straightforward, however—that it requires familiarity with GDI+ objects and methods is one complication. But drawing elements is now surely easier than it is under Visual Basic 6. (Creating custom ListBox and ComboBox controls with previous language versions requires a good amount of subclassing wizardry.)

The key to this new feature is the DrawMode property, used together with the ItemHeight property and the DrawItem event. To create an owner-draw ListBox, you set its DrawMode property to OwnerDrawFixed, set the ItemHeight property to the height of individual items (in pixels), and fill the control with all your items, as you would do with a regular ListBox. For example, the following routine uses reflection methods to fill the control with the names of all known colors (which the Color class exposes as shared properties):

```
Private Sub FillListBoxWithColors()
    ' Make the ListBox owner-draw.
    ListBox1.DrawMode = DrawMode.OwnerDrawFixed
    ListBox1.ItemHeight = 24

    ' Avoid flickering.
    ListBox1.BeginUpdate()
    ListBox1.Items.Clear()

    ' Create a list of all the properties in the Color class.
    Dim pi As Reflection.PropertyInfo
    For Each pi In GetType(Color).GetProperties( _
        Reflection.BindingFlags.Static Or Reflection.BindingFlags.Public)
        ' Add the name of the property (that is, the color) to the ListBox.
        ListBox1.Items.Add(pi.Name)
    Next
    ' Now display the result.
    ListBox1.EndUpdate()
End Sub
```

An owner-draw ListBox object fires a DrawItem event just before displaying each element. Your job is to trap this event and draw the element on the ListBox control's surface. You decide how to render the element by checking a few properties of the second argument passed to the event: Index is the index of the element in question; State is a bit-code value that lets you determine the element's state, such as whether the element is selected or disabled. Other properties tell you where the item should be rendered (Bounds) and what its attributes are (Font, ForeColor, BackColor). All the graphic operations must be performed on the Graphics object exposed by the property of the same name. The following procedure completes the preceding example and actually displays all the colors in the ListBox object, as shown in Figure 17-3:

```
Private Sub ListBox1_DrawItem(ByVal sender As Object, _
    ByVal e As DrawItemEventArgs) Handles ListBox1.DrawItem

    ' Get the rectangle to be drawn.
    Dim rect As Rectangle = e.Bounds

    ' Draw the background of the proper color.
    If (e.State And DrawItemState.Selected) Then
        ' Fill the rectangle with the highlight system color.
        e.Graphics.FillRectangle(SystemBrushes.Highlight, rect)
    Else
        ' Else, fill the rectangle with the Window system color.
        e.Graphics.FillRectangle(SystemBrushes.Window, rect)
    End If

    ' Get the color of the item to be drawn.
    Dim colorName As String = ListBox1.Items(e.Index)
    ' Build a brush of that color.
    Dim b As New SolidBrush(Color.FromName(colorName))

    ' Shrink the rectangle by some pixels.
    rect.Inflate(-16, -2)
    ' Draw the rectangle interior with the color.
    e.Graphics.FillRectangle(b, rect)
    ' Draw the rectangle outline with a black pen.
    e.Graphics.DrawRectangle(Pens.Black, rect)

    ' Decide the color of the text (black or white).
    Dim b2 As Brush
    If CInt(b.Color.R) + CInt(b.Color.G) + CInt(b.Color.B) > 128 * 3 Then
        b2 = Brushes.Black
    Else
        b2 = Brushes.White
    End If

    ' Draw the name of the color using the default font.
    e.Graphics.DrawString(colorName, e.Font, b2, rect.X + 4, rect.Y + 2)

    ' Destroy the custom brush.
    ' (Don't dispose of b2 because it is a system brush.)
    b.Dispose()
End Sub
```

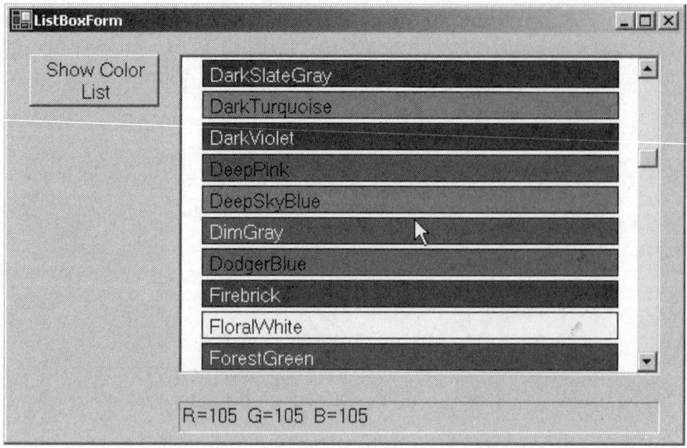

Figure 17-3. An owner-draw ListBox control.

The DrawMode property of the ListBox, ComboBox, and MainMenu controls supports the OwnerDrawVariable setting, which lets you create elements with varying height. When such a control is created, it fires one MeasureItem event for each element. You're expected to return the height of each element, given its index.

If you create owner-draw ListBox controls with the HorizontalScrollBar property set to True, you should also assign a suitable value in pixels to the HorizontalExtent property to inform the control about the width of the largest element.

The CheckedListBox Control

The CheckedListBox control is a variant of the ListBox control that displays a check box to the left of each element. (See Figure 17-4.) In Visual Basic 6, you can create this control by setting a ListBox control's Style property to 1-Checkboxes.

The CheckedListBox control inherits from ListBox, so it exposes the same properties, methods, and events. As its name implies, this control lets users check one or more items. However, the CheckedListBox control doesn't support multiple selected items, so you use the SelectionMode property only to decide whether one or no elements can be selected. For the same reason, the SelectedItems and SelectedIndices collections have been replaced by two collections, CheckedItems and CheckedIndices.

The CheckedListBox control exposes two new properties: ThreeDCheckBoxes can be set to True to display three-dimensional check boxes, whereas CheckOnClick can be set to True to let users check or uncheck elements by means of a single click. The default value for both properties is False.

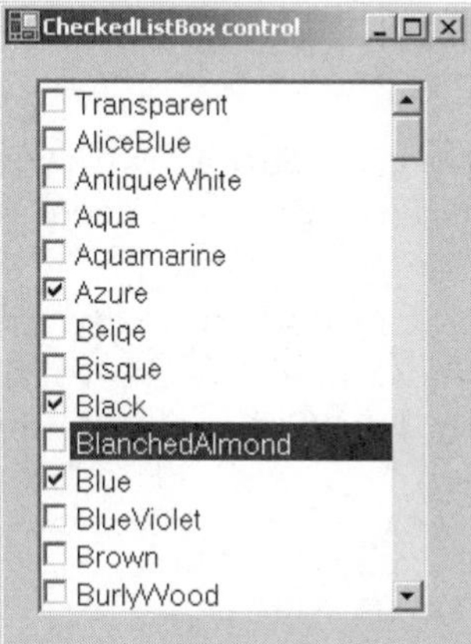

Figure 17-4. A CheckedListBox with the ThreeDCheckBoxes property set to True. When an element is checked or unchecked, the control fires an ItemCheck event, as it does under Visual Basic 6.

The individual check boxes can be in three possible states, like a CheckBox control whose ThreeState property is set to True. However, a click on the check box can only select or clear it, and the Indeterminate state can be set only by means of code, when you use the SetItemCheckState method. The control also exposes the GetItemCheckState, GetItemChecked, and SetItemChecked methods to read and write the state of individual check boxes. To iterate over all checked elements, you can use the CheckedItems and CheckedIndices collections, as I mentioned previously.

The ComboBox Control

Both the ComboBox and the ListBox controls derive from the same class, ListControl; this fact explains why these controls have so many properties in common. Moreover, because a ComboBox also has an editable area, it exposes many of the members that you can find in a TextBox control, such as the SelectedText, SelectionStart, SelectionLength, and MaxLength properties; the SelectAll method; and the TextChanged event. Here are a few properties peculiar to the ComboBox control:

- The Visual Basic 6 Style property has been renamed DropDownStyle (can be DropDown, Simple, or DropDownList).
- The MaxDropDownItems property specifies the maximum number of items to be displayed in the drop-down area, whereas the DropDownWidth property specifies the width of the drop-down area. (Values less than the control's width have no effect.)

- The DroppedDown property can be set to True or False to programmatically open or close the drop-down area.

As with the old Visual Basic 6 control, you get a DropDown event when the drop-down area opens. You get a SelectedIndexChanged event when a new element is selected.

The ComboBox control supports the DrawMode property and the DrawItem event, so you can create a user-draw ComboBox control that displays icons, items in a different color, and so on. For this reason, the ImageCombo control isn't supported any longer.

Provider Controls

The Windows Forms architecture is quite extensible. For example, you can create so-called *provider controls*, which add new properties to all the controls on the form. The Windows Forms namespace includes three such controls: ToolTip, ErrorProvider, and HelpProvider.

The ToolTip Control

The ToolTip control enables any control on a form to display a ToolTip when the mouse hovers over it.

The ToolTip control isn't visible at run time, so it appears in the designer's component tray area. This action creates a new control named ToolTip1. If you now select the control, you'll see the few properties that it exposes at design time: InitialDelay, AutoPopDelay, ReshowDelay, and AutomaticDelay. (You can read a short description of each in the Properties window.) In most cases, you can leave them at their default value.

If you next select another control on the form, you'll see that a new property is now visible in the Properties window: ToolTip on ToolTip1. (All the provider controls add properties whose names are in the "*propername* on *controlname*" format.) You can assign this property at design time the same way you used to assign the ToolTipText property under Visual Basic 6.

You see the difference from previous language versions when you have to assign this property in code. In fact, the new property doesn't truly belong to the control associated with the ToolTip; instead, it's just a string that's stored inside the ToolTip control.

In general, all provider controls expose a pair of methods for each of the properties they provide to other controls. The names of these methods are Get*propertyname* and Set*propertyname*, and they follow a similar syntax:

```
' Assign a ToolTip to the TextBox1 control.
ToolTip1.SetToolTip(TextBox1, "Enter the name of the product")
' Read it back.
Debug.WriteLine(ToolTip1.GetToolTip(TextBox1))
```

All provider controls expose the CanExtend method, which lets you test whether a control of a given type can be extended using the new properties (only the ToolTip property in this specific case). This method is useful when you're writing generic routines:

```
' Clear the ToolTip for all the controls on this form.
Dim ctrl As Control
For Each ctrl In Me.Controls
    If ToolTip1.CanExtend(ctrl) Then ToolTip1.SetToolTip(ctrl, "")
Next
```

The ErrorProvider Control

The ErrorProvider control lets you implement Windows Forms applications that use a validation method now familiar to all users who spend their time on the Internet. Typical Internet applications validate all the controls on the form when the user clicks the OK or Save button, and they display a red icon (or some other icon) near all the controls that failed the validation. This approach to validation leaves end users free to skip among fields and fill them in the order they prefer.

You can drop an ErrorProvider control on a form and then set its few properties in the Properties window: BlinkStyle tells whether the icon should blink; BlinkRate is the blink frequency in milliseconds; Icon is of course the icon that will be displayed beside each control that contains an invalid value. All the controls use the same icon, but you can use multiple ErrorProvider controls on the same form to provide different icons for different types of errors.

The ErrorProvider control adds two properties to controls on forms. (See Figure 17-5.) IconAlignment tells where the icon should be displayed, and IconPadding is the distance from the control's edge. In most cases, the default values are OK.

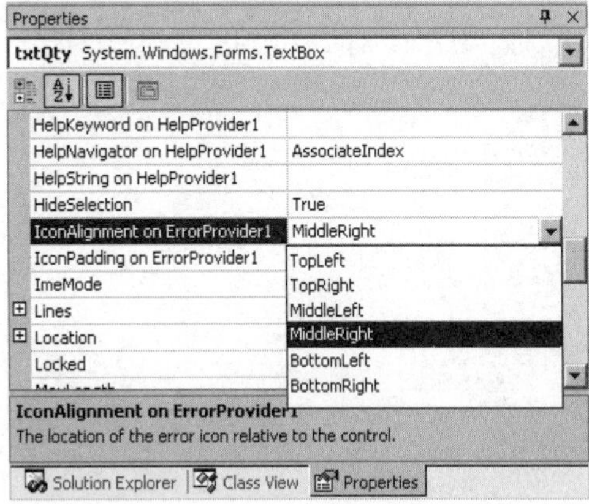

Figure 17-5. The properties added by the HelpProvider and ErrorProvider controls.

You actually display an error icon beside a control by using the ErrorProvider's SetError method, which takes a reference to the control and an error description that will be used as a ToolTip for the icon itself. You hide the icon by calling SetError again with a null string argument. The following code is behind the simple form you see in Figure 17-6:

```
Private Sub btnOK_Click(ByVal sender As System.Object, _
    ByVal e As System.EventArgs) Handles btnOK.Click

    ' Assume it's OK to close the form.
    Me.DialogResult = DialogResult.OK
    ' Clear all error icons.
    ErrorProvider1.SetError(txtProduct, "")
    ErrorProvider1.SetError(txtQty, "")

    ' Check that first field contains something.
    If txtProduct.Text = "" Then
        ErrorProvider1.SetError(txtProduct, "Must enter a product name")
        Me.DialogResult = DialogResult.None
    End If

    Try
        ' Attempt to get a valid quantity in second field (might throw).
        Dim qty As Integer = CInt(txtQty.Text)
        ' Throw a generic error if out of range.
        If qty < 1 Or qty > 100 Then Throw New Exception()
    Catch
        ' Regardless of the exception type, use the same error message.
        ErrorProvider1.SetError(txtQty, "Enter a valid number in range 1-100")
        Me.DialogResult = DialogResult.None
    End Try

    ' Close the form only if validation passed.
    ' (This line isn't really required if this is a dialog box.)
    If Me.DialogResult = DialogResult.OK Then Me.Close()
End Sub
```

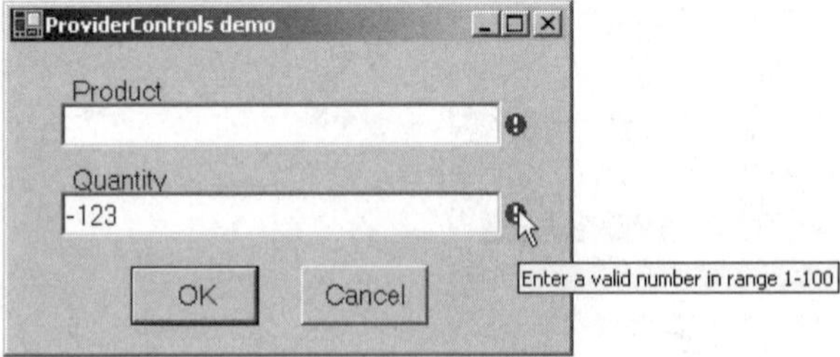

Figure 17-6. The ErrorProvider control in action.

The HelpProvider Control

The HelpProvider control works as a bridge between your program and the Help class so that you can display either simple help messages or more complex help pages when the user presses the F1 key and the focus is on a control in your form. (Review Chapter 16 for more information about the Help class.)

The only property of the HelpProvider control is HelpNamespace, which should be assigned the name of the compiled Help file (.chm) or raw HTML file. The HelpProvider control adds three properties to each control on your form. (See Figure 17-5.)

- The HelpNavigator property tells what kind of action must be performed when the end user presses the F1 key. It can be one of the following enumerated values: Find, Index, TableOfContents, Topic, KeywordIndex, and AssociateIndex.
- The HelpKeyword property specifies the keyword or the topic to be searched.
- The HelpString property is a short message that is displayed in a ToolTip-like window when the user presses the F1 key. (See Figure 17-7.) This property is used only if HelpKeyword is left blank.

Figure 17-7. The pop-up message produced by the HelpString property of the HelpProvider control.

In most cases, you don't need to assign these properties in code. But if you must, you can do so by using the SetHelpNavigator, SetHelpKeyword, and SetHelpString methods. You can leave the HelpNamespace property blank if you use just the HelpString property and never access an actual help file.

The Splitter Control

The Splitter control makes it incredibly easy to create splitter bars, that is, those dividers that you use to partition the space on a form among different controls.

A minor problem with this control is that it is somewhat tricky to change the layout of a form once you have created it, so you should think long and hard about what controls you want to have on the form and how they should be arranged. Let's take as an example the form visible in Figure 17-8, which contains a ListBox, a TextBox, a PictureBox, and two Splitter controls. The following list shows the right sequence for building the form's layout:

1. Drop the ListBox control on the form, and dock it to the left border.
2. Drop the first Splitter control; since the default value for its Dock property is Left, it will automatically stick to the ListBox.
3. Drop the TextBox control in the unoccupied area of the form, and dock it to the top border; set its Multiline property to True, and make it taller than its default height.
4. Drop the second Splitter control in the available area of the form. It will dock to the left, so you have to change its Dock property to Top so that it sticks to the bottom border of the TextBox.
5. Finally, drop the PictureBox in the empty area on the form, and set its Dock property to Fill.

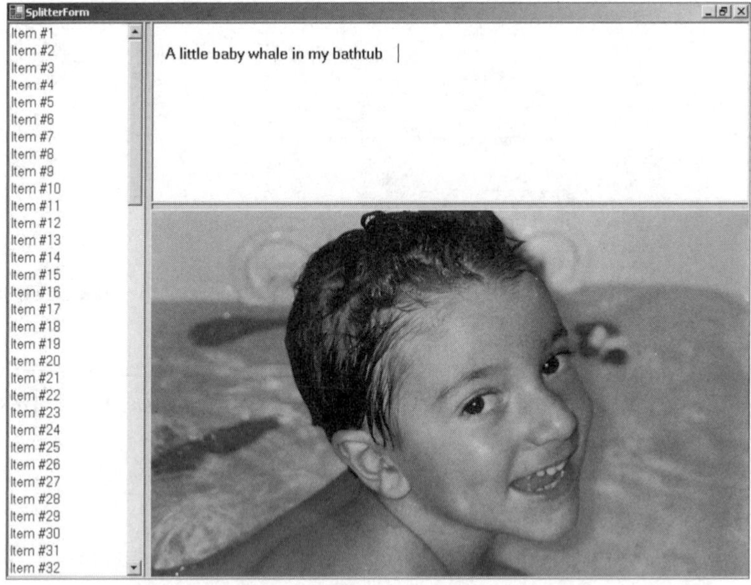

Figure 17-8. A form with two Splitter controls.

Now you can run the program and check that the controls resize correctly when you drag the splitter bars.

For more complex layouts, you can drop Panel controls on the form's surface and use them as containers for other controls. You can set the Dock and Anchor properties of controls inside each panel to achieve many different effects.

You can set the minimum and maximum sizes of controls being resized by means of the Splitter's MinSize and MinExtra properties. The former specifies the minimum size of the docked control; the latter, the minimum size of the part of the form that was empty when you dropped the Splitter. For example, in the case of the vertical Splitter in Figure 17-8, MinSize is the minimum width of the ListBox control to its left, whereas MinExtra is the minimum width of the TextBox and PictureBox to its right.

At run time, you can use the Splitter's Move event to determine when the splitter bar has been moved, and you can check the position of the splitter by using the SplitPosition property.

Common Dialog Controls

The Windows Forms namespace contains six controls that replace the functionality of the CommonDialog control, which you can find in previous language versions. In this section, I'll quickly explain how you can use these controls. (I assume that you're familiar with the corresponding Visual Basic 6 control; if this isn't the case, please refer to my *Programming Microsoft Visual Basic 6*, provided on the companion CD.)

These controls have very little in common with one another, and this is presumably the reason Microsoft decided to split the original CommonDialog control. In practice, these are the only members that all of them expose:

- The ShowDialog method, which brings up the dialog box and returns DialogResult.OK if the user confirmed the action, or DialogResult.Cancel if the user canceled it
- The ShowHelp property, which can be set to True to display a Help button
- The HelpRequest event, which fires if the end user asks for help
- The Reset method, which brings all properties back to their default value

The OpenFileDialog Control

This control shows an Open File dialog box. Instead of setting the bit-coded Flags property, as you do under Visual Basic 6, you can count on self-describing Boolean properties, such as CheckFileExists, CheckPathExists, MultiSelect, ShowReadOnly, ReadOnlyChecked, AddExtension, RestoreDirectory, ValidateNames, and DereferenceLinks. Other properties have retained their old name, and you now have the FileNames property that returns a String array with all the files that have been selected in a multiple-selection dialog box. The following example asks for a bitmap file and loads it into a PictureBox control:

```
With OpenFileDialog1
    .CheckFileExists = True
    .ShowReadOnly = False
    .Filter = "All Files|*.*|Bitmap Files (*)|*;*.gif;*.jpg"
    .FilterIndex = 2
    If .ShowDialog = DialogResult.OK Then
        ' Load the specified file into a PictureBox control.
        PictureBox1.Image = Image.FromFile(.FileName)
    End If
End With
```

The control also exposes an OpenFile method, which opens the file and returns a Stream object, so you can load the image using this syntax as well:

```
Dim st As System.IO.Stream = .OpenFile
    PictureBox1.Image = Image.FromStream(st)
    st.Close
```

Interestingly, the control exposes a FileOk event that lets you cancel a click on the Open button:

```
Private Sub OpenFileDialog1_FileOk(ByVal sender As Object, _
    ByVal e As System.ComponentModel.CancelEventArgs) _
    Handles OpenFileDialog1.FileOk

    ' Check the Hidden attribute of the currently selected file.
    If System.IO.File.GetAttributes(OpenFileDialog1.FileName) _
        And IO.FileAttributes.Hidden Then
        ' Reject hidden files.
        MessageBox.Show("You can't select hidden files")
        e.Cancel = True
    End If
End Sub
```

The SaveFileDialog Control

The SaveFileDialog control is similar to OpenFileDialog, with a slightly different set of properties. For example, you can set the CreatePrompt or OverwritePrompt property to True to display a warning when a new file would be created or an existing file would be overwritten. You can use the OpenFile method to create a Stream object, and the FileOk event to cancel the user's selection.

The ColorDialog Control

You can set a few Boolean properties before opening a common dialog with the ColorDialog control: AllowFullOpen, SolidColorOnly, and AnyColor. The FullOpen property can be set to True to display an open custom color pane.

When the user closes the dialog box, the Color property returns the selected color, whereas the CustomColors array contains all the custom colors defined by the user:

```
' Let the user select the BackColor of a TextBox control.
With ColorDialog1
    .Color = TextBox1.BackColor
    .SolidColorOnly = True
    If .ShowDialog() = DialogResult.OK Then
        TextBox1.BackColor = .Color
    End If
End With
```

The FontDialog Control

The FontDialog control exposes a set of properties whose meaning should be immediately clear to programmers who have worked with the Visual Basic 6 CommonDialog control: FontMustExist, ShowColor, ShowEffects, AllowVectorFonts, FixedPitchOnly, MinSize, and MaxSize. Of course, there's also a Font property, which sets or returns the selected font:

```
' Let the user select Font and ForeColor for a TextBox control.
With FontDialog1
    ' Enable the selection of effects and color.
    .ShowEffects = True
    .ShowColor = True
    ' Set a limit to font size.
    .MinSize = 8
    .MaxSize = 72
    ' Initialize with font and color from a TextBox control.
    .Font = TextBox1.Font
    .Color = TextBox1.ForeColor
    ' Display the Apply button. (See next code snippet.)
    .ShowApply = True
    If .ShowDialog = DialogResult.OK Then
        ' Apply to TextBox properties.
        TextBox1.Font = .Font
        TextBox1.ForeColor = .Color
    End If
End With
```

The ShowApply property enables a great feature of the FontDialog control, which is the ability to trap clicks on the Apply button. All you have to do is write some code for the Apply event:

```
Private Sub FontDialog1_Apply(ByVal sender As Object, _
    ByVal e As System.EventArgs) Handles FontDialog1.Apply
    ' Enforce font properties without closing the dialog.
    TextBox1.Font = FontDialog1.Font
    TextBox1.ForeColor = FontDialog1.Color
End Sub
```

The PrintDialog Control

Before you use the PrintDialog control, you need to know a few things about the PrinterSettings object. This object exposes all the settings you see in a Print dialog box as properties, the most important of which are PrinterName, FromPage, ToPage, Copies, PrintToFile, and PrintRange (can be AllPages, SomePages, or Selection). You can also set the MinimumPage and MaximumPage properties to the lowest and highest valid page numbers. The following code snippet should give you an idea of how you can set up a Print dialog box:

```
' This code assumes the following Imports statement:
'    Imports System.Drawing.Printing

With PrintDialog1
    ' Set a few basic properties.
    .AllowPrintToFile = True
    .AllowSelection = True
    .AllowSomePages = True

    ' Create the PrinterSettings object, and set its properties.
    .PrinterSettings = New PrinterSettings()
    With .PrinterSettings
        .PrintRange = PrintRange.SomePages
        .FromPage = 1
        .ToPage = 10
        .MinimumPage = 1
        .MaximumPage = 10
    End With

    ' Exit if the user canceled the operation.
    If .ShowDialog <> DialogResult.OK Then Exit Sub

    ' Get the values entered by the user.
    If .PrinterSettings.PrintRange = PrintRange.SomePages Then
        Dim firstPage As Integer = .PrinterSettings.FromPage
        Dim lastPage As Integer = .PrinterSettings.ToPage
        ' Call the procedure that does the printing. (See next code.)
        PrintDocumentPages(firstPage, lastPage)
    End If
End With
```

At this point, you're just halfway through your task because you still have to print the document or a selected portion of it. Printing under .NET isn't as simple as it was under Visual Basic: you have to create a PrintDocument object, set up a handler for its PrintPage event, and do the actual printing from inside that event. Here's a simple example of how you implement the PrintDocumentPages routine called from the preceding code:

```
Dim WithEvents PrintDoc As PrintDocument
Dim currPage As Integer
Dim lastPage As Integer

Sub PrintDocumentPages(ByVal firstPage As Integer, ByVal lastPage As Integer)
    ' Move arguments into variables for sharing them with other procedures.
    Me.currPage = firstPage
    Me.lastPage = lastPage
    Me.PrintDoc = New PrintDocument()

    ' Start a print operation.
    Try
        PrintDoc.Print()
    Catch ex As Exception
        MessageBox.Show(ex.Message, "Print error")
    End Try
End Sub

Private Sub PrintDoc_PrintPage(ByVal sender As Object, _
    ByVal e As System.Drawing.Printing.PrintPageEventArgs) _
    Handles PrintDoc.PrintPage

    ' This demo prints a rectangle on the printable area of the sheet.
    e.Graphics.DrawRectangle(Pens.Black, e.MarginBounds)

    ' Increment the page number.
    currPage += 1
    ' Let the print engine know whether there are more pages.
    e.HasMorePages = (currPage <= lastPage)
End Sub
```

You can take advantage of two more events of the PrintDocument object: BeginPrint and EndPrint, which fire before printing the first page and after printing the last page of the document, respectively.

The PageSetupDialog Control

The PageSetupDialog control displays the Page Setup dialog box and lets the user select things such as print orientation (portrait or landscape), paper size, and the four page margins. (See Figure 17-9.) All these values are held in a PageSettings object, which you must initialize before showing the dialog:

```
With PageSetupDialog1
    ' Initialize the PageSettings property.
    .PageSettings = New PageSettings()

    ' Allow the user to select paper size and margins.
```

(continued)

```
    .AllowPaper = True
    .AllowMargins = True
    ' Disable the Printer button.
    .AllowPrinter = False
    ' Set minimum margins (100 units = 1 inch).
    .MinMargins = New Margins(50, 50, 50, 50)

    ' Display the dialog; exit if user canceled the action.
    If .ShowDialog() <> DialogResult.OK Then Exit Sub

    ' Save some of the page settings in variables.
    Dim leftMargin As Single = .PageSettings.Margins.Left
    Dim rightMargin As Single = .PageSettings.Margins.Right
    Dim landscapeOrientation As Boolean = .PageSettings.Landscape
    Dim paperSize As PaperKind = .PageSettings.PaperSize.Kind
    ' Do something with these values.
    ⋮
End With
```

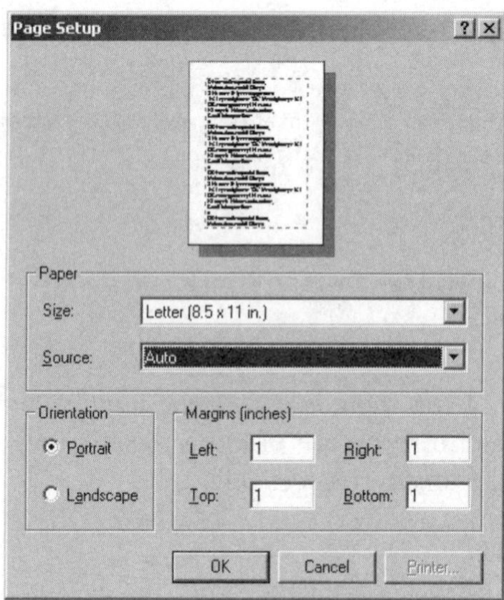

Figure 17-9. The Page Setup common dialog box.

If you enable the Printer button, you can also set and read back a PrinterSettings object, as I explained in the section about the PrintDialog control.

The ImageList Control

This control is essentially the same control you have under Visual Basic 6 and works as a repository for images. You can associate an ImageList control with any control that supports the Image property, not just Windows common controls such as TreeView or ListView (as you can in Visual Basic 6). Creating the list of images at design time is simple, thanks to the new Image Collection Editor dialog box. (See Figure 17-10.) In an important difference from previous versions, you can't assign a key to an image, and you can reference an image only by its index.

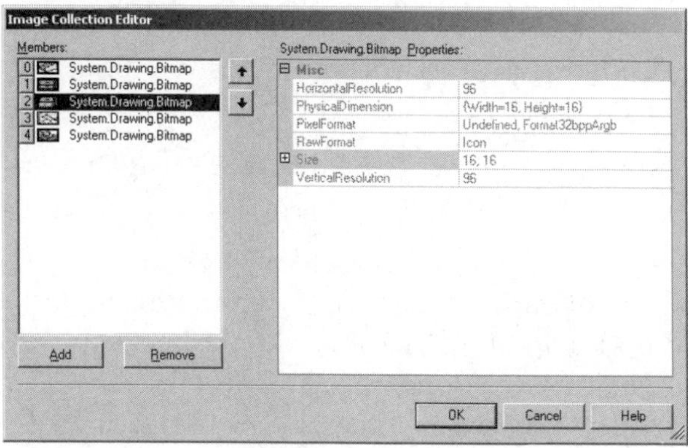

Figure 17-10. The Image Collection Editor lets you add images to an ImageList control at design time.

The new ColorDepth property specifies the number of colors to use when rendering the images (8, 16, 24, or 32 bits). The TransparentColor property defines the transparent color. (This property replaces MaskColor.) The ImageSize property returns a Size object that defines the dimension of the images in the control and therefore replaces the ImageHeight and ImageWidth properties.

At run time, you can access all the images through the Images collection (which replaces the ListImages collection you have under Visual Basic 6). This object inherits from IList, so it exposes the usual members—for example, Count, Item, Add, RemoveAt, and Clear. You can add an image via code this way:

```
ImageList1.Images.Add(Image.FromFile("c:\myimage")
```

You can render images on a graphic surface by using the Draw method. This method takes a Graphics object (the destination device context), the target coordinates, and the index of the image to be displayed:

```
Dim gr As System.Drawing.Graphics = Me.CreateGraphics
' Display the first image on the form's surface, at coordinates (100, 200).
ImageList1.Draw(gr, 100, 200, 0)
' Display the second image at coordinates (200, 300) - alternate syntax.
ImageList1.Draw(gr, New Point(200, 300), 1)
' Stretch the third image to fill a rectangle 160 x 160 at upper left corner.
ImageList1.Draw(gr, 0, 0, 160, 160, 2)
```

The TreeView Control

If you have worked with the Visual Basic 6 TreeView control, you'll feel at ease immediately with this new version. The great news is that you can edit the

Nodes collection at design time by using the TreeNode Editor dialog box. (See Figure 17-11.) You see the effect in the control placed on the form. These are the most important new properties:

- The ShowLines, ShowRootLines, and ShowPlusMinus Boolean properties replace the enumerated Style property.
- The Indent property replaces Indentation. (This value is the indentation width of child nodes.)
- The Scrollable property replaces Scroll. (If True, the control displays the scroll bars if necessary.)
- The ImageIndex and SelectedImageIndex properties contain the index in the companion ImageList control of the image to be used for unselected nodes and the selected node, respectively. (You can override this default image for individual nodes, though.) The Properties window lets you browse all the images in the ImageList control, so selecting the right one is easy.
- The new ItemHeight property affects the height of individual nodes.
- At run time, you can query the VisibleCount read-only property to get the number of visible nodes, and the TopNode read-only property to get a reference to the first visible TreeNode object.

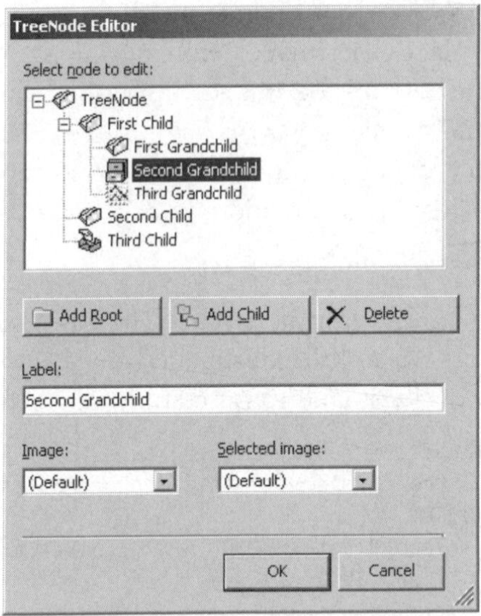

Figure 17-11. You can display the TreeNode Editor dialog box by clicking on the ellipsis button beside the Nodes element in the Properties window.

You can build the Nodes collection by means of code by adding new TreeNode objects to it. The constructor for this object can take the Text for the node, the image index, and the selected image index:

```
' Append two new nodes at the root level.
TreeView1.Nodes.Add(New TreeNode("A new node"))
TreeView1.Nodes.Add(New TreeNode("Another new node"))
' Create a new root-level node after the first root node.
' (The first argument becomes the index of the new node.)
TreeView1.Nodes.Insert(1, New TreeNode("Another root node"))
```

In a significant difference from previous versions of this control, each TreeNode object exposes its own Nodes collection, which greatly simplifies the creation and deletion of nodes at any level in the hierarchy:

```
' Get a reference to the first node.
Dim firstNode as TreeNode = TreeView1.Nodes(0)
' Insert a new node as the first child node.
firstNode.Nodes.Insert(0, New TreeNode("The new first child node"))

' Create a new node, and append it as the last child node.
Dim lastChild As TreeNode = New TreeNode("A new child node")
firstNode.Nodes.Add(lastChild)
' Create a grandchild node.
lastChild.Nodes.Add(New TreeNode("A new grandchild node"))
```

> **Tip** When adding a large number of nodes, you should bracket your code within a BeginUpdate and EndUpdate pair of methods to speed up operations and reduce flickering.

Thanks to the truly hierarchical structure, you can easily create recursive procedures that perform a given operation over all or a subset of the TreeView nodes. For example, the following procedure calculates and displays (or hides if the second argument is False) the number of child nodes in the Text property of all the nodes in the control:

```
Sub DisplayChildrenCount(ByVal nodes As TreeNodeCollection, _
    ByVal display As Boolean)

    Dim node As TreeNode
    For Each node In nodes
        ' Remove any child count at the end of the Text, if there.
        node.Text = System.Text.RegularExpressions.Regex.Replace( _
```

(continued)

```
            node.Text, " \[.*\]$", "")
        ' Add it again if so requested.
        If display Then
            node.Text &= " [" & CStr(node.Nodes.Count) & "]"
        End If
        ' Recurse over child nodes.
        DisplayChildrenCount(node.Nodes, display)
    Next
End Sub
```

To see this procedure in action, add some nodes to a TreeView control, and then create a Button control and add this code:

```
Private Sub Button1_Click(ByVal sender As System.Object, _
    ByVal e As System.EventArgs) Handles Button1.Click
    ' Toggle current display status.
    Static display As Boolean
    display = Not display
    ' Display or hide children count.
    DisplayChildrenCount(TreeView1.Nodes, display)
End Sub
```

If you have a reference to a TreeNode object, you can navigate the node hierarchy by using the Parent, FirstNode, LastNode, NextNode, PreviousNode, NextVisibleNode, and PrevVisibleNode properties. You can expand or collapse a node by using its Expand, ExpandAll, Collapse, and Toggle methods, and you can test its current state by using the IsExpanded, IsSelected, IsVisible, and IsEditing properties.

You can control the many other attributes of a TreeNode object with the Text, Checked, ForeColor, BackColor, ImageIndex, and SelectedImageIndex properties. Or you can let the user edit the node's label by using the BeginEdit method and terminate the edit operation by using EndEdit.

The new TreeView control offers several pairs of events, which fire immediately before and after a node is edited, selected, expanded, collapsed, or checked. In all cases, you can examine the node in question and decide whether to cancel the operation. The following event procedure ensures that the user can't edit a node's label that contains the count of children nodes. (See the preceding code example.)

```
Private Sub TreeView1_BeforeLabelEdit(ByVal sender As Object, _
    ByVal e As System.Windows.Forms.NodeLabelEditEventArgs) _
    Handles TreeView1.BeforeLabelEdit

    ' Refuse to edit a node that has a children count on its Text.
    If System.Text.RegularExpressions.Regex.IsMatch(e.Node.Text, _
        " \[.*\]$") Then
        e.CancelEdit = True
```

```
        MessageBox.Show("You can't edit while children count is displayed")
    End If
End Sub
```

The ListView Control

The new ListView control exposes most of the properties and methods that the Visual Basic 6 version does, and you have to account only for a few different names. The Properties window lets you add new ListViewItem objects and one or more subitems (see Figure 17-12), as well as define all the ColumnHeader objects that you want to define. Another great improvement is the ability to resize column width at design time.

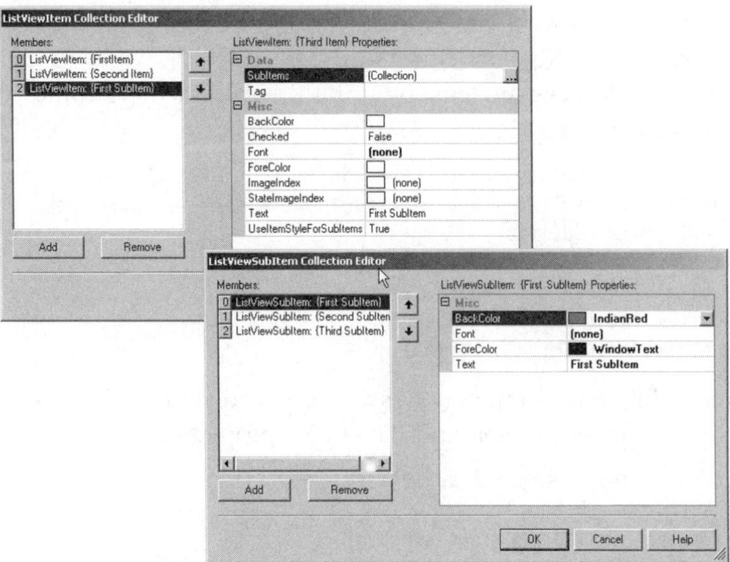

Figure 17-12. At design time, you can edit ListView items using the ListViewItem Collection Editor and subitems using the ListViewSubItem Collection Editor.

The ListView control exposes only a few new properties. This group includes Activation (whether items are activated with one or two clicks), HeaderStyle (whether column headers are clickable), Scrollable (should be set to False to prevent scrolling), LargeImageList (the ImageList control used for the images in large icon mode), and SmallImageList (the ImageList control used for all other modes). Note that the View property defines the display mode, as in Visual Basic 6, but the Report mode has been renamed Details mode. (Details is the mode that displays column headers and subitems.)

You create new ListView items—displayed as rows when in details mode or icons in all other modes—by adding ListViewItem objects to the control's Items collection. The constructor for the ListViewItem object can take a string (the caption of the icon) and an optional integer used as an index for the companion ListImage controls:

```
' Append a new list item; use the first icon in companion ListImage controls.
ListView1.Items.Add(New ListViewItem("Another list item", 0))
' Insert a new item at the beginning of the collection, with no icons.
ListView1.Items.Insert(0, New ListViewItem("A new first item"))
```

The ListViewItem object exposes many of the properties of the Visual Basic 6 ListItem object. The Bounds property returns a Rectangle object that tells where the item is on the screen, and the Focused property returns True if the item has the focus. Unfortunately, a few properties have been lost in the transition, such as Key and Ghosted.

You create new subitems by using the Add method of the ListViewItem's SubItems collection:

```
' Create a ListViewItem object, and add it to the ListView.
Dim lvi As ListViewItem = New ListViewItem("A new list item", 0)
ListView1.Items.Add(lvi)
' Next add three subitems.
lvi.SubItems.Add("First subitem")
lvi.SubItems.Add("Second subitem")
lvi.SubItems.Add("Third subitem")
```

In a difference from previous versions, individual subitems can have their own Text, Font, ForeColor, and BackColor properties:

```
' ...(Continuing previous code snippet)...
' Add a fourth subitem.
With lvi.SubItems.Add("Fourth subitem")
    ' Change text and background colors.
    .ForeColor = Color.Red
    .BackColor = Color.Yellow
    ' Use standard form font, but make it bold and italic.
    .Font = New Font(Me.Font, FontStyle.Bold Or FontStyle.Italic)
End With
```

(As is the case under Visual Basic 6, subitems from the second one onward are visible only in Details mode and only if you have defined sufficient numbers of ColumnHeader objects.) The following routine fills a ListView control with information about files in a given directory, so it mimics the contents of the right pane in Windows Explorer:

```
' Show files in specified directory.
Sub ShowFilesInListView(ByVal lv As ListView, ByVal path As String)
    ' Get the DirectoryInfo object corresponding to the path.
    Dim di As New DirectoryInfo(path)

    lv.BeginUpdate()        ' Suppress refresh.
    lv.Items.Clear()

    ' Get data about all the files.
    Dim fi As FileInfo
    For Each fi In di.GetFiles()
        ' Create a new ListViewItem object, and add to the Items collection.
        Dim item As New ListViewItem(fi.Name)
        lv.Items.Add(item)
        ' Create all subitems.
        item.SubItems.Add(fi.Length)
        item.SubItems.Add(fi.CreationTime)
        item.SubItems.Add(fi.LastWriteTime)
        item.SubItems.Add(fi.LastAccessTime)
    Next
    lv.EndUpdate            ' Reenable refresh.
End Sub
```

This routine paints the rows with alternating background color. (See Figure 17-13.)

```
' Display alternating color for background.
Sub PaintAlternatingBackColor(ByVal lv As ListView, _
    ByVal color1 As Color, ByVal color2 As Color)

    Dim item As ListViewItem
    Dim subitem As ListViewItem.ListViewSubItem

    For Each item In lv.Items
        ' Set the color for this Item object.
        If (item.Index Mod 2) = 0 Then
            item.BackColor = color1
        Else
            item.BackColor = color2
        End If

        ' Assign same color to all subitems.
        For Each subitem In item.SubItems
            subitem.BackColor = item.BackColor
        Next
    Next
End Sub
```

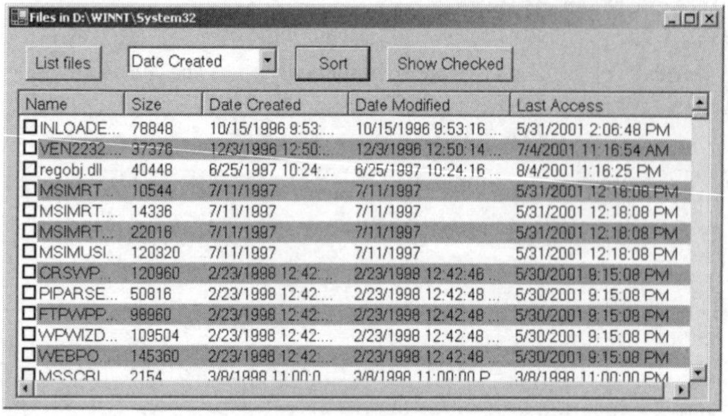

Figure 17-13. The demo application shows how to sort elements in a ListView according to different sort criteria.

The demo program uses the following code to display files in the Windows system directory:

```
ShowFilesInListView(ListView1, System.Environment.SystemDirectory)
PaintAlternatingBackColor(ListView1, Color.White, Color.Cyan)
```

A great feature of this control is the ability to sort its contents according to the sort criterion that you decide. You just have to define a class that implements the IComparer interface, assign an instance of this class to the ListView's ListViewItemSorter property, and then invoke the Sort method. The CompareTo function of this class receives a reference to the two ListViewItem objects being compared, so you can access their properties and the properties of their subitems. Following is the code in the demo application that sorts the items according to the filename, size, creation date, write date, and last access date (depending on the selected criterion in the cboSort ComboBox control). Note that you can reuse the same CompareByDate class for all the sorts on date values because the only difference is the index of the subitem element, a piece of data that we pass to the class constructor:

```
Private Sub btnSort_Click(ByVal sender As System.Object, _
    ByVal e As System.EventArgs) Handles btnSort.Click

    ' Use the correct sort object.
    Dim index As Integer = cboSort.SelectedIndex
    Select Case index
        Case 0
            ' Sort by name.
            ListView1.ListViewItemSorter = New CompareByName()
        Case 1
            ' Sort by size.
            ListView1.ListViewItemSorter = New CompareBySize()
```

```
        Case 2, 3, 4
            ' Sort by one of the date properties.
            ListView1.ListViewItemSorter = New CompareByDate(index)
    End Select
    ' Now we can sort the ListView and repaint the background.
    ListView1.Sort()
    PaintAlternatingBackColor(ListView1, Color.White, Color.Cyan)
End Sub

' These classes are nested inside the form class.

Class CompareByName
    Implements IComparer

    Function Compare(ByVal x As Object, ByVal y As Object) As Integer _
        Implements System.Collections.IComparer.Compare
        ' Cast the two arguments to ListViewItem objects.
        Dim item1 As ListViewItem = CType(x, ListViewItem)
        Dim item2 As ListViewItem = CType(y, ListViewItem)
        ' Compare their text property.
        Return String.Compare(item1.Text, item2.Text)
    End Function
End Class

Class CompareBySize
    Implements IComparer

    Function Compare(ByVal x As Object, ByVal y As Object) As Integer _
        Implements System.Collections.IComparer.Compare
        ' Cast the two arguments to ListViewItem objects.
        Dim item1 As ListViewItem = CType(x, ListViewItem)
        Dim item2 As ListViewItem = CType(y, ListViewItem)
        ' Compare their second subitem as a Long.
        Return Math.Sign(CLng(item1.SubItems(1).Text) _
            - CLng(item2.SubItems(1).Text))
    End Function
End Class

' We can use one class for all date comparisons,
' just by passing a different subitem index.
Class CompareByDate
    Implements IComparer

    Dim Index As Integer

    Sub New(ByVal subitemIndex As Integer)
        Me.Index = subitemIndex
    End Sub
```

(continued)

```
    Function Compare(ByVal x As Object, ByVal y As Object) As Integer _
        Implements System.Collections.IComparer.Compare
        ' Cast the two arguments to ListViewItem objects.
        Dim item1 As ListViewItem = CType(x, ListViewItem)
        Dim item2 As ListViewItem = CType(y, ListViewItem)
        ' Compare their Nth subitem as a date.
        Return Date.Compare(Date.Parse(item1.SubItems(Index).Text), _
            Date.Parse(item2.SubItems(Index).Text))
    End Function
End Class
```

The CheckedItems and CheckedIndices properties return information about all the checked elements. The SelectedItems and SelectedIndices collections return the list of selected items. To use these collections, you should set the value of the CheckBoxes and MultiSelect properties correctly.

Other Controls

This section summarizes the changes in the controls that I haven't discussed in previous sections. In most cases, I don't discuss them in depth because there are only minimal differences from the corresponding Visual Basic 6 control or because I assume that you're smart enough to understand how they work by just using my hints. (And I want to devote the remainder of this chapter to more interesting things.)

The PictureBox Control

The PictureBox control is less powerful and complex than the corresponding Visual Basic 6 control in that you can't use it as a container. The Image property replaces the Picture property, and you can also load an image in the BackgroundImage property. (In the latter case, the image is tiled to cover the entire control.)

You can load images in the following formats: bitmap, icon, metafiles, enhanced metafiles, GIF, JPEG, and PNG. You can center or stretch the image to fit the control or stretch the control to fit the image by using the SizeMode property.

The HScrollBar and VScrollBar Controls

There are no relevant differences from the corresponding Visual Basic 6 controls except that the Change event isn't supported any longer and you can trap user actions with the Scroll event exclusively. The new ValueChanged event fires whenever the Value property changes, either programmatically or because of UI interaction.

Note that these controls don't support a flat appearance, so you can't create flat scroll bars in this Windows Forms version.

The Timer Control

The Timer control is virtually identical to the Visual Basic 6 control, with these exceptions:

- The Tick event replaces the Timer event.
- You can enable or disable the timer using the Start and Stop methods or by setting the Enabled property; you can't prevent a Timer from ticking by setting its Interval property to 0, as you can in previous language versions.

The Panel Control

The Panel control is similar to the old Frame control, but it has no caption. The Panel control provides a container for other controls, and it can support AutoScroll and all the related properties so that the end user can scroll its contents. You can also dock one or more controls on its borders, and you can control the distance of contained controls from the edge by using the DockPadding property.

The GroupBox Control

The GroupBox control is identical to the old Frame control. In practice, the only properties that you usually modify after you drop it on a form are Text and FlatStyle. Unlike the Frame control, you can't hide the border. (Use a Panel control if you need to group controls without a visible border.)

The NotifyIcon Control

This new control makes it easy to add an icon to the Windows taskbar tray area, as many recent programs do. It has only a handful of properties: Icon is the icon being used, Text is the ToolTip being displayed when the mouse hovers over the icon, Visible lets you hide the icon, and ContextMenu is a menu that appears when the user clicks the icon. The control fires the Click, DoubleClick, MouseDown, MouseUp, and MouseMove events, so you can control exactly what happens when the user interacts with the icon in the tray area.

The ToolBar Control

The new version of this control comes with a Buttons collection that you can populate at design time. Elements in this collection can be push buttons, toggle buttons, separators, or drop-down buttons with which you can associate a MainMenu object that you've defined in the form's component tray area. Each button can have text, ToolTip text, and an image taken from a companion ImageList control. When a button is clicked, the control fires a ButtonClicked event, and you can react to it by writing this kind of code:

```
Private Sub ToolBar1_ButtonClick(ByVal sender As Object, _
    ByVal e As ToolBarButtonClickEventArgs) Handles ToolBar1.ButtonClick

    Select Case e.Button.Text
        Case "Open"
            ' Open the document.
        Case "Save"
            ' Save the document.
        ⋮
    End Select
End Sub
```

The TabControl Control

This control replaces the Visual Basic 6 TabStrip control, as well as the other tab control, named SSTab, provided with previous versions of the language. The new control is remarkably simple to use because you define all the tabs at design time by using properties such as Text, ToolTipText, and ImageIndex (the icon that appears near the tab). Each tab you create is an instance of the TabPage class, which is a scrollable container for other controls.

You rarely need to interact with this control at run time by means of code. You might need to check the control's SelectedIndex property (the index of the active TabPage object) and trap the SelectedIndexChanged event to detect when the user activates another tab, but these would be the only operations you'd need to perform. You can also receive events from individual TabPage objects if necessary.

The StatusBar Control

By default, the status bar displays the value assigned to its Text property, and you have to explicitly set the ShowPanels property to True to see the panels. Each Panel object has text, ToolTip text, an icon, and a minimum width; you can add these objects to the Panels collection from the Properties window or with code. The control fires a PanelClick event when the user clicks on a panel, as under Visual Basic 6, but the PanelDblClick event isn't supported any longer.

Panels can have an owner-draw style, so you can define their appearance in the DrawItem event. For example, you might use this feature to display an animated icon or a progress bar inside the StatusBar control.

The NumericUpDown and DomainUpDown Controls

The NumericUpDown control displays a numeric value that the user can edit directly or increment and decrement by using the arrow keys. The DomainUp-

Down control is conceptually similar to a ListBox control with only one visible element: you can scroll through all the elements of the list by using the arrow keys, and you can cycle through them if the Wrap property is True. These controls have several members in common, such as UpDownAlign (the position of the arrow buttons) and InterceptArrowKeys (True if arrow keys are processed automatically). You can also programmatically click the arrow buttons by using the UpButton and DownButton methods.

The NumericUpDown control lets you set a minimum and maximum value, an increment value, the number of decimal places, and whether thousand separators should be displayed. You extract the numeric contents (as a Decimal) by using the Value property, and you get a ValueChanged event when this property changes.

The DomainUpDown control is more similar to a ListBox control in that it exposes an Items collection that you can initialize at design time or by means of code. The control fires a SelectedIndexChanged event when the user selects another item in the list.

The RichTextBox Control

This control has several new properties and methods that make it remarkably more powerful than the Visual Basic 6 version. For example, the new version of the control has a ZoomFactor property that can apply a zoom level in the range of 0.64 to 64. The DetectURLs property, if True, makes the control automatically recognize and format URLs in text. (You receive a LinkClicked event when one of those URLs is clicked.) If the new AutoWordSelection is True, a mouse click selects entire words. The new Protected event fires when the user attempts to edit text that has been protected.

The TrackBar Control

Except for the name, this control is identical to the Visual Basic 6 Slider control. In addition, it exposes the SetRange method (for setting both the Minimum and Maximum properties in one operation) and the ValueChanged event (similar to Scroll but fires also when the Value property is set programmatically).

The ProgressBar Control

This control is very similar to the Visual Basic 6 version; it has only two new methods: PerformStep (which increments the Value property by the quantity defined by the Step property) and Increment (which takes the increment as an argument). Not very exciting, after all.

Data Binding

Data binding allows you to link a control to a data source so that the control automatically displays (and possibly updates) the data without your having to write any specific code. Data binding has been a feature of Visual Basic since version 3.0. The underlying mechanism was significantly improved with ADO data binding (introduced with Visual Basic 6) and has been further perfected in Visual Basic .NET. Unlike previous versions, however, Visual Basic .NET doesn't offer a Data control, and you have to create your navigational buttons. (It doesn't take much to create a custom control that does exactly that, however.)

You can choose from two types of data binding, depending on whether the data source is updated when the user enters a new value in the bound control. In *one-way data binding*, the control is bound in read-only fashion and the data source isn't automatically updated. In *two-way data binding*, the control is bound in read/write fashion and notification of any change to the bound property is sent to the data source.

You can also classify data binding according to how many items or properties of the bound control are bound to the data source. In *simple data binding*, only one property of the control is bound to a given column of the database (or, more generally, to a single value in the data source). This situation arises, for example, when you have the Text property of a TextBox control bound to a string or a numeric column in a database table. In *complex data binding*, you bind multiple items of a control to the same or different fields in the data source. For example, you have complex data binding when you fill the Items collection of a ListBox or ComboBox control with the values coming from a column in the data source or when you display multiple fields of the data source in a DataGrid control.

In a difference from previous versions of Visual Basic, the data-binding mechanism lets you bind a control to virtually any potential data source. In fact, the minimum prerequisite for an object to qualify as a data source is that it must expose the IList interface, so you can bind a control to an array and to most of the collection-like objects I described in Chapter 9. And of course you can bind them to ADO.NET sources, including DataTable, DataSet, and DataView objects.

Binding to an Array of Objects

As you might expect, you pay for all this flexibility in the amount of code you have to write to set up the binding mechanism correctly. For starters, four different object types cooperate in a form that contains bound controls, here listed from the simplest to the most complex. (See Figure 17-14.)

- The Binding object binds a single property of a control to a single field of the data source. You rarely interact directly with this object unless you want to trap its Format or Parse event. The Format and Parse events give you the highest flexibility in how individual values are displayed or stored back in the data source.
- The ControlBindingCollection object gathers all the Binding objects associated with a given control; in practice, you can create a new Binding object only by invoking the Add method of this collection. You can access this collection through the DataBindings property, which all Windows Forms controls expose. Thanks to the DataBindings property, you can bind multiple properties to different fields of a given control. For example, a TextBox control might have its Text property bound to the Model field and its BackColor property bound to the Color field of the Cars class.
- The BindingManagerBase object gathers all the Binding objects associated with the same data source. When its Position property changes, the BindingManagerBase object notifies all the Binding objects that they should transfer current values of controls into the data source and retrieve the values at the new position. As these changes occur, this object also fires a PositionChanged event, which you can trap to perform additional processing (such as updating a calculated field).
- The BindingContext object is returned by the property of the same name exposed by the Form object (and more generally by all classes derived from ContainerControl). This object is necessary because a form or a container control might contain multiple sets of bound controls, with each group associated with a different data source. For example, a form might contain a group of controls bound to the Employees array and another group of controls bound to the Cars array.

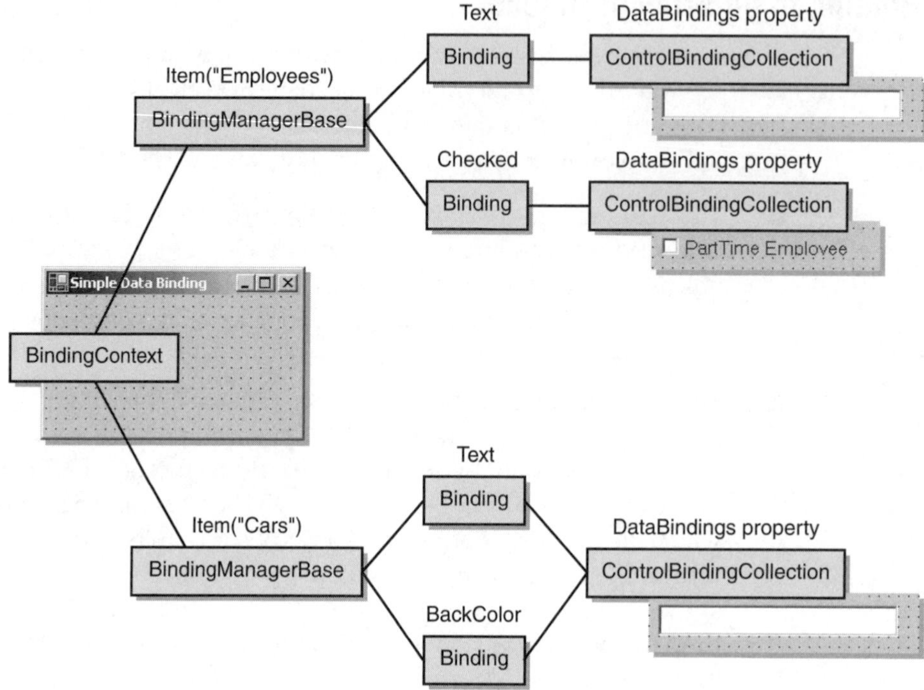

Figure 17-14. Data-binding objects.

Simple Data-Bound Form

Let's see a complete example of a form with four controls, in which each control binds to one of the properties of the Employee class: FirstName, LastName, BirthDate, and PartTimeEmployee. (The code of the Employee class is omitted because of its simplicity, but you can browse it in the complete source code on the companion CD.) The form is shown in Figure 17-15; it also contains all the buttons to navigate in the data source, which in this case is an array of Employee objects.

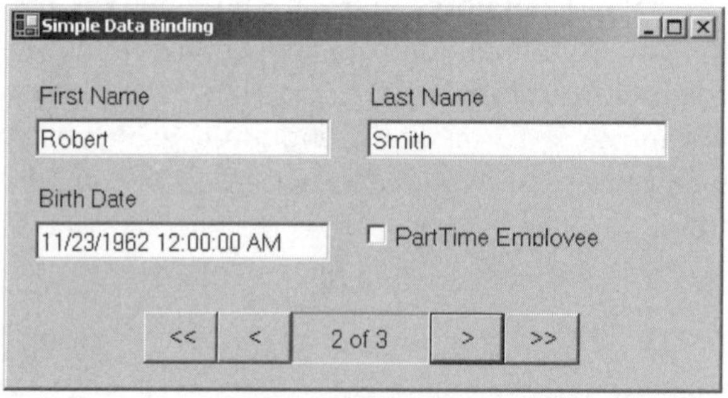

Figure 17-15. The Simple Data Binding demo form.

As you see in the following code, you create the individual Binding objects by using the DataBindings.Add method, which takes the name of the bound property, a reference to the data source (the employees array in this case), and the name of the member in the data source. The last argument is the name of a field when you're binding to a database table or the name of a property when you're binding to an object:

```
' This is the data source.
Dim employees() As Employee = {New Employee("Joe", "Doe", #1/3/1960#), _
    New Employee("Robert", "Smith", #11/23/1962#), _
    New Employee("Ann", "Ross", #2/5/1965#, True)}
' This is the BindingManagerBase object that manages all the bindings.
Dim WithEvents bmb As BindingManagerBase

' Initialize the binding when the form loads.
' (You can move the call to InitializeBinding to the Sub New procedure.)
Private Sub SimpleBindingForm_Load(ByVal sender As Object, _
    ByVal e As EventArgs) Handles MyBase.Load
    InitializeBinding()
End Sub

' Create all the necessary bindings.
Sub InitializeBinding()
    ' Create the Binding object for each bound field.
    txtFirstName.DataBindings.Add("Text", employees, "FirstName")
    txtLastName.DataBindings.Add("Text", employees, "LastName")
    txtBirthDate.DataBindings.Add("Text", employees, "BirthDate")
    chkPartTime.DataBindings.Add("Checked", employees, "PartTimeEmployee")

    ' Save a reference to the BindingManagerBase object.
    bmb = Me.BindingContext(employees)
    ' Force a refresh of buttons.
    bmb.Position = bmb.Count
    bmb.Position = 0
End Sub
```

The remainder of the code manages the actions performed when someone clicks on the navigational buttons. As you see, this code just changes the value of the Position property of the BindingManagerBase object and traps the PositionChanged event to display the correct record number:

```
Private Sub btnFirst_Click(ByVal sender As Object, _
    ByVal e As EventArgs) Handles btnFirst.Click
    bmb.Position = 0
End Sub

Private Sub btnPrevious_Click(ByVal sender As Object, _
    ByVal e As EventArgs) Handles btnPrevious.Click
```

(continued)

```
    bmb.Position -= 1
End Sub

Private Sub btnNext_Click(ByVal sender As Object, _
    ByVal e As EventArgs) Handles btnNext.Click
    bmb.Position += 1
End Sub

Private Sub btnLast_Click(ByVal sender As Object, _
    ByVal e As EventArgs) Handles btnLast.Click
    bmb.Position = bmb.Count - 1
End Sub

' Display current position in label.
Private Sub bmb_PositionChanged(ByVal sender As Object, _
    ByVal e As EventArgs) Handles bmb.PositionChanged
    lblRecord.Text = String.Format("{0} of {1}", bmb.Position + 1, bmb.Count)
End Sub
```

When you bind to an IList object, you get two-way binding and any new value the user enters in bound fields is assigned to the underlying data source. You can also support AddNew and Delete operations, even though you must implement them manually—for example, by writing the code that adds or deletes elements in the source array.

Formatting Events

You can enforce much finer control over how values are transferred to and from the data source by using the two events that individual Binding objects fire. The Format event fires when data is transferred from the data source to the bound control, whereas the Parse event fires when data is moved back into the data source. (The latter control fires only if the data in the control has been modified after the most recent Format event.)

Typically you take advantage of these events to change the display format of one or more values—for example, to display data as uppercase but store it as lowercase. Or you might store currency values in a currency unit (such as U.S. dollars or Euros) and display the values in the unit selected by the end user. The demo application uses these two events to display the BirthDate value in dd-mm-yyyy format instead of the default long date format. To trap the two events you must modify the code in the InitializeBinding procedure:

```
Sub InitializeBinding()
    ⋮
    ' Get a reference to this binding and bind it to two events.
    Dim bnd As Binding
    bnd = txtBirthDate.DataBindings.Add("Text", employees, "BirthDate")
    AddHandler bnd.Format, AddressOf DataFormat
    AddHandler bnd.Parse, AddressOf DataParse
    ⋮
```

```
End Sub

' Change format of BirthDate value.
Private Sub DataFormat(ByVal sender As Object, ByVal e As ConvertEventArgs)
    If sender Is txtBirthDate Then
        e.Value = String.Format("{0:dd-MM-yyyy}", e.Value)
    End If
End Sub

' Convert BirthDate string back to a Date value.
Private Sub DataParse(ByVal sender As Object, ByVal e As ConvertEventArgs)
    If sender Is txtBirthDate Then
        e.Value = CDate(e.Value)
    End If
End Sub
```

The preceding code uses the AddHandler statement to create event handlers dynamically because this technique gives more flexibility than a WithEvents variable does and lets you have two procedures that serve the Format or Parse event from multiple controls. The code in event handlers shows how you can discern which control is the destination (for Format) or the source (for Parse) of the operation.

Data-Bound ListBox and ComboBox Controls

As I've explained, the complex data-binding mechanism lets you bind a data source to multiple items in a control. Three Windows Forms controls support complex data binding: the ListBox control, the ComboBox control, and the DataGrid control.

Data binding to a ListBox or ComboBox control is especially useful because these controls can be used to display lookup tables. Say that you define a Department class with two properties, Name and ID. You can extend the Employee class with a new property, DepartmentID, which holds the numeric ID value of the department for a given employee. In this case, you can consider the array of Employee objects the main data source and the array of Department objects the lookup data source.

A data entry form could include a ListBox or ComboBox control that lists all the department names so that the operator can see or change the department where each employee works, as shown in Figure 17-16. (Such a control is therefore similar to the DataList or DataCombo control that was available in Visual Basic 6.) Binding a ListBox or ComboBox control in this fashion requires that you assign three of its properties:

- The DisplayMember property must be assigned the name of the property in the lookup class that's used to fill the list area of the control. (In our example, this is the Name property of the Department class.)

- The ValueMember property must be assigned the name of the property in the lookup class whose value is actually stored in the main data source when the end user selects an element from the ListBox or ComboBox control. (In our example, this is the ID property of the Department class.)
- The DataSource property must be assigned the lookup data source, which can be an IList object or one of the ADO.NET objects that can work as a data source, such as DataTable or DataSet. (In our example, this is the array of Department objects.)

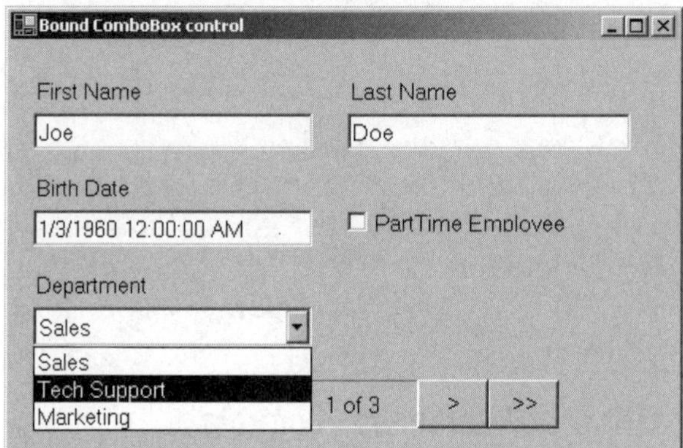

Figure 17-16. The improved version of the data-bound form includes a bound ComboBox control.

Once you've correctly assigned these properties, you can bind the SelectedValue property of the ListBox or ComboBox control to the field in the main data source. (In our example, this field is the DepartmentID property of the Employee class.) In practice, you can extend the original code to support a lookup ComboBox control by adding just four lines of code in the InitializeBinding procedure:

```
' An array of three Department objects
Dim departments() As Department = {New Department("Sales", 1), _
    New Department("Tech Support", 2), _
    New Department("Marketing", 3)}

Sub InitializeBinding()
    ' Load the Departments array in the ComboBox control's list area.
    cboDepartments.DisplayMember = "Name"
    cboDepartments.ValueMember = "ID"
    cboDepartments.DataSource = departments

    ' Bind the ComboBox control to the main data source.
```

```
    cboDepartments.DataBindings.Add("SelectedValue", employees, _
        "DepartmentID")

    ' ...(The remainder of the procedure is unchanged)...
    ⋮
End Sub
```

ADO.NET Data Binding

Although binding to an array is useful, most of the time you'll use Windows Forms data binding with ADO.NET objects. You can implement this kind of data binding either by using designable components that you add to the form's component tray or by creating ADO.NET objects and defining the binding mechanism via code.

Using Designable Components

In this section, I'll show you how you can use the features of the Visual Studio IDE to bind controls to fields in a data table using a RAD approach, almost without writing code. Follow this sequence of actions:

1. Open the Server Explorer window, and define a new data connection to a database of your choice; to follow the remainder of this example, you should create a connection to Biblio.mdb, but any Access or SQL Server database can be used. You can then open the data connection node to browse the tables in the selected database. (See Figure 17-17.)

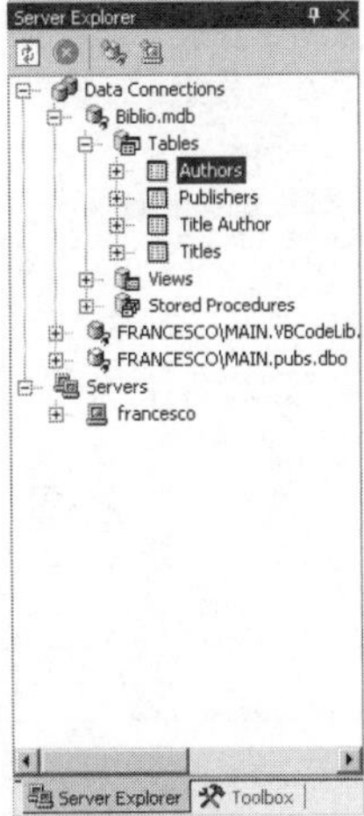

Figure 17-17. The Server Explorer window after you've added a data connection to Biblio.mdb.

2. Expand Biblio.mdb and then the Tables nodes in the Server Explorer window, select the Publishers table, and drop it onto the form. This action creates in the component tray two objects, which are named OleDbConnection1 and OleDbAdapter1. Select the former, and in the Properties window change its name to cnBiblio; repeat the same operation with the latter component to change its name to daPublishers.

3. Right-click on the daPublishers component, and click Generate Dataset on the shortcut menu; this action brings up the Generate Dataset dialog box. Ensure that the New radio button is selected and that the check box near the Publishers (daPublishers) element is selected, and then click OK. This operation creates a third component named DataSet11, but you should change its name to dsBiblio. At the end of this operation, the component tray should look like the one in Figure 17-18. You can see that a new DataSet1.xsd file has been added to the Solution Explorer window.

4. Create three TextBox controls on the form; name them txtName, txtCity, and txtState; and place appropriate labels on top of them. Next create the usual four navigation buttons, and name them btnFirst, btnPrevious, btnNext, and btnLast. (You can arrange them as you see in Figure 17-18.)

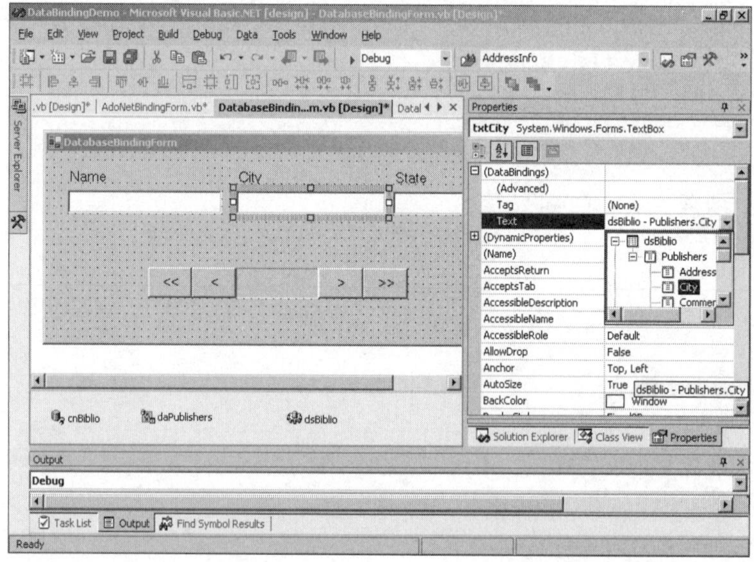

Figure 17-18. A data-bound form that uses ADO.NET components.

5. Select the txtName control; in the Properties window, expand the DataBinding node; and click the down arrow button near the Text item to associate this control with the dsBiblio.Publishers.Name field. Repeat this operation to bind the txtCity control to the City field and the txtState control to the State field in the Publishers data table.

To make the binding mechanism fully operational, you have to write the code that fills the dsBiblio DataSet object with data from the database, gets a reference to the BindingManagerBase object associated with the Publishers table, and reacts to clicks on navigational controls.

```
Private Sub Form_Load(ByVal sender As Object, _
    ByVal e As EventArgs) Handles MyBase.Load
    ' Fill the DataSet using the defined DataAdapter.
    Me.daPublishers.Fill(dsBiblio, "Publishers")
    ' Get a reference to the BindingManagerBase object.
    bmb = Me.BindingContext(dsBiblio, "Publishers")
End Sub

Dim bmb As BindingManagerBase

' ...(Navigational code as in preceding example)...
⋮
```

Data Binding via Code

If you open the region of source code automatically generated by the form designer, you can see how to set up the binding to an ADO.NET data source by means of code only, without resorting to any components in the component tray. The code-only approach requires more time and attention, but in general it's more flexible and slightly more efficient. Here's the code-only version of the same bound form created in the preceding example:

```
Private Sub Form_Load(ByVal sender As Object, ByVal e As EventArgs) _
    Handles MyBase.Load
    CreateDataSet()
    InitializeBinding()
End Sub

Dim dsBiblio As New DataSet()
Dim bmb As BindingManagerBase
```

(continued)

```
Sub CreateDataSet()
    ' Open a connection to the Biblio.mdb database.
    ' (You might have to provide a different connection string or path.)
    Dim cn As New OleDbConnection("Provider=Microsoft.Jet.OLEDB.4.0;Data " _
        & " Source=C:\Program Files\Microsoft Visual Studio\VB98\BIBLIO.MDB")
    cn.Open()
    ' Create a data adapter for the Publishers table.
    Dim daPublishers As New OleDbDataAdapter("SELECT * FROM Publishers", cn)
    ' Fill the DataSet object with data from the Publishers table.
    da.Fill(dsBiblio, "Publishers")

    ' Close the connection.
    cn.Close()
End Sub

Sub InitializeBinding()
    ' Bind controls to database fields.
    txtName.DataBindings.Add("Text", dsBiblio, "Publishers.Name")
    txtCity.DataBindings.Add("Text", dsBiblio, "Publishers.City")
    txtState.DataBindings.Add("Text", dsBiblio, "Publishers.State")

    ' Get a reference to the BindingManagerBase object.
    bmb = Me.BindingContext(dsBiblio, "Publishers")
    ' Force a refresh.
    bmb.Position = bmb.Count
    bmb.Position = 0
End Sub

' ...(Navigational code as in preceding example)...
:
```

Note that ADO.NET data binding is two-way, in the sense that when you modify a value in a bound field, the new value is stored in the data source. However, don't forget that the data source is the DataSet object, not the database table, so the data in the database isn't automatically updated. (Read Chapter 21 to learn more about how you can update data modified in a disconnected DataSet object.)

Master-Detail Bound Forms

A common type of data-bound form is the one that displays data coming from two tables between which a relation exists. For example, you can create a form like the one in Figure 17-19, with the DataGrid control displaying all the titles related to the publisher currently shown in the topmost TextBox controls.

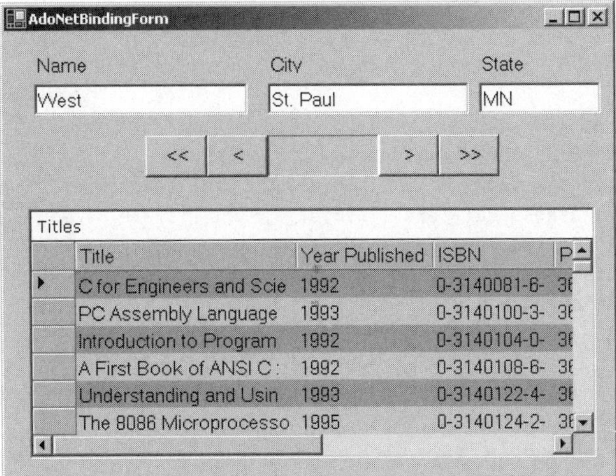

Figure 17-19. A master-detail form.

Creating such a master-detail form is a breeze with the great data-binding features of Windows Forms. In fact, you only have to drop a DataGrid control, name it grdTitles on the form, and add a few statements to the CreateDataSet and InitializeBinding procedures. (Added statements are in boldface.)

```
Sub CreateDataSet()
    ' Open a connection to the Biblio.mdb database.
    ' (You might have to provide a different connection string or path.)
    Dim cn As New OleDbConnection("Provider=Microsoft.Jet.OLEDB.4.0;Data " _
        & " Source=C:\Program Files\Microsoft Visual Studio\VB98\BIBLIO.MDB")
    cn.Open()
    ' Create a data adapter for the Publishers table.
    Dim daPublishers As New OleDbDataAdapter("SELECT * FROM Publishers", cn)
    ' Fill the DataSet object with data from the Publishers table.
    daPublishers.Fill(dsBiblio, "Publishers")

    ' Create a data adapter for the Titles table.
    Dim daTitles As New OleDbDataAdapter("SELECT * FROM Titles", cn)
    ' Fill the DataSet object with data from the Titles table.
    daTitles.Fill(dsBiblio, "Titles")

    ' Create a Relation between the two tables.
    dsBiblio.Relations.Add("PubTitles", _
        dsBiblio.Tables("Publishers").Columns("PubID"), _
        dsBiblio.Tables("Titles").Columns("PubId"))
```

(continued)

```
    ' Close the connection.
    cn.Close()
End Sub

Sub InitializeBinding()
    ' Bind fields to database fields.
    txtName.DataBindings.Add("Text", dsBiblio, "Publishers.Name")
    txtCity.DataBindings.Add("Text", dsBiblio, "Publishers.City")
    txtState.DataBindings.Add("Text", dsBiblio, "Publishers.State")
    ' Bind the DataGrid.
    grdTitles.DataSource = dsBiblio
    grdTitles.DataMember = "Publishers.PubTitles"

    ' Get a reference to the BindingManagerBase object.
    bmb = Me.BindingContext(dsBiblio, "Publishers")
    ' Force a refresh.
    bmb.Position = bmb.Count
    bmb.Position = 0
End Sub
```

Notice that the DataMember property of the DataGrid control usually takes the name of the table to which you're binding the grid. However, when you're creating detail grids, the value of the DataMember property becomes the complete name of the relation, in the format *mastertablename.relationname* (Publishers.PubTitles in the preceding example).

The last example of the master-detail form has two DataGrid controls on it: grdPublishers, displaying data from the Publishers table; and grdTitles, displaying data from the Titles table, as shown in Figure 17-20. Because the database data is the same as in the preceding example, you don't have to modify the CreateDataSet procedure and the only changes are inside the InitializeBinding procedure. This procedure is actually simpler than before because you don't have to create a BindingManagerBase object to manage the navigational buttons:

```
Sub InitializeBinding()
    ' Bind the master grid to the Publishers table.
    grdPublishers.DataSource = dsBiblio
    grdPublishers.DataMember = "Publishers"
    ' Don't allow navigation to child tables (optional).
    grdPublishers.AllowNavigation = False
    ' Bind the detail grid to the Titles table.
    grdTitles.DataSource = dsBiblio
    grdTitles.DataMember = "Publishers.PubTitles"
End Sub
```

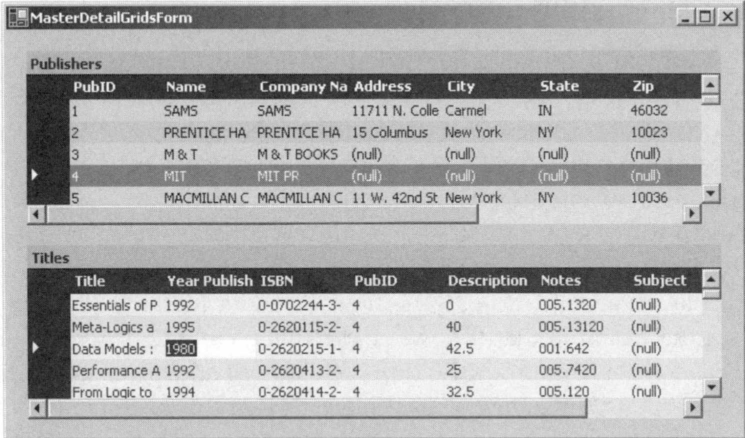

Figure 17-20. Two DataGrid controls in master-detail relationship.

Custom Control Creation

As if the controls in the Windows Forms package weren't enough, you can create your own controls. As a matter of fact, Visual Studio makes the creation of new controls a breeze. In this section, I'll show how you can create custom controls using one of the following approaches:

- Inheriting from an existing control
- Composing multiple controls
- Creating a control from scratch

If you have some familiarity with ActiveX control creation under Visual Basic 6, you'll probably agree after reading the remainder of this chapter that the Visual Basic .NET approach is more linear and easier to understand than the Visual Basic 6 approach and requires far less code because it relies on inheritance. You'll also see that, thanks to the superior features of Windows Forms, you don't have to resort to the many tricks and advanced programming techniques that were necessary under previous language versions.

Deploying a custom control is also considerably simpler than deploying an ActiveX control. In fact, you can deploy the control as a private assembly or install it in the GAC. The latter solution is preferable if the control must be used by many applications, but using private assemblies is OK in many cases. The control must not be installed in the GAC if it is being displayed from inside Internet Explorer. (See the section "Hosting Custom Controls in Internet Explorer" at the end of this chapter.)

Inheriting from an Existing Control

The easiest way to author a new Windows Forms control is by inheriting it from an existing control. This approach is the right one when you want to extend an existing control with new properties, methods, or events but without changing its appearance significantly. For example, you can create a ListBox that supports icons by using the owner-draw mode internally and exposing an Images collection to the outside. Here are other examples: an extended PictureBox control that supports methods for graphic effects and a TreeView-derived control that automatically displays the file and folder hierarchy for a given path.

In the example that follows, I use this technique to create an extended TextBox control named TextBoxEx, with several additional properties that perform advanced validation chores. I have chosen this example because it's relatively simple without being a toy control and because it's complete and useful enough to be used in a real application.

The TextBoxEx control has a property named IsRequired, which you set to True if the control must be filled before moving to another control, and the ValidateRegex property, which is a regular expression that the field's contents must match. There's also an ErrorMessage property and a Validate method, which returns True or False and can display a message box. Our control will take advantage of the Validating event of the standard TextBox control to cancel the focus shift if the current value can't be validated.

Creating the Control Project

Create a new Windows Control Library project named CustomControlsDemo. A project of this type is actually a Class Library project (that is, it generates a DLL) and contains a file named UserControl1.vb. Rename the file TextBoxEx.vb, then switch to its code portion, and replace the template created by Visual Studio with what follows:

```
Public Class TextBoxEx
    Inherits System.Windows.Forms.TextBox

End Class
```

This is just the skeleton of our new control, but it already has everything it needs to behave like a TextBox control. Because you want to expand on this control, let's begin by adding the new IsRequired property. Note the couple of Imports statements. (They'll be useful later.)

```
Imports System.Text.RegularExpressions
Imports System.ComponentModel

Public Class TextBoxEx
```

```
    Inherits System.Windows.Forms.TextBox

    Sub New()
        MyBase.New()
    End Sub

    ' The IsRequired property
    Dim m_IsRequired As Boolean

    Property IsRequired() As Boolean
        Get
            Return m_IsRequired
        End Get
        Set(ByVal Value As Boolean)
            m_IsRequired = Value
        End Set
    End Property
End Class
```

Note that you can't use a Public field to expose a property in the Properties window, in contrast with what you do with Visual Basic 6 ActiveX controls. Only properties appear in this window, so you must use a Property procedure even if you don't plan to validate the value entered by the user, as in the preceding case.

The Sub New constructor isn't strictly required in this demo, but it doesn't hurt either. In a more complex custom control, you can use this event to initialize a property to a different value; for example, you might set the Text property to a null string so that the developer who uses this control doesn't have to do it manually.

The control doesn't do anything useful yet, but you can compile it by selecting Build on the Build menu. This action produces a DLL executable file: take note of the path of this file because you'll need it very soon.

Creating the Client Application

On the File menu, point to Add Project and then click New Project to add a Windows Application project named CustomControlsTest to the same solution as the existing control. You can also create this test application using another instance of Visual Studio, but having both projects in the same solution has an important advantage, as I'll explain shortly.

Next make CustomControlsTest the start-up project so that it will start when you press F5. You can do this by right-clicking the project in the Solution Explorer window and clicking Set As Startup Project on the shortcut menu. Visual Studio confirms the new setting by displaying the new start-up project in boldface.

Right-click the Toolbox and click Add Tab on the shortcut menu to create a new tab named My Custom Controls, on which you'll place your custom controls. This step isn't required, but it helps you keep things well ordered.

Right-click the new Toolbox tab (which is empty), and click Customize Toolbox on the shortcut menu. Switch to the .NET Framework Components page in the Customize Toolbox dialog box that appears, click Browse, and select the CustomControlsDemo.dll file that you compiled previously. The TextBoxEx control appears now in the Customize Toolbox dialog box, so you can ensure that its check box is selected and that it is ready to be added to the custom tab you've created in the Toolbox. (See Figure 17-21.)

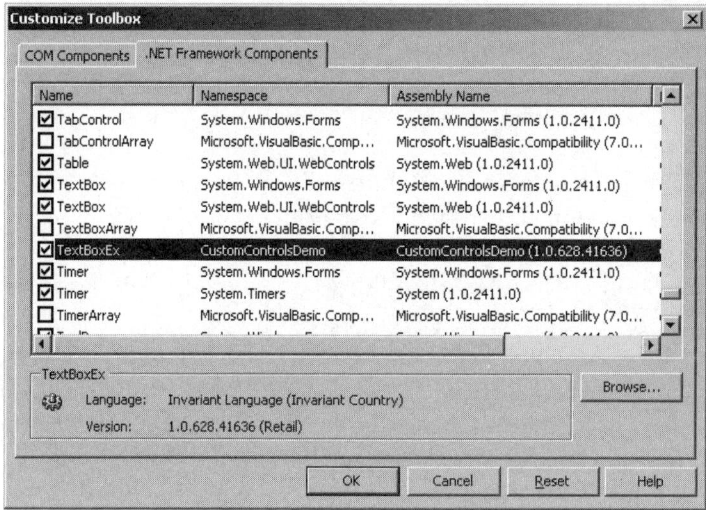

Figure 17-21. Adding a new control to the Toolbox.

Drop an instance of the control on the form, and switch to the Properties window: you'll see all the properties of the TextBox control, which should be no surprise because the TextBoxEx control inherits them from its base class. Scroll the Properties window to ensure that the new IsRequired property is also there: the designer has detected that it's a Boolean property, so the designer knows that the property can be set to True or False.

Adding the Validation Logic

Now that you know that your control is going to work correctly on a form's surface, you can go back to the TextBoxEx code module and add the remaining two properties. Note that the code checks that the regular expression assigned to the ValidateRegex property is correct by attempting a search on a dummy string:

```
' The ErrorMessage property

    Dim m_ErrorMessage As String

    Property ErrorMessage() As String
        Get
            Return m_ErrorMessage
        End Get
        Set(ByVal Value As String)
            m_ErrorMessage = Value
        End Set
    End Property

    ' The ValidateRegex property

    Dim m_ValidateRegex As String

    Property ValidateRegex() As String
        Get
            Return m_ValidateRegex
        End Get
        Set(ByVal Value As String)
            ' Check that this is a valid regular expression.
            Try
                If Value <> "" Then
                    Dim dummy As Boolean = Regex.IsMatch("abcde", Value)
                End If
                ' If no error assignment, value is OK.
                m_ValidateRegex = Value
            Catch ex As Exception
                MessageBox.Show(ex.Message, "Invalid Property", _
                    MessageBoxButtons.OK, MessageBoxIcon.Error)
            End Try
        End Set
    End Property
```

You now have all you need to implement the Validate method, which returns False if the current value doesn't pass the validation test. Note that the code uses the MyBase.Text property to access the control's contents.

```
' The Validate method

    Function Validate() As Boolean
        ' Assume control passed the validation.
        Validate = True

        ' Apply the IsRequired property.
        If Me.IsRequired And Me.Text = "" Then
```

(continued)

```
            Validate = False
        End If

        ' Apply the ValidateRegex property if specified.
        If Validate = True And Me.ValidateRegex <> "" Then
            Validate = Regex.IsMatch(Me.Text, Me.ValidateRegex)
        End If
    End Function
```

The structure of the Validate method permits you to add other validation tests just before the End Function statement. Having a single place in which the validation occurs means that this is the only point to modify when you want to extend the control with new properties.

You still need to write the code that actually validates the current value when the user moves the input focus to a control that has CausesValidation set to True. The inner TextBox control fires a Validating event when this happens, so you can implement the validation by using the following naive approach:

```
' NOTE: CancelEventArgs is defined in System.ComponentModel.
Private Sub TextBoxEx_Validating(ByVal sender As Object, _
    ByVal e As CancelEventArgs) Handles MyBase.Validating
    ' If the validation fails, cancel the focus shift.
    If Me.Validate() = False Then e.Cancel = True
End Sub
```

This technique works, in the sense that it does prevent the focus from leaving the TextBoxEx control. The problem, however, is that you can't prevent the Validating event from propagating to your client form. In other words, the developer who uses this control will see a Validating event even if the focus shift is going to be canceled anyway.

A far better technique consists of intercepting the validation action *before* the inner TextBox object fires the event. You can do this by overriding the OnValidating protected method in the base class. You can create the template for the overridden method by clicking Overrides in the Class Name combo box in the code editor and then clicking the method in question in the Method Name combo box. (See Figure 17-22.) The following is the correct code for performing the internal validation; it correctly raises the Validating event only if the validation passed:

```
Protected Overrides Sub OnValidating(ByVal e As CancelEventArgs)
    If Me.Validate() Then
        ' If validation is OK, let the base class fire the Validating event.
        MyBase.OnValidating(e)
    Else
        ' Else, cancel the focus shift.
        e.Cancel = True
    End If
End Sub
```

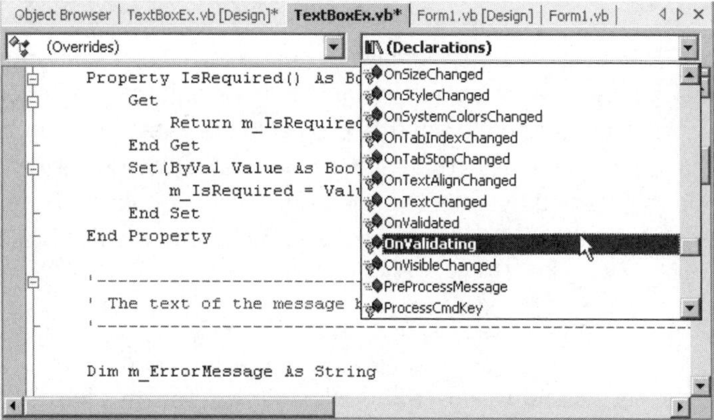

Figure 17-22. Using the code editor and the Class Name and Method Name combo boxes to create an overridden method.

The focal point here is the call to MyBase.OnValidating, where the base class fires the Validating event and possibly performs additional actions.

Recompiling Both Projects

Having both projects in the same solution offers an important advantage: you recompile both of them in one operation, and you can be sure that the client Windows Forms application always uses the latest version of the control. It's interesting to learn what Visual Studio does for you behind the scenes because this knowledge can help you get out of trouble in many cases.

As you might remember from the section "The Binding Process" in Chapter 14, a .NET application can use a private assembly only if the private assembly is located in the application's main directory or in a subdirectory under it. You haven't signed the CustomControlsDemo.dll; therefore, it's a private assembly. So the question is, how can the CustomControlsTest.exe program reference the CustomControlsDemo.dll assembly in another directory? It turns out that when you added the custom control to the Toolbox in the client application, Visual Studio automatically copied the CustomControlsDemo.dll into the CustomControlsTest\bin subdirectory, the same place the CustomControlsTest.exe file is located. Even more interesting, each time you recompile the CustomControlsDemo project, the new DLL is automatically copied to a location in which the CustomControlsTest application can see it. This is why the control on the form always sees the most recent version of the control. If you've struggled with binary compatibility problems under Visual Basic 6, you'll surely love this feature.

> **Note** The ability to automatically update references to other projects works with any type of project, not just custom controls. In general, if a project has a reference to another project in the same solution, the reference is automatically refreshed as needed. If necessary, you can disable this feature by selecting the referenced DLL in the References folder of the Solution Explorer window, switching to the Properties window, and setting the Copy Local property to False.

Even the schema I just described allows room for problems, however. For example, what happens if Visual Studio recompiles the CustomControlsTest project before CustomControlsDemo? In this case, the CustomControlsTest project would use an outdated version of the DLL. So the real question is this: how can you be sure that the projects in a solution are compiled in the correct order? The answer is that *you* decide what is the correct order by using the Project Dependencies command on the Project menu. This command brings up the Project Dependencies dialog box shown in Figure 17-23. On the Dependencies tab, you indicate which other projects a given project depends on; on the Build Order tab, you check that the resulting order is exactly the one you want.

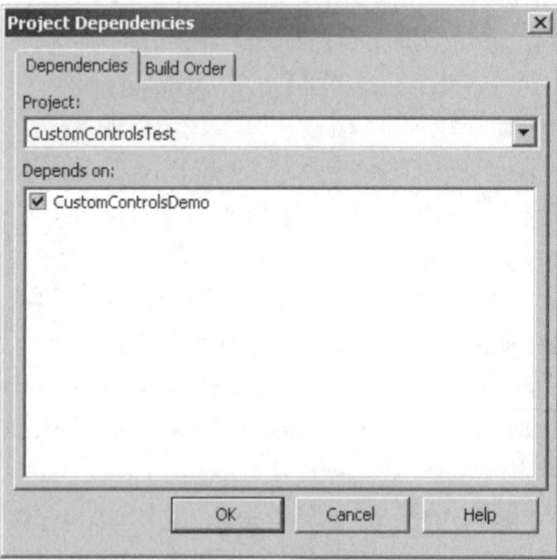

Figure 17-23. The Project Dependencies dialog box.

Testing the Control

You can test your control in the client form at last. Create a new form, and drop the following controls on it: a TextBoxEx control, a regular TextBox control, and a Label control that you'll use for displaying messages. Next set the TextBoxEx properties as follows:

```
' A required field that can contain only digits
TextBoxEx1.IsRequired = True
TextBoxEx1.ValidateRegex = "\d+"
```

Run the program; you'll see that you can't move the focus from the TextBoxEx control to the TextBox control unless you enter one or more digits (or you set the TextBox control's CausesValidation property to False). You can also add a Validating event procedure that proves that the form receives this event only if the internal validation passed:

```
Private Sub TextBoxEx1_Validating(ByVal sender As Object, _
    ByVal e As CancelEventArgs) Handles TextBoxEx1.Validating
    Label1.Text = "Validating event in form"
End Sub
```

Improving the Custom Control

You can add many other properties to the TextBoxEx control to increase its usefulness and flexibility. Each property is an occasion to discuss additional advanced capabilities of custom control creation.

Working with Other Types

It is interesting to see how the Properties browser works with properties that aren't plain numbers or strings. For example, you can add a DisplayControl and an ErrorForeColor property: the former takes a reference to a control that will be used to display the error message, and the latter is the color used for the error message itself. Implementing these properties is straightforward: you add a couple of Property procedures and add a few statements to the Validate method. (New statements are shown in boldface.)

```
Dim m_ErrorForeColor As Color = SystemColors.ControlText

Property ErrorForeColor() As Color
    Get
        Return m_ErrorForeColor
    End Get
    Set(ByVal Value As Color)
        m_ErrorForeColor = Value
    End Set
End Property

Dim m_DisplayControl As Control

Property DisplayControl() As Control
```

(continued)

```
    Get
        Return m_DisplayControl
    End Get
    Set(ByVal Value As Control)
        m_DisplayControl = Value
    End Set
End Property

Function Validate() As Boolean
    ' Assume control passed the validation.
    Validate = True

    ' Apply the IsRequired property.
    If Me.IsRequired And Me.Text = "" Then
        Validate = False
    End If

    ' Apply the ValidateRegex property.
    If Validate = True And Me.ValidateRegex <> "" Then
        Validate = Regex.IsMatch(Me.Text, Me.ValidateRegex)
    End If

    ' If the validation failed but the client defined a display control
    ' and an error message, show the message in the control.
    If DisplayMessage And Not (DisplayControl Is Nothing) _
        And Me.ErrorMessage <> "" Then
        If Validate Then
            ' Delete any previous error message.
            DisplayControl.Text = ""
        Else
            ' Display error message, and enforce color.
            DisplayControl.Text = Me.ErrorMessage
            DisplayControl.ForeColor = m_ErrorForeColor
        End If
    End If
End Function
```

Next rebuild the solution, select the TextBoxEx control, and switch to the Properties window, where you'll see a couple of interesting things. First, the ErrorForeColor property displays the same color palette that all other color properties expose. Second, the Properties window recognizes the nature of the new DisplayControl property and displays a drop-down list that lets you select one of the controls on the current form. In this particular example, you can set this property to the Label1 control so that all error messages appear there. Also, remember to store a suitable message in the ErrorMessage property. Of course, you can do these operations from code as well, which is necessary if the target control is on another form:

```
TextBoxEx1.ErrorMessage = "This field must contain a positive number"
TextBoxEx1.ErrorForeColor = Color.Red
TextBoxEx1.DisplayControl = Label1
```

You can see another smart behavior of the Properties window if you have an enumerated property. For example, you can create a ValueType property that states the type of variable to which the contents of the field will be assigned. Because most enumerated values are Visual Basic keywords, you must enclose them in square brackets. (You can also use this trick when the name contains spaces or other symbols.)

```
Enum ValidTypes
    Any = 0
    [Byte]
    [Short]
    [Integer]
    [Long]
    [Single]
    [Double]
    [Decimal]
    [DateTime]
End Enum


Dim m_ValidType As ValidTypes

Property ValidType() As ValidTypes
    Get
        Return m_ValidType
    End Get
    Set(ByVal Value As ValidTypes)
        m_ValidType = Value
    End Set
End Property
```

You can browse the demo application to see how this feature is implemented, but for now just rebuild the solution and go to the Properties window again to check that the ValueType property corresponds to a combo box that lets the user select the valid type among those available.

Adding Attributes

If you have ever created ActiveX controls under Visual Basic, you surely remember the large number of properties you had to set for each property from inside the Procedure Attributes dialog box. Faithful to the .NET philosophy—which dictates that everything related to applications should be rendered as plain code—these properties correspond now to attributes that you assign to property procedures or methods.

For example, all properties are displayed in the Properties window by default. This isn't desirable for read-only properties (which are visible but grayed by default) or for properties that should be assigned only at run time via code. You can control the visibility of elements in the Properties window by using the Browsable attribute; the default value for this attribute is True, so you must set it to False to hide the element:

```
' This property has the same semantics as the Validate method.
' (Just an example to show how you can hide a property.)

<Browsable(False)> _
ReadOnly Property IsValid() As Boolean
    Get
        Return Validate()
    End Get
End Property
```

Another frequently used attribute is Description, which defines the string displayed near the bottom edge of the Properties window:

```
<Description("The control that will display the error message")> _
Property DisplayControl() As Control
    ⋮
End Property
```

You put a property into a category in the Properties window by using the Category attribute. You can specify one of the existing categories—Layout, Behavior, Appearance—or define a new one. If a property doesn't belong to a specific category, it appears in the Misc category:

```
<Description("The control that will display the error message"), _
    Category("Validation")> _
Property DisplayControl() As Control
    ⋮
End Property
```

By default, properties aren't localizable and the form designer doesn't save their values in a separate source file when the user selects a language other than the default one. You can change this default behavior by using the Localizable attribute:

```
<Localizable(True) > _
Property HeaderCaption() As String
    ⋮
End Property
```

The DefaultProperty attribute tells the environment which property should be selected when the user creates a new instance of the control and then activates the Properties window. Similarly, the DefaultEvent attribute specifies the event handler that's automatically created when you double-click on a control in the designer. (For example, TextChanged is the default event for the TextBox control.) You apply these attributes to the class and pass them the name of the property or the event:

```
<DefaultProperty("IsRequired"), DefaultEvent("InvalidKey")> _
Public Class TextBoxEx
    Inherits System.Windows.Forms.TextBox

    Event InvalidKey(ByVal sender As Object, ByVal e As EventArgs)
    ⋮
End Class
```

The MargableProperty attribute tells whether a property is visible in the Properties window when multiple controls are selected. The default value of this attribute is True, so you must include it explicitly only if you don't want to allow the user to modify this property for all the selected controls. In practice, you use this attribute when a property can't have the same value for multiple controls on a form (as in the case of the TabIndex or Name property):

```
<MargableProperty(False)> _
Property ProcessOrder() As Integer
    ⋮
End Class
```

The RefreshProperties attribute is useful if a new value assigned to a property can affect other properties in the Properties window. The default behavior of the Properties window is that only the value of the property being edited is updated, but you can specify that all properties should be requeried and refreshed by using this attribute:

```
<RefreshProperties(RefreshProperties.All)> _
Property MaxValue() As Long
    Get
        Return m_MaxValue
    End Get
    Set(ByVal Value As Long)
        m_MaxValue = Value
        ' This property can affect the Value property.
        If Value > m_MaxValue Then Value = m_MaxValue
    End Set
End Property
```

The last attribute you might want to add to your first custom control is ToolboxBitmap, which you apply at the class level. In its simplest form, this attribute takes the path of a file that contains a 16-by-16-pixel bitmap or icon:

```
<ToolboxBitmap("C:\CustomControlsDemo\FileTextBox.ico")> _
Public Class FileTextBox
    ⋮
End Class
```

An overloaded syntax variation of this attribute's constructor lets you specify the name of a type and the name of a resource compiled in that type's executable. For more information, read the .NET Platform SDK documentation.

Working with Default Values

You have surely noticed that the Properties window displays in boldface values different from the property's default value, so you might have wondered where the default value is defined. As you might guess, you define the default value with yet another attribute, appropriately named DefaultValue. This example is taken from the demo application:

```
Dim m_BeepOnError As Boolean = True

<Description("If True, a beep will be emitted if validation fails"), _
    DefaultValue(True)> _
Property BeepOnError() As Boolean
    Get
        Return m_BeepOnError
    End Get
    Set(ByVal Value As Boolean)
        m_BeepOnError = Value
    End Set
End Property
```

Note that the default value is just a directive to the Properties window: it doesn't actually initialize the property itself. For that, you must use an initializer or use the necessary code in the Sub New procedure.

Unfortunately, the DefaultValue attribute has a problem: it can take only constant values, and in several cases the default value isn't a constant. For example, the value SystemColors.ControlText, which is the initial value for the ErrorForeColor property, isn't a constant, so you can't pass it to the DefaultValue attribute's constructor. To resolve this difficulty, the author of the custom control can create a special Reset*xxxx* procedure, where *xxxx* is the property name. Here is the code in the TextBoxEx class that the form designer implicitly calls to initialize the two color properties:

```
Sub ResetErrorForeColor()
    ErrorForeColor = SystemColors.ControlText
End Sub
```

If a property is associated with a Reset*xxxx* method, you can reset the property by clicking Reset on the context menu that you bring up by clicking on the property name in the Properties window.

The DefaultValue attribute has another, less obvious, use: if a property is set to its default value—as specified by this attribute—this property isn't persisted, and the designer generates no code for it. This behavior is highly desirable because it avoids the generation of a lot of useless code that would slow down the rendering of the parent form. Alas, you know that you can't specify a nonconstant value, a color, a font, or another complex object in the DefaultValue attribute. In this case, you must implement a method named ShouldSerialize*xxxx* (where *xxxx* is the name of the property) that returns True if the property must be serialized and False if its current value is equal to its default value:

```
Function ShouldSerializeErrorForeColor() As Boolean
    ' We can't use the = operators on objects, so we use
    ' the Equals method.
    Return Not Me.ErrorForeColor.Equals(SystemColors.ControlText)
End Function
```

Composing Multiple Controls

More complex custom controls require that you combine multiple controls by using an approach more like the one available under Visual Basic 6. You can think of several custom controls of this type, such as

- TreeView, ListView, and Splitter controls that work together to provide Windows Explorer–like functionality
- Two ListBox controls that let you move items from one ListBox to the other, using auxiliary buttons or drag-and-drop (This type is the typical control used in many wizards.)
- A scrollable image viewer, made up of a PictureBox and two scroll bar controls
- A calculator control, made up of one TextBox and several Button controls

In this section, I build a composite custom control named FileTextBox, which lets the user enter a filename by typing its name in a field or by selecting it in an OpenFile common dialog box.

Creating the UserControl Component

Add a new UserControl module named FileTextBox to the CustomControlsDemo project by selecting the project and then selecting Add UserControl on the Project menu. Ensure that you've selected the CustomControlsDemo project before you perform this action—otherwise, the custom control will be added to the test application instead.

The UserControl class derives from the ContainerControl class, so it can work as a container for other controls. In this respect, the UserControl object behaves very much like the Form object, and in fact, the programming interface of these classes is very similar, with properties such as Font, ForeColor,

AutoScroll, and so on. A few typical form properties are missing because they don't make sense in a control—for example, MainMenu and TopMost—but by and large, you code against a UserControl as if you were working with a regular form.

You can therefore drop on the UserControl's surface the three child controls you need for the FileTextBox control. These are a TextBox for the filename (named txtFilename, with a blank Text property); an OpenFileDialog control to display the dialog box (named OpenFileDialog1); and a Button control to let the user bring up the common dialog (named btnBrowse, with the Text property set to three dots). You can arrange these controls in the manner of Figure 17-24. Don't pay too much attention to their alignment, however, because you're going to move them on the UserControl's surface by means of code.

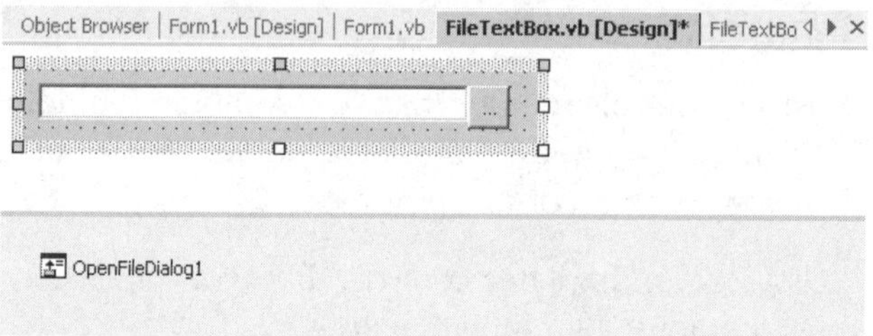

Figure 17-24. The FileTextBox custom control at design time.

Before you start adding code, you should compile the CustomControlsDemo project to rebuild the DLL and then switch to the client project to invoke the Customize ToolBox command. You'll see that the FileTextBox control doesn't appear yet in the list of available .NET controls in the Toolbox, so you have to click on the Browse button and select CustomControlsDemo.dll once again.

If all worked well, the new FileTextBox is in the Toolbox and you can drop it on the test form. You can resize it as usual, but its contents don't resize correctly because you haven't written any code that handles resizing.

Adding Properties, Methods, and Events

The FileTextBox control doesn't expose any useful properties yet, other than those provided by the UserControl class. The three child controls you placed on the UserControl's surface can't be reached at all because by default they have a Friend scope and can't be seen from code in the client project. Your next step is to provide programmatic access to the values in these controls. In most cases, all you need to do is create a property procedure that wraps directly around a child control's property. For example, you can implement the Filename and Filter properties, as follows:

```
' This code assumes that you added the following statement:
'    Imports System.ComponentModel
```

```
<Description("The filename as it appears in the textbox")> _
Property Filename() As String
    Get
        Return Me.txtFilename.Text
    End Get
    Set(ByVal Value As String)
        Me.txtFilename.Text = Value
    End Set
End Property

<Description("The list of file filters"), _
    DefaultValue("All files (*.*)|*.*")> _
Property Filter() As String
    Get
        Return OpenFileDialog1.Filter
    End Get
    Set(ByVal Value As String)
        OpenFileDialog1.Filter = Value
    End Set
End Property
```

If you wrap your property procedures around child controls' properties, you must be certain that you properly initialize the child controls so that the initial values of their properties match the values passed to the DefaultValue attribute. In this case, you must ensure that you set the OpenFileDialog1.Filter property correctly.

You don't create wrappers around child controls' properties only. For example, you can implement a ShowDialog method that wraps around the OpenFileDialog1 control method of the same name:

```
Function ShowDialog() As DialogResult
    ' Show the OpenFile dialog, and return the result.
    ShowDialog = OpenFileDialog1.ShowDialog
    ' If the result is OK, assign the filename to the TextBox.
    If ShowDialog = DialogResult.OK Then
        txtFilename.Text = OpenFileDialog1.FileName
    End If
End Function
```

You can also provide wrappers for events. For example, exposing the FileOk event gives the client code the ability to reject invalid filenames:

```
Event FileOk(ByVal sender As Object, ByVal e As CancelEventArgs)

Private Sub OpenFileDialog1_FileOk(ByVal sender As Object, _
    ByVal e As CancelEventArgs) Handles OpenFileDialog1.FileOk
    RaiseEvent FileOk(Me, e)
End Sub
```

Bear in mind that the client will receive the event from the FileTextBox control, not from the inner OpenFileDialog control, so you must pass Me as the first argument of the RaiseEvent method, as in the preceding code snippet. In some cases, you also need to change the name of the event to meet the client code's expectations, as in the following example:

```
Event FilenameChanged(ByVal sender As Object, ByVal e As EventArgs)

Private Sub txtFilename_TextChanged(ByVal sender As Object, _
    ByVal e As EventArgs) Handles txtFilename.TextChanged
    RaiseEvent FilenameChanged(Me, e)
End Sub
```

Not all events should be exposed to the outside, however. The Button's Click event, for example, is handled internally to automatically fill the txtFilename field when the user selects a file from the common dialog box:

```
Private Sub btnBrowse_Click(ByVal sender As Object, _
    ByVal e As EventArgs) Handles btnBrowse.Click
    ' Just delegate to the ShowDialog method.
    ShowDialog()
End Sub
```

Shadowing and Overriding UserControl Properties

If you modify the Font property of the FileTextBox control, you'll notice that the new settings are immediately applied to the inner txtFilename control, so you don't have to manually implement the Font property. The custom control behaves this way because you never assign a specific value to txtFilename.Font, so it automatically inherits the parent UserControl's settings. This feature can often save you a lot of code and time. The group of properties that you shouldn't implement explicitly includes Enabled and TabStop because all the constituent controls inherit these properties from their UserControl container.

You're not always that lucky. For example, TextBox controls don't inherit automatically the ForeColor of their container, and you have to implement this property manually. A minor annoyance is that the UserControl already exposes a property of this name, so you receive a compilation warning. You can get rid of this warning by using the Shadows keyword. Note that you must use explicit shadowing also with the Reset*xxxx* procedure:

```
Shadows Property ForeColor() As Color
    Get
        Return txtFilename.ForeColor
    End Get
    Set(ByVal Value As Color)
        txtFilename.ForeColor = Value
    End Set
End Property
```

```
Shadows Sub ResetForeColor()
    Me.ForeColor = SystemColors.ControlText
End Sub

Function ShouldSerializeForeColor() As Boolean
    Return Not Me.ForeColor.Equals(SystemColors.ControlText)
End Function
```

If your custom control exposes a property with the same name, return type, and default value as a property in the base UserControl, you can override it instead of shadowing it. For example, the FileTextBox control overrides the ContextMenu property so that the pop-up menu appears also when the end user right-clicks on constituent controls:

```
Overrides Property ContextMenu() As ContextMenu
    Get
        Return MyBase.ContextMenu
    End Get
    Set(ByVal Value As ContextMenu)
        MyBase.ContextMenu = Value
        ' Propagate the new value to constituent controls.
        ' (This generic code works with any UserControl.)
        Dim ctrl As Control
        For Each ctrl In Me.Controls
            ctrl.ContextMenu = Me.ContextMenu
        Next
    End Set
End Property
```

In many cases, however, you really have to go as far as overriding a property in the base UserControl only if you need to cancel its default behavior. If you just want a notification that a property has changed, you can be satisfied by simply trapping the *xxxx*Changed event. For example, the following code displays the btnBrowse button control with a flat appearance when the FileTextBox control is disabled:

```
Private Sub FileTextBox_EnabledChanged(ByVal sender As Object, _
    ByVal e As EventArgs) Handles MyBase.EnabledChanged
    If Me.Enabled Then
        btnBrowse.FlatStyle = FlatStyle.Standard
    Else
        btnBrowse.FlatStyle = FlatStyle.Flat
    End If
End Sub
```

Note that *xxxx*Changed events don't fire at design time, so you can't use this method to react to setting changes in the Properties window.

You often need to shadow properties in the base class for the sole purpose of hiding them in the Properties window. For example, the demo FileTextBox control can't work as a scrollable container, so it shouldn't display the AutoScroll, AutoScrollMargins, AutoScrollPosition, and DockPadding items in the Properties window. You can achieve this by shadowing the property and adding a Browsable(False) attribute:

```
<Browsable(False)> _
Shadows Property AutoScroll() As Boolean
    Get
        ' Don't really need to delegate to inner UserControl.
    End Get
    Set(ByVal Value As Boolean)
        ' Don't really need to delegate to inner UserControl.
    End Set
End Property
```

Although you can easily hide a property in the Properties window, inheritance rules prevent you from completely wiping out a UserControl property from the custom control's programming interface. However, you can throw an exception when this property is accessed at run time programmatically so that the developer using this custom control learns the lesson more quickly. You can discern whether you're in design mode or run-time mode with the DesignMode property, which the UserControl inherits from the System.ComponentModel.Component object:

```
<Browsable(False)> _
Shadows Property AutoScroll() As Boolean
    Get
        If Not Me.DesignMode Then
            Throw New NotImplementedException()
        End If
    End Get
    Set(ByVal Value As Boolean)
        If Not Me.DesignMode Then
            Throw New NotImplementedException()
        End If
    End Set
End Property
```

You must check the DesignMode property before throwing the exception—otherwise, the control doesn't work correctly in design-time mode. You can use this property for many other purposes, such as displaying a slightly different user interface at design time or run time.

Adding Resize Logic

The code inside your UserControl determines how its constituent controls are arranged when the control is resized. In the simplest cases, you don't have to write code to achieve the desired effect because you can simply rely on the Anchor and Dock properties of constituent controls. However, this approach is rarely feasible with more complex custom controls. For example, the btn-Browse button in FileTextBox should always be square, and so its height and width depend on the txtFilename control's height, which in turn depends on the current font. Besides, the height of the FileTextBox control should always be equal to the height of its inner fields. All these constraints require that you write custom resize logic in a private RedrawControls procedure and call this procedure from the UserControl's Resize event:

```
Private Sub FileTextBox_Resize(ByVal sender As Object, _
    ByVal e As System.EventArgs) Handles MyBase.Resize
    RedrawControls()
End Sub

Private Sub RedrawControls()
    ' This is the width of the control.
    Dim width As Integer = Me.ClientRectangle.Width
    ' This is the (desired) height of the control.
    Dim btnSide As Integer = txtFilename.Height

    ' Adjust the height of the UserControl if necessary.
    If Me.ClientRectangle.Height <> btnSide Then
        ' Resize the UserControl.
        Me.SetClientSizeCore(Me.ClientRectangle.Width, btnSide)
        ' The above statement fires a nested Resize event, so exit right now.
        Exit Sub
    End If

    ' Resize the constituent controls.
    txtFilename.SetBounds(0, 0, width - btnSide, btnSide)
    btnBrowse.SetBounds(width - btnSide, 0, btnSide, btnSide)
End Sub
```

Don't forget that the custom control's height should also change when its Font property changes, so you must override the OnFontChanged method as well. (You can't simply trap the FontChanged event because it doesn't fire at design time.)

```
Protected Overrides Sub OnFontChanged(ByVal e As System.EventArgs)
    ' Let the base control update the TextBox control.
    MyBase.OnFontChanged(e)
    ' Now we can redraw controls if necessary.
    RedrawControls()
End Sub
```

Creating a Control from Scratch

The third technique for creating a custom control is building it from scratch, by inheriting from the Control class and painting directly on its surface using graphic methods in the GDI+ package. This technique corresponds to creating owner-draw ActiveX controls in Visual Basic 6. In general, it's a more complex approach than the other two techniques you've seen so far.

In this section, I'll illustrate a relatively simple example: a custom control named GradientControl, which can be used to provide a gradient background for other controls. Figure 17-25 shows this control at design time, but most of the time, you'll set its Docked property to Fill so that it spreads over the entire form. This control has only three properties: StartColor, EndColor, and GradientMode. This is the complete source code for this control:

```
Imports System.ComponentModel
Imports System.Drawing.Drawing2D

Public Class GradientBackground
    Inherits System.Windows.Forms.Control

    ' The StartColor property
    Dim m_StartColor As Color = Color.Blue

    <Description("The start color for the gradient")> _
    Property StartColor() As Color
        Get
            Return m_StartColor
        End Get
        Set(ByVal Value As Color)
            m_StartColor = Value
            ' Redraw the control when this property changes.
            Me.Invalidate()
        End Set
    End Property

    Sub ResetStartColor()
        m_StartColor = Color.Blue
    End Sub

    Function ShouldSerializeStartColor() As Boolean
        Return Not m_StartColor.Equals(Color.Blue)
    End Function

    ' The EndColor property
    Dim m_EndColor As Color = Color.Black

    <Description("The end color for the gradient")> _
    Property EndColor() As Color
```

```
        Get
            Return m_EndColor
        End Get
        Set(ByVal Value As Color)
            m_EndColor = Value
            ' Redraw the control when this property changes.
            Me.Invalidate()
        End Set
    End Property

    Sub ResetEndColor()
        m_EndColor = Color.Black
    End Sub

    Function ShouldSerializeEndColor() As Boolean
        Return Not m_EndColor.Equals(Color.Black)
    End Function

    ' The GradientMode property
    Dim m_GradientMode As LinearGradientMode = _
        LinearGradientMode.ForwardDiagonal

    <Description("The gradient mode"), _
        DefaultValue(LinearGradientMode.ForwardDiagonal)> _
    Property GradientMode() As LinearGradientMode
        Get
            Return m_GradientMode
        End Get
        Set(ByVal Value As LinearGradientMode)
            m_GradientMode = Value
            ' Redraw the control when this property changes.
            Me.Invalidate()
        End Set
    End Property

    ' Render the control background.

    Protected Overrides Sub OnPaint(ByVal e As PaintEventArgs)
        ' Create a gradient brush as large as the client area, with specified
        ' start/end color and gradient mode.
        Dim br As New LinearGradientBrush(Me.ClientRectangle, _
            m_StartColor, m_EndColor, m_GradientMode)
        ' Paint the background.
        e.Graphics.FillRectangle(br, Me.ClientRectangle)
        ' Destroy the brush in an orderly manner.
        br.Dispose()
        ' Let the base control do its chores (e.g., raising the Paint event).
        MyBase.OnPaint(e)
    End Sub
```

(continued)

```
    Private Sub GradientBackground_Resize(ByVal sender As Object, _
        ByVal e As EventArgs) Handles MyBase.Resize
        Me.Invalidate()
    End Sub
End Class
```

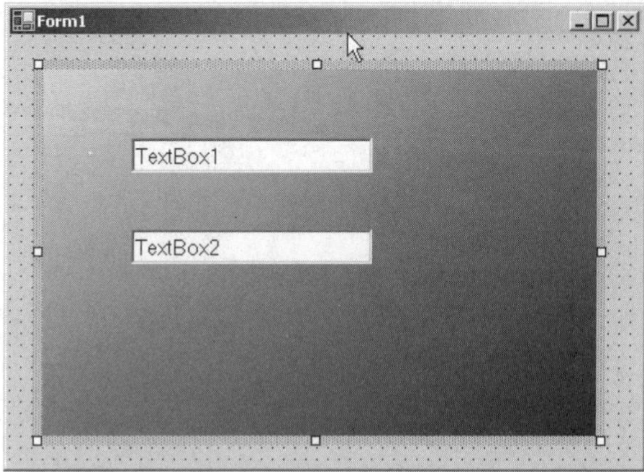

Figure 17-25. You can use the GradientControl to create eye-catching backgrounds by just setting three properties.

A custom control implemented by inheriting from the Control class must render itself in the overridden OnPaint method. In this particular case, redrawing the control is trivial because the System.Drawing.Drawing2d namespace exposes a LinearGradientBrush object that does all the work for you. In practice, you only have to create a gradient brush as large as the control itself and then use this brush to paint the control's client rectangle. The last argument you pass to the brush's constructor is the gradient mode, an enumerated value that lets you create horizontal, vertical, forward diagonal (default), and backward diagonal gradients. The GradientMode property is opportunely defined as type LinearGradientMode so that these four modes appear in a drop-down list box in the Properties window.

The only other detail to take care of is refreshing the control whenever a property changes. The best way to do so is by invalidating the control appearance with its Invalidate method so that the form engine can refresh the control at the first occurrence. This is considered a better practice than invoking the Refresh method directly because the form engine can delay all repaint operations until it's appropriate to perform them.

Advanced Topics

Windows Forms control creation is a complex topic, and I don't have space enough to cover every little detail. But what you've learned in previous chapters and the techniques I am covering in this section are more than sufficient to enable you to author useful and complex controls with relatively little effort.

Multithreaded Controls

Creating a multithreaded control class isn't different from creating a new thread in a regular application, and you have several options: you can create a new Thread object, use a thread from the thread pool, or just use asynchronous method invocation. (Threading is covered in Chapter 13.) The only potential glitch you should watch for is that the control you have created—whether it's inherited from a Control, a UserControl, or another control—must be accessed *exclusively* from the thread that created it. In fact, all the Windows Forms controls rely on the single-threaded apartment (STA) model because windows and controls are based on the Win32 message architecture, which is inherently apartment-threaded. This means that a control (or a form, for that matter) can be created on any thread, but all the methods of the control must be called from the thread that created the control. This constraint can create a serious problem because other .NET portions use the free-threading model, and carelessly mixing the two models isn't a wise idea.

The only methods that you can call on a control object from another thread are Invoke, BeginInvoke, and EndInvoke. You already know from Chapter 13 how to use the latter two methods for calling a method asynchronously, so in this section I'll focus on the Invoke method exclusively. This method takes a delegate pointing to a method (Sub or Function) and can take an Object array as a second argument if the method expects one or more arguments.

To illustrate how to use this method, I've prepared a CountdownLabel control, which continuously displays the number of seconds left until the countdown expires. (See Figure 17-26.) The code that updates the Label runs on another thread. You start the countdown by using the StartCountdown method, and you can stop it before the end by using the StopCountdown method.

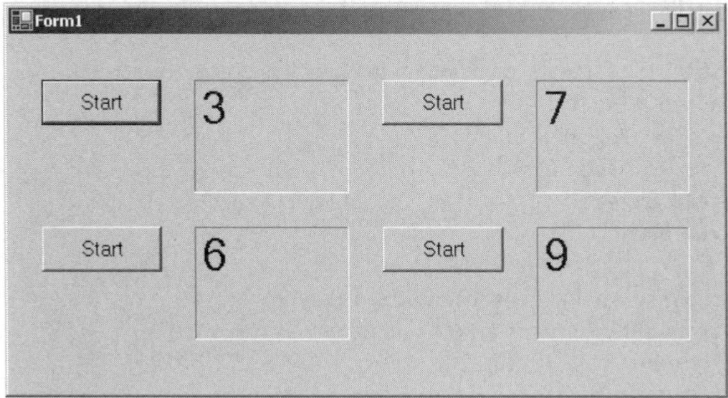

Figure 17-26. A form with four CountdownLabel instances.

Here are the steps you must take to correctly implement multithreading in a control:

1. Define a private method that operates on the control or its properties. This method runs in the control's main thread and can therefore access all the control's members. In the sample control, this method is named SetText and takes the string to be displayed in the Label control.
2. Declare a delegate patterned after the method defined in step 1; in the sample control, this is called SetTextDelegate.
3. Declare a delegate variable and make it point to the method defined in step 1; this value is passed to the Invoke method. In the sample control, this variable is named SetTextMarshaler: the name comes from the fact that this delegate actually marshals data from the new thread to the control's main thread.
4. Create a method that spawns the new thread using one of the techniques described in Chapter 13. For simplicity's sake, the sample application uses the Thread object; in the sample control, this task is performed by the StartCountdown method.

Here's the complete listing of the CountdownLabel control:

```
Imports System.Threading

Public Class CountdownLabel
    Inherits System.Windows.Forms.Label

    ' A delegate that points to the SetText procedure
    Delegate Sub SetTextDelegate(ByVal Text As String)

    ' An instance of this delegate that points to the SetText procedure
    Dim SetTextMarshaler As SetTextDelegate = AddressOf Me.SetText

    ' The internal counter for number of seconds left
    Dim secondsLeft As Integer
    ' The end time for countdown
    Dim endTime As Date
    ' The thread object: if nothing, no other thread is running.
    Dim thr As Thread

    Sub StartCountdown(ByVal seconds As Integer)
        ' Wait until all variables can be accessed safely.
        SyncLock Me
            ' Save values where the other thread can access them.
            secondsLeft = seconds
            endTime = Now.AddSeconds(seconds)
```

```
            ' Create a new thread, and run the procedure on that thread
            ' only if the thread isn't running already.
            If (thr Is Nothing) Then
                thr = New Thread(AddressOf CountProc)
                thr.Start()
            End If
        End SyncLock

        ' Display the initial value in the label.
        SetText(CStr(seconds))
    End Sub

    Sub StopCountdown()
        SyncLock Me
            ' This statement implicitly causes CountProc to exit.
            endTime = Now
        End SyncLock
    End Sub

    ' This procedure is just a wrapper for a simple property set and must run
    ' on the control's creation thread. The other thread(s) must call it
    ' through the control's Invoke method.
    Private Sub SetText(ByVal Text As String)
        Me.Text = Text
    End Sub

    ' This procedure runs on another thread.
    Private Sub CountProc()
        Do
            ' Ensure that this is the only thread that is accessing variables.
            SyncLock Me
                ' Calculate the number of seconds left.
                Dim secs As Integer = CInt(endTime.Subtract(Now).TotalSeconds)

                ' If different from current value, update the Text property.
                If secs <> secondsLeft Then
                    ' Never display negative numbers.
                    If secs < 0 Then secs = 0
                    secondsLeft = secs

                    ' Arguments must be passed in an Object array.
                    Dim args() As Object = {CStr(secondsLeft)}
                    ' Update the Text property with current number of seconds.
                    MyBase.Invoke(SetTextMarshaler, args)

                    ' Terminate the thread if countdown is over.
                    If secondsLeft <= 0 Then
                        ' Signal that no thread is running, and exit.
```

(continued)

```
                    thr = Nothing
                    Exit Do
                End If
            End If
        End SyncLock

        ' Wait for 100 milliseconds.
        Thread.Sleep(100)
    Loop
End Sub

End Class
```

As usual in multithreaded applications, you must pay a lot of attention to how you access variables shared among threads to prevent your control from randomly crashing after hours of testing. Other problems can arise if the user closes the form while the other thread is running because this extra thread attempts to access a control that doesn't exist any longer and would prevent the application from shutting down correctly. You can work around this obstacle by killing the other thread when the control is being destroyed, which you do by overriding the OnHandleDestroyed method:

```
' Kill the other thread if the control is being destroyed.
    Protected Overrides Sub OnHandleDestroyed(ByVal e As System.EventArgs)
        SyncLock Me
            If Not (thr Is Nothing) AndAlso thr.IsAlive Then
                thr.Abort()
                thr.Join()
            End If
        End SyncLock
        MyBase.OnHandleDestroyed(e)
    End Sub
```

Remember that you can't use the RaiseEvent statement from another thread. To have the CountdownLabel control fire an event when the countdown is complete, you must adopt the same technique described previously. You must create a method that calls RaiseEvent and runs on the main thread, define a delegate that points to it, and use Invoke from the other thread when you want to raise the event.

> **Tip** The techniques described in this section should be used whenever you access a Windows Forms control from another thread and not just when you're creating a custom control.

Extender Provider Controls

You can create property extender controls similar to those provided with the Windows Forms package, such as ToolTip and HelpProvider. In this section, I'll guide you through the creation of a component named UserPropExtender, which adds a property named UserRole to all the visible controls on the form. The developer can assign a user role to this list, or even a semicolon-separated list of roles, such as Manager;Accountants. At run time, the UserPropExtender control makes invisible those controls that are associated with a user role different from the current role (information that you assign to the UserPropExtender control's CurrentUserRole property). Thanks to the UserPropExtender control, you can provide different control layouts for different user roles without writing any code. Here are the steps you must follow when creating an extender provider control:

1. You define a class for your extender provider, making it inherit from System.Windows.Forms.Control (if the new control has a user interface) or from System.ComponentModel.Component (if the new control isn't visible at run time and should be displayed in the component tray of the form designer).

2. Associate a ProvideProperty attribute with the class you've created in the preceding step. The constructor for this attribute takes the name of the property that's added to all the controls on the form and a second System.Type argument that defines which type of objects can be extended by this extender provider. In this example, the new property is named UserList and can be applied to Control objects.

3. All extender providers must implement the IExtenderProvider interface, so you must add a suitable Implements statement. This interface has only one method, CanExtend, which receives an Object and is expected to return True if that object can be extended with the new property. The code in the sample control returns True for all control classes except its own class.

4. Declare and initialize a class-level Hashtable object that stores the value of the UserName property for all the controls on the form, where the control itself is used as a key in the Hashtable. In the sample project, this collection is named userListValues.

5. Define two methods, Get*xxxx* and Set*xxxx*, where *xxxx* is the name of the property that the extender provider adds to all other controls. (These methods are named GetUserName and SetUserName in the sample control.) These methods can read and write values in the Hashtable defined in the preceding step and modify the control's user interface as necessary. (The Set*xxxx* method is invoked from the code that is automatically generated by the form designer.)

Armed with this knowledge, you should be able to decode the complete listing for the UserPropExtender component quite easily:

```
Imports System.ComponentModel

' Let the form know that this control will add the UserRole property.
<ProvideProperty("UserRole", GetType(Control))> _
Public Class UserPropExtender
    Inherits System.ComponentModel.Component

    Implements IExtenderProvider

    ' Return True for all controls that can be extended with
    ' the UserRole property.
    Public Function CanExtend(ByVal extendee As Object) As Boolean _
        Implements System.ComponentModel.IExtenderProvider.CanExtend
        ' Extend all controls except this one. (Not really necessary in
        ' this case because this is a component, not a control.)
        If Not (TypeOf extendee Is UserPropExtender) Then
            Return True
        End If
    End Function

    ' The Hashtable object that associates controls with their UserRole
    Dim userRoleValues As New Hashtable()

    ' These are the Get/Set methods related to the property being added.

    Function GetUserRole(ByVal ctrl As Control) As String
        ' Check whether a property is associated with this control.
        Dim value As Object = userRoleValues(ctrl)
        ' Return the value found or an empty string.
        If value Is Nothing Then
            Return ""
        Else
            Return value.ToString
        End If
    End Function

    Sub SetUserRole(ByVal ctrl As Control, ByVal value As String)
        ' In case Nothing is passed
        If Value Is Nothing Then Value = ""

        If Value.Length = 0 And userRoleValues.Contains(ctrl) Then
            ' Remove the control from the hash table.
            userRoleValues.Remove(ctrl)
            ' Remove event handlers, if any
            ' (none in this example).
        ElseIf Value.Length > 0 Then
```

```
        If Not userRoleValues.Contains(ctrl) Then
            ' Add event handlers here
            ' (none in this example).
        End If
        ' Assign the new value, and refresh the control.
        userRoleValues.Item(ctrl) = Value
        SetControlVisibility(ctrl)
    End If
End Sub

' This property is assigned the name of the current user.

Dim m_CurrentUserRole As String

Property CurrentUserRole() As String
    Get
        Return m_CurrentUserRole
    End Get
    Set(ByVal Value As String)
        m_CurrentUserRole = Value
        RefreshAllControls()      ' Redraw all controls.
    End Set
End Property

' Hide/show all controls based on their UserRole property.

Sub RefreshAllControls()
    Dim ctrl As Control
    For Each ctrl In userRoleValues.Keys
        SetControlVisibility(ctrl)
    Next
End Sub

' Hide/show a single control based on its UserRole property.

Private Sub SetControlVisibility(ByVal ctrl As Control)
    ' Do nothing if no current role.
    If CurrentUserRole = "" Then Exit Sub
    ' Do nothing if the control isn't in the hash table.
    If Not userRoleValues.Contains(ctrl) Then Exit Sub

    ' Get the value in the hash table.
    Dim value As String = userRoleValues(ctrl).ToString
    ' Check whether current role is among the role(s) defined
    ' for this control.
    If InStr(";" & value & ";", ";" & CurrentUserRole & ";", _
        CompareMethod.Text) > 0 Then
        ctrl.Visible = True
```

(continued)

```
        Else
            ctrl.Visible = False
        End If
    End Sub
End Class
```

The UserPropExtender control is fully functional and uses many of the techniques you should know about when writing extender providers. But because of its simplicity, it doesn't need to trap events coming from other controls on the form, which is often a requirement for extender providers. For example, the ToolTip control intercepts mouse events for all controls that have a nonempty ToolTip property, and the HelpProvider control intercepts the HelpRequested event to display the associated help page or string.

Intercepting events from controls isn't difficult, however: when the control is added to the Hashtable (typically in the Set*xxxx* method), you use the AddHandler command to have one of its events trapped by a local procedure, and you use RemoveHandler to remove the event added dynamically when the control is removed from the Hashtable. Remarks in the preceding listing clearly show where these statements should be inserted.

Custom Property Editors

If you're familiar with custom control authoring under Visual Basic 6, you might have noticed that I haven't mentioned property pages, either when describing built-in controls or in this section devoted to custom control creation. Property pages aren't supported in the .NET architecture and have been replaced by custom property editors.

The most common form of property editor displays a Windows Forms control in a drop-down area inside the Properties window. You can display any control in the drop-down area, such as a TrackBar, a ListBox, or even a complex control such as a TreeView or a DataGrid, but the limitation is that you can display only *one* control. If you want to display more controls, you'll have to create a custom control with multiple child controls for the sole purpose of using it in the drop-down area. For example, the editors used by Anchor and Dock properties work in this way.

The Windows Form designer also supports property editors that display modal forms. Because you're in charge of drawing the appearance of such modal forms, you can display tab pages and multiple controls, and even modify more than one property. For example, you can add OK, Cancel, and Apply buttons and have a Visual Basic 6–like property page. Because these forms are modal, the Property window should be updated only when the user closes them, but you can offer a preview of what the custom control being edited will look like when the property or properties are assigned. As a matter of fact, it's perfectly legal to use your custom control inside the property editor you create for one of its properties, regardless of whether these editors use the drop-down area or a modal form.

Implementing a custom property editor isn't simple. Worse, as of this writing the documentation in the .NET Platform SDK is less than perfect—to use a euphemism—so I had to dig deep in the samples provided with the .NET Framework and use some imagination. On the companion CD, you'll find a GradientBackgroundEx control that extends GradientBackground with a new RotateAngle property, which permits you to rotate the gradient brush. (I have purposely chosen to extend an existing control so that I don't need to lead you through all the steps necessary to create a brand-new custom control.) The new property is associated with a custom property editor that uses a TrackBar control in a drop-down area of the Properties window to let the user select the angle with the mouse.

Thanks to inheritance, the code for the GradientBackgroundEx control is quite concise and includes only the new Property procedure and a redefined OnPaint procedure, which differs from the original OnPaint procedure by one statement only, here shown in boldface:

```
Imports System.Drawing.Design
Imports System.Drawing.Drawing2D
Imports System.Windows.Forms.Design

Class GradientBackgroundEx
    Inherits GradientBackground

    Dim m_RotateAngle As Single

    <Description("The rotation angle for the brush"), DefaultValue(0)> _
    Property RotateAngle() As Single
        Get
            Return m_RotateAngle
        End Get
        Set(ByVal Value As Single)
            m_RotateAngle = Value
            Me.Invalidate()
        End Set
    End Property

    ' Redefine the OnPaint event to account for the new property.

    Protected Overrides Sub OnPaint(ByVal e As PaintEventArgs)
        ' Create a gradient brush as large as the client area, with specified
        ' start/end color and gradient mode.
        Dim br As New Drawing2D.LinearGradientBrush(Me.ClientRectangle, _
            Me.StartColor, Me.EndColor, Me.GradientMode)
```

```
        ' Apply the rotation angle.
        br.RotateTransform(Me.RotateAngle)
        ' Paint the background.
        e.Graphics.FillRectangle(br, Me.ClientRectangle)
        ' Destroy the brush in an orderly manner.
        br.Dispose()
    End Sub
End Class
```

The first step in defining a custom editor for a given property is to specify the editor itself in the Editor attribute associated with the property procedure itself. The editor we're going to create is named RotateAngleEditor, so the new version of the RotateAngle Property procedure becomes

```
<Description("The rotation angle for the brush"), DefaultValue(0), _
    Editor(GetType(RotateAngleEditor), GetType(UITypeEditor))> _
Property RotateAngle() As Single
    ⋮
End Property
```

Note that the attribute's constructor takes two System.Type arguments, so you must use the GetType function. In this version of the .NET Framework, the second argument is always GetType(UITypeEditor).

The property editor is a class that you define. If you don't plan to reuse this property editor for other custom controls, you can avoid namespace pollution by making the editor a nested class of the custom control class.

The property editor class inherits from System.Drawing.Design.UITypeEditor and must override two methods in its base class, GetEditStyle and EditValue. The form designer calls the GetEditStyle method when it's filling the Properties window with the values of all the properties of the control currently selected. This method must return an enumerated value that tells the designer whether your property editor is going to display a single control in a drop-down area or a modal form. In the former case, a down-arrow button is displayed near the property name; in the latter case, a button with an ellipsis is used instead.

The form designer calls the EditValue method when the user clicks the button beside the property name. This method is overloaded, but we don't have to override all the overloaded versions of the method. In the most general overloaded version—the only one I override in the demo program—this method receives three arguments:

- The first argument is an ITypeDescriptorContext type that can provide additional information about the context in which the editing action is being performed. For example, Context.Instance returns a reference to the control whose property is being edited, and Context.Container returns a reference to the control's container.

- The second argument is an IServiceProvider type. You can query the GetService method of this object to get the editor service object that represents the Properties editor; this is an IWindowsFormEditor-Service object that exposes the three methods that let you open the drop-down area (DropDownControl), close it (CloseDropDown), or display a modal form (ShowDialog).
- The third argument is the current value of the property being edited. You should use this value to correctly initialize the control about to appear in the drop-down area (or the controls on the modal form). The EditValue method is expected to return the new value of the property being edited.

Here's the complete listing of the RotateAngleEditor class. Its many remarks and the details I have already given should suffice to let you understand how it works:

```
Class RotateAngleEditor
    Inherits UITypeEditor

    ' Override the GetEditStyle method to tell that this editor supports
    ' the DropDown style.
    Overloads Overrides Function GetEditStyle( _
        ByVal context As ITypeDescriptorContext) As UITypeEditorEditStyle
        If Not (context Is Nothing) AndAlso _
            Not (context.Instance Is Nothing) Then
            ' Return DropDown if you have a context and a control instance.
            Return UITypeEditorEditStyle.DropDown
        Else
            ' Otherwise, return the default behavior, whatever it is.
            Return MyBase.GetEditStyle(context)
        End If
    End Function

    ' This is the TrackBar control that is displayed in the editor.
    Dim WithEvents tb As TrackBar
    ' This the editor service that creates the drop-down area
    ' or shows a dialog.
    Dim wfes As IWindowsFormsEditorService

    ' Override the EditValue function,
    ' and return the new value of the property.

    Overloads Overrides Function EditValue( _
        ByVal context As ITypeDescriptorContext, _
        ByVal provider As IServiceProvider, _
        ByVal value As Object) As Object
```

(continued)

```
        ' Exit if no context, instance, or provider is provided.
        If (context Is Nothing) OrElse (context.Instance Is Nothing) _
            OrElse (provider Is Nothing) Then
            Return value
        End If
        ' Get the Editor Service object; exit if not there.
        wfes = CType(provider.GetService( _
            GetType(IWindowsFormsEditorService)), IWindowsFormsEditorService)
        If (wfes Is Nothing) Then
            Return value
        End If

        ' Create the TrackBar control, and set its properties.
        tb = New TrackBar()
        tb.Size = New Size(50, 150)
        tb.TickStyle = TickStyle.TopLeft
        tb.TickFrequency = 45
        tb.SetRange(0, 360)
        tb.Orientation = Orientation.Vertical
        ' Initalize its Value property.
        tb.Value = CInt(value)

        ' Show the control. (It returns when the drop-down area is closed.)
        wfes.DropDownControl(tb)

        ' The return value must be of the correct type.
        EditValue = CSng(tb.Value)
        ' Destroy the TrackBar control.
        tb.Dispose()
        tb = Nothing
    End Function

    ' Close the drop-down area when the mouse button is released.
    Private Sub TB_MouseUp(ByVal sender As Object, _
        ByVal e As MouseEventArgs) Handles tb.MouseUp
        If Not (wfes Is Nothing) Then
            wfes.CloseDropDown()
        End If
    End Sub
End Class
```

The RotateAngleEditor class automatically closes the drop-down area when the user releases the mouse button, but this isn't strictly necessary because the Properties window closes the drop-down area when the user clicks somewhere else. I implemented this detail only to show you how you can react to user selections in the drop-down area. Figure 17-27 shows the new property editor in action.

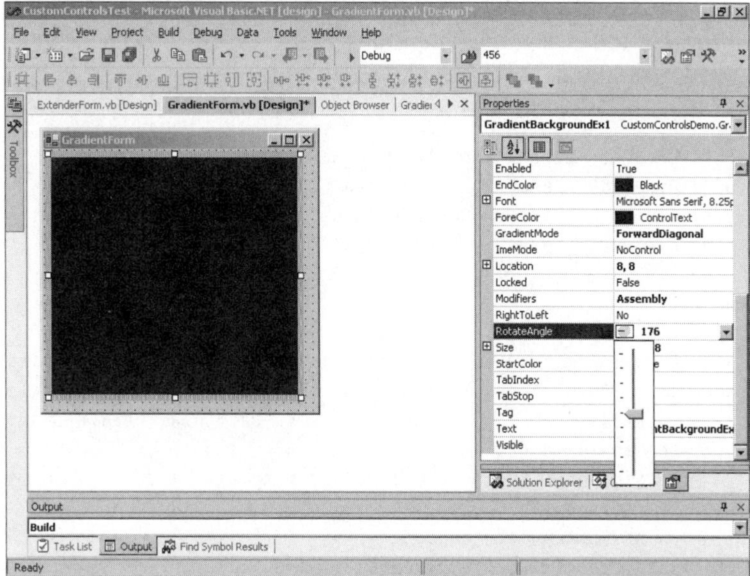

Figure 17-27. The RotateAngle property of a GradientBackgroundEx control is being edited with a custom property editor.

The steps you must take to display a modal form instead of the drop-down area are the same as those you've seen so far, with only two differences:

- The GetEditStyle method must return the UITypeEditorEditStyle.Modal value to let the Property window know that an ellipsis button must be displayed beside the property name.
- Your class library project must contain a form class in which you drop the controls that make up the editor interface. In the EditValue method, you create an instance of this form and pass it to the Show-Modal method of the IWindowsFormsEditorService object (instead of the DropDownControl method, as in the preceding code example).

Custom property editors provide support for one more feature: the ability to offer the visual representation of the current value in the Properties window in a small rectangle to the left of the actual numeric or string value. (You can see how the form designer uses such rectangles for the ForeColor, BackColor, and BackgroundImage properties.) In this case, you must override two more methods of the base UITypeEditor class: GetPaintValueSupported (which should return True if you want to implement this feature) and PaintValue (where you place the code that actually draws inside the small rectangle). The latter method receives a PaintValueEventArgs object, whose properties give you access to the Graphics object on which you can draw, the bounding rectangle, and the value to be printed. The following code extends the RotateAngleEditor class with the ability to display a small yellow circle, plus a black line that shows the current value of the RotateAngle property in a visual manner:

```
' Let the property editor know that we want to paint the value.
Overloads Overrides Function GetPaintValueSupported( _
    ByVal context As System.ComponentModel.ITypeDescriptorContext) As Boolean
    ' In this demo, we return True regardless of the actual editor.
    Return True
End Function

' Display a yellow circle to the left of the value in the Properties window
' with a line forming the same angle as the value of the RotateAngle property.
Overloads Overrides Sub PaintValue(ByVal e As Design.PaintValueEventArgs)
    ' Get the angle in radians.
    Dim a As Single = CSng(e.Value) * CSng(Math.PI) / 180!
    ' Get the rectangle in which we can draw.
    Dim rect As Rectangle = e.Bounds
    ' Evaluate the radius of the circle.
    Dim r As Single = Math.Min(rect.Width, rect.Height) / 2!
    ' Get the center point.
    Dim p1 As New PointF(rect.Width / 2!, rect.Height / 2!)
    ' Calculate where the line should end.
    Dim p2 As New PointF(CSng(p1.X + Math.Cos(a) * r), _
        CSng(p1.Y + Math.Sin(a) * r))
    ' Draw the yellow-filled circle.
    e.Graphics.FillEllipse(Brushes.Yellow, rect.Width / 2! - r, _
        rect.Height / 2! - r, r * 2, r * 2)
    ' Draw the line.
    e.Graphics.DrawLine(Pens.Black, p1, p2)
End Sub
```

You can see the effect in Figure 17-27.

Object Properties

A few common properties, such as Font and Location, return objects instead of scalar values. These properties are displayed in the Properties window with a plus sign (+) to the left of each of their names so that you can expand those items to edit the individual properties of the object. If you implement properties that return objects defined in the .NET Framework (such as Font, Point, and Size objects), your control automatically inherits this behavior. However, when your control exposes an object defined in your application, you must implement a custom TypeConverter class to enable this feature.

The demo application on the companion CD contains an AddressControl custom control, which lets the user enter information such as street, city, zip code, state, and country. (See the form on the left in Figure 17-28.) Instead of exposing this data as five independent properties, this control exposes them as a single Address object, which is defined in the same application:

```
Public Class Address
    ' This event fires when a property is changed.
    Event PropertyChanged(ByVal propertyName As String)

    ' Private members
    Dim m_Street As String
    Dim m_City As String
    Dim m_Zip As String
    Dim m_State As String
    Dim m_Country As String

    Property Street() As String
        Get
            Return m_Street
        End Get
        Set(ByVal Value As String)
            If m_Street <> Value Then
                m_Street = Value
                RaiseEvent PropertyChanged("Street")
            End If
        End Set
    End Property

    ' ...(Property procedures for City, Zip, State, and Country
    '     omitted because substantially identical to Street property)...
    :

    Overrides Function ToString() As String
        Return "(Address)"
    End Function
End Class
```

Note that property procedures in the Address class are just wrappers for the five private variables and that they raise a PropertyChanged event when any property changes. The ToString method is overridden to provide the text that will appear as a dummy value for the Address property in the Properties window. The AddressControl control has an Address property that returns an Address object:

```
Imports System.ComponentModel

Public Class AddressControl
    Inherits System.Windows.Forms.UserControl
```

(continued)

```
#Region " Windows Form Designer generated code "
    ⋮
#End Region

    ' The member variable for the Address property
    Dim WithEvents m_Address As New Address()

    <TypeConverter(GetType(AddressTypeConverter))> _
    Property Address() As Address
        Get
            Return m_Address
        End Get
        Set(ByVal Value As Address)
            m_Address = Value
            RefreshControls()
        End Set
    End Property

    ' Refresh controls when any property changes.
    Private Sub Address_PropertyChanged(ByVal propertyName As String) _
        Handles m_Address.PropertyChanged
        RefreshControls()
    End Sub

    ' Display Address properties in the control's fields.
    Private Sub RefreshControls()
        txtStreet.Text = m_Address.Street
        txtCity.Text = m_Address.City
        txtZip.Text = m_Address.Zip
        txtState.Text = m_Address.State
        txtCountry.Text = m_Address.Country
    End Sub
End Class
```

The key statement in the preceding code is the TypeConverter attribute, which tells the form designer that a custom TypeConverter object is associated with the Address property. Or you can associate this attribute with the Address class itself, in which case all the controls that expose a property of type Address will automatically use the AddressTypeConverter class. (The .NET Framework uses this approach for common classes such as Point and Font.)

The AddressTypeConverter class derives from TypeConverter and overrides two methods. The GetPropertiesSupported method must return True to let the editor know that a plus symbol must be displayed to the left of the Address property in the Properties window; the GetProperties method must return a PropertyDescriptorCollection object, which describes the items that will appear when the plus symbol is clicked:

```
' The TypeConverter class for the Address property
' (It can be a nested class of AddressControl.)

Public Class AddressTypeConverter
    Inherits TypeConverter

    Overloads Overrides Function GetPropertiesSupported( _
        ByVal context As ITypeDescriptorContext) As Boolean
        ' Tell the editor to display a + symbol near the property name.
        Return True
    End Function

    Overloads Overrides Function GetProperties( _
        ByVal context As ITypeDescriptorContext, ByVal value As Object, _
        ByVal attributes() As Attribute) As PropertyDescriptorCollection

        ' Use the GetProperties shared method to return a collection of
        ' PropertyDescriptor objects, one for each property of Address.
        Return TypeDescriptor.GetProperties(GetType(Address))
    End Function
End Class
```

You see the effect of this custom TypeConverter class in the right portion of Figure 17-28.

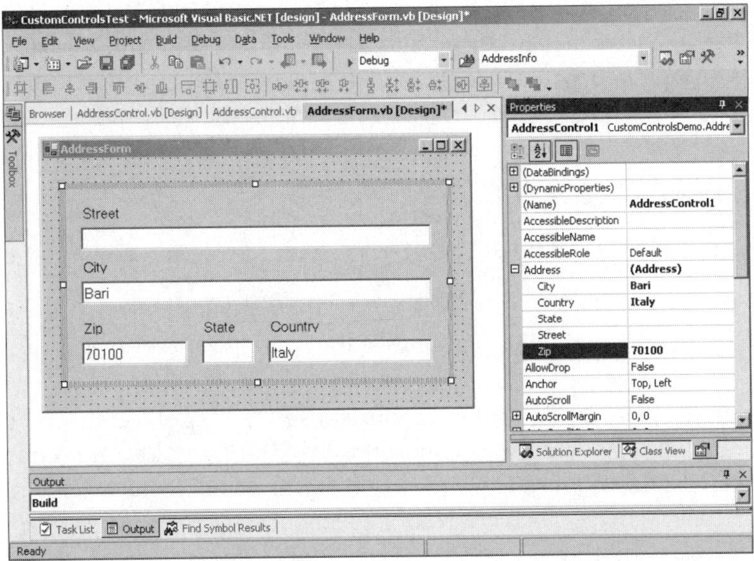

Figure 17-28. The AddressControl control includes a TypeConverter for its custom property, Address.

To keep code as concise as possible, the AddressTypeConverter class uses the TypeDescriptor.GetProperties shared method to create a PropertyDescriptorCollection object that describes all the properties of the Address class. In some cases, you might need to create this collection manually, or at least change the properties of its members. You must take this step, for example, when not all the properties should be made available in the Properties window, when you want to sort them in a different order, or when you need to define a custom editor for one of them.

A custom TypeConverter object can do more than add support for object properties. For example, you can use a custom TypeConverter class to validate the string entered in the Properties window or to convert this string to a value type other than a standard numeric and date .NET type. For more information about custom TypeConverter classes, see the .NET Platform SDK documentation.

Design-Time and Run-Time Licensing

If you plan to sell your custom controls and components, you probably want to implement some type of licensing for them to enforce some restriction on their use. The good news is that the .NET Framework already comes with a built-in licensing scheme, but you can override it to create your own licensing method.

To explain how licensing works, I'll start by showing the built-in licensing scheme, which is based on the LicFileLicenseProvider class provided by the .NET Framework. This class ensures that there's a file named *controlname*.lic in the same directory as the control's directory, where *controlname* is the complete name of the control class. For example, the license file for the AddressControl class in the CustomControlsDemo assembly should be called CustomControlsDemo.AddressControl.lic. This .lic file must be a text file that contains a string in the following format: controlname *is a licensed component.* For example, the AddressControl's licensing file should contain this text:

```
CustomControlsDemo.AddressControl is a licensed component.
```

If this file is missing, the control is unusable both at design time (that is, inside Visual Studio) and at run time. You bind a custom control, or any component for that matter, to the LicFileLicenseProvider object or any other license provider class by using the LicenseProvider attribute. You then query the .NET licensing infrastructure from inside the control's constructor method by using the LicenseManager.Validate shared method, which throws an exception if the .lic file can't be found or its contents aren't correct. If successful, the method returns a License object, which you later dispose of when the object is destroyed. Here's a revised version of the AddressControl class that employs the built-in licensing mechanism. (Added lines are in boldface.)

```
<LicenseProvider(GetType(LicFileLicenseProvider))> _
Public Class AddressControl
    Inherits System.Windows.Forms.UserControl

    ' The License object
    Private lic As License

    Public Sub New()
        MyBase.New()
        ' Validate the License.
        lic = LicenseManager.Validate(GetType(AddressControl), Me)

        ' This call is required by the Windows Form Designer.
        InitializeComponent()
    End Sub

    ' Destroy the License object without waiting for the garbage collection.

    Protected Overloads Overrides Sub Dispose(ByVal disposing As Boolean)
        If disposing Then
            ' Destroy the license.
            If Not (lic Is Nothing) Then
                lic.Dispose()
                lic = Nothing
            End If
        End If
        MyBase.Dispose(disposing)
    End Sub

    ⋮
End Class
```

Obviously, the built-in licensing mechanism is quite easy to violate, in that you only need to copy the .lic file in the same directory as the control's assembly. For more robust licensing, you must devise some other mechanism. For example, you might add a key to the registry or store encrypted information about the computer on which the control is first installed so that malicious users can't simply copy the file to another machine. In addition, you can decide how to react if the control doesn't come with a correct license. The more common behavior is to throw an exception, but you might decide to run the control in demo mode, use nag screens, or throw an exception only after a random timeout (which would make the job of breaking the licensing mechanism more difficult).

Implementing a custom licensing scheme requires that you pass the name of a custom license provider class as an argument to the LicenseProvider attribute, as in

```
<LicenseProvider(GetType(LicWindowsFileLicenseProvider))> _
Public Class AddressControl
    ⋮
End Class
```

A custom license provider is a class that derives from the abstract LicenseProvider class and overrides the virtual GetLicense method. This method is indirectly called by the LicenseManager.Validate method (in the custom control's constructor method) and receives several arguments that let you determine the name of the control or component in question, whether you're at design time or run time, and other pieces of information. The Windows Forms infrastructure expects the GetLicense method to return a license object if it's OK to use the custom control or component; otherwise, it should return Nothing or throw a LicenseException object. (You decide whether the method returns Nothing or throws the exception by inspecting the allowException argument passed to the GetLicense method.)

The following code shows how to implement a license provider class that's similar to the built-in LicFileLicenseProvider class except that it checks the license only at design time and looks for the .lic file in the Windows system directory instead of in the assembly's directory:

```
Class LicWindowsFileLicenseProvider
    Inherits LicenseProvider

    Public Overrides Function GetLicense(ByVal context As LicenseContext, _
        ByVal typ As System.Type, ByVal instance As Object, _
        ByVal allowExceptions As Boolean) As License

        ' This is the name of the control.
        Dim ctrlName As String = typ.FullName

        If context.UsageMode = LicenseUsageMode.Designtime Then
            ' We are in design mode.
            ' Check that there is a .lic file in Windows system directory.
            ' Build the full path of the .lic file.
            Dim filename As String = Environment.SystemDirectory() _
                & "\" & ctrlName & ".lic"
            Dim fs As System.IO.StreamReader

            Try
                ' Open the license file (throws exception if not found).
                fs = New System.IO.StreamReader(filename)
                ' Read its contents.
```

```
            Dim licText As String = fs.ReadToEnd
            ' Compare with the expected license text.
            If licText <> ctrlName & " is a licensed component." Then
                ' Any exception object activates the Catch clause.
                Throw New ArgumentException()
            End If
        Catch ex As Exception
            ' Throws a LicenseException object, if possible;
            ' else just returns Nothing.
            If allowExceptions Then
                Throw New LicenseException(typ, instance, _
                    "Can't find design-time license for " & ctrlName)
            Else
                Return Nothing
            End If
        Finally
            ' In all cases, close the StreamReader.
            If Not (fs Is Nothing) Then fs.Close()
        End Try

        ' If we get here, we can return a RuntimeLicense object.
        Return New DesignTimeLicense(Me, typ)
    Else
        ' We enforce no licensing at run time,
        ' so we always return a RunTimeLicense.
        Return New RuntimeLicense(Me, typ)
    End If
End Function
End Class
```

In general, you should return two different license objects, depending on whether you're at design time or run time. (Otherwise, a malicious user might use the run-time license at design time.) A license object is an instance of a class that derives from System.ComponentModel.License and overrides its LicenseKey and Dispose virtual methods. Here's a simple implementation of the DesignTimeLicense and RuntimeLicense classes referenced by the preceding code snippet. (These classes can be nested inside the LicWindowsFileLicenseProvider class.)

```
Class LicWindowsFileLicenseProvider
    ⋮

    ' Nested class for design-time license

    Public Class DesignTimeLicense
        Inherits License
```

(continued)

```
        Private owner As LicWindowsFileLicenseProvider
        Private typ As Type

        Sub New(ByVal owner As LicWindowsFileLicenseProvider, _
            ByVal typ As Type)
            Me.owner = owner
            Me.typ = typ
        End Sub

        Overrides ReadOnly Property LicenseKey() As String
            Get
                ' Just return the type name in this demo.
                Return typ.FullName
            End Get
        End Property

        Overrides Sub Dispose()
            ' There is nothing to do here.
        End Sub
    End Class

    ' Nested class for run-time license

    Public Class RuntimeLicense
        Inherits License

        Private owner As LicWindowsFileLicenseProvider
        Private typ As Type

        Sub New(ByVal owner As LicWindowsFileLicenseProvider, _
            ByVal typ As Type)
            Me.owner = owner
            Me.typ = typ
        End Sub

        Overrides ReadOnly Property LicenseKey() As String
            Get
                ' Just return the type name in this demo.
                Return typ.FullName
            End Get
        End Property

        Overrides Sub Dispose()
            ' There is nothing to do here.
        End Sub
    End Class

End Class
```

Read the remarks in the demo project on the companion CD to see how to test the LicWindowsFileLicenseProvider class with the AddressControl custom control. Figure 17-29 shows the kind of error message that you see in Visual Studio if you attempt to load a form that contains a control for which you don't have a design-time license.

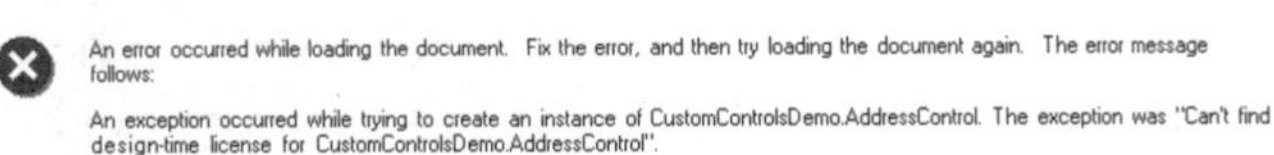

An error occurred while loading the document. Fix the error, and then try loading the document again. The error message follows:
An exception occurred while trying to create an instance of CustomControlsDemo.AddressControl. The exception was "Can't find design-time license for CustomControlsDemo.AddressControl".

Figure 17-29. The error message that Visual Studio displays when you load a form containing a control for which you don't have a design-time license.

Hosting Custom Controls in Internet Explorer

Windows Forms controls have one more intriguing feature that I haven't discussed yet: you can host a Windows Forms control in Internet Explorer in much the same way that you can use an ActiveX control, with an important improvement over ActiveX controls—Windows Forms controls don't require any registration on the client machine. However, the .NET Framework must be installed on the client, so in practice you can adopt this technique only for intranet installations.

You specify a Windows Forms control in an HTML page using a special <OBJECT> tag that contains a CLASSID parameter pointing to the DLL containing the control. For example, the following HTML page hosts an instance of the TextBoxEx control; you can see the effect in Figure 17-30.

```
<HTML>
<BODY>
<H2>Loading the TextBoxEx custom control in IE</H2>

Enter a 5-digit value:<BR>
<OBJECT ID="TextBoxEx1"
    CLASSID="/CustomControlDemo.dll#CustomControlDemo.TextBoxEx"
    HEIGHT=80" WIDTH="300" VIEWASTEXT>
        <PARAM NAME="Text" VALUE="12345">
        <PARAM NAME="ValidateRegEx" VALUE="\d{5}" >
</OBJECT>
<P><INPUT type="button" value="Clear Text" onclick="ClearText()">
</BODY></HTML>
```

(continued)

```
<SCRIPT>
function ClearText() {
        TextBoxEx1.Text = "";
}
</SCRIPT>
```

The boldface portions show how you insert the control in the page, initialize its properties using the <PARAM> tag, and access its properties programmatically from a JScript function. The value of the CLASSID attribute is the path of the DLL hosting the control, followed by a pound sign and the complete name of the control in question. In the preceding example, the DLL is in the root virtual directory, but it can be located anywhere in the virtual directory tree of Internet Information Services (IIS). When testing the preceding code, remember that you must deploy the HTML file in an IIS directory and access it from Internet Explorer using HTTP: nothing happens if you display it by double-clicking the file from inside Windows Explorer.

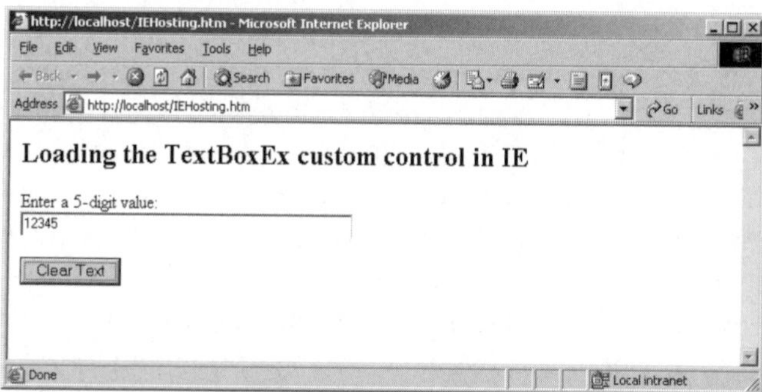

Figure 17-30. Hosting the TextBoxEx control in Internet Explorer 6.

Using a control hosted in Internet Explorer has other limitations. For example, you can't use a control stored in the local machine's GAC and can't use a CAB file to host multiple assemblies because Internet Explorer 6 is able to deal only with CAB files containing only one assembly. There are limitations also when accessing the control programmatically: for one, you can't access object properties—such as the Address property of the AddressControl sample described in this chapter—because the runtime creates a COM Callable Wrapper (CCW) to make the control visible to the script, but it doesn't create a CCW for dependent properties.

Finally, the IIS virtual directory containing the control must have its security set to Scripts only: any other value, including Scripts and Executables, will prevent the control from loading. The code running in the control appears to the runtime as downloaded from the Internet; therefore, many operations won't be allowed unless you grant this executable broader privileges.

> **Note** An ASP.NET page can check whether the client browser supports the .NET runtime by querying the HTTPRequest.Browser.ClrVersion property. A well-behaved ASP.NET application might use ActiveX controls, DHTML, or plain HTML if the browser isn't able to host Windows Forms controls.

At the end of our exploration of Windows Forms controls, you should be able to make the best of existing controls as well as create your own custom controls, should the need arise. To create a truly functional and eye-catching user interface, however, you need to leverage the GDI+ portion of the .NET Framework. This is the topic of the next chapter, so keep reading.

Front
Top
Left
Back

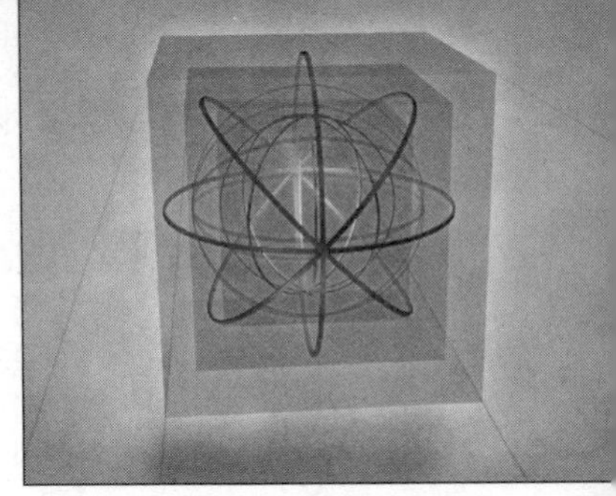

18

GDI+

GDI+ is the technology in the .NET Framework that you produce text and graphic output and deal with bitmaps and other kinds of images. I've already used GDI+ methods in previous chapters, but without engaging in a thorough description of this important part of the new architecture. Broadly speaking, you can subdivide GDI+ into three parts:

- **2-D vector graphics** This subset of GDI+ includes objects for drawing lines, polygons, ellipses, and arcs, possibly filled with color. GDI+ supports sophisticated features in this area, such as gradient brushes (as you've seen in the "Creating a Control from Scratch" section in Chapter 17), complex cardinal and Bézier spline curves, scalable regions, persistent paths, and more. Most of the objects for doing 2-D vector graphics are in the System.Drawing and System.Drawing.Drawing2D namespaces.
- **Imaging** This subset gathers objects for displaying and processing image formats such as bitmaps and icons. The .NET capabilities for working with raster images are really outstanding and include image stretching, conversion to and from the most common graphic formats, and support for semitransparent regions by means of alpha blending. The objects that you use for making images are in the System.Drawing.Imaging namespace.
- **Typography** This subset includes all the objects you use to display text in a variety of forms, colors, and styles. You have complete control over how text is displayed, and you can even activate anti-aliasing and special techniques for better text rendering on LCD displays, such as those of PDAs. The objects for typography are in the System.Drawing.Text namespace.

2-D Vector Graphics

The three segments of GDI+ have many objects in common, and above all, they employ a similar programming model. In this section, I'll cover 2-D vector graphics, but most concepts apply to other parts of GDI+ as well.

> **Note** For the sake of brevity, all the code samples that follow assume that you have added the following statements at the top of your code modules:
>
> ```
> Imports System.Drawing
> Imports System.Drawing.Drawing2D
> Imports System.Drawing.Imaging
> Imports System.Drawing.Text
> ```

The Graphics Object

The very first operation you must perform to draw a graphic primitive on a drawing surface is get a reference to a Graphics object, which represents the canvas on which you'll draw your lines and other shapes even though it isn't necessarily a visible surface. (The Graphics object broadly corresponds to a device context in "classic" GDI programming.) This object doesn't have a public constructor method, so you can't create it by using the New keyword. Instead, you must use one of these two techniques: get a Graphics object from the argument of an event or get a Graphics object by using the CreateGraphics method that the form and all control objects expose.

Here's an example that uses the first technique to display a circle as large as the form inside the Paint event of a form. The PaintEventArgs object passed to this event has a property that exposes the Graphics object that represents the visible surface of the object being repainted:

```
Private Sub Form1_Paint(ByVal sender As Object, _
    ByVal e As PaintEventArgs) Handles MyBase.Paint
    ' Get the Graphics object that corresponds to the form's surface.
    Dim gr As Graphics = e.Graphics
    ' Clear the background with azure color.
    gr.Clear(Color.Azure)
    ' Draw a red ellipse as large as the form.
    gr.DrawEllipse(Pens.Red, 0, 0, Me.ClientSize.Width, Me.ClientSize.Height)
End Sub
```

Other events let you get a reference to the Graphics object in this way—for example, the DrawItem event that you use for owner-draw controls. But if your code runs inside the handler of an event that doesn't make this object available, you must use the CreateGraphics method of the form or the control to get a valid Graphics object. The main difference with the technique that uses the object received as an argument is that you must destroy the Graphics object before exiting the procedure—otherwise, the corresponding Windows resource (that is, the underlying device context) will be destroyed only at the next garbage collection. The following example shows how you can draw an ellipse as large as the form, which will be automatically redrawn when the form is resized:

```
Private Sub Form1_Resize(ByVal sender As Object, _
    ByVal e As EventArgs) Handles MyBase.Resize
    ' Get the Graphics object corresponding to the form's surface.
    Dim gr As Graphics = Me.CreateGraphics
    ' Clear the background with azure color.
    gr.Clear(Color.Azure)
    ' Draw a red ellipse as large as the form.
    gr.DrawEllipse(Pens.Red, 0, 0, Me.ClientSize.Width, Me.ClientSize.Height)
    ' Destroy the Graphics object.
    gr.Dispose()
End Sub
```

The Graphics object exposes many properties and methods, and I will illustrate most of them in the sections that follow.

Lines, Rectangles, Polygons, Ellipses, and Arcs

The Graphics object exposes methods for drawing graphic primitives such as lines, rectangles, and ellipses. Each method is overloaded and therefore several syntax forms are available, but as a rule you pass a Pen object as the first argument and a set of coordinates or a bounding rectangle in the remaining arguments. In a difference from Visual Basic 6, there's no concept of current foreground color, and you must pass the Pen object at each call. Moreover, the Graphics object doesn't remember the last point drawn. Putting it another way, the Graphics object is stateless— although this statement isn't completely accurate because the object does maintain some important values that you can assign to its properties, as I'll explain later.

```
' Create a Graphics object.
Dim gr As Graphics = Me.CreateGraphics
' Draw a red line from (100, 30) to (500, 300).
gr.DrawLine(Pens.Red, 100, 30, 500, 300)
' Draw a white square with left-top corner at (130, 50) and side=300 pixels.
gr.DrawRectangle(Pens.White, New Rectangle(130, 50, 300, 300))
' Draw a green circle with radius=200 and center at (350,250).
Dim r As Integer = 200
gr.DrawEllipse(Pens.Green, 350 - r, 250 - r, r * 2, r * 2)
' Destroy the Graphics object.
gr.Dispose()
```

Drawing an arc of an ellipse using the DrawArc method is similar to drawing an ellipse, but you must supply two additional arguments: the starting angle and the sweep angle, both of which are measured in degrees. The starting angle is measured clockwise from the X axis; the sweep angle is also measured clockwise. For example, the following statement

```
' Draw a quarter of a circle, whose center is at (200, 150)
' with radius equal to 100.
Dim r2 As Integer = 100
gr.DrawArc(Pens.Blue, 200 - r2, 150 - r2, r2 * 2, r2 * 2, 0, 90)
```

draws the following arc:

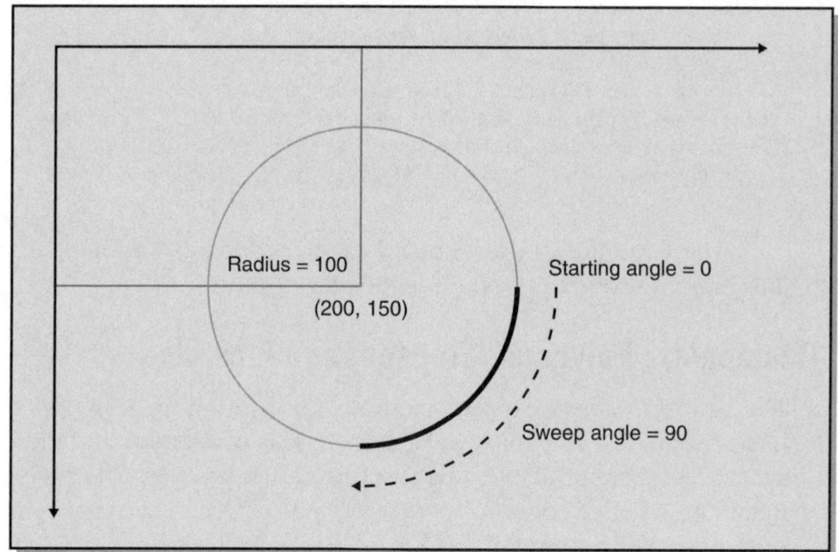

A few methods let you create multiple lines with one call. The DrawLines method draws a series of connected lines; it takes an array of Point or PointF objects. (The only difference between these two objects is that PointF expresses the two coordinates as Single numbers.)

```
' Draw three straight lines.
Dim points() As Point = {New Point(10, 10), _
    New Point(100, 80), New Point(200, 20), New Point(300, 100)}
gr.DrawLines(Pens.Black, points)
```

If the end point of the last line coincides with the first point of the first line, you're actually drawing a polygon and you can use the DrawPolygon method:

```
' Draw a rhombus.
' Note that we build the array of Point objects on the fly.
gr.DrawPolygon(Pens.Red, New Point() {New Point(200, 50), _
    New Point(300, 100), New Point(200, 150), New Point(100, 100)})
```

You can also quickly draw multiple rectangles using the DrawRectangles method:

```
' Draw three rectangles.
Dim rects() As Rectangle = {New Rectangle(50, 30, 200, 100), _
    New Rectangle(70, 40, 220, 110), New Rectangle(90, 50, 240, 120)}
gr.DrawRectangles(Pens.Green, rects)
```

Cardinal and Bézier Splines

GDI+ supports two different forms of a complex curve that can't be represented as an arc of a circle or an ellipse: a cardinal spline and a Bézier spline. A cardinal spline is the curve that you would create by taking a piece of flexible material—such as a thin strip of iron or wood—and making it pass through a given set of fixed points on the X-Y plane. Unless the material you're using is infinitely flexible (as would be a string of rope or rubber), the path drawn by the material would be a curve that doesn't create any sharp angles at the connecting points. Depending on the degree of flexibility (also known as *tension*) of the material used, a given set of points can generate different curves. The default tension is 0.5. The following code snippet draws five cardinal splines, with a tension that goes from 0 (which corresponds to a material with infinite flexibility, which therefore draws straight lines) to 2:

```
Dim points() As Point = {New Point(100, 100), New Point(200, 200), _
    New Point(250, 30), New Point(350, 100)}
Dim tension As Single
For tension = 0 To 2 Step 0.5
    gr.DrawCurve(Pens.Blue, points, tension)
Next
```

Figure 18-1 shows the resulting cardinal splines. You can also draw a closed cardinal spline by using the DrawClosedCurve method, which takes an array of Point objects.

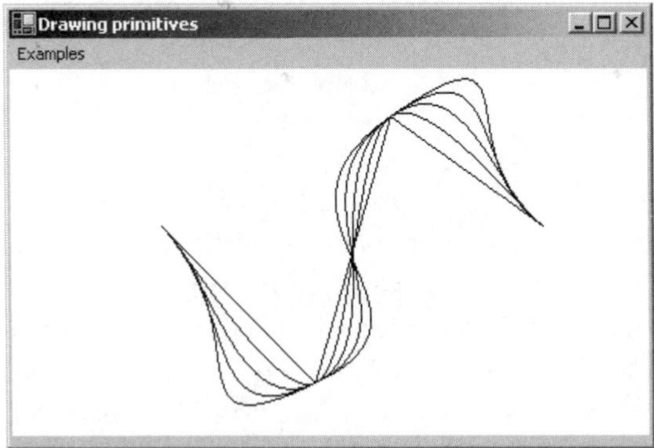

Figure 18-1. Five cardinal splines, with tensions from 0 (the straight line) to 2.

A Bézier spline is a curve specified by four points: the initial point, the ending point, and two control points. The curve doesn't pass through the control points, but they influence the direction of the curve at the starting and ending points. More precisely, the Bézier spline begins in the direction indicated by the imaginary line that joins the starting point and the first control point and ends in the direction indicated by the imaginary line that joins the second control point and the ending line. Figure 18-2 is an example of a Bézier curve that also shows these two tangent lines. You can draw this kind of curve by using the DrawBezier method, which takes four Point objects (in this order): the starting point, the first control point, the second control point, and the ending point. For example, here's the code that draws the curve shown in the figure:

```
gr.DrawBezier(Pens.Black, New Point(10, 30), New Point(100, 20), _
    New Point(140, 190), New Point(200, 200))
```

You can also draw multiple connected Bézier curves with the DrawBeziers method. This method takes an array of Point objects. The first four objects define the first curve, and then each subsequent group of three objects defines the control points and the ending point for the next curve.

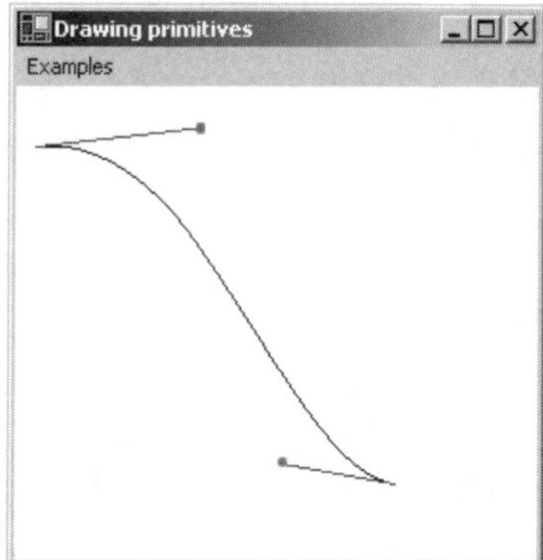

Figure 18-2. A Bézier curve, with two tangent lines joining its end points to its control points.

The Pen Object

All the examples I've shown you so far used a Pen object taken from predefined objects exposed by the Pens class, such as Pens.Black. You can also use one of the Pen objects that correspond to a system color using the SystemPens class—for example, SystemPens.ActiveCaptionText to use the color defined for the title bar of the active window. In many cases, however, you need to create a custom Pen object yourself if you want to use one of the colors not available in the Pens or SystemPens class, define a width larger than 1 pixel, define a dashed line, or in general have more control over the appearance of the lines or curves being drawn. A key difference between predefined and custom Pen objects is that you must always destroy the latter objects by calling their Dispose method. Here are a couple of examples:

```
' Draw the inner rectangle with a pen of custom color.
Dim p1 As New Pen(Color.FromArgb(128, 0, 60))
gr.DrawRectangle(p1, 50, 50, 100, 50)
' Draw the outer rectangle with a blue pen 4 pixels wide.
Dim p2 As New Pen(Color.Blue, 4)
gr.DrawRectangle(p2, 10, 10, 200, 100)
' Destroy Pen objects.
p1.Dispose()
p2.Dispose()
```

When you're working with a Pen object wider than 1 pixel, you must also account for its alignment, which affects how the line is drawn in respect to its beginning and ending points. For example, Figure 18-3 shows two squares with sides of the same length but drawn with pens aligned differently:

```
Dim p As New Pen(Color.Yellow, 12)
Dim rect As New Rectangle(20, 20, 100, 100)
' Draw first square, with alignment = center (default).
gr.DrawRectangle(p, rect)
' Draw also the theoretical line as a reference.
gr.DrawRectangle(Pens.Black, rect)

' Move the rectangle to the right.
rect.Offset(150, 0)
' Change the alignment to inset, and draw the two squares once again.
p.Alignment = Drawing.Drawing2D.PenAlignment.Inset
gr.DrawRectangle(p, rect)
gr.DrawRectangle(Pens.Black, rect)
' Destroy the custom Pen object.
p.Dispose()
```

Note that the PenAlignment enumeration defines three more settings—Left, Outset, and Right—but as of this writing, they aren't functional and deliver the same result as the default setting (Center).

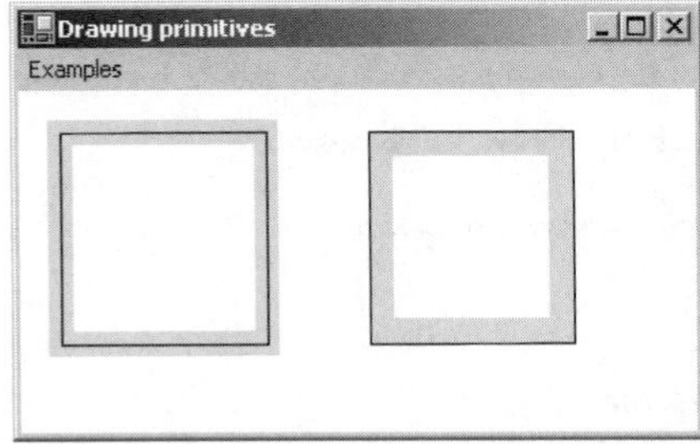

Figure 18-3. Two squares drawn with different pen alignment.

You can set other properties of the Pen object to create custom lines. For example, you can use the DashStyle enumerated property to draw dashed lines using a predefined pattern, and you can even create custom dash patterns by assigning an array of Single values to the DashPattern property. The StartCap and EndCap properties can take an enumerated value and let you change the shape of the starting and ending points of the line so that you can easily create arrows or other common shapes. Figure 18-4 shows some of the many different line variations that you can achieve using these properties. Here's the source code that creates that output:

```
Dim p1 As New Pen(Color.Black, 3)
p1.DashStyle = Drawing.Drawing2D.DashStyle.Dash
gr.DrawLine(p1, 10, 10, 200, 10)
p1.DashStyle = Drawing.Drawing2D.DashStyle.DashDot
gr.DrawLine(p1, 10, 30, 200, 30)
p1.DashStyle = Drawing.Drawing2D.DashStyle.DashDotDot
gr.DrawLine(p1, 10, 50, 200, 50)
p1.DashStyle = Drawing.Drawing2D.DashStyle.Dot
gr.DrawLine(p1, 10, 70, 200, 70)

' Create a custom dash pattern.
Dim sngArray() As Single = {4, 4, 8, 4, 12, 4}
p1.DashPattern = sngArray
gr.DrawLine(p1, 10, 90, 200, 90)

' Display pens with nondefault caps.
Dim p2 As New Pen(Color.Black, 8)
p2.StartCap = Drawing.Drawing2D.LineCap.DiamondAnchor
p2.EndCap = Drawing.Drawing2D.LineCap.ArrowAnchor
gr.DrawLine(p2, 280, 30, 500, 30)

p2.StartCap = Drawing.Drawing2D.LineCap.RoundAnchor
p2.EndCap = Drawing.Drawing2D.LineCap.Round
gr.DrawLine(p2, 280, 70, 500, 70)

' Destroy custom Pen objects.
p1.Dispose()
p2.Dispose()
```

Figure 18-4. Dashed lines and lines with different starting and ending caps.

Paths

A GraphicPath object is a collection of graphic primitives that are drawn and manipulated as a single entity. A path can contain lines, arcs, rectangles, ellipses, polygons, and in general any shape that I've described so far. A path can also contain one or more closed figures, but this isn't a requirement. Before you can draw a GraphicPath object, you must create it and define its contents, using one or more Add*xxxx* methods. Even though you can add individual lines to a path, you should keep in mind that the end point of each segment is automatically connected to the start point of the next unless you explicitly invoke the StartFigure method between the two AddLine methods. Here's an example of a path that contains a parallelepiped and a triangle:

```
' Create a new Path object.
Dim pa As New GraphicsPath()
' Start a figure.
pa.StartFigure()
pa.AddRectangle(New Rectangle(20, 20, 200, 150))
pa.AddRectangle(New Rectangle(50, 50, 200, 150))
pa.AddLine(20, 20, 50, 50)
pa.StartFigure()    ' Avoid connecting the two segments.
pa.AddLine(220, 20, 250, 50)
pa.StartFigure()    ' Avoid connecting the two segments.
pa.AddLine(220, 170, 250, 200)
pa.StartFigure()    ' Avoid connecting the two segments.
pa.AddLine(20, 170, 50, 200)

' Start another triangular (closed) figure.
pa.StartFigure()
pa.AddLine(300, 20, 400, 20)
pa.AddLine(400, 20, 400, 120)
pa.CloseFigure()
```

Notice that the CloseFigure method automatically closes the most recently opened polygonal shape. Once you have defined a path, you can draw it with the pen of your choice, using the DrawPath method:

```
' ...(Continuing the preceding code snippet)...
' Draw the path, using a thick red pen.
Dim p As New Pen(Color.Red, 3)
gr.DrawPath(p, pa)
' Destroy both the Path and the Pen object.
pa.Dispose()
p.Dispose()
```

Figure 18-5 shows the effect of the code sample just completed.

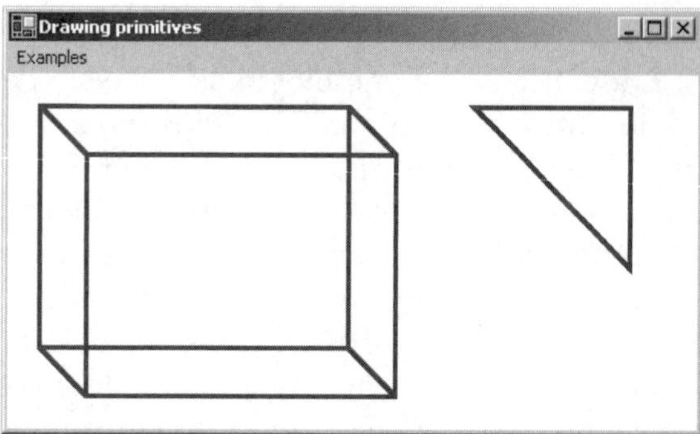

Figure 18-5. A GraphicPath object containing two figures.

Filled Shapes

The Graphics object exposes eight methods that create filled geometrical shapes: FillRectangle, FillRectangles, FillEllipse, FillPolygon, FillPie, FillClosedCurve, FillPath, and FillRegion. These methods support several overloaded variations, but all of them take a Brush object as a first argument, which determines how the shape is filled. Several types of brush classes are available—solid brushes, hatch brushes, gradient brushes, and texture brushes—but all of them derive from the System.Drawing.Brush class, so you can use any of these types whenever a generic brush is expected. I discuss the several types of brushes in the next section, so for now I will use only predefined solid color brushes:

```
' Draw a green-filled rectangle.
gr.FillRectangle(Brushes.Green, New Rectangle(20, 10, 200, 100))
' Draw a blue-filled ellipse.
gr.FillEllipse(Brushes.Blue, 20, 150, 200, 100)
' Draw a red pie (portion of an ellipse).
gr.FillPie(Brushes.Red, 320, 150, 200, 100, -45, 90)
' Draw the remainder of the ellipse in pink.
gr.FillPie(Brushes.Pink, 320, 150, 200, 100, 45, 270)
' Note that you don't have to dispose of system brushes.
```

You can fill irregular polygonal shapes by using the FillPolygon method, which takes an array of Point objects, each defining a vertex of the polygon. An optional fill mode argument lets you specify how intersecting areas are filled, and you can choose between alternate mode (the default) and winding mode. Figure 18-6 shows the effects of the two modes on a similar polygon; it was produced by the following code:

```
Dim points() As Point = {New Point(200, 100), New Point(300, 300), _
    New Point(50, 170), New Point(350, 170), New Point(100, 300)}
gr.FillPolygon(Brushes.Gray, points, Drawing.Drawing2D.FillMode.Alternate)
```

```
Dim points2() As Point = {New Point(600, 100), New Point(700, 300), _
    New Point(450, 170), New Point(750, 170), New Point(500, 300)}
gr.FillPolygon(Brushes.Green, points2, Drawing.Drawing2D.FillMode.Winding)
```

You can fill irregular curves by using the FillClosedCurve method, which takes an array of Point objects, a tension value, and an optional fill mode argument. The FillPath method can be used to paint complex paths, and the FillRegion method paints a Region object. (I'll talk about region objects a little later in this chapter.)

Figure 18-6. You can produce the filled starlike shape on the left by using the alternate fill mode, and the one on the right by using the winding fill mode.

Brush Objects

All the examples I've shown you so far use one of the predefined Brush objects exposed as properties of the Brushes or the SystemBrushes class. You can create a custom brush yourself by using one of the many available classes in the GDI+ subsystem. The most notable difference between custom and predefined brushes is that you must dispose of your custom brushes before you set them to Nothing or let them go out of scope. The simplest type of custom brush is the SolidBrush object, whose constructor takes a color:

```
' Create a solid brush with a custom color, and use it to fill a rectangle.
Dim br As New SolidBrush(Color.FromArgb(128, 30, 100))
gr.FillRectangle(br, New Rectangle(10, 10, 200, 100))
' Destroy the brush.
br.Dispose()
```

The HatchBrush class (in the System.Drawing.Drawing2D namespace) is a simple way to create two-color brushes that use one of the 56 predefined motifs available. The following listing shows the code that generates the upper left hatched rectangle in Figure 18-7:

```
Dim br1 As New HatchBrush(HatchStyle.BackwardDiagonal, _
    Color.White, Color.Blue)
gr.FillRectangle(br1, New Rectangle(10, 10, 200, 100))
br1.Dispose()
```

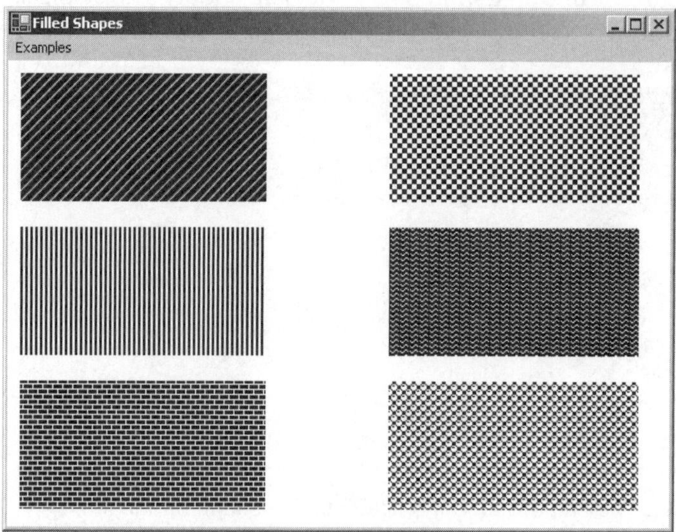

Figure 18-7. Six of the 56 available styles for hatch brushes.

You've seen the LinearGradientBrush class in action in the section "Creating a Control from Scratch" in Chapter 17, but there are many other aspects of the class to learn about. To begin with, a gradient brush is a brush that contains all the color nuances that vary from a starting color to an ending color, like the typical background screen of many installation procedures or Microsoft PowerPoint slides. The simplest way to create a linear gradient brush is to pass its size (by means of a Rectangle object), the two colors, and a direction to the brush's constructor. You can then use this brush to paint any filled shape:

```
Dim br As New LinearGradientBrush(New Rectangle(0, 0, 200, 100), _
    Color.Blue, Color.Black, LinearGradientMode.ForwardDiagonal)
gr.FillRectangle(br, 0, 0, 200, 100)
gr.FillRectangle(br, 220, 0, 200, 100)
br.Dispose()
```

The constructor that you see in the preceding code lets you indicate four directions for the gradient: horizontal, vertical, forward diagonal, and backward diagonal. If the shape being painted is larger than the brush rectangle, the brush is tiled to cover the shape. If the shape's coordinates aren't exact multiples of the rectangle's size, the color of the shape's upper left corner won't coincide with the brush's first color, as is the case with the rightmost rectangle in Figure 18-8 (which shows the outcome of the preceding code snippet). You can influence how the brush is used to fill the shape by using the WrapMode property, which can be Tile (the default), TileFlipX, TileFlipY, TileFlipXY, and Clamp.

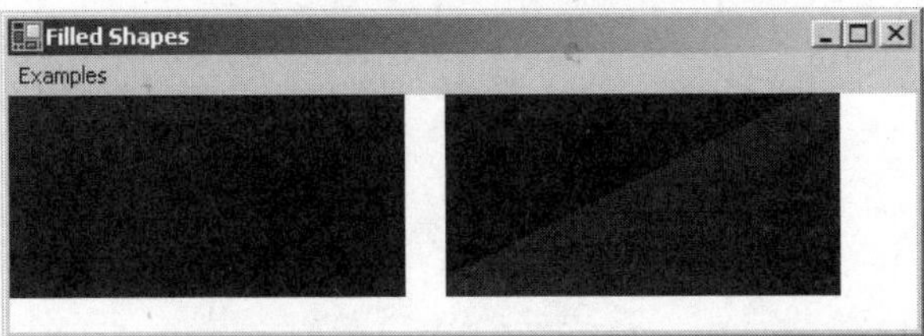

Figure 18-8. Two rectangles painted with linear gradient brushes.

By default, this type of brush uses a linear gradient, in which intermediate pixels change linearly from starting to ending color. However, you can use the Blend property to define a nonlinear progression. (See the .NET Platform SDK documentation for more details about nonlinear gradient brushes.)

Yet another type of brush is the TextureBrush class, whose constructor takes an Image object and an optional argument that tells how the image must be tiled if the painted shape is larger than the image. By default, the image is tiled as is, but you can also decide to flip it on the horizontal axis, the vertical axis, or both, as the following code illustrates. (See Figure 18-9.)

```
' These examples use a bitmap loaded in a PictureBox control.
Dim br1 As New TextureBrush(PictureBox1.Image)
gr.FillRectangle(br1, New Rectangle(20, 20, 250, 150))
br1.Dispose()

Dim br2 As New TextureBrush(PictureBox1.Image, WrapMode.TileFlipY)
gr.FillRectangle(br2, New Rectangle(300, 20, 250, 150))
br2.Dispose()

Dim br3 As New TextureBrush(PictureBox1.Image, WrapMode.TileFlipX)
gr.FillRectangle(br3, New Rectangle(20, 220, 250, 150))
br3.Dispose()

Dim br4 As New TextureBrush(PictureBox1.Image, WrapMode.TileFlipXY)
gr.FillRectangle(br4, New Rectangle(300, 220, 250, 150))
br4.Dispose()
```

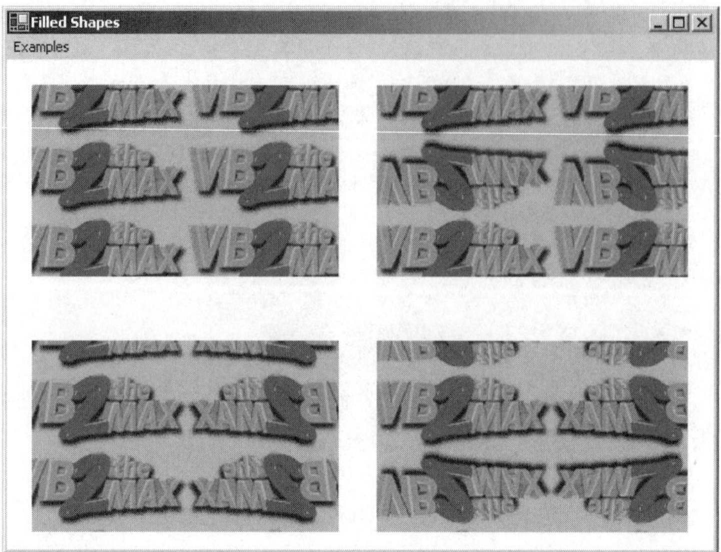

Figure 18-9. Texture brushes that tile a bitmap and flip it on one or both axes.

The one type of brush class left to be examined is PathGradientBrush, which patterns a gradient brush after a GraphicsPath object. Unlike other rectangular brushes, which are automatically tiled to cover surfaces of any size and shape, this type of brush doesn't extend over the boundaries of the path object used to define it, and in practice it should be used only to paint a specific path surface. In its simplest form, a PathGradientBrush is defined by a GraphicsPath object, the color of the center point, and the color at the path's borders:

```
' Define an elliptical path.
Dim pa As New GraphicsPath()
pa.AddEllipse(10, 10, 200, 100)
' Create the Brush shaped after the Path.
Dim br As New PathGradientBrush(pa)
br.CenterColor = Color.Yellow
' Define a one-element array of colors.
Dim colors() As Color = {Color.Blue}
br.SurroundColors = colors
' Paint the path.
gr.FillPath(br, pa)
' Destroy the Brush and Path objects.
br.Dispose()
pa.Dispose()
```

The ellipse in Figure 18-10 shows the result of the preceding code.

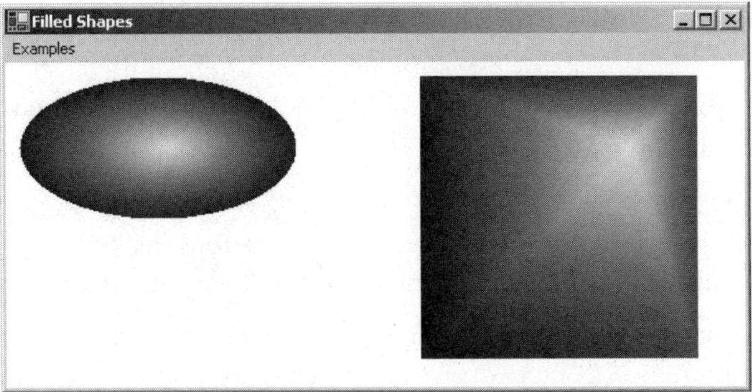

Figure 18-10. Two examples of path gradient brushes.

You can create fancier path gradient brushes by specifying multiple colors on the path's border. In practice, you can use a Point array for defining the path's vertices, then define a Color array with an equal number of elements, and then pass the array to the brush's SurroundColors property:

```
Dim pa2 As New GraphicsPath()
' This defines a square path.
Dim points() As Point = {New Point(300, 10), New Point(500, 10), _
    New Point(500, 210), New Point(300, 210)}
pa2.AddLines(points)
pa2.CloseFigure()
' Create a brush patterned after that path.
Dim br2 As New PathGradientBrush(pa2)
' Define color and position of the center.
br2.CenterColor = Color.Yellow
br2.CenterPoint = New PointF(450, 60)
' Define an array of colors, one for each vertex.
Dim colors2() As Color = {Color.Blue, Color.Green, Color.Red, Color.Black}
br2.SurroundColors = colors2
' Paint the path.
gr.FillPath(br2, pa2)
' Destroy the Brush and Path objects.
br2.Dispose()
pa2.Dispose()
```

You can see the effect of the preceding code on the right of Figure 18-10. Path gradient brushes can be customized in many other ways—for example, you can add an intermediate color (so that the color varies from the beginning color to the intermediate color and from the intermediate color to the end color), or you can specify a nonlinear variation between the beginning and end colors. (For more information, see the .NET Platform SDK documentation.)

Regions

A Region object consists of a combination of other, simpler, shapes, such as rectangles and paths. You can combine these shapes using many different methods, such as the following:

- **Union** The shape is added (ORed) to the current region. The resulting region contains all the points belonging to the original region and all the points belonging to the specified shape.
- **Intersect** The shape is intersected (ANDed) with the region. The resulting region contains only the points common to both the original region and the specified shape.
- **Exclude** The shape is subtracted from the region. The resulting region includes only the points in the original region that aren't also in the specified shape.
- **Xor** The resulting region contains all the points belonging to either the original region or the specified shape but not to both of them.
- **Complement** The resulting region contains only the points in the specified shape that don't belong to the original region.

Two more methods affect a region's size: MakeEmpty and MakeInfinite. The former reinitializes the region to an empty region; the latter initializes it to the entire X-Y plane. Once you have defined a Region object, you can paint it with the FillRegion method of the Graphics object, using any predefined or custom brush:

```
' Start with a square region.
Dim reg As New Region(New Rectangle(20, 20, 300, 300))
' Create a circular hole in it.
Dim pa As New GraphicsPath()
pa.AddEllipse(120, 120, 100, 100)
reg.Exclude(pa)
' Add another, smaller, square in the center.
reg.Union(New Rectangle(150, 150, 40, 40))
' Paint the region.
gr.FillRegion(Brushes.Green, reg)
' Destroy the Path and Region objects.
pa.Dispose()
reg.Dispose()
```

Regions are most useful for hit testing and clipping. The goal of hit testing is to determine whether a point or another shape is contained by the region: you might want to check whether the mouse cursor is over a given shape, but you can exploit the concept of regions for other purposes as well. The IsVisible method is overloaded to take a Point object, an X-Y pair of coordinates, or a Rectangle object as an argument:

```
' This code assumes that the reg variable references a Region object.
If reg.IsVisible(Me.MousePosition) Then
    ' The mouse cursor is over the region.
    ⋮
End If
```

If you define a clipping region for the Graphics object, all the pixels that would fall outside the region aren't drawn at all. You define a clipping region by using the SetClip method, which takes a Rectangle, a Path, or a Region object as its first argument, and a second argument that tells whether the shape in question must replace the current clipping region or must augment, complement, or intersect with the current clipping region. The following code uses the Region object specified earlier as a clipping region and then draws a series of circles with random colors. (You can see the result in Figure 18-11.)

```
' Use the Region as a clipping region (replaces any current region).
gr.SetClip(reg, CombineMode.Replace)
' Display circles with random colors.
Dim x As Integer, y As Integer, r As New Random()
For x = 10 To 400 Step 40
    For y = 10 To 400 Step 40
        Dim br As New SolidBrush( _
            Color.FromArgb(r.Next(0, 255), r.Next(0, 255), r.Next(0, 255)))
        gr.FillEllipse(br, x, y, 30, 30)
        br.Dispose()
    Next
Next
```

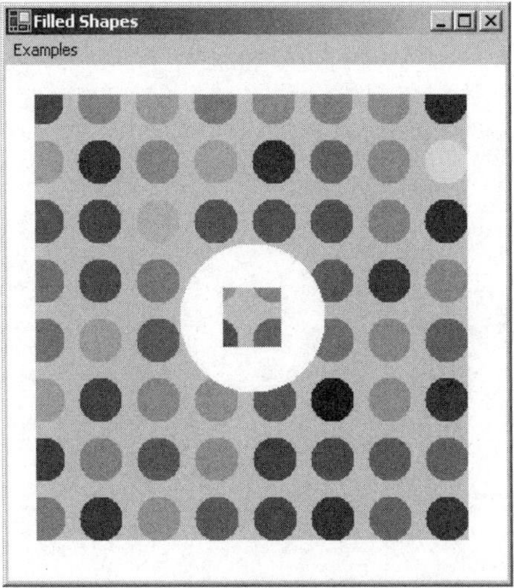

Figure 18-11. Using a region for clipping.

The Graphics object exposes the VisibleClipBounds property, which returns a RectangleF object that represents the visible area of the corresponding window. You can use this property to optimize your graphic routines by not processing shapes that are completely outside this rectangular area. When used with the printer, this property returns the printable area of the page.

Alpha Blending

One of the great features of GDI+ is *alpha blending*, which is the ability to define semitransparent colors and then use them to draw or paint all kinds of shapes. You define the transparency degree in the first argument of the Color.FromArgb method, passing a number in the range from 255 (opaque) to 0 (completely transparent). Any value less than 255 causes the background to show behind the figure being drawn. For example, the result visible in Figure 18-12 was produced by the following code:

```
' A solid green square
gr.FillRectangle(Brushes.Green, 20, 20, 200, 200)
' A semitransparent red ellipse
Dim br1 As New SolidBrush(Color.FromArgb(128, 255, 0, 0))
gr.FillEllipse(br1, 120, 50, 200, 120)
' An even more transparent blue rectangle
Dim br2 As New SolidBrush(Color.FromArgb(30, 0, 0, 255))
gr.FillRectangle(br2, 160, 80, 120, 200)
' A semitransparent thick yellow ellipse
Dim p As New Pen(Color.FromArgb(128, 128, 128, 128), 5)
gr.DrawEllipse(p, 100, 100, 200, 200)

' Destroy brushes and pens.
br1.Dispose()
br2.Dispose()
p.Dispose()
```

Figure 18-12. Alpha blending with outline and filled shapes.

Transformations

All the code samples seen so far assumed that that the coordinate origin was the upper left corner of the client area and that all values were in pixels. However, the Graphics object is highly flexible and lets you change these default settings as your needs dictate. To take advantage of this ability, you should understand that three different coordinate systems come into play whenever you draw any graphic object (including bitmaps and text):

- **The world coordinate system** This is the system that you use to model your "graphic world," and all the coordinates that you pass to graphic methods are expressed in this system.
- **The page coordinate system** This is the system used by the surface on which you're drawing, be it a form, a control, or a printer document. By default, the origin and the scale of this system coincide with the world coordinate system, but they don't have to. For example, you can have the origin of the world system at the center of the form, which might be convenient if you're plotting a mathematical function. The conversion between world and page coordinates is called *world transformation*.
- **The device coordinate system** This is the system used by the physical device on which the drawing operation occurs—that is, the actual window if you're drawing on the screen or the sheet of paper if you're sending output to the printer. You can define precisely the unit of measure of the system (inches, millimeters, and so on), the ratio between the horizontal and vertical axes, and more. The conversion between page and device coordinates is called *page transformation*. Note that you can't perform translations along the X or Y axis, nor can you reverse the direction along these axes. (In other words, you can't flip an image using page transformation.)

The Graphics object exposes several methods for affecting how world transformation is performed. The TranslateTransform method lets you change the origin of the coordinate system, so, for example, you can draw the same GraphicsPath object in a different location by simply translating the origin of the X-Y axes:

```
' Create a Path that we can draw multiple times.
Dim pa As New GraphicsPath()
pa.AddRectangle(New Rectangle(20, 20, 200, 100))
pa.AddEllipse(New Rectangle(30, 30, 180, 80))
' Draw the path without any transformation.
```

(continued)

```
gr.DrawPath(Pens.Black, pa)
' Apply a translation, and redraw the object in another position.
gr.TranslateTransform(30, 200)
gr.DrawPath(Pens.Red, pa)
```

The two leftmost shapes in Figure 18-13 show the effect of the preceding code.

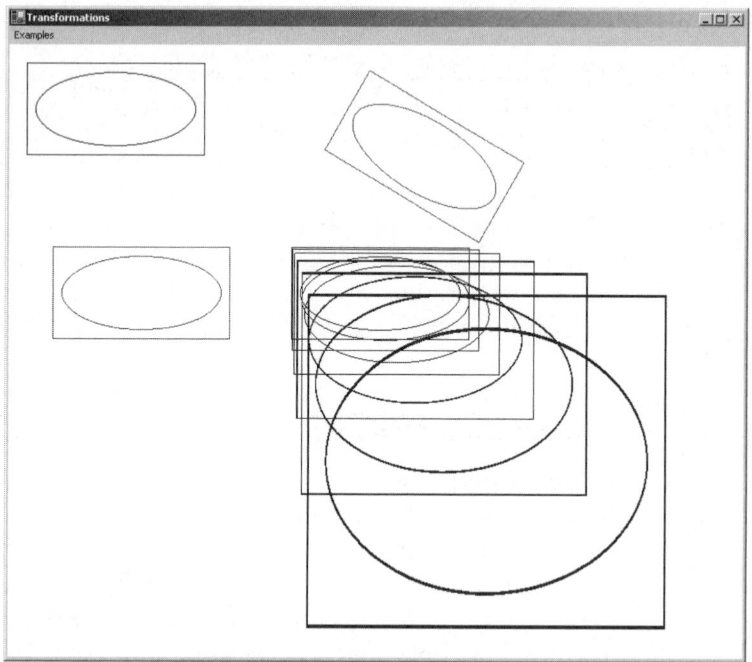

Figure 18-13. Effects of translation, rotation, and scaling world transformation.

The RotateTransform method lets you rotate all the shapes you draw on the Graphics object by the angle you specify:

```
' Ensure that we start with default values (that is, no transformations).
gr.ResetTransform()
' Apply both a translation and a rotation, and redraw the Path.
gr.TranslateTransform(400, 0)
gr.RotateTransform(30)
gr.DrawPath(Pens.Green, pa)
```

See the result in the rotated shape near the upper right corner in Figure 18-13.

You can also vary the scale used to draw along the two axes by using the ScaleTransform method:

```
gr.ResetTransform()
gr.TranslateTransform(300, 200)
' Create multiple shapes that vary in angle and scale.
Dim i As Integer
Dim scaleX As Single = 1
Dim scaleY As Single = 1
For i = 1 To 6
    gr.ScaleTransform(scaleX, scaleY)
    gr.DrawPath(Pens.Blue, pa)
    scaleX += 0.05
    scaleY += 0.1
Next
```

See the result in the lower right corner of Figure 18-13.

You can also combine multiple transformations in the Transform property, which takes a Matrix object that defines all the translations, rotations, and scaling that you want to apply. Correctly initializing a Matrix object takes some knowledge in the math theory behind scale transformations (you can read more about this object in the .NET Platform SDK documentation), but even without going so much in depth you can still use the Transform property to save and restore the current state of world transformation:

```
' Save current world transformation state.
Dim mat As Matrix = gr.Transform
' Apply any xxxxTransform method here.
⋮
' Restore original world transformation settings.
gr.Transform = mat
```

You can control how page transformation is carried out by means of the PageUnit and PageScale properties. The PageUnit property takes a GraphicsUnit enumerated value, which can be Pixel (the default for video), Inch, Millimeter, Point (1/72 inch), Display (1/75 inch), or Document (1/300 inch):

```
' Use inches as the unit of measure.
gr.PageUnit = GraphicsUnit.Inch
```

PageScale is a Single value that lets you reduce or magnify the output on the screen or printer by a given factor:

```
' Shrink output to 10 percent of the original size.
gr.PageScale = 0.1
```

Setting a page unit value other than pixels requires special attention because by default Pen objects are 1 unit wide (as measured in device coordinates). So if you use inches as your graphic unit by default, lines and curves are drawn with a pen 1 inch wide. You can address this problem by using the

DpiX and DpiY read-only properties to determine the value to pass to the Pen's constructor:

```
' Create a Pen that is 1 pixel wide, regardless of current graphic unit.
Dim p As New Pen(1 / gr.DpiX)
```

Sometimes you might want to see how one or more points would be affected by the current transformation settings, but without actually drawing the points. You can do this by using the TransformPoints method of the Graphics object, which takes two CoordinateSpace enumerated values to specify from which system and to which system you're converting, and an array of PointF objects:

```
' Define an array of points (in World system).
Dim points() As PointF = { New PointF(10, 20), New PointF(190, 220)}
' Convert then from World to Device systems.
gr.TransformPoints(CoordinateSpace.World, CoordinateSpace.Device, points)
' The result is now in the points array.
```

Here are a few more tips about coordinate transformations:

- The DrawImage method of the Graphics object is affected by world transformation but not by page transformation. (See the "Imaging" section, which immediately follows, for more details about this method.)
- Hatched brushes aren't affected by either world or page transformation.
- TextureBrush and LinearGradientBrush classes have their own Translate property and TranslateTransform, RotateTransform, MultiplyTransform, and ResetTransform methods, so you can modify their appearance independently of the Graphics object on which you use them.

Imaging

A portion of GDI+ lets you display and process raster images as well metafiles. The two most important objects for working with images are the Image class (which offers methods to save and load images from disk) and the Bitmap class (which inherits from Image and lets you access the individual pixels and other features of the image). Both these objects are in the System.Drawing namespace, but the imaging subsystem uses a few other objects in the System.Drawing.Imaging namespace, such as Metafile and ColorPalette.

Loading and Saving Images

The LoadFromFile and LoadFromStream methods of the Image and the Bitmap classes allow you to load an image from a file or from an open Stream object (not necessarily a file stream). The following code snippet shows how you can use an OpenFileDialog control to ask the user for an image name and then display it on the surface related to a Graphics object with a DrawImage method:

```
With OpenFileDialog1
    .Filter = "Image files|*;*.jpg;*.jpeg;*.gif;*.png;*.tif"
    If .ShowDialog = DialogResult.OK Then
        ' Load a file into a Bitmap object.
        Dim bmp As Bitmap = Bitmap.FromFile(.FileName)
        ' Create a Graphics object and draw the bitmap on it.
        Dim gr As Graphics = Me.CreateGraphics
        gr.DrawImage(bmp, 0, 0)
        ' Destroy both the Bitmap and the Graphics objects.
        bmp.Dispose()
        gr.Dispose()
    End If
End With
```

An even simpler way to load an image into a Bitmap object is by taking advantage of its constructor:

```
' (This statement can replace the FromFile call in preceding code.)
        Dim bmp As New Bitmap(.Filename)
```

GDI+ can load images in the following formats: bitmaps (BMP); Graphics Interchange Format (GIF, for compressing images with up to 8 bits per pixel); Joint Photographic Experts Group (JPEG, for compressed images with adjustable compression ratios); Exchangeable Image File (EXIF, an extended JPEG format that can also store additional information about the photo, such as date, exposure, and so on); Portable Network Graphics (PNG, a compression format similar to GIF that can also store images with 24 or 48 bits per pixel); and Tag Image File Format (TIFF, a compressed format that can also carry additional information by means of tags).

You can save an image stored in an Image or Bitmap object using its Save method, which takes the filename and an argument that specifies the target format. The following code shows how you can prompt the user to save the contents of a Bitmap object in several different formats by using a SaveFileDialog control:

```
' This code assumes that you have a bmp Bitmap variable holding an image.
With SaveFileDialog1
    .Title = "Select target image and format"
    .Filter = "Bitmap|*|GIF|*.gif|TIFF|*.tif"
    .OverwritePrompt = True
    If .ShowDialog = DialogResult.OK Then
        Select Case System.IO.Path.GetExtension(.FileName).ToUpper
            Case ""
                bmp.Save(.FileName, ImageFormat)
```

(continued)

```
            Case ".GIF"
                bmp.Save(.FileName, ImageFormat.Gif)
            Case ".TIF"
                bmp.Save(.FileName, ImageFormat.Tiff)
            Case Else
                MessageBox.Show("Unrecognized extension", "Error", _
                    MessageBoxButtons.OK, MessageBoxIcon.Error)
        End Select
    End If
End With
```

You can save an image in any format, but in some cases you might need to specify additional details, such as the compression ratio. (Read the .NET Platform SDK documentation for additional information.)

Displaying an Image

As you've seen in the preceding section, you display an image on a Graphics object by using the DrawImage method. In its simplest syntax, this method takes the image to be displayed and the coordinates of the upper left corner of the destination area:

```
' Display an image at coordinates 100,200.
gr.DrawImage(bmp, 100, 200)
```

The DrawImage method supports 30 overloaded variations. One of such variations allows you to specify the rectangular portion of the image that must be drawn:

```
' Draw only the left half of the image to coordinates 20,20.
gr.DrawImage(bmp, 20, 20, _
    New RectangleF(0, 0, bmp.Width / 2, bmp.Height), GraphicsUnit.Pixel)
```

Another overloaded variation copies the entire image to the specified destination rectangle. By changing the size of the target rectangle, you can therefore zoom or reduce the image during the copy operation:

```
' Create a destination rectangle 3 times as wide and twice as tall.
Dim rect As New RectangleF(20, 120, bmp.Width * 3, bmp.Height * 2)
' Draw the enlarged bitmap.
gr.DrawImage(bmp, rect)
```

You can also combine the two effects by specifying both the destination rectangle and the source rectangle:

```
Dim destRect As New RectangleF(20, 320, bmp.Width * 1.5, bmp.Height)
' Create a rectangle corresponding to the upper left quarter of the image.
Dim sourceRect As New RectangleF(0, 0, bmp.Width / 2, bmp.Height / 2)
' Draw the portion of bitmap in the destination rectangle.
gr.DrawImage(bmp, destRect, sourceRect, GraphicsUnit.Pixel)
```

Figure 18-14 shows the effect of the last three code snippets. As I mentioned in the previous section about coordinate transformations, the DrawImage method is affected by world transformation but not by page transformation.

Figure 18-14. Copy all or part of an image, with optional stretching of the result.

You can draw on an image by getting a Graphics object (with the Graphics.FromImage static method), as in the following code snippet:

```
' This code assume that the bmp holds a reference to a bitmap.
Dim gr As Graphics = Graphics.FromImage(bmp)
' Draw directly on the Graphics object, and then release it.
gr.FillRectangle(Brushes.Red, 20, 20, 100, 100)
gr.Dispose()
```

You can do more sophisticated processing on a bitmap by using the Bitmap class's LockBits method, which returns a BitmapData object. Among other pieces of information, the BitmapData object exposes the memory address of actual pixels. Unfortunately, you can't access the bitmap's memory in Visual Basic because this language doesn't support pointers, so you have to either use C# or call unmanaged code. Bitmaps locked with this method should be unlocked with the UnlockBits method.

Flipping, Rotating, and Skewing an Image

The DrawImage method can also take an array of three Point elements as an argument; these points define a parallelogram on the target Graphics object that will be used as the destination area for the image being painted. More specifically, the three points define where on the destination surface the upper left, upper right, and lower left points in the original image are copied to. You can flip, rotate, or skew the image by arranging these points appropriately, as the following diagram shows:

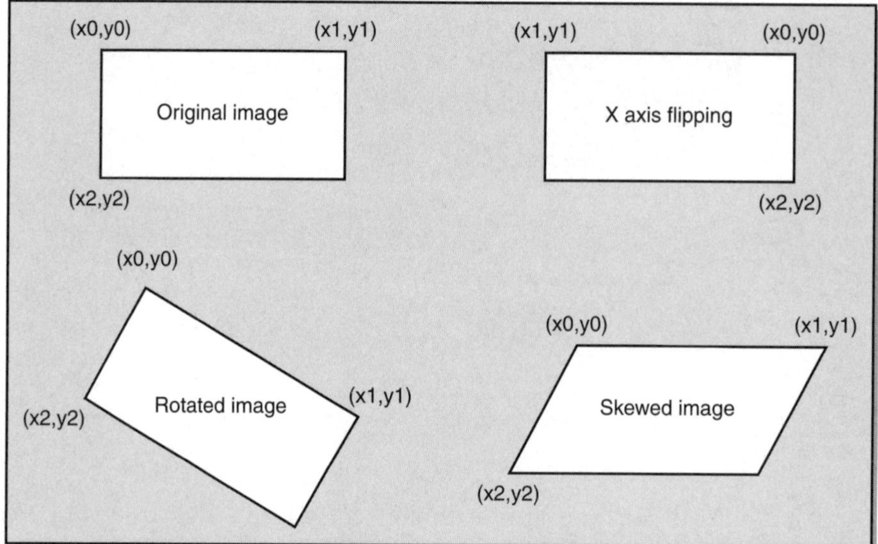

Understanding how you must specify these three points to achieve the desired effect isn't immediate. For example, the rotation effect requires some trigonometric calculations. So I have prepared three reusable routines that let you flip an image on one or both axes, rotate it by a specified angle (in degrees), and skew it by a given amount along one or both axes:

```
Sub DrawFlipImage(ByVal gr As Graphics, ByVal bmp As Bitmap, _
    ByVal x As Single, ByVal y As Single, _
    ByVal flipX As Boolean, ByVal flipY As Boolean)
    ' Start with values of parallelogram's vertices as if no flipping occurs.
    Dim x0 As Single = x
    Dim y0 As Single = y
    Dim x1 As Single = x + bmp.Width
    Dim y1 As Single = y
    Dim x2 As Single = x
    Dim y2 As Single = y + bmp.Height
```

```
    ' Account for horizontal flipping.
    If flipX Then
        x0 = x + bmp.Width
        x1 = x
        x2 = x0
    End If
    ' Account for vertical flipping.
    If flipY Then
        y0 = y + bmp.Height
        y1 = y0
        y2 = y
    End If
    ' Create the points array.
    Dim points() As Point = _
        {New Point(x0, y0), New Point(x1, y1), New Point(x2, y2)}
    ' Draw the flipped image.
    gr.DrawImage(bmp, points)
End Sub

Sub DrawRotateImage(ByVal gr As Graphics, ByVal bmp As Bitmap, _
    ByVal x As Single, ByVal y As Single, ByVal angle As Single)
    ' Convert the angle in degrees.
    angle = angle / (180 / Math.PI)
    ' Find the position of (x1,y1) and (x2,y2).
    Dim x1 As Single = x + bmp.Width * Math.Cos(angle)
    Dim y1 As Single = y + bmp.Width * Math.Sin(angle)
    Dim x2 As Single = x - bmp.Height * Math.Sin(angle)
    Dim y2 As Single = y + bmp.Height * Math.Cos(angle)

    ' Create the points array.
    Dim points() As Point = _
        {New Point(x, y), New Point(x1, y1), New Point(x2, y2)}
    ' Draw the rotated image.
    gr.DrawImage(bmp, points)
End Sub

Sub DrawSkewImage(ByVal gr As Graphics, ByVal bmp As Bitmap, _
    ByVal x As Single, ByVal y As Single, _
    ByVal dx As Single, ByVal dy As Single)
    ' Find the position of (x1,y1) and (x2,y2).
    Dim x1 As Single = x + bmp.Width
    Dim y1 As Single = y + dy
    Dim x2 As Single = x + dx
    Dim y2 As Single = y + bmp.Height
    ' Create the points array.
    Dim points() As Point = _
        {New Point(x, y), New Point(x1, y1), New Point(x2, y2)}
    ' Draw the skewed image.
    gr.DrawImage(bmp, points)
End Sub
```

Using these three routines, drawing a flipped, rotated, or skewed image is a breeze. For example, the following code produces the effects you can see in Figure 18-15:

```
DrawFlipImage(gr, bmp, 100, 20, False, False)
DrawFlipImage(gr, bmp, 300, 20, True, False)
DrawFlipImage(gr, bmp, 100, 120, False, True)
DrawFlipImage(gr, bmp, 300, 120, True, True)

DrawRotateImage(gr, bmp, 100, 220, 45)
DrawRotateImage(gr, bmp, 300, 220, 90)
DrawRotateImage(gr, bmp, 500, 220, 135)

DrawSkewImage(gr, bmp, 100, 400, -50, 0)
DrawSkewImage(gr, bmp, 300, 400, 0, 50)
DrawSkewImage(gr, bmp, 500, 400, -50, 50)
```

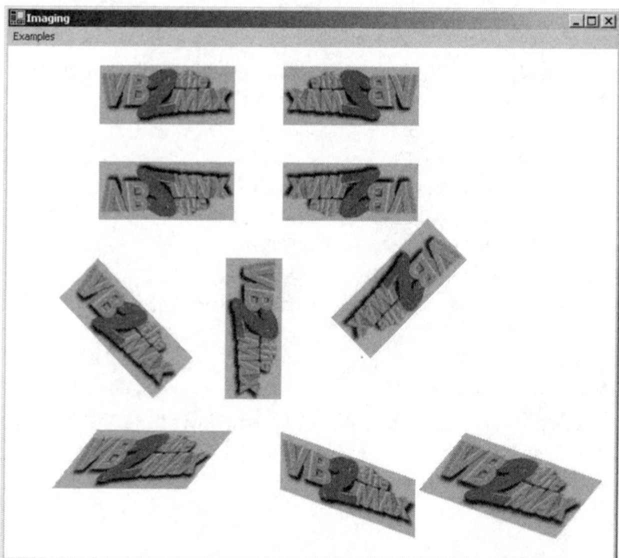

Figure 18-15. Flipped, rotated, and skewed images.

When you're stretching or shrinking an image, in some cases one point in the source image maps to multiple points in the destination image or vice versa. So GDI+ must determine the color of the destination pixel by interpolating the colors of more than one pixel. You can control how this interpolation is performed by assigning a value to the Graphics.InterpolationMode property. The available modes are Low, High, Bilinear, Bicubic, NearestNeighbor, HighQualityBilinear, and HighQualityBicubic. (Read the .NET Platform SDK documentation for additional details on these modes.)

When you don't need to transform anything, you can improve the performance of the DrawImage method by specifying explicitly that the destination rectangle have the same size as the source image, thereby preventing any transformation that takes place if the number of dots per inch on the destination Graphics object is different from the number of dots on the device where the image was created. Here's a simple way to ensure that the image is copied as fast as possible:

```
gr.DrawImage(bmp, 20, 50, bmp.Width, bmp.Height)
```

Or you can use the DrawImageUnscaled method, which draws the image in its original size at the location specified by the target Point or X,Y pair of coordinates:

```
gr.DrawImageUnscaled(bmp, 20, 50)
```

You can also specify a Rectangle object, which works as a clipping region for the image:

```
gr.DrawImageUnscaled(bmp, New Rectangle(20, 50, 200, 100))
```

Transparent and Semitransparent Bitmaps

GDI+ gives you three ways to create a transparent or semitransparent bitmap. You can select one of the colors in the bitmap to be transparent, you can select a degree of transparency for the entire bitmap (in much the same way you can select the degree of transparency of a form using its Opacity property), or you can set a different degree of transparency for each individual pixel in the bitmap.

Creating a bitmap with a transparent color is the simplest technique of the three: You just have to invoke the MakeTransparent method, which takes the transparent color as an argument:

```
' Create a clone bitmap, and make it transparent.
Dim bmp As New Bitmap("logo")
bmp.MakeTransparent(Color.FromArgb(140, 195, 247))
gr.DrawImage(bmp, 20, 20)
```

The leftmost image in Figure 18-16 shows the effect of this operation.

Figure 18-16. Transparent and semitransparent bitmaps.

Creating a bitmap with a fixed degree of transparency for all its pixels requires that you pass an appropriate ImageAttributes object to the DrawImage method. Before you do so, however, you must assign a 5-by-5-pixel color matrix to the ImageAttributes object by using the SetColorMatrix method. The code that you need to write to perform this operation isn't trivial because the color matrix actually is an array of Single arrays. Here's a code example that draws an image using a transparency level equal to 0.8. (This code produces the images in the middle of Figure 18-16.)

```
Dim bmp As New Bitmap("logo")
' Define the transparency level common to all pixels in the bitmap.
Dim transparency As Single = 0.8
' Create a 5x5 matrix with the transparency value in position (4,4).
Dim values()() As Single = {New Single() {1, 0, 0, 0, 0}, _
    New Single() {0, 1, 0, 0, 0}, _
    New Single() {0, 0, 1, 0, 0}, _
    New Single() {0, 0, 0, transparency, 0}, _
    New Single() {0, 0, 0, 0, 1}}
' Use the matrix to initialize a new colorMatrix object.
Dim colMatrix As New ColorMatrix(values)
' Create an ImageAttributes object, and assign its color matrix.
Dim imageAttr As New ImageAttributes()
imageAttr.SetColorMatrix(colMatrix, ColorMatrixFlag.Default, _
    ColorAdjustType.Bitmap)
' Draw the bitmap using the specified ImageAttributes object.
gr.DrawImage(bmp, New Rectangle(200, 20, bmp.Width, bmp.Height), _
    0, 0, bmp.Width, bmp.Height, GraphicsUnit.Pixel, imageAttr)
```

The last way to create a semitransparent bitmap is the most flexible of the three because you control the alpha component of each individual pixel in the image. You can access the color of an individual pixel in an image with the GetPixel method and modify the color (and possibly its alpha blend component) with the SetPixel method. As you can probably guess, it's also the slowest method of the group, but on the other hand it lets you achieve truly stunning results, such as the rightmost image in Figure 18-16, which was created by means of the following code:

```
Dim bmp As New Bitmap("logo")
Dim x, y As Single
' This loop visits all the pixels in the bitmap.
For x = 0 To bmp.Width - 1
    For y = 0 To bmp.Height - 1
        ' Get the current color.
        Dim oldColor = bmp.GetPixel(x, y)
        ' Enforce a transparency value that goes from 0 (the left border)
        ' to 1 (the rightmost border).
```

```
        Dim newColor As Color = Color.FromArgb(x / bmp.Width * 256, oldColor)
        bmp.SetPixel(x, y, newColor)
    Next
Next
gr.DrawImage(bmp, 400, 20)
```

Icons

An icon is like a small bitmap that contains a transparent color and whose size is determined by the system. The System.Drawing namespace contains an Icon class, which is the one you must use to load and draw icons. This class doesn't inherit from Image, so you can't use any of the methods you've seen so far. In fact, the operations you can perform on an Icon object are fairly limited. You load an icon by passing a filename or a Stream object to the icon's constructor:

```
Dim icon As New Icon("W95MBX01.ICO")
```

Another way to get an icon is by using the objects exposed by the SystemIcons class, which exposes properties that return the icons that you can display in a message box and a few others:

```
Dim icon2 As Icon = SystemIcons.Exclamation()
Dim icon3 As Icon = SystemIcons.WinLogo()
```

Once you have an Icon object, you can display it on a Graphics surface by using the DrawIcon method, which can take either a target coordinate pair or the destination rectangle:

```
' Draw the icon in its original size.
gr.DrawIcon(icon, 20, 20)
' Draw the icon with a 400% zoom.
gr.DrawIcon(icon, New Rectangle(100, 20, icon.Width * 4, icon.Height * 4))
' All icons must be destroyed.
icon.Dispose()
```

Most of the time, loading an icon and displaying it is all you need to do. If you want to achieve more sophisticated graphics effects, such as rotating an icon or defining another transparent color, you must convert the icon to a bitmap:

```
Dim icon As New Icon("W95MBX01.ICO")
' Convert the icon to a bitmap.
Dim bmp As Bitmap = icon.ToBitmap
' Make red the second transparent color, and draw the image.
bmp.MakeTransparent(Color.Red)
gr.DrawImage(bmp, 20, 200)
' Destroy both the bitmap and the icon.
icon.Dispose()
bmp.Dispose()
```

The Graphics object also exposes the DrawIconUnstretched method, which takes the icon to be displayed and a Rectangle object. The icon isn't stretched to fit the target rectangle, but it's clipped if it's larger than the rectangle itself.

Metafiles

A metafile is akin to a Path object in that it stores a sequence of drawing actions on a Graphics surface, including imaging and text operations. The main difference between a Metafile object and a Path object is that a Metafile object lets you save and reload this sequence of operations from a disk file. The Metafile class's constructor offers as many as 39 overloaded variations, but in the most common case you pass the name of the file you want to create and a handle to the device context on which the metafile will be drawn:

```
' Get the Graphics object associated with the current form.
Dim gr As Graphics = Me.CreateGraphics
' Create a new metafile object, with the same features as the form's Graphics.
Dim mf As New Metafile("sample.emf", gr.GetHdc)
```

The next step is to retrieve the inner Graphics object associated with the metafile. This object lets you draw any shape or text on the metafile's invisible graphic surface:

```
' Retrieve the metafile's internal Graphics object.
Dim mfgr As Graphics = Graphics.FromImage(mf)
' Draw some graphics on the metafile's Graphics.
mfgr.DrawLine(Pens.Blue, 20, 20, 200, 200)
mfgr.DrawRectangle(Pens.Red, 50, 50, 200, 120)
mfgr.FillEllipse(Brushes.Green, 70, 20, 200, 120)
' Draw a text string in Arial 20 font.
Dim fnt As New Font("Arial", 20, FontStyle.Bold Or FontStyle.Italic)
mfgr.DrawString("Test
```

When the Metafile object is destroyed, the associated file is updated. Playing back the drawing instructions in a metafile is very simple:

```
' Retrieve the form's Graphics object.
Dim gr As Graphics = Me.CreateGraphics
' Read the metafile from the file.
Dim mf As New Metafile("sample.emf")
' Draw the metafile in two different positions.
gr.DrawImage(mf, 0, 0)
gr.DrawImage(mf, 300, 100)
' Destroy all objects.
mf.Dispose()
gr.Dispose()
```

You can see the result of these operations in Figure 18-17.

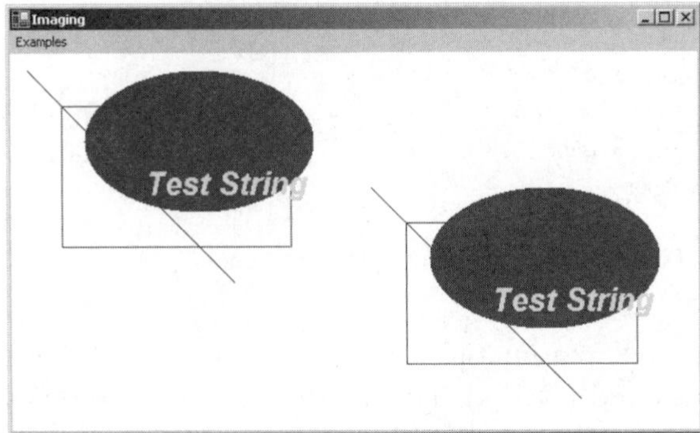

Figure 18-17. Displaying a metafile.

One last note about metafiles: when you're playing back a metafile, the properties of the Graphics object used for world transformation, clipping, and so on are those that were active when the metafile was recorded, not those currently active.

Typography

Typography is the portion of the .NET Framework that has to do with printing text in various fonts or style. You've already seen how to create textual output in several code samples earlier in this chapter, but I haven't yet explained the operational details.

GDI+ supports only TrueType and OpenType fonts; these fonts are continuously scalable, rotatable, and shareable and can be used on both video and printer without any limitation.

Font Families

In GDI+ parlance, a *font family* is a group of fonts with the same typeface and different styles. For example, the Tahoma font family includes Tahoma Regular, Tahoma Bold, Tahoma Italic, and Tahoma Bold Italic. You can enumerate all the installed font families using the Families property of the InstalledFontCollection object. This property returns an array of FontFamily objects, which you can then enumerate to extract properties of individual font families:

```
' Get the collection of installed Fonts.
Dim fonts As New System.Drawing.Text.InstalledFontCollection()
```

(continued)

```
' Get an array with all installed font families.
Dim fontFamilies() As FontFamily = fonts.Families
' Create a comma-delimited list of font family names.
Dim list As String
Dim fontFam As FontFamily
For Each fontFam In fontFamilies
    If list <> "" Then list &= ", "
    list &= fontFam.Name
Next
' Display the list of fonts in the Debug window.
Debug.WriteLine(list)
```

Another way to get an array of installed font families is by using the FontFamily.GetFamilies shared method. This method takes a Graphics object and returns only the font installed for that device, so you can use it to enumerate only the fonts installed for the screen or for the printer:

```
' Enumerate fonts installed for the screen.
Dim gr As Graphics = Me.CreateGraphics
Dim fontFamilies() As FontFamily = FontFamily.GetFamilies(gr)
gr.Dispose
```

You can get a reference to a standard font family by using three static properties of the FontFamily class: GenericMonospace returns a generic monospace FontFamily object; GenericSansSerif returns a generic sans serif FontFamily; and GenericSerif returns a generic serif FontFamily.

Once you have a FontFamily object, you can determine whether a given style is available by means of a call to the IsStyleAvailable method:

```
If fontFam.IsStyleAvailable(FontStyle.Bold) Then
    ' This font family supports bold style.
    ⋮
End If
```

Note that for some fonts the Regular style might be unavailable. You can determine font metrics information by using other methods of the FontFamily class, such as GetEmHeight, GetCellAscent, GetCellDescent, and GetLineSpacing. (Read the .NET Platform SDK documentation for more details about these methods.)

Drawing Text

You can't use FontFamily objects in printing operations, however, because they don't have a specific size or other attributes, such as underline or strikethrough.

You can create a Font object in many ways, as demonstrated by the following code snippet:

```
' Create a font from a family and a size in points.
Dim font1 As New Font("Arial", 12)
' Create a font from a family, a size, and a style.
Dim font2 As New Font("Arial", 14, FontStyle.Bold)
' Create a font from a family, a size, and two combined styles.
Dim font3 As New Font("Arial", 16, FontStyle.Italic Or FontStyle.Underline)
' Create a font from a family and a size in another unit.
Dim font4 As New Font("Arial", 10, FontStyle.Regular, GraphicsUnit.Millimeter)
' Create a font family and then a font of that family.
Dim fontFam As New FontFamily("Courier New")
Dim font5 As New Font(fontFam, 18, FontStyle.Italic)
```

The size argument you pass to the Font's constructor is a metrical size, not a pixel size, and the result for a given size isn't affected by the current page transforms. (Text size is subject to world transformation, however.) You can specify a given GraphicsUnit by passing an extra argument to the constructor, as you see here:

```
Dim font1 As New Font("Arial", 12, GraphicsUnit.Pixel)
Dim font2 As New Font("Arial", 14, FontStyle.Bold, GraphicsUnit.Pixel)
⋮
```

You can't use the GraphicsUnit.Display setting for a font size.

You draw text by using the DrawString method of the Graphics object. In its simplest form, this method takes the string to be printed, a Font object, a Brush object, and the coordinates of the point where the string must be drawn:

```
' ...(Continuing preceding code snippet)...
Dim gr As Graphics = Me.CreateGraphics
gr.DrawString("Arial 12 Regular", font1, Brushes.Black, 20, 20)
gr.DrawString("Arial 14 Bold", font2, Brushes.Black, 20, 60)
gr.DrawString("Arial 16 Italic & Underline", font3, Brushes.Black, 20, 100)
gr.DrawString("Arial 10 millimeters", font4, Brushes.Black, 20, 140)
' Note that the destination point can be a PointF object.
gr.DrawString("Courier 18 Italic", font5, Brushes.Black, New PointF(20, 200))
' Always destroy Font objects when you don't need them any longer.
font1.Dispose()
font2.Dispose()
font3.Dispose()
font4.Dispose()
font5.Dispose()
```

You can see the result of this code in Figure 18-18.

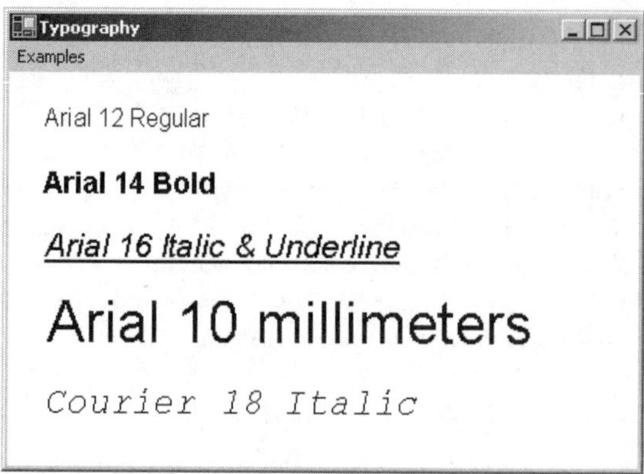

Figure 18-18. Displaying fonts with different sizes and attributes.

When displaying strings on consecutive lines, you can take advantage of the Font's GetHeight method, which returns the height of the font on the specified Graphics object. For example, this code is similar to the preceding snippet except that it displays individual lines closer to one another:

```
' Redraw the same font output with a more compact line spacing.
Dim y As Integer = 20
gr.DrawString("Arial 12 Regular", font1, Brushes.Black, 20, y)
y += font1.GetHeight(gr)
gr.DrawString("Arial 14 Bold", font2, Brushes.Black, 20, y)
y += font2.GetHeight(gr)
gr.DrawString("Arial 16 Italic & Underline", font3, Brushes.Black, 20, y)
y += font3.GetHeight(gr)
gr.DrawString("Arial 10 millimeters", font4, Brushes.Black, 20, y)
y += font4.GetHeight(gr)
gr.DrawString("Courier 18 Italic", font5, Brushes.Black, New PointF(20, y))
```

Because you draw text using a Brush (and not a Pen) object, you can easily create dazzling effects by using textured, hatched, or gradient brushes, as in the following code. (See the result in Figure 18-19.)

```
' Create a textured brush.
Dim br As New TextureBrush(Image.FromFile("greenstone"))
' Create a large font.
Dim fnt As New Font("Arial", 50, FontStyle.Bold, GraphicsUnit.Millimeter)
' Paint a string with textured pattern.
gr.DrawString("Textured", fnt, br, 20, 20)
gr.DrawString("Text", fnt, br, 20, 200)
```

Figure 18-19. Drawing text with a textured brush.

Aligned Text

The DrawString method can also take a RectangleF object as an argument, in which it draws the text inside the specified rectangle, as you see in this code:

```
Dim msg As String = "This is a long string whose purpose is to show how" _
    & " you can format a message inside a rectangle."
Dim fnt As New Font("Arial", 12)
Dim rectF As RectangleF

' Draw the text inside the rectangle.
rectF = New RectangleF(20, 20, 140, 160)
gr.DrawString(msg, fnt, Brushes.Black, rectF)
' Also display the bounding rectangle.
gr.DrawRectangle(Pens.Red, 20, 20, 140, 160)
```

You can determine both the horizontal and vertical alignment of the text inside the bounding rectangle by initializing a StringFormat object and passing it to the DrawString method. The Alignment property of the StringFormat object affects the horizontal alignment and can be Near (default), Center, or Far (which corresponds to left, center, right in all languages that write text from left to right, such as all Western ones). The LineAlignment property affects the vertical alignment and again can be Near (top, the default), Center (middle), or Far (bottom).

```
' ...(Continuing the preceding code snippet)...

' Draw the text again, but align it to the right.
Dim strFormat As New StringFormat()
```

(continued)

```
strFormat.Alignment = StringAlignment.Far
' Draw the text inside the rectangle with the format string.
rectF = New RectangleF(220, 20, 140, 160)
gr.DrawString(msg, fnt, Brushes.Black, rectF, strFormat)
' Also, display the bounding rectangle.
gr.DrawRectangle(Pens.Red, 220, 20, 140, 160)

' Draw the text again, but center it horizontally AND vertically.
strFormat.Alignment = StringAlignment.Center
strFormat.LineAlignment = StringAlignment.Center
' Draw the text inside the rectangle with the format string.
rectF = New RectangleF(420, 20, 140, 160)
gr.DrawString(msg, fnt, Brushes.Black, rectF, strFormat)
' Also, display the bounding rectangle.
gr.DrawRectangle(Pens.Red, 420, 20, 140, 160)
```

You can see the result of this code sample in Figure 18-20.

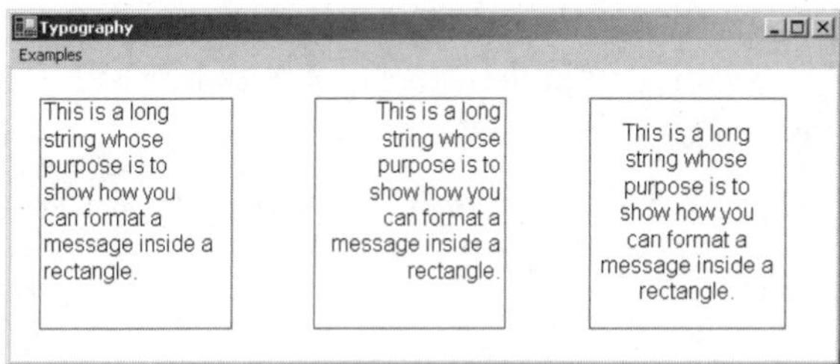

Figure 18-20. Text alignment inside a bounding rectangle.

When you're deciding how large the bounding rectangle should be, you can use the MeasureString method of the Graphics object, which at a minimum takes a string and a Font object:

```
' Determine the room necessary to print the text as one long line.
Dim size As SizeF = gr.MeasureString(msg, fnt)
Debug.WriteLine(size.ToString)
```

Most of the time, you want to wrap the text so that it doesn't extend beyond a given width, so you must pass an additional width argument:

```
' Determine how tall the bounding rectangle must be if the
' text can't extend wider than 200 pixels.
Dim size As SizeF = gr.MeasureString(msg, fnt, 200)
Debug.WriteLine(size.ToString)
```

Textual Variations

Other properties of the StringFormat object affect how the text is displayed. For example, the Trimming property tells whether text that is too long to be displayed entirely should be trimmed at the character boundary or at the word boundary, or whether an ellipsis should be inserted at the end of the visible portion of the string:

```
' Text is trimmed at the last whole word.
strFormat.Trimming = StringTrimming.Word
' Text is trimmed at the last visible character,
' and an ellipsis is inserted after it.
strFormat.Trimming = StringTrimming.EllipsisCharacter
' An ellipsis is used in the center of the string.
' (Useful to display long files' paths.)
strFormat.Trimming = StringTrimming.EllipsisPath
```

The FormatFlags property is a bit-coded field that gives you even more control over how text is printed:

```
' Ensure that only whole lines are displayed. (The last line isn't
' displayed if it isn't completely visible in the bounding rectangle.)
strFormat.FormatFlags = StringFormatFlags.LineLimit

' Display the text vertically.
strFormat.FormatFlags = StringFormatFlags.DirectionVertical
gr.DrawString(msg, fnt, Brushes.Black, 20, 20, strFormat)
```

(Note that you can rotate text to any angle by using the RotateTransform method of the Graphics object.)

One more thing you can do when displaying text is use tab stops so that you can align columns of data, as in Figure 18-21. You can make tab stops by preparing a string containing tab and carriage return characters, preparing a Single array that holds the position of each tab stop, and then passing the array to the StringFormat object's SetTabStops method:

```
' Prepare a message with tabs and carriage returns.
Dim msg As String = String.Format("{0}Column 1{0}Column 2{0}Column 3{1}" _
    & "Row 1{0}Cell (1,1){0}Cell (1,2){0}Cell (1,3){1}" _
    & "Row 2{0}Cell (2,1){0}Cell (2,2){0}Cell (3,3){1}", _
    ControlChars.Tab, ControlChars.CrLf)

Dim fnt As New Font("Arial", 12)
Dim strFormat As New StringFormat()
' Set the tab stops.
Dim tabStops() As Single = {80, 140, 200}
strFormat.SetTabStops(0, tabStops)
' Draw the text with specified tab stops.
gr.DrawString(msg, fnt, Brushes.Black, 20, 20, strFormat)
' Destroy the Font object.
fnt.Dispose()
```

Typography
Examples

	Column 1	Column 2	Column 3
Row 1	Cell (1,1)	Cell (1,2)	Cell (1,3)
Row 2	Cell (2,1)	Cell (2,2)	Cell (3,3)

Figure 18-21. Using tab stops.

Anti-Aliasing

Anti-aliasing is a technique that allows you to process graphic output so that lines don't appear jagged. You achieve this smoothing effect by using a color halfway between those of the line and the background. For example, if you draw a jagged black line over a white background, you can smooth it by using gray pixels for the points near the boundary.

The small ellipse on the right in Figure 18-22 is the anti-aliased version of the ellipse on the left. It looks better defined, even though you probably can't really say why. But if you enlarge the two ellipses (see bottom part of figure), you see that the anti-aliased version uses gray pixels to smooth its edges.

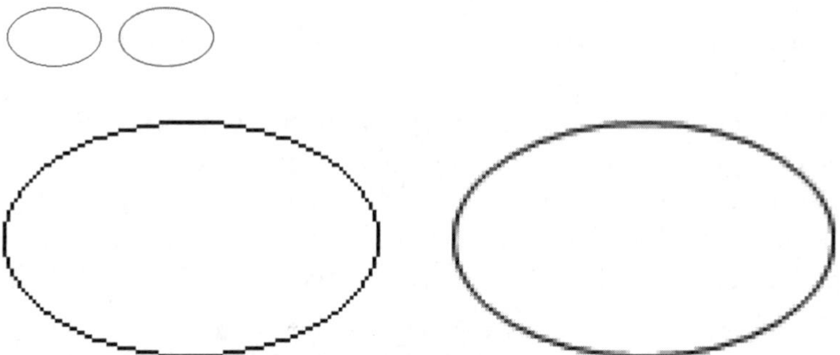

Figure 18-22. Using anti-aliasing on shapes.

GDI+ supports anti-aliasing of both text and shapes. You can choose between two types of smoothing modes: anti-aliasing and high quality. The former works well on any type of display, whereas the latter takes advantage of the subpixel resolution of LCD screens. A pixel on an LCD screen is subdivided into three stripes that can be turned on or off individually, so you can achieve even more refined effects. (This is the smoothing mode used by the Microsoft ClearType display technology.) High-quality mode has no effect on regular CRT displays. Because of the required extra processing time, anti-aliasing is slower than regular display, and high-quality rendering is even slower than standard anti-aliasing.

You use two different properties of the Graphics object to activate anti-aliasing, depending on whether you want to smooth lines or text. The SmoothingMode property affects how lines and curves are drawn. For example, this is the code that produces the two ellipses in Figure 18-22:

```
' Draw a first ellipse in regular mode.
gr.DrawEllipse(Pens.Black, 20, 20, 100, 60)
' Draw a second ellipse in anti-aliasing mode.
gr.SmoothingMode = Drawing.Drawing2D.SmoothingMode.AntiAlias
gr.DrawEllipse(Pens.Black, 140, 20, 100, 60)
```

You can further influence graphic anti-aliasing by using the PixelOffsetMode property. (Read the .NET Platform SDK documentation for more details.)

Text anti-aliasing is controlled by the TextRenderingHint property. Here's a code example, which produces the result visible in Figure 18-23:

```
Dim fnt As New Font("Arial", 14)
gr.DrawString("Regular Text", fnt, Brushes.Black, 20, 200)
' Standard anti-aliasing
gr.TextRenderingHint = Drawing.Text.TextRenderingHint.AntiAlias
gr.DrawString("Standard Anti-aliasing", fnt, Brushes.Black, 20, 260)
' ClearType anti-aliasing
gr.TextRenderingHint = Drawing.Text.TextRenderingHint.ClearTypeGridFit
gr.DrawString("ClearType Anti-aliasing", fnt, Brushes.Black, 20, 320)
' Destroy the Font object.
fnt.Dispose()
```

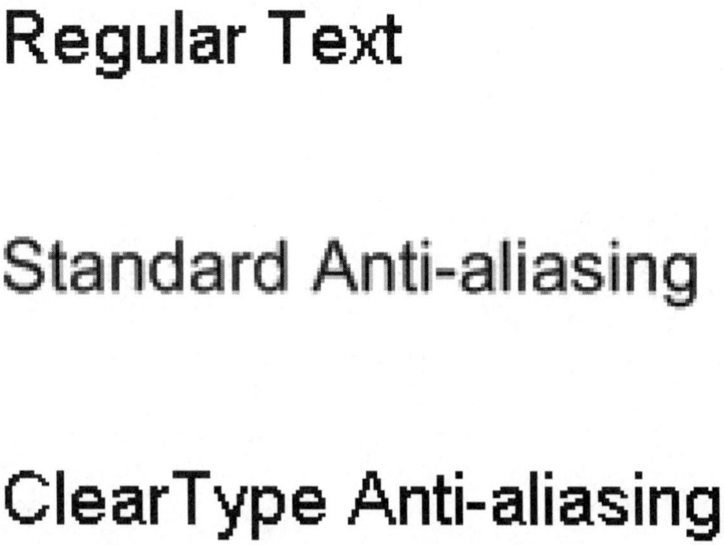

Regular Text

Standard Anti-aliasing

ClearType Anti-aliasing

Figure 18-23. The two flavors of anti-aliasing methods compared with regular text output.

Alas, I don't have enough pages to cover all the great features of GDI+, so I have to stop here. For example, I haven't explained transformation matrix objects, graphic containers, or advanced color manipulations. However, I believe that you now know enough to leverage the great potential of this portion of the .NET Framework. Now it's time to explore more of what you can do in Win32 applications.

19

Advanced Win32 Techniques

Creating a Windows application involves more than just making a nice user interface with Windows Forms controls. The .NET Framework offers many nonvisual objects that you can use to empower your Win32 applications. In this chapter, we'll have a look at some such objects, including these:

- The Registry and RegistryKey classes, to read and write registry keys and values
- The FileSystemWatcher component, to get a notification when a file or a directory is created, deleted, or modified
- The Process, ProcessModule, and ProcessThread components, to get information about running processes, their modules, and their threads
- The PerformanceCounter component, to read and write performance counters and list all the performance counters installed on a local or remote machine
- The EventLog component, to read existing entries in an event log on a local or remote machine
- The ServiceController component, to list, start, stop, pause, and resume any Windows service on a local or remote machine

The last portion of this chapter is devoted to the creation of Windows service applications using Visual Basic .NET.

The Registry and RegistryKey Classes

The Registry and RegistryKey classes belong to the Microsoft.Win32 namespace rather than to the System namespace because they're platform-specific classes that would be very difficult to port to non-Windows operating systems. As their name suggests, these classes provide an easy, object-oriented way to access the system registry. If you've ever played with the limited registry commands that Visual Basic 6 offers or the rather complex functions exposed by the Windows API, you'll surely appreciate the power and the simplicity of the Registry and RegistryKey classes. However, keep in mind that these classes are provided only for interoperability with existing applications or for the gradual porting of legacy code—for example, to read what a legacy application wrote in the registry or to write data that a legacy application expects to find in the registry. Developers of applications for the .NET platform should avoid using the registry as a repository for their own data.

> **Note** For the sake of brevity, all the code samples in this section assume that you have used the following Imports statement at the top of your source file:
>
> ```
> Imports Microsoft.Win32
> ```

Reading Registry Keys

The Registry class's only purpose is to expose six read-only shared properties, each returning a RegistryKey object that represents one of the main registry subtrees (also known as hives).

```
' Define the RegistryKey objects for the registry hives.
Dim regClasses As RegistryKey = Registry.ClassesRoot
Dim regCurrConfig As RegistryKey = Registry.CurrentConfig
Dim regCurrUser As RegistryKey = Registry.CurrentUser
Dim regDynData As RegistryKey = Registry.DynData
Dim regLocalMachine As RegistryKey = Registry.LocalMachine
Dim regPerfData As RegistryKey = Registry.PerformanceData
Dim regUsers As RegistryKey = Registry.Users
```

Each RegistryKey object has only three instance properties, whose names are entirely self-explanatory: Name, SubKeyCount, and ValueCount. If SubKeyCount is higher than 0, you can use the GetSubKeyNames method to return an array of strings that contains the names of all the subkeys, and then you can use the OpenSubKey method to retrieve the RegistryKey object corresponding to each subkey. If the key doesn't exist, this method returns Nothing without throwing an exception:

```
' Check whether Microsoft Word is installed on this computer
' by searching the HKEY_CLASSES_ROOT\Word.Application key.
Dim regWord As RegistryKey = regClasses.OpenSubKey("Word.Application")
If regWord Is Nothing Then
    Console.WriteLine("Microsoft Word isn't installed")
Else
    Console.WriteLine("Microsoft Word is installed")
End If
' Always close registry keys after using them.
regWord.Close
```

If the ValueCount property is greater than 0, you can use the GetValueNames method to retrieve an array of all the value names under the current key, and then you can use the GetValue method to retrieve the data associated with a given value. The following reusable routine peeks in the registry to retrieve the CLSID associated with the specified COM component:

```
' Return the CLSID of a COM component, or "" if not found.
Function GetCLSID(ByVal ProgId As String) As String
    ' Open the key associated with the ProgID.
    Dim regProgID As RegistryKey = Registry.ClassesRoot.OpenSubKey(ProgId)
    If Not (regProgID Is Nothing) Then
        ' If found, open the CLSID subkey.
        Dim regClsid As RegistryKey = regProgID.OpenSubKey("CLSID")
        If Not (regClsid Is Nothing) Then
            ' If found, get its default value. 2nd optional argument is the
            ' string to be returned if the specified value doesn't exist.
            ' (Returns an Object that we must convert to a string.)
            GetCLSID = CStr(regClsid.GetValue(""))
            ' Always close registry keys.
            regClsid.Close()
        End If
        ' Always close registry keys.
        regProgId.Close()
    End If
End Function

' A usage example: get the CLSID of the ADODB.Recordset object.
Console.WriteLine(GetCLSID("ADODB.Recordset"))
    ' => {00000514-0000-0010-8000-00AA006D2EA4}
```

Remember always to close any RegistryKey object that you opened using the OpenSubKey method or CreateSubKey (which I discuss shortly). You don't have to close the registry keys corresponding to the upper-level hives returned by shared methods of the Registry class.

The GetValue method returns an Object, which can contain a number, a string, an array of bytes, or Nothing if the value doesn't exist. If you want to tell a nonexistent value from a value whose associated data is a null string, you can pass a second argument, which is the data returned if the value hasn't been found:

```
' Return the data, or "<not found>" if the value isn't there.
Console.Write(regClsid.GetValue("", "<not found>")
```

The following snippet demonstrates how these classes let you implement routines that extract information from the registry with few lines of code:

```
' Print ProgID, CLSID, and path of all the COM components
' installed on this computer.
Sub DisplayCOMComponents()
    ' Open the HKEY_CLASSES_ROOT\CLSID key.
    Dim regClsid As RegistryKey = Registry.ClassesRoot.OpenSubKey("CLSID")

    ' Iterate over all the subkeys.
    Dim clsid As String
    For Each clsid In regClsid.GetSubKeyNames
        ' Open the subkey.
        Dim regClsidKey As RegistryKey = regClsid.OpenSubKey(clsid)

        ' Get the ProgID. (This is the default value for this key.)
        Dim ProgID As String = CStr(regClsidKey.GetValue(""))
        ' Get the InProcServer32 key, which holds the DLL path.
        Dim regPath As RegistryKey = regClsidKey.OpenSubKey("InprocServer32")
        If regPath Is Nothing Then
            ' If not found, it isn't an in-process DLL server;
            ' let's see if it's an out-of-process EXE server.
            regPath = regClsidKey.OpenSubKey("LocalServer32")
        End If
        If Not (regPath Is Nothing) Then
            ' If either key has been found, retrieve its default value.
            Dim filePath As String = CStr(regPath.GetValue(""))
            ' Display all the relevant info gathered so far.
            Console.WriteLine(ProgId & " " & clsid & " -> " & filePath)
            ' Always close registry keys.
            regPath.Close()
        End If
        ' Always close registry keys.
        regClsidKey.Close()
    Next
End Sub
```

Figure 19-1 shows the output produced by a similar routine in the demo application, which displays the result in a TextBox control instead of the console window.

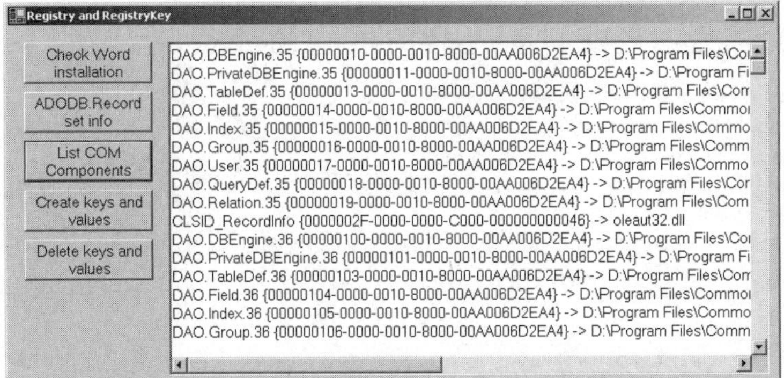

Figure 19-1. The demo application parses the registry and lists all installed COM components.

> **More Info** For background information about the system registry, its structure, and how information is stored in it, see the appendix of my *Programming Microsoft Visual Basic* book, provided on the companion CD.

The RegistryKey class also lets you modify the registry—for example, by creating or deleting subkeys and values. When you plan to write data under a key, you must open it for writing, which you do by passing True as the second argument to the OpenSubKey method:

```
' The following code snippets, taken together, add company/product
' keys under the HKEY_LOCALMACHINE\SOFTWARE key, as many Windows apps do.

' Open the HKEY_LOCALMACHINE\SOFTWARE key.
Dim regSoftware As RegistryKey = _
    Registry.LocalMachine.OpenSubKey("SOFTWARE", True)
```

The CreateSubKey method creates a registry key or opens an existing key; you don't need to specify that you're opening in writing mode:

```
' Add a key for the company name (or open it if it exists already).
Dim regCompany As RegistryKey = regSoftware.CreateSubKey("VB2TheMax")
' Add another key for the product name (or open it if it exists already).
Dim regProduct As RegistryKey = regCompany.CreateSubKey("VBMaximizer")
```

The SetValue method creates a new value and associates data with it; the second argument can be any data type that can be stored in the registry:

```
' Create three Values under the Product key.
regProduct.SetValue("Path", "C:\VBMaximizer\Bin")    ' A string value
regProduct.SetValue("MajorVersion", 2)               ' A numeric value
regProduct.SetValue("MinorVersion", 1)               ' A numeric value
```

You can delete values by using the DeleteValue method and delete keys by using the DeleteSubKey method:

```
' Delete the three values just added.
regProduct.DeleteValue("Path")
regProduct.DeleteValue("MajorVersion")
regProduct.DeleteValue("MinorVersion")
' Delete the Product key after closing it.
regProduct.Close()
regCompany.DeleteSubKey("VBMaximizer")
' Delete the Company key after closing it.
regCompany.Close()
regSoftware.DeleteSubKey("VB2TheMax")
```

The RegistryKey object also exposes the DeleteSubTreeKey, which deletes an entire registry subtree. So the previous code snippet could be replaced by the following one-liner:

```
regSoftware.DeleteSubKeyTree("VB2TheMax")
```

> **Warning** Writing to the registry is a dangerous activity, and you must know very well what you're doing. Otherwise, you might damage sensitive data and be forced to reinstall one or more applications or the complete operating system. At a minimum, you should back up your registry before proceeding.

The FileSystemWatcher Component

The System.IO.FileSystemWatcher component lets you monitor a directory or a directory tree and get a notification when something happens inside it—for example, when a file or a subdirectory is created, deleted, or renamed or when its attributes are changed. This component can be useful in many circumstances. For example, say that you're creating an application that automatically encrypts all the files stored in a given directory. Without this component, you should poll the directory at regular time intervals (typically using a Timer), but the FileSystemWatcher component makes this task easy. Unfortunately, this component works only on Microsoft Windows Me, Microsoft Windows NT, Microsoft Windows 2000, and Microsoft Windows XP. Another good example of how this component can be useful is when you cache a text or an XML file in memory to access its contents very quickly but need to reload it when another application modifies the data.

> **Note** All the code samples in this section assume that you've used the following Imports statement at the top of your source file:
>
> ```
> Imports System.IO
> ```

Initializing a FileSystemWatcher Component

You can create a FileSystemWatcher component in either of two ways: by means of code or by dragging it from the Components tab of the Toolbox to the form's component tray area. There's no noticeable difference in performance or flexibility, so any method is fine. The demo application included on the companion CD uses a component in the form's component tray area, which I have renamed *fsw* (see Figure 19-2), but creating it through code is equally simple:

```
' Use WithEvents to be able to trap events from this object.
Dim WithEvents fsw As New FileSystemWatcher()
```

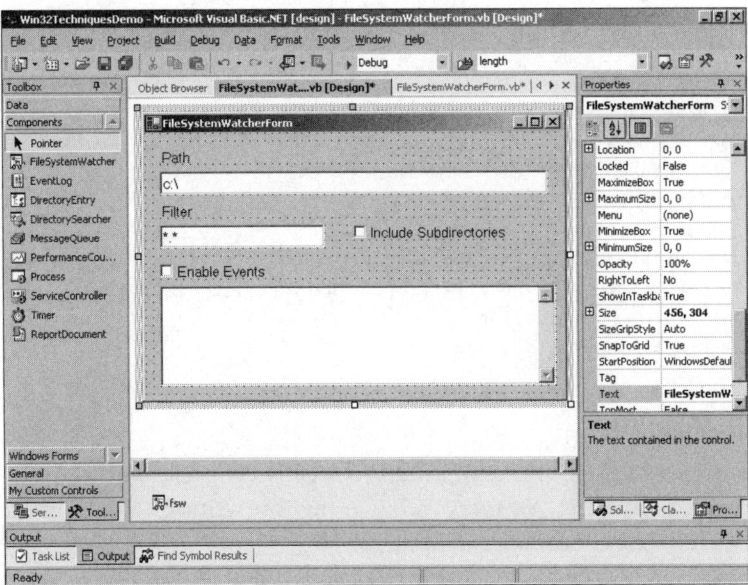

Figure 19-2. The demo application lets you experiment with the FileSystemWatcher component.

Before you use this component, you must initialize a few important properties:

- The Path property is the name of the directory that you want to watch; note that you're notified of changes occurring inside this directory but not of changes to this directory's attributes (such as its Hidden or ReadOnly attribute).
- The IncludeSubdirectories property should be set to False if you want to be notified of any change inside the specified directory only, or to True if you want to watch for changes in the entire directory tree whose root is the directory specified by the Path property.
- The Filter property lets you specify which files you're interested in; for example, use *.* to get notifications about all the files in the directory or *.txt to watch only files with the .txt extension. The default value for this property is a null string, which means all files (same as *.*).
- The NotifyFilter property is a bit-coded value that specifies which kind of modifications are announced by means of the component's Changed event. This property can be a combination of one or more NotifyFilters enumerated values: Attributes, CreationTime, DirectoryName, FileName, LastAccess, LastWrite, Security, and Size. The initial value of this property is LastWrite Or FileName Or DirectoryName, so by default you don't get notifications when an attribute is changed.

Here's an example of how you can set up a FileSystemWatcher component to watch for events in the C:\WinNT directory and its subdirectories:

```
Dim WithEvents fsw As New FileSystemWatcher()
fsw.Path = "c:\winnt"
fsw.IncludeSubdirectories = True
' Watch only DLL files.
fsw.Filter = "*.dll"
' Add attribute changes to the list of changes that can fire events.
fsw.NotifyFilter = fsw.NotifyFilter Or NotifyFilters.Attributes
' Enable event notification.
fsw.EnableRaisingEvents = True
```

Getting Notifications

Once you've set up the component correctly, you can get a notification when something happens. You can achieve this by writing event handlers or using the WaitForChanged method.

Events

The simplest way to get a notification from the FileSystemWatcher component is by writing handlers for the component's events. However, events don't fire until you set EnableRaisingEvents to True. The Created, Deleted, and Changed events receive a FileSystemEventArgs object, which exposes two important properties: Name (the name of the file that has been created, deleted, or changed) and FullPath (its complete path):

```
Private Sub fsw_Created(ByVal sender As Object, _
    ByVal e As FileSystemEventArgs) Handles fsw.Created
    LogMessage("File created: " & e.FullPath)
End Sub

Private Sub fsw_Deleted(ByVal sender As Object, _
    ByVal e As FileSystemEventArgs) Handles fsw.Deleted
    LogMessage("File deleted: " & e.FullPath)
End Sub

Private Sub fsw_Changed(ByVal sender As Object, _
    ByVal e As FileSystemEventArgs) Handles fsw.Changed
    LogMessage("File changed: " & e.FullPath)
End Sub

' Add a string to the txtLog TextBox control.
Sub LogMessage(ByVal msg As String)
    txtLog.AppendText(msg & ControlChars.CrLf)
End Sub
```

Note that the Changed event receives no information about the type of change that fired the event (such as a change in the file's LastWrite date or attributes). The FileSystemEventArgs object also exposes a ChangeType enumerated property, which tells whether the event is a create, delete, or change event. You can use this property to use a single handler to manage all three events, as in this code:

```
Private Sub fsw_All(ByVal sender As Object, _
    ByVal e As FileSystemEventArgs) _
    Handles fsw.Changed, fsw.Created, fsw.Deleted
    ' Transform changeType into a readable string.
    Dim changeType As String = _
        [Enum].GetName(GetType(WatcherChangeTypes), e.ChangeType)
    LogMessage("File event: " & e.FullPath & " (" & changeType & ")")
End Sub
```

Finally, the Renamed event receives a RenamedEventArgs object, which exposes two additional properties: OldName (the name of the file before being renamed) and OldFullPath (its complete path):

```
Private Sub fsw_Renamed(ByVal sender As Object, _
    ByVal e As RenamedEventArgs) Handles fsw.Renamed
    LogMessage("File renamed: " & e.OldFullPath & " => " & e.FullPath)
End Sub
```

You can also have multiple FileSystemWatcher components forward their events to the same event handler. In this case, you can use the first argument to detect which specific component raised the event:

```
' ...(Inside an event handler)...
    ' Get a reference to the component that raised this event.
    Dim fsw As FileSystemWatcher = DirectCast(sender, FileSystemWatcher)
```

The FileSystemWatcher component raises one event for each file and for each action on the file. For example, if you delete 10 files, you receive 10 distinct Deleted events. If you move 10 files from one directory to another, you receive 10 Deleted events from the source directories and 10 Created events from the destination directory.

The WaitForChanged Method

If your application doesn't perform any operation other than waiting for changes in the specified path, you can write simpler and more efficient code by using the WaitForChanged method. This method is synchronous, in the sense that it doesn't return until a file change is detected or the (optional) timeout expires. This method returns a WaitForChangedResult structure, whose fields let you determine whether the timeout elapsed, the type of the event that occurred, and the name of the involved file:

```
' Create a *new* FileSystemWatcher component with values from
' the txtPath and txtFilter controls.
Dim tmpFsw As New FileSystemWatcher(txtPath.Text, txtFilter.Text)
' Wait max 10 seconds for any file event.
Dim res As WaitForChangedResult
res = tmpFsw.WaitForChanged(WatcherChangeTypes.All, 10000)

' Check whether the operation timed out.
If res.TimedOut Then
    LogMessage("10 seconds have elapsed without an event")
Else
    Dim ct As String
    ct = [Enum].GetName(GetType(WatcherChangeTypes), res.ChangeType)
    LogMessage("Event: " & res.Name & " (" & changeType & ")")
End If
```

The WaitForChanged method traps changes only in the directory pointed to by the Path property and ignores the IncludeSubdirectories property. For this reason, the WaitForChangedResult structure includes a Name field but not a FullPath field. The first argument you pass to the WaitForChanged method lets you further restrict the kind of file operation you want to intercept:

```
' Pause the application until the c:\temp\temp.dat file is deleted.
Dim tmpFsw As New FileSystemWatcher("c:\temp", "temp.dat")
tmpFsw.WaitForChanged(WatcherChangeTypes.Deleted)
```

Buffer Overflows

You should be aware of potential problems when too many events fire in a short time. The FileSystemWatcher component uses an internal buffer to keep track of file system actions so that events can be raised for each one of them even if the application can't serve them fast enough. By default, this internal buffer is 8 KB long and can store about 160 events: each event takes 16 bytes plus 2 bytes for each character in the filename. (Filenames are stored as Unicode characters.) If you anticipate a lot of file activity, you should perform one or more of the following actions to prevent the buffer from overflowing:

- You increase the size of the buffer by setting the InternalBufferSize to a larger value. The size should be an integer multiple of the operating system's page size (4 KB under Windows 2000).
- You use the NotifyFilter property to limit the number of change operations that fire the Changed event.
- You set IncludeSubdirectories to False if you don't really need to monitor an entire directory tree. (Use multiple FileSystemWatcher components to monitor individual subdirectories if you aren't interested in monitoring all the subdirectories under a given path.)

You can't use the Filter property to prevent the internal buffer's overflow because this property filters out files only after they've been added to the buffer. When the internal buffer overflows, you get an Error event:

```
Private Sub fsw_Error(ByVal sender As Object, _
    ByVal e As ErrorEventArgs) Handles fsw.Error
    LogMessage("FileSystemWatcher error")
End Sub
```

Troubleshooting

By default, the Created, Deleted, Renamed, and Changed events run in a thread taken from the system thread pool. (See Chapter 13 for more information about the thread pool.) Because Windows Forms controls aren't thread safe, you should avoid accessing any control or the form itself from inside the FileSystem-Watcher component's event handlers. If you find this limitation unacceptable, you should assign a Windows Form control to the component's Synchronizing-Object property, as in this code:

```
' Use the Form object as the synchronizing object.
fsw.SynchronizingObject = Me
```

The preceding code ensures that all event handlers run in the same thread that serves the form itself. When you create a FileSystemWatcher component using the Visual Studio .NET designer, this property is automatically assigned the hosting form object.

Here are a few more tips about the FileSystemWatcher component and the problems you might find when using it:

- The FileSystemWatcher component starts raising events when the Path property is nonempty and the EnableRaisingEvents property is True. You can also prevent the component from raising unwanted events during the initialization phase by bracketing your setup statements between a call to the BeginInit method and a call to the EndInit method. (This is the approach used by the Visual Studio designer.)
- As I mentioned before, this component works only on Windows Me, Windows NT, Windows 2000, and Windows XP. It raises an error when it points to a path on machines running earlier versions of the operating system. Remote machines must have one of these operating systems to work properly, but you can't monitor a remote Windows NT system from another Windows NT machine. You can use UNC-based directory names only on Windows 2000 or Windows XP systems. The FileSystemWatcher component doesn't work on CD-ROM and DVD drives because their contents can't change.
- In some cases, you might get multiple Created events, depending on how a file is created and on the application that creates it. For example, when you create a new file with Notepad, you see the following sequence of events: Created, Deleted, Created, and Changed. (The first event pair fires because Notepad checks whether the file exists by attempting to create it.)
- A change in a file can generate an extra event in its parent directory as well because the directory maintains information about the files it contains (their size, last write date, and so on).

- If the directory pointed to by the Path property is renamed, the FileSystemWatcher component continues to work correctly. However, in this case the Path property returns the old directory name, so you might get an error if you use it. (This happens because the component references the directory by its handle, which doesn't change if the directory is renamed.)
- If you create a directory inside the path being watched and the IncludeSubdirectories property is True, the new subdirectory is watched as well.
- When a large file is created in the directory, you might not be able to read the entire file immediately because it's still owned by the process that's writing data to it. You should protect any access to the original file with a Try block and, if an exception is thrown, attempt the operation again some milliseconds later.
- When the user deletes a file in a directory, a new file is created in the Recycle Bin directory.

The Process Component

The System.Diagnostics.Process component lets you start and stop processes on the local computer and query a running process for information (such as the names of its modules and the number of its threads) on either the local or a remote computer. You can use the Process component on any Windows platform, but you must have sufficient rights to stop a process or query it for information.

> **Note** For the sake of brevity, all the code samples in this section assume that you have used the following Imports statement at the top of your source file:
>
> ```
> Imports System.Diagnostics
> ```

Running and Stopping a Process

You can create a Process component by dragging the corresponding item on the Components tab of the Toolbox or by instantiating it by means of code. In the following code samples, I follow the latter approach because it's the most frequently used in real-world applications:

```
Dim proc As New Process()
```

Starting a Process

Creating a new Process component doesn't create or start a new process on the local computer. You should think of this component as a means through which your application can start a new process or retrieve information from a running process.

Before you start a new process, you must set the StartInfo property. This property is itself an object (of the ProcessStartInfo class) and exposes members such as Filename (the name of the executable file), WorkingDirectory (the initial directory), and Arguments (a string passed to the executable). Once all the necessary information is in place, you can actually run the other application by using the Start method:

```
Dim proc As New Process()
' Prepare to run Notepad and load C:\Autoexec.bat in it.
proc.StartInfo.FileName = "Notepad.exe"
' (Change the following statement to match your system.)
proc.StartInfo.WorkingDirectory = "c:\winnt"
proc.StartInfo.Arguments = "c:\autoexec.bat"
' Run it.
proc.Start()
```

A great feature of the Process component is its ability to run the application associated with a data file so that you can simulate the action that occurs when the end user double-clicks on a file in Windows Explorer. In this case, you specify a document file in the FileName member of the StartInfo property and ensure that the UseShellExecute property is True:

```
' Use an OpenFileDialog control to ask the user for a data file,
' and load it in the application associated with that extension.
OpenFileDialog1.CheckFileExists = True
OpenFileDialog1.Filter = "All Files|*.*"
If OpenFileDialog1.ShowDialog = DialogResult.OK Then
    proc = New Process()
    proc.StartInfo.FileName = OpenFileDialog1.FileName
    proc.UseShellExecute = True
    ' In case no application is associated with this extension
    Try
        proc.Start()
    Catch ex As Exception
        MessageBox.Show(ex.Message, "Error")
    End Try
End If
```

You can also start a process by using the Process.Start shared method, which takes only two arguments (the name of the file and the command-line arguments) and returns the Process object associated with the application being launched:

```
Dim proc As Process = Process.Start("Notepad.exe", "c:\autoexec.bat")
```

If the process you've started has a graphical user interface, you can use the WaitForInputIdle method to pause the current application until the launched process enters the idle state and is therefore able to process other messages. For example, you should use the WaitForInputIdle method before sending keystrokes to the other application:

```
' Run Notepad on an empty file.
proc = Process.Start("Notepad.exe")
' Wait until its main window is ready to receive keystrokes.
proc.WaitForInputIdle()
SendKeys.Send("Hello from VB.NET")
```

Setting Other Startup Properties

You can decide whether you want Windows to display its standard error dialog box if the executable pointed to by FileName can't be found or can't run for some other reason. If you're loading a document and no application has been registered for that extension, the standard error dialog box is replaced by the Open With dialog box, which lets the user select the application that should open the data file. You enable this feature by setting the ErrorDialog property to True and ErrorDialogParentHandle to the handle of the parent form, and by ensuring that the UseShellExecute property is True:

```
proc.StartInfo.ErrorDialog = True
proc.StartInfo.ErrorDialogParentHandle = Me.Handle
proc.StartInfo.UseShellExecute = True
Try
    proc.Start()
Catch ex As Exception
    ' No need to display an error message in case of error.
End Try
```

The ProcessStartInfo class exposes many other interesting properties. For example, you can enumerate all the environment variables that the child process is going to inherit from the current process (and even create new ones) by means of the EnvironmentVariables property:

```
Dim de As DictionaryEntry
For Each de In proc.StartInfo.EnvironmentVariables
    Debug.WriteLine(de.Key.ToString & "=" & de.Value.ToString)
Next
```

The WindowStyle enumerated property determines the state of the child process's main window and can be Normal, Minimized, Maximized, or Hidden. (This property corresponds to the second argument you pass to the Shell function in Visual Basic 6.)

Stopping a Process

You can terminate the application associated with a Process component in two ways: by calling the CloseMainWindow method or by invoking the Kill method. The former method is the better way because it simulates the user's action of closing the application main window and so gives the application a chance to save data and release resources in an orderly fashion:

```
proc.CloseMainWindow()
```

The latter method abruptly terminates an application, so it might cause data loss; however, it's the only way to stop an application without a graphical user interface and an application that isn't responding. You can determine whether an application isn't responding by using the Responding property, so you might use Kill only when strictly necessary, as the following code snippet shows:

```
If proc.Responding Then
    ' The application is responding: CloseMainWindow should be OK.
    proc.CloseMainWindow()
Else
    proc.Kill()
End If
```

In a real application, however, you should always enclose a call to the CloseMainWindow or Kill method in a Try block because they aren't guaranteed to work and might throw an exception.

You can learn whether a process has exited by querying the HasExited read-only property. If a process has terminated, you can determine when it ended by querying the ExitTime property:

```
If proc.HasExited Then
    lblStatus.Text = "Process terminated at " & proc.ExitTime
End If
```

Redirecting the Input, Output, and Error Channels

As I mentioned earlier, the UseShellExecute property determines whether you should start the process by using the Windows shell. This property must be True (the default value) to start the application associated with a document or to display the standard error message if the application can't run. By setting this property to False, however, you can redirect the standard input, output, and error channel of the child process, which is useful when you launch command-line system commands or utilities. Depending on which channels you want to redirect, you must also set the RedirectStandardInput, RedirectStandardOutput, or RedirectStandardError member of the StartInfo property to True, and you must set the CreateNoWindow member to True to suppress the creation of a console window:

```
' Search all the lines in C:\AUTOEXEC.BAT that contain an "x" character.
proc.StartInfo.FileName = "find ""x"""
proc.StartInfo.Arguments = "c:\autoexec.bat"
' UseShellExecute must be False.
proc.StartInfo.UseShellExecute = False
' Redirect the standard output channel.
proc.StartInfo.RedirectStandardOutput = True
' Suppress the creation of the console window.
proc.StartInfo.CreateNoWindow = True
proc.Start()
```

When the process terminates, you can read the output it sent to its standard output channel by using the Process component's StandardOutput property, which returns a StreamReader object that you can use to read the output data:

```
' Get the StreamReader that points to output data.
Dim sr As System.IO.StreamReader = proc.StandardOutput
' Display the output data in a TextBox control.
txtOutput.Text = sr.ReadToEnd
' Close the stream.
sr.Close()
```

Similarly, the StandardError property returns a StreamReader object that lets you read any error message, whereas the StandardInput property returns a StreamWriter object that lets you write data to the standard input channel of the child process.

Querying a Process for Information

The Process class exposes a few shared methods that enable you to get a reference to a process that is already running on the local or a remote computer. Once you have a reference to the other process, you can stop it or query for its properties.

Getting a Reference to a Running Process

The simplest way to get a reference to a running process is by using the Process.GetCurrentProcess shared method, which returns the Process object that represents the current application:

```
Dim currProc As Process = Process.GetCurrentProcess
```

You can easily list all the processes running on the local computer by using the Process.GetProcesses shared method, which returns an array of Process objects. For example, the following code fills a ListBox control with all the Process objects and displays the name of each process:

```
' Start with an empty ListBox.
lstProcesses.Items.Clear()
' Display ProcessName property in the list area.
lstProcesses.DisplayMember = "ProcessName"

' Load info on all running processes in the ListBox control.
Dim p As Process
For Each p In Process.GetProcesses
    lstProcesses.Items.Add(p)
Next
```

The Process.GetProcessById shared method returns the Process object associated with the process with a given ID. The Process.GetProcessByName shared method returns an array of Process objects associated with the processes with the specified name. (The process name is the name of the executable file without its path and extension.) The ID and the name of a process correspond to the Id and ProcessName instance properties of the Process object. The ID uniquely identifies a process on a given system, but because you can have multiple processes with a given name, the Process.GetProcessByName method returns an array:

```
' Get an array with all running instances of Notepad.
Dim procs() As Process = Process.GetProcessesByName("notepad")

If procs.Length = 0 Then
    ' No matching process has been found.
    MessageBox.Show("Notepad isn't running")
Else
    ' Load all matching processes in a ListBox control.
    lstProcesses.Items.Clear()
    ' Display ProcessName property in the list area.
    lstProcesses.DisplayMember = "ProcessName"

    Dim p As Process
    For Each p In procs
        lstProcesses.Items.Add(p)
    Next
End If
```

The GetProcesses, GetProcessById, and GetProcessByName methods are overloaded and can take an extra String argument, which is taken as the name of the remote computer on which the processes that interest you are running.

Getting Information About Processes

The Process class exposes many instance properties that make it easy to collect information about a running process, once you've retrieved a reference to a running process using one of the methods outlined in the preceding section. Table 19-1 summarizes all the properties of the Process class. (Properties inherited from the Component class aren't shown.) The meaning of most properties should be clear, but the correct usage and interpretation of a few properties—for example, those related to the working set memory, virtual memory, and processor usage—might require detailed knowledge of Windows internals. All the properties are read-only unless otherwise stated.

Getting Information About Threads

The Threads property returns a collection of ProcessThread objects, each one representing a thread of the specified process. The ProcessThread class exposes several properties that are useful for diagnostic purposes.

The Id property returns an integer value that uniquely identifies the thread in the system; because the system reuses thread IDs, however, the uniqueness is guaranteed only during the thread's lifetime. The ThreadState read-only property tells in which state the thread currently is; it can be Initialized (not yet running), Ready, Running, StandBy, Wait, Terminated, Transition (switching between states), and Unknown.

If a thread is in a wait state, you can query its WaitReason property to determine what the thread is waiting for. The most common wait states are Suspended, Executive (waiting for the scheduler), UserRequest (waiting for a user request), PageIn (waiting for a virtual memory page to arrive in memory), and PageOut (waiting for a virtual memory page to be written to disk).

Most other properties of the ProcessThread class are similar to properties of the same name as the Process class. For example, you can check the processor time spent by a thread by means of the UserProcessorTime, PrivilegedProcessorTime, and TotalProcessorTime properties. You can check the thread priority by using the BasePriority and CurrentPriority properties and even change it by using the PriorityLevel and PriorityBoostEnabled properties. Finally, you can learn when a thread started its execution by means of its StartTime property, and you can get the address of its startup function by using the StartAddress property.

Table 19-1 Main Properties of the Process Class

Category	Property	Description
Identity	ProcessName	The friendly name of the process.
	Id	The unique process ID.
	MachineName	The name of the machine the process is running on.
	Handle	The process handle. (Available only if the current application started the process.)
	MainWindowTitle	The caption of the process's main window.
	MainWindowHandle	The handle of the process's main window.
Priority	PriorityClass	The overall priority category for the process, as an enumerated value. It can be Idle, BelowNormal, Normal, AboveNormal, High, RealTime (read/write).
	BasePriority	The base priority for the process—that is, the starting priority of its threads. It's an integer that corresponds to one of the values of the PriorityClass property: 4 (idle), 8 (normal), 13 (high), 24 (real-time).
	PriorityBoostEnabled	A Boolean value that determines whether the process's priority should be temporarily boosted when its main window has the focus (read/write).
Working set	WorkingSet	The amount of physical memory the process is currently using.
	MinWorkingSet	The minimum allowable working set size (read/write).
	MaxWorkingSet	The maximum allowable working set size (read/write).
	PeakWorkingSet	The maximum amount of physical memory that the process has requested all at once.
Memory	VirtualMemorySize	The amount of virtual memory that the process has requested.
	PrivateMemorySize	The amount of memory allocated by the process that can't be shared with other processes.
	PagedMemorySize	The amount of memory allocated by the process that can be written to the virtual memory paging file.

Table 19-1 Main Properties of the Process Class *(continued)*

Category	Property	Description
	PagedSystemMemorySize	The amount of memory that the operating system allocated for the process and that can be written to the virtual memory paging file.
	NonpagedSystemMemorySize	The amount of memory that the operating system allocated for the process and that can't be written to the virtual memory paging file.
	PeakVirtualMemorySize	The maximum amount of virtual memory that the process has requested.
	PeakPagedMemorySize	The maximum amount of memory allocated by the process that could be written to the virtual memory paging file.
Processor	UserProcessorTime	A TimeSpan value equal to the amount of CPU time spent by the process running the operating system's code.
	PrivilegedProcessorTime	A TimeSpan value equal to the amount of CPU time spent by the process running the application's code.
	TotalProcessorTime	A TimeSpan value equal to the total amount of CPU time spent by the process. (It's the sum of the UserProcessorTime and PrivilegedProcessTime values.)
	ProcessorAffinity	A bit-coded IntPtr value that represents the processors on which the process's threads can run (read/write). For example, the value 3 means that threads can run on processors 1 and 2.
Modules and threads	MainModule	The ProcessModule object that represents the module that was used to start the process.
	Modules	A collection of all the ProcessModule objects that represents all the modules loaded by the process.
	Threads	A collection of all the ProcessThread objects that represents all the threads running inside the process.
Start/Exit information	StartInfo	The ProcessStartInfo object that was used to start the process.

(continued)

Table 19-1 Main Properties of the Process Class *(continued)*

Category	Property	Description
	StartTime	The time when the process was started.
	ExitTime	The time when the process exited. It throws an exception if the process is still running.
	HasExited	Returns True if the process has exited.
	ExitCode	The exit code of a terminated process; it throws an exception if the process is still running.
	SynchronizingObject	The object used to marshal the event handler calls that are issued when the process exits.
Redirection	StandardInput	Returns a StreamWriter object that can be used to write to the process's standard input channel.
	StandardOutput	Returns a StreamRead object that can be used to read from the process's standard output channel.
	StandardError	Returns a StreamRead object that can be used to read from the process's standard error channel.
Miscellaneous	HandleCount	The number of handles the process has opened. Throws an exception under Windows 95/98 if the process was started with UseShellExecuted equal to True.
	EnableRaisingEvents	True if the Process object should raise an Exited event when the associated process exits (read/write).
	Responding	Returns True if the process is responding.

Getting Information About Modules

The Modules property returns a collection of all the modules loaded in the address spaces of a process. This list includes the main module (typically the .exe file that started the process, represented by the value returned by the MainModule property) and all the DLLs that the process has loaded. Each element in this collection is a ProcessModule object, which exposes properties such as ModuleName (the name of the module), BaseAddress (an IntPtr value that tells where in memory the module is loaded), ModuleMemorySize (the amount of bytes of memory allocated for the module), and EntryPointAddress (an IntPtr value that specifies the address of the function that runs when the system loads the module).

The FileVersionInfo property returns a FileVersionInfo object that exposes detailed information about the module's file:

- The FileVersionNumber property returns the complete version number as a string. You can also check individual portions of the version number by using the FileMajorPart, FileMinorPart, FileBuildPart, and FilePrivatePart properties. The Language property returns the default language string for the version information block.
- The ProductName property returns the name of the product a file is distributed with. You can learn more about this product by querying the ProductVersion, ProductMajorPart, ProductMinorPart, ProductBuildPart, and ProductPrivatePart properties.
- The CompanyName property returns the name of the company that produced this file. You can also query the LegalCopyright and LegalTrademarks properties for additional information about who legally owns this file.
- The IsDebug property returns True if an executable file has been compiled with debug information. The IsPatched property returns True if the file has been modified and isn't identical to the original shipping file.
- You can get additional information about the file by means of the OriginalFilename, Comments, and FileDescription properties.

The FileVersionInfo class has no instance methods (other than those inherited by System.Object) and has one shared method, GetVersionInfo, that lets you retrieve version information on any file, not just process module files. This method replaces the long sequence of API calls you had to perform under Visual Basic 6 to get version information.

```
Dim fvi As FileVersionInfo
fvi = FileVersionInfo.GetVersionInfo("c:\winnt\myapp.exe")
Console.WriteLine("Version {0}.{1}", fvi.FileMajorPart, fvi.FileMinorPart)
```

Putting Information Together

At this point, you know enough to create an advanced reporting utility that scans the local or a remote system and displays detailed information about running processes, their threads, and their modules. The core of this program is a function that returns information about a given Process object:

```
' Return a string describing a process.
Function GetProcessInfo(ByVal proc As Process) As String
    Dim res As String
    Dim crlf As String = ControlChars.CrLf
    Dim mo As ProcessModule
    Dim th As ProcessThread

    ' Ignore properties that raise an error.
    On Error Resume Next

    ' Ensure that data is up-to-date.
    proc.Refresh()

    res &= "=== PROCESS " & proc.ProcessName & crlf
    res &= "ID = " & proc.Id & crlf
    res &= "BasePriority = " & proc.BasePriority.ToString & crlf
    ' Get main window information.
    res &= "MainWindowTitle = " & proc.MainWindowTitle & crlf
    res &= "MainWindowHandle = " & Hex(proc.MainWindowHandle.ToInt32) & crlf
    res &= crlf

    ' Get CPU time information.
    res &= "StartTime = " & proc.StartTime.ToString & crlf
    res &= "UserProcessorTime = " & proc.UserProcessorTime.ToString & crlf
    res &= "PrivilegedProcessorTime = " & _
        proc.PrivilegedProcessorTime.ToString & crlf
    res &= "TotalProcessorTime = " & proc.TotalProcessorTime.ToString & crlf
    res &= crlf

    ' Get Working set information.
    res &= "WorkingSet = " & proc.WorkingSet.ToString & crlf
    res &= "MinWorkingSet = " & proc.MinWorkingSet.ToString & crlf
    res &= "MaxWorkingSet = " & proc.MaxWorkingSet.ToString & crlf
    res &= "PeakWorkingSet = " & proc.PeakWorkingSet & crlf
    res &= crlf

    ' Get memory information.
    res &= "VirtualMemorySize = " & proc.VirtualMemorySize & crlf
    res &= "NonpagedSystemMemorySize = " & _
        proc.NonpagedSystemMemorySize & crlf
    res &= "PagedMemorySize = " & proc.PagedMemorySize & crlf
    res &= "PagedSystemMemorySize = " & proc.PagedSystemMemorySize & crlf
```

```
    res &= "PeakPagedMemorySize = " & proc.PeakPagedMemorySize & crlf
    res &= "PeakVirtualMemorySize = " & proc.PeakVirtualMemorySize & crlf
    res &= "PrivateMemorySize = " & proc.PrivateMemorySize & crlf
    res &= crlf

    ' Get information on all modules.
    res &= "MODULES : " & crlf
    res &= "MainModule = " & proc.MainModule.ModuleName & crlf
    For Each mo In proc.Modules
        res &= "   Module Name = " & mo.ModuleName & crlf
        res &= "      FileName = " & mo.FileName & crlf
        res &= "      BaseAddress = " & Hex(mo.BaseAddress.ToInt32) & crlf
        res &= "      Version = " & mo.FileVersionInfo.FileVersion & crlf
        res &= "      Memory size = " & mo.ModuleMemorySize & crlf
    Next
    res &= crlf

    ' Get information on all threads.
    res &= "THREADS : " & crlf
    For Each th In proc.Threads
        res &= "   Thread ID = " & th.Id.ToString & crlf
        res &= "      StartTime = " & th.StartTime.ToString & crlf
        res &= "      BasePriority = " & th.BasePriority & crlf
        res &= "      PriorityLevel = " & th.PriorityLevel & crlf
        res &= "      ThreadState = " & th.ThreadState.ToString & crlf
        res &= "      UserProcessorTime = " & _
            th.UserProcessorTime.ToString & crlf
        res &= "      TotalProcessorTime = " & _
            th.TotalProcessorTime.ToString & crlf
    Next
    Return res & crlf
End Function
```

The preceding routine uses an On Error Resume Next statement to work around exceptions that some properties might raise in certain circumstances. For example, the BasePriority, PriorityClass, HandleCount, and Responding properties aren't available under Windows 95 and Windows 98 if the process wasn't started from the Windows shell.

In the "Getting a Reference to a Running Process" section earlier in this chapter, you saw how you can load the names of all the running processes (or just the processes with a given name) in a ListBox control. The following code snippet traps the SelectedIndexChanged event and displays information about the highlighted process in a TextBox control. (See Figure 19-3.)

```
' Display information about the selected process.
Private Sub lstProcesses_SelectedIndexChanged(ByVal sender As Object, _
    ByVal e As EventArgs) Handles lstProcesses.SelectedIndexChanged
    ' Get the selected process.
    Dim proc As Process = CType(lstProcesses.SelectedItem, Process)
    ' Display information about this process.
    txtOutput.Text = GetProcessInfo(proc)
End Sub
```

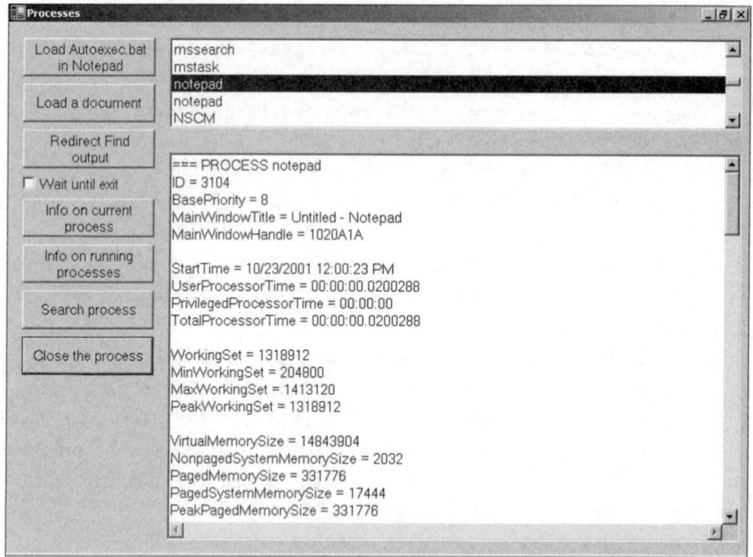

Figure 19-3. Displaying detailed information about all running processes, their threads, and their modules.

When querying a process for information, you should bear in mind that dynamic data—such as WorkingSet, VirtualMemorySize, and the list of threads and processes—is loaded the first time you read any property and is then cached in the Process object. The information that you read might therefore be stale. For this reason, the GetProcessInfo routine issues a Refresh method before reading process data.

Waiting for a Process to End

One of the most frequent questions among Visual Basic 6 developers is, "How can I run another process and wait until it ends?" The answer to this question involves several calls to Windows API functions and solid knowledge of how processes and handles work internally. You can perform the same task under any .NET language with just one call to the WaitForExit method of the Process class, or you can wait until the associated Process object raises an Exited event.

Using the WaitForExit Method

Using the WaitForExit method is a breeze, as this code snippet demonstrates:

```
' Run Notepad and load a file in it.
Dim proc As Process = Process.Start("notepad.exe", "c:\autoexec.bat")
' Wait until Notepad exits.
proc.WaitForExit()
' Get exit code.
MessageBox.Show("Notepad exited. Exit code is " & proc.ExitCode.ToString)
```

You can also pass an optional timeout in milliseconds. In this case, the method returns True if the process exited and False if it's still running. This overloaded variation is useful when you don't want to block the calling thread until the other process terminates:

```
Do Until proc.WaitForExit(1000)
    ' Do something every 1 second while waiting.
    ⋮
Loop
```

When a process exits, you can query its ExitCode and ExitTime properties. Because the process isn't running any longer, all properties—except these two properties and the HasExited and Handle properties—are invalid and shouldn't be queried. Better yet, after you've collected the information you need, you should call the Close method to release the resources associated with the Process object.

Using the Exited Event

Instead of polling for process termination, you can trap the Exited event. However, you must explicitly enable this event by setting the EnableRaisingEvent property to True:

```
Dim WithEvents proc As Process

Sub StartNotepad()
    proc = Process.Start("notepad.exe", "c:\autoexec.bat")
    proc.EnableRaisingEvents = True
End Sub

Private Sub proc_Exited(ByVal sender As Object, ByVal e As EventArgs) _
```

(continued)

```
        Handles proc.Exited
    MessageBox.Show("Notepad has exited. Exit code = " _
        & proc.ExitCode.ToString)
End Sub
```

You can trap events from both the processes that you started and from Process objects that represent running processes. In the latter case, you probably want to use dynamic event handlers because you don't know in advance how many processes you're going to monitor:

```
Sub ListProcesses()
    ' Clear list box elements.
    lstProcesses.Items.Clear()
    ' Display ProcessName property in the list area.
    lstProcesses.DisplayMember = "ProcessName"

    ' This is necessary because some processes might prevent your
    ' setting the EnableRaisingEvents property to True.
    On Error Resume Next

    ' Load info on all running process in the ListBox control.
    Dim p As Process
    For Each p In Process.GetProcesses
        lstProcesses.Items.Add(p)
        ' Bind each element to the event handler.
        AddHandler p.Exited, AddressOf Process_Exited
        p.EnableRaisingEvents = True
    Next
End Sub

Private Sub Process_Exited(ByVal sender As Object, ByVal e As EventArgs)
    ' Get a reference to the process.
    Dim proc As Process = CType(sender, Process)
    MessageBox.Show(String.Format( _
        "Process {0} has exited - Exit code is {1}", proc.Id, proc.ExitCode)
End Sub
```

When you attach multiple Process objects to the same event handler, you don't have an immediate way to determine which process has exited because when the Exited event fires, only a few properties can be queried—namely, Id, ExitCode, and ExitTime. To get more informative data, such as the name of the process that terminated, you should maintain all the (id, name) pairs of values in the Hashtable object so that you can easily retrieve the name of a process from its Id property.

The PerformanceCounter Component

Performance counters are values that the operating system or individual applications set whenever something relevant occurs. (Performance counters are supported under the Windows NT, Windows 2000, and Windows XP platforms.) Examples of common performance counters are the number of processes running in the system, the number of file write operations per second, and the number of lock requests per second in SQL Server. You can even read performance counters on a remote machine if you're granted sufficient permissions to do so.

> **Note** All the code samples in this section assume that you have used the following Imports statement at the top of your source file:
>
> ```
> Imports System.Diagnostics
> ```

Introduction to Performance Counters

Classes in the .NET Framework let you read the value of existing performance counters and create your own counters as well. If your application creates and updates one or more performance counters, you can then use standard tools—such as the Performance utility (see Figure 19-4)—to monitor the performance of your code. Or you can create another .NET application to check periodically the performance counters of your main application, create logs, and maybe automatically fine-tune one or more critical settings while the application is running on the end user's machine.

Categories, Counters, and Instances

A performance counter is completely identified by its category, name, and instance. A performance counter category is useful for gathering related counters. For example, the Memory category includes all the counters related to memory management, such as Page Reads/sec, Committed Bytes, and Page Faults/sec. Windows comes with several built-in categories, such as Cache, Memory, Physical Disk, Processor, System, and Thread. Many applications, especially applications that run as services, add one or more categories—for example, the Active Server Pages category, the MSMQ Queue category, and the SQL Server: SQL Statistics category. (SQL Server and a few other applications add many categories.)

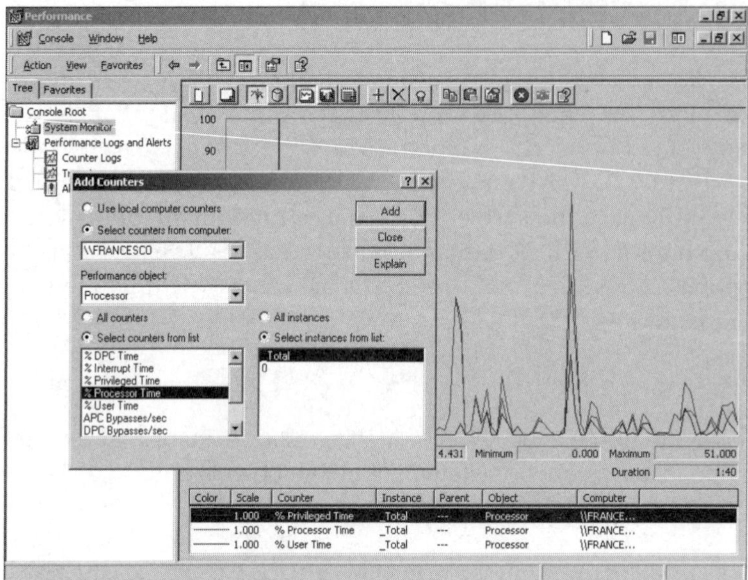

Figure 19-4. The Performance utility.

A category might expose multiple instances for each performance counter. For example, the counters in the Processor category have multiple instances, each one associated with an individual CPU. These instances enable you to check values and statistics for each distinct processor, such as % Processor Time, % User Time, and Interrupts/sec. (The Processor category also exposes a _Total_ instance, which lets you read values averaged on all the installed CPUs.) Similarly, the counters in the Process category have multiple instances, one for each running process, plus a _Total_ instance that averages all processes.

Other categories don't expose instances because it doesn't make any sense to do so: this is the case with categories such as Cache, Indexing Service, Memory, Server, and most SQL Server categories.

.NET Performance Counters

The .NET Framework creates and manages several categories and counters, the most interesting of which are summarized in Table 19-2. (This table doesn't include ASP.NET counters, which are described in the "ASP.NET Performance Counters" section of Chapter 24.) For a detailed description of these counters and for the complete list of all the available .NET counters, see the .NET Platform SDK documentation.

Table 19-2 Partial List of .NET CLR Performance Counters

Category	Counter	Description
.NET CLR Exceptions	# of Exceps Thrown	Total number of exceptions being thrown. Exceptions should occur only in rare situations and not in the normal control flow of the program.
	# of Exceps Thrown/sec	Rate at which exceptions are being thrown.
.NET CLR Interop	# of CCWs	Current number of existing COM-Callable Wrappers (CCWs). A CCW wraps a CLR class and allows it to be called from COM.
	# of marshalling	Number of times marshaling is done for arguments and return values. Custom marshaling is not counted.
.NET CLR Jit	# of Methods Jitted	Number of methods JIT-compiled.
	% Time in Jit	Percent of total time spent in the JIT compiler since the last sample.
	Total # of IL Bytes Jitted	Total number of IL bytes JIT-compiled since the beginning of the application.
.NET CLR Loading	% Time Loading	Percentage of execution time spent loading assemblies, application domains, classes, etc.
	Current appdomains	Current appdomains loaded in this application.
	Current assemblies	Current assemblies loaded in this application.
	Current Classes Loaded	Current classes loaded in all appdomains.
	Total # of Load Failures	Total number of classes that failed to load since the beginning of the application's execution.
.NET CLR LocksAndThreads	# of current logical Threads	Total number of existing logical threads created by the runtime. Some of these might not have a physical thread associated.
	# of current physical Threads	Total number of native OS threads created by the runtime.
	Contention Rate/sec	Rate at which threads in the runtime attempt to acquire a lock unsuccessfully.
	Current Queue Length	Average number of threads currently waiting to acquire a lock.

(continued)

Table 19-2 Partial List of .NET CLR Performance Counters *(continued)*

Category	Counter	Description
	Queue Length Peak	Average peak number of threads that waited to acquire a lock.
.NET CLR Memory	# Bytes in all Heaps	Total bytes in heaps for generation 0, 1, and 2 and from the large object heap. This indicates how much memory the garbage collector is using to store allocated objects.
	# Gen 0 Collections	Number of collections of generation 0 (youngest) objects.
	# Gen 1 Collections	Number of collections of generation 1 objects.
	# Gen 2 Collections	Number of collections of generation 2 (oldest) objects.
	% Time in GC	Percentage of elapsed time that was spent in doing a Garbage Collection since the last Garbage Collection cycle.
	Get 0 heap size	Size of generation 0 (youngest) heap in bytes.
	Get 1 heap size	Size of generation 1 heap in bytes.
	Get 2 heap size	Size of generation 2 (oldest) heap in bytes.
	Large Object Heap size	Size of the Large Object Heap in bytes.
.NET CLR Remoting	Channels	Current number of remoting channels.
	Contexts	Current number of remoting contexts.
	Remote Calls/sec	Rate of remote calls being made. Remote calls are calls between processes, between appdomains, or between machines.
	Total Remote Calls	Total number of remote calls since the start of the application.
.NET CLR Security	Total Runtime Checks	Number of runtime security checks performed.

Reading Performance Counter Values

The System.Diagnostics namespace includes several classes that let you read the value of any performance counter defined on the local or remote system. The namespace also contains classes to list all the categories, counters, and instances defined on a given machine.

Reading Raw Values

If you know exactly which performance counter you're interested in, reading its value is just a matter of instantiating a PerformanceCounter object that points to the specific category and counter (and instance name if that category exposes multiple instances) and then reading the object's RawValue property. For example, the following code reads a few counters from the System and Server categories:

```
' Create a few performance counters.
Dim pcProcesses As New PerformanceCounter("System", "Processes")
Dim pcThreads As New PerformanceCounter("System", "Threads")
Dim pcFilesOpen As New PerformanceCounter("Server", "Files Opened Total")
' Display their values.
Console.WriteLine("Processes = {0}", pcProcesses.RawValue)
Console.WriteLine("Threads = {0}", pcThreads.RawValue)
Console.WriteLine("Files Open Total = {0}", pcFilesOpen.RawValue)
```

If the category exposes multiple categories, you must pass a third argument to the PerformanceCounter object's constructor:

```
' Display handle count of Devenv process (that is, Visual Studio).
Dim pcHandles As New PerformanceCounter("Process", "Handle Count", "devenv")
Console.WriteLine("Devenv Handle Count = {0}", pcHandles.RawValue)
```

You can also pass a fourth argument to specify the name of the machine from which the counter must be retrieved. (Use "." for the local machine.) You don't have to create a different object for each distinct instance exposed by its category because you can simply assign a new value to the InstanceName property and read the new value, as in the following code:

```
' ...(continuing the preceding code sample)...
pcHandles.InstanceName = "WINWORD"
Console.WriteLine("WinWord Handle Count = {0}", pcHandles.RawValue)
```

Similarly, you can have the PerformanceCounter object point to a different category or counter by assigning a new value to the object's CategoryName or CounterName.

> **Note** You can also create a PerformanceCounter object at design time, either by dragging it from the Server Explorer window or by dragging a PerformanceCounter item from the Components tab in the Toolbox. In both cases, you end up with an object in the component tray area and you can read or modify its CategoryName, CounterName, InstanceName, and MachineName properties in the Properties window.

Reading Calculated Values

Although the RawValue property is appropriate when the value of the performance counter is a simple integer value—such as the number of processes, threads, and open files—for many cases, the value this property returns should be processed in some way—as when you're evaluating quantities such as percentages or rates of operations per second. In these instances, you need to use either the NextValue or the NextSample property.

The NextValue property returns the current value of a calculated value. The first time you retrieve this property, you might get the value 0; but after the first time, you start receiving meaningful values:

```
Dim pcCpu As New PerformanceCounter("Process", "% Processor Time", "myapp")
Console.WriteLine("Devenv % Processor Time = {0}", pcCpu.NextValue)
```

The problem with the NextValue property is that you might receive unusually high or low values, depending on when you invoke it. In these cases, you should use the NextSample property instead, which returns a CounterSample object. This object exposes several properties, including RawValue (the value just read) and TimeStamp (when the value was sampled). You can use these objects in your application by storing a first sample object and then comparing it with another sample taken later. The actual (averaged) value of the performance counter is returned by the Calculate method of the CounterSample class:

```
Dim pcSwitches As New _
    PerformanceCounter("Thread", "Context Switches/sec", "_Total")
' Read the first sample.
Dim cs1 As CounterSample = pcSwitches.NextSample
' Wait for some time.
System.Threading.Thread.Sleep(1000)
' Read the second sample.
Dim cs2 As CounterSample = pcSwitches.NextSample
' Evaluate the result.
Dim result As Single = CounterSample.Calculate(cs1, cs2)
Console.WriteLine("Thread switches/sec = {0}", result)
```

Because you decide when to read the samples, the value that you actually calculate is averaged over the period of time that you decide. For example, you might want to display both the average in the most recent second and the average since the program started:

```
' ...(continuing preceding code snippet)...
Dim i As Integer
For i = 1 To 10
    System.Threading.Thread.Sleep(1000)
    ' Get a new sample after one second.
    Dim cs3 As CounterSample = pcSwitches.NextSample
    ' Evaluate "instantaneous" (moving) average.
    result = CounterSample.Calculate(cs2, cs3)
    Console.WriteLine("Thread switches/sec = {0}", result)
```

```
    ' Evaluate average value since the first sample.
    result = CounterSample.Calculate(cs1, cs3)
    Console.WriteLine("Average Thread switches/sec = {0}", result)
    ' Use most recent sample as the basis for next moving average.
    cs2 = cs3
Next
```

Enumerating Existing Counters

The techniques that I've shown you so far assume that you know the category name, counter name, and instance name of the performance counter you want to monitor. When this information isn't available or when you want to let the end user select one or more performance counters among the available ones, you must enumerate all the existing categories and the counters and instances inside each category. Getting the list of all the performance counter categories on a computer requires a call to the PerformanceCounterCategory.GetCategories shared method. The following code is taken from the demo application provided on the CD (see Figure 19-5) and loads the names of all categories in a ComboBox control:

```
Private Sub btnGetCategories_Click(ByVal sender As Object, _
    ByVal e As EventArgs) Handles btnGetCategories.Click
    cboCategories.Items.Clear()
    ' Store categories in the ComboBox control, but display their names.
    cboCategories.DisplayMember = "CategoryName"
    ' Load the combo box with all category names.
    Dim pcc As PerformanceCounterCategory
    For Each pcc In PerformanceCounterCategory.GetCategories
        cboCategories.Items.Add(pcc)
    Next
End Sub
```

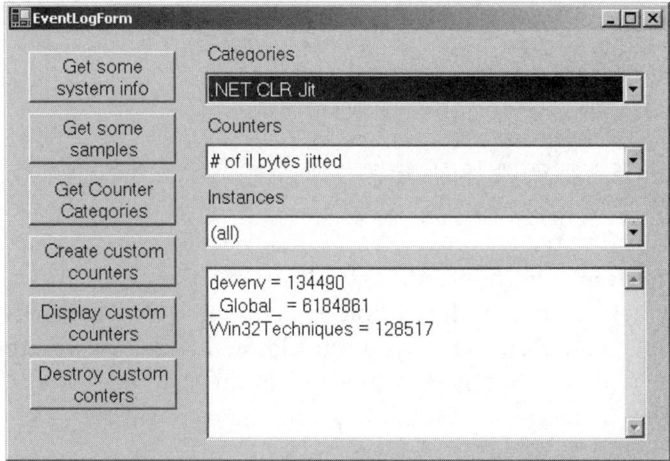

Figure 19-5. The demo application lists all the performance counter categories, counters, and instances.

Retrieving the list of counters and instances in each category requires a call to the ReadCategory and GetInstanceNames methods, respectively. The following code runs when the user selects a category in the cboCategories control (filled by the preceding snippet) and loads the names of all the counters and instances in the selected category in two ComboBox controls:

```
' Populate the other two ComboBox controls when a category is selected.
Private Sub cboCategories_SelectedIndexChanged(ByVal sender As Object, _
    ByVal e As EventArgs) Handles cboCategories.SelectedIndexChanged

    Dim pcCat As PerformanceCounterCategory
    Dim pCnt As PerformanceCounter
    Dim instName As String

    ' Get a reference to the selected category.
    pcCat = CType(cboCategories.SelectedItem, PerformanceCounterCategory)

    ' Fill cboCounters with the list of counters.
    cboCounters.Items.Clear()
    ' Get a collection of counters for this category.
    Dim idcc As InstanceDataCollectionCollection = pcCat.ReadCategory
    ' Each element of this collection is associated with a counter.
    Dim cntName As String
    For Each cntName In idcc.Keys
        cboCounters.Items.Add(cntName)
    Next

    ' Fill cboInstances with the list of instances.
    cboInstances.Items.Clear()
    Try
        ' Not all categories have multiple instances.
        For Each instName In pcCat.GetInstanceNames
            cboInstances.Items.Add(instName)
        Next
    Catch ex As Exception
        ' There's nothing to do in this case.
    End Try
End Sub
```

The PerfomanceCounterCategory class also exposes the GetCounters method, which returns all the PerformanceCounter objects associated with a given instance name. However, you must know in advance whether the category has one or more instances, which makes this method less usable than the ReadCategory method, as seen in the preceding code snippet.

Working with Custom Performance Counters

Your .NET applications can create new performance counter objects and write data to them so that you or the end user can check these values by using the standard Performance utility or a custom application that you've written. For example, you might write a service that continuously monitors these counters and do something when they go below or above a given threshold. (For example, it might adjust your application's settings or send an e-mail to the tech support folks.)

Creating Custom Performance Counters

You can't create new performance counters in an existing category, even if you've created the category yourself: all the counters in a category must be created when the category itself is created. To create a category and its counters, you begin by creating a CounterCreationDataCollection object. This collection will hold one or more CounterCreationData objects, where each object describes an individual counter associated with the category. When you've filled this collection with data related to all the counters that you want, you can pass it to the Create shared method of the PerformanceCounterCategory class. The following sample code shows how you can create a new category named MyApp, which contains two counters:

```
Sub CreateCounters()
    Dim counters As New CounterCreationDataCollection()
    Dim ccd As CounterCreationData

    ' Exit if the category exists already.
    If PerformanceCounterCategory.Exists("MyApp") Then Exit Sub

    ' Define the first counter, and then add it to the collection.
    ccd = New CounterCreationData("Flush operations", _
        "Total number of flush operations", _
        PerformanceCounterType.NumberOfItems32)
    counters.Add(ccd)

    ' Define the second counter, and then add it to the collection.
    ccd = New CounterCreationData("Flush operations / sec", _
        "Number of flush operations per second", _
        PerformanceCounterType.RateOfCountsPerSecond32)
    counters.Add(ccd)

    ' Create the category and the counters in one operation.
    PerformanceCounterCategory.Create("MyApp", _
        "Counters for MyApp program", counters)
End Sub
```

The second argument of the CounterCreationData object's constructor is the help string associated with the new counter, whereas the second argument of the PerformanceCounterCategory.Create method is the help string of the new category. These help strings appear when you browse available counters with the Performance utility.

The last argument you pass to the CounterCreationData object's constructor is the type of the new counter, expressed as an enumerated PerformanceCounterType value. The most frequent types are NumberOfItems32 (a 32-bit count value), NumberOfItems64 (a 64-bit count value), RateOfCountsPerSecond32 (the amount per second stored as a 32-bit number), RateOfCountsPerSecond64 (the amount per second stored as a 64-bit number), and AverageTimer32 (the average time to perform an operation). For the complete list of types, see the .NET Platform SDK documentation.

> **Note** New counter categories that you create through code don't appear immediately in the Performance utility unless you close and restart the utility. But they do appear in the list of categories that you retrieve via the PerformanceCounterCategory.GetCategories shared method.

Writing Values

Writing values to a custom performance counter you've created is easy, thanks to a few methods of the PerformanceCounter class. The Increment and Decrement methods increase and decrease the current value by 1; the IncrementBy method increases the counter by the specified value (or decreases it if the argument is negative); the RawValue property assigns a new value to the counter. Before you can apply any of these methods, though, you must create a writable instance of the PerformanceCounter object:

```
' Create a writable instance of the two counters created previously.
' (The last argument is the ReadOnly mode. If omitted, it's True.)
Dim pc1 As New PerformanceCounter("MyApp", "Flush operations", False)
Dim pc2 As New PerformanceCounter("MyApp", "Flush operations / sec", False)
' Assign a starting value to both counters.
' (Not really needed in this case since this value is 0.)
pc1.RawValue = 0
pc2.RawValue = 0
' Store an initial sample for the latter counter.
Dim cs1 As CounterSample = pc2.NextSample
```

(You must evaluate an initial CounterSample object for the latter counter because it represents a rate per second value.) Now you can use the Increment, Decrease, and IncrementBy methods to update the counters. In this specific example, the two counters are just two different ways of seeing the same data, so you must always assign and increment them at the same time:

```
Dim res As Single
' Wait some time, and increment values.
System.Threading.Thread.Sleep(200)
pc1.IncrementBy(15)
pc2.IncrementBy(15)
' Display current values.
res = CounterSample.Calculate(cs1, pc2.NextSample)
Console.WriteLine("Flush operations = {0}", pc1.RawValue)
Console.WriteLine("Flush operations / sec = {0}", res)

' Wait some time, and increment values.
System.Threading.Thread.Sleep(200)
pc1.IncrementBy(25)
pc2.IncrementBy(25)
' Display current values.
res = CounterSample.Calculate(cs1, pc2.NextSample)
Console.WriteLine("Flush operations = {0}", pc1.RawValue)
Console.WriteLine("Flush operations / sec = {0}", res)
```

In the preceding demo code, the same application increments the two performance counters and then queries their values. Most real-world applications, however, perform only the first kind of operation, leaving the task of sampling the counters to the Performance utility or another application.

You don't have to explicitly create instances of a given counter. Just assigning the RawValue property of a PerformanceCounter object that points to a given instance creates that instance if necessary, as this code demonstrates:

```
Dim pc1 As New PerformanceCounter("MyApp", "Flush operations", False)
' Create a first instance.
pc1.InstanceName = "First"
pc1.RawValue = 10
' Create a second instance.
pc1.InstanceName = "Second"
pc1.RawValue = 20
' Display the value of the two instances.
pc1.InstanceName = "First"
Console.WriteLine("First Instance = {0}", pc1.RawValue)
pc1.InstanceName = "Second"
Console.WriteLine("Second Instance = {0}", pc1.RawValue)
```

Deleting Instances and Counters

You can remove an instance by assigning its name to the InstanceName property and then invoking the RemoveInstance method:

```
pc1.InstanceName = "Second"
pc1.RemoveInstance()
```

You can delete a category and all the counters it contains by using the PerformanceCounterCategory.Delete shared method:

```
' Check whether the category exists.
If PerformanceCounterCategory.Exists("MyApp") Then
    PerformanceCounterCategory.Delete("MyApp")
End If
```

The EventLog Component

The .NET Framework gives you the classes to read and write from one of the event logs installed on a local or remote machine, and even to create new logs. This feature overcomes one of the limitations of Visual Basic 6 and offers a standard way for applications to record the success or failure of key operations.

> **Note** For the sake of brevity, all the code samples in this section assume that you have used the following Imports statement at the top of your source file:
>
> ```
> Imports System.Diagnostics
> ```

Introduction to Event Logging

When something relevant happens in an application—particularly, in applications that don't have a user interface, such as components, ASP.NET applications, and Windows services—your code should record an event in one of the system logs so that the user or the administrator can then check whether something went wrong. For example, an application might write to the event log when it can't start correctly, when it can't complete a critical operation, or when a low-memory situation is degrading performance.

Event logs are available only on Windows NT, Windows 2000, and Windows XP machines. By default, three event logs are available: the System log (which records events occurring on system components, such as drivers), the Security log (which records security changes and attempts to violate of security permissions), and the Application log (which records events coming from registered applications). Applications can create their own logs, as is the case with the Active Directory and the DNS Server programs, but in most cases they write their events to the Application log. Five different types of events are available:

- **Information** A significant successful operation—for example, when a service starts or when a complex backup operation has completed. (This is the default type if you don't specify otherwise.)
- **Warning** A problem has occurred, but the application can recover from it without having to shut down. A typical warning records a low-resource situation, which might later cause problems, such as loss of performance.
- **Error** A significant problem has occurred, such as loss of data or functionality; for example, Windows writes an error event when it can't load a service.
- **Success audit** A security event that occurs when an access attempt is successful, such as when a user successfully logs on to the machine.
- **Failure audit** A security event that occurs when an access attempt fails, such as when a user can't log on or when a file can't be opened because the user has insufficient security permissions.

The main tool for browsing the current state of all event logs is the Event Viewer, a Microsoft Management Console (MMC) snap-in that's installed with the operating system. (See Figure 19-6.) In most cases, you want to filter events by their source—that is, the program that wrote them. You can achieve this filtering by using the Filter command in the View menu.

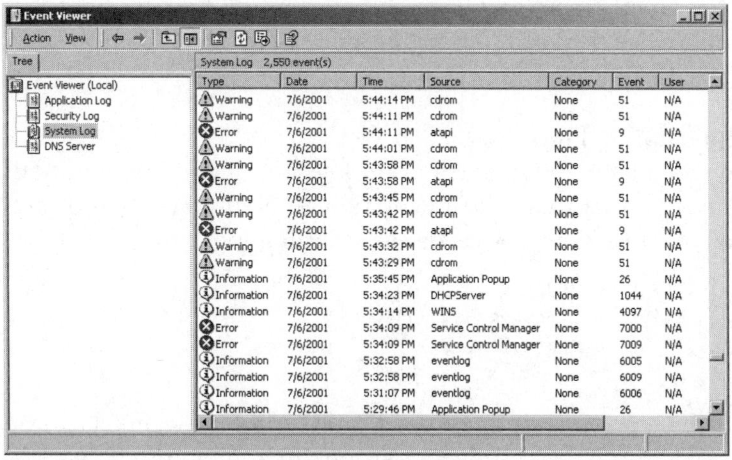

Figure 19-6. The Event Viewer MMC snap-in.

You can manage the event logs also from the Visual Studio .NET Server Explorer window, which lets you browse existing entries grouped by their source application, as you can see in Figure 19-7.

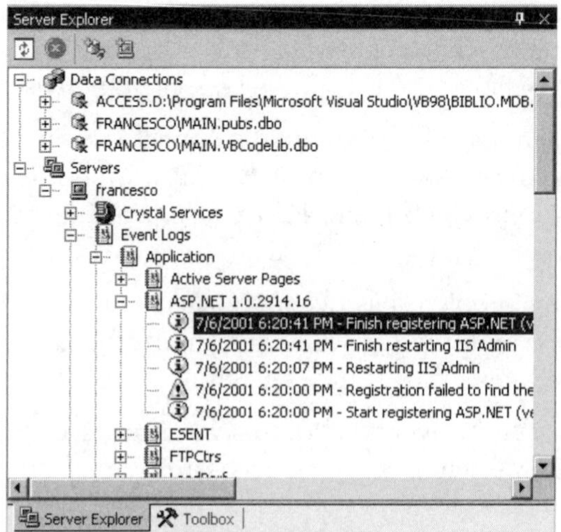

Figure 19-7. The Server Explorer window in Visual Studio .NET.

Reading Event Log Entries

You can read event log entries by defining a System.Diagnostics.EventLog object that points to a specific event log—for example, the Application log or the System log. You can create such an object in three ways: by dragging an element from the Server Explorer window to the form's component tray area, by dragging an item from the Component tab of the Toolbox to the form's component tray area, or entirely through code. In this section, I'll focus on the last method, which works also from inside classes and modules, but the concepts apply to the other two cases as well.

Listing Existing Logs

If you aren't sure about which event logs are defined on the local or a remote machine, you can use the EventLog.GetEventLogs shared method, which returns one EventLog object for each existing log:

```
Dim evlog As EventLog
For Each evlog In EventLog.GetEventLogs
    Console.WriteLine(evlog.Log)
Next
```

The GetEventLogs method takes the machine name as an optional argument, so you can also list event logs on any remote machine. (Use "." to point to the local machine.) You can also check whether a log exists on the local or remote machine with the Exists shared method:

```
If EventLog.Exists("CustomLog", "DomainServer") Then
    Console.Write("The CustomLog log exists on the DomainServer machine.")
End If
```

The name of the log is case insensitive.

Reading Existing Event Log Entries

Most of the time, you already know which log you're interested in, so you can just create an instance of the EventLog class and use it to read existing entries by using its Entries property. This property returns an array of EventLogEntry objects, each one representing an individual entry in the log. These objects expose properties whose names are self-explanatory, such as EntryType, TimeGenerated, TimeWritten, Source, Category, EventID, UserName, MachineName, Message, and Data. The following code snippet is adapted from the demo application (Figure 19-8) and lists all the entries in the Application log on the local machine:

```
Private Sub ListApplicationEntries()
    ' Get a reference to the Application event log.
    Dim elApp As New EventLog("Application")
    Dim entry As EventLogEntry

    For Each entry In elApp.Entries
        Console.WriteLine(GetEntryInfo(entry))
    Next
End Sub

' Return readable information about an event log entry.
Private Function GetEntryInfo(ByVal entry As EventLogEntry) As String
    ' This schema is similar to the info you see in Event Viewer
    ' but also includes the logged message.
    Dim sb As New System.Text.StringBuilder(200)
    sb.Append(entry.EntryType.ToString)
    sb.Append("  ")
    sb.Append(entry.TimeGenerated)
    sb.Append("  ")
    sb.Append(entry.Source)
    sb.Append("  ")
    sb.Append(entry.Category)
    sb.Append("  ")
    sb.Append(entry.EventID)
    sb.Append("  ")
    sb.Append(entry.UserName)
```

(continued)

```
    sb.Append("  ")
    sb.Append(entry.Message)
    sb.Append("  ")
    Return sb.ToString
End Function
```

Even if you can specify a source when you instantiate the EventLog object, the Entries property always returns all the items in that log. In other words, you must filter events according to their source (or any other property) manually, as in this code:

```
' Display information about SQL Server events only.
For Each entry In elApp.Entries
    If entry.Source = "MSSQLServer" Then
        Console.WriteLine(GetEntryInfo(entry))
    End If
Next
```

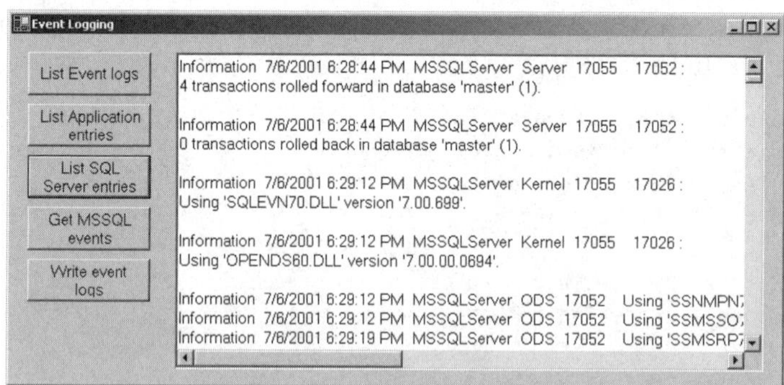

Figure 19-8. The demo application lets you list all the entries in the Application log or just the ones coming from Microsoft SQL Server.

Handling EntryWritten Events

The ability to read existing log entries is fine when you want to build a log viewer application—for example, a custom version of the Event Viewer system utility. In many cases, however, you really need to get a notification when an entry is written to the event log by a specific source. You can achieve this functionality in a relatively simple way, thanks to the EntryWritten event of the EventLog component. (An important limitation: you can receive notifications only from event logs on the local machine, not from remote machines.)

You first need to check that the application you're interested in is actually registered as an event source on the machine; to do this, use the SourceExists shared method. Next, by using the LogNameFromSourceName shared method, you retrieve the name of the log that contains entries written by that specific event source. At this point, you're ready to create an EventLog object that points to the log in question, and you can use the AddHandler command or a WithEvents variable to bind the EntryWritten event to a specific event handler in your application. To actually receive events, however, you must set the EnableRaisingEvents property to True:

```
Private Sub StartLogging()
    ' We're interested in SQL Server events on the local machine only.
    Dim source As String = "MSSQLServer"

    ' Exit if the source isn't registered.
    If Not EventLog.SourceExists(source) Then Exit Sub
    ' Get the name of the log that contains entries from SQL Server.
    ' (Note that you must specify the computer name.)
    Dim logName As String = EventLog.LogNameFromSourceName(source, ".")
    ' Get the corresponding EventLog object.
    Dim evLog As New EventLog(logName)
    ' Associate it with an event handler.
    AddHandler evLog.EntryWritten, AddressOf EntryWritten
    ' This statement is very important.
    evLog.EnableRaisingEvents = True
End Sub

Private Sub EntryWritten(ByVal sender As Object, _
    ByVal e As System.Diagnostics.EntryWrittenEventArgs)
    ' Filter out events from sources we aren't interested in.
    If e.Entry.Source = "MSSQLServer" Then
        ' (GetEntryInfo has been defined previously.)
        Console.WriteLine(GetEntryInfo(e.Entry))
    End If
End Sub
```

As the preceding code shows, the EntryWritten event fires when *any* source writes to the specified log, regardless of the source argument you might have specified in the constructor of the EventLog component. For this reason, you have to manually filter out events from sources you aren't interested in.

Writing Event Log Entries

The EventLog class makes it simple to write to an event log as well, even though an application can write to an event log only if it's registered as a valid event source.

Registering Your Application as an Event Source

You can register your application as a valid event source by means of the CreateEventSource shared method of the EventLog class. This method takes the source name (the string that will identify messages from this application in the log) and the name of the log your application will write to (typically the Application log):

```
' Register your demo app as an event source.
EventLog.CreateEventSource("DemoApp", "Application")
```

If you skip this registration step, however, your application will be registered on the fly when you write the first entry to the log. The DeleteEventSource shared method unregisters an event source. Note that you don't have to specify the name of the log because the system can deduce it from the name of the source:

```
' Delete this event source.
EventLog.DeleteEventSource("DemoApp")
```

The DeleteEventSource method can be useful when you want to change the destination log for events written by your application. Note that deleting an event source doesn't remove the existing log entries associated with that source.

Creating a Custom Log

Creating a custom log is much simpler than you probably think it is, and you might argue that it's a bit *too* simple. In fact, if the log name that you pass to the second argument of the CreateEventSource method or to the EventLog's constructor doesn't correspond to an existing log, a new log is automatically created for you. This means that you might accidentally create new logs just because you misspelled the name of the log in one of these calls:

```
' Create a new custom log named MyLog.
EventLog.CreateEventSource("MyDemoApp", "MyLog")
```

Only the first eight characters of the log name are significant; if the first eight characters in your custom log's name match the name of an existing log (as in ApplicationNew), you won't create a new log. You can create a custom log on a remote machine by passing a third argument to the CreateEventSource method, provided you have sufficient administrative rights on the remote system.

You delete a custom log using the EventLog.Delete shared method. Pay attention when using this method because it deletes all the event entries and all the event sources associated with the deleted log. Also note that you might accidentally delete one of the predefined system logs, in which case you might have to reinstall the operating system:

```
' Delete the custom log.
EventLog.Delete("MyLog")
```

A less radical operation consists of removing all the entries from a given log, which you can do by invoking the Clear method:

```
Dim evLog As New EventLog("MyLog", ".")
evLog.Clear()
```

Clearing an event log periodically—possibly after saving its current contents to a file from inside the Event Viewer utility—helps you avoid problems when the event log becomes full. (The default behavior when this happens is to start overwriting the oldest entries with the newest entries.) By default, the Application, System, and Security logs can grow up to 4992 KB, whereas custom logs have a default maximum size of 512 KB. You can change these default values and modify the default behavior from inside the Event Viewer utility.

Writing to the Event Log

Once your application is a registered event source, you only have to instantiate an EventLog object that points to the correct log on the target machine. The constructor for this class takes a third argument, which is the name of the source and must match the event source argument you specified in the CreateEventSource method. Now you can invoke the WriteEntry method, which at the very least takes the message associated with the event you're writing:

```
' Create an EventLog object connected to that event log.
Dim evLog As New EventLog("Application", ".", "DemoApp")

' Write two entries to the Application log.
evLog.WriteEntry("First message")
System.Threading.Thread.Sleep(500)
evLog.WriteEntry("Second message")
```

(The message you write can't be longer than 16 KB.) If you're using the Event Viewer utility, you have to refresh the display to see the new entries added by your application.

The WriteEntry method is overloaded to take additional arguments, such as an event type, an application-defined event identifier, an application-defined category identifier, and a Byte array containing binary data to be associated with the event:

```
' Write an error message.
evLog.WriteEntry("Third message", EventLogEntryType.Error)
' Write a warning error with an application-defined event ID.
evLog.WriteEntry("Fourth message", EventLogEntryType.Warning, 123)
' Write a warning error with an application-defined event ID and category ID.
```

(continued)

```
evLog.WriteEntry("Fifth message", EventLogEntryType.Warning, 123, 456)
' Write a warning error with an application-defined event ID and category ID,
' plus associated binary data.
Dim bytes() As Byte = {0, 2, 4, 6, 8, 10, 12}
evLog.WriteEntry("Fifth message", EventLogEntryType.Warning, 123, 456, bytes)
```

Dealing with Security Issues

Because event logs are such a critical part of the system, not all applications are allowed to read, write, or clear them. The operations actually permitted depend on the identity under which the code is running and are summarized in Table 19-3. The LocalSystem account is the account under which most services run, and it's the most powerful account in terms of the operations it can perform on system logs.

Table 19-3 Operations Allowed on System Logs from Different Accounts

Account	Application Log	System Log	Security Log
LocalSystem	Read, Write, Clear	Read, Write, Clear	Read, Write, Clear
Administrator	Read, Write, Clear	Read, Write, Clear	Read, Write
ServerOperator	Read, Write, Clear	Read	(none)
World	Read, Write	Read, Clear	(none)

In addition to the rights listed in Table 19-3, users have the right to read and clear the Security log if they have been granted the Manage Auditing And Security Log user right or the SE_AUDIT_NAME privilege. (See the Windows SDK documentation for additional information.)

The ServiceController Component

Service applications are programs that are designed to run unattended. They typically start as soon as the operating system completes the bootstrap phase and can run even if no interactive user has logged in, even though you can configure them to be started manually. Windows services are available only on Windows NT, Windows 2000, and Windows XP. They are used for many server-side tasks, such as running Internet Information Services, Microsoft SQL Server, the Microsoft Search engine, and so on.

The System.ServiceProcess.ServiceController component lets you programmatically control any service on a local or remote machine. You can list all the existing services as well as start, stop, pause, and resume them (provided you have sufficient administrative permissions on the system).

As with most components described in this chapter, you can create an instance of the ServiceController class in three distinct ways: by dragging an element from the Server Explorer window to the form's component tray area, by dropping an item from the Component tab of the Toolbox, or simply by means of code. The three techniques are equivalent, but I'll focus exclusively on the last one because it can also be used from inside classes and modules.

> **Note** For the sake of brevity, all the code samples in this section assume that you have used the following Imports statement at the top of your source file:
>
> ```
> Imports System.ServiceProcess
> ```
>
> In most project types, this namespace isn't included among the available references and you must manually add a reference to the System.ServiceProcess.dll component.

Listing Installed Services

Listing installed services on local or remote machines is trivial if you use the GetServices and GetDevices shared methods of the ServiceController class. These methods return an array of all the nondevice services and all the device services installed on the specified machine, respectively, or the local machine if the argument is omitted:

```
Dim sc As ServiceController

' List all nondevice services on local machines.
Console.WriteLine("--- NON-DEVICE SERVICES:")
For Each sc In ServiceController.GetServices
    Console.WriteLine(sc.ServiceName & " (" & sc.DisplayName & ")")
Next

' List all device services on local machines.
Console.WriteLine ("--- DEVICE SERVICES:")
For Each sc In ServiceController.GetDevices
    Console.WriteLine(sc.ServiceName & " (" & sc.DisplayName & ")")
Next
```

The demo application contains a routine that displays the list of installed services, as shown in Figure 19-9.

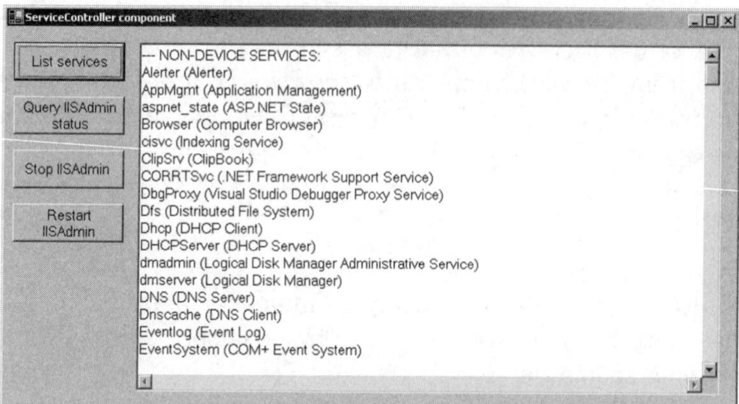

Figure 19-9. The demo application lists all installed services.

Querying a ServiceController Object

Once you have a reference to a ServiceController object, you can query its many properties to learn more about the related service:

- The ServiceName property is the short name of the service, whereas the DisplayName property returns the longer, descriptive, name of the service. For example, the service name of the Internet Information Services service is IISADMIN, whereas its display name is IIS Admin Service.
- The MachineName property is the name of the machine on which the service is running.
- The Status property is an enumerated value that indicates the state the service is in. It can be one of the following values: Running, Paused, Stopped, StartPending, PausePending, ContinuePending, or StopPending. A service is in one of the *xxx*Pending states when a command has been issued but not yet completed.
- The CanStop property is True if the service can be stopped; the CanPauseAndContinue property is True if the service can be paused and resumed; the CanShutdown property is True if the service should be notified when the service shuts down.
- The ServiceType property is a bit-coded value that lets you determine other features of the service. It can be a combination of the following values: Adapter (a service for a hardware device that requires

its own driver); FileSystemDriver (a file system driver, which is also a kernel device driver); InteractiveProcess (a service that can communicate with the desktop); KernelDriver (a kernel device driver such as a hard disk or other low-level hardware device driver); RecognizerDriver (a file system driver used during startup to determine the file systems present on the system); Win32OwnProcess (a Win32 program that can be started by the Service Controller, obeys the service control protocol, and is a type of Win32 service that runs in a process by itself); and Win32ShareProcess (a Win32 service that can share a process with other Win32 services).

- The ServicesDependedOn property returns an array of ServiceController objects, each one identifying a service that must be running for the related service to run. If any of these services isn't running, you won't be able to start the related service.

The following code snippet creates a ServiceController object that points to the IISADMIN service and displays information about it:

```
' Get a reference to the IISADMIN service on the local machine.
Dim scIISAdmin As New ServiceController("IISADMIN", ".")

Console.WriteLine("ServiceName = " & scIISAdmin.ServiceName)
Console.WriteLine("DisplayName = " & scIISAdmin.DisplayName)
Console.WriteLine("MachineName = " & scIISAdmin.MachineName)
Console.WriteLine("Status = " & scIISAdmin.Status.ToString)
Console.WriteLine("CanStop = " & scIISAdmin.CanStop)
Console.WriteLine("CanPauseAndContinue = " & scIISAdmin.CanPauseAndContinue)
Console.WriteLine("CanShutDown = " & scIISAdmin.CanShutdown)
Console.WriteLine("ServiceType = " & scIISAdmin.ServiceType.ToString)

' List services IISADMIN depends on.
Dim sc As ServiceController
Console.WriteLine ("Services this service depends on:")
For Each sc In scIISAdmin.ServicesDependedOn
    Console.WriteLine("  {0} ({1})", sc.ServiceName, sc.DisplayName)
Next

' List services that depend on IISADMIN.
Console.WriteLine("Services that depend on this service:")
For Each sc In scIISAdmin.DependentServices
    Console.WriteLine("  {0} ({1})", sc.ServiceName, sc.DisplayName)
Next
```

Managing a Service

The ServiceController class exposes a few methods that let you manage Windows services:

- The Start method starts the service. When you invoke this method, the status of the service changes into StartPending and then into Running; you can't stop a service until it has reached the running status. The Start method is overloaded to take an optional String array for services that take arguments.
- The Stop method stops the service and all the services that depend on this service. You should test the CanStop property before invoking this method. (If CanStop returns False, the Stop method throws an exception.)
- The Pause method pauses the service. When you invoke this method, the status of the service changes into StartPending and then into Paused. You can't resume a service until it has reached the paused status.
- The Continue method restarts the paused service. When you invoke this method, the status of the service changes into ContinuePending and then into Running.
- The ExecuteCommand method executes an application-defined command. This method takes an Integer argument and passes it to the service but doesn't change the status of the service. See the documentation of each service about supported custom commands. (Also read the "Managing Custom Commands" section later in this chapter to see how you can write a service that reacts to custom commands.)
- The Refresh method reads again all the properties of the ServiceController object.

The following code shows how you can stop and restart the IISADMIN service on the local machine. Note that you should ensure that all the services on which the IISADMIN service depends are running before you attempt to invoke the Start method:

```
Sub StopService()
    ' Get a reference to the IISADMIN service on the local machine.
    Dim scIISAdmin As New ServiceController("IISADMIN", ".")
```

```
    ' Check that the service can be stopped.
    If scIISAdmin.CanStop Then
        scIISAdmin.Stop()
    Else
        Console.WriteLine("Unable to stop the service at this time")
    End If
End Sub

Sub RestartService()
    ' Get a reference to the IISADMIN service on the local machine.
    Dim scIISAdmin As New ServiceController("IISADMIN", ".")

    ' Ensure that all the services this service depends on are running.
    Dim sc As ServiceController
    For Each sc In scIISAdmin.ServicesDependedOn
        If sc.Status <> ServiceControllerStatus.Running Then
            sc.Start()
        End If
    Next
    ' Now you can start this service.
    scIISAdmin.Start()
End Sub
```

The only other method that the ServiceController class exposes is WaitForStatus, which waits until the service reaches a given status:

```
scIISAdmin.Stop()
' Wait until the service has stopped.
scIISAdmin.WaitForStatus(ServiceControllerStatus.Stopped)
Console.WriteLine("The service has stopped")
```

You can also use a timeout so that your application isn't blocked if the service can't reach the specified status. The WaitForStatus method doesn't return any value, so you must manually check the state of the service when the application regains control:

```
' Start this service.
scIISAdmin.Start()
' Wait until the service is running (timeout = 5 seconds)
scIISAdmin.WaitForStatus(ServiceControllerStatus.Running, _
    New TimeSpan(0, 0, 5))
If scIISAdmin.Status = ServiceControllerStatus.Running Then
    Console.WriteLine("The service is running")
Else
    Console.WriteLine("Unable to start the service")
End If
```

Here are two additional notes on the ServiceController component:

- The component passes the start, stop, pause, and continue commands to the Service Control Manager, not to the service itself. The method returns after the request has been acknowledged, without waiting for the Service Control Manager to pass the request to the service. For this reason, you don't need to catch exceptions inside the code that uses the ServiceController component, but at the same time, you can't assume that the operation was successful.
- Don't use this component to manipulate a service contained in the same project. The code in a project that creates a service can't control the service itself. The service must be controlled from another context.

Windows Service Applications

The .NET Framework makes it exceedingly easy to create a Windows service application, and Visual Studio .NET offers a template project that saves you even more time. (By comparison, you can't create a service using Visual Basic 6 unless you resort to third-party components.)

The System.ServiceProcess namespace contains several classes that let you deal with services. In the preceding section, I illustrated the ServiceController component and how to start, stop, pause, and resume an existing service. In this section, you'll see how to create a Windows service and how to apply many of the concepts you learned when exploring the ServiceController class. Remember that you can create and install services only on Windows NT, Windows 2000, and Windows XP systems.

> **Note** For the sake of brevity, all the code samples in this section assume that you have used the following Imports statement at the top of your source file:
>
> ```
> Imports System.ServiceProcess
> ```

Windows Service Basics

From the perspective of .NET developers, a Windows service application is just a class that inherits from the System.ServiceProcess.ServiceBase abstract class. In practice, all you have to do to implement a service is create a class that derives from this abstract class, set its properties, and override a few of its methods so that your code can react appropriately when the service is started or stopped.

Creating the Project

Our demo application will be a service named Encryptor, which monitors a directory on the hard disk and automatically encrypts all the files that the user copies to it. The encryption algorithm is a simple one: it won't resist the cracking attempts of a determined hacker but is sufficient for most ordinary situations. (Of course, once you've understood the underlying principles, you can replace the provided encryption routine with a more robust one—for example, you can use the cryptographic services offered by the .NET Framework.)

Start by creating a new project of type Windows Service. (You'll have to scroll down the Templates list to see this type of project in the New Project dialog box.) Assign a suitable name to the project. (Use EncryptorService to parallel the code in the demo application provided on the companion CD.) Then click OK. This action creates a new project with two files: Service1.vb and the ubiquitous AssemblyInfo.vb. You can rename the former Encryptor.vb.

If you select the now-renamed Encryptor file, you'll see that it has a designer surface. This is where you can drop any component this service uses. For example, you can add the FileSystemWatcher component that you'll use to detect any files added to the watched directory. In most cases, however, you'll work mostly with the code module behind this designer.

Setting Service Properties

Before you start working with code, you should assign a few key properties of the service component you've just created. To do so, right-click on the designer's surface and click Properties on the shortcut menu, which will bring you to the Properties window (shown in Figure 19-10), where you should modify the following properties as follows:

1. Set the Name property equal to Encryptor. This is the name of the class that the designer generates.
2. Set the ServiceName property equal to Encryptor. This is the name of the service that will be created; it's usually the same as the name of the class, but nothing prevents you from using a different name.
3. Ensure that the CanStop property is True. This property determines whether the service can be stopped once started.
4. Set the CanPauseAndContinue property to True. This property determines whether the service can be paused and resumed.

5. Ensure that the AutoLog property is True. When this property is True, the service automatically writes entries in the Application event log when it starts and stops successfully, when it's paused and resumed, and when any command fails to complete correctly. The messages sent to the event log are rather generic (for example, "Service started successfully"), and you have no control over their contents, but they're OK in most cases and very useful, especially during the debug phase.

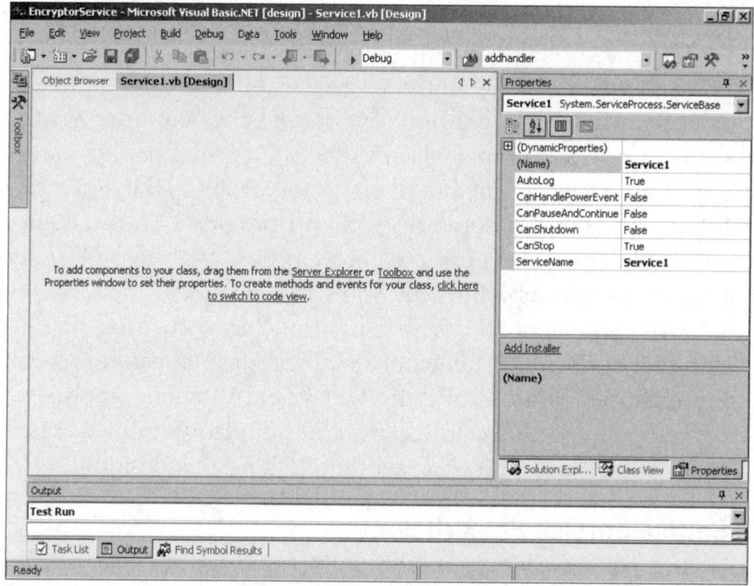

Figure 19-10. The designer window of a service component.

Browsing and Fixing the Code

After you've set these properties, you can switch to the code editor. Here's an abridged version of the code the designer has generated for you:

```
Public Class Encryptor
    Inherits System.ServiceProcess.ServiceBase

#Region " Component Designer generated code "
    Public Sub New()
        MyBase.New()

        ' This call is required by the Component Designer.
        InitializeComponent()

        ' Add any initialization after the InitializeComponent() call.
    End Sub
```

```
    ' The main entry point for the process
    Shared Sub Main()
        Dim ServicesToRun() As System.ServiceProcess.ServiceBase

        ' More than one NT Service may run within the same process. To add
        ' another service to this process, change the following line to
        ' create a second service object. For example,
        '
        '   ServicesToRun = New System.ServiceProcess.ServiceBase () _
        '        {New Service1, New MySecondUserService}
        '
        ServicesToRun = New System.ServiceProcess.ServiceBase() _
            {New Service1()}
        System.ServiceProcess.ServiceBase.Run(ServicesToRun)
    End Sub

    'Required by the Component Designer
    Private components As System.ComponentModel.Container

    ' NOTE: The following procedure is required by the Component Designer.
    ' It can be modified using the Component Designer.
    ' Do not modify it using the code editor.
    <System.Diagnostics.DebuggerStepThrough()> _
        Private Sub InitializeComponent()
        '
        'Encryptor
        '
        Me.CanPauseAndContinue = True
        Me.ServiceName = "Encryptor"
    End Sub
#End Region

    Protected Overrides Sub OnStart(ByVal args() As String)
        ' Add code here to start your service. This method should set things
        ' in motion so your service can do its work.
    End Sub

    Protected Overrides Sub OnStop()
        ' Add code here to perform any tear-down necessary to stop
        ' your service.
    End Sub
End Class
```

The preceding code reveals how your service class actually works. The code in the Shared Sub Main procedure creates an array of all the service classes that share the same process space and then passes this array to the ServiceBase.Run shared method:

```
System.ServiceProcess.ServiceBase.Run(ServicesToRun)
```

Thanks to this approach, your project can include multiple service classes that run in the same process (and therefore save system resources) yet can be stopped, paused, and resumed independently of one another.

A careful examination of the preceding code shows a minor bug in the code generated by the designer. Although the name of the class correctly reflects the Name property you've set in the Properties window, the name of the class instantiated in the Shared Sub Main procedure is still Service1 (the statement in boldface in the preceding listing), so you must change it manually as follows:

```
ServicesToRun = New System.ServiceProcess.ServiceBase() _
        {New Encryptor()}
```

Overriding ServiceBase Methods

A nontrivial service application must typically execute code when the service starts and stops, as well as when the service is paused and resumed (if you set the CanPauseAndContinue property to True). When these events occur, the .NET runtime invokes one of the public methods of the ServiceBase class, so you have to override these methods to execute your custom code instead.

The Encryptor service uses a FileSystemWatcher component to be notified when a new file is created in a given directory on the hard disk. As you saw earlier in this chapter, you can create this component by means of code or by dropping it from the Components tab of the Toolbox. In our demo Encryptor service, we'll use the latter approach.

After you drop an instance of the FileSystemWatcher component on the designer's surface, you should set its EnableRaisingEvents property to False so that the component won't raise events before the service starts. You can leave all the other properties at their default value. Next you can switch to the code editor and add the following code inside the OnStart and OnStop methods:

```
' The path of the watched directory
Dim Path As String = "C:\Encrypt"

Protected Overrides Sub OnStart(ByVal args() As String)
    ' Ensure that the directory exists.
    If Not System.IO.Directory.Exists(Path) Then
        System.IO.Directory.CreateDirectory(Path)
    End If
    ' Start receiving file events.
    FileSystemWatcher1.Path = Path
    FileSystemWatcher1.EnableRaisingEvents = True
End Sub

Protected Overrides Sub OnStop()
    ' Stop receiving file events.
```

```
    FileSystemWatcher1.EnableRaisingEvents = False
End Sub
```

Because this service can also be paused and resumed, you should override the OnPause and OnContinue methods as well:

```
Protected Overrides Sub OnPause()
    ' Stop receiving file events.
    FileSystemWatcher1.EnableRaisingEvents = False
End Sub

Protected Overrides Sub OnContinue()
    ' Start receiving file events.
    FileSystemWatcher1.EnableRaisingEvents = True
End Sub
```

Implementing the Encryption Algorithm

The Encryptor service sleeps until the FileSystemWatcher component detects that a new file is created in the directory and fires a Created event. When this happens, the service invokes the EncryptFile custom routine, which reads the contents of the file (in blocks of 8 KB each) and creates a temporary encrypted file with a .$$$ extension. When the encryption is completed, the service deletes the original file and renames the temporary file as the original file. The encryption routine simply uses an XOR operation on each byte in the original file with a byte specified in a password:

```
' This is the binary password.
Dim pwBytes() As Byte = {123, 234, 12, 9, 78, 89, 212}
' This is the extension used for temporary files.
Dim tempExt As String = ".$$$"

Private Sub FileSystemWatcher1_Created(ByVal sender As Object, _
    ByVal e As System.IO.FileSystemEventArgs) _
    Handles FileSystemWatcher1.Created
    ' Ignore temporary files created by the encryption process.
    If System.IO.Path.GetExtension(e.FullPath) = tempExt Then Exit Sub
    ' Encrypt the file being created.
    EncryptFile(e.FullPath, pwBytes)
End Sub

' This is the encryption/decryption routine.
Private Sub EncryptFile(ByVal Filename As String, ByVal pwBytes() As Byte)
    ' This is the size of each input block.
    ' (Files must be decrypted using the same block size.)
    Const BLOCKSIZE = 8192

    ' Determine the name of the temporary file.
```

(continued)

```
    Dim tempFile As String = Filename & tempExt
    ' Open the source file as a binary input stream.
    Dim inStream As New System.IO.FileStream(Filename, IO.FileMode.Open)
    ' Open the temporary output file as a binary input stream.
    Dim outStream As New System.IO.FileStream(tempFile, IO.FileMode.Create)
    ' Determine the number of bytes to read.
    Dim bytesLeft As Long = inStream.Length
    ' Prepare an input buffer.
    Dim buffer(BLOCKSIZE - 1) As Byte

    ' Loop until there are bytes to read.
    Do While bytesLeft > 0
        ' Read max 8 KB at a time.
        Dim bytesToRead As Long = Math.Min(BLOCKSIZE, bytesLeft)
        ' Read into the input buffer.
        inStream.Read(buffer, 0, bytesToRead)
        ' Encrypt this buffer.
        EncryptArray(buffer, pwBytes)
        ' Output to the temporary file.
        outStream.Write(buffer, 0, bytesToRead)
        ' We have fewer bytes to read now.
        bytesLeft -= bytesToRead
    Loop

    ' Close the two streams.
    inStream.Close()
    outStream.Close()
    ' Delete the source file.
    System.IO.File.Delete(Filename)
    ' Rename the temporary file as the original file.
    System.IO.File.Move(tempFile, Filename)
End Sub

' This routine encrypts an array of bytes.
Sub EncryptArray(ByVal buffer() As Byte, ByVal pwBytes() As Byte)
    ' This index points to the buffer.
    Dim index As Integer
    ' This index points to the password array.
    Dim i As Integer
    ' The max value for i
    Dim maxval As Integer = pwBytes.Length

    For index = 0 To buffer.Length - 1
        ' XOR each element with the corresponding element in the password.
        buffer(index) = buffer(index) Xor pwBytes(i)
        ' Ensure that the index is always in the valid range.
        i = (i + 1) Mod maxval
    Next
End Sub
```

Installing the Service

Windows services can't be launched as regular Windows applications. You must first install the service on the computer on which it must run, and then you must actually start the process by using the Services MMC snap-in or the NET START command from the command prompt.

The first step in making a service installable is to add an installer class. You can choose from two ways of doing this: by using an automatic tool that Visual Studio provides or by manually creating the installer class in code.

The former method is the easiest one and versatile enough in most cases. Switch to the designer of the Encryptor component, and ensure that the Properties window is visible. Near the bottom of this window, you'll see an Add Installer hyperlink. Click on this link, and Visual Studio adds a new component, named ProjectInstaller.vb, to the current project. The designer of this component hosts two more objects, named ServiceProcessInstaller1 and ServiceInstaller1. (See Figure 19-11.) You don't need to change the names of these objects.

Setting the Service's Main Properties

By setting the properties of the ServiceInstaller object appropriately, you define how your service behaves. The key properties of this object are the following:

- **ServiceName** This property *must* match the ServiceName property of the service class that you have defined in the project (Encryptor, in our case). Visual Studio correctly initializes this property, so in most cases you don't have to worry about it.
- **DisplayName** This property is the descriptive string that appears in the Services MMC snap-in and is retrieved by means of the DisplayName property of the ServiceController class.
- **StartType** This property tells whether the service is started automatically or manually or is disabled; the default value is Manual.
- **ServicesDependedOn** This property is a String array in which each array element contains the name of a service that must be running for this service to be successfully started. (Go back to the section titled "The ServiceController Component" to read more about this property.)

For our Encryptor service, you can assign the string Simple Encrypting Service for the DisplayName property and ensure that StartType is set to Manual. Because the Encryptor service doesn't depend on any other service, you don't have to modify the ServicesDependedOn property. Figure 19-11 shows what the Properties window looks like after you've set these properties.

> **Tip** If your project contains multiple services, you should create multiple ServiceInstaller objects, one for each service to be installed.

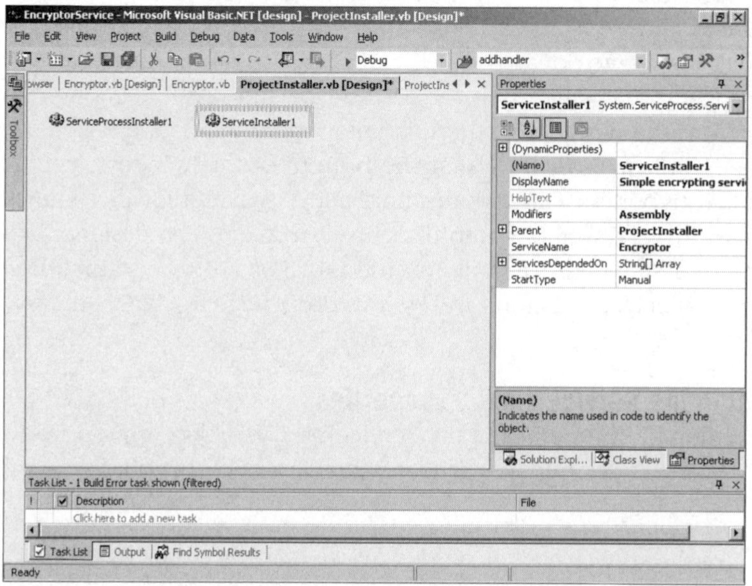

Figure 19-11. Setting the properties of a ServiceInstaller component.

Setting the Service's Security Context

The ServiceProcessInstaller object determines the identity under which the service runs. It exposes only three properties:

- **Account** This property specifies the type of the account used by the service and can be User (default), LocalSystem, LocalService, or NetworkService. Note that your service won't be able to display a message box or a user interface, even if you specify a user account. In most cases, using the LocalSystem account is the wiser choice.
- **Username and Password** These properties specify the user account and password to be used if the service runs under a user account; otherwise, they're ignored. The username can refer to a registered user in the local machine or a registered user in the domain, provided that account has sufficient privileges on the machine on which the service is installed.

If the service runs under a user account and you leave the username or the password empty, they aren't requested during the installation and the installation itself fails.

Running InstallUtil

When you've set all the properties of the ServiceInstaller and ServiceProcessInstaller components correctly, you can finally build the project. In the case of our demo service, this action creates an executable file named EncryptorService.exe in the Bin subdirectory under the project's main directory. At this point, you're ready to install this service by using the InstallUtil utility provided with the .NET Framework. (You can find it in the \WinNT\Microsoft.NET\Framework\v*x.y.zzzz* directory, where *x.y.zzzz* is the version of the installed Framework.) Before proceeding, ensure that this directory is on the system path. For example, you can run the Corvars.bat batch file provided with the .NET Framework (as suggested in the section "The Visual Basic .NET Compiler" in Chapter 1).

Open a command prompt window, navigate to the Bin directory, and issue this command to install the service:

```
InstallUtil EncryptorService.exe
```

If everything goes well, you'll see a message that says that the service has been installed correctly. The InstallUtil runs a transacted installation, so if something goes wrong, the utility will clean up any partial actions that couldn't be completed because of an error, such as writes to the registry. If an error occurs, a detailed message is displayed and a log file is created.

You can uninstall the service using the /U option of the InstallUtil program:

```
InstallUtil EncryptorService.exe /u
```

The service must be stopped for the uninstall operation to be successful.

> **Note** The InstallUtil program looks for all the Installer classes that are marked with the RunInstaller attribute set to True. This attribute is created by the Visual Studio code generator, so everything works correctly as long as you don't delete it. In advanced scenarios, you might build service applications containing services that aren't installed by the InstallUtil program. In this case, the installation of the service is up to you.

Starting and Stopping the Service

If the installation went well, you can now start the service and check that it behaves as expected. You can start and stop a service in two ways: by using the

Services system utility (actually an MMC snap-in under Windows 2000 or later) or by using the NET command from the system prompt. Here's how you start:

```
NET START Encryptor
```

Stopping the service is also easy:

```
NET STOP Encryptor
```

Similarly, you can use the NET PAUSE and NET CONTINUE commands to pause and continue a service from the command prompt. All these commands display a message that tells you that the operation was successful or explains why it failed.

Using the Services MMC snap-in is even simpler. (See Figure 19-12.) You can start, stop, pause, and resume any service by right-clicking on the corresponding item, and you can even change all the service's settings by double-clicking on the service.

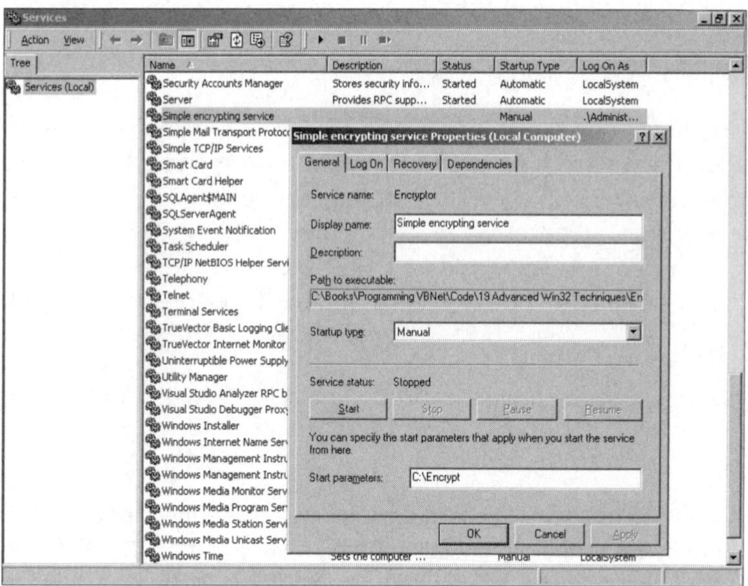

Figure 19-12. You can change the settings of any service with the Services MMC snap-in.

Once the service is running, you can test its functionality by copying one or more files in the C:\Encrypt directory and then trying to read them back. You'll see that the copy of the file in that directory has been automatically encrypted. You can then send it as an e-mail attachment to your friends who have installed the Encryptor service. When they receive the attachment, they'll have to copy the file into their C:\Encrypt directory to have the file automatically decrypted. (This technique works because the encryption mechanism is symmetrical.) To test how the encryption mechanism works without having two distinct machines, you can copy a file to the C:\Encrypt directory to encrypt it, then copy the encrypted file to another directory, and finally copy it back to the C:\Encrypt directory. The file that you obtain at the end of this sequence should be the same as the original file.

More Service Programming Techniques

In this last section, I've gathered a few tips that you might find useful when you're writing and debugging Windows service applications.

Custom Event Log Messages

As I explained earlier, if you set the AutoLog property to True, your service class automatically records important events in the Application log, such as when the service is started and stopped or when a problem occurs.

To suppress the standard start/stop log messages or to produce more informative messages, you should set the AutoLog property to False and send custom messages yourself. This is an especially easy thing to do, thanks to the ServiceBase class's EventLog property. This property returns an EventLog object that lets you send a message to the Application log:

```
' From inside the service class...
Me.EventLog.WriteEntry("Message from the Encryptor service")
```

Here's one caveat, however: don't attempt to send a message to a log before setting your service's ServiceName property in code because this is the moment in time when the service registers itself as an event source.

To send messages to a log other than the Application log, you must register an event source manually, as I explained in the section titled "The EventLog Component" earlier in this chapter.

Reacting to Shutdown and Power Events

Most service applications contain cleanup code in their OnStop and (sometimes) OnPause methods so that the service doesn't take resources while it isn't running. In some cases, you should run special code also when the system shuts down, when the system enters suspend mode, or when another power-related event occurs—for example, when batteries are low.

You can execute a custom routine when the system shuts down by setting the CanShutdown property to True and then overriding the OnShutdown protected method. Similarly, you can run a routine when a power event occurs by setting the CanHandlePowerEvent property to True and overriding the OnPowerEvent method. This method receives an enumerated value that explains what specific event happened. The following routine shows how you can take advantage of these methods:

```
' This method is called only if the CanShutdown property is True.
Protected Overrides Sub OnShutdown()
    ' Add the code that executes when the system shuts down here.
End Sub

' This method is called only if the CanHandlePowerEvent property is True.
Protected Overrides Function OnPowerEvent( _
    ByVal powerStatus As PowerBroadcastStatus) As Boolean
    Select Case powerStatus
        Case PowerBroadcastStatus.Suspend
            ' Add the code to execute when the system enters suspend mode.
        Case PowerBroadcastStatus.ResumeSuspend
            ' Add the code to execute when the system exits suspend mode.
        Case PowerBroadcastStatus.BatteryLow
            ' Add the code to execute when batteries are low.
    End Select
    ' This method must return True.
    Return True
End Function
```

Managing Custom Commands

In the section "The ServiceController Component," I mentioned that you could send a custom command to a service. (A custom command is just an Integer value whose value is defined by the application.) Some system services react to custom commands, but you can implement a similar mechanism in your services by simply overriding the OnCustomCommand protected method, which fires when another application sends a custom command to your service:

```
' This method is called when a custom command is sent to the service.
Protected Overrides Sub OnCustomCommand(ByVal command As Integer)
    Select Case command
        Case 1
            ' React to custom command #1.
        Case 2
            ' React to custom command #2.
        ⋮
    End Select
End Sub
```

Again, the meaning and the effect of each custom command depend on the specific service exclusively. For example, the Encryptor service might use a custom command to select a different encryption algorithm.

Passing and Receiving Arguments

A great feature of Windows services is their ability to receive arguments. You specify one or more arguments for your service in the General tab of the Properties dialog box in the Services MMC snap-in. For example, the final version of the Encryptor service on the companion CD receives the name of the directory in which files are automatically encrypted in this way. (See Figure 19-12.)

The arguments that you specify are converted to a String array and passed as an argument to the OnStart method. So you need only one statement to implement this feature in the Encryptor service. (Added lines are in boldface.)

```
Protected Overrides Sub OnStart(ByVal args() As String)
    ' If an argument has been specified, use it as the path
    ' of the directory being watched.
    If args.Length > 0 Then Path = args(0)
    ⋮
End Sub
```

Debugging a Windows Service

The easiest way to debug a Windows service is to attach the Visual Studio debugger to it. To use this technique, compile the service project in Debug mode, start the process as usual, and switch back to Visual Studio. Next select the Processes command from the Debug menu, and double-click on the EncryptorService element in the list of running processes. This action brings up the Attach To Process dialog box, which lets you confirm that you want to debug the service application. (At this point, the screen looks like Figure 19-13.) Click OK to close this dialog box.

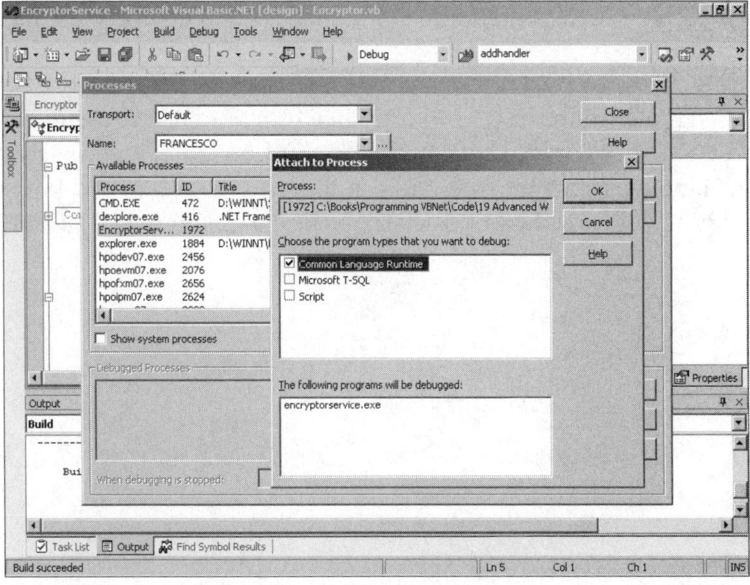

Figure 19-13. Attaching the Visual Studio debugger to a running Windows service application.

In the Processes dialog box, you can decide what happens when the debugging is stopped: you can choose the Detach From This Process option (in which case, the service will continue to run when the debugger stops) and the Terminate This Process option (in which case, the service will terminate). Finally click Close to start debugging the service application.

You can now set one or more breakpoints, as you would in a regular application. For example, you might set a breakpoint at the beginning of the FileSystemWatcher1_Created procedure to trace code in the service application and see what happens when a new file is created in the directory being monitored.

When debugging a service in this fashion, you should keep one limitation in mind: you can attach a debugger only to a service that's already running. For this reason, you can't debug the code in the Main or OnStart procedure. In theory, you might add a pause in the OnStart method to give you the time necessary to set up the debugger immediately after the service is started; however, Windows imposes a 30-second timeout on all attempts to start a service. If your debugging chores take longer than that, the system assumes that the service can't run.

One way to debug the code in the OnStart method is to add another "dummy" service to your service project. You can therefore start the dummy process so that its process appears in the list of processes that can be debugged in Visual Studio. At this point, you can attach the debugger to that process and trace through all its initialization code. Even in this case, however, you're subject to the 30-second timeout mentioned in the preceding paragraph.

All the code samples you've seen so far have focused on language features, the user interface, or some other functionality of Windows programs. However, the majority of real-world applications deal with databases, and the .NET Framework has much to offer in that field as well. Read on to learn more about how you read and update databases using the new ADO.NET classes.

Part V

Database Applications

Front
Top
Left
Back

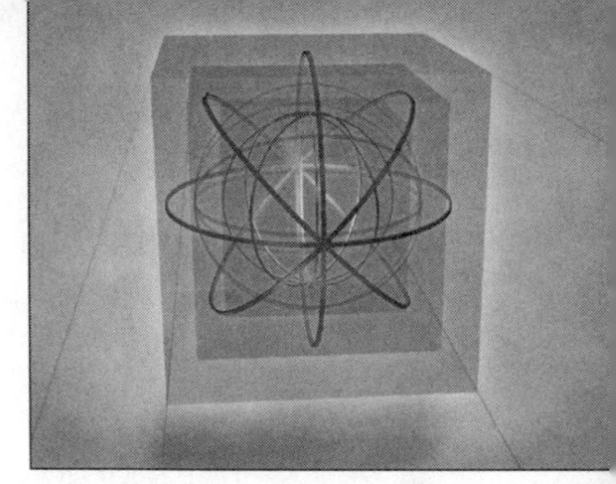

20

ADO.NET in Connected Mode

It's time to get your hands dirty with database programming. If you're a .NET developer, this means writing code against a few classes in System.Data and its child namespaces, which are collectively known as ADO.NET. These classes and their methods let you retrieve data from Microsoft SQL Server or a more generic OLE DB data source, process it, and update the original database tables.

ADO.NET is a vast topic, so I decided to address it in two chapters to keep it manageable. This chapter introduces ADO.NET and illustrates how to use it in a connected mode scenario—that is, while keeping the database connection open—whereas in Chapter 21, I focus on using ADO.NET in disconnected mode. In addition, some sections in Chapter 22 explore the ADO.NET features that are related to XML.

The Transition to ADO.NET

Generally speaking, ADO.NET is remarkably simpler than ActiveX Data Objects (ADO), both because its object model is more straightforward and because it has a narrower field of application. ADO.NET doesn't support server-side cursors, so Visual Basic .NET developers don't have to worry about table locks, or at least not as much as Visual Basic 6 programmers using ADO have to. At first glance, the lack of server-side cursors might be perceived as a defect, but in the next chapter you'll discover that the ADO.NET way of doing things is far superior to the ADO way in terms of performance and scalability.

ADO.NET has a novel approach to data processing, which might appear limited when compared with ADO's. For this reason, I believe that the best introduction to ADO.NET is an explanation of why Microsoft decided to switch from the old programming model to the new one.

The Limits of ADO

In my opinion, ADO is a great technology, much superior to whatever came before it, such as Data Access Objects (DAO) and Remote Data Objects (RDO). However, in some areas ADO clearly shows its limits:

- Because it's based on COM, ADO can't be used on any platform other than Windows. Moreover, the native binary of ADO data sent over the wire is in a proprietary format, which impedes interoperability with other systems, even for simply exchanging data.
- The support of XML in ADO is little more than an afterthought: XML is just an output format, and the schema used for exporting XML data has actually changed from ADO 2.1 to ADO 2.5. In practice, you can't use XML as a means to exchange data with other platforms, a feature that would have been a (partial) solution to the interoperability problem mentioned in the preceding point.
- Although ADO promotes (and permits, to an extent) the adoption of heterogeneous data sources—such as database tables, directory entries, and simple text files—thanks to the abstraction level provided by OLE DB providers, ADO is clearly based on a programming model that doesn't account for the countless ways data can be stored in nonrelational formats, such as the hierarchical structure implied by XML.
- ADO lets you work with data from different sources in the same application but provides no support for creating links and relationships among them. For example, if you have a database of customers running on a mainframe and a database of sales agents on a SQL Server running on a Windows workstation, ADO lets you read and update both databases but doesn't let you easily associate customers with agents.
- ADO is an object-oriented wrapper on OLE DB, a lower-level technology that's unusable in Visual Basic and script languages such as VBScript. This extra layer causes overhead that might have a negative impact on the performance of applications (even though in most cases this overhead is admittedly negligible).

- Even if ADO is based on COM and is therefore language-agnostic, in practice using it from C++ is more difficult than it should be. As a matter of fact, most C++ developers prefer to access the OLE DB layer, also because of its superior performance.

The last point might not be perceived as a serious issue by C++ developers, but clearly this limitation is unacceptable in the .NET world—which promotes equivalence among all programming languages.

Introducing ADO.NET

ADO.NET is revolutionary by many measures. Nevertheless, if you're familiar with ADO it won't take much effort and time to learn ADO.NET and become as productive as you were using Visual Basic 6.

Major Changes from ADO

From an architectural perspective, the most important change from "classic" ADO is that ADO.NET doesn't rely on OLE DB providers and uses .NET managed providers instead. A .NET Data Provider works as a bridge between your application and the data source, so you see that it can be considered an evolution of the OLE DB provider concept. However, the inner implementation details are very different. ADO.NET and .NET managed data providers don't use COM at all, so a .NET application can access data without undergoing any performance penalty deriving from the switch from managed and unmanaged code. (Unfortunately, this isn't 100 percent true at the time of this writing because you still need COM to access any data source other than SQL Server, but this problem will be gone when new managed providers are released.)

From a programmer's perspective, the most important difference between ADO.NET and ADO is that dynamic and keyset server-side cursors aren't supported any longer. ADO.NET supports only forward-only, read-only resultsets (known as firehose cursors, even though they aren't really a type of cursor) and disconnected resultsets. Server-side cursors have been dumped because they consume resources on the server and create a large number of locks on database tables. Taken together, these two factors can hinder application scalability more than anything else.

Personally, I would have preferred a less drastic alteration because server-side cursors are easy to use and are useful in many cases—for example, I use server-side cursors for administrative tasks that run once in a while. But I agree that too many developers have used server-side cursors to create applications that perform poorly and don't scale well. Fortunately, ADO.NET uses an extensible architecture, and Microsoft has announced support for server-side cursors at a later time. In the meantime, you can still use server-side cursors through the ADO library, which you can access through the COM Interoperability layer of .NET. You go through an additional layer, and performance will be less than optimal, but this condition shouldn't be a serious problem because you would use these cursors only in exceptional cases.

Retrieving Data

Many of the concepts you learned in ADO have survived the .NET revolution and are still valid today, even though classes and their methods often have different names and syntax.

For example, ADO.NET exposes a Connection object that's conceptually identical to the ADO Connection object. Before you can perform any operation on a data source, you *must* open a Connection object that points to that data source, and you must close the Connection object when you don't need it any longer. Fortunately, Microsoft didn't change the syntax of the connection string, so you can reuse all the arguments you used with ADO under Visual Basic 6. Creating a correct connection string was probably the hardest part of establishing a connection, so this instance of backward compatibility will make most programmers happy. (For sure, it made *me* happy.)

Of the two ways that ADO.NET provides for dealing with data, forward-only, read-only resultsets give you the best performance, as all experienced ADO developers know. In ADO.NET, you create this type of resultset by creating a Command object for the connection in question, defining the SELECT query to be executed, and finally performing an ExecuteReader method.

The second way to retrieve data from a data source is conceptually similar to the way you work with disconnected ADO recordsets: you open a connection, retrieve a block of data and store it on the client, and then close the connection to release the server-side resources associated with it. After you have downloaded the data to the client, you can perform all types of processing on it, including modifying values, adding new rows, and deleting existing rows. You can then reopen the connection and reconcile your local data with the actual data source. This approach to data handling is exactly the same that you follow when working with ADO client-side recordsets in optimistic batch update mode and has proved to be the key to most scalable client/server applications.

The similarities with ADO stop here, however. ADO uses the Recordset object for accessing all types of data—data stored both in a server-side cursor and in a client-side cursor—whereas ADO.NET introduces a new object, the DataSet, whose specific purpose is to store and process client-side data. You can think of a DataSet as a recordset on steroids: it can hold multiple resultsets (instead of just one), it can create relationships between resultsets, and it can export and import data from multiple data sources. A better way to think of the DataSet is to consider it a scaled-down relational database that you keep on the client and that contains a local (and partial) copy of data read from one or more data sources (not necessarily databases).

An important feature of the DataSet object is that it's *completely* disconnected from any particular data source, both physically and logically. For example, you might fill a single DataSet with a resultset coming from SQL Server, a resultset coming from Microsoft Access, a third resultset coming from an XML stream, and maybe a table of data that you build in code. Then you can create relations among these different resultsets, navigate through them with ease, and maybe use the DataSet to update an Oracle table. The independence from a specific data source is achieved by means of the DataAdapter object, the component that actually reads data into a DataSet and is capable of updating a data source with the data that the client application has added or modified. Compare these features with the limitations of ADO disconnected recordsets—which can store only a single resultset and update only the same data source from which data had been read—and you'll appreciate the extra flexibility that the DataSet gives you.

In the transition from ADO disconnected recordsets to the more powerful DataSet object, something has been lost, however. First, ADO.NET doesn't support the notion of hierarchical resultsets as ADO does, although this isn't a serious problem because ADO hierarchical recordsets were difficult to use and not flexible enough for most real-world applications (even though they looked so nice in demonstrations!). In my opinion, the relational capabilities of the DataSet object will keep you from pining for ADO hierarchical recordsets. The second noteworthy limitation is that ADO.NET offers less built-in support for updates than ADO does, so you have to write more code to reconcile a modified DataSet with the data source. Nevertheless, the ADO.NET approach is superior in terms of flexibility and performance because you're in control of virtually every detail of the synchronization process.

New XML Features

As I mentioned already, ADO.NET offers superb support for XML sources. As a matter of fact, you can consider XML as the native format for ADO.NET data, even though data is stored in memory in a different format to maximize throughput. You can define the schema of the imported or exported XML stream by using XSD schemas, a feature that simplifies interoperability with other platforms and data sources. For example, you can have a .NET application read and update a data source residing on a non-Windows system by using XML as a common denominator between the two worlds.

The tight integration with XML means that you can process your data according to the familiar relational model by using the DataSet object or according to the hierarchical model promoted by XML when it is more convenient to do so. By comparison, Visual Basic 6 developers using ADO don't have this choice and must opt for one of the two models early in the development stage.

Being able to exchange data in XML format also allows you to overcome problems that occur when sending information over the Internet. In theory, you can send an ADO resultset through the Internet using the Remote Data Services programming model. (See Chapter 19 of my *Programming Microsoft Visual Basic 6* on the companion CD.) In practice, however, sending binary data over the Internet is easier said than done if there's a firewall in the middle. With ADO.NET, you can send plain XML data as text by means of the HTTP protocol, so exchanging data over a firewall isn't a problem any longer. You can send an entire DataSet object and all the data it contains as XML and rebuild it on the target machine.

ADO.NET also supports strongly typed datasets, which simplify how your code refers to tables and fields in a resultset. This feature is built on XML, which is the reason I mention it in this section. You see the convenience of strongly typed DataSet objects when you compare the usual way of referring to a column in a given table,

```
id = myDataSet.Tables("Authors").Fields("au_id").Value
```

with the more concise (even though not faster) code you can write against a strongly typed DataSet that exposes all the tables as nested classes and all the fields as properties:

```
id = myDataSet.Authors.au_id
```

.NET Data Providers

.NET data providers play the same role that OLE DB providers play under ADO: they enable your application to read and write data stored in a data source. ADO.NET currently supports three providers:

- **The OLE DB .NET Data Provider** This provider lets you access a data source for which an OLE DB provider exists, although at the expense of a switch from managed to unmanaged code and the performance degradation that ensues.
- **The SQL Server .NET Data Provider** This provider has been specifically written to access SQL Server 7.0 or later versions using Tabular Data Stream (TDS) as the communication medium. TDS is SQL Server's native protocol, so you can expect this provider to give you better performance than the OLE DB Data Provider. Additionally, the SQL Server .NET Data Provider exposes SQL Server–specific features, such as named transactions and support for the FOR XML clause in SELECT queries.

- **The ODBC .NET Data Provider** This provider works as a bridge toward an ODBC source, so in theory you can use it to access any source for which an ODBC driver exists. However, as of this writing, this provider officially supports only the Access, SQL Server, and Oracle ODBC drivers, so there's no clear advantage in using it instead of the OLE DB .NET Data Provider. The convenience of this provider will be more evident when more ODBC drivers are added to the list of those officially supported.

> **Note** I won't cover the ODBC .NET Data Provider in this book.

Which Provider to Choose

Because of its superior performance, you should use the SQL Server .NET Data Provider whenever you work with SQL Server 7.0 or later versions. The only requirement for this provider is that you install Microsoft Data Access Components (MDAC) version 2.6 or later.

If you don't work with SQL Server 7.0 or later, you must use the OLE DB Data Provider. Unfortunately, as of this writing, the OLE DB Data Provider has a few limitations, the most serious of which are the following:

- It's guaranteed to be compatible with only the following OLE DB providers: Microsoft OLE DB Provider for SQL Server (SQLOLEDB), Microsoft OLE DB Provider for Oracle (MSDAORA), and OLE DB Provider for Microsoft Jet (Microsoft.Jet.OLEDB.4.0). It might be compatible with other OLE DB providers, but at this time Microsoft assures its operation with only the aforementioned providers.
- It doesn't support the OLE DB 2.5 interfaces, and therefore, it doesn't work with OLE DB providers that require these interfaces. The group of incompatible providers includes the Microsoft OLE DB Provider for Microsoft Exchange and the Microsoft OLE DB Provider for Internet Publishing.
- It doesn't work with the OLE DB provider for ODBC sources (MSDASQL). This is a major obstacle that might prevent the adoption of ADO.NET in many cases. As mentioned previously, Microsoft is working on an ODBC .NET Data Provider: it's currently being beta tested but might be released by the time Visual Studio .NET is published.

If you want to reach a data source that isn't compatible with the OLE DB .NET Data Provider, you must give up ADO.NET and read data using the good old ADO object model through the COM Interoperability layer (and accept the performance hit that will ensue). Even in this case, however, you can use the ADO.NET DataSet object to work in disconnect mode. Microsoft engineers anticipated this situation and extended the OleDbDataAdapter object with a Fill method that takes an ADO Recordset as an argument so that you can easily open an ADO connection, read some data into an ADO Recordset, and then move the data into a DataSet to process in disconnected mode.

Using ADO via COM Interop

Before we dive into ADO.NET and its object model, I want to briefly mention using classic ADO objects through the COM Interop layer. You might need to do this to accomplish the few things that aren't possible in ADO.NET yet, such as the following:

- Working with server-side keysets and dynamic cursors
- Accessing an OLE DB provider that the OLE DB .NET Data Provider doesn't support yet
- Using the Data Definition Language (DDL) and security features of the ADO Extensions for DDL and Security (ADOX) library, none of which is supported in ADO.NET

As you know, server-side cursors generally should be avoided, but in some cases it's OK to use them. For example, you might have an administrative utility (or an ASP.NET page that's accessible only to the site administrator) that the user runs once in a while. Using a server-side cursor can save you coding time without having an impact on overall scalability and performance.

Using ADO objects is actually very simple because this library has been installed in the global assembly cache (GAC) already, together with the .NET Framework, so it's just a matter of adding a reference to it. You can add a reference to the library by invoking the Add Reference command on the Project menu and selecting the adodb component on the .NET tab (and not the COM tab) of the Add Reference dialog box. The following code shows how to use the ADO Connection and Recordset objects to create a server-side keyset cursor and use it to modify a database table using optimistic locking:

```
' Open an ADO Connection.
Dim adoCn As New ADODB.Connection()
adoCn.Open("Provider=SQLOLEDB.1;Integrated Security=SSPI;" _
    & "Persist Security Info=False;Initial Catalog=pubs;Data Source=(local)")
```

```
' Open an ADO Recordset.
Dim adoRs As New ADODB.Recordset()
adoRs.Open("SELECT * FROM Publishers", adoCn, _
    ADODB.CursorTypeEnum.adOpenKeyset, ADODB.LockTypeEnum.adLockOptimistic)

' Convert Publisher names to uppercase.
Do Until adoRs.EOF
    adoRs("pub_name").Value = UCase(adoRs("pub_name").Value)
    adoRs.MoveNext()
Loop
' Close objects to release resources.
adoRs.Close()
adoCn.Close()
```

Even though it looks as if it's using the original COM objects, the preceding code is actually referencing .NET wrappers around the original ADO Connection and Recordset objects, so you must manually close them to release the associated resources as soon as possible. If you omit the last two statements, the connection will be kept open until the next garbage collection, which is something you should avoid.

You can't use the adodb library installed in the GAC to exploit the DDL and security features of ADOX. Instead you must add a reference to the Microsoft ADO Ext. 2.7 For DDL And Security library, from the COM tab of the Add Reference dialog box. The following code uses the ADOX library to list all the tables in a SQL Server database:

```
' Open an ADO connection to SQL Server.
Dim adoCn As New ADODB.Connection()
adoCn.Open("Provider=SQLOLEDB.1;Integrated Security=SSPI;" _
    & "Persist Security Info=False;Initial Catalog=pubs;Data Source=(local)")
' Create an ADOX Catalog on that connection.
Dim cat As New ADOX.Catalog()
cat.ActiveConnection = adoCn
' Enumerate all the database tables and their columns.
Dim tbl As ADOX.Table, col As ADOX.Column
For Each tbl In cat.Tables
    Debug.WriteLine(tbl.Name)
    For Each col in tbl.Columns
        Debug.WriteLine("    " & col.Name)
    Next
Next
' Close the connection, and release resources.
adoCn.Close()
```

You can learn more about the ADOX library and its object model in Chapter 13 of my *Programming Microsoft Visual Basic 6*, provided on the companion CD.

The ADO.NET Object Model

It's time to have a closer look at the individual objects that make up the ADO.NET architecture and that I've illustrated in Figure 20-1. You see that objects have been divided into two groups: the objects included in the .NET Data Provider and those that belong to the ADO.NET disconnected architecture. (In practice, the second group includes only the DataSet and its secondary objects.)

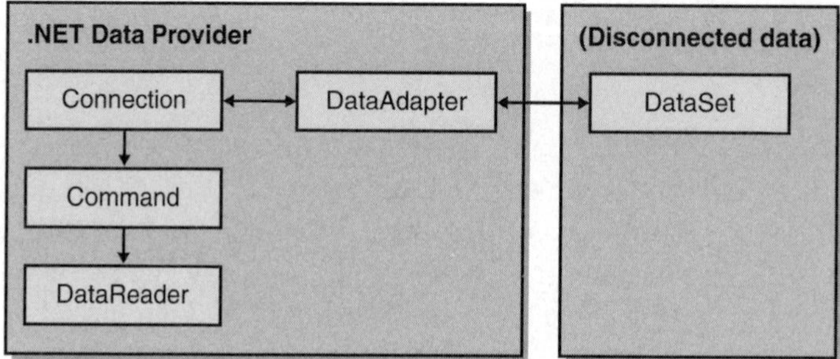

Figure 20-1. The relationships among the main ADO.NET objects.

ADO.NET Objects at a Glance

The Connection object has the same function it has under ADO: establishing a connection to the data source. Like its ADO counterpart, it has the ConnectionString property, the Open and Close methods, and the ability to begin a transaction using the BeginTransaction method. The Execute method isn't supported, and the ADO.NET Connection object lacks the ability to send a command to the database.

The Command object lets you query the database, send a command to it, or invoke one of its stored procedures. You can perform these actions by using one of the object's Execute*xxxx* methods. For example, you use the ExecuteNonQuery method to send an action query to the database (for example, an INSERT or DELETE SQL statement) and an ExecuteReader method to perform a SELECT query that returns a resultset. Other properties let you set the command timeout and prepare the parameters for a call to a stored procedure. You must manually associate a Command object with the Connection object that has been previously connected to the data source, as you do under ADO (even though the syntax is different).

The DataReader object is the object returned by the ExecuteReader method of the Command object and represents a forward-only, read-only resultset. A new row of results becomes available each time you invoke the DataReader's Read method, after which you can query each individual field using the GetValue method or one of the strongly typed Get*xxxx* methods, such as GetString or GetFloat. Remember that you can't update the database by means of a DataReader object.

The DataSet object is the main object in the ADO.NET disconnected architecture. It works as a sort of small relational database that resides on the client and is completely unrelated to any specific database. It consists of a collection of DataTable objects, with each DataTable object holding a distinct resultset (typically the result of a query to a different database table). A DataTable object contains a collection of DataRow objects, each one holding data coming from a different row in the result. A DataSet also contains a collection of DataRelation objects, in which each item corresponds to a relationship between different DataTable objects, much like the relationships you have between the tables of a relational database. These relations let your code navigate among tables in the same DataSet using a simple and very effective syntax.

The DataAdapter object works as a bridge between the Connection object and the DataSet object. Its Fill method moves data from the database to the client-side DataSet, whereas its Update method moves data in the opposite direction and updates the database with the rows that your application has added, modified, or deleted from the DataSet.

ADO.NET Namespaces

I must clarify one point: most of the names described in the preceding section—more precisely, the names of the objects in the .NET Data Provider portion of the figure—are generic names that you never use as is in your code. Not only do different .NET data providers use different namespaces, but they also use different names for these objects:

- The System.Data namespace gathers the ADO.NET objects that don't belong to a specific data provider. For example, this namespace contains the DataSet object and all its secondary objects, such as DataTable, DataRow, and DataRelation. The System.Data namespace also contains several ADO.NET interfaces.
- The System.Data.Common namespace contains the DataAdapter objects and other virtual classes. These classes are used as base classes for several objects in the namespaces that follow. You rarely have to reference items from this namespace in your code.
- The System.Data.OleDb namespace contains the objects associated with the OLE DB .NET Data Provider, such as OleDbConnection, OleDbCommand, OleDbDataReader, and OleDbDataAdapter.
- The System.Data.SqlClient namespace contains the objects associated with the SQL Server .NET Data Provider, such as SqlConnection, SqlCommand, SqlDataReader, and SqlDataAdapter.

Even if you never explicitly use the DataAdapter object in your code, it's convenient to think in terms of the abstract DataAdapter class because both the OleDbDataAdapter and SqlDataAdapter objects inherit from it and therefore expose the same methods and exhibit the same behavior.

Similar objects in different providers share a common interface rather than inherit from the same class. For example, the OleDbConnection and SqlConnection objects implement the IDBConnection interface. Similarly, the OleDbCommand and SqlCommand objects implement the IDBCommand interface, and the IDBDataReader interface is the common trait between the OleDbDataReader and the SqlDataReader object. As you'll see in the next section, this information is very useful in some circumstances.

Note To keep the code as concise as possible, all the code samples in this chapter assume that you have added the following Imports statements at the top of your source files:

```
Imports System.Data
Imports System.Data.OleDb
Imports System.Data.SqlClient
```

Database Independence with ADO.NET

Classic ADO promotes the reuse of data-related code from different data sources by having the Connection, Recordset, and Command objects work equally well with any data source. For example, the only point in code at which you must decide the actual data source you're using is when you build the connection string. Because all the ADO objects work with any data source, you're able to write programs that work with any data source for which an OLE DB provider exists just by providing a suitable connection string.

This approach works well in practice with small- or medium-size database applications. For example, I developed the source code of my VB-2-The-Max Web site (*www.vb2themax.com*) using Access because I wanted to take advantage of Access's ease of use and reporting capabilities. The real production site runs on SQL Server, however, and the only point at which the two versions differ is where the code defines the connection string.

When you turn to large-scale applications, however, ADO's database-agnostic approach shows its greatest limitation: you can't take advantage of the specific features of a given database. ADO partly copes with this limitation by having its main objects expose a Properties collection, which is filled with the dynamic properties that are specific to each provider. For example, you can use

ADO's dynamic properties to decide how the ODBC driver behaves when login information isn't complete (the Prompt property) or to set an Access password (the Jet OLEDB:Database Password property). However, dynamic properties don't allow you to execute commands against the database, so you can't access all the peculiar features of a given database.

ADO.NET solves this problem in an ingenious way. On the one hand, each provider uses a different object to perform database-related tasks, so Microsoft (or the author of the data provider) can enhance each object with specific methods and properties that are meaningful only to that database. For example, the SqlConnection object has the PacketSize and ServerVersions properties (which are missing in the OleDbConnection object) and a BeginTransaction overloaded method that lets you create named transactions (which can't be used with the OLE DB .NET Data Provider).

On the other hand, because the objects in a specific .NET data provider must inherit from an ADO.NET base class or implement one of the IDb*xxxx* interfaces, you can create polymorphic code that works equally well with any provider. Here's a fragment of code that works well with either a SQL Server connection or a connection to an OLE DB source:

```
Dim cn As IDBConnection

' (UseSqlServerProvider is a Boolean defined and assigned elsewhere.)
If UseSqlServerProvider Then
    ' Create a connection using the SQL Server provider.
    ' (SqlPubsConnString is a string defined and initialized elsewhere.)
    cn = New SqlConnection(SqlPubsConnString)
Else
    ' Create a connection using the OLE DB provider.
    ' (BiblioConnString is a string defined and initialized elsewhere.)
    cn = New OleDbConnection(BiblioConnString)
End If

' (The following code works well with both providers.)
' Open the connection.
cn.Open
⋮
' Close the connection.
cn.Close
```

Even if the preceding code snippet is incomplete—for one thing, it doesn't show how to define the connection strings for the two providers—it should prove the point I want to make: ADO.NET lets you achieve database independence through common base classes and interfaces but without renouncing specific and more powerful features of each individual database engine. You pay for this extra flexibility in terms of the larger amount of code you have to write, however.

By comparison, ADO offers almost-free database-agnostic code and doesn't introduce any complexity into the code you write, but it prevents you from exploiting the best features of specific databases. Because the number of applications that really need to be database independent is relatively small, I believe that the ADO.NET approach is more reasonable because it delivers the best results in terms of performance and flexibility and adds complexity only to those few applications for which database independence is a requirement.

Even if you aren't writing a database-agnostic program but you often work with both providers, you might want to write procedures that you can easily reuse in different applications. In the "Writing Provider-Agnostic Code" section in Chapter 21, I illustrate a few techniques that you can use to pursue this goal.

The Connection Object

Whether you work in connected or in disconnected mode, the first action you need to perform when working with a data source is to open a connection to it. In ADO.NET terms, this means that you create a Connection object that connects to the specific database.

The Connection object is similar to the ADO object of the same name, so you'll feel immediately at ease with the new ADO.NET object if you have any experience with ADO programming. Table 20-1 summarizes the properties, methods, and events of the ADO.NET Connection object and indicates the few members that are supported solely by either the OLE DB or the SQL Server .NET Data Provider.

Table 20-1 Properties, Methods, and Events of the Connection Object

Category	Name	Description
Properties	ConnectionString	The string used to connect to the data source.
	ConnectionTimeout	The number of seconds after which an unsuccessful connection times out. This property is read-only because you set this value in the ConnectionString property. (Default is 15 seconds.)
	Database	Returns the name of the database, as specified in the ConnectionString property (read-only).
	DataSource	Returns the name of the Data Source attribute, as specified in the ConnectionString property (read-only).

Table 20-1 Properties, Methods, and Events of the Connection Object *(continued)*

Category	Name	Description
	ServerVersion	Returns the version of the connected server in the format *xx.yy.zzzz*, or an empty string if this information can't be retrieved. (The provider can also append a product-specific version string after the version number.)
	State	Returns the current state of the database. Can be an enumerated value in the following list: Closed, Connecting, Open, Executing, Fetching, and Broken.
(OleDb provider only)	Provider	Returns the value of the Provider attribute, as specified in the ConnectionString property (read-only).
(SQL Server provider only)	PacketSize	Returns the size in bytes of network packets used to communicate with SQL Server, as specified in the ConnectionString property. It can be any value in the range 512 to 32767. (Default is 8192.)
	WorkstationId	Returns a string that identifies the client, as specified by the Workstation ID attribute in the ConnectionString property.
Methods	Open	Opens the connection.
	Close	Closes the connection and releases all related resources.
	BeginTransaction	Begins a database transaction, using the isolation level specified in the optional argument.
	ChangeDatabase	Changes the name of the database for the current connection.
	CreateCommand	Creates a Command object related to the current connection.
(OleDb provider only)	GetOleDbSchemaTable	Returns the schema table and associated restriction columns of the schema whose GUID is passed as an argument.
	ReleaseObjectPool	A shared method that says the OLE DB connection pool can be released when the last connection is closed.
Events	StateChange	Fires when the State property changes.
	InfoMesssage	Fires when the database or the provider sends an informational or a warning message.

Setting the ConnectionString Property

The key property of the Connection object is ConnectionString, a string that defines the type of the database you're connecting to, its location, and other semicolon-delimited attributes. When you work with the OleDbConnection object, the connection string matches the connection string that you use with the ADO Connection object. Such a string typically contains the following information:

- The Provider attribute, which specifies the name of the underlying OLE DB Provider used to connect to the data. As of this writing, the only valid values are SQLOLEDB (the OLE DB provider for Microsoft SQL Server), Microsoft.Jet.OLEDB.4.0 (the OLE DB provider for Microsoft Access), and MSDAORA (the OLE DB provider for Oracle).
- The Data Source attribute, which specifies where the database is. It can be the path to an Access database or the name of the machine on which the SQL Server or the Oracle database is located.
- The User ID and Password attributes, which specify the user name and the password of a valid account for the database.
- The Initial Catalog attribute, which specifies the name of the database when you're connecting to a SQL Server or an Oracle data source.

Once you've set the ConnectionString property correctly, you can open the connection by invoking the Open method:

```
Dim BiblioConnString As String = "Provider=Microsoft.Jet.OLEDB.4.0;" _
    & "Data Source=C:\Program Files\Microsoft Visual Studio\VB98\BIBLIO.MDB;"
' Open the Biblio.mdb database.
Dim cn As New OledbConnection()
cn.ConnectionString = BiblioConnString
cn.Open()
```

You can make your code more concise by passing the connection string to the Connection object's constructor method:

```
' Another, more concise, way to open the Biblio.mdb database.
Dim cn As New OledbConnection(BiblioConnString)
cn.Open()
```

The same description applies as well to the SqlConnection object, with just one difference: you must omit the Provider attribute from the connection string. In fact, you don't need this attribute in this case because you can connect only to a SQL Server database if you use the SQL Server .NET Data Provider. Also note that you can specify **(local)** as the Data Source attribute if you're connecting to the SQL Server on the local machine:

```
Dim SqlPubsConnString As String = "Data Source=(local); User ID=sa;" _
    & "Initial Catalog=pubs"
Dim cn As New SqlConnection(SqlPubsConnString)
cn.Open()
```

The connection string can include other attributes. For example, the Connection Timeout attribute sets the number of seconds after which the attempt to open the connection fails with an error. (The default value is 15 seconds.) After you open the connection, you can query the current value of this timeout with the ConnectionTimeout property:

```
' Specify a longer timeout when connecting to Pubs.
Dim cn As New SqlConnection("Data Source=(local); User ID=sa;" _
    & "Initial Catalog=pubs;Connection Timeout=30")
cn.Open()
Debug.WriteLine(cn.ConnectionTimeout)       ' => 30
```

Other values that you pass in the connection string depend on the specific OLE DB provider to which you're connecting. For example, the provider Microsoft.Jet.OLEDB.4.0 supports attributes for setting the database password or specifying the system database that contains information about groups and users. (For additional information, read Chapters 13 and 14 of *Programming Microsoft Visual Basic 6*, on the companion CD).

When you're working with the SQL Server .NET Data Provider, you can specify two additional attributes in the connection string: Packet Size and Workstation ID. The former value sets the size of the network packet used to communicate with SQL Server; the latter is a string that can be later used to identify the client. (Read the description of the related PacketSize and WorkstationId properties in Table 20-1.) The Packet Size attribute is sometimes useful for optimizing the flux of data to and from SQL Server. For example, you might increase it if your application deals with large BLOB fields (such as images) or decrease it if you often query the server for a small amount of data.

```
' Optimize the connection for large BLOB fields.
Dim cn As New SqlConnection("Data Source=(local); User ID=sa;" _
    & "Initial Catalog=pubs;Packet Size=32767")
cn.Open()
Debug.WriteLine(cn.PacketSize)       ' => 32767
```

Note All the code routines in this chapter open a connection to either the Biblio.mdb database using the OLE DB .NET Data Provider (which comes with Visual Studio 6 and Access) or the Pubs database using the SQL Server .NET Data Provider (which is installed with any version of SQL Server). To keep code as concise as possible, the demo application defines these three connection strings at the module level:

```
' For Biblio.mdb using the OLE DB .NET Data Provider
Public BiblioConnString As String = "Provider=" _
    & "Microsoft.Jet.OLEDB.4.0;Data Source=" & _
    "C:\Program Files\Microsoft Visual Studio\VB98\Biblio.mdb"

' For SQL Server's Pubs using the OLE DB .NET Data Provider
Public OleDbPubsConnString As String = "Provider=" _
    & "SQLOLEDB.1;Data Source=.;" _
    & "Integrated Security=SSPI:Initial Catalog=Pubs"

' For Pubs using the SQL Server .NET Data Provider
Public SqlPubsConnString As String = "Data Source=.;" _
    & "Integrated Security=SSPI:Initial Catalog=Pubs"
```

Obviously, you should edit these connection strings to match your system's configuration. For example, you should change the Data Source value in BiblioConnString to assign it the actual path of Biblio.mdb.

Opening and Closing the Connection

You've already seen that the Open method takes no arguments, unlike the Open method of the ADO Connection object:

```
Dim cn As New OledbConnection(BiblioConnString)
cn.Open()
```

The State Property and the StateChange Event

The State property is a bit-coded field that indicates the current state of the database connection. It can be the combination of one or more of the following ConnectionState enumerated values: Closed, Connecting, Open, Executing, Fetching, and Broken. You typically check the State property to ensure that you're opening a closed connection or closing an open connection, as in this snippet:

```
' Close the connection only if it was opened.
If (cn.State And ConnectionState.Open) <> 0 Then
    cn.Close()
End If
```

Whenever the State property changes from Open to Close or vice versa, the Connection object fires a StateChange event:

```
Dim WithEvents cn As SqlConnection

Private Sub cn_StateChange(ByVal sender As Object, _
    ByVal e As System.Data.StateChangeEventArgs) Handles cn.StateChange
    ' Show the status of the connection in a Label control.
    If (e.CurrentState And ConnectionState.Open) <> 0 Then
        lblStatus.Text = "The connection has been opened"
    ElseIf e.CurrentState = ConnectionState.Closed Then
        lblStatus.Text = "The connection has been closed"
    End If
End Sub
```

Note that ConnectionState.Closed is equal to 0, so you can't use the And bitwise operator to test this state, unlike all the other values. Be careful not to throw an exception from inside this event handler because it would be returned to the code that issued the Open or Close method.

Although it's a good habit to test the state of the database before performing any operation on it, ADO.NET is much more forgiving than classic ADO in some cases. For example, you can execute the Close method of the Connection object (or any other ADO.NET object that exposes this method) without throwing any exception if the object is already closed:

```
' This statement never throws an exception.
cn.Close()
```

Dealing with Errors

As in ADO, you should protect your code from unexpected errors when attempting a connection to a database as well as while processing data coming from the database itself. However, when working with ADO.NET you have an added responsibility: because of the garbage collection mechanism intrinsic in .NET, the connection isn't automatically closed when the Connection object goes out of scope. In this case, in fact, the connection is closed in the Finalize protected method of the Connection object, and you know that the garbage collector might call this method several minutes after the object goes out of scope. (This situation is just another form of the *nondeterministic* finalization problem that I discuss in Chapter 4.)

Because an error can occur virtually anywhere you're working in a database, you should protect your code with a Try block and ensure that you close the connection in the Finally section in an orderly way:

```
Dim cn As New SqlConnection(SqlPubsConnString)
Try
    cn.Open()
    ' Process the data here.
    ⋮
Catch ex As Exception
    MessageBox.Show(ex.Message)
Finally
    ' Ensure that the connection is closed.
    ' (It doesn't throw an exception even if the Open method failed.)
    cn.Close()
End Try
```

Most of the exceptions that you catch when working with the OLE DB .NET Data Provider are of class OleDbException. In addition to all the members it has in common with other exception classes, this class exposes the Errors collection that contains one or more OleDbError objects, each one describing how the original error in the database (for example, a violation of the referential integrity rules) has been reported to the many software layers that sit between the database and the application. (This concept is the same one on which the Errors collection of the ADO Connection object is based.) The following code shows how you can explore the OleDbException.Errors collection to show details about the caught exception:

```
' Run a query that references a table that doesn't exist.
Dim cmd As New OleDbCommand("UPDATE xyz SET id=1", cn)

Try
    cmd.ExecuteNonQuery()
Catch ex As OleDbException
    ' An OleDbException has occurred - display details.
    Dim i As Integer, msg As String
    For i = 0 To ex.errors.Count - 1
        Dim oledbErr As OleDbError = ex.Errors(i)
        msg = "Message = " & oledbErr.Message & ControlChars.CrLf
        msg &= "Source = " & oledbErr.Source & ControlChars.CrLf
        msg &= "NativeError = " & oledbErr.NativeError & ControlChars.CrLf
        msg &= "SQLState = " & oledbErr.SQLState & ControlChars.CrLf
```

```
    Next
    MessageBox.Show(msg)

Catch ex As Exception
    ' A generic exception has occurred.
    MessageBox.Show(ex.Message)
Finally
    ' Close the connection.
    cn.Close()
End Try
```

The SqlException object also exposes an Errors collection, containing one or more SqlError objects. The SqlError object doesn't support the NativeError and SQLState properties but exposes a few members that aren't in OleDbError:

- **Server** The name of the SQL Server that generated the error
- **Procedure** The name of the stored procedure or remote procedure call that generated the error
- **LineNumber** The line number within the T-SQL batch or stored procedure where the error occurred
- **Number** A number that identifies the type of error
- **Class** The severity level of the error, in the range 1 through 25

Severity level values in the range 1 through 10 are informational and indicate problems deriving from mistakes in the information the user entered. Values in the range 11 through 16 are caused by the user and can be corrected by the user. Severity levels 17 and higher indicate serious software or hardware errors. In general, errors with severity levels equal to 20 or higher automatically close the connection. For this reason, you should always test the State property of the Connection object when an exception is thrown, regardless of the data provider you're working with.

Opening a Database Asynchronously

One of the great innovations of ADO was its ability to perform a few methods—most notably, the opening of a connection and the querying of data—in an asynchronous fashion, that is, without blocking the current application. Asynchronous operations were pretty difficult to set up correctly, but they were a great tool in the hands of experienced programmers.

Don't look for asynchronous options in ADO.NET because you won't find any. Does this mean that ADO.NET is less capable than good old ADO? Of course not: it only means that asynchronous operation support is offered at the

.NET Framework level through asynchronous delegates. (See Chapter 13.) Moving the support for asynchronous operations out of ADO.NET makes the object model cleaner and simpler, and even more flexible dealing with asynchronous operations. In fact, you can perform *any* ADO.NET operation, not just a few methods, while the main program does something else.

The following code snippet shows how you can open a connection asynchronously. You can use the same code pattern for any other database operation involving the Connection object or any other ADO.NET object:

```
Delegate Sub OpenMethod()

Sub OpenAsyncConnection()
    ' Define the Connection object.
    Dim cn As New OleDbConnection(BiblioConnString)
    ' Create a delegate that points to the Open method.
    Dim asyncOpen As New OpenMethod(AddressOf cn.Open)
    ' Call it asynchronously - pass the delegate as the cookie.
    Dim ar As IAsyncResult
    ar = asyncOpen.BeginInvoke(AddressOf OpenComplete, asyncOpen)
    ' Show a message in a Label control.
    lblStatus.Text = "Waiting ..."
    ' Do something else here.
    ⋮
End Sub

Sub OpenComplete(ByVal ar As IAsyncResult)
    ' Retrieve a reference to the delegate, passed in the cookie.
    Dim asyncOpen As OpenMethod = CType(ar.AsyncState, OpenMethod)

    Try
        ' Complete the operation.
        asyncOpen.EndInvoke(ar)
        ' Let the user know that the operation completed.
        MessageBox.Show("The connection has been opened")
    Catch ex As Exception
        ' Show an error message otherwise.
        MessageBox.Show(ex.Message)
    End Try
End Sub
```

Leveraging Connection Pooling

Connection pooling is a great feature of ADO.NET; it lets you transparently reuse a database connection when an application doesn't need it any longer. The mechanism works this way: when the first connection to the database is opened, a pool of identical connections is created, so subsequent requests don't have to wait to get a valid connection. When an application completes its database chores, it should explicitly close the Connection object so that it can be returned to the pool and made available for other applications. (Note that you must explicitly close the connection to return it to the pool.)

ADO.NET creates a number of connection pools equal to the number of distinct connection strings that your program uses, so the necessary condition for exploiting the connection pool is that you open all your database connections using *exactly* the same connection string. Even just an extra space or semicolon makes a connection string different, so pay attention.

This requirement means that you can't take advantage of connection pooling if you specify a different user name and password in the connection string. You're better off, therefore, using Windows integrated security instead of database security whenever it's feasible to do so:

```
Dim cn As New SqlConnection("Data Source=MyServer;" _
    & "Integrated Security=SSPI;Initial Catalog=pubs")
```

Another viable approach to reliable connection pooling is to encapsulate all the database access in a .NET component that logs in to the database using a special account and therefore uses the same connection string for all its open connections.

The OLE DB .NET Data Provider creates a connection pool based on the OLE DB session pooling. Connection pooling is enabled by default, but you can turn it off by specifying a special OLE DB Services value in the connection string:

```
Dim cn As New OleDbConnection("Provider=SQLOLEDB;" _
    & "Data Source=MyServer;Integrated Security=SSPI;OLE DB Services=-4")
```

The OleDbConnection object exposes a ReleaseObjectPool method that discards all unused connections from the pool. You might call it and then invoke the GC.Collect method to free as many resources as possible.

The SQL Server .NET Data Provider offers connection pooling based on Windows 2000 Component Services, using an implicit pooling model by default. This arrangement means that if the current thread has already opened a transaction using this provider, any new transaction opened will match the same transactional context. When the thread requests a connection, the pool is searched for a matching connection object. To be eligible for reuse, a connection in the pool must have exactly the same connection string, must have a matching transaction context (or not be associated with any transaction context), and must have a valid link to the specified server.

You can control the behavior of connection pooling under the SQL Server .NET Data Provider by using several values in the connection string. For example, you can disable automatic enlistment in the pooling by setting the Pooling attribute to False:

```
Dim cn As New SqlConnection("Data Source=MyServer;" _
    & "Integrated Security=SSPI;Initial Catalog=pubs;Pooling=false")
```

You can also avoid automatic enrollment in the current transaction if no transactions are required on the current connection, by setting the Enlist attribute to False:

```
Dim cn As New SqlConnection("Data Source=MyServer;" _
    & "Integrated Security=SSPI;Initial Catalog=pubs;Enlist=False")
```

You can set the minimum and maximum size of the pool by using the Min Pool Size and Max Pool Size attributes, whose default values are 0 and 100 respectively:

```
' If this is the first connection with this connection string, a
' pool with 10 identical connections is prepared.
Dim cn As New SqlConnection("Data Source=MyServer;" _
    & "Integrated Security=SSPI;Initial Catalog=pubs;" _
    & "Min Pool Size=10;Max Pool Size=120")
```

If the pool has reached its maximum size and all the connections are currently active and serving other applications, a request for an available connection is queued until another application releases one of the connections. If no connection is made available within the connection timeout period, an exception is thrown.

The Connection Lifetime attribute is useful in a clustered environment for taking advantage of any new server activated after the connection pool has already been created. As you know, all the connections in the pool link to the server on which they were originally opened. So by default they would never attempt to use any new server brought up after the pool has reached its maximum size. The Connection Lifetime sets the lifetime of a connection in the pool (in seconds). After this period, the connection is destroyed automatically; presumably, it will be replaced in the pool by a new connection that points to the server activated in the meantime.

```
' Destroy a connection in the pool after 2 minutes.
Dim cn As New SqlConnection("Data Source=MyServer;" _
    & "Integrated Security=SSPI;Initial Catalog=pubs;" _
    & "Connection Lifetime=120")
```

Connection pooling is a mixed blessing: on the one hand, it can dramatically improve the performance and scalability of your applications; on the other, it can give you headaches if you don't use it correctly. When you see that a database-intensive piece of code performs with suspicious sluggishness, you should double-check to see that it's using connection pooling correctly. To help you in this task, ADO.NET defines a few performance counters that you might want to monitor while searching for unexpected behaviors in the SQL Server .NET Data Provider. All the counters belong to the .NET CLR Data Performance object:

- **SqlClient: Current # connection pools** Number of pools associated with the process
- **SqlClient: Current # pooled and nonpooled connections** Number of connections, pooled or not
- **SqlClient: Current # pooled connections** Number of connections in pools associated with the process
- **SqlClient: Peak # pooled connections** Highest number of connections in all pools since the application started
- **SqlClient: Total # failed connects** Number of connection attempts that failed for any reason

The .NET CLR Data Performance object exposes a sixth counter that isn't directly related to connection pooling but is useful in many other circumstances:

- **SqlClient: Total # failed commands** Number of commands that failed for any reason

You can monitor these counters using the Performance utility or by reading them via code, using the technique described in the "Reading Performance Counter Values" section of Chapter 19.

Working with Transactions

The way you work with transactions has changed in the transition from ADO to ADO.NET. The ADO Connection class exposes the BeginTrans, CommitTrans, and RollbackTrans methods, which let you start, commit, or abort a transaction. The isolation level of the transaction is determined by the current value of the IsolationLevel property.

Creating a Transaction Object

The ADO.NET Connection object exposes only the BeginTransaction method, which takes an optional argument that specifies the isolation level of the transaction being started. As in ADO, the isolation level is an enumerated value that tells how locks are created and honored during the transaction. In a difference from ADO, the BeginTransaction method is a function that returns a Transaction object: more precisely, it returns either an OleDbTransaction or a SqlTransaction object, depending on the .NET provider you're using:

```
' Opening a transaction with the OLE DB .NET Data Provider
Dim cn As New OleDbConnection(BiblioConnString)
Dim tr As OleDbTransaction = cn.BeginTransaction(IsolationLevel.Serializable)

' Opening a transaction with the SQL Server .NET Data Provider
Dim cn2 As New SqlConnection(SqlPubsConnString)
Dim tr2 As SqlTransaction = cn2.BeginTransaction(IsolationLevel.Serializable)
```

You then use the Transaction object to control the outcome of the transaction: you invoke the Commit method to confirm all the changes in the transaction and the Rollback method to cancel them:

```
Dim tr As OleDbTransaction
Try
    ' Start a transaction.
    tr = cn.BeginTransaction(IsolationLevel.Serializable)
    ' Insert here database processing code.
    ⋮
    ' If we get here, we can confirm all changes.
    tr.Commit()
Catch ex As Exception
    ' Display an error message, and roll back all changes.
    MessageBox.Show(ex.Message)
    tr.Rollback()
End Try
```

Selecting the Isolation Level

The IsolationLevel property returns an enumerated value that specifies the level of the current transaction and that's equal to the value passed to the BeginTransaction method, as you can see in the preceding code example. Here's a brief description of the isolation levels that ADO.NET supports:

- **Chaos** The pending changes from the more highly isolated transactions can't be overridden. SQL Server doesn't support this isolation level.

- **ReadUncommitted** No shared (read) locks are issued, and no exclusive (write) locks are honored, which means that an application can read data that has been written from inside a transaction but not committed yet. If the transaction is then rolled back, the data that was read doesn't correspond to the data now in the database, a phenomenon known as *dirty reads*.
- **ReadCommitted (default)** Shared (read) locks are issued, and exclusive (write) locks are honored; this isolation level avoids dirty reads, but an application isn't guaranteed to retrieve a given row if the same query is reexecuted (a problem known as *nonrepeatable reads*). Moreover, a reexecuted query might find additional rows because in the meantime the code running in another transaction has inserted one or more records (*phantom rows*).
- **RepeatableRead** Exclusive locks are placed on all the rows being read so that code running in a transaction can't even read the data being read from inside another transaction. This isolation level degrades the scalability of the application but prevents the nonrepeatable reads problem. Phantom rows are still possible, however.
- **Serializable** This level is similar to the RepeatableRead level, but an exclusive lock is issued on the entire range, and therefore code running in another transaction can't even add a new record in the same range. This isolation level is the least efficient one, but it also solves the phantom row problem: each transaction truly runs in complete isolation.

For more information about the implications of each isolation level, you should read a good database book. If you work primarily with SQL Server, I highly recommend *Inside SQL Server 2000*, by Kalen Delaney (Microsoft Press).

It should be noted that transactions offer a way to implement pessimistic concurrency in ADO.NET, even though ADO.NET doesn't directly support this type of concurrency, unlike classic ADO. While a transaction is held open, no other user can read the data you have modified (if the transaction level is ReadCommitted) or just read (if the transaction is RepeatableRead or Serializable). Transactions are often the only way you have to ensure that the read and write operations work in a consistent way, but misused transactions can quickly degrade the overall performance and scalability of entire applications. So it's your responsibility to commit or roll back the transaction as soon as possible.

Nesting Transactions

The OleDbTransaction object exposes a Begin method, which lets you start a transaction that's nested in the current transaction. The Begin method takes an optional isolation level and returns another OleDbTransaction object:

```
' Open an OLE DB connection.
Dim cn As New OleDbConnection(BiblioConnString)
cn.Open()

' Open the first (outer) transaction.
Dim tr As OleDbTransaction = cn.BeginTransaction(IsolationLevel.ReadCommitted)
' Do some work here.
:
' Open a nested (inner) transaction.
Dim tr2 As OleDbTransaction = tr.Begin(IsolationLevel.ReadUncommitted)
:
' Roll back the inner transaction.
tr2.Rollback()
:
' Commit the outer transaction.
tr.Commit()
' Close the connection.
cn.Close()
```

Not all databases support nested transactions. For example, Access supports them, but SQL Server doesn't. In fact, if you run the preceding code on a connection opened using the SQLOLEDB provider, you get the following error:

```
Cannot start more transactions on this session.
```

Working with Named Transactions

SQL Server doesn't support true nested transactions—that is, transactions that can be rolled back or committed independently of outer (pending) transactions—and for this reason, the SqlTransaction object doesn't expose the Begin method. However, SQL Server supports named transactions. A *named transaction* is a sort of bookmark that remembers the state of the database at a given moment so that you can restore that state by using a named rollback command. You can create as many bookmarks as you need with the SQL Server SAVE TRAN command. Here's a fragment of a T-SQL routine that shows how to work with named transactions:

```
BEGIN TRAN MainTran
-- Insert, delete, or modify rows here.
:
```

```
SAVE TRAN EndOfFirstPart
-- Do some more work here.
⋮
-- Restore the database contents as they were before the second SAVE TRAN.
ROLLBACK TRAN EndOfFirstPart
⋮
-- Commit all changes.
COMMIT TRAN
```

To support named transactions, the BeginTransaction method of the SqlConnection object takes an optional transaction name. In addition, the SqlTransaction object exposes a Save method: both this method and the Rollback method can take an optional transaction name. Here's a Visual Basic .NET snippet that performs the same task as the preceding T-SQL fragment:

```
Dim cn As New SqlConnection(SqlPubsConnString)
cn.Open()

' Open a transaction named MainTran.
Dim tr As SqlTransaction = _
    cn.BeginTransaction(IsolationLevel.ReadCommitted, "MainTran")
' Insert, delete, or modify rows here.
⋮
' Create a named save point.
tr.Save("EndOfFirstPart")
' Do some more work here.
⋮
' Restore the database contents as they were before the second SAVE TRAN.
tr.Rollback("EndOfFirstPart")
⋮
' Commit all changes.
tr.Commit()
```

The Command Object

After you've opened a connection, you can decide whether you want to work in connected or disconnected mode. In the former case, you typically create a Command object that contains a select query (to read data from the database) or an action query (to update data) and then run one of its Execute*xxxx* methods, for which the exact name depends on the type of query.

Table 20-2 summarizes all the main properties and methods of the Command object. Except for the Disposed event inherited from the Component class, the Command object has no events.

Table 20-2 Properties and Methods of the Command Object

Category	Name	Description
Properties	CommandText	The SQL text of the query.
	CommandType	An enumerated value that specifies the type of the query: Text, StoredProcedure, or TableDirect. (The last value is supported only by the OLE DB .NET Data Provider when working with Microsoft Access.)
	Connection	The Connection object associated with this command.
	Transaction	The Transaction object corresponding to the transaction in which this command is executing.
	CommandTimeout	The number of seconds after which the query times out; default is 30 seconds. The value 0 means an infinite timeout and should be avoided.
	Parameters	The collection of parameters associated with this command.
	UpdatedRowSource	Specifies how command results are applied to the DataRow object. It's meaningful only when Command is associated with a DataAdapter object that performs an Update method.
Methods	ExecuteNonQuery	Executes the action query specified by CommandText and returns the number of rows affected.
	ExecuteReader	Executes the select query specified by CommandText and returns the DataReader object that lets you access the resultset. This method can take an optional CommandBehavior bit-coded value that further specifies how the command works—for example, whether it returns a single row or whether the connection should be closed when the method returns.
	ExecuteScalar	Executes the select query specified by CommandText and returns the scalar value in the first column of the first row, ignoring all other values.
	Cancel	Cancels the execution of the Command object; no error occurs if the command isn't running.

Table 20-2 Properties and Methods of the Command Object *(continued)*

Category	Name	Description
	CreateParameter	Creates a Parameter object connected to this parameterized command.
	ResetCommandTimeout	Resets the CommandTimeout property to its default value (30 seconds).
	Prepare	Creates a compiled version of the command on the data source; it can work only if CommandType is StoredProcedure, even though it might have no effect.
(SQL Server provider only)	ExecuteXmlReader	Performs that select query specified by CommandText (usually a SELECT FOR XML query) and returns an XmlReader object that lets you read the values in the resultset.

Creating a Command Object

The key properties of the Command object are CommandText (the SQL text of the action or select query) and Connection (the connection on which the query should run). You can set these properties individually, as in the following code snippet:

```
' Open a connection.
Dim cn As New OleDbConnection(BiblioConnString)
cn.Open()

' Define the command to insert a new record in the Authors table.
Dim sql As String = _
    "INSERT INTO Authors (Author, [Year Born]) VALUES ('Joe Doe', 1955)"

' Create an action command on that connection.
Dim cmd As New OleDbCommand()
cmd.Connection = cn
cmd.CommandText = sql

' Run the query; get the number of affected records.
Dim records As Integer = cmd.ExecuteNonQuery()
Debug.WriteLine(records)                          ' => 1

' Close the connection.
cn.Close()
```

Or you can pass these two values to the Command object's constructor, which makes for more-concise code:

```
Dim cmd As New OleDbCommand(sql, cn)
```

If you've opened a transaction on the connection, you must enlist the command in the transaction by assigning the Transaction object to the property with the same name or you must pass this object to the Command's constructor:

```
' (This code assumes that you've opened a connection and defined a query.)
' Begin a transaction.
Dim tr As OleDbTransaction = cn.BeginTransaction

' Create an action command, and enlist it in the transaction.
Dim cmd As New OleDbCommand(sql, cn, tr)
' Run the query; get the number of affected records.
Dim records As Integer = cmd.ExecuteNonQuery()
' Commit (or roll back) the transaction.
tr.Commit()
```

You get an error if you don't enlist the Command object in the existing transaction (more precisely, the most nested transaction being opened on that connection). Therefore, you can't help passing the Transaction object to the constructor method or to the Transaction property. This operation could be performed implicitly by ADO.NET when the Command object is associated with the connection, so you might wonder why you have to do it manually. The only reasonable explanation for this behavior I can think of is that in the future it might be possible to associate the command with a transaction obtained in some other way—for example, a distributed transaction created by the Microsoft Distributed Transaction Coordinator (MS DTC). At this time, however, nothing in the documentation confirms or rejects this hypothesis.

Issuing Database Commands

As you've seen in the preceding code snippets, you can perform insert, update, and delete operations through a Command object by means of the ExecuteNonQuery method, which returns the number of records that were affected by the statement:

```
Dim sql As String = _
    "INSERT INTO Authors (Author, [Year Born]) VALUES ('Joe Doe', 1955)"
Dim cmd As New OleDbCommand(sql, cn)
' Run the query; get the number of affected records.
Dim records As Integer = cmd.ExecuteNonQuery()
```

Of course, you can update existing records by using the UPDATE SQL statement and delete existing records with the DELETE statement. (You can read a complete tutorial on the SQL language in Chapter 8 of my *Programming Microsoft Visual Basic 6* book, on the companion CD.) There isn't much else to say about this method except that—as with all database operations—you should protect it with a Try block:

```
Try
    ' Run the query; get the number of affected records.
    Dim records As Integer = cmd.ExecuteNonQuery()
Catch ex As Exception
    ' Process the error here.
    :
Finally
    ' Always close the connection.
    cn.Close()
End Try
```

Reading Data

You can read data from a data source in three ways: by using the ExecuteReader method and the DataReader object to read complete resultsets; by using the ExecuteScalar method to read individual values; or by using the ExecuteXmlReader method and the XmlReader object to read the results of a FOR XML query on a SQL Server 2000 data source.

Using the ExecuteReader Method

The most common way to query the database in connected mode is through the ExecuteReader method of the Command object. This method returns a DataReader object, which you then use to read the resultset one row at a time, as you'd do with a forward-only, read-only Recordset under classic ADO. There are actually two versions of this object, OleDbDataReader and SqlDataReader.

```
' Create a query command on the connection.
Dim cmd As New OleDbCommand("SELECT * FROM Publishers", cn)
' Run the query; get the DataReader object.
Dim dr As OleDbDataReader = cmd.ExecuteReader()
' Read the names of all the publishers in the resultsets.
Do While dr.Read()
    Debug.WriteLine(dr.Item("Name"))
Loop
' Close the DataReader.
dr.Close
```

I discuss the DataReader object and its methods in greater detail in the section "The DataReader Object" later in this chapter. For now, let me focus on how you can affect the query by passing an optional CommandBehavior bit-coded value to the ExecuteReader method. The available values for this argument are

- **CloseConnection** The connection should be closed immediately after the DataReader object is closed.

- **SingleRow** The SQL statement is expected to return a single row of data. The OLE DB .NET Data Provider uses this information to optimize the data retrieval operation.
- **SingleResult** The SQL statement is expected to return a single scalar value. (In this case, however, you should use the ExecuteScalar method instead of ExecuteReader, as I explain in the next section.)
- **KeyInfo** The query returns column and primary key information and is executed without locking the selected rows. In this case, the SQL Server .NET Data Provider appends a FOR BROWSE clause to the SQL statement, which requires that the table have a time-stamp field and a unique index. (See SQL Server Books Online for additional information.)
- **SequentialAccess** The query results are read sequentially at the column level instead of being returned as a whole block to the caller. You should use this option when the table contains very large text and binary fields that you read in chunks using the GetChars and GetBytes methods of the DataReader object. In these circumstances, this option can improve the performance of your read operations significantly.
- **SchemaOnly** The query returns column information only and doesn't affect the database state.

Here's an example that uses the CloseConnection value:

```
' Run the query; get the DataReader object.
Dim dr As OleDbDataReader = cmd.ExecuteReader(CommandBehavior.CloseConnection)
' Process the data.
⋮
' Close the DataReader and (implicitly) the connection.
dr.Close()
```

The SingleRow option is useful when you're absolutely sure that the resultset contains only one row. This is often the case when the WHERE clause of the query filters a single record by its primary key, as in this example:

```
' Read a single line from the Publishers table.
Dim sql As String = "SELECT * FROM Publishers WHERE PubID=1"
Dim cmd As New OleDbCommand(sql, cn)
' Open a DataReader that contains one single row.
Dim dr As OleDbDataReader = cmd.ExecuteReader(CommandBehavior.SingleRow)
' Show name and city of this publisher.
dr.Read()
Debug.WriteLine(dr("Name") & " - " & dr ("City"))
dr.Close
```

Note that the argument is bit-coded, so you can combine multiple values using the Or operator:

```
Dim dr As OleDbDataReader = cmd.ExecuteReader(CommandBehavior.SingleRow _
    Or CommandBehavior.CloseConnection)
```

Using the ExecuteScalar Method

The ExecuteScalar method lets you perform a database query that returns a single scalar value in a more efficient way because it doesn't go through the overhead to build a resultset:

```
' Define the command to read a single scalar value
Dim sql As String = "SELECT Name FROM Publishers WHERE PubID=1"
' Create a command on that connection.
Dim cmd As New OleDbCommand(sql, cn)
' Read the value.
Dim pubName As String = cmd.ExecuteScalar().ToString
```

Another good occasion to use the ExecuteScalar method is for reading the result of aggregate functions, as in this code snippet:

```
' Read the number of records in the Publishers table.
Dim cmd As New OleDbCommand("SELECT COUNT(*) FROM Publishers", cn)
Dim recCount As Integer = CInt(cmd.ExecuteScalar())
```

Remember that the ExecuteScalar method works with *any* SQL query, and in all cases it returns the first field of the first row without raising an error if the query returns multiple columns or multiple rows.

Using the ExecuteXmlReader Method

SQL Server 2000 is able to process FOR XML queries and return data in XML format. If you connect to the database by using the SQL Server .NET Data Provider, you can leverage this capability with the ExecuteXmlReader of the SqlCommand object, which returns a System.Xml.XmlReader object that lets you walk through the resultset. Here's a code example that uses this feature:

```
' Open a connection to SQL Server 2000.
Dim cn As New SqlConnection(SqlPubsConnString)
cn.Open()
' Prepare a FOR XML command.
Dim sql As String = "SELECT pub_name FROM Publishers FOR XML AUTO, ELEMENTS"
Dim cmd As New SqlCommand(sql, cn)
' Create the XmlReader.
Dim reader As System.Xml.XmlReader = cmd.ExecuteXmlReader()
' Display XML data in a TextBox control.
Do While reader.Read
    txtOut.AppendText(reader.Value & ControlChars.CrLf)
Loop
' Close the XmlReader and the connection.
reader.Close()
cn.Close()
```

As you see, the XmlReader works similarly to the DataReader object, with a Read method that returns True if there are more elements and False when you arrive at the end of the resultset. I describe the XmlReader and XmlTextReader objects in Chapter 22.

Working with Parameters and Stored Procedures

The SQL command that you pass to a Command object can contain parameters, an especially useful feature when you're working with stored procedures. The exact syntax you can use in the SQL command depends on which data provider you're working with, so we'll examine the two providers separately.

Parameterized Commands

A common misconception is that parameters are useful only when you're working with stored procedures. But in fact, you can define a parameterized SQL command that contains one or more question marks as placeholders, as in this line of code:

```
SELECT * FROM Titles WHERE PubId=? AND [Year Published]=?
```

When you use this syntax—which is valid only with the OLE DB .NET Data Provider—you must manually create one or more Parameter objects and add them to the Command object's Parameters collection in the exact order in which the parameter appears in the SQL command. You can choose from three ways of creating a Parameter object: you can use the Parameter's constructor, use the Command's CreateParameter method, or invoke the Add method of the Parameters collection:

```
' First method: the Parameter's constructor
Dim par As New OleDbParameter("PubId", OleDbType.Integer)
par.Value = 156                  ' Set the parameter's value.
cmd.Parameters.Add(par)          ' Add to the collection of parameters.
Dim par2 As New OleDbParameter("YearPub", OleDbType.SmallInt)
par2.Value = 1992
cmd.Parameters.Add(par2)

' Second method: the Command's CreateParameter method
Dim par As OleDbParameter = cmd.CreateParameter
' Note that setting the name and the type isn't mandatory.
par.Value = 156
cmd.Parameters.Add(par)
par = cmd.CreateParameter        ' Reuse the same variable.
par.Value = 1992
cmd.Parameters.Add(par)

' Third method: passing name and value to the Parameters.Add method
cmd.Parameters.Add("PubId", 156)
cmd.Parameters.Add("YearPub", 1992)
```

(The Parameters collection implements the IList interface, so it exposes all the usual methods for adding, inserting, and removing elements.) The syntax with the SQL Server .NET Data Provider is different: it doesn't support question marks in queries and requires you to use @ parameters, as in this line of code:

```
SELECT * FROM Titles WHERE title_id=@TitleId
```

The code for creating the Parameters collection is similar, but of course you must use a SqlParameter object instead:

```
' First method: the Parameter's constructor
Dim par As New SqlParameter("TitleId", SqlDbType.VarChar)
par.Value = "BU1032"                ' Set the parameter's value.
cmd.Parameters.Add(par)             ' Add to the collection of parameters.

' Second method: the Command's CreateParameter method
Dim par As SqlParameter = cmd.CreateParameter
par.Value = "BU1032"
cmd.Parameters.Add(par)

' Third method: passing name and value to the Parameters.Add method
cmd.Parameters.Add("TitleId", "BU1032")
```

After the Parameters collection is set up, you can call the ExecuteReader method to retrieve the resultset as usual, or the ExecuteNonQuery method if it is an action query that doesn't return data rows. Parameterized commands are useful when you must perform the same type of query more than once, each time with different parameter values. The following example shows how you can extract different rows from the same table without having to create a different Command object:

```
' Create a SQL command with one parameter.
Dim sql As String = "SELECT * FROM Publishers WHERE PubID=?"
Dim cmd As New OleDbCommand(sql, cn)
' Define the first (and only) parameter, and assign its value.
cmd.Parameters.Add("PubID", 156)

' Read the result.
Dim dr As OleDbDataReader = cmd.ExecuteReader()
' No need to loop because we know there is only one row.
dr.Read()
Debug.WriteLine(dr("Name"))
dr.Close()

' Change the parameter's value, and reexecute the query.
cmd.Parameters(0).Value = 10
dr = cmd.ExecuteReader
dr.Read()
Debug.WriteLine(dr("Name"))
dr.Close()
```

Stored Procedures

The substantial difference between executing a simple parameterized SQL command and calling a stored procedure is that in the latter case, you just specify the name of the stored procedure in the command text and set the CommandType property to StoredProcedure:

```
' Run the byroyalty stored procedure in SQL Server's Pubs database.
Dim cmd As New SqlCommand("byroyalty", cn)
cmd.CommandType = CommandType.StoredProcedure
' Create the first parameter, and assign it the value 100.
' (Note that the parameter name must match the name used in the procedure.)
cmd.Parameters.Add("@percentage", 100)
' Read the result.
Dim dr As SqlDataReader = cmd.ExecuteReader()
```

You can execute a SQL Server stored procedure by using either the OLE DB .NET Data Provider or the SQL Server .NET Data Provider, the only difference being that the former provider doesn't require that the name you use for a parameter match the parameter's name as defined in the stored procedure itself.

In another difference from parameterized commands, when you're working with stored procedures you must account for the type and the direction of each parameter. In general, the type of each Parameter must match the type of the argument that the stored procedure accepts; if this doesn't happen, you might have problems passing and retrieving a value from that stored procedure. You can pass the type as the second argument to the Parameter's constructor by using an enumerated OleDbType value, which is similar to the data types that ADO supports:

```
' Create a Parameter of type Single.
Dim param1 As New OleDbParameter("param1", OleDbType.Single)
```

When working with strings, you can also specify a size:

```
Dim param2 As New OleDbParameter("param2", OleDbType.VarChar, 100)
```

The same syntax applies to SqlParameter objects, except that you specify the type by using a SqlDbType enumeration value. In some cases, the name of this value differs from its OLE DB counterpart:

```
' Create a Single parameter for SQL Server.
Dim param3 As New SqlParameter("param3", SqlDbType.Float)
```

By default, all parameters are created as input parameters. If you're calling a stored procedure that returns a value through an argument, you must set the Direction property to either InputOutput or Output. If the stored procedure returns a value, you must define an additional parameter: the name of this parameter doesn't matter as long as it's the first parameter appended to the Parameters collection and its Direction property is set to ReturnValue.

To test how to work with output parameters and return values, you can define a new byroyalty2 stored procedure in SQL Server's Pubs database by running this script in SQL Server's Query Analyzer:

```
CREATE PROCEDURE byroyalty2 @percentage int, @avgprice float output
AS
-- Return the average price for all titles in the second argument.
SELECT @avgprice= AVG(Price) FROM Titles
-- Return a resultset.
SELECT au_id FROM titleauthor
    WHERE titleauthor.royaltyper = @percentage
-- Return the number of titles in the second argument.
DECLARE @numtitles Int
SELECT @numtitles=COUNT(*) FROM titles
RETURN @numtitles
```

Here's the complete source code of a routine that invokes the byroyalty2 stored procedure and displays its results in a multiline TextBox control:

```
Dim cn As New SqlConnection(SqlPubsConnString)
cn.Open()

Dim sql As String = "byroyalty2"
Dim cmd As New SqlCommand(sql, cn)
cmd.CommandType = CommandType.StoredProcedure

' Define the return value parameter.
cmd.Parameters.Add("@numtitles", OleDbType.Integer)
cmd.Parameters(0).Direction = ParameterDirection.ReturnValue
' Define the first (input) parameter, and assign its value.
cmd.Parameters.Add("@percentage", 100)

' Define the second (output) parameter, and set its direction.
' (A better method for setting the direction and other properties.)
With cmd.Parameters.Add("@avgprice", SqlDbType.Float)
    .Direction = ParameterDirection.Output
End With

' Read the result.
Dim dr As SqlDataReader = cmd.ExecuteReader()
Do While dr.Read
    txtOut.AppendText(dr(0).ToString & ControlChars.CrLf)
Loop
dr.Close()
```

(continued)

```
' You can read the return value and output argument only after
' closing the DataReader object.
txtOut.AppendText("Number of titles = " & _
    cmd.Parameters("@numtitles").Value.ToString & ControlChars.CrLf)
txtOut.AppendText("Average price = " & _
    cmd.Parameters("@avgprice").Value.ToString & ControlChars.CrLf)
' Close the connection.
cn.Close()
```

As a remark in the preceding code snippet explains, you can read output arguments and return values only after you've closed the DataReader object. This is a known problem of SQL Server and doesn't depend on ADO.NET. (As a matter of fact, you have the same problem also when calling a SQL Server stored procedure from ADO.)

When invoking a SQL Server stored procedure that doesn't have output parameters or a return value, you can take the following shortcut: just create an EXEC statement that contains the name of the stored procedure followed by all its input parameters, as in this code snippet:

```
Dim sql As String = "EXEC byroyalty 100"
Dim cmd As New SqlCommand(sql, cn)
cmd.CommandType = CommandType.Text
```

Note that in this case you don't have to set the CommandType property to StoredProcedure because from the perspective of ADO.NET, you're executing a regular SQL command.

Automatic Population of the Parameters Collection

When working with stored procedures, you can save some time by having ADO.NET populate the Parameters collection of the Command object automatically by means of the DeriveParameters shared method of the OleDbCommandBuilder or SqlCommandBuilder class:

```
' Get the parameters for the byroyalty stored procedure in Pubs.
Dim cmd As New SqlCommand("byroyalty", cn)
cmd.CommandType = CommandType.StoredProcedure

' Let the CommandBuilder object populate the Parameters collection.
SqlCommandBuilder.DeriveParameters(cmd)

' Show number and names of parameters.
Debug.WriteLine(cmd.Parameters.Count & " parameters")   ' => 2 parameters
Debug.WriteLine(cmd.Parameters(0).ParameterName)        ' => @RETURN_VALUE
Debug.WriteLine(cmd.Parameters(1).ParameterName)        ' => @percentage
```

ADO supports a similar technique based on the Parameters.Refresh method, but Microsoft initially decided not to make this technique available to ADO.NET developers because of its horrible performance. In fact, both ADO's Refresh method and the ADO.NET DeriveParameters method require a round-trip to the SQL Server database to acquire the metadata needed to fill the Parameters collection. Because the signature of a stored procedure rarely changes after the application is deployed, it makes sense that you burn the names and the type of the parameters in code to speed up execution.

Even if you don't count performance problems, filling the Parameters collection automatically isn't usually a good idea. For example, the preceding code snippet shows that the DeriveParameters method incorrectly detects a return value parameter, even when the stored procedure doesn't really have a return value. In some circumstances, this method isn't smart enough to read the exact type and direction of parameters. For example, if you run the DeriveParameters method on the byroyalty2 stored procedure that we've defined in the preceding section, you'll see that the @avgprice output parameter is incorrectly retrieved as an input/output parameter. You can remedy this problem either by manually adjusting the Direction property to Output or by assigning a dummy value to the @avgprice parameter before calling the stored procedure, even if this value will never be used. If you fail to take either of these steps, the ExecuteReader method will throw an exception.

Despite its defects, the DeriveParameters method fits the bill during the prototyping phase, but be prepared to replace it with code that populates the Parameters collection manually before you ship the application. Here's a tip: you should always reference your parameters by their names rather than by their indexes in the Parameters collection so that you don't have to change your code if you switch from automatic to manual creation of the Parameters collection. And don't include the return value parameter (if the stored procedure doesn't have one).

```
' This statement works regardless of how you fill the Parameters collection.
cmd.Parameters("@percentage").Value = 100
```

The DeriveParameters method works in a slightly different way in the two .NET data providers. As you've seen, the parameter names that the SQL Server .NET Data Provider retrieves have a leading @ character and match their definitions in the stored procedure. This character is missing when you retrieve the collection of parameters using the OLE DB .NET Data Provider. (The present or missing @ character is an issue only if you want to change the provider during the development phase.)

> **Note** The DeriveParameters method was added rather late in the beta process, which explains why earlier articles and books on ADO.NET don't cover it. I suspect that the main reason for its introduction was the disappointed feedback from earlier adopters who would have liked to have a mechanism similar to the ADO Parameters.Refresh method. However, remember that you should use the DeriveParameters method only during the testing step, and you should populate the Parameters collection manually in the definitive version of your application to avoid an unnecessary round-trip to the server.

The DataReader Object

I summarize the most important properties and methods of the DataReader object in Table 20-3. The most important of these members are described in the following sections.

Iterating over Individual Rows

Using the DataReader object couldn't be simpler: you invoke its Read method to advance to the next row in the resultset and check its return value to see whether you have more results (if True) or are at the end of the resultset (if False). Because of this double function, you can create tight loops based on the DataReader object:

```
Do While dr.Read()
    ' Process the current row here.
    :
Loop
dr.Close()
```

It's important that you close the DataReader object when you don't have to process any more rows, to release resources on both the client and the server and make the connection available again for other commands. In fact, you can't issue any other command on a connection while a DataReader object is active on that connection. The only command you can perform on a connection actively serving a DataReader is the Close method.

You can check whether a connection is available by using its State property. The DataReader object doesn't expose this property, but you can check whether it has been closed by means of its IsClosed property.

Table 20-3 Properties and Methods of the DataReader Object

Category	Name	Description
Properties	IsClosed	Returns True if the DataReader is closed.
	FieldCount	Returns the number of columns in the current row.
	Item	Returns the value of the column with the specified index or name.
	RecordsAffected	Returns the number of rows inserted, deleted, or updated by the SQL statement.
	Depth	Returns the depth of nesting of the current row. (The outermost table has a depth of 0.)
Methods	Read	Advances to the next row and returns True if there are more rows, False if the end of the resultset has been found.
	Close	Closes the DataReader object, releases all the resources allocated to it, and makes the connection available for other commands.
	NextResult	Advances to the next resultset and returns True if there is another resultset. Use this method to process multiple resultset results, such as those returned by batch SQL statements and stored procedures.
	GetName	Returns the name of the column with the specified index.
	GetOrdinal	Returns the index of a column corresponding to the field name passed as an argument.
	IsDBNull	Returns True if the column at the specified index contains a DBNull value.
	GetValue	Returns the value of a column at the specified index in its native format.
	GetValues	Takes an Object array and fills it with the values from all the columns in the resultset; returns the number of Object instances in the array.
	GetBoolean, GetByte, GetChar, GetDateTime, GetDecimal, GetDouble, GetFloat, GetGuid, GetInt16, GetInt32, GetInt64, GetString, GetTimeSpan	Retrieves the strongly typed value of the field at the specified column index. (GetTimeSpan isn't supported by the SQL Server .NET Data Provider.)

Table 20-3 Properties and Methods of the DataReader Object *(continued)*

Category	Name	Description
	GetBytes	Fills a Byte array (or a portion thereof) with the contents of a binary field; returns the number of bytes read.
	GetChars	Fills a Char array (or a portion thereof) with the contents of a long text field; returns the number of characters read.
	GetFieldType	Returns the System.Type object that describes the type of the field at a given index.
	GetDataTypeName	Returns the name of the source data type for the column whose index is passed as an argument.
	GetSchemaTable	Returns a DataTable that describes the column metadata.
(SQL Server provider only)	GetSqlBinary, GetSqlBoolean, GetSqlByte, GetSqlDateTime, GetSqlDecimal, GetSqlDouble, GetSqlGuid, GetInt16, GetInt32, GetInt64, GetSqlMoney, GetSqlSingle, GetSqlString	Retrieve the strongly typed value of the field at the specified column index as one of the SqlTypes.Sql*xxxx* data types.
	GetSqlValue	Gets an Object that's a representation of the underlying Data.SqlDbTypeVariant value.
	GetSqlValues	Takes an Object array and fills it with the value from all the columns in the resultset; returns the number of Object instances in the array.

Reading Column Values

A quick look at Table 20-3 shows that the DataReader object provides many properties and methods that let you read the value of the columns in the resultset.

The Item read-only property gives you a means to access any field by either its name or its (zero-based) column index in a way that resembles the kind of access you perform with the Fields collection of the ADO Recordset:

```
' Read the result into a DataReader object.
Dim dr As OleDbDataReader = cmd.ExecuteReader(CommandBehavior.CloseConnection)

' Display the names of all publishers.
Do While dr.Read()
    Dim res As String = String.Format("{0} - {1}", _
        dr.Item("Name"), dr.Item("City"))
    ' Append the result to the current contents of a TextBox control.
    txtOut.AppendText(res & ControlChars.CrLf)
Loop
' Close the DataReader and the connection.
dr.Close()
```

Item is the default member, so you can make your code more concise by omitting it:

```
Dim res As String = String.Format("{0} - {1}", dr("Name"), dr("City"))
```

You can iterate over all the columns in the resultset by using an index that goes from 0 to FieldCount <–1; then you can use the GetName method to retrieve the name of the field and the GetValue method (or the Item property) to read the field's value. If you're dealing with a nullable field, however, you should protect your code from exceptions by checking a field with the IsDBNull method:

```
' Read the result into a DataReader object.
Dim dr As OleDbDataReader = cmd.ExecuteReader(CommandBehavior.CloseConnection)

' Display the value of all fields.
Do While dr.Read
    ' Prepare the buffer for the values of this row.
    Dim res As String = ""
    Dim i As Integer

    ' Iterate over all fields.
    For i = 0 To dr.FieldCount - 1
        ' Insert a comma if necessary.
        If res.Length > 0 Then res &= ", "
        ' Append field name and value.
        res &= dr.GetName(i) & "="
        ' Protect the code from null values.
        If dr.IsDBNull(i) Then
            res &= "<NULL>"
        Else
```

(continued)

```
            res &= dr.GetValue(i).ToString
        End If
    Next
    ' Append to the result text box.
    txtOut.AppendText(res & ControlChars.CrLf)
Loop
' Close the DataReader and the Connection.
dr.Close()
```

When you read all the fields in the current row, you can optimize your code by using the GetValues method, which returns all the fields' values in an Object array. The following code snippet uses this method and makes the code even faster by retrieving the names of all fields once and for all outside the main loop and by using a StringBuilder object instead of a regular String. After the value has been moved to an element of the Object array, you must test it using the IsDBNull function instead of the DataReader's IsDBNull method:

```
' Run the query; get the DataReader object.
Dim dr As OleDbDataReader = cmd.ExecuteReader(CommandBehavior.CloseConnection)

' Build the array of all fields.
Dim fldNames(dr.FieldCount - 1) As String
Dim i As Integer
For i = 0 To dr.FieldCount - 1
    fldNames(i) = dr.GetName(i)
Next

' Display all fields.
Do While dr.Read
    Dim res As New System.Text.StringBuilder(256)
    ' Get all the values in one shot.
    Dim values(dr.FieldCount - 1) As Object
    dr.GetValues(values)

    ' Iterate over all fields.
    For i = 0 To dr.FieldCount - 1
        ' Insert a comma if necessary.
        If res.Length > 0 Then res.Append(", ")
        ' Append field name and equal sign.
        res.Append(fldNames(i))
        res.Append("=")
        ' Append the field value, or <NULL>.
        If IsDBNull(values(i)) Then
            res.Append("<NULL>")
        Else
```

```
                res.Append(values(i).ToString)
            End If
        Next
        ' Append to the result text box.
        res.Append(ControlChars.CrLf)
        txtOut.AppendText(res.ToString)
    Loop
    ' Close the DataReader and the Connection.
    dr.Close()
```

The OLE DB .NET Data Provider offers several Get*xxxx* methods to retrieve field values in their native format, saving you the overhead of going through a more generic Object variable. Compare how you can retrieve an integer value with the generic GetValue method and the more specific GetInt32 method:

```
' The generic GetValue method requires type casting.
Dim res As Integer = CInt(dr.GetValue(0))
' The specific GetInt32 method does not.
Dim res2 As Integer = dr.GetInt32(0)
```

Using Specific SQL Server Types

The SQL Server .NET Data Provider also provides the same Get*xxxx* methods as the OLE DB provider, with one glaring exception: it doesn't support the GetTimeSpan method. On the other hand, the SQL Server provider supports more specific GetSql*xxxx* methods, which behave much like their Get*xxxx* counterparts except that they return specific SQL Server types defined in the System.Data.SqlTypes namespace:

```
' This code assumes that dr is a SqlDataReader object.
Dim res As Integer = dr.GetSqlInt32(0)
```

When you're working with the SQL Server .NET Data Provider, you should always use these more specific types because they prevent conversion errors caused by loss of precision and provide faster code as well. This advice is especially important to follow with the SqlDecimal data type, which provides a precision of 38 digits instead of the 28 digits that the .NET Decimal type provides.

Table 20-4 summarizes the data types in the System.Data.SqlTypes namespace and aligns them with the corresponding SQL Server type and with the corresponding value of the enumerated SqlDbType (defined in System.Data). As you see, some of the SqlTypes correspond to more than one native SQL Server type.

Table 20-4 SqlTypes and the Corresponding Native SQL Server Types and SqlDbType Enumerated Values

SqlTypes	Native SQL Server	SqlDbType Enumerated Value
SqlBoolean	bit	Bit
SqlByte	tinyint	TinyInt
SqlInt16	smallint	SmallInt
SqlInt32	int	Int
SqlInt64	bigint	BigInt
SqlSingle	real	Real
SqlDouble	float	Float
SqlDecimal	decimal	Decimal
SqlDateTime	datetime	DateTime
	smalldatetime	SmallDateTime
SqlMoney	money	Money
	smallmoney	SmallMoney
SqlString	char	Char
	nchar	NChar
	ntext	NText
	nvarchar	NVarChar
	sysname	VarChar
	text	Text
	varchar	VarChar
SqlBinary	binary	Binary
	varbinary	VarBinary
	image	Image
	timestamp	TimeStamp
SqlGuid	uniqueindentifier	UniqueIdentifier
Object	sql_variant	Variant

Reading Multiple Resultsets

Some databases support multiple statements in one query. For example, you can send multiple commands to SQL Server, using the semicolon as a separator:

```
SELECT Name FROM Publishers WHERE PubId=10;
SELECT Name FROM Publishers WHERE PubId=12
```

Multiple queries let you create batch commands, which minimize the number of round-trips to the server and network traffic. (One batch command uses a single network packet to carry multiple queries that would otherwise require multiple packets.) The DataReader object supports multiple resultsets by means of the NextResult method, which returns True if there is one more resultset and False otherwise. The following code snippet shows how to use this method with any number of resultsets:

```
' Open a connection to the Pubs database on SQL Server.
Dim cn As New SqlConnection(SqlPubsConnString)
cn.Open()

' Define a SQL statement with multiple queries.
Dim sql As String = "SELECT pub_name FROM Publishers;SELECT Title FROM titles"
Dim cmd As New SqlCommand(sql, cn)
Dim dr As SqlDataReader = cmd.ExecuteReader()

Dim resCount As Integer
Do
    ' Process the next resultset.
    resCount += 1
    txtOut.AppendText("RESULTSET #" & resCount.ToString)
    txtOut.AppendText(ControlChars.CrLf)

    ' Process all the rows in the current resultset.
    Do While dr.Read
        txtOut.AppendText(dr(0).ToString)
        txtOut.AppendText(ControlChars.CrLf)
    Loop
    txtOut.AppendText(ControlChars.CrLf)
Loop While dr.NextResult
' Close the DataReader and the connection.
dr.Close()
cn.Close()
```

Figure 20-2 shows the outcome of this code.

If the SQL statement contains action queries—such as an INSERT, a DELETE, or an UPDATE statement—they're correctly ignored by the NextResult method because they don't return any resultsets. (Under the same circumstances, the NextResultset method of the ADO Recordset object returned a closed Recordset, so you had to write additional code to handle this special case.)

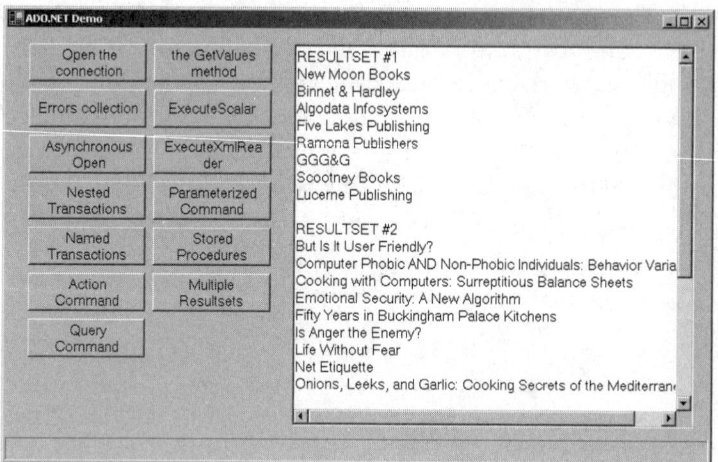

Figure 20-2. The demo program lets you test several features of the DataReader object.

We've come to the end of the first part of ADO.NET coverage, which is about using the Connection, Command, and DataReader objects. Even though the name and syntax of these objects and their methods differ from what you had in classic ADO, you'll probably agree that few things have changed: using ADO.NET in connected mode is much like using ADO (except that you can't count on keysets and dynamic cursors). However, things are very different in a disconnected scenario, as I explain in the following chapter.

21

ADO.NET in Disconnected Mode

In the preceding chapter, you saw how to work with ADO.NET in connected mode, processing data coming from an active connection and sending SQL commands to one. ADO.NET in connected mode behaves much like classic ADO, even though the names of the involved properties and methods (and their syntax) are often different.

You see how ADO.NET differs from its predecessor when you start working in disconnected mode. ADO 2.*x* permits you to work in disconnected mode using client-side static recordsets opened in optimistic batch update mode. This was one of the great new features of ADO that has proved to be a winner in client/server applications of any size. As a matter of fact, working in disconnected mode is the most scalable technique you can adopt because it takes resources on the client (instead of on the server) and, above all, it doesn't enforce any locks on database tables (except for the short-lived locks that are created during the update operation).

> **Note** To make code samples in this chapter less verbose, all of them assume that the following Imports statements have been specified at the top of each source file:
>
> ```
> Imports System.Data
> Imports System.Data.OleDb
> Imports System.Data.SqlClient
> ```

The DataSet Object

Because ADO.NET (and .NET in general) is all about scalability and performance, the disconnected mode is the preferred way to code client/server applications. Instead of a simple disconnected recordset, ADO.NET gives you the DataSet object, which is much like a small relational database held in memory on the client. As such, it provides you with the ability to create multiple tables, fill them with data coming from different sources, enforce relationships between pairs of tables, and more.

Even with all its great features, however, the DataSet isn't always the best answer to all database programming problems. For example, the DataSet object is great for traditional client/server applications—for example, a Windows Forms application that queries a database on a networked server—but is almost always a bad choice in ASP.NET applications and, more generally, in all stateless environments. An ASP.NET page lives only a short lifetime, just for the time necessary to reply to a browser's request, so it rarely makes sense to use a DataSet to read data from a database, then send the data to the user through HTML, and destroy the DataSet immediately afterward. (Yes, you might save the DataSet in a Session variable, but this technique takes memory on the server and might create server affinity, two problems that impede scalability, as I explain in the "State Management and Caching" section of Chapter 24.)

Exploring the DataSet Object Model

The DataSet is the root and the most important object in the object hierarchy that includes almost all the objects in the System.Data namespace. Figure 21-1 shows the most important classes in this hierarchy, with the name of the property that returns each object.

An important feature of the DataSet class is its ability to define relationships between its DataTable objects, much like what you do in a real database. For example, you can create a relationship between the Publishers and the Titles DataTable objects by using the PubId DataColumn that they have in common. After you define a DataRelation object, you can navigate from one table to another, using the DataTable's ChildRelations and ParentRelations properties.

A DataSet object consists of one or more DataTable objects, each one containing data coming from a database query, an XML stream, or code added programmatically. Table 21-1 summarizes the most important members of the DataSet class.

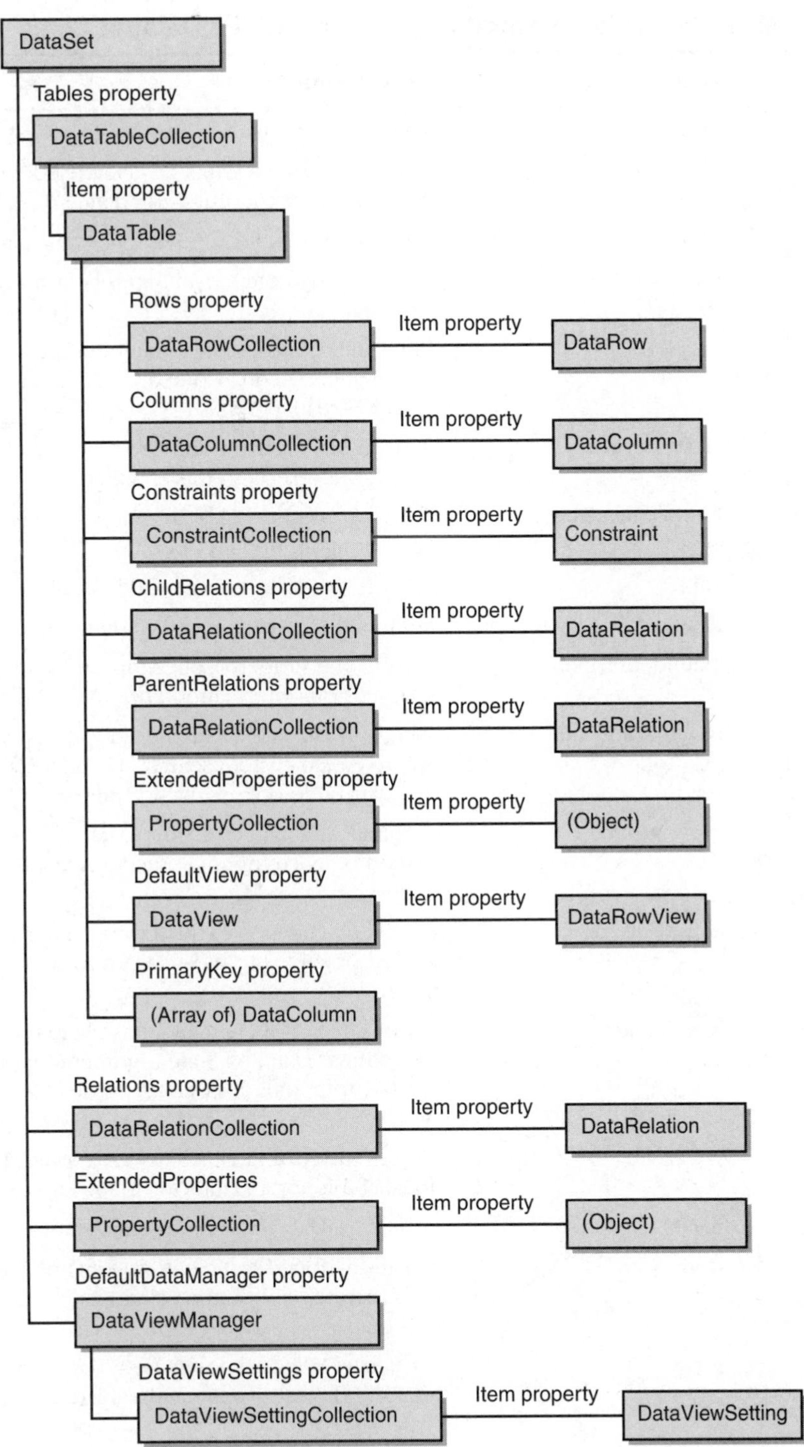

Figure 21-1. The DataSet object hierarchy.

Table 21-1 Main Properties, Methods, and Events of the DataSet Class

Category	Name	Description
Properties	DataSetName	The name of this DataSet object.
	Namespace	The namespace for this DataSet, used when importing or exporting XML data.
	Prefix	The XML prefix for the DataSet namespace.
	CaseSensitive	True if string comparisons in this DataSet are case sensitive.
	Locale	The CultureInfo object containing the locale information used to compare strings in the DataSet (read/write).
	HasErrors	Returns True if there are errors in any of the DataTable objects in this DataSet.
	EnforceConstraints	True if constraint rules are enforced when attempting an update operation.
	Tables	Returns the collection of child DataTable objects.
	Relations	Returns the collection of DataRelation objects.
	ExtendedProperties	Returns the PropertyCollection object used to store custom information about the DataSet.
	DefaultViewManager	Returns a DataViewManager object that allows you to create custom search and filter settings for the DataTable objects in the DataSet.
Methods	AcceptChanges	Commits all changes to this DataSet after it was loaded or since the most recent AcceptChanges method.
	RejectChanges	Rejects all changes to this DataSet after it was loaded or since the most recent AcceptChanges method.
	HasChanges	Returns True if the DataSet has changed. It takes an optional DataRowState argument that lets you check for modified, inserted, or deleted rows only.
	Merge	Merges the current DataSet with another DataSet, a DataTable, or a DataRow array.
	Reset	Resets the DataSet to its original state.
	Clone	Creates a cloned DataSet that contains the identical structure, tables, and relationships as the current one.
	Copy	Creates a DataSet that has both the same structure and the same data as the current one.

Table 21-1 Main Properties, Methods, and Events of the DataSet Class *(continued)*

Category	Name	Description
	Clear	Clears all the data in the DataSet.
	GetChanges	Gets a DataSet that contains all the changes made to the current one since it was loaded or since the most recent AcceptChanges method, optionally filtered using the DataRowState argument.
	ReadXml	Reads an XML schema and data into the DataSet.
	ReadXmlSchema	Reads an XML schema into the DataSet.
	GetXml	Returns the XML representation of the contents of the DataSet.
	InferXmlSchema	Infers the XML schema from the TextReader or from the file into the DataSet.
	WriteXml	Writes the XML schema and data from the current DataSet.
	WriteXmlSchema	Writes the current DataSet's structure as an XML schema.
Events	MergeFailed	Fires when two DataSet objects being merged have the same primary key value and the EnforceConstraints property is True.

In the remainder of this section, I'll briefly introduce all the major classes in the DataSet hierarchy, with a list of their most important properties, methods, and events. Once you have an idea of the purpose of each object, I'll describe how to perform the most common operations in disconnected mode.

The DataTable Class

A DataTable object resembles a database table and has a collection of DataColumn instances (the fields) and DataRow instances (the records). It can also have a primary key based on one or more columns and a collection of Constraint objects, which are useful for enforcing the uniqueness of the values in a column. DataTable objects in a DataSet class are often tied to each other through relationships, exactly as if they were database tables. A DataTable object can also exist outside a DataSet class, the main limitation being that it can't participate in any relationships.

Table 21-2 summarizes the most important members of the DataTable object. As you see, some of the properties and methods have the same names and meaning as properties and methods in the DataSet class.

Table 21-2 Main Properties, Methods, and Events of the DataTable Class

Category	Name	Description
Properties	TableName	The name of this DataTable object.
	Namespace	The namespace for this DataTable, used when importing or exporting XML data.
	Prefix	The XML prefix for the DataTable namespace.
	CaseSensitive	Returns True if string comparisons in this DataTable are case sensitive.
	Locale	The CultureInfo object containing the locale information used to compare strings in the DataTable (read/write).
	HasErrors	Returns True if there are errors in any of the DataRow objects in this DataTable.
	DataSet	Returns the DataSet this DataTable belongs to.
	Rows	Returns the collection of child DataRow objects.
	Columns	Returns the collection of child DataColumn objects.
	ChildRelations	Returns the collection of DataRelation objects in which this DataTable is the master table.
	ParentRelations	Returns the collection of DataRelation objects in which this DataTable is the detail table.
	Constraints	Returns the collection of the Constraint objects for this DataTable (for example, foreign key constraints or unique constraints).
	ExtendedProperties	Returns the PropertyCollection object used to store custom information about the DataTable.
	MinimumCapacity	The initial number of rows for this DataTable (read/write).
	PrimaryKey	An array of DataColumn objects that represent the primary keys for the DataTable.
	DefaultView	Returns the DataView object that you can use to filter and sort this DataTable.
	DisplayExpression	A string expression used to represent this table in the user interface. The expression supports the same syntax defined for the DataColumn's Expression property.
Methods	AcceptChanges	Commits all changes to this DataTable after it was loaded or since the most recent AcceptChanges method.
	RejectChanges	Rejects all changes to this DataTable after it was loaded or since the most recent AcceptChanges method.

Table 21-2 Main Properties, Methods, and Events of the DataTable Class *(continued)*

Category	Name	Description
	Reset	Resets the DataTable to its original state.
	Clone	Creates a cloned DataTable that contains the identical structure, tables, and relationships as the current one.
	Copy	Creates a DataTable that has both the same structure and the same data as the current one.
	Clear	Clears all the data in the DataTable.
	GetChanges	Gets a DataTable that contains all the changes made to the current one after it was loaded or since the most recent AcceptChanges method, optionally filtered by the DataRowState argument.
	NewRow	Creates a DataRow with the same schema as the current table.
	ImportRow	Copies the DataRow passed as an argument into the current table. The row retains its original and current values, its DataRowState values, and its errors.
	Select	Returns the array of all the DataRow objects that satisfy the filter expression. It takes optional arguments that specify the desired sort order and the DataViewRowState to be matched.
	GetErrors	Returns the array of all the DataRow objects that have errors.
	Compute	Calculates the expression specified by the first argument for all the rows that satisfy the filter expression specified in the second argument.
	BeginLoadData	Turns off notifications, index maintenance, and constraints while loading data; to be used in conjunction with the EndLoadData and LoadDataRow methods.
	EndLoadData	Ends a load data operation started with BeginLoadData.
	LoadDataRow	Finds and updates a specific row or creates a new row if no matching row is found.
Events	ColumnChanging	Fires when a DataColumn is changing. The event handler can inspect the new value.
	ColumnChanged	Fires after a DataColumn has changed.
	RowChanging	Fires when a DataRow is changing.
	RowChanged	Fires after a DataRow has changed.
	RowDeleting	Fires when a DataRow is being deleted.
	RowDeleted	Fires after a DataRow has been deleted.

The DataRow Class

The DataRow class represents an individual row (or record) in a DataTable. Each DataRow contains one or more fields, which can be accessed through its Item property. (Because it's the the default member, the name of this property can be omitted.) Table 21-3 lists the main properties and methods of the DataRow object.

Table 21-3 Main Properties and Methods of the DataRow Class

Category	Name	Description
Properties	Item	Gets or sets the data stored in the specified column. The argument can be the column name, the column index, or a DataColumn object. An optional DataRowVersion argument lets you retrieve the current, original, proposed, or default value for the column.
	ItemArray	Gets or sets the values of all the columns, using an Object array.
	RowState	The current state of this row; can be Unchanged, Modified, Added, Deleted, or Detached.
	HasErrors	Returns True if there are errors in the column collection.
	RowError	Gets or sets a string containing the custom error description for the current row.
Methods	AcceptChanges	Commits all changes to this DataRow after it was loaded or since the most recent AcceptChanges method.
	RejectChanges	Rejects all changes to this DataRow after it was loaded or since the most recent AcceptChanges method.
	BeginEdit	Marks the beginning of an edit operation on a DataRow.
	EndEdit	Confirms all the changes to the DataRow since the most recent BeginEdit method.
	CancelEdit	Cancels all the changes to the DataRow since the most recent BeginEdit method.
	Delete	Deletes this row.

Table 21-3 Main Properties and Methods of the DataRow Class *(continued)*

Category	Name	Description
	GetColumnError	Returns the error description for the error in the column specified by the argument, which can be the column name, the column index, or a DataColumn object.
	GetColumnsInError	Returns the array of DataColumn objects that have an error.
	SetColumnError	Sets an error description for the specified column.
	ClearErrors	Clear all errors for this row, including the RowError property and errors set with the SetColumnError method.
	IsNull	Returns True if the specified column has a null value. The argument can be a column name, a column index, or a DataColumn. An optional second argument lets you refer to a specific DataRowVersion value (original, current, etc.).
	GetChildRows	Returns an array of the DataRow objects that are the child rows of the current row, following the relationship specified by the argument, which can be a relationship name or a DataRelation object. An optional second argument lets you refer to a specific DataRowVersion (original, current, etc.) for the row to be retrieved.
	GetParentRow	Returns the parent DataRow object, following the relationship specified by the argument (which can be one of the values accepted by the GetChildRows method).
	GetParentRows	Returns an array of the parent DataRow objects, following the relationship specified by the argument (which can be one of the values accepted by the GetChildRows method).
	SetParentRow	Sets the parent DataRow for the current row.

The DataColumn Class

The DataColumn class represents a single column (field) in a DataRow or in a DataTable. Not counting the methods inherited from System.Object, this class exposes only the properties summarized in Table 21-4. All properties are read/write except where otherwise stated.

Table 21-4 Main Properties of the DataColumn Class

Name	Description
ColumnName	The name of this column.
DataType	The System.Type object that defines the data type of this column.
MaxLength	The maximum length of a text column.
AllowDBNull	A Boolean that determines whether null values can be accepted for this column (for rows belonging to a table).
Unique	A Boolean that determines whether duplicated values are accepted in this column (for rows belonging to a table).
ReadOnly	A Boolean that determines whether values in this column can be modified after the row has been added to a table.
DefaultValue	The default value for this column when a new row is added to the table.
Expression	The expression to be used for calculated columns.
AutoIncrement	A Boolean that determines whether this is an auto-incrementing column (for rows added to a table).
AutoIncrementSeed	The starting value for an auto-incrementing column.
AutoIncrementStep	The increment value for an auto-incrementing column.
Caption	The caption to be used for this column in the user interface.
Namespace	The namespace for this DataTable, used when importing or exporting XML data.
Prefix	The XML prefix for the DataTable namespace.
ColumnMapping	The MappingType of this column, which is how this column is rendered as XML. It can be Element, Attribute, SimpleContent, or Hidden.
Table	The DataTable this column belongs to (read-only).
Ordinal	The position of this column in the DataColumnCollection (read-only).
ExtendedProperties	Returns the PropertyCollection object used to store custom information about the DataTable (read-only).

The DataView Class

The DataView class represents a view over a DataTable object, a concept that doesn't really match any ADO object you might already know. For example, you can filter the data in a table or sort it without affecting the values in the original DataTable object. Or you can create a view on a table that does (or doesn't) allow insertions, deletions, or updates.

A DataView object contains a collection of DataRowView objects, which are views over the rows in the underlying DataTable object. You can insert, delete, or update these DataRowView objects, and your changes are reflected in the original table as well. Another major function of the DataView class is to provide data binding to Windows Forms and Web Forms. Table 21-5 summarizes the most important members of the DataView class.

Table 21-5 Main Properties, Methods, and Events of the DataView Class

Category	Name	Description
Properties	AllowDelete	True if rows can be deleted.
	AllowEdit	True if values in the DataView can be modified.
	AllowNew	True if new rows can be added.
	Item	Returns the Nth DataRow (default member).
	Count	Returns the number of rows in this view.
	RowFilter	An expression that determines which rows appear in this view.
	RowStateFilter	A DataViewRowState enumerated value that determines how rows are filtered according to their state. It can be None, CurrentRows, OriginalRows, ModifiedCurrent, ModifiedOriginal, Added, Deleted, or Unchanged.
	Sort	A string that specifies the column or columns used as sort keys.
	ApplyDefaultSort	True if the default sort order should be used.
	Table	The source DataTable.
	DataViewManager	The DataView associated with this view (read-only).
Methods	AddNew	Adds a new row and returns a DataRowView object that can be used to set fields' values.
	Delete	Deletes the row at the specified index.
	Find	Finds a row in the DataView given the value of its key column(s); returns the row index.
Events	ListChanged	Fires when the list managed by the DataView changes, that is, when an item is added, deleted, moved, or modified.

The DataRelation Class

The DataRelation class represents a relationship between two DataTable objects in the same DataSet. The relationship is established between one or more fields in the parent (master) table and an equal number of fields in the child (detail) table. Table 21-6 lists the main properties of the DataRelation class. (This class doesn't expose methods other than those inherited from System.Object.) Note that all properties except Nested are read-only.

Table 21-6 Main Properties of the DataRelation Class

Name	Description
RelationName	The name of this relationship.
DataSet	The DataSet object this relationship belongs to.
ParentTable	The parent DataTable object.
ChildTable	The child DataTable object.
ParentColumns	An array of DataColumn objects representing the keys in the parent table that participates in this relationship.
ChildColumns	An array of DataColumn objects representing the keys in the child table that participates in this relationship.
ParentKeyConstraint	The UniqueConstraint object that ensures that values in the parent column are unique.
ChildKeyConstraint	The ForeignKeyConstraint object that ensures that values in the child table's foreign key column are equal to a value in the parent table's key field.
Nested	A Boolean value that specifies whether child columns should be rendered as nested elements when the DataSet is saved as XML text (read/write).

Building a DataSet

Most applications fill a DataSet with data coming from a database query. However, you can use a DataSet in stand-alone mode as well: in this case, you define its structure, set the relationships between its DataTable objects, and fill it with data exclusively through code. Even though this way of working with a DataSet is less frequently used in real-world applications, I'll describe it first because it reveals many inner details of the DataSet class. (Filling a DataSet with data coming from a database is described in the "Reading Data from a Database" section later in this chapter.)

Here's the sequence that you typically follow when you're creating a DataSet:

1. Create a DataSet object.
2. Create a new DataTable object with the desired name. You can set its CaseSensitive property to decide how strings are compared inside the table.

3. Create a new DataColumn object with a given name and type, and optionally set other properties such as AllowDBNull, DefaultValue, and Unique; you can also create calculated columns by setting the Expression property.
4. Add the DataColumn object to the DataTable's Columns collection.
5. Repeat steps 3 and 4 for all the columns in the table.
6. Assign an array of DataColumn objects to the PrimaryKey property of the DataTable. This step is optional but often necessary to leverage the full potential of a DataTable with a primary key.
7. Create one or more constraints for the table, which you do by creating either a UniqueConstraint or a ForeignKeyConstraint object, setting its properties, and then adding it to the DataTable's Constraints collection.
8. Add the DataTable object to the DataSet's Tables collection.
9. Repeat steps 2 through 8 for all the tables in the DataSet.
10. Create all the necessary relationships between tables in the DataSet; you can create a relationship by passing its properties to the Add method of the DataSet's Relations collection or by explicitly creating a DataRelation object, setting its properties, and then adding it to the Relations collection.

Sometimes you can omit some of the steps in the preceding list—for example, when you don't need table constraints or relationships. You can also make your code more concise by creating a DataTable and adding it to the parent DataSet's Tables collection in a single step or by adding a column to the parent DataTable's Columns collection without explicitly creating a DataColumn object. In the following sections, I'll provide examples for each of these techniques.

You create a DataSet by calling its constructor method, which can take the DataSet name. This name is used only in a few cases—for example, when you're outputting data to XML. If the name is omitted, your new DataSet's name defaults to NewDataSet:

```
Dim ds As New DataSet("MyDataSet")
```

As a rule, your application creates and manages only one DataSet object at a time because you can create relationships between tables only if they belong to the same DataSet. In some circumstances, however, working with multiple DataSet objects can be convenient—for example, when you want to render as XML only some of the DataTable objects you're working with or when you want to create a clone of the main DataSet at a given moment in time so that you can restore it later.

Creating a DataTable Object

The code that follows creates a DataSet object that contains an Employees table:

```
' This is at the form level, to be shared among all procedures.
Dim ds As New DataSet()

Sub CreateEmployeesTable()
    ' Create a table; set its initial capacity and case sensitivity.
    Dim dtEmp As New DataTable("Employees")
    dtEmp.MinimumCapacity = 100
    dtEmp.CaseSensitive = False

    ' Create all columns.
    ' You can create a DataColumn and then add it to the Columns collection.
    Dim dcFName As New DataColumn("FirstName", GetType(String))
    dtEmp.Columns.Add(dcFName)
    ' Or you can create an implicit DataColumn with the Columns.Add method.
    dtEmp.Columns.Add("LastName", GetType(String))
    dtEmp.Columns.Add("BirthDate", GetType(Date))

    ' When you have to set additional properties, you can use an explicit
    ' DataColumn object, or you can use a With block.
    With dtEmp.Columns.Add("HomeAddress", GetType(String))
        .MaxLength = 100
    End With
    ' (When you must set only one property, you can be more concise,
    '  even though the result isn't very readable.)
    dtEmp.Columns.Add("City", GetType(String)).MaxLength = 20

    ' Create a calculated column by setting the Expression
    ' property or passing it as the third argument to the Add method.
    dtEmp.Columns.Add("CompleteName", GetType(String), _
        "FirstName + ' ' + LastName")

    ' Create an ID column.
    Dim dcEmpId As New DataColumn("EmpId", GetType(Integer))
    dcEmpId.AutoIncrement = True          ' Make it auto-increment.
    dcEmpId.AutoIncrementSeed = 1
    dcEmpId.AllowDBNull = False           ' Default is True.
    dcEmpId.Unique = True                 ' All key columns should be unique.
    dtEmp.Columns.Add(dcEmpId)            ' Add to Columns collection.

    ' Make it the primary key.
    Dim pkCols() As DataColumn = {dcEmpId}
    dtEmp.PrimaryKey = pkCols
```

```
    ' You can also use a more concise syntax, as follows:
    dtEmp.PrimaryKey = New DataColumn() {dcEmpId}

    ' This is a foreign key, but we haven't created the other table yet.
    dtEmp.Columns.Add("DeptId", GetType(Integer))

    ' Add the DataTable to the DataSet.
    ds.Tables.Add(dtEmp)
End Sub
```

The MinimumCapacity property offers an opportunity to optimize the performance of the application: the first rows that you create—up to the number defined by this property—won't require any additional memory allocation and therefore will be added more quickly.

As you see in the listing, you define the type of a DataColumn by using a System.Type object. So most of the time you'll use the Visual Basic GetType function for common data types such as String, Integer, and Date. The many remarks explain the several syntax variations that you might adopt when you're adding a new column to the table's schema.

Some columns might require that you set additional properties. For example, you should set the AllowDBNull property to False to reject null values, set the Unique property to True to ensure that all values in the column are unique, or set the MaxLength property for String columns. You can create auto-incrementing columns (which are often used as key columns) by setting the AutoIncrement property to True and optionally setting the AutoIncrementSeed and AutoIncrementStep properties:

```
' Create an ID column.
    Dim dcEmpId As New DataColumn("EmpId", GetType(Integer))
    dcEmpId.AutoIncrement = True            ' Make it auto-increment.
    dcEmpId.AutoIncrementSeed = 1
    dcEmpId.AllowDBNull = False             ' Default is True.
    dcEmpId.Unique = True                   ' All key columns should be unique.
```

You can set the primary key by assigning a DataColumn array to the PrimaryKey property of the DataTable object. In most cases, this array contains just one element, but you can create compound keys made up of multiple columns if necessary:

```
' Create a primary key on the FirstName and LastName columns.
' (Create the DataColumn arrays on the fly.)
dtEmp.PrimaryKey = New DataColumn() _
    {dtEmp.Columns("FirstName"), dtEmp.Columns("LastName")}
```

The DataTable built in the CreateEmployeesTable procedure also contains a calculated column, CompleteName, evaluated as the concatenation of the

FirstName and LastName columns. You can assign this expression to the Expression property or pass it as the third argument of the Add method. The "Working with Expressions" section later in this chapter describes which operators and functions you can use in an expression.

> **Note** Interestingly, you can store any type of object in a DataSet, including forms, controls, and your custom objects. When using a column to store an object, you should specify the column type with GetType(Object). If the object is serializable, it will be restored correctly when you write the DataSet to a file and read it back. (If the object isn't serializable, you get an error when you attempt to serialize the DataSet.) Note that the object state isn't rendered correctly as XML when you issue the WriteXml method, however. (See the "Writing XML Data" section in Chapter 22 for more information about this method.)

Adding Rows

The only significant operation that you can perform on an empty DataTable is the addition of one or more DataRow objects. The sequence to add a new row is as follows:

1. Use the DataTable's NewRow method to create a DataRow object with the same column schema as the table.
2. Assign values to all the fields in the DataRow (at least, to all fields that aren't nullable and that don't support a default value).
3. Pass the DataRow to the Add method of the table's Rows collection.

You should ensure that the new row doesn't violate the constraints defined for the table. For example, you must provide a value for all non-nullable columns and set a unique value for the primary key and for all the keys whose Unique property is True. Here's an example that adds a row to the Employees table defined previously. (Note that it doesn't set the primary key because you've defined an auto-incrementing column.)

```
' Get a reference to the Employees table.
Dim dtEmp As DataTable = ds.Tables("Employees")
' Create a new row with the same schema.
Dim dr As DataRow = dtEmp.NewRow()

' Set all the columns.
dr("FirstName") = "Joe"
dr("LastName") = "Doe"
```

```
dr("BirthDate") = #1/15/1955#
dr("HomeAddress") = "1234 A Street"
dr("City") = "Los Angeles"
dr("DeptId") = 1
' Add to the Rows collection.
dtEmp.Rows.Add(dr)
```

The Rows collection also supports an InsertAt method, which apparently would let you insert the new row in any position of the DataTable.

When adding a large number of rows, you can optimize the performance of your code by using the LoadDataRow method (which takes an array of the values to be assigned) and bracketing your code in the DataTable's BeginLoadData and EndLoadData methods. (These methods temporarily disable and then reenable notifications, index maintenance, and constraints while loading data.) For example, suppose you want to import data into the Employees table from a semicolon-delimited file structured as follows:

```
"Andrew";"Fuller";2/19/1952;"908 W. Capital Way";"Tacoma"
"Janet";"Leverling";8/30/1963;"722 Moss Bay Blvd.";"Kirkland"
```

Here's how you can solve the problem with a concise routine that's also as efficient as possible:

```
' Open the file, and read its contents.
Dim sr As New System.IO.StreamReader("employees.dat")
Dim fileText As String = sr.ReadToEnd
sr.Close()

' This regular expression defines a row of elements and assigns a name
' to each group (that is, a field in the text row).
Dim re As New System.Text.RegularExpressions.Regex( _
    """(?<fname>[^""]+)"";""(?<lname>[^""]+)"";(?<bdate>[^;]+);" _
    & """(?<addr>[^""]+)"";""(?<city>[^""]+)""")
Dim ma As System.Text.RegularExpressions.Match

' Turn off index maintenance and constraints.
dtEmp.BeginLoadData()
' Repeat for each match (that is, each line in the file).
For Each ma In re.Matches(fileText)
    ' A new line has been found, so add a row to the table.
    ' Create an array of values.
    Dim values() As Object = {ma.Groups("fname").Value, _
        ma.Groups("lname").Value, ma.Groups("bdate").Value, _
        ma.Groups("addr").Value, ma.Groups("city").Value}
    ' Load all fields in one operation.
    dtEmp.LoadDataRow(values, True)
Next
' Turn on index maintenance and constraints.
dtEmp.EndLoadData()
```

The syntax of the regular expression used to parse the file is maybe the most complex part of this code, but it's simpler than you might imagine. The purpose of this regular expression is to define the structure of each line in the data file and assign a distinct name to each group of characters delimited by semicolons and (in some cases) enclosed in double quotation marks. The meaning of the pattern becomes clearer if you get rid of the repeated double quotation marks that you see inside the string itself and split the expression according to each of the fields referenced:

```
"(?<fname>[^"]+)";
"(?<lname>[^"]+)";
(?<bdate>[^;]+);
"(?<addr>[^""]+)";
"(?<city>[^""]+)"
```

Thanks to the groups defined in the regular expression, you can then reference each field by its name when you create the array of values:

```
Dim values() As Object = {ma.Groups("fname").Value, _
    ma.Groups("lname").Value, ma.Groups("bdate").Value, _
    ma.Groups("addr").Value, ma.Groups("city").Value}
```

Be aware that the LoadDataRow method adds a new row only if the key field isn't already in the table. If you're passing the primary key as a value and the table already contains a record with that key, the LoadDataRow method replaces the existing row with the new values. For this reason, it's important that you correctly set the DataTable's primary key to avoid duplicate keys.

The BeginLoadData and EndLoadData methods are also useful for performing changes in a DataTable that would result in a temporary violation of the referential integrity rules or other constraints such as the uniqueness of a column—for example, when you have to exchange the primary keys of two rows in a table.

Updating and Deleting Rows

One important difference between an ADO disconnected Recordset and a DataTable is that the latter doesn't support the concept of navigation through its rows. If you think about it, the inability to access any row other than the current one is a limitation that the ADO Recordset has only because it must serve server-side cursors. This limitation makes little sense when all the data has been transferred to the client application. Because the DataSet and its DataTable objects have been designed specifically for client-side operations, they get rid of the current record concept and appear to the developer like an array of DataRow objects, which you can access through their positional index. For example, the following loop converts the FirstName and LastName columns to uppercase in the first 10 records of the Employees table:

```
Dim i As Integer
For i = 0 To 9
    Dim dr As DataRow = dtEmp.Rows(i)
    dr("FirstName") = dr("FirstName").ToString.ToUpper
    dr("LastName") = dr("LastName").ToString.ToUpper
Next
```

You can also avoid the temporary DataRow object, as in this code snippet:

```
' Clear the name fields of all the records in the DataTable.
For i = 0 To dtEmp.Rows.Count - 1
    dtEmp.Rows(i)("FirstName") = ""
    dtEmp.Rows(i)("LastName") = ""
Next
```

You can also use a For Each loop when looping over all the DataRow items in a DataTable:

```
Dim dr As DataRow
For Each dr In dtEmp.Rows
    dr("FirstName") = ""
    dr("LastName") = ""
Next
```

Deleting a row is as easy as issuing a Delete method on the corresponding DataRow object:

```
' Delete the last DataRow in the table.
dtEmp.Rows(dtEmp.Rows.Count - 1).Delete
```

However, deleted rows aren't physically deleted from the DataSet. In fact, the only effect of the Delete method is to mark the row as deleted: the row is still in the DataTable, even though you can perform only a small number of operations on it. You can detect whether a row is deleted by means of the RowState property, which is described in the following section.

The Rows collection supports the Remove method, which removes the DataRow from the collection. Unlike the DataRow's Delete method, the row is immediately removed from the DataSet and not just marked for deletion:

```
' Remove the last DataRow in the table. (Can't be undeleted.)
dtEmp.Rows.Remove(dtEmp.Rows.Count - 1)
```

Accepting and Rejecting Changes

Because the DataSet is just a client-side repository of data and is physically disconnected from any data source, it should be clear that the operations you perform on the DataSet, its tables, and its rows aren't reflected in the data source you used to fill it, at least not automatically, as happens with ADO keysets and dynamic recordsets. (I discuss how you update a database from a DataSet later in this chapter.)

I mentioned in the preceding section that when you delete a row you're actually marking it for deletion, but the row is still in the DataSet. You can test the current state of a DataRow object by querying its RowState property, which can return one of the following values:

- **Detached** The row has been created but hasn't been added to a DataTable.
- **Added** The row has been added to a DataTable.
- **Modified** The row has been updated.
- **Deleted** The row has been deleted.
- **Unchanged** The row hasn't been modified.

You can use the DataTable's Select method to filter the rows in a table depending on their current state, as I explain in the "Filtering, Searching, and Sorting" section later in this chapter.

The RowState property is read-only, but the DataRow class exposes two methods that affect this property. You invoke the AcceptChanges method to confirm your changes on the current row and the RejectChanges method to cancel them. (Once again, these methods don't really update any data source outside the DataSet.) The effect of the AcceptChanges method is to physically delete rows marked for deletion and then set the RowState property of all the remaining rows to Unchanged. The RejectChanges method drops all the rows that have been added since the DataTable was loaded and then sets the RowState property of all the remaining rows to Unchanged.

To see in greater detail how these methods affect the state of a row, consider the following code:

```
Dim dr As DataRow = dtEmp.NewRow
Debug.WriteLine(dr.RowState)          ' => Detached
dr("FirstName") = "Joe"
dr("LastName") = "Doe"
dtEmp.Rows.Add(dr)
Debug.WriteLine(dr.RowState)          ' => Added

' AcceptChanges marks all records as unchanged.
dr.AcceptChanges()
Debug.WriteLine(dr.RowState)          ' => Unchanged
dr(0) = ""
```

```
Debug.WriteLine(dr.RowState)        ' => Modified
dr.Delete()
Debug.WriteLine(dr.RowState)        ' => Deleted

' RejectChanges undeletes the row and restores its unchanged status.
dr.RejectChanges()
Debug.WriteLine(dr.RowState)        ' => Unchanged
dr.Delete()
Debug.WriteLine(dr.RowState)        ' => Deleted

' AcceptChanges definitively deletes the row,
' which now appears to be detached.
dr.AcceptChanges()
Debug.WriteLine(dr.RowState)        ' => Detached
```

Also, the DataTable and the DataSet classes expose the AcceptChanges and RejectChanges methods, so you can easily accept or undo changes that you've made in all the rows in a table and all the tables in a DataSet. Note that the second argument of the LoadDataRow method specifies whether the method should execute an implicit AcceptChanges.

Validating Values in Rows and Columns

All robust applications should validate data entered by the end user. Doing this is easy when you add data programmatically—you just avoid entering invalid values. But validation is less easy when the end user enters or modifies records through the user interface—for example, by means of a bound DataGrid control. Fortunately, validating data entered by this route is also relatively simple thanks to the events that the DataTable object exposes. (See Table 21-2.) These events are of two types: *xxx*Changing (which occur before a column is changed, a row is changed, or a row is deleted) and *xxx*Changed (which occur after the column has changed, the row has changed, or the row has been deleted).

The demo application displays the Employees table in the lowest grid and then assigns the Employees table to a DataTable variable marked with the WithEvents keyword so that any editing action on the table underlying the DataGrid control can be handled through code:

```
Dim WithEvents DataTable As DataTable

Private Sub btnEvents_Click(ByVal sender As Object, _
    ByVal e As EventArgs) Handles btnEvents.Click
    ' Demonstrate how to deal with events from the Employees table.
    DataTable = ds.Tables(0)
End Sub
```

Validating a new value in a column is as easy as trapping the ColumnChanging event, checking the new value (which can be found in the ProposedValue property of the object passed in the second argument to the event handler), and throwing an exception if it can't be accepted. For example, the following code rejects future dates assigned to the BirthDate column:

```
Private Sub DataTable_ColumnChanging(ByVal sender As Object, _
    ByVal e As DataColumnChangeEventArgs) Handles DataTable.ColumnChanging
    If e.Column.ColumnName = "BirthDate" Then
        If CDate(e.ProposedValue) > Date.Now Then
            Throw New ArgumentException("Invalid birth date value")
        End If
    End If
End Sub
```

If the user attempts to enter an invalid birth date in the DataGrid, the old value is automatically restored when the caret leaves the grid cell. Note that the DataGrid absorbs the exception and no error message is shown to the user. Interestingly, you can check the value and throw the exception even in the ColumnChanged event handler: in this case, the value is rejected only when the caret leaves the row (not the column).

Often you can't validate columns individually and must consider two or more columns at a time. The typical case is when the value in a column must be greater or lower than the value in another column. In this case, you must validate both columns in the RowChanging event handler. This event fires when a row is changed or added to the table. You can determine the action being performed by checking the Action property of the second argument passed to the event handler. For example, you can use the following code to ensure that State and Country columns can't both be null strings:

```
Private Sub DataTable_RowChanging(ByVal sender As Object, _
    ByVal e As DataRowChangeEventArgs) Handles DataTable.RowChanging
    If CStr(e.Row("State")) = "" And CStr(e.Row("Country")) = "" Then
        Throw New ArgumentException("State and Country can't both be empty")
    End If
End Sub
```

In this case, the DataGrid catches the exception when the user moves the caret to another row, displays the error message you've passed to the ArgumentException's constructor, and restores the original values in the row's fields.

The *xxx*Changed events aren't just for validation chores, and you can use them in a variety of other situations as well. For example, you might use them to update a calculated column that depends on one or more other columns but whose value can't be expressed using the operators allowed by ADO.NET for calculated columns. (See the "Working with Expressions" section later in this chapter.)

Setting, Retrieving, and Fixing Errors

Instead of throwing exceptions when a column or a row doesn't contain valid values, you can opt for a different error handling strategy and just mark the column or the row with an error message. This approach lets you show end users a list of all the existing errors so that they can decide to fix the invalid values or cancel the update operation as a whole. (This alternative strategy is more feasible when you're importing data from a file or when the user has submitted all changes together, as is the case when he or she fills out a form in the browser and then clicks the Submit button.)

If you opt for this strategy, you can still use the *xxx*Changing and *xxx*-Changed events as before; what changes is the way to react to an invalid value. When you detect an invalid column value, you use the DataRow's Set-ColumnError method to associate an error message with that column. When you detect an invalid row, you assign an error message to the DataRow's RowError property:

```
Private Sub DataTable_ColumnChanging(ByVal sender As Object, _
    ByVal e As DataColumnChangeEventArgs) Handles DataTable.ColumnChanging
    If e.Column.ColumnName = "BirthDate" Then
        If CDate(e.ProposedValue) > Date.Now Then
            e.Row.SetColumnError(e.Column.ColumnName, _
                "Invalid birth date value")
        End If
    End If
End Sub

Private Sub DataTable_RowChanging(ByVal sender As Object, _
    ByVal e As DataRowChangeEventArgs) Handles DataTable.RowChanging
    If CStr(e.Row("State")) = "" And CStr(e.Row("Country")) = "" Then
        e.Row.RowError = "State and Country can't both be null"
    End If
End Sub
```

It's interesting to see that the DataGrid control reacts to columns and rows marked with an error by displaying an error icon in the column's cell or in the row indicator, respectively, but without automatically restoring the original values. You can then move the mouse cursor over the icon to read the error message you've set via code. (See Figure 21-2.)

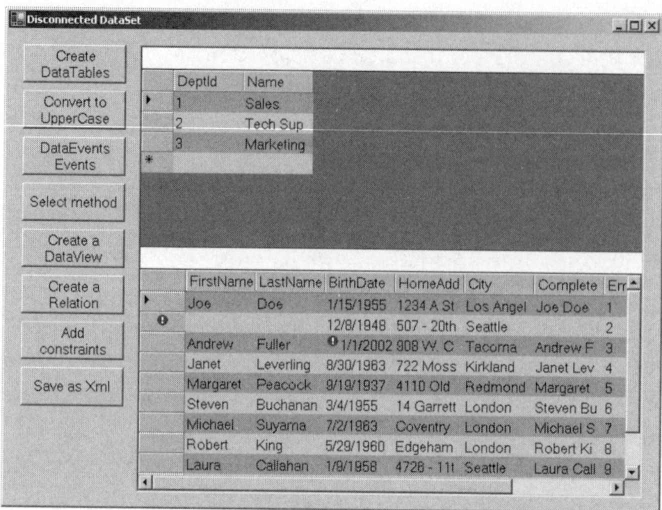

Figure 21-2. The DataGrid control displays error icons near invalid columns and rows.

You can check via code whether a DataRow, a DataTable, or a DataSet contains any error through its HasErrors read-only property, without having to go through each column of each row of each table in the DataSet. For example, you can use the following loop to evaluate the number of rows that contain one or more errors:

```
Dim dt As DataTable, dr As DataRow, numErrors As Integer
If ds.HasErrors Then
    ' There is at least one DataTable with an invalid row.
    For Each dt In ds.Tables
        If dt.HasErrors Then
            ' There is at least one DataRow with an invalid column.
            For Each dr In dt.Rows
                If dr.HasErrors Then numErrors += 1
            Next
        End If
    Next
End If
' Now numErrors contains the number of rows with errors.
```

You can retrieve the actual error message associated with a column by means of the DataRow's GetColumnError method. And you can clear all the error messages associated with a row by using the ClearErrors method. You can get the array of all the columns that have an error with GetColumnsInError.

```
' Gather all the error messages associated with individual columns.
' (dr is the DataRow under examination.)
```

```
Dim messages As String, dc As DataColumn
For Each dc In dr.GetColumnsInError()
    Messages &= dr.GetColumnError(dc) & ControlChars.CrLf
Next
```

Your application might even attempt to resolve some errors without the assistance of end users. For example, you might keep a numeric or date value within its valid range, and you can use the spelling checker and automatically correct the name of a state or country. When you attempt to fix the errors each row contains, you can take advantage of the DataRow's ability to preserve both the original value and the current version of the value in each column. You can access these versioned values by passing a DataRowVersion argument to the Item property, after checking with the HasVersion method that the row supports the versioned value you're looking for:

```
' This code attempts to resolve errors in the BirthDate column
' by restoring the original value if there is one.
Dim dr As DataRow
For Each dr In dtEmp.Rows
    If dr.GetColumnError("BirthDate") <> "" Then
        If dr.HasVersion(DataRowVersion.Original) Then
            dr("BirthDate") = dr("BirthDate", DataRowVersion.Original)
            ' This statement hides the error icon in the DataGrid.
            dr.SetColumnError("BirthDate", "")
        End If
    End If
Next
```

When you issue the DataRow's AcceptChanges method, the proposed value becomes the current value and the original value persists. Conversely, when you issue the DataTable's AcceptChanges method, the original value is lost and both the DataRowVersion.Original and DataRowVersion.Current values for the second argument return the same result. The reasons for this behavior will become apparent in the "Updating the Database" section later in this chapter.

If you enclose your edit operations between BeginEdit and EndEdit (or CancelEdit) methods, you can query the value being assigned but not yet commited using the DataRowVersion.Proposed value for the argument. When you issue the EndEdit method, the proposed value becomes the current value.

Filtering, Searching, and Sorting

You can choose from two different techniques for filtering, searching, and sorting the rows of a DataTable: you can use its Select method, or you can define a DataView object. The Select method takes up to three arguments: a filter expression, a sort criterion, and a DataViewRowState enumerated argument that lets you filter rows on their current state and decide which value you see in the columns of modified rows. In its simplest form, the Select method takes a filter expression and returns an array of matching DataRow elements:

```
' Retrieve all employees whose first name is Joe.
Dim drows() as DataRow = dtEmp.Select("FirstName = 'Joe'")
```

The second (optional) argument is the list of fields on which the result array should be sorted:

```
' Retrieve all employees born in 1960 or later, and
' sort the result on their (LastName, FirstName) fields.
drows = dtEmp.Select("BirthDate >= #1/1/1960#", "LastName, FirstName")
```

You can also sort in descending mode using the DESC qualifier, as in this code snippet:

```
' Retrieve all employees born in 1960 or later, and
' sort the result on their birth date. (Younger employees come first.)
drows = dtEmp.Select("BirthDate >= #1/1/1960#", "BirthDate DESC")
```

Finally, you can filter rows depending on their state by passing a DataViewRowState value that specifies whether you're interested in changed, unchanged, added, or deleted rows:

```
' Retrieve all deleted rows, sorted by (FirstName, LastName) values.
drows = dtEmp.Select("", "FirstName, LastName", DataViewRowState.Deleted)
```

The third argument can take any of the values listed in Table 21-7; if you omit this argument, you see rows with their current values and deleted rows aren't returned. The Select method is therefore able to access the values that were in the DataTable after the most recent AcceptChanges or RejectChanges method or after reading them from a data source by using a DataAdapter object (as I explain in a later section).

The following code uses the Select method to extract a subset of rows from the Employees table and loads them into another table with the same column structure by means of ImportRow, a method that imports a DataRow object into a table without resetting the row's original and current values and its RowState property:

```
' Copy only the structure of the Employees table in the new table.
Dim newDt As DataTable = dtEmp.Clone()
newDt.TableName = "YoungEmployees"

' Select a subset of all employees, sorted on their names;
' extract only modified rows, with their current values.
Dim drows() As DataRow = dtEmp.Select("BirthDate >= #1/1/1960#", _
    "LastName, FirstName", DataViewRowState.ModifiedCurrent)
' Import the array of DataRows into the new table.
```

```
Dim dr As DataRow
For Each dr In drows
    newDt.ImportRow(dr)
Next
```

Table 21-7 Allowed Values for the DataViewRowState Argument

Name	Description
CurrentRows	Current rows, including unchanged, new, and modified rows. Deleted rows aren't visible.
OriginalRows	Original rows as they were after the most recent AcceptChanges or RejectChanges method, including unchanged and deleted rows. Added rows aren't visible.
Unchanged	Unchanged rows only.
Added	Added rows only.
Deleted	Deleted rows only.
ModifiedCurrent	Changed rows only. Columns contain the current (modified) value.
ModifiedOriginal	Changed rows only. Columns contain the original value.
None	No rows are returned.

Using the DataView Object

Another way for you to filter or sort the rows in a DataTable is to use an auxiliary DataView object. As its name suggests, this object works as a view over an existing DataTable. You can decide which records are visible by means of the DataView's RowFilter property, sort its rows with the Sort property, and decide which column values are displayed by assigning a DataViewRowState enumerated value to the DataView's RowStateFilter property. These properties give you the same filtering and sorting capabilities as the Select method:

```
' Display a subset of all employees, sorted on their names;
' show only modified rows, with their current values.

' Create a DataView on this table.
Dim dv As New DataView(dtEmp)
' Set its filter and sort properties.
dv.RowFilter = "BirthDate >= #1/1/1960#"
dv.Sort = "LastName, FirstName"
dv.RowStateFilter = DataViewRowState.ModifiedCurrent
```

You can add, delete, and modify rows in a DataView by using the same methods you'd use with a regular DataTable, and your edit operation will affect the underlying table. You can also use the Find method to retrieve a DataRow given its primary key value.

The DataView object is especially useful when you bind it to a Windows Form control or Web Form control. For example, you might have two DataGrid controls displaying data from two DataView objects, each one containing a different view of the same table—for example, the original and the edited rows or two different sorted views of the same data. You bind a DataView to a DataGrid by assigning it to the control's DataSource property and then calling its DataBind method:

```
DataGrid1.DataSource = dv
DataGrid1.DataBind()
```

Even when you have an unfiltered and unsorted set of data, binding a DataView instead of a DataTable is usually a better idea because you can finely control what operations the end user can perform on data by means of the DataView's AllowDelete, AllowEdit, and AllowNew properties. See Table 21-5 for the list of the main properties, methods, and events of the DataView class.

Creating Relationships

A great feature of the DataSet is its ability to create relationships between its DataTable objects. Like real relational databases, a DataSet allows a relationship between two tables if they have a field in common. For example, you can establish a relationship between the Publishers and Titles tables if they have the PubId field in common. In this case, there would be a one-to-many relationship from the Publishers table (the parent or master table) to the Titles table (the child or detail table).

Lookup tables often use relationships, such as when you use the DeptId field in the Employees table to retrieve the name of the department in the Departments table. This is the case shown in the following diagram.

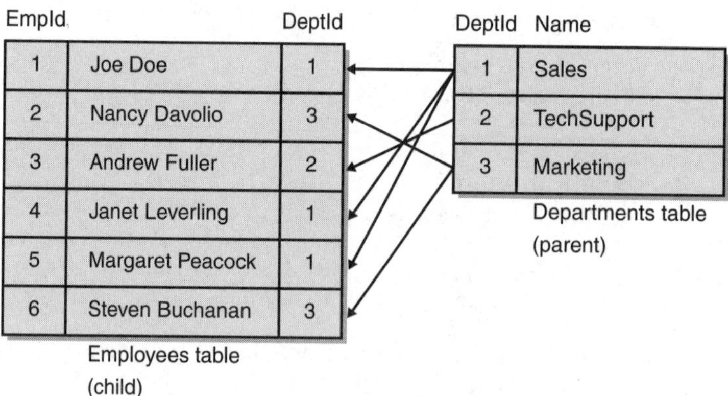

Let's see how to build such a relationship. First of all, let's create the Departments table and add some rows to it:

```
' Create the Departments table.
Dim dtDept As New DataTable("Departments")

' The DeptId field must be marked as unique.
Dim dcDeptId As DataColumn = dtDept.Columns.Add("DeptId", GetType(Integer))
dcDeptId.Unique = True
' The department name must be unique as well.
Dim dcName As DataColumn = dtDept.Columns.Add("Name", GetType(String))
dcName.MaxLength = 50
dcName.Unique = True
' Make DeptId the primary key of the table.
dtDept.PrimaryKey = New DataColumn() {dcDeptId}
' Add this table to the DataSet.
ds.Tables.Add(dtDept)

' Add a few rows.
Dim values() As Object = {1, "Sales"}
dtDept.LoadDataRow(values, True)
' You can do the same in just one statement.
dtDept.LoadDataRow(New Object() {2, "Tech Support"}, True)
dtDept.LoadDataRow(New Object() {3, "Marketing"}, True)
```

Next let's ensure that the DeptId field in the Employees table points to an existing row in the Departments table:

```
' Ensure that all Employees are associated with a Department.
Dim i As Integer
For i = 0 To dtEmp.Rows.Count - 1
    ' Assign a DeptId value in the range 1-3.
    dtEmp.Rows(i).Item("DeptId") = CInt((i Mod 3) + 1)
Next
dtEmp.AcceptChanges()
```

Now we can create the relationship between the Departments and Employees tables. You can choose from a couple of ways to create a relationship: you can create a DataRelation object explicitly and then add it to the DataSet's Relations collection, or you can create a relationship directly with the Add method of the Relations collection. The following code snippet uses the first approach:

```
' The DataRelation constructor takes the name of the relationship and
' a reference to the DataColumn in the parent and in the child table.
Dim relDeptEmp As New DataRelation("DeptEmp", _
    dtDept.Columns("DeptId"), dtEmp.Columns("DeptId"))
ds.Relations.Add(relDeptEmp)
```

The upper grid in Figure 21-3 shows how a DataGrid control displays a DataTable that works as a parent table in a relationship.

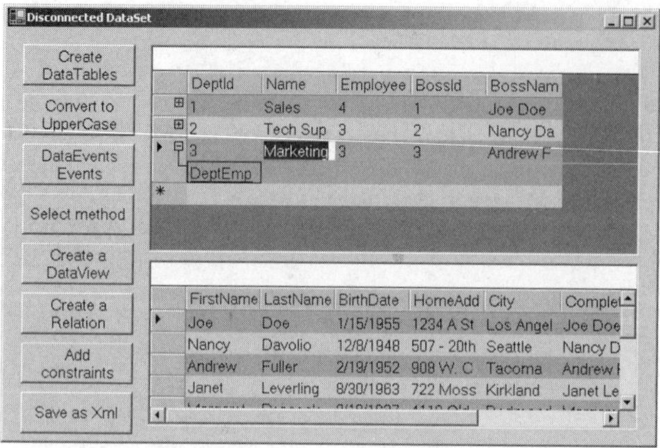

Figure 21-3. The DataGrid control lets you navigate through DataTable objects linked by relationships.

Once you have created a relationship, you can easily navigate from one table to the other using the GetParentRow and GetChildRows methods of the DataRow class. You use the former method to get the row in the parent table that corresponds to the current row in the child table. For example, you can retrieve the name of the department associated with the first row in the Employees table as follows:

```
' Retrieve the name of the department of the first employee.
Dim drDepartment As DataRow = dtEmp.Rows(0).GetParentRow("DeptEmp")
Dim deptName As String = CStr(drDepartment("Name"))
```

You use the GetChildRows method when navigating from a row in the parent table to the corresponding rows in the child table. However, because this is a one-to-many relationship, the GetChildRows method returns an array of rows taken from the child table:

```
' Display the names of the employees in the first department.
Dim drEmployees() As DataRow = dtDept.Rows(0).GetChildRows("DeptEmp")
Dim drEmp As DataRow
For Each drEmp in drEmployees
    Debug.WriteLine(drEmp("LastName"))
Next

' Display the number of employees in each department.
Dim dr As DataRow
For Each dr In dtDept.Rows
    Debug.WriteLine(dr("Name").ToString & ", " & _
        dr.GetChildRows("DeptEmp").Length.ToString)
Next
```

A DataSet can contain multiple relationships and can even contain more than one relationship between the same pair of tables. For example, the Departments table might have a BossId field that contains the ID of the row in Employees corresponding to the department's boss. Here's how you can set the corresponding relationship:

```
' Add a new BossId column to the Departments table, and fill it with the
' ID of the first 3 employees.
dtDept.Columns.Add("BossId", GetType(Integer))
For i = 0 To dtDept.Rows.Count - 1
    dtDept.Rows(i)("BossId") = dtEmp.Rows(i)("EmpId")
Next
dtDept.AcceptChanges()

' Create another relationship between the Departments and Employees tables.
ds.Relations.Add("DeptBoss", dtEmp.Columns("EmpId"), dtDept.Columns("BossId"))
```

Here's the code that leverages the new relationship to print the list of departments and the names of their bosses:

```
' List the name of each department and the name of its boss.
Dim dr As DataRow
For Each dr In dtDept.Rows
    Debug.WriteLine(dr("Name").ToString & ", " & _
        dr.GetParentRow("DeptBoss")("LastName").ToString)
Next
```

The GetChildRows method supports a second DataRowVersion argument that lets you decide whether you want to extract the original or current versions of the child rows. In the next section, you'll learn how to create calculated columns that take advantage of the relationships existing in the DataSet.

You can remove an existing relationship by using the Remove or RemoveAt method of the DataSet's Relations collection. However, these methods throw an exception if the DataRelation object can't be removed from the collection. To avoid this exception, you should test whether the relationship can be removed by means of the CanRemove method:

```
' ds is the DataSet that holds the relationship.
Dim relDeptEmp As DataRelation = ds.Relations("DeptEmp")
If ds.Relations.CanRemove(relDeptEmp) Then
    ' Remove the relationship only if it is safe to do so.
    ds.Relations.Remove(relDeptEmp)
End If
```

Working with Expressions

Many ADO.NET properties and methods support custom expressions. For example, you can assign an expression to the Expression property of a calculated DataColumn or pass an expression to the Filter method of a DataTable to extract a subset of all the rows. In all cases, the syntax of the expression you create must obey the few simple rules that I summarize in this section.

The expression can contain numeric, string, and date constants; string constants must be enclosed in single quotes, and date constants must be enclosed in # characters. You can reference another column in the same table by using its ColumnName property. If a column name contains special punctuation characters, you should enclose the name between square brackets.

The four math operations are supported, as well as the modulo operation (use the % symbol) and the string concatenation operator (use the + sign). All the comparison operators are supported. When applied to strings, they perform case-sensitive or case-insensitive comparisons depending on the CaseSensitive property of the DataTable object. Here are a few examples of valid expressions:

```
FirstName + ' ' + LastName
UnitPrice * 0.80
BirthDate > #1/4/1980#
```

The LIKE operator is similar to the SQL operator of the same name; you can use either the % or the * character as a wildcard, and they can appear anywhere in the second operand. For example, both the following expressions filter all employees whose last name starts with "A":

```
LastName LIKE 'A*"
LastName LIKE 'A%"
```

The IN operator is also similar to the SQL operator of the same name and lets you check that a column's value is among those specified. For example, you can filter only those employees whose DeptId is equal to 2, 3, or 4:

```
DeptId IN (2, 3, 4)
```

The expression evaluator also supports a few functions, which are listed in Table 21-8. For example, suppose you want to create a calculated column named Discount, whose value is equal to Total * .90 when Total is less than or equal to 1000 and Total *.85 if Total is higher than 1000. The IIF function is what you need:

```
dt.Columns.Add("Discount", GetType(Double), _
    "IIF(Total <= 1000, Total * 0.9, Total * 0.85)")
```

An expression can refer also to a field in another table if a relationship exists between the current table and the other table. When working with relationships, you can use two different syntaxes, depending on whether the other table is the parent table or the child table in the relationship. For example, if there is a relationship named DeptEmp between the Departments and the Employees tables in the DeptId column that they have in common, you can add a calculated column to the Employees table that returns the name of the department, as follows:

```
' Extend the Employees table with a calculated column that
' returns the name of the department for that employee.
dtEmp.Columns.Add("Department", GetType(String), "Parent(DeptEmp).Name)")
```

The following example uses the DeptBoss relationship to extend the Departments table with a calculated field equal to the name of the department's boss:

```
dtDept.Columns.Add("BossName", GetType(String), _
    "Parent(DeptBoss).CompleteName")
```

If the current table is the parent table of the relationship and you want to reference a field in the child table, you use Child(relname).fieldname syntax. However, because most relationships are of the one-to-many kind when seen from the perspective of the parent table, in most cases what you really want is to evaluate an aggregate function on the matching rows in the child table. The expression engine supports all the usual aggregation functions, including Count, Sum, Min, Max, Avg (average), StDev (standard deviation), and Var (variance).

For example, you can leverage the DeptEmp relationship to extend the Departments table with a calculated column that returns the count of employees in each department:

```
' Add a calculated column to the Departments table
' that returns the number of employees for each department.
dtDept.Columns.Add("EmployeesCount", GetType(Integer), _
    "Count(Child(DeptEmp).EmpID)")
```

Assuming that the Employees table has a Salary column, you can add other calculated fields in the Departments table that evaluate to the minimum, maximum, and average salary for the employees in each department:

```
dtDept.Columns.Add("MinSalary", GetType(Double), _
    "Min(Child(DeptEmp).Salary)")
dtDept.Columns.Add("MaxSalary", GetType(Double), _
    "Max(Child(DeptEmp).Salary)")
dtDept.Columns.Add("AvgSalary", GetType(Double), _
    "Avg(Child(DeptEmp).Salary)")
```

You often use aggregate functions together with the DataTable's Compute method, which offers a simple method to extract data from all or a subset of the rows in a DataTable object. This method takes an expression and a filter that specifies the rows that are used to compute the expression: Evaluate the average salary of all employees.

```
Debug.WriteLine(dtEmp.Compute("Avg(Salary)", Nothing))
' Evaluate the average salary for employees in a given department.
Debug.WriteLine(dtEmp.Compute("Avg(Salary)", "DeptId = 2"))
```

Table 21-8 Functions Allowed in Expressions

Syntax	Description	Example
Convert(expr, type)	Converts an expression to a .NET type.	Convert(salary, 'System.Double')
Len(string)	Returns the length of a string.	Len(FirstName)
IsNull(expr, ifnullexpr)	Returns the first operand if it isn't DBNull or Nothing. Otherwise, it returns the second value.	IsNull(DeptId, −1)
IIf(expr, truevalue, falsevalue)	Returns the second argument if the expression is True. Otherwise, it returns the third argument.	IIf(total >= 0, 100, −100)
Substring(string, start, length)	Extracts a portion of a string expression. The start index is 1-based.	Substring(MiddleName, 1, 2)

Enforcing Constraints

The DataTable object supports the creation of constraints, where a constraint is a condition that must be met when you add or modify a row in the table. Two different types of constraints are supported: unique constraints and foreign-key constraints.

A unique constraint mandates that all the values in a column or a collection of columns must be unique—in other words, you can't have two rows that contain the same value for the column or combination of columns specified in the constraint. In the majority of cases, the constraint affects only one column: this is the case with the EmpId field in the Employees table. You can enforce this type of constraint by simply setting the column's Unique property to True when you create the column:

```
' The DeptId field must be unique.
Dim dcDeptId As DataColumn = dtDept.Columns.Add("DeptId", GetType(Integer))
dcDeptId.Unique = True
```

In more complex cases, you have multiple columns whose combination must be unique. For example, let's say that the combination of FirstName and LastName columns must be unique. (In other words, you can't have two people with the same name.) To enforce this type of constraint, you must create a UniqueConstraint object, pass an array of columns to its constructor, and add the constraint to the table's Constraints collection:

```
' Prepare the array of involved DataColumn objects.
Dim cols() As DataColumn = { dtEmp.Columns("LastName"), _
    dtEmp.Columns("FirstName") }
' Create the UniqueConstraint object, assigning it a name.
Dim uc As New UniqueConstraint("UniqueName", cols)
' Add it to the table's Constraints collection.
dtEmp.Constraints.Add(uc)
```

Or you can do everything with a single (but less readable) statement:

```
dtEmp.Constraints.Add(New UniqueConstraint(New DataColumn() _
    { dtEmp.Columns("LastName"), dtEmp.Columns("FirstName")}))
```

Now you get an error if you attempt to add a new employee who has the same first name and last name as an employee already in the table:

```
Dim dr As DataRow = dtEmp.NewRow
dr("FirstName") = dtEmp.Rows(0)("FirstName")
dr("LastName") = dtEmp.Rows(0)("LastName")
dtEmp.Rows.Add(dr)              ' This statement causes an error.
```

Constraints are active only if the DataSet's EnforceConstraints property is True (the default value).

You have a foreign-key constraint when the values in a column of a table must match one of the existing values in a column in another table. For example, you can decide that the user isn't able to add an employee whose DeptId field is null or doesn't point to an existing row in the Departments table. You would create such a constraint this way:

```
' Create a foreign-key constraint.
Dim fkrelDeptEmp As New ForeignKeyConstraint("FKDeptEmp", _
    dtDept.Columns("DeptId"), dtEmp.Columns("DeptId"))
' Add it to the child table's Constraints collection.
dtEmp.Constraints.Add(fkrelDeptEmp)
```

Most of the time, however, you don't have to explicitly create a ForeignKeyConstraint object because you can use the foreign-key constraint that's implicitly defined by a relationship between tables and that's available through the ChildKeyConstraint property. (A relationship also creates a unique constraint on the parent table and makes it available through the ParentKeyConstraint property.) The following line of code retrieves a reference to the ForeignKeyConstraint object implied by the relationship between Departments and Employees:

```
Dim fkrel As ForeignKeyConstraint = ds.Relations("DeptEmp").ChildKeyConstraint
```

Note If you have defined a relationship between two tables, the attempt to set another foreign-key constraint over the same columns throws an exception. Creating the foreign-key constraint first and then the relationship on the same columns doesn't raise an error because the relationship reuses the existing constraints. (You can prove it by checking that the relationship's ChildKeyConstraint property returns the original DataConstraint object.)

A foreign-key constraint lets you exert more control over what happens when the end user deletes a row or updates the key field of a row in the parent table. Three properties of the ForeignKeyConstraint object come into play in this case:

- **DeleteRule** This property determines what happens to the rows in the child table when a row in the parent table is deleted. The valid values for this property are Cascade (default, child rows are deleted); None (no action is taken); SetDefault (child column is set to its default value); and SetNull (child column is set to DBNull).
- **UpdateRule** This property specifies what happens to rows in the child table when the key field of a row in the parent table is modified. The valid values for this property are Cascade (default, child column is modified to reflect the new key value); None (no action is taken); SetDefault (child column is set to its default value); and SetNull (child column is set to DBNull).
- **AcceptRejectRule** This property tells how changes in the child table are rolled back when an update operation in the parent table fails because of an error or because the application calls the RejectChanges method. This property can take only one of two values: None (no action occurs) or Cascade (changes are cascaded across the relationship).

Constraints associated with relationships are temporarily suspended during an edit operation until changes are confirmed with the AcceptChanges method. When this happens, constraints are reenabled and an error can occur if the new data doesn't comply with existing constraints. The AcceptRejectRule property determines what happens to child rows when such an error occurs.

You must observe some limitations to the settings that you can assign to the DeleteRule and UpdateRule properties. For example, you can't really use the None value. In fact, after the delete or edit operation, the child row would point to a nonexistent row in the parent table, and this condition would violate the foreign-key constraint itself. In addition, if the child table contains calculated properties that use the relationship, you can't use the SetNull value for most cases.

Let's see how you can set up a foreign-key constraint that automatically updates child rows when the parent row is changed and sets the foreign key in child rows to DBNull if the parent row is deleted:

```
' Note: this code throws an exception if there is already a relationship
'       between the Department.DeptId and Employees.DeptId fields.
Dim fkrelDeptEmp As New ForeignKeyConstraint("FKDeptEmp", _
    dtDept.Columns("DeptId"), dtEmp.Columns("DeptId"))
dtEmp.Constraints.Add(fkrelDeptEmp)

fkrelDeptEmp.DeleteRule = Rule.SetNull
fkrelDeptEmp.UpdateRule = Rule.Cascade
fkrelDeptEmp.AcceptRejectRule = AcceptRejectRule.None
```

Figure 21-4 shows what happens when the user deletes a row in the parent table when the DeleteRule property is set as in the preceding code snippet.

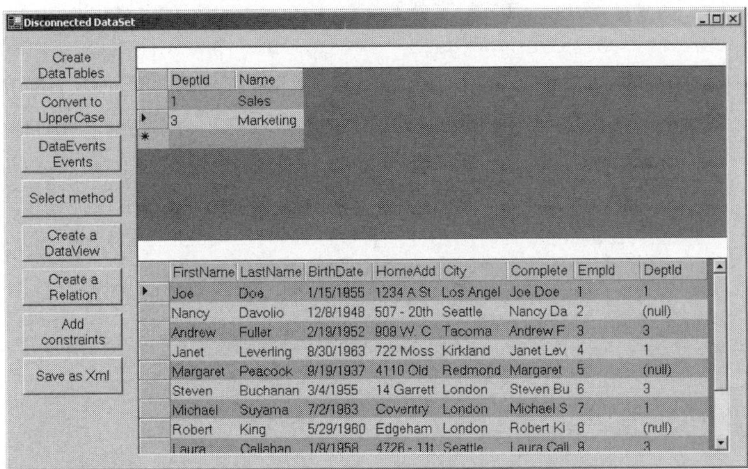

Figure 21-4. When the end user deletes a department in the upper grid, the DeptId fields of the child rows in the Employees table become null (lower grid).

The DataAdapter Class

In the first portion of this chapter, I showed you how to create a DataSet object, load it with data produced by your application (or read from a text file), create constraints and relationships, and define calculated fields. In other words, I showed you how to use the DataSet as a sort of scaled-down client-side database that your code defines and fills with data. While this functionality can be very useful in many scenarios, the majority of .NET applications have to process data coming from a real database, such as Access, SQL Server, or Oracle.

The key to using the DataSet in this way is the DataAdapter object, which works as a connector between the DataSet and the actual data source. The DataAdapter is in charge of filling one or more DataTable objects with data taken from the database so that the application can then close the connection and work in a completely disconnected mode. After the end user has performed all his or her editing chores, the application can reopen the connection and reuse the same DataAdapter object to send changes to the database.

Admittedly, the disconnected nature of the DataSet makes life for us developers more complex, but it greatly improves its versatility, in my opinion. You can now fill a DataTable with data taken from any data source—whether it's SQL Server, a text file, or a mainframe—and process it with the same routines, regardless of its origin. The decoupled architecture based on the DataSet and the DataAdapter makes it possible to read data from one source and send updates to another source, should it be necessary. You have a lot more freedom when working with ADO.NET but also many more responsibilities.

All the code samples that follow assume that a proper connection string has been defined previously and stored in one of the following global variables:

```
' Connection string to Biblio.mdb using the OLE DB .NET Data Provider
Public BiblioConnString As String = "Provider=Microsoft.Jet.OLEDB.4.0;" _
    & "Data Source=C:\Program Files\Microsoft Visual Studio\VB98\Biblio.mdb"
' Connection string to SQL Server's Pubs using the OLE DB .NET Data Provider
Public OledbPubsConnString As String = "Provider=SQLOLEDB.1;Data Source=.;" _
    & "Integrated Security=SSPI:Initial Catalog=Pubs"
' Connection string to Pubs using the SQL Server .NET Data Provider
Public SqlPubsConnString As String = "Data Source=.;" _
    & "Integrated Security=SSPI:Initial Catalog=Pubs"
```

Introducing the DataAdapter

The first thing you need to know about the DataAdapter is that there's actually one DataAdapter class for each .NET data provider, so you have the OleDbDataAdapter and the SqlDataAdapter classes. All DataProvider objects expose the same set of properties and methods because they inherit from the DbDataAdapter abstract class. All the .NET data providers that are to be released in the future will include their own DataAdapter because the DataAdapter must know how to read from and update a specific data source. Except for their names and a few other details—such as how they deal with parameters—you use the OleDbDataAdapter and the SqlDataAdapter in exactly the same way. (See Table 21-9 for their main properties, methods, and events.)

Table 21-9 Main Properties, Methods, and Events of the OleDbDataAdapter and SqlDataAdapter Classes

Category	Name	Description
Properties	SelectCommand	The SQL statement used to read the data source.
	DeleteCommand	The SQL statement used to delete rows in the data source.
	InsertCommand	The SQL statement used to insert rows in the data source.
	UpdateCommand	The SQL statement used to update rows in the data source.
	TableMappings	The collection of table mappings, which maintain the correspondence between columns and tables in the data source and columns and tables in the DataSet.
	MissingMappingAction	The action to take when incoming data doesn't have a matching table or column.
	MissingSchemaAction	The action to take when an existing DataSet schema doesn't match incoming data.
	AcceptChangesDuringFill	Determines whether the AcceptChanges method is called after a DataRow has been added to the DataTable.
Methods	Fill	Adds or refreshes rows in a DataSet with data coming from a DataAdapter or an ADO Recordset.
	FillSchema	Adds a DataTable to the DataSet and configures the schema of the new table based on schema in the data source.
	Update	Updates the data source with the appropriate insert, update, and delete SQL statements.
	GetFillParameters	Gets the parameters set by the user when executing a SQL SELECT statement.
Events	RowUpdating	Fires before sending a SQL command that updates the data source.
	RowUpdated	Fires after sending a SQL command that updates the data source.
	FillError	Fires when an error occurs during a Fill operation.

Reading Data from a Database

The DataAdapter's constructor is overloaded to take zero, one, or two arguments. In its most complete form, you pass to it a SQL SELECT statement (or an

ADO.NET Command object containing a SQL SELECT statement) and a Connection object, as in this code snippet:

```
Dim cn As New OleDbConnection(BiblioConnString)
cn.Open()

' Create a DataAdapter that reads and writes the Publishers table.
Dim sql As String = "SELECT * FROM Publishers"
Dim da As New OleDbDataAdapter(sql, cn)
```

Or you can create a DataAdapter and then assign an ADO.NET Command object to its SelectCommand property:

```
da = New OleDbDataAdapter()
da.SelectCommand = New OleDbCommand(sql, cn)
```

Filling a DataTable

Once you've created a DataAdapter object and defined its SELECT command, you can use the object to fill an existing or new DataTable of a DataSet with the Fill method, which takes the name of the target DataTable in its second argument:

```
' Create a DataSet.
Dim ds As New DataSet()
' Read the Publishers database table into a local DataTable.
da.Fill(ds, "Publishers")
' Close the connection.
cn.Close()
```

Because of the disconnected nature of the DataSet, the action of opening a connection only for the short time necessary to read data from a single database table is so frequent that Microsoft engineers provided the DataAdapter object with the ability to open the connection automatically and close it immediately at the completion of the Fill method. For this reason, the preceding code can be written in a more concise way, as you see here:

```
' Define the connection; no need to open it.
Dim cn As New OleDbConnection(BiblioConnString)
Dim da As New OleDbDataAdapter("SELECT * FROM Publishers", cn)
Dim ds As New DataSet()
' Read the Publishers table; no need to open or close the connection.
da.Fill(ds, "Publishers")
```

(Of course, you shouldn't use this technique when reading data from multiple tables, and you should open the connection manually once and close it afterward.) The Fill method is overloaded to take a variety of arguments, including a reference to an existing DataTable object. You can also omit the name of the target table, in which case a DataTable object named Table is created by default. However, I strongly advise you against doing this because it makes your code less readable to other programmers who aren't aware of this detail.

In most real-world applications, you should avoid reading resultsets containing more than a few hundred rows. You can do this by refining the WHERE clause of the SELECT command or by using an overloaded form of the Fill method that takes the starting record and the maximum number of rows to read. To determine how many rows were actually read, you can check the method's return value:

```
' Read only the first 100 rows of the Publishers table.
Dim numRows As Integer = da.Fill(ds, 0, 100, "Publishers")
```

You can then provide the user with the ability to navigate through pages of the resultset, possibly by using the usual Previous, Next, First, and Last buttons:

```
' Read Nth page; return number of rows on the page.
' (Assuming that the da and ds variables have been correctly initialized)
Function ReadPage(ByVal n As Integer) As Integer
    ReadPage = da.Fill(ds, (n - 1) * 100, 100, "Publishers")
End Sub
```

Another simple way to limit the amount of information read from the database is by using parameters in the WHERE clause of the SQL command. In this case, you can create a parameterized OleDbCommand or SqlCommand object by using the guidelines I describe in the "Parameterized Commands" section in Chapter 20, and you can pass it to the constructor or the SelectCommand property of the DataAdapter, as in the following example:

```
Dim cn As New OleDbConnection(BiblioConnString)

' Create a Command object with parameters.
Dim sql As String = "SELECT * FROM Publishers WHERE Name LIKE ?"
Dim cmd As New OleDbCommand(sql, cn)
' Create the parameter with an initial value.
cmd.Parameters.Add("PubNameLike", "S%")

' Create the DataAdapter based on the parameterized command.
Dim da As New OleDbDataAdapter(cmd)
' Get publishers whose name begins with "S".
da.Fill(ds, "Publishers")

' Add publishers whose name begins with "M".
cmd.Parameters(0).Value = "M%"
da.Fill(ds, "Publishers")
```

The Fill method of the OleDbDataAdapter object can even take an ADO Record or Recordset object as an argument. This lets your .NET application use a method in an existing COM component that reads data from the database and returns it as an ADO Recordset. Keep in mind, however, that this is a one-way operation: you can read the contents of an ADO Recordset or a Record object, but you can't update them. The following code fills a DataSet by using an ADO Recordset created with the adodb library and COM Interop, which is something that you'll never do in a real application, but the example shows how you can proceed when you have a middle-tier component that returns a query result as an ADO Recordset:

```
' Open an ADO DB connection toward SQL Server's Pubs database.
Dim adoCn As New ADODB.Connection()
adoCn.Open(OledbPubsConnString)
' Read the Publishers table using a firehose cursor.
Dim adoRs As New ADODB.Recordset()
adoRs.Open("SELECT * FROM Publishers", adoCn)

' Use the Recordset to fill a DataSet table.
Dim ds As New DataSet()
Dim da As New OleDb.OleDbDataAdapter()
' (The following line automatically closes the Recordset.)
da.Fill(ds, adoRs, "Publishers")
' Close the connection.
adoCn.Close()
```

A great feature of the Fill method is its ability to support SQL batch commands that return multiple resultsets if the back-end database supports them. For example, you can retrieve multiple tables of data from SQL Server (regardless of the .NET data provider you're using) as follows:

```
' Access SQL Server using the OLE DB .NET Data Provider.
Dim cn As New OleDbConnection(OledbPubsConnString)

' Create a DataAdapter that reads three tables.
Dim sql As String = "SELECT * FROM Publishers;SELECT * FROM Titles;" _
    & "SELECT * FROM Authors"
Dim da As New OleDbDataAdapter(sql, cn)
' Create and fill the DataSet's tables.
da.Fill(ds, "Publishers")

' Change the names of the generated tables.
ds.Tables(1).TableName = "Titles"
ds.Tables(2).TableName = "Authors"
```

In the preceding code, the Fill method creates three tables named Publishers, Publishers1, and Publishers2, so we need to change the last two names manually. If you're retrieving data from SQL Server, you should use this technique because it minimizes the number of round-trips to the server.

Dealing with Filling Errors

Most of the time, the Fill method shouldn't raise any error, especially if the structure of the DataSet perfectly mirrors the metadata in the data source. In some cases, however, this method can throw an exception, such as when the row being read violates the constraints of a DataColumn or the data being read can't be converted to a .NET data type without losing precision. When such a problem occurs, ADO.NET throws an InvalidCastException exception. You can handle this exception the way you would any other exception, but you can get even better control of the read operation if you write a handler for the FillError event.

The second argument passed to this event is a FillErrorEventArgs object, which exposes the following information: DataTable (the table being filled), Errors (the error that occurred), Values (an Object array that contains values for all the columns in the row being updated), and Continue (a Boolean value that you can set to True to continue the fill operation despite the error). Here's an example that sets up a FillError handler to deal with overflow errors gracefully:

```
Sub FillData()
    Dim cn As New OleDbConnection(OledbPubsConnString)
    Dim da As New OleDbDataAdapter("SELECT * FROM Publishers", cn)
    ' Create a handler for the FillError event.
    AddHandler da.FillError, AddressOf FillError
    ' Create and fill the DataSet's table.
    da.Fill(ds, "Publishers")
End Sub

Sub FillError(ByVal sender As Object, ByVal args As FillErrorEventArgs)
    If TypeOf args.Errors Is System.OverflowException Then
        ' Add here the code that handles overflow errors.
        ⋮
        ' Continue to fill the DataSet.
        args.Continue = True
    End If
End Sub
```

Note that the FillError event fires only for errors that occur when filling the DataSet. No event fires if the error occurs at the database level.

Mapping DataBase Tables

By default, the DataAdapter's Fill method creates a DataTable whose columns have the same name and type as the columns in the source database table. However, there are occasions when you need more control over how columns are imported—for example

- You want to establish a DataTable name that's different from the name that the table has in the database. This difference can be useful when you're importing the same table more than once, each time with a different WHERE clause.

- You want to change the names of the source columns to make them more readable. This change might be necessary when you want to create a strongly typed DataSet (see later in this chapter) and the original names contain invalid characters.
- You need to assign a name to calculated expressions that don't have an AS clause in the original SQL SELECT statement (as in SELECT @@IDENTITY FROM MyTable).

You can perform all of these tasks, and a few others, by means of the DataAdapter's TableMappings collection. This collection contains zero or more DataTableMapping objects, each one defining the name of the source database table (the SourceTable property) and the name of the corresponding DataTable (the DataSetTable property). Each DataTableMapping object exposes also a collection of DataColumnMapping objects, which store the mapping between columns in the database table (the SourceColumn property) and columns in the DataTable (the DataSetColumn property). Figure 21-5 illustrates the relationships among all these objects and their properties. All these objects are in the System.Data.Common namespace.

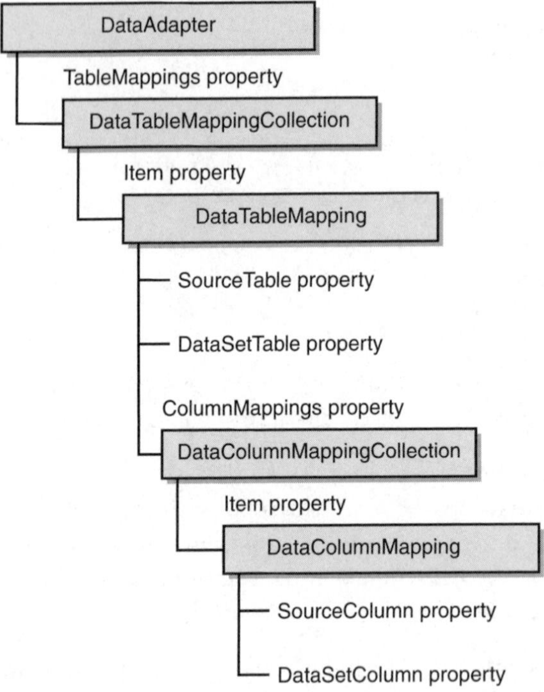

Figure 21-5. The TableMappings collection and its dependent classes.

If the meaning of these objects is clear, creating a mapping between a database and a DataSet is simple and ultimately resolves to calling the Add method of the right collection. For example, let's see how you can map the Publishers table in SQL Server's Pubs database to a client-side DataTable named PublishersData and change the names of a few columns in the process:

```
Dim cn As New SqlConnection(SqlPubsConnString)
Dim sql As String = "SELECT * FROM Publishers"
Dim da As New SqlDataAdapter(sql, cn)

' Adds an element to the TableMappings collection.
' (Returns a DataTableMapping object.)
With da.TableMappings.Add("Publishers", "DataPublishers")
    ' Add two elements to the ColumnMappings collection.
    .ColumnMappings.Add("pub_id", "ID")
    .ColumnMappings.Add("pub_name", "Name")
End With

' Fill the DataSet, using the prepared mappings.
' (Note that the second argument is the source database table's name.)
da.Fill(ds, "Publishers")
```

(Note that any column that isn't explicitly mapped is imported with its original name.) Two more properties of the DataAdapter object define what happens if the mapping isn't complete or correct:

- The MissingMappingAction property determines what happens if a table or a column defined in the mapping is missing from the database. It can take three values: Passthrough (the behavior depends on the MissingSchemaAction property), Ignore (missing columns are ignored), and Error (an exception is thrown).
- The MissingSchemaAction property determines what happens if the DataSet doesn't match incoming data. The valid values are Add (adds the necessary columns to complete the schema), AddWithKey (adds the necessary columns and primary key to complete the schema), Ignore (extra columns are ignored), and Error (an exception is thrown).

The default values are Passthrough for MissingMappingAction and Add for MissingSchemaAction, which means that the DataAdapter extends the DataSet with all the necessary columns. Another common combination of values is Ignore for both properties, which means that a column is imported only if it exists already in the DataSet. For example, consider the following code:

```
Dim cn As New SqlConnection(SqlPubsConnString)
Dim sql As String = "SELECT * FROM Publishers"
```

(continued)

```
Dim da As New SqlDataAdapter(sql, cn)

' Adds an element to the TableMappings collection.
With da.TableMappings.Add("Publishers", "DataPublishers")
    .ColumnMappings.Add("pub_id", "ID")
    .ColumnMappings.Add("pub_name", "Name")
End With

' Define the structure of the DataPublishers table in advance.
' (Note that column names must match target names defined by the mapping.)
With ds.Tables.Add("DataPublishers")
.Columns.Add("ID", GetType(String))
.Columns.Add("Name", GetType(String))
End With
' Ignore any other column.
da.MissingSchemaAction = MissingSchemaAction.Ignore

' Fill the DataSet, using the prepared mappings.
da.Fill(ds, "Publishers")
```

The effect of the preceding routine is to fill only the ID and Name columns of the DataPublishers table, ignoring all other columns implied by the SELECT command. Remember that you need to include the key column in the list of fields being retrieved only if you plan to later update the data source or to issue another Fill method to refresh the contents of the DataTable object. (If key columns aren't included in the DataTable, any subsequent Fill method *adds* the rows being read instead of using them to replace the rows already in the DataTable.)

Preloading the Database Structure

You might often want to fill the DataSet with the structure of the database without being interested in getting any data. This is the case when the end user wants to enter new records but isn't interested in the records already in the database. The solution that classic ADO offered for this very common problem was sort of a hack: you had to retrieve an empty Recordset to minimize the amount of data you sent along the wires, typically by using a SELECT command with a WHERE expression that always evaluated to False.

The ADO.NET DataAdapter object offers a more streamlined solution, in the form of the FillSchema method. This method takes the target DataSet; an argument that specifies whether the original table names are used (SchemaType.Source, the default value) or the current table mappings are honored (SchemaType.Mapped); and the name of the DataTable that must be created. Here are two examples:

```
' Fill the Publishers DataTable with the schema of the Publishers
' database table, using original column names.
da.FillSchema(ds, SchemaType.Mapped, "Publishers")
```

```
' Fill the DataPublishers DataTable with the schema of the Publishers
' database table, using mapped column names.
With da.TableMappings.Add("Publishers", "DataPublishers")
    ' Add two elements to the ColumnMappings collection.
    .ColumnMappings.Add("pub_id", "ID")
    .ColumnMappings.Add("pub_name", "Name")
End With
da.FillSchema(ds, SchemaType.Mapped, "Publishers")
```

The FillSchema method correctly sets the name, type, MaxLength, AllowDBNull, ReadOnly, Unique, and AutoIncrement properties of each column. (You must set the AutoIncrementSeed and AutoIncrementStep properties manually, however.) The method also retrieves existing table constraints and sets the PrimaryKey and Constraints properties accordingly.

Preloading the database schema is important because it ensures that primary key fields are always retrieved and stored in the DataSet. When subsequent Fill methods are issued, new rows are matched with existing rows on their primary key and new rows replace old rows accordingly. If the DataSet held no primary key information, new rows would always be appended to existing ones and duplicate rows would result. If you don't preload a DataSet with the database structure, you should ensure that all your SELECT commands include the primary key column or a column whose Unique property is True. If in doubt, you should set the MissingSchemaAction property to AddWithKey to ensure that primary key information is automatically retrieved if necessary.

If the SQL command associated with the SqlDataAdapter contains multiple SELECT statements, the SQL Server .NET Data Provider creates multiple tables whose names are obtained by appending an ordinal to the name of the table specified in the FillSchema method. This procedure is similar to what happens with the Fill method. For example, the following code fills three DataTable objects with the structure of three tables in the Pubs database:

```
Dim cn As New SqlConnection(SqlPubsConnString)
Dim sql As String = "SELECT * FROM Publishers;SELECT * FROM Titles;" _
    & "SELECT * FROM authors"
Dim da As New SqlDataAdapter(sql, cn)
da.FillSchema(ds, SchemaType.Source, "Publishers")

' Change the names of the second and third tables.
ds.Tables(1).TableName = "Titles"
ds.Tables(2).TableName = "Authors"
```

When you're working with the OLE DB .NET Data Provider, the FillSchema method ignores any resultset after the first one, regardless of whether the back-end database supports multiple resultsets. To load the structure of all the tables, use the Fill method with the MissingSchemaAction property set to AddWithKey.

> **Warning** The FillSchema method of the OleDbDataAdapter object doesn't work well with the Oracle OLE DB Provider (MSDAORA) because it *always* retrieves primary key and indexed columns, even if the original SELECT command doesn't include them. The problem occurs when you subsequently use the Fill method to fill the DataTable because this method reads only the columns specified in the SELECT command and would therefore leave the primary key columns blank. If the extra columns are not nullable, as is often the case, this results in an error. The solution is simple: always include primary key or indexed columns in the SELECT statement when working with Oracle.

Updating the Database

Most applications that work with databases need to update data in the original tables sooner or later. With ADO.NET, you have two choices when it's time to update a database:

- You can use ADO.NET Command objects with appropriate INSERT, DELETE, and UPDATE SQL statements. This is what you usually do when you work in connected mode and read data by means of a DataReader object.
- You can use the Update method of the DataAdapter object to send changed rows in a DataSet to a database. In this case, you usually use the same DataAdapter object that you created to read data into the DataSet, even though this isn't a requirement. (For example, you might have filled the DataSet manually via code without using a DataAdapter object.)

The DataAdapter's Update method is conceptually similar to the ADO Recordset object's UpdateBatch method, which you might have used with optimistic batch update locking in pre-.NET days. If you're familiar with disconnected ADO programming, you'll find yourself at ease with the ADO.NET conceptual model, even though the two models differ in many details. (If you aren't familiar with disconnected ADO Recordsets, you should read Chapter 14 of my *Programming Microsoft Visual Basic 6*, on the companion CD.)

The real issue when working in disconnected mode is that you have to detect and resolve update conflicts. You have a conflict when another user has modified or deleted the same record that you want to update or delete or has inserted a new record that has the same primary key as a record that you have inserted. How your application reacts to a conflict depends on the application's own logic: for example, you might follow the simple strategy by which the first update wins and subsequent ones are ignored; or you might decide that the last update wins. I'll explain these conflict-resolution strategies later in this chapter; for now, let's focus on the basics of update operations under the simplistic assumption that there are no update conflicts, an assumption that's realistic only when you're working with single-user applications.

> **Warning** The code in the following sections modifies the Biblio.mdb demo database or SQL Server's Pubs database. Before running this code, you might want to make a copy of the database so that you can restore it later. Also note that you might need to restore it before running the same sample again—for example, if you want to compare the outcomes of different update strategies.

Getting Familiar with Update Concepts

You can update data in a DataSet by means of the DataAdapter's Update method, which takes one of the following sets of arguments:

- **A DataTable object** The designated table is used as the source for the update operation.
- **A DataSet plus the name of a DataTable** This is just another way to indicate the table to be used as the source for the update operation. (If you omit the table name, the command attempts to use the default DataTable named Table.)
- **An array of DataRow objects** Only these rows are used as a source for the update operation. This variant is useful when you need more control over the order in which rows of a table are sent to the database.

In all cases, the Update method returns the number of rows that have been successfully updated. The key to performing batch updates with ADO.NET is a group of three properties of the DataAdapter object: InsertCommand, UpdateCommand, and DeleteCommand. Here's how the update mechanism works.

When an Update command is issued, the DataAdapter checks the RowState property of each row specified as a source for the update operation. If the state is Added, the DataAdapter issues the SQL command specified in the InsertCommand property. If the state is Modified, the DataAdapter uses the SQL command in the UpdateCommand property. If the state is Deleted, the command in the DeleteCommand property is used instead. (See Figure 21-6.)

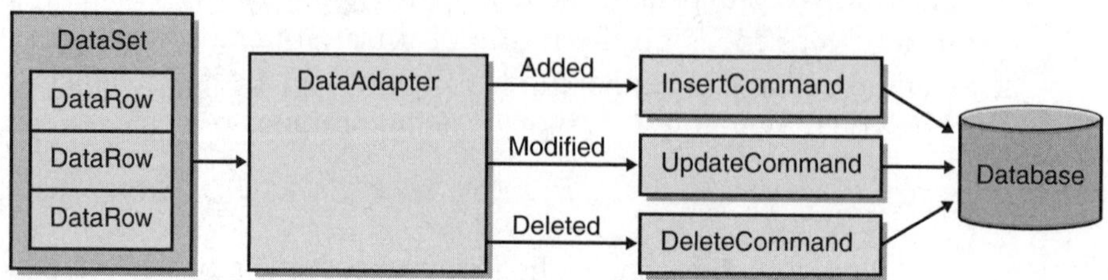

Figure 21-6. How the DataAdapter's Update method works.

The InsertCommand, UpdateCommand, and DeleteCommand properties must be assigned actual ADO.NET Command objects with parameters. You can create these commands yourself or generate them more easily by using an auxiliary CommandBuilder object. The main drawbacks of the latter technique are that the auxiliary CommandBuilder object must execute the SELECT command to retrieve the metadata, so it requires an additional round-trip to the server and adds overhead to your application. Because of its simplicity, however, I'll explain the technique based on the CommandBuilder object first.

Each .NET data provider comes with its own CommandBuilder class, so you'll work with either the OleDbCommandBuilder or the SqlCommandBuilder object. The following code snippet creates a DataAdapter from a simple SELECT statement and then uses the CommandBuilder object to generate the three *xxx*-Command properties:

```
' Connect to Pubs using the OLE DB .NET Data Provider.
Dim cn As New OleDbConnection(OledbPubsConnString)
cn.Open()
Dim sql As String = "SELECT * FROM Publishers"
Dim da As New OleDbDataAdapter(sql, cn)
' Ensure that the primary key is set correctly.
Dim ds As New DataSet()
da.FillSchema(ds, SchemaType.Source, "Publishers")
' Fill the DataTable.
da.Fill(ds, "Publishers")

' Create an auxiliary CommandBuilder object for this DataAdapter.
Dim cmdBuilder As New OleDbCommandBuilder(da)
' Use it to generate the three xxxCommand objects.
da.InsertCommand = cmdBuilder.GetInsertCommand
```

```
da.DeleteCommand = cmdBuilder.GetDeleteCommand
da.UpdateCommand = cmdBuilder.GetUpdateCommand
```

We're now able to modify the local DataSet and send the updated rows to the database:

```
With ds.Tables("Publishers")
    ' Modify the first record (just append 3 asterisks to the pub_name field).
    .Rows(0)("pub_name") = .Rows(0)("pub_name").ToString & " ***"
    ' Add a new record.
    Dim dr As DataRow = .NewRow
    dr("pub_id") = "9988"
    dr("pub_name") = "VB2TheMax"
    dr("city") = "Bari"
    dr("country") = "Italy"
    .Rows.Add(dr)
End With

' Send changes to the database, and disconnect.
da.Update(ds, "Publishers")
cn.Close()
```

If you now browse the Publishers table in Pubs, you see that the first record has been changed and that a new record has been added near the end.

> **Note** The code should *not* invoke the AcceptChanges method on the DataSet. This is a very important detail: this method resets the RowState property of all rows to Unchanged, thus making the rows appear as if they have never been modified by the application.

The preceding code snippet keeps the connection open while the application adds, modifies, and deletes rows. This approach makes sense when the editing operations are performed through code, but it works against the overall scalability if editing operations are performed by end users (who seem to have a steady habit of taking a coffee break in the middle of an editing session). Most of the time, it makes sense to close the connection immediately after the Fill method and reopen it immediately before the Update method. You don't even need to explicitly open and close the connection if you're reading and updating a single table because these two methods can do it for you. In the end, your typical code in a disconnected environment becomes

```
Dim cn As New OleDbConnection(OledbPubsConnString)
Dim da As New OleDbDataAdapter("SELECT * FROM Publishers", cn)
' Fill the DataSet table.
' (No need to explicitly open and close the connection.)
da.Fill(ds, "Publishers")

' Add, modify, or remove rows here, or let the user do it.
⋮

' Send changes to the database.
' (Again, no need to explicitly open and close the connection.)
da.Update(ds, "Publishers")
```

Remember, however, that this code works well only if you're reading and updating a single table. When multiple tables are used, you should open the connection before the read operation and close it immediately afterward to avoid a useless close and reopen operation:

```
Dim cn As New OleDbConnection(OledbPubsConnString)
Dim da As New OleDbDataAdapter("SELECT * FROM Publishers", cn)
Dim da2 As New OleDbDataAdapter("SELECT * FROM Authors", cn)
' Fill the DataSet table.
cn.Open()                           ' Open the connection explicitly.
da.Fill(ds, "Publishers")
da2.Fill(ds, "Authors")
cn.Close()                          ' Close the connection explicitly.

' Add, modify, or remove rows here, or let the user do it.
⋮

' Send changes to the database.
cn.Open()                           ' Open the connection explicitly.
da.Update(ds, "Publishers")
da2.Update(ds, "Authors")
cn.Close()                          ' Close the connection explicitly.
```

A last tip: you can query the DataSet's HasChanges property to detect whether it contains one or more DataTable objects with modified rows. If this property returns True, you can use the GetChanges method to build a second DataSet that contains only the rows that are actually modified and then update only those tables whose Rows collection contains elements:

```
If ds.HasChanges Then
    ' Build another DataSet that contains only modified rows.
    Dim ds2 As DataSet = ds.GetChanges()
    Dim dt As DataTable
    ' Update each data table individually.
    For Each dt in ds2.Tables
        If dt.Rows.Count > 0 Then
```

```
            ' This table contains modified rows.
            Debug.WriteLine("Updating table " & dt.TableName)
            ' Proceed with the update operation.
            ⋮
        End If
    Next
End If
```

You can achieve the same result in other ways as well. For example, you can use the DataTable's GetChanges method to retrieve the modified rows in a table. You can also pass an argument to both the DataSet's GetChanges method and the DataTable's GetChanges method to retrieve only the rows that have been added, deleted, or modified:

```
' Check whether there are deleted rows in the Publishers table.
Dim dt2 As DataTable = _
    ds.Tables("Publishers").GetChanges(DataRowState.Deleted)
If dt2.Rows.Count > 0 Then
    ' Process deleted rows in the Publishers table.
    ⋮
End If
```

Understanding the CommandBuilder Object

To understand the benefits and disadvantages of using the CommandBuilder object, you need to take a closer look at the SQL commands that it generates for the insert, delete, and update operations in the preceding code example. Let's start with the INSERT command that the OleDbCommandBuilder object has created for us to manage insertions in the Publishers table:

```
INSERT INTO Publishers ( pub_id, pub_name, city, state, country )
    VALUES ( ? , ?, ?, ?, ?)
```

As you see, this command is straightforward: it just inserts a new record and fills its fields with the arguments that will be passed to the InsertCommand object. (The CommandBuilder object has conveniently created and initialized the Parameters collection.)

The DELETE command is also relatively simple, but its WHERE clause has to account for the fact that some fields (other than the primary key pub_id) might be null when the record is read from the database, so you can't simply use the equality operator (which by default the T-SQL language would evaluate to Null instead of True):

```
DELETE FROM Publishers
    WHERE ( (pub_id = ?)
    AND ((? IS NULL AND pub_name IS NULL) OR (pub_name = ?))
    AND ((? IS NULL AND city IS NULL) OR (city = ?))
    AND ((? IS NULL AND state IS NULL) OR (state = ?))
    AND ((? IS NULL AND country IS NULL) OR (country = ?))
```

The need to account for null values makes the syntax of the SQL command overly complex and forces the creation of duplicates in the Parameters collection. In fact, the same argument value is inserted twice in the WHERE clause, the first time to test whether it's null and the second time to compare its value with the current value stored in the database. Oddly, the CommandBuilder generates this sort of code for all database fields, including those that aren't nullable. When a field isn't nullable, this precaution is unnecessary, but it doesn't have a noticeable impact on performance either.

The UPDATE command is the most complicated of the lot because its WHERE clause uses the new values for all fields plus all the (repeated) original values that are needed to locate the record that must be updated:

```
UPDATE Publishers
    SET pub_id = ?, pub_name = ?, city = ?, state = ?, country = ?
    WHERE ( (pub_id = ?)
    AND ((? IS NULL AND pub_name IS NULL) OR (pub_name = ?))
    AND ((? IS NULL AND city IS NULL) OR (city = ?))
    AND ((? IS NULL AND state IS NULL) OR (state = ?))
    AND ((? IS NULL AND country IS NULL) OR (country = ?))
```

The SQL commands that the CommandBuilder object produces depend on the .NET data provider that you're using. You see the difference when you access the same database table using the native SQL Server .NET Data Provider:

```
INSERT INTO Publishers ( pub_id, pub_name, city, state, country )
    VALUES ( @p1 , @p2, @p3, @p4, @p5)

DELETE FROM Publishers
    WHERE ( (pub_id = @p1)
    AND ((pub_name IS NULL AND @p2 IS NULL) OR (pub_name = @p3))
    AND ((city IS NULL AND @p4 IS NULL) OR (city = @p5))
    AND ((state IS NULL AND @p6 IS NULL) OR (state = @p7))
    AND ((country IS NULL AND @p8 IS NULL) OR (country = @p9))

UPDATE Publishers
    SET pub_id = @p1, pub_name = @p2, city = @p3, state= @p4, country = @p5
    WHERE ( (pub_id = @p6)
    AND ((pub_name IS NULL AND @p7 IS NULL) OR (pub_name = @p8))
    AND ((city IS NULL AND @p9 IS NULL) OR (city = @p10))
    AND ((state IS NULL AND @p11 IS NULL) OR (state = @p12))
    AND ((country IS NULL AND @p13 IS NULL) OR (country = @p14))
```

Even if the actual SQL text is different, delete, insert, and update commands work in the same way in both providers:

- The INSERT command adds a new record and uses the *current* value of columns in the DataRow for its parameters. (Note that identity values are correctly omitted from the list because they're generated by the database.)

- The DELETE command locates the record that was originally read by passing the *original* column values in the DataRow to the WHERE clause, and deletes it.
- The UPDATE command locates the record that was originally read (using the *original* column values in the WHERE clause) and updates all fields with the *current* column values in the DataRow in the SET clause.

You need to understand the difference between using original column values and current column values. You can determine which version of the column value is used by browsing the Parameters collection and checking the SourceColumn and SourceVersion properties of each parameter:

```
' Display information about each parameter of the UpdateCommand command.
Dim par As SqlParameter
For Each par In da.UpdateCommand.Parameters
    Debug.WriteLine(par.ParameterName & " => " & par.SourceColumn _
        & " (" & par.SourceVersion.ToString & ")")
Next
```

This is the output in the Debug window:

```
@p1 => pub_id (Current)
@p2 => pub_name (Current)
@p3 => city (Current)
@p4 => state (Current)
@p5 => country (Current)
@p6 => pub_id (Original)
@p7 => pub_name (Original)
@p8 => pub_name (Original)
@p9 => city (Original)
@p10 => city (Original)
@p11 => state (Original)
@p12 => state (Original)
@p13 => country (Original)
@p14 => country (Original)
```

Oddly, the SqlCommandBuilder object generates duplicates in the Parameters collection that might be avoided by simply using the same parameter name twice in the text for the DELETE and UPDATE commands. This behavior doesn't affect the result of the command but might introduce some overhead when working with many fields. (Using duplicated parameters is necessary only when you're working with the OLE DB .NET Data Provider because it doesn't support named parameters.)

Here are a few more details about the CommandBuilder object and some of its limitations:

- The original SELECT command assigned to the DataAdapter (which is also exposed by the SelectCommand property) can reference only one table.
- The source table must include a primary key or at least a column with a unique constraint, and the result returned by the SELECT statement must include that column. Primary keys consisting of multiple columns are supported.
- The InsertCommand object inserts only the columns that are updatable and correctly omits identity, timestamp, and calculated columns and in general all columns that are generated by the database engine.
- The UpdateCommand object uses the values of all the original columns in the WHERE clauses, including the primary key, but correctly omits timestamp and calculated columns from the SET clause.
- The DeleteCommand object uses the values of all the original columns in the WHERE clause to locate the row that has to be deleted.
- The CommandBuilder generates invalid commands when the name of a table or a column contains a space or a special character.

You can solve the last problem easily by forcing the CommandBuilder to use a prefix and a suffix for all the table and column names used in the generated command. You can do this by assigning a string to the QuotePrefix and QuoteSuffix properties so that the resulting SQL text conforms to the syntax expected by the target database. For example, you must use this technique when generating commands for Biblio's Authors, Publishers, and Titles tables, all of which contain one column with a space in its name:

```
Dim cn As New OleDbConnection(BiblioConnString)
Dim da As New OleDbDataAdapter("SELECT * FROM Authors", cn)
' Create builder and enclose field names in square brackets.
Dim cmdBuilder As New OleDbCommandBuilder(da)
cmdBuilder.QuotePrefix = "["
cmdBuilder.QuoteSuffix = "]"
' Generate insert, delete, and update commands.
da.InsertCommand = cmdBuilder.GetInsertCommand
da.DeleteCommand = cmdBuilder.GetDeleteCommand
da.UpdateCommand = cmdBuilder.GetUpdateCommand
```

Here's the text generated for the INSERT command:

```
INSERT INTO [Authors] ( [Author], [Year Born] ) VALUES (?, ?)
```

Keep in mind that the CommandBuilder executes the SQL command assigned to the SelectCommand's CommandText property to generate the other three commands, so if you later change the SELECT command, the read and update commands will be out of sync. For this reason, you should always invoke the CommandBuilder's RefreshSchema method any time you modify the SELECT command.

Customizing Insert, Update, and Delete Commands

After you understand how the InsertCommand, UpdateCommand, and DeleteCommand properties work, it's relatively easy to create your custom commands. This technique requires that you write a lot more code than you have to when using the CommandBuilder object, but it lets you generate faster and more scalable code, both because you avoid one round-trip to the server and because a well-written command can reduce the number of update conflicts. In general, the InsertCommand object produced by the CommandBuilder is OK for most purposes. So in the following discussion, I'll focus only on the UpdateCommand and DeleteCommand objects.

The DELETE command generated by the CommandBuilder uses the original values of all the columns in its WHERE clause to locate the record that has to be deleted. This approach is the safest one because it ensures that no record is deleted if another user has changed one or more columns in the meantime. In some applications, however, it might make sense to adopt a different strategy for deletions and decide to delete the record even if another user has modified any of its fields (other than the primary key). According to this strategy, the most recent edit operation always wins and successfully updates the record (unless another user has changed the primary key field). You can enforce this strategy simply by using only the primary key field in the WHERE clause. This technique is faster and more scalable, but you should ensure that it doesn't invalidate the business logic of your application.

For example, you might decide that it's legal for a user to delete the record of an employee who has left the company even though another user has modified the employee's address in the meantime. You can enforce this strategy by manufacturing the DeleteCommand yourself:

```
Dim cn As New OleDbConnection(BiblioConnString)
cn.Open()
Dim da As New OleDbDataAdapter("SELECT * FROM Authors", cn)
da.FillSchema(ds, SchemaType.Source, "Authors")
da.Fill(ds, "Authors")

' Add here all insert/update/delete operations.
:

' Create a delete command that filters records by their Au_id field only.
Dim cmdDelete As New OleDbCommand("DELETE FROM Authors WHERE Au_ID = ?", cn)
' Create an Integer parameter, and set its properties.
```

(continued)

```
With cmdDelete.Parameters.Add("@p1", GetType(Integer))
    ' This is the name of the column in the DataTable.
    .SourceColumn = "Au_id"
    ' We want to use the original value in each DataRow.
    .SourceVersion = DataRowVersion.Original
End With
' Assign command to the DeleteCommand property of the DataAdapter.
da.DeleteCommand = cmdDelete
```

You can enforce a similar strategy for the UpdateCommand object as well by deciding that changes by the current user always overwrite changes by other users who have modified the same record after the current user imported the record into the DataSet:

```
' Create a custom update command.
Dim cmdUpdate As New OleDbCommand( _
    "UPDATE Authors SET Author = ?, [Year Born] = ? WHERE Au_ID = ?", cn)
' Add arguments for the SET clause. (They use current field values.)
With cmdUpdate.Parameters.Add("@p1", GetType(String))
    .SourceColumn = "Author"
    .SourceVersion = DataRowVersion.Current
End With
With cmdUpdate.Parameters.Add("@p2", GetType(Integer))
    .SourceColumn = "Year Born"
    .SourceVersion = DataRowVersion.Current
End With
' Add the argument in the WHERE clause. (It uses the original field value.)
With cmdUpdate.Parameters.Add("@p3", GetType(Integer))
    .SourceColumn = "Au_id"
    .SourceVersion = DataRowVersion.Original
End With
' Assign the command to the DataAdapter's UpdateCommand property.
da.UpdateCommand = cmdUpdate
```

You can often create DELETE and UPDATE commands better than those generated by the CommandBuilder without making them less safe. For example, the au_fname, au_lname, phone, and contract columns in the Pubs database's Authors table aren't nullable, so you can update this table with a command that's simpler (and slightly faster) than the one generated by the CommandBuilder object:

```
UPDATE Authors
    SET au_id = @p1, au_fname = @p2, au_lname = @p3, phone = @p4,
        address = @p5, city = @p6, state = @p7, zip = @p8, contract = @p9
    WHERE ( (au_id = @p10)
    AND (au_fname = @p11) AND (au_lname = @p12) AND (phone = @p13)
    AND ((address IS NULL AND @p14 IS NULL) OR (address = @p14))
    AND ((city IS NULL AND @p15 IS NULL) OR (city = @p15))
```

```
AND ((state IS NULL AND @p16 IS NULL) OR (state = @p16))
AND ((zip IS NULL AND @p17 IS NULL) OR (zip = @p17))
AND (contract = @p18)
```

Note that the preceding custom command correctly reuses the same named parameter for the original value of nullable columns, unlike the SQL statement produced by the CommandBuilder. This custom command works correctly as long as the current value isn't null, so your code must never use a null value as a parameter.

The knowledge of how your application works often lets you simplify the structure of the UPDATE command. For example, you might have an application that displays all the columns in the records but prevents users from modifying a few columns (typically, the primary key or other keys that might work as foreign keys in other tables). As a result, you can omit such fields in the SET clause of the UPDATE command.

If the database table contains a timestamp field, you have an opportunity to improve the performance of both delete and update operations in a safe way because in this case you can detect whether another user has modified the record in question without verifying that all columns still contain their original values. In fact, a timestamp field is guaranteed to change whenever a database record is changed, so you can shrink the WHERE clause to include only the primary key (which serves to locate the record) and the timestamp field (which serves to ensure that no user has modified the record after it was imported into the DataSet). To see how this technique works in practice, extend the Authors table in SQL Server's Pubs database with a timestamp field named LastUpdate, and then run this code:

```
' Connect to SQL Server's Pubs using the OLE DB .NET Data Provider.
Dim cn As New OleDbConnection(OledbPubsConnString)
' Read a few fields, but ensure that you include the timestamp column.
Dim sql As String = "SELECT au_id,au_fname,au_lname,lastupdate FROM Authors"
Dim da As New OleDbDataAdapter(sql, cn)
da.Fill(ds, "Authors")

' Create a custom delete command that uses the timestamp field.
Dim cmdDelete As New OleDbCommand( _
    "DELETE FROM Authors WHERE Au_ID = ? And LastUpdate=?", cn)
With cmdDelete.Parameters.Add("@p1", GetType(Integer))
    .SourceColumn = "Au_id"
    .SourceVersion = DataRowVersion.Original
End With
' Timestamp values are saved as arrays of Byte.
With cmdDelete.Parameters.Add("@p2", GetType(Byte()))
    .SourceColumn = "LastUpdate"
```

(continued)

```
    .SourceVersion = DataRowVersion.Original
End With
da.DeleteCommand = cmdDelete

' Create a custom update that uses the timestamp column.
' (Note that primary key and timestamp columns don't appear in the SET clause.)
Dim cmdUpdate As New OleDbCommand("UPDATE Authors SET au_fname=?, " _
    & "au_lname=? WHERE au_id = ? AND LastUpdate=?", cn)
' Add the arguments for the SET clause. (They use the current field value.)
With cmdUpdate.Parameters.Add("@p1", GetType(String))
    .SourceColumn = "au_fname"
    .SourceVersion = DataRowVersion.Current
End With
With cmdUpdate.Parameters.Add("@p2", GetType(Integer))
    .SourceColumn = "au_lname"
    .SourceVersion = DataRowVersion.Current
End With
' Add the arguments in the WHERE clause. (They use the original field values.)
With cmdUpdate.Parameters.Add("@p3", GetType(Integer))
    .SourceColumn = "Au_id"
    .SourceVersion = DataRowVersion.Original
End With
' Timestamp values are saved as arrays of Byte.
With cmdUpdate.Parameters.Add("@p4", GetType(Byte()))
    .SourceColumn = "LastUpdate"
    .SourceVersion = DataRowVersion.Original
End With
da.UpdateCommand = cmdUpdate
```

Yet another reason for customizing the InsertCommand, UpdateCommand, and DeleteCommand properties is to take advantage of any stored procedure in the database that has been specifically designed to insert, modify, and delete records. By delegating these editing operations to a stored procedure and preventing users and applications from directly accessing the database tables, you can enforce greater control over data consistency. Inserting, updating, and deleting records through a stored procedure isn't conceptually different from what I have described so far. Please refer to the "Stored Procedures" section in Chapter 20 to review how to create parameters for Command objects that call stored procedures.

Changing the Order of Insert, Update, and Delete Operations

By default, all the rows in each table are processed according to their primary key order. Most of the time, the order in which commands are sent to the database doesn't affect the outcome of the operation, but this isn't always the case. For example, suppose you change the primary key of a row from 10 to 20 and then add a new row whose primary key is 10. Because this new row is processed before the old one, the Update method will attempt to insert a record with a primary key of 10 before the key of the existing database record is changed. This attempt raises an error.

You can avoid this problem by sending all the delete operations first, then all the update operations, and finally all the insert operations. This strategy is possible because the Update method takes an array of DataRow objects as an argument, so you can pass the result of a Select method whose third argument is an appropriate DataViewRowState value:

```
Dim dt As DataTable = ds.Tables("Authors")
' First process deletes.
da.Update(dt.Select(Nothing, Nothing, DataViewRowState.Deleted))
' Next process updates.
da.Update(dt.Select(Nothing, Nothing, DataViewRowState.ModifiedCurrent))
' Finally process inserts.
da.Update(dt.Select(Nothing, Nothing, DataViewRowState.Added))
```

Another good time to send delete, update, and insert operations separately is when you're updating tables in a parent-child relationship. You must insert a record in the parent table *before* adding the corresponding records in the child table; however, you must delete a record in the parent table *after* deleting the corresponding records in the child table. Here's a piece of code that takes these constraints into account:

```
' This code shows how to update the Publishers (parent) and
' Titles (child) tables correctly.

Dim cn As New OleDbConnection(BiblioConnString)
cn.Open()
' Fill both tables.
Dim daPub As New OleDbDataAdapter("SELECT * FROM Publishers", cn)
Dim daTit As New OleDbDataAdapter("SELECT * FROM Titles", cn)
daPub.Fill(ds, "Publishers")
daTit.Fill(ds, "Titles")

' Insert, update, and delete records in both tables.
⋮

' Send updates to both tables without any referential integrity error.
Dim dtPub As DataTable = ds.Tables("Publishers")
Dim dtTit As DataTable = ds.Tables("Titles")

' First process deleted rows in the child table.
daTit.Update(dtTit.Select(Nothing, Nothing, DataViewRowState.Deleted))
' Next process deleted rows in the parent table.
```

(continued)

```
daPub.Update(dtPub.Select(Nothing, Nothing, DataViewRowState.Deleted))

' Next process inserted rows in the parent table and then in the child table.
daPub.Update(dtPub.Select(Nothing, Nothing, DataViewRowState.Added))
daTit.Update(dtTit.Select(Nothing, Nothing, DataViewRowState.Added))

' Finally process updates in the two tables.
daPub.Update(dtPub.Select(Nothing, Nothing, DataViewRowState.ModifiedCurrent))
daTit.Update(dtTit.Select(Nothing, Nothing, DataViewRowState.ModifiedCurrent))
```

Merging Changes in Another DataSet

The examples I've shown you so far were based on the assumption that the code that modifies the DataSet is the same that updates the actual data source. This holds true in most traditional client/server applications, but multitier systems can adopt a different pattern. For example, consider an application consisting of a middle-tier component (for example, an XML Web service) that sits between the database and the user interface layer (a Windows Forms program):

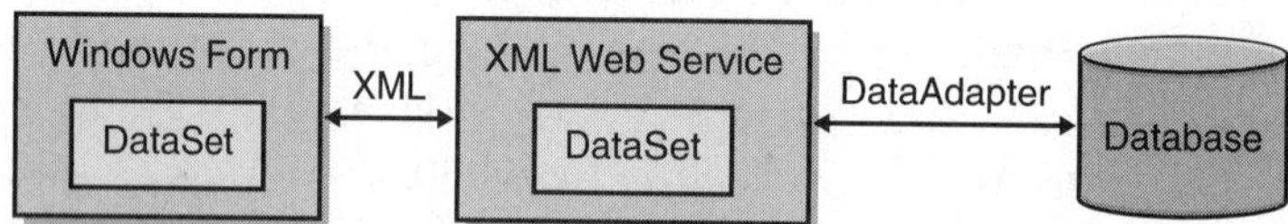

In this arrangement, the XML Web service reads data from the database using a DataAdapter object, manufactures a DataSet object, and sends it as XML to the Windows Form client, which therefore gets a perfect copy of the DataSet originally held in the XML Web service. The client code can now update, insert, and delete one or more rows and can send the modified DataSet back to the XML Web service, which can finally update the data source using the same DataAdapter that was used to read data into the DataSet.

Most of the time, however, the client application doesn't really need to send back the entire DataSet because the middle-tier component needs to know only which tables and which rows were changed after the DataSet was sent to the client user interface layer. You can reduce the amount of data sent over the wire by using the GetChanges method of the DataSet or the DataTable object. This method returns another DataSet or DataTable object that contains only the modified rows:

```
' Produce a DataSet with only the modified tables and rows.
Dim modDs As DataSet = ds.GetChanges()
```

When this new DataSet is sent to the XML Web service in the middle tier, two things can happen:

- The XML Web service rebuilds the DataAdapter object (or objects) that was created to extract data from the database, initializes its UpdateCommand, InsertCommand, and DeleteCommand properties as you want, and applies the DataAdapter to the DataSet containing only the modified rows. This behavior is the most scalable one, but it can be adopted only when the changes coming from the client don't need any additional processing.
- The XML Web service merges the modified DataSet just received with the original DataSet, processes the resulting DataSet as required, and then invokes the DataAdapter's Update method to update the data source. This technique requires that the XML Web service save the original DataSet somewhere while the client is processing the data. Of course, you get the best performance if the original DataSet is kept in memory, but this arrangement reduces the fault tolerance of the entire system and raises affinity issues when you're working with a cluster of servers (because only one server can reply to a given client's request).

To merge the original DataSet with the modified DataSet received by the user-interface layer, the XML Web service can use the Merge method:

```
' ds is the original DataSet.
' modDs is the modified DataSet received by the Windows Form client.
ds.Merge(modDs)
```

The Merge method can take two additional arguments: a Boolean that tells whether current changes in the original DataSet should be maintained and a MissingSchemaAction enumerated value that specifies what happens if the schema of the two DataSet objects aren't identical:

```
' Preserve changes in the original DataSet (ds), and
' add any new column found in the modified DataSet (modDs).
ds.Merge(modDs, True, MissingSchemaAction.Add)
```

Before merging data, the Merge method attempts to merge the schema of the two DataSet objects, and it modifies the schema of the original DataSet with any new column found in the DataSet being merged if the third argument is MissingSchemaAction.Add.

While data is being merged, all constraints are disabled. If a constraint can't be reenforced at the end of the merge operation, a ConstraintException object is thrown. In this case, the merged data is preserved, but the EnforceConstraints property is left as False. The middle-tier component should programmatically resolve all conflicts before setting EnforceConstraints back to True and performing the actual update on the data source.

Resolving Update Conflicts

All the update samples you've seen so far were based on the simplistic assumption that the current user was the only one updating the database and that no other user was allowed to modify the records in the database after the application had read data into the DataSet. At last, it's time to see how you can resolve the unavoidable conflicts that occur in all multiuser systems.

By default, if an Update command finds a conflict and can't process a row, it throws an exception, skipping all the remaining rows. This means that you should always protect an Update command with a Try...End Try block:

```
Try
    da.Update(ds, "Authors")
Catch ex As Exception
    MessageBox.Show(ex.Message)
End Try
```

In many cases, however, you want to try the update operation on all the rows in the DataTable instead of stopping the operation at the first row that fails to update. You can do this by simply setting the DataAdapter's ContinueUpdateOnErrors property to True. In this case, you can test whether one or more rows failed to update by checking the DataSet or DataTable's HasChanges property:

```
da.ContinueUpdateOnErrors = True
da.Update(ds, "Authors")
If ds.HasChanges() Then
    ' One or more rows failed to update.
End If
```

You can get a more granular control over what happens when an update is attempted by trapping the RowUpdated event. This event lets you detect the conflict and decide to continue the update operation with the remaining rows if possible.

Handling the RowUpdated Event

When an Update command is issued, the DataAdapter object fires a pair of events for each inserted, modified, or deleted row in the table being updated. The RowUpdating event fires before sending the command to the database, whereas the RowUpdated event fires immediately after the database has processed the command. Table 21-10 describes the properties of the object passed to the second argument of these events.

Table 21-10 Values Passed to the RowUpdating and RowUpdated Events

Event	Property	Description
RowUpdating and RowUpdated	StatementType	An enumerated value that specifies the type of SQL command just executed. It can be SELECT, INSERT, UPDATE, or DELETE. (You'll never see the SELECT value from inside these events, however.)
	Command	The ADO.NET Command object sent to the database.
	Row	The DataRow being updated.
	TableMapping	The DataTableMapping object used for the update operation.
	Status	An UpdateStatus enumerated value that specifies how to handle the current row and the remaining rows. It can be Continue (continue the processing of rows), ErrorsOccurred (this update operation must be treated as an error), SkipCurrentRow (don't update the current row), and SkipAllRemainingRows (don't update the current row and all remaining rows).
RowUpdated only	RecordsAffected	Returns the number of records affected during the update.
	Errors	Returns the error generated by the .NET data provider during the update. (In spite of its name, this property returns a single Exception object.)

The key value is the RecordsAffected property, which returns the number of records that were affected by the update command. Any value less than 1 in this property means that the command failed and that we have an update conflict. This is the usual sequence of operations you perform inside a RowUpdated event handler:

1. If the Status property is equal to Continue and the value of the RecordsAffected property is 1, the update operation was successful. In most cases, you have little else to do, and you can exit the event handler.
2. If the Status property is equal to ErrorsOccurred, you can check the Errors property to understand what went wrong. Frequent causes of errors are violations of database constraints or referential integrity rules, such as a duplicated value in a primary key or a unique column or a foreign key that doesn't point to any row in the parent table.

3. If you get a System.Data.DBConcurrencyException exception, it means that the WHERE clause in the SQL command failed to locate the row in the data source. What you do next depends on your application's business logic. Typically, you test the StatementType property to determine whether it was an insert, delete, or update operation; in the latter two cases, the conflict is likely to be caused by another user who has deleted or modified the record you're trying to delete or update.

4. You can issue a SELECT query against the database to determine what columns caused the conflict, in an attempt to resynchronize the DataSet with the data source and reconcile the conflicting row. For example, if you have a conflict in an update operation (the most frequent case), you can issue a SELECT command to read again the values now in the database table. If you have a conflict in a delete operation, you can issue a SELECT command to check whether the DELETE command failed because the record was deleted or because another user changed one of the fields listed in your WHERE clause.

5. In all cases, you must decide whether the update operation should continue. You can set the Status property to Continue or SkipCurrentRow to ignore the conflict for now, or SkipAllRemainingRows to end the update operation without raising an error in the application. You can also leave the value set to ErrorsOccurred, in which case the Update method is terminated right away and an exception is thrown to the main application.

You don't have to perform all the preceding operations from inside a RowUpdate event handler, however, and you don't even need to write this event handler in some cases. For example, you can postpone the resychronization step until after the Update method has completed, and you might even decide not to resynchronize at all. The sections that follow illustrate three possible resynchronization strategies that you can adopt when dealing with update conflicts:

- You don't reconcile at all and just display a warning to the user, mentioning which rows failed to be updated correctly. In this case, you just set the ContinueUpdateOnErrors property to True and don't have to intercept the RowUpdated event.
- You reconcile with the data source after the Update method, using a SELECT command that reads again all the rows that failed to update. In this case, you place the resync code in the main application after the Update method and set the ContinueUpdateOnErrors property to True to avoid an exception when a conflicting row is found.

- You reconcile with the data source on a row-by-row basis for each row that failed to update correctly. In this case, you place the resync code right inside the RowUpdated event handler and set the Status property of its argument to Continue. (Otherwise, the Update method will fail when the first conflict is found.)

Displaying Conflicting Rows

In the first strategy for managing conflicts, you don't even try to reconcile them and limit your actions to just displaying the records that failed the update operation. This strategy can be implemented quite simply, as this code demonstrates:

```
' A class-level DataAdapter that has been correctly initialized
Dim da As OleDbDataAdapter

Sub UpdateRecords()
    ' Ensure that conflicting rows don't throw an exception.
    da.ContinueUpdateOnErrors = True
    ' Send changes to the database.
    da.Update(ds, "Publishers")

    ' Exit if all rows were updated correctly.
    If Not ds.HasChanges Then Exit Sub

    ' If we get here, there's at least one conflicting row.
    Dim dt As DataTable = ds.Tables("Publishers")

    ' Here's a simple way to evaluate the number of conflicting rows.
    Dim rowCount As Integer = dt.GetChanges().Rows.Count
    Debug.WriteLine(rowCount & " rows failed to update correctly")

    ' Mark all conflicting rows with the proper error message.
    Dim dr As DataRow
    For Each dr In dt.Rows
        If dr.RowState = DataRowState.Added Then
            dr.RowError = "Failed INSERT operation"
        ElseIf dr.RowState = DataRowState.Modified Then
            dr.RowError = "Failed UPDATE operation"
        ElseIf dr.RowState = DataRowState.Deleted Then
            dr.RowError = "Failed DELETE operation"
            ' Undelete this record, else it wouldn't show in the table.
            dr.RejectChanges()
        End If
    Next
End Sub
```

This code works because the Update method automatically invokes AcceptChanges on all the rows that were updated correctly without any conflict but leaves the conflicting rows in the state they were before the update. As a result, you can use the DataSet's HasChanges property to quickly determine whether at least one row is still marked as modified, and then you can iterate over all the rows in the DataTable to mark each row with a proper error message, which shows up in the DataGrid control. (See Figure 21-7.) The only precaution you have to take is to reject changes on deleted rows. Otherwise, these deleted rows won't be included in the DataTable object and won't be displayed in the DataGrid control.

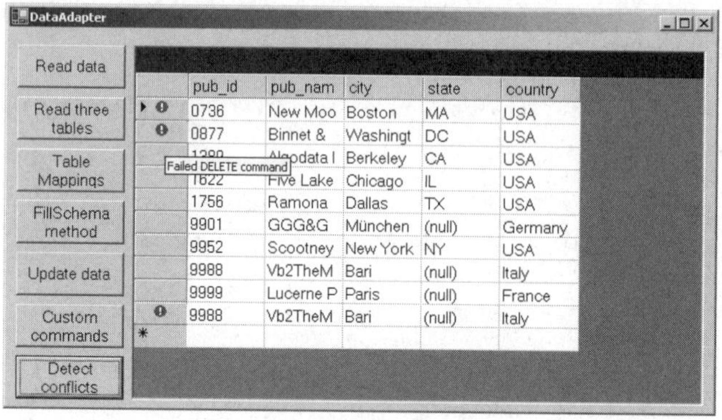

Figure 21-7. Marking conflicting rows with an error message.

Resynchronizing After the Update Method

In most cases, you can (and should) try to understand why each update operation failed, instead of just showing the user the list of conflicting rows. You typically do this by rereading rows from the data source and comparing the values found in the database with those read when you filled the DataTable. If you find different values, you're likely to have found the cause of the conflict because the default WHERE clause in the DELETE and UPDATE commands searches for a record that contains the original column values, as I explain in "Understanding the CommandBuilder Object" earlier in this chapter. (If you used custom update commands, you have to retouch the code in this section.)

When synchronizing the DataTable with the data source, you might keep things simple by reapplying the same DataAdapter to fill another DataTable and then comparing this new DataTable with the original one. (Note that you can't fill the same DataTable again because you would reset the status of all inserted and updated rows to Unchanged.) However, this simple technique requires the transfer of a lot of rows from the server, even though only a small fraction of such rows—that is, the conflicting ones—are actually needed for your purposes.

A much better approach is to read only those rows that caused an update conflict. You can do this by repeatedly calling a parameterized SELECT command or by manufacturing a single SELECT that returns all and only the rows in question. In most cases, you should adopt the latter approach because of its greater efficiency and scalability, even though it requires more code on your part. The code I'm showing here isn't exactly trivial, but it's well commented and has been designed with ease of reuse in mind:

```
Sub UpdateRecords()
    ' Ensure that conflicting rows don't throw an exception.
    da.ContinueUpdateOnErrors = True
    ' Send changes to the database.
    da.Update(ds, "Publishers")

    If Not ds.HasChanges Then Exit Sub

    ' Not all rows were updated successfully.
    Dim dt As DataTable = ds.Tables("Publishers")

    ' Keeping key column name in a variable helps make this code reusable.
    Dim keyName As String = "pub_id"

    ' Build the list of the key values for all these rows.
    Dim values As New System.Text.StringBuilder(1000)
    Dim keyValue As String
    Dim dr As DataRow

    For Each dr In dt.Rows
        ' Consider only modified rows.
        If dr.RowState <> DataRowState.Unchanged Then
            ' The key to be used depends on the row state.
            If dr.RowState = DataRowState.Added Then
                ' Use the current key value for inserted rows.
                keyValue = dr(keyName, DataRowVersion.Current).ToString
            Else
                ' Use the original key value for deleted and modified rows.
                keyValue = dr(keyName, DataRowVersion.Original).ToString
            End If
            ' Append to the list of key values. (Assume it's a string field.)
            If values.Length > 0 Then values.Append(",")
            values.Append("'")
            values.Append(keyValue)
            values.Append("'")
        End If
    Next
```

(continued)

```
    ' Create a new SELECT that reads only these records,
    ' using the DataAdapter's SELECT command as a template.
    Dim sql2 As String = da.SelectCommand.CommandText
    ' Delete the WHERE clause if there is one.
    Dim k As Integer = sql2.ToUpper.IndexOf(" WHERE ")
    If k > 0 Then sql2 = sql2.Substring(0, k - 1)
    ' Add the WHERE clause that contains the list of all key values.
    sql2 &= " WHERE " & keyName & " IN (" & values.ToString & ")"

    ' Read only the conflicting rows.
    ' (Assume that cn holds a reference to a valid OleDbConnection object.)
    Dim da2 As New OleDbDataAdapter(sql2, cn)
    ' Fill a new DataTable. (It doesn't have to belong to the DataSet.)
    Dim dt2 As New DataTable()
    da2.Fill(dt2)
```

The remainder of the UpdateRecords routine compares rows in the original DataTable with those that have just been read from the data source and marks both the conflicting rows and modified columns with a suitable error message:

```
' Loop on all the rows that failed to update.
    Dim dr2 As DataRow
    For Each dr In dt.Rows
        If dr.RowState <> DataRowState.Unchanged Then
            ' Mark the row with a proper error message,
            ' and retrieve the key value to be used for searching in DT2.
            If dr.RowState = DataRowState.Added Then
                dr.RowError = "Failed INSERT command"
                keyValue = dr(keyName, DataRowVersion.Current).ToString
            ElseIf dr.RowState = DataRowState.Deleted Then
                dr.RowError = "Failed DELETE command"
                keyValue = dr(keyName, DataRowVersion.Original).ToString
            ElseIf dr.RowState = DataRowState.Modified Then
                dr.RowError = "Failed UPDATE command"
                keyValue = dr(keyName, DataRowVersion.Original).ToString
            End If

            ' Find the matching row in the new table.
            Dim rows() As DataRow
            rows = dt2.Select(keyName & "='" & keyValue & "'")

            If (rows Is Nothing) OrElse rows.Length = 0 Then
                ' We can't find the conflicting row in the database.
                dr.RowError &= " - Unable to resync with data source"
                ' Check whether the user changed the primary key.
                If dr.RowState <> DataRowState.Added AndAlso _
                    dr(keyName, DataRowVersion.Current).ToString <> _
                    dr(keyName, DataRowVersion.Original).ToString Then
```

```
                    ' This is a probable source of the conflict.
                    dr.SetColumnError(keyName, "Modified primary key")
                End If

            Else
                ' We have found the conflicting row in the database, so
                ' we can compare current values in each column.
                dr2 = rows(0)

                Dim i As Integer
                For i = 0 To dr.Table.Columns.Count - 1
                    ' The type of comparison we do depends on the row state.
                    If dr.RowState = DataRowState.Added Then
                        ' For inserted rows, we compare the current value
                        ' with the database value.
                        If dr(i).ToString <> dr2(i).ToString Then
                            ' Show the value now in the database.
                            dr.SetColumnError(i, "Value in database = " _
                                & dr2(i).ToString)
                        End If
                    Else
                        ' For deleted and modified rows, we compare the
                        ' original value with the database value.
                        If dr(i, DataRowVersion.Original).ToString <> _
                            dr2(i).ToString Then
                            Dim msg As String = ""
                            If dr(i, DataRowVersion.Original).ToString <> _
                                dr(i).ToString Then
                                msg = "Original value = " & dr(i).ToString
                                msg &= ", "
                            End If
                            msg &= "Value in database = " & dr2(i).ToString
                            dr.SetColumnError(i, msg)
                        End If
                    End If
                Next
            End If
        End If

        ' If a deleted row, reject changes to make it visible in the table.
        If dr.RowState = DataRowState.Deleted Then
            dr.RejectChanges()
        End If
    Next
End Sub
```

Figure 21-8 shows how row and column error messages are displayed in a DataGrid control.

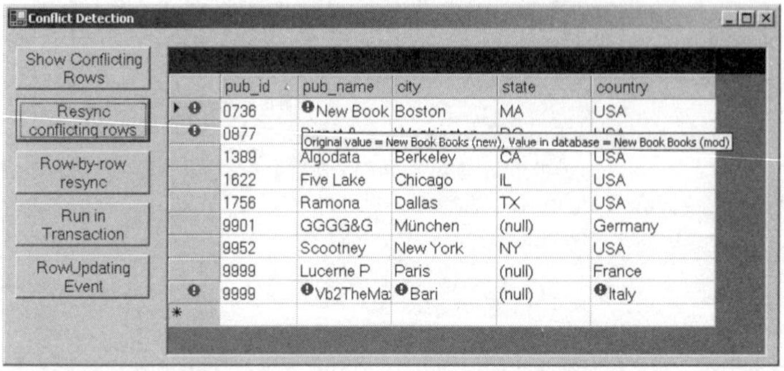

Figure 21-8. Resynchronization with the data source lets you display which columns caused the conflict.

Resolving Conflicts on a Row-by-Row Basis

Reconciling the DataTable on a row-by-row basis can be the most appropriate strategy when the application's business logic allows you to resolve conflicts automatically, without asking the intervention of the user. In this scenario, you reread each conflicting row from inside the RowUpdated event handler. When this event fires, the connection is surely open, so you can execute the SELECT command using a regular Command object.

Because you're going to repeat the same query for all the conflicting rows, it makes sense to build a parameterized command and reuse it from inside the event handler. This task is common to many ADO.NET applications that update the data source using the DataSet object, so I've prepared a reusable function that takes a DataAdapter and a list of one or more key DataColumn objects and returns a parameterized Command object. This Command object contains a SELECT query that returns the only row with the given key:

```
' Create a Command that retrieves a single record from a table.
Function GetCurrentRowCommand(ByVal da As OleDbDataAdapter, _
    ByVal ParamArray keyColumns() As DataColumn) As OleDbCommand
    ' Get the SELECT statement in the DataAdapter.
    Dim sql As String = da.SelectCommand.CommandText
    ' Truncate the statement just before the WHERE clause if there is one.
    Dim i As Integer = sql.ToUpper.IndexOf("WHERE ")
    If i > 0 Then sql = sql.Substring(0, i - 1)

    ' Prepare the WHERE clause on all primary key fields.
    Dim dc As DataColumn
    Dim sb As New System.Text.StringBuilder(100)
    For Each dc In keyColumns
        If sb.Length > 0 Then sb.Append(" AND ")
```

```
            sb.Append("[")
            sb.Append(dc.ColumnName)
            sb.Append("]=?")
        Next
        sql &= " WHERE " & sb.ToString

        ' Create the Command object on the same connection.
        Dim cmd As New OleDbCommand(sql, da.SelectCommand.Connection)

        ' Create the collection of parameters.
        For Each dc In keyColumns
            cmd.Parameters.Add(dc.ColumnName, dc.DataType)
        Next
        ' Return the command object.
        Return cmd
    End Function
```

Here's a quick example that shows how to use the GetCurrentRowCommand function:

```
Dim cn As New OleDbConnection(OledbPubsConnString)
Dim da As New OleDbDataAdapter( _
    "SELECT * FROM Publishers WHERE City='Seattle'", cn)
' You must pass the list of key columns after the first argument.
Dim resyncCmd As OleDbCommand = GetCurrentRowCommand(da, _
    ds.Tables("Publishers").Columns("pub_id"))
' Display the resulting command.
Debug.WriteLine(resyncCmd.CommandText)
    ' => SELECT * FROM Publishers WHERE [pub_id]=?
```

The following code shows how to build a RowUpdated handler event that attempts to resolve conflicts on a row-by-row basis, using the parameterized Command object just initialized. The code that flags rows and columns with an error message is similar to the one I showed you in the preceding section, so I won't comment on it again.

The key point in this routine is when the code checks whether an update operation failed because the current user has changed one or more fields by assigning exactly the same value as another user. For example, say that a publisher moves to another city and that two operators attempt to enter new values in the City, State, and possibly Country fields. The first operator updates the record successfully, but the second one receives a conflict error because the UPDATE command can't locate the original row in the database. In such circumstances, you might argue that this error isn't a real update conflict because, after all, the row in the database contains exactly the values that the second operator meant to enter. The following code correctly detects this case and manually performs an AcceptChanges method on the row in question, effectively clearing any update conflict. (Related statements are in boldface.)

```
' The code in this event handler uses the resyncCmd object
' initialized in the preceding code snippet.

Sub OnRowUpdated(ByVal sender As Object, _
    ByVal args As OleDbRowUpdatedEventArgs)
    If args.Status <> UpdateStatus.ErrorsOccurred Then
        ' Update was OK.
    ElseIf Not TypeOf args.Errors Is DBConcurrencyException Then
        ' An error occurred (maybe an RI violation).
        args.Row.RowError = "ERROR: " & args.Errors.Message
        ' Continue the update operation.
        args.Status = UpdateStatus.Continue
    Else
        ' An update conflict occurred.
        Dim dr As DataRow = args.Row
        Dim keyValue As String
        Dim keyName As String = "pub_id"

        Select Case args.StatementType
            Case StatementType.Insert
                dr.RowError = "Conflict on an INSERT operation"
                keyValue = dr(keyName, DataRowVersion.Current).ToString
            Case StatementType.Delete
                dr.RowError = "Conflict on a DELETE operation"
                keyValue = dr(keyName, DataRowVersion.Original).ToString
            Case StatementType.Update
                dr.RowError = "Conflict on an UPDATE operation"
                keyValue = dr(keyName, DataRowVersion.Original).ToString
        End Select

        ' Read the current row. Use the original key value in WHERE clause.
        ' (Otherwise, you get an error if the row has been deleted.)
        resyncCmd.Parameters(keyName).Value = keyValue
        Dim dre As OleDbDataReader = _
            resyncCmd.ExecuteReader(CommandBehavior.SingleRow)
        ' Advance to first record, and remember whether there's a record.
        Dim recordFound As Boolean = dre.Read

        If recordFound And args.StatementType = StatementType.Insert Then
            ' We attempted an insert on a record that's already there.
            dr.RowError &= "- There is a record with key = " & keyValue
        ElseIf Not recordFound AndAlso _
            args.StatementType <> StatementType.Insert Then
            ' We tried to update/delete a record that isn't there any longer.
            dr.RowError &= "Can't find a record with key = " & keyValue
        Else
```

```
' The operation failed for some other reason.

' After the loop, this variable is 0 only if the current value
' and the database value are the same for all conflicting columns.
Dim nonMatchingColumns As Integer = 0

Dim i As Integer
For i = 0 To dre.FieldCount - 1
    Dim dbValue, origValue, currValue As Object
    ' Get value in database if there is a matching record.
    If recordFound Then
        dbValue = dre(i)
    End If
    ' Get original value if not an Insert operation.
    If args.StatementType <> StatementType.Insert Then
        origValue = args.Row(i, DataRowVersion.Original)
    End If
    ' Get the current value if not a Delete operation.
    If args.StatementType <> StatementType.Delete Then
        currValue = args.Row(i, DataRowVersion.Current)
    End If

    ' Decide whether this field might be a source for a conflict.
    Dim conflicting As Boolean = False
    If Not recordFound Then
        ' If couldn't find the record, any modified column can be
        ' considered as a potential cause for conflict.
        If Not (origValue Is Nothing) AndAlso _
            Not (currValue Is Nothing) AndAlso _
            (origValue.ToString <> currValue.ToString) Then
            conflicting = True
        End If
    Else
        ' If the record was found, but original and database value
        ' differ, we've found a cause for the conflict.
        If Not (origValue Is Nothing) AndAlso _
            (dbValue.ToString <> origValue.ToString) Then
            conflicting = True
            If Not (currValue Is Nothing) AndAlso _
            (dbValue.ToString <> currValue.ToString) Then
                ' We've found a column for which the database and
                ' current values don't match.
                nonMatchingColumns += 1
            End If
        End If
    End If
```

(continued)

```
                If conflicting Then
                    ' Display field name and all related values.
                    Dim msg As String = ""
                    If Not (origValue Is Nothing) Then
                        msg = "Original value = " & origValue.ToString & ","
                    End If
                    If Not (dbValue Is Nothing) Then
                        msg &= "Value in database =" & dbValue.ToString
                    End If
                    dr.SetColumnError(i, msg)
                End If
            Next

            ' If we've found a record in the database and all values in the
            ' database match the current values, it means that we can consider
            ' this record successfully updated because another user had
            ' inserted exactly the same values this user wanted to change.
            If recordFound And nonMatchingColumns = 0 Then
                dr.AcceptChanges()
                dr.ClearErrors()
            End If
        End If

        ' Close the DataReader.
        dre.Close()
        ' In all cases, swallow the exception and continue.
        args.Status = UpdateStatus.Continue
    End If
End Sub
```

Another type of conflict that can be resolved automatically occurs when two operators insert the same record, with the same values in all fields. In this case, the second operator receives an OleDbException or a SqlException error, whose exact message depends on the database server. With SQL Server, you get an error message like this:

```
Violation of PRIMARY KEY constraint 'UPKCL_pubind'.
Cannot insert duplicate key in object 'publisher'.
```

The code in the RowUpdated event might intercept this error, compare the values in the current row with the values in the database table, and cancel the conflict if they match perfectly. The code that reads the database table and compares all fields is similar to the code in the preceding snippet, so I leave this task to you as an exercise.

Rolling Back Multiple Updates

As you know, the Update method sends an individual INSERT, DELETE, or UPDATE command to the data source for each modified row in the DataTable.

However, an exception is thrown and no more commands are sent if there is an update conflict and you neither set the ContinueUpdateOnErrors property to True nor set the Status property to Continue inside the RowUpdated event. If an exception is thrown, you must be prepared to catch it in a Try…End Try block.

However, it should be made clear that when the exception is thrown and the Update method returns the execution flow to the main code, some rows might have been already updated in the database. In the majority of cases, this effect is undesirable because usually you want to update either all the rows (at least those that don't cause any conflict) or no row at all. For example, if you get an exception after inserting an Order record but before adding the first OrderDetail row, you'll end up with a database in an inconsistent state.

In the preceding sections, I've shown how you can continue to perform updates when a conflict arises, so what's left to learn is how to use transactions to completely roll back any update operation on the database before the first conflict occurred. Protecting your application from partial updates is actually simple: you just have to open a transaction on the connection and commit it if the Update method completes successfully, or roll it back if an exception is thrown. To do so, you must explicitly assign the Transaction object to all the Command objects in the DataAdapter's UpdateCommand, InsertCommand, and DeleteCommand properties. Here's an example of this technique:

```
' Run the Update method inside a transaction.
Dim tr As OleDbTransaction
' Comment next line to see how updates behave without a transaction.
tr = cn.BeginTransaction()

' Enroll all the DataAdapter's commands in the same transaction.
da.UpdateCommand.Transaction = tr
da.DeleteCommand.Transaction = tr
da.InsertCommand.Transaction = tr

' Send changes to the database.
Try
    da.Update(ds, "Publishers")
Catch ex As Exception
    ' Roll back the transaction if there is one.
    If Not (tr Is Nothing) Then
        tr.Rollback()
        tr = Nothing
        ' Let the user know that there was a problem.
        MessageBox.Show(ex.Message, "Update error", MessageBoxButtons.OK, _
            MessageBoxIcon.Error)
    End If
Finally
```

(continued)

```
    ' Commit the transaction if there is one.
    If Not (tr Is Nothing) Then
        tr.Commit()
        tr = Nothing
    End If
End Try

' Close the connection.
cn.Close()
```

Transactions can be useful even if you protect your code from exceptions by setting the ContinueUpdateOnErrors property to True or by setting the Status property to Continue from inside the RowUpdated event. For example, you might show the user all the conflicts that you have detected and possibly resolved via code and then ask for his or her approval to commit all changes or roll them back as a whole.

Advanced Techniques

What I've described so far covers the fundamentals of update operations in a disconnected fashion, but there's much more to know. In fact, I dare say that each application poses its special challenges, and it's up to you to find the best solution in each specific circumstance. Fortunately, the more I work with ADO.NET the more I realize that it's far more flexible than I suspected at first. In this section, I've gathered a few sophisticated techniques that can improve your application's performance and scalability even further.

Reducing Conflicts with the RowUpdating Event

The RowUpdating event fires before the DataAdapter sends an insert, update, or delete command to the data source. The RowUpdating event isn't as important as the RowUpdated event because you can't fix a conflict before the conflict has occurred. Nevertheless, this event gives you something that the RowUpdated event doesn't give you: the ability to change the command being sent to the database, which in some scenarios is important.

For example, say that two users are modifying different columns of the same employee record at the same time: one user is changing the employee's address, city, and state values, while another user is changing the employee's salary. By default, the second user receives a conflict notification when she attempts to save the new salary value, but you can also decide that this operation is valid for your application's logic. If you decide that it's OK for two users to modify different fields, the second user shouldn't experience any update conflict.

To achieve this result, you must build an UPDATE command whose WHERE clause contains only the primary key and the fields that have been modified (as opposed to all the fields in the row). You can't solve this problem with a custom command in the DataAdapter's UpdateCommand property because each row might have been modified in different ways. So your only choice is to create a new Command on the fly from inside the RowUpdating event handler.

As you can see in Table 21-10, both the RowUpdating and RowUpdated events can access the command being sent to the data source through the argument's Command property. However, when you're inside a RowUpdating event, you can even *assign* a new Command object to this property, which effectively allows you to plug your custom update commands into the DataAdapter's row-by-row update mechanism. Moreover, you can access the DataRow being updated, so it's relatively easy to create an UPDATE command that uses only the modified fields in the SET and WHERE clauses. (The latter clause must always include the primary key—otherwise, the command might affect multiple rows.)

The following code is a sample RowUpdating event handler that implements this technique. It creates a parameterized command instead of a plain SQL command that contains constant values so that it doesn't have to account for setting field delimiters, doubling embedded quotes, and the like. If nothing else, this example should convince you that ADO.NET gives you incredible flexibility, even if it doesn't give it for free:

```
' A DataAdapter object that has been correctly initialized.
Dim WithEvents da As OleDbDataAdapter

Sub OnRowUpdating(ByVal sender As Object, _
    ByVal args As OleDbRowUpdatingEventArgs) Handles da.RowUpdating
    ' Exit if this isn't an Update operation.
    If args.StatementType <> StatementType.Update Then Exit Sub

    Dim keyName As String = "pub_id"
    Dim dr As DataRow = args.Row

    Dim i As Integer
    Dim numColumns As Integer = dr.Table.Columns.Count
    Dim setText As String = ""
    Dim whereText As String = ""
    Dim setParams As New ArrayList()
    Dim whereParams As New ArrayList()
    Dim param As OleDbParameter
```

(continued)

```
For i = 0 To dr.Table.Columns.Count - 1
    Dim dc As DataColumn = dr.Table.Columns(i)
    Dim colName As String = dc.ColumnName

    ' Check whether this column must be added to the SET part.
    If dr(i).ToString <> dr(i, DataRowVersion.Original).ToString Then
        ' Add this column to the SET text.
        If setText.Length > 0 Then setText &= ","
        setText &= "[" & colName & "]=?"
        ' Add a parameter in the corresponding position of the SET list.
        param = New OleDbParameter(colName, dc.DataType)
        param.SourceVersion = DataRowVersion.Current
        param.Value = dr(i)
        setParams.Add(param)
    End If

    ' Check whether this column must be added to the WHERE part.
    ' (Primary keys are always added to the WHERE part.)
    If colName = keyName Or dr(i).ToString <> _
        dr(i, DataRowVersion.Original).ToString Then
        If whereText.Length > 0 Then whereText &= " AND "
        whereText &= "[" & colName & "]=?"
        ' Add a parameter in the corresponding position of the WHERE list.
        param = New OleDbParameter(colName, dc.DataType)
        param.SourceVersion = DataRowVersion.Original
        param.Value = dr(i, DataRowVersion.Original)
        whereParams.Add(param)
    End If
Next

' Assemble the SQL string.
Dim sql As String = "UPDATE " & dr.Table.TableName & " SET " _
    & setText & " WHERE " & whereText
' Create a command on the same connection as the original command.
Dim cmd As New OleDbCommand(sql, args.Command.Connection)
' Enroll the new command in the same transaction as well.
cmd.Transaction = args.Command.Transaction

' Assemble the collection of parameters.
' (SET parameters first; then WHERE parameters.)
For Each param In setParams
    cmd.Parameters.Add(param)
Next
For Each param In whereParams
    cmd.Parameters.Add(param)
Next
```

```
    ' Assign the command to the DataAdapter command.
    args.Command = cmd
End Sub
```

Improving Performance with JOIN Queries

All the examples we've seen so far were based on rather simple queries. Possibly they retrieved all the records in a database table or perhaps they attempted to reduce the network traffic and database activity by selecting a subset of rows with a WHERE clause or a subset of columns, as in these two examples:

```
-- Only the titles published on or after 10/1/1992.
SELECT title_id, title, pub_id, pubdate FROM Titles WHERE pubdate>'10/1/1992'
-- Only the publishers from the U.S.A.
SELECT pub_id, pub_name, city FROM Publishers WHERE country='USA'
```

Alas, in the real world very few queries are that simple, as all database programmers know. For example, consider a query that must return all (and only) the titles published after October 1, 1991, from all (and only) the publishers based in the United States. No problem, you might say: just fill two DataTable objects using the preceding two SELECT queries, and then create a relationship between them. Well, this can work with tables with a few hundred rows, but you aren't going to use this naive technique with tables of 100,000 rows, are you? The point is, you would read a lot of records that you don't really want—such as titles published by publishers not in the United States and U.S. publishers who haven't published any books since October 1991.

Obviously, you must filter rows before the resultset leaves the server if you want to reduce both network traffic and the load on the database engine. The ideal solution would be to issue a JOIN command like this:

```
-- QUERY A: Retrieve data on titles and publishers satisfying
-- the query criteria in one resultset, sorted by Publishers.
SELECT pub_name, city, Publishers.pub_id, title_id, title, pubdate
    FROM Publishers INNER JOIN Titles ON Publishers.pub_id = Titles.pub_id
    WHERE country = 'USA' AND pubdate > '10/1/1991'
    ORDER BY Publishers.pub_id
```

In fact, this is the statement that you would have used in the good old ADO days. Unfortunately, the DataSet update model requires a one-to-one mapping between DataTable objects on the client and a database table on the server. For example, the CommandBuilder can work only if the DataAdapter's SELECT command references only one table.

Even if you can't use a single JOIN like the preceding one, certainly you can use *two* JOIN commands to fill the two DataTable objects without reading more rows than strictly necessary:

```
-- QUERY B: Only the titles published in or after Oct 1991 by a U.S. publisher
SELECT Titles.pub_id, title_id, title, pubdate FROM Titles
    INNER JOIN Publishers ON Publishers.pub_id = Titles.pub_id
    WHERE country = 'USA' AND pubdate > '10/1/1991'
-- QUERY C: Only the publishers from the USA that published a book since 1992
-- (The GROUP BY clause is necessary to drop duplicate rows.)
SELECT pub_name, city, Publishers.pub_id FROM Publishers
    INNER JOIN Titles ON Publishers.pub_id = Titles.pub_id
    WHERE country='USA' AND pubdate > '10/1/1991'
    GROUP BY Publishers.pub_id, pub_name, city
```

This solution is *much* better than the first one, but it still suffers from a couple of problems that negatively affect the resulting scalability. First, you're asking the database engine to perform basically the same filtering operation twice—in fact, the two WHERE clauses are identical—so you can expect that these two JOINs take longer than the single JOIN seen before (even though not twice as long). The second problem is subtler: to be *absolutely* certain that the two returned resultsets are consistent with each other, you must run the two SELECT queries inside a transaction with the level set to Serializable, thus holding a lock on both tables until you complete the read operation and commit the transaction.

To see why you need to wrap these commands in a transaction, imagine what would happen if another user deleted a publisher immediately after your first SELECT query and before your second SELECT query. The modified publisher wouldn't be returned by your second SELECT, and a row in the Titles DataTable would point to a parent row that didn't exist in the Publishers DataTable. This condition would raise an error when you attempted to establish a relationship between these two DataTable objects, and you'd have a title in your DataSet for which you couldn't retrieve the corresponding publisher. Reversing the order of the two queries wouldn't help much because you'd get a similar error if a title from a U.S. publisher were added to the database after the SELECT on the Publishers table and before the query on the Titles table. Again, the only way to avoid this consistency problem is to run the two SELECT queries inside a serializable transaction, which degrades overall scalability.

Now that the problem is clear, let's see whether we can find a better solution. Have a look at Figure 21-9. At the top, it shows the result of the JOIN statement that returns fields from both tables (labeled as query A in previous code snippets); at the bottom, you see the results from the two JOINs that return fields from a single table (queries B and C). Now it's apparent that you can duplicate the effect of query C by dropping a few columns from the result of query A, which you can do simply by invoking the Remove or RemoveAt method of the Columns collection.

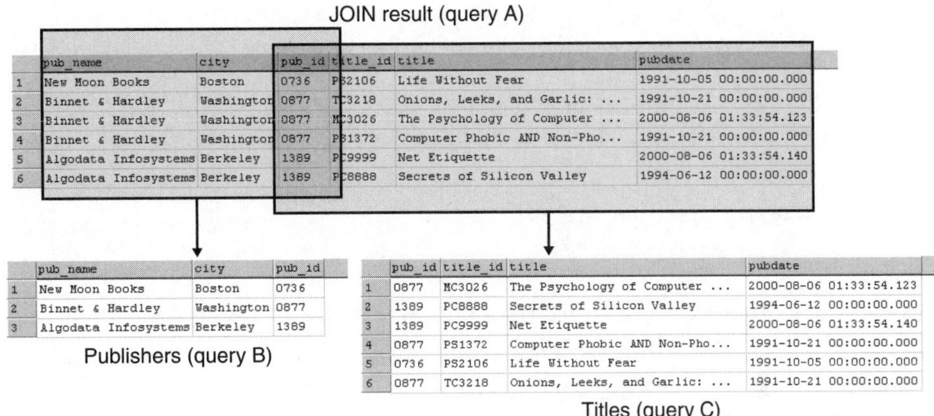

	pub_name	city	pub_id	title_id	title	pubdate
1	New Moon Books	Boston	0736	PS2106	Life Without Fear	1991-10-05 00:00:00.000
2	Binnet & Hardley	Washington	0877	TC3218	Onions, Leeks, and Garlic: ...	1991-10-21 00:00:00.000
3	Binnet & Hardley	Washington	0877	MC3026	The Psychology of Computer ...	2000-08-06 01:33:54.123
4	Binnet & Hardley	Washington	0877	PS1372	Computer Phobic AND Non-Pho...	1991-10-21 00:00:00.000
5	Algodata Infosystems	Berkeley	1389	PC9999	Net Etiquette	2000-08-06 01:33:54.140
6	Algodata Infosystems	Berkeley	1389	PC8888	Secrets of Silicon Valley	1994-06-12 00:00:00.000

	pub_name	city	pub_id
1	New Moon Books	Boston	0736
2	Binnet & Hardley	Washington	0877
3	Algodata Infosystems	Berkeley	1389

	pub_id	title_id	title	pubdate
1	0877	MC3026	The Psychology of Computer ...	2000-08-06 01:33:54.123
2	1389	PC8888	Secrets of Silicon Valley	1994-06-12 00:00:00.000
3	1389	PC9999	Net Etiquette	2000-08-06 01:33:54.140
4	0877	PS1372	Computer Phobic AND Non-Pho...	1991-10-21 00:00:00.000
5	0736	PS2106	Life Without Fear	1991-10-05 00:00:00.000
6	0877	TC3218	Onions, Leeks, and Garlic: ...	1991-10-21 00:00:00.000

Figure 21-9. Splitting the result of a JOIN into two DataTable objects.

Deriving the results of query B from query A is slightly more difficult because you must loop through all the rows in a large resultset to filter out duplicate values. However, the GROUP BY clause in query A ensures that the same values are consecutive, so it's easy to filter out all rows with duplicate values in the primary key column. The following code shows how to perform the splitting in an optimized way:

```
' Define all the involved SQL commands.
' NOTE: the code below assumes that the first column in the child
'       table is its foreign key.
Dim titSql As String = "SELECT pub_id, title_id, title, pubdate FROM Titles"
Dim pubSql As String = "SELECT pub_id, pub_name, city FROM Publishers"
Dim joinSql As String = "SELECT Publishers.pub_id, pub_name, city, " _
    & "title_id, title, pubdate FROM Publishers " _
    & "INNER JOIN Titles ON Publishers.pub_id=Titles.pub_id " _
    & "WHERE country = 'USA' AND pubdate > '10/1/1991'" _
    & "ORDER BY Publishers.pub_id"

' Create the connection and all the involved DataAdapter objects.
Dim cn As New SqlConnection(SqlPubsConnString)
Dim titDa As New SqlDataAdapter(titSql, cn)
Dim pubDa As New SqlDataAdapter(pubSql, cn)
Dim joinDa As New SqlDataAdapter(joinSql, cn)
```

(continued)

```
' Open the connection.
cn.Open()

' Manually create the parent and child tables in the DataSet.
Dim ds As New DataSet
Dim pubDt As DataTable = ds.Tables.Add("Publishers")
Dim titDt As DataTable = ds.Tables.Add("Titles")

' Fill the schema of the master table.
pubDa.FillSchema(pubDt, SchemaType.Mapped)

' Execute the JOIN, using the child DataTable as a target.
' (It creates additional columns that belong to the parent table.)
joinDa.Fill(titDt)

' This variable holds the last value found in the master table.
Dim keyValue As String
Dim i As Integer
Dim dr As DataRow

' Extract rows belonging to the parent table, and discard duplicate values.
For Each dr In titDt.Rows
    ' If we haven't seen this value yet, create a record in the parent table.
    If dr(0).ToString <> keyValue Then
        ' Remember the new key value.
        keyValue = dr(0).ToString
        ' Add a new record.
        Dim pubRow As DataRow = pubDt.NewRow
        ' Copy only the fields belonging to the parent table.
        For i = 0 To pubDt.Columns.Count - 1
            pubRow(i) = dr(i)
        Next
        pubDt.Rows.Add(pubRow)
    End If
Next

' Remove columns belonging to the master table,
' but leave the foreign key (assumed to be in the zeroth column).
For i = pubDt.Columns.Count - 1 To 1 Step -1
    titDt.Columns.RemoveAt(i)
Next

' Now we can fill the schema of the child table and close the connection.
titDa.FillSchema(titDt, SchemaType.Mapped)
cn.Close()

' Add the relationship manually. Note that this statement is based on the
' assumption that the foreign key is in the zeroth column in the child table.
```

```
ds.Relations.Add("PubTitles", pubDt.Columns(0), titDt.Columns(0))

' Bind to the DataGrid controls.
DataGrid1.DataSource = pubDt
DataGrid2.DataSource = titDt
```

Figure 21-10 shows the result of the preceding code. This solution solves all the problems mentioned previously because SQL Server evaluates only one statement and you don't have to use a transaction to ensure consistent results. (Individual statements run inside an implicit transaction.) The only minor defect of this technique is that it retrieves some duplicated data for the parent table (the rows that you discard in the For Each loop in the previous code), which causes slightly more network traffic. If you're retrieving many columns from the parent table and each parent row has many child records, this extra traffic becomes noticeable, and you might find it preferable to fall back on the solution based on the two JOIN statements running inside a transaction. Only a benchmark based on the actual tables and the actual network configuration can tell which technique is more efficient or scalable.

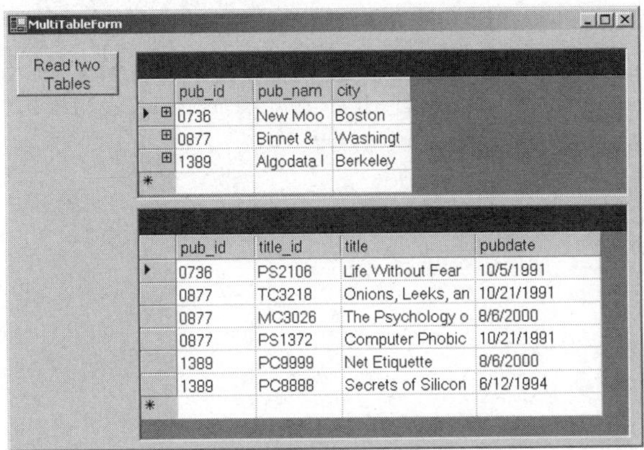

Figure 21-10. The two DataGrid controls contain only the data really needed.

A final note: the preceding code defines two DataAdapter objects, one for each table, and uses them only to retrieve the database table's schema. Even if the DataTable objects weren't filled using these DataAdapters, you could still pass them to a CommandBuilder object to generate the usual INSERT, DELETE, and UPDATE statements that you then use to update either table.

Paginating Results

Even though a DataTable object can contain up to slightly more than 16 million rows, you shouldn't even try loading more than a few hundred rows in it, for two good reasons. First, you'd move just too much information through the wire; second, the user won't browse all those rows anyway. So you should attempt to reduce the number of records read—for example, by refining the WHERE clause of your query. If this remedy isn't possible, you should offer a pagination mechanism that displays results only one page at a time, without reading more rows than strictly needed each time.

Implementing a good paging mechanism isn't trivial. For example, you can easily implement a mediocre paging mechanism by passing a starting record and a number of records as arguments to the DataAdapter's Fill method, as in this code snippet:

```
' Read page N into Publishers table. (Each page contains 10 rows.)
da.Fill(ds, (n - 1) * 10, 10, "Publishers")
```

(I explained this syntax in the "Filling a DataTable" section earlier in this chapter.) What actually happens is that the DataAdapter reads all the records before the ones you're really interested in, and then it discards them. So this approach is OK for small resultsets, but you should never use it for tables containing more than a few hundred rows. You have to roll up your sleeves and start writing some smart SQL code to implement a better paging mechanism.

Let's start by having a look at the following graph, which depicts a small Publishers table of just 12 records, divided into three pages of four rows each. The resultset is sorted on the PubId numeric key.

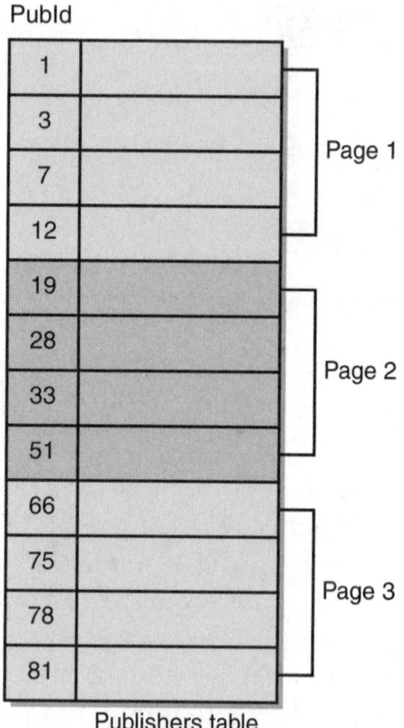

Getting the first page is easy, thanks to the TOP clause offered by both Access's SQL and T-SQL dialects:

```
SELECT TOP 4 * FROM Publishers ORDER BY PubId
```

Moving to the next page is also simple. Say that you're currently positioned on a page in the middle of the table, such as the one that appears in gray in the preceding diagram, and you want to read the next four rows. These rows are the first four records whose key value is higher than the value of the key at the last record in the current page:

```
-- 51 is the value of the key at the last row in the current page.
SELECT TOP 4 * FROM Publishers WHERE Pubs > 51 ORDER BY PubId
```

Getting the last page is also simple: we just need to retrieve rows in *reverse* order and select the first four rows of the result. To keep things simple, let's assume that the resultset contains an integer multiple of the page size:

```
SELECT TOP 4 * FROM Publishers ORDER BY PubId DESC
```

The problem here is that we get the result in reverse order and therefore must reverse the rows. We might do this after we load the rows into the DataTable, but it's better to have the database engine do the job for us so that we can bind the resultset directly to a DataGrid control. So we need to run the preceding query as a subquery of another SELECT command that puts all rows in the correct order:

```
SELECT * FROM Publishers WHERE PubId IN
   (SELECT TOP 4 PubId FROM Publishers ORDER BY PubId DESC)
   ORDER BY PubId
```

Implementing the Previous button is slightly more complex because we want the four records that come immediately before the key value in the first row of the current page, as in this code snippet:

```
-- 19 is the value of the key at the first row in the current page.
SELECT TOP 4 * FROM Publishers WHERE PubId < 19 ORDER BY PubId DESC
```

Again, this query returns a resultset whose rows are in reverse order, so we need to run the query as a subquery of another SELECT that puts everything right again:

```
SELECT * FROM Publishers WHERE PubId IN
   (SELECT TOP 4 PubId FROM Publishers WHERE PubId < 19 ORDER BY PubId DESC)
   ORDER BY ISBN
```

We're now able to implement the First, Previous, Next, and Last buttons in our Windows Form or Web Form. We can also add a Goto button that displays the Nth page. For example, showing the fifth page would mean reading the first 20 rows and extracting the last 4 rows of the result:

```
SELECT TOP 4 * FROM Publishers WHERE PubId IN
    (SELECT TOP 20 PubId FROM Publishers ORDER BY PubId)
    ORDER BY PubId DESC
```

This query returns the rows in reverse order, so we must run it as a subquery of another query that re-sorts the result in the correct order:

```
SELECT * FROM Publishers WHERE PubId IN
    (SELECT TOP 4 PubId FROM Publishers WHERE PubId IN
        (SELECT TOP 20 PubId FROM Publishers ORDER BY PubId)
        ORDER BY PubId DESC)
    ORDER BY PubId
```

I told you that implementing paging isn't a trivial task, remember? Anyway, at this point creating the application has become just a matter of running the right queries against the database. Here's an abridged version of the demo program you'll find on the companion CD. (See Figure 21-11.)

```
Dim cn As New OleDbConnection(BiblioConnString)
Dim cmd As New OleDbCommand(sql, cn)
Dim da As OleDbDataAdapter

' You can change the page size as you prefer.
Dim pageSize As Integer = 10
' This is the number of records.
Dim recCount As Integer
' This is the number of pages.
Dim pageCount As Integer
' This is the current page number.
Dim currPage As Integer

Dim ds As New DataSet()
Dim dt As DataTable = ds.Tables.Add("Titles")
Dim sql As String

Private Sub PagingForm_Load(ByVal sender As System.Object, _
    ByVal e As System.EventArgs) Handles MyBase.Load
    ' Evaluate number of pages.
    GetPageNumber()
    ' Bind the Titles table.
    DataGrid1.DataSource = dt
    ' Show the first page of results.
    btnFirst.PerformClick()
End Sub
```

```
' Evaluate number of pages in the results.
Sub GetPageNumber()
    Dim closeOnExit As Boolean
    ' Open the connection if necessary.
    If cn.State = ConnectionState.Closed Then
        cn.Open()
        closeOnExit = True
    End If

    ' Evaluate number of records.
    cmd.CommandText = "SELECT COUNT(*) FROM Titles"
    recCount = CInt(cmd.ExecuteScalar())
    ' Close the connection if it was closed.
    If closeOnExit Then cn.Close()

    ' Evaluate number of pages, and display the count.
    pageCount = (recCount + pageSize - 1) \ pageSize
    lblRecords.Text = " of " & pageCount.ToString
End Sub

' Run the specified query, and display the Nth page of results.
Sub DisplayPage(ByVal n As Integer, ByVal sql As String)
    ' Perform the query, and display the results.
    cn.Open
    Dim da As New OleDbDataAdapter(sql, cn)
    dt.Clear()
    da.Fill(dt)
    ' Uncomment next statement to update page count each time
    ' a new page is displayed.
    ' GetPageNumber()
    cn.Close

    ' Remember current page number, and display it.
    currPage = n
    lblCurrPage.Text = n.ToString

    ' Enable or disable buttons.
    btnFirst.Enabled = (n > 1)
    btnPrevious.Enabled = (n > 1)
    btnNext.Enabled = (n < pageCount)
    btnLast.Enabled = (n < pageCount)
End Sub

' Manage the four navigational buttons.
```

(continued)

```
Private Sub btnFirst_Click(ByVal sender As System.Object, _
    ByVal e As System.EventArgs) Handles btnFirst.Click
    sql = String.Format("SELECT TOP {0} * FROM Titles ORDER BY ISBN", _
        pageSize)
    DisplayPage(1, sql)
End Sub

Private Sub btnPrevious_Click(ByVal sender As System.Object, _
    ByVal e As System.EventArgs) Handles btnPrevious.Click
    sql = String.Format("SELECT * FROM Titles WHERE ISBN IN " _
        & "(SELECT TOP {0} ISBN FROM Titles WHERE ISBN < '{1}' " _
        & "ORDER BY ISBN DESC) ORDER BY ISBN", pageSize, dt.Rows(0)("ISBN"))
    DisplayPage(currPage - 1, sql)
End Sub

Private Sub btnNext_Click(ByVal sender As System.Object, _
    ByVal e As System.EventArgs) Handles btnNext.Click
    sql = String.Format("SELECT TOP {0} * FROM Titles WHERE ISBN > '{1}' " _
        & "ORDER BY ISBN", pageSize, dt.Rows(dt.Rows.Count - 1)("ISBN"))
    DisplayPage(currPage + 1, sql)
End Sub

Private Sub btnLast_Click(ByVal sender As System.Object, _
    ByVal e As System.EventArgs) Handles btnLast.Click
    ' Evaluate number of records on last page.
    Dim num As Integer = recCount - pageSize * (pageCount - 1)
    sql = String.Format("SELECT * FROM Titles WHERE ISBN IN (SELECT TOP " _
        & " {0} ISBN FROM Titles ORDER BY ISBN DESC) ORDER BY ISBN", num)
    DisplayPage(pageCount, sql)
End Sub

' Go to Nth page.
Private Sub btnGoto_Click(ByVal sender As System.Object, _
    ByVal e As System.EventArgs) Handles btnGoto.Click
    Try
        ' txtPageNum contains the page number we want to jump to.
        Dim pageNum As Integer = CInt(txtPageNum.Text)
        sql = String.Format("SELECT * FROM Titles WHERE ISBN IN " _
            & "(SELECT TOP {0} ISBN FROM Titles WHERE ISBN IN " _
            & "(SELECT TOP {1} ISBN FROM Titles ORDER BY ISBN) ORDER BY " _
            & " ISBN DESC) ORDER BY ISBN", pageSize, pageSize * pageNum)
        DisplayPage(pageNum, sql)
    Catch ex As Exception
        MessageBox.Show("Page # must be in the range [1," & _
            pageCount.ToString & "]")
    End Try
End Sub
```

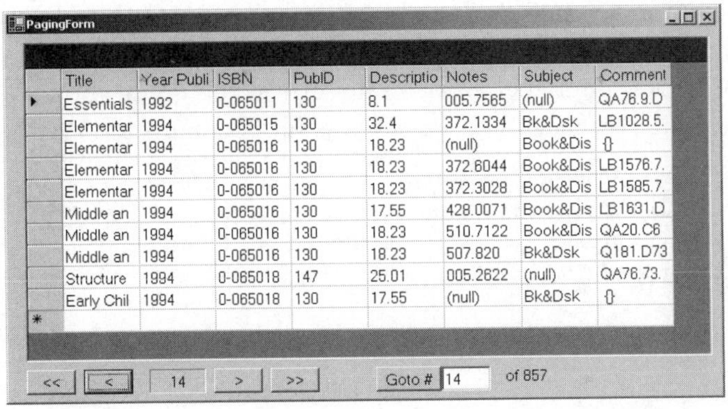

PagingForm

Title	Year Publi	ISBN	PubID	Descriptio	Notes	Subject	Comment
Essentials	1992	0-065011	130	8.1	005.7565	(null)	QA76.9.D
Elementar	1994	0-065015	130	32.4	372.1334	Bk&Dsk	LB1028.5.
Elementar	1994	0-065016	130	18.23	(null)	Book&Dis	{}
Elementar	1994	0-065016	130	18.23	372.6044	Book&Dis	LB1576.7.
Elementar	1994	0-065016	130	18.23	372.3028	Book&Dis	LB1585.7.
Middle an	1994	0-065016	130	17.55	428.0071	Book&Dis	LB1631.D
Middle an	1994	0-065016	130	18.23	510.7122	Book&Dis	QA20.C6
Middle an	1994	0-065016	130	18.23	507.820	Bk&Dsk	Q181.D73
Structure	1994	0-065018	147	25.01	005.2622	(null)	QA76.73.
Early Chil	1994	0-065018	130	17.55	(null)	Bk&Dsk	{}

<< < 14 > >> Goto # 14 of 857

Figure 21-11. The demo program shows how to navigate among pages of the Titles table in Biblio.mdb (over 8000 records).

The program evaluates the number of pages when the form is loaded, but a more robust implementation should execute the GetPageNumber procedure each time a new page is displayed. (See remarks in the DisplayPage routine.) Updating a DataTable that contains paged results doesn't require any special technique—define a DataAdapter based on a generic SELECT statement:

```
Dim titDa As New OleDbDataAdapter("SELECT * FROM Titles", cn)
```

and then use a CommandBuilder object to generate the INSERT, DELETE, and UPDATE commands. Or create your custom update commands, as I described earlier in this chapter.

Writing Provider-Agnostic Code

In Chapter 20, I explain that ADO and ADO.NET provide different solutions to the problem of creating code that works with any provider and any database. In ADO, the solution to this problem comes for free because you can use the same ADO Connection, Command, and Recordset objects regardless of the OLE DB provider you're using, and you only have to correctly build the connection string that you pass to the Connection object's Open method.

The ADO.NET objects defined in the System.Data.OleDb and System.Data.SqlClient namespaces inherit the same core set of members from a common base class or a common interface but are otherwise free to define new properties and methods to better leverage the features of each provider. You can take advantage of the common base class or the common interface to create generic routines that work with either provider, even though the code you write isn't straightforward. Here are a few examples that perform common operations in a provider-agnostic way.

Creating a procedure that opens and returns either an OleDbConnection or a SqlConnection object is relatively easy because these objects implement the IDbConnection interface. You can discern which connection should be created by checking whether the connection string contains the Provider attribute:

```
' Create a suitable connection object for a given connection string.
Function CreateConnection(ByVal connString As String) As IDbConnection
    If connString.ToLower.IndexOf("provider=") >= 0 Then
        Return New OleDbConnection(connString)
    Else
        Return New SqlConnection(connString)
    End If
End Function
```

The Connection object exposed by both providers exposes a CreateCommand method that returns either an OleDbConnection or a SqlConnection object. The Command object exposed by both providers implements the IDbCommand interface, so you can perform a command in a database-independent way, as follows:

```
' Start with the connection string.
Dim connStr As String = BiblioConnString
' Uncomment next line to check that it works also with the SQL provider.
' connStr = SqlPubsConnString

' Create a connection object, and assign to a generic IDbConnection variable.
Dim cn As IDbConnection = CreateConnection(connStr)
' Create a command on this connection.
Dim cmd As IDbCommand = cn.CreateCommand
' The CommandText must be assigned separately.
cmd.CommandText = "DELETE Publishers WHERE City='Boston'"
cmd.ExecuteNonQuery()
```

You can read data returned from a SELECT command by assigning the result of an ExecuteReader method to an IDataReader variable:

```
' Get a DataReader object. (Assumes the cmd contains a SELECT query.)
Dim dr As IDataReader = cmd.ExecuteReader
' Write field values, and close the DataReader.
Do While dr.Read
    Dim i As Integer
    For i = 0 To dr.FieldCount - 1
        Debug.Write(dr(i))
    Next
    Debug.WriteLine("")
Loop
dr.Close()
```

(Of course, you can't access the ExecuteXmlReader method through a generic IDbCommand object because only the SQL Server provider exposes this method.) Working with transactions in a database-independent way is also simple, but keep in mind that you can't use nested transactions (with the OLE DB .NET Data Provider) or named transactions (with the SQL Server .NET Data Provider) when you work with a generic IDbTransaction variable:

```
' Open a transaction.
Dim tr As IDbTransaction = cn.BeginTransaction
Try
    ' Perform your database task here.
    ⋮
Catch ex As Exception
    ' Roll back everything in case of error.
    tr.Rollback()
    tr = Nothing
Finally
    ' If the transaction is still active, commit it.
    If Not (tr Is Nothing) Then tr.Commit()
End Try
```

You can create parameterized Command objects that work equally well with both providers, but in general this approach isn't easy because the two providers require a different syntax for the arguments in the CommandText string. If you don't consider the difficulty of building the command text, however, you'll find it simple to create individual parameters in a way that works with both providers:

```
' cmd is an IDbCommand variable.
cmd.Parameters.Add("PubId", 1)
```

To assign additional properties, use the return value of the preceding statement in a With block:

```
With cmd.Parameters.Add("Total")
    .DbType = DbType.Double
    .Direction = ParameterDirection.Output
End With
```

Most of the objects you need when working in disconnected mode—such as the DataSet, DataTable, and DataRow objects—belong to the System.Data namespace and therefore don't depend on any specific provider. The only other object that you must have to create database-agnostic code is the generic DbDataAdapter object. Unfortunately, there's no direct way to create a DbDataAdapter object from a connection (as we do, for example, with CreateCommand for the generic Command object), nor is there a way to create a generic CommandBuilder object. So we must define a helper routine that performs both these tasks:

```
' This code requires that you have used the following Imports statement:
'    Imports System.Data.Common

' Create a suitable DataAdapter object for a given connection object.
Function CreateDataAdapter(ByVal sql As String, _
    ByVal cn As IDbConnection) As DbDataAdapter
    If TypeOf cn Is OleDbConnection Then
        ' Create an OleDbDataAdapter, and initialize its properties.
        Dim da As New OleDbDataAdapter(sql, DirectCast(cn, OleDbConnection))
        Dim cb As New OleDbCommandBuilder(da)
        da.UpdateCommand = cb.GetUpdateCommand
        da.DeleteCommand = cb.GetDeleteCommand
        da.InsertCommand = cb.GetInsertCommand
        Return da

    ElseIf TypeOf cn Is SqlConnection Then
        ' Create a SqlDataAdapter, and initialize its properties.
        Dim da As New SqlDataAdapter(sql, DirectCast(cn, SqlConnection))
        Dim cb As New SqlCommandBuilder(da)
        da.UpdateCommand = cb.GetUpdateCommand
        da.DeleteCommand = cb.GetDeleteCommand
        da.InsertCommand = cb.GetInsertCommand
        Return da
    Else
        Throw New ArgumentException()
    End If
End Function
```

Filling a DataSet is now simple:

```
Dim da As OleDbDataAdapter = CreateDataAdapter("SELECT * FROM Titles", cn)
Dim ds As New DataSet
da.Fill(ds, "Titles")
```

Now we're left with the problem of writing events that work with any type of provider. In some cases, this job is simple because the event handler doesn't take any argument from the System.Data.OleDb or System.Data.SqlClient namespace, so it can serve events from any provider. The Connection's StateChange event is an example of such events:

```
Sub OnStateChange(ByVal sender As Object, _
    ByVal e As System.Data.StateChangeEventArgs)
    Dim cn As IDbConnection = DirectCast(sender, IDbConnection)
    ⋮
End Sub
```

Unfortunately, this approach doesn't work with all possible events because the type of their second argument often depends on the specific provider, and therefore, an event routine has no way to serve events coming from objects belonging to just any provider. The best you can do is write two separate event procedures that call the same helper routine, as in this code snippet:

```
' An example of two event procedures that delegate to a common routine
Sub OnOleDbRowUpdated(ByVal sender As Object, _
    ByVal e As System.Data.OleDb.OleDbRowUpdatedEventArgs)
    OnRowUpdated(sender, e)
End Sub

Sub OnSqlRowUpdated(ByVal sender As Object, _
    ByVal e As System.Data.SqlClient.SqlRowUpdatedEventArgs)
    OnRowUpdated(sender, e)
End Sub

Sub OnRowUpdated(ByVal sender As Object, _
    ByVal e As System.Data.Common.RowUpdatedEventArgs)
    ⋮
End Sub
```

The preceding code works because both the OleDbRowUpdatedEventArgs and the SqlRowUpdatedEventArgs class inherit from RowUpdatedEventArgs. The following code selects one of the preceding procedures as the target for the *xxx*RowUpdated event:

```
If TypeOf da Is OleDbDataAdapter Then
    AddHandler DirectCast(da, OleDbDataAdapter).RowUpdated, _
        AddressOf OnOleDbRowUpdated
ElseIf TypeOf da Is SqlDataAdapter Then
    AddHandler DirectCast(da, SqlDataAdapter).RowUpdated, _
        AddressOf OnSqlRowUpdated
Else
    Throw New ArgumentException()
End If
```

Or you can create a generic routine that takes an object, the name of one of its events, and an array of delegates that point to a potential event handler and then uses .NET reflection to perform an AddHandler command on the first delegate that matches the expected type:

```
' A routine that takes an object, an event name, and a list of potential
' delegates to event handlers and selects the first delegate that matches the
' expected signature of the event handler
```

(continued)

```
Sub AddHandlerByName(ByVal obj As Object, ByVal eventName As String, _
    ByVal ParamArray events() As [Delegate])

    ' Get the type of the object argument.
    Dim ty As System.Type = obj.GetType
    ' Get the EventInfo corresponding to the requested event.
    Dim evInfo As System.Reflection.EventInfo = ty.GetEvent(eventName)
    ' Get the delegate class that represents the event procedure.
    Dim evType As System.Type = evInfo.EventHandlerType

    ' Compare this type with arguments being passed.
    Dim del As [Delegate]
    For Each del In events
        If del.GetType Is evType Then
            ' If this is the correct delegate, use AddHandler on it.
            ' (This corresponds to a reflection's AddEventHandler method.)
            evInfo.AddEventHandler(obj, del)
            Exit Sub
        End If
    Next
End Sub
```

Here's how you can use the preceding routine:

```
' Dynamically add an event to the DataAdapter.
AddHandlerByName(da, "RowUpdated", _
    New OleDbRowUpdatedEventHandler(AddressOf OnOleDbRowUpdated), _
    New SqlRowUpdatedEventHandler(AddressOf OnSqlRowUpdated))
' Update the data source.
da.Update(ds, "Titles")
```

As you've seen in this section, writing database-independent code with ADO.NET isn't as simple as it used to be with ADO. You have to adopt several polymorphic techniques based on common base classes and interfaces, and you even need to resort to reflection for some thorny tasks. On the other hand, well-written code that performs well with any provider is surely a great form of code reuse, and it will become more important when other .NET data providers are introduced. Of course, deciding whether the added complexity is worth the savings in coding is entirely up to you.

At this point, you know enough to build great database-centric applications. Yet there are a few more ADO.NET features that I haven't covered yet. I discuss them at the end of the next chapter, after I introduce the new XML-related classes in the .NET Framework.

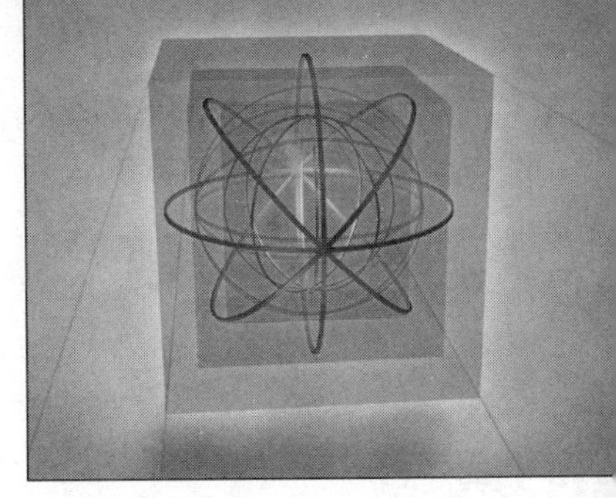

22

XML and ADO.NET

In recent years, the Extensible Markup Language, better known as XML, has emerged as a leading technology for storing data of any complexity and exchanging it among applications or even different operating systems. Because of the high degree of interoperability that it allows, XML is used nearly everywhere in the .NET Framework. For example, you saw in Chapter 11 that you can serialize the state of an object to Simple Object Access Protocol (SOAP) (which is an XML-based format) or to custom-defined XML.

Paradoxically, XML is so deeply buried in the .NET Framework that in most cases you don't even see it, and you don't have to process it directly. XML Web services are the perfect example of this concept: you send requests and receive results from an XML Web service using SOAP (and therefore XML) without having to learn anything about .NET XML classes.

However, you'll come across situations in which you must work with XML directly, so I'm covering the most important .NET classes and namespaces related to XML in this chapter. I'm also covering all the XML-related features of ADO.NET—for example, the support for strongly typed DataSet objects.

> **Note** To keep the code as concise as possible, all code samples in this chapter assume that you have added the following Imports statement at the top of your source files:
>
> ```
> Imports System.Xml
> ```

Reading and Writing XML Files

The .NET Framework supports different techniques for working with XML data. When you need to simply parse an XML file to process its contents as you read it, you can achieve the best performance with the XmlTextReader class. Similarly, you should use the XmlTextWriter class if you write XML data as you produce it. For more complex tasks, such as loading entire XML files into memory and processing them, you should use the XmlDocument class, which implements the XML Document Object Model (DOM). The XmlDocument class is described later in this chapter.

The XmlTextReader Class

The System.Xml.XmlTextReader class offers a fast way for reading XML data into memory. This object works a bit like the forward-only DataReader object in that the XML stream is consumed as it's being read and parsed, and you cannot backtrack to reread any preceding node. As is the case with a DataReader object, the XML data retrieved by an XmlTextReader object is read-only, so you never affect the original XML file. This object is clearly less powerful than a full-featured XML DOM parser—which can traverse the XML data in both directions and change its structure—but in many situations, using the XmlTextReader is the best choice you can make, especially with very large documents that would seriously tax the memory.

Note Because the XmlTextReader never reads the entire document into memory, it's somewhat akin to Simple API for XML (SAX) parsers. The similarities between these types of parsers stop here, however, and many important differences exist between these two tools—for example:

- A SAX parser works in *push* mode: after the application starts the parsing, the SAX parser actively pushes data to the application through a set of methods of the IContent-Handler interface; the application passively replies to such interface methods (which appear as events to the main application).

(continued)

- The XmlTextReader object works in *pull* mode: the application is in charge of pulling data out of the XML stream, therefore playing a more active role. Many programmers might find this programming model more intuitive because of its active role and also because the application doesn't have to remember the current parsing state. In addition, the application can skip one or more XML items it isn't interested in and speed up the parsing process.

You pass the name of the XML file to be parsed to the XmlTextReader constructor:

```
Dim xtr As New XmlTextReader("mydata.xml")
```

(Other overloaded versions of the constructor can take a Stream-derived object or a TextReader object.) Next you enter a loop that checks the return value from the Read method, similar to what you do with a DataReader object—inside the loop, you usually test the NodeType property of the current element and proceed appropriately:

```
Do While xtr.Read
    Select Case xtr.NodeType
        Case XmlNodeType.Document
            ' The root element in the XML data
        Case XmlNodeType.Element
            ' An XML element
        Case XmlNodeType.EndElement
            ' A closing XML tag
        Case XmlNodeType.Text
            ' Text value
        Case XmlNodeType.CDATA
            ' A CDATA section
    End Select
Loop
' Close the XML stream.
xtr.Close()
```

All the possible values of the NodeType property are listed in Table 22-1; this table will also be useful when we explore the XML DOM using the Xml-Document class.

Table 22-1 XmlNodeType Enumerated Values and Corresponding XML Class

XmlNode Type Value	XML Class	Description	Can Be a Child Of	Can Have These Nodes as Children	Example
Attribute	Xml-Attribute	An attribute	None (It isn't considered the child of an element.)	Text, EntityReference	id='123'
CDATA	XmlCData-Section	A CDATA section	Document-Fragment, Entity-Reference, Element	None	<![CDATA [mydata]]>
Comment	Xml-Comment	A comment	Document, Document-Fragment, Entity-Reference, Element	None	<!-- mycomment -->
Document	Xml-Document	A document root object	None (It works as the root node of the document.)	Xml-Declaration, Element, Processing-Instruction, Comment, Document-Type	
Document-Fragment	Xml-Document-Fragment	A document fragment used to process a node subtree	None	Element, Processing-Instruction, Comment, Text, CDATA, Entity-Reference	
Document-Type	Xml-Document-Type	The document type declaration indicated by the DOC-TYPE tag	Document	Notation, Entity	<!DOCTYPE ...>

Table 22-1 XmlNodeType Enumerated Values and Corresponding XML Class

XmlNode Type Value	XML Class	Description	Can Be a Child Of	Can Have These Nodes as Children	Example
Element	Xml-Element	An XML element	Document, Document-Fragment, Entity-Reference, Element	Element, Text, Comment, Processing-Instruction, CDATA, Entity-Reference	<myelement> ⋮ </myelement>
EndElement	n/a	An end element tag; it's returned when an XmlReader gets to the end of an element	n/a	n/a	</myelement>
EndEntity	n/a	The end of an entity declaration; it's returned by the XmlReader	n/a	n/a	
Entity	XmlEntity	An entity declaration	Document-Type	Text, EntityReference, or any node that represents an expanded entity	<!ENTITY ...>
Entity-Reference	XmlEntity-Reference	A reference to an entity	Attribute, Document-Fragment, Element, Entity-Reference	Element, Processing-Instruction, Comment, Text, CDATA, Entity-Reference	&ref
None	n/a	It's returned by Xml-Reader if the Read method hasn't been called yet	n/a	n/a	

(continued)

Table 22-1 XmlNodeType Enumerated Values and Corresponding XML Class

XmlNode Type Value	XML Class	Description	Can Be a Child Of	Can Have These Nodes as Children	Example
Notation	Xml-Notation	A notation in the document type declaration	Document-Type	None	<!NOTATION ...>
Processing-Instruction	XmlPro-cessing-Instruction	A processing instruction	Document, Document-Fragment, Element, Entity-Reference	None	<?instr data?>
Significant-Whitespace	Xml-Significant-White-space	White space between markup in mixed content model or within the xml:space= 'preserve' scope	None	None	
Text	XmlText	The text content of a node	Attribute, Document-Fragment, Element, Entity-Reference	None	<myelement> mytext </myelement>
Whitespace	XmlWhite-space	Whitespace between markup	n/a	n/a	
Xml-Declaration	XmlDecla-ration	The XML declaration	Document (Must be the first node in the document.)	None (But it has attributes that provide version and encoding information.)	<?xml version='1.0' ?>

The following program displays the names of all the publishers in the pubs.xml file (which I obtained by saving a DataSet filled with data from the Publishers table in the Pubs database):

```
Dim xtr As New XmlTextReader("pubs.xml")
Do While xtr.Read
    If xtr.NodeType = XmlNodeType.Element Then
       ' Publisher names are inserted as text immediately
       ' after an element named pub_name.
       If xtr.Name = "pub_name" Then
           ' Move to the next element, and display its value.
           xtr.Read()
           Console.WriteLine(xtr.Value)
       End If
    End If
Loop
xtr.Close()
```

Attributes are usually skipped over when XML data is parsed, but you can use the HasAttributes property to check whether the current element has any attributes and then iterate over them with the MoveToNextAttribute method, which returns True if attributes are found, and False otherwise:

```
' Display elements and attributes in an XML file.
Dim xtr As New XmlTextReader("mydata.xml")
Do While xtr.Read
    If xtr.NodeType = XmlNodeType.Element Then
        ' Display the name of the current node.
        Console.Write("<" & xtr.Name)
        ' Display name and value of attributes, if any.
        If xtr.HasAttributes Then
            Do While xtr.MoveToNextAttribute()
                Console.Write(" " & xtr.Name & "='" & xtr.Value & "'")
            Loop
        End If
        ' Go back to the main element.
        xtr.MoveToElement()
        ' Print the ending / if this is an empty element.
        If xtr.IsEmptyElement Then Console.Write("/")
        ' Close the tag.
        Console.WriteLine(">")
    End If
Loop
xtr.Close()
```

The following two tables, Tables 22-2 and 22-3, list the most important properties and methods of the XmlTextReader class.

Table 22-2 Main Properties of the XmlTextReader Class

Category	Syntax	Description
Current node properties	Name	The name of current node, including the namespace.
	LocalName	The name of current node, without the namespace.
	Prefix	The namespace prefix of the current node.
	BaseURI	The base Uniform Resource Identifier (URI) of the current node.
	NamespaceURI	The namespace URI of the current node.
	NodeType	The type of the current node, as an XmlNodeType enumerated value. (See Table 22-1.)
	Value	The text value of the current node.
	HasValue	True if the current node has a value. Only these node types have a value: Attribute, Text, CDATA, Comment, DocumentType, XmlDeclaration, ProcessingInstruction, Whitespace, SignificantWhitespace.
	IsEmptyElement	True if the current node is an empty element, such as <ELEM/>.
	Depth	The nesting depth of the current node.
Attribute management	HasAttributes	True if the current node has attributes.
	AttributeCount	The number of attributes in the current node.
	QuoteChar	The quotation mark character used to enclose the attribute's value (single or double quotes).
State properties	ReadState	The current state for the reader. It can be Initial (the Read method hasn't been called), Interactive (the Read method has been called), EndOfFile, Error, or Closed.
	EOF	True if the reader has reached the end of the XML data.
	LineNumber	The line number in the source XML data.
	LinePosition	The column number in the source XML data.

Table 22-2 Main Properties of the XmlTextReader Class *(continued)*

Category	Syntax	Description
Parsing behavior (read/write)	Encoding	The encoding attribute of the XML document being parsed.
	WhitespaceHandling	An enumerated value that specifies how whitespace is handled: can be All, None, or Significant.
	Namespaces	True if the parser should provide namespace support. (This is the default behavior.)
	Normalization	True if whitespace and attribute values should be normalized.

Table 22-3 Main Methods of the XmlTextReader Class

Category	Syntax	Description
Move methods	Read	Reads the next node; returns True if successful, False if at the end of the XML data.
	Skip	Skips the children of the current node.
	MoveToFirstAttribute	Moves to the first attribute of an element node.
	MoveToNextAttribute	Moves to the next attribute.
	MoveToAttribute(index)	Moves to a given attribute of an element node; argument can be an attribute name or a numeric index.
	MoveToElement	Moves to the element node that contains the current attribute; should be used after visiting one or more attributes.
	MoveToContent	If the current node isn't a content element (nonwhitespace text, CDATA, Element, EndElement, EntityReference, EndEntity) it skips the current node and subsequent nodes until a content node is found (or the end of stream is reached).
Read methods	GetAttribute(index)	Reads the value of the specified attribute; the argument can be a name or a numeric index.

Table 22-3 Main Methods of the XmlTextReader Class *(continued)*

Category	Syntax	Description
	GetRemainder	Reads the XML data not read yet and sets EOF to True.
	ReadInnerXml	Reads all content, including markup.
	ReadOuterXml	Reads all content for this node and its children, including markup.
	ReadString	Reads the content of an element or a text node as a string.
	ReadStartElement or ReadStartElement(name)	Checks that the current element is a start element and advances to the next element.
	ReadEndElement or ReadEndElement(name)	Checks that the current element is an end element and advances to the next element.
Other methods	Close	Closes the XmlTextReader object.
	IsStartElement	Returns True if the current node is a start element tag, such as <ELEM>.
	ResetState	Resets the ReadState property to Initial.

The XmlTextWriter Class

The XmlTextWriter class is the writing counterpart of the XmlTextReader class in the sense that it lets you write to an XML file using a forward-only mechanism. Of course, you can output XML text yourself, but this class offers some advantages, such as ensuring that the output is well-formed XML, that special characters are correctly stored as character entities, and that element names comply with XML specifications.

You create an XmlTextWriter object by passing a filename to its constructor (but you can also pass a Stream-derived object or a TextWriter object). The second argument is an Encoding value that specifies how data is encoded:

```
Dim xtw As New XmlTextWriter("mydata.xml", System.Text.Encoding.UTF8)
```

Before you start outputting data, you can set a few properties that determine whether tags are indented (Formatting), the indent length (Indentation), and the character used to enclose attribute values (QuoteChar):

```
' Indent tags by 2 characters.
xtw.Formatting = Formatting.Indented
xtw.Indentation = 2
' Enclose attributes' values in double quotes.
xtw.QuoteChar = """"c
```

The first method you must call is WriteStartDocument, which outputs the XML declaration for the document; its argument specifies whether the standalone attribute is set to "yes":

```
' Create the following XML declaration for this XML document:
'    <?xml version="1.0" standalone="yes" ?>
xtw.WriteStartDocument(True)
```

You can now write elements and attributes by using the many methods that the XmlTextWriter class exposes, which I summarize in Table 22-4. The most useful methods are WriteStartElement, which writes the start tag of an XML element; and WriteEndElement, which writes the end tag of the most recently opened XML element. Interestingly, the latter method doesn't require the element name (because the XmlTextWriter object keeps a stack of pending XML elements) and is able to use the short form for the end tag if the element doesn't contain anything else, as in:

```
<Invoice id="1" />
```

Another method that you'll use quite often is WriteAttributeString, which outputs the name and the value of an attribute using the correct quote delimiters.

Table 22-4 Main Methods of the XmlTextWriter Class

Category	Syntax	Description
Stream	Close	Closes the writer and the underlying stream.
	Flush	Flushes the data in the output stream.
Document	WriteStartDocument(standalone)	Writes the XML declaration at the top of the document.
	WriteEndDocument	Closes all open elements and attributes.
Elements	WriteStartElement(localname)	Writes an XML element start tag; this method is overloaded to take a namespace and a prefix if necessary.
	WriteEndElement	Closes the current element and pops the corresponding namespace scope; if the element has no contents, a short end tag /> is used.
	WriteFullEndElement	Closes the current element and pops the corresponding namespace scope; it never uses the short end tag, so it's useful for adding </SCRIPT> tags and other tags that can't be shortened.

Table 22-4 Main Methods of the XmlTextWriter Class *(continued)*

Category	Syntax	Description
	WriteElementString(localname, value)	Writes an element that contains only a text node; you don't have to use Write-EndElement after a call to this method; this method is overloaded to take a namespace argument.
Other XML entities	WriteAttributeString(localname, value)	Writes an attribute and its value; this method is overloaded to take a prefix and a namespace argument.
	WriteComment(text)	Writes a comment.
	WriteCData(text)	Writes a CDATA section.
	WriteProcessingInstruction(name, text)	Writes a processing instruction, as in <?name text?>.
	WriteCharEntity(char)	Writes a character entity.
	WriteEntityRef(name)	Writes an entity reference, as &name.
Raw text	WriteName(name)	Writes a name, ensuring it's valid according to W3C XML 1.0 recommendations.
	WriteQualifiedName(localname, namespace)	Writes a qualified name, looking up the prefix that's in scope for the given namespace.
	WriteString(text)	Writes the given text, replacing special characters <, >, &, and quotes with the corresponding escape sequence.
	WriteRaw(text)	Writes text without converting special characters; it's useful for writing markup text.
	WriteChars(chararr, index, count)	Writes a portion of a Char array.
	WriteWhitespace(spaces)	Writes the given white space; it's useful for manually formatting the document.
Binary values	WriteBase64(bytearr, index, count)	Writes a portion of a Byte array as Base64.
	WriteBinHex(bytearr, index, count)	Writes a portion of a Byte array as binhex.
Copying from an Xml-Reader	WriteNode(xmlreader, copydefault)	Copies a node from an XmlReader and moves the reader at the start of the next element.
	WriteAttributes(xmlreader, copydefault)	Writes all the attributes found at the current position in an XmlReader object.

The following code shows how you can read a comma-delimited file and convert it to an XML document. I illustrated how to use regular expressions to parse a comma-delimited file in the section "Adding Rows" in Chapter 21, so I won't explain it again here. The remarks in code should make clear how the XmlTextWriter class works.

```
' Convert a semicolon-delimited text file to XML.

' Open the file, and read its contents.
Dim sr As New System.IO.StreamReader("employees.dat")
Dim fileText As String = sr.ReadToEnd
sr.Close()

' Create the output XML file.
Dim xtw As New XmlTextWriter("employees.xml", System.Text.Encoding.UTF8)
' Indent tags by 2 spaces.
xtw.Formatting = Formatting.Indented
xtw.Indentation = 2
' Enclose attributes' values in double quotes.
xtw.QuoteChar = """"c
' Create the following XML declaration for this XML document:
'    <?xml version="1.0" standalone="yes" ?>
xtw.WriteStartDocument(True)
' Add a comment.
xtw.WriteComment("Data converted from employees.dat file")
' The root element is <Employees>.
xtw.WriteStartElement("Employees")

' This regular expression defines a row of elements and assigns a name
' to each group (that is, a field in the text row).
Dim re As New System.Text.RegularExpressions.Regex( _
    """(?<fname>[^""]+)"";""(?<lname>[^""]+)"";(?<bdate>[^;]+);" _
    & """(?<addr>[^""]+)"";""(?<city>[^""]+)""")
Dim ma As System.Text.RegularExpressions.Match

' This variable will provide a unique ID for each employee.
Dim id As Integer

For Each ma In re.Matches(fileText)
    ' A new line has been found, increment employee ID.
    id += 1
    ' Write a new <Employee id="nnn"> element.
    xtw.WriteStartElement("Employee")
    xtw.WriteAttributeString("id", id.ToString)
    ' Write fields as nested elements containing text.
    xtw.WriteElementString("firstName", ma.Groups("fname").Value)
```

(continued)

```
    xtw.WriteElementString("lastName", ma.Groups("lname").Value)
    xtw.WriteElementString("birthDate", ma.Groups("bdate").Value)
    xtw.WriteElementString("address", ma.Groups("addr").Value)
    xtw.WriteElementString("city", ma.Groups("city").Value)
    ' Close the <Employee> element.
    xtw.WriteEndElement()
Next
' Close the root element (and all pending elements, if any).
xtw.WriteEndDocument()
' Close the underlying stream (never forget this).
xtw.Close()
```

Figure 22-1 shows the resulting XML file loaded in Microsoft Internet Explorer.

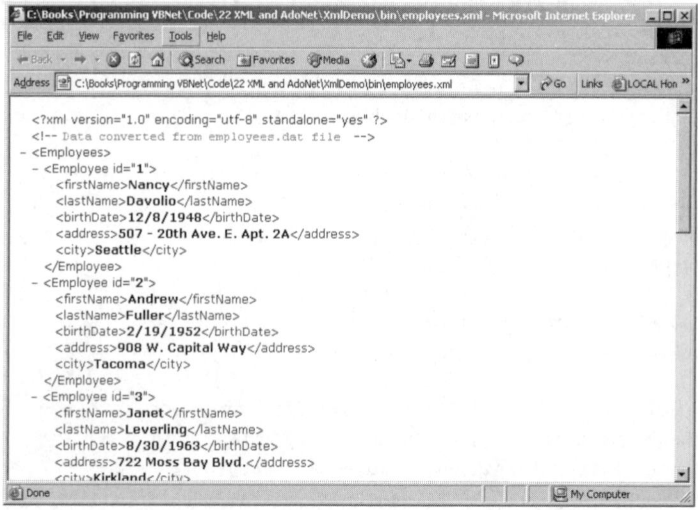

Figure 22-1. An XML file produced by the XmlTextWriter class.

Working with the XML DOM

The XmlTextReader and XmlTextWriter classes are OK for parsing or writing XML files, but they can't be used to manipulate the structure of an XML document—for example, to add or remove nodes, search for nested nodes, extract node subtrees, and the like. In cases like these, you must instantiate a full-fledged XmlDocument object and use it to access the XML Document Object Model (DOM).

An XmlDocument object can contain several child objects, each one representing a different node in the DOM. The names of these secondary classes are quite self-explanatory: XmlElement, XmlAttribute, XmlComment, XmlDeclaration, XmlEntityReference, XmlProcessingInstruction, XmlCDataSection, XmlCharacterData, XmlText, and a few others. (See Table 22-1.) But before having a look at these classes, you should get acquainted with the XmlNode class.

The XmlNode Class

XmlNode is a virtual class that works as the base class for several classes in the System.Xml namespace, including the XmlDocument class itself and most of its secondary classes. The XmlNode class represents a generic node in the DOM and exposes several properties and methods that are inherited by other DOM classes—thus, studying this class first means simplifying the exploration of other classes described in later sections.

The most important property of this class is NodeType, which you use to determine the type of a given node. The NodeType property returns an XmlNodeType enumerated value, which can be one of the values listed in Table 22-1. Table 22-5 contains the complete list of properties of the XmlNode class, and Table 22-6 lists its methods.

Note that XmlNode is a virtual class and I can't instantiate it, so I will defer showing you a complete code example until I introduce the XmlDocument class in the next section.

Table 22-5 Main Properties of the XmlNode Class

Category	Syntax	Description
Identity	NodeType	The type of this node, as an XmlNodeType enumerated value.
	Name	The qualified name of this node; returns a significant value only for elements, attributes, processing instructions, entities, entity references, and document types.
	LocalName	The local name of this node.
	BaseURI	The base URI of this node.
	NamespaceURI	The namespace URI of this node.
	Prefix	The prefix of this node (read/write).
Value	Value	The value of this node (read/write). It's significant only for attributes, comments, CDATA sections, text nodes, processing instructions, XML declarations, and whitespace nodes.
	InnerXml	The markup that represents the child nodes of this node (read/write).

Table 22-5 Main Properties of the XmlNode Class *(continued)*

Category	Syntax	Description
	InnerText	The concatenated values of all the children of this node. If modified, the new value replaces all the children nodes.
	OuterXml	The markup representing the current node and its children; unlike InnerXml, this property is read-only.
	IsReadOnly	True if this node's properties, attributes, and children can't be modified.
Navigation	HasChildNodes	True if this node has children.
	ChildNodes	The child nodes of this node, as an Xml-NodeList collection.
	Attributes	The attributes of the node, as an XmlAttribute-Collection. It's different from Nothing only for element nodes.
	OwnerDocument	The XmlDocument this node belongs to, or Nothing if this is an XmlDocument object.
	ParentNode	The parent node of this node. It's significant only for elements, CDATA sections, comments, text, processing instructions, entity references, and document nodes; returns Nothing for other node types.
	FirstChild	The first child of this node.
	NextSibling	The next sibling node after this node.
	PreviousSibling	The previous sibling node before this node.
	LastChild	The last child of this node.
	Item(name)	The child node with the specified name.

Table 22-6 Main Methods of the XmlNode Class

Category	Syntax	Description
Insert and delete methods	AppendChild(node)	Appends a new child node at the end of the list of children of this node.
	InsertAfter(newnode, refnode)	Inserts a new node (or a DocumentFragment object) after the child node specified in the second argument, or at the beginning of the list if this argument is Nothing.

Table 22-6 Main Methods of the XmlNode Class *(continued)*

Category	Syntax	Description
	InsertBefore(newnode, refnode)	Inserts a new node (or a DocumentFragment object) before the child node specified in the second argument, or at the end of the list if the second argument is Nothing.
	PrependChild(newnode)	Adds a new node (or a DocumentFragment object) at the beginning of the child node list.
	ReplaceChild(newnode, oldnode)	Replaces a child node with another node.
	RemoveChild(node)	Removes a child node.
	RemoveAll	Removes all the children and attributes of this node.
Search methods	SelectNodes(xpath)	Returns the XmlNodeList collection of child nodes that match an XPath expression.
	SelectSingleNode(xpath)	Returns the first child node that matches an XPath expression.
	GetNamespaceOfPrefix (prefix)	Returns the namespace URI in the closest xmlns declaration for the given prefix that is in scope for this node.
	GetPrefixOfNamespace (namespace)	Returns the prefix in the closest xmlns declaration for the given namespace that is in scope for this node.
Write methods	WriteContentTo(xmlwriter)	Writes all the child nodes to an XmlWriter object.
	WriteTo(xmlwriter)	Writes the current node to an XmlWriter object.
Clone methods	Clone	Creates a duplicate of this node.
	CloneNode(deepcopy)	Creates a duplicate of this node; if the argument is True, it also recursively clones all the child nodes.
Miscellaneous methods	CreateNavigator	Creates an XPathNavigator object for navigating this node.
	Normalize	Puts all the text child nodes in normalized format, merging adjacent text nodes; it ensures that the DOM view of a document is the same as if it were saved and reloaded.
	Supports(feature, version)	Tests whether the DOM implementation supports a specific feature.

The XmlDocument Class

You can't do much with the XmlNode class alone because you need to create a DOM in memory before you can create and manipulate its nodes. You create the DOM by instantiating the XmlDocument class, which also inherits from XmlNode:

```
Dim xmldoc as New XmlDocument()
```

What you do next depends on whether you want to process an existing XML data source or create a new document from scratch. In the first case, you typically use the Load method to load XML data from a file, a Stream, a TextReader, or an XmlReader object:

```
' In a real application, this should be protected in a Try block.
xmldoc.Load("employees.xml")
```

If you already have the XML text in a string, you can use the LoadXml method:

```
' This code assumes that the txtXml TextBox control contains XML data.
xmldoc.LoadXml(txtXml.Text)
```

Table 22-7 lists the main properties, methods, and events of the XmlDocument class (other than those inherited from XmlNode); the sections following the table illustrate how you can use a few of these members.

Table 22-7 Main Members of the XmlDocument Class

Category	Syntax	Description
Properties	DocumentElement	The root XmlElement object for this document.
	DocumentType	The XmlDocumentType object containing the DOCTYPE declaration.
	NameTable	Returns the XmlNameTable associated with this implementation. This is a list of all the atomized strings used in the document and makes it possible to perform fast string comparisons.
	PreserveWhitespace	A Boolean value that says whether whitespace should be preserved (read/write).
	XmlResolver	The XmlResolver object used to resolve external references.
Create methods	CreateAttribute(name)	Creates an attribute and returns an XmlAttribute object. It takes optional arguments for prefix and namespace values.

Table 22-7 Main Members of the XmlDocument Class *(continued)*

Category	Syntax	Description
	CreateCDataSection(text)	Creates a CDATA section and returns an XmlCDataSection object.
	CreateComment(text)	Creates a comment and returns an XmlComment object.
	CreateDocumentFragment	Creates an empty document fragment and returns an XmlDocumentFragment object.
	CreateDocument-Type(name, publicId, systemId, internalSubset)	Creates a DOCTYPE section and returns an XmlDocumentType object.
	CreateElement(name)	Creates an element and returns an XmlElement object. It takes optional arguments for prefix and namespace values.
	CreateEntity-Reference(name)	Creates an entity reference and returns an XmlEntityReference object.
	CreateNode(nodetype, name, namespace)	Creates a node with the specified node type, name, and namespace URI and returns an XmlNode object; the first argument can be an XmlNodeType value or string.
	CreateProcessing-Instruction(target, data)	Creates a processing instruction and returns an XmlProcessingInstruction object.
	CreateSignificant-Whitespace(spaces)	Creates significant whitespace and returns an XmlSignificantNamespace object; the argument can contain only space, tab, carriage return, and line feed characters.
	CreateTextNode(text)	Creates a text node and returns an XmlText object.
	CreateWhitespace(spaces)	Creates whitespace and returns an XmlNamespace object; the argument can contain only space, tab, carriage return, and line feed characters.
	CreateXmlDeclaration (version, encoding, standalone)	Creates a declaration and returns an XmlDeclaration object; if the XML document is saved to an XmlTextWriter, this declaration is discarded and the XmlTextWriter's declaration is used instead.

Table 22-7 Main Members of the XmlDocument Class *(continued)*

Category	Syntax	Description
	ImportNode(node, deep)	Imports a node from another document to the current document; a deep copy is performed if the second argument is True.
Search methods	GetElementById(id)	Returns the XmlElement with the specified attribute ID, or Nothing if the search fails.
	GetElementsByTagName(name)	Returns an XmlNodeList collection holding all the descendant elements with the specified name.
File methods	Load(filename)	Loads the specified XML from a file, a Stream, a TextReader, or an XmlReader object.
	LoadXml(string)	Loads the XML contained in the string argument.
	Save(filename)	Saves the XML to a file, a Stream, a TextWriter, or an XmlWriter object; the file is overwritten if it exists already.
	ReadNode(xmlreader)	Creates an XmlNode object based on the information at the current position in an XmlReader object (which must be positioned on a node or an attribute).
Events	NodeInserting	A node belonging to this document is about to be inserted into another node. The second argument of this and all following events exposes these properties: Action, Node, NewParent, and OldParent.
	NodeInserted	A node belonging to this document has been inserted into another node.
	NodeChanging	A node belonging to this document is about to be changed.
	NodeChanged	A node belonging to this document has been changed.
	NodeRemoving	A node belonging to this document is about to be removed.
	NodeRemoved	A node belonging to this document has been removed.

Exploring the DOM

After you've loaded XML data into an XmlDocument object, you might want to explore all the nodes it contains. The two main entry points for exploring the DOM hierarchy are the Children collection of the XmlDocument itself, which lets you discover any XML declaration, processing instruction, and comment at the top level of the document; and the XmlDocument's DocumentElement property, which jumps directly to the main XML element that contains the real data:

```
' Access the root XML element in the DOM.
Dim xmlEl As XmlElement = xmldoc.DocumentElement
```

The following code shows how you can load an XML file into an XmlDocument object and then traverse the DOM hierarchy and display the data in a TreeView control. (See Figure 22-2.) Not surprisingly, the core routine is a recursive procedure that adds an element to the Nodes collection of the TreeView and then calls itself over all the child nodes of the current XmlNode object. You can iterate over all the child nodes of an XmlNode object in either of two ways: by indexing the ChildNodes collection or by using the FirstChild and NextSibling properties. The second technique is slightly faster and is the one that the following routine uses.

```
Sub DisplayXmlTree()
    ' Load an XML file into an XmlDocument object.
    Dim xmldoc As New XmlDocument()
    xmldoc.Load("employees.xml")
    ' Add it to the Nodes collection of the TreeView1 control.
    DisplayXmlNode(xmldoc, TreeView1.Nodes)
End Sub

' A recursive procedure that displays an XmlNode object in a TreeView
' control and then calls itself for each child node
Sub DisplayXmlNode(ByVal xmlnode As XmlNode, _
    ByVal nodes As TreeNodeCollection)

    ' Add a TreeView node for this XmlNode.
    ' (Using the node's Name is OK for most XmlNode types.)
    Dim tvNode As TreeNode = nodes.Add(xmlnode.Name)

    ' Specific code for different node types
    Select Case xmlnode.NodeType
        Case XmlNodeType.Element
            ' This is an element: check whether there are attributes.
            If xmlnode.Attributes.Count > 0 Then
```

(continued)

```
                ' Create an ATTRIBUTES node.
                Dim attrNode As TreeNode = tvNode.Nodes.Add("(ATTRIBUTES)")
                ' Add all the attributes as children of the new node.
                Dim xmlAttr As XmlAttribute
                For Each xmlAttr In xmlnode.Attributes
                    ' Each node shows name and value.
                    attrNode.Nodes.Add(xmlAttr.Name & " = '" & _
                        xmlAttr.Value & "'")
                Next
            End If
        Case XmlNodeType.Text, XmlNodeType.CDATA
            ' For these node types, we display the value.
            tvNode.Text = xmlnode.Value
        Case XmlNodeType.Comment
            tvNode.Text = "<!--" & xmlnode.Value & "-->"
        Case XmlNodeType.ProcessingInstruction, XmlNodeType.XmlDeclaration
            tvNode.Text = "<?" & xmlnode.Name & " " & xmlnode.Value & "?>"
        Case Else
            ' Ignore other node types.
    End Select

    ' Call this routine recursively for each child node.
    Dim xmlChild As XmlNode = xmlnode.FirstChild
    Do Until xmlChild Is Nothing
        DisplayXmlNode(xmlChild, tvNode.Nodes)
        ' Continue with the next child node.
        xmlChild = xmlChild.NextSibling
    Loop
End Sub
```

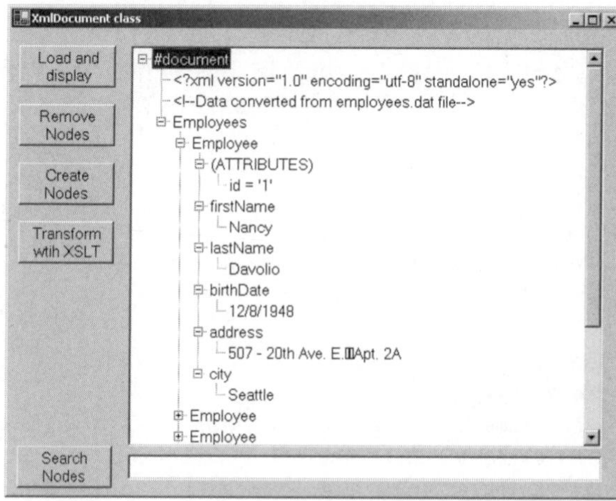

Figure 22-2. Using the XmlDocument object to display the XML DOM in a TreeView control.

Adding and Removing Nodes

Usually you don't use the XmlDocument object just to read and display the structure of a piece of XML data, as the real power of this object (and the DOM in general) is its ability to modify the structure of an XML document by adding and removing nodes and then saving the result back to a file (or whatever data source you read it from).

To remove a node, you simply use the RemoveChild method of its parent element node. This method takes the element to be deleted as an argument, so you must find it first by iterating over the ChildNodes collection, by using the SelectSingleNode method of the generic XmlNode class, or by using the GetElementsByTagName method of the XmlElement class (which is the technique adopted by the code shown below). Likewise, to remove an attribute, you can use the Remove method of the XmlNode's Attributes collection or simply use the RemoveAttribute method of the XmlElement class. The following code snippet loads the XML file, shown in Figure 22-1, in memory and deletes the id attribute and the birthDate subelement under all Employee elements:

```
' Load the XML document.
Dim xmldoc As New XmlDocument()
xmldoc.Load("employees.xml")

' Remove the id attribute and the birthDate subelement from all
' Employee elements.
Dim xmlEl As XmlElement
For Each xmlEl In xmldoc.DocumentElement.ChildNodes
    ' Remove the attribute with a given name.
    xmlEl.RemoveAttribute("id")
    ' Get a reference to the birthDate subelement.
    Dim xmlList As XmlNodeList = xmlEl.GetElementsByTagName("birthDate")
    ' The GetElementsByTagName method returns a collection, so we must take
    ' the result's first element.
    If xmlList.Count > 0 Then
        xmlEl.RemoveChild(xmlList(0))
    End If
Next
```

In theory, you can manipulate the DOM using only the properties and methods exposed by the generic XmlNode class. In practice, however, you'll often want to cast the XmlNode object to a more specific class (such as XmlElement or XmlAttribute) to leverage the additional members it exposes:

- The XmlElement class exposes several additional methods for working on attributes (other than those inherited from XmlNode). (See Table 22-8.)

- The XmlAttribute class exposes the OwnerElement property (the owner XmlElement object) and the Specified property (True if the attribute was explicitly set; False if the attribute exists only because it has a default value).
- The XmlText class exposes the SplitText method, which creates two text elements by splitting the string at the specified offset.
- The XmlProcessingInstruction class exposes the Target and Data properties, which get or set the target and the data of the processing instruction.

Table 22-8 Main Methods of the XmlElement Class

Category	Syntax	Description
Search	GetAttribute(name)	Returns the value of the attribute with a given name.
	GetAttributeNode(name)	Returns the XmlAttribute object corresponding to the attribute with a given name.
	GetElementsByTagName(name)	Returns an XmlNodeList collection of all the descendant elements with the specified name.
Create attributes	SetAttribute(name, value)	Sets the value of the specified attribute; an overloaded version lets you specify both the local name and the namespace.
	SetAttributeNode(name,value)	Creates a new attribute and returns the XmlAttribute object; an overloaded version accepts an XmlAttribute object.
Delete attributes	RemoveAllAttributes	Removes all the attributes.
	RemoveAttribute(name)	Removes the attribute with a given name; if the attribute has a default name, it's immediately replaced.
	RemoveAttributeAt(index)	Removes the attribute at the specified index; if the attribute has a default name, it's immediately replaced.
	RemoveAttributeNode(xmlattr)	Like RemoveAttribute but can take an XmlAttribute argument.

Adding a node is a three-step process:

1. Call one of the Create*xxxx* methods of the XmlDocument object to generate an XmlNode-derived object (such as an XmlElement or XmlText object).
2. Set any additional properties of the object just created if necessary.
3. Add the new node in the correct place in the DOM, using the AppendChild, InsertAfter, InsertBefore, or PrependChild method, which all DOM objects expose.

The following code sample shows how you can add a new Employee element (and all its attributes and subelements) to the employees.xml file. The remarks in the listing explain several of the coding techniques you can adopt to make your code more concise:

```
' Load the XML document.
Dim xmldoc As New XmlDocument()
xmldoc.Load("employees.xml")

' Create a new Employee element.
Dim xmlEl As XmlElement = xmldoc.CreateElement("Employee")
' Append it to the children collection of the DOM root element.
xmldoc.DocumentElement.AppendChild(xmlEl)

' Set the id attribute of the new element.
xmlEl.SetAttribute("id", "100")
' Create all its subelements.
' (Each subelement is created with a different technique.)
Dim xmlChildEl As XmlElement

' This is the firstName subelement.
xmlChildEl = xmldoc.CreateElement("firstName")
' Create a child XmlText element for the firstName element.
Dim xmlText As XmlText = xmldoc.CreateTextNode("Joe")
xmlChildEl.AppendChild(xmlText)
' Append the firstName element to the new Employee element.
xmlEl.AppendChild(xmlChildEl)

' This is the lastName subelement.
xmlChildEl = xmldoc.CreateElement("lastName")
' Create a child XmlText element, and append it in one operation.
xmlChildEl.AppendChild(xmldoc.CreateTextNode("Doe"))
' Append the lastName subelement to the new Employee element.
xmlEl.AppendChild(xmlChildEl)
```

(continued)

```
' This is the address subelement.
xmlChildEl = xmldoc.CreateElement("address")
' This time we use the InnerText property (a Microsoft extension of WC3 DOM).
xmlChildEl.InnerText = "1234 North Street"
' Append the address subelement to the new Employee element.
xmlEl.AppendChild(xmlChildEl)

' This is the city subelement.
xmlChildEl = xmldoc.CreateElement("city")
xmlChildEl.InnerText = "Boston"
xmlEl.AppendChild(xmlChildEl)

' Save to a different XML file.
xmldoc.Save("employees2.xml")
```

To make your code even more concise, you can prepare a helper routine for creating subelements and their inner text and append them to a parent element as one operation:

```
'  Create an XmlElement object with inner text, and make it
'  a child of another XmlNode.
Function CreateAppendElement(ByVal parentNode As XmlNode, _
    ByVal name As String, Optional ByVal innerText As String = Nothing) _
    As XmlElement
    ' Create a new XmlElement object, and set the return value.
    Dim xmlEl As XmlElement = parentNode.OwnerDocument.CreateElement(name)
    ' Set its inner text if provided.
    If Not (innerText Is Nothing) Then xmlEl.InnerText = innerText
    ' Make it a child of its parent node.
    parentNode.AppendChild(xmlEl)
    ' Return the new node to the caller.
    Return xmlEl
End Function
```

The CreateAppendElement routine makes the job of adding a new Employee element much easier:

```
' Create a new Employee element.
Dim xmlEl As XmlElement
xmlEl = CreateAppendElement(xmldoc.DocumentElement, "Employee")
' Set the id attribute of the new element.
xmlEl.SetAttribute("id", "100")
' Create all its subelements.
CreateAppendElement(xmlEl, "firstName", "Joe")
CreateAppendElement(xmlEl, "lastName", "Doe")
CreateAppendElement(xmlEl, "address", "1234 North Street")
CreateAppendElement(xmlEl, "city", "Boston")
```

You can create similar helper routines for adding other types of XML nodes, such as comments, processing instructions, and CDATA sections.

Searching Nodes

The XmlNode class exposes two search methods that take an XPath expression. Use the SelectNodes method if the XPath expression can return more than one match or the SelectSingleNode method if it can return only one node (or you're interested in its first matching node only). Since this isn't an XML textbook, I won't go into many details about XPath, but I'll provide a few XPath examples based on the employees.xml file that we've been using most recently.

Select all the <Employee> descendant nodes:

```
//Employee
```

Select all the <lastName> child nodes of any Employee descendant node:

```
//Employee/lastName
```

Select the <Employee> descendant node whose id attribute is equal to 3:

```
//Employee[id='3']
```

Select the <lastName> child node of the first <Employee> element:

```
//Employee[position() = 1]/lastName
```

Select the text child node of the <lastName> child node of the last <Employee> element:

```
//Employee[position() = last()]/lastName/text()
```

Select the <firstName> child node of the <Employee> element whose <lastName> child element is equal to Davolio:

```
//Employee[lastName='Davolio']/firstName
```

Although writing down a search expression can be difficult if you aren't familiar with the XPath syntax, using the expression to select one or more nodes in an XmlDocument is easy:

```
' Select a single node.
Dim xpath As String = "//Employee[lastName='Davolio']/firstName"
Dim xn As XmlNode = xmldoc.SelectSingleNode(xpath)
' Display its text content.
Debug.WriteLine(xn.innerText)           ' => Nancy

' Select all elements whose id attribute is <= 4.
Dim xnl As XmlNodeList = xmldoc.SelectNodes("//Employee[@id <= 4]")
```

(continued)

```
' Display number of matches.
Debug.WriteLine(xnl.Count)                ' => 4
For Each xn In xnl
    ' Cast result to an XmlElement object.
    Dim xmlEl As XmlElement = DirectCast(xn, XmlElement)
    ' Display the innerText property of the <lastName> child element.
    ' (We know that there is only one <lastName> child node.)
    Debug.WriteLine(xmlEl.GetElementsByTagName("lastName")(0).InnerText())
Next
```

The XslTransform Class

The System.Xml.Xsl.XslTransform class is the key for working with Extensible Stylesheet Language Transformations (XSLT), which allow you to transform an XML document into another XML document. Typically, you use an XSLT to change the layout of existing XML data—for example, to change the order of XML elements, to transform XML elements into attributes, or to produce a browsable file in XHTML format (the XML-compliant version of HTML).

To see how this class works, let's start by creating an XSLT file named Employees.xslt, which transforms the Employee.xml file into an .html file that you can then view inside a browser. You can create an .xslt file using Notepad or by pointing to New on the File menu in Visual Studio .NET, then selecting File, and finally clicking the General category in the New File dialog box and double-clicking XSLT File. Unlike source code files, XSLT documents are created in memory, and you'll be asked for their path only when you save them.

```
<?xml version="1.0" encoding="UTF-8" ?>
<xsl:stylesheet version="1.0"
    xmlns:xsl="http://www.w3.org/1999/XSL/Transform">
  <xsl:template match="/">
    <HTML>
    <TITLE>Employees Table</TITLE>
    <TABLE BORDER='1'>
      <THEAD>
        <TH>First Name</TH>
        <TH>Last Name</TH>
        <TH>Birth Date</TH>
        <TH>Address</TH>
        <TH>City</TH>
      </THEAD>
      <xsl:for-each select="//Employee">
        <TR>
          <TD><xsl:value-of select="firstName" /></TD>
          <TD><xsl:value-of select="lastName" /></TD>
          <TD><xsl:value-of select="birthDate" /></TD>
          <TD><xsl:value-of select="address" /></TD>
          <TD><xsl:value-of select="city" /></TD>
```

```
      </TR>
    </xsl:for-each>
  </TABLE>
  </HTML>
 </xsl:template>
</xsl:stylesheet>
```

Once you have an .xslt file, applying an XSLT transform is easy: you create an XslTransform object, load the .xslt file into it with its Load method, and finally invoke the Transform method, passing the input XML file and the output XML file as arguments:

```
' Load the XSLT into an XslTransform.
Dim xslTran As New System.Xml.Xsl.XslTransform()
' Load the .xslt file into it.
xslTran.Load("Employees.xslt")
' Convert the XML file to another XML file.
xslTran.Transform("employees.xml", "employees.html")
```

Figure 22-3 shows how the resultant employees.html file appears when loaded into Internet Explorer.

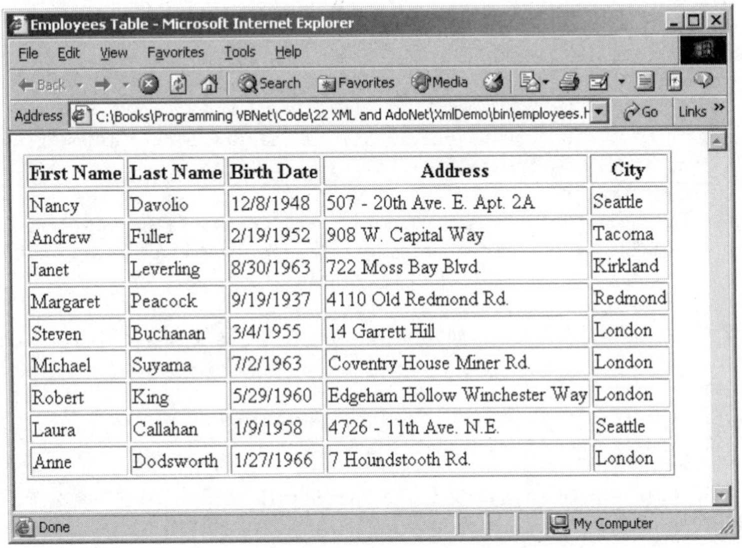

First Name	Last Name	Birth Date	Address	City
Nancy	Davolio	12/8/1948	507 - 20th Ave. E. Apt. 2A	Seattle
Andrew	Fuller	2/19/1952	908 W. Capital Way	Tacoma
Janet	Leverling	8/30/1963	722 Moss Bay Blvd.	Kirkland
Margaret	Peacock	9/19/1937	4110 Old Redmond Rd.	Redmond
Steven	Buchanan	3/4/1955	14 Garrett Hill	London
Michael	Suyama	7/2/1963	Coventry House Miner Rd.	London
Robert	King	5/29/1960	Edgeham Hollow Winchester Way	London
Laura	Callahan	1/9/1958	4726 - 11th Ave. N.E.	Seattle
Anne	Dodsworth	1/27/1966	7 Houndstooth Rd.	London

Figure 22-3. An .html file produced by the XslTransform class.

If the input XML data is held in an XmlDocument object rather than in a file, you can use an overloaded version of the Transform method that takes a System.Xml.XPath.XPathNavigator object to indicate the input data and an XmlTextWriter object to indicate where the result must be written. You create the XPathNavigator object using the CreateNavigator method of the XmlDocument class:

```
' Load the XML document.
Dim xmldoc As New XmlDocument()
xmldoc.Load("employees.xml")
' Process the XML data as needed.
⋮
' Create the XslTransform object, and load the .xslt file into it.
Dim xslTran As New System.Xml.Xsl.XslTransform()
xslTran.Load("Employees.xslt")
' Open the resultant XML file with an XmlTextWriter object.
Dim xtw As New XmlTextWriter("employees.html", System.Text.Encoding.UTF8)
' Pass the XPathNavigator and XmlTextWriter objects to the Transform method.
xslTran.Transform(xmldoc.CreateNavigator, Nothing, xtw)
xtw.Close()
```

Another overloaded version of the Transform method transforms the DOM contained in an XmlDocument into another XmlDocument; this version takes an XPathNavigator and returns an XmlReader object, which you can pass to the resultant XmlDocument object's Load method:

```
' Load the XML document.
Dim xmldoc As New XmlDocument()
xmldoc.Load("employees.xml")
' Process the XML data as needed.
⋮
' Create the XslTransform object, and load the .xslt file into it.
Dim xslTran As New System.Xml.Xsl.XslTransform()
xslTran.Load("Employees.xslt")
' Transform the data in the XmlDocument, and get an XmlReader.
Dim xr As XmlReader = xslTran.Transform(xmldoc.CreateNavigator, Nothing)
' Create another XmlDocument that will hold the result.
Dim xmldoc2 As New XmlDocument()
' Load the resultant XML in this XmlDocument using the XmlReader object.
xmldoc2.Load(xr)
xr.Close
' Display the resultant XML in the TreeView object.
DisplayXmlNode(xmldoc2, TreeView1.Nodes)
```

You can use other classes in the System.Xml.Xsl namespace, such as the XmlResolver class, to resolve external references. For more information, read the .NET SDK documentation.

XML Features in ADO.NET

In this portion of the chapter, I'll describe the XML features supported by ADO.NET and, more specifically, by the DataSet class and its dependent classes. As you'll see in a moment, the contents of a DataSet can be easily saved to and reloaded from an XML file or, more generally, an XML stream. Additionally, you can save the structure of the DataSet to an XML schema.

> **Note** To keep the code as concise as possible, all code samples in this chapter assume that you have added the following Imports statements at the top of your source files:
>
> ```
> Imports System.Data
> Imports System.Data.OleDb
> Imports System.Data.SqlClient
> Imports System.IO
> ```

Writing XML Data

The main DataSet method for writing XML data is WriteXml. Like most of the methods described in this section, WriteXml is overloaded to take different types of arguments, including a Stream object (and therefore any object that inherits from this class, such as a FileStream), a TextWriter, and an XmlWriter (and therefore, any object that inherits from this class, such as an XmlTextWriter):

```
' Save the current contents of the DataSet to C:\Dataset.xml.
' (ds is a DataSet defined and initialized elsewhere.)
ds.WriteXml("C:\Dataset.xml")
```

The preceding command saves all the tables in the DataSet in the order in which they appear in the Tables collection. The metadata of the DataSet—that is, the structure of its tables, its relations, and its constraints—isn't saved. For example, consider this code:

```
' Fill the data set with data from two tables.
Dim cn As New OleDbConnection(OledbPubsConnString)
cn.Open()
Dim daPub As New OleDbDataAdapter("SELECT * FROM Publishers", cn)
Dim daTit As New OleDbDataAdapter("SELECT * FROM Titles", cn)
daPub.Fill(ds, "Publishers")
daTit.Fill(ds, "Titles")
cn.Close()
' Create a relationship between the tables.
ds.Relations.Add("PubTitles", ds.Tables("Publishers").Columns("pub_id"), _
    ds.Tables("Titles").Columns("pub_id"))
ds.WriteXml("ds.xml")
```

This is an abridged version of the ds.xml file that the WriteXml method produces. As you see, the contents of the two tables are listed one after the other, and no schema information is supplied:

```
<?xml version="1.0" standalone="yes"?>
<NewDataSet>
  <Publishers>
    <pub_id>0736</pub_id>
    <pub_name>New Book Books (mod)</pub_name>
    <city>Boston</city>
    <state>MA</state>
    <country>USA</country>
  </Publishers>
  <Publishers>
    <pub_id>0877</pub_id>
    <pub_name>Binnet &amp;</pub_name>
    <city>Washington</city>
    <state>DC</state>
    <country>USA</country>
  </Publishers>
  ⋮
  <Publishers>
    <pub_id>9999</pub_id>
    <pub_name>Lucerne P</pub_name>
    <city>Paris</city>
    <country>France</country>
  </Publishers>
  <Titles>
    <title_id>BU1032</title_id>
    <title>The Busy Executive's Database Guide</title>
    <type>business    </type>
    <pub_id>1389</pub_id>
    <price>19.99</price>
    <advance>5000</advance>
    <royalty>10</royalty>
    <ytd_sales>4095</ytd_sales>
    <notes>An overview of available database systems with emphasis on
        common business applications. Illustrated.</notes>
    <pubdate>1991-06-12T00:00:00.0000000+02:00</pubdate>
  </Titles>
  ⋮
  <Titles>
    <title_id>TC7777</title_id>
    <title>Sushi, Anyone?</title>
    <type>trad_cook   </type>
    <pub_id>0877</pub_id>
    <price>14.99</price>
    <advance>8000</advance>
    <royalty>10</royalty>
```

```
    <ytd_sales>4095</ytd_sales>
    <notes>Detailed instructions on how to make authentic
        Japanese sushi in your spare time.</notes>
    <pubdate>1991-06-12T00:00:00.0000000+02:00</pubdate>
  </Titles>
</NewDataSet>
```

Note that the main node in this output is the name of the DataSet. (NewDataSet is the default value for the DataSetName property.) You can affect the output in several ways—for example, by assigning a value to the Namespace and Prefix properties of the DataSet, DataTable, and DataColumn objects. Or you can create a treelike structure by setting the Nested property of existing relationships to True:

```
ds.Relations("PubTitles").Nested = True
ds.WriteXml("ds.xml")
```

This is the kind of result you obtain with nested relationships:

```
<?xml version="1.0" standalone="yes"?>
<NewDataSet>
  <Publishers>
    <pub_id>0736</pub_id>
    <pub_name>New Book Books (mod)</pub_name>
    <city>Boston</city>
    <state>MA</state>
    <country>USA</country>

    <Titles>
      <title_id>BU2075</title_id>
      <title>You Can Combat Computer Stress!</title>
      <type>business     </type>
      <pub_id>0736</pub_id>
      <price>2.99</price>
      <advance>10125</advance>
      <royalty>24</royalty>
      <ytd_sales>18722</ytd_sales>
      <notes>The latest medical and psychological techniques for living
          with the electronic office. Easy-to-understand explanations.</notes>
      <pubdate>1991-06-30T00:00:00.0000000+02:00</pubdate>
    </Titles>
    ⋮
  </Publishers>
  <Publishers>
    <pub_id>0877</pub_id>
    <pub_name>Binnet &amp;</pub_name>
    <city>Washington</city>
    <state>DC</state>
    <country>USA</country>
```

(continued)

```
    <Titles>
      <title_id>MC2222</title_id>
      <title>Silicon Valley Gastronomic Treats</title>
      <type>mod_cook    </type>
      <pub_id>0877</pub_id>
      <price>19.99</price>
      <advance>0</advance>
      <royalty>12</royalty>
      <ytd_sales>2032</ytd_sales>
      <notes>Favorite recipes for quick, easy, and elegant meals.</notes>
      <pubdate>1991-06-09T00:00:00.0000000+02:00</pubdate>
    </Titles>
    ⋮
  </Publishers>
  <Publishers>
  ⋮
  </Publishers>
</NewDataSet>
```

The ColumnMapping property of the DataColumn class lets you customize the output even more. This property is a MappingType enumerated value that can be Element (the default), Attribute (the column is mapped to an XmlAttribute node), SimpleContent (the column is mapped to an XmlText node), or Hidden (the column doesn't appear in the XML output). For example, consider this code:

```
' Set the ColumnMapping property for some columns.
With ds.Tables("Publishers")
    .Columns("pub_id").ColumnMapping = MappingType.Attribute
    .Columns("country").ColumnMapping = MappingType.Hidden
End With
```

This is the XML text produced for a row in the Publishers table:

```
  <Publishers pub_id="0736">
    <pub_name>New Book Books</pub_name>
    <city>Boston</city>
    <state>MA</state>
  </Publishers>
```

The GetXml method returns the XML that you would write to disk with the WriteXml method:

```
Dim xml As String = ds.GetXml()
```

The only relevant difference in the output produced by the WriteXml method is that GetXml doesn't produce the <?xml > processing instruction at the beginning of the XML text.

Writing the Schema and the DiffGram

All the overloaded versions of WriteXml take an additional (optional) XmlWriteMode argument, which can be one of the following values:

- **IgnoreSchema** Doesn't write the schema (This is the default.)
- **WriteSchema** Writes the schema and the table data
- **DiffGram** Writes the current contents of the DataSet but preserves information about rows that were modified since the most recent AcceptChanges method

(The GetXml method doesn't support these arguments.) For example, the following statement produces an XML file that contains both the DataSet data and its schema:

```
ds.WriteXml("ds.xml", XmlWriteMode.WriteSchema)
```

This is a condensed version of the resultant file. (I have added a blank line between the schema and the data section.)

```
<?xml version="1.0" standalone="yes"?>
<NewDataSet>
  <xs:schema id="NewDataSet" xmlns=""
       xmlns:xs="http://www.w3.org/2001/XMLSchema"
       xmlns:msdata="urn:schemas-microsoft-com:xml-msdata">
    <xs:element name="NewDataSet" msdata:IsDataSet="true">
      <xs:complexType>
        <xs:choice maxOccurs="unbounded">
          <xs:element name="Publishers">
            <xs:complexType>
              <xs:sequence>
                <xs:element name="pub_id" type="xs:string" minOccurs="0" />
                <xs:element name="pub_name" type="xs:string" minOccurs="0" />
                <xs:element name="city" type="xs:string" minOccurs="0" />
                <xs:element name="state" type="xs:string" minOccurs="0" />
                <xs:element name="country" type="xs:string" minOccurs="0" />
              </xs:sequence>
            </xs:complexType>
          </xs:element>
          <xs:element name="Titles">
            <xs:complexType>
              <xs:sequence>
                <xs:element name="title_id" type="xs:string" minOccurs="0" />
                <xs:element name="title" type="xs:string" minOccurs="0" />
                <xs:element name="type" type="xs:string" minOccurs="0" />
```

(continued)

```
                <xs:element name="pub_id" type="xs:string" minOccurs="0" />
                <xs:element name="price" type="xs:decimal" minOccurs="0" />
                <xs:element name="advance" type="xs:decimal" minOccurs="0" />
                <xs:element name="royalty" type="xs:int" minOccurs="0" />
                <xs:element name="ytd_sales" type="xs:int" minOccurs="0" />
                <xs:element name="notes" type="xs:string" minOccurs="0" />
                <xs:element name="pubdate" type="xs:dateTime" minOccurs="0" />
              </xs:sequence>
            </xs:complexType>
          </xs:element>
        </xs:choice>
      </xs:complexType>
      <xs:unique name="Constraint1">
        <xs:selector xpath=".//Publishers" />
        <xs:field xpath="pub_id" />
      </xs:unique>
      <xs:keyref name="PubTitles" refer="Constraint1">
        <xs:selector xpath=".//Titles" />
        <xs:field xpath="pub_id" />
      </xs:keyref>
    </xs:element>
  </xs:schema>

  <Publishers>
    <pub_id>0736</pub_id>
    <pub_name>New Book Books (mod)</pub_name>
    <city>Boston</city>
    <state>MA</state>
    <country>USA</country>
  </Publishers>
  ⋮
  <Titles>
    <title_id>BU1032</title_id>
    <title>The Busy Executive's Database Guide***</title>
    <type>business    </type>
    <pub_id>1389</pub_id>
    <price>19.99</price>
    <advance>5000</advance>
    <royalty>10</royalty>
    <ytd_sales>4095</ytd_sales>
    <notes>An overview of available database systems with
       emphasis on common business applications. Illustrated.</notes>
    <pubdate>1991-06-12T00:00:00.0000000+02:00</pubdate>
  </Titles>
  <Titles>
  ⋮
  </Titles>
</NewDataSet>
```

You can also write only the schema (without the data) by using the WriteXmlSchema method. Like WriteXml, the WriteXmlSchema method can take a filename, a Stream, a TextWriter, or an XmlWriter object:

```
ds.WriteXmlSchema("ds.xml")
```

You can retrieve only the schema with the GetXmlSchema method:

```
Dim xml As String = ds.GetXmlSchema
```

A DiffGram is a piece of XML that describes changes in a DataSet. Consider the following code:

```
' Make some changes to the Titles table.
With ds.Tables("Titles")
    ' Delete the first row.
    .Rows(0).Delete()
    ' Modify two fields in the second row.
    .Rows(1)("price") = 49.99
    .Rows(1)("advance") = 12300
    ' Insert a new row.
    Dim dr As DataRow = .NewRow
    dr("title") = "Programming VB .NET"
    dr("type") = "technical"
    dr("price") = 59.99
End With
' Write only the changed rows to disk.
ds.WriteXml("ds.xml", XmlWriteMode.DiffGram)
```

This is the resultant XML DiffGram. (The most important differences are in boldface.)

```
<?xml version="1.0" standalone="yes"?>
<diffgr:diffgram xmlns:msdata="urn:schemas-microsoft-com:xml-msdata"
      xmlns:diffgr="urn:schemas-microsoft-com:xml-diffgram-v1">
  <NewDataSet>
    <Publishers diffgr:id="Publishers1" msdata:rowOrder="0">
      <pub_id>0736</pub_id>
      <pub_name>New Book Books (mod)</pub_name>
      <city>Boston</city>
      <state>MA</state>
      <country>USA</country>
    </Publishers>
    <Publishers diffgr:id="Publishers2" msdata:rowOrder="1">
      ⋮
    </Publishers>
    ⋮
    </Publishers>
    <Titles diffgr:id="Titles2" msdata:rowOrder="1"
            diffgr:hasChanges="modified">
```

(continued)

```
    <title_id>BU1111</title_id>
    <title>Cooking with Computers: Surreptitious Balance Sheets</title>
    <type>business    </type>
    <pub_id>1389</pub_id>
    <price>49.99</price>
    <advance>12300</advance>
    <royalty>10</royalty>
    <ytd_sales>3876</ytd_sales>
    <notes>Helpful hints on how to use your electronic resources
         to the best advantage.</notes>
    <pubdate>1991-06-09T00:00:00.0000000+02:00</pubdate>
  </Titles>
  <Titles diffgr:id="Titles3" msdata:rowOrder="2">
    ⋮
  </Titles>
  ⋮
  <Titles diffgr:id="Titles19" msdata:rowOrder="18"
        diffgr:hasChanges="inserted">
    <title>Programming VB .NET</title>
    <type>technical</type>
    <price>59.99</price>
  </Titles>
</NewDataSet>

<diffgr:before>
  <Titles diffgr:id="Titles1" msdata:rowOrder="0">
    <title_id>BU1032</title_id>
    <title>The Busy Executive's Database Guide***</title>
    <type>business    </type>
    <pub_id>1389</pub_id>
    <price>19.99</price>
    <advance>5000</advance>
    <royalty>10</royalty>
    <ytd_sales>4095</ytd_sales>
    <notes>An overview of available database systems with
         emphasis on common business applications. Illustrated.</notes>
    <pubdate>1991-06-12T00:00:00.0000000+02:00</pubdate>
  </Titles>
  <Titles diffgr:id="Titles2" msdata:rowOrder="1">
    <title_id>BU1111</title_id>
    <title>Cooking with Computers: Surreptitious Balance Sheets</title>
    <type>business    </type>
    <pub_id>1389</pub_id>
    <price>11.95</price>
    <advance>5000</advance>
    <royalty>10</royalty>
    <ytd_sales>3876</ytd_sales>
```

```
      <notes>Helpful hints on how to use your electronic resources
           to the best advantage.</notes>
      <pubdate>1991-06-09T00:00:00.0000000+02:00</pubdate>
    </Titles>
  </diffgr:before>
</diffgr:diffgram>
```

When you write a DiffGram, all rows are marked with a unique ID so that it's possible to compare the current state of the DataSet (which is found near the beginning of the XML file) and its state before any change was applied (as described in the <diffgr:before> section). Here's how the modified rows have been reflected in the DiffGram:

1. The first row in the Titles table appears in the <diffgr:before> section but doesn't appear in the first section because it has been deleted.
2. The second row is marked in the first section with the diffgr:hasChanges attribute set to the "modified" value. The original version of this row can be found in the <diffgr:before> section; the correspondence between the two versions is provided by the msdata:rowOrder attribute.
3. The new row appears in the current section with a diffgr:hasChanged attribute set to the "inserted" value.

If you want only the DiffGram related to changed rows and you aren't interested in records that haven't changed, you can use the DataSet's GetChanges method before saving it to file:

```
Dim ds2 As DataSet = ds.GetChanges()
ds2.WriteXmlSchema("ds.xml")
```

Reading XML Data and Schema

The ReadXml method can read XML data into a DataSet. It can take a filename, a Stream, a TextReader, or an XmlReader object (or any object that inherits from it, such as an XmlTextReader object). Each of these overloaded versions can take a second, optional, XmlReadMode argument that can be one of the following values:

- **DiffGram** Reads a DiffGram and applies all the changes to the DataSet, behaving as the Merge method. If the schema of the data being read is different from the DataSet's schema, an exception is thrown.

- **IgnoreSchema** Ignores any schema embedded in the XML and reads only the data. If the data being read doesn't match the DataSet's schema (including data from different namespaces), the data in excess is discarded. If the XML being read is a DiffGram, this option behaves as the preceding one does.
- **ReadSchema** Reads any inline schema and then loads the data. New tables can be added to the DataSet, but an exception is thrown if the schema defines a table already in the DataSet.
- **InferSchema** Ignores any inline schema, deduces the schema from the data, and loads the data into the DataSet. The DataSet can be extended with new tables or new columns, but an exception is thrown if the new columns conflict with the existing ones or if the inferred new table exists already in another namespace.
- **Fragment** Reads XML documents such as those produced by a SQL Server's FOR XML query.
- **Auto** The ReadXml method understands the structure of the data being read and behaves as if the DiffGram, ReadSchema, or InferSchema value had been specified. (This is the default behavior.)

Here are a few examples:

```
' Write a DataSet as XML, and load it into another DataSet.
ds.WriteXml("ds.xml")
Dim ds2 As New DataSet
ds2.ReadXml("ds.xml")

' Create a new DataSet that has the same schema as the current one.
ds.WriteXmlSchema("ds.xml")
Dim ds3 As New DataSet
ds3.ReadXml("ds.xml", XmlReadMode.ReadSchema)
```

The ability to read the schema of a DataSet from an XML file can be useful for reducing the number of round-trips to the server. For example, say that you're creating a data-entry application that lets end users add new rows to a database table using a DataGrid control bound to a DataSet. You can initialize the DataSet by using the ReadXml method with the ReadSchema option to read the schema from a local XML file without using a DataAdapter's FillSchema method (which requires an open connection).

The WriteXml and ReadXml methods allow you to send a DataSet in XML format over HTTP, for example to an XML Web service. In most cases, however, these methods are implicitly called by the .NET serialization infrastructure.

Working with Strongly Typed DataSets

ADO.NET allows you to create a strongly typed DataSet object that exposes its tables as properties instead of members of the Tables collection. Similarly, a field in a DataRow can be accessed as a member with a given name rather than by the passing of a numeric index or a string to the Item property. To understand the difference that this can make to your coding style, consider the code that you typically write to access a column in a DataSet table:

```
value = ds.Tables("Publishers").Rows(0).Item("pub_id")
```

Now see how you can rewrite the same assignment if you are working with a strongly typed DataSet:

```
value = ds.Publishers(0).pub_id
```

Using strongly typed DataSets offers you several advantages, such as these:

- You can write more concise code.
- You can display the list of tables and columns when writing code in Visual Studio, thanks to the support from IntelliSense.
- You have more control over how the DataSet is saved as XML by adding custom attributes. (See the "XML Serialization" section in Chapter 11.)

Note that you don't get better performance when you use a strongly typed DataSet because it internally stores and accesses data using an internal (standard) DataSet, as will be clear in a moment.

Creating a Strongly Typed DataSet with the XSD Utility

You can create a strongly typed DataSet from inside Visual Studio .NET (as I explain in the next section) or manually using the XSD utility that comes with the .NET Framework SDK. (You can find this utility in the \Program Files\Microsoft.NET\FrameworkSDK\Bin folder.) To see how the manual approach works, create the schema for the DataSet using the WriteXmlSchema method:

```
ds.WriteXmlSchema("pubs.xsd")
```

Next run the XSD utility on the .xsd file just produced, using the following syntax:

```
XSD /d /l:VB pubs.xsd
```

The XSD utility creates a pubs.vb file in the current directory, so you can now add this file to the current project and browse it. The pubs.vb file is too long for all of its contents to be published here, so I'll just display the more interesting sections:

```
Public Class NewDataSet
    Inherits DataSet

    Private tablePublishers As PublishersDataTable
    Private tableTitles As TitlesDataTable
    Private relationPubTitles As DataRelation

    Public ReadOnly Property Publishers As PublishersDataTable
        Get
            Return Me.tablePublishers
        End Get
    End Property

    Public ReadOnly Property Titles As TitlesDataTable
        Get
            Return Me.tableTitles
        End Get
    End Property

    ⋮

    Public Class PublishersDataTable
        Inherits DataTable
        Implements System.Collections.IEnumerable

        Private columnpub_id As DataColumn
        Private columnpub_name As DataColumn
        Private columncity As DataColumn
        Private columnstate As DataColumn
        Private columncountry As DataColumn
        ⋮
    End Class
    ⋮
End Class
```

As you can see, a strongly typed DataSet is nothing more than a custom class that inherits from System.Data.DataSet and that includes several nested classes. The first thing to do after importing this file in your project is to change the name of the class to something other than NewDataSet (which is the default name assigned to all DataSets)—for example, PubsDataSet. You need to change this name in two places in the class:

```
Public Class PubsDataSet
    ⋮
    Public Overrides Function Clone() As DataSet
        Dim cln As PubsDataSet = CType(MyBase.Clone, PubsDataSet)
    ⋮
```

> **Tip** Use the Class View window to explore the structure of the new class.

Or you can assign the desired name to the DataSet's DataSetName property before saving the XML schema. Now you can code against this class using its strongly typed nature:

```
Dim pubsDs As New PubsDataSet()
' Add a new row to the Publishers table.
Dim pubsRow As PubsDataSet.PublishersRow = pubsDs.Publishers.NewPublishersRow
pubsRow.pub_id = "1234"
pubsRow.pub_name = "VB2TheMax"
pubsRow.city = "Bari"
pubsRow.country = "Italy"
pubsDs.Publishers.AddPublishersRow(pubsRow)
```

The strongly typed DataSet defines one Is*xxx*Null function and one Set*xxx*Null method for each column. The former tests whether a field is DBNull; the latter stores a DBNull value in a column:

```
' If the city column is null, set the country column to null as well.
If pubsDs.Publishers(0).IscityNull Then
    pubsDs.Publishers(0).SetcountryNull()
End If
```

Creating a Strongly Typed DataSet with Visual Studio .NET

Although it's useful to know how the XSD utility works, in most cases you will create a strongly typed DataSet using Visual Studio .NET. Here's how you can proceed:

1. Open the Server Explorer window and create a database connection to the Microsoft Access Biblio.mdb file if you haven't done so already. Next drag the Publishers table to the form's surface; this operation creates two components in the component tray area: OleDbConnection1 and OleDbDataAdapter1. Repeat the drag operation with the Titles database table: in this case, only one component will be created (OleDbDataAdapter2) because the connection object is already available.
2. To improve readability of the code that the designer is going to produce, change the names of the components to cnBiblio, daPubs, and daTitles. The result should look like Figure 22-4.

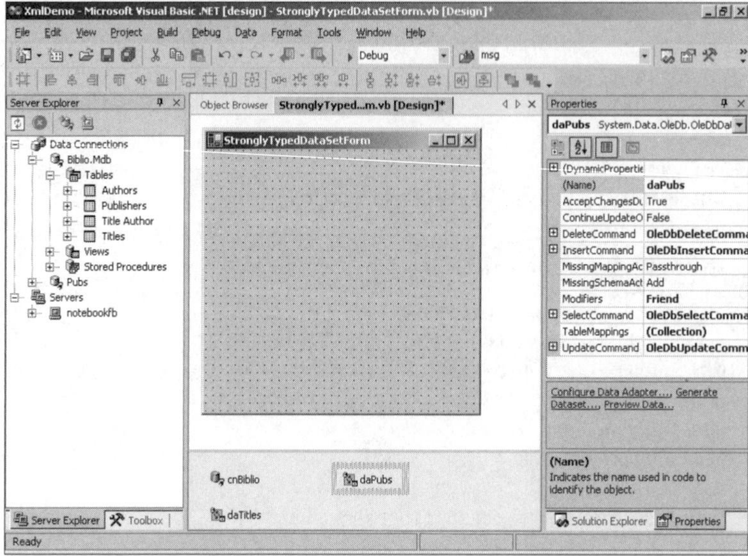

Figure 22-4. Creating Connection and DataAdapter objects with the Visual Studio designer.

3. Right-click one of the two DataAdapter components, and select the Generate Dataset command from the Properties window. (This command is also available in the DataAdapter's shortcut menu and in the top-level Data menu.) The Generate Dataset dialog box shown in Figure 22-5 will appear.

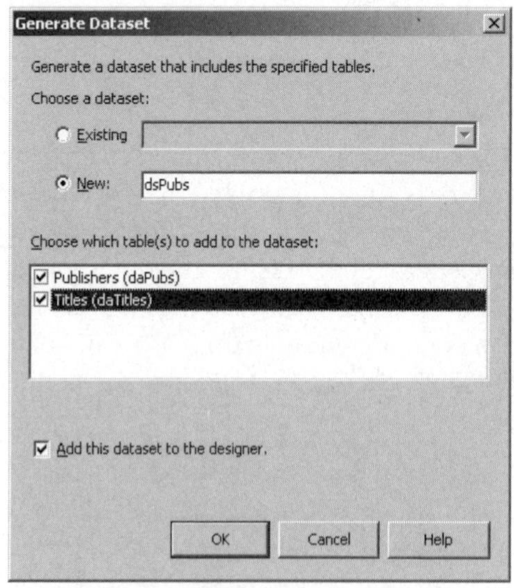

Figure 22-5. Selecting the tables that make up the strongly typed DataSet.

4. Type the name of the strongly typed DataSet class about to be created (dsBiblio, in this example), ensure that both tables are included in the list, and finally click OK to generate the DataSet. This action adds a new file named dsBiblio.xsd to the Solution Explorer window and a new component named DsBiblio1 to the component tray area.

You can now use the DsBiblio1 variable or create another instance of the DsBiblio class as you would use any strongly typed DataSet object. You can double-click the dsBiblio.xsd file to display the schema of the strongly typed DataSet in a graphic fashion, as shown in Figure 22-6. This diagram view lets you perform many interesting operations on the XML schema using a RAD approach; for example, you can

- Add new elements to the schema (and the underlying DataSet) by pointing to Add on the Schema menu and clicking New Element. Figure 22-6 shows two elements, Price and DiscountedPrice, added to the Titles table. Note that DiscountedPrice is a calculated column (as you can see from the corresponding Expression element in the Properties window).

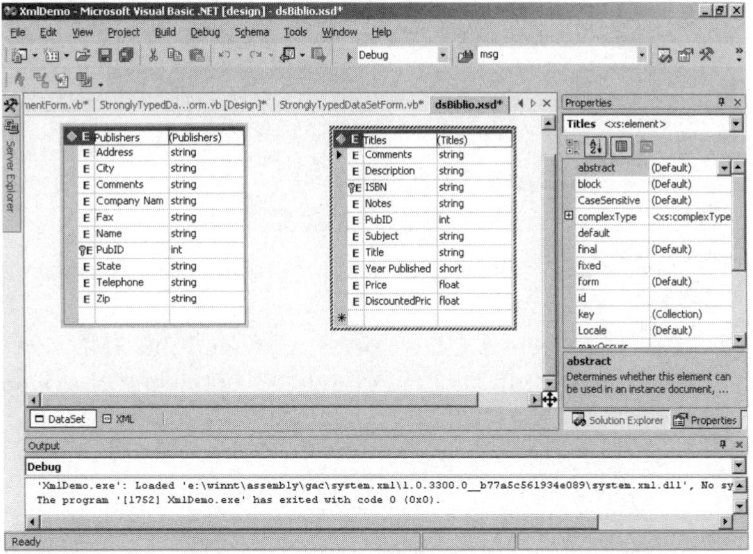

Figure 22-6. Adding new elements to the XSD schema; note that DiscountedPrice is a calculated element.

- Change the way a field is rendered in XML (for example, to render it as an attribute instead of an XML element) by clicking in the leftmost column and selecting an item from the drop-down list.

- Create a relationship between two tables by selecting the two tables, pointing to Add on the Schemu menu, and then clicking Add Relation. (You can also reach this command from the shortcut menu of a table in the schema.) This command brings up the Edit Relation dialog box. Next, to ensure that the relationship is between the primary key in the parent table and the foreign key in the child table, determine the behavior to be applied when a row in the parent table is modified or deleted. You can enter all these values as shown in Figure 22-7, and you can finally click OK to enforce the relationship. The two tables will appear connected in the schema.

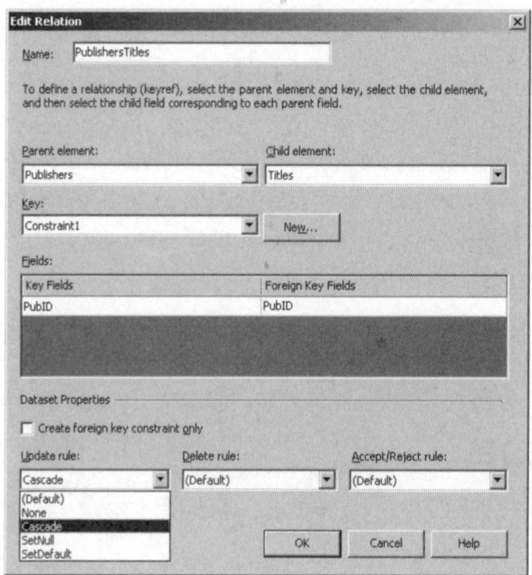

Figure 22-7. Creating a relationship between two tables in the XML schema.

- Alternate between the DataSet view and the XML view by clicking buttons near the bottom of the XSD designer. For example, you can use the XML view of the schema to alter the order of the columns in each DataTable, which affects the order in which fields are shown in a DataGrid control. (You can change this order also by arranging fields in the SelectCommand property of the DataAdapter before generating the DataSet.)

Let's see how to create a form with two DataGrid controls in a parent-child relationship on the form that hosts the strongly typed DataSet instance:

1. Place the first DataGrid control in the upper half of the form, change its CaptionText property to Publishers, and set its DataSource property to DsBiblio1 and its DataMember property to Publishers.

2. Place the second DataGrid control in the lower half of the form, change its CaptionText property to Titles, and set its DataSource property to DsBiblio1 and its DataMember property to Publishers. PublishersTitles.

3. Add the following code to the Load event handler of the hosting form:

```
' Open the connection.
cnBiblio.Open()
' Fill the two DataTables.
daPubs.Fill(DsBiblio1, "Publishers")
daTitles.Fill(DsBiblio1, "Titles")
' Close the connection.
cnBiblio.Close()
```

Figure 22-8 shows the two DataGrid controls in action.

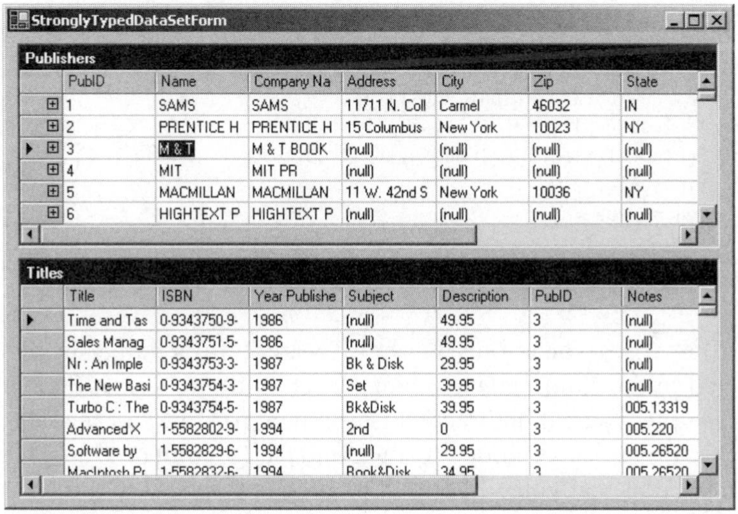

StronglyTypedDataSetForm

Publishers

PubID	Name	Company Na	Address	City	Zip	State
1	SAMS	SAMS	11711 N. Coll	Carmel	46032	IN
2	PRENTICE H	PRENTICE H	15 Columbus	New York	10023	NY
3	M & T	M & T BOOK	(null)	(null)	(null)	(null)
4	MIT	MIT PR	(null)	(null)	(null)	(null)
5	MACMILLAN	MACMILLAN	11 W. 42nd S	New York	10036	NY
6	HIGHTEXT P	HIGHTEXT P	(null)	(null)	(null)	(null)

Titles

Title	ISBN	Year Publishe	Subject	Description	PubID	Notes
Time and Tas	0-9343750-9-	1986	(null)	49.95	3	(null)
Sales Manag	0-9343751-5-	1986	(null)	49.95	3	(null)
Nr : An Imple	0-9343753-3-	1987	Bk & Disk	29.95	3	(null)
The New Basi	0-9343754-3-	1987	Set	39.95	3	(null)
Turbo C : The	0-9343754-5-	1987	Bk&Disk	39.95	3	005.13319
Advanced X	1-5582802-9-	1994	2nd	0	3	005.220
Software by	1-5582829-6-	1994	(null)	29.95	3	005.26520
MacIntosh Pr	1-5582832-6-	1994	Book&Disk	34.95	3	005.26520

Figure 22-8. Two DataGrid controls bound to the strongly typed DataSet in a parent-child relationship.

The XmlDataDocument Class

The DataSet and the XmlDocument classes are two different ways to store data. The DataSet is the better choice for relational structures, whereas the XmlDocument class (and the XML DOM in general) excels at describing hierarchical data. The relational and XML-like hierarchical worlds have always been completely distinct, and you traditionally had to decide the structure that fits your data needs better in the early stages of development. However, the .NET Framework gives you a degree of freedom that was inconceivable before in that you can process a relational set of data stored in a DataSet using a hierarchical approach when necessary.

This little magic is made possible by the XmlDataDocument class. This class derives from XmlDocument, so it inherits all the properties and methods that you're already familiar with. Usually you create an XmlDataDocument object by passing a DataSet to its constructor method, as in this code snippet:

```
Dim cn As New OleDbConnection(OledbPubsConnString)
Dim daPubs As New OleDbDataAdapter("SELECT * FROM Publishers", cn)
Dim daTitles As New OleDbDataAdapter("SELECT * FROM Titles", cn)
Dim ds As New DataSet

' Fill the DataSet with data from two tables.
cn.Open()
daPubs.Fill(ds, "Publishers")
daTitles.Fill(ds, "Titles")
cn.Close()

' Create a (nested) relationship between the two tables.
Dim rel As New DataRelation("PubsTitles", _
    ds.Tables("Publishers").Columns("pub_id"), _
    ds.Tables("Titles").Columns("pub_id"))
ds.Relations.Add(rel)
rel.Nested = True

' Associate an XmlDataDocument with the DataSet.
Dim xdd As New XmlDataDocument(ds)
```

After the association has been created, any change in the DataSet is reflected in the XmlDataDocument object, and vice versa. (See Figure 22-9.) For example, you can indirectly insert a new row into a DataTable by adding an appropriate set of nodes to the XmlDataDocument. The only (obvious) requirement is that you add only XML elements that fit in the DataSet schema and that don't violate any null, unique, or relation constraint. Since you add one element at a time, the only way to avoid an exception when adding a row is by temporarily setting EnforceConstraints to False. This code uses the CreateAppendElement helper routine (defined earlier in this chapter) to add a row to the Publishers table:

```
' Before proceeding, you must set EnforceConstraints to False.
ds.EnforceConstraints = False
' It is advisable to normalize before any XML operation.
xdd.Normalize()
' Add a new node to the XmlDataElement.
Dim xmlEl As XmlElement
xmlEl = CreateAppendElement(xdd.DocumentElement, "Publishers")
CreateAppendElement(xmlEl, "pub_id", "9997")
```

```
CreateAppendElement(xmlEl, "pub_name", "Sci-Fi Publications")
CreateAppendElement(xmlEl, "city", "Boston")
CreateAppendElement(xmlEl, "state", "MA")
CreateAppendElement(xmlEl, "country", "USA")
' Reenable constraints.
ds.EnforceConstraints = True
```

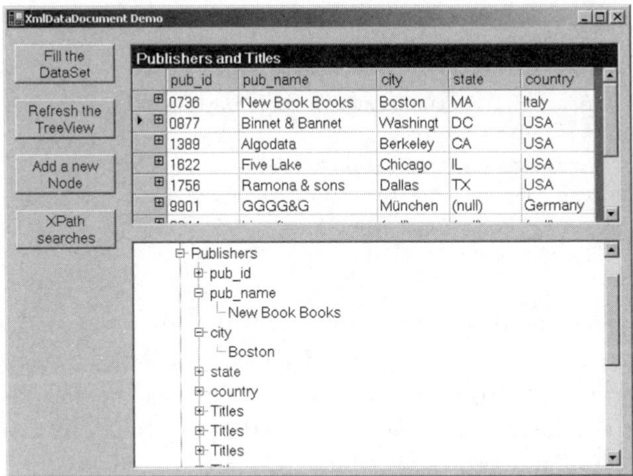

Figure 22-9. An XmlDataDocument is a synchronized hierarchical view of a DataSet.

You see the great benefits in accessing the DataSet using a hierarchical structure when performing complex queries. For example, this code uses the SelectNodes method to display the list of all the titles published by publishers based in Boston:

```
' This is the XPath search expression.
' (Note that node name matches are case sensitive.)
Dim xpath As String = "//Publishers[city = 'Boston']/Titles/title/text()"
Dim xnl As XmlNodeList = xdd.SelectNodes(xpath)
Dim xt As XmlText
For Each xt In xnl
    Debug.WriteLine(xt.Value)
Next
```

The XmlDataDocument object adds only three members to those defined in the base XmlDocument class, namely:

- The DataSet read-only property, which returns a reference to the associated DataSet instance.
- The GetElementFromRow method, which takes a DataRow object and returns the corresponding XmlElement object in the DOM.

- The GetRowFromElement method, which takes an XmlElement object and returns the corresponding DataRow in the DataSet.

For example, the following code snippet applies the GetRowFromElement method to the result of a SelectSingleNode method:

```
' This XPath expression searches for the Publishers XML element
' that has a title descendant whose text is 'Net Etiquette.'
Dim xpath As String = "//Publishers[Titles/title/text() = 'Net Etiquette']"
' Get the only XmlNode that matches the expression, and cast it to XmlElement.
Dim xmlEl As XmlElement = DirectCast(xdd.SelectSingleNode(xpath), XmlElement)
' Retrieve the corresponding DataRow.
Dim dr As DataRow = xdd.GetRowFromElement(xmlEl)
' Display the name and the city of this publisher.
Debug.WriteLine("Name = " & dr("pub_name"))
Debug.WriteLine("City = " & dr("city"))
```

This chapter concludes the part of the book devoted to database techniques. You've seen that the Visual Basic .NET way of handling data in disconnected mode is different from anything you've learned in the past, so you'll probably have to redesign most of your existing applications when moving them to the .NET Framework, especially if you made heavy use of server-side cursors. Although you can still use classic ADO through the COM Interop layer, switching to ADO.NET gives you much better integration with other .NET features—for example, data binding. This is especially true when working with Web Forms and XML Web services, which I'll cover in the next portion of this book.

Part VI

Internet Applications

Front
Top
Left
Back

23

Web Forms and Controls

ASP.NET is the portion of the .NET Framework that lets you create Internet applications. It has been the first part of the Framework to be completed, and to many developers it's still the most innovative part of the .NET initiative. ASP.NET comprises two different but closely related technologies:

- Web Forms, for creating Internet applications with user interfaces that can be accessed via a browser. These are the heirs to Active Server Pages (ASP) applications.
- XML Web services, for creating nonbrowsable Internet applications that can be accessed only programmatically.

In this chapter and in Chapter 24, I explain Web Forms applications; I cover XML Web services in Chapter 26.

> **Note** This and the following chapter assume that you're familiar with "classic" ASP programming. If you aren't, you might want to read Chapter 20 of my *Programming Microsoft Visual Basic 6* book, on the companion CD.

Basic Web Forms Concepts

At installation time, the .NET Framework registers several new file extensions with Internet Information Services (IIS). One of these extensions is .aspx, which identifies a Web Forms page. When a client browser requests a file with this extension, the aspnet_isapi.dll component is loaded in memory (if not already loaded) and processes the request. Because they use a different file extension, Web Forms applications (and ASP.NET applications in general) can coexist on the same IIS with older ASP sites.

As with all types of .NET applications, the .NET Framework comes with all the tools you need to create Web Forms applications, so in theory you can get along with just an editor as simple as Notepad. In practice, however, you'll want to use Visual Studio .NET and its integrated tools for most real applications, as you'll see countless times while reading this chapter.

Your First Web Forms Project

Load Visual Studio .NET, point to New on the File menu and choose Project; this series of actions brings up the familiar New Project dialog box. (See Figure 23-1.) When you select the ASP.NET Web Application icon, however, the Name field is grayed and the Location field contains something like http://localhost/WebApplication1, where WebApplication1 is the name of a subdirectory under the main directory for IIS projects (c:\inetpub\wwwroot for a default installation). You can specify the name of any virtual IIS directory in the default IIS Web site or in another Web site hosted on the local machine. For your first Web Forms application, you can change this location to http://localhost/FirstWebForm. When you click OK, Visual Studio creates a new project in the directory you specified; the project contains several new types of files:

- The WebForm1.aspx file is an empty ASP.NET Web Forms page, on which you can drop controls and components. (The components go to the component tray area, as for Windows Forms.)
- AssemblyInfo.vb is the usual source code file that contains all the assembly attributes.
- Global.asax is the first file loaded when the application starts. It contains event handlers that are executed when a new client connects to the application and any time a new request is posted. (It has the same function as the Global.asa file in classic ASP applications.)
- Styles.css is the stylesheet used by default for all the pages in this application. By editing this file, you can modify how common HTML tags are rendered on the client browser. For example, you can select the default color and font used for headings; the colors used for regular, active, and visited links; and the margin left around images.

- The Web.config file is the configuration file for this ASP.NET application. This XML file is functionally similar to the .config files that I described in Chapter 14, even though it contains different entries.

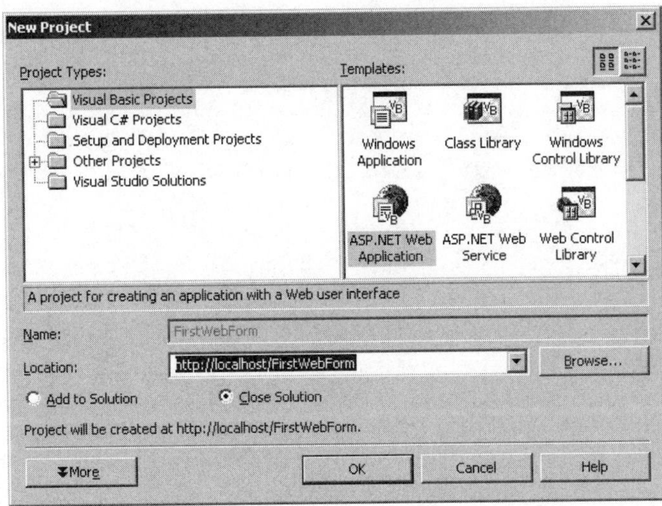

Figure 23-1. Creating a new ASP.NET Web application.

I cover the Global.asax and Web.config files in detail in Chapter 24. For now, let's focus on the WebForm1.aspx file. Web Forms files come with a designer and a code portion, much like Windows Forms files. A Web Forms designer can work in two modes: design and HTML. In design mode, you drop controls taken from the HTML or Web Forms tabs of the Toolbox, as well as from other tabs that contain items that go to the component tray area, such as Data or Components. In HTML mode, you can write plain HTML code as you do with any HTML editor; you often need to switch to this mode to add HTML elements that don't correspond to an item on any Toolbox tab.

Setting Main Page Properties

You should set the pageLayout, targetSchema, and defaultClientScript properties of the page document immediately after creating the form because they affect how your application sends output to the various browsers. Changing these properties in the middle of the development stage usually requires that you recheck how the form behaves, possibly testing it with different browsers. You can also set these properties in the project Property Pages dialog box to have all new Web Forms inherit them automatically. (See Figure 23-2.)

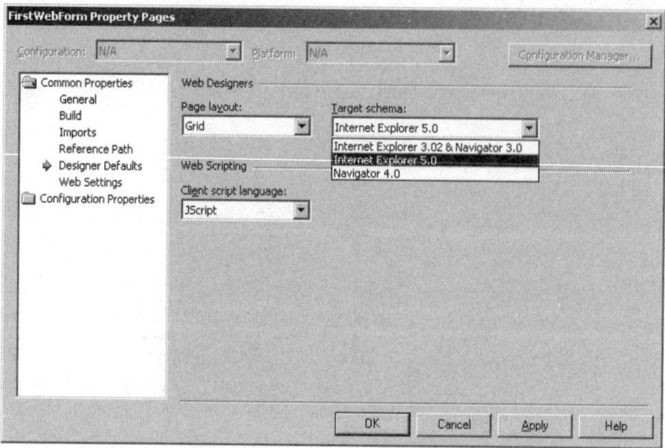

Figure 23-2. The Designer Defaults page of the project Property Pages dialog box.

The pageLayout property can be set to FlowLayout or GridLayout. The first value renders HTML elements in a flowing manner, a bit like words in a word processor: if the user resizes the browser's window, the layout of the HTML contents automatically changes to accommodate the new window's dimensions. The GridLayout value sets absolute coordinates for all HTML elements; in this mode, the designer works like the Windows Forms designer.

The targetSchema property tells which HTML flavor to use: it can be Microsoft Internet Explorer 3.02, Netscape Navigator 3.0, Navigator 4.0, or Internet Explorer 5.0. Needless to say, you get extended functionality when you select a more recent version of Internet Explorer or Navigator, but you lose compatibility with previous versions. In practice you should use the Internet Explorer 3.02/Navigator 3.0 setting when you create an Internet site, and use one of the other settings only for intranets. For example, when pageLayout is set to GridLayout and you select the Internet Explorer 5.0 target schema, the ASP.NET code that Visual Studio produces sets the position of HTML elements by using a style attribute. If you select the Explorer 3.02/Navigator 3.0 target schema, the ASP.NET code arranges controls on the page by using HTML tables, which require that more HTML text is sent over the wire and is rendered slowly in the browser.

The defaultClientScript property determines which script language is used to activate client-side functionality, such as script code that supports validation controls. By default, this property is set to JScript (which is compatible with all browsers), but you can change it to VBScript if you're sure that only Internet Explorer users are accessing your application.

Other page properties are less critical, and most of the time you can leave them at their default values, or you can change them later without a serious impact on the application's testing and debugging. For example, the language property is the language used to compile inline code blocks in the page. It's automatically set to VB because you've created this Web Forms page in a Visual Basic .NET project; other valid values are C# and JScript.

Dropping Controls onto the Page

Your first Web Forms application is a simple calculator that takes two numbers and displays their sum in another field. This sample program requires very little code but provides a good opportunity to understand a few basic principles of Web Forms.

Ensure that the form's pageLayout property is set to FlowLayout, open the Web Forms tab on the Toolbox, and drop three TextBox controls, two Label controls, and one Button control, as shown in the upper portion of Figure 23-3. The two Label controls are used for the title at the top of the page and the plus symbol between the two TextBox controls. You can see their captions by setting their Text properties as you would do with a Label control in a Windows Forms application. You can change the size of the first Label by setting its Font.Bold property to True and its Font.Size property to X-Large. (Font sizes for Web controls aren't measured in points.) Unlike Windows Forms, however, you can just type text whenever you want in the HTML designer, if it's in FlowLayout mode, exactly as you do with a word processor.

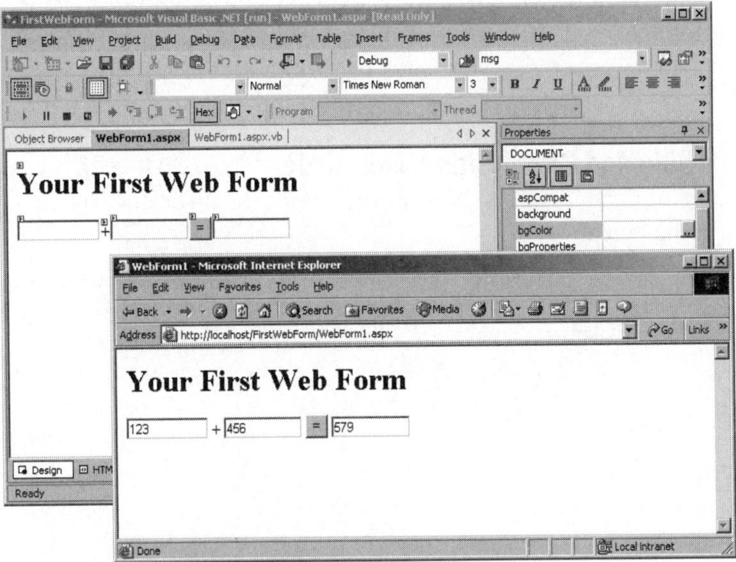

Figure 23-3. Your first Web Forms application in design mode (top) and inside Internet Explorer (bottom).

Next change the names of the three TextBox controls to txtOne, txtTwo, and txtResult. You use these names when referencing these controls in code. You must set them by using the (ID) property because Web controls don't expose a Name property. Similarly, set the ID property of the button to btnAdd and its Text property to the equal sign.

Finally you can double-click the Button control to bring up the code editor and enter the following code:

```
Private Sub btnAdd_Click(ByVal sender As System.Object, _
    ByVal e As System.EventArgs) Handles btnAdd.Click
    Dim res As Double = CDbl(txtOne.Text) + CDbl(txtTwo.Text)
    txtResult.Text = res.ToString
End Sub
```

As you see, you're using plain Visual Basic .NET code to define what happens when the user clicks the button. The interesting thing—which is also one of the fundamental concepts in ASP.NET programming—is that this code runs on the server, not on the client, so the client machine doesn't need to be running the .NET Framework. More precisely, the client machine doesn't even need to be a Windows computer because the communication with the server is done through plain HTML and HTTP exclusively.

To see this program in action, press the F5 key to run the application. Visual Studio .NET automatically runs Internet Explorer, which in turn asks IIS for the page you've written, and displays it. Enter two numbers in the first two fields, and click on the button: a progress bar in the status bar of the browser shows that a request is posted back to IIS, which returns the same form with the result in the third field.

Server-Side and Client-Side HTML Code

To better understand how Web Forms work, let's see the HTML code that the designer has created for us:

```
<%@ Page Language="vb" AutoEventWireup="false" Codebehind="WebForm1.aspx.vb"
  Inherits="FirstWebForm.WebForm1"%>
<!DOCTYPE HTML PUBLIC "-//W3C//DTD HTML 4.0 Transitional//EN">
<HTML>
  <HEAD>
    <title>WebForm1</title>
    ⋮
  </HEAD>
  <body>
    <form id="Form1" method="post" runat="server"><P>
      <asp:Label id="Label1" runat="server" Font-Bold="True"
        Font-Size="X-Large">Your First Web Form</asp:Label></P>
```

```
      <P>
      <asp:TextBox id="txtOne" runat="server" Width="88px"></asp:TextBox>
      <asp:Label id="Label2" runat="server"> + </asp:Label>
      <asp:TextBox id="txtTwo" runat="server" Width="84px"></asp:TextBox>
      <asp:Button id="btnAdd" runat="server" Text=" = "></asp:Button>
      <asp:TextBox id="txtResult" runat="server" Width="84px">
        </asp:TextBox></P>
    </form>
  </body>
</HTML>
```

As you see, all the components we've dropped onto the designer's surface have been translated to <asp:*xxxx*> tags inside a <form> block. Both the form and the individual controls contain a runat="server" attribute, which makes it clear that the corresponding element is processed on the server, not on the client. Each control has an id attribute that corresponds to the name you've assigned to it. Finally, at the top of the page you'll see an @Page directive that contains information on the page being processed.

No browser is able to interpret this HTML code, and in fact, this isn't plain HTML. More precisely, it's an XML block that's processed before being sent to the browser, in a way that depends on the targetSchema and other properties. For example, this is the HTML code that Internet Explorer 5.0 or later versions receive:

```
<!DOCTYPE HTML PUBLIC "-//W3C//DTD HTML 4.0 Transitional//EN">
<HTML>
  <HEAD>
    <title>WebForm1</title>
    ⋮
  </HEAD>
  <body>
    <form name="Form1" method="post" action="WebForm1.aspx" id="Form1">
    <input type="hidden" name="__VIEWSTATE" value="dDwxNDE4MjA3OTY2Ozs+" />
    <P>
    <span id="Label1" style="font-size:X-Large;font-weight:bold;">
      Your First Web Form</span></P>
    <P>
    <input name="txtOne" type="text" id="txtOne" style="width:88px;" />
    <span id="Label2"> + </span>
    <input name="txtTwo" type="text" id="txtTwo" style="width:84px;" />
    <input type="submit" name="btnAdd" value=" = " id="btnAdd" />
    <input name="txtResult" type="text" id="txtResult" style="width:84px;" />
    </P>
    </form>
  </body>
</HTML>
```

A few points are worth noting here:

- All <asp:*xxxx*> elements have been morphed into plain HTML tags. TextBox controls have been translated to <input type="text"> elements, Label controls have been rendered as <span> elements, and the Button control has been translated to an <input type="submit"> element.
- An action attribute has been added to the <form> element. This attribute causes the submit button to repost the form contents to the same .aspx page, which processes the values in the two text boxes and sends the modified page back again to the client. Forms that behave this way are called *self-posting forms*. As you'll learn shortly, the code in the form can detect whether it's running because of a postback operation.
- A hidden field named __VIEWSTATE has been added to the form. This field contains the values of all the controls when the form has been sent to the client in an encoded format.

The __VIEWSTATE hidden field is central to the ASP.NET architecture. When the form is posted back to the server, ASP.NET compares the current value of each control with its original value (which is encoded in the hidden field), and raises the corresponding event on the server. For example, if the end user has modified the value of a TextBox control, a TextChanged event is fired on the server. In contrast to what happens in Windows Forms applications, this event isn't fired immediately and is postponed until the form is posted back to the server.

> **Note** Unlike standard HTML and classic ASP pages, an ASP.NET page can contain only one <form> tag.

Web Forms Dynamics

Let's consider in more detail what happens when a client browser interacts with a Web Forms application. You need this information to understand what you can do with Web Forms, as well as which actions are to be performed on the server and which ones on the client.

Code-Behind Classes

One of the major defects of classic ASP was the inability to separate the user interface (the HTML text) and the script code that does the actual page processing. This obstacle prevented a clear separation between the job of the graphic designer and the job of the programmer, and most ASP developers had to become experts in user interface issues as well programming, with overall results less than exciting in most cases. (Results certainly weren't exciting in *my* case.) Web Forms take a completely new approach that, while not perfect, is a great step in the right direction.

When a browser posts a request to an .aspx file, the ASP.NET DLL intercepts the request, loads the file, and parses its @Page directive looking for the Inherits attribute. This attribute's value is the name of the class that contains the code associated with server-side events for that page—for example, the event handlers that execute when a button is clicked. This class must be in a DLL that's stored in the /Bin subdirectory under the application's root directory, or in another subdirectory that can be found by using the usual probing rules applied to all .NET assemblies (as I explained in Chapter 14). The association between event handlers and user interface elements is based on the interface elements' id attributes.

Interestingly, ASP.NET doesn't really load the original DLL. Instead, it copies the DLL to another location and then loads this copy, which is called the *shadow copy*. This operation slows the processing of the very first request but has a great advantage: you can overwrite the original DLL without getting an error because IIS isn't locking it. When another request comes, ASP.NET checks that the shadow copy still matches the original DLL and performs the copy operation again if necessary to keep the two versions in sync. This shadow copying feature is a great improvement over the way classic ASP deals with compiled DLLs. As many ASP developers know, you have to restart the IIS application (and at times the entire IIS) to replace a compiled COM DLL that's being used by IIS.

On-Demand Compilation

Visual Studio .NET builds the compiled DLL before running the browser on the .aspx page, but ASP.NET works well even if no DLL has been created for the code-behind portion of the form. You can deploy only the .aspx and the .vb (or .cs) source file, in which case the latter file is automatically compiled the first time a browser posts a request for the companion .aspx file. ASP.NET looks at the file's extension to decide which compiler—Visual Basic, C#, or any other valid .NET language—must be used to compile the source file, so it's crucial that you use the .vb extension for your Visual Basic .NET files.

The association between the .aspx file and its code-behind source module is held in the Src attribute of the @Page directive:

```
<%@ Page Src="WebForm1.aspx.vb" Inherits="FirstWebForm.WebForm1"%>
```

The on-demand compilation model doesn't offer any advantages over the Visual Studio .NET approach, other than the ability to create Web Forms pages using a tool as simple as Notepad, and it has a couple of drawbacks. First, the compilation step adds a short delay the very first time a page is requested. Second, and more important, you must deploy the source code file to have it compiled on the fly, so you might not be able to protect your intellectual property if you aren't in full control of the server computer.

ASP.NET supports also a third code model, in which the .aspx file contains both the HTML text and the server-side code. In this model, server-side code is enclosed in <script> blocks with a runat="server" attribute, exactly as you find in classic ASP:

```
<%@ Page Language="VB" %>
⋮
<SCRIPT RUNAT="server">
Private Sub btnAdd_Click(ByVal sender As System.Object, _
    ByVal e As System.EventArgs) Handles btnAdd.Click
    Dim res As Double = CDbl(txtOne.Text) + CDbl(txtTwo.Text)
    txtResult.Text = res.ToString
End Sub
</SCRIPT>
```

This code model is often adopted in the SDK documentation and in many ASP.NET books and articles because it shows the HTML and the language code in a single place. But because this book is about using Visual Studio .NET, all my code samples uses separate listings for the HTML and the Visual Basic portions.

The Page Life Cycle

The great innovation of Web Forms is that they let you adopt the same event-driven programming model that made Visual Basic the most popular programming language under Windows. By and large, Web Forms controls expose the same events of their Windows Forms counterparts: Button controls expose a Click event, TextBox controls expose a TextChanged event, ListBox controls expose the SelectedIndexChanged event, and so on. The Page class is the ASP.NET equivalent of the form, and exposes events such as Load and Unload.

Even if the event-driven model is similar, you find an important difference between the Windows Forms and the Web Forms worlds. Events in Win32 applications fire as soon as end users operate on the user interface element—that is, when they click on buttons, type something in a TextBox, or select another element in a ListBox control. On the other hand, Web Forms events fire on the server, not inside the browser, so their handlers run only when the form is posted back to the server. This usually occurs when the user clicks on the Submit button, even though other controls can fire a postback.

This is what happens when a form is posted back to the server:

1. ASP.NET loads the code-behind class and fires the Page_Init event. At this time, your code can't determine whether this is the first time the form is requested, nor can it retrieve the values the user typed in controls.
2. After the page object and all its controls have been initialized, the Page_Load event fires. At this time, you can determine whether the page is executing because of a postback operation (by checking the IsPostBack property) and can access current values in controls. Typically, you use this event to initialize controls and bind them to data sources. In other words, you use it for the kind of operations you perform in a Windows Forms Load event.
3. All the events related to controls fire at this time, if this is a postback. For example, TextChanged events for TextBox controls that have been modified by the end user fire now, as well as CheckedChanged events for CheckBox and RadioButton controls that have been clicked.
4. The last control event that fires is the one that caused the postback action; usually this is the Click event of a Button or ImageButton control.
5. Finally the Page object fires an Unload event, when you're expected to release all resources, close files and database connections, and so on.

The order in which control events fire isn't necessarily the order in which the end user operated on the corresponding controls. The Web Forms object fires these events by analyzing the current state of all the controls on the form posted back to the server and comparing it with the control's state at the time when the form was sent to the browser. (This information is stored in the hidden __VIEWSTATE field.) For example, a TextBox's TextChanged event fires if the control contains a string other than its original value. Of course, you receive a single TextChanged event even if the end user modified the control's value several times before posting the form back to the server.

Web Forms controls fire fewer events than their Windows Forms counterparts. For example, Web Forms controls don't expose events such as MouseEnter, MouseExit, GotFocus, and LostFocus because these events are typically used to provide instantaneous feedback to the end user. It makes little sense to cache them and fire them when the form is posted back to the server.

The EnableViewState Property

From the description I gave in the preceding section, it appears that the Page_Load event fires both when it's the first request for the page and when it's a result of a postback. Unless you're jumping to another page, you typically want to restore the values that the user typed in each control before sending the page back to the browser. This simple task was overly difficult in classic ASP but requires no action on your part under ASP.NET because ASP.NET automatically saves the value of all controls.

As a matter of fact, you must explicitly do something only if you do *not* want these values to be saved. More precisely, you can disable the persistence mechanism for a given control by setting its EnableViewState property to False:

```
' Don't save the value of ListBox1 between postbacks.
' (You can set this property also in the Property window at design time.)
ListBox1.EnableViewState = False
```

If you don't need to save the value of any control on the form, you can disable the ViewState mechanism completely by setting the Page object's EnableViewState property to False:

```
' Don't save any control between postbacks.
Me.EnableViewState = False
```

The value of controls whose EnableViewState property is False isn't included in the hidden __VIEWSTATE field, which results in fewer bytes sent to the client browser and then back to the server. For this reason, you should disable the ViewState mechanism for all the controls that don't really need to be saved between postbacks.

The IsPostBack Property

Consider the following code, which loads a DropDownList control with the list of all the states for which there is at least one publisher:

```
Private Sub Page_Load(ByVal sender As Object, ByVal e As EventArgs) _
    Handles MyBase.Load
    InitializeStateList()
End Sub

' BiblioConnString is the connection string that points to Biblio.mdb.
Dim cn As New OleDbConnection(BiblioConnString)

' Display unique state strings in the ddlStates DropDownList control.
Sub InitializeStateList()
    cn.Open()
    Dim cmd As New OleDbCommand("SELECT DISTINCT State FROM Publishers", cn)
    Dim dr As OleDbDataReader = cmd.ExecuteReader()
    ddlStates.DataSource = dr
```

```
    ' The State field is used for filling the list of the DropDownList control.
    ddlStates.DataTextField = "State"
    ' Bind the control to the data source.
    ddlStates.DataBind()
    dr.Close
    cn.Close
End Sub
```

(I'll explain data binding in the "Data Binding with Web Forms Controls" section later in this chapter.) In the preceding code snippet, the InitializeStateList routine runs each time the page is requested. However, running this code for any request after the first one is useless because the contents of the ddlStates control are embedded in the hidden __VIEWSTATE field and are restored automatically when the page is reloaded after a postback. You can choose from two ways to avoid this overhead:

- Set the EnableStateView property of the ddlStates control to False so that its contents aren't added to the __VIEWSTATE hidden field.
- Run the InitializeStateList routine only the very first time the browser requests the page and skip it during a postback operation.

Choosing between these two approaches isn't an easy decision: sometimes recalculating the contents of a control (or reloading it from a database query) is faster than bloating each page with a large __VIEWSTATE field. In the majority of cases, however, the best approach is to load the data once and store it in the __VIEWSTATE field.

To load the data only once, you must distinguish the first page request from postbacks, which you do by means of the page's IsPostBack read-only property. Here's an improved version of the Page_Load event handler that takes advantage of this property:

```
Private Sub Page_Load(ByVal sender As Object, ByVal e As EventArgs) _
    Handles MyBase.Load
    If Not Page.IsPostBack Then
        InitializeStateList()
    End If
End Sub

' ...(The remainder of the code is unchanged)...
```

The AutoPostBack Property

By default, only a few controls can start a postback operation—namely, the Button control and its ImageButton and LinkButton variations. This behavior is OK most of the time because the user is usually expected to fill in all the fields in a form and then click the submit button.

Occasionally, however, you might want to offer immediate feedback when the user selects an item from a list or clicks a check box or a radio button. You can achieve this different behavior by setting the AutoPostBack property to True for the controls that can initiate a postback operation. This property is exposed by the following controls: TextBox, CheckBox, RadioButton, CheckBoxList, RadioButtonList, DropDownList, and ListBox.

To see the AutoPostBack property in action, create a new Web Forms component (from the Project menu) and name it AutoPostBackForm. Add a DropDownList and a DataGrid control plus a couple of Label controls on the new form, as shown in the upper portion of Figure 23-4. Rename the DropDownList control ddlStates and the DataGrid control dgrPublishers, and set the DropDownList control's AutoPostBack property to True. You're already familiar with a few routines in the code behind the form:

```
Private Sub Page_Load(ByVal sender As Object, ByVal e As EventArgs) _
    Handles MyBase.Load
    If Not Page.IsPostBack Then
        InitializeStateList()
    End If
End Sub

' BiblioConnString is the connection string that points to Biblio.mdb.
Dim cn As New OleDbConnection(BiblioConnString)

' Display unique state strings in the ddlStates DropDownList control.
Sub InitializeStateList()
    cn.Open()
    Dim cmd As New OleDbCommand("SELECT DISTINCT State FROM Publishers", cn)
    Dim dr As OleDbDataReader = cmd.ExecuteReader()
    ddlStates.DataSource = dr
    ' The State field is used for filling the list of the DropDownList control.
    ddlStates.DataTextField = "State"
    ' Bind the control to the data source.
    ddlStates.DataBind()
    dr.Close
    cn.Close
End Sub

Private Sub ddlStates_SelectedIndexChanged(ByVal sender As Object, _
    ByVal e As EventArgs) Handles ddlStates.SelectedIndexChanged
    ' Create the query string.
    Dim sql As String = "SELECT Name, Address, City, State FROM Publishers"
    If ddlStates.SelectedIndex >= 0 Then
        sql &= " WHERE State = '" & ddlStates.SelectedItem.Text & "'"
    End If

    ' Display publishers in the DataGrid.
    cn.Open()
```

```
    Dim cmd As New OleDbCommand(sql, cn)
    Dim dr As OleDbDataReader = cmd.ExecuteReader()
    ' Bind the control to the data source.
    dgrPublishers.DataSource = dr
    dgrPublishers.DataBind()
    dr.Close()
    cn.Close()
End Sub
```

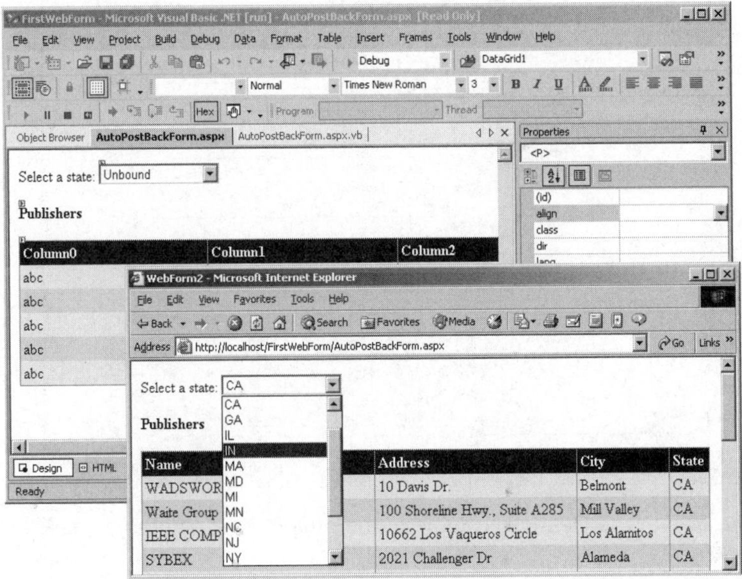

Figure 23-4. The AutoPostBackForm.aspx page.

Note Here's an important point about connection strings in ASP.NET. As you'll learn in Chapter 24, by default an ASP.NET application runs under the identity of a user named ASPNET. If you want to use integrated security when you access SQL Server, you must make this ASPNET account a valid user account for SQL Server. If you don't, you can establish a valid SQL Server connection only if you provide a specific User ID and Password in the connection string, as in this line of code:

```
Data Source=.;User ID=sa;Password=sapwd;Initial Catalog=pubs
```

Similar security issues might arise when you're working with other databases.

To test this Web Forms page from inside Visual Studio, you must modify the start page—that is, the .aspx page shown in Internet Explorer when you run the application. You can do this in the Debugging page of the project Property Pages dialog box. (See Figure 23-5.)

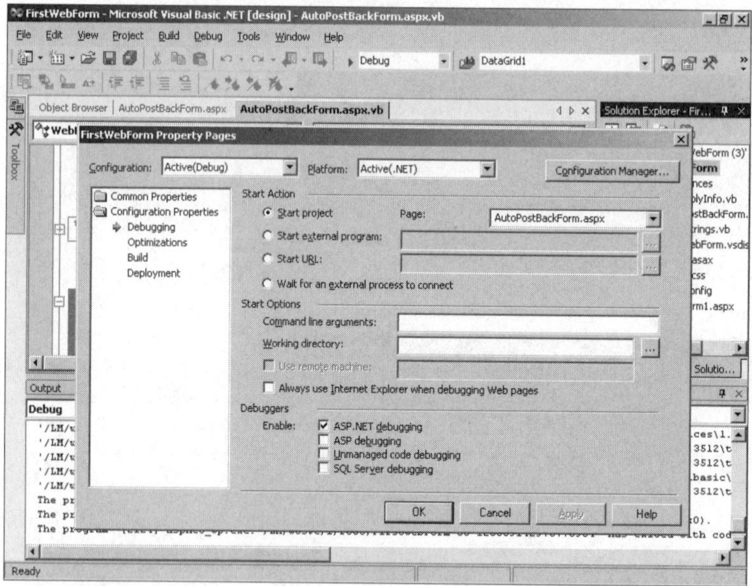

Figure 23-5. The Debugging page of the project Property Pages dialog box.

It's interesting to see that the AutoPostBack property is implemented by means of a short client-side JavaScript routine and a couple of hidden fields. When the user selects a new item in the combo box, the routine loads the name of the control that fired the postback in the first control, loads an additional argument in the second hidden field (an empty string in this specific case), and finally submits the form. Here's the abridged version of the HTML form sent to the browser:

```
<form name="Form1" method="post" action="AutoPostBackForm.aspx" id="Form1">
<input type="hidden" name="__EVENTTARGET" value="" />
<input type="hidden" name="__EVENTARGUMENT" value="" />
<input type="hidden" name="__VIEWSTATE"
  value="dDwtMTc3Nzk0Nzg4NDt0PDtsPGk8MT47PjtsPHQ8O2w8aTwxPjtpPDU+Oz47bDx0PHQ8c
  DxwPGw8RGF0YVRleHRGaWVsZDs+O2w8U3RhdGU7Pj47Pjt0PGk8MTc+O0A8XGU7QUs7Q0E7R0E7S
  Uw7SU47TUEgO01EO01JO01OO05DO05KO05ZO09SO1BBO1RYO1dBOz47QDxcZTtBSztDQTtHQTtJT
  DtJTjtNQSA7TUQ7TUk7TU47TkM7Tko7Tlk7T1I7UEE7VFg7V0E7Pj47Pjs7Pjt0PEAwPDs7Ozs7O
  zs7Ozs+Ozs+Oz4+Oz4+Oz4=" />
```

```
<script language="javascript">
<!--
   function __doPostBack(eventTarget, eventArgument) {
      var theform = document.Form1;
      theform.__EVENTTARGET.value = eventTarget;
      theform.__EVENTARGUMENT.value = eventArgument;
      theform.submit();
   }
// -->
</script>
<P>Select a state:
<select name="ddlStates" id="ddlStates"
   onchange="__doPostBack('ddlStates','')"
   language="javascript" style="width:130px;">
   <option value="AK">AK</option>
   <option value="CA">CA</option>
   ⋮
</select></P>
⋮
</form>
```

> **Note** For the AutoPostBack property to work correctly, the user's browser must allow scripting. This is the default setting for all browsers, but users might turn this feature off for security reasons. In that case, the AutoPostBack property doesn't work. If in doubt, include a Submit button on the form to cover these cases. (Or at least add a warning to your users that they must enable scripting to navigate your site.)

The Page Class

The Page class represents the Web Forms page itself, and its members affect how the .aspx page is displayed in the browser. For this reason, you should become familiar with its properties, methods, and events.

Page Properties

Table 23-1 lists the most important properties of the Page class. I've already discussed a few of them, such as EnableViewState and IsPostBack. The meaning of other properties will become clearer as you read this chapter—for example, as you read about the properties related to validation—or the next chapter.

Table 23-1 Main Properties of the Page Class

Category	Syntax	Description
ASP objects	Request	Returns the HttpRequest object that describes the current request posted to the server.
	Response	Returns the HttpResponse object that lets you control how data is sent to the client browser.
	Server	Returns the HttpServerUtility object that represents the server.
	Application	Returns the HttpApplicationState object that you can use to store data shared by all clients of this application.
	Session	Returns the HttpSessionState object that you can use to store data belonging to the current user.
Behavior	ClientTarget	You can assign an HttpBrowserCapabilities object to this property to override the automatic browser detection; if you don't set this property, the HttpBrowserCapabilities object associated with the Page.Request object is used instead.
	EnableStateView	True (the default) if all controls retain their values between consecutive requests to the same page; if False, it supersedes individual controls' settings.
	SmartNavigation	Set this property to True to enable smart navigation (works only with Internet Explorer 5.0 or later versions).
	IsPostBack	False if this is the first time the client requests the page, True if the page is doing a postback to itself.
	ErrorPage	The URL of the page that's displayed in case of an unhandled page exception.
Validation	Validators	Returns the collection of all the validation controls on the page.
	IsValid	Returns True if the conditions specified by all the validation controls on the page are met.
Trace	Trace	The TraceContext object you can use to output trace information and diagnostic information.
	TraceEnabled	Set this property to True to enable tracing on this page.
	TraceMode	Specifies how trace messages are ordered; it can be SortByTime or SortByCategory.

Table 23-1 Main Properties of the Page Class *(continued)*

Category	Syntax	Description
Miscellaneous	Controls	The collection of controls on the page.
	ViewState	Returns the ViewState dictionary object that preserves values between postbacks (protected scope).
	TemplateSource-Directory	Returns the virtual directory in which the page resides.
	Cache	The System.Web.Caching.Cache object that you can use to cache a large amount on the server and share it among all the clients of this application.
	User	Returns an IPrincipal object containing information about the current user. The main property of this object is Identity, which in turn exposes the Name, IsAuthenticated, and AuthenticationType properties.

Smart Navigation

During a postback, the page is redrawn and users see a short but annoying flickering. Worse, the scroll position isn't preserved during postbacks (the page scrolls to its top) and the first control on the page takes the input focus. This behavior contrasts with the experience that users have with regular Windows applications and tends to be confusing. If you're working with Internet Explorer 5.0 or a later version, you can overcome all these shortcomings by setting the SmartNavigation property to True, which performs the following tasks:

- Eliminates the flashing that usually occurs when a page is reloaded.
- Preserves the scroll position in longer pages.
- Maintains the input focus between postbacks.
- Retains only the last page state in the browser's history.

This property is especially useful for forms that do a lot of postbacks but whose contents don't change much between postbacks. Remember that it works only with Internet Explorer 5.0 or later versions, even though you can safely set the SmartNavigation property to True even for Internet sites because ASP.NET checks the browser version and ignores this property for down-level browsers, such as earlier versions of Internet Explorer or Navigator.

You can set the SmartNavigation property from the Properties window or by using an @Page directive (as I'll explain later). You can also set it for the entire application by adding a line to the web.config file:

```
<configuration>
    <system.web>
        <pages smartNavigation="true" />
    </system.web>
</configuration>
```

The ViewState Dictionary Object

In classic ASP, the only way to preserve information—for example, the value of a variable—between consecutive client requests is by means of Session variables, cookies, or other awkward techniques, such as arguments on the query string or values in hidden fields.

ASP.NET gives you yet another method in the form of the ViewState property of the Page object. (More precisely, this is a protected property that the Page class inherits from the Control class.) This property represents the contents of the __VIEWSTATE hidden field and works as a StateBag dictionary of key-value pairs. The following example uses the ViewState property to preserve the number of requests to the current page:

```
Private Sub Page_Load(ByVal sender As Object, ByVal e As EventArgs) _
    Handles MyBase.Load

    ' Number of requests to this page posted so far
    Dim count As Integer
    If Not Me.ViewState("count") Is Nothing Then
        count = CInt(Me.ViewState("count")) + 1
    End If
    ' Store the value back in the ViewState dictionary.
    Me.ViewState("count") = count
    ' Display in a Label control.
    lblCount.Text = count.ToString
End Sub
```

Keep in mind that this property works only if you left the EnableViewState property set to True.

Page Methods

Table 23-2 lists the most useful methods of the Page class. You already saw the DataBind method in action, and the meaning of many other methods should be clear if you've worked with classic ASP before. For example, the MapPath method converts a virtual path into a physical path, so it's useful for passing arguments to objects that don't work with virtual paths:

```
Dim sr As New System.IO.StreamReader(Me.MapPath("/data/values.dat"))
```

You can also use MapPath to retrieve information about the current ASP.NET application, as you see in this snippet:

```
' The current directory (same as TemplateSourceDirectory property)
Dim currDir As String = Me.MapPath(".")
' The parent directory
Dim parentDir As String = Me.MapPath("..")
' The root directory
Dim rootDir As String = Me.MapPath("/")
```

The ResolveUrl method converts a relative virtual path into an absolute virtual path, so it's useful for building URLs to be passed to the client (for example, as hyperlinks). Note that the domain name isn't returned by this function, so you must add it explicitly if necessary:

```
' Provide the complete URL to a file.
' (Assumes that the domain URL is www.vb2themax.com.)
Dim url As String = "www.vb2themax.com" & Me.ResolveUrl("/data/values.dat")
```

Table 23-2 Main Methods of the Page Class

Category	Syntax	Description
Path	MapPath(virtualpath)	Converts a virtual path to a physical path (same as the MapPath method of the Server object in classic ASP).
	ResolveUrl(url)	Converts a relative URL to an absolute URL, implicitly using the value of the TemplateSourceDirectory property.
Controls	HasControls	Returns True if the page contains controls.
	FindControl(id)	Returns the server control with the specified id, or Nothing if the control doesn't exist.
	LoadControl(virtualpath)	Loads a UserControl from an .ascx file.
	DataBind	Binds all the child controls to their data source.
	Validate	Forces all the validation controls to validate their associated control; this method is called automatically when the end user clicks a Button, ImageButton, or LinkButton control (and its HTML counterpart) whose CausesValidation property is True.

Page Events

The Page class inherits several events from the Control and TemplateControl classes. (See Table 23-3.) All these events receive a plain EventArgs object in their second argument, so in practice no additional information is passed to the event.

I've already covered a few of these events in the section "The Page Life Cycle" earlier in this chapter. Not counting events raised by transactional pages, the only other event worth mentioning is Error, which fires when an unhandled exception is thrown by code in the page. This event lets you clear the error and redirect the execution flow, if you want, to another page:

```
Private Sub Page_Error(ByVal sender As Object, ByVal e As EventArgs) _
    Handles MyBase.Error
    ' Clear the server error (optional).
    Server.ClearError()
    ' Redirect to another page.
    Server.Transfer("Instructions.aspx")
End Sub
```

Table 23-3 Main Events of the Page Class

Category	Syntax	Description
Inherited from Control class	Init	The page is initialized. This is the first event in the page's life cycle; when this event fires controls are available, but they haven't been initialized yet from the ViewState object.
	Load	The page is being loaded. This event fires after all controls have been initialized from the ViewState object.
	PreRender	Fires before the page sends HTML text to the client.
	Unload	The page is being unloaded.
	Disposed	The page and its controls are being released from memory.
Inherited from TemplateControl class	Error	An unhandled exception is thrown.
	CommitTransaction	A transaction completes (only for transactional pages).
	AbortTransaction	A transaction aborts (only for transactional pages).

Page Directives

Many of the properties that you set inside the Properties window in Visual Studio are converted into attributes of the @Page directive, at the top of the .aspx file. Some of these values appear also as properties of the Page object (and as such they are listed in Table 23-1) and can also be set in code. In some cases, however, they can be set only in the @Page directive.

The .aspx file can host other types of directives, such as @Import and @Implements, which I also cover briefly in this section. Remember that when working with Visual Studio .NET, you rarely have to manage these directives directly.

The @Page Directive

Only one @Page directive can be in an .aspx file, and it's generally placed at the top of the file. Table 23-4 lists all the valid attributes for this directive.

If you create pages with Visual Studio, the Inherits attribute is added automatically, and you never have to use any other attribute in the Dynamic compilation category. I've already shown you page properties that map to attributes in the @Page directive, for example EnableViewState and SmartNavigation. A few other attributes, including Buffer and ContentType, should be clear if you're familiar with classic ASP programming.

The ErrorPage attribute is interesting, in that it lets you redirect any unhandled exception to a custom page, rather than to the default page supplied by ASP.NET. This attribute gives you much greater flexibility than ASP did, in which you had to set the error page's URL using an IIS dialog box. Here's an example of the @Page directive that sets this and a few other attributes:

```
<%@ Page Language="vb" AutoEventWireup="false"
    Codebehind="AutoPostBackForm.aspx.vb" Inherits="FirstWebForm.WebForm2"
    smartNavigation="True" errorPage="/ErrorPage.asp" %>
```

Note that ASP.NET considers any <%@ that lacks an explicit name an @Page directive (or an @Control directive if inside a user control, which I cover in Chapter 25), so the following syntax is legal:

```
<%@ Language="vb" AutoEventWireup="false"
    Codebehind="AutoPostBackForm.aspx.vb" Inherits="FirstWebForm.WebForm2"
       smartNavigation="True" errorPage="/ErrorPage.asp" %>
```

Table 23-4 Attributes for the @Page Directive

Category	Syntax	Description
Behavior	EnableSession-State=value	Determines the kind of access this page has to the Session object. The value can be True (default), False, or ReadOnly.
	EnableViewState=bool	Enables or disables ViewState for all the controls on the page. (Default is True.)
	EnableView-StateMac=bool	If True, ASP.NET runs a machine authentication check (MAC) on the page's ViewState to ensure that the state hasn't been tampered with. (Default is False.)

(continued)

Table 23-4 Attributes for the @Page Directive *(continued)*

Category	Syntax	Description
	SmartNavigation=bool	Enables or disables smart navigation for this page. (Default is False.)
	ErrorPage=url	The URL of the page that's displayed when an unhandled exception is thrown.
Page rendering	Buffer=bool	Enables or disables HTTP buffering; same as the Response.Buffer property in ASP. (Default is True.)
	ContentType=mime-type	The HTTP content type of the response, as a MIME type; same as the Response.ContentType in ASP.
	ResponseEncoding=encoding	The response encoding for this page.
	CodePage=code	The code page value for the response. You must set this attribute only if you're creating a page that uses a code page different from the default code page of the Web server.
	LCID=locale	The locale identifier for this page.
	Culture=string	The culture setting for this page. It takes the same values as the CultureInfo class. (See the section "The CultureInfo Auxiliary Class" in Chapter 8.)
	UICulture=id	The user interface culture setting for this page.
COM and COM+ Compatibility	AspCompat=bool	If True, the page runs in a single-threaded apartment (STA) and can use STA components, such as those authored with Visual Basic 6. You must set it to True also for calling COM+ 1.0 components that access the unmanaged ASP objects through the ObjectContext object. (Default is False.)
	Transaction=mode	Indicates whether transactions are supported for this page. The value can be Disabled (default), NotSupported, Supported, Required, or RequiresNew.
Debug and trace	Debug=bool	Enables or disables the generation of debug symbols for this page. (Default is False.)
	Trace=bool	Enables or disables tracing for this page. (Default is False.)
	TraceMode=value	Determines how trace messages are displayed. The value can be SortByTime (default) or SortByCategory.

Table 23-4 Attributes for the @Page Directive *(continued)*

Category	Syntax	Description
Dynamic compilation	ClassName=name	The name of the class that is compiled automatically the first time the page is requested. The name must not contain spaces.
	Inherits=classname	The code-behind class for the page; can be any class derived from the Page class.
	Language=langname	The language used for inline code enclosed by <% and %> delimiters.
	Src=path	The source filename for the code-behind class.
	Compiler-Options=string	A string containing valid options for the Visual Basic compiler; these options are used when dynamically compiling the page the first time a browser requests it.
	WarningLevel=level	The compiler warning level used when compiling this page dynamically. The level is an integer between 0 and 4.
	Explicit=bool	The Option Explicit setting for dynamically compiled .aspx files authored in Visual Basic .NET. This attribute is set to True in the machine.config file.
	Strict=bool	The Option Strict setting for dynamically compiled .aspx files authored in Visual Basic .NET. (Default is False.)
Miscellaneous	AutoEvent-Wireup=bool	If True, event handlers are automatically associated with the page or the control based on the ObjectName_EventName naming convention, as in Visual Basic 6. (Default is False.)
	ClientTarget=user-agentname	The User Agent name for which server-side controls should render their contents; same as the ClientTarget property.
	Description=text	A description for this page; this value is ignored by the ASP.NET parser.

The @Import Directive

This directive imports a namespace in an .aspx page and is therefore equivalent to a Visual Basic .NET Imports statement. Each @Import directive can specify only one namespace, so you need multiple directives to import more than one namespace:

```
<%@ Import namespace="System.Xml" %>
<%@ Import namespace="System.Xml.Xsl" %>
```

The following namespaces are automatically imported in all pages, and therefore don't need this directive:

- System, System.Collections, System.IO
- System.Collections.Specialized
- System.Text, System.Text.RegularExpressions
- System.Web, System.Web.Caching, System.Web.Security, System.Web.SessionState
- System.Web.UI, System.Web.UI.HtmlControls, System.Web.UI.WebControls

The @Assembly Directive

This directive links an assembly to the current page during compilation so that all the types in the assembly are available to the code in the page. This directive must include either the Name attribute (the name of the assembly) or the Src attribute (the path to a source file that's dynamically compiled and linked to the current page):

```
<%@ Assembly Name="Functions.dll" %>
<%@ Assembly Src="Functions.vb" %>
```

Assemblies that reside in your application's \Bin directory don't need to be referenced by an @Assembly directive because they're automatically linked to pages in the application. You can't include the path to an assembly in this directive.

The @Register Directive

This directive associates an alias with a namespace or a class name to let the developer use a concise notation when referring to custom server controls. You can reference the other namespace or class using two different syntax formats:

```
<%@ Register tagprefix="alias" Namespace="namespace" Assembly="asmname" %>
<%@ Register tagprefix="alias" Tagname="tagname" Src="path" %>
```

In the first case, you associate the alias with the namespace contained in the specified compiled assembly. (Don't include a filename extension in the assembly name.) In the second case, you associate the alias with a custom control contained in a source file that is dynamically compiled when the page is loaded.

The meaning of this directive will be clear when I explain how to create and use custom controls in Web Forms pages, in Chapter 25. For now, let me provide a simple example. Say that you have a compiled assembly named Controls that contains a control named Calculator inside a namespace named MyCompany. Here's how you can reference that control inside an .aspx page:

```
<%@ Register tagprefix="MyComp" Namespace="MyCompany" Assembly="Controls" %>
⋮
<form runat="server">
   <MyComp:Calculator id="Calc1" runat="server" />
</form>
```

The @Reference Directive

This directive tells ASP.NET that another control or page source file should be dynamically compiled and linked to the current page. Two syntax forms are supported, depending on whether you're linking another page or a control:

```
<%@ Reference page=anotherpage.aspx" %>
<%@ Reference control=mycontrol.ascx" %>
```

This directive adds a reference to the other page or control so that the current page can reference it using early binding, even if the control is added dynamically by means of a LoadControl method:

```
<%@ Reference control=mycontrol.ascx" %>
⋮
Private Sub Page_Load(ByVal sender As Object, ByVal e As EventArgs) _
   Dim ctrl As MyControl
   ctrl = DirectCast(Page.LoadControl("mycontrol.ascx"), MyControl)
End Sub
```

Other Directives

The @Implements directive indicates that the current page implements a given interface and so is equivalent to a Visual Basic .NET Implements statement:

```
<%@ Implements Interface="System.Web.UI.IPostBackEventHandler" %>
```

The @Control directive is used to specify attributes of a custom control and can be used only inside .ascx files. It supports many of the attributes that are valid for the @Page directive, such as EnableViewState, Debug, AutoEventWireup, and all the attributes that control dynamic compilation features.

The @OutputCache directive activates one of the most effective features of ASP.NET: the ability to cache the output from a page and use it in subsequent requests for the same page. I'll cover this feature in detail in the "Page Caching" section of Chapter 24.

Web Forms Controls

All the controls in the Web Forms portion of the Framework can be subdivided into the following six groups:

- **HTML Server controls** These 18 controls are the ASP.NET, server-side versions of the standard HTML controls.
- **Web Forms controls** These are the native ASP.NET controls, most of which duplicate and extend the functionality of an HTML server control.
- **Validation controls** This is a group of six controls that are used to validate the contents of other controls (typically text fields).
- **List controls** This group includes all the list box–like ASP.NET controls, namely the DropDownList, ListBox, CheckBoxList, and RadioButtonList controls.
- **Template controls** This group includes the DataList, DataGrid, and Repeater controls. You can customize their appearance and behavior by using templates.
- **Other controls** These controls don't fall into any of the preceding categories: Calendar, AdRotator, and Xml.

All the controls in these groups are server-side controls, which means that they can be initialized and processed by code running on the server. However, a Web Forms page might include plain HTML controls too, which might call client-side controls to distinguish them from the controls in the preceding groups.

You can drop any item from the HTML tab of Visual Studio's Toolbox onto a Web Forms page to create a client-side HTML control. After you've dropped a client-side HTML control onto the form, you can set its properties in the Property window but you can't write code against it, as you'll realize if you double-click on it. A client-side HTML control is rendered on the browser as a plain HTML tag, as you can see here:

```
<INPUT type="text">
<INPUT type="button" value="Button"></P>
```

You might wonder why you should use client-side HTML controls if you can use their more powerful server-side versions. The answer is simple: performance. Client-side controls aren't processed by ASP.NET and are rendered more efficiently. There are several cases for which you don't really need the full power of HTML Server controls—for example, when you have a hyperlink that points to a different page or a button whose only purpose is to run a client-side script.

> **Note** I'm covering all the controls categories in the sections that follow except the template controls, which require a whole section of their own and are covered later in this chapter.

HTML Server Controls

All HTML Server controls are defined in the System.Web.UI.HtmlControls namespace. This group of controls includes the ASP.NET version of the most common HTML controls, and in fact it has been included in the Web Forms portion of the framework to ease the migration from HTML forms. Strictly speaking, you don't need to use HTML Server controls because most HTML Server controls have a corresponding Web Forms control with extended functionality (with the notable exception of the HtmlInputFile control). HTML Server controls expose a limited set of properties whose names match the attributes of the corresponding HTML tag, so they'll look familiar to all HTML and ASP developers.

HTML Server controls are available on the HTML tab of the toolbox (see Figure 23-6), but when you drop one of these items onto the form you don't get an HTML Server control. As I explained previously, this action creates a plain client-side control. To transform a client-side HTML control into its corresponding server-side version, you must add a runat=server attribute. You can do that by editing the actual HTML code in the designer or more simply by right-clicking on the control and clicking Run As Server Control on the shortcut menu.

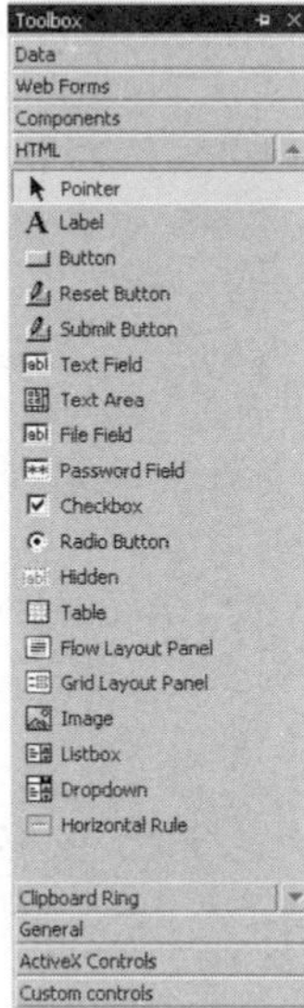

Figure 23-6. The HTML tab of the Toolbox.

The HtmlControl and HtmlContainerControl Base Classes

All the controls in the System.Web.UI.HtmlControls namespace derive from the HtmlControl class. This base class offers basic functionality that's shared by all the HTML Server controls. A few controls—more specifically, those that always have a closing tag, such as <select> and <table>—derive from the HtmlContainerControl (which in turn inherits from HtmlControl). Table 23-5 lists the main properties, methods, and events of these base classes.

Table 23-5 Main Members of the HtmlControl and HtmlContainerControl Base Classes

Category	Syntax	Description
Properties	Attributes	The AttributeCollection that describes all the attributes associated with this control. You can create a new attribute by using the Add method of this collection.
	ClientID	The server control identifier generated by ASP.NET.
	Controls	The collection of all child controls for this server control.
	Disabled	A Boolean value that indicates whether the control is disabled.
	EnableViewState	A Boolean value that indicates whether the value of this control is saved in the parent page's ViewState.
	ID	The programmatic identifier assigned to the control.
	Page	Returns the Page object to which this control belongs.
	Parent	Returns the parent control of this control.
	Style	Returns a collection of Cascading Style Sheet (CSS) properties applied to the control.
	TagName	Returns the name of the HTML tag used to render this control.
	Visible	A Boolean that determines whether the control is visible.
Properties derived from HtmlContainerControl	InnerHtml	Sets or gets the HTML and text contents embedded between the opening and closing tags for this control.
	InnerText	Sets or gets the text contents embedded between the opening and closing tags for this control.

Table 23-5 Main Members of the HtmlControl and HtmlContainerControl Base Classes *(continued)*

Category	Syntax	Description
Methods	DataBind	Binds a data source to the control.
	Dispose	Releases resources used by the control.
	FindControl(name)	Returns the child control with the specified name.
	HasControls	Returns True if the control has child controls.
Events	DataBinding	Fires when the control binds to a data source.
	Disposed	Fires when the control is being disposed.
	Init	Fires when the control is being initialized.
	Load	Fires when the control is being loaded in its parent page.
	PreRender	Fires when the control is about to render its contents to its containing page.
	Unload	Fires when the control is being unloaded from memory.

I've already described many of the properties, methods, and events in common among HTML Server controls, so I won't explain them again here. A couple of collection properties require a more complete description, however.

The Attributes collection gathers all the attributes associated with the HTML Server control. You can use it to iterate over existing attributes, as this code does:

```
Dim key As String
Dim res As String = ""
' Iterate over the Attributes collection of the Text1 control.
For Each key In Text1.Attributes.Keys
    If res.Length > 0 Then res &= ", "
    res &= key & "=" & Text1.Attributes.Item(key)
Next
' Show the result in a Label control.
lblResult.InnerText = res
```

The Add method lets you add new items to the Attributes collection:

```
' Add a size attribute and set it equal to 30.
Text1.Attributes.Add("size", "30")
```

Browsers ignore HTML attributes that they don't recognize. This behavior lets you use the Attributes collection as a sort of grab bag for values that are related to the control and that you want to persist between postbacks but don't want to store in the page's ViewState. Say that you want to store the first nonempty value that the user types in the Text1 control so that you can compare it with the value found in subsequent postbacks:

```
Private Sub Page_Load(ByVal sender As Object, ByVal e As EventArgs) _
    Handles MyBase.Load

    ' Check whether the InitialValue attribute is still empty.
    If Text1.Attributes("InitialValue") = "" Then
       ' If the control's value isn't an empty string
       If Text1.Value.Length > 0 Then
           ' Store the initial value in the Attributes collection.
           Text1.Attributes.Add("InitialValue", Text1.Value)
       End If
    End If
End Sub
```

The Style property returns a collection of style attributes; you can iterate over this collection or add new items to it, as you do with the Attributes collection:

```
' Change the background color of the Text1 control.
Text1.Style.Add("background-color", "Aqua")
```

You don't have to use the Add method because the default Item property will do:

```
Text1.Style("font-family") = "Tahoma"
Text1.Style("font-size") = "20px"
Text1.Style("color") = "red"
```

Main Properties and Events

Table 23-6 lists all the HTML Server controls, the corresponding HTML tags, and their main properties and events. No HTML Server control exposes any method in addition to those defined in the base HtmlControl class. The last three classes in the table don't correspond to any element in the HTML tab of the Toolbox, so these controls can be created only programmatically or by inserting HTML text directly. A few properties are common to several controls:

- The Type property returns the value of the type attribute, such as text or password.
- The Size property determines the width of single-line text and input file fields, whereas the MaxLength property tells how many characters the user can type in these controls.
- The CausesValidation property determines whether a click on the control activates the form validation.

Check boxes and radio buttons don't expose a Text property, unlike their Windows Forms and Web Forms counterparts. To provide such a control with a caption, you must add a label or type some text to its right. Also, no HTML Server control exposes the AutoPostBack property; to leverage this feature you must use Web Forms controls.

HTML Server controls can expose only one of these two events: ServerChange (for controls that contain a textual value) or ServerClick (for button-like controls). Their use is straightforward:

```
Private Sub Password1_ServerChange(ByVal sender As Object, _
    ByVal e As EventArgs) Handles Password1.ServerChange
    ' Save the current password value.
    myPwd = Password1.Value
End Sub
```

Table 23-6 HTML Controls and Their Main Properties and Events

Class	HTML Tag	Properties	Events
HtmlInputText	<input type="text"> <input type="password">	Name, Type, Size, MaxLength, Value	ServerChange
HtmlInputCheck-Box	<input type="checkbox">	Name, Type, Checked, Value	ServerChange
HtmlInputRadio-Button	<input type="radio">	Name, Type, Checked, Value	ServerChange
HtmlInputButton	<input type="button"> <input type="submit"> <input type="reset">	Name, Type, Value, CausesValidation	ServerClick
HtmlInput-Hidden	<input type="hidden">	Name, Type, Value	ServerChange
HtmlInputFile	<input type="file">	Name, Type, Value, Size, MaxLength, Value, Accept, PostedFile	(none)
HtmlTextArea	<textarea>...</textarea>	Name, Type, Cols, Rows, Value	ServerChange
HtmlSelect	<select>...</select>	Name, Size, Multiple, Value, SelectedIndex, Items, DataSource, DataMember, DataTextField, DataValueField	ServerChange
HtmlImage	<img>	Src, Align, Border, Width, Height, Alt	(none)

(continued)

Table 23-6 HTML Controls and Their Main Properties and Events *(continued)*

Class	HTML Tag	Properties	Events
HtmlTable	<table>...</table>	Width, Height, Align, BgColor, Border, BorderColor, CellPadding, CellSpacing, Rows	(none)
HtmlTableRow	<tr>...</tr>	Height, Align, VAlign, BgColor, BorderColor, Cells	(none)
HtmlTableCell	<td>...</td> <th>...</th>	Width, Height, Align, VAlign, BgColor, BorderColor, RowSpan, ColSpan, NoWrap	(none)
HtmlAnchor	<a>...</a>	Name, HRef, Target, Title	ServerClick
HtmlGenericControl	(any)	TagName	(none)
HtmlInputImage	<input type="image">	Name, Type, Src, Align, Border, CausesValidation	ServerClick

The HtmlGeneric control is a generic object used to render any HTML tag that isn't included in the table. Its peculiarity is that its TagName property is writable. For more information, read the .NET SDK documentation.

The HTML tab of the Toolbox contains three controls that don't appear in Table 23-6 and that map to the <div> tag. The Label control offers a simple way to enter aligned or data-bound text. The Flow Layout Panel and the Grid Layout Panel controls define an area in the form in which controls are laid out as if the pageLayout property is set to FlowLayout or GridLayout, respectively.

I don't mean to devote many pages to HTML Server controls because, as I mentioned previously, they're provided mainly to ease the migration from classic ASP forms. For new ASP.NET applications, you should use Web Forms controls exclusively. For this reason and for the self-describing nature of most properties of these controls, I'll focus exclusively on the features that are less obvious.

The HtmlSelect Class

You can assign most properties of an HtmlSelect control from the Properties window: for example, you set its Size property equal to the number of desired rows, or to 0 to create a drop-down list. (In fact, this property is what makes the difference between a list box and a drop-down list box HTML control.)

You can add elements programmatically by using the Add method of the Items collection. This method takes either a string or a ListItem element. If you pass a string, it works as both the caption of the element and its value. If instead you pass a ListItem element, you can specify different strings for the caption and its value:

```
' Add three elements - caption and value are the same string.
' (Tip: Always clear the Items collection first.)
Select1.Items.Clear
Select1.Items.Add("Computer")
Select1.Items.Add("Monitor")
Select1.Items.Add("Keyboard")

' Fill the control with the list of month names.
Select2.Items.Clear()
Dim i As Integer
For i = 1 To 12
    ' Create a ListItem object on the fly.
    Select2.Items.Add(New ListItem(MonthName(i), CStr(i)))
Next
```

At run time, you can determine which element has been selected by checking the SelectedIndex property or the Value property, which returns the value attribute of the selected element. If you want to see the selected element's caption, you must query the Text property of the selected ListItem element:

```
With Select1.Items(Select1.SelectedIndex)
    System.Diagnostics.Debug.WriteLine(.Text)     ' The caption
    System.Diagnostics.Debug.WriteLine(.Value)    ' The value
End With
```

You can create multiple selection list box controls by setting the Multiple property to True. In this case, you retrieve the caption and value of selected items by checking the Selected property of each element in the Items collection:

```
Dim li As ListItem
For Each li In Select2.Items
    If li.Selected Then
        System.Diagnostics.Debug.WriteLine(li.Text & " (" & li.Value & ")")
    End If
Next
```

The HtmlTable, HtmlTableRow, and HtmlTableCell Classes

An HTML table consists of an HtmlTable object, which exposes a Rows collection. Each element of this collection is an HtmlTableRow object, which in turn exposes a Cells collection of HtmlTableCell elements. The properties that these classes expose let you finely control the appearance of the table and its cells:

- The Width and Height properties affect the size of the table or an individual cell. The HtmlTableRow class doesn't expose these properties because a row is as wide as the table and as tall as its tallest cell.
- The BgColor property affects the background color of the table, its rows, or its individual cells. This property can be assigned a value in the format #RRGGBB (the red, green, and blue components in hex format) or a predefined color name in the following list: Black, Blue, Cyan, Gray, Green, Lime, Magenta, Maroon, Navy, Olive, Purple, Red, Silver, Teal, White, or Yellow.
- You can control the appearance of the border by using the Border property (border width in pixels) and the BorderColor property.
- The Align property can be Left, Center, or Right and affects the horizontal alignment of the table, its rows, and its individual cells. The VAlign property can be Top, Middle, or Bottom and is used with table rows and cells to control their vertical alignment.
- The CellPadding property sets the distance in pixels between a table cell and the table border. The CellSpacing property sets the distance between adjacent cells in the table.
- The ColSpan property determines how many table columns a given cell takes. The RowSpan property determines how many table rows a cell takes.

You create a table programmatically by adding HtmlTableCell objects to an HtmlTableRow, and then adding the HtmlTableRow object to the table. Here's a code snippet that creates a table with 3 rows of 4 cells each. (See Figure 23-7.)

```
Dim row, col As Integer
For row = 0 To 2
    ' Add a new row to the table.
    Dim tr As New HtmlTableRow()
    For col = 0 To 3
        ' Define a new table cell.
        Dim tc As New HtmlTableCell()
        tc.InnerText = "(" & CStr(row) & "," & CStr(col) & ")"
        ' Add the cell to the table row.
        tr.Cells.Add(tc)
    Next
    ' Add the row to the table.
    Table1.Rows.Add(tr)
Next
```

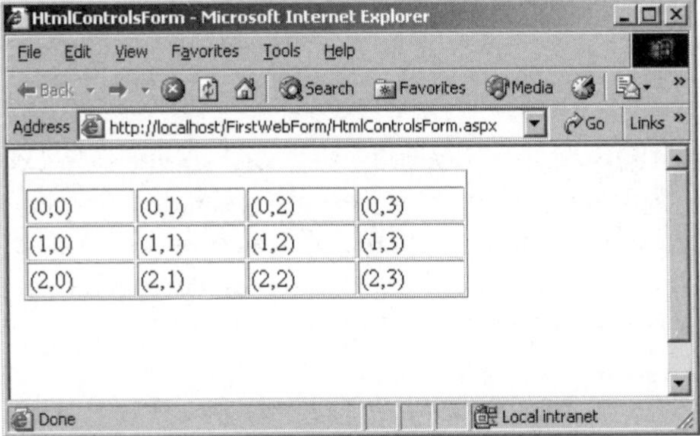

Figure 23-7. An HtmlTable control rendered in Internet Explorer.

You set the text inside each cell by means of the InnerText or InnerHtml property. You can also affect its background color with the BgColor property, and the alignment of the text with the Align and VAlign properties.

The HtmlInputFile Class

The HtmlInputFile control is a combination of a text box field and a button. (See Figure 23-8.) It lets the user upload a file to the Web server so that your ASP.NET code can grab it and save it locally for further processing. This control works on Internet Explorer 3.02 or later, and compatible browsers.

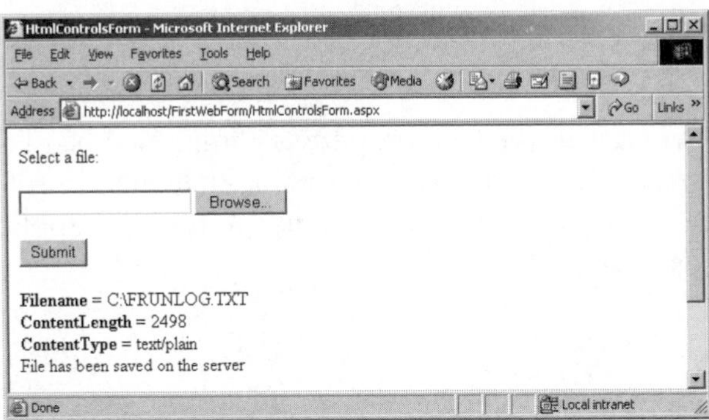

Figure 23-8. The HtmlInputFile control in action.

The HtmlInputFile control requires that the Enctype property of the form be set to multipart/form-data. You can't set this property in the Properties window if you're in design mode, so you must switch to HTML mode and click on the <form> tag. At this point, all the form properties appear in the Properties window and you can assign the property. The <form> tag should now look like this:

```
<form id="Form1" method="post" runat="server" enctype="multipart/form-data">
```

The HtmlInputFile control doesn't raise any server-side events, so you must add at least a Submit button to process it. You can determine name, size, and type of the file being posted by means of the control's PostedFile property, which exposes also a SaveAs method to save the file on the server. Here's some demo code that shows how to work with this control:

```
' Button1 is the submit button on the form.
Private Sub Button1_ServerClick(ByVal sender As Object, _
    ByVal e As EventArgs) Handles Button1.ServerClick
    Dim msg As String
    If Not File1.PostedFile Is Nothing Then
        ' Determine properties of the posted file.
        msg = "Filename = " & File1.PostedFile.FileName & "<br>"
        msg &= "ContentLength = " & File1.PostedFile.ContentLength & "<br>"
        msg &= "ContentType = " & File1.PostedFile.ContentType & "<br>"
        ' Save it on the server.
        File1.PostedFile.SaveAs("C:\file.dat")
        msg &= "File has been saved on the server"
    Else
        ' No file has been posted.
        msg = "No file has been posted"
    End If
    ' Show the message in a Label control.
    DIV1.InnerHtml = msg
End Sub
```

You can set the control's Accept property to limit the type of files that can be posted to the server. This property is a comma-delimited list of valid MIME types—for example, image/* for accepting all image types or application/octet-stream to accept .exe files.

Web Forms Controls

All the Web Forms controls are located on the Web Forms tab of the Visual Studio Toolbox and belong to the System.Web.UI.WebControls namespace. However, in this section I'll describe only the simplest controls in this group, namely those that extend the functionality of basic HTML controls. Template controls aren't in this group and are discussed later in this chapter. Figure 23-9 shows how these controls appear in the Visual Studio .NET designer.

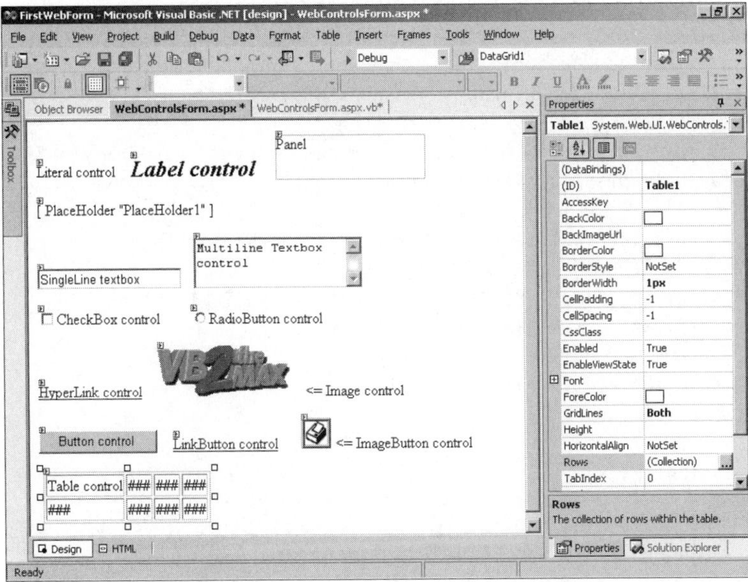

Figure 23-9. The Web Forms controls at design time.

Although HTML Server controls are rendered in the Visual Studio HTML editor as plain HTML tags, Web Forms controls create special XML tags in the <asp:*classname*> format. For example, this is how the controls in Figure 23-9 appear in the HTML editor, after I've trimmed some portions to make the text more concise:

```
<form id="Form1" method="post" runat="server">
  <asp:Literal id="Literal1" runat="server"
    Text="Literal control"></asp:Literal>
  <asp:Label id="Label1" runat="server" Font-Bold="True"
    Font-Italic="True" Font-Size="Large">Label control</asp:Label>
  <asp:Panel id="Panel1" runat="server" Width="160px"
    Height="47px">Panel</asp:Panel>
  <asp:PlaceHolder id="PlaceHolder1" runat="server"></asp:PlaceHolder>
  <asp:TextBox id="TextBox1" runat="server">SingleLine textbox</asp:TextBox>
  <asp:TextBox id="TextBox2" runat="server" TextMode="MultiLine"
    Rows="3">Multiline Textbox control</asp:TextBox>
  <asp:CheckBox id="CheckBox1" runat="server"
    Text="CheckBox control"></asp:CheckBox>
  <asp:RadioButton id="RadioButton1" runat="server"
    Text="RadioButton control"></asp:RadioButton>
  <asp:HyperLink id="HyperLink1" runat="server">
```

(continued)

```
    HyperLink control</asp:HyperLink>   
  <asp:Image id="Image1" runat="server" ImageUrl="\logo.gif"></asp:Image>
  <asp:Button id="Button1" runat="server" Text="Button control"></asp:Button>
  <asp:LinkButton id="LinkButton1" runat="server">
    LinkButton control </asp:LinkButton>
  <asp:ImageButton id="ImageButton1" runat="server" BorderStyle="Ridge"
    ImageUrl="print.gif"></asp:ImageButton>

  <asp:Table id="Table1" runat="server" BorderWidth="1px" GridLines="Both">
    <asp:TableRow>
      <asp:TableCell Text="Table control"></asp:TableCell>
      <asp:TableCell></asp:TableCell>
        <asp:TableCell></asp:TableCell>
      <asp:TableCell></asp:TableCell>
    </asp:TableRow>
    ⋮
  </asp:Table></P>
</form>
```

Unlike HTML Server controls, Web Forms controls expose a consistent set of properties, whose names don't necessarily reflect the name of the HTML attribute to which they map. For example, all the Web Forms controls expose a Text property that determines the string displayed in the control. Even HTML controls that don't display a caption—for example, check boxes and radio buttons—expose the Text property (which in this case is opportunely translated into plain text adjacent to the control). Another example: all controls expose the BorderStyle and BorderColor properties for controlling the border drawn around the control. If the control doesn't have a native border, it's embedded in a <span> tag with an appropriate Border-style style attribute.

The WebControl Base Class

All visible Web Forms controls derive from the WebControl class and therefore inherit its properties, methods, and events. So it makes sense to have a look at this abstract class before I describe more specific controls. I summarized the main members of the WebControl class in Table 23-7 but omitted members of interest only to control authors.

You're already familiar with the methods and events exposed by the WebControl class because they're inherited from the Control class (which is also the base class for the Page object). Most of the properties are self-explanatory—such as ForeColor, BackColor, and ToolTip—or have been described previously, such as EnableViewState and Attributes.

You might have problems working with the Width, Height, and BorderWidth properties because they must be assigned a Unit object. This auxiliary class exposes shared methods to convert from pixels, points (1/72 inch), and from a percentage value (relative to the container's width).

```
MyControl.Width = Unit.Pixel(100)      ' 100 pixels
MyControl.Width = Unit.Point(144)      ' 144 points (2 inches)
MyControl.Width = Unit.Percentage(50) ' 50% of the parent's width
```

You can also use the Parse method to convert from a string, as in this code snippet:

```
MyControl.Width = Unit.Parse("170px") ' 170 pixels
MyControl.Width = Unit.Parse("60%")   ' 60% of the parent's width
```

Table 23-7 Main Members of the WebControl Class

Category	Syntax	Description
Identification properties	ClientID	The server control identifier generated by ASP.NET.
	ID	The programmatic identifier assigned to the control.
	Page	Returns the Page object to which this control belongs.
	Parent	Returns the parent control of this control.
Behavior properties	AccessKey	The access key that lets you move the focus to this control by using an Alt-key combination.
	TabIndex	The tab index for this control.
	Enabled	A Boolean that determines whether the control is enabled.
	EnableViewState	A Boolean that indicates whether the value of this control is saved in the parent page's ViewState.
	Controls	The collection of all the child controls for this server control.
Appearance properties	Width	The width of this control.
	Height	The height of this control.
	Visible	A Boolean that determines whether the control is visible.
	ForeColor	The foreground color.
	BackColor	The background color.
	Font	The FontInfo object that describes the font used by this control. This object exposes the following properties: Names, Name, Size, Bold, Italic, Strikeout, Underline, and Overline.

(continued)

Table 23-7 Main Members of the WebControl Class *(continued)*

Category	Syntax	Description
	ToolTip	The text of the ToolTip for this control.
	Attributes	The AttributeCollection that describes all the attributes associated with this control. You can create a new attribute by using the Add method of this collection.
	Style	Returns a collection of Cascading Style Sheet (CSS) properties applied to the control.
	CssClass	The name of the CSS class rendered by the control on the client.
Border properties	BorderColor	The border color.
	BorderStyle	The border style. It can be NotSet (default), None, Dotted, Dashed, Solid, Double, Groove, Ridge, Inset, or Outset.
	BorderWidth	The border width, expressed as a Unit object.
Methods	DataBind	Binds a data source to the control.
	Dispose	Releases resources used by the control.
	FindControl(name)	Returns the child control with the specified name.
	HasControls	Returns True if the control has child controls.
Events	DataBinding	Fires when the control binds to a data source.
	Disposed	Fires when the control is being disposed of.
	Init	Fires when the control is being initialized.
	Load	Fires when the control is being loaded in its parent page.
	PreRender	Fires when the control is about to render its contents to its containing page.
	Unload	Fires when the control is being unloaded from memory.

Main Properties and Events

Table 23-8 lists the basic Web Forms controls, the corresponding HTML tags, and their main properties and events. (These Web Forms controls don't expose any methods other than those inherited by the WebControl class.) You already know how to use many of these properties, either because I have already described them—as is the case with the AutoPostBack and MaxLength properties—or because their names and meanings are the same as in the Windows Forms package (for example, the Text, Checked, Wrap, and TextAlign properties).

Table 23-8 Web Forms Controls and Their Main Properties and Events

Class	HTML Tag	Properties	Events
Literal	plain text	Text	(none)
Label	<span>...</span>	Text	(none)
Panel	<div>...</div>	BackImageUrl, HorizontalAlign, Wrap	(none)
PlaceHolder	(none)	(none)	(none)
TextBox	<input type="text"> <input type="password"> <textarea>...</textarea>	AutoPostBack, TextMode, ReadOnly, MaxLength, Rows, Columns, Wrap, Text	TextChanged
CheckBox	<input type="checkbox">	AutoPostBack, Checked, Text, TextAlign	CheckedChanged
RadioButton	<input type="radio">	AutoPostBack, Checked, Text, TextAlign, GroupName	CheckedChanged
Image	<img>	ImageUrl, ImageAlign, AlternateText	(none)
HyperLink	<a>...</a>	ImageUrl, Text, NavigateUrl, Target	(none)
Button	<input type="submit"> <input type="button">	Text, CausesValidation, CommandName, CommandArgument	Click, Command
LinkButton	<a>...</a>	Text, CausesValidation, CommandName, CommandArgument	Click, Command
ImageButton	<a><img ...></a>	ImageUrl, ImageAlign, AlternateText, CausesValidation, CommandName, CommandArgument	Click, Command
Table	<table>...</table>	BackImageUrl, GridLines, HorizontalAlign, CellPadding, CellSpacing, Rows	(none)
TableRow	<tr>...</tr>	HorizontalAlign, VerticalAlign, Cells	(none)
TableCell	<td>...</td>	Text, HorizontalAlign, VerticalAlign, Wrap, ColumnSpan, RowSpan	(none)

The Literal, Label, Panel, and PlaceHolder Controls

The Literal control is undoubtedly the simplest Web Forms control because it exposes only one property and no events. You can use it to insert any HTML text you want by using its Text property. Your insertion can be an HTML tag or just text:

```
Literal1.Text = "Just plain text"
Literal2.Text = "<I><B>Bold Italic Text</I></B>
```

Also the Label control exposes only the Text property, which it renders inside a <span> and </span> pair of tags. Unlike the Literal control (which derives from Control), the Label control inherits many style properties from its WebControl base class, so you can display a message with a foreground and background color, your preferred font, and so on.

The Panel can be used to define an HTML region enclosed between <div> and </div> tags. The BackImageUrl property lets you specify a background image that's automatically tiled to fill the screen portion assigned to the Panel, and you can decide how the contents are aligned by using the HorizontalAlign and Wrap properties.

The PlaceHolder control doesn't generate any HTML text. Rather, it simply provides a way for you to insert new controls in a specific position on the form dynamically at run time by using its Controls collection:

```
' Use a Literal control to display static text.
PlaceHolder1.Controls.Add(New LiteralControl("Enter the name of the user"))
' Create a TextBox control, and set its main properties.
Dim tb As New TextBox()
tb.Width = Unit.Pixel(100)
tb.ID = "txtUser"
' Show it on the form using the PlaceHolder control.
PlaceHolder1.Controls.Add(tb)
```

The HyperLink, Image, Button, LinkButton, and ImageButton Controls

These controls offer similar functionality and it's easy to get confused, so I'll describe them together and compare their properties.

The Image control is the simplest of the group because it maps to the <img> HTML tag. It exposes only three properties and no events. ImageUrl is the URL of the image. ImageAlign is an enumerated value that tells how the image must be aligned. AlternateText is the text displayed if the browser has disabled graphics rendering. When you're assigning the ImageUrl property from the Properties window, you can select an image by using the Select Image dialog box. (See Figure 23-10.)

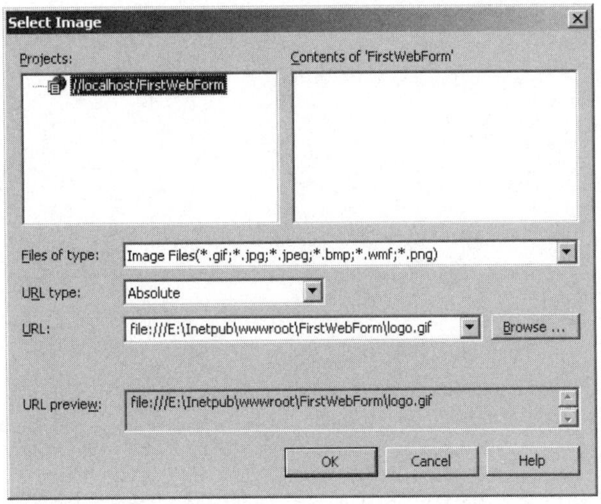

Figure 23-10. The Select Image dialog box.

The HyperLink control maps to the <a> HTML tag. As a nice touch, you can specify either a string (with the Text property) or an image (with the ImageUrl property) for the visible portion of the hyperlink. You can assign both the ImageUrl and the NavigateUrl property using a dialog box. The Target property indicates the target frame in the page pointed to by the NavigateUrl property. Like the Image control, the HyperLink control never does a postback: when the user clicks on it, the browser jumps to the new URL without raising any server-side events.

The Button control implements the standard submit button, with a few additional capabilities. You can place multiple buttons on the form, each one with a different CommandName property (for example, Edit, Sort, GroupBy) and possibly a different CommandArgument property as well (for example, Ascending or Descending to specify the direction of the sort operation). These properties are especially useful when the button is used inside a template control such as DataList, but they simplify programming even when the button is placed directly on the form's surface.

You can trap clicks on a Button control by means of either its Click or Command event. A click fires both events in all cases, but the latter event lets you access the values of the CommandName or CommandArgument properties to determine the action that the user requested:

```
' This routine handles the Command event from three Button controls.
Private Sub Button_Command(ByVal sender As Object, _
    ByVal e As CommandEventArgs) _
    Handles btnEdit.Command, btnSortAsc.Command, btnSortDesc.Command
```

(continued)

```
    Select Case e.CommandName
        Case "Edit"
            ' Start an edit operation.
            ⋮
        Case "Sort"
            If e.CommandArgument = "Ascending" Then
                ' Perform an ascending sort.
                ⋮
            ElseIf e.CommandArgument = "Descending" Then
                ' Perform a descending sort.
                ⋮
            Else
                ' (This should never happen.)
            End If
    End Select
End Sub
```

The LinkButton appears to the user as a textual hyperlink but works more like a Button control in that it supports the CommandName and CommandArgument properties and raises both a Click and a Command server-side event. It doesn't support the NavigateUrl and the Target properties, and if you want to redirect the browser to another page you must do it manually using a Response.Redirect or a Server.Transfer method from inside the server-side event.

Finally, the ImageButton control implements a graphical, clickable button that raises both the Click and the Command server-side events. You can therefore consider it a mix between the Image control (its base class, from which it inherits the ImageUrl, ImageAlign, and AlternateText properties) and the Button control (from which it borrows the CausesValidation, CommandName, and CommandArgument properties, but not the Text property). Here's a summary of when to use each control described in this section:

- Use an Image control to display an image that doesn't react to clicks.
- Use a HyperLink control to display a link to another page that doesn't require any server-side processing.
- Use a Button control for the usual push button control that must fire a server-side event when clicked.
- Use a LinkButton control for a hyperlink element that must fire a server-side event when clicked.
- Use an ImageButton control for a clickable image that must fire a server-side event.

Other Web Forms Controls

The TextBox control exposes the TextMode property, an enumerated value that can be SingleLine, MultiLine, or Password. If it's a multiline TextBox, you can use the Rows and Columns properties to affect its size and the Wrap property to enable or disable word wrapping.

The RadioButton control exposes a GroupName property. All the RadioButton controls on a form with the same value for this property comprise a group of options that are mutually exclusive. You must always assign a non-empty string to this property, even if there's only a group of radio buttons on the form, else each control will be considered a group by itself and won't work as expected.

The Table, TableRow, and TableCell controls work exactly like their HTML Server control counterparts, including the ability to add new rows and columns using the Rows and Columns collection. You can, however, assign the contents of a table cell using the Text property (instead of the InnerText or InnerHtml properties for HTML controls). Another important difference is how the Visual Studio designer deals with the Table control: by clicking on the Rows item in the Properties window you can add rows and cells at design time, using the dialog boxes shown in Figure 23-11 and without writing any code at all.

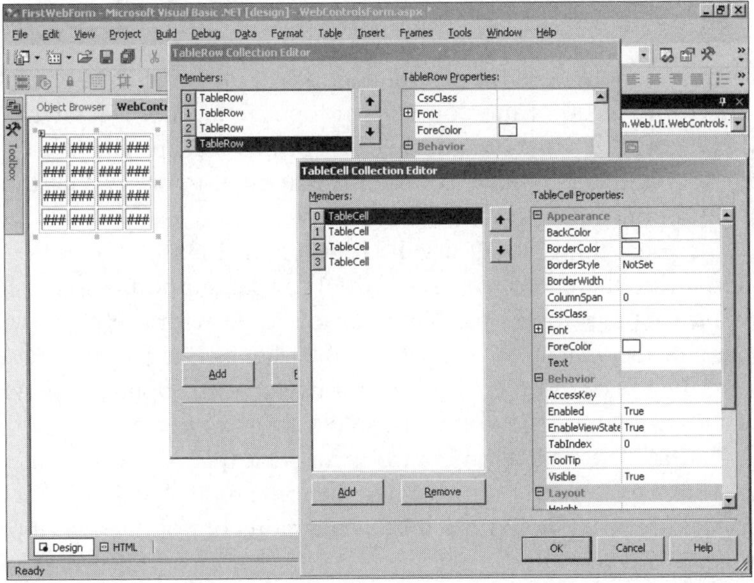

Figure 23-11. Creating TableRow and TableCell elements at design time.

Validation Controls

The Web Forms portion of the framework support six validation controls, whose purpose is to perform the most common type of validation on other controls on the form, typically TextBox controls:

- The RequiredFieldValidator control checks that a given input control isn't empty.
- The RangeValidator control checks that the value of an input control is within a specified range of valid values.
- The CompareValidator control checks that the value of an input control is equal to, lower than, or higher than another value, which can be a constant or the contents of another control.
- The RegularExpressionValidator control checks that the value in an input control matches a given regular expression.
- The CustomValidator control defines a client-side or server-side function (or both) that validates the contents of an input control.
- The ValidationSummary control gathers the error messages from all the validation controls on the same form and displays them in a region of the form or in a message box.

An important note: all the validation controls except RequiredFieldValidator check the value of the companion input field only if it isn't empty; if the field is empty, the validation succeeds. For this reason, you must use an additional RequiredFieldValidator control if you want to check that the input field contains a nonempty value.

The great thing about a validation control is that the validation is performed inside the client browser if the browser supports scripts. If client-side scripting isn't supported (or has been disabled with the page's ClientTarget property or the validation control's EnableClientScript property), the validation is performed on the server. The test for client-side scripting is performed automatically, and your code will work smoothly in all cases.

The first five validation controls can send their error message to the ValidationSummary control on the same page or can display their own message. In the latter case, you should place the validation control near the input control it validates.

Properties, Methods, and Events

All the validation controls except ValidationSummary derive from the BaseValidator base class, from which they inherit the properties and methods they have in common:

- The ControlToValidate property is the name of the input control to be validated.
- The EnableClientScript property is a Boolean value that determines whether validation can be performed via client-side scripts, if possible. (The default is True.)
- The Enabled property is a Boolean value that tells whether the validation must be performed. (The default is True.)
- The ErrorMessage property is the string displayed in the validation control or in the ValidationSummary control if the validation fails.
- The Display property is an enumerated value that specifies whether and how the error message is displayed in the validation control. It can be Static (the default, space for the message is allocated on the form), Dynamic (the validation control takes screen space only when it displays the error message), or None (the error message is never displayed in the validation control).
- The IsValid property is a Boolean that tells whether the validation failed and the error message should be displayed. It can be set programmatically to suppress unwanted error messages.
- The Validate method performs the validation on the associated input control and updates the IsValid property.

The Display property tells whether the error message appears in the validation control. When you use the Static setting (the default), the validation control is resized to contain the error message, but the message itself is initially hidden. This setting ensures that the form layout doesn't suddenly change when the error message is actually displayed. (Most validation controls display the error message as soon as the user moves the focus from the input control containing the value that fails the validation.) The error message is made visible by the client-side script code that performs the validation. If client-side scripts are disabled, the Static setting is ignored because the page must be rebuilt anyway on the server, and the validation control behaves as if the Dynamic setting had been specified.

The BaseValidator class derives from the Label control and therefore inherits all the usual display properties, such as BackColor, BorderStyle, BorderColor, and Font. By default, the ForeColor property of validation controls is set to red, but you can change it to match your form's color scheme.

The Text property behaves in a peculiar way with validation controls, however. Even if you specify a nonempty string for this property, it becomes visible only when the associated input control fails to validate (and only if the Display property isn't None). If you leave the Text property empty, the ErrorMessage value is shown instead. However, the string shown inside the ValidationSummary control is always taken from the ErrorString property, not the Text property. Therefore you can implement several different behaviors:

- You can display the same message near the input control and in the ValidationSummary control by assigning the message to the ErrorMessage property and leaving the Text property empty.
- You can display a message near the input control and a different message in the ValidationSummary control by assigning these messages to the Text and ErrorMessage properties, respectively. For example, you might assign an asterisk to the Text property so that the user can immediately see which fields failed the validation and read a more descriptive error message in the ValidationSummary control.
- You can display just a message near the input control by storing it in the Text property and assigning an empty string to the ErrorMessage property.
- You can display just a message in the ValidationSummary control by assigning the message to the ErrorMessage property and setting the Display property to None.

In addition to the common members inherited from BaseValidator, each validation control exposes its own specific properties and events, which I explain in the following sections.

I've prepared a form that contains one example of each validation control, plus a ValidationSummary control at the top of the page. (See Figure 23-12.) As you'll see, in all cases except the CustomValidator control you don't have to write any code to perform validation chores.

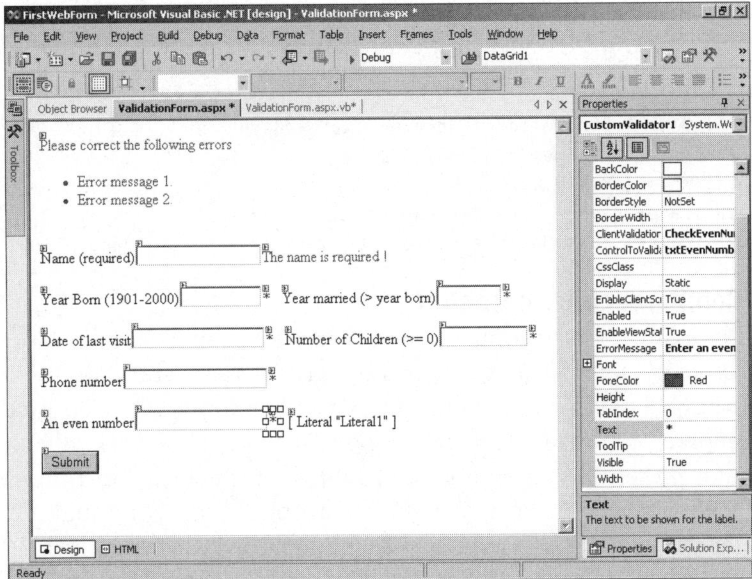

Figure 23-12. A demo form for testing all the validation controls, at design time and run time.

The RequiredFieldValidator Control

The RequiredFieldValidator control is the simplest of the group; you just assign the name of the control that must contain a value to its ControlToValidate property and set a suitable error message:

```
' Check that the txtUserName control contains a nonempty string.
RequiredFieldValidator1.ControlToValidate = "txtUserName"
RequiredFieldValidator1.ErrorMessage = "User name is a required field"
```

The RequiredFieldValidator control checks that the value of the input control differs from the value of its InitialValue property (which is a null string by default), so you can still use this validation control if the initial value of the input field isn't a null string. This feature is useful if a TextBox control is initialized with a message such as "(Enter your email address)".

```
RequiredFieldValidator1.ControlToValidate = "txtEMailAddress"
RequiredFieldValidator1.InitialValue = "(Enter your email address)"
```

The RangeValidator Control

The RangeValidator control exposes three properties: MinimumValue, MaximumValue, and Type. The third property determines the type of the value and affects how the values are compared. It can be String (the default), Integer,

Double, Date, and Currency. This code uses a RangeValidator control to check whether a txtYearBorn field contains a value in the range 1901 to 2000 (inclusive):

```
RangeValidator1.ControlToValidate = "txtYearBorn"
RangeValidator1.MinimumValue = "1901"
RangeValidator1.MaximumValue = "2000"
RangeValidator1.Type = ValidationDataType.Integer
RangeValidator1.ErrorMessage = "Year Born must be in the range [1901,2000]"
```

The CompareValidator Control

The CompareValidator control can compare the contents of the associated input control with another value, either the constant value specified by the ValueToCompare property or the contents of another control specified by the ControlToCompare property. The Type property tells the type of both values, and the Operator property is an enumerated value that specifies the comparison operator to be applied to the two values (can be Equal, NotEqual, GreaterThan, GreaterThanEqual, LessThan, LessThanEqual, or DataTypeCheck). The following code checks that the txtYearMarried control contains an integer value that's greater than the value of the txtYearBorn control:

```
CompareValidator1.ControlToValidate = "txtYearMarried"
CompareValidator1.ControlToCompare = "txtYearBorn"
CompareValidator1.Type = ValidationDataType.Integer
CompareValidator1.Operator = ValidationCompareOperator.GreaterThan
```

You can assign DataTypeCheck to the Operator property if you just want to verify that the contents of the input field can be safely converted to the data type specified by the Type property. In this case, the ControlToCompare and ValueToCompare properties are ignored:

```
' Check that txtLastVisit contains a valid date.
CompareValidator2.ControlToValidate = "txtLastVisit"
CompareValidator2.Type = ValidationDataType.Date
CompareValidator2.Operator = ValidationCompareOperator.DataTypeCheck
CompareValidator2.ErrorMessage = "Last visit isn't a valid date."
```

When comparing the contents of your control to a constant value, you must use the ValueToCompare property:

```
CompareValidator3.ControlToValidate = "txtChildren"
CompareValidator3.ValueToCompare = "0"
CompareValidator3.Type = ValidationDataType.Integer
CompareValidator3.Operator = ValidationCompareOperator.GreaterThanEqual
CompareValidator3.ErrorMessage = "Number of children must >= 0"
```

The following are a few potential problems that you might encounter when using the CompareValidator control:

- No validation is performed if the input control is empty, so you should use a RequiredFieldValidator control to ensure that an empty field displays an error message.
- If the value in the input control can be converted to the data type specified by the Type property but the value in the control specified by the ControlToCompare property can't be converted, the input control passes the validation. For this reason, you might need an additional RangeValidator or CompareValidator control to check that the other control contains a valid value.
- If the value specified in the ValueToCompare property can't be converted to the data type specified by the Type property, an exception is thrown.
- In general, you should never specify both the ControlToCompare and ValueToCompare properties. If you do, the ControlToCompare property has the priority.

The RegularExpressionValidator Control

If you're familiar with regular expressions—which I cover in Chapter 12—using the RegularExpressionValidator control is a breeze. You just have to set the ControlToValidate and the ValidationExpression properties:

```
' Ensure that a field contains a phone number in the (###)###-#### format.
RegularExpressionValidator1.ControlToValidate = "txtPhoneNumber"
RegularExpressionValidator1.ValidationExpression = "\(\d{3}\)\d{3}-\d{4}"
RegularExpressionValidator1.ErrorMessage = _
    "Please enter the phone number in (###)###-#### format"
```

In many cases, you don't even have to be a regular expression wizard to use this validation control effectively. In fact, Visual Studio .NET lets you pick the regular expressions for the most common field types, such as phone numbers, postal codes, URLs, e-mail addresses, and social security numbers. (See Figure 23-13.) Here are other useful regular expressions:

```
' A one-character Yes/No/True/False field
' (rev1 is a RegularExpressionValidator control.)
rev1.ValidationExpression = "[YyNnTtFf]"

' 16-digit credit card number, with or without spaces
rev1.ValidationExpression = "(\d{4}( \d{4}){3}|\d{16})"

' A month/year expiration date in the format mm/yy
rev1.ValidationExpression = "(0[1-9]|1[0-2])/\d\d"

' An alphanumeric password of at least 8 characters
rev1.ValidationExpression = "[A-Za-z0-9]{8,}"
```

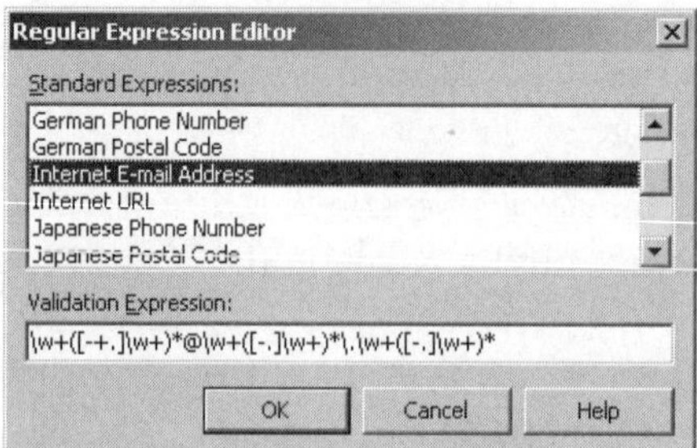

Figure 23-13. Visual Studio lets you select the most common regular expressions from a dialog box.

Keep in mind these particulars when working with the RegularExpressionValidator:

- If the input control is empty, the validation always succeeds. Therefore, you might need to add a RequiredFieldValidation to display an error message if the end user didn't type anything in the field.
- The regular expression is applied either on the client side (using the JScript regular expression engine) or on the server side (using the .NET regular expression engine) if client-side scripts are disabled. The JScript syntax is a subset of the .NET syntax, so in general the same regular expression works well in both cases. But you should either avoid .NET syntax forms that aren't supported by JScript—for example, the (?i) option for case-insensitive comparison—or disable client-side scripting with the EnableClientScript property.

The CustomValidator Control

If none of the validator controls I've shown you so far fulfills your validation needs, you can write your own validation routine and enforce it with the CustomValidator control. This control supports both client-side validation functions (through the ClientValidationFunction property) and server-side validation functions (through the ServerValidate event). The client-side validation function must be written in any script language supported by the browser—typically JScript, but it can also be VBScript if you're sure that you're working with Internet Explorer.

Both the client-side validation routine and the ServerValidate event receive two arguments: an Object value that contains a reference to the validation control and a ServerValidateEventArgs object that expose two properties. Value is the value in the input control to be validated, and IsValid is a property that you must set to True to accept the value or False to reject it. For example, consider this JScript function, which checks whether a number is even:

```
<script language="JScript">
<!--
function CheckEvenNumber(source, args) {
    var theNumber = args.Value;
    if (theNumber % 2 == 0)
        args.IsValid = true;
    else
        args.IsValid = false;
}
//-->
</script>
```

(Note that we can check evenness also with regular expressions.) You can enter this code right in the HTML editor, or you can dynamically assign it to the Text property of a Literal control on the form:

```
Literal1.Text = "<script language=""JScript""><!-- " & ControlChars.CrLf _
    & "function CheckEvenNumber(source, args) {" & ControlChars.CrLf _
    & "  var theNumber = args.Value;" & ControlChars.CrLf _
    & "  if (theNumber % 2 == 0) " & ControlChars.CrLf _
    & "    args.IsValid = true;" & ControlChars.CrLf _
    & "  else " & ControlChars.CrLf _
    & "    args.IsValid = false;" & ControlChars.CrLf _
    & "} " & ControlChars.CrLf _
    & "//--> " & ControlChars.CrLf _
    & "</script>" & ControlChars.CrLf
```

You can (and should) perform the same validation task in a ServerValidate event as well. As you see, the code is the same except for the language used and the fact that you can use early binding on the server:

```
Private Sub CustomValidator1_ServerValidate(ByVal source As Object, _
    ByVal args As System.Web.UI.WebControls.ServerValidateEventArgs) _
    Handles CustomValidator1.ServerValidate

    Dim theNumber As Integer = CInt(args.Value)
    If (theNumber Mod 2) = 0 Then
        args.IsValid = True
    Else
        args.IsValid = False
    End If
End Sub
```

Both the client-side and the server-side functions should implement exactly the same validation strategy—otherwise, your application might perform differently, depending on whether client-side scripting is supported. Also, you should always implement the server-side validation routine, or a clever user might edit the received HTML code to discard or disable the client-side validation routine.

To enable a CustomValidator control you must assign the ControlToValidate and the ClientValidationFunction properties:

```
CustomValidator1.ControlToValidate = "txtEvenNumber"
CustomValidator1.ClientValidationFunction = "CheckEvenNumber"
CustomValidator1.ErrorMessage = "Enter an even number in this field"
```

If the control referenced by the ControlToValidate property is empty, no validation occurs, so you might need a RequiredFieldValidator control to cover that case as well. Also, it's legal to leave the ControlToValidate property blank, in which case the validation function will be called when the user submits the form. This practice can be useful for performing validation tasks that involve multiple controls. (In this case, the args.Value property always receives a null string.)

The ValidationSummary Control

You use this control to gather the error message strings for all the other controls on the form and display them to the end user:

- If the ShowSummary property is True (the default), the error messages are displayed within the ValidationSummary control itself.
- If the ShowMessageBox property is True, the error messages are displayed in a message box (the default value for this property is False). To display the message box, the EnableClientScript property must be True as well.
- The HeaderText property is a string displayed just before the first error message, both on the page and in the message box; you typically assign it a string like "Please correct the following errors."
- The DisplayMode property is an enumerated value that specifies how the individual error messages are arranged on the control or the message box. Available options are BulletList (default), List, and SingleParagraph; if you select the single paragraph mode you should append a suitable punctuation symbol at the end of each error message.

The result shown in Figure 23-14 has been produced by setting these properties:

```
ValidationSummary1.ShowMessageBox = True
ValidationSummary1.ShowSummary = True       ' (the default)
ValidationSummary1.DisplayMode = ValidationSummaryDisplayMode.BulletList
ValidationSummary1.HeaderText = "Please correct the following errors"
```

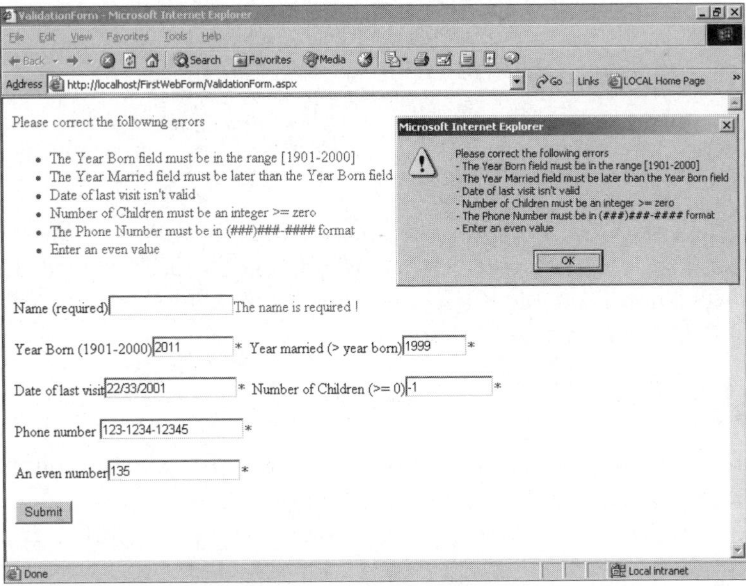

Figure 23-14. A screen full of error messages, both in the Validation-Control and in a message box.

Note that the ErrorMessage property of the first validation control in the demo program—the RequiredFieldValidator associated with the txtUserName control—is set to an empty string, and for this reason it doesn't appear in the ValidationSummary control or in the message box.

Forcing Server-Side Validation

If a form contains one or more validation controls, you should force them to validate the companion controls in the Page_Load event or in the Click event of the button that fires the postback. This strategy ensures that input values are validated even if client-side scripts are disabled.

You can force the validation of all controls by invoking the Validate method. Then you can check the page's IsValid property and, if False, iterate over all the validation controls to detect which fields contain invalid values:

```
Private Sub Button1_Click(ByVal sender As Object, ByVal e As EventArgs) _
    Handles Button1.Click
    ' Force the validation of all controls.
    Me.Validate()

    If Not Me.IsValid Then
        Dim ctrl As BaseValidator
        Dim errorCount As Integer
        ' Count how many errors were found.
```

(continued)

```
            For Each ctrl In Me.Validators
                If Not ctrl.IsValid Then errorCount += 1
            Next
            ' Display a suitable error message.
            lblStatus.Text = "There are " & errorCount.ToString & " errors."
        End If
    End Sub
```

Note that the message prepared by the preceding code is actually displayed only if the browser doesn't support client-side scripts. In fact, if client-side validation is enabled the form can't be posted back to the server until all input fields contain a valid value.

List Controls

All the controls in this group—DropDownList, ListBox, RadioButtonList, CheckBoxList—inherit from the ListControl class and therefore have several members in common (listed in Table 23-9) in addition to those inherited from the WebControl base class.

Table 23-9 Main Members of the ListControl Class

Category	Syntax	Description
General properties	Items	The collection of child ListItem objects.
	SelectedIndex	The index of the currently selected item (read/write).
	SelectedItem	The currently selected ListItem object (read-only).
	AutoPostBack	If True, the control fires a postback when the SelectedIndex value changes.
Data binding properties	DataSource	The source used for data binding.
	DataMember	The source member used for data binding.
	DataTextField	The name of the data source field used to fill the list area of the control.
	DataTextFormatString	The format string that affects how data bound to the list control is displayed.
	DataValueField	The name of the data source field used as the value attribute for the control's items.
Events	SelectedIndexChanged	Fires when the value of the SelectedIndex property changes.

Filling the Items Collection

The Items property returns a collection of ListItem objects, each one exposing four properties. The Text property is the string displayed in the control for that item. The Value property is the item's value attribute. The Selected property is a Boolean that tells whether the element is selected or not. (It's useful with the ListBox and CheckBoxList controls, the only controls that support multiple selections.) The Attributes property is of course the collection of attributes for that item, which you can use as a repository for additional values associated with the element. You can fill the Items collection in three ways:

- At design time, by clicking on the Items element of the Properties window and adding elements in the ListItem Collection Editor dialog box.
- Through code, by using the Add method of the Items collection; this method takes either a string or a ListItem object.
- By using data binding to fill the controls with the values in a DataReader, a DataTable, a DataView, or any data structure that exposes the IEnumerable interface, such as an ArrayList or a Hashtable object.

The code needed to fill a list control is similar to the code I showed you for the HtmlSelect control. For example, this code creates an array of seven radio buttons displaying the weekday names:

```
Private Sub Page_Load(ByVal sender As Object, ByVal e As EventArgs) _
    Handles MyBase.Load
    If Not Page.IsPostBack Then
        ' Creating the collection of radio buttons via code.
        Dim i As Integer
        For i = 1 To 7
            Dim li As New ListItem(WeekdayName(i), i.ToString)
            RadioButtonList1.Items.Add(li)
        Next
    End If
End Sub
```

Note Regardless of the technique you adopt to fill the Items collection, you should perform this action only the very first time the page is requested—hence the use of the IsPostBack function in the preceding code snippet—because the EnableStateView property is set to True by default. Therefore the content of a control is automatically preserved in subsequent postbacks. In some cases, you might optimize your application's performance by disabling the ViewState feature for specific controls, and filling the control anytime the page is loaded.

Figure 23-15 shows the demo program at design time and inside the browser. All the controls but the RadioButtonList have been filled using data binding, as I explain in the "Data Binding with List Controls" section later in this chapter.

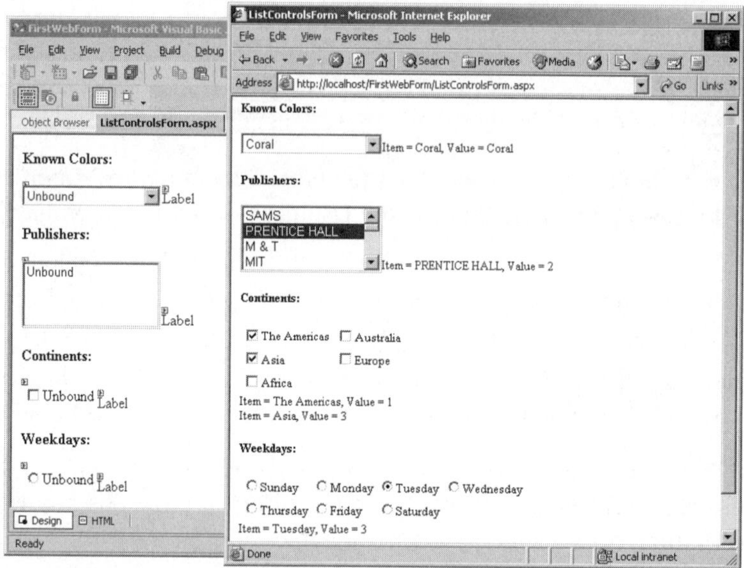

Figure 23-15. The four list controls, as they appear in Visual Studio at design time and inside Internet Explorer at run time.

The ListBox and DropDownList Controls

From the programmer's perspective, these two controls are very similar. The only difference between a DropDownList control and a ListBox control is that the latter exposes two additional properties: Rows (the number of visible elements in the list area) and SelectionMode (which can be Single or Multiple and serves to enable multiple selections). Both controls expose the BorderStyle, BorderWidth, BorderColor, and all the other members inherited from the ListControl base class.

When the page is posted back to the server, a SelectedIndexChanged event fires if the end user has selected a new element in the control. Inside this event's handler, you can retrieve the selected item by using the SelectedItem property:

```
Private Sub lstPublishers_SelectedIndexChanged(ByVal sender As Object, _
    ByVal e As EventArgs) Handles lstPublishers.SelectedIndexChanged
    ' Update a Label control with information on the selected item.
    Dim li As ListItem = lstPublishers.SelectedItem
    Label1.Text = String.Format("Text={0}, Value={1}", li.Text, li.Value)
End Sub
```

If the SelectionMode property of a ListBox control is set to Multiple, you must iterate over the Items collection and test the Selected property of each ListItem element:

```
Private Sub lstPublishers_SelectedIndexChanged(ByVal sender As Object, _
    ByVal e As System.EventArgs) Handles lstPublishers.SelectedIndexChanged
    Dim li As ListItem, msg As String
    ' Display information on all the selected elements.
    For Each li In lstPublishers.Items
        If li.Selected Then
            msg &= String.Format("Text={0}, Value={1}<br>", li.Text, li.Value)
        End If
    Next
    Label1.Text = msg
End Sub
```

The RadioButtonList and CheckBoxList Controls

A RadioButtonList control is functionally similar to a DropDownList or a ListBox control whose SelectionMode property is set to Single, in the sense that it allows the user to select only one of the items in the control. A CheckBoxList control is similar to a ListBox control whose SelectionMode property is set to Multiple.

Even if these two controls don't look like a DropDownList or a ListBox control, you fill their Items collection exactly as you do with the other controls in this group. Likewise, you check which elements are selected by using the SelectedIndex and SelectedItem properties of the control, or the Selected property of individual ListItem objects in the case of the CheckBoxList control. The only properties that these two controls have in addition to the ListControl base control affect how they're laid out on the form:

- The TextAlign property tells whether the text is aligned to the right (the default) or the left of the check box or radio button.
- The RepeatLayout property is an enumerated value that specifies whether the elements are displayed in a table (RepeatedLayout.Table value, the default) or not (RepeatedLayout.Flow value).
- The RepeatColumns property specifies how many columns are displayed. By default, elements are displayed in a single column.
- The RepeatDirection property is an enumerated value that specifies whether elements are displayed horizontally (the default) or vertically. If elements are displayed in a single column, this property has no effect.
- The CellPadding and CellSpacing properties specify the distance in pixels between the cells and the border and between individual cells, respectively.

For example, the CheckBoxList control in Figure 23-15 has the RepeatColumns property set to 2 and the RepeatDirection property set to Vertical, whereas the RadioButtonList control has the RepeatColumns property set to 4 and the RepeatDirection property set to Horizontal.

Other Controls

Not counting the template controls, which are described at the end of this chapter, the only three controls that I haven't discussed yet are the Calendar control, the AdRotator control, and the Xml control.

The Calendar Control

If you consider the number of properties and events it exposes, the Calendar control is among the most complex controls in ASP.NET, perhaps second only to the DataGrid control. This isn't surprising, when you realize that the Calendar control lets you customize the appearance of any visual element; select individual days, weeks, or months; add text or images to individual day cells; finely control whether a day can be selected; and more.

You can determine how the calendar looks by setting the properties in the Style and Appearance categories listed in Table 23-10. All properties in the Style category are actually TableItemStyle style objects, which derive from the Style class and expose properties such as ForeColor, BackColor, Font, BorderColor, BorderWidth, HorizontalAlign, VerticalAlign, and Wrap. For example, this code changes a few properties of the title bar:

```
' Use a big white title on a red background.
With Calendar1.TitleStyle
    .BackColor = System.Drawing.Color.Red
    .ForeColor = System.Drawing.Color.White
    .Font.Size = New FontUnit(FontSize.XLarge)
End With
' Display only the month name.
Calendar1.TitleFormat = TitleFormat.Month
```

Table 23-10 Main Properties and Events of the Calendar Control

Category	Syntax	Description
Style properties	DayStyle	The style for days in current month. Today, weekends, and the selected date can have a different style (see below).
	TodayDayStyle	The style for today's date.
	WeekendDayStyle	The style for weekend days.
	SelectedDayStyle	The style for the selected days.

Table 23-10 Main Properties and Events of the Calendar Control *(continued)*

Category	Syntax	Description
	OtherMonthDayStyle	The style for days in previous or next month.
	DayHeaderStyle	The style for the row above day numbers, where weekday names appear.
	TitleStyle	The style for the title bar at the top of the calendar, where the month name and year number appear.
	NextPrevStyle	The style for the month navigation LinkButton controls.
	SelectorStyle	The style for the leftmost column of the selector, which is visible only if week or month selectors are enabled.
Appearance properties	ShowDayHeader	If False, the section containing the weekday names isn't displayed. (Default is True.)
	ShowGridLines	If False (the default) the grid lines between days aren't displayed.
	ShowNextPrevMonth	If False, buttons to navigate to other months aren't displayed. (Default is True.)
	ShowTitle	If False, the title section isn't displayed. (Default is True.)
	CellPadding	The distance between cells and the control's border.
	CellSpacing	The distance between individual cells.
Format properties	DayNameFormat	The format for the names of the days; can be FirstLetter, FirstTwoLetters, Short, or Full.
	FirstDayOfWeek	An enumerated value that specifies the day to be shown in the first column. The default value depends on current system settings.
	TitleFormat	The format for the title section; can be MonthYear (the default) or Month.
	NextPrevFormat	The format for month navigation buttons. Can be ShortMonth, FullMonth, or CustomText.

(continued)

Table 23-10 Main Properties and Events of the Calendar Control *(continued)*

Category	Syntax	Description
	PrevMonthText, NextMonthText	The text for the month navigation buttons. They're used only if NextPrevFormat is set to CustomText.
	SelectMonthText	The text used for the month selection element in the selector column. The default is >>, which is rendered as >>.
Date properties	SelectionMode	An enumerated value that determines what the end user can select in the calendar. It can be Day (single date), DayWeek (single day or week), DayWeekMonth (single day, week, or month), or None (selection is disabled).
	TodayDate	The day to be highlighted as the current date.
	SelectedDate	The date that's currently selected.
	SelectedDates	A collection of dates that appear as selected in the calendar—its elements are automatically sorted. Use the Add method to select new dates, and the Clear method to clear the selection.
	VisibleDate	A date value that affects the month that's visible in the calendar.
Events	SelectionChanged	Fires when the user selects a different date.
	DayRender	Fires when a day cell is about to be rendered to the browser. It receives the Day argument (the day being rendered) and the Cell argument (the TableCell object being rendered).
	VisibleMonthChanged	Fires when a new month is becoming visible. It receives the PreviousDate argument (the month that was visible previously) and the NewDate argument (the month that is about to become visible).

Fortunately, you don't have to assign these properties individually, at least if you're satisfied with the predefined styles that Visual Studio .NET displays when you click on the Auto Format command in the Properties window or in the control's shortcut menu. (See Figure 23-16.)

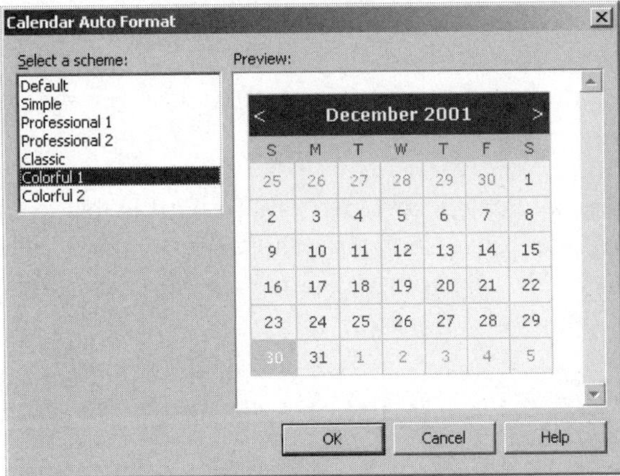

Figure 23-16. Visual Studio .NET predefined calendar styles.

You can customize how each individual day cell is rendered by trapping the DayRender event. The second argument for this event exposes two properties:

- Day is the CalendarDay object that describes the day being rendered, and exposes properties such as Date, DayNumberText (the text used to render the day), IsToday, IsWeekend, IsOtherMonth, IsSelected, and IsSelectable. You can set the IsSelectable property to False to prevent the user from selecting this date. All other properties are read-only.
- Cell is the TableCell object that affects the appearance of the cell. This object derives from WebControl and therefore exposes all the usual properties, such as ForeColor, BackColor, and the like, plus a few additional properties such as HorizontalAlign and VerticalAlign.

For example, see how you can use the DayRender event to change the background color of the days in the range from 12/24 to 12/26 and make them nonselectable:

```
Private Sub Calendar1_DayRender(ByVal sender As Object, _
    ByVal e As DayRenderEventArgs) Handles Calendar1.DayRender
    ' Ensures that days 12/24 to 12/26 are displayed with yellow background.
```

(continued)

```
        If Not e.Day.IsOtherMonth Then
            ' Consider only days in the current month.
            If e.Day.Date.Month = 12 AndAlso e.Day.Date.Day >= 24 _
                AndAlso e.Day.Date.Day <= 26 Then
                ' Change the cell background color.
                e.Cell.BackColor = System.Drawing.Color.Yellow
                ' Prevent the user from selecting this day.
                e.Day.IsSelectable = False
            End If
        End If
End Sub
```

You can even display images and load other controls inside each individual cell by leveraging the cell's Controls collection. For example, this code replaces the usual text with a custom image for all the cells corresponding to the first day of the month:

```
Private Sub Calendar1_DayRender(ByVal sender As Object, _
    ByVal e As DayRenderEventArgs) Handles Calendar1.DayRender
    If e.Day.Date.Day = 1 Then
        Dim imgCtrl As New System.Web.UI.WebControls.Image()
        imgCtrl.ImageUrl = "/images/warning.gif"
        imgCtrl.Width = Unit.Percentage(100)
        imgCtrl.Height = Unit.Percentage(100)
        e.Cell.Text = ""
        e.Cell.Controls.Add(imgCtrl)
    End If
End Sub
```

Figure 23-17 shows a calendar based on the preceding code, together with an instance of the other two controls discussed in this section. Compared to the DayRender event, the other two events that the Calendar exposes are pretty simple. The event you'll use more frequently is SelectionChanged, which occurs when the user clicks on a day hyperlink:

```
Private Sub Calendar1_SelectionChanged(ByVal sender As Object, _
    ByVal e As EventArgs) Handles Calendar1.SelectionChanged
    ' Display the selected date in a Label control.
    Label1.Text = "Current Selected Date is " & _
        Calendar1.SelectedDate.ToLongDateString
End Sub
```

The Calendar control doesn't support data binding, so you must manually assign the SelectedDate property in the Page_Load event and update the data source in the SelectionChanged event handler.

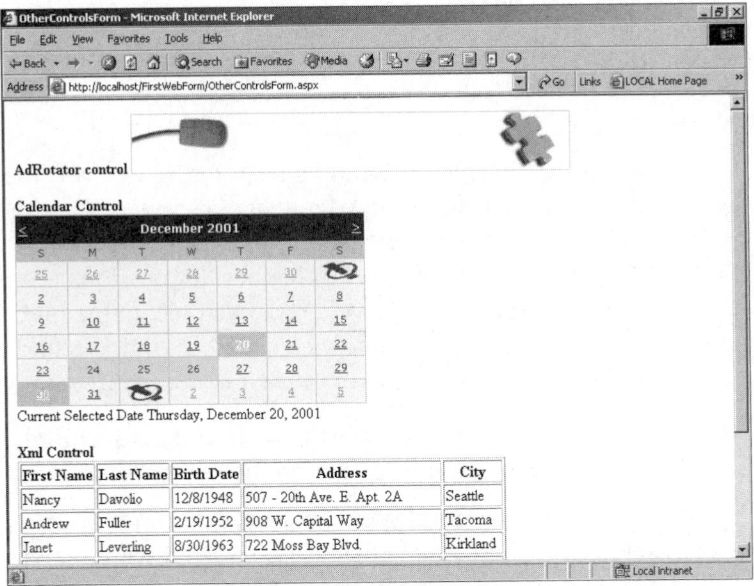

Figure 23-17. A page containing an AdRotator, a Calendar, and an Xml control.

The AdRotator Control

The AdRotator control offers the same functionality as the component of the same name included in ASP—that is, the ability to display advertisement banners in a random manner. The most important difference from the ASP component is that the file that contains information about the banners is now in XML format. Here's an example of such a data file:

```
<?xml version="1.0" encoding="utf-8" ?>
<Advertisements
    xmlns="http://schemas.microsoft.com/AspNet/AdRotator-Schedule-File">
  <Ad>
    <ImageUrl>/foo_banner.gif </ImageUrl>
    <NavigateUrl>www.foo.com</NavigateUrl>
    <AlternateText>Visit www.foo.com</AlternateText>
    <Keyword>shopping</Keyword>
    <Impressions>20</Impressions>
  </Ad>
  <Ad>
    <ImageUrl>bar_banner.gif</ImageUrl>
    <NavigateUrl>www.bar.com</NavigateUrl>
    <AlternateText>Visit www.bar.com</AlternateText>
```

(continued)

```
    <Keyword>travels</Keyword>
    <Impressions>10</Impressions>
  </Ad>
  ⋮
</Advertisements>
```

Most elements in this file are self-explanatory. ImageUrl is the URL of the image; NavigateUrl is the URL of the page that's displayed if the user clicks on the banner; AlternateText is the text used if the image is unavailable; Keyword is the (optional) category assigned to this banner; Impressions is a number that affects how often the banner is displayed. (For example, in the preceding advertisement file, the first banner appears twice as often as the second one.) Using the AdRotator control is quite simple because it exposes only three properties:

- The AdvertisementFile property is the path to the advertisement file in XML format. This file must reside on the same Web server.
- The KeywordFilter property specifies a keyword and forces the control to select only the banners that are associated with this keyword. If the XML file defines no banners with this keyword, the control doesn't display anything.
- The Target property sets or gets the browser window or frame that displays the content of the Web page that appears when the banner is clicked.

For example, here's how you can filter banners so that only shopping-related ones are displayed:

```
AdRotator1.AdvertisementFile = "/advertisement.xml"
AdRotator1.KeywordFilter = "shopping"
```

Note that you can specify only one keyword in both the XML file and the KeywordFilter property. The control exposes the AdCreated event, which fires each time a new banner is displayed. You might trap this event to keep a log of which banners were actually displayed.

The AdRotator control doesn't offer any support for detecting when the user clicks a banner and jumps to the site pointed to by the NavigateUrl property. Implementing this feature is simple, however: instead of pointing directly to the site's URL, you can have the NavigateUrl property point to a page in your site, which reads the target URL on the query string, updates a log file, and finally redirects the browser to the real destination. Here's an example of how you might retouch the XML file to redirect clicks to your redirector.aspx page:

```
<Ad>
  <NavigateUrl>/redirector.aspx?url=www.foo.com</NavigateUrl>
  ⋮
</Ad>
```

The Xml Control

The Xml control is simply a component that lets you implement XSL transformation using a declarative code style instead of explicitly creating an XmlDocument and an XslTransform object (as we did in Chapter 22). To use this control, you typically need to set the source XML document that contains the data to be displayed and the XSL document that contains the XSL style sheet that specifies how data must be rendered.

You can specify the XML source document in three ways: by assigning an XmlDocument object to the Document property, by assigning a file path to the DocumentSource property, or by storing the raw XML data in the DocumentContent property. Likewise, you can specify the XSL style sheet by assigning an XslTransform object to the Transform property or a file path to the TransformSource property. The only other property, TransformArgumentList, serves to pass arguments to the style sheet.

Here's a simple example that uses the employees.xslt XSL file to render the data in the employees.xml data file:

```
Xml1.DocumentSource = "employees.xml"
Xml1.TransformSource = "employees.xslt"
```

Data Binding with Web Forms Controls

Web Forms controls support data binding differently from the way Windows Forms controls implement it. For starters, data binding on Web Forms is one-directional: it can fill a control with data coming from a data source, but it can't update the data source with what the user types inside a control. This limitation is due to the stateless nature of Web Forms and you must circumvent it by doing the update manually through code. Depending on the type of control and the property you're binding, data binding requires different syntax forms:

- If you're binding a single-value property—such as Text, ForeColor, and BackColor—you must use the <%# ...%> syntax to embed a binding expression in the HTML code. This is the only binding mode supported by simple controls like TextBox, Label, Literal, CheckBox, and RadioButton, but it can be used with single-value properties of any control (for example, the ForeColor property of a DataGrid control).
- If you're binding the list area of a list control, you must assign the DataSource and the DataTextField properties (and optionally the DataValueField property). You can use this binding technique to fill the Items collection of a ListBox, DropDownList, CheckBoxList, or RadioButtonList control.

- If you're binding the content area of a template control—namely the DataGrid, DataList, or Repeater control—you must assign the DataSource property and provide one <%# ...%> expression for each bound column. The DataGrid control is also able to automatically create one bound column for each field in the data source.

Regardless of the technique you use to do the binding, you must explicitly activate the data binding for all the controls on the form by calling the DataBind method of the Page object. This method is also exposed by individual bindable controls:

```
' Activate data binding for the TextBox1 control.
TextBox1.DataBind()
' Activate data binding for all the controls on the form.
Me.DataBind()
```

Binding Single-Value Properties

Binding single-value properties requires that you switch to the HTML view in the form editor, locate the attribute that you want to bind to a data source, and replace its value with an expression enclosed between <%# and %> delimiters. For example, this HTML code binds the Text property of the TextBox1 control to the UserName field or property of the page object:

```
<asp:TextBox id="TextBox1" runat="server" Text="<%# UserName %>" />
```

The expression between delimiters is any valid expression that can be evaluated correctly in the context of the current page object. For example, if GetValue is a method that takes an integer value you might use this syntax:

```
<asp:TextBox id="TextBox1" runat="server" Text="<%# GetValue(0) %>" />
```

If the code-behind class exposes a DataTable object as a public variable, you can access its rows and fields as well:

```
<asp:TextBox id="TextBox1" runat="server"
   Text="<%# myDataTable.Rows(0)("Name").ToString %>" />
```

As I mentioned previously, you can bind any property using this syntax. For example, the BackColor property might be bound to a field in a DataTable as follows:

```
<asp:TextBox id="TextBox1" runat="server"
   BackColor="<%# myDataTable.Rows(0)("Color").ToString %>" />
```

Another example: you might bind the width of an Image control as a cheap way to display a horizontal histogram that reflects the value in the data source. If you work with Visual Studio .NET, you don't have to edit the HTML code by hand; just click on the ellipsis button to the right of the (DataBindings) element in the Properties window to bring up the DataBindings dialog box shown in Figure 23-18, where you can type the binding expression in the Custom binding expression field. As you see, all bound properties are marked with a small database yellow icon, both in this dialog and in the Properties window. This dialog also supports binding to designable components dropped onto the form's component tray area, such as a DataSet or a DataAdapter object.

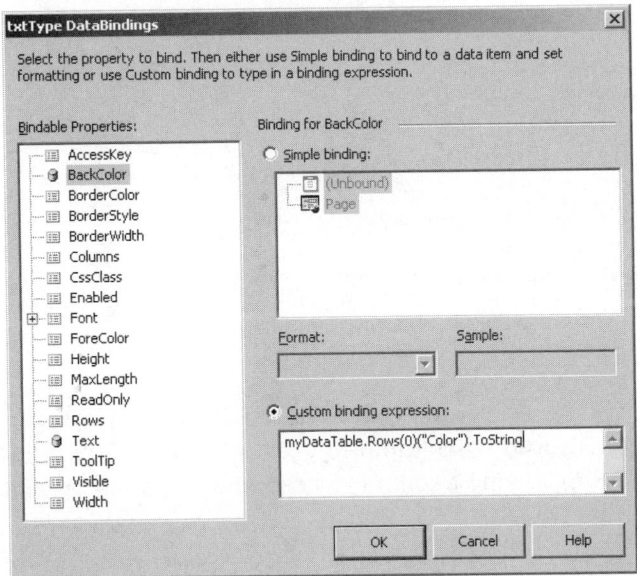

Figure 23-18. Typing a custom binding expression in Visual Studio .NET.

If you don't want to use any designable component on the form, you must write some code in the Page_Load event handler to prepare the public variable that bound controls can reference in their bound attributes. The following code example loads a DataTable from the Titles table in the Pubs database, fills a DropDownList control with the list of all available titles, and then prepares a public DataRow variable named Titles, which contains the row that is currently selected in the DropDownList control:

```
' Define a public DataRow variable that is visible from <%# %> expressions.
Public Titles As DataRow

Private Sub Page_Load(ByVal sender As Object, ByVal e As EventArgs) _
    Handles MyBase.Load
    If Not Page.IsPostBack Then
        ' Fill the data table and then close the connection.
```

(continued)

```
        Dim cn As New SqlConnection(SqlPubsConnString)
        Dim da As New SqlDataAdapter("SELECT * FROM Titles", cn)
        Dim dt As New DataTable()
        da.Fill(dt)
        ' Store the DataTable in a Session variable.
        Session("TitlesDataTable") = dt

        ' Manually fill the Items collection of the ddlTitles control.
        ' (We might use data binding for this job as well.)
        Dim dr As DataRow
        For Each dr In dt.Rows
            ddlTitles.Items.Add(dr("title").ToString)
        Next
        ddlTitles.SelectedIndex = 0

        ' Prepare the Titles variable for binding.
        Titles = dt.Rows(0)
        ' Bind all controls on the form.
        Me.DataBind()
    End If
End Sub
```

As you see, the DataTable object is stored in a Session variable, from which it can be retrieved when the user causes a postback by selecting a new element in the DropDownList control (whose AutoPostBack property has been opportunely set to True):

```
Private Sub ddlTitles_SelectedIndexChanged(ByVal sender As Object, _
    ByVal e As EventArgs) Handles ddlTitles.SelectedIndexChanged
    ' Retrieve the DataTable object from the session variable.
    Dim dt As DataTable = DirectCast(Session("TitlesDataTable"), DataTable)
    ' Prepare the Titles variable and activate the data binding.
    Titles = dt.Rows(ddlTitles.SelectedIndex)
    Me.DataBind()
End Sub
```

The form contains three databound TextBox controls, whose binding expressions reference the Titles variable:

```
<asp:textbox id="txtTitle" runat="server" Text='<%# Titles("title") %>' />
<asp:textbox id="txtPrice" runat="server" Text='<%# Titles("price") %>' />
<asp:textbox id="txtType" runat="server"  Text='<%# Titles("type") %>' />
```

Figure 23-19 shows the result in the browser.

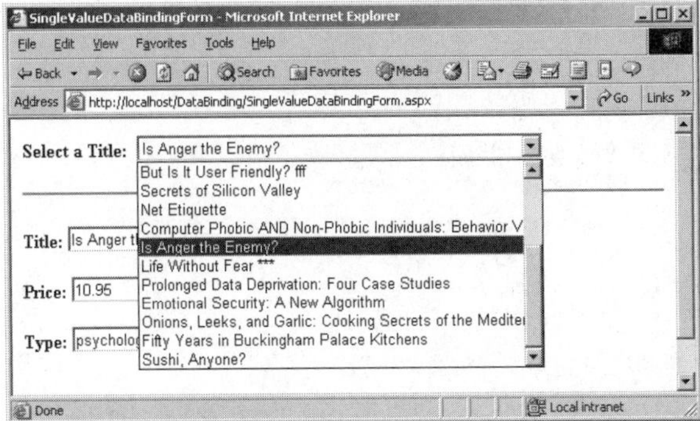

Figure 23-19. A simple form with three bound controls; data binding is one-directional and the data source isn't updated.

Binding expressions can use the Eval method of the DataBinder object for even more flexibility. This method takes two arguments—a reference to a public object and the name of one of its properties—plus an optional argument that affects how the value is formatted before being assigned to the bound control. For example, the following binding expression displays the price field as a currency value with four decimals:

```
<asp:textbox id="txtPrice" runat="server"
    Text='<%# DataBinder.Eval(Titles, "(""price"")", "{0:C4}") %>' />
```

See the "Formatting Numeric Values" and "Formatting Date Values" sections in Chapter 8 for a list of valid format symbols.

Data Binding with List Controls

When you're using data binding with a list control, at the very minimum you must assign the data source object to the DataSource property and the name of the field to be displayed in the control to the DataTextField property. You must also assign the DataValueField property if you want to associate a value with each element. For example, this code uses data binding to display continent names stored in a Hashtable object:

```
Private Sub Page_Load(ByVal sender As Object, ByVal e As EventArgs) _
    Handles MyBase.Load
    If Not Page.IsPostBack Then
        ' Create a Hashtable with continent names.
        Dim continents As New Hashtable(5)
        continents.Add("The Americas", 1)
```

(continued)

```
            continents.Add("Europe", 2)
            continents.Add("Asia", 3)
            continents.Add("Africa", 4)
            continents.Add("Australia", 5)
            ' Bind it to the cblContinents CheckBoxList control.
            cblContinents.DataSource = continents
            ' Each element in the Hashtable has a Key and a Value property.
            cblContinents.DataTextField = "Key"
            cblContinents.DataValueField = "Value"
            :
            ' Bind all the controls on this page.
            Me.DataBind()
        End If
    End Sub
```

If you're binding to an array of strings, you don't even need to set the DataTextField property:

```
' Fill a string array with the names of all known colors.
Dim colors() As String = [Enum].GetNames(GetType(System.Drawing.KnownColor))
' Bind it to the ddlColors DropDownList control.
ddlColors.DataSource = colors
```

Finally, you can fill a list control by assigning an ADO.NET object, such as a DataReader, a DataTable, a DataView, or a DataSet object, to the control's DataSource property. (You must assign also the DataMember property if you're binding to a DataSet object.) This code shows how you can display a list of publishers' names in a ListBox control and associate each element with the corresponding PubID value:

```
' Open a connection to Biblio.mdb and create a DataReader.
Dim cn As New OleDbConnection(BiblioConnString)
Dim cmd As New OleDbCommand("SELECT PubId,Name FROM Publishers", cn)
cn.Open()
Dim dr As OleDbDataReader = cmd.ExecuteReader(CommandBehavior.CloseConnection)
' Bind the DataReader to the ListBox control.
lstPublishers.DataSource = dr
lstPublishers.DataTextField = "Name"
lstPublishers.DataValueField = "PubId"
' Bind the ListBox and close the DataReader (and the Connection).
lstPublishers.DataBind()
dr.Close()
```

This code produces the output shown in Figure 23-15. If you can, you should bind an ASP.NET control to a DataReader object, which takes less memory than a DataTable or DataView object. Using a DataTable or DataView object is necessary when you're binding multiple controls because you read the data from the database once and reuse it for all the controls. You can store a DataTable or DataView object in a Session variable between consecutive postbacks, even though I don't recommend this technique because it creates server affinity and doesn't work on Web farms (unless you use out-of-process sessions, which I describe in the "Session State" section of Chapter 24) and also because it isn't appropriate when you're working with more than a few hundred rows.

Remember that you aren't limited to displaying a single database field in a list control. For example, you might tweak the SELECT command to display the first and last name of all authors in Pubs by using this code:

```
Dim cn As New OleDbConnection(OledbPubsConnString)
Dim cmd As New OleDbCommand( _
    "SELECT au_id, au_lname+', '+au_fname As Name FROM Authors", cn)
cn.Open()
Dim dr As OleDbDataReader = cmd.ExecuteReader(CommandBehavior.CloseConnection)
' Bind the DataReader to the ListBox control.
lstAuthors.DataSource = dr
lstAuthors.DataTextField = "Name"
lstAuthors.DataValueField = "Au_id"
```

The DataTextFormatString property lets you exert some control over how bound elements are displayed in the control and is especially useful with numeric and date fields. You can assign this property any format string accepted by the String.Format property:

```
' Display a date using a LongDatePattern.
lstDeadlineDates.DataTextField = "deadline_date"
lstDeadlineDates.DataTextFormatString = "{0:D}"
```

Simulating Two-Way Data Binding

As you've seen, ASP.NET data binding for simple controls and list controls is less powerful than Windows Forms data binding because ASP.NET data binding is one-directional and offers no automatic way to store modified values back into the data source. In this section, I'll show how you can extend the previous code sample to implement bidirectional data binding. (See Figure 23-20.)

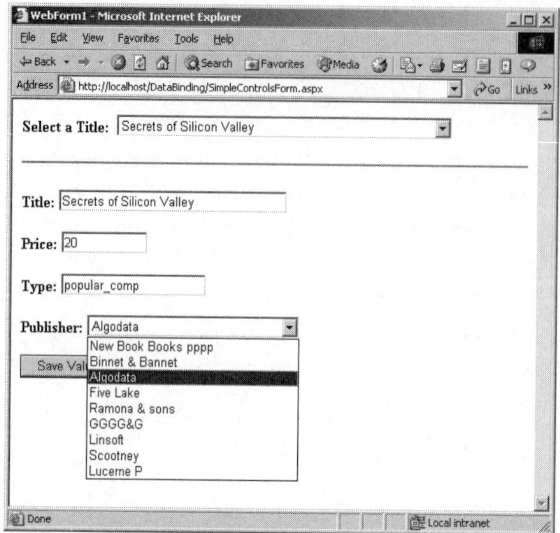

Figure 23-20. An ASP.NET page that implements (simulated) bidirectional data binding.

In this sample, data binding for most controls is just simulated via code. More precisely, I use data binding to fill the list portion of the two DropDownList controls but not to associate values in controls to the corresponding field in the Titles table. As an additional touch, I'll demonstrate how you can have the ddlPublishers DropDownList control look up a value in another table. The code behind this form isn't exactly trivial:

```
' Define a connection object that points to Pubs.
Dim cn As New SqlConnection(SqlPubsConnString)

Private Sub Page_Load(ByVal sender As Object, ByVal e As EventArgs) _
    Handles MyBase.Load
    If Not IsPostBack Then
        ' Fill the two DropDownList (lookup) controls.
        FillListControl(ddlTitles, cn, "Titles", "title", "title_id")
        FillListControl(ddlPublishers, cn, "Publishers", "pub_name", "pub_id")
        ' Display the first record.
        ShowTitleInfo(ddlTitles.Items(0).Value)
    End If
End Sub

' Bind a List control to a table in a database (provider-agnostic code).
Sub FillListControl(ByVal ctrl As ListControl, ByVal cn As IDbConnection, _
    ByVal tableName As String, ByVal textField As String, _
```

```
    ByVal valueField As String)
    ' Open the connection if necessary.
    If cn.State = ConnectionState.Closed Then cn.Open()
    ' Read the text and the value field.
    Dim cmd As IDbCommand = cn.CreateCommand
    cmd.CommandText = String.Format("SELECT {0},{1} FROM {2}", _
        textField, valueField, tableName)
    Dim dr As IDataReader = cmd.ExecuteReader

    ' Bind the control.
    ctrl.DataSource = dr
    ctrl.DataTextField = textField
    ctrl.DataValueField = valueField
    ctrl.DataBind()
    ' Close the DataReader.
    dr.Close()
End Sub

' Simulate binding by reading field values of "current" record.
Sub ShowTitleInfo(ByVal titleId As String)
    ' Open the connection if necessary.
    If cn.State = ConnectionState.Closed Then cn.Open()
    Dim cmd As New SqlCommand("SELECT * FROM Titles WHERE title_id='" _
        & titleId & "'", cn)
    Dim dr As SqlDataReader = cmd.ExecuteReader(CommandBehavior.SingleRow)
    ' Read field values into controls on the form.
    dr.Read()
    txtTitle.Text = dr("title").ToString
    txtPrice.Text = dr("price").ToString
    txtType.Text = dr("type").ToString
    SelectItemFromValue(ddlPublishers, dr("pub_id").ToString)
    ' Close the DataReader.
    dr.Close()
End Sub

' Select the ListControl element with a given value.
Sub SelectItemFromValue(ByVal lst As ListControl, ByVal value As String)
    Dim i As Integer
    For i = 0 To lst.Items.Count - 1
        If lst.Items(i).Value = value Then
            ' We've found the element - select it and exit.
            lst.SelectedIndex = i
            Exit Sub
        End If
    Next
End Sub
```

(continued)

```
Private Sub ddlTitles_SelectedIndexChanged(ByVal sender As Object, _
    ByVal e As EventArgs) Handles ddlTitles.SelectedIndexChanged
    ' Display the value of current row.
    ShowTitleInfo(ddlTitles.SelectedItem.Value)
End Sub

Private Sub btnSave_Click(ByVal sender As Object, ByVal e As EventArgs) _
    Handles btnSave.Click
    ' Retrieve title_id and pub_id of visible record.
    Dim titleId As String = ddlTitles.SelectedItem.Value
    Dim pubId As String = ddlPublishers.SelectedItem.Value
    ' Update this record.
    UpdateTitle(titleId, txtTitle.Text, txtPrice.Text, txtType.Text, pubId)
    ' Ensure that the title in the DropDownList control matches the new title.
    ddlTitles.SelectedItem.Text = txtTitle.Text
End Sub

' Update a record in the Titles table.
Sub UpdateTitle(ByVal title_id As String, ByVal title As String, _
    ByVal price As String, ByVal type As String, ByVal pub_id As String)
    ' Prepare the Update command.
    Dim sql As String = "UPDATE Titles SET title=@title, price=@price, " _
        & " type=@type, pub_id=@pub_id WHERE title_id=@title_id"
    Dim cmd As New SqlCommand(sql, cn)
    cmd.Parameters.Add("@title", title)
    cmd.Parameters.Add("@price", CDec(price))
    cmd.Parameters.Add("@type", type)
    cmd.Parameters.Add("@pub_id", pub_id)
    cmd.Parameters.Add("@title_id", title_id)
    ' Open the connection if necessary, and execute the Update command.
    If cn.State = ConnectionState.Closed Then cn.Open()
    cmd.ExecuteNonQuery()
End Sub

Private Sub Page_Unload(ByVal sender As Object, ByVal e As EventArgs) _
    Handles MyBase.Unload
    ' Close the connection if still open.
    If cn.State <> ConnectionState.Closed Then cn.Close()
End Sub
```

While the one-directional binding sample that I showed you previously uses a DataTable object stored in a Session variable to store the individual records, the preceding code reopens the connection each time and reads the data from the database using a DataReader object. This technique offers two important benefits: it's faster and more scalable with large tables, and it can be used with Web farms because no Session variables are used. All the information that the code needs, such as the key value of the record that must be updated, is stored in the form itself.

The code contains a couple of routines that you can reuse in your applications. The FillListControl routine uses binding to fill a list control with data coming from a database table. The demo program uses this routine to fill both the ddlTitles control (which lets the user navigate among available records) and the ddlPublishers control (which works as a lookup control in the Publisher foreign table). Note that the routine can work with any .NET data provider.

The other reusable routine is SelectItemFromValue, which takes a value stored in a list control and selects the first element with that value. You must use this routine when you need to display a publisher's name in the ddlPublisher control, given the pub_id value read from the Titles table.

The final detail worth noting in the preceding listing is that each routine opens the connection if it isn't open already, but never closes it. The connection is closed in the Page_Unload event handler if necessary, when all other routines have completed. This technique ensures that the connection is opened as late as possible, that it's never opened twice during the page processing, and that it's correctly released when the page has been completely processed.

Text Formatting in Visual Studio .NET

Before we move to more advanced topics, I want to draw your attention to the formatting capabilities of the HTML editor in Visual Studio .NET.

If you don't need to create server-side Web Forms controls, you can just drop HTML elements on the page's surface as you'd do with any HTML editor. In fact, when you're in design mode, four new top-level menus appear in Visual Studio .NET:

- The Format menu lets you apply standard formatting to selected text, justify text, align controls, and so on. (See Figure 23-21.)
- The Insert menu lets you insert <DIV>, <SPAN>, and <FORM> elements, images, and <A> elements (bookmarks). It also lets you transform a portion of text into a hyperlink.
- The Table menu lets you create a new table, add and delete rows, columns, and cells, and so on. (See Figure 23-22.)
- The Frames menu lets you add and delete frames.

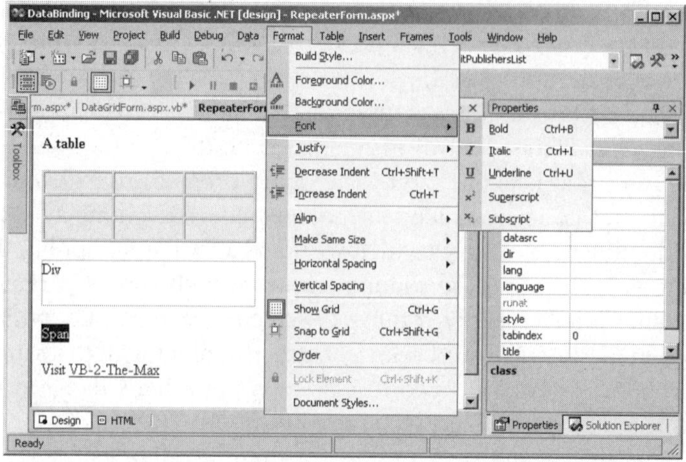

Figure 23-21. Visual Studio offers four additional top-level menus (Format, Table, Insert, and Frames) when the HTML editor is active.

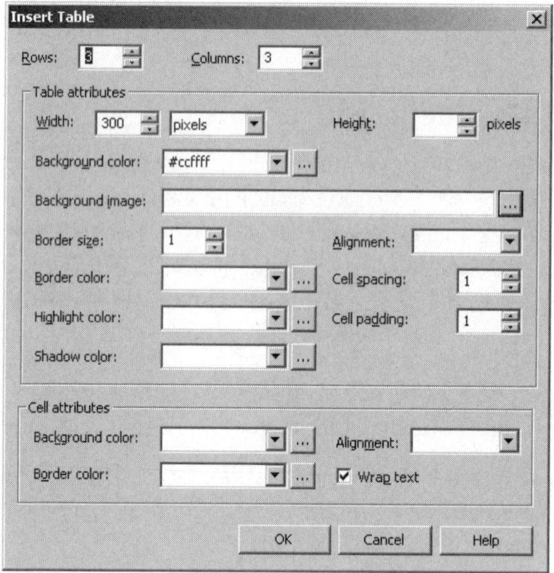

Figure 23-22. The Insert Table dialog box.

Instead of applying separate format operations to an HTML element, you can select it and choose Style Builder from the Format menu or in the shortcut menu to display the Style Builder dialog box shown in Figure 23-23. (You can reach this dialog also from the Style element in the Properties window.) The dialog is in practice a very sophisticated builder for the style HTML attribute of an element, and it lets you create font properties, foreground and background colors, text alignment, flow or absolute position, edges, and bulleted lists.

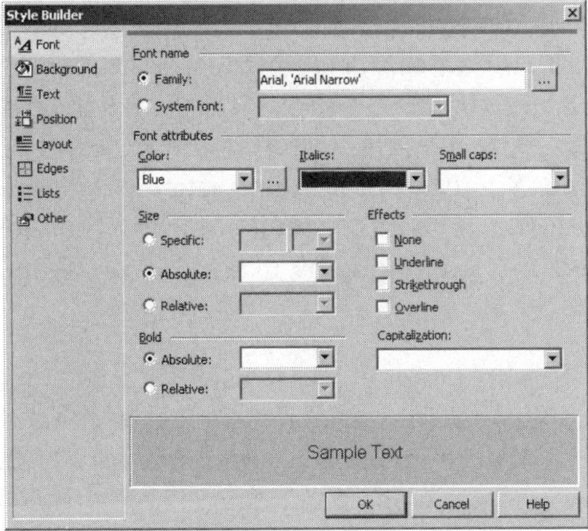

Figure 23-23. The Style Builder dialog box.

Template Controls

The only Web Forms controls that I haven't covered yet are the Repeater, DataList, and DataGrid controls. The main feature these controls have in common is their support for templates, which provide a simple way to affect the appearance and behavior of the elements they contain, their header and footer, and so on. Another point in common among these controls is that you can fill their contents only by using data binding.

The Repeater control is a simple way to display multiple elements taken from a data source. It provides no default appearance, and you're in complete control of the HTML tags generated for each element. Visual Studio doesn't offer any tools to help you edit the elements of a Repeater control in a WYSIWYG manner. You can decide whether elements are laid out vertically, horizontally, all in one line, or in any other format you like; you can specify the format for the header, the footer, the generic item, the alternate row item, and the separator between items. The control doesn't offer support for selecting or editing elements, or for paging through them.

The DataList control displays elements taken from a data source using a default table appearance that you can customize using templates. As with the Repeater control, you can specify the format for the header, the footer, the regular and the alternate row element, and the separator between items. The

DataList control also supports custom appearance for items that are in selected or edit mode, and Visual Studio .NET offers a WYSIWYG tool to edit how each element is displayed. This control doesn't support paging.

The DataGrid control is the most powerful control of the lot. It renders its contents as an HTML grid that you can customize by using templates for the header, the footer, regular and alternating row items, and selected and edited items. This control can do everything the DataList control can do, and it also supports sorting and paging. You can opt for automatic generation of columns (based on fields of the data source), or be in full control of how each column appears in regular, selected, and edit mode by using column templates.

Templates

To tap the power of the controls in this group, you must become familiar with the concept of templates. Each template is a container for HTML code and affects how a given portion of the control appears. There are eight different types of templates, whose names are self-explanatory. (See Figure 23-24.) All the templates except ItemTemplate are optional: if omitted, the corresponding control visual element isn't displayed; if you omit the AlternatingItemTemplate, all rows have the appearance defined by the ItemTemplate.

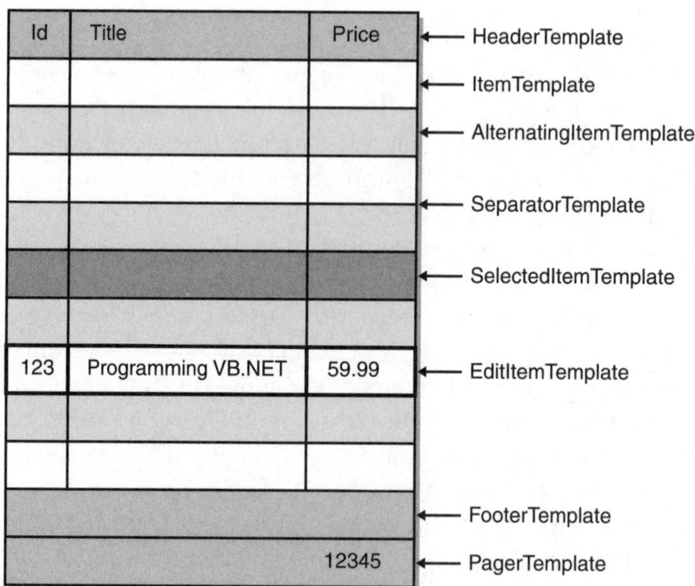

Figure 23-24. The eight types of templates.

The SelectedItemTemplate and EditItemTemplate are applied when an element is in selected or edit mode, respectively. Typically a selected item has a different background color or a visible row selector in the leftmost column, whereas an item in edit mode contains TextBox and CheckBox controls for all the fields that can be edited. In theory, you might select an item while another item is being edited, but in practice you'll never want to do so because it would disorient the end user.

The DataList control supports all types of templates except PagerTemplate. The Repeater control doesn't support SelectedItemTemplate, EditItemTemplate, and PagerTemplate, and you can't apply the SeparatorTemplate to the DataGrid control. The SeparatorTemplate is applied only between items but not before the first line or after the last line: if you want to display a separator in these positions, you must include it in the HeaderTemplate and FooterTemplate.

A template can contain really any type of ASP.NET control—including buttons, check boxes, images, and hyperlinks—so there are few limits to how you can customize the appearance and behavior of a Repeater, DataList, or DataGrid control.

The Repeater Control

The Repeater control is the simplest template control. It doesn't expose any custom properties and therefore works well to demonstrate the potential of templates. On the other hand, Visual Studio doesn't support visual editing of Repeater templates, so we must manually type its templates in the HTML code editor.

Inserting Templates in HTML Text

Each template is a <templatename> block inside the main <asp:Repeater> block. For example, the following HTML code creates a Repeater control that shows a list of publishers as bulleted items, with a <br> tag as a separator between elements, a header on top of the control, and a closing horizontal line. To make things more interesting and to show how to use all the five templates that the Repeater supports, I added an AlternatingItemTemplate element that displays every other row with a yellow background. (See Figure 23-25.)

```
<asp:repeater id="Repeater1" runat="server">
  <HeaderTemplate>
    <b>Bulleted list of publishers: </b><br /><hr />
  </HeaderTemplate>
  <ItemTemplate>
    <li><%# Container.DataItem("Name") %></li>
  </ItemTemplate>
```

(continued)

```
  <AlternatingItemTemplate>
    <span style="BACKGROUND-COLOR: #ffff99">
      <li><%# Container.DataItem("Name") %></li>
    </span>
  </AlternatingItemTemplate>
  <SeparatorTemplate><br /></SeparatorTemplate>
  <FooterTemplate><hr /></FooterTemplate>
</asp:repeater>
```

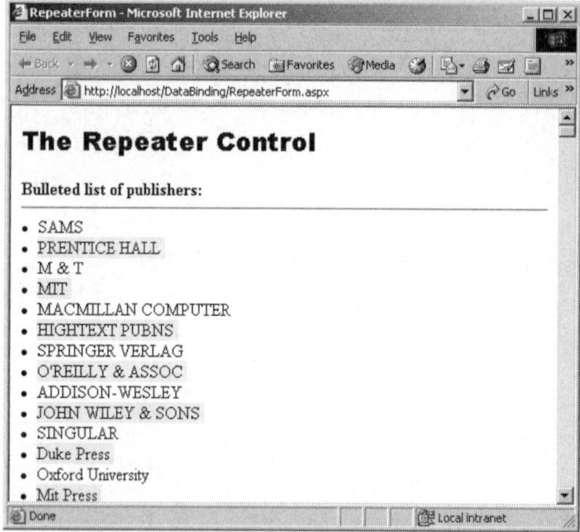

Figure 23-25. A Repeater control that displays a bulleted list of items with alternating background colors.

The key point here is that you must bind the content of each item to the data source using a Container.DataItem("fieldname") expression in a <%# ...#> block. Note that the Repeater control doesn't expose the DataField property, so you must access any field exposed by the data source using this syntax. You can also use the DataBinder.Eval method, as in this code snippet:

```
<ItemTemplate>
  <li><%# DataBinder.Eval(Container, "DataItem(""Name"")") %></li>
</ItemTemplate>
```

Of course, you must bind the control to a proper data source—such as the Publishers table in Biblio.mdb—to have this code work properly:

```
Private Sub Page_Load(ByVal sender As Object, ByVal e As EventArgs) _
    Handles MyBase.Load
    If Not Page.IsPostBack Then
        ' Open the connection to Biblio.mdb.
        Dim cn As New OleDbConnection(BiblioConnString)
        cn.Open()
        ' Read the Name column into a DataReader.
```

```
        Dim cmd As New OleDbCommand("SELECT * FROM Publishers", cn)
        Dim dr As OleDbDataReader = cmd.ExecuteReader()
        ' Bind the control, close the DataReader and the connection.
        Repeater1.DataSource = dr
        Repeater1.DataBind()
        dr.Close()
        cn.Close()
    End If
End Sub
```

You aren't limited to displaying a single data field in each item. For example, you might display the publisher's name and city by using this syntax:

```
<ItemTemplate>
  <li><%# Container.DataItem("Name")+" - "+Container.DataItem("City") %></li>
</ItemTemplate>
```

or this syntax:

```
<ItemTemplate>
  <li><%# Container.DataItem("Name") %> -
      <%# Container.DataItem("City") %></li>
</ItemTemplate>
```

The preceding expression displays a trailing hyphen if the City field is Null for a given publisher. You'll see how to solve this problem by using the ItemDataBound event, which I discuss in its own section shortly. Also, remember that there's no need to retrieve all the fields from the database table if you're going to use only a subset of them. For example, if you're displaying only the publisher's name and city, you should use the following SELECT command:

```
SELECT name, city FROM Publishers
```

You can use a Repeater control's Items collection to iterate over its elements. This collection holds a series of RepeaterItem objects, and each object exposes the following properties: ItemIndex (the index of the item in the control), ItemType (an enumerated value that can be Item, AlternatingItem, Header, Footer, or Separator), and DataItem (an object that represents the item itself), plus all the members of the Control base class. The most important of such members is the Controls collection, which gathers all the elements contained in the RepeaterItem. I'll show how to use this collection in the following section.

The ItemCreated Event

The ItemCreated event fires when an item in the Repeater control is created. The second argument of this event has an Item property pointing to the RepeaterItem object being created. You can trap this event to modify the style or the contents of items as they're created. For example, the following code counts items being displayed and then shows the total number in the footer element. Note that you can't display a string in the footer simply by assigning it to the Text property because this property isn't exposed. Instead, you must add a Literal control to the RepeaterItem's Controls collection:

```
Dim itemCount As Integer

Private Sub Repeater1_ItemCreated(ByVal sender As Object, _
    e As RepeaterItemEventArgs) Handles Repeater1.ItemCreated
    Select Case e.Item.ItemType
        Case ListItemType.Item, ListItemType.AlternatingItem
            ' Count repeater items carrying publisher's data.
            itemCount += 1
        Case ListItemType.Footer
            ' Create a Literal control and add it to the current item.
            Dim lc As New Literal()
            lc.Text = itemCount & " publishers."
            e.Item.Controls.Add(lc)
    End Select
End Sub
```

The ItemDataBound Event

The ItemDataBound event fires each time an item of the Repeater control is bound to a field of the data source. The second argument passed to this event has an Item property that returns a reference to the RepeaterItem object being bound, so you can query its properties and manipulate it as you need.

The DataItem property of the RepeaterItem exposes the object that's providing the bound data. This property has a generic Object type because it can really be anything, depending on what the data source is (a Hashtable, an ArrayList, a DataReader, and so on). For example, the DataItem property returns a System.Data.Common.DbDataRecord object when you're binding to a DataReader, and it returns a DataRowView object when you're binding to a DataTable or a DataView object. The following code leverages the ItemDataBound event to display the city in which a publisher resides, but only if the City field isn't Null:

```
Private Sub Repeater1_ItemDataBound(ByVal sender As Object, _
    ByVal e As RepeaterItemEventArgs) Handles Repeater1.ItemDataBound
    Select Case e.Item.ItemType
        Case ListItemType.Item, ListItemType.AlternatingItem
            ' Get the DbDataRecord that is providing the bound data.
            Dim dbr As System.Data.Common.DbDataRecord
            dbr = DirectCast(e.Item.DataItem, System.Data.Common.DbDataRecord)
            ' Retrieve the city field.
            Dim city As String = dbr("city").ToString
```

```
            If city.Length > 0 Then
                ' If the city isn't null or an empty string, show it in
                ' a Literal control added to the current item.
                Dim lc As New Literal()
                lc.Text = " - " & city
                e.Item.Controls.Add(lc)
            End If
    End Select
End Sub
```

The ItemCommand Event

Each row in the Repeater can contain one or more button controls, which let the user perform actions on the element displayed in that row. For example, you might display a More Info button to the left of each publisher's name so that the user can jump to another page that displays more detailed information about that publisher. (See Figure 23-26.) Because Visual Studio doesn't support WYSIWYG editing of the Repeater templates, you can add a new control only in the HTML editor:

```
<asp:repeater id="Repeater2" runat="server">
  <HeaderTemplate>List of publishers with MoreInfo button</HeaderTemplate>
  <ItemTemplate>
    <asp:Button runat=server Text='more info' CommandName='moreinfo'
      CommandArgument='<%# Container.DataItem("PubId") %>' />
    <%# Container.DataItem("Name") %>
  </ItemTemplate>
  <SeparatorTemplate><br /></SeparatorTemplate>
  <FooterTemplate><hr /></FooterTemplate>
</asp:repeater>
```

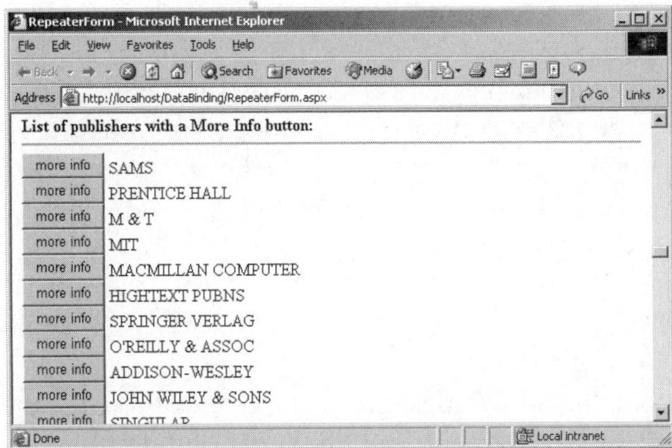

Figure 23-26. A Repeater control can display one or more buttons for each element.

You must set the CommandName attribute to detect which button was clicked, and you must store a unique value in the CommandArgument attribute so that you can later understand which publisher you must apply the command to. (In this specific example there's just one button in each row and you might omit the CommandName attribute, but specifying it is a good programming rule.) Keep in mind that if the Repeater control has an AlternatingItemTemplate element, you must add the button to it as well.

A click on the button causes a postback, and an ItemCommand event is fired on the server. The second argument passed to this event receives an object that exposes all the properties you need to react correctly to the user's action. The Item property is the RepeaterItem that contains the button, CommandSource is the clicked button, and CommandName and CommandArgument are the button's attributes:

```
Private Sub Repeater2_ItemCommand(ByVal source As Object, _
    ByVal e As RepeaterCommandEventArgs) Handles Repeater2.ItemCommand
    Select Case e.CommandName
        Case "moreinfo"
            ' Show additional info about the selected publisher.
            Dim pubId As String = e.CommandArgument
            ' Use the PubId key value to retrieve additional information.
            ' ...(omitted for brevity)...
        Case "showtitles"
            ' Add the code that reacts to other buttons here.
            ⋮
    End Select
End Sub
```

You don't need to set the CommandArgument attribute if you're binding to an ArrayList or a Hashtable object because you can use the e.Item.ItemIndex property to retrieve the index of the element whose button has been clicked.

You can think of other mechanisms to associate one or more commands with elements of a Repeater control. For example, you might use a hyperlink control that carries information about the clicked element on its query string:

```
<ItemTemplate>
  <%# Container.DataItem("Name") %>
  (<asp:HyperLink Runat=server NavigateUrl='ShowTitles.aspx?pubid=
      <%# Container.DataItem("PubId") %>' >Show Titles</asp:HyperLink>)
</ItemTemplate>
```

In this example, the ShowTitle.aspx page is executed when the user clicks on the hyperlink. This page should retrieve the ID of the publisher in question using the following statement in its Page_Load event handler:

```
Dim pubId as String = Me.Request.QueryString("pubid")
```

The DataList Control

The DataList control supports all the available templates except PagerTemplate. The DataList control usually displays data in an HTML table, but you can change its default appearance if you want. Unlike the Repeater control, the DataList templates are editable in a visual manner inside Visual Studio .NET. (See Figure 23-27.)

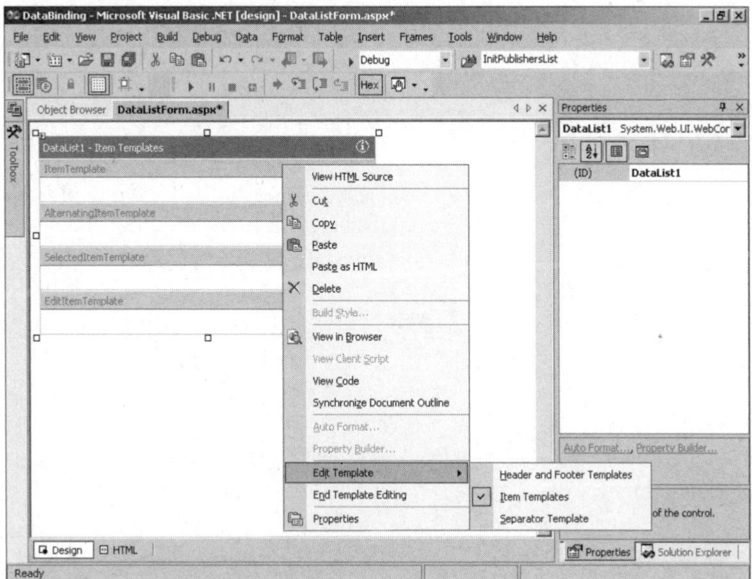

Figure 23-27. Visual Studio .NET lets you edit DataList templates in a WYSIWYG editor.

Each of the seven templates that the DataList control supports corresponds to both an *xxxx*Template property and an *xxxx*Style property. You don't usually have to manipulate these properties in code because it's simpler to set them at design time: just right-click a template and click Build Style on the shortcut menu. You can also assign a visual style quickly by using the Auto Format command on the DataList's shortcut menu. Table 23-11 summarizes all the properties and events that the DataList control doesn't inherit from the WebControl base class.

Table 23-11 Main Properties and Events of the DataList Control

Category	Syntax	Description
Template properties	ItemStyle, AlternatingItem-Style, EditItemStyle, Selected-ItemStyle, HeaderStyle, FooterStyle, SeparatorStyle	A TableItemStyle object that affects how the corresponding visual element is rendered. This object exposes properties such as ForeColor, BackColor, Font, Border-Color, BorderWidth, CssClass, Horizontal-Align, VerticalAlign, and Wrap.
	ShowFooter	True if the footer section is visible (default).
	ShowHeader	True if the header section is visible (default).
Layout properties	RepeatLayout	Determines whether elements are displayed in flow or table mode.
	RepeatColumns	The number of columns displayed in the DataList. The default value is 0, which causes all the elements to be displayed as a single row or a single column.
	RepeatDirection	Determines the direction in which elements are displayed. It can be Horizontal or Vertical.
Data binding properties	DataSource	The data source for this control.
	DataMember	The data member for this control.
	DataKeyField	The key field in the data source.
	DataKeys	A collection that stores the key value of each record displayed in the control.
Appearance properties	HorizontalAlign	The horizontal alignment of the DataList inside its container. It can be NotSet, Left, Center, or Right.
	GridLines	The grid line style used when the Repeat-edLayout property is set to Table. It can be None, Horizontal, Vertical, or Both.
	CellPadding	The distance between cells from the control's border.
	CellSpacing	The distance between adjacent cells.

Table 23-11 Main Properties and Events of the DataList Control *(continued)*

Category	Syntax	Description
	ExtractTemplateRows	True if the rows of a Table control, defined in each template of this DataList, are extracted and displayed. The default is False. This property allows you to create a single table from other smaller tables.
Run time–only properties	Items	The collection of DataListItem objects that represent individual DataList elements.
	EditItemIndex	The index of the element being edited, or −1 if no element is in edit mode.
	SelectIndex	The index of the selected item in the DataList, or −1 if no item is selected.
	SelectedItem	Returns the DataListItem object that represents the selected item.
Events	ItemCreated	Fires when an item is created.
	ItemDataBound	Fires when an item is being bound to the data source.
	ItemCommand	Fires when a button in the DataList control is clicked.
	CancelCommand	Fires when the user clicks a button whose CommandName is cancel.
	DeleteCommand	Fires when the user clicks a button whose CommandName is delete.
	UpdateCommand	Fires when the user clicks a button whose CommandName is update.
	EditCommand	Fires when the user clicks a button whose CommandName is edit.
	SelectedIndexChanged	Fires when a different item is selected, which occurs when the user clicks a button whose CommandName is select.

Data Binding with the DataList Control

The DataList control supports two new properties related to data binding. The DataKeyField is the name of the key column in the data source. The DataKeys collection contains the key value for each element in the DataList after you've bound the control. These properties let you retrieve the key of each row without having to display it in a control in the DataList:

```
Dim cmd As New OleDbCommand("SELECT title_id,title FROM Titles", cn)
Dim dr As OleDbDataReader = cmd.ExecuteReader
' Bind the DataReader to the DataList control.
dlstBooks.DataSource = dr
dlstBooks.DataKeyField = "title_id"      ' Name of key field
dlstBooks.DataBind()
```

Now you can access key values in the DataKeys collection:

```
' The key value for the first visible element in the DataList
Dim key As String = dlstBooks.DataKeys(0).ToString
```

Labels, images, and other controls in the ItemTemplate and AlternatingItemTemplate can be bound to the data source if you use the same syntax that I showed you for the Repeater control, and you can do the binding right in the Visual Studio editor. For example, this is the HTML code that defines the DataList control visible in Figure 23-28. (Data binding expressions are in boldface.)

```
<asp:datalist id="dlstBooks" runat="server" Width="538px">
  <HeaderTemplate>
    <DIV style="COLOR: white; FONT-FAMILY: 'Arial Black';
      BACKGROUND-COLOR: navy">
      Click on [X] to select and edit a book</DIV>
  </HeaderTemplate>
  <ItemTemplate>
    <asp:LinkButton id="Linkbutton3" runat="server" CommandName="select">
      [X]</asp:LinkButton> 
    <asp:Label id=Label5 runat="server" Width="559px"
      Text='<%# Container.DataItem("Title") %>' />
  </ItemTemplate>
  <AlternatingItemTemplate>
    <DIV style="BACKGROUND-COLOR: yellow">
    <asp:LinkButton id="Linkbutton4" runat="server" CommandName="select">
      [X]</asp:LinkButton> 
    <asp:Label id=Label6 runat="server" Width="561px"
      Text='<%# Container.DataItem("Title") %>' />
    </DIV>
  </AlternatingItemTemplate>
  <FooterTemplate>
    <DIV style="COLOR: white; FONT-FAMILY: 'Arial Black';
      BACKGROUND-COLOR: navy">
      End of list</DIV>
  </FooterTemplate>
</asp:datalist>
```

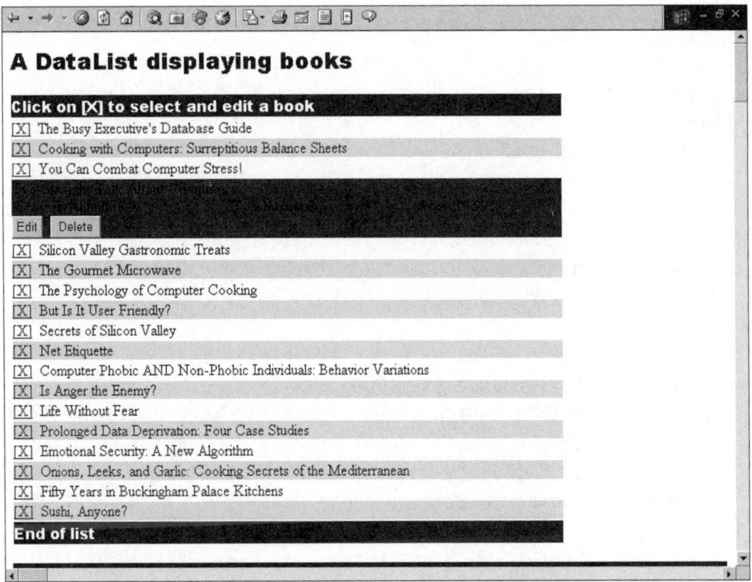

Figure 23-28. A DataList control with alternating styles for rows and a selected element.

The Select and Edit Templates

DataList controls support templates for selected and edited elements. A selected row might display additional information about the element and perhaps include buttons for additional commands (such as the control displayed in Figure 23-28), whereas the EditTemplate should include editable controls, such as TextBox, CheckBox, and DropDownList controls. (See Figure 23-29.) Here are the two templates that implement the selection and edit states:

```
<asp:datalist id="dlstBooks" runat="server" Width="538px">
  ⋮
  <SelectedItemTemplate>
    <DIV style="BACKGROUND-COLOR: blue">Title:
    <asp:Label id=Label7 runat="server" Width="547px" Font-Bold="True"
      Text='<%# Container.DataItem("Title") %>' /><BR>
    Publisher:
    <asp:Label id=Label4 runat="server" Width="170px" Font-Bold="True"
      Text='<%# Container.DataItem("pub_name") %>' />
    Type:
    <asp:Label id=Label8 runat="server" Width="168px" Font-Bold="True"
      Text='<%# Container.DataItem("Type") %>' />
    Price:
    <asp:Label id=Label9 runat="server" Width="83px" Font-Bold="True"
      Text='<%# Container.DataItem("Price") %>' />
```

(continued)

```
      <asp:Button id="Button2" runat="server" Text="Edit"
        CommandName="Edit" /> 
      <asp:Button id="Button4" runat="server" Text="Delete"
        CommandName="delete" /> 
      </DIV>
    </SelectedItemTemplate>

    <EditItemTemplate>
      <DIV style="BACKGROUND-COLOR: blue">Title:
      <asp:TextBox id="txtTitle" runat="server" Width="500px"
        Text='<%# Container.DataItem("Title") %>' /><BR>
      Publisher:
      <asp:Literal id=PubId runat=server Visible=False
        Text='<%# Container.DataItem("pub_id") %>' />
      <asp:DropDownList id="ddlPublishers" runat="server" Width="170px"
        DataTextField='pub_name' DataValueField='pub_id' />
      <asp:TextBox id="txtType" runat="server" Width="168px"
        Text='<%# Container.DataItem("Type") %>' />
      Price:
      <asp:TextBox id="txtPrice" runat="server" Width="83px"
        Text='<%# Container.DataItem("Price") %>' />
      <asp:Button id="Button1" runat="server" Text="Update"
        CommandName="update" /> 
      <asp:Button id="Button3" runat="server" Text="Cancel"
        CommandName="cancel" /> 
      </DIV>
    </EditItemTemplate>
  </asp:datalist>
```

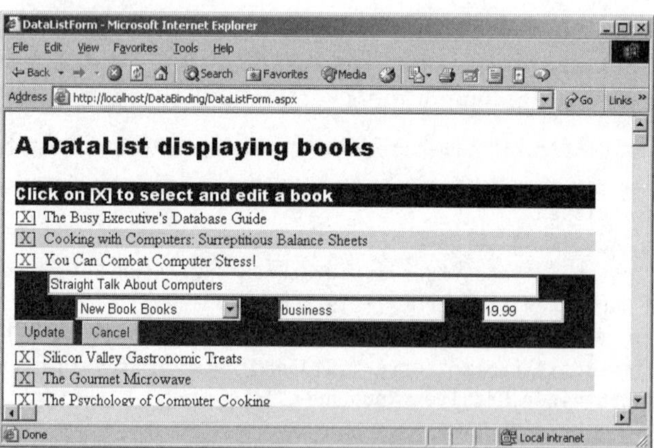

Figure 23-29. A DataList control in edit mode.

Note that the EditItemTemplate contains a Literal control whose Visible attribute is set to False; I'll explain the role of this control in the "Managing the Select and Edit States" section later in this chapter.

The DataList control doesn't offer any support for switching into select or edit mode, so you must provide one or more Button or LinkButton controls on each row to enter these modes. The demo application you'll find on the companion CD uses an [X] label in ItemTemplate to select an element and an Edit button in SelectedItemTemplate to enter the edit mode. (Of course, you're free to enter edit mode directly without passing through select mode.) The EditItemTemplate should include buttons to save the modified values in the data source and to cancel the edit operation.

At any moment, you can have zero or one selected element and zero or one edited element. Most of the time, you shouldn't have a selected element if another element is being edited because the end user might be confused, but there are exceptions to this rule. (See the next note.) You decide which element is in select state by assigning the SelectedIndex property:

```
' Select the first element in the DataList.
dlstBooks.SelectedIndex = 0
```

Similarly, you decide which element is in edit state by assigning the EditItemIndex property. When you do so, you might want to reset SelectedIndex to –1 to ensure that only one element is highlighted with a style different from the standard one:

```
' Enter the edit mode for the second element.
dlstBooks.EditItemIndex = 1
' Ensure that no other element is selected.
dlstBooks.SelectedIndex = -1
```

You exit the edit mode for an element by assigning the value –1 to the EditItemIndex property:

```
' Cancel edit mode.
dlstBooks.EditItemIndex = -1
```

Note The terms *select mode* and *edit mode* are completely arbitrary. For example, the *edit* mode might not include editable controls, and you might use it just for an element that should have a visual appearance different from the default one. Say that you're using the DataList control to display the elements in an array and you want to provide the end user with a command for swapping two elements. You might apply SelectedItemTemplate to the first element and EditItemTemplate to the second element about to be swapped, to highlight each with a different style. (This technique lets you work around the limitation that you can't have two elements in the selected state.)

Command Buttons and Command Events

The Button, LinkButton, or ImageButton controls that you place inside a DataList control should have an appropriate CommandName attribute so that you can trap a click on them from inside an ItemCommand event, as you did with the Repeater control. The DataList control automatically recognizes a button whose CommandName is set to select and fires a SelectedIndexChanged event when that button is clicked:

```
Private Sub dlstBooks_SelectedIndexChanged(ByVal sender As Object, _
    ByVal e As EventArgs) Handles dlstBooks.SelectedIndexChanged
    ' End the edit operation, if any is active.
    dlstBooks.EditItemIndex = -1
    ' Rebind the DataList control.
    BindBookList()
End Sub
```

(The BindBookList routine binds the DataList control to its data source; I describe this routine in the next section.) Note that you don't need to explicitly assign the SelectedIndex property because it already points to the selected element—that is, the element that contains the button that fired the event. However, you still need to trap this event because you must rebind the DataList control to ensure that it correctly renders the element just selected.

The DataList control recognizes four more special CommandName values: edit, cancel, update, and delete. A click on a button assigned one of these CommandName values automatically translates to an EditCommand, CancelCommand, UpdateCommand, or DeleteCommand event. (See Table 23-11.) The second argument for each of these events is an object that exposes properties related to the button being clicked. The Item property returns a reference to the DataListItem where the button resides. CommandSource is a reference to the button. CommandName and CommandArgument are each button's same-name properties.

The handler for the EditCommand event typically sets the EditItemIndex property and rebinds the control. It uses the e.Item.ItemIndex property to determine which element should enter the edit state:

```
Private Sub dlstBooks_EditCommand(ByVal source As Object, _
    ByVal e As DataListCommandEventArgs) Handles dlstBooks.EditCommand
    ' Hide any selected item, if any.
    dlstBooks.SelectedIndex = -1
    ' Have the current element enter the edit state.
    dlstBooks.EditItemIndex = e.Item.ItemIndex
    ' Rebind the DataList control.
    BindBookList()
End Sub
```

The code in the CancelCommand event handler is simple: it sets the EditItemIndex property to –1 to exit edit mode and then rebinds the control:

```
Private Sub dlstBooks_CancelCommand(ByVal source As Object, _
    ByVal e As DataListCommandEventArgs) Handles dlstBooks.CancelCommand
    ' End any edit operation and rebind the control.
    dlstBooks.EditItemIndex = -1
    BindBookList()
End Sub
```

The code you write in the DeleteCommand event handler should delete the element from the data source. Implementing this command is easy because you can retrieve the key value for the selected element from the DataKeys collection:

```
Private Sub dlstBooks_DeleteCommand(ByVal source As Object, _
    ByVal e As DataListCommandEventArgs) Handles dlstBooks.DeleteCommand

    ' Retrieve the ID of the record to be deleted.
    Dim id As String = dlstBooks.DataKeys(e.Item.ItemIndex).ToString
    ' Open the connection if necessary.
    If cn.State = ConnectionState.Closed Then cn.Open()
    ' Delete this row.
    Dim cmd As New OleDbCommand("DELETE Titles WHERE title_id='" _
        & id & "'", cn)
    cmd.ExecuteNonQuery()
    ' Rebind the control.
    BindBookList()
End Sub
```

The code that you write in the UpdateCommand event handler should update the current element with the values that the user typed in the controls. We'll look at it in the next section.

> **Note** The ItemCommand event fires even for buttons whose CommandName property is set to select, edit, cancel, delete, or update. If you don't keep track of these details, you might process a command twice—for example, once in the DeleteCommand and once in the ItemCommand event handler.

Managing the Select and Edit States

The demo program that comes on the companion CD uses select mode to display additional information about the title that the user has selected and uses edit mode to let the user modify these fields. Displaying data in select mode is simple, and in many cases you can get along with simple data binding expressions in SelectedItemTemplate. However, in our specific example one of the fields (the publisher's name) comes from another table, so you must specify a JOIN query instead of a single-table SELECT query. Here's the first version of the code that does the data binding and optimizes the SQL query, depending on whether you're in select or edit mode:

```
' The connection to the Pubs database
Dim cn As New OleDbConnection(OledbPubsConnString)

Private Sub Page_Load(ByVal sender As Object, ByVal e As EventArgs) _
    Handles MyBase.Load
    If Not Me.IsPostBack Then
        BindBookList()
    End If
End Sub

Private Sub Page_Unload(ByVal sender As Object, ByVal e As EventArgs) _
    Handles MyBase.Unload
    ' Close the connection if still open.
    If cn.State = ConnectionState.Open Then cn.Close()
End Sub

Sub BindBookList()
    ' Open a connection to Pubs, if necessary.
    If cn.State = ConnectionState.Closed Then cn.Open()

    ' Read title name and key from the Titles table.
    Dim sql As String = "SELECT title_id, title FROM Titles"
    ' If we are in select or edit mode, we must read more data.
    If dlstBooks.SelectedIndex >= 0 Or dlstBooks.EditItemIndex >= 0 Then
        sql = "SELECT Titles.*, Publishers.pub_name FROM Titles " _
            & "INNER JOIN Publishers ON Titles.pub_id=Publishers.pub_id"
    End If

    ' Bind the DataReader to the DataList control.
    Dim cmd As New OleDbCommand(sql, cn)
    Dim dr As OleDbDataReader = cmd.ExecuteReader
    dlstBooks.DataSource = dr
    dlstBooks.DataKeyField = "title_id"
    dlstBooks.DataBind()
    dr.Close()

    If dlstBooks.EditItemIndex >= 0 Then
        ' Get a reference to the DataListItem.
        Dim dli As DataListItem = dlstBooks.Items(dlstBooks.EditItemIndex)
        ' Get a reference to the ddlPublishers DropDownList control.
        Dim ddlPublishers As DropDownList = _
```

```
            DirectCast(dli.FindControl("ddlPublishers"), DropDownList)
        ' Get a reference to the PubId hidden Literal control.
        Dim litPubId As Literal = _
            DirectCast(dli.FindControl("litPubId"), Literal)

        ' Fill the list of publishers.
        cmd = New OleDbCommand("SELECT pub_id, pub_name FROM Publishers", cn)
        dr = cmd.ExecuteReader
        ddlPublishers.DataSource = dr
        ddlPublishers.DataTextField = "pub_name"
        ddlPublishers.DataValueField = "pub_id"
        ddlPublishers.DataBind()
        dr.Close()

        ' Highlight the element corresponding to the title's publisher.
        SelectItemFromValue(ddlPublishers, litPubId.Text)
    End If
End Sub
```

We must solve a couple of additional problems when we enter edit mode, however. First, we must fill the ddlPublishers control with the names of all the publishers. The problem emerges from the fact that we can't reference the ddl-Publishers control directly because it isn't a child control of the page. Worse, it isn't even a child control of the DataList control. In fact, all the controls you place on a DataList control are actually children of the many DataListItem objects contained in the DataList. Therefore, we must first use the Items collection to get a reference to the DataListItem object and then use the FindControl method to obtain a reference to the actual control:

```
' Get a reference to the selected DataListItem.
Dim dli As DataListItem = dlstBooks.Items(dlstBooks.EditItemIndex)
' Get a reference to the ddlPublishers DropDownList control.
Dim ddlPublishers As DropDownList = _
    DirectCast(dli.FindControl("ddlPublishers"), DropDownList)
```

The second problem to solve is selecting the ddlPublishers element that corresponds to the publisher of the titles being edited. To do so, we need the value of the pub_id column for the title being edited, but unfortunately this value isn't available in any field in this row. You can choose from several ways to solve this problem. For example, you might bind to a DataTable or a Data-View object (instead of a DataReader, as we did in this example) and retrieve the value of the pub_id column of the row whose index is equal to the Edit-ItemIndex value. However, DataTable or DataView objects consume more memory and are less scalable than a DataReader, so I suggest that you stay clear of these objects if possible.

The demo program solves this problem by creating an invisible Literal control inside EditItemTemplate and binding it to the pub_id field:

```
<asp:Literal id=litPubId Runat=server Visible=False
    Text='<%# Container.DataItem("pub_id")' %> />
```

Now we can retrieve the pub_id field for the current element simply by querying the Text property of this Literal control. Because the control is buried inside the DataList control, we must use the FindControl method to get a reference to it, as we did for the ddlPublishers control. Once we have the value of the pub_id foreign key, we call the SelectItemFromValue routine to highlight the name of the corresponding publisher:

```
Sub BindBookList()
    ' ...(Introduction code as before)...

    If dlstBooks.EditItemIndex >= 0 Then
        ' Get a reference to the DataListItem.
        Dim dli As DataListItem = dlstBooks.Items(dlstBooks.EditItemIndex)
        ' Get a reference to the ddlPublishers DropDownList control.
        Dim ddlPublishers As DropDownList = _
            DirectCast(dli.FindControl("ddlPublishers"), DropDownList)

        ' Fill the list of publishers.
        cmd = New OleDbCommand("SELECT pub_id, pub_name FROM Publishers", cn)
        dr = cmd.ExecuteReader
        ddlPublishers.DataSource = dr
        ddlPublishers.DataTextField = "pub_name"
        ddlPublishers.DataValueField = "pub_id"
        ddlPublishers.DataBind()
        dr.Close()

        ' Get a reference to the PubId hidden Literal control.
        Dim litPubId As Literal = _
            DirectCast(dli.FindControl("litPubId"), Literal)
        ' Highlight the element corresponding to the title's publisher.
        SelectItemFromValue(ddlPublishers, litPubId.Text)
    End If
End Sub
```

Because the Control class exposes the Controls collection, you can easily implement a generic function that returns a reference to the first control in a form or control with the specified ID. You can use this routine when you don't exactly know which DataListItem contains the control you're looking for:

```
' Find a control in a hierarchy of controls.
Function FindControlRecursive(ByVal ctrl As Control, id As String) As Control
    ' Exit if this is the control we're looking for.
    If ctrl.ID = id Then Return ctrl
```

```
    ' Else, look in the control hierarchy.
    Dim childCtrl As Control
    For Each childCtrl In ctrl.Controls
        Dim resCtrl As Control = FindControlRecursive(childCtrl, id)
        ' Exit if we've found the result.
        If Not resCtrl Is Nothing Then Return resCtrl
    Next
End Function
```

We need to implement the Update command to complete the sample application. This command reads the string in the txtTitle, txtType, and txtPrice controls, and the value associated with the current element in the ddlPublishers control. Once again, we can solve this problem by using the FindControl method of the DataListItem object:

```
Private Sub dlstBooks_UpdateCommand(ByVal source As Object, _
    ByVal e As DataListCommandEventArgs) Handles dlstBooks.UpdateCommand
    ' Get the ID of the record to be deleted.
    Dim title_id As String = dlstBooks.DataKeys(e.Item.ItemIndex).ToString

    ' This is the DataListItem being edited.
    Dim dli As DataListItem = dlstBooks.Items(e.Item.ItemIndex)

    ' Get the values of the txtTitle child control.
    Dim tb As TextBox = DirectCast(dli.FindControl("txtTitle"), TextBox)
    Dim title As String = tb.Text
    ' Do the same with txtType & txtPrice controls, but use a shorter syntax.
    Dim type As String = DirectCast(dli.FindControl("txtType"), TextBox).Text
    Dim price As Decimal = CDec(DirectCast(dli.FindControl("txtPrice"), _
        TextBox).Text)
    ' Get the value of the selected element in ddlPublishers.
    Dim ddlPublishers As DropDownList = _
        DirectCast(dli.FindControl("ddlPublishers"), DropDownList)
    Dim pub_id As String = ddlPublishers.SelectedItem.Value

    ' Prepare to update this record.
    Dim cmd As New OleDbCommand("UPDATE Titles SET title=?, pub_id=?, " _
        & "type=?, price=? WHERE title_id=?", cn)
    cmd.Parameters.Add("@title", title)
    cmd.Parameters.Add("@pub_id", pub_id)
    cmd.Parameters.Add("@type", type)
    cmd.Parameters.Add("@price", price)
    cmd.Parameters.Add("@title_id", title_id)

    ' Open the connection if necessary, and execute the command.
    If cn.State = ConnectionState.Closed Then cn.Open()
    cmd.ExecuteNonQuery()
```

(continued)

```
    ' End the edit mode and rebind the control.
    dlstBooks.EditItemIndex = -1
    dlstBooks.SelectedIndex = e.Item.ItemIndex
    BindBookList()
End Sub
```

A final note: the demo application deletes and updates the data source without worrying about update conflicts based on editing actions performed by other users. To take these conflicts into account, you *must* read the database table in a DataTable or a DataView object and store it in a Session variable. Then you must use one of the update techniques I explained in Chapter 21. Again, storing DataTable or DataView objects in Session variables kills scalability and might introduce server affinity (unless you use out-of-process sessions, which I describe in the next chapter), so you must weigh your decision carefully.

Multiple Columns in DataList Controls

The only feature of the DataList control that I haven't covered yet is its ability to display data in multiple columns, using either a vertical or horizontal layout. You can control this feature by means of the RepeatColumns, RepeatDirection, and RepeatLayout properties. Figure 23-30 shows a DataList control that hosts an Image and a CheckBox control in its ItemTemplate and displays all the graphic files in the directory specified by the user in the txtPath TextBox control. This code does the binding when the user clicks the Display button:

```
Private Sub btnDisplay_Click(ByVal sender As Object, _
    ByVal e As EventArgs) Handles btnDisplay.Click
    ' This is the directory we want to browse.
    Dim path As String = txtPath.Text
    ' This is the ArrayList that works as the data source.
    Dim arrFiles As New ArrayList(100)

    ' Fill the ArrayList with complete filenames.
    Dim file As String
    For Each file In System.IO.Directory.GetFiles(path)
        ' Filter files on their extension.
        Select Case System.IO.Path.GetExtension(file).ToLower
            Case ".gif", ".ico", ".bmp", ".jpg", ".jpeg"
                arrFiles.Add(file)
        End Select
    Next

    ' Bind the ArrayList to the DataList.
    dlstFiles.DataSource = arrFiles
    dlstFiles.DataBind()
End Sub
```

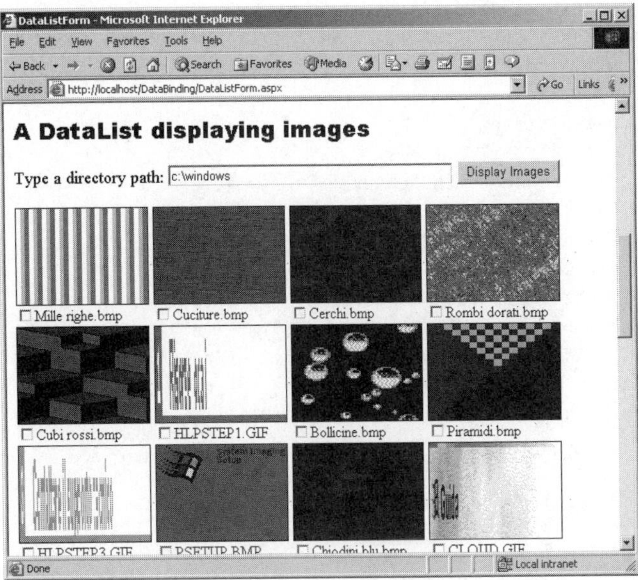

Figure 23-30. A DataList control displaying images in multiple columns.

The ImageUrl property of the Image control has to be bound to complete file paths, but we want to display only the filename in the CheckBox control. Here's how to define the binding expression to solve the problem:

```
<asp:DataList id="dlstFiles" runat="server"
    RepeatDirection="Horizontal" RepeatColumns="4">
  <ItemTemplate>
    <asp:Image id=imgFile runat="server" Width="140px"
       ImageUrl="<%# Container.DataItem %>"
       BorderWidth="1" Height="100px" /><BR>
    <asp:CheckBox id=Checkbox1 runat="server"
       Text='<%# System.Io.Path.GetFileName(Container.DataItem) %>' />
  </ItemTemplate>
</asp:DataList>
```

As the preceding code shows, you must reference the current item by using the Container.DataItem expression when you bind to an ArrayList object. Similarly, you can reference the properties of the current item by using Container.DataItem.Key and Container.DataItem.Value when you bind to a Hashtable object.

The demo program doesn't process the selected images—that is, the images whose companion CheckBox control has been flagged—but it's quite a simple thing to do, now that you know how to use the FindControl method to get a reference to controls contained in a DataList control. Here's a routine that returns an ArrayList containing the complete path of all selected images:

```
' Return the list of selected files.
Function GetSelectedFiles() As ArrayList
    Dim arr As New ArrayList(100)

    Dim dli As DataListItem
    For Each dli In dlstFiles.Items
        ' Get a reference to the CheckBox control.
        Dim chkFile As CheckBox = _
            DirectCast(dli.FindControl("chkFile"), CheckBox)
        If chkFile.Checked Then
            ' If check box is checked, get a reference to the Image control.
            With DirectCast(dli.FindControl("imgFile"), WebControls.Image)
                ' Add the filename to the list of results.
                arr.Add(.ImageUrl)
            End With
        End If
    Next
    ' Return the result array.
    Return arr
End Function
```

The DataGrid Control

The DataGrid control is by far the most complex Web Forms control: it supports several templates, automatic edit mode, and sorting and paging capabilities. Yet it shares many of its properties and events with the DataList control, so you already know how to use most of its features. Table 23-12 lists the main members of the DataGrid control.

Table 23-12 Main Properties and Events of the DataGrid Control

Category	Syntax	Description
Template properties	ItemStyle, AlternatingItemStyle, EditItemStyle, SelectedItemStyle, HeaderStyle, FooterStyle, PagerStyle	A TableItemStyle object that affects how the corresponding visual element is rendered. This object exposes properties such as ForeColor, BackColor, Font, BorderColor, BorderWidth, CssClass, HorizontalAlign, VerticalAlign, and Wrap.
	ShowFooter	True if the footer section is visible (default).
	ShowHeader	True if the header section is visible (default).
Data binding properties	DataSource	The data source for this control.
	DataMember	The data member for this control.
	DataKeyField	The key field in the data source.
	DataKeys	A collection that stores the key value of each record displayed in the control.

Table 23-12 Main Properties and Events of the DataGrid Control *(continued)*

Category	Syntax	Description
Columns properties	Columns	The collection of columns. Columns created automatically aren't added to this collection.
	AutoGenerateColumns	If True (default), the DataGrid automatically creates one column for each bound field.
Appearance properties	HorizontalAlign	The horizontal alignment of the DataGrid inside its container. It can be NotSet, Left, Center, or Right.
	GridLines	The grid line style used when the Repeated-Layout property is set to Table. It can be None, Horizontal, Vertical, or Both.
	CellPadding	The distance between cells and the control's border.
	CellSpacing	The distance between individual cells.
	BackImageUrl	The URL of the image displayed in the background of the DataGrid.
Sorting and paging properties	AllowSorting	True if sorting is enabled. In this case, column headers are rendered as hyperlinks.
	AllowPaging	True if paging is enabled.
	AllowCustomPaging	True if custom paging is allowed.
	VirtualItemCount	The number of items when custom paging is used.
	PageSize	The number of elements in each page.
	PageCount	The number of pages.
	CurrentPageIndex	The index of the current page.
Run time–only properties	Items	The collection of DataGridItem objects that represent individual grid rows.
	EditItemIndex	The index of the element being edited, or –1 if no element is in edit mode
	SelectedIndex	The index of the selected item in the Data-List, or –1 if no item is selected.
	SelectedItem	Returns the DataGridItem object that represents the selected row.
Events	ItemCreated	Fires when an item is created.
	ItemDataBound	Fires when an item is being bound to the data source.
	ItemCommand	Fires when any button in the DataGrid control is clicked.

(continued)

Table 23-12 Main Properties and Events of the DataGrid Control *(continued)*

Category	Syntax	Description
	CancelCommand	Fires when the user clicks a button whose CommandName is Cancel.
	DeleteCommand	Fires when the user clicks a button whose CommandName is Delete.
	UpdateCommand	Fires when the user clicks a button whose CommandName is Update.
	EditCommand	Fires when the user clicks a button whose CommandName is Edit.
	SortCommand	Fires when the user clicks on the hyperlink in a column header to request a sorting operation. The event receives the CommandSource and SortExpression values.
	SelectedIndexChanged	Fires when a different item is selected, which occurs when the user clicks a button whose CommandName is Select.
	PageIndexChanged	Fires when the user navigates to a different page.

Don't be intimidated by the large number of properties of this control. Visual Studio provides both an Auto Format command that lets you select the control's appearance from a gallery of available styles (see Figure 23-31) and a Property Builder command that lets you access a paged dialog box where you can set virtually any property of the control. (See Figure 23-32.) Both commands are available on the control's shortcut menu and in the bottom portion of the Properties window.

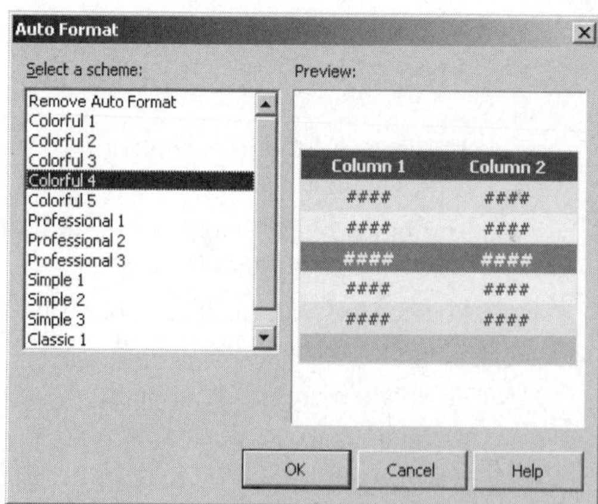

Figure 23-31. The Auto Format dialog box of the DataGrid control.

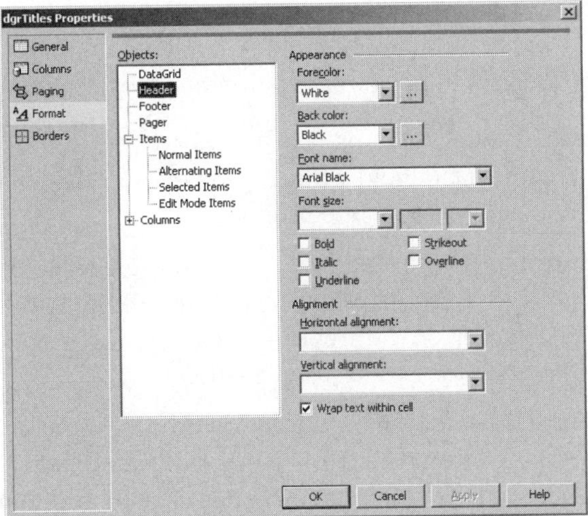

Figure 23-32. The Format page of the Properties dialog box of the DataGrid control.

Columns and Templates

You can display a DataGrid control simply by binding it to a data source and leaving its AutoGenerateColumns property set to True (the default value). In this case, the control generates one bound column for each field in the data source:

```
DataGrid1.DataSource = ds.Tables("Titles")
DataGrid1.DataBind()
```

Even if you don't customize the contents of each grid cell, you still have a lot of control over the appearance of the control by means of *xxxx*Style properties. The DataGrid control supports different styles for seven different visual elements. You can set them using Visual Studio's dialog boxes or by inserting them right in the HTML code:

```
<asp:datagrid id="dgrTitles" runat="server" Width="679px" Height="183px" >
  <HeaderStyle Font-Names="Arial Black" ForeColor="White" _
     BackColor="Black" />
  <ItemStyle BackColor="White" />
  <AlternatingItemStyle BackColor="Khaki" />
  <SelectedItemStyle BackColor="Orange" />
  <EditItemStyle BackColor="Orange" />
  <FooterStyle ForeColor="Blue" />
  <PagerStyle BackColor="Gray" />
  <Columns>
    ⋮
  </Columns>
</asp.datagrid>
```

The items in the <Columns> block define the columns in the DataGrid. You need to specify these columns only if the AutoGenerateColumns property is False. The DataGrid control supports five different types of columns:

- **Bound columns** These columns are bound to the data source's field specified by their DataField property. They automatically display a TextBox control for rows in edit mode.
- **Hyperlink columns** These columns are rendered as hyperlinks that display either a constant caption or a string taken from a data source's field. The target of the hyperlink can be a fixed URL or, more often, a URL based on a data source's field.
- **Button columns** These columns are rendered as Button or LinkButton controls. The button's Text property can be constant or be taken from the data source. When the button is clicked, an ItemCommand event fires on the server and your code can detect which button has been clicked by looking at the CommandName and the e.Item.ItemIndex properties. If CommandName is Select, a click on the button fires a server-side SelectedIndexChanged event and activates the edit mode for the current row. If CommandName is Delete, it fires a server-side DeleteCommand event.
- **Edit, Update, and Cancel columns** These columns are rendered with a Button whose caption is Edit. When clicked, this button fires a server-side EditCommand event. Your code inside this event should set the EditItemIndex property to activate the edit mode for the current row; when you do so, the Edit button is replaced by a pair of buttons labeled Update and Cancel. (You can opt for different captions for the Edit, Update, and Cancel buttons, and you can also use LinkButton controls instead of push buttons.)
- **Template columns** You are in full control of template controls, and in fact you must specify templates for normal items, alternate items, selected items, and edited items. Each template can contain literal HTML text and one or more controls that can be bound to the data source. For example, you can use a template column to render a Boolean field by means of a CheckBox control, a lookup field with a DropDownList control, an enumerated value with a set of RadioButton controls, an Image control for a field that contains a picture, and so on.

Figure 23-33 shows the DataGrid control created by the demo application. This is the column collection used to generate its columns:

```
<asp:datagrid id="dgrTitles" runat="server" AutoGenerateColumns="False">
  ⋮
```

```
 <Columns>
   <asp:TemplateColumn HeaderText="[ ]">
     <ItemTemplate>
       <asp:CheckBox id="chkSelect" runat="server" />
     </ItemTemplate>
   </asp:TemplateColumn>
   <asp:BoundColumn DataField="title" HeaderText="Title" />
   <asp:TemplateColumn HeaderText="Publisher">
     <ItemTemplate>
       <asp:Label id=lblPublisher runat="server" Text=
       '<%# Container.DataItem.Row.GetParentRow("PubsTitles")("pub_name") %>'
         />
     </ItemTemplate>
     <EditItemTemplate>
        <asp:DropDownList id="ddlPublishers" runat="server"
          DataTextField="pub_name" DataValueField="pub_id" />
     </EditItemTemplate>
   </asp:TemplateColumn>
   <asp:BoundColumn DataField="type" HeaderText="Type">
       <HeaderStyle Width="80px" />
   </asp:BoundColumn>
   <asp:BoundColumn DataField="price" HeaderText="Price">
     <HeaderStyle Width="50px" />
   <asp:EditCommandColumn ButtonType="PushButton" UpdateText="Update"
     HeaderText="Edit" CancelText="Cancel" EditText="Edit" />
   <asp:ButtonColumn Text="Delete" ButtonType="PushButton"
     HeaderText="Delete" CommandName="Delete" />
   <asp:HyperLinkColumn Text="Publisher" DataNavigateUrlField="pub_id"
     DataNavigateUrlFormatString="/showpubs.aspx?pub_id={0}"
     HeaderText="More info" />
 </Columns>
</asp:datagrid>
```

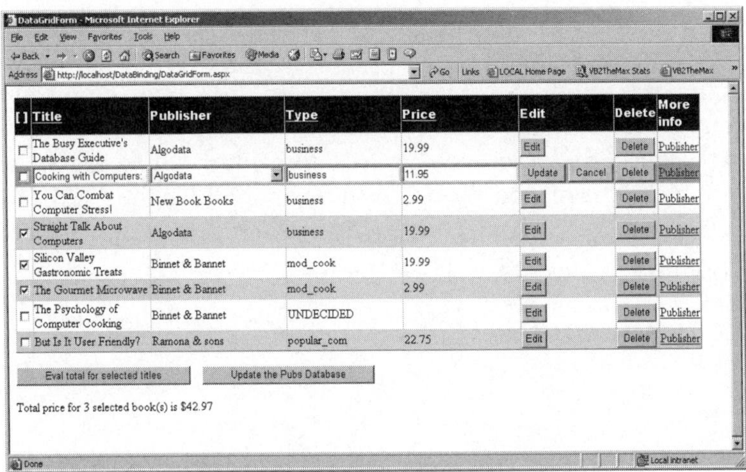

Figure 23-33. The DataGrid created by the demo application.

The Publisher column is a template column because we want to use a DropDownList control to let the user select a publisher when the element is being edited. The first column is also a template column, which we use to display a CheckBox control: the user can select one or more titles and then click the leftmost button at the bottom to evaluate the sum of the prices of selected titles.

The easiest way to set column properties is by right-clicking the DataGrid, clicking Property Builder on the shortcut menu and using the Columns page of the Properties dialog box. (See Figure 23-34.) After you create one or more template columns, you can right-click the DataGrid control, point to Edit Template and click the column on the shortcut menu to edit the template in a visual way, as you did with the DataList control.

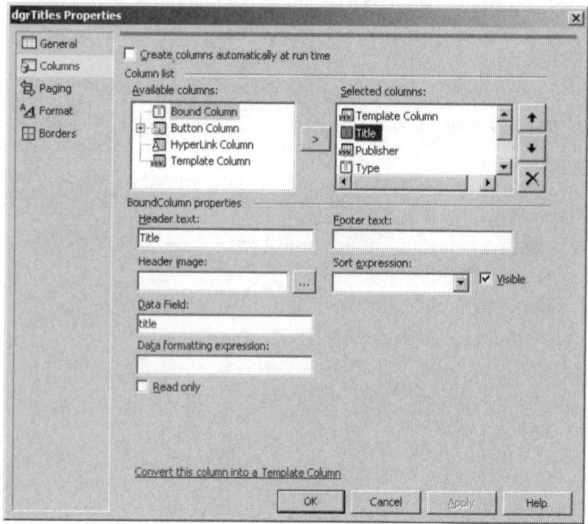

Figure 23-34. The Columns page of the Properties dialog box.

The last column is a hyperlink column. It's interesting to see how the hyperlink is generated for each row in the DataGrid. The value of the DataNavigateUrlFormatString attribute is a .NET formatting string; it contains a {0} element, which is replaced by the value provided by the field pointed to by DataNavigateUrlField. For example, this column generates URLs like these:

```
/showpubs.aspx?pub_id=0736
/showpubs.aspx?pub_id=0877
/showpubs.aspx?pub_id=1389
⋮
```

Command Event Handlers

To simplify the code behind Edit, Update, and Delete, the code reads both the Titles and Publishers table in a DataSet object and then stores it in a Session variable. (Of course, all my warnings against storing a DataSet or a DataTable in a Session variable are still valid, but I needed to simplify the code to keep it manageable enough for this demo.)

```
' The DataSet that contains the data.
Dim ds As New DataSet()

Private Sub Page_Load(ByVal sender As Object, ByVal e As EventArgs) _
    Handles MyBase.Load
    If Not Me.IsPostBack Then
        ' If this is the first time the form is displayed, read the DataSet
        ' and store it in a Session variable.
        FillDataSet()
        Session("DataSet") = ds
        ' Bind the DataGrid control.
        BindDataGrid()
    Else
        ' Or just retrieve the DataSet from the Session variable.
        ds = DirectCast(Session("DataSet"), DataSet)
    End If
End Sub

' Fill the DataSet from the Pubs database.
Sub FillDataSet()
    Dim cn As New OleDbConnection(OledbPubsConnString)
    cn.Open()
    ' Fill the Titles DataTable.
    Dim daTitles As New OleDbDataAdapter("SELECT * FROM Titles", cn)
    daTitles.Fill(ds, "Titles")
    ' Fill the Publishers DataTable (with only the fields we need).
    Dim daPubs As New OleDbDataAdapter( _
        "SELECT pub_id,pub_name FROM Publishers", cn)
    daPubs.Fill(ds, "Publishers")
    ' Close the connection.
    cn.Close()
    ' Create the relation between the two tables.
    ds.Relations.Add("PubsTitles", _
        ds.Tables("Publishers").Columns("pub_id"), _
        ds.Tables("Titles").Columns("pub_id"))
End Sub
```

Thanks to the relation between the Titles and the Publishers table, we can display the name of the publisher in each row by using the following data binding expression for the Label control in the third column:

```
<asp:Label id=lblPublisher runat="server"
  Text='<%# Container.DataItem.Row.GetParentRow("PubsTitles")("pub_name") %>'
/>
```

An explanation is in order: the Container.DataItem operand returns a DataRowView object, which doesn't allow you to traverse relationships. However, it exposes the Row property, which returns the corresponding DataRow object and makes it possible for you to use the GetParentRow method to choose the publisher name by using the PubsTitles relationship.

Inside the BindDataGrid procedure, the program actually binds the dgrTitles control. If the DataGrid is in edit mode, it also binds the ddlPublishers DropDownList control and fills it with the list of available publishers:

```
' Bind the DataGrid control.
Sub BindDataGrid()
    ' Bind the data source to the DataGrid.
    dgrTitles.DataSource = ds.Tables("Titles")
    dgrTitles.DataKeyField = "title_id"
    dgrTitles.DataBind()

    ' If we are in edit mode, also bind the ddlPublishers control.
    If dgrTitles.EditItemIndex >= 0 Then
        ' Get a reference to the ddlPublishers control.
        Dim dgi As DataGridItem = dgrTitles.Items(dgrTitles.EditItemIndex)
        Dim ddlPublishers As DropDownList = _
            DirectCast(dgi.FindControl("ddlPublishers"), DropDownList)
        ' Bind it to the Publishers DataTable.
        ddlPublishers.DataSource = ds.Tables("Publishers")
        ddlPublishers.DataTextField = "pub_name"
        ddlPublishers.DataValueField = "pub_id"
        ddlPublishers.DataBind()

        ' Highlight the publisher of the current title.
        Dim dr As DataRow
        dr = GetDataRow(dgrTitles.DataKeys(dgrTitles.EditItemIndex).ToString)
        SelectItemFromValue(ddlPublishers, dr("pub_id").ToString)
    End If
End Sub
```

The preceding code is very similar to the BindBookList routine that we saw in the section devoted to the DataList control; the main difference is a call to the GetDataRow function to retrieve the DataRow object from the Titles DataTable with a given key value. This detail is important: you might be tempted to use the EditItemIndex value as an index into the DataTable to extract the DataRow corresponding to a given DataGrid element, but this technique fails if the end user has deleted one or more rows. Such deleted rows don't appear in the DataGrid any longer but are still in the DataTable, so the index of a DataGrid element might be less than the index of the corresponding row in the DataTable. The only safe way to retrieve the correct DataRow is by using its key value:

```
' Return the DataRow with a given key value.
Function GetDataRow(ByVal id As String) As DataRow
    ' Select the DataTable rows with this key value.
    Dim drows() As DataRow
    drows = ds.Tables("Titles").Select("title_id='" & id & "'")
    ' Return the DataRow if found.
    If drows.Length > 0 Then
        Return drows(0)
    End If
End Function
```

The following code for the Edit and Cancel buttons is similar to the code that I already described for the DataList control:

```
Private Sub dgrTitles_EditCommand(ByVal source As Object, _
    ByVal e As DataGridCommandEventArgs) Handles dgrTitles.EditCommand
    ' Enter the edit mode and rebind the control.
    dgrTitles.EditItemIndex = e.Item.ItemIndex
    BindDataGrid()
End Sub

Private Sub dgrTitles_CancelCommand(ByVal source As Object, _
    ByVal e As DataGridCommandEventArgs) Handles dgrTitles.CancelCommand
    ' Exit edit mode and rebind the control.
    dgrTitles.EditItemIndex = -1
    BindDataGrid()
End Sub
```

The code for the Update command is not so simple because it has to retrieve the value stored in the bound controls, and therefore it needs a reference to these controls. We can get a reference to a child control in a template column by using the FindControl method of the DataGridItem object, using a technique similar to the one we used with child controls in the DataList control. But this technique doesn't work with child controls in bound columns because in that case we don't know what name we should pass to the FindControl method. To access controls in bound columns, we must first use the Cells collection of the DataGridItem object to retrieve a reference to the table cell that contains the control we're interested in and then use Controls(0) to get a reference to the first (and only) control contained in that cell. Here's the code that implements this technique:

```
Private Sub dgrTitles_UpdateCommand(ByVal source As Object, _
    ByVal e As DataGridCommandEventArgs) Handles dgrTitles.UpdateCommand
    ' Get a reference to the DataGridItem being edited.
    Dim dgi As DataGridItem = dgrTitles.Items(e.Item.ItemIndex)
    ' Get the DataRow with the corresponding key value.
    Dim dr As DataRow = _
        GetDataRow(dgrTitles.DataKeys(e.Item.ItemIndex).ToString)

    ' Update DataRow columns.
    ' The title value is the only control in the 2nd cell in this row.
    dr("title") = DirectCast(dgi.Cells(1).Controls(0), TextBox).Text
    ' The pub_id field is the current value of the ddlPublishers control.
    Dim ddlPublishers As DropDownList = _
        DirectCast(dgi.FindControl("ddlPublishers"), DropDownList)
    dr("pub_id") = ddlPublishers.SelectedItem.Value
    ' The type field is the only control in the 4th cell in this row.
    dr("type") = DirectCast(dgi.Cells(3).Controls(0), TextBox).Text
    ' The price field is the only control in the 5th cell in this row.
    dr("price") = CDec(DirectCast(dgi.Cells(4).Controls(0), TextBox).Text)

    ' Exit edit mode and rebind the DataGrid.
    dgrTitles.EditItemIndex = -1
    BindDataGrid()
End Sub
```

The handler for the DeleteCommand event calls the GetDataRow function to retrieve a reference to the current DataRow and then invokes the Delete method on it:

```
Private Sub dgrTitles_DeleteCommand(ByVal source As Object, _
    ByVal e As DataGridCommandEventArgs) Handles dgrTitles.DeleteCommand
    ' Get a reference to the DataGridItem being deleted.
    Dim dgi As DataGridItem = dgrTitles.Items(e.Item.ItemIndex)
    ' Get the DataRow with the corresponding key value.
    Dim dr As DataRow = _
        GetDataRow(dgrTitles.DataKeys(e.Item.ItemIndex).ToString)
    ' Delete it and rebind the control.
    dr.Delete()
    BindDataGrid()
End Sub
```

The code behind the btnEval button scans the Items collection of the DataGrid control and sums the price value for all the titles whose CheckBox controls in the first column have been flagged. Here's an example of what you can do with this technique:

```
Private Sub btnEval_Click(ByVal sender As System.Object, _
    ByVal e As EventArgs) Handles btnEval.Click
    ' Sum the price of all titles that have a selected checkbox.
    Dim totalPrice As Decimal
    Dim count As Integer

    Dim dgi As DataGridItem
    For Each dgi In dgrTitles.Items
        ' Get a reference to the CheckBox control in this item.
        Dim cb As CheckBox = _
            DirectCast(dgi.FindControl("chkSelect"), CheckBox)
        ' If checked, delete this element.
        If cb.Checked Then
            ' Get the title_id key value for this row.
            Dim id As String = dgrTitles.DataKeys(dgi.ItemIndex).ToString
            ' Select the DataTable row with this key value.
            Dim dr As DataRow = GetDataRow(id)
            If Not dr.IsNull("price") Then
                ' Add the price to the running total.
                totalPrice += CDec(dr("price"))
                count += 1
            End If
        End If
    Next

    ' Display the total.
    lblTotal.Text = String.Format( _
        "Total price for {0} selected book(s) is ${1}", count, totalPrice)
End Sub
```

For simplicity's sake, the demo program doesn't contain the code that updates the Pubs database from the modified DataSet. But it's easy to implement this code by adopting one of the update techniques outlined in Chapter 21.

Sorting Rows

The DataGrid provides support for sorting its rows. To enable this feature, you must do the following:

- Set the AllowSorting property to True.
- Set the SortExpression property for one or more columns to a suitable string (most often, the name of the field that works as the sort key). You can initialize this property in the Columns page of the Property Builder page. (See Figure 23-34.)

When these properties are properly set, the text in the column's header becomes a hyperlink that the user can click to sort the DataGrid's contents on that field. (For example, the DataGrid in Figure 23-33 can be sorted on the Title,

Type, and Price fields.) A click on these hyperlinks fires a server-side SortCommand event that receives the column's sort expression in the SortExpression property of the second argument. You must trap this event, sort the rows as requested, and rebind the control. Typically you implement sorting by binding the DataGrid control to a DataView object (instead of a DataTable) and setting its Sort property appropriately.

To make things more interesting, the demo application supports sorting in both ascending and descending directions. A first click on a column sorts in ascending order, and a second click on the same column reverses the direction. This technique requires that we preserve the current sort expression between postbacks. We can store this value in the page's ViewState or as a custom attribute of the DataGrid. The demo program adopts the latter technique, which lets you set the attribute at design time by editing the HTML code. For example, the following HTML code sorts titles from the priciest to the least expensive:

```
<asp:datagrid id="dgrTitles" SortExpr="price DESC" runat="server"
    AutoGenerateColumns="False" AllowSorting="True">
  ⋮
</asp:datagrid>
```

To implement sorting in our program, we must trap the SortCommand event and set the SortExpr attribute correctly:

```
Private Sub dgrTitles_SortCommand(ByVal source As Object, _
    ByVal e As DataGridSortCommandEventArgs) Handles dgrTitles.SortCommand
    ' Extract current sort expression and set the new one.
    Dim currSortExpr As String = dgrTitles.Attributes("SortExpr")
    Dim newSortExpr As String = e.SortExpression

    ' If the expression is the same, just reverse the direction.
    If Not (currSortExpr Is Nothing) AndAlso _
        currSortExpr.ToString = e.SortExpression Then
            newSortExpr &= " DESC"
    End If

    ' Remember the new sort expression and rebind.
    dgrTitles.Attributes("SortExpr") = newSortExpr
    BindDataGrid()
End Sub
```

To complete the implementation of the sort command, we must check the SortExpr attribute just before binding the control and use a sorted DataView object if the attribute isn't a null string. The following listing shows the statements (in boldface) that we must add to the BindDataGrid procedure:

```
Sub BindDataGrid()
    ' Bind the data source to the DataGrid.
    dgrTitles.DataSource = ds.Tables("Titles")
    dgrTitles.DataKeyField = "title_id"
```

```
    ' Retrieve the SortExpression.
    Dim sortExpr As String = dgrTitles.Attributes("SortExpr")
    If Not (sortExpr Is Nothing) AndAlso sortExpr.ToString <> "" Then
        ' We must bind to a sorted DataView object instead.
        Dim dv As DataView = ds.Tables("Titles").DefaultView
        dv.Sort = sortExpr.ToString
        dgrTitles.DataSource = dv
    End If
    ' Do the binding.
    dgrTitles.DataBind()

    ' ...(The remainder of the routine is as before)...
    ⋮
End Sub
```

Because you're binding to a DataView object instead of a DataTable, you can implement several other features. For example, you can use the RowFilter and RowStateFilter properties to display only a subset of all the rows, find rows with the Find and FindRows methods, and so on.

Default and Custom Paging

We've arrived at the last DataGrid feature I cover. The DataGrid control allows the user to navigate through pages of results, which is essential when a table displays more than a few dozen rows. The DataGrid control supports three paging techniques:

- **Default paging with default navigation buttons** The DataGrid displays a set of hyperlink buttons that let you navigate through its pages. You can display either Previous and Next buttons (with any caption you wish) or page numbers.
- **Default paging with custom navigation buttons** You provide the navigation buttons and trap their server-side Click event to move to the page the user requested.
- **Custom paging** You're in complete control of how data is loaded in the DataGrid control, as well as how navigation buttons are displayed.

Not surprisingly, the first technique is the simplest one. You just set the AllowPaging property to True and set the PageSize property to a suitable value (for example, 10 rows). You can quickly set these and other properties related to paging in the DataGrid's Properties dialog box. (See Figure 23-35.) Ensure that the Show Navigation Buttons check box is selected, decide where you want to display the buttons (Top, Bottom, or Top and Bottom), and whether you want to display Previous and Next buttons or page-number buttons. If you want Previous and Next buttons, you can set the buttons' captions (default is <

and >). If you want page-number buttons, you can decide how many buttons are visible. (Default is 10.)

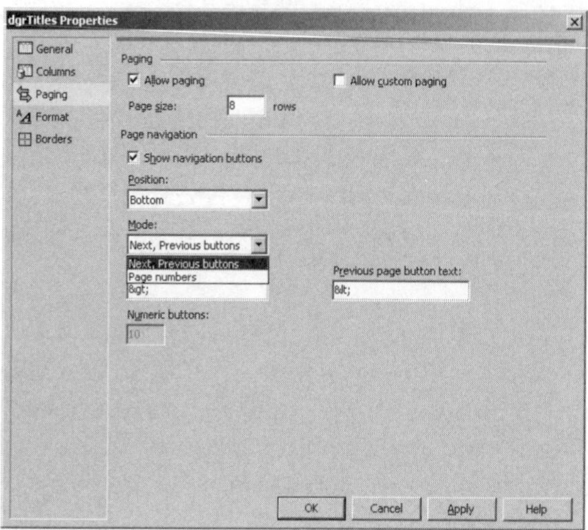

Figure 23-35. The Paging section of the DataGrid's Properties dialog box.

When a navigation button is clicked, a PageIndexChanged event is fired on the server. Inside this event's handler, you must assign a new value to the DataGrid's CurrentPageIndex property and rebind the control:

```
Private Sub dgrTitles_PageIndexChanged(ByVal source As Object, _
    ByVal e As DataGridPageChangedEventArgs) _
    Handles dgrTitles.PageIndexChanged
    ' Navigate to another page and rebind the DataGrid.
    dgrTitles.CurrentPageIndex = e.NewPageIndex
    BindDataGrid()
End Sub
```

Implementing the second technique, default paging with custom navigation controls, is only a little more complex. Because you're providing the navigation buttons, you must clear the Show Navigation Buttons check box in the Properties dialog box and place suitable navigation buttons elsewhere on the form. The demo application displays the usual four navigation buttons, plus a Go button that lets you jump to any page. The text box in the center always displays the current page, and buttons are correctly disabled if their action wouldn't move to another page. (See Figure 23-36.)

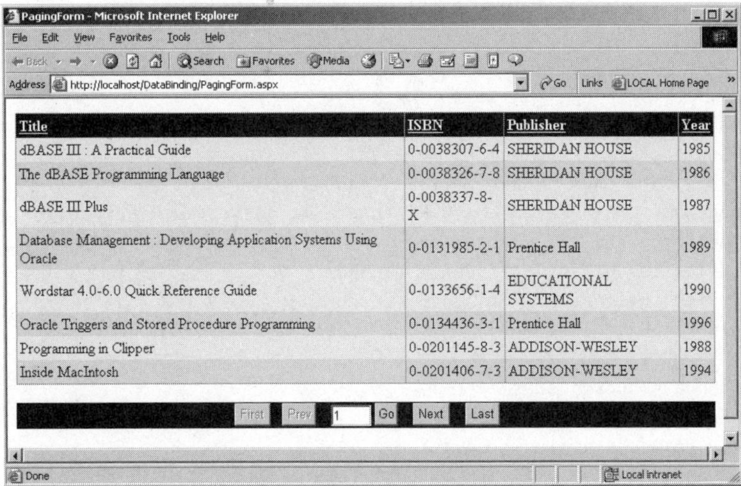

Title	ISBN	Publisher	Year
dBASE III : A Practical Guide	0-0038307-6-4	SHERIDAN HOUSE	1985
The dBASE Programming Language	0-0038326-7-8	SHERIDAN HOUSE	1986
dBASE III Plus	0-0038337-8-X	SHERIDAN HOUSE	1987
Database Management : Developing Application Systems Using Oracle	0-0131985-2-1	Prentice Hall	1989
Wordstar 4.0-6.0 Quick Reference Guide	0-0133656-1-4	EDUCATIONAL SYSTEMS	1990
Oracle Triggers and Stored Procedure Programming	0-0134436-3-1	Prentice Hall	1996
Programming in Clipper	0-0201145-8-3	ADDISON-WESLEY	1988
Inside MacIntosh	0-0201406-7-3	ADDISON-WESLEY	1994

Figure 23-36. The demo application supports five navigation buttons.

Here's the code that traps the buttons' server-side Click event, modifies the DataGrid's CurrentPageIndex property as required, and rebinds the control. Each control has been assigned a different CommandName property, so detecting the navigation command being invoked is simple:

```
Private Sub ButtonClick(ByVal sender As Object, ByVal e As EventArgs) _
    Handles btnFirst.Click, btnPrevious.Click, btnNext.Click, _
    btnLast.Click, btnGo.Click

    ' The current page number
    Dim pageNum As Integer = dgrTitles.CurrentPageIndex

    Select Case DirectCast(sender, Button).CommandName.ToLower
        Case "first"
            pageNum = 0
        Case "prev"
            pageNum -= 1
        Case "next"
            pageNum += 1
        Case "last"
            pageNum = dgrTitles.PageCount - 1
        Case "go"
            Try
                ' Visible page number is 1-based.
                pageNum = CInt(txtPage.Text) - 1
            Catch
                Exit Sub
            End Try
    End Select
```

(continued)

```
        ' Show the page.
        ShowPage(pageNum)
    End Sub

    ' Display a page.
    Sub ShowPage(ByVal pageNum As Integer)
        ' Keep the page number in valid range.
        pageNum = Math.Max(0, Math.Min(pageNum, dgrTitles.PageCount - 1))
        ' Enforce the new page number.
        dgrTitles.CurrentPageIndex = pageNum
        ' Bind the control.
        BindDataGrid()

        ' Update button state.
        btnFirst.Enabled = (pageNum > 0)
        btnPrevious.Enabled = (pageNum > 0)
        btnNext.Enabled = (pageNum < dgrTitles.PageCount - 1)
        btnLast.Enabled = (pageNum < dgrTitles.PageCount - 1)
        ' Display the current page number (1-based).
        txtPage.Text = (pageNum + 1).ToString
    End Sub
```

When you're doing default paging—using either default or custom navigation buttons—you must bind the DataGrid control to a DataView or DataTable object, as you'd do if paging were disabled so that the control can use the CurrentPageIndex property to display only the requested page. The demo application reduces database activity by creating the DataSet object the first time the page is requested and storing it in a Session variable. Here's the code that does the binding and provides support for column sorting as well:

```
' Bind the DataGrid control.
Sub BindDataGrid()
    ' Retrieve the DataSet from the session variable.
    Dim ds As DataSet = DirectCast(Session("DataSet"), DataSet)

    ' Read data from database if this is the first time we do it.
    If ds Is Nothing Then
        Dim cn As New OleDbConnection(BiblioConnString)
        cn.Open()
        ' Read data from Titles table, plus the publisher's name.
        Dim sql As String
        sql = "SELECT Titles.*, Publishers.Name As PubName FROM Titles " _
            & " INNER JOIN Publishers ON Titles.PubId=Publishers.PubId"
        Dim da As New OleDbDataAdapter(sql, cn)
        ds = New DataSet()
        da.Fill(ds, "Titles")
        cn.Close()
        ' Store the DataSet in a Session variable.
        Session("DataSet") = ds
    End If
```

```
    ' Get a DataView object sorted on the required sort expression.
    Dim dv As DataView = ds.Tables("Titles").DefaultView
    dv.Sort = dgrTitles.Attributes("SortExpr")
    dgrTitles.DataSource = dv

    ' Do the data binding.
    dgrTitles.DataBind()
End Sub

Private Sub dgrTitles_SortCommand(ByVal source As Object, _
    ByVal e As DataGridSortCommandEventArgs) Handles dgrTitles.SortCommand
    ' Extract current sort column and order.
    Dim currSortExpr As String = dgrTitles.Attributes("SortExpr")
    Dim newSortExpr As String = e.SortExpression

    ' If the sort field is the same, just reverse the direction.
    If Not (currSortExpr Is Nothing) AndAlso _
        currSortExpr.ToString = e.SortExpression Then
        newSortExpr &= " DESC"
    End If

    ' Remember the new sort expression and show the first page.
    dgrTitles.Attributes("SortExpr") = newSortExpr
    ShowPage(0)
End Sub
```

Default paging has a great shortcoming: you must load *all* the data in a DataTable or DataView object to let the DataGrid control select only the rows that belong to the current page. This approach might be OK when the data source contains a few hundred rows, but it won't work in real-world applications that manage thousands (or even millions) of rows. In cases like these, custom paging is the only reasonable solution.

You activate custom paging by setting both the AllowPaging and the AllowCustomPaging properties to True. You then assign the total number of rows to the VirtualItemCount property so that the control can correctly evaluate the PageCount value. You can either use default buttons or provide your own.

Unlike our practice in all the samples I've shown you so far, when in custom paging mode we bind the DataGrid control to a data source that contains *only* the data we want to display in the current page. Fortunately, we already know how to page through a large resultset by using the DataAdapter's Fill method. Thanks to the high modularity of the code we've written so far, implementing custom paging is just a matter of replacing the BindDataGrid procedure with a new version that takes the CurrentPageIndex and PageSize properties into account. The following code also takes the current sort order into account: note that when doing custom paging, we implement sorting by means of an ORDER BY clause in the SQL query so that we can then extract the correct page from the sorted resultset:

```
Sub BindDataGrid()
    ' Open the connection.
    Dim cn As New OleDbConnection(BiblioConnString)
    cn.Open()

    ' If necessary, initialize VirtualItemCount with number of records.
    If Not Me.IsPostBack Then
        Dim cmd As New OleDbCommand("SELECT COUNT(*) FROM Titles", cn)
        dgrTitles.VirtualItemCount = CInt(cmd.ExecuteScalar)
    End If

    ' Prepare to read from Titles table plus Name of publisher.
    Dim sql As String = "SELECT Titles.*, Publishers.Name As PubName FROM " _
        & "Titles INNER JOIN Publishers ON Titles.PubId=Publishers.PubId"
    ' Append sort expression, if there is one.
    Dim sortExpr As String = dgrTitles.Attributes("SortExpr")
    If Not (sortExpr Is Nothing) AndAlso sortExpr.ToString <> "" Then
        sql &= " ORDER BY " & sortExpr
    End If
    ' Fill a DataSet only with data for the current page.
    Dim ds As New DataSet()
    Dim da As New OleDbDataAdapter(sql, cn)
    da.Fill(ds, dgrTitles.CurrentPageIndex * dgrTitles.PageSize, _
        dgrTitles.PageSize, "Titles")
    ' Close the connection and release resources.
    cn.Close()

    ' Do the binding.
    dgrTitles.DataSource = ds.Tables("Titles")
    dgrTitles.DataBind()
End Sub
```

If you really want to squeeze the best performance out of your code, you should use the technique described in the section "Paginating Results" of Chapter 21, which performs better than the Fill method with large resultsets.

Dynamic Templates

All the templates we've dealt with in this chapter were static templates: they were defined in HTML code buried inside the .aspx page and couldn't be changed at run time. For the highest degree of flexibility, ASP.NET supports the ability to load templates at run time, using one of the following two mechanisms:

- You can use the LoadTemplate method of the Page object to load a template file (which must have an .ascx extension) and assign it to one of the *xxxx*Template properties that the Repeater, DataList, and DataGrid controls expose.
- You can define a template class in code, and then instantiate it at run time and assign it to an *xxxx*Template property. A template class is a class that implements the ITemplate interface.

Loading a Template File

A template file is simply an .ascx file that contains the text that you would place inside an <*xxxx*Template> block. For example, you might save the following text in a file named blue_on_orange.ascx and later apply it to display a DataList item with blue foreground color and orange background color, which displays the title and price fields from its data source:

```
<div style="COLOR: Blue; BACKGROUND-COLOR: Orange">
  <b>
  <%# DataBinder.Eval(CType(Container, DataListItem).DataItem, "title") %>
  </b> -
  <%# DataBinder.Eval(CType(Container, DataListItem).DataItem, "price") %>
</div>
```

An important note: you must use the DataBinder.Eval syntax and early binding when you create a dynamic template; hence you need the CType operator to convert from the generic Container reference to a more specific DataListItem or DataGridItem object to invoke the DataItem property. Unfortunately, this requirement means that a single template file containing bound expressions can't serve different types of controls.

Loading an .ascx file at run time into a template control is trivial. For example, this code applies different templates to regular and alternate items in a DataList control:

```
DataList1.ItemTemplate = Me.LoadTemplate("blue_on_orange.ascx")
DataList1.AlternatingItemTemplate = Me.LoadTemplate("blue_on_white.ascx")
DataList1.DataBind()
```

I prepared a demo application that lets you experiment with dynamic template loading. (See Figure 23-37.) The two DropDownList controls are loaded with four template names, and you can select separate templates for the regular and the alternate item. You can use this code as a boilerplate for building applications that users can customize with the templates you provide. The template must belong to the same ASP.NET application as the page that loads it.

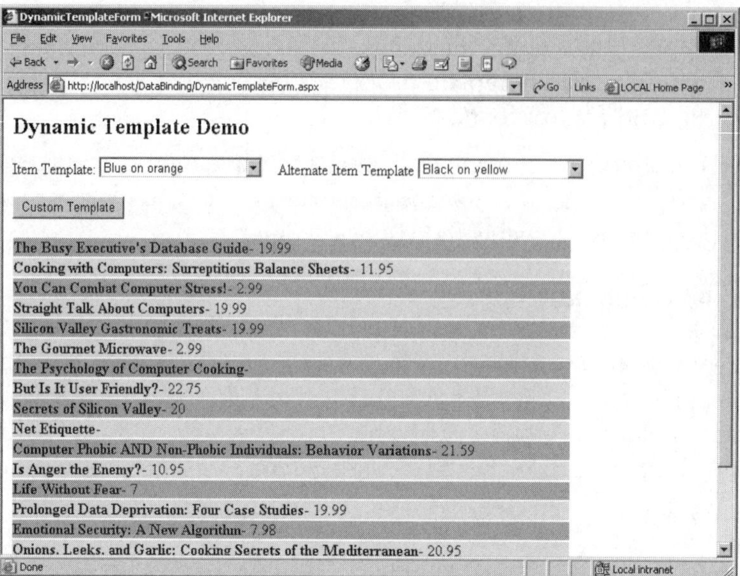

Figure 23-37. The demo application lets you select different custom templates for regular and alternate items.

Template Classes

For maximum flexibility, you can write a template class and assign one of its instances to the *xxxx*Template properties that the Repeater, DataList, and DataGrid controls expose. A template class is just a class that implements the ITemplate interface, which in turn exposes just one method: InstantiateIn. This method is called once for each item in the control and receives a reference to the RepeaterItem, DataListItem, or DataGridItem object. You typically react to this method by creating a child control inside the item:

```
Class MyTemplate
    Implements ITemplate

    Dim WithEvents pan As Panel

    Public Sub InstantiateIn(ByVal container As Control) _
        Implements ITemplate.InstantiateIn

        ' Get a strongly typed reference to the containing item.
        Dim dli As DataListItem = DirectCast(container, DataListItem)
        ' Create a new Panel control.
        pan = New Panel()
        ⋮
        ' Add the Panel control to the DataListItem control.
        dli.Controls.Add(pan)
    End Sub
End Class
```

You must be able to trap events from the control being added (the Panel control in the preceding code) because you must process its DataBinding event, which fires once for every item in the template control:

```
Private Sub pan_DataBinding(ByVal sender As Object, _
    ByVal e As EventArgs) Handles pan.DataBinding
    ⋮
End Sub
```

The demo application uses a custom template class to perform a few tasks that wouldn't be possible with a standard template. First the template paints items with three different colors. Next it replaces Null values in the data source with a custom string. Finally it changes the style of a data-bound element, depending on its contents. (See Figure 23-38.) Here's the complete source code of the template class:

```
Class MyCustomTemplate
    Implements ITemplate

    Public ForeColor As Color
    Public BackColor As Color
    Public AltBackColor As Color
    Public AltBackColor2 As Color

    Sub New(ByVal foreColor As Color, ByVal backColor As Color, _
        ByVal altBackColor As Color, ByVal altBackColor2 As Color)
        Me.ForeColor = foreColor
        Me.BackColor = backColor
        Me.AltBackColor = altBackColor
        Me.AltBackColor2 = altBackColor2
    End Sub

    ' We must trap the DataBinding event for this control.
    Dim WithEvents pan As Panel

    Public Sub InstantiateIn(ByVal container As Control) _
        Implements ITemplate.InstantiateIn

        ' Get a strongly typed reference to the containing item.
        Dim dli As DataListItem = DirectCast(container, DataListItem)

        ' Create a panel with specified colors.
        pan = New Panel()
        pan.ForeColor = Me.ForeColor
        ' Use alternate colors for background.
        Select Case dli.ItemIndex Mod 3
            Case 0 : pan.BackColor = Me.BackColor
            Case 1 : pan.BackColor = Me.AltBackColor
            Case 2 : pan.BackColor = Me.AltBackColor2
        End Select
```

(continued)

```
        ' Adapt to the container's size.
        pan.Width = dli.Width
        pan.Height = dli.Height

        ' Add child controls to this panel.
        pan.Controls.Add(New LiteralControl("<b>"))
        pan.Controls.Add(New Label())          ' This is the title field.
        pan.Controls.Add(New LiteralControl("</b> - "))
        pan.Controls.Add(New Label())          ' This is the price field.

        ' Add the Panel control to the DataListItem control.
        dli.Controls.Add(pan)
    End Sub

    Private Sub pan_DataBinding(ByVal sender As Object, _
        ByVal e As EventArgs) Handles pan.DataBinding
        ' Get a reference to the item container.
        ' (Note: cast to a DataGridItem if working with a DataGrid.)
        Dim dli As DataListItem = _
            DirectCast(pan.NamingContainer, DataListItem)
        ' Get a reference to the data source row.
        ' (Note: cast to a DataRowView if binding to a DataTable/DataView.
        Dim dbr As System.Data.Common.DbDataRecord = _
            DirectCast(dli.DataItem, System.Data.Common.DbDataRecord)

        ' Get the values of all the fields you're interested in,
        ' and display them in the Panel child controls.
        Dim lblTitle As Label = DirectCast(pan.Controls(1), Label)
        lblTitle.Text = dbr("title").ToString
        ' This is the price Label control.
        Dim lblPrice As Label = DirectCast(pan.Controls(3), Label)

        If dbr("price").ToString.Length > 0 Then
            ' Display price if this field isn't Null.
            lblPrice.Text = "$" & dbr("price").ToString
            ' Use special attributes for expensive titles.
            If CDec(dbr("price")) > 20 Then
                lblPrice.ForeColor = Color.Red
                lblPrice.Font.Bold = True
            End If
        Else
            ' Display special message for Null values.
            lblPrice.Text = "(unknown price)"
            lblPrice.Font.Italic = True
        End If
    End Sub
End Class
```

This is the code behind the button's Click event that activates the custom template:

```
Private Sub btnCustom_Click(ByVal sender As System.Object, _
    ByVal e As EventArgs) Handles btnCustom.Click
    ' Set the alternate item template to Nothing so that the control
    ' uses the custom template for all its elements.
    DataList1.AlternatingItemTemplate = Nothing
    ' Create a custom template and assign it to the ItemTemplate property.
    DataList1.ItemTemplate = New MyCustomTemplate(Color.Blue, Color.White, _
        Color.Cyan, Color.LightGreen)
    BindDataList()
End Sub

Sub BindDataList()
    Dim cn As New OleDbConnection(OleDbPubsConnString)
    cn.Open()
    Dim cmd As New OleDbCommand("SELECT * FROM Titles", cn)
    Dim dr As OleDbDataReader = cmd.ExecuteReader
    DataList1.DataSource = dr
    DataList1.DataBind()
    dr.Close()
    cn.Close()
End Sub
```

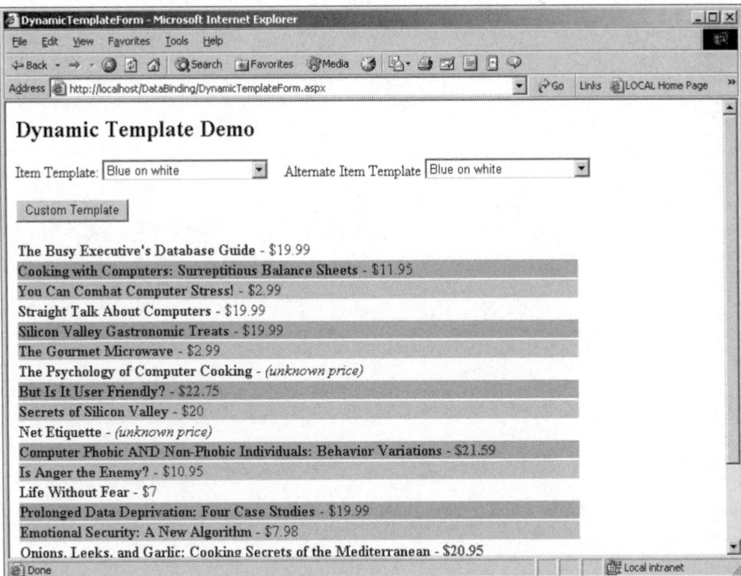

Figure 23-38. The MyCustomTemplate class paints items with alternate background colors, displays high prices in red, and replaces Null values with a custom string.

In this chapter, you've seen how to create a rich and functional user interface for your Web Forms applications. However, ASP.NET isn't just about a pretty interface, and you still have to learn several important details about caching, error handling, configuration, and debugging. I discuss those topics in the next chapter.

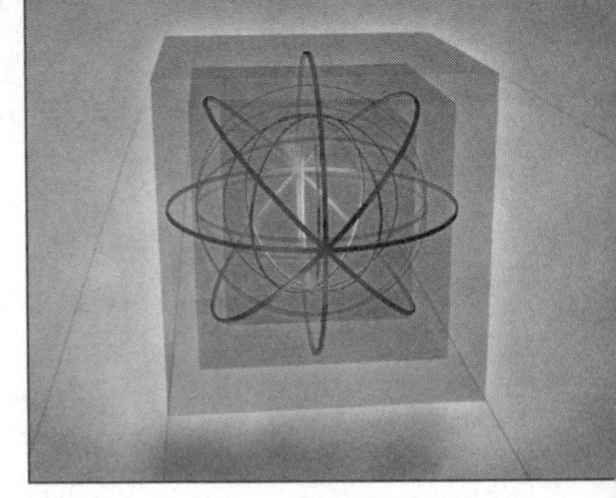

24

ASP.NET Applications

Knowing the ins and outs of Web Forms and controls is a good starting point for creating great Internet applications, but you have to learn more to leverage the full potential of ASP.NET. This chapter covers such missing details as these and unveils the essentials of ASP.NET configuration, caching, security, error handling, debugging, and tracing.

Configuration files play an essential role in any ASP.NET application. These are XML files that hold critical information about the ASP.NET runtime or individual ASP.NET applications—for example, how state sessions are implemented and which users are granted access to the application. There are three types of configuration files:

- **machine.config** is the main configuration file and contains the settings related to ASP.NET as a whole. All the ASP.NET applications inherit these settings, but they can override them. This file resides in the c:\winnt\Microsoft.Net\Framework\v*x.y.zzzz*\Config directory. There's one machine.config file for each installed version of the .NET Framework.
- **web.config** is the configuration file that you place in an ASP.NET application's root directory. It often overrides machine.config settings related to session state, page directives, security, and tracing. Visual Studio .NET automatically generates this file when you create a new Web Forms project.
- **secondary web.config files** can reside in any subdirectory belonging to the application. Each additional configuration file can override values in the application's main web.config file, and can assign different settings to files that are located in that subdirectory.

All the web.config files in an application form a hierarchy: each directory inherits all the settings from its parent directory, but it can override them by using a local web.config file. This hierarchical structure makes possible the so-called XCOPY deployment and sharply contrasts with the way you install complex ASP applications, which requires that you manually set Microsoft Internet Information Services (IIS) settings on a directory-by-directory basis (or create a script that does it on your behalf). A few settings can't be overridden by secondary configuration files—for example, those related to state sessions and a few security settings. Regardless of their position, all configuration files have the same basic structure:

```
<?xml version="1.0" encoding="utf-8" ?>
<configuration>
  <system.web>
    ⋮
  </system.web>
</configuration>
```

I'll cover configuration files in much detail in the "ASP.NET Configuration Files" section near the end of this chapter, but I needed to make this introduction so that you can fully understand the topics in between.

ASP.NET Intrinsic Objects

In the section "Page Properties" of Chapter 23, I hinted at the fact that the five "classic" Active Server Pages objects—namely, Request, Response, Server, Session, and Application—have now become properties of the Page object. Because your code runs in the page's context, you can access these objects under ASP.NET exactly as you did under ASP. For example, you can still send raw output to the browser by using the Response.Write method, and you can read arguments passed to the page by using the Request.QueryString collection.

```
' These two statements are equivalent.
Response.Write("<h1>Welcome to ASP.NET</h1>")
Me.Response.Write("<h1>Welcome to ASP.NET</h1>")
```

Here's the source code of a simple ASP.NET page that redirects the browser to another page whose URL is passed as an argument and keeps a running total of redirections performed so far:

```
Public Class RedirectPage
    Inherits System.Web.UI.Page

    Private Sub Page_Load(ByVal sender As Object, ByVal e As EventArgs) _
        Handles MyBase.Load
        ' Read the target URL on the query string.
        Dim url As String = Request.QueryString("url")
```

```
        ' Increment the number of redirections so far.
        Dim appVarName As String = "redirections_count"
        Application.Lock()
        If Application(appVarName) Is Nothing Then
            Application(appVarName) = 1
        Else
            Application(appVarName) = CInt(Application(appVarName)) + 1
        End If
        Application.UnLock()

        ' Redirect to the specified URL (on this Web server).
        Server.Transfer(url)
    End Sub
End Class
```

You can use the RedirectPage.aspx page as follows:

```
http://www.tailspintoys.com/RedirectPage.aspx?url=/productinfo.aspx
```

Although on the surface the preceding code looks similar to old ASP scripts, these five objects have been greatly enhanced in ASP.NET. Let's see how.

> **Note** The following sections assume that you're familiar with classic ASP programming. Remember: you can refresh your knowledge of this subject by reading Chapter 20 of *Programming Microsoft Visual Basic 6*, included on the companion CD.

The HttpRequest Class

The page's Request property returns an instance of the System.Web.HttpRequest class. The main difference from the old ASP Request object is the addition of many properties that were previously exposed as members of the ServerVariables collection. (See Table 24-1.) For example, we can enhance the previous redirection example to store a different counter for each referrer URL; all we need to do is replace the line of code that defines which Application variable holds the number of redirections:

```
Dim appVarName As String = "redirections_from_" & Request.UrlReferrer
```

In classic ASP, you can pass a string as an argument to the Request object as a quick way to look for a value in the QueryString, Form, ServerVariables, and Cookies collections:

```
itemValue = Request("itemname")
```

This syntax isn't supported in ASP.NET. You can port your legacy code quite easily, however, thanks to the new Params collection:

```
itemValue = Request.Params("itemname")
```

The HttpRequest class inherits the BinaryRead method from ASP and adds a few new ones. The MapPath method is similar to Server.MapPath in classic ASP, but it can take a base virtual directory and can work across ASP.NET applications:

```
' The physical location corresponding to the /default.aspx virtual
' path belonging to the /MyAspNetApp application.
' (Last argument must be true to support cross-app references.)
Dim path As String = Request.MapPath("/default.aspx", "/MyAspNetApp", True)
```

Table 24-1 Properties of the HttpRequest Class

Syntax	Description
AcceptTypes	A string array that contains all the MIME types accepted by the browser.
ApplicationPath	The application's virtual root path on the server.
Browser	The HttpBrowserCapabilities object that describes the client browser capabilities.
ClientCertificate	The current request's client security certificate.
ContentEncoding	The character set of the encoding body.
ContentLength	The size of the client request (in bytes).
ContentType	The MIME content type of the client request.
Cookies	The collection of cookies sent by the client.
CurrentExecutionFilePath	The virtual path of the current executing page. This can be different from FilePath if the page has been invoked using a Transfer or Execute method.
FilePath	The virtual path of the current page.
Files	An HttpFileCollection object representing all the files uploaded by the client (for Multipart MIME format).
Filter	Gets or sets the Stream used to filter the current input stream.
Form	The collection of form variables.
Headers	The collection of HTTP headers, as a NameValueCollection object.
HttpMethod	A string that specifies the HTTP method (GET, POST, or HEAD).
InputStream	A Stream that represents the contents of the incoming HTTP content body.
IsAuthenticated	True if the user has been authenticated.

Table 24-1 Properties of the HttpRequest Class *(continued)*

Syntax	Description
IsSecureConnection	True if the connection is using secure sockets (HTTPS).
Params	A collection that combines the values in QueryString, Form, ServerVariables, and Cookies. (This was the default member in ASP.)
Path	The virtual path of the current request.
PathInfo	Additional path information for a resource containing a URL extension.
PhysicalApplicationPath	The physical file system path of the application's root directory.
PhysicalPath	The physical file system path of the current page.
QueryString	The collection of query string arguments.
RawUrl	The portion of the URL string that follows the domain name.
RequestType	Gets or sets the HTTP method used by the client (GET or POST).
ServerVariables	The collection of server variables.
TotalBytes	The number of bytes in the current input stream.
Url	The System.Uri object containing information about the URL of the current request.
UrlReferrer	The System.Uri object containing information about the URL of the client's previous request that linked to the current request.
UserAgent	The raw user agent string of the client browser.
UserHostAddress	The IP address of the remote user.
UserHostName	The DNS name of the remote user.
UserLanguages	The sorted string array of client language preferences.

Working with URLs

The Url and UrlReferrer properties return a System.Uri object. You can query the properties of this object to learn more about the address in question, so you don't have to parse the string yourself:

```
' Get information on the referrer for this request.
Dim url As System.Uri = Request.UrlReferrer
Debug.WriteLine(url.AbsoluteUri)    ' => http://www.tailspintoys.com/
default.aspx
Debug.WriteLine(url.AbsolutePath)   ' => /default.aspx
Debug.WriteLine(url.Host)           ' => http:/www.tailspintoys.com
Debug.WriteLine(url.Port)           ' => 80
Debug.WriteLine(url.IsLoopback)     ' => False
```

You can also use a Uri object to parse a URL string that the user typed in a field or that you've received in an argument:

```
Dim url As New System.Uri("http://www.tailspintoys.com/index.aspx?id=123")
Dim path As String = url.AbsolutePath          ' => /index.aspx
Dim queryString As String = url.Query          ' => id=123
```

Saving HTTP Requests

The new SaveAs method saves the current HTTP request to a file, which can be very useful for logging and debugging reasons. You should pass True to its second argument if you want to save HTTP headers as well:

```
Request.SaveAs "c:\lastrequest.txt", True
```

The saved file contains something like this:

```
GET /AspObjects/RequestForm.aspx HTTP/1.1
Connection: Keep-Alive
Accept: */*
Accept-Encoding: gzip, deflate
Accept-Language: en-us
Cookie: LastVisitDate=12%2F6%2F2001+5%3A02%3A46+PM;
   ASP.NET_SessionId=ee4mi0ugensntgvkfjt0v4nd
Host: localhost
User-Agent: Mozilla/4.0 (compatible; MSIE 6.0; Windows NT 5.0; .NET CLR
   1.0.3512)
```

Testing Browser Capabilities

The Browser property returns an HttpBrowserCapabilities object that lets you check whether the client browser supports a given functionality. (You needed an external component to perform this test under ASP.) This class exposes 25 properties, including Browser (the user agent string), MajorVersion and MinorVersion (the browser's version), Platform (the client operating system), JavaApplets, JavaScript, VBScript, ActiveXControls, BackgroundSounds, and Frames:

```
' Check whether the request comes from a search engine robot.
If Request.Browser.Crawler Then
    ' Adapt the response to the search engine.
    ⋮
End If

' Check whether the client supports VBScript.
If Request.Browser.VBScript Then
    ' Send VBScript code to the browser.
    ⋮
End If
```

Reading Uploaded Files

The Files collection gives you access to all uploaded files in a multipart/form-data page. Each element in this collection is an HttpPostedFile object that exposes properties such as FileName, ContentType, and ContentLength. You can read the file's contents using the InputStream property or by calling the SaveAs method:

```
Dim file As HttpPostedFile
Dim counter As Integer
For Each file In Request.Files
    ' Display the original filename.
    Debug.WriteLine(file.FileName)
    ' Save on the server with a unique file.
    counter += 1
    file.SaveAs("PostedFile" & counter.ToString & ".dat")
Next
```

For more information about file uploading, see the section "The HtmlInputFile Class" in Chapter 23.

The HttpResponse Class

The page's Response property returns an instance of the System.Web.HttpResponse class. This class has several new properties and methods that are missing in the corresponding ASP object. (See Tables 24-2 and 24-3.) Some properties and methods—namely Buffer, CacheControl, Expires, ExpiresAbsolute, AddHeader, and Clear—are maintained for backward compatibility but have been deprecated in favor of new ones. Other methods have survived the transition from ASP without any noticeable change—as in the case of CharSet, Cookies, IsClientConnected, Status, AppendToLog, Close, End, Flush, and Redirect—and for this reason I won't cover them here.

The main method in this class is still Write, which has been overloaded to work with any object and with an array of Chars. However, the ASP.NET Response object has been greatly expanded in its ability to send output to the client browser. For example, the WriteFile method can send the contents of any text, HTML, or XML file to the browser. In classic ASP, you have to load the file in memory and then pass its contents to a Write method to achieve the same effect. For example, you can use this method to apply a common frame and style, typically a menu bar or footer, to any .txt file:

```
' Get the name of the requested document (passed on the query string).
Dim path As String = Request.QueryString("doctitle") & ".txt"
' Convert to a physical path.
path = Request.MapPath(path)
If System.IO.File.Exists(path) Then
    ' If the file exists, send it to the browser as HTML.
```

(continued)

```
    Response.Write("<HTML><BODY>")
    Response.Write("<H1>Here's the document you've requested</H1>")
    Response.WriteFile(path)
    Response.Write("</BODY></HTML>")
Else
    ' Else display an error message.
    Response.Write("Sorry, no document with this name.")
End If
```

Table 24-2 Properties of the HttpResponse Class

Syntax	Description
Buffer	True (default) if output is buffered and sent when the page has been completely processed. This ASP property is now deprecated in favor of BufferOutput.
BufferOuput	True (default) if output is buffered and sent when the page has been completely processed.
Cache	An HttpCachePolicy object that describes the current caching policy.
CacheControl	A string that affects the Cache-Control HTTP header. Can be Public or Private; this property has been deprecated in favor of the HttpCachePolicy class.
CharSet	Gets or sets the character set of the output stream.
ContentEncoding	Gets or sets the Encoding object that describes the characters sent to the browser.
ContentType	Gets or sets the string that represents the MIME type of the output stream (for example, "text/html" or "text/xml").
Cookies	The collection of cookies being sent to the client browser.
Expires	Gets or sets the number of minutes after which a cached page expires; this property has been deprecated in favor of the HttpCachePolicy class.
ExpiresAbsolute	Gets or sets the absolute date and time when a cached page expires; this property has been deprecated in favor of the HttpCachePolicy class.
Filter	Gets or sets the Stream object that filters all the data being sent to the browser.
IsClientConnected	Returns True if the client is still connected to the server and waiting for an answer.
Output	Returns the TextStream object that sends text output to the client browser.
OutputStream	Returns the Stream object that sends binary output to the client.

Table 24-2 Properties of the HttpResponse Class *(continued)*

Syntax	Description
Status	The string representing the status line being returned to the client; the default is "200 OK".
StatusCode	Gets or sets the status code being returned to the client; the default is 200.
StatusDescription	The string representing the status description being returned to the client; the default is the "OK" string.
SuppressContent	If True, no content will be sent to the client.

Table 24-3 Main Methods of the HttpResponse Class

Syntax	Description
AddCacheItem-Dependency (cacheKey)	Makes the cached response of this page dependent on the specified cached item.
AddCacheItem-Dependencies (cacheKeys)	Makes the cached response of this page dependent on all the cached items specified by the ArrayList passed as an argument.
AddFile-Dependency (filename)	Makes the cached response of this page dependent on the specified file.
AddFile-Dependencies (filenames)	Makes the cached response of this page dependent on all the files whose names are specified in the ArrayList passed as an argument.
AddHeader (name, value)	Adds an HTTP header to the output stream; this method has been deprecated in favor of AppendHeader.
AppendHeader (name, value)	Adds an HTTP header to the output stream.
Append-ToLog(text)	Adds custom log information to the IIS log file.
ApplyAppPath-Modifier (virtualpath)	Combines a virtual path with the session ID; it is used to build absolute HREFs when cookieless sessions are enabled.
BinaryWrite (bytearr)	Writes the contents of a Byte array to the output stream.
Clear	Clears the content of the output stream; this method has been deprecated in favor of ClearContent.
ClearContent	Clears the content of the output stream.
ClearHeaders	Clears all the headers from the output stream.
Close	Closes the socket connection to a client.

Table 24-3 Main Methods of the HttpResponse Class *(continued)*

Syntax	Description
End	Stops execution of the page and sends buffered output to the client.
Flush	Sends buffered output to the client.
Pics(label)	Appends a Platform for Internet Content Selection (PICS) label HTTP header to the output stream.
Redirect(url [,bool])	Redirects the client to a new URL. If the second (optional) argument is True, the execution of the current page is terminated.
RemoveOutput-CacheItem(path)	Removes from the cache all the cached methods associated with a given physical path (shared methods).
Write(string) Write(chararr, index, count)	Writes a string, an object, or a portion of a Char array to the output stream.
WriteFile(path)	Write the contents of a file directly to the output stream.

Working with Cookies

The importance of cookies has dramatically decreased under ASP.NET because now you can choose from so many other ways to store information between consecutive requests—for example, by using the page's ViewState property. However, there are still many cases when you want to send a cookie to the browser, especially if you mean for the cookie to persist on the client's system to be read back in future visits that the client makes to a site. You can use cookies in this fashion to store user names, passwords, color schemas, and other preferences, or partially filled shopping carts for orders that can be completed in subsequent sessions.

As in ASP, both the Request and the Response objects expose a Cookies collection, but the way you interact with these collections is slightly different in ASP.NET. The Request.Cookies collection is the collection of HttpCookie objects that the browser is submitting with the current request. As in ASP, this collection is read-only and you can choose to only enumerate its contents or read the value of a specific cookie:

```
Sub ShowCookies()
    ' Display name and value of all cookies.
    Dim msg, cookieName As String

    For Each cookieName In Request.Cookies.AllKeys
        ' Get the cookie with a given name.
        Dim cookie As HttpCookie = Request.Cookies(cookieName)
        ' Add information on this cookie.
```

```
        msg &= String.Format("<b>{0}</b> = {1}<br>", cookieName, _
            cookie.Value)
    Next
    ' Display the result in a Literal control.
    litCookieValues.Text = msg
End Sub
```

You create a new cookie and send it to the client browser by creating an HttpCookie object and adding it to the Response.Cookies collection. Here's a code snippet that creates a cookie that expires in two weeks:

```
' Create a cookie with a given name and value.
Dim cookie As New HttpCookie("color", "red")
' Set its expiration date (2 weeks from now).
cookie.Expires = Now.AddDays(14)
' Send it to the client.
Response.Cookies.Add(cookie)
```

The HttpCookie class exposes a few other properties, such as Domain and Path (the domain and path associated with the cookie); HasKeys (a read-only property that returns True if the cookie is multikey); Values (a collection of values for multikey cookies); and Secure (True if the cookie should be transmitted only over HTTPS). Except for HasKeys, you set these properties when you create the cookie.

Generating Graphics Dynamically

The OutputStream property is a Stream object that you can use to send binary output to the client browser. This feature is especially powerful when used together with graphic images generated dynamically on the server. Typically, you create an in-memory Bitmap object of the size and color depth that you want. Then you draw your image in it using GDI+ methods. (See Chapter 18.) Finally you use the Bitmap's Save method to serialize the image in your choice of format to the Stream object returned by Response.OutputStream. Here's the code that produces the image shown in Figure 24-1:

```
Private Sub Page_Load(ByVal sender As Object, ByVal e As EventArgs) _
    Handles MyBase.Load
    If Request.QueryString("imgtitle") <> "" Then
        ShowImage(Request.QueryString("imgtitle"))
    End If
End Sub

Sub ShowImage(ByVal imgTitle As String)
    ' Create a bitmap with given width, height, and color depth.
    Dim bmp As New Bitmap(400, 200, Imaging.PixelFormat.Format16bppRgb565)
    ' Get the underlying Graphics object.
    Dim gr As Graphics = Graphics.FromImage(bmp)
    ' Clear its background.
    gr.Clear(Color.Red)
```

(continued)

```
    ' Create a font.
    Dim fnt As New Font("Arial", 16, FontStyle.Regular, GraphicsUnit.Point)

    ' Draw a series of rotated strings.
    Dim angle As Single
    For angle = 0 To 360 Step 30
        ' Reset coordinate transforms.
        gr.ResetTransform()
        ' Translate and rotate the coordinate system.
        gr.TranslateTransform(200, 100)
        gr.RotateTransform(angle)
        ' Draw the (rotated) string.
        gr.DrawString(imgTitle, fnt, Brushes.Black, 0, 0)
    Next

    ' Clear current content and set returned content type.
    Response.Clear()
    Response.ContentType = "image/jpeg"
    ' Save to the Response.OutputStream object.
    bmp.Save(Response.OutputStream, Imaging.ImageFormat.Jpeg)

    ' Release resources.
    fnt.Dispose()
    gr.Dispose()
    bmp.Dispose()

    Response.End()
End Sub
```

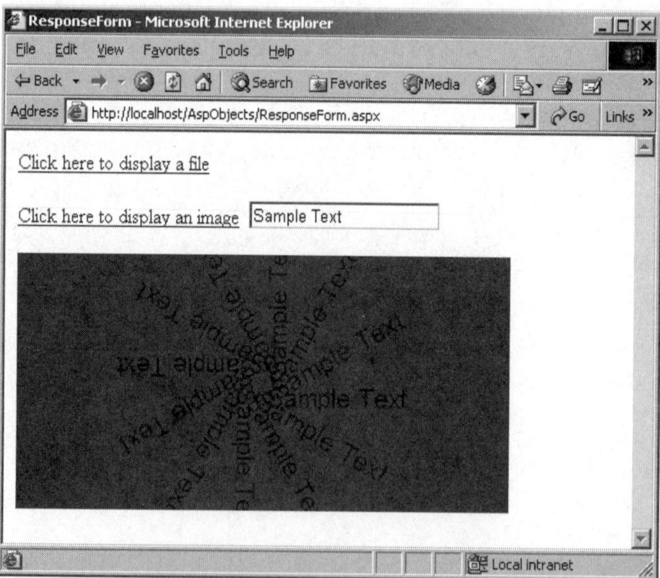

Figure 24-1. An image generated dynamically with ASP.NET.

It's essential that the Response.ContentType property matches the type of the graphic contents that you're sending to the client browser (image/jpeg in this case). Just as important, the routine must stop processing the page by using a Response.End method immediately after sending the graphic data. The code reads the query string to retrieve the text to be displayed in the image, so you can see an image if you navigate to the page using an address like this:

```
http://localhost/AspObjects/ResponseForm.aspx?imgtitle=sample text
```

However, a page like this isn't meant to work as the target of browser navigation; more likely you'll use this page as the SRC attribute of an <IMG> tag, or the ImageUrl property of an Image or ImageButton control. This is exactly how the page in Figure 24-1 works, and this is the server-side code behind the Click event for the hyperlink:

```
Private Sub btnImage_Click(ByVal sender As Object, _
    ByVal e As EventArgs) Handles btnImage.Click
    ' Change the ImageUrl of the Image control, so that it makes
    ' a request to this same page.
    Image1.ImageUrl = Request.Url.AbsolutePath & "?imgtitle=sample text"
End Sub
```

Note that the Request.Url.AbsolutePath property returns the URL of the running page. In other words, this page has a dual function: when the user navigates to it, the page returns only the HTML code for the two hyperlinks and the Image control; but the SRC attribute in the Image control causes a second request to be posted to the page, this time with an imgtitle argument on the query string. The code in the Page_Load event detects that this time the image is requested and returns only the bitmap that's dynamically generated, which is why you must end the page processing and prevent other code in the page from executing.

This (admittedly contorted) technique lets you keep both the controls and the image generation code in the same page and lets you accomplish a lot of intriguing things. You might take data from a database and display it in a graph—for example, a histogram or a pie. Or you might store and retrieve bitmaps stored in database BLOB fields, such as photos, and process them on the fly to adjust their size, color depth, transparency, and so on. Best of all, you can adapt this technique to data formats other than images and generate other types of documents—for example, Microsoft Word or Microsoft Excel documents—based on data stored in a database or returned by an XML Web service.

Filtering Response Output

The last feature of the Response object I am covering is the ability it gives you to filter its output. To implement this feature, you must define a class that inherits from Stream and assign an object of this class to the Response's Filter property before any response is sent to the client browser:

```
Private Sub Page_Load(ByVal sender As Object, ByVal e As EventArgs) _
    Handles MyBase.Load
    ' Filter all output.
    Response.Filter = New ConvertTagFilter(Response.Filter)
End Sub
```

Your class must store a reference to the original filter stream and must override the Write method to intercept all the HTML text data sent to the client (although it might be any type of content, such as XML or binary). The demo application on the companion CD uses a ConvertTagFilter class to convert all <b> and </b> tags into <strong> and </strong>. As you see, the code in the Write method converts from a Byte array to a Char array, then to a string, and then to a Byte array again:

```
Class ConvertTagFilter
    Inherits System.IO.Stream

    Private m_stream As System.IO.Stream
    Private m_position As Long

    ' Store the original filter Stream in a private variable.
    Public Sub New(ByVal stream As System.IO.Stream)
        m_stream = stream
    End Sub

    ' This is the method that actually does the filtering.
    Public Overrides Sub Write(ByVal bytes() As Byte, _
        ByVal offset As Integer, ByVal count As Integer)

        ' Copy the Byte array into an array of chars.
        Dim chars(count - 1) As Char
        Dim i As Integer
        For i = 0 To count - 1
            chars(i) = Convert.ToChar(bytes(i + offset))
        Next

        ' Create a string from the Char array.
        Dim output As New String(chars)
        ' Replace all <BR> with <P>, in case-insensitive mode.
        output = Replace(output, "<b>", "<strong>", , , CompareMethod.Text)
        output = Replace(output, "</b>", "</strong>", , , CompareMethod.Text)

        ' Copy the string back into an array of chars.
        chars = output.ToCharArray
        Dim newBytes(chars.Length - 1) As Byte
        ' Copy the array of chars into another array of bytes.
```

```
        For i = 0 To chars.Length - 1
            newBytes(i) = Convert.ToByte(chars(i))
        Next
        ' Output the bytes.
        m_stream.Write(newBytes, 0, count)
    End Sub

    ' ...(Other overridden methods are omitted.)...

End Class
```

The ConvertTagFilter class must also override all the methods that are marked as MustOverride in the Stream base class—namely, CanRead, CanWrite, Seek, Length, and a few others. The implementation of these methods is really easy because most of the time you just return a True value or delegate the method to the inner Stream object stored in the m_stream variable. See the demo application for the complete source code.

This technique isn't simple, but it allows rather intriguing results. You can use it to implement several advanced features, including content encryption, tag substitution, XML rendering, and dynamic modifications of the URLs embedded in HREF and SRC attributes.

The HttpServerUtility Class

The page's Server property returns an object of the System.Web.HttpServerUtility class. This object is similar to the ASP Server object, with just a few minor differences and improvements.

The HttpServerUtility class exposes only two properties: ScriptTimeout (the timeout in seconds for a request) and the new MachineName property, which returns the name of the server computer. You can use the latter property to understand whether the ASP.NET application is running on the development box or on the production server. This information might be useful if you want to adopt slightly different parameters (for example, the connection string to the database).

Class methods haven't changed much in the transition to ASP.NET, so you can still use Execute, Transfer, MapPath, HtmlEncode, UrlEncode, and UrlPathEncode. The CreateObject method has been overloaded to support a System.Type argument, and you also have a CreateObjectFromClsid method that instantiates a COM object with a given CLSID. The new HtmlDecode method decodes a string that has been encoded, so it reverses the effect of the HtmlEncode method:

```
Dim text As String = "A <tag>"
Dim encoded As String = Server.HtmlEncode(text)    ' => A &lt;tag&gt;
Dim decoded As String = Server.HtmlDecode(encoded) ' => A <tag>
```

Similarly, the new UrlDecode method reverses the action of the UrlEncode method. The only other new method of this object is ClearError, which clears the most recently thrown exception. You typically use it after trapping an exception in a Page_Error event handler, as you saw in the "Page Events" section of Chapter 23.

The HttpSessionState Class

The Session property of the Page object returns an instance of the System.Web.SessionState.HttpSessionState class. You use this object for storing values that are logically related to a specific user (as opposed to values shared by all users of the application), in much the same way you used the Session object under ASP:

```
Session("counter") = CInt(Session("counter")) + 1
```

You can create a new session variable by using the Add method:

```
' This statement overwrites the previous value of counter, if there is one.
Session.Add("counter", 0)
```

The Remove and RemoveAt methods remove a single session variable. You can also delete all the session variables by using either the RemoveAll or the Clear method.

Table 24-4 lists the properties of the HttpSessionState class. A few new properties might become useful, such as Count (number of variables) and IsNewSession (True if this is the first request from this user). The Keys property returns the collection of the names of all session variables:

```
' Display the list of all session variables.
Dim key As String
For Each key In Session.Keys
    Response.Write(String.Format("<b>{0}</b> = {1}<br>", key, Session(key)))
Next
```

I'll explain the meaning of other new properties—such as IsCookieless, IsReadOnly, and Mode—in the "Session State" section, later in this chapter.

Table 24-4 Properties of the HttpSessionState Class

Syntax	Description
CodePage	The code page identifier for the current session (read/write).
Contents	Returns a reference to the current session-state object. It's provided for compatibility with ASP.
Count	Returns the number of items in the session-state collection.
IsCookieless	Returns True if the current session ID is embedded in the URL instead of being stored in a cookie.

Table 24-4 Properties of the HttpSessionState Class

Syntax	Description
IsNewSession	Returns True if the session has been created with the current request.
IsReadOnly	Returns True if the session is read-only.
IsSynchronized	Returns True if access to the session collection is synchronized (or thread-safe).
Item(indexOrName)	Gets or sets a session variable. This is the default member for the class.
Keys	Returns a KeysCollection that contains the names of all the session variables.
LCID	Gets or sets the locale identifier for the current session.
Mode	Returns the current session mode. It can be InProc (default), Off, SqlServer, or StateServer.
SessionID	Returns the ID of the current session.
StaticObjects	Returns the collection of objects that are declared with <object runat=server> tags in Global.asax.
SyncRoot	Returns an object that can be used to synchronize access to the collection of session values.
Timeout	Gets or sets the session timeout (in minutes). If no request arrives for this session in the specified timeout, the session is terminated.

The HttpApplicationState Class

The Page's Application property returns an instance of the HttpApplicationState class. This object is created when the very first request is posted to an ASP.NET application and an Application_Start event fires in Global.asax. A single HttpApplicationState object is created for all the clients of an ASP.NET application on a Web server, but it isn't shared across a Web garden (an application hosted in multiple worker processes on the same multi-CPU machine) or a Web farm (an application hosted in multiple computers on the same network).

You use this object in the same way that you use the Session object, except that application variables are shared between all clients of the application. You should use these variables only for data that doesn't change often after the application has been created. In a difference from the way you use session variables, you must lock the Application object before accessing its variables, and you must unlock the object when you're done with them:

```
Application.Lock()
Application("items") = CInt(Application("items")) + _
    CInt(Application("newitems"))
Application.Unlock()
```

After a piece of code has locked the Application object, no other ASP.NET pages can access its variables until the Application object is unlocked. So working with application variables can easily become a bottleneck. Fortunately, if you don't unlock the Application explicitly, the Unlock method is called automatically when the current request has been completed, when it timeouts, or when an unhandled exception occurs. The Application object also supports the Add method:

```
Application.Add("connectionstring", BiblioConnString)
```

In this case, the variable is created even if there's already another variable with this name and you'd see both variables in the Keys collection. The Application object exposes a subset of the properties and methods of the Session object, including Contents, StaticObjects, Add, Clear, Remove, RemoveAt, and RemoveAll.

Don't forget that application variables are lost when the ASP.NET process is stopped or recycled. If you want to preserve the application's state when this happens, you should write code for the Application_OnEnd event in Global.asax to save it to a persistent medium and restore it in the Application_Start event handler.

Application recycling is a great feature that lets you configure an application so that ASP.NET automatically shuts it down and restarts it after a given period or a given number of client requests, or when it consumes more memory than the specified threshold. This feature is a lifesaver if the application progressively degrades its performance because of memory leaks—which might happen if the application uses unmanaged resources. You control application recycling by means of one or more settings in the <processModel> tag in web.config. For example, this setting recycles the ASP.NET application every hour:

```
<configuration>
  <system.web>
    <processModel timeout="60" />
  </system.web>
</configuration>
```

For more information about application recycling, read the section about the <processModel> tag, later in this chapter.

State Management and Caching

ASP.NET developers have several options for places they can store values used by applications. In fact, unlike traditional Win32 applications, ASP or ASP.NET programming is stateless, which means that variables aren't preserved between consecutive requests to the same (or a different) page of the same application. Let me quickly review the advantages and shortcomings of the techniques available to ASP developers for storing state between consecutive requests:

- **Client-side cookies** Because data travels back and forth at each request to a page of the application, you can use this technique only for small amounts of data. Of course, it doesn't work at all if the end user has disabled cookie support in the browser. A great advantage of this technique is that values can be persisted between consecutive visits to the same site.
- **Session variables** You can use Session variables for larger amounts of data than cookies, but each variable takes memory on the server, so this technique impedes scalability. Worse, ASP sessions don't work on Web gardens or Web farms, so your application can't easily scale out to multiple processes or multiple servers. Finally, sessions are implemented by means of cookies, so they aren't available when cookies are disabled (even though the IIS SDK contains a utility that helps you work around this problem by storing the user ID in the URL instead of a client-side cookie).
- **Application variables** You can use this technique only for data shared by all the clients that are connected to the application, so its usefulness is limited, in practice, to caching read-only data such as a database connection string or the table of product codes and prices. Finally, Application values aren't shared among Web gardens and farms.
- **Hidden fields or the query string** This approach doesn't require cookie support but can't be implemented easily and usually requires rather contorted coding techniques. Moreover, unlike cookies and session variables, values stored in hidden fields or the query string are lost when the user hits the Back button to return to a page visited previously.
- **Database records plus a cookie or a Session variable that holds the key associated with each user** This technique is the only one that scales well even with large amounts of data and that can scale out to Web farms. It has some drawbacks: it requires extra coding, is slower than all other techniques, and still requires client-side cookie support.

Although all these techniques are still available under ASP.NET, you'll rarely use some of them directly because ASP.NET offers a few great alternatives. For example, the Page's ViewState property works exactly like hidden fields, but it's remarkably simpler to use. As you'll see shortly, ASP.NET supports additional session modes that work across Web farms, can use a database to store user data, and can even function without cookie support. Almost unbelievably, you can switch from regular sessions to these enhanced session modes by simply changing a configuration setting without editing a single line in code.

Another important facet of ASP.NET programming is using its caching features correctly. As you'll learn later in this chapter, ASP.NET supports different types of cache techniques: you can cache the ouput generated by a page and you can cache large data structures in the Cache object. In both cases, you can enforce very sophisticated expiration policies. And you can still use other forms of caching as well—for example, Application and Session variables.

Session State

As I mentioned in the previous section, ASP.NET extends Session state management with two new features:

- **Cookieless sessions** When you enable this feature, the session ID token is burned into the URL instead of being stored in a cookie. This setting slows down execution a little but ensures that your application works flawlessly even if the end user disabled cookie support in the browser.
- **Out-of-process sessions** ASP.NET can store session data in its process's memory (the default behavior, the same as in ASP), in a separate process running as a Windows service, or in a SQL Server database. The last two options let you share session data among all the components of a Web garden or a Web farm, at the cost of slower execution.

You can combine these new features, if necessary, by having cookieless sessions whose data is stored in a Windows service or a SQL Server database. As in classic ASP, you can even disable sessions completely, either for individual pages or the entire application, to reduce memory consumption on the server machine. In addition, ASP.NET supports a new read-only mode at the page level, which enables you to improve the performance of individual pages that read but don't need to modify Session variables.

You enable most of the new session state features by setting one or more attributes in machine.config or in the web.config file stored in the root directory of the application:

```
<configuration>
  <system.web>
    <sessionState
        mode="InProc"
        stateConnectionString="tcpip=127.0.0.1:42424"
        sqlConnectionString="data source=127.0.0.1;user id=sa;password="
        cookieless="false"
        timeout="20"
    />
    ⋮
  </system.web>
</configuration>
```

You can edit the web.config file right inside Visual Studio .NET. This file is automatically created with each new ASP.NET application, and it contains several sections with default settings and many remarks that explain how you can change them.

Cookieless Sessions

Enabling cookieless sessions is as simple as setting the cookieless attribute to true:

```
cookieless="true"
```

If you now run the application, you'll notice that the session ID is embedded in the URL and enclosed in parentheses (as you see in Figure 24-2). Of course, all the hyperlinks embedded in the page take this extra item into account, as you see here:

```
<a href="/AspObjects/(3s5e3p551hk0mn55znkurpmv)/AnotherPage.aspx>
Click here to display a file</a>
```

Most of the time, you don't have to do anything else to leverage this feature. An exception to this laissez-faire practice is when you want to pass a URL to another application—for example, an external component. In this case, you should build the URL properly to ensure that the correct session ID is found when the other component accesses the application. You can test whether you're in a cookieless session by using the IsCookieless property and call the Response.ApplyAppPathModifier method to produce the correct URL:

```
Dim url As String = "/AnotherPage.aspx"
If Session.IsCookieless Then
    url = Response.ApplyAppPathModifier(url)
End If
' You can now safely pass the URL to another component.
```

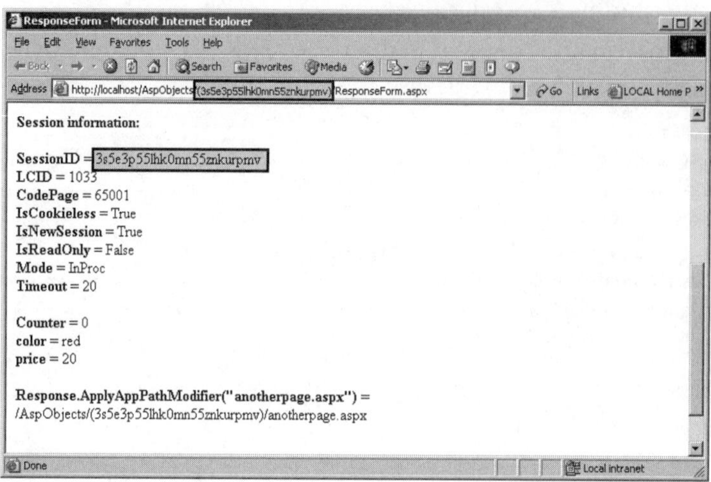

Figure 24-2. Cookieless sessions in Microsoft Internet Explorer.

Out-of-Process Sessions Based on a Windows Service

To activate out-of-process sessions based on a Windows service, you must do two things. First, you must start the Windows service named aspnet_state, which has been installed with ASP.NET. You can use the NET START command from the command prompt to begin aspnet_state:

```
net start aspnet_state
```

In production sites, however, you'll probably want to run this service automatically when the server reboots. You can do this by setting the start-up–type setting for this service to Automatic in the Properties window of the Services snap-in for Microsoft Management Console. (See Figure 24-3.)

Services

Action View

Tree: Services (Local)

Name	Description	Status	Startup Type	Log On As
Alerter	Notifies selected users and computers of ad…	Started	Automatic	LocalSystem
Application Management	Provides software installation services such …		Manual	LocalSystem
ASP.NET State Service	Provides support for out-of-process session…		Automatic	.\ASPNET
ClipBook	Supports ClipBook Viewer, which allows pag…		Manual	LocalSystem
COM+ Event System	Provides automatic distribution of events to…	Started	Manual	LocalSystem
Computer Browser	Maintains an up-to-date list of computers o…	Started	Automatic	LocalSystem
DHCP Client	Manages network configuration by registeri…	Started	Automatic	LocalSystem
Distributed File System	Manages logical volumes distributed across …	Started	Automatic	LocalSystem
Distributed Link Tracking Cl…	Sends notifications of files moving between …	Started	Automatic	LocalSystem
Distributed Link Tracking S…	Stores information so that files moved betw…		Manual	LocalSystem
Distributed Transaction Co…	Coordinates transactions that are distribute…	Started	Automatic	LocalSystem
DNS Client	Resolves and caches Domain Name System …	Started	Automatic	LocalSystem
Event Log	Logs event messages issued by programs a…	Started	Automatic	LocalSystem
Fax Service	Helps you send and receive faxes		Manual	LocalSystem
File Replication	Maintains file synchronization of file director…		Manual	LocalSystem
FTP Publishing Service	Provides FTP connectivity and administratio…	Started	Automatic	LocalSystem
IIS Admin Service	Allows administration of Web and FTP servic…	Started	Automatic	LocalSystem
Indexing Service			Manual	LocalSystem
Infrared Monitor	Supports infrared devices installed on the c…	Started	Automatic	LocalSystem
Internet Connection Sharing	Provides network address translation, addr…		Manual	LocalSystem

Figure 24-3. The start-up mode for the aspnet_state Windows service should be set to Automatic in production sites.

The second step in activating out-of-process sessions is to modify the configuration file so that the mode attribute is set to the StateServer value and the stateConnectionString attribute points to the IP address and port of the machine on which the service is running. If the service is running on the local machine, you can use the loopback address 127.0.0.1, but in real life, this attribute will point to the one computer in the LAN that stores the session variables for all the other machines in the Web farm:

```
<sessionState
    mode="StateServer"
    stateConnectionString="tcpip=192.168.0.4:42424"
    cookieless="false"
    timeout="20"
/>
```

By default, the aspnet_state service listens to port 42424, so this is the port number you specify in the stateConnectionString attribute. (And you can omit it if you want.) You can configure the service to use a different port by editing the Port value under the HKEY_LOCAL_MACHINE\SYSTEM\CurrentControlSet\Services\aspnet_state\Parameters key in the registry. You shouldn't change the default port unless you have a good reason to do it, such as if the default port is already being used by another application.

Using out-of-process sessions is the best setting for Web gardens, and it also provides a viable setting for Web farms. If the machine that runs the aspnet_state service isn't one of the machines that are part of the farm, this technique offers increased robustness because session state will survive restarts of the IIS machines.

One important note: all the machines in a Web farm should have the same machine key settings in their machine.config files or in the web.config files of individual applications. These settings are used to encrypt and validate the session ID sent through cookies. By default, machine key settings are autogenerated, so each computer uses a different key. To have multiple servers take part in a Web farm, however, all of them should have the same machine key—otherwise, one computer couldn't decypher the session cookie generated by another computer in the farm:

```
<configuration>
   <system.web>
      <machineKey
      validationKey="0123456789abcdef0123456789abcdef0123456789abcdef"
      decryptionKey="fedcba9876543210fedcba9876543210fedcba9876543210"
      validation="SHA1" />
    ⋮
  </system.web>
</configuration>
```

Out-of-Process Sessions Based on SQL Server

Before you can use ASP.NET sessions based on SQL Server, you must run the InstallSqlState.sql script in the c:\WinNT\Microsoft.Net\v*x.x.xxxx* directory. The simplest way to run this script is by dragging it inside the SQL Query Analyzer program or running it from the command prompt using the OSQL utility. ASP.NET also comes with the UninstallSqlState.sql script, should you wish to remove this database.

The script creates a new database named ASPState, containing all the stored procedures that ASP.NET requires. (See Figure 24-4.) It also installs a start-up procedure named ASPState_Startup, which ensures that all the necessary TempDB tables used for storing session data are correctly re-created when SQL Server restarts. Because TempDB is used, write operations are slightly faster but session data won't survive a reboot. If you feel brave enough, you might attempt to modify the script so that a nontemporary table is used instead.

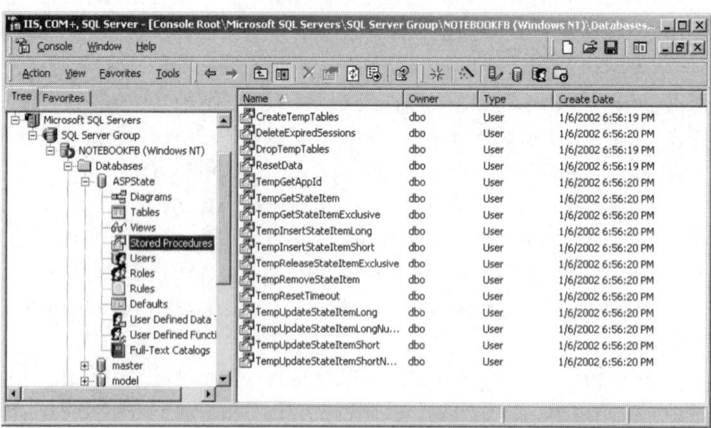

Figure 24-4. The SQL Server database created by the InstallSqlState.sql script.

To actually configure ASP.NET to use a SQL Server–based session, you must change the web.config file so that the mode attribute is set to SQLServer and the sqlConnectionString attribute contains all the parameters required to connect to SQL Server:

```
<sessionState
    mode="SQLServer"
    sqlConnectionString="data source=127.0.0.1;user id=sa;password=mypwd"
    cookieless="false"
    timeout="20"
/>
```

Of course, all the machines in a Web farm should have the sqlConnectionString attribute point to the same SQL Server, so that they can share session values.

In general, you can write your ASP.NET code without worrying about which session mode your application is using, even though you might experience a performance hit when using out-of-process sessions. The only exception to this general rule is when you store an object in a SQL Server–based session variable: the object must be serializable—otherwise, it can't be stored in the database. (See Chapter 11 for a review of serializable objects.)

Disabled or Read-Only Sessions

Because sessions take memory and other resources, you should disable them if you can live without them. You can disable sessions for the entire application or just for selected pages. In the former case, you set the mode attribute to Off in the web.config file:

```
<sessionState
    mode="Off"
/>
```

You can disable sessions for individual pages by setting the EnableSessionState attribute in the @Page directive to False, either by editing the HTML file or by setting a property of the page in Visual Studio .NET's Properties window:

```
<%@ Page Language="vb" EnableSessionState="False" %>
```

ASP.NET also supports read-only sessions, which weren't available under classic ASP:

```
<%@ Page Language="vb" EnableSessionState="ReadOnly" %>
```

Read-only sessions can slightly improve the performance of your code because ASP.NET doesn't have to store new values in memory (or in the aspnet_state service or in SQL Server) when the page completes its execution. If you attempt to write a read-only session variable, no exception is thrown but a new session ID is generated. This undocumented behavior is confusing and can create subtle bugs in your code. For this reason, you might want to check the IsReadOnly property before assigning a session variable:

```
If Not Session.IsReadOnly Then
    Session("price") = 345
End If
```

Page Caching

Even though the main goal of ASP.NET is the generation of dynamic pages, the actual HTML text being sent to the client browser doesn't change often for many sites. A typical online newspaper is updated only once a day, and even highly dynamic sites—for example, those providing stock quotes—aren't usually updated more often than every minute or two. In these circumstances, you might want to cache the page content and serve it again to other clients until the data in the cache is out-of-date. This technique can save frequent trips to the database and improve both performance and scalability.

Unlike classic ASP—which supported page caching only through third-party, often quite expensive, tools—ASP.NET supports a very flexible page caching mechanism on a page-by-page basis. Not only can you decide when the cached content expires, but you can also create different cached versions that depend on the value of one or more arguments passed on the query string, the value of an HTTP header, or the type of the client browser.

The @OutputCache Directive

The key to page caching is the @OutputCache directive, which can take several attributes:

```
<%@ OutputCache Duration="#ofseconds"
    Location="Any|Client|Downstream|Server|None"
    VaryByControl="controlname"
    VaryByCustom="browser|customstring"
    VaryByHeaders="headerlist|*"
    VaryByParam="paramlist|*|none"   %>
```

You often want to cache a page for a given number of seconds, which you do by setting the Duration attribute to the desired timeout and the VaryByParam attribute to none. This directive caches the current page for 10 seconds:

```
<%@ OutputCache Duration="10" VaryByParam="none" %>
```

You can check that caching works as expected by creating a page with a Label and a Submit control and then adding this code:

```
Private Sub Page_Load(ByVal sender As Object, ByVal e As EventArgs) _
    Handles MyBase.Load
    ' Append current time to the current contents of the Label control.
    lblTime.Text &= "Current time is " & Date.Now.ToLongTimeString & "<br>"
End Sub
```

If the page weren't cached, you'd see the time value of the Label control increase each time you clicked the submit button. Because caching is enabled, however, you'll see that most of your clicks return an unmodified page, as shown in Figure 24-5.

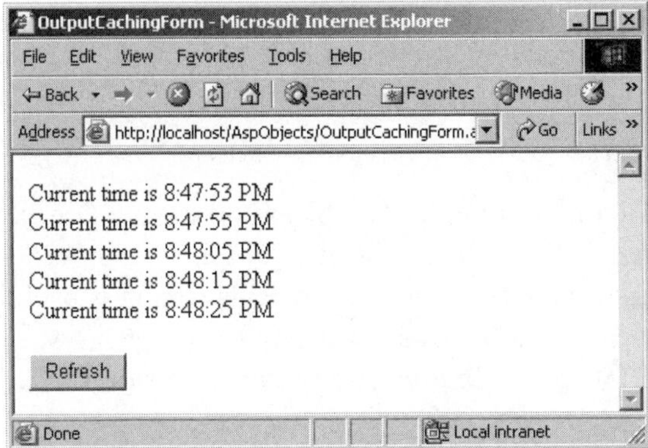

Figure 24-5. The demo application proves that page caching actually works.

The VaryByParam attribute lets you specify a semicolon-separated list of arguments, which can be either query string arguments or arguments passed by means of the POST method. This argument list lets you create different cached versions of the same page, each version associated with a different value for that argument. For example, consider this directive:

```
<%@ OutputCache Duration="10" VaryByParam="id" %>
```

and suppose the users send these requests in sequence:

```
http://www.tailspintoys.com/mypage.aspx?id=1
http://www.tailspintoys.com/mypage.aspx?id=1
http://www.tailspintoys.com/mypage.aspx?id=2
http://www.tailspintoys.com/mypage.aspx?id=1
http://www.tailspintoys.com/mypage.aspx?id=2
```

The effect is that the page is cached twice, at the first and the third request, and all other requests use a cached version of it (unless the cached version has expired in the meantime, of course). Interestingly, because ASP.NET sends control values as POST arguments, in practice you can vary the cached version by the name of a control. For example, the following directive creates a different cached version for each different value that users type in either txtValue or txtDate controls:

```
<%@ OutputCache Duration="10" VaryByParam="txtValue;txtDate" %>
```

You can also vary the cached page according to the value of any parameter, using an asterisk:

```
<%@ OutputCache Duration="10" VaryByParam="*" %>
```

The most frequent value of the VaryByCustom attribute is browser, which causes a different cached version of the page to be created for each different brand and version of the browser that requests the page:

```
<%@ OutputCache VaryByParam="none" VaryByCustom="browser" %>
```

(Note that the VaryByParam attribute is required in all cases.) For example, there would be a cached page for Internet Explorer 5, another for Internet Explorer 6, yet another for Netscape Navigator 6, and so on. This setting is useful when your ASP.NET code uses the Request.Browser property to query browser capabilities and return different HTML depending on the browser version.

> **Note** You can store a custom string other than browser in this attribute, but you have to override the GetVaryByCustomString method in Global.asax to specify the behavior of the cache for the custom string.

The VaryByHeader attribute can take a semicolon-delimited list of HTTP headers and create a different cached page for each different value of any of these headers. For example, the following directive creates a different cached page, depending on the value of the Accept-Language HTTP header:

```
<%@ OutputCache VaryByParam="none" VaryByHeader="Accept-Language" %>
```

You typically use this attribute when the code in your page delivers different HTML code depending on the value of a header found in the Request.ServerVariables collection. In the case of the Accept-Language header, you'll probably output text in different languages (English if the header is en-us, French if it is fr-fr, and so on). You can also specify an asterisk to generate a cached page when the value of any header changes, but this setting usually doesn't make sense because you'd end up with too many items in the page cache.

The Location attribute specifies where the page will be cached. The default setting is Any, which allows ASP.NET to cache the page in the most convenient place. Other valid settings are Client (the page is cached on the client); Server (the page is cached on the server that's serving the request); Downstream (the page is cached on a machine other than the server that's serving the request, which can be a proxy server or the client that made the request).

```
<%@ OutputCache Duration="60" Location="Downstream"
    VaryByParam="none" VaryByCustom="browser"   %>
```

The @OutputCache directive is also supported in ASP.NET user controls and permits you to implement caching for portions of the page. When this directive appears in user controls, the VaryByHeader and Location attributes aren't supported. For more information, see the "Caching with the @Output-Cache Directive" section in Chapter 25.

The HttpCachePolicy Class

Although the @OutputCache directive is easy to use, in some circumstances it isn't as flexible as your requirements dictate. For example, it doesn't support absolute expiration time (use the cached page until midnight) and you can't specify complex conditions on arguments' or controls' values (recache the page when both the txtName and txtDate controls have a new value). In these cases, you must control the page caching feature via code. The key to programmatic control of page caching is the HttpCachePolicy object, which is exposed by the Response.Cache property. This object exposes many methods, but I'll cover only the most useful ones.

If the page contains an @OutputCache directive, you can query the Vary-ByParams and VaryByHeaders properties, which return a dictionary of all the headers or parameters specified in the directive. In most cases, however, you want to use the HttpCachePolicy methods to enforce your custom cache policy. The first step in doing so is to invoke the SetCacheability method, which takes one of the following values: Private, Public, Server, or NoCache. (Any value other than the last one activates the caching.) Next, you can set an absolute expiration time by using the SetExpires method (which therefore corresponds to the Duration attribute of the @OutputCache directive):

```
Private Sub Page_Load(ByVal sender As Object, ByVal e As EventArgs) _
    Handles MyBase.Load
    ' Use the cached page for the next 20 seconds.
    Response.Cache.SetCacheability(HttpCacheability.Server)
    Response.Cache.SetExpires(Now.AddSeconds(20))
End Sub
```

Often you'll cache the page until a given time:

```
' Refresh the cached page until 10 PM today.
    Response.Cache.SetExpires(Date.Parse("10:00:00PM"))
```

The HttpCachePolicy exposes many other features. See the .NET SDK documentation for the complete list of its properties and methods.

The Cache Class

Another frequently used technique for improving performance is to cache large amounts of data in memory to avoid an expensive read operation from a file or a database each time you need it. For example, you might want to read an XML file into an XmlDocument object once and share it among all the pages that use the data. This approach is surely better than reloading the file in each page because it skips both the read operation and the overhead that is necessary to re-create the DOM in memory.

When you cache data, you must decide *where* in memory to store it. ASP developers had only a couple of choices: Application variables for data shared among all users, or Session variables for data unique to each user. In all cases, you're trading memory for speed, and you get the best results from this tradeoff if you're caching data shared by all users. A shortcoming of the Application object is that it's up to you, the programmer, to correctly refresh its contents when the original data—the file, the database table—changes.

Sometimes refreshing the data isn't simple. For example, assume that you'd like to cache currency exchange rates read from a third-party Web service and you want these values to be read every 30 minutes. This scenario requires that every time you're about to access the cached data, you compare the current time with the time of the most recent call to the XML Web service. (This information should be stored in another Application variable.) And then you call the XML Web service again if necessary. Wouldn't it be great if you could refresh the cached data automatically, without needing to check each time you use it?

The ASP.NET answers to all the problems I've mentioned come in the form of the new System.Web.Caching.Cache object. As with the Application object, all the users share the same instance of the Cache object. In a difference from the way you use the Application object, however, you can enforce very sophisticated expiration policies for the Cache object to have it automatically refreshed when a timeout expires, the original file is updated, or another object in the cache expires.

Inserting Items in the Cache

There's only one instance of the Cache object for each AppDomain. When you're inside an ASP.NET page, you can reach this instance through the Cache property of the Page object. When you're inside Global.asax, no Page object is available and you must use the Cache property of the Context object.

In the simplest scenario, you use the Cache object as you'd use the Application object: you check whether an object is already in the cache and load it if necessary. The following code shows how you can use the Cache object to store an XmlDocument object that stores the DOM of a given XML file; the code uses a second Cache variable to keep track of when the XML data was read:

```
Private Sub Page_Load(ByVal sender As Object, ByVal e As EventArgs) _
    Handles MyBase.Load
    ' Check whether XML data is cached already.
    If Cache("Employees") Is Nothing Then
        CacheEmployeesData()
    End If
    ' Get the cached data.
    Dim xmldoc As System.Xml.XmlDocument = _
        DirectCast(Cache("Employees"), System.Xml.XmlDocument)
End Sub

Sub CacheEmployeesData()
    ' Read an XML document.
    Dim filename As String = MapPath("Employees.xml")
    Dim xmldoc As New System.Xml.XmlDocument()
    xmldoc.Load(filename)
    ' Store it in the Cache object.
    Cache("Employees") = xmldoc
    ' Remember caching time as well.
    Cache("EmployeesCacheTime") = Date.Now
End Sub
```

When used in this fashion, the Cache object offers no clear advantages over the Application object. Each item in the cache is a DictionaryEntry object, so you can enumerate all the cached items by using this loop:

```
Sub DisplayCacheContents()
    Dim de As DictionaryEntry
    Dim msg As String
    For Each de In Cache
        msg &= String.Format("<b>{0}</b> = {1}<br>", de.Key, de.Value)
    Next
    ' Display the result in a Label control.
    lblMessage.Text = msg
End Sub
```

Figure 24-6 shows what the cache looks like after you add two custom items (one of which is highlighted). As you see, ASP.NET uses the Cache object for its own purposes as well, for example page caching.

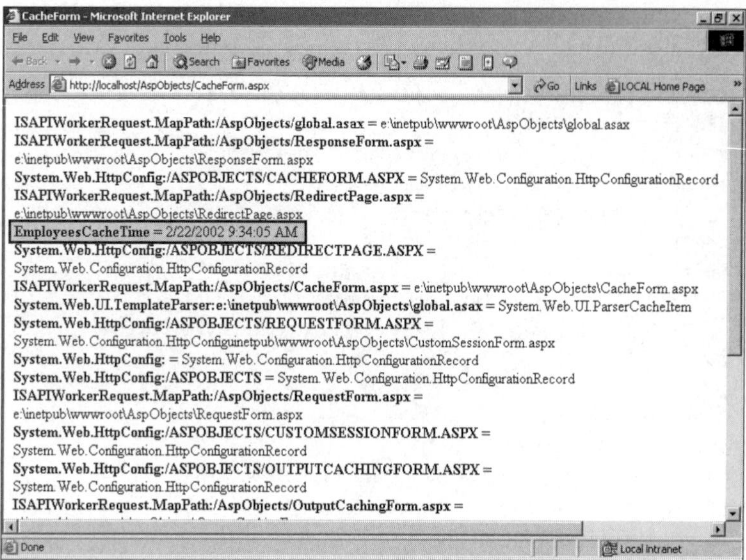

Figure 24-6. The contents of the Cache object include ASP.NET's own data.

The Cache object does internal synchronization, and for this reason it doesn't expose any Lock and Unlock methods. Even so, you still have to synchronize access to this object when you're performing multistep operations that should be considered atomic, as in this code snippet:

```
SyncLock counterLock
    If CInt(Cache("counter")) > 1 Then
        Cache("counter") = CInt(Cache("counter"))-1
    End If
End SyncLock
```

where counterLock is a non-Nothing object variable defined in a module to make it visible to all threads and pages.

Of course you can also use all the synchronized objects that I discussed in Chapter 13, as the circumstances dictate. For example, you can use a ReaderWriterLock object to allow multiple read operations to be performed at the same time.

Enforcing File and Key Dependencies

You see the higher flexibility of the Cache object when you use its Insert method, which takes a CacheDependency object in its third argument. Depending on how you create this dependency object, you can have a cache item expire when a given file is updated or when the value of another cache item changes (or is removed). For example, the following code makes the Employees cached item expire when the Employees.xml file is updated:

```
' ...(Inside CacheEmployeesData) ...
' Add XML data to the cache, making it dependent on the specified filename.
Dim xmldocDep As New System.Web.Caching.CacheDependency(filename)
Cache.Insert("Employees", xmldoc, xmldocDep)
```

The constructor of the CacheDependency object is overloaded to let you specify more than one file, in which case the element is removed from the cache when any of these files are updated:

```
' Remove an element from the cache when any of these files are updated.
Dim filenames() As String = { MapPath("Employees.xml"), _
    MapPath("Employees.xsl"), MapPath("Orders.xml") }
Dim xmldocDep As New System.Web.Caching.CacheDependency(filenames)
Cache.Insert("Employees", xmldoc, xmldocDep)
```

Because the EmployeesCacheTime element is expected to expire when the Employees element is removed from the cache, you should create a CacheDependency object that makes this dependency explicit:

```
' Create an array of cache keys (only one in this case).
Dim cacheKeys() As String = {"Employees"}
' Pass Nothing in the first argument of the constructor because
' there's no file dependency in this case.
Dim timeDep As New System.Web.Caching.CacheDependency(Nothing, cacheKeys)
' Add the current time to the cache.
Cache.Insert("EmployeesCacheTime", Date.Now, timeDep)
```

You see the real power of key-based dependencies when you work with calculated elements that are based on other numeric or string values, as in this code snippet:

```
' The size of a rectangle.
Cache("rect_width") = 123
Cache("rect_height") = 45
' Cache the area value, and make it dependent on size values.
Dim keys() As String = { "rect_width", "rect_height" }
' Create the CacheDependency on the fly.
Cache.Insert("rect_area", 123 * 45, _
    New System.Web.Caching.CacheDependency(Nothing, keys))
```

Whenever either the rect_width or rect_height value is modified (not just removed), the rect_area element is removed from the cache. When you combine this feature with callback routines (which I'll explain in a moment), you can ensure that a calculated value dependent on other values in the cache is always up-to-date.

The CacheDependency object has only one property, HasChanged, which you can query when you want to know whether the dependency condition has been met.

Enforcing Time Dependencies

The fourth and fifth arguments in the Insert method let you remove an element from the cache when a timeout expires. You can choose from two ways of removing the element. In the first case, you specify an absolute expiration date in the fourth argument and the Cache.NoSlidingExpiration constant in the fifth argument:

```
' Remove this element from the cache after 10 minutes.
Cache.Insert("Employees", xmldoc, Nothing, _
    Now.AddMinutes(10), Cache.NoSlidingExpiration)
```

In the second case, you require that the element be removed from the cache if it hasn't been requested for the amount of time specified by the fifth argument (which can't be negative or higher than one year). You typically use this mode to release memory when an object isn't used frequently:

```
' Make this item expire after 5 minutes of inactivity.
Cache.Insert("Employees", xmldoc, Nothing, _
    Cache.NoAbsoluteExpiration, New TimeSpan(0, 5, 0))
```

You must specify either Cache.NoAbsoluteExpiration for the fourth argument or Cache.NoSlidingExpiration for the fifth argument—otherwise an exception is thrown.

Keep in mind that items might be removed from the cache when ASP.NET runs short of memory, regardless of the expiration policy you enforce. You have some control over which items are removed first by setting their priority in the sixth argument of the Insert method. For example, if rereading a cached element isn't expensive, you might set a low priority for it:

```
' Note that you must pass a seventh argument in this case.
Cache.Insert("Employees", xmldoc, Nothing, _
    Cache.NoAbsoluteExpiration, New TimeSpan(0, 5, 0), _
    Caching.CacheItemPriority.Low, Nothing)
```

The available values for the priority argument are (from lower to higher priorities) Low, BelowNormal, Normal or Default, AboveNormal, High, and NotRemovable. You should use NotRemovable exclusively for items that never expire and can't be accessed a second time.

The Cache class exposes also an Add method that's very similar to Insert, with only two differences. First, it supports only the seven-argument syntax; second, if the item specified in the first argument already exists in the cache, the

Add method is ignored. (The Insert method always overwrites an item of the same name.)

```
' Add this element only if it has expired or was removed in the meantime.
Cache.Add("Employees", xmldoc, Nothing, _
    Cache.NoAbsoluteExpiration, New TimeSpan(0, 0, 10), _
    Caching.CacheItemPriority.Low, Nothing)
```

You can also explicity remove an element from the cache by using the Remove method:

```
Cache.Remove("Employees")
```

Setting Up a Remove Callback

In all the examples I've shown you so far, the application's code had to manually check that the cached element was already in the cache and hadn't been removed in the meantime; the code then had to read the cached element again if necessary:

```
If Cache("Employees") Is Nothing Then
    CacheEmployeesData()
End If
' Get the cached data.
Dim xmldoc As System.Xml.XmlDocument = _
    DirectCast(Cache("Employees"), System.Xml.XmlDocument)
```

This coding style is clumsy and adds a slight overhead each time you access an object. Fortunately, you can solve both problems by specifying a delegate to a callback procedure in the last argument of the Insert and Add methods. This procedure is invoked by ASP.NET immediately after removing the element from the cache. Here's a prototype of the callback procedure that's invoked when the element is removed. As you see, its last argument lets you understand what exactly happened:

```
Sub OnRemoveItem(ByVal key As String, ByVal value As Object, _
    ByVal reason As Caching.CacheItemRemovedReason)
    Select Case reason
        Case Caching.CacheItemRemovedReason.Expired
            ' The element expired.
        Case Caching.CacheItemRemovedReason.DependencyChanged
            ' The element depends on files/keys that have changed.
        Case Caching.CacheItemRemovedReason.Removed
            ' The element has been removed by a Remove method, or by an
            ' Insert method on the same key.
        Case Caching.CacheItemRemovedReason.Underused
            ' The element has been removed because of memory shortage.
    End Select
End Sub
```

The following code shows how you can update the sample application to use this feature. Note that I moved both functions into a module and that I'm accessing the Cache object by using the HttpRuntime.Cache property because I'm outside a Page class:

```
Module CacheFunctions
    ' Save a reference to the Cache object.
    Dim Cache As System.Web.Caching.Cache = HttpRuntime.Cache
    ' This is the XML file.
    Dim filename As String = "C:\Inetpub\wwwroot\AspObjects\employees.xml"

    Sub CacheEmployeesData()
        ' Read an XML document.
        Dim filename As String = MapPath("employees.xml")
        Dim xmldoc As New System.Xml.XmlDocument()
        xmldoc.Load(filename)

        ' Make this item expire when the file is modified, and
        ' call a callback procedure when this happens.
        Dim xmldocDep As New System.Web.Caching.CacheDependency(filename)
        Cache.Insert("Employees", xmldoc, xmldocDep, Nothing, Nothing, _
            Caching.CacheItemPriority.Default, AddressOf OnRemoveItem)
    End Sub

    Sub OnRemoveItem(ByVal key As String, ByVal value As Object, _
        ByVal reason As Caching.CacheItemRemovedReason)
        ' Always refresh the XML file when the cached item expires.
        CacheEmployeesData()
    End Sub
End Module
```

The technique based on callbacks is most effective when the data is cached the first time inside the Application_Start event in Global.asax. Because the code is in a module (and not in a Page class), you can access these routines from Global.asax:

```
' Global.asax partial listing

Public Class Global
    Inherits System.Web.HttpApplication

    Sub Application_Start(ByVal sender As Object, ByVal e As EventArgs)
        ' Cache the XML file when the application starts.
        CacheEmployeesData()
    End Sub

    ⋮
End Class
```

You can now reference the cached element from anywhere in your ASP.NET application without testing it for Nothing first because the XML file is automatically recached when it's modified:

```
' You can place this statement in any .aspx page.
Public xmldoc As System.Xml.XmlDocument = _
    DirectCast(Cache("Employees"), System.Xml.XmlDocument)
```

Static Variables

ASP.NET offers another means for storing application-wide values that wasn't available under ASP and can work as a viable alternative to standard Application variables. Because your code is compiled and runs inside the aspnet_wp working process until the process is shut down or recycled, any static variable in your project will preserve its value between client requests. Consider this simple Module block:

```
Module GlobalVars
    Public PageViewCount As Integer
    Public Counter As Integer
End Module
```

You can then access the fields from any page in the application as a regular variable:

```
Private Sub Page_Load(ByVal sender As Object, ByVal e As EventArgs) _
    Handles MyBase.Load
    ' Increment page view counter.
    PageViewCount += 1
End Sub
```

In other words, you've created an application-wide variable, akin to the items in the Application object. Why should you use these module variables instead of a standard Application variable? Well, the answer is simple: performance. In fact, these variables don't require a lookup in the Application collection of variables and, just as important, they're strongly typed, so you don't need to convert their contents as you do with Application variables (or unbox the contents of a variable if it's a value type). An informal benchmark shows that incrementing the PageViewCount variable is about 500 times faster than the following statement:

```
' Increment a counter in an Application variable.
Application("counter") = CInt(Application("counter")) + 1
```

Of course, you aren't limited to shared fields and you can also implement shared properties and methods. Unlike Application variables, which can be locked and unlocked only as a whole, shared variables allow you to implement a much finer granular locking strategy.

The Global.asax File

As I've already explained in Chapter 23, the Global.asax file is the ASP.NET counterpart of Global.asa in ASP and is used to host the handlers of the Application object's events. As you'll see, however, the contents of this file are quite different in ASP.NET. For example, this is a simple Global.asax file (created in Visual Studio) that keeps a counter of how many client sessions are in memory:

```
Imports System.Web
Imports System.Web.SessionState

Public Class Global
    Inherits System.Web.HttpApplication

    Sub Application_Start(ByVal sender As Object, ByVal e As EventArgs)
        ' We start with zero sessions.
        Application("SessionCount") = 0
    End Sub

    Sub Session_Start(ByVal sender As Object, ByVal e As EventArgs)
        ' A new session is being created.
        Application.Lock
        Application("SessionCount") = CInt(Application("SessionCount")) + 1
        Application.Unlock
    End Sub

    Sub Session_Start(ByVal sender As Object, ByVal e As EventArgs)
        ' A session is being destroyed.
        Application.Lock
        Application("SessionCount") = CInt(Application("SessionCount")) - 1
        Application.Unlock
    End Sub
End Class
```

A couple of things are worth noticing here. First, the events take the usual two arguments and are named Start and End, not OnStart and OnEnd (as they are under classic ASP), even though the old names are still recognized correctly. Second, they're contained in a class named Global, which inherits from the HttpApplication class. The original ASP Application class has been split into two classes under ASP.NET: HttpApplicationState provides support for application-wide variables, whereas HttpApplication is the class instantiated when the ASP.NET application starts.

The ASP.NET Application object exposes many new events that were missing in the ASP object. The majority of these new events normally fire once at *every* request posted to the server, not just when the application starts or ends. The exception to this frequent firing is the Error event (which one would *hope* doesn't fire for all requests). I've listed all the Application events in Table 24-5, in their firing order.

You can create an empty handler for all these events using the Method Name combo box at the top of the Visual Studio .NET editor, as you do with control events. At first, it's rather confusing that the event templates provided with the default Global.asax are in the form Application_eventname:

```
Sub Application_BeginRequest(ByVal sender As Object, ByVal e As EventArgs)
    ' Fires at the beginning of each request
    ⋮
End Sub
```

whereas the event templates created with the combo box in the editor are in the form Global_eventname and have a Handles clause:

```
Sub Global_BeginRequest(ByVal sender As Object, ByVal e As EventArgs) _
    Handles MyBase.BeginRequest
    ⋮
End Sub
```

Even though they look different, these event handlers work in exactly the same way. In fact, both of them fire if they're contained in the same Global.asax file, an arrangement that you'll probably want to avoid in real applications because it adds overhead to each page request and might introduce bugs. An exception to this rule: the Start and End events (as well as their OnStart and OnEnd aliases) can be trapped only if you use the Application_eventname syntax. These events, in fact, aren't exposed by the HttpApplication object and therefore don't correspond to any valid Handles clause.

I'm not going to discuss every Application event, mainly because most of them exist only to let ASP.NET implement some of their advanced features, such as distributed sessions and page caching. In most applications, you never need to play with these events (except, as I've said, for the Error event), so I'll cover only the most interesting ones in this section.

Table 24-5 Events of the HttpApplication Class*

Syntax	Description
Start	Fires when the ASP.NET application starts—that is, when the first request for an .aspx file is posted to the server. (Same as the OnStart event.)
BeginRequest	Fires as the first event when ASP.NET receives a request from a client; the event provides the developer with the opportunity to process the request before the page does it.
AuthenticateRequest	Fires when ASP.NET has established the identity of the user but before authorization is enforced; it gives you the means to implement a custom authentication and authorization mechanism.

Table 24-5 Events of the HttpApplication Class* *(continued)*

Syntax	Description
AuthorizeRequest	Fires when ASP.NET has verified user authorization.
ResolveRequestCache	Fires when ASP.NET determines whether the request should be served using a page stored in the cache. (The page caching mechanism uses this event, for example.)
AcquireRequestState	Fires after ASP.NET acquires the current state associated with the current request; if this is the first request from a client, the Session_Start event fires just before the AcquireRequestState event. ASP.NET traps this event to implement distributed sessions.
PreRequestHandlerExecute	Fires one instant before executing the code in the page or the XML Web service (more generally, the registered handler for the requested resource).
PostRequestHandlerExecute	Fires after the page or the XML Web service has completed its processing. At this point, the Response object contains the text being sent to the client.
ReleaseRequestState	Fires when ASP.NET completes the execution of all request handlers and is ready to store session state. ASP.NET traps this event to implement distributed sessions.
UpdateRequestCache	Fires when caching handlers are able to store data being sent to the client in the page output cache.
EndRequest	Fires when the page has been completely processed. This event is the last in the chain if buffering has been disabled.
PreSendRequestHeaders	Fires when ASP.NET is about to send HTTP headers to the client. If buffering is enabled, this and the following event are raised after the EndRequest event.
PreSendRequestContent	Fires when ASP.NET is about to send content to the client. This event can fire multiple times during the same request.
End	Fires when ASP.NET is about to shut down. (Same as the OnEnd event.)
Disposed	Fires when the ASP.NET application is being disposed of.
Error	Fires when an unhandled exception is thrown.

* All events except Error are in the order in which they fire.

Global Error Handlers

Of all the application events, the majority of ASP.NET applications need to trap only the Error event. This event lets you implement a global error handler that fires when an unhandled exception fires in any page of the current application. In other words, you can enforce a common error resolution strategy by using the same code you'd insert in the Page_Error event but without having to modify each and every .aspx file in the application.

The code inside the Application's Error event can use the Server.GetLastError property to access the exception object being thrown most recently. However, this property always returns an HttpUnhandledException object, and you must query the InnerException property of this object to retrieve the actual exception that was thrown. The code inside the Error event handler can access all the usual properties in the Request object to understand what went wrong and the methods of the Response object to send an alternative error message. For example, the following error handler displays the custom error message shown in Figure 24-7:

```
Private Sub Global_Error(ByVal sender As Object, ByVal e As EventArgs) _
    Handles MyBase.Error
    ' Prepare an error report.
    Response.Clear()
    Response.Write("<H1>An exception has occurred:</H1>")
    ' Display information on the page being processed.
    Response.Write("<b>URL = </b>" & Request.Path & "<br />")
    Response.Write("<b>QueryString = </b>" & Request.QueryString.ToString _
        & "<p>")
    Response.Write("<b>Error details</b><p>")

    ' Get a reference to the (real) error that occurred.
    Dim ex As Exception = Server.GetLastError.InnerException
    ' Convert the string in a format that is suitable for HTML output.
    Dim errMsg As String = Server.HtmlEncode(ex.ToString)
    errMsg = errMsg.Replace(ControlChars.CrLf, "<BR />")
    Response.Write(errMsg)
    Response.End()
End Sub
```

Or you can redirect the execution to another .aspx page by using a Response.Redirect method. In general, the standard error page that ASP.NET displays when an unhandled exception is thrown contains a lot of detailed information, so as a rule you shouldn't override it while testing and debugging an application. However, the Error event can be a precious resource in a production site for logging error information to a file or the system log.

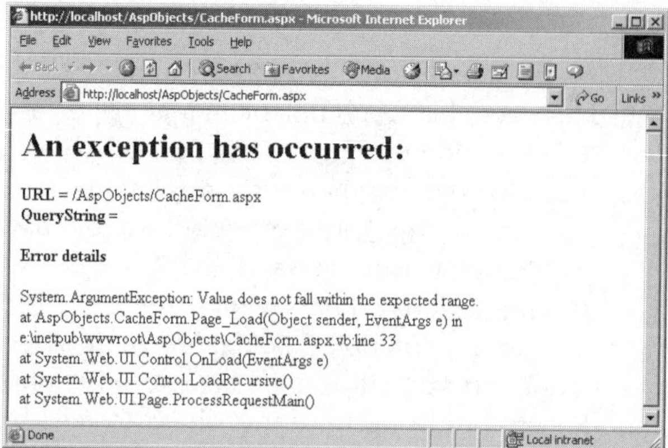
http://localhost/AspObjects/CacheForm.aspx - Microsoft Internet Explorer

An exception has occurred:

URL = /AspObjects/CacheForm.aspx
QueryString =

Error details

System.ArgumentException: Value does not fall within the expected range.
at AspObjects.CacheForm.Page_Load(Object sender, EventArgs e) in e:\inetpub\wwwroot\AspObjects\CacheForm.aspx.vb:line 33
at System.Web.UI.Control.OnLoad(EventArgs e)
at System.Web.UI.Control.LoadRecursive()
at System.Web.UI.Page.ProcessRequestMain()

Figure 24-7. An example of a custom error page.

Application-Wide Response Filter

In the "Filtering Response Output" section earlier in this chapter, you saw how an ASP.NET page can assign a custom filter to the Response.Filter property to postprocess HTML code being sent to the client browser:

```
Private Sub Page_Load(ByVal sender As Object, ByVal e As EventArgs) _
    Response.Filter = New ConvertTagFilter(Response.Filter)
End Sub
```

Of course, inserting the preceding lines of code in each and every .aspx file is a nuisance, and fortunately you don't have to do that. In fact, the PreRequestHandlerExecute application event fires after the Response object has been created and immediately before the code in a page has a chance to execute, so you just have to assign the Filter property in this event to create a filter for all the pages in an ASP.NET application:

```
' Inside Global.asax file
Private Sub Application_PreRequestHandlerExecute(ByVal sender As Object, _
    ByVal e As EventArgs)
    Response.Filter = New ConvertTagFilter(Response.Filter)
End Sub
```

This technique is very powerful, and lets you implement advanced features with relatively little code.

Persistent Session Variables

You learned earlier in this chapter that ASP.NET greatly improves session state management and supports both cookieless sessions and out-of-process sessions. However, there's still one thing that ASP.NET doesn't offer: persistent sessions. For example, it would be great if you could decide whether Session values should be persisted between client visits to the site. Imagine an e-commerce site that lets its users keep items in their shopping carts for, say, a week so that users can choose their purchases without any hurry.

As you'll see in a moment, implementing persistent sessions isn't trivial, but it isn't overly difficult either. The technique I am about to illustrate makes use of the AquireRequestState and ReleaseRequestState events: the former fires immediately after loading data from memory into the "regular" Session variables, the latter fires before saving Session variables in memory. The code in the AcquireRequestState event handler attempts to read a special client-side cookie named PermSessionID. The value of this cookie is considered to be the name of an XML file (on the server machine) that contains the values of Session variables as stored at the end of the previous request, so the code can populate the Session collection before the page sees the new values. If this cookie doesn't exist yet, you're seeing the first request from this client. So the code creates the cookie and stores a random unique string in it. (For simplicity's sake, it uses the Session.SessionID value, but you can help ensure its uniqueness by appending the current date or the value of a count that you increment each time.)

```
' NOTE: this code requires a reference to the
' System.Runtime.Serialization.Formatters.Soap.dll assembly.

Const SESSIONDATAPATH = "C:\SessionData\"

Private Sub Application_AcquireRequestState(ByVal sender As Object, _
    ByVal e As EventArgs)

    Dim fs As System.IO.FileStream
    Dim sf As New System.Runtime.Serialization.Formatters.Soap.SoapFormatter()

    Try
        ' Get the special cookie, or exit if not found.
        Dim cookie As HttpCookie = Request.Cookies("PermSessionID")
        If (cookie Is Nothing) Then
            ' If not found, generate it now (use pseudo-random SessionID).
            cookie = New HttpCookie("PermSessionID", Session.SessionID)
            ' Let this cookie expire after one week.
            cookie.Expires = Now.AddDays(7)
            ' Send it to the client browser.
            Response.Cookies.Add(cookie)
            ' There's nothing else to do for now.
            Exit Try
        End If

        ' The filename is equal to the value of this cookie.
        Dim permSessionId As String = cookie.Value
```

(continued)

```
        ' Build the name of the data file.
        Dim filename As String = _
            SESSIONDATAPATH & permSessionID.ToString & ".xml"
        ' Open the file, or exit if error.
        fs = New System.IO.FileStream(filename, IO.FileMode.Open)
        ' Deserialize the Hashtable that contains values.
        Dim ht As Hashtable = DirectCast(sf.Deserialize(fs), Hashtable)

        ' Move data into the Session collection.
        Dim key As String
        Session.Clear()             ' Clear regular Session values.
        For Each key In ht.Keys
            Session(key) = ht(key)
        Next
    Catch ex As Exception
        ' Ignore any exceptions.
    Finally
        ' Close the stream on exit.
        If Not (fs Is Nothing) Then fs.Close()
    End Try
End Sub
```

When the request has been served, the code in the ReleaseRequestState event handler creates a server-side XML file whose name is taken from the PermSessionID cookie that was read or created previously. It then serializes all Session variables to the XML file and clears the Session collection to minimize server's memory usage:

```
Private Sub Application_ReleaseRequestState(ByVal sender As Object, _
    ByVal e As EventArgs)

    ' Get the special cookie.
    Dim cookie As HttpCookie = Request.Cookies("PermSessionID")
    ' The value of the cookie is the name of the .xml file.
    Dim permSessionID As String = cookie.Value

    ' Move data from the Session collection into a Hashtable.
    Dim ht As New Hashtable(Session.Count)
    Dim key As String
    For Each key In Session.Keys
        ht(key) = Session(key)
    Next
    ' Clear the regular session collection, to save memory.
    Session.Clear()

    Dim fs As System.IO.FileStream
    Dim sf As New System.Runtime.Serialization.Formatters.Soap.SoapFormatter()
    Try
        ' Build the name of the data file.
```

```
        Dim filename As String = _
            SESSIONDATAPATH & permSessionID.ToString & ".xml"
        ' Open the file for output, or exit if error.
        fs = New System.IO.FileStream(filename, IO.FileMode.Create)
        ' Serialize the Hashtable that contains values.
        sf.Serialize(fs, ht)
    Catch ex As Exception
        ' Ignore any exceptions.
    Finally
        ' Close the stream on exit.
        If Not (fs Is Nothing) Then fs.Close()
    End Try
End Sub
```

Note that the c:\SessionData directory shouldn't be accessible from the outside world, for obvious security reasons, so it isn't under the Inetpub\wwwroot directory tree. Moreover, this directory will be accessed by the ASP.NET process, so it must be located on a non-NTFS partition or it must have been configured to allow access to the ASPNET account (the identity under which ASP.NET runs).

Next create a simple test page that increments a Session variable:

```
Private Sub Page_Load(ByVal sender As System.Object, ByVal e As EventArgs) _
    Handles MyBase.Load
    If Session("counter") Is Nothing Then
        Session("counter") = 0
    Else
        Session("counter") = CInt(Session("counter")) + 1
    End If
    ' Display current value of the variable.
    lblCounter.Text = "Counter = " & Session("counter").ToString
End Sub
```

Each time you refresh the page, the counter is incremented. However, if you now close the browser and restart the application, you'll see that the counting doesn't restart at 0 because the session state is restored from the XML file on the server!

This technique has another great advantage: if XML data files are stored on a network shared directory, you can implement Session variables distributed over a Web farm without using SQL Server (which might be an issue if your site uses another database server) and without the single-point-of-failure problem that you have if you manage distributed sessions with the aspnet_state Windows service. The performance of the preceding code is in the same range as those achieved with SQL Server, and you can make it faster if you persist Session values as binary data instead of XML.

As provided, the code doesn't address a minor problem: when the client-side code expires (for example, after one week) you should delete the corresponding data file on the server to reclaim disk memory and make file searches faster. You can solve this problem by creating a Windows service that periodically checks the date of the last access to XML files and deletes those that are older than one week. This isn't a critical issue, however, because session data files that aren't deleted as soon as they expire don't take any server resource except disk space, so the site administrator might even perform these cleanup chores manually, once every few days.

Tracing

Tracing plays an important role in debugging and fine-tuning any application, and ASP.NET applications are no exception. Unlike classic ASP, whose tracing capabilities were limited to cluttering the script code with Response.Write statements to display the value of variables and properties, ASP.NET comes with powerful tracing features built in.

The Trace Property

The great thing about ASP.NET tracing is that you can activate it just by adding a new attribute in the @Page directive:

```
<%@ Page Language="vb" trace="True" %>
```

If you're working in Visual Studio .NET, you don't even need to edit this directive manually because you can just set the Trace property of the Page object to True from inside the Properties window.

When tracing is enabled, ASP.NET appends a lot of additional information to the regular content of the page, as seen in Figure 24-8. This information includes request details (such as session ID), time spent in page processing steps, information about each control on the form (including size of HTML produced and bytes used in ViewState), session and application variables, cookies, headers, and the collection of server variables.

This information is really precious when you're debugging a page that doesn't behave as it should. For example, I used tracing extensively when I was working with a DataGrid control containing templates to understand the relationship among parent and child controls.

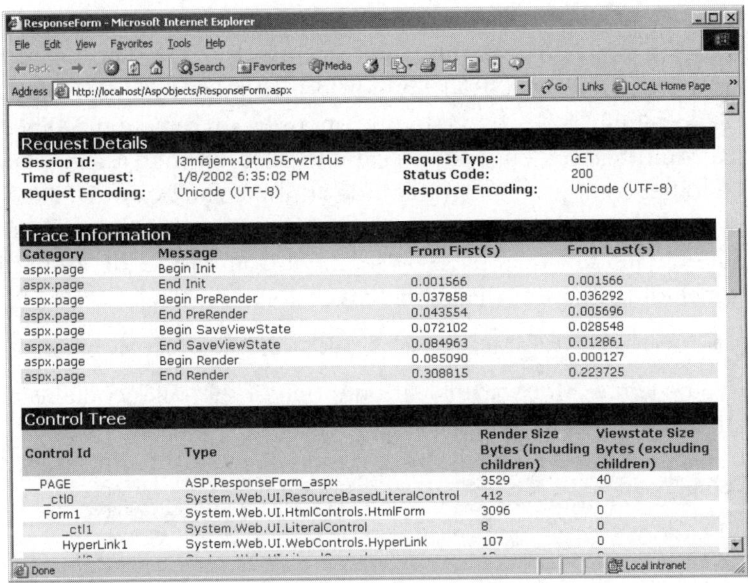

Figure 24-8. Tracing information appended to the regular page content.

Application-Level Tracing

You can enable tracing for all the pages in your application by setting a few values in the web.config file, either in the application root directory (if you want to trace all pages) or in a specific directory (to trace only the pages in that directory):

```
<configuration>
  <system.web>
    <trace enabled="false"
        requestLimit="10" pageOutput="false"
        traceMode="SortByTime" localOnly="true" />
      ⋮
  </system.web>
</configuration>
```

You enable application-level tracing by setting the enabled attribute to true. When you do that, however, tracing information isn't appended to the page's regular contents, as you saw in the preceding section. Instead, you must point your browser to a special page named trace.axd. ASP.NET intercepts the request for this .axd page (regardless of the directory in which you look for it) and displays a result like the one shown in Figure 24-9, with the 10 most recent requests processed by the application. You can display details about each request by clicking on the View Details link on the right. Or you can enforce output in each page by setting the pageOutput attribute to true.

The remaining attributes of the trace section in web.config let you control other tracing details. The requestLimit attribute is the number of requests whose details are cached by ASP.NET when not in page mode. (Default is 10.) By default, localOnly is set to true to prevent users on remote machines from viewing trace information, but you can set it to false if you're tracing the application from another computer. The traceMode attribute can be SortByTime (default) or SortByCategory, and affects how trace information is produced. You can set this attribute on an individual page by setting it from inside the Properties window or by including it in the @Page directive:

```
<%@ Page Language="vb" trace="true" traceMode="SortByCategory" %>
```

You see the effect of this attribute only if the page contains custom trace output, as I explain in the following section.

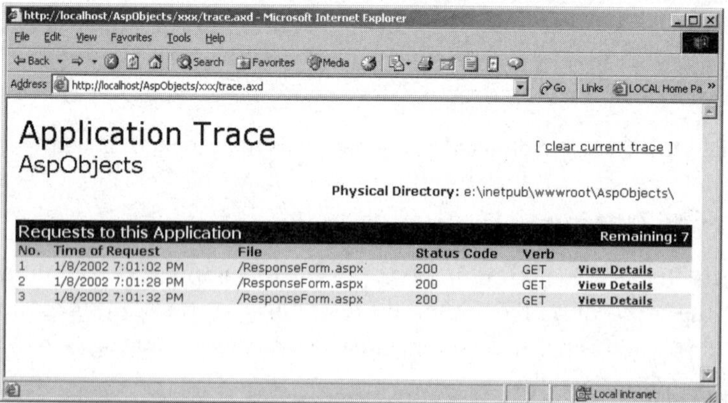

Figure 24-9. The Application Trace page; you must press F5 to refresh the page and see more recent requests.

The TraceContext Class

The Page class exposes the Trace property, which returns a System.Web.TraceContext object and lets you send custom strings to the trace page. Don't confuse this object with the System.Diagnostics.Trace class that you use in Windows Forms programs (and that's still available in ASP.NET applications to display values in the Visual Studio output window). The TraceContext object is also accessible from anywhere in an ASP.NET application, not just from a page, when you use the HttpContext.Current.Trace syntax.

The TraceContext class has only two properties and two methods. The IsEnabled property gets or sets the current page mode, so you can activate tracing programmatically if you wish; the TraceMode property gets or sets the attribute with the same name. You can output trace information by using either the Write or Warn method, the only difference between them being that the latter displays its message in red instead of black. These methods are overloaded to support three different syntax forms:

```
Trace.Write(message)
Trace.Write(category, message)
Trace.Write(category, message, exception)
```

Here's an example that uses these methods:

```
Sub DoSomething(ByVal arg As String)
    Trace.Write("FLOW", "Entering Sub DoSomething")
    Trace.Write("arg = " & arg)

    Try
        ⋮
    Catch ex As Exception
        Trace.Warn("ERRORS", "A fatal error has occurred", ex)
        Response.End
    Finally
        Trace.Write("FLOW", "Exiting Sub DoSomething")
    End Try
End Sub
```

Figure 24-10 shows how these trace messages appear in the trace output when traceMode is set to SortByTime (the default).

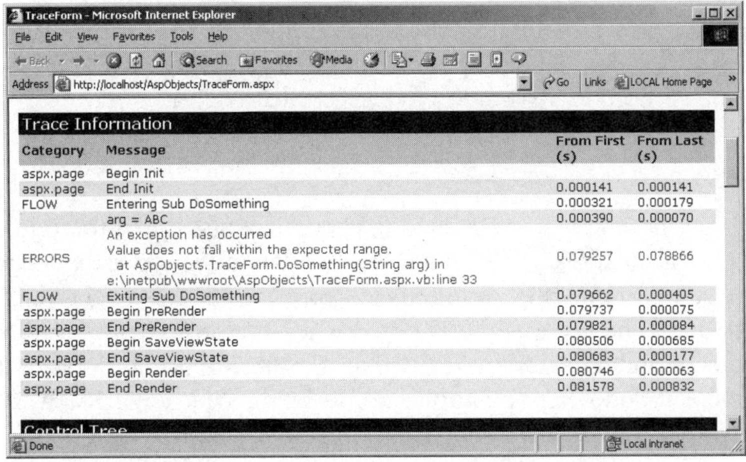

Figure 24-10. Custom message in the trace page; the output from the Warn method is in red.

HTTP Modules and Handlers

The beauty of ASP.NET is that its architecture is extensible. This claim is true also for classic ASP, but you had to be a C++ wizard to create ISAPI filters for IIS. Things are one or two orders of magnitude simpler with ASP.NET, and you can implement all these features in your good old Visual Basic!

For starters, let's compare the two extension mechanisms that ASP.NET provides:

- HTTP handlers are components that handle requests for a given resource type. For example, ASP.NET uses a handler to manage requests for plain .aspx files and another handler to redirect requests for the special trace.axd resource. (Note that we must use the term resource here because trace.axd isn't a physical file; handlers can trap requests for resources before ASP.NET checks that these resources actually exist.)
- HTTP modules are filters that are notified when a request is posted to the ASP.NET application; they loosely correspond to ISAPI filters in IIS. A module can trap a request only if it has been already accepted by ASP.NET, so there must be a registered handler for it. A module can trap the request both before and after the handler associated with it has processed it. ASP.NET uses modules to implement authentication and session state services.

I'll begin with a discussion of HTTP modules, the simpler of the two. As a matter of fact, implementing HTTP modules is a breeze if you have carefully read the section on application events in Global.asax.

HTTP Modules

An HTTP module is a .NET class that implements the IHttpModule interface. This interface exposes only two methods, Init and Dispose, which are invoked by the ASP.NET runtime and therefore appear as events to the implementor of the module. The Init method is called when the ASP.NET application is loaded in memory and receives a reference to the HttpApplication object; the Dispose method is called when the application is being shut down.

Your job in regard to an HTTP module is simple: you take the HttpApplication object passed to the Init method and store it in a variable declared with the WithEvents keyword. From now on, your HTTP module class will listen to all the application events listed in Table 24-5 and can therefore perform all the actions you could perform by writing code right in Global.asax. For example, this simple HTTP module traps all unhandled exceptions and stores details about them in an ArrayList:

```
Public Class ErrorLoggerModule
    Implements IHttpModule

    ' The Application object
    Dim WithEvents Application As HttpApplication

    ' This is where all error messages are stored.
    Public Shared ErrorMessages As New ArrayList()

    Public Sub Init(ByVal context As System.Web.HttpApplication) _
        Implements System.Web.IHttpModule.Init
        ' Store the Application object in a local variable.
        Application = context
    End Sub

    Private Sub Application_Error(ByVal sender As Object, _
        ByVal e As EventArgs) Handles Application.Error
        Dim msg As String
        msg &= "<B>An exception occurred at</B> " & Now.ToString & "<BR />"
        msg &= "<B>URL</B> =" & Application.Request.Path & "<BR />"
        msg &= "<B>QueryString</B> = " & _
            Application.Request.QueryString.ToString & "<BR /><BR />"

        ' Append details about the error, but convert CR-LF pairs.
        msg &= Application.Server.GetLastError.ToString.Replace( _
            ControlChars.CrLf, "<BR />")

        ' Prepend to the collection of error messages.
        SyncLock ErrorMessages.SyncRoot
            ErrorMessages.Insert(0, msg)
        End SyncLock
    End Sub

    Public Sub Dispose() Implements System.Web.IHttpModule.Dispose
        ' The application is being shut down.
        Application = Nothing
    End Sub
End Class
```

Because all the messages are in a global ArrayList object in reverse order, it's easy to display them in a separate page by using a bound DataList control:

```
' The ErrorMessages ArrayList can be reached from anywhere in the application.
DataList1.DataSource = ErrorLoggerModule.ErrorMessages
DataList1.DataBind()
```

An administrator might navigate to such a page and browse all the unhandled exceptions that have occurred recently. (You should also provide a button or some other means to clear the ErrorMessages ArrayList.)

An HTTP module must be listed in the web.config file to be instantiated when the application starts.

```
<configuration>
  <system.web>
    ⋮
    <httpModules>
      <add name="ErrorLogger"
         type="AspnetApplications.ErrorLoggerModule,AspnetApplications" />
    </httpModules>
  </system.web>
</configuration>
```

Note that the type argument has a value in the format *classname,assemblyname*. If you're using a private assembly, it should be stored in the \bin directory under the application's root directory.

> **Note** Assembly binding under ASP.NET works in the manner I described in the section "The Binding Process" of Chapter 14. In addition, ASP.NET automatically finds and binds any assembly stored in the \bin directory under the application's root directory.

Thanks to the hierarchical structure of configuration files, you can have a module that filters all the requests to the application by adding it to the web.config file in the application's root, or you can have a module that filters just the requests for the files in a given directory. If you add an HTTP handler in machine.config, it filters all requests for all the installed ASP.NET applications on the local computer. In fact, by peeking at the <httpModules> section in machine.config, you can get an idea of which ASP.NET features are implemented through HTTP modules. (Some of these features are related to security, which I haven't discussed yet.)

```
<httpModules>
  <add name="OutputCache" type="System.Web.Caching.OutputCacheModule" />
  <add name="Session" type="System.Web.SessionState.SessionStateModule" />
  <add name="WindowsAuthentication"
     type="System.Web.Security.WindowsAuthenticationModule" />
  <add name="FormsAuthentication"
     type="System.Web.Security.FormsAuthenticationModule" />
```

```
  <add name="PassportAuthentication"
     type="System.Web.Security.PassportAuthenticationModule" />
  <add name="UrlAuthorization"
     type="System.Web.Security.UrlAuthorizationModule" />
  <add name="FileAuthorization"
     type="System.Web.Security.FileAuthorizationModule" />
</httpModules>
```

HTTP Handlers

HTTP handlers are .NET components that are instantiated when a client requests the resource associated with it. For example, an HTTP handler associated with .xyz files is instantiated whenever a client requests a file with this extension. As I mentioned previously, ASP.NET itself uses HTTP handlers to process .aspx files (Web Forms) and .asmx files (XML Web services), the special trace.axd request, and a few other resource types. Again, you should reason in terms of resources, not files: there's no trace.axd file anywhere on your system, but ASP.NET uses a component of the class System.Web.Handlers.TraceHandler to handle requests for this resource.

Mapping File Extensions in IIS

You might want to create a handler for files that are already associated with ASP.NET—namely, .aspx, .asmx, .ascx, .asax, .axd, and a few others—or you can create a handler for a file extension not yet handled by ASP.NET, such as .xyz. In the latter case, however, you have to inform IIS that requests for .xyz resources must be passed to the aspnet_isapi.dll component. Otherwise, ASP.NET will never have a chance to pass the request to your handler. The association of a file extension with the aspnet_isapi.dll component is a manual operation that you must perform by using the MMC snap-in for Internet Information Services. (See Figure 24-11.)

1. In the Internet Information Services window, expand the computer node, right-click Web Sites in the console tree and click Properties in the shortcut menu; the Properties dialog box appears. (In Windows 2000, you must use the Properties dialog box of the computer node, ensure that WWW Service is selected in the Master Properties combo box, and click the Edit button.) You can also use the Properties dialog box of a specific Web site, if you don't want to affect all the sites on the server.

2. Click the Home Directory tab and click the Configuration button. This action opens the Application Configuration dialog box, where you can see all the file extensions associated with ASP and ASP.NET.

3. Click the Add button to display the Add/Edit Application Extension Mapping dialog box, in which you can associate the .xyz extension with the aspnet_isapi.dll executable file. (This file is in the C:\WinNT\Microsoft.NET\Framework\v*x*.*y*.*zzzz* directory.). If your handler processes only files that exist, you should select the Check That File Exists option. (Leave it deselected for this example, however.)

4. Click OK: you'll see that the .xyz extension has been included in the list of Application Mappings. Click OK twice to close the open dialog boxes.

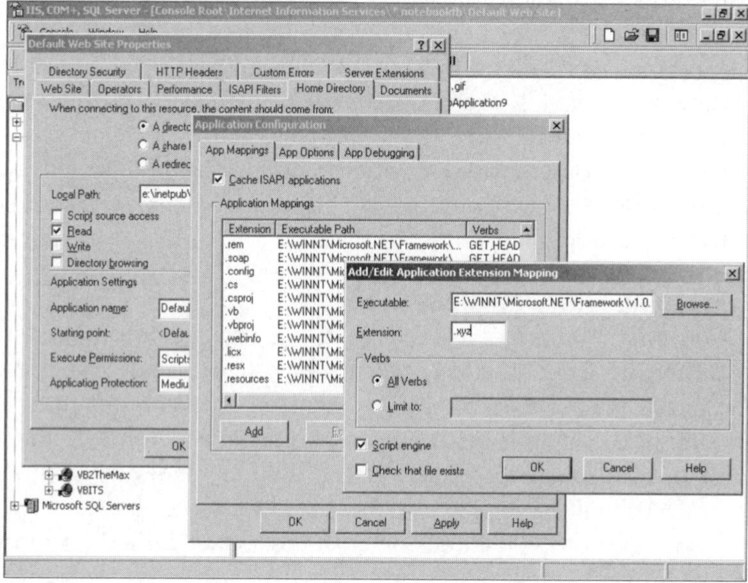

Figure 24-11. All the dialog boxes you need to traverse to map a file extension in IIS.

To help you avoid the nuisance of registering a file extension in IIS for the sole purpose of writing a handler against it, ASP.NET registers the .ashx extension in IIS but leaves it available to your handlers. If you write a handler for this extension, you just have to add an entry in the web.config file, as I explain in the following section.

Adding the HTTP Handler to Configuration Files

The second step that you must take is to modify the web.config file (or the machine.config file, if your handler must be used by all the ASP.NET applications on the local computer) so that ASP.NET knows that requests for a given resource type—files with the .xyz extension in this example—must be passed along to your handler. All HTTP handlers are listed in the <httpHandlers> section. For example, here's what this section of machine.config looks like:

```
<configuration>
  <system.web>
    ⋮
    <httpHandlers>
      <add verb="*" path="trace.axd" type="System.Web.Handlers.TraceHandler"/>
      <add verb="*" path="*.aspx" type="System.Web.UI.PageHandlerFactory" />
      <add verb="*" path="*.asmx"
       type="System.Web.Services.Protocols.WebServiceHandlerFactory,
             System.Web.Services, Version=1.0.3300.0, Culture=neutral,
             PublicKeyToken=b03f5f7f11d50a3a" validate="false" />
      <add verb="*" path="*.asax" type="System.Web.HttpForbiddenHandler" />
      <add verb="*" path="*.ascx" type="System.Web.HttpForbiddenHandler" />
      <add verb="*" path="*.config" type="System.Web.HttpForbiddenHandler" />
      <add verb="*" path="*.cs" type="System.Web.HttpForbiddenHandler" />
      <add verb="*" path="*.vb" type="System.Web.HttpForbiddenHandler" />
      ⋮
    </httpHandlers>
  </system.web>
</configuration>
```

Let's see what each attribute in the <add> block stands for:

- The verb attribute is the HTTP verb that the handler can process. It can be a single verb (Get), a semicolon-delimited list of verbs (Get;Post;Head), or an asterisk for all verbs.
- The path attribute tells which files must be passed to the HTTP handler. It's usually a wildcard expression (*.aspx), but it can also be a filename (trace.axd) or a directory name plus a wildcard expression (/MyApp/MySubDir/*.aspx) if you want your handler to process only files with a given extension in the specified directory.
- The type attribute is the name of your class, in the format *classname,assemblyname*, where the name of the assembly can be a fully qualified or a partial name. All ASP.NET standard handlers are in the GAC, but you can use private assemblies in the \bin subdirectory for handlers that are used by only one application.

The name of the class associated with each extension provides some clues for what ASP.NET does with each file type. For example, .aspx files are managed by the PageHandlerFactory class (which creates a Page object that handles the request), and .asmx files are passed to the WebServiceHandlerFactory class, which replies by instantiating an XML Web service. Interestingly, requests for .asax, .ascx, .vb, and .cs files (and a few others) are processed by a class named HttpForbiddenHandler, which correctly prevents remote users from downloading source files.

Now that you know the meaning of the attributes for the <add> tag, it's easy to come up with the correct <httpHandlers> section for the sample application's web.config file:

```
<httpHandlers>
   <add verb="*" path="*.xyz"
      type="AspnetApplications.XyzHandler,AspnetApplications" />
</httpHandlers>
```

If you have multiple <add> tags for the same path or extension, the last one takes precedence. You can slightly improve performance by setting the optional validate attribute to false for handlers that are used infrequently. This setting speeds up start-up time by loading the handler only when a request for the specified resource comes:

```
<add verb="*" path="*.xyz" validate="false"
     type="AspnetApplications.XyzHandler,AspnetApplications" />
```

You can also insert <remove> tags to disable a handler that was defined in machine.config, or in the web.config file stored in the root directory of the current application. In this case, you use the verb and path attributes only:

```
<httpHandlers>
   <remove verb="*" path="*.xyz" />
</httpHandlers>
```

Writing the HTTP Handler Class

An HTTP Handler is a class that implements the IHttpHandler interface, which consists of just two members. The IsReusable read-only property should return True if another request can use the same instance of the handler class. The ProcessRequest method is invoked when a client requests a resource for which your handler has been registered. This method receives an HttpContext object as an argument, which lets your code access all the ASP.NET intrinsic objects such as Request, Response, and so on.

To show you the power of HTTP handlers, I've prepared a class that processes requests for .xyz resources and maps them to a Biblio.mdb table named after the requested page. For example, a request for the Publishers page returns a table with all the records in the Publishers table:

```
http://www.tailspintoys.com/anypath/publishers.xyz
```

Whatever is passed on the query string is considered to be a WHERE clause to restrict the database query, so here's how you can display all the publishers in a given U.S. state:

```
http://www.tailspintoys.com/anypath/publishers.xyz?state='MA'
```

The result of this query is shown in Figure 24-12.

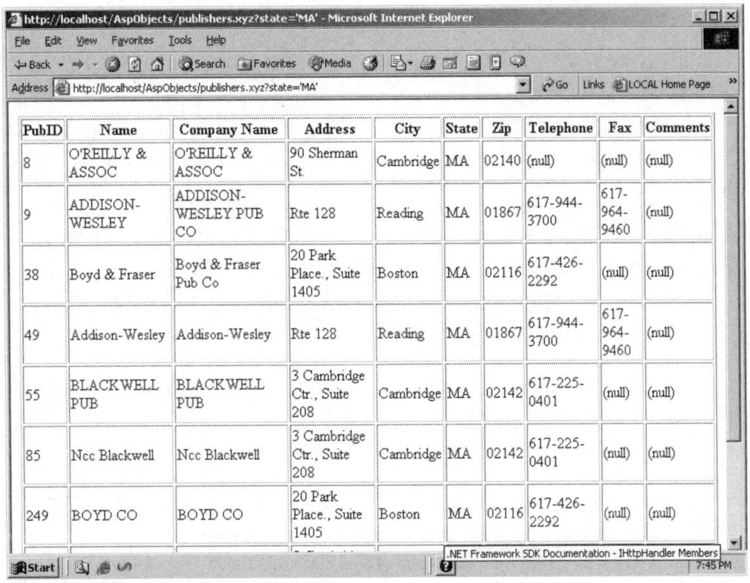

Figure 24-12. An HTTP handler can map a request to a database table.

Here's the complete source code of the XyzHandler class. As you see, its heart is in the ProcessRequest method, which extracts the table name and the WHERE clause from the URL string:

```
Public Class XyzHandler
    Implements IHttpHandler

    ' This method is called for every request for .xyz resources.
    Public Sub ProcessRequest(ByVal context As System.Web.HttpContext) _
        Implements System.Web.IHttpHandler.ProcessRequest

        ' The name of the page is the table's name.
        Dim tableName As String = context.Request.Path
        ' Drop directory name, if any, and the extension.
        tableName = System.IO.Path.GetFileNameWithoutExtension(tableName)
        ' The query string is an optional WHERE clause.
        Dim whereClause As String = context.Request.QueryString.ToString
        ' Build the SQL query.
        Dim sql As String = "SELECT * FROM " & tableName
        If whereClause.Length > 0 Then sql &= " WHERE " & whereClause

        ' Send the table to the client.
        context.Response.Write("<HTML><BODY>")
        context.Response.Write(MakeHtmlTable(sql, context))
        context.Response.Write("</BODY></HTML>")
    End Sub
```

(continued)

```
' This property is queried before this handler is reused.
Public ReadOnly Property IsReusable() As Boolean _
    Implements System.Web.IHttpHandler.IsReusable
    Get
        Return True                 ' Just return True in this demo.
    End Get
End Property
```

The bulk of the work is done in the MakeHtmlTable function. This routine takes a reference to the HTTP context, which it uses to encode the HTML being sent to the client. (Otherwise any special character in fields, like < or &, would be mistakenly interpreted as HTML.)

```
' Perform an SQL query, and return the result as an HTML table.
Function MakeHtmlTable(ByVal sql As String, _
    ByVal context As HttpContext) As String

    Dim cn As New System.Data.OleDb.OleDbConnection(BiblioConnString)
    Dim cmd As New System.Data.OleDb.OleDbCommand(sql, cn)
    Dim dr As System.Data.OleDb.OleDbDataReader

    ' Use a StringBuilder to create the output.
    Dim sb As New System.Text.StringBuilder(10240)

    Try
        ' Open a connection to Biblio and process the query.
        cn.Open()
        dr = cmd.ExecuteReader

        ' Create an HTML table with correct header row.
        sb.Append("<TABLE Border='1'><THEAD>")
        Dim i As Integer
        For i = 0 To dr.FieldCount - 1
            sb.Append("<TH>")
            sb.Append(dr.GetName(i))
            sb.Append("</TH>")
        Next
        sb.Append("</THEAD>")

        ' Output data for each record.
        Do While dr.Read
            sb.Append("<TR>")                   ' Row start delimiter
            For i = 0 To dr.FieldCount - 1
                sb.Append("<TD>")               ' Cell start delimiter
                If Not dr.IsDBNull(i) Then
                    ' A single field value (must be encoded for html)
                    sb.Append(context.Server.HtmlEncode(dr(i).ToString))
                Else
```

```
                    ' Special treatment for Null values
                    sb.Append("(null)")
                End If
                sb.Append("</TD>")              ' Cell end delimiter
            Next
            sb.Append("</TR>")                  ' Row end delimiter
        Loop
        ' Close the table.
        sb.Append("</TABLE>")

    Catch ex As Exception
        sb.Append("<h1>Unable to process the request</h1>")
    Finally
        ' Close the data reader and the connection, if necessary.
        If Not (dr Is Nothing) Then dr.Close()
        cn.Close()
    End Try

    ' Return the HTML text to the caller.
    Return sb.ToString
  End Function
End Class
```

It's easy to expand on this example to create a fully hierarchical system that appears to remote users as a complex tree of directories but that in reality takes all its data from database tables or XML files. As usual with ASP.NET, the possibilities are virtually endless.

ASP.NET Security

ASP.NET security is a complex topic because it's actually the convergence of three different security models: Windows security, Internet Information Services security, and ASP.NET's own security. Not surprisingly, therefore, you need to know the rudiments of how security works in Windows and IIS to fully comprehend ASP.NET security issues.

Basic Concepts

Before we begin our security tour, let's make it clear that we're going to discuss two different but closely tied topics here: authentication and authorization.

Authentication is the process through which a Web application detects the identity of the user posting the request and associates the request with the user's Windows account, if the user has one. In most Internet sites, users don't have a Windows account on the server, and IIS is configured to accept anonymous requests. In the case of an anonymous posting, the request is considered to be coming from a user named IUSR_machinename, a fictitious identity created when IIS was installed. If anonymous requests aren't enabled and the user can't prove that she has a valid Windows account, the request fails and the user sees an error page, "You are not authorized to view this page," in the browser.

The authentication process ends after the identity of the user posting the request has been ascertained. If the request was for one of the resources associated with ASP.NET, IIS passes the request to the ASP.NET process.

Authorization is the process during which Windows, IIS, or ASP.NET makes sure that the user identity associated with the request (or the identity associated with anonymous requests) has enough privileges to access the requested resource. In this context, a *resource* is usually an .aspx file, but it can be any other file on the server—for example, a GIF image pointed to by an <img> tag. If the user identity has enough privileges on the .aspx file, the ASP.NET code is given a chance to run. Otherwise an error message is sent back to the user.

The authorization process doesn't complete when the .aspx file is read and executed because its code might attempt to access other resources on the Web server—for example, an XML data file. Or it might attempt to connect to a SQL Server database using the current user identity. Again, if the identity under which the current request is executing doesn't have enough privileges on the resource, an exception is thrown and an error is returned to the client. The exact identity under which the request runs inside ASP.NET depends on several factors, including the authentication settings in IIS and whether impersonation is enabled.

IIS Authorization

As soon as the request arrives at the server, IIS performs its own authorization chores. IIS supports two different levels of authorizations. Neither of them takes user identity into account, so they can be carried out before the authentication process starts.

First IIS lets you prevent access to the Web server from unauthorized or unknown users by means of IP address and domain name restrictions. For example, you can reject requests from any IP address other than those associated with recognized users or sites. Domain restrictions are applied before the authentication process begins; you enable them by clicking the button in the middle section of the Directory Security tab, in the IIS Properties dialog box. For example, the settings shown in Figure 24-13 allow access to a resource only from the local computer (127.0.0.1) and all the computers in a group (192.168.0.nnn). You can apply this type of authorization to the entire site, selected directories, or individual files.

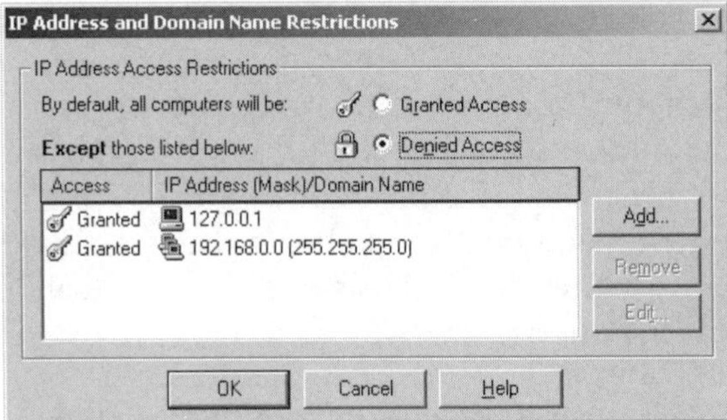

Figure 24-13. IP address and domain name restrictions in IIS.

The second type of IIS authorization checks that only permissible operations are performed on the site, a directory, or a file. By default, files can only be read, and you need to change these authorization settings if you want to let users write files, allow them to browse the contents of a directory, or prevent them from accessing the directory or the file. You typically apply this type of authorization to individual files or directories because you'll rarely want to make the entire Web site writable (not to mention nonreadable). For example, IIS uses this type of authorization to hide its own private directories under wwwroot. (See Figure 24-14.) Any attempt to read a resource protected in this way results in an error page entitled "The page cannot be displayed" being sent to the browser.

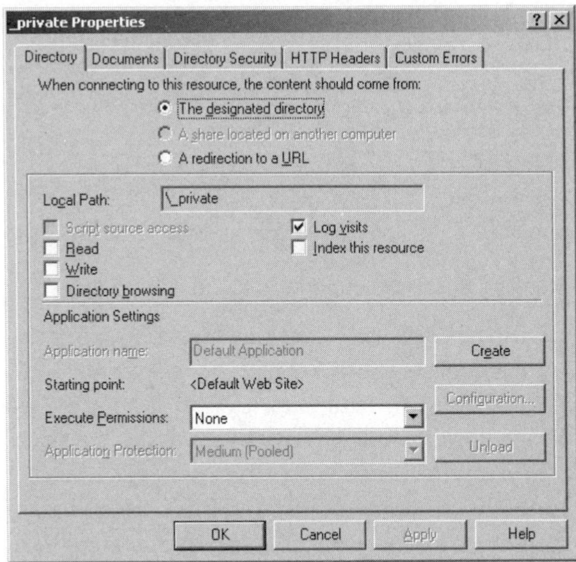

Figure 24-14. Preventing read, write, or directory browsing access to a private directory.

IIS Authentication

After you've enforced satisfactory IIS authentication settings, you must decide what kind of authentication IIS can perform on incoming requests. You set these settings inside the Authentication Methods dialog box (Figure 24-15, center), which you reach by clicking the Edit button on the Directory Security tab of the Web Site Properties dialog box (to the left in the same figure). You can apply these settings to the entire site, its directories, or individual files. Here's a brief description of available modes.

- **Anonymous access** Any incoming request is accepted, and it's associated with the identity you specify in the Anonymous User Account dialog box (Figure 24-15, right). By default, this account is IUSR_machinename, and you shouldn't change it if you don't have a good reason to do so.

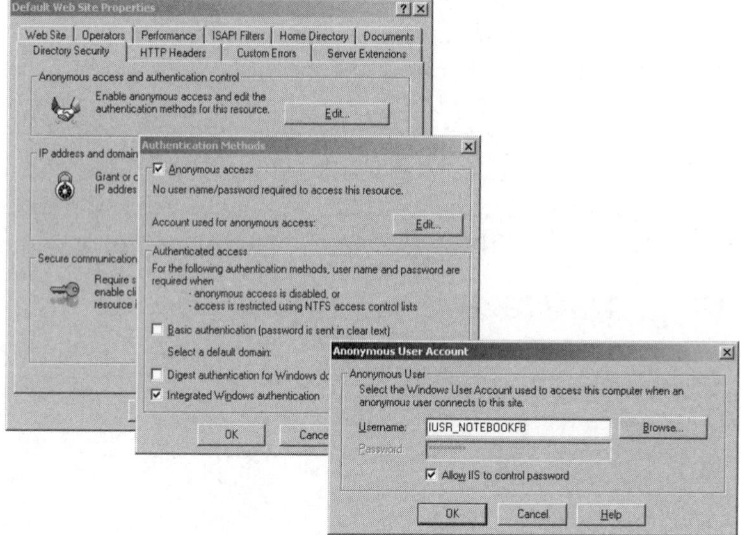

Figure 24-15. Mapping anonymous requests to a user account.

- **Basic authentication** The browser displays the Enter Network Password dialog box that asks the user for her name and password. (See Figure 24-16.) This information is then sent to IIS, which attempts a Windows login for a user with this name and password. This authentication method is compatible with all browsers and works across firewalls and proxy servers, but the user name and password aren't encrypted and can be spoofed relatively easily. For this reason, Basic authentication should be used only when security issues aren't critical or for resources that can be accessed only through an encrypted channel such as HTTPS.

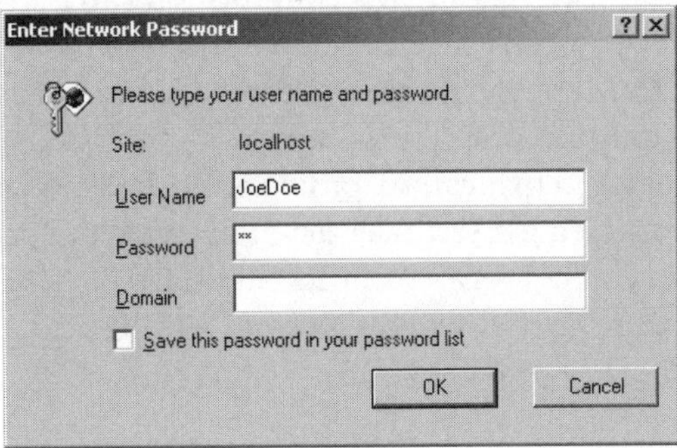

Figure 24-16. The dialog box that the browser displays when accessing a resource for which anonymous access is disabled.

- **Digest authentication** Also in this case, a remote user enters a user name and password in a dialog box that the browser displays. Unlike Basic authentication, however, Digest authentication encrypts the password by using a hash value sent by the Web server and therefore offers a good degree of security. It works well with firewalls and proxy servers but has a couple of serious shortcomings: it works only with Internet Explorer 5 or later versions and requires that passwords be stored in clear text on the server. (For security reasons, most Windows servers hash the password and store only the hashed value.)
- **Windows authentication** This method is very secure because user credentials are never passed on the wire and can't be spoofed. This method is also known as NTLM authentication or Challenge/Response authentication because IIS challenges the browser to provide a hash value that depends on the user name and password. The browser sends IIS information based on the identity specified by the user when she logged on the client machine, and it displays a dialog box only if this identity isn't authorized to access the requested resource. Unlike the previous two authentication methods, Windows authentication is a Microsoft proprietary standard, works only on Windows and with Internet Explorer (version 2 or later), and doesn't work over firewalls. For these reasons, this authentication method is more suitable for intranet sites than as the only authentication method used on Internet sites.

Any authentication method other than anonymous access requires that, in one way or another, remote users prove that they have a valid account on the Windows server. This requirement makes sense when you're running an intranet site, but could hardly be met in large Internet sites that everyone can visit. This doesn't mean that you can't mix these authorization methods, however: for example, you might have a public portion of the site that uses anonymous access and a restricted portion that only the company's employees can access from inside the local network and that can be protected with Windows authentication.

I suggest that you create a test user account to try out security settings in IIS and ASP.NET, such as the JoeDoe user in Figure 24-17. The highlighted user accounts in the figure are crucial when working with IIS and ASP.NET security, as I'll explain in the next section:

- IUSR_machinename is the user account that IIS associates with anonymous requests.
- ASPNET is the default user account for the ASP.NET worker process.

There's also a third account related to IIS security, IWAM_machinename. This account is assigned to IIS applications that run out of process, and I won't describe it here.

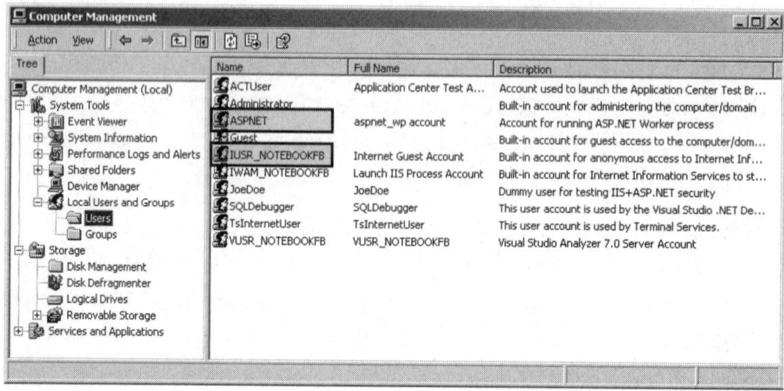

Figure 24-17. Setting users in Windows 2000.

Windows Authorization

If the authentication process finishes successfully, the remote user has been associated with a Windows account, whether it's a real user's account or the IUSR_machinename built-in account used for anonymous accesses. At this point, the Windows authorization process can begin.

During the Windows authorization process, the operating system checks that the user is allowed to access the resource. This step is performed only if the resource resides on an NTFS drive and has been protected with an access control list (ACL), which specifies which operations (read, write, and so on) a specific user can perform on the resource. To edit an ACL, right-click a file or a directory inside Windows Explorer, click Properties to open the Properties dialog box, and click the Security tab. (See Figure 24-18.)

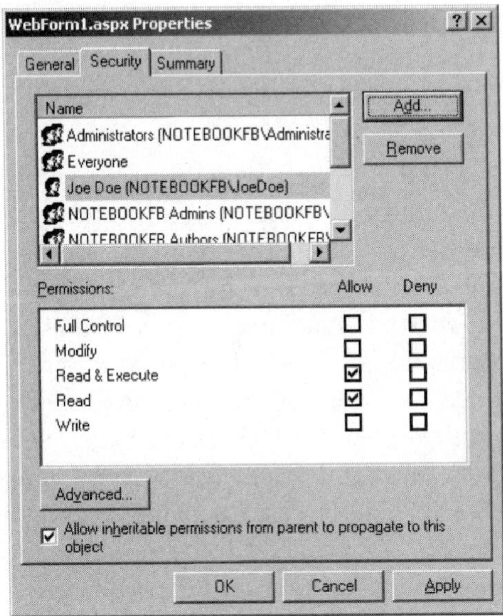

Figure 24-18. The Security property page of a file on an NTFS drive.

ASP.NET Impersonation

When the authentication process finishes, IIS checks whether there's an ISAPI filter that's willing to process the request. For example, requests for .asp files are passed to ASP (asp.dll) and requests for .aspx files are passed to ASP.NET. If no ISAPI filter is associated with the extension of the requested file, IIS processes the request by itself and sends the file's content to the client; this is the normal process for .html, .gif, .jpg, and .txt files.

Let's say that the request is for an .aspx file and is therefore passed to the aspnet_isapi.dll filter. In turn, this DLL passes the request to the ASP.NET worker process (aspnet_wp.exe), launching it from disk if it's not running already. Now the question is: under which identity does the aspnet_wp process run? The answer to this question is important because this is the identity that will be considered during the authorization process. For example, if ASP.NET runs under an account that doesn't have write privileges for the \Temp directory, your code will fail when attempting to create a temporary file there. The process will run under one of three identities, depending on the value of these two tags in the configuration file:

```
<configuration>
  <system.web>
     <identity impersonate="false"/>
     <processModel userName="ASPNET" password="AutoGenerate" />
  </system.web>
</configuration>
```

If impersonation isn't enabled (the default setting), the ASP.NET worker process runs under the identity indicated by the username attribute in the <processModel> block in machine.config. By default, this identity is ASPNET, an account that was created when ASP.NET was installed. (See Figure 24-15.) This account has more privileges than IUSR_machinename, and ASP.NET leverages them to perform dynamic compilations of .aspx files, among other things.

If impersonation is enabled, the ASP.NET worker process runs under the identity of the remote authenticated user. This can be the user's Windows account if she was authenticated through Basic, Digest, or Integrated Windows authentication methods, or it can be IUSR_machinename if anonymous access was used. In impersonation mode, your ASP.NET code is allowed to do what the remote user could do if she were logged on locally. You'll typically use impersonation together with ACLs to deny access to sensitive information.

It's also possible to enable impersonation but opt for a user account other than the authenticated user's account. You can make this choice by specifying a user name and a password in the <identity> block:

```
<identity impersonate="true"
  userName="MyComputer\JoeDoe" password="jdpwd" />
```

As you'll see shortly, in practice impersonation should be enabled only when you use Windows mode for ASP.NET authentication.

Putting Things Together

I wouldn't be surprised if all these security settings have confused you, so let me summarize what conditions must be met for a generic HTTP request to pass IIS and Windows authentication and authorization tests:

1. The request comes from an IP address or domain that's granted access.
2. The requested resource is readable in IIS.
3. IIS allows anonymous access to the resource, or the user can provide a user name and password for a valid Windows account on the server by using one of the enabled IIS authentication methods (Basic, Digest, or Integrated Windows).
4. If the resource is on an NTFS drive, its ACL specifies that the user has read access to the file.

If the request is for a resource associated with ASP.NET, two more tests are performed:

1. The resource's ACL grants read permissions to the identity under which the ASP.NET worker process runs. This identity depends on whether impersonation is enabled and on other settings in configuration files.
2. If the resource is an .aspx file, any other file or resource the page uses is accessible from the identity under which the ASP.NET worker process runs.

I prepared a diagram that shows what happens when a request is posted to IIS and the points where the request might be rejected, in which case the client browser is redirected to an error page (Figure 24-19). The last steps in the diagram are related to ASP.NET authentication and authorization, the topic of following sections.

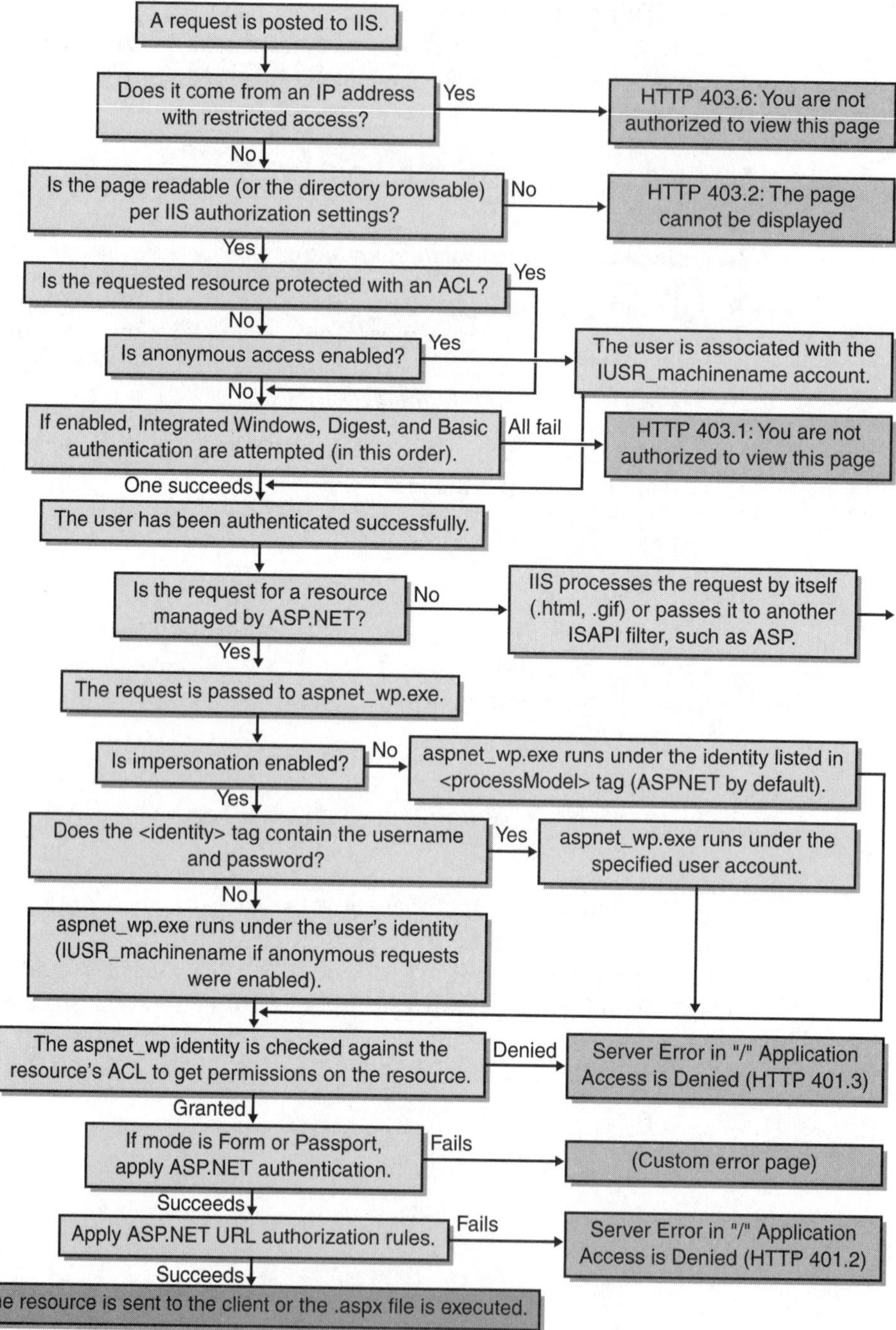

Figure 24-19. The path of requests sent to IIS.

ASP.NET Authentication Modes

With IIS and Windows authentication and authorization methods out of the way, we can finally focus on ASP.NET's own security model. Unlike classic ASP, ASP.NET can use configuration files to specify which users can access a given resource or directory and what happens if the user isn't granted access.

ASP.NET supports four authentication modes, and each one corresponds to different authorization techniques. For this reason, I'll cover ASP.NET authentication and authorization together. You decide which mode to enforce by setting the mode attribute of the <authentication> tag in the machine.config or web.config file:

```
<configuration>
  <system.web>
    <authentication mode="authmode">
      ⋮
    </authentication>
  </system.web>
</configuration>
```

where authmode can be None, Windows, Forms, or Passport. Let's briefly see what each option is all about:

- **None** ASP.NET doesn't perform any authentication and authorization steps other than those that IIS has already carried out. All resources are accessed by means of the identity assigned to the ASP.NET worker process.
- **Windows** ASP.NET uses the user identity (as authenticated by IIS) to decide whether the resource is accessible. Settings in web.config let you authorize individuals or groups of users to access the entire application or portions of it, without having to write any code whatsoever. The drawback of this mode is that each user must map to a Windows account, so it works especially well only in intranets. This is the default mode in ASP.NET, but you can change it by editing the machine.config file.
- **Forms** ASP.NET redirects the first request from unauthenticated users to a custom .aspx login page that asks remote users for their user name and password. You author this login page, so it can have the same look and feel as other pages in the site. The code in the login page then compares the user's name and password against a list of user credentials kept in web.config or another repository (most likely a database). If your code authenticates the user, ASP.NET issues a cookie that will travel with each subsequent request so that the login form isn't shown again.

- **Passport** ASP.NET uses the centralized Passport service that Microsoft provides and that's able to authenticate users across all the sites that subscribe to this service. A user can log in to one site and browse any other Passport-enabled site, without having to log in to each one. Passport is a secure authentication method—because user credentials can travel on encrypted channels—and makes for a great user experience.

I'm not discussing Passport authentication in this book. Those who are interested can find more information and download the Passport SDK at *http://www.passport.com*.

ASP.NET Windows Authentication

Let's restrict our focus to Windows and Forms authentication modes. In this section, I describe the first mode and postpone the discussion about ASP.NET Forms authentication to later in this chapter.

Configuration Settings for Windows Authentication

You activate Windows authentication by adding this line in machine.config or web.config:

```
<configuration>
  <system.web>
    <authentication mode="Windows" />
  </system.web>
</configuration>
```

(No other tag is used in the authentication block when you're using Windows authentication mode.) In Windows authentication mode, it usually makes sense to have ASP.NET impersonate the remote user. If impersonation is enabled, ASP.NET accesses files and other resources on the server under the remote user's account, and all usual ACL constraints must be satisfied. If impersonation is disabled, a remote user might have access to fewer (or more) resources than when he logs in locally, and you'll probably want to avoid this discrepancy. As I already showed you, you enable impersonation by means of the <identity> tag in the configuration file:

```
<configuration>
  <system.web>
    <authentication mode="Windows" />
    <identity impersonate="true"/>
  </system.web>
</configuration>
```

You can also have ASP.NET impersonate a given user if you add the username and password attributes to the <identity> tag, but this rarely makes sense because the main goal of impersonation is to enable different behavior depending on the identity of the remote user.

Once the user has been recognized by means of Windows authentication, you can finally apply ASP.NET authorization rules to allow or deny the user access to specific areas on the site. You can make such distinctions by means of URL authorization rules.

URL Authorizations

Each .config file can include a section named <authorization>, which lists the users who are allowed or denied access to the portion of the site that the .config file is related to. This section can contain a series of <allow> and <deny> elements, each one specifying which users or groups are or aren't granted access:

```
<configuration>
  <system.web>
    <authorization>
      <allow users="userlist" roles="grouplist" verb="verblist" />
      <deny users="userlist" roles="grouplist" verb="verblist" />
    </authorization>
  </system.web>
</configuration>
```

where

- **userlist** is a comma-separated list of users, in the format *domainname\username* or *machinename\username*. A question mark (?) stands for anonymous users, and an asterisk (*) means all users.
- **grouplist** is a comma-separated list of Windows account groups, in the format *domainname\rolename* or *machinename\rolename*. An asterisk (*) means all roles.
- **verblist** is a comma-separated list of HTTP verbs. Verbs registered to ASP.NET are GET, POST, HEAD, and DEBUG. An asterisk (*) means all verbs. The verb attribute is optional, and if omitted all verbs are considered.

<allow> and <deny> tags must contain at least one user's or role's attribute. Note that user and role names must include either a domain name or the name of the local machine, which means that you must edit the configuration file when you move the application to another machine or another domain. The default settings in machine.config grant access to all users:

```
<authorization>
  <allow users="*" />
</authorization>
```

Of course, you can override these settings in web.config files. For example, these settings grant access to administrators and managers only, and deny access to everybody else:

```
<authorization>
  <allow roles="MyDomain\administrators,MyDomain\managers" verb="*" />
  <deny users="*" />
</authorization>
```

The following example denies access only to anonymous users:

```
<authorization>
  <deny users="?" />
  <allow users="*" />
</authorization>
```

Here's an example that employs user names instead of group names:

```
<authorization>
  <allow users="MyComputer\FrancescoB,MyComputer\JoeDoe" />
  <deny users="*" />
</authorization>
```

The <allow> and <deny> tags are processed in order until one element in the list of users or roles matches the identity of the user. Therefore, the order of entries is significant: for example, if you reverse the order of the two elements in the <authorization> block in the preceding sample, no user is allowed to access any resource controlled by this web.config file (or any ASP.NET resource, if these entries are in machine.config):

```
<deny users="*" />
      <allow roles="MyDomain\administrators,MyDomain\managers" verb="*" />
```

ASP.NET processes a web.config file in the directory where the requested resource is, then proceeds towards the application's root directory, and stops as soon as it finds a user or group list that matches the user's identity. This means that you can have a \Documents directory visible only to authors and managers, and a \Documents\Public directory that can be accessed by anyone, including anonymous users:

```
<!-- settings in \Documents\web.config -->
  <allow roles="MyDomain\Authors,MyDomain\Managers" />
  <deny users="*" />

<!-- settings in \Documents\Public\web.config -->
  <allow users="*" />
```

If the current user isn't granted access to the requested page or resource, ASP.NET sends an error page to the client browser, mentioning HTTP error code 401.2.

Forms Authentication Mode

ASP.NET Windows authentication mode is fine and provides a fairly understandable authentication model that's also easily coupled with URL authorizations. However, Windows authentication isn't a practical solution when you're building an Internet site that must authenticate thousands of remote users. When selecting the authentication model for such a site, you must ask yourself *why* you want to authenticate your users. If you authenticate users to carry out secure transactions or arbitrate access to highly confidential information, you must resort to advanced techniques, such as client certificates and communications over Secure Sockets Layer (SSL), which I don't cover in this book. In the vast majority of cases, you authenticate users only to customize your site accordingly without too severe security constraints. In these circumstances, ASP.NET Forms authentication mode fits the bill very nicely.

Forms authentication works as follows: if the remote user requests a protected resource managed by ASP.NET—typically, an .aspx page—the ASP.NET infrastructure checks whether the request carries a special authentication cookie, also known as an authentication ticket. If yes, the user has been authenticated and ASP.NET can display the page. If the cookie isn't there, ASP.NET redirects the request to a custom login page, an .aspx page that you've prepared and that typically asks the user for her user name and password and compares them with the list of registered users. (This list can be kept in web.config or, more frequently, in a database.) If your code successfully authenticates the user, it must issue an authentication cookie so that from that point on the user can visit any other page in the site without being redirected to the login page. You decide whether the authentication ticket is a session cookie (which expires when the user closes the browser or a timeout elapses) or a persistent cookie stored on disk. An easy tip: always give users the ability to choose whether the cookie is persistent; otherwise, no one will ever want to log in to your site from a public computer.

Keep this in mind when you consider using Forms authentication for your site: You can protect only resources directly managed by ASP.NET, such as .aspx files. You can't use Forms authentication for, say, preventing the download of GIF or JPEG files. If protecting these files is a requirement, you should opt for another protection mechanism, such as using Windows authentication and protecting those resources with ACLs. Another easy technique is storing all the files in a directory that can be accessed only from the ASP.NET worker process (but not directly from remote users), and use a special .aspx page that reads the file and returns it to the client, for example, by using the Response.WriteFile method:

```
http://www.tailspintoys.com/gettext.aspx?file=instructions.txt
```

Configuration Settings for Forms Authentication

You enforce Forms authentication by setting the mode attribute and adding a <forms> section inside the <authentication> section, as follows:

```
<configuration>
  <system.web>
    <authentication mode="Forms">
       <forms loginUrl="/LoginPage.aspx"
           name="MySiteName" path="/"
           protection="All"  timeout="10">
         <credentials passwordFormat="Clear" >
           <user name="JoeDoe" password="jdpwd" />
           <user name="AnnSmith" password="aspwd" />
         </credentials>
       </forms>
    </authentication>

    <authorization>
        <deny users="?" />
    </authorization>
  </system.web>
</configuration>
```

The <deny> tag is very important: you must explicitly deny access to anonymous users. If you omit this step, Forms authentication won't work. Let's see what each attribute in the <forms> section stands for:

- **loginUrl** is the URL of the custom login page you've prepared for the user to enter her user name and password. Its default value is login.aspx.
- **name** is the name of the authentication cookie. Most of the time, you can omit it and use its .ASPXAUTH default value.
- **path** is the path of your site where the cookie is valid; its default value is /, which makes the cookie visible to the entire site. You can specify a more specific path, such as /Reserved, if only a portion of your site is protected. This setting prevents the browser from sending the cookie when a user is requesting pages that aren't protected.
- **protection** is the protection level to be used for the cookie. It can be Validation (the cookie is validated against tampering but not encrypted), Encryption (the cookie is encrypted using Triple-DES or DES but not validated), All (the default; the cookie is both encrypted and validated), or None.
- **timeout** is the number of minutes of inactivity after which the session cookie expires. (Default is 30 minutes.) If a request is posted to the Web site within this interval, the authentication cookie is automatically renewed.

The default values for all these attributes are those defined in machine.config, so you can change them if you want.

The <forms> section can contain a <credentials> subsection that stores names and passwords of all recognized users. Many real-world ASP.NET applications don't use this section, however, and store user data in a database, where the data can be processed more easily and can be associated with additional information (such as e-mail addresses and whether users subscribe to the site's newsletter). If you omit this section and accept the default value for most of the attributes in the <forms> section, this is all you really need to activate Forms authentication:

```
<authentication mode="Forms">
   <forms loginUrl="/LoginPage.aspx" />
</authentication>
```

You must be aware of a few potential problems with <forms> settings in web.config. First, setting a path for the cookie other than "/" requires that *all* the links to pages in the reserved section—for example, the NavigateUrl property in Hyperlink controls or HREF attributes in <a> tags—are in the correct case because a few browsers compare paths in case-sensitive mode and don't send the cookie when they're accessing a URL in the wrong case.

The second potential problem is with cookie timeout. To improve performance and avoid multiple warnings in browsers that have cookie warning activated, ASP.NET refreshes this cookie only when half the timeout has expired (15 minutes, if you use default settings). This fact can cause a loss of precision. Imagine the following scenario: The user logs on to the site and spends 14 minutes visiting several pages, during which time the cookie is never renewed. Next the user stays on a long page for 20 minutes, but when she attempts to read another page the authentication cookie (which is now 34 minutes old) has expired and the user is brought again to the login page.

A third potential problem: you must pay attention to authentication cookies if you are in a Web farm. As I explained in the "Out-of-Process Sessions Based on a Windows Service" section earlier in this chapter, each server validates and encrypts cookies with two keys whose value is stored in the <machineKey> section of the machine.config file or of the main web.config file of individual applications. By default, these keys are autogenerated and each computer uses a different key, so a server on the Web farm won't recognize an authentication cookie issued by another server. To avoid this problem, ensure that all the computers on the farm use the same validation and decryption key:

```
<configuration>
   <system.web>
      <machineKey
         validationKey="0123456789abcdef0123456789abcdef0123456789abcdef"
```

(continued)

```
        decryptionKey="fedcba9876543210fedcba9876543210fedcba9876543210"
        validation="SHA1" />
  </system.web>
</configuration>
```

Or you can set the protection level for the authentication cookie to None, but that would mean sending the authentication cookie in clear text.

I've already hinted at the fact that the <credentials> section is rarely used in real-world applications because it's highly impractical to store user data in web.config. Worse, you surely noticed that passwords are stored in clear text, which makes them visible to anyone who has read access to the web.config file. Most of the time, you don't have to worry about this detail because you'll often prefer to store user credentials in a database, but it's good to know that you can encrypt passwords in the web.config file:

```
<credentials passwordFormat="SHA1">
  <user name="JoeDoe" password="7C9690380BB6A10B886AEFF2202F94C5C8FFCB92" />
  <user name="AnnSmith" password="D69DCC3EABAF925EF64BD625B0F045EACE4F0478" />
</credentials>
```

The passwordFormat attribute specifies the encryption algorithm used to encode the password and can be either SHA1, MD5, or Clear. SHA1 is more secure than MD5, but it's slower and produces longer passwords. Of course, you must encode the passwords before storing them in web.config. You do the encryption with the HashPasswordForStoringInConfigFile shared method of the System.Web.Security.FormsAuthentication class. The name of this method says it all: you pass the password and a string indicating the encryption method, and the method returns the encrypted password:

```
' The txtPassword control contains the password as entered by the user.
Dim encryptedPassword As String
encryptedPassword = System.Web.Security.FormsAuthentication. _
    HashPasswordForStoringInConfigFile(txtPassword.Text, "SHA1")
```

The value of the passwordFormat attribute is inherited from machine.config if you omit it. You might believe that it defaults to Clear and be tempted to omit it when you're storing passwords in clear text; unfortunately, machine.config sets SHA1 as the default password format, so you must specify this attribute when you're using unencrypted passwords.

The Login Page

To complete the Forms authentication implementation, you must prepare the login page to which unauthenticated users are redirected before they can access any protected resource on the site. The appearance of this login page can vary, but essentially it should look like the one in Figure 24-20 and contain a field for the user name, a field for the password, and a check box to make the authorization cookie persistent. You also have to provide a Login (or Submit) button and a link to a page where new users can register themselves. You should also add a Label control for displaying error messages.

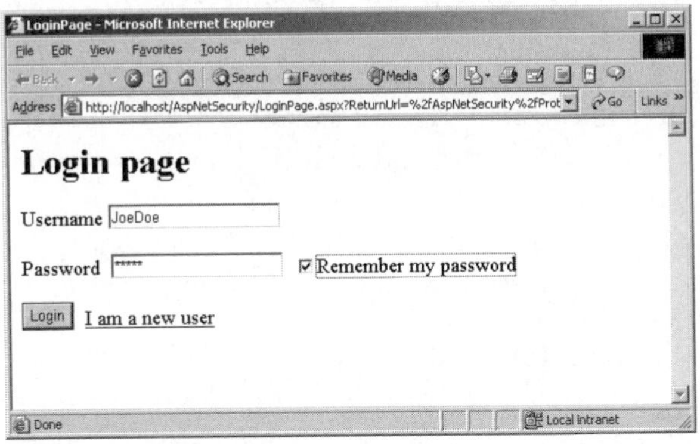

Figure 24-20. A typical login form.

The code you write for the Login button's Click event depends on where you've stored the list of user names and passwords. In the simplest case, the user list is stored in the web.config file (with passwords in clear text or encrypted format), and you simply need to check whether the provided name and password are valid. You can do this by using the Authenticate shared method of the FormsAuthentication class:

```
' This code assumes that you have the following Imports statement:
'    Imports System.Web.Security

Private Sub btnLogin_Click(ByVal sender As Object, ByVal e As EventArgs) _
    Handles btnLogin.Click
    If FormsAuthentication.Authenticate(txtUsername.Text, _
        txtPassword.Text) Then
        FormsAuthentication.RedirectFromLoginPage(txtUsername.Text, _
            chkRemember.Checked)
    Else
        lblMessage.Text = "Invalid user name or password"
    End If
End Sub
```

If the Authenticate method returns True, you usually call the Redirect-FromLoginPage method, passing the user name and a Boolean that specifies whether the authentication cookie is persistent. In our demo program, the user decides whether the cookie is persistent by selecting a CheckBox control, so the preceding code simply passes the Checked property of this control in the second argument to the method.

A persistent cookie is valid for 50 years, so the user will be automatically authenticated when she visits the same site again from the same computer. Note that modern browsers keep a separate list of cookies for each Windows user, so the authentication cookie isn't found if the user logs in to the operating system under a different identity.

The user name you pass to the RedirectFromLoginPage method is then used to perform URL authorization against the resource being requested. If the requested resource is denied to the authenticated user, the RedirectFromLoginPage method works partially: it does authenticate the user but the redirection fails and the user will be looking again at the login form, without a clue about what happened because no error message is shown in this case.

Custom Forms Authentication

The great thing about Forms authorization is the degree of customization it allows. For example, you can easily change the standard behavior to store user data in a place other than web.config; or you can change the expiration date for a persistent cookie if 50 years sounds like too long a period for you. The FormsAuthentication class exposes all the methods you need to perform these tasks.

The most common reason to switch to custom Forms authorization is when you store user data in a database. In that case, you replace the call FormsAuthentication.Authenticate with a call to a custom function that you provide:

```
If AuthenticateUser(txtUsername.Text, txtPassword.Text) Then
    FormsAuthentication.RedirectFromLoginPage(txtUsername.Text, _
        chkRemember.Checked)
End If
```

Here's an example of how you might implement the custom authenticate function:

```
' This code assumes that you have the following Imports statement:
'     Imports System.Data.OleDb

Function AuthenticateUser(ByVal username As String, _
    ByVal password As String) As Boolean
    ' Open the connection to the database holding user names and passwords.
    Dim cn As New OleDbConnection(PasswordDBConnString)
    cn.Open()
    ' Read the record for this user.
    ' (A parameterized query to avoid errors if username contains quotes.)
    Dim cmd As New OleDbCommand("SELECT * FROM Users WHERE UserName=?", cn)
    cmd.Parameters.Add("username", username)
    Dim dr As OleDbDataReader = cmd.ExecuteReader(CommandBehavior.SingleRow)

    If dr.Read AndAlso dr("Password") = password Then
        ' Authenticate user if there's a record and the password is correct.
```

```
        AuthenticateUser = True
    End If
    ' Close the DataReader and the connection.
    dr.Close()
    cn.Close()
End Function
```

Notice that the preceding code reads all the fields in the Users table, even though it uses just the Password field. This slight inefficiency makes the procedure ready for situations when you offer customization features. For example, you can read the preferred color scheme and store this data in Session variables before closing the DataReader:

```
Session("ForeColor") = CInt(dr("ForeColor"))
Session("BackColor") = CInt(dr("BackColor"))
```

Another reason to override the Forms authorization's standard behavior is for precisely specifying the authentication cookie's lifetime. In fact, the standard method lets you choose only between temporary (session) cookies and persistent cookies. If you want to create a cookie that expires in, say, one month, you must replace the RedirectFromLoginPage method with a custom routine:

```
' A custom routine that works like FormsAuthentication.RedirectFromLoginPage
' but lets you control the authentication cookie's expiration date.

Function RedirectFromLoginPageEx(ByVal username As String, _
    ByVal persistentCookie As Boolean, _
    Optional ByVal expirationDays As Integer = -1) As Boolean

    ' Get the URL of the requested resource.
    Dim url As String = _
        FormsAuthentication.GetRedirectUrl(username, persistentCookie)
    ' Create the authentication cookie.
    FormsAuthentication.SetAuthCookie(username, persistentCookie)

    If persistentCookie And expirationDays > 0 Then
        ' Get a reference to the cookie just created.
        Dim cookie As HttpCookie = _
            Response.Cookies(FormsAuthentication.FormsCookieName)
        ' Set its expiration date.
        cookie.Expires = Now.AddDays(expirationDays)
    End If
    ' Redirect to the resource that was requested originally.
    Response.Redirect(url)
End Function
```

Another reason for creating authentication cookies programmatically is to ensure that these cookies can travel only through encrypted channels, a trick that makes Forms authentication infinitely more secure. To implement this technique, you place the login form in a directory that can be accessed only through HTTPS:

```
<forms loginUrl="https://www.tailspintoys.com/protected/login.aspx />
```

You can improve this technique by having the cookie transmitted only when the user navigates to a page of the /Protected subdirectory. You do so by passing a third argument to the SetAuthCookie method:

```
FormsAuthentication.SetAuthCookie(username, persistentCookie, "/Protected")
```

Finally, you ensure that the cookie can travel only over secure lines by setting its Secure property to True:

```
' Add this statement to the RedirectFromLoginPageEx routine.
cookie.Secure = True
```

The FormsAuthentication class exposes other shared members that are useful for customizing the authentication process:

- The FormsCookieName and FormsCookiePath properties return the name and the path of the authentication cookie as defined in configuration files.
- The GetAuthCookie method returns the HttpCookie object without adding it to the Response.Cookies collection.
- The SignOut method removes the authentication cookie. You can provide a Sign Out hyperlink in your pages to let users of public computers safely exit your site without having to close the browser to remove the temporary cookie.

Programmatic Security

ASP.NET also offers you the ability to write code that determines whether a user has been authenticated, retrieves her name and role, and so on. Programmatic security can be useful for implementing more sophisticated security options—for example, by preventing a group of users from accessing the system during weekends. Or you can use programmatic security simply for customizing the Web site depending on the user's identity, such as when you hide or show controls and hyperlinks that can be used only by users with broader permissions.

The key to programmatic security is the User property of the Page object. Code that isn't running inside a Page class can access the User object by means of the HttpContext.Current.User property instead.

The IPrincipal and IIdentity Interfaces

You must become familiar with a few classes and two interfaces in the System.Security.Principal namespace to master programmatic security. The Page.User property returns an IPrincipal object—that is, an object that implements the IPrincipal interface. This interface exposes only two members, the IsInRole method and the Identity property.

The IsInRole method returns True if the authenticated user belongs to the Windows group passed in the argument. (This method doesn't work with users authenticated through Forms authentication because authenticated users don't belong to groups.) For example, this code checks whether the user is a manager:

```
If User.IsInRole("MyDomain\Managers") Then
    ' The user is a manager.
End If
```

You can also check whether the user belongs to one of the predefined Windows groups (Administrators, Users, Guests, and so on) with this syntax:

```
If User.IsInRole("BUILTIN\Administrators") Then
    ' The user is a system administrator.
End If
```

Remember that you need programmatic security only to implement sophisticated security options or customize the site. If you want to always forbid access to a page, you can just rely on settings in web.config. For example, here's how you can deny access to users other than administrators during weekends:

```
If Today.DayOfWeek=DayOfWeek.Saturday Or Today.DayOfWeek=DayOfWeek.Sunday Then
    If Not User.IsInRole("BUILTIN\Administrators") Then
        ' Refuse access to non-administrators on weekends.
        Response.Redirect("/AccessDenied.htm")
    End If
End If
```

The User.Identity property returns an IIdentity interface—that is, an object that implements the IIdentity interface. The actual class of the object depends on the type of authentication that has been performed, and can be WindowsIdentity, FormsIdentity, PasswordIdentity, or GenericIdentity.

The IIdentity interface exposes three read-only properties, which are therefore inherited by all the *xxxx*Identity classes:

- IsAuthenticated returns True if the user has been authenticated by means of any of the authentication methods that ASP.NET supports.
- AuthenticationType returns a string that specifies which authentication method has been used; it can be NTLM, Basic, Forms, or Passport, or any other string passed to the .NET runtime by the authentication provider (Kerberos, for instance).

- Name returns the user name under which the user logged in. This is the user name if the user was authenticated by means of the Forms method, or a string in the format *domainname\username* or *machinename\username* if the user was authenticated by means of the Windows authentication method.

Properties in the IIdentity interface let you gather information about the logged user, a precious piece of information when you're debugging odd behaviors related to security:

```
Dim msg As String
If Not User.Identity.IsAuthenticated Then
    ' You can see this only if the site doesn't require authentication.
    msg = "Unauthenticated user"
Else
    msg = "User name = " & User.Identity.Name & "<br />"
    msg &= "Authentication type = " & User.Identity.AuthenticationType _
        & "<br />"
End If
lblUserInfo.Text = msg
```

The WindowsIdentity Class

If the user has been authenticated via Windows authentication, the IPrincipal object returned by Page.User is actually a WindowsPrincipal object, and the IIdentity object returned by Page.User.Identity is actually a WindowsIdentity object. Because the string returned by User.Identity.AuthenticationType can vary depending on the authentication provider, the more robust way to check whether the user was authenticated through Windows is to attempt a cast to a WindowsIdentity variable or to use a TypeOf operator:

```
' This code assumes that you have the following Imports statement:
'     Imports System.Security.Principal

Dim wp As WindowsPrincipal
If Page.User.Identity.IsAuthenticated AndAlso _
    TypeOf User.Identity Is WindowsIdentity Then
    wp = DirectCast(Page.User, WindowsPrincipal)
End If
```

A WindowsPrincipal object offers very little in addition to a generic IPrincipal object. For example, you can test whether the user is in one of the Windows built-in roles by using an enumerated value instead of a string, so it works even if roles have been localized or renamed:

```
' ...(Continuing the preceding code example)...
If wp.IsInRole(WindowsBuiltInRole.Administrator) Then
    ' The user is an administrator.
End If
```

The WindowsIdentity class exposes a few members in addition to those inherited from IIdentity interface:

```
Dim wi As WindowsIdentity = DirectCast(Page.User.Identity, WindowsIdentity)
Dim msg As String = "Anonymous = " & wi.IsAnonymous & "<br />"
msg &= "Guest = " & wi.IsGuest & "<br />"
msg &= "System = " & wi.IsSystem & "<br />"
Response.Write(msg)
```

> **Note** You can use the WindowsIdentity object also in regular console or Windows Forms applications. The WindowsIdentity.GetCurrent shared method returns the identity of the currently logged user, so you can check the name of the current user with this code:
>
> ```
> Dim username As String = WindowsIdentity.GetCurrent.Name
> ```

When using Forms authentication, you can cast the value of User.Identity to a FormsIdentity object; however, this object doesn't offer any significant extensions to the methods in IIdentity.

ASP.NET Configuration Files

Configuration files are a key aspect of ASP.NET programming and are a huge improvement over classic ASP. Thanks to configuration files, you can set virtually all features of an ASP.NET application without interacting with IIS and its dialog boxes, except when you're creating the application in IIS and setting its security features. The only other task for which you need to assign values in IIS dialog boxes is for associating a new file extension to the ASP.NET ISAPI filter, an infrequent operation that you perform only when you create HTTP handlers.

Except for the aforementioned tasks, you can deploy an ASP.NET application or replicate it on another machine, by using a simple XCOPY command. This procedure works despite the fact that a few configuration settings might require fixing after this operation—for example, the machine or domain name in the list of users granted access to the application or the connection string for SQL Server–based sessions.

You can change a configuration file even while the application is running, in which case the new settings are immediately used for each new request arriving on the server. This is possible because ASP.NET listens to modifications to these files and can detect when a .config file is created or updated.

ASP.NET then creates a new AppDomain and launches another aspnet_wp.exe executable based on the new settings: the existing application continues to process the requests already accepted and shuts down as soon as the last of such requests has been served. This is an important difference from classic ASP, which forces the administrator to stop and restart the application to enforce any new setting.

Configuration files are extensible, thanks to custom configuration handlers. Odds are that you'll never take advantage of this feature, but it's good to know that you can store any information you want in a configuration file and write your own class that handles the new setting. It's a bit like storing data in an .ini or .xml file, with an important difference: the ASP.NET runtime automatically detects when the file is updated and informs your handler that new settings are available and should be processed.

Configuration Basics

As I explained at the beginning of this chapter, ASP.NET relies on three types of configuration files:

- The machine.config main configuration file stored in the c:\WinNT\Microsoft.Net\Framework\v*x.y.zzzz*\Config directory. This file affects any ASP.NET application running on the local computer unless its settings aren't overridden by other settings in the web.config files.
- The web.config configuration file that you place in an ASP.NET application's root directory. This file can override all settings in machine.config except the processModel tags.
- Any secondary web.config file that resides in a subdirectory of an ASP.NET application. This file can override all settings in the main web.config file except the authentication, sessionState, trust, and securityPolicy tags.

Configuration Sections

As you know, all configuration files have a top-level tag named <configuration>. The data inside this tag can be roughly subdivided into two halves:

- The <configSections> portion defines all the sections and section groups that you can find in the second half of the configuration file and indicates the handler class for each section.
- Section groups and individual sections contain the actual configuration data. Each section group or individual section must correspond to an entry in <configSections>, otherwise the .NET runtime doesn't know how to process data in the section.

This organization is quite confusing at first, so an example is in order. Here's a condensed listing from machine.config that shows just one individual section and one section group, preceded by the <configSections> entries that define the handler class for the individual section and section group:

```
<?xml version="1.0" encoding="UTF-8"?>
<configuration>
  <configSections>
    <section name="appSettings"
       type="System.Configuration.NameValueFileSectionHandler, System,
             Version=1.0.3300.0, Culture=neutral,
             PublicKeyToken=b77a5c561934e089" />
    <sectionGroup name="system.web">
      <section name="trace"
               type="System.Web.Configuration.TraceConfigurationHandler,
                     System.Web, Version=1.0.3300.0, Culture=neutral,
                     PublicKeyToken=b03f5f7f11d50a3a" />
        ⋮
    </sectionGroup>
  </configSections>

  <appSettings>
    <add key="XML File Name" value="myXmlFileName.xml" />
  </appSettings>
  <system.web>
    <trace enabled="false" localOnly="true" pageOutput="false"
           requestLimit="10" traceMode="SortByTime" />
      ⋮
  </system.web>
</configuration>
```

The <configSections> portion can contain two different elements:

- A <section> tag defines a one-level data section, such as the <appSettings> section. Each tag defines the name of the section and the .NET type that can manage the contents in that section.
- A <sectionGroup> tag defines a two-level data section that in turn contains several one-level sections, such as the <system.web> section that contains the <trace> section.

In the machine.config file, several configuration data sections follow the <configSections> block:

- **<appSettings>** is a one-level data section that contains user-defined, application-specific data. For more information, see the "Dynamic Properties" section of Chapter 14.

- **<system.Diagnostics>** is a two-level section that contains settings related to application tracing; I discussed its <switches>, <trace>, and <assert> tags in the "Trace Switches" section of Chapter 3.
- **<system.net>** is a two-level data section that contains network-related settings. It contains subsections that define what kind of authentication modules are installed (Basic, NTLM, Digest, Kerberos, and so on) and what protocols are recognized (HTTP, HTTPS, FILE, and so on). I don't cover this section anywhere in this book because developers rarely have to interact with these settings.
- **<system.web>** is the two-level data section containing settings for ASP.NET, as you've seen in this chapter.
- **<system.runtime.remoting>** is a two-level section that contains settings related to .NET remoting. I don't cover remoting in this book, so I won't describe this section in any more detail.
- **<runtime>** is a two-level section that contains settings about assembly versioning and binding. I cover these settings in detail in Chapter 14.

Application .config files and main web.config files can also contain this section:

- **<startup>** is a two-level section that contains data about the version of the .NET runtime that's necessary to run the application. I cover this section in the "Runtime Version" section of Chapter 14.

Configuration Inheritance

You need to understand how value overriding works with configuration files. Let's say that we have an ASP.NET application in the c:\MyApp directory and that it contains a subdirectory named Public. Consider these settings:

```
<!-- in machine.config -->
<authentication mode="Windows">
<authorization>
    <allow users="*" />
</authorization>

<!-- in c:\MyApp\web.config -->
<authorization>
    <allow roles="MyDomain\Administrator" />
    <deny users="*" />
</authorization>

<!-- in c:\MyApp\Public\web.config -->
<authorization>
```

```
  <allow users="?" />
</authorization>
```

Because neither web.config file redefines the <authentication> tag, the entire application uses Windows authentication mode. The main application directory grants access only to domain administrators, and the Public subdirectory is visible to both anonymous users and administrators.

Centralized Configuration Files

Although ASP.NET lets you distribute web.config files over all the application's subdirectories, it surely doesn't force you to do so. You can keep all the application settings in its main web.config file, while enforcing different settings on a directory-by-directory basis, if you want. The key to this useful feature is the <location> tag.

For example, let's see how an application's configuration file can specify different authorization settings for its different subdirectories. This web.config file enforces the same settings as the example seen in the preceding section:

```
<configuration>
  <system.web>
    <authorization>
      <allow roles="MyDomain\Administrator" />
      <deny users="*" />
    </authorization>
  </system.web>

  <location path="/Public">
    <system.web>
      <authorization>
        <allow users="?" />
      </authorization>
    </system.web>
  </location>
</configuration>
```

You can use a <location> tag also in machine.config to affect settings in individual ASP.NET applications and their subdirectories. In this case, the path attribute must begin with the IIS site name, as read in the MMC snap-in. For example, here's how you can enable tracing for the .aspx files in the /MyApp virtual directory of the default Web site:

```
<location path="Default Web Site/MyApp">
  <system.web>
    <trace enabled="true" localOnly="true" pageOutput="true" />
  </system.web>
</location>
```

Some ASP.NET settings are so critical that the system administrator should prevent them from being changed by individual applications. This ability is especially crucial for servers that host multiple applications written by different developers. In this case, the administrator can prevent undesired changes by adding an allowOverride attribute to the <location> tag:

```
<location path="Default Web Site/MyApp" allowOverride="false">
  <system.web>
    <authorization>
      <allow roles="MyDomain\Administrator" />
      <deny users="*" />
    </authorization>
  </system.web>
</location>
```

Another way to prevent a set of values from being redefined is by adding an allowDefinition attribute to a <section> tag in the <configSections> portion of the configuration file. For example, the following entry in machine.config effectively prevents the <processModel> key from appearing in application's web.config files:

```
<section name="processModel"
    type="System.Web.Configuration.ProcessModelConfigurationHandler,
          System.Web, Version=1.0.3300.0, Culture=neutral,
          PublicKeyToken=b03f5f7f11d50a3a"
    allowDefinition="MachineOnly" />
```

The allowDefinition attribute can take three values: MachineOnly for settings that can appear only in machine.config; MachineToApplication for settings that can appear in machine.config and the application's main web.config file, but not in secondary web.config files; and Everywhere for settings that can appear in any .config file. (This is the default behavior if this attribute setting is omitted.)

ASP.NET Configuration Settings

In the remainder of this chapter, I'll focus on <system.web> settings, with a list of its sections in alphabetical order. I'll provide a detailed description of those settings that I haven't covered yet or mention exactly where each tag has been discussed earlier in this chapter.

<authentication>

This tag configures ASP.NET authentication. (I covered this tag in the "ASP.NET Authentication Modes" section of this chapter.)

```
<authentication mode="Windows|Forms|Passport|None">
   <forms name="name"
         loginUrl="url"
```

```
        protection="All|None|Encryption|Validation"
        timeout="30" path="/" >
      <credentials passwordFormat="Clear|SHA1|MD5">
        <user name="username" password="password" />
      </credentials>
   </forms>
   <passport redirectUrl="internal"/>
</authentication>
```

<authorization>

This tag configures ASP.NET authorization support. (I covered this tag in the "URL Authorizations" section of this chapter.)

```
<authorization>
  <allow users="userlist" roles="grouplist" verb="verblist" />
  <deny users="userlist" roles="grouplist" verb="verblist" />
</authorization>
```

<browserCaps>

This tag controls the settings of the browser capabilities component. When a request arrives, ASP.NET compares the HTTP_USER_AGENT or another server variable with the entries in this tag, using regular expressions to find the best match.

```
<browserCaps>
   <result type="class" />
   <use var="HTTP_USER_AGENT" />
        browser=Unknown  version=n.m  majorver=n  minorver=m
        frames=false tables=false
        <!-- other browser settings -->
        …
   <filter>
     <case match="Windows 98|Win98">platform=Win98</case>
     <case match="Windows NT|WinNT">platform=WinNT</case>
   </filter>
   <!-- other filters and cases -->
   ⋮
</browserCaps>
```

The syntax of this part of the configuration file is convoluted. Because you won't modify these settings for most cases, I decided not to cover them in more detail. The most curious of you can learn more from the .NET SDK documentation.

<clientTarget>

This tag adds or removes one or more aliases for specific user agents to or from the collection of aliases known to ASP.NET.

```
<clientTarget>
   <add alias="aliasname" userAgent="useragentstring" />
   <remove alias="aliasname" />
   <clear />
</clientTarget>
```

For example, this section of machine.config adds an alias named ie4 to the collection of ASP.NET aliases:

```
<clientTarget>
 <add alias="ie4"
  userAgent="Mozilla/4.0 (compatible; MSIE 4.0; Windows NT 4.0)" />
</clientTarget>
```

You typically assign browser aliases to the ClientTarget property of the Page object to override automatic detection of browser capabilities and to specify for which browser a page should render its ouput:

```
' (Inside a Page class)
' Output HTML for Internet Explorer 4.0.
Me.ClientTarget = "ie4"
```

<compilation>

This tag configures all the compilation settings for ASP.NET. Here's how this tag appears in machine.config:

```
<compilation debug="false" explicit="true" defaultLanguage="vb">
  <compilers>
    <compiler language="vb;vbs;visualbasic;vbscript" extension=".vb"
       type="Microsoft.VisualBasic.VBCodeProvider, System,
             Version=1.0.3300.0, Culture=neutral,
             PublicKeyToken=b77a5c561934e089" />
    <compiler language="c#;cs;csharp" extension=".cs"
       type="Microsoft.CSharp.CSharpCodeProvider, System,
             Version=1.0.3300.0, Culture=neutral,
             PublicKeyToken=b77a5c561934e089" warningLevel="1" />
    <compiler language="js;jscript;javascript" extension=".js"
       type="Microsoft.JScript.JScriptCodeProvider, Microsoft.JScript,
             Version=7.0.3300.0, Culture=neutral,
             PublicKeyToken=b03f5f7f11d50a3a" />
  </compilers>
  <assemblies>
    <add assembly="mscorlib" />
    <add assembly="System, Version=1.0.3300.0, Culture=neutral,
         PublicKeyToken=b77a5c561934e089" />
    ⋮
  </assemblies>
</compilation>
```

The most important settings for us developers are the debugMode attribute (true if ASP.NET debugging is enabled by default), defaultLanguage (the default language used when compiling ASP.NET applications), and the list of assemblies that are always visible to compiled ASP.NET applications. When you create a project with Visual Studio .NET, the environment creates a web.config file that overrides the default settings as required, so most of the time you don't have to worry about these settings.

<customErrors>

This tag affects how error pages are managed in an ASP.NET application and whether developers can redirect users to their custom error pages when an exception is thrown.

```
<customErrors mode="On|Off|RemoteOnly" defaultRedirect="url">
   <error statusCode="statuscode" redirect="url"/>
</customErrors>
```

As you've learned, ASP.NET produces an error page like the one shown in Figure 24-21 when an application throws an unhandled exception or when you deploy an .aspx file whose source contains a syntax error without compiling it inside Visual Studio .NET first. Most of the time, you don't want this page to be visible to your site's visitors because the source code might contain confidential information, such as the password to access a database. So you should redirect the browser to a custom error page on which you instruct users about error causes and possible remedies.

The mode attribute is required and can be one of the following values:

- **Off** ASP.NET always displays its own error pages.
- **On** ASP.NET never displays its own error pages, and developers can define their own custom error pages.
- **RemoteOnly** ASP.NET displays its error pages only for requests from the local computer and allows custom error pages for requests from remote users. This is the default setting in machine.config and allows you to perform debugging chores while remote users are accessing the site.

Unless the mode attribute is Off, you should provide a defaultRedirect attribute pointing to your custom error page. You can also indicate different URLs for specific HTTP status codes by using one or more <error> subtags, as in this example:

```
<customErrors> mode="RemoteOnly" defaultRedirect="ErrorPage.aspx" >
   <error statusCode="500" redirect="InternalError.htm"/>
</customErrors>
```

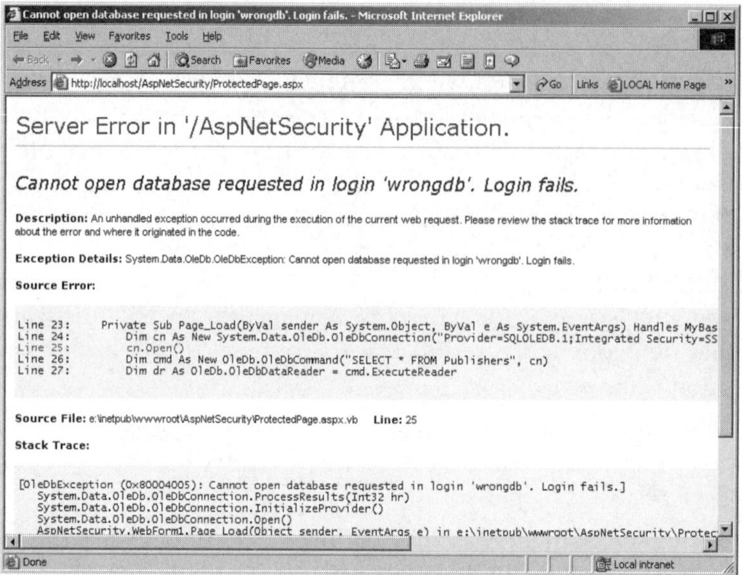

Figure 24-21. An ASP.NET error page.

<globalization>

This tag configures the default globalization settings of an application or a portion thereof.

```
<globalization requestEncoding="encodestring"
               responseEncoding="encodestring"
               fileEncoding="encodestring"
               culture="culturestring"
               uiCulture="culturestring" />
```

The values of the requestEncoding and responseEncoding attributes specify how the request data and the response data are expected to be encoded: they can be a string such as UTF-8 or Unicode and are overridden by an Accept-Charset attribute contained in the request header. The fileEncoding attribute is the default encoding method for .aspx, .asax, and .asmx files.

The culture and uiCulture attributes specify the default culture for processing incoming requests and server-side resource searches and can be any valid argument for the constructor of the System.Globalization.CultureInfo class—for example, en-US or fr-FR. The former attribute affects the output of format functions for dates and numbers.

<httpHandlers>

This tag maps incoming requests to the appropriate HTTP handler.

```
<httpHandlers>
   <add verb="verblist" path="path|wildcard"
```

```
        type="type,assemblyname" validate="true|false" />
    <remove verb="verblist"  path="path|wildcard" />
    <clear />
</httpHandlers>
```

The <remove> and <clear> subtags allow you to remove one or all installed handlers in a nested directory. (I covered this tag in the section "Adding the HTTP Handler to Configuration Files" earlier in this chapter.)

<httpModules>

This tag adds or removes HTTP modules in an application.

```
<httpModules>
    <add type="classname,assemblyname" name="modulename" />
    <remove name="modulename" />
    <clear />
</httpModules>
```

The <remove> and <clear> subtags allow you to remove one or all installed modules in a nested directory. (I covered this topic earlier in the "HTTP Modules" section.)

<httpRuntime>

This tag affects important configuration settings of the ASP.NET runtime.

```
<httpRuntime executionTimeout="seconds"
             maxRequestLength="kbytes"
             minFreeThreads="numberOfThreads"
             minLocalRequestFreeThreads="numberOfThreads"
             appRequestQueueLimit="numberOfRequests"
             useFullyQualifiedRedirectUrl="true|false"  />
```

Here's a brief description of each attribute:

- **executionTimeout** is the maximum time an .aspx page can run before timing out. The default is 90 seconds, but you should extend this value for pages that perform long database queries or remote calls to an XML Web service. This attribute corresponds to the Server.ScriptTimeout property.
- **maxRequestLength** is the maximum length of a request. All requests longer than this value are rejected. The default value is 4096 KB, so it should suffice for most practical purposes, but you have to increase this value for pages that accept posted files larger than 4 megabytes. Or you can reduce this value to prevent denial of service attacks caused by posting very large files to the server for all the pages that don't accept uploaded files.

- **minFreeThreads** is the minimum number of threads that must be free for ASP.NET to accept a request. The default value is 8, so ASP.NET normally rejects a request if there are 7 or fewer free threads. This setting lets you prevent stalls when your site accepts a request that creates additional threads.
- **minLocalRequestFreeThreads** is like the minFreeThreads attribute, but it's applied to local requests, which often issue child requests.
- **appRequestQueueLimit** is the maximum number of requests that ASP.NET can queue for the application when there aren't enough free threads to serve it. Any request that arrives when the queue is full is rejected with a 503—Server Too Busy error.
- **useFullyQualifiedRedirectUrl** specifies whether a Request.Redirect method is processed to use a fully qualified URL that contains also the server name. Fully qualified URLs are required by some mobile controls. The default setting is False.

<identity>

This tag controls the impersonation features of ASP.NET. (I covered this tag in the "ASP.NET Impersonation" section.)

```
<identity impersonate="true|false"
          userName="username"
          password="password"/>
```

<machineKey>

This tag specifies how cookies are validated and encrypted. It can appear in machine.config and application's main web.config files only. (I covered this tag in the "Out-of-Process Sessions Based on a Windows Service" and "Configuration Settings for Forms Authentication" sections.)

```
<machineKey validationKey="autogenerate|value"
            decryptionKey="autogenerate|value"
            validation="SHA1|MD5|3DES" />
```

<pages>

This tag specifies default values for page configuration settings.

```
<pages buffer="true|false"
       enableSessionState="true|false|ReadOnly"
       enableViewState="true|false"
       enableViewStateMac="true|false"
       autoEventWireup="true|false"
       smartNavigation="true|false"
       pageBaseType="typename, assembly"
       userControlBaseType="typename" />
```

The values of the buffer, enableSessionState, enableViewState, enableViewStateMac, autoEventWireup, or smartNavigation attribute affect the page properties or directive of the same name. The last two attributes define the code-behind class that pages and user controls inherit by default. These are the default values as defined in machine.config:

```
<pages buffer="true" enableSessionState="true" enableViewState="true"
      enableViewStateMac="false" autoEventWireup="true" />
```

The enableSessionState can also be set to readonly, but it makes sense to do so only inside secondary web.config files. The autoEventWireup attribute is reset to false inside the @Page directive of all .aspx pages created inside Visual Studio .NET.

<processModel>

This tag configures the ASP.NET worker process aspnet_wp.exe.

```
<processModel enable="true|false" idleTimeout="mins"
              timeout="mins"  shutdownTimeout="hrs:mins:secs"
              requestLimit="num"
              requestQueueLimit="Infinite|num"
              restartQueueLimit="Infinite|num"
              memoryLimit="percent"
              cpuMask="num"  webGarden="true|false"
              userName="username"  password="password"
              logLevel="All|None|Errors"
              clientConnectedCheck="HH:MM:SS"
              comAuthenticationLevel=
                 "Default|None|Connect|Call|Pkt|PktIntegrity|PktPrivacy"
              comImpersonationLevel=
                 "Default|Anonymous|Identify|Impersonate|Delegate"
              maxWorkerThreads="num"
              maxIoThreads="num" />
```

The most intriguing feature that you can control with these settings is process recycling, which lets you automatically launch another worker process after a timeout, after processing a given number of requests, or when free memory goes below the specified threshold. (I briefly mentioned application recycling in the section "The HttpApplicationState Class" earlier in this chapter.)

Table 24-6 contains a brief explanation of the attributes in this tag. I already covered the username and password attributes in the "ASP.NET Impersonation" section.

Table 24-6 Main Attributes of the processModel Configuration Tag

Category	Name	Description
General	enable	Tells whether ASP.NET runs outside IIS (True, the default) or inside IIS (False). If you change this setting, you're going to miss many of the advantages of the process model mechanism.
	username	The Windows account under which the worker process runs. The default is ASPNET.
	password	The password for the identity adopted for the worker process. The special System and Machine accounts don't require a password.
Process shutdown	idleTimeout	The period of inactivity after which the worker process is shut down. The default value is infinite.
	shutdownTimeout	The timeout after which ASP.NET forces the shutdown of the working process that refuses to shut down itself gracefully. The default value is 5 seconds.
Process recycling	timeout	The number of minutes after which the worker process is automatically shut down and restarted.
	requestLimit	The number of requests processed before the worker process is automatically shut down and restarted. The default value is infinite.
	memoryLimit	The percentage of the total system memory that the worker process can consume before being automatically recycled. The default is 60 percent.
	responseDeadlock-Interval	The interval after which the process is restarted if there hasn't been a response even though there are requests in the queue. The default value is 3 minutes.
	responseRestart-DeadlockInterval	How much time must elapse after the last restart to cure a deadlock before the process is restarted to cure a deadlock again. This setting prevents problems with processes that require a long start-up time. Its value can be infinite or a timeout in the format hh:mm:ss.
	pingFrequency	How often ASP.NET pings the worker process to check whether it's active and restart it if it isn't. The default is 30 seconds.
	pingTimeout	How long an ASP.NET ping waits for an unresponsive worker process before restarting it. The default is 5 seconds.
Threads	maxWorker-Threads	The maximum number of worker threads that each CPU can run; it must be in the range 5 to 100. The default is 25.
	maxIoThreads	The maximum number of IO threads that each CPU can run. It must be in the range 5 to 100. Default is 25.

Table 24-6 Main Attributes of the processModel Configuration Tag *(continued)*

Category	Name	Description
Multi CPU systems	webGarden	If True, the application works as a Web garden, and the operating system schedules CPU usage. If False, the cpuMask affects CPU usage.
	cpuMask	A bit-coded value that specifies which CPUs on a multi-CPU system can run a copy of the worker process.
COM interaction	comAuthentica-tionLevel	The authentication level for COM security; can be None, Connect (default), Call, Pkt, PktIntegrity, PktPrivacy, or Default.
	comImperson-ationLevel	The COM impersonation level; can be Anonymous, Identify, Impersonate, Delegate, or Default.
Miscellaneous	clientConnected-Check	The period after which ASP.NET checks that the client for a queue request is still connected. An ASP.NET page can check whether the client is connected by using the Request.IsClientConnected property.
	requestQueueLimit	The number of requests allowed in the queue before ASP.NET returns a 503—Server Too Busy error. Default is 5000.
	serverError-MessageFile	The file path to use instead of the default "Server Unavailable" message in the event of a fatal error; the file location is relative to the machine.config file or is an absolute path.
	logLevel	Specifies which application events must be recorded to the event log. It can be All, Errors (the default), or None.

An ASP.NET application can use the ProcessModelInfo.GetCurrentProcess-Info shared method to get a reference to the ProcessInfo object that contains information about the running worker process:

```
' Get a reference to the current worker process.
Dim pi As ProcessInfo = ProcessModelInfo.GetCurrentProcessInfo
' Get information from the process.
Dim msg As String = "ProcessID = " & pi.ProcessID.ToString & "<br />"
msg &= "Status = " & pi.Status.ToString & "<br />"
msg &= "StartTime = " & pi.StartTime & "<br />"
msg &= "Age = " & pi.Age.ToString & "<br />"
msg &= "RequestCount = " & pi.RequestCount & "<br />"
msg &= "PeakMemoryUsed = " & pi.PeakMemoryUsed.ToString & "<br />"
' Display them in a Label control.
lblProcessInfo.Text = msg
```

You can also get a reference to a ProcessInfo object by means of the ProcessModelInfo.GetHistory method, which lets you access information for the up to 100 last processes launched. For testing and debugging, you can even replace internal variables with your own values by means of the SetAll method. See the .NET SDK documentation for additional details.

<securityPolicy>

This tag defines the mapping between named security levels and policy files.

```
<securityPolicy>
   <trustLevel name="value" policyFile="configfilename" />
</securityPolicy>
```

The machine.config file defines four security levels, which are named Full, High, Low, and None. Each level corresponds to a security configuration file in the c:\WinNT\Microsoft.Net\Framework\v*x.y.zzzz*\Config directory:

```
<securityPolicy>
  <trustLevel name="Full" policyFile="internal" />
  <trustLevel name="High" policyFile="web_hightrust.config" />
  <trustLevel name="Low" policyFile="web_lowtrust.config" />
  <trustLevel name="None" policyFile="web_notrust.config" />
</securityPolicy>
```

This tag is used in conjunction with the <trust> tag, which I mention shortly.

<sessionState>

This tag configures how sessions are managed in the current application. (I covered this tag in the "Session State" section.)

```
<sessionState mode="Off|Inproc|StateServer|SQLServer"
              cookieless="true|false"
              timeout="numberOfMinutes"
              stateConnectionString="tcpip=server:port"
              sqlConnectionString="sql connection string" />
```

<trust>

This tag configures the code access security level applied to an ASP.NET application; it can appear in all types of configuration files.

```
<trust level="Full|High|Low|None" originUrl="url" />
```

The level attribute defines the security zone under which the application runs and is one of the named security policies defined in the <securityPolicies> tag. The default is Full, which specifies that ASP.NET doesn't restrict security policy.

<webServices>

This tag controls the configuration of XML Web services.

```
<webServices>
   <protocols>
```

```
        <add name="protocolName" />
    </protocols>
    <serviceDescriptionFormatExtensionTypes>
    </serviceDescriptionFormatExtensionTypes>
    <soapExtensionTypes>
        <add type="type" />
    </soapExtensionTypes>
    <soapExtensionReflectorTypes>
        <add type="type" />
    </soapExtensionReflectorTypes>
    <soapExtensionImporterTypes>
        <add type="type" />
    </soapExtensionImporterTypes>
    <wsdlHelpGenerator href="helpGeneratorFile"/>
</webServices>
```

You'll see how to use this tag in Chapter 26. I mention it here only for the sake of completeness.

ASP.NET Performance Counters

ASP.NET creates many performance counters that you can use to monitor its activity. All these counters are grouped in two performance objects:

- ASP.NET, for values related to the ASP.NET runtime.
- ASP.NET Applications, for values related to individual applications. (See Figure 24-22.)

Tables 24-7 and 24-8 list the most important performance counters exposed by these objects.

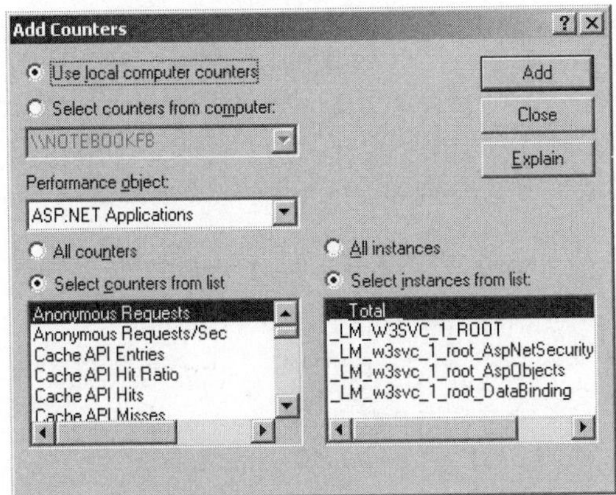

Figure 24-22. Adding ASP.NET counters to the Performance Monitor window.

Table 24-7 Main Counters in the ASP.NET Performance Object

Counter	Description
Application Restarts	Number of times the application (or IIS) has been restarted during the Web server's lifetime
Applications Running	Number of currently running Web applications
Request Execution Time	The number of milliseconds that it took to execute the most recent request
Request Wait Time	The number of milliseconds the most recent request was waiting in the queue
Requests Disconnected	The number of requests that were disconnected due to communication errors or user sessions terminated
Requests Queued	The number of requests waiting to be processed
Requests Rejected	The number of requests rejected because the request queue was full
State Server Sessions Abandoned	The number of sessions that have been explicitly abandoned
State Server Sessions Active	The number of sessions currently active
State Server Sessions Timed Out	The number of sessions timed out
State Server Sessions Total	The total number of sessions
Worker Process Restarts	Number of times a worker process has restarted on the machine
Worker Processes Running	Number of worker processes running on the machine

Table 24-8 Main Counters in the ASP.NET Applications Performance Object

Counter	Description
Anonymous Requests/Sec	Number of Authentication Anonymous Requests/Sec.
Cache API Entries	Total number of entries within the cache added by the user.
Cache API Hit Ratio	Ratio of hits called from user code.
Cache Total Entries	Total number of entries within the cache (both internal and user added).
Cache Total Hit Ratio	Ratio of hits from all cache calls.
Compilations Total	Number of .asax, .ascx, .ashx, .asmx, or .aspx source files dynamically compiled.

Table 24-8 Main Counters in the ASP.NET Applications Performance Object *(continued)*

Counter	Description
Errors During Execution	Number of errors that have occurred during the processing of a request.
Errors During Preprocessing	Number of errors that have occurred during parsing and configuration.
Errors Total	Total number of errors occurred.
Errors Total/Sec	Rate of errors occurred.
Errors Unhandled During Execution	Number of errors not handled by user code, but by the default error handler.
Output Cache Entries	Current number of entries in the output cache.
Output Cache Hit Ratio	Ratio of hits to requests for output cacheable requests.
Request Bytes In Total	The total size, in bytes, of all requests.
Request Bytes Out Total	The total size, in bytes, of responses sent to a client. This value doesn't include standard HTTP response headers.
Requests Executing	The number of requests currently executing.
Requests Failed	Total number of failed requests.
Requests Not Authorized	The number of requests failed due to unauthorized access.
Requests Not Found	The number of requests for resources that were not found.
Requests Succeeded	The number of requests that executed successfully.
Requests Timed Out	The number of requests that timed out.
Requests Total	The total number of requests since the application was started.
Requests/Sec	The number of requests executed per second.
Sessions Abandoned	The number of sessions that have been explicitly abandoned.
Sessions Active	The number of sessions currently active.
Sessions Timed Out	The number of sessions timed out.
Sessions Total	The total number of sessions since the application was started.

This chapter completes the discussion about ASP.NET applications and their advanced features, such as session state, caching, and security. But I haven't yet covered one ASP.NET-related topic: user controls. This is what the next chapter is all about.

Front
Top
Left
Back

This organization is quite confusing at first, so an example is in order. Here's a condensed listing from machine.config that shows just one individual section and one section group, preceded by the <configSections> entries that define the handler class for the individual section and section group:

```
<?xml version="1.0" encoding="UTF-8"?>
<configuration>
  <configSections>
    <section name="appSettings"
       type="System.Configuration.NameValueFileSectionHandler, System,
             Version=1.0.3300.0, Culture=neutral,
             PublicKeyToken=b77a5c561934e089" />
    <sectionGroup name="system.web">
      <section name="trace"
               type="System.Web.Configuration.TraceConfigurationHandler,
                     System.Web, Version=1.0.3300.0, Culture=neutral,
                     PublicKeyToken=b03f5f7f11d50a3a" />
      ⋮
    </sectionGroup>
  </configSections>

  <appSettings>
    <add key="XML File Name" value="myXmlFileName.xml" />
  </appSettings>
  <system.web>
    <trace enabled="false" localOnly="true" pageOutput="false"
           requestLimit="10" traceMode="SortByTime" />
    ⋮
  </system.web>
</configuration>
```

The <configSections> portion can contain two different elements:

- A <section> tag defines a one-level data section, such as the <appSettings> section. Each tag defines the name of the section and the .NET type that can manage the contents in that section.
- A <sectionGroup> tag defines a two-level data section that in turn contains several one-level sections, such as the <system.web> section that contains the <trace> section.

In the machine.config file, several configuration data sections follow the <configSections> block:

- **<appSettings>** is a one-level data section that contains user-defined, application-specific data. For more information, see the "Dynamic Properties" section of Chapter 14.

- **<system.Diagnostics>** is a two-level section that contains settings related to application tracing; I discussed its <switches>, <trace>, and <assert> tags in the "Trace Switches" section of Chapter 3.
- **<system.net>** is a two-level data section that contains network-related settings. It contains subsections that define what kind of authentication modules are installed (Basic, NTLM, Digest, Kerberos, and so on) and what protocols are recognized (HTTP, HTTPS, FILE, and so on). I don't cover this section anywhere in this book because developers rarely have to interact with these settings.
- **<system.web>** is the two-level data section containing settings for ASP.NET, as you've seen in this chapter.
- **<system.runtime.remoting>** is a two-level section that contains settings related to .NET remoting. I don't cover remoting in this book, so I won't describe this section in any more detail.
- **<runtime>** is a two-level section that contains settings about assembly versioning and binding. I cover these settings in detail in Chapter 14.

Application .config files and main web.config files can also contain this section:

- **<startup>** is a two-level section that contains data about the version of the .NET runtime that's necessary to run the application. I cover this section in the "Runtime Version" section of Chapter 14.

Configuration Inheritance

You need to understand how value overriding works with configuration files. Let's say that we have an ASP.NET application in the c:\MyApp directory and that it contains a subdirectory named Public. Consider these settings:

```
<!-- in machine.config -->
<authentication mode="Windows">
<authorization>
    <allow users="*" />
</authorization>

<!-- in c:\MyApp\web.config -->
<authorization>
    <allow roles="MyDomain\Administrator" />
    <deny users="*" />
</authorization>

<!-- in c:\MyApp\Public\web.config -->
<authorization>
```

25

User Controls and Custom Controls

The information in Chapters 23 and 24 is sufficient to help you create very sophisticated Web Form applications, which use advanced features such as out-of-process sessions, caching, HTTP modules, and handlers. ASP.NET lets you trim down development time and effort even more by letting you encapsulate and reuse pieces of UI functionality as well as business logic in user-defined controls. There are two types of reusable ASP.NET controls: *user* controls and *custom* controls:

- **User controls** are portions of HTML and script code stored in .ascx files. User controls are similar to .aspx files, and in fact you can easily convert a functioning .aspx page into a user control. ASP.NET compiles .ascx files on the fly the first time they're referenced from inside a page, which is similar to what happens to .aspx pages the first time they're requested by the client browser. User controls are also useful for implementing so-called *partial* or *fragment caching*, in which only the output from a portion of an .aspx page is cached.
- **Custom controls** are compiled components that can encapsulate complex functionality and contain simpler controls. Custom controls use inheritance to gain the functionality of a simpler class, such as Control, WebControl, or an existing Web control, such as the TextBox. Authoring custom controls is more complex than writing user controls, but custom controls let you precisely define what the browser receives.

Having two different types of user-defined controls to choose from can be confusing, and the fact that they have similar names surely doesn't help. As a general guideline, you should think of user controls as rather like subforms that contain multiple controls that you want to reuse in multiple pages or that produce HTML text that you want to cache separately from the remainder of the page that hosts them. Custom controls, on the other hand, are conceptually more similar to the classic third-party controls that you've used under Visual Basic for years.

The ways that you deploy user controls and custom controls are very different. User controls are .ascx files (with an optional code-behind class in source or compiled format) that are part of the same ASP.NET application. Custom controls are usually deployed as compiled DLLs and can be installed in the global assembly cache (GAC) so that every ASP.NET application on the computer can use them.

User Controls

Declarative user controls are the simplest user-defined controls that you can build for ASP.NET. User controls are similar to pages deployed in .aspx files in that they can contain a block of HTML text and controls, with the following differences:

- User controls are contained in .ascx files.
- User controls can't contain <html>, <body>, or <form> HTML tags because these tags are provided by the page that hosts the control.
- User controls can't contain the @Page directive. Instead they can contain the @Control directive, which takes a subset of the attributes of the @Page directive.

In a sense, user controls are the ASP.NET counterpart of classic ASP include files (which are still supported by ASP.NET), except that they can encapsulate only user interface elements. No code element or procedure in a user control is accessible from the client .aspx page.

Your First User Control

To see how simple creating a User control is, let's author an .aspx page that has a group of controls on it, which we'll then convert to a user control.

Some ASP.NET settings are so critical that the system administrator should prevent them from being changed by individual applications. This ability is especially crucial for servers that host multiple applications written by different developers. In this case, the administrator can prevent undesired changes by adding an allowOverride attribute to the <location> tag:

```
<location path="Default Web Site/MyApp" allowOverride="false">
  <system.web>
    <authorization>
      <allow roles="MyDomain\Administrator" />
      <deny users="*" />
    </authorization>
  </system.web>
</location>
```

Another way to prevent a set of values from being redefined is by adding an allowDefinition attribute to a <section> tag in the <configSections> portion of the configuration file. For example, the following entry in machine.config effectively prevents the <processModel> key from appearing in application's web.config files:

```
<section name="processModel"
    type="System.Web.Configuration.ProcessModelConfigurationHandler,
          System.Web, Version=1.0.3300.0, Culture=neutral,
          PublicKeyToken=b03f5f7f11d50a3a"
    allowDefinition="MachineOnly" />
```

The allowDefinition attribute can take three values: MachineOnly for settings that can appear only in machine.config; MachineToApplication for settings that can appear in machine.config and the application's main web.config file, but not in secondary web.config files; and Everywhere for settings that can appear in any .config file. (This is the default behavior if this attribute setting is omitted.)

ASP.NET Configuration Settings

In the remainder of this chapter, I'll focus on <system.web> settings, with a list of its sections in alphabetical order. I'll provide a detailed description of those settings that I haven't covered yet or mention exactly where each tag has been discussed earlier in this chapter.

<authentication>

This tag configures ASP.NET authentication. (I covered this tag in the "ASP.NET Authentication Modes" section of this chapter.)

```
<authentication mode="Windows|Forms|Passport|None">
   <forms name="name"
          loginUrl="url"
```

```
    <allow users="?" />
</authorization>
```

Because neither web.config file redefines the <authentication> tag, the entire application uses Windows authentication mode. The main application directory grants access only to domain administrators, and the Public subdirectory is visible to both anonymous users and administrators.

Centralized Configuration Files

Although ASP.NET lets you distribute web.config files over all the application's subdirectories, it surely doesn't force you to do so. You can keep all the application settings in its main web.config file, while enforcing different settings on a directory-by-directory basis, if you want. The key to this useful feature is the <location> tag.

For example, let's see how an application's configuration file can specify different authorization settings for its different subdirectories. This web.config file enforces the same settings as the example seen in the preceding section:

```
<configuration>
  <system.web>
    <authorization>
      <allow roles="MyDomain\Administrator" />
      <deny users="*" />
    </authorization>
  </system.web>

  <location path="/Public">
    <system.web>
      <authorization>
        <allow users="?" />
      </authorization>
    </system.web>
  </location>
</configuration>
```

You can use a <location> tag also in machine.config to affect settings in individual ASP.NET applications and their subdirectories. In this case, the path attribute must begin with the IIS site name, as read in the MMC snap-in. For example, here's how you can enable tracing for the .aspx files in the /MyApp virtual directory of the default Web site:

```
<location path="Default Web Site/MyApp">
  <system.web>
    <trace enabled="true" localOnly="true" pageOutput="true" />
  </system.web>
</location>
```

Converting an .aspx Page to a User Control

For my example, I'll use the group of one Literal and four Button controls shown in Figure 25-1. These controls can be used to navigate through all the pages of a database query result. (You've seen an example of paging techniques in the "Default and Custom Paging" section of Chapter 23.) Adding code behind the buttons would be easy, but for now let's focus on just the user interface.

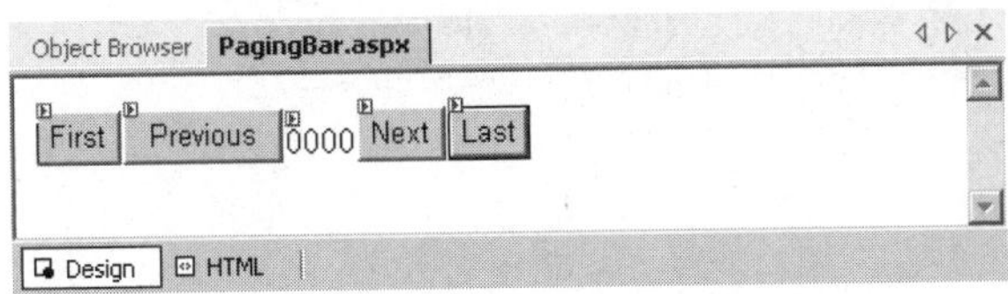

Figure 25-1. An .aspx page with five controls on it.

This is the HTML code behind this .aspx page:

```
<%@ Page Language="vb" %>
<HTML>
  <HEAD><title>WebForm1</title></HEAD>
  <body>
    <form id="Form1" method="post" runat="server">
      <asp:Button id="btnFirst" runat="server" Text="First" />
      <asp:Button id="btnPrevious" runat="server" Text="Previous" />
      <asp:Literal id="litNumber" runat="server" Text="0000" />
      <asp:Button id="btnNext" runat="server" Text="Next" />
      <asp:Button id="btnLast" runat="server" Text="Last" />
    </form>
  </body>
</HTML>
```

To convert this page to a user control, we must convert the @Page directive into an @Control directive and delete everything except the controls inside the form. Here's the result of these transformations:

```
<%@ Control Language="vb" %>
<asp:Button id="btnFirst" runat="server" Text="First" />
<asp:Button id="btnPrevious" runat="server" Text="Previous" />
<asp:Literal id="litNumber" runat="server" Text="0000" />
<asp:Button id="btnNext" runat="server" Text="Next" />
<asp:Button id="btnLast" runat="server" Text="Last" />
```

Save this text in the PagingBar.ascx file, and you're done: you've written your first user control!

The .ascx file must be located in the same ASP.NET application as the .aspx pages that use it.

Writing a Test Page

We now need to reuse our control inside a page. Use Notepad to create the following text and save it in a file named TestPagingBar.aspx:

```
<%@ Page Language="vb" %>
<%@ Register TagPrefix="ProgVB" TagName="PagingBar" src="PagingBar.ascx" %>
<HTML>
  <body>
    <form id="Form1" method="post" runat="server">
      <ProgVB:PagingBar name="PagingBar1" runat="server" />
    </form>
  </body>
</HTML>
```

I introduced the @Register directive in Chapter 23—together with @Page and other directives—but I never actually showed you how to use it with a user control. The meaning of its three attributes is simple:

- The TagPrefix attribute specifies the prefix for the complete name of the user control. This prefix corresponds to the asp prefix in all ASP.NET control names, as in <asp:Label>, and should be a unique string that makes your control (or group of controls) different from any other user control you're likely to use on the same page. (For example, it can be your company name.)
- The TagName attribute specifies the second part of the complete name of the control, which is therefore in the form tagprefix:tagname.
- The Src attribute is the virtual path to the .ascx file that contains the user control.

Once you've registered the user control, you can use it anywhere in the page exactly as you would any built-in ASP.NET control. If you navigate to this page, you'll see the PagingBar control in the browser. (See Figure 25-2.)

Note that you can author .aspx and .ascx files with Notepad (or a regular HTML editor) and then import them into a Visual Studio .NET project. When you do so, Visual Studio detects that the new file has no class file associated with the .aspx or .ascx file and asks whether you want to create the new class. Click yes if you want to extend the user control with properties, methods, and event handlers.

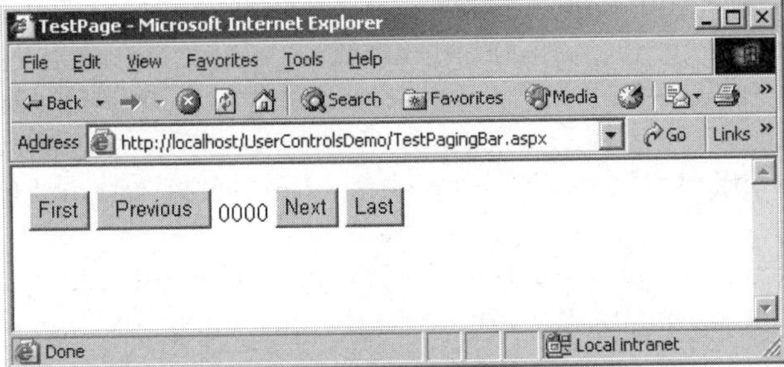

Figure 25-2. An .aspx page that hosts the PagingBar user control.

Of course you can create multiple instances of the PagingBar control in the same page by inserting additional <ProgVB:PagingBar> elements. Even if you include multiple instances of the control, you still need a single @Register directive.

This first version of the user control can't do more than display itself because it doesn't expose any property to the outside and doesn't process clicks on the navigational buttons. You could implement all these features using a script inside the .ascx file, but I won't waste your time showing you how to do it because in real development you'd use Visual Studio .NET and its code-behind programming model. This is exactly what I'm showing you next.

User Controls in Visual Studio .NET

Creating a user control inside Visual Studio .NET requires that you abandon the simple script-based approach that I showed you in the preceding section and adopt the code-behind programming model that you already use for .aspx forms.

Adding a Web User Control File

Create a new ASP.NET Web Forms application project, name it UserControls-Demo, and then choose Add Web User Control on the Project menu. Name the new file PagingBar.ascx, and click the Open button. Using the editor in design mode, re-create the controls shown in Figure 25-1 and assign them the following IDs (from left to right): btnFirst, btnPrevious, litPageNumber, btnNext, and btnLast. The UI portion of the user control has been completed.

Next, create a Web Form file named TestPage.aspx—or just rename the default WebForm1.aspx file created with the project—and make sure that it's the start page for the project. You can create an instance of the user control on this form by simply dragging the PagingBar item from the Solution Explorer window. Unfortunately, the Visual Studio HTML editor isn't able to show you the actual appearance of the .ascx file, so it displays a gray rectangle labeled UserControl-PagingBar1. If you switch to the Properties window, you can change the PagingBar1 ID to something else and set its Visible and EnableViewState properties.

If you switch from the Design to the HTML view in the editor, you see that Visual Studio has automatically added both the @Register directive and the actual control tag inside the form. This is an abridged version of the resulting HTML text:

```
<%@ Page Language="vb" AutoEventWireup="false" Codebehind="TestPage.aspx.vb"
    Inherits="UserControlsDemo.TestPage"%>
<%@ Register TagPrefix="uc1" TagName="PagingBar" src="PagingBar.ascx" %>
<HTML>
  <body>
    <form id="Form1" method="post" runat="server">
      <uc1:pagingbar id="PagingBar1" runat="server"></uc1:pagingbar>
    </form>
  </body>
</HTML>
```

If you don't like the uc1 tag prefix, you can change it to something else in the @Register directive—for example, ProgVB, provided that you also change the prefix in the start and end <uc1:pagingbar> tags. You need to change the prefix only once because all the other PagingBar controls added to the page from now on will use the new prefix.

To ensure that everything works as expected, run the project and make certain that the user control is correctly displayed in the TestPage.aspx page. We've now achieved the same result we got by working with Notepad, but now we can continue and add code to the user control's code-behind module.

Adding Code

Click anywhere on the PagingBar.ascx component, and choose Code on the View menu (or just press the F7 key) to display the PagingBar.ascx.vb code-behind module. This is the code you'll find in the editor:

```
Public MustInherit Class PagingBar
    Inherits System.Web.UI.UserControl

    Protected WithEvents btnLast As System.Web.UI.WebControls.Button
    Protected WithEvents btnNext As System.Web.UI.WebControls.Button
    Protected WithEvents btnPrevious As System.Web.UI.WebControls.Button
    Protected WithEvents litPageNumber As System.Web.UI.WebControls.Literal
    Protected WithEvents btnFirst As System.Web.UI.WebControls.Button
```

```
#Region " Web Form Designer Generated Code "
    ⋮
#Region

    Private Sub Page_Load(ByVal sender As Object, ByVal e As EventArgs) _
        Handles MyBase.Load
        ' Put user code to initialize the page here.
    End Sub
End Class
```

The code-behind class for a user control is similar to the code-behind class for a Web form, with one important difference: it inherits from UserControl instead of Page. Except for this detail, however, you write code in this class as you'd do in an .aspx page. For example, you can add a public property named PageNumber, manage the Click event handlers for the four buttons, and use them to change the Text property of the Literal control:

```
Const PageCount As Integer = 100

' The PageNumber property
Private m_PageNumber As Integer = 1

Public Property PageNumber() As Integer
    Get
        Return CInt(litPageNumber.Text)
    End Get
    Set(ByVal Value As Integer)
        ' Ensure that new value is in valid range.
        If Value >= 1 And Value <= PageCount Then
            litPageNumber.Text = Value.ToString
        End If
    End Set
End Property

Private Sub btnFirst_Click(ByVal sender As Object, ByVal e As EventArgs) _
    Handles btnFirst.Click
    PageNumber = 1
End Sub

Private Sub btnLast_Click(ByVal sender As Object, ByVal e As EventArgs) _
    Handles btnLast.Click
    PageNumber = PageCount
End Sub

Private Sub btnPrevious_Click(ByVal sender As Object, ByVal e As EventArgs) _
    Handles btnPrevious.Click
    PageNumber -= 1
End Sub
```

(continued)

```
Private Sub btnNext_Click(ByVal sender As Object, ByVal e As EventArgs) _
    Handles btnNext.Click
    PageNumber += 1
End Sub
```

If you now run the application, you'll see that clicking on one of the four buttons actually causes a postback and that the number in the Literal control is updated correctly. The mechanism works because the user control receives the Click event for the button that was actually clicked. Notice that you *must* handle events from constituent controls inside the user control's code-behind class; you can't trap them from inside the host page.

A user control might need to cause a postback when a control other than a Button is clicked. For example, a user control containing a ListBox and a CheckBox control might cause a postback when the end user selects a new element in the ListBox or clicks on the CheckBox control. You can achieve this behavior by simply setting the AutoPostBack property for these constituent controls to True.

Saving Variables and Properties

The first version of the PagingBar user control needs to save only one piece of information between postbacks—that is, the value of the PageNumber property. In the preceding code snippet, I used a trick to have this information moved to the client and then back to the server: I stored it in the Text property of the litPageNumber control. This solution works, but it isn't elegant or efficient (because I have to convert a number to the string and back), and above all it doesn't work with properties that don't correspond to any user interface elements.

To see how to work around this issue, let's improve the user control by morphing the PageCount constant into a property of the same name. The value of this property—which doesn't correspond to any UI element—would be lost between postbacks, so I used the page's ViewState to preserve it.

```
' The PageCount property
Private m_PageCount As Integer = 100

Public Property PageCount() As Integer
    Get
        Return m_PageCount
    End Get
    Set(ByVal Value As Integer)
        If Value >= 1 Then
            m_PageCount = Value
            ' Save in the page's ViewState.
            Me.ViewState("PageCount") = Value
        End If
    End Set
End Property
```

```
Private Sub Page_Load(ByVal sender As Object, ByVal e As EventArgs) _
    Handles MyBase.Load
    ' Restore variables from the page's ViewState.
    If Not (Me.ViewState("PageCount") Is Nothing) Then
        PageCount = CInt(Me.ViewState("PageCount"))
    End If
End Sub
```

This solution works but isn't well encapsulated, and it's also slightly inefficient because the code retrieves the value from ViewState (which requires an unboxing operation) even if the PageCount property isn't actually used. Here's a better solution, which moves all the code related to the PageCount property inside its Property procedure and doesn't require any statements in the Page_Load event:

```
' The PageCount property
Private m_PageCount As Integer = -1      ' An invalid value

Public Property PageCount() As Integer
    Get
        If m_PageCount < 0 Then
            ' Restore variables from the page's ViewState only
            ' the first time this property is read.
            Dim objValue As Object = Me.ViewState("PageCount")
            If Not (objValue Is Nothing) Then
                m_PageCount = CInt(objValue)
            Else
                m_PageCount = 100         ' Use a default value.
            End If
        End If
        Return m_PageCount
    End Get
    Set(ByVal Value As Integer)
        If Value >= 1 Then
            m_PageCount = Value
            ' Save in the page's ViewState.
            Me.ViewState("PageCount") = Value
        End If
    End Set
End Property
```

Of course, you can also leverage any other available technique for remembering values between postbacks. For example, Session variables are a wise choice when you have to store a large amount of data and don't want to send it back and forth along the wire. The problem with using Session variables or cookies is that you must devise a naming mechanism that ensures that the names you select are unique for each different instance of the control on the form.

Accessing the User Control from the Client Page

In a real application, the PageCount property must be initialized from inside the host page, but when you switch to the code module behind the TestPage.aspx page you have an unpleasant surprise: you can't reference the PagingBar1 control as if it were a regular ASP.NET control such as a TextBox or a Button control.

You can easily observe another difference between user controls and regular controls. Drop any Web control on the TestPage.aspx—for example, a TextBox control—then switch to the code module and expand the #Region block. You see that a variable pointing to the TextBox control has been automatically created for you:

```
Protected WithEvents TextBox1 As System.Web.UI.WebControls.TextBox
```

However, no similar variable exists for the PagingBar1 user control that you have dropped from the Solution Explorer window. To reach the control programmatically, you must declare the variable yourself and initialize it by using a FindControl method. You can do this initialization from inside the Page_Load or the Page_Init event:

```
Protected WithEvents pbar As PagingBar

Private Sub Page_Load(ByVal sender As Object, ByVal e As EventArgs) _
    Handles MyBase.Load
    ' Get a reference to the PagingBar1 user control.
    pbar = DirectCast(FindControl("PagingBar1"), PagingBar)
End Sub
```

Now that you have a correct reference for the user control, you can access its properties and methods via code as you'd do with a standard Web control. For example, you can initialize the PageCount property the first time the page is visited:

```
Private Sub Page_Load(ByVal sender As Object, ByVal e As EventArgs) _
    Handles MyBase.Load
    pbar = DirectCast(FindControl("PagingBar1"), PagingBar)
    ⋮
    If Not Me.IsPostBack Then
        pbar.PageCount = 50
    End If
End Sub
```

Creating the User Control Dynamically

A page can also load a user control dynamically by means of the LoadControl method of the Page object. A control added in this way becomes visible only when you add it to the Controls collection of the Page itself or of another control container. In practice, you often drop a PlaceHolder control on the page on which you want to insert the new control and add the user control to the PlaceHolder's Controls collection:

```
Protected WithEvents pbar2 As PagingBar

Private Sub Page_Load(ByVal sender As Object, ByVal e As EventArgs) _
    Handles MyBase.Load
    ⋮
    ' Add a new PagingBar control dynamically.
    pbar2 = DirectCast(LoadControl("PagingBar.ascx"), PagingBar)
    pbar2.PageCount = 25
    ' Insert it where the PlaceHolder control is now.
    PlaceHolder1.Controls.Add(pbar2)
End Sub
```

Keep in mind that controls added with LoadControl aren't persisted in the page automatically between postbacks. In other words, if you don't take precautions, those controls disappear when the page is posted back. For this reason, user controls are usually added dynamically from inside the Page_Load event handler, possibly after you have checked the state of other variables or controls. For example, you might have a CheckBox control on the page that determines whether one or more additional controls are to be loaded:

```
If chkShowAdditionalControls.Checked Then
    ' Add a new PagingBar control dynamically.
    pbar2 = DirectCast(LoadControl("PagingBar.ascx"), PagingBar)
    ' Insert it where the PlaceHolder control is now.
    PlaceHolder1.Controls.Add(pbar2)
End If
```

Raising Events in the Page

A user control can expose properties, methods, and events. You've already seen how to implement properties (such as PageNumber and PageCount), and I won't discuss methods because you implement methods in user controls as you do any other type of component. This leaves us only the task of understanding how a user control can raise events.

In simpler cases, you implement events in a user control the same way that you implement them in other components. For example, the PagingBar control might expose a PageChanged event that the client page can trap to update its content when the user navigates to another page. You need only a handful of additional statements to implement this new feature: an Event statement and a RaiseEvent call when the value of the PageNumber property actually changes:

```
' ...(inside the .ascx file)...

Public Event PageChanged(ByVal sender As Object, ByVal e As EventArgs)

Public Property PageNumber() As Integer
    Get
        Return CInt(litPageNumber.Text.TrimStart)
    End Get
```

(continued)

```
        Set(ByVal Value As Integer)
            If Value >= 1 And Value <= PageCount AndAlso Value <> PageNumber Then
                ' Update the state of the Literal and Button controls.
                litPageNumber.Text = Value.ToString
                UpdateButtonState()
                ' Let the parent form know that the page has changed.
                RaiseEvent PageChanged(Me, EventArgs.Empty)
            End If
        End Set
    End Property
```

In this case, you don't need to pass any additional information in the second argument, so you can declare it as an EventArgs object and pass the special EventArgs.Empty shared field in the call to RaiseEvent. Thanks to the WithEvents keyword in the variable declaration, the client page can trap the event exactly like any event from a regular Web control:

```
' ...(Inside the .aspx file)...

Private Sub pbar_PageChanged(ByVal sender As Object, _
    ByVal e As EventArgs) Handles pbar.PageChanged
    ' Display a new page of results.
    ' (Just update a Label control in this demo.)
    lblPageData.Text = "( showing page #" & pbar.PageNumber.ToString & " )"
End Sub
```

Run the demo application and check for yourself that the PageChanged event is fired when you click on a navigation button and that the lblPageData control on the page is correctly updated with the new page number.

In this particular case, using this simple way of raising events is acceptable because the PageChanged event is fired when the PageNumber property is modified, and this can happen only from inside the Click event of a navigation button. Because it's the event that causes the postback, the Click event is guaranteed to fire last, after all other controls on the page have fired their own events and have been updated accordingly. When the property isn't updated from a postback event, however, you can't guarantee that this condition is met, and you would incur subtle bugs caused by the user control firing an event before all other controls have been updated. You'll learn how to avoid this problem in the "Raising Server-Side Events" section later in this chapter.

Fragment Caching

User controls let you leverage a great feature of ASP.NET: *partial* or *fragment caching*. This feature is the natural complement to page caching and the @OutputCache directive (which you read about in the "Page Caching" section in Chapter 24) in that it allows you to cache only selected portions of the page—that is, the HTML generated by the user control.

Caching with the @OutputCache Directive

To see when partial caching can be useful, consider the home page of a portal that displays weather information, local news, and stock quotes. Weather information is updated every hour, local news every five minutes, and stock quotes every two minutes. If you want to take advantage of page caching, you obviously must have an @OutputCache directive with a Duration attribute set to two minutes (the lowest value of the three) or just one minute to avoid any delay in displaying local news (which otherwise would be updated after six minutes in some cases). This approach forces you to re-create several portions of the page even if no new content is available for that section.

Fragment caching enables you to solve this issue quite nicely: just encapsulate the different sections of the page in three user controls: one for weather information, another for local news, and a third for stock quotes. Each user control should contain an @OutputCache directive with a different value for its Duration attribute. For example, this is the directive for the weather.ascx file:

```
<%@ OutputCache Duration="3600" VaryByParam="*" %>
```

Everything I've explained about the @OutputCache directives with pages applies when this directive is used inside an .ascx file, except that Location and VaryByHeader attributes aren't supported in user controls.

The @OutputCache directive in user controls supports a new attribute that isn't supported in pages: VaryByControl. This attribute can be assigned a semicolon-delimited list of the user control's properties, and the cached content is invalidated when any of the list properties takes a different value. The VaryByControl attribute is required if you omit the VaryByParam attribute:

```
<%@ OutputCache Duration="3600" VaryByControl="Name;Value" %>
```

Caching with the PartialCaching Attribute

You can enable fragment caching also by applying the PartialCaching attribute to the code-behind class of the user control. The constructor for this attribute takes either the value for the Duration attribute or the duration followed by the value for the VaryByParam, VaryByCustom, and VaryByControls properties:

```
' Cache the output of this user control for 1 minute.
<PartialCaching(60)> _
Public MustInherit Class MyUserControl
    Inherits System.Web.UI.UserControl
    ⋮
End Class
```

(continued)

```
' Cache for 1 minute or until the Name or Value properties change.
<PartialCaching(60, "none", "Name;Value", "")> _
Public MustInherit Class MyUserControl2
    Inherits System.Web.UI.UserControl
    ⋮
End Class
```

Note that the attribute's property is named VaryByControls (plural), whereas the corresponding directive attribute is named VaryByControl (singular).

Regardless of whether you use the @OutputCache directive or the PartialCaching attribute, you should pay a lot of attention when you use fragment caching in an application. For example, the user control's appearance isn't updated if the cached version is used, even if one or more properties have been assigned by code in the client page.

Custom Controls

User controls are fine when you can deploy your control as an .ascx and its code-behind class or when you want to reuse the HTML and the code in an .aspx page. For more powerful Web controls, you must switch to custom controls, which come in at least three flavors:

- Custom controls that extend an existing Web control with new properties, methods, events, or just a different behavior. In this case, you create a control class that inherits directly from the control to be extended.
- Custom controls that don't extend any existing Web control. In this case, you create a control class that inherits from either the Control or WebControl classes. (The latter class should be used for custom controls that expose a user interface and style attributes.)
- Custom controls that are made of two or more constituent controls, such as one TextBox and one ListBox control. In this case, you create a class that inherits from the Control class and creates all the constituent controls programmatically. Custom controls of this type are called composite controls.

Custom controls are harder to create than user controls but deliver more power and flexibility and are especially suited for highly dynamic output. For example, you need to deploy just one copy of the compiled custom control in the GAC to make it usable by all the ASP.NET applications running on the computer. (By comparison, you must deploy an .ascx file with each application that uses it.) Additionally, Visual Studio .NET offers better design-time support for custom controls. You can add a custom control to Visual Studio's Toolbox and you actually see how the control is rendered on an .aspx page at design time—two things that you can't do with user controls.

Your First Custom Control

Visual Studio .NET makes the creation of a custom control a very easy task. Just carefully follow this sequence of actions:

1. Create a new project of type Web Control Library. To match the code that follows, you should name the project CustomControlLibrary. (See Figure 25-3.)
2. Delete the WebCustomControl1.vb module that Visual Studio has created.
3. Choose Add New Item on the Project menu. In the Add New Item dialog box, select Web Custom Control in the Templates list; name the new module FirstControl.vb, and click Open. (After you become familiar with custom controls, you'll be able to customize the default WebCustomControl1 module instead of creating a new one.)

   The module just created in the Solution Explorer implements a functioning custom control that mimics a Label control. In following sections, you'll learn how to make it more interesting and useful, but for now let's see how you can add this control to the Toolbox and then drop it on an .aspx page.

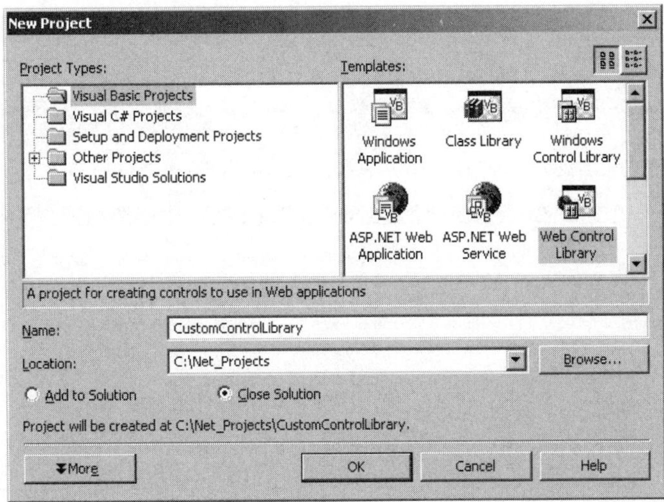

Figure 25-3. Creating a Web Control Library project.

4. Compile the CustomControlLibrary project by selecting Build Solution on the Build menu. This action creates the CustomControlLibrary.dll file in the \bin directory under the main project directory.

5. Point to Add Project on the File menu, and click New Project. Create an ASP.NET Web Forms Application project named CustomControls-Demo in the same solution. Right-click the project in the Solution Explorer window, and click Set As StartUp Project on the shortcut menu.

6. Right-click the Toolbox, and click Add Tab on the shortcut menu to create a new tab for all the custom controls you're going to create. Name this new tab Custom Controls or whatever you like.

7. Right-click in the new tab in the Toolbox, and click Customize Toolbox on the shortcut menu. In the Customize Toolbox dialog box, click the .NET Framework Components tab, click Browse, and select the CustomControlLibrary.dll file that we compiled earlier; this action imports all the controls contained in the DLL—only FirstControl, in this example—into the list of components. (See Figure 25-4.) Click OK to add the FirstControl to the Toolbox.

8. Drag the FirstControl item from the Toolbox to the WebForm1.aspx page in the CustomControlsDemo project, as you'd do with a built-in Web control. The FirstControl appears on the page as a Label. Switch to the Properties window to assign a string to its Text property and see how the new string is immediately rendered on the .aspx page.

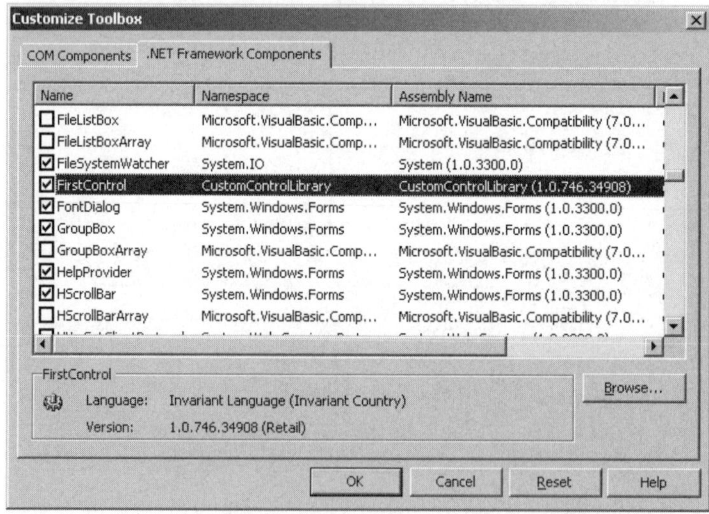

Figure 25-4. Adding the FirstControl custom control to the Toolbox.

The Render Method

Let's have a look at the source code that Visual Studio has created for the First-Control class:

```
Imports System.ComponentModel
Imports System.Web.UI

<DefaultProperty("Text"), _
    ToolboxData("<{0}:FirstControl runat=server></{0}:FirstControl>")> _
Public Class FirstControl
    Inherits System.Web.UI.WebControls.WebControl

    Dim _text As String

    <Bindable(True), Category("Appearance"), DefaultValue("")> _
    Property [Text]() As String
        Get
            Return _text
        End Get
        Set(ByVal Value As String)
            _text = Value
        End Set
    End Property

    Protected Overrides Sub Render(ByVal output As HtmlTextWriter)
        output.Write([Text])
    End Sub
End Class
```

The Render method is the means by which the control generates its own appearance. This method is inherited from the WebControl base class and is invoked by the ASP.NET infrastructure when the control must render itself as HTML text. By overriding this method, you're actually in control of how exactly the control appears on the client page. For example, let's have the FirstControl render itself as a button with a given caption:

```
Protected Overrides Sub Render(ByVal output As HtmlTextWriter)
    ' Pay attention to (repeated) double quotes in the string below.
    output.Write("<input type=""button"" Value=""" & [Text] & """>")
End Sub
```

Now that you have a broad idea of how a custom control works, let's focus on the main classes and interfaces you'll have to become familiar with to get the most out of custom controls.

The HtmlTextWriter Class

The argument passed to the Render method is an HtmlTextWriter object. As its name suggests, it's an auxiliary class that can help you write formatted HTML text. In practice, however, the support it offers is minimal; it does very little that you wouldn't do manually.

Its main methods are Write and WriteLine, which output raw HTML text to the stream. You can write an open tag with WriteBeginTag and close it with WriteEndTag, as in:

```
output.WriteBeginTag("textarea")
output.Write("Type a comment in this box")
output.WriteEndTag("textarea")
```

The HtmlTextWriter class offers better support when you have to write nested tags. In that case, you output the open tag using the RenderBeginTag method and close it with the RenderEndTag method. The latter method doesn't take an argument because the HtmlTextWriter remembers the most recent open tag. The following code is taken from the TableControl demo on the companion CD:

```
' Output an HTML table.
Public Rows As Integer = 3
Public Columns As Integer = 4

Protected Overrides Sub Render(ByVal output As HtmlTextWriter)
    Dim r, c As Integer

    output.RenderBeginTag("table")
    For r = 1 To Rows
        output.RenderBeginTag("tr")
        For c = 1 To Columns
            output.RenderBeginTag("td")
            output.Write(r.ToString & "," & c.ToString)
            output.RenderEndTag()      ' </td>
        Next
        output.RenderEndTag()          ' </tr>
    Next
    output.RenderEndTag()              ' </table>
End Sub
```

The AddAttribute method outputs the name and value of an attribute. Its peculiarity is that you must invoke it *before* the RenderBeginTag method that outputs the main tag:

```
' These statements output this html: <table border="1">
output.AddAttribute("border", "1")
output.RenderBeginTag("table")
```

The HtmlTextWriter doesn't indent its result automatically, but it offers an Indent property that specifies how many tab characters are added at the beginning of any new line. These tab characters are added only after a WriteLine method. Let's see how to revise the code snippet seen previously to create the indented text for an HTML table. Added statements are in boldface:

```
Protected Overrides Sub Render(ByVal output As HtmlTextWriter)
    output.AddAttribute("border", "1")
    output.RenderBeginTag("table")
    output.WriteLine()
    output.Indent += 1
    For r = 1 To Rows
        output.RenderBeginTag("tr")
        output.WriteLine()
        output.Indent += 1
        For c = 1 To Columns
            output.RenderBeginTag("td")
            output.Write(r.ToString & "," & c.ToString)
            output.RenderEndTag()
            output.WriteLine()
        Next
        output.Indent -= 1
        output.RenderEndTag()
        output.WriteLine()
    Next
    output.Indent -= 1
    output.RenderEndTag()
End Sub
```

Figure 25-5 shows how the table appears to the end user. The following is the HTML source code received by the browser:

```
<table border="1">
    <tr>
        <td>1,1</td>
        <td>1,2</td>
        ⋮
    </tr>
    <tr>
        <td>2,1</td>
        <td>2,2</td>
        ⋮
</table>
```

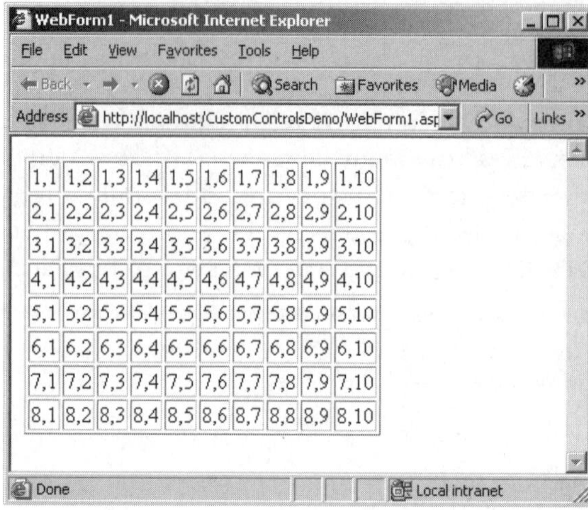

Figure 25-5. A custom control that produces an HTML table.

The Control and WebControl Classes

As I explained previously, a custom control can inherit from the System.Web.UI.Control class when it exposes a very simple user interface or no UI at all. Table 25-1 lists the most important properties, methods, and events of this class from the perspective of a custom control author. Notice that all the methods and a couple of properties have Protected scope, so you can use them only when you're writing a class that inherits from the Control class.

Table 25-1 Main Members of the Control Class Used in Custom Control Authoring

Category	Syntax	Description
Properties	Controls	The collection of child controls.
	Page	The parent Page object.
	Parent	The parent control for this control. It can be the Page object.
	ID	Gets or sets the programmatic identifier assigned to the control. This property must be set to enable server-side access to the control.
	UniqueID	The unique, hierarchical qualified identifier assigned to this control (read-only).
	ClientID	The read-only, unique ID assigned to the control by ASP.NET, regardless of whether the ID property has been assigned. This property is used to identify the control in client-side scripts.

Table 25-1 Main Members of the Control Class Used in Custom Control Authoring

Category	Syntax	Description
	Visible	Determines whether the control is visible.
	EnableViewState	Determines whether the control maintains its ViewState between postback. (The default is True.)
	ViewState	The StateBag collection that can be used to store values between postbacks. (This is a protected property.)
	ChildControlsCreated	Returns True if the child controls for this control have been created. (This is a protected property.)
Methods (protected)	Render	Sends the contents of this control to the provided HtmlTextWriter object.
	EnsureChildControls	Ensures that child controls of this control have been created.
	RenderChildren	Causes the content of all child controls to be output to the provided HtmlTextWriter object.
	SaveViewState	Save any ViewState value that has changed since the page was posted back.
	LoadViewState	Restores values from ViewState that were saved by the SaveState method.
	OnInit	Raises the Init event.
	OnPreRender	Raises the PreRender event.
Events	Init	Fires when the control is initialized.
	PreRender	Fires when the control is ready to render its contents.
	Load	Fires when the control is loaded on the page.
	Unloaded	Fires when the control is unloaded from memory.
	DataBinding	Fires when the control binds to a data source.

Most of the time, however, you'll inherit your custom control from the System.Web.UI.WebControls.WebControl base class, which offers more support to controls that have a rich user interface. The WebControl class inherits from Control and adds UI-related properties, such as ForeColor, BackColor, and Font. Table 25-2 lists the main properties and a couple of protected methods of this class that are of interest to custom control authors. (The WebControl class doesn't add any events to those defined in the Control class.)

The meaning and usage of a few properties and methods will become clear in the following sections.

Table 25-2 Main Members of the WebControl Class Used in Custom Control Authoring

Category	Syntax	Description
Properties	ForeColor	The foreground color of the control.
	BackColor	The background color of the control.
	Font	The font used by the control.
	Attributes	The collection of attributes.
	Width	The width of the control.
	Height	The height of the control.
	BorderStyle	The style of the border.
	BorderWidth	The width of the border.
	BorderColor	The color of the border.
	Enabled	True if the control is enabled.
	Style	A collection of text attributes that will be rendered as a style attribute.
Methods (protected)	AddAttributesToRender	Outputs attributes and styles to the HtmlTextWriter object passed as an argument.
	RenderContents	Renders the contents of the control into the HtmlTextWriter passed as an argument.

Improving the Custom Control

You can already create functioning controls by applying what you've learned so far, but of course there's a lot more to know. For example, you need to know how your control can participate in postback events and how it can expose events to its client page.

Adding Properties

You can add properties to a custom control as you do with any other class—that is, by implementing a Property procedure. You typically prefix the Property procedure with a Description attribute, which sets the text that appears in Visual Studio's Properties window:

```
Dim m_Rows As Integer = 3

<Description("The number of rows")> _
Property Rows() As Integer
    Get
        Return m_Rows
    End Get
```

```
        Set(ByVal Value As Integer)
            If Value > 0 Then
                m_Rows = Value
            End If
        End Set
    End Property
```

Other common attributes are DefaultValue (the initial value of the property), Category (the category it belongs to in the Properties window), and Bindable (True if the property can be bound to a data source):

```
<Bindable(True), Category("Appearance"), DefaultValue(3), _
  Description("The number of rows")> _
Property Rows() As Integer
    ⋮
End Property
```

Remember that Visual Studio uses the DefaultValue attribute only to decide whether the property value should be marked as modified (in bold) in the Properties window, but it's up to you to correctly initialize the property to the given value. By default, all properties appear in the Properties window, but you can control the visibility of a property with the Browsable attribute; this is what you usually do with run-time-only properties:

```
<Browsable(False)> _
Property CurrRow() As Integer
    ⋮
End Property
```

The properties that you set for an ASP.NET control in the Properties window are actually translated to attributes inside the .aspx file. For example, the TableControl demo stores the values of the Rows and Columns properties in the .aspx file, as follows:

```
<cc1:TableControl id="TableControl1" runat="server"
    Width="72px" Height="33px" Columns="10" Rows="8">
</cc1:TableControl>
```

Because all your custom properties are ultimately translated to text, you should know more about how this translation is carried out. In general, properties that return a primitive type (Boolean, numeric, date, and String) are translated to text as you'd expect and never create any problems.

ASP.NET works well also with enumerated properties. It stores their textual value in the page if you set the property from the Properties window but is also able to parse a new value that you enter directly in the HTML editor. For example, let's add a property that returns a BorderStyle enumerated value:

```
Dim m_CellBorderStyle As System.Web.UI.WebControls.BorderStyle
```

(continued)

```
<Description("The border style of table cells")> _
Property CellBorderStyle() As System.Web.UI.WebControls.BorderStyle
    Get
        Return m_CellBorderStyle
    End Get
    Set(ByVal Value As System.Web.UI.WebControls.BorderStyle)
        m_CellBorderStyle = Value
    End Set
End Property
```

This is how this property is rendered in the .aspx page:

```
<cc1:TableControl id="TableControl1" runat="server" Width="72px" Height="33px"
    Columns="10" Rows="8" CellBorderStyle="Dotted">
</cc1:TableControl>
```

You can now modify the CellBorderStyle attribute and enter another valid enumeration value—for example, Double or Inset—and it's correctly recognized when you switch the editor back to Design mode. If you type a value that doesn't correspond to any element in the enum type, you get a parsing error.

ASP.NET also supports a special syntax for object properties in the format *propertyname-membername*. For example, you can set the Bold and Size members of the Font property as follows:

```
<cc1:TableControl id="TableControl1" runat="server"
    Font-Bold="True" Font-Size="Larger">
</cc1:TableControl>
```

This behavior is applied to your custom object properties as well. For example, let's say that you define the following class:

```
Public Class CellStyle
    Dim m_ForeColor As System.Drawing.Color
    Dim m_BackColor As System.Drawing.Color

    Property ForeColor() As Drawing.Color
        Get
            Return m_ForeColor
        End Get
        Set(ByVal Value As Drawing.Color)
            m_ForeColor = Value
        End Set
    End Property

    Property BackColor() As Drawing.Color
        Get
            Return m_BackColor
        End Get
```

```
        Set(ByVal Value As Drawing.Color)
            m_BackColor = Value
        End Set
    End Property
End Class
```

The custom control can implement a CellStyle property that returns an instance of the preceding class:

```
' ...(inside the TableControl.vb module)...

Dim m_CellStyle As New CellStyle()

Property CellStyle() As CellStyle
    Get
        Return m_CellStyle
    End Get
    Set(ByVal Value As CellStyle)
        m_CellStyle = Value
    End Set
End Property
```

Thanks to ASP.NET support for object properties, you can now set the CellStyle property in the HTML editor as follows:

```
<cc1:TableControl id="TableControl1" runat="server"
    CellStyle-ForeColor="black" CellStyle-BackColor="yellow">
</cc1:TableControl>
```

Note, however, that you can't edit the CellStyle property in the Properties window because Visual Studio doesn't know how to display an object property unless it's associated with a TypeConverter object. Many .NET Framework objects—for example, Size and FontInfo—are associated with a TypeConverter, and that's why they can be edited in the Properties window. Interestingly, if you define a custom property that returns one of these standard .NET objects, your property can also be set from inside the Properties window. For example, consider a property that returns a FontInfo object:

```
' The CellFont property
Dim m_CellFont As System.Web.UI.WebControls.FontInfo = MyBase.Font

Property CellFont() As System.Web.UI.WebControls.FontInfo
    Get
        Return m_CellFont
    End Get
    Set(ByVal Value As System.Web.UI.WebControls.FontInfo)
        m_CellFont = Value
    End Set
End Property
```

Because this property returns a FontInfo object, it's correctly rendered in the Properties window. (See Figure 25-6.) You can read the "Object Properties" section in Chapter 17 to learn how you can implement a TypeConverter for properties that return a user-defined class.

Figure 25-6. The CellFont property is displayed correctly in the Properties window, but the CellStyle property isn't, because it has no associated TypeConverter.

Occasionally you might want to display a special editor for your properties, even if they don't return an object. The ImageUrl property of the Image control is a good example of this concept: it's a plain String property, but it lets you select the target file using a special editor. (See Figure 25-7.) Although implementing a custom property editor isn't a breeze, you can often "borrow" one that's already defined in the .NET Framework. Just locate a property that uses the editor you need in the object browser, and copy its Editor attribute, as in this code:

```
' The full name of the assembly depends on the installed .NET version.
<EditorAttribute("System.Web.UI.Design.ImageUrlEditor, System.Design, " _
    & "Version=1.0.3300.0, Culture=neutral, " _
    & "PublicKeyToken=b03f5f7f11d50a3a", _
    GetType(System.Drawing.Design.UITypeEditor))> _
Property ImageUrl As String
    ⋮
End Property
```

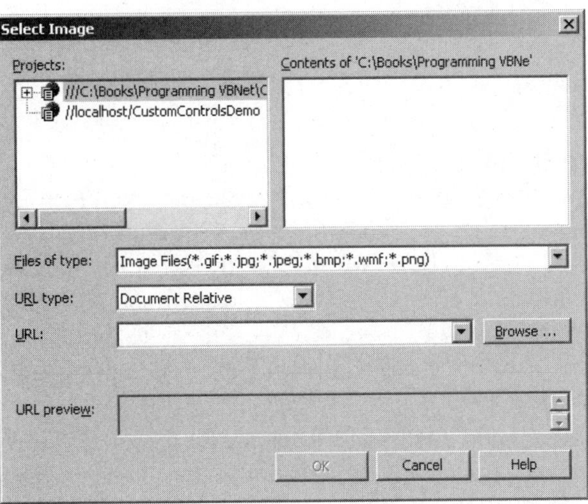

Figure 25-7. You can easily associate your properties with existing custom editors.

You can associate many other common properties with existing editors. A great example is the Items property of the ListBox and DropDownList controls, which returns a ListItemCollection object. A trip to the object browser unveils the type of the editor associated with this object:

```
<Editor("System.Web.UI.Design.WebControls.ListItemsCollectionEditor, " _
    & "System.Design, Version=1.0.3300.0, Culture=neutral, " _
    & "PublicKeyToken=b03f5f7f11d50a3a", _
    & "GetTypeSystem.Drawing.Design.UITypeEditor,System.Drawing)> _
Property Items() As ListItemsCollection
    ⋮
End Property
```

By default, all the properties you inherit from Control and WebControl classes appear in the Properties window, but sometimes you won't like this behavior. For example, let's say that your control has a fixed white background color and you don't want to allow users to change it. You can't remove the BackColor property from the class interface of your control, but at least you should override it to apply a Browsable attribute that hides it in the Property window and to nullify any assignment to it done programmatically:

```
<Browsable(False)> _
Overrides Property BackColor() As System.Drawing.Color
    Get
        ' Always return white.
        Return System.Drawing.Color.White
    End Get
```

(continued)

```
    Set(ByVal Value As System.Drawing.Color)
        ' Ignore this assignment.
    End Set
End Property
```

Rendering Style Attributes

If your control inherits from WebControl, it exposes several properties related to the user interface, such as Font, ForeColor, and BackColor. In the Render method you should output these values as attributes of the main tag in an orderly fashion, with multiple calls to the AddAttribute or AddStyleAttribute methods of the HtmlTextWriter object. To keep the HTML sent to the client as slim as possible, you should output those properties only if they're different from their default value.

The WebControl class offers a helper method called AddAttributesToRender, which lets you render all the attributes that have a nondefault value with a single call. To show this method in action, I've prepared a ComboBoxEx custom control, which is similar to a DropDownList control but exposes an ItemList property that takes a comma-delimited list of elements in the control:

```
ComboBoxEx1.ItemList = "First,Second,Third"
```

Because the ComboBoxEx control inherits from WebControl, the user can set properties such as Width or BackColor. Let's have a look at the Render method of this custom control:

```
Protected Overrides Sub Render(ByVal output As System.Web.UI.HtmlTextWriter)
    ' Split the elements in an array.
    Dim items() As String = ItemList.Split(","c)

    ' Output the <select> tag and its attributes.
    output.AddAttribute("name", Me.ID)
    Me.AddAttributesToRender(output)
    output.RenderBeginTag("select")

    Dim index As Integer
    For index = 0 To items.Length - 1
        ' Prepare the Value attribute, equal to the element index.
        output.AddAttribute("value", index.ToString)
        ' If this is the selected element, add "selected" attributes.
        If index = SelectedIndex Then
            output.AddAttribute("selected", "selected")
        End If
        ' Output the <option> tag.
        output.RenderBeginTag("option")
        output.Write(parts(0))
        output.RenderEndTag()
```

```
    Next
    ' Close the </select> tag.
    output.RenderEndTag()
End Sub
```

(Note that the name attribute must be added separately and should be taken from the UniqueID property.) This is the HTML rendered to the browser when the user selects a nondefault value for the BackColor property:

```
<select name="cboItems" id="cboItems"
        style="background-color:#C0FFFF;width:217px;">
   <option value="1">First</option>
   <option value="2">Second</option>
   <option value="3">Third</option>
</select>
```

Handling Postback Data

The ComboBoxEx custom control displays its contents with the correct style attributes but still lacks an important feature: it doesn't remember the SelectedIndex property between postbacks. To see what I mean, place a ComboBoxEx and a Button control on the form, run the program, select the second element in the ComboBoxEx control, and click on the push control. This action causes a postback, but in the page now returned to the browser the ComboBoxEx control displays the first (default) item.

To correctly implement the behavior of the control during postbacks, you must do two things:

- Preserve property values between callbacks, which you do by storing them in the ViewState collection.
- Implement the IPostBackDataHandler interface to receive a notification when a postback occurs.

You already know how to store control properties between postbacks, so this code shouldn't look new to you:

```
' The SelectedIndex property
Property SelectedIndex() As Integer
    Get
        ' If not a postback, the value isn't in the ViewState collection.
        Dim objValue As Object = Me.ViewState("SelectedIndex")
        If objValue Is Nothing Then
            Return 0              ' The default value
        Else
            Return CInt(objValue)
        End If
    End Get
```

(continued)

```
    Set(ByVal Value As Integer)
        If Value >= 0 Then
            Me.ViewState("SelectedIndex") = Value
        End If
    End Set
End Property
```

The IPostBackDataHandler interface exposes only two methods, LoadPostData and RaisePostDataChangedEvent. For now let's focus on LoadPostData, the more important of the two. ASP.NET calls this method when a postback occurs and passes it the post collection that the form posted to itself:

```
Public Function LoadPostData(ByVal postDataKey As String, _
    ByVal postCollection As NameValueCollection) As Boolean _
    Implements IPostBackDataHandler.LoadPostData
    ⋮
End Function
```

Understanding how the postCollection argument is built is crucial. All ASP.NET forms use the POST action method and send the values of all the controls on the form in the request header. The postCollection argument passed to the LoadPostData method contains the name and value pairs posted with the form, and the postDataKey argument is the key of the element in this collection that contains the new value of your custom control. (This argument is actually equal to the control's ID.)

The value being posted back in the collection for the ComboBoxEx custom control is the value associated with the element that's currently selected in the combo box. Because each element in our custom combo box has a value equal to its index in the list, we can take this value from the collection and assign it to the SelectedIndex property:

```
Public Function LoadPostData(ByVal postDataKey As String, _
    ByVal postCollection As NameValueCollection) As Boolean _
    Implements IPostBackDataHandler.LoadPostData

    ' The posted value is equal to the index of the selected element.
    SelectedIndex = CInt(postCollection(postDataKey))
End Function

Public Sub RaisePostDataChangedEvent() _
    Implements IPostBackDataHandler.RaisePostDataChangedEvent
    ' Nothing to do for now.
End Sub
```

If you now rebuild the ComboBoxEx control and run the demo application (or just run the complete project on the companion CD), you'll see that the

SelectedIndex property is correctly preserved between postbacks and that the ComboBoxEx control works as expected. You might have noticed that we've left the RaisePostDataChangedEvent method of the IPostBackDataHandler interface empty. The purpose of this method will become clear in the next section.

Raising Server-Side Events

The ComboBoxEx control still lacks a SelectedIndexChanged event. You already know how to declare an event in a class:

```
Event SelectedIndexChanged(ByVal sender As Object, ByVal e As EventArgs)
```

If your event uses the standard EventArgs object in its second argument—as most ASP.NET events do—you can also recycle the definition of the EventHandler delegate class:

```
Event SelectedIndexChanged As EventHandler
```

The next step is of course to raise the event when the SelectedIndex property changes. You might be tempted to do this from inside the Set block in the SelectedIndex property procedure or from the LoadPostData event if you detect that a new value is being assigned to the SelectedIndex property. However, as I explained in the "Raising Events in the Page" section earlier in this chapter, this technique might create subtle bugs because the client page might receive the event when not all controls on the page have been completely updated after the postback. For example, the code in the event handler might use the SelectedIndex property of another ComboBoxEx control and would get the wrong value if that control hadn't processed its own LoadPostData method yet. The purpose of the second method in the IPostBackDataHandler interface is to avoid this kind of problem. Here's how it works.

When the page is posted back, ASP.NET calls the LoadPostData method of all the controls that have a value in the post collection and remembers the Boolean value that this method returns. When this first round of calls is completed, ASP.NET calls the RaisePostDataChangedEvent method of those controls whose LoadPostData method had returned True. The code in the LoadPostData method should compare the new value of the property (as taken from the post collection) with the previous value of the same property (as retrieved from the ViewState collection) and return True if the two values differ. Here's a new implementation of the LoadPostData method that follows these guidelines:

```
Public Function LoadPostData(ByVal postDataKey As String, _
    ByVal postCollection As NameValueCollection) As Boolean _
    Implements IPostBackDataHandler.LoadPostData

    ' The posted value is equal to the index of the selected element.
    Dim newSelectedIndex As Integer = CInt(postCollection(postDataKey))
```

(continued)

```
    If SelectedIndex <> newSelectedIndex Then
        ' If the new value is different, store it in the property.
        SelectedIndex = newSelectedIndex
        ' Tell ASP.NET to call the RaisePostDataChangedEvent method.
        Return True
    End If
End Function
```

The code in the RaisePostDataChangedEvent method could contain the RaiseEvent statement. However, if you want to allow other developers to derive from your ComboBoxEx control you should delegate that action to an On*xxxx* method, as in the following example:

```
Public Sub RaisePostDataChangedEvent() _
    Implements IPostBackDataHandler.RaisePostDataChangedEvent
    OnSelectedIndexChanged(EventArgs.Empty)
End Sub

Protected Overridable Sub OnSelectedIndexChanged(ByVal e As EventArgs)
    RaiseEvent SelectedIndexChanged(Me, e)
End Sub
```

Now you can finally trap the SelectedIndexChanged event in the client page as you'd do for a standard DropDownList control:

```
' ...(Inside the client .aspx page)...

Private Sub cboItems_SelectedIndexChanged(ByVal sender As Object, _
    ByVal e As EventArgs) Handles cboItems.SelectedIndexChanged
    ' Update a Label with the new value of the SelectedIndex property.
    lblMessage.Text = "Element index = " & cboItems.SelectedIndex.ToString
End Sub
```

Generating Postback Events

The ComboBoxEx control is getting closer to a standard DropDownList control, but it still lacks the ability to perform postback events as the standard control does when you set its AutoPostBack property to True. Adding this property to a custom control is relatively simple, but before looking at the actual implementation, let's see how the AutoPostBack property is implemented in a standard DropDownList control.

Try this simple experiment: create a Web Form, drop a DropDownList control on it, add a couple of elements to its Items collection, set the control's AutoPostBack property to True, run the project, and see what source code the browser receives (here in a concise version):

```
<form name="Form1" method="post" action="WebForm1.aspx" id="Form1">
<input type="hidden" name="__EVENTTARGET" value="" />
```

```
<input type="hidden" name="__EVENTARGUMENT" value="" />
<input type="hidden" name="__VIEWSTATE" value="dDw5NTg10TIyODQ70z4=" />

<script language="javascript">
<!--
    function __doPostBack(eventTarget, eventArgument) {
        var theform = document.Form1;
        theform.__EVENTTARGET.value = eventTarget;
        theform.__EVENTARGUMENT.value = eventArgument;
        theform.submit();
    }
// -->
</script>

<select name="DropDownList1" id="DropDownList1" style="width:105px;"
    onchange="__doPostBack('DropDownList1','')" language="javascript" >
    <option value="one">one</option>
    <option value="two">two</option>
</select>
</form>
```

Three things should draw your attention in the preceding code:

- The form contains two new hidden fields, named __EVENTTARGET and __EVENTARGUMENT.
- The form also contains a JavaScript function named __doPostBack, which saves its two arguments in the hidden fields and programmatically causes a postback.
- The <select> tag (which renders the original DropDownList controls) contains an onchange attribute that points to the __doPostBack routine and passes it a reference to itself (the DropDownList1 name) and an empty argument.

Even if you aren't an expert in client-side JavaScript programming, it should be clear how the AutoPostBack feature works: when the user selects a new element in the DropDownList control, the onchange attribute causes the __doPostBack routine to run. This routine loads the control name into the __EVENTTARGET field, loads the second argument (a null string in this case) in the __EVENTARGUMENT field, and submits the form via code. When the request gets to the server, the ASP.NET infrastructure can check the value of the __EVENTTARGET field and, if the field isn't empty, ASP.NET can determine which control caused the postback.

Of all the additional elements on the page—the hidden fields, the JavaScript routine, and the attribute in the HTML tag—you only have to care about the onchange attribute in the <select> tag because ASP.NET adds the hidden fields and the JavaScript routine automatically if it recognizes that one or more controls on the form rely on the AutoPostBack feature. The only necessary condition for this to happen is that you use the Page.GetPostBackEventReference method when you build the HTML attribute, as I'll explain in a moment.

Let's start by correctly implementing the AutoPostBack property. This step is simple because this code does nothing but save and restore the value of the property from the ViewState collection:

```
' The AutoPostBack property
Property AutoPostBack() As Boolean
    Get
        Dim objValue As Object = Me.ViewState("AutoPostBack")
        If objValue Is Nothing Then
            Return False
        Else
            Return CBool(objValue)
        End If
    End Get
    Set(ByVal Value As Boolean)
        Me.ViewState("AutoPostBack") = Value
    End Set
End Property
```

We can now focus on the code that emits the onchange attribute from inside the Render method. You need to add only four lines of code to implement this feature:

```
Protected Overrides Sub Render(ByVal output As System.Web.UI.HtmlTextWriter)
    ' Split the elements in an array.
    Dim items() As String = ItemList.Split(","c)

    ' Output the <select> tag and its attributes.
    output.AddAttribute("name", Me.UniqueID)
    Me.AddAttributesToRender(output)

    ' If this control requires AutoPostBack
    If Me.AutoPostBack Then
        output.AddAttribute("onchange", Page.GetPostBackEventReference(Me))
        output.AddAttribute("language", "javascript")
    End If

    ' ...(The remainder of the routine is unchanged.)...
```

As I anticipated, this code works as expected because it uses the GetPostBackEventReference method of the Page object. This method does two things. The first and the most evident: it returns a string in the format expected by the onchange attribute, as in

```
onchange="__doPostBack('clientsidename','')"
```

where *clientsidename* is the client-side ID of the control. (It corresponds to the ClientID property.) In addition to returning this string, the GetPostBackEvent-Reference method remembers that it has been called by a control in the page so that ASP.NET can output the two hidden fields and the JavaScript code of the __doPostBack routine when it sends back the page to the client browser. This method ensures that only one routine and one pair of hidden fields are created, regardless of how many controls on the page have their AutoPostBack property set to True.

The GetPostBackEventReference method takes a control reference in its first argument and a string in its second (optional) argument. The second argument is the string stored in the __EVENTARGUMENT field when the postback occurs. For simpler controls you can leave this argument blank, but sometimes you need this additional argument to figure out which operation should be performed on callback. I'll show an example of a custom control that uses this feature in the next section.

Handling Postback Events

In many cases, controls that expose the AutoPostBack property should also implement the IPostBackEventHandler interface. This interface contains only one method, RaisePostBackEvent, which ASP.NET invokes when the postback actually occurs. There are two main reasons why you should implement this interface:

- Your control must raise a particular server-side event—say, Click—when it causes a postback.
- Your control must access the value contained in the __EVENT-ARGUMENT field—that is, the second argument passed to the __doPostBack function.

Extending the ComboBoxEx control to fire a Click event when it causes a postback is really simple. You only have to define the event, raise the event from inside an overridable OnClick procedure, and call this OnClick routine from inside the IPostBackEventHandler.RaisePostBackEvent method:

```
Public Class ComboBoxEx
    Inherits System.Web.UI.WebControls.WebControl
    Implements IPostBackDataHandler
    Implements IPostBackEventHandler

    ⋮

    Public Event Click As EventHandler
```

(continued)

```
    Public Sub RaisePostBackEvent(ByVal eventArgument As String) _
        Implements IPostBackEventHandler.RaisePostBackEvent
        ' Invoke the (overridable) procedure that fires the event
        ' when this control causes a postback.
        OnClick(EventArgs.Empty)
    End Sub

    Protected Overridable Sub OnClick(ByVal e As EventArgs)
        ' Raise the server-side Click event.
        RaiseEvent Click(Me, e)
    End Sub
End Class
```

In the next example, I'll show you a custom control that uses both arguments of the __doPostBack procedure and therefore needs to implement the IPostBackEventHandler interface. This new custom control, named NavigateRibbon, is similar to the PagingBar user control that you saw earlier in this chapter, but it uses hyperlinks instead of buttons. (See Figure 25-8.)

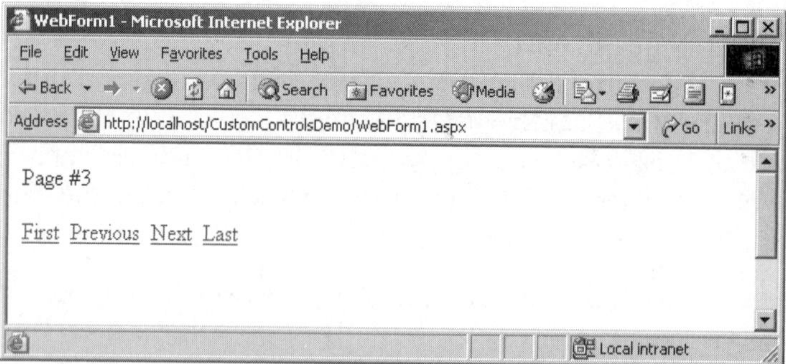

Figure 25-8. The NavigateRibbon custom control.

In general, you can't use plain <A HREF="url"> tags when working with custom controls because a click on these hyperlinks doesn't post the values in the form's fields. However, the solution is easy: you let the __doPostBack routine perform the post for you:

```
<A HREF="javascript:__doPostBack('NavigateRibbon1', 'first')">First</A>
```

Once you understand the trick, it's easy to write the code for the Render method of the NavigateRibbon custom control. Here's the control's source code, after I omit a couple of property procedures to save space. Note that this control implements the IPostBackEventHandler interface but doesn't need to implement IPostBackDataHandler:

```
Public Class NavigateRibbon
    Inherits System.Web.UI.WebControls.WebControl
    Implements IPostBackEventHandler
```

```
' ...(The implementation of these properties is omitted here)...
Property PageCount() As Integer
    ⋮
End Property
Property PageNumber() As Integer
    ⋮
End Property

Protected Overrides Sub Render(ByVal output As HtmlTextWriter)
    Dim items() As String = {"First", "Previous", "Next", "Last"}

    Dim s As String
    For Each s In items
        ' Create the <A HREF="javascript:__doPostBack(....)"> tag
        output.AddAttribute("id", Me.ClientID)
        output.AddAttribute("href", "javascript:" & _
            Page.GetPostBackEventReference(Me, s))
        output.RenderBeginTag("a")
        ' Display the caption.
        output.Write(s)
        ' Close the tag.
        output.RenderEndTag()
        ' Add a couple of spaces.
        output.Write("  ")
    Next
End Sub

' Process the postback.
Public Sub RaisePostBackEvent(ByVal eventArgument As String) _
    Implements IPostBackEventHandler.RaisePostBackEvent

    ' Update the page number, but keep it within valid range.
    Dim pageNum As Integer = PageNumber
    Select Case eventArgument.ToLower
        Case "first"
            pageNum = 1
        Case "previous"
            pageNum = Math.Max(pageNum - 1, 1)
        Case "next"
            pageNum = Math.Min(pageNum + 1, PageCount)
        Case "last"
            pageNum = PageCount
    End Select

    If PageNumber <> pageNum Then
        ' If the page number changed, fire a PageChanged event.
        PageNumber = pageNum
        OnPageChanged(EventArgs.Empty)
    End If
End Sub
```

(continued)

```
    Event PageChanged As EventHandler

    ' Raise the event in the client page.
    Protected Overridable Sub OnPageChanged(ByVal e As EventArgs)
        RaiseEvent PageChanged(Me, e)
    End Sub
End Class
```

A client page can react to a click on the four navigation links as follows:

```
Private Sub NavigateRibbon1_PageChanged(ByVal sender As Object, _
    ByVal e As EventArgs) Handles NavigateRibbon1.PageChanged
    ' (Just update a Label control in this demo.)
    lblMessage.Text = "Page #" & NavigateRibbon1.PageNumber
End Sub
```

Composite Controls

Custom controls that render themselves by emitting HTML in the Render method are very efficient but fail to take advantage of the functionality embedded in standard ASP.NET controls. For example, say that you want to create a control that contains 10 text fields. Wouldn't it be simpler to instantiate 10 TextBox controls and rely on their properties instead of emitting HTML code for each one of them? Composite controls exist exactly to fulfill this necessity.

A composite control is a custom control that inherits from Control or WebControl, with a few differences from the examples we've seen so far:

- It overrides the CreateChildrenControls method of the base class. Inside this method, it instantiates all the constituent controls and adds them to its own Controls collection.
- It implements the INamingContainer interface. This interface is just a marker interface that exposes no methods. Its only purpose is to inform ASP.NET that this control has child controls, and each control must receive a unique ID.

From a conceptual point of view, composite custom controls are similar to user controls in that you build them by composing simpler controls. Unlike user controls, however, composite controls have all the advantages of custom controls: they are compiled, they can be used in Visual Studio designers in a WYSIWYG fashion, and they give you better control over how they render HTML code to the client.

Creating a composite control is generally simpler than creating a regular custom control with the same functionality for at least a couple of reasons. First, you don't have to worry about rendering each child control: you just call the RenderChildren method and each child control will render itself. Second, you don't have to take any special steps for persisting the state of child controls or implementing additional interfaces, such as IPostBackDataHandler and IPostBackEventHandler.

The key to building composite controls is the CreateChildControls method. ASP.NET invokes this method on all the controls on a page when it's time for them to create child controls, if they have any. We didn't worry about this method in previous examples because our controls had no child controls, but in this case we can't ignore it any longer.

The problem with composite controls is that you can't be sure about *when* the collection of child controls must be created. Depending on many factors, it might occur early in the life cycle of the control or just when the Render method is called. For this reason, you can't assume that a child control is available when you reference it in code. To avoid null reference exceptions, you should always call the EnsureChildControls method before accessing any child control: this method invokes the CreateChildControls method if it hasn't been invoked already. Or you can check the ChildControlsCreated property, a Boolean that tells whether the collection of child controls has been created already. (You can also reset this property to False if you want the control to refresh itself.)

To illustrate how to create a composite control, I wrote a Multiplier control that multiplies the numbers entered in two text fields and shows the result in a third field. (See Figure 25-9.) This control contains (in this order) a TextBox control, a Label control, another TextBox control, a Button, and finally a third TextBox control with its ReadOnly property set to True.

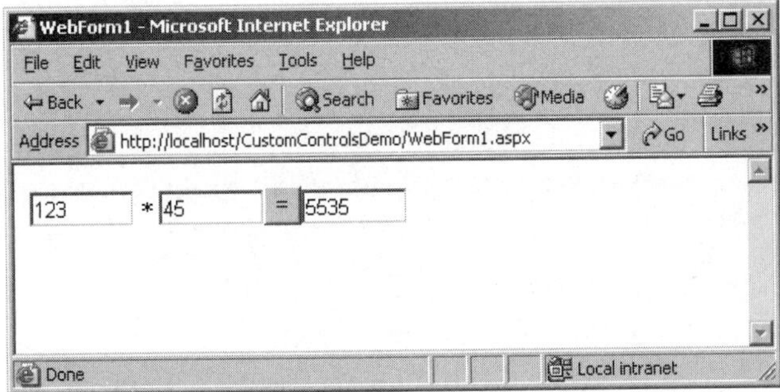

Figure 25-9. The Multiplier composite custom control.

Here's the complete source code of the Multiplier control:

```
Public Class Multiplier
    Inherits System.Web.UI.WebControls.WebControl
    Implements INamingContainer
```

(continued)

```
' These variables hold a reference to child controls.
Dim txtFirst As TextBox
Dim txtSecond As TextBox
Dim txtResult As TextBox
Dim WithEvents btnEval As Button

Sub New()
    MyBase.New()
    Me.Width = Unit.Pixel(200)
End Sub

Protected Overrides Sub CreateChildControls()
    ' Create all child controls.
    txtFirst = New TextBox()
    txtSecond = New TextBox()
    Dim lblAsterisk As New Label()
    btnEval = New Button()
    txtResult = New TextBox()

    ' Set their properties.
    lblAsterisk.Text = " * "
    btnEval.Text = " = "
    txtResult.ReadOnly = True
    ' Establish correct width for text controls.
    AdjustControlWidth()

    ' Add to the Controls collection.
    Controls.Add(txtFirst)
    Controls.Add(lblAsterisk)
    Controls.Add(txtSecond)
    Controls.Add(btnEval)
    Controls.Add(txtResult)
End Sub

Protected Overrides Sub Render(ByVal output As HtmlTextWriter)
    ' Ensure the child controls exist and then render them.
    EnsureChildControls()
    RenderChildren(output)
    ' Adjust their width.
    AdjustControlWidth()
End Sub

' Adjust controls' width.
Private Sub AdjustControlWidth()
    ' Evaluate the space available for the three text boxes.
    Dim w As Unit = Unit.Pixel(CInt(Me.Width.Value - 50) \ 3)
    txtFirst.Width = w
    txtSecond.Width = w
```

```
        txtResult.Width = w
    End Sub

    Private Sub btnEval_Click(ByVal sender As Object, ByVal e As EventArgs) _
        Handles btnEval.Click
        EnsureChildControls()
        Try
            ' Multiply the two numbers.
            Dim res As Double = CDbl(txtFirst.Text) * CDbl(txtSecond.Text)
            txtResult.Text = res.ToString
        Catch
            ' Do nothing if there's an error.
        End Try
    End Sub

    ' The value of the result field
    <Browsable(False)> _
    Property Result() As Double
        Get
            EnsureChildControls()
            Try
                Return CDbl(txtResult.Text)
            Catch
                Return 0
            End Try
        End Get
        Set(ByVal Value As Double)
            EnsureChildControls()
            txtResult.Text = Value.ToString
        End Set
    End Property
End Class
```

Several details in this listing are worth noticing:

- You must create class-level variables for all the controls that you want to later reference in code, and use the WithEvents keyword if you also want to trap events raised by them. All the other controls, typically Literal and Label controls, can be created on the fly in the CreateChildControls method.
- You must invoke the EnsureChildControls method before accessing any control's property to prevent NullReference exceptions being thrown because the object hasn't been created yet.
- Your code inside the Render method must ensure that controls have been created and then call the RenderChildren method, which in turn will call the CreateChildControls method if necessary.

You must arrange the dimension and position of children controls from inside both the CreateChildControls method and the Render method; otherwise, your control won't react to resizing operations inside the Visual Studio designer. For this reason, I've encapsulated the resizing logic in the AdjustControlWidth private procedure, which the code calls from both the CreateChildControls method and the Render method.

Client-Side Script Code

Custom controls can be greatly enhanced with blocks of script code that run on the client machine. For example, all the ASP.NET validation controls take advantage of client-side script blocks. Client-side scripts improve performance and scalability as well because they lessen the workload on the server and make for a better user experience.

Client-side code should be written in JavaScript language, which is the only script language supported by all major browsers, but you can also use VBScript if you know that your application will be seen on Internet Explorer. In general, custom controls that use client-side script code should work correctly even when the end user has disabled client-side scripting. These custom controls usually expose an EnableClientScript property; in most applications, developers will leave this property set to True, but it's useful to test how the control behaves on down-level browsers, such as earlier versions of Internet Explorer.

The example I've prepared to illustrate how you can leverage client-side scripting is a custom control that expands on the Multiplier control you saw in the preceding section. If the browser supports scripting and the programmer has left the EnableClientScript property set to True (its default value), this control performs the multiplication on the client without firing a postback on the server.

HTML and JavaScript Code on the Client

Because the real action occurs on the client in this case, let's see the HTML and script code that the MultiplierEx class has to generate first. Only when it's clear what we need to produce, we'll have a look at the source code of the class. This is the text produced by an HTML form that contains an instance of the MultiplierEx control:

```
<form name="Form1" method="post" action="WebForm1.aspx" id="Form1">
<input type="hidden" name="__VIEWSTATE" value="dDw2MzYwNDk3MTk7Oz4=" />

<script language="javascript"><!--
function MultiplierExecute(txt1, txt2, txt3) {
   var op1 = parseFloat( txt1.value );
   var op2 = parseFloat( txt2.value );
```

```
    txt3.value = (op1 * op2).toString();
  }
-->></script>

<input name="MultiplierEx1:_ctl0" type="text" id="MultiplierEx1__ctl0"
    style="width:82px;" />
<span> * </span>
<input name="MultiplierEx1:_ctl2" type="text" id="MultiplierEx1__ctl2"
    style="width:82px;" />
<input type="button" name="MultiplierEx1__ctl3" value=" = "
    onClick="javascript:MultiplierExecute(MultiplierEx1__ctl0,
    MultiplierEx1__ctl2, MultiplierEx1__ctl4);" />
<input name="MultiplierEx1:_ctl4" type="text" readonly="readonly"
    id="MultiplierEx1__ctl4" style="width:82px;" /></P>
</form>
```

As you see, the key to client-side functionality of the control is the onClick attribute of the button control, which cancels the default submit action and redirects the execution to the MultiplierExecute JavaScript procedure. This procedure receives a reference to the three text fields, so it can multiply the value of the first control by the value of the second control and store the result in the third control. Before you can correctly generate this HTML from inside the MultiplierEx class, you must solve the following problems:

- How do you generate the MultiplierExecute procedure and send it to the browser? How do you ensure that this procedure appears only once in the page, even if the form contains multiple MultiplierEx controls?
- How do you force ASP.NET to generate the id attribute for the three text fields?

The second point is important: without the id attribute, the JavaScript code wouldn't have a valid reference for accessing the controls' values. Unfortunately, you can't use the name attribute that ASP.NET generates for this purpose because the default name attribute string contains a colon, which is an invalid character inside JavaScript variables.

The MultiplierEx Custom Control

Let's see how to address the first issue, the one related to the generation of the client-side code block. The Page class exposes several methods that help developers implement client-side functionality in custom controls. (See Table 25-3.) The Register*xxxx* methods can add pieces of script code in specific positions on the page, and above all they ensure that the same piece of script is sent to the client only once even if there are multiple instances of the same control on the page. Needless to say, you should select a very unlikely name for the key value passed to the first argument, in the hope that no other custom control from a different author uses it.

The best place to output pieces of client-side scripts is in the OnPreRender method. This method is defined in the base Control class and is called by ASP.NET immediately before it calls the Render method of all the controls on the form.

Table 25-3 Members of the Page Class That Are Related to Client-Side Script Generation

Syntax	Description
RegisterClientScriptBlock(key,script)	Emits a block of script code immediately after the <form> tag. It registers the code with a key so that subsequent requests with the same key are ignored.
IsClientScriptBlockRegistered(key)	Returns True if a script block with a given key has been registered for this page.
RegisterStartupScript(key,script)	Emits a block of script code at the bottom of the page so that the elements it references are guaranteed to exist when the script runs.
IsStartupScriptRegistered(key)	Returns True if a script block with a given key has been registered as a start-up script for this page.
RegisterHiddenField(fieldname,initialvalue)	Creates and registers a hidden field on the page. The field is accessible to client script and to server-side code as postback data. (This method is useful when a server control must make a value visible to client scripts.)
RegisterOnSubmitStatement(key,script)	Associates a script code with the onSubmit attribute of the form so that the code runs when the form is submitted. The code can be an inline statement or a call to a script routine registered separately.
RegisterArrayDeclaration(arrayname,value)	Registers the name of a client-side array that will be declared in the page and adds the specified value to the array. (This method is useful when all the instances of a given custom control must be processed together, as is the case with validation controls.)

The design of the MultiplierEx class poses an interesting design problem that comes up regularly when you're attaching client-side script functionality to composite controls. On the one hand, you must override the custom control's Render method to insert the correct value for the onClick attribute of the btnEval constituent control. On the other hand, overriding the Render method means that you give up the convenience offered by composite controls, revert to using the IPostBackDataHandler interface to trap postbacks, manage the state of individual constituent controls manually, and so on.

Fortunately, you can implement custom code generation for a single constituent control—the Button, in our example—while continuing to use the composition technique for all others. The trick is actually simple: instead of instantiating a regular Button object, you create an instance of a custom Button class that you have defined. This custom Button class derives its functionality from the "real" Button but overrides two methods: in the Render method you output the custom <input> tag with a proper onClick attribute, while in the OnPreRender method you emit the code for the MultiplierExecute script routine.

The custom Button class appears as a nested class inside the main MultiplierEx class so that the name Button now refers to the nested custom class instead of the standard Button class in the System.Web.UI.WebControls namespace. This trick enables you to reuse all the code in the main class because the nested Button class shadows the ASP.NET Button class.

Not counting the implementation of the EnableClientScript property, which is just a wrapper around a ViewState collection, the only addition to the main MultiplierEx class is a block of three lines in the CreateChildControls routine (emphasized in boldface in the following listing). These statements ensure that the name attribute that ASP.NET generates for the three text fields is a valid variable name in JavaScript. This can be achieved easily by assigning the ClientID property to the ID property.

```
<ToolboxData("<{0}:MultiplierEx runat=server></{0}:MultiplierEx>")> _
Public Class MultiplierEx
    Inherits System.Web.UI.WebControls.WebControl
    Implements INamingContainer

    ' ...(All variable declarations and procedures as in Multiplier class
    '     except the ones that follow)...

    Protected Overrides Sub CreateChildControls()
        ' Create all child controls.
        txtFirst = New TextBox()
        txtSecond = New TextBox()
        btnEval = New Button()    ' <= It refers to the nested class!!
        txtResult = New TextBox()
        Dim lblAsterisk As New Label()

        ' This is necessary to achieve syntactically correct ID properties.
        txtFirst.ID = txtFirst.ClientID
        txtSecond.ID = txtSecond.ClientID
        txtResult.ID = txtResult.ClientID
```

(continued)

```
    ' ...(The remainder of the procedure as in Multiplier control)...
End Sub

Property EnableClientScript() As Boolean
    Get
        Dim objValue As Object = Me.ViewState("EnableClientScript")
        If objValue Is Nothing Then
            Return True            ' The default value
        Else
            Return CBool(objValue)
        End If
    End Get
    Set(ByVal Value As Boolean)
        Me.ViewState("EnableClientScript") = Value
    End Set
End Property

' The custom Button control

Friend Class ButtonEx
    Inherits System.Web.UI.WebControls.Button

    Protected Overrides Sub Render(ByVal writer As HtmlTextWriter)
        ' If client scripts are disabled, render as usual and exit.
        If Not IsClientScriptEnabled() Then
            MyBase.Render(writer)
            Exit Sub
        End If

        ' Get a reference to the parent control.
        Dim parCtrl As MultiplierEx = DirectCast(Me.Parent, MultiplierEx)
        ' Prepare the code that invokes the script.
        Dim scriptInvoke As String = _
            String.Format("javascript:MultiplierExecute({0},{1},{2});", _
            parCtrl.txtFirst.ClientID, parCtrl.txtSecond.ClientID, _
            parCtrl.txtResult.ClientID)

        ' Output standard attributes plus the onClick attribute.
        writer.AddAttribute("type", "button")
        writer.AddAttribute("name", Me.ClientID)
        writer.AddAttribute("value", Me.Text)
        writer.AddAttribute("onClick", scriptInvoke)
        ' Enclose attributes in <input> tag.
        writer.RenderBeginTag("input")
        writer.RenderEndTag()
    End Sub

    ' Output the client script code if requested.
    Protected Overrides Sub OnPreRender(ByVal e As System.EventArgs)
```

```
            ' Let the base class do what it needs to do.
            MyBase.OnPreRender(e)
            ' Nothing else to do if client scripts are disabled.
            If Not IsClientScriptEnabled() Then Exit Sub

            ' Prepare the script routine.
            Dim s As String
            s &= "<script language=""javascript""><!--{0}" & ControlChars.CrLf
            s &= "function MultiplierExecute(txt1, txt2, txt3) {" & _
                ControlChars.CrLf
            s &= "    var op1 = parseFloat( txt1.value );" & ControlChars.CrLf
            s &= "    var op2 = parseFloat( txt2.value );" & ControlChars.CrLf
            s &= "    txt3.value = (op1 * op2).toString(); " & _
                ControlChars.CrLf
            s &= "    }" & ControlChars.CrLf
            s &= "--></script>" & ControlChars.CrLf
            ' Register the script on the page.
            Page.RegisterClientScriptBlock("MultiplierExecute", s)
        End Sub

        ' Return True if client script support is requested and possible.
        Private Function IsClientScriptEnabled() As Boolean
            ' We need a Try block because accessing the Browser
            ' property at design time may throw an exception.
            Try
                ' Return False if DOM version is too low.
                If Page.Request.Browser.W3CDomVersion.Major < 1 Then
                    Return False
                End If

                ' Return False if EcmaScript version is too low.
                If Page.Request.Browser.EcmaScriptVersion.CompareTo( _
                    New Version(1, 2)) < 0 Then
                    Return False
                End If

                ' If all tests passed, return the EnableClientScript property
                ' of the parent MultiplierEx control
                Dim parCtrl As MultiplierEx = DirectCast(Me.Parent,
                    MultiplierEx)
                IsClientScriptEnabled = parCtrl.EnableClientScript
            Catch
                ' Return False if any error occurs.
                Return False
            End Try
        End Function

    End Class                      ' ButtonEx class

End Class                          ' MultiplierEx class
```

Because it's a nested class, the custom Button class is able to access Private variables in its container class, which it must do to read the ClientID property of the txtFirst, txtSecond, and txtResult controls.

You can use the IsClientScriptEnabled auxiliary to decide whether the client-side script code should be emitted or not. For example, you must not output script code when the control is running inside the designer, when the request comes from a browser that doesn't support scripting, and of course when the developer using your control has turned the EnableClientScript property to False. You can easily reuse this code in all your controls that rely on client-side scripting.

Client-side script programming is a complex topic, and I have just scratched the surface here. For example, you can use the Page.Request.Browser object to test specific browser features and generate HTML and the client-side script code that take advantage of these features. You can perform very sophisticated validation chores right in the browser to increase your site's scalability even more. You can take advantage of Dynamic HTML to do eye-catching animations. You can open secondary windows for showing help messages or subforms, and so on.

You now know enough to create valuable user and custom controls, and it's time to move on to the last chapter of this book: XML Web services, where we'll apply many of the concepts learned in the past two chapters. We can do this because XML Web services are just a different kind of ASP.NET application, as you'll see in a moment.

26

XML Web Services

As you might remember from Chapter 1, an XML Web service is a .NET component that replies to HTTP requests that are formatted using the SOAP syntax. XML Web services are one of the cornerstones of the .NET initiative in that they allow a degree of interoperability among applications over the Internet that was inconceivable before.

Given the importance of XML Web services, you might be surprised by the relatively little space devoted to them in this book. The explanation is simple, however: XML Web services leverage many features of the .NET Framework that I've already covered in depth in previous chapters. First and foremost, XML Web services are just ASP.NET applications—more precisely, they're implemented as HTTP handlers that intercept requests for .asmx files—so you can apply most of what you've learned in Chapter 24, including state management, output caching, and authentication. You'll also see that you can create better XML Web services by applying your knowledge of XML serialization from Chapter 11 and of asynchronous operations from Chapter 13.

Note To keep the code as concise as possible, all the code samples in this chapter assume that you have added the following Imports statements at the top of your source files:

```
Imports System.Web.Services
Imports System.Web.Services.Protocols
Imports System.Net
Imports System.Threading
Imports System.Web.Security
Imports System.IO
```

Introduction to XML Web Services

Instead of illustrating the XML Web service theory first, I'll start by showing you how to create a simple XML Web service and access it from a Visual Basic .NET program. As with any other .NET application, you can build an XML Web service by using Notepad and the command-line tools provided with the .NET Framework. However, Visual Studio .NET makes everything so easy that it's difficult to resist the temptation to use it exclusively. In the following sections, I'll show how to create a simple XML Web service for converting from dollar to euro currencies and back. (To keep things simple, I hard coded the conversion rate in code.)

Building the XML Web Service Project

Launch Visual Studio and create a new ASP.NET Web Service project named MoneyConverter, as shown in Figure 26-1. Visual Studio creates a subdirectory under IIS's main directory and names it after your project, exactly as it does when you create an ASP.NET Web Forms project. Like Web Forms applications, the new project contains its own web.config and global.asax files. It also includes two files that can't be found in Web Forms projects, however: MoneyConverter.vsdisco and Service1.asmx. For now, let's focus on the latter file.

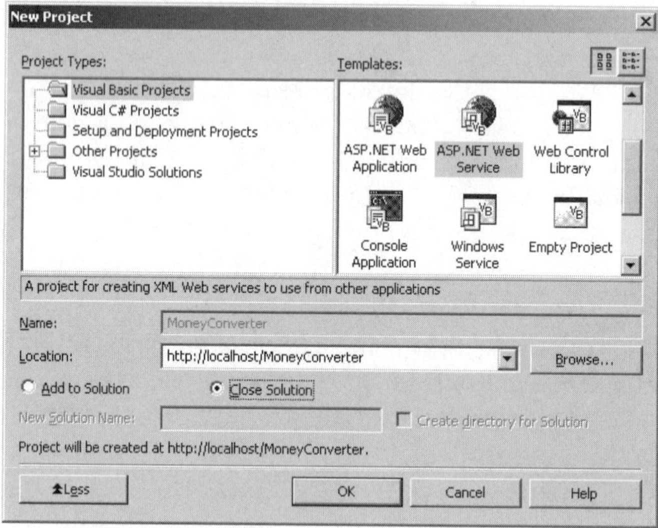

Figure 26-1. Creating an ASP.NET Web Service project.

The Service1.asmx file contains the code of your XML Web service that—once again—is just a .NET component that's accessed through the Internet via HTTP. Before continuing with our example, you should give this file a more descriptive name, such as Converter.asmx. Because an .asmx page is usually accessed programmatically, renaming it isn't as important as for an .aspx page, but it's good to keep your files sorted anyway.

Like Web Forms files, .asmx files each have a designer's surface on which you can drop .NET components. Because an XML Web service doesn't have a user interface, you'll use this feature only for nonvisual components, such as ADO.NET connections or FileSystemWatcher objects. Next, press the F7 key and switch to the code editor: as you see, Visual Studio has already created for us a working XML Web service class named Service1, with a sample HelloWorld method ready to be uncommented.

Let's rename the class Converter to keep it in sync with the filename, and let's add two methods that convert currencies, patterned after the commented sample procedure. Following is the source code of our first XML Web service. To save space, I omitted the automatically generated code in the #Region block:

```
<WebService(Description:="A web service for converting currencies",
    Namespace:="http://tempuri.org/") > _
Public Class Converter
    Inherits System.Web.Services.WebService

#Region " Web Services Designer Generated Code "
    ⋮
#End Region

    <WebMethod(Description:="Convert from Euro to Dollar currency")> _
    Function EuroToDollar(ByVal amount As Decimal) As Decimal
        Return amount * GetEuroToDollarConversionRate()
    End Function

    <WebMethod(Description:="Convert from Dollar to Euro currency")> _
    Function DollarToEuro(ByVal amount As Decimal) As Decimal
        Return amount / GetEuroToDollarConversionRate()
    End Function

    Private Function GetEuroToDollarConversionRate() As Decimal
        ' A real application would read this number from a file or a database.
        Return 0.9@
    End Function
End Class
```

The actual code for the two worker methods is so simple that I won't comment it. Instead, I want to draw your attention to the attributes used in the preceding listing:

- The WebService attribute qualifies the Converter class as an XML Web service class. This attribute isn't really required because the .asmx file extension and the fact that the Converter class inherits from System.Web.Services.WebService is enough to inform the ASP.NET infrastructure that we're building an XML Web service. However, the WebService attribute is useful for passing additional information about the XML Web service, such as its description and namespace, and in practice you should never omit it.
- The WebMethod attribute makes a method of the class accessible through the Internet. Only methods marked with this attribute are seen from remote clients, so you can't omit it. You can use this attribute to associate a description with the method and to define other important properties, such as session-state support and caching. (See the section "The WebMethod Attribute" later in this chapter.)

Testing the XML Web Service Within the Browser

The simplest way to test the XML Web service that you've just created is by running the project, after ensuring that Converter.asmx is defined as its start page. Visual Studio will then launch a new instance of Microsoft Internet Explorer and have it point to the .asmx page. Figure 26-2 shows what you see in the browser. The title of the page is the name of the class, and the description property of the WebService attribute appears immediately below it, followed by the list of all available methods and their descriptions.

Where does this information come from? When ASP.NET intercepts a request for an .asmx page without anything on the query string, it uses reflection to extract the attributes and the method names of the first class in the .asmx file, and then it synthesizes this HTML page for you. (If the file contains multiple classes deriving from System.Web.Services.WebService, only the first class is visible in the browser.) In a real application, clients access the service programmatically, but this nice feature lets you test the service interactively during the debugging phase.

The page that produces the output you've seen is nothing but an .aspx page. More precisely, it's the DefaultWsdlHelpGenerator.aspx file stored in the C:\WinNT\Microsoft.NET\Framework\v*x.y.zzzz*\Config directory. Because it's a standard .aspx page, you can customize it if you want. You could add your own company logo, for example, or use it to hide information about your XML Web services. You can also modify a few constants defined near the top of this page to enable debugging mode or other features.

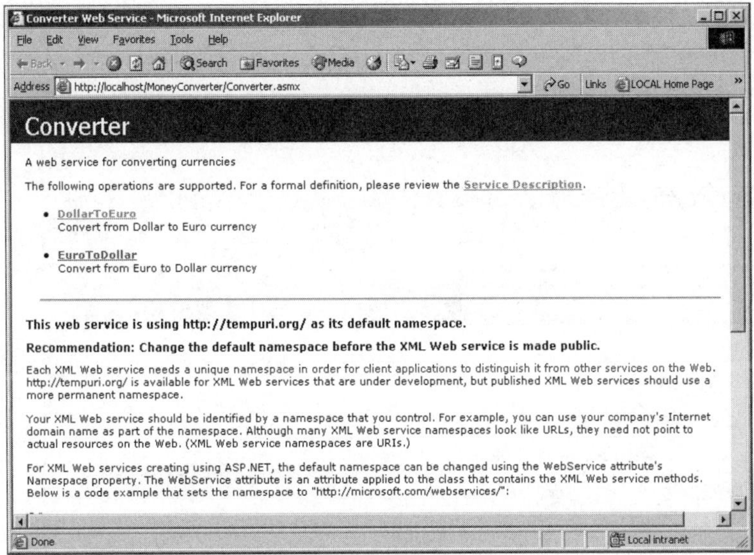

Figure 26-2. The HTML page that ASP.NET creates on the fly when accessing an .asmx file without passing any parameters.

Changing the DefaultWsdlHelpGenerator.aspx file affects all the XML Web services running on the machine. For a more granular control of which page should be used, you can add a <wsdlHelpGenerator> tag to the web.config file in your application's root directory or in the directory that contains the .asmx file:

```
<configuration>
   <system.web>
      <webServices>
         <wsdlHelpGenerator href="LocalWsdlHelpGenerator.aspx" />
      </webServices>
   </system.web>
</configuration>
```

The standard help page offers more than just a description of the XML Web service and its methods: it also lets you interactively call individual methods and pass them all the required attributes. Not all methods can be tested in this way—for example, you can't test methods that take object or ByRef arguments—but it's surely a great bonus when you're testing the service.

Figure 26-3 shows the page that appears when you click on a method's name (DollarToEuro, in this example). You can enter any value in the Amount box and click the Invoke button. The return value from the method is displayed as XML inside a new instance of Internet Explorer. (See Figure 26-4.) Notice that the URL used to get the result is in the following format:

```
http://servername/webservicename/pagename.asmx/methodname?arg=value
```

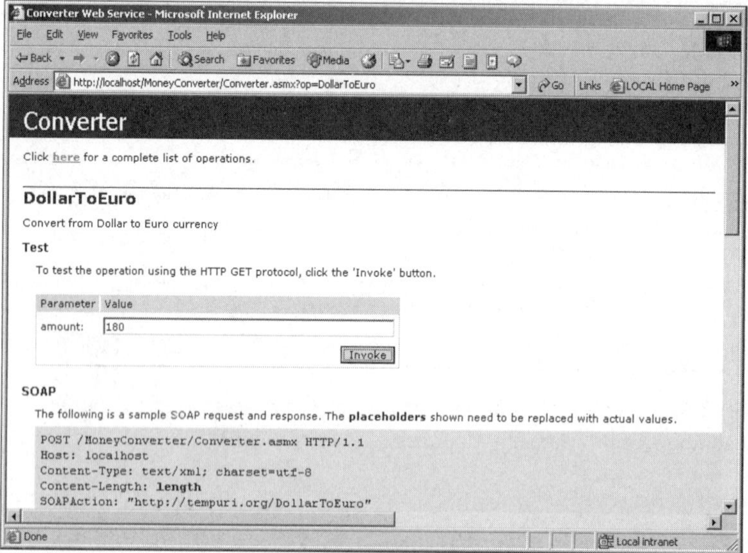

Figure 26-3. You can invoke an XML Web service method from inside the browser.

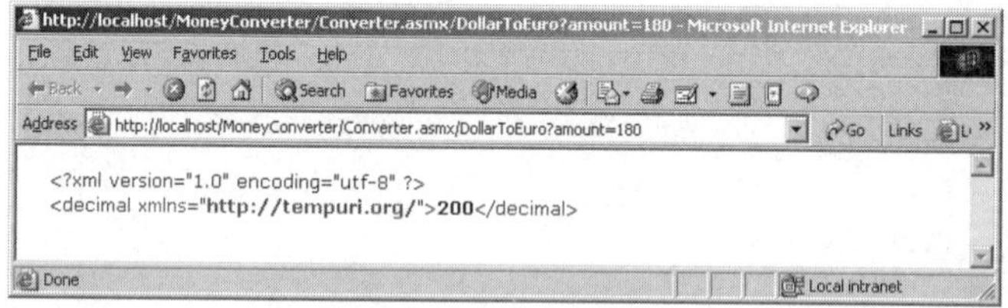

Figure 26-4. The return value from an XML Web service method is formatted as XML.

Any remote client that knows where to look for this XML Web service and what arguments to pass can call a method remotely by posting an HTTP GET request. As you'll learn later in this chapter, this is just one of the three protocols you can use to query an XML Web service through the Internet, the other two being HTTP POST and SOAP.

The main XML Web service help page contains one more link of interest. If you click on the Service Description link, the browser displays the Web Service Description Language (WSDL) contract. This is an XML file that describes the XML Web service you've just created, with information about each method and the arguments it expects. You can browse the WSDL contract for an .asmx page directly from the browser by appending the ?WSDL argument to the .asmx page's URL.

Although XML Web services rely heavily on WSDL files, most of the time you don't have to worry about them and the information they contain because Visual Studio .NET can handle these files transparently.

Creating an XML Web Service Client

Now that you know that the MoneyConverter XML Web service works correctly from inside a browser, let's see how to create a client application that uses it. Any application that can post an HTTP request can be a client of the XML Web service, and it doesn't need to be a .NET application or even a Windows application. If we limit our attention to managed applications only, typically an XML Web service client is one of the following application types: a Windows Forms application, a Web Forms application, or another XML Web service application. In the following steps, I'll show how to create a Windows Forms client, but keep in mind that the procedure to follow is the same when you're creating other types of clients.

1. Add a Windows Forms project to the current solution, name it MoneyConverterClient, and make it the start-up project of the solution.

2. Select the Add Web Reference command from the Project menu or from the shortcut menu that you open by right-clicking the project's node in the Solution Explorer.

3. The dialog box that appears lets you select a Web service from among those registered in a Universal Description, Discovery, and Integration (UDDI) directory. (See Figure 26-5.) UDDI directories are a bit like the Web services' yellow pages in that they list XML Web services distributed across the Internet. (Visit *http://www.uddi.org* for more information about UDDI.)

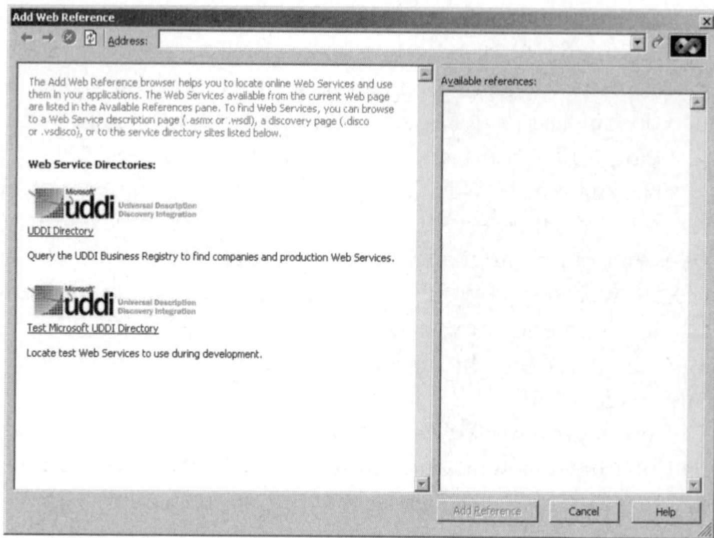

Figure 26-5. The Add Web Reference dialog box.

4. Type the path to the .asmx file on the local machine—that is, http://localhost/MoneyConverter/converter.asmx—in the Address box, and press the Enter key. If you entered the path correctly, the left pane will display the description page associated with the XML Web service. (See Figure 26-6.)

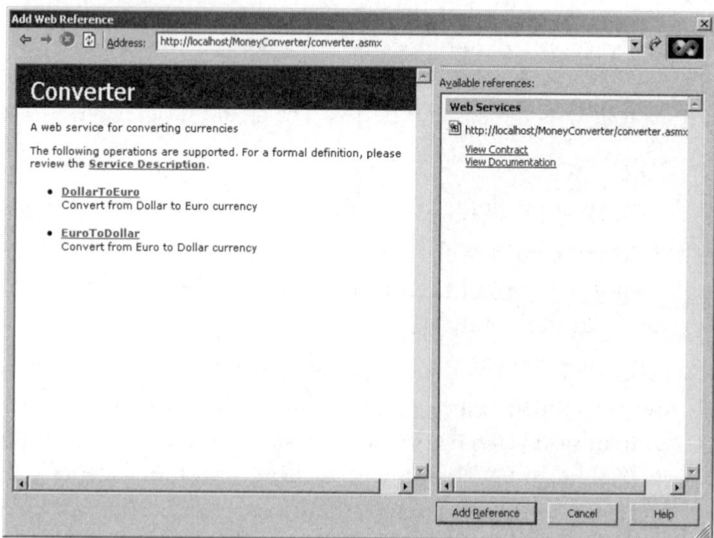

Figure 26-6. Entering the address of an .asmx page enables the Add Reference button.

5. The right pane contains additional links to view the WSDL contract and the default help page. Because you already know that your XML Web service works correctly, you can proceed to click the Add Reference button.

Visual Studio adds a new Web References folder to the project, with a localhost node that gathers all the files that Visual Studio has created or downloaded from the XML Web service—for example, the WSDL contract file. The most important file, from the perspective of the client application, is the Reference.vb file. (You must click the Show All Files button in the Solution Explorer, expand Web References, Localhost, and Reference.map to access this file.) This file contains a Converter class that exposes the same methods as the original XML Web services (and a few additional ones) and that works as a proxy between the Windows Forms application and the XML Web service running somewhere in the Internet. (See Figure 26-7.) Instead of sending the HTTP requests directly to the XML Web service, the client application invokes the methods of this proxy class, and the proxy class routes the call to the XML Web service through the HTTP protocol.

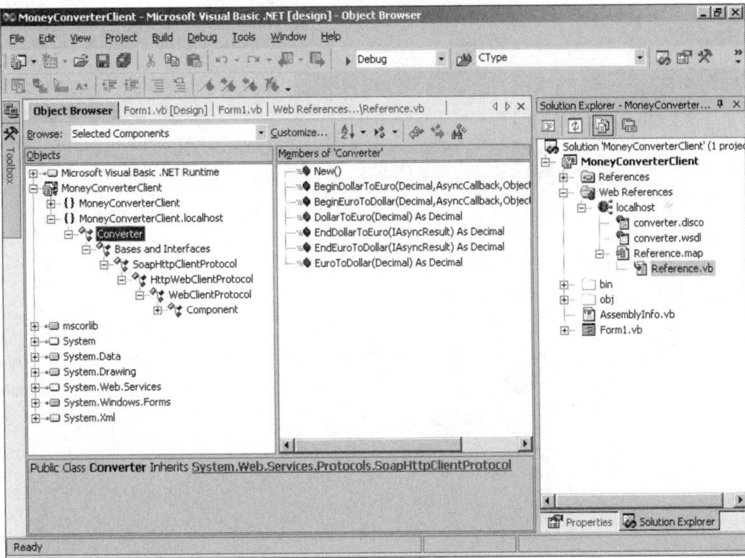

Figure 26-7. How a Web reference appears in the Solution Explorer and in the Object Browser.

As often happens in the .NET world, this little magic is made possible by inheritance. The Converter proxy class inherits many of its methods from the System.Web.Services.Protocols.SoapHttpClientProtocol base class. The most important of these inherited methods is Invoke, which performs a sort of late-bound call to the remote XML Web service class. The class that Visual Studio has generated automatically contains wrapper procedures that allow the client application to call remote methods using a strongly typed syntax:

```
' ...(From inside the Converter class in Reference.vb file)...

Public Function EuroToDollar(ByVal amount As Decimal) As Decimal
    Dim results() As Object = Me.Invoke("EuroToDollar", New Object() {amount})
    Return CType(results(0), Decimal)
End Function
```

Once you understand how the mechanism works, invoking the XML Web service is just a matter of creating an instance of the proxy class and calling one of its methods, without worrying about what happens behind the scenes. Figure 26-8 shows a simple form that lets you convert dollars to euros and back. This is the code behind the two push buttons:

```
Private Sub btnToEuros_Click(ByVal sender As Object, ByVal e As EventArgs) _
    Handles btnToEuros.Click
    Dim conv As New localhost.Converter()           ' Create the proxy.
    Dim value As Decimal = CDec(txtDollars.Text)    ' Get the argument.
    Dim result As Decimal = conv.DollarToEuro(value) ' Call the remote method.
    txtEuros.Text = result.ToString                 ' Display the result.
End Sub

Private Sub btnToDollars_Click(ByVal sender As Object, ByVal e As EventArgs) _
    Handles btnToDollars.Click
    Dim conv As New localhost.Converter()           ' Create the proxy.
    Dim value As Decimal = CDec(txtEuros.Text)      ' Get the argument.
    Dim result As Decimal = conv.EuroToDollar(value) ' Call the remote method.
    txtDollars.Text = result.ToString               ' Display the result.
End Sub
```

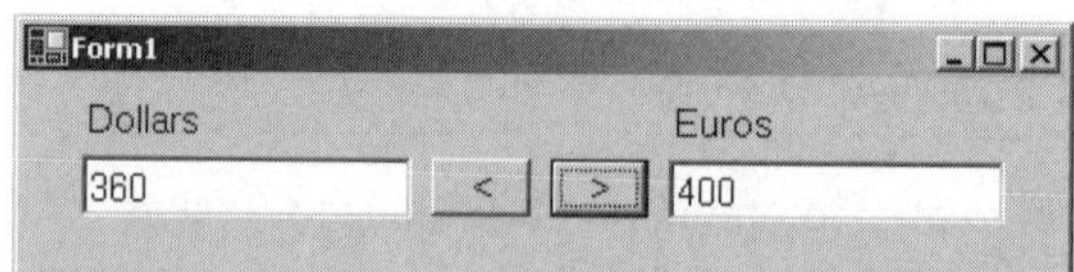

Figure 26-8. The demo client application.

> **Note** During the test phase, you'll often change the structure of the XML Web service class—for example, by adding new methods or changing the signature of existing ones. After any change to the class interface, you should rebuild the proxy class in the client project. The easiest way to do this is with the Update Web Reference command on the shortcut menu of the individual reference (localhost, if you haven't renamed it) in the Web References folder of the Solution Explorer window.

XML Web Services Protocols

As I mentioned earlier, XML Web services built with ASP.NET automatically support three protocols: HTTP GET, HTTP POST, and SOAP. In practice, however, you'll use the SOAP protocol in virtually all your applications, and you should consider the other two as helper protocols that let you test the XML Web service from the browser or invoke its methods from legacy ASP applications. The help page that ASP.NET creates on the fly for XML Web services contains information about how data is sent to and returned from an XML Web service using these three protocols. (See Figure 26-3.)

The HTTP GET Protocol

You invoke an XML Web service using the HTTP GET protocol by passing all arguments on the query string, as Figure 26-4 shows. When you invoke the DollarToEuro method through the HTTP GET method, this is the text sent to the .asmx page:

```
GET /MoneyConverter/Converter.asmx/DollarToEuro?amount=180 HTTP/1.1
Host: localhost
```

and this is what is returned to the caller:

```
HTTP/1.1 200 OK
Content-Type: text/xml; charset=utf-8
Content-Length: 94

<?xml version="1.0" encoding="utf-8"?>
<decimal xmlns="http://www.vb2themax.com/">200</decimal>
```

The HTTP GET protocol prevents you from passing structures and objects as arguments; it won't let you pass ByRef arguments either, even though it's legal to return an object (provided that it can be serialized to XML). In addition, you must encode arguments that contain special characters, such as the = symbol. On the plus side, you can easily access an XML Web service via HTTP GET even from legacy applications, such as those written in Visual Basic 6 or classic ASP. For example, the following Visual Basic 6 routine uses the MSXML component to provide a wrapper around the DollarToEuro method:

```
' A Visual Basic 6 routine
' NOTE: requires a reference to the Microsoft XML v3.0 type library.

Function ConvertDollarToEuro(ByVal amount As Currency) As Currency
    ' This is the XML Web service's URL.
    Const url As String = "http://localhost/MoneyConverter/Converter.asmx/" _
        & "DollarToEuro?amount="

    Dim httpReq As New MSXML2.XMLHTTP30
    ' Append the argument to the query string, and make a synchronous request.
    httpReq.open "GET", url & CStr(amount), False
    ' Send the HTTP GET request.
    httpReq.send

    ' Read the returned XML text.
    Dim xmlResp As MSXML2.DOMDocument30
    Set xmlResp = httpReq.responseXML
    ' The returned result is the Text of the main document XML element.
    ConvertDollarToEuro = CCur(xmlResp.documentElement.Text)
End Function
```

You can also convert this code to VBScript and call it from ASP. This is so easy that I'll leave it to you as an exercise.

The HTTP POST Protocol

The HTTP POST protocol is similar to the HTTP GET protocol. The main difference between them is that arguments in the HTTP POST protocol are passed in the HTTP body instead of the query string. As with the HTTP GET protocol, you can't pass ByRef arguments, structures, or objects with the HTTP POST protocol, and in practice you should consider this protocol only when invoking the XML Web service from a legacy application. The following is an example of a call to the DollarToEuro method through the HTTP POST protocol:

```
POST /MoneyConverter/Converter.asmx/DollarToEuro HTTP/1.1
Host: localhost
Content-Type: application/x-www-form-urlencoded
Content-Length: 13

amount=string
```

I don't show the text returned to the client because it's the same as when you're using the HTTP GET protocol. Like the HTTP GET protocol, you can call a method that returns a serializable object by means of the HTTP POST protocol.

The SOAP Protocol

The majority of real-world XML Web services should use the SOAP protocol, which employs SOAP messages for both the input arguments and for the return value. The SOAP protocol doesn't have any of the limitations you saw for the HTTP GET and POST protocols.

The root node of any SOAP message is the message envelope, which contains the message body; in turn, the body contains an XML tag named after the target method, and all arguments are sent inside this block. For example, this is the text sent to the XML Web service when the DollarToEuro method is invoked through the SOAP protocol:

```
POST /MoneyConverter/Converter.asmx HTTP/1.1
Host: localhost
Content-Type: text/xml; charset=utf-8
Content-Length: 341
SOAPAction: "http://tempuri.org/DollarToEuro"

<?xml version="1.0" encoding="utf-8"?>
<soap:Envelope xmlns:xsi="http://www.w3.org/2001/XMLSchema-instance"
    xmlns:xsd="http://www.w3.org/2001/XMLSchema"
    xmlns:soap="http://schemas.xmlsoap.org/soap/envelope/">
  <soap:Body>
    <DollarToEuro xmlns="http://tempuri.org/">
      <amount>180</amount>
    </DollarToEuro>
  </soap:Body>
</soap:Envelope>
```

The text returned from the method is another SOAP message with its own envelope and body blocks. In this case, however, the body contains a tag named *MethodName*Response, which in turn contains a nested tag named *MethodName*Result, whose text is the return value:

```
HTTP/1.1 200 OK
Content-Type: text/xml; charset=utf-8
Content-Length: 381

<?xml version="1.0" encoding="utf-8"?>
<soap:Envelope xmlns:xsi="http://www.w3.org/2001/XMLSchema-instance"
    xmlns:xsd="http://www.w3.org/2001/XMLSchema"
    xmlns:soap="http://schemas.xmlsoap.org/soap/envelope/">
  <soap:Body>
```

(continued)

```
    <DollarToEuroResponse xmlns="http://tempuri.org/">
      <DollarToEuroResult>200</DollarToEuroResult>
    </DollarToEuroResponse>
  </soap:Body>
</soap:Envelope>
```

Any SOAP message can contain an optional header, which might contain additional information not strictly related to the method being called. For example, a client might use the header to send its credentials so that the XML Web service can record who accessed its methods and when. The body of a SOAP message can be replaced by a <soap:Fault> section if the message is carrying error information, such as when you call a method with the wrong number of arguments or when the code in the method has thrown an exception.

SOAP is the only protocol that supports objects and structures as arguments. The only requirement for an object fed to or returned from an XML Web service is that it must be serializable. In addition, only the SOAP protocol supports output arguments. In other words, if the method takes one or more ByRef arguments, you can invoke that method only by using the SOAP protocol. You can easily prove this point by changing the DollarToEuro method's signature and replacing the ByVal keyword with ByRef. If you visit the help page that shows the syntax supported by this method, you'll see that only the SOAP protocol is mentioned.

> **Note** The remainder of this chapter focuses only on SOAP-based XML Web services.

Enabling Protocols in Configuration Files

By default, .NET XML Web services support all three protocols. However, you can disable one or more of them by editing the machine.config file or a local web.config file in the scope of the .asmx file that you want to control. The default machine.config file contains the following section, which enables all three protocols and allows an XML Web service to automatically document itself in the browser:

```
<configuration>
  <system.web>
    <webServices>
      <protocols>
        <add name="HttpSoap" />
        <add name="HttpPost" />
        <add name="HttpGet" />
```

```
        <add name="Documentation" />
      </protocols>
    </webServices>
  </system.web>
</configuration>
```

In a production XML Web service, you might decide to drop all the <add> tags except the one that defines support for the SOAP protocol and possibly the one that enables the automatic generation of the documentation.

Building XML Web Services Without Visual Studio

As you know, everything you need to leverage the power of the .NET Framework is provided with the .NET SDK, and that includes what you need to create XML Web services. Even though you're going to use Visual Studio for most of your development work, it's good to know how to create XML Web services with Notepad and the command line utilities installed with .NET. If nothing else, you'll appreciate even more what Visual Studio does for you behind the scenes.

In this section, you'll also learn how to create a .disco file, which allows remote clients to discover all the XML Web services that the local computer hosts. This is an operation that you need to perform whether or not you create your XML Web services using Visual Studio.

Creating the .asmx File

The first step in building an XML Web service from scratch is entering the XML Web service source code using any editor, including Notepad. Like .aspx pages, .asmx files are compiled on the fly the very first time a client posts a request for them. ASP.NET supports code-behind classes for .asmx files too. When you're writing an .asmx file with a text editor, you should add an @WebService directive whose attributes indicate the name of the class and the language used. Here's a simple MathService class that contains two methods for adding and subtracting integers:

```
<%@ WebService Language="VB" Class="MathService" %>

Imports System
Imports System.Web.Services

< WebService (Description:="Yet another math web service", _
    Namespace:="www.vb2themax.com")> _
Public Class MathService
    Inherits WebService

    <WebMethod (Description:="Add two Integers")> _
```

(continued)

```
    Public Function Add(ByVal n1 As Integer, ByVal n2 As Integer) _
        As Integer
        Return n1 + n2
    End Function

    <WebMethod (Description:="Subtract two Integers")> _
    Public Function Subtract(ByVal n1 As Integer, ByVal n2 As Integer) _
        As Integer
        Return n1 - n2
    End Function
End Class
```

You can save the preceding code in the MathService.asmx file in IIS's root directory and then navigate to it by using your browser. Figure 26-9 shows the usual help page, from which you can test both methods. If you compare this figure with Figure 26-2, you can see that the warning about the default namespace (tempuri.org) has been suppressed because the .asmx page contains a namespace that ensures that its classes have a unique name on the Internet. For example, you might use your company's Web site address in the Namespace attribute.

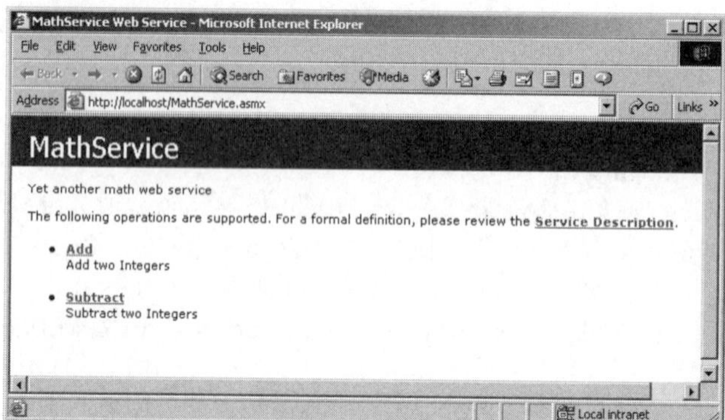

Figure 26-9. The help page omits the warning if the XML Web service uses a specific namespace.

You can also browse the WSDL contract by appending ?wsdl to the query string, as in this code snippet:

```
http://localhost/MathService.asmx?wsdl
```

Enabling XML Web Service Discovery

If you've built a cool Web service, you probably want to let other people access it. A programmer can easily download the .wsdl file containing the contract by appending ?wsdl to the XML Web service's URL, or she can follow the procedure outlined in the previous section "Creating an XML Web Service Client." But what if the programmer doesn't know the exact URL of your XML Web service? This is where XML Web service discovery comes into play.

Discovery lets you determine the URL through which you can find one or more XML Web services located on a specific server or spread over the Internet. There are several types of discovery, including these:

- **Static discovery** You create a .disco XML file that lists all the XML Web services available on the local machine and save it in the root directory of your Web server.
- **Dynamic discovery** You create an XML file named default.vsdisco and save it in the root directory of your Web server. This file enables remote clients to discover all the XML Web services installed on the machine, but you can list a series of subdirectories that shouldn't be searched when someone is doing dynamic discovery. For security reasons, you should never enable dynamic discovery on production servers, and use it on nonproduction servers exclusively.
- **Universal Description, Discovery, and Integration (UDDI)** As I explained in the section "Creating an XML Web Service Client," UDDI offers a standard way to expose information about Web services located anywhere on the Internet.

In this section, I'll focus on static discovery exclusively. You can read more about dynamic discovery in the Visual Studio .NET documentation. You can read a detailed description of UDDI at *www.uddi.org*.

Each XML Web service project should have a companion .disco file that describes where its help page and its .wsdl contract file are. As you know, ASP.NET creates a standard help page on the fly when you navigate to the .asmx file, and it can manufacture a WSDL contract by simply appending ?wsdl to the .asmx file's URL. Sometimes, however, you might want to create a custom .htm file that explains how to use your XML Web service and a static .wsdl file that contains its WSDL contract. In this case, you need to create a .disco file.

You can see what a standard .disco file looks like by asking ASP.NET to create one on the fly, which you do by appending ?disco to an .asmx file's URL:

```
http://localhost/MathService.asmx?disco
```

This is what appears in the browser:

```
<?xml version="1.0" encoding="utf-8" ?>
<discovery xmlns:xsd="http://www.w3.org/2001/XMLSchema"
           xmlns:xsi="http://www.w3.org/2001/XMLSchema-instance"
           xmlns="http://schemas.xmlsoap.org/disco/">
  <contractRef ref="http://localhost/mathservice.asmx?wsdl"
               docRef="http://localhost/mathservice.asmx"
               xmlns="http://schemas.xmlsoap.org/disco/scl/" />
  <soap address="http://localhost/mathservice.asmx"
        xmlns:q1="www.vb2themax.com" binding="q1:MathServiceSoap"
        xmlns="http://schemas.xmlsoap.org/disco/soap/" />
</discovery>
```

The ref attribute in the <contractRef> tag specifies where the .wsdl contract is, and the docRef attribute specifies where human beings can read a description of your XML Web service, so you can improve your site's performance by having these attributes point to physical files that you've prepared instead of forcing ASP.NET to build them dynamically at each request.

Now you're ready to create a master .disco file that describes all the XML Web services available on this Web server (only one so far). By convention, this file is named default.disco. It contains a <disco:discovery> root element, which contains one or more pairs of <discoveryRef> and <contractRef> tags that, taken together, point to all the .disco, .wsdl, and help pages of all the XML Web services available on the local machine. For example, this might be the default.disco file that describes the two XML Web services that we've created so far:

```
<?xml version="1.0" ?>
<disco:discovery xmlns:disco="http://schemas.xmlsoap.org/disco/">
  <discoveryRef ref="/MathService.asmx?disco" />
  <contractRef ref="http:/MathService.asmx?WSDL"
               docRef="/MathService.asmx"
               xmlns="http://schemas.xmlsoap.org/disco/scl/" />
  <discoveryRef ref="/MoneyConverter/Converter.asmx?disco" />
  <contractRef ref="http:/MoneyConverter/converter.asmx?WSDL"
               docRef="ConverterService.htm"
               xmlns="http://schemas.xmlsoap.org/disco/scl/" />
</disco:discovery>
```

You should save the default.disco file in the Web server's root directory so that anyone can download it. For example, you can now see both the MathService and the MoneyConverter XML Web services when you enter the URL *http://localhost/default.disco* in Visual Studio's Add Web Reference dialog box. (See Figure 26-10.)

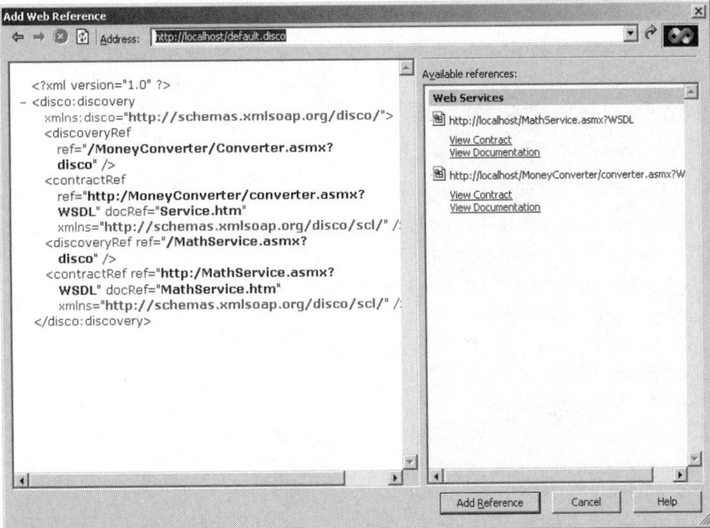

Figure 26-10. The default.disco file lets you view the contract and documentation of all the XML Web services that you want to expose to the outside world.

You can do one more thing to help developers locate and use your default.disco file: you can make it the default file for your Web server. You can achieve this by bringing up the Documents page of the IIS's Default Web Site Properties dialog box and clicking the Add button to add a new default document. (See Figure 26-11.) If default.disco is the default document for the Web server, you can list all the XML Web services from inside the Add Web Reference dialog box by simply typing **http://localhost**.

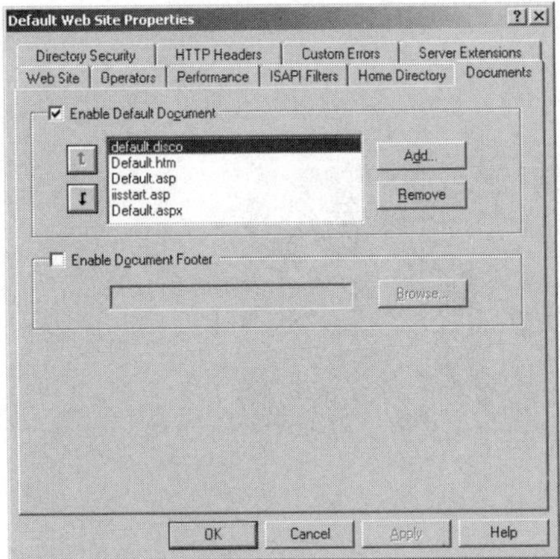

Figure 26-11. You can make default.disco the default document for your Web server.

In many cases, however, a Web server hosts both a regular Web site (that outputs HTML text) and one or more XML Web services, so you can't simply make default.disco the default document for the entire site because it would be the document that visitors would receive when they typed the URL of your site in their browsers. The solution to this problem is simple, however: you must embed a special <link> tag inside your .htm or .aspx file, as follows:

```
<HTML>
  <HEAD>
    <LINK TYPE='text/xml' REL='alternate' HREF='default.disco'/>
  </HEAD>
<BODY>
  Welcome to my default page.
</BODY>
</HTML>
```

Using the Disco Utility

In the preceding section, I described how you can create a .disco file and use it to discover all the available XML Web services on the local machine from inside Visual Studio. However, as you know, everything you do from inside Visual Studio can also be done by using the utilities that the .NET Framework provides.

In the next step, you use the disco.exe utility to discover (hence the name) any XML Web service registered at a given URL. The following command discovers XML Web services on the local machine, but you can also use this utility for remote servers:

```
DISCO http://localhost/default.disco
```

(If default.disco is the default document for the Web site, you can omit it and just type the URL of the site.) If the discovery process is successful, the Disco utility downloads the .disco file and all the .wsdl files pointed to by the .disco file and creates a results.discomap file that holds the links to each of these files. (See Figure 26-12.)

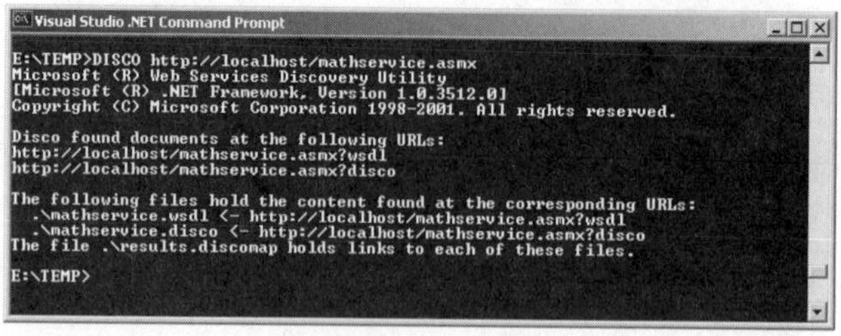

```
Visual Studio .NET Command Prompt

E:\TEMP>DISCO http://localhost/mathservice.asmx
Microsoft (R) Web Services Discovery Utility
[Microsoft (R) .NET Framework, Version 1.0.3512.0]
Copyright (C) Microsoft Corporation 1998-2001. All rights reserved.

Disco found documents at the following URLs:
http://localhost/mathservice.asmx?wsdl
http://localhost/mathservice.asmx?disco

The following files hold the content found at the corresponding URLs:
  .\mathservice.wsdl <- http://localhost/mathservice.asmx?wsdl
  .\mathservice.disco <- http://localhost/mathservice.asmx?disco
The file .\results.discomap holds links to each of these files.

E:\TEMP>
```

Figure 26-12. Using the Disco utility.

Other command line switches let you save the downloaded files in a different directory, or access Web servers that require authentication. (Type

Disco /? for a complete list of available options.) You can also create the .wsdl file of an XML Web service by passing its complete URL as an argument to the disco utility:

```
DISCO http://localhost/MathService.asmx
```

As you'll see in a moment, the .wsdl file is essential to creating the client proxy class.

Using the Wsdl Utility

Once you have a .wsdl file that contains the description of the XML Web service class and its methods, you can use the Wsdl.exe utility to generate the source code for the proxy class that clients can use to access the remote XML Web service. The syntax of the Wsdl utility is simple:

```
WSDL MathService.wsdl /l:vb
```

where the /l switch specifies the language to be used for the proxy class. (If omitted, it defaults to C#.) Unless you use the /out switch to change the destination file, the Wsdl utility creates a .vb or .cs file with the same name as the .wsdl file (MathService.vb in this example). The .vb class created by the preceding command is exactly the same class that you generate using the Add Web Reference command from inside Visual Studio.

The Wsdl utility has one additional feature that doesn't correspond to any Visual Studio command. If you pass the /server switch, the Wsdl utility creates a MustInherit class that has the same methods as the original XML Web service class instead of creating the client proxy class:

```
WSDL MathService.wsdl /l:vb /server /out:BaseClass.vb
```

Here are the contents of the BaseClass.vb file, after stripping down all comments and superfluous attributes:

```
Public MustInherit Class MathService
    Inherits System.Web.Services.WebService

    <System.Web.Services.WebMethodAttribute()> _
    Public MustOverride Function Add(ByVal n1 As Integer, _
        ByVal n2 As Integer) As Integer

    <System.Web.Services.WebMethodAttribute() > _
    Public MustOverride Function Subtract(ByVal n1 As Integer, _
        ByVal n2 As Integer) As Integer
End Class
```

Both the Disco and Wsdl utilities support several command switches that I haven't covered here—for example, the /domain, /username, and /password options for accessing protected servers. For additional information, run the utility with the /? option, or read the .NET SDK documentation.

XML Web Services Up Close

You can create functional and useful XML Web services with what you've learned in the first part of this chapter, but of course you can learn much more. In the sections that follow, you'll see how you can improve the performance of XML Web services through caching, how to deal with exceptions, and how to take advantage of the ASP.NET infrastructure.

The XML Web Service Class

The class that exposes the methods of the XML Web service usually inherits from System.Web.Services.WebService class, even though this isn't a requirement because the presence of the WebMethod attribute is enough to make one or more methods of the class callable by remote clients. In practice, however, you always build an XML Web service class that inherits from the WebService base class because this arrangement lets you access the ASP.NET context and other useful objects, such as Application and Session variables.

The WebService Attribute

As I've just explained, the WebService attribute is optional in the sense that ASP.NET can determine that a class can work as an XML Web service without it. However, you should always apply this attribute for specifying a namespace other than http://tempuri.org/ before the XML Web service goes public.

The constructor of the WebService attribute can take three arguments: Description, Namespace, and Name. You've already seen how to use the first two:

```
<WebService(Description:="A web service for converting currencies",
    Namespace:="http://www.vb2themax.com/") > _
Public Class Converter
    Inherits System.Web.Services.WebService
    ⋮
End Class
```

Remember that the namespace value is only a means to make the XML Web service name unique and doesn't have to correspond to a physical URL. The common convention of using the URL of your company's Web site ensures that the namespace+name combination is unique.

The Name argument affects the name of the class as it appears in the WSDL contract, and it ultimately becomes the name of the proxy class that you create with the Add Web Reference command in Visual Studio or with the Wsdl utility. If you omit this argument, the proxy class has the same name as the original XML Web service class:

```
<WebService(Description:="A web service for converting currencies",
    Namespace:="http://www.vb2themax.com/", Name:="MoneyConv") > _
Public Class Converter
    Inherits System.Web.Services.WebService
    ⋮
End Class
```

Access to ASP.NET Objects

One of the benefits of creating an XML Web service by deriving a class from System.Web.Services.WebService is the ability to access any ASP.NET intrinsic object from inside the class. More precisely, the WebService base class exposes the following properties:

- The Application, Session, and Server properties return the ASP.NET object of the same name. You can use the Application object to cache values in common to all clients, as you do in a Web Forms application. Keep in mind that the Session object is available only if you have specified the EnableState argument in the WebMethod attribute, as I explain in the "Enabling Session State" section later in this chapter.
- The User property returns the IPrincipal object that represents an authenticated user. For example, this property returns a Windows-Principal object if users are authenticated through Windows authentication. You can decide which authentication method the XML Web service supports by editing the web.config file for the XML Web service application, exactly as you do for Web Forms applications. (See the "ASP.NET Security" section in Chapter 24 for details about ASP.NET authentication.)
- The Context property returns the HttpContext object for the current request. This object exposes the five ASP.NET intrinsic objects, the Trace object, the Error object, and a few other properties.

Among the most useful objects you can access from inside an XML Web service are Application and Cache, which can cache values and share them among clients. Here's a very simple example that uses an Application variable to keep track of how many times a given method has been called:

```
<WebMethod(Description:="Return the server time")> _
Function GetTime(ByVal arg As Integer) As Date
    Me.Application.Lock()
```

(continued)

```
    Me.Application("GetTimeCounter") = GetTimeCounter() + 1
    Me.Application.Unlock()
    Return Date.Now
End Function

<WebMethod(Description:="The number of times GetTime has been called")> _
Function GetTimeCounter() As Integer
    Dim o As Object = Me.Application("GetTimeCounter")
    If o Is Nothing Then
        Return 0
    Else
        Return CInt(o)
    End If
End Function
```

You can review how to use the Application and Cache objects in the sections "The HttpApplicationState Class" and "The Cache Class" in Chapter 24.

Simple and Complex Data Types

The great thing about XML Web services is their ability to receive and return any .NET data type, including your custom type, provided that it's serializable. (Read Chapter 11 to refresh your knowledge about object serialization.) For example, you can pass and return ADO.NET DataSet objects—either generic or strongly typed—because they're serializable.

Most of the time, you don't have to do anything special to marshal a data type because the definition of all the types taken or returned by the XML Web service project and exposed as arguments or return values is included in the WSDL contract. When you add a Web reference in Visual Studio or run the Wsdl utility, a proxy class for each of these types is generated and the client can therefore use them. In a few cases, however, you must force Visual Studio or the Wsdl utility to include the right types in the WSDL contract. For example, consider the following XML Web service class:

```
Imports System.Xml.Serialization

<WebService(Description:="A web service with methods for doing tests", _
    Namespace:="http://www.vb2themax.com/")> _
Public Class SampleService
    Inherits System.Web.Services.WebService

    <WebMethod()> _
    Function GetDocument(ByVal docname As String) As Document
        Select Case docname.ToLower
            Case "invoice"
                Return New Invoice()
            Case "purchaseorder"
                Return New PurchaseOrder()
```

```
        End Select
    End Function
End Class

Public MustInherit Class Document
    Public [Date] As Date
    Public Number As Integer
End Class

Public Class Invoice
    Inherits Document
    Public Total As Decimal
End Class

Public Class PurchaseOrder
    Inherits Document
    Public AuthorizedBy As String
End Class
```

The problem in the preceding listing is that the GetDocument method can return either an Invoice or a PurchaseOrder object, although the WSDL contract will contain the definition of only the Document abstract class. To force the WSDL contract to include the definition of the two concrete classes, you must flag the method with the SoapRpcMethod attribute and add two instances of the SoapInclude attribute, as follows:

```
<WebMethod(),SoapRpcMethod(),SoapInclude(GetType(Invoice)), _
    SoapInclude(GetType(PurchaseOrder))> _
Function GetDocument(ByVal docname As String) As Document
    :
End Function
```

You should use the SoapInclude attribute in other similar cases—for example, when a method takes or returns an ArrayList or a collection of objects and the actual class name of the returned object doesn't appear explicitly anywhere in public method signatures:

```
' The following method takes an ArrayList of Book objects
' but no other method explicitly takes or returns a Book object.

<WebMethod(),SoapRpcMethod(),SoapInclude(GetType(Book)) > _
Sub ProcessProducts(ByVal books As ArrayList)
    :
End Function
```

The System.Xml.Serialization namespace includes other Soap*xxxx* attributes, such as SoapType, SoapElement, SoapAttributeAttribute, SoapIgnore, and SoapEnum. These attributes can be used to define how structures and classes are serialized to XML and work much like the Xml*xxxx* attributes

I illustrated in the "XML Serialization" section of Chapter 11. Unless you need to control the shape of the XML sent or received from the XML Web service, you don't need to apply these attributes to work with XML Web services.

The WebMethod Attribute

Unlike the WebService attribute, the WebMethod attribute is mandatory and you must use it to flag all the methods that must be accessible to clients. This arrangement lets you build a component that exposes a set of methods to its local clients, but it makes only a subset of those methods available to remote clients that connect to it through an XML Web service. All the arguments for this attribute are optional, but in practice you should at least specify the Description for the method, which appears in the XML Web service help page:

```
<WebMethod(Description:="Convert from Euro to Dollar currency")> _
Function EuroToDollar(ByVal amount As Decimal) As Decimal
    Return amount * GetEuroToDollarConversionRate()
End Function
```

Working with Overloaded Methods

The MessageName argument specifies the name clients can use to invoke the method. This argument is necessary only when the XML Web service class exposes overloaded methods of the same name. Because the XML Web service infrastructure can't resolve calls to overloaded methods, you must specify different external names for them:

```
<WebMethod (Description:="Add two Integers")> _
Public Function Add(ByVal n1 As Integer, ByVal n2 As Integer) _
    As Integer
    Return n1 + n2
End Function

<WebMethod (Description:="Add two floating point numbers", _
    MessageName:="AddDouble")> _
Public Function Add(ByVal n1 As Double, ByVal n2 As Double) _
    As Double
    Return n1 + n2
End Function
```

Buffering the Response

The BufferResponse argument is similar to the BufferOutput property of the HttpResponse object in that it affects whether the output from the XML Web service is sent to the client as a single XML block or split in smaller chunks that are sent while the returned object is being serialized to XML. In practice, you'll want to leave this argument set to True (its default value) and set it to False only when you're returning large quantities of XML, as when you're returning a large DataSet to the client:

```
<WebMethod(BufferResponse:="False")> _
Public Function GetPublishers() As DataSet
    ⋮
End Function
```

When BufferResponse is False, SOAP extensions are disabled for the method. (See the "SOAP Extensions" section later in this chapter for a description of SOAP extensions.)

Caching Results

Because they're ASP.NET applications, XML Web services support output caching, much like Web Forms and Web User controls. XML Web services don't support the @OutputCache directive, however, and the output from each individual method can be cached with a different duration by means of the CacheDuration argument of the WebMethod attribute. For example, the following code caches the output of the GetPublishers method for one minute:

```
<WebMethod(CacheDuration:=60)> _
Public Function GetPublishers() As DataSet
    ⋮
End Function
```

If the method takes arguments, ASP.NET maintains a different cached version for each combination of argument values. For example, the following method stores a cached image for each distinct value of the State argument passed to the method in its argument:

```
<WebMethod(CacheDuration:=60, MesssageName:="GetPublishersByState")> _
Public Function GetPublishers(ByVal State As String) As DataSet
    ⋮
End Function
```

If used wisely, the CacheDuration attribute can improve the XML Web service performance more than any other technique available. However, you should always consider carefully the impact on resource consumption on the server. This technique is especially effective for small results that require a lot of processing on the server—for example, computation of database statistics—and can become a bottleneck if the method takes arguments whose value can vary greatly or if the method returns a large amount of data.

Enabling Session State

XML Web services can take advantage of session state support, like all ASP.NET applications, even though session support is disabled for XML Web services by default because most XML Web service calls are stateless and don't need to store data in a session variable. This arrangement avoids the need to populate the Session collection at each call, reduces memory consumption on the server, and avoids server affinity.

Sometimes, however, enabling session variables can be useful or desirable—for example, in an XML Web service that has a method for ordering individual products and another method that confirms the order, evaluates shipping charges, and returns the total cost. Such an XML Web service isn't stateless and has to store details of the order being built in one or more session variables. You enable session support by setting the EnableSession argument of the WebMethod attribute to True; if you omit this argument or set it to False, any reference to the Session object throws a NullReference exception. Here's a simple example of an XML Web service method that relies on session variables:

```
<WebMethod(EnableSession:=True)> _
Function IncrementCounter() As Integer
    If Session("counter") Is Nothing Then
        Session.Add("counter", 1)
    Else
        Session("counter") = CInt(Session("counter")) + 1
    End If
    Return CInt(session("counter"))
End Function

<WebMethod(EnableSession:=True)> _
Function GetSessionID() As String
    Return Session.SessionId
End Function
```

XML Web services that rely on session state have a serious shortcoming. If you test the IncrementCounter method from the browser by using the standard help page, you'll see that each call to the method increments the result, which proves that session state is correctly preserved between method invocations. You can double-check that this feature works well by seeing that the return value from the GetSessionID method doesn't change, at least until you close the browser or the session expires after its natural timeout (20 minutes of inactivity by default).

However, be prepared for an unpleasant surprise when you call the method from a Windows Forms application that uses a proxy class. In this case, the IncrementCounter method always returns 1 and the GetSessionID method returns a different string at each invocation. To explain this odd behavior, you must remember that session support depends on a nonpersistent cookie sent to the client the first time the client sends a request to the ASP.NET application. If the client is a browser, the session cookie is preserved in the browser's memory and resubmitted at each subsequent request so that the application can recognize the client and associate it with the proper set of session variables. If the client is a Windows Forms application, however, the session cookie can't be stored anywhere, and each new request appears as if it were the first request coming from that client. In the section "The CookieContainer Property" later in this chapter, you'll see how to work around this issue.

Building Transactional XML Web Services

You can use the TransactionOption argument of the WebMethod attribute to create transactional XML Web services, which can call transactional COM+ components and take advantage of Microsoft Distributed Transaction Coordinator (MS DTC) support. I don't cover transactional components in this book, so I am describing this attribute here only for the sake of completeness.

Due to the stateless nature of XML Web services, an XML Web service method can be only the root of a transaction. In other words, you can't start a transaction in a client—which might be a Windows Forms application, a Web Forms page, or another XML Web service method—and propagate the transaction through a call to the XML Web service. In this respect, transactional XML Web services behave like transactional ASP and ASP.NET pages.

The TransactionOption argument can take five different values—Disabled, NotSupported, Supported, Required, and RequiresNew—but because of the limitation I just mentioned, only two different behaviors are available. You have a transactional XML Web service if you specify Required or RequiresNew, and a regular, nontransactional XML Web service if you use any other value for this argument. Here's the typical structure of a transactional XML Web service method:

```
' This code assumes that you've added the following Imports statement:
'    Imports System.Data.OleDb

<WebMethod(TransactionOption:=TransactionOption.RequiresNew)> _
Function UpdateDatabase() As Boolean
    Dim cn As New OleDbConnection(myConnString)
    Try
        cn.Open()
        ' Perform all the required update operations.
        :
        ' If everything went well, commit the transaction.
        ContextUtil.SetComplete()
        ' Let the client know that everything is OK.
        Return True
    Catch
        ' If an update error occurred, abort the transaction.
        ContextUtil.SetAbort()
        ' Let the client know that something went wrong.
```

(continued)

```
        Return False
    Finally
        ' Close the connection in all cases.
        cn.Close()
    End Try
End Function
```

You can also flag the method with the AutoComplete attribute, in which case the transaction is rolled back if the method throws an exception but committed otherwise, so you can omit the call to the SetComplete and SetAbort methods. For more information, see the .NET SDK documentation.

The XML Web Service Proxy Class

The proxy class that Visual Studio .NET or the Wsdl utility creates inherits from the System.Web.Protocols.SoapHttpClientProtocol class and exposes additional methods that mirror the methods exposed by the original XML Web service class. Table 26-1 lists the main members of the SoapHttpClientProtocol class, with a brief description of each one.

Table 26-1 Main Properties and Methods of the SoapHttpClientProtocol Class

Category	Syntax	Description
Properties	AllowAutoRedirect	If False (the default), the proxy throws an exception if a server redirection is attempted. If the message contains authentication information or other confidential information, you should prohibit redirections, which would compromise security.
	ClientCertificates	The collection of client certificates.
	CookieContainer	Gets or sets the collection of cookies.
	Credentials	An ICredential object containing the credentials used for XML Web service client authentication.
	PreAuthenticate	True if all the requests must contain authentication credentials. If False (the default), the credentials are sent only if the XML Web service disallows anonymous access and returns a 401 HTTP return code when the request is initially attempted.
	Proxy	Gets or sets proxy information. This property allows the XML Web service to be invoked through a firewall that would prevent direct calls.

Table 26-1 Main Properties and Methods of the SoapHttpClientProtocol Class

Category	Syntax	Description
	RequestEncoding	A System.Text.Encoding enumerated value that specifies the encoding to be used when you're submitting requests (for example, Encoding.UTF8). The default value is Nothing, in which case the underlying protocol's default encoding is used.
	Timeout	The timeout in milliseconds for a synchronous request to an XML Web service method.
	Url	The base URL of the XML Web service—for example, *http://www.tailspintoys.com/your-service.asmx*. Assign this property to redirect the request to another XML Web service with the same interface as an XML Web service that's currently unavailable.
	UserAgent	The user agent header used in the request to the XML Web service. The default is Mozilla/4.0 (compatible; MSIE 6.0; MS Web Services Client Protocol w.*x.yyyy.z*), where w.*x.yyyy.z* is the version of the common language runtime.
Methods	Abort	Cancels a synchronous XML Web service method invocation. This method must be called from another thread; the blocked thread receives a WebException.
	Discover	Dynamically binds the proxy class to the XML Web service whose discovery document is located at the address contained in the Url property.
Methods (protected)	Invoke(name, args)	Invokes a method synchronously using SOAP. The first argument is the method name, and the second argument is an array containing the arguments to be passed to the XML Web service.
	BeginInvoke(name, args, callback, state)	Starts an asynchronous method using SOAP; returns an IAsyncResult object.
	EndInvoke(iasyncres)	Ends an asynchronous method started with a BeginInvoke method.
	GetWebResponse(webrequest)	Returns a response from a synchronous request to the XML Web service.

Late-Bound and Early-Bound Method Calls

All proxy classes inherit from the SoapHttpClientProtocol base class the ability to invoke methods synchronously and asynchronously by means of the Invoke, BeginInvoke, and EndInvoke protected methods.

In addition to these generic, late-bound methods, Visual Studio and the Wsdl utility create three strongly typed methods in the proxy class for each method in the XML Web service component. These methods are public and can be invoked from the client application. For example, the EuroToDollar method in the Converter.asmx file causes the following methods to be created in the proxy class:

```
' Strongly typed method for synchronous calls
Public Function DollarToEuro(ByVal amount As Decimal) As Decimal
    Dim results() As Object = Me.Invoke("DollarToEuro", New Object() {amount})
    Return CType(results(0),Decimal)
End Function

' Strongly typed method for starting asynchronous calls
Public Function BeginDollarToEuro(ByVal amount As Decimal, _
    ByVal callback As AsyncCallback, ByVal asyncState As Object) _
    As IAsyncResult
    Return Me.BeginInvoke("DollarToEuro", _
        New Object() {amount}, callback, asyncState)
End Function

' Strongly typed method for ending asynchronous calls
Public Function EndDollarToEuro(ByVal asyncResult As IAsyncResult) As Decimal
    Dim results() As Object = Me.EndInvoke(asyncResult)
    Return CType(results(0),Decimal)
End Function
```

Let's see how you can make a synchronous and an asynchronous call to an XML Web service.

Synchronous Method Calls

Because you're making a call to an XML Web service running on a computer across the Internet, you should always protect your synchronous calls with a timeout. If the timeout specified by the Timeout property is exceeded, a System.Net.WebException object is thrown. So you should protect the method invocation with a Try…End Try block:

```
Dim service As New localhost.SampleService
Try
    ' Set a timeout of 5 seconds.
    service.Timeout = 5000
    ' Invoke a method that takes 10 seconds to complete.
    service.LengthyMethodCall(10)
```

```
Catch ex As WebException
    If ex.Status = WebExceptionStatus.Timeout Then
        ' The operation timed out.
        ⋮
    End If
Catch ex As Exception
    ' Another exception has occurred.
End Try
```

The LengthyMethodCall method in the SampleService.asmx XML Web service contains just a Thread.Sleep method, so we can use it to test how the proxy class behaves when the call times out:

```
<WebMethod(Description:="A lengthy method")> _
Sub LengthyMethodCall(ByVal seconds As Integer)
    ' Wait for the specified number of seconds.
    Thread.Sleep(seconds * 1000)
End Sub
```

You can use the Timeout property in combination with the Url property to provide alternate addresses. Suppose, for example, that you have a list of XML Web services that offer the same functionality (and have the same WSDL contract). You can then call the default XML Web service—whose URL is stored in the WSDL and hard coded into the proxy class's source code—after setting an adequate timeout. If the timeout expires, you can have the Url property point to an alternate XML Web service and retry the method call.

The proxy class also exposes the Abort method, which allows you to cancel a synchronous XML Web service method call. Because a synchronous call blocks the thread, you can call the Abort method only from another thread, so this technique makes sense if your application has at least two threads. (If you create the additional thread with the only purpose of calling the Abort method, you should consider calling the method asynchronously.) If a synchronous method call is canceled, the thread on which it runs receives a WebException object.

The Abort method enables you to cancel a synchronous method call depending on conditions other than timeout expiration, as in the following example:

```
Dim service As New localhost.SampleService

Sub RunTheMethod()
    ' Run another thread.
    Dim tr As New Thread(AddressOf CallWebMethod)
    tr.Start()
    ' Abort the method call when a condition becomes true. For example,
```

(continued)

```
        ' a file is updated or a process is terminated.
        ⋮
        ' (In this demo we just wait for some seconds.)
        Thread.Sleep(5000)
        service.Abort()
    End Sub

    Sub CallWebMethod()
        Try
            ' Invoke a method that takes 10 seconds to complete.
            service.LengthyMethodCall(10)
        Catch ex As WebException
            If ex.Status = WebExceptionStatus.RequestCanceled Then
                ' The method call has been canceled.
                ⋮
            End If
        End Try
    End Sub
```

Asynchronous Method Calls

As I've shown you before, the proxy class exposes a Begin*xxxx* and End*xxxx* pair of methods for each procedure in the XML Web service component marked with the WebMethod attribute. You can use these two methods for calling the XML Web service asynchronously.

The actions necessary to invoke an XML Web service method asynchronously are identical to the actions needed to invoke an asynchronous delegate. I covered asynchronous delegates in Chapter 13, so in this section I'll give you just an example of asynchronous invocation of an XML Web service method.

```
Sub CallAsyncMethod()
    Dim service As New localhost.SampleService
    ' Call a lengthy method that takes about 5 seconds to complete.
    ' Note that the proxy object is passed in the third argument.
    Dim ar As IAsyncResult = service.BeginLengthyMethodCall(5, _
        AddressOf MethodCallback, service)
End Sub

' This is the callback method.
Sub MethodCallback(ByVal ar As IAsyncResult)
    ' Retrieve the proxy object from the AsyncState property.
    Dim service As localhost.SampleService = _
        DirectCast(ar.AsyncState, localhost.SampleService)
    ' Complete the method call.
    service.EndLengthyMethodCall(ar)
End Sub
```

Aborting an XML Web service asynchronous call is slightly more difficult than aborting a synchronous call. You must cast the IAsyncResult object returned by the Begin*xxxx* method to a WebClientAsyncResult object and then call the Abort method of the WebClientAsyncResult object:

```
Sub AbortAsyncMethodCall()
    Dim service As New localhost.SampleService()
    ' Run a method that takes 10 seconds to complete.
    Dim ar As IAsyncResult = service.BeginLengthyMethodCall(5, _
        Nothing, Nothing)

    ' Do something else here.
    ⋮

    If ar.IsCompleted Then
        ' If the method completed, complete the call.
        service.EndLengthyMethodCall(ar)
    Else
        ' Else abort the method call
        Dim wcar As WebClientAsyncResult = CType(ar, WebClientAsyncResult)
        wcar.Abort()
    End If
End Sub
```

One-Way Methods

A special case of asynchronous calls occurs when the client doesn't really care about the return value from the XML Web service. For example, you might build an XML Web service that exposes one or more methods that clients call only to signal that something has occurred or to issue commands (for example, to start a lengthy batch compilation). In such a case, you can reach perfect asynchronicity by flagging the XML Web service method using a SoapDocumentMethod attribute with its OneWay argument set to True:

```
<WebMethod(), SoapDocumentMethod(OneWay:=True)> _
Sub OneWayLengthyMethodCall(ByVal seconds As Integer)
    ' Simulate a lengthy method.
    Thread.Sleep(seconds * 1000)
End Sub
```

Methods flagged in this way must have neither a return value nor ByRef arguments. Also, they can't access their HttpContext object, and any property of the XML Web service class returns Nothing.

The CookieContainer Property

As you might remember from the "Enabling Session State" section earlier in this chapter, the standard proxy class doesn't work well with XML Web service methods that rely on session state—that is, methods whose EnableSession attribute is set to True—because the proxy class can't work as a cookie container. Therefore, it can't store the session cookie that ASP.NET sends to the client when a new session is detected.

Fortunately, making the proxy class a valid cookie container is just a matter of ensuring that its CookieContainer property holds a reference to a System.Net.CookieContainer object:

```
Dim service As New localhost.SampleService()

Sub TestIncrementCounterMethod()
    ' Make the proxy object a cookie container, if necessary.
    If service.CookieContainer Is Nothing Then
        service.CookieContainer = New CookieContainer()
    End If
    ' Each time this method is called, the value in the Label
    ' control is incremented by 1.
    Label1.Text = service.IncrementCounter()
End Sub
```

After setting the CookieContainer property, the proxy object is able to store the session cookie. The session is terminated when the proxy object is set to Nothing or when the session timeout expires without invoking any method in the XML Web service. (The default session timeout is 20 minutes.)

The CookieContainer property returns a collection of cookies, so you can read the cookies it contains and you can add your own cookies. In particular, you can read the special session cookie named ASP.NET_SessionId, save it in a variable or on disk, and add it to the cookies collection in a subsequent call:

```
Dim saveCookie As System.Net.Cookie

Sub CallStatefulWebServiceMethod()
    Dim service As New localhost.SampleService()
    ' Make the proxy object a cookie container.
    service.CookieContainer = New CookieContainer()

    ' If we already have the cookie, let's add it to the cookies collection.
    If Not (saveCookie Is Nothing) Then
        service.CookieContainer.Add(saveCookie)
    End If

    ' Call the XML Web service method.
    Label1.Text = service.IncrementCounter()

    ' Save the cookie if this is the first call.
    If saveCookie Is Nothing Then
        ' Replace the argument with the actual XML Web service's URL.
        Dim cookieUri As New Uri("http://localhost")
        ' Save the ASP.NET_SessionId cookie belonging to the localhost URI.
```

```
        saveCookie = service.CookieContainer.GetCookies(cookieUri).Item _
            ("ASP.NET_SessionId")
    End If
End Sub
```

This technique has two important applications. First, two Windows Forms applications can share the same session, regardless of whether they're running on the same or different client machines as long as they have a means for exchanging the contents of the session cookie. Second, all the pages in a Web Forms ASP.NET application can invoke methods in an XML Web service and share the same set of session variables. (In this case, the individual .aspx pages should save the cookie in a Session or Application variable.)

SOAP Exceptions

XML Web services methods can throw exceptions, either directly with a Throw statement or indirectly when they perform an invalid operation. When interacting with an XML Web service, you must account for other types of errors as well, such as those caused by a client using an outdated version of the WSDL contract (and of the proxy class).

Whenever an error occurs while an XML Web service is processing a request, the SOAP message returned to the client contains a <soap:Fault> block inside its body instead of the usual <soap:Body> block. On the client side, this fault block is translated into a SoapException object, which is the type to look for in the Catch clause of the Try...End Try block. The SoapException class inherits from SystemException all the usual properties, to which it adds a few specific ones. The most significant members of the SoapException class are the following:

- **Message** is the message property of the original exception.
- **Actor** is the URL of the XML Web service that threw the exception.
- **Code** is an XmlQualifiedName object that specifies the SOAP fault code that describes the general cause of the error.
- **Detail** is an XmlNode object representing application-specific error information. This property is set only if the error occurred when the XML Web service was processing the body of the message and is Nothing in other cases (such as when the problem was in the header or in the format of the message).

Most of the time, the properties you should focus your attention on are Message and Code. A minor problem is that the original error string is buried inside the value returned by the Message property. For example, if the XML

Web service method throws a NullReferenceException, this is the string you'll find in the Message property:

```
System.Web.Services.Protocols.SoapException: Server was unable to
process request. ---> System.NullReferenceException: Object reference
not set to an instance of an object.
   at MoneyConverter.SampleService.ThrowAnException()
   --- End of inner exception stack trace ---
```

The simplest way to extract the name of the real exception is to use regular expressions. Here's a reusable routine that does the job:

```
' This code assumes that you've used the following Imports statement:
'    Imports System.Text.RegularExpression

' Extract the name of the "inner" exception.
Function GetWSException(ByVal ex As SoapException) As String
    ' Parse the exception's Message property.
    Dim mc As MatchCollection = Regex.Matches(ex.Message, "---> ([^:]+):")
    If mc.Count >= 1 Then
        ' We've found a match - the first group contains the value.
        Return mc.Item(0).Groups(1).Value
    End If
End Function
```

You can use the GetWSException function inside a Try...End Try block as follows:

```
Try
    Dim service As New localhost.SampleService()
    service.ThrowAnException()
Catch ex As SoapException _
    When GetWSException(ex) = "System.NullReferenceException"
    ' A null reference exception
    ⋮
Catch ex As SoapException _
    When GetWSException(ex) = "System.DivideByZeroException"
    ' A divide-by-zero exception
    ⋮
End Try
```

The Code property of the SoapException class is useful in that it lets you quickly classify the type of exception you've received. This property returns an XmlQualifiedName object, whose Name property can be one of the following:

- **VersionMismatch** An invalid namespace was found.
- **MustUnderstand** The client sent an element whose MustUnderstand attribute was 1, but the server was unable to process it.

- **Client** The client request wasn't formatted properly or didn't contain appropriate information. This exception is an indication that the message shouldn't be sent again without change.
- **Server** An error occurred on the server but wasn't caused by the message contents; this is the Code returned when the code running in the XML Web service throws an exception.

To help you test the Code property, the SoapException class defines four constants, named VersionMismatchFaultCode, MustUnderstandFaultCode, ClientFaultCode, and ServerFaultCode. The following code uses these constants to determine what kind of error occurred, by means of the When clause of the Try...End Try block:

```
Try
    Dim service As New localhost.SampleService()
    service.ThrowAnException()
Catch ex As SoapException _
    When ex.Code.Equals(SoapException.VersionMismatchFaultCode)
    ' An invalid namespace has been used.
    ⋮
Catch ex As SoapException _
    When ex.Code.Equals(SoapException.ServerFaultCode)
    ' An invalid namespace has been used.
    ⋮
End Try
```

Advanced Topics

In the last part of this chapter, I cover three advanced topics that can be useful when implementing real-world XML Web services: SOAP headers, security, and SOAP extensions.

SOAP Headers

As you might remember from the section "The SOAP Protocol" near the beginning of this chapter, a SOAP message can contain additional information in its header. The message header is optional, and in fact all the examples I've shown you so far haven't used this portion of the SOAP message.

I've prepared an example that shows how you can pass a SOAP header and how an XML Web service can use this header to format date and other information in the format expected by the client. To prepare an XML Web service class to work with a SOAP header, you must do three things:

1. Define a class that contains the fields that you want to pass through the header. This class must inherit from the System.Web.Services.Protocols.SoapHeader class.
2. Define a public field in the class typed after the class defined in the previous point.
3. Add a SoapHeader attribute to all the methods that you want to read the SOAP header. The argument of this attribute is the name of the field defined in the previous point.

Here's an example of an XML Web service that exposes a method named GetClientTime, which returns the client's local time formatted according to the client's locale. The locale information and the offset from Coordinated Universal Time (UTC) are passed in an instance of the UserInfoHeader class:

```
Public Class SampleService
    Inherits System.Web.Services.WebService

    ' This is the Public variable that receives the userInfo header.
    Public userInfo As UserInfoHeader

    <WebMethod(), SoapHeader("userInfo")> _
    Function GetClientTime() As String
        ' The server's local time in Coordinated Universal Time
        Dim serverTime As Date = Date.Now.ToUniversalTime
        ' Convert to client's time zone.
        Dim clientTime As Date = serverTime.AddHours(userInfo.TimeOffset)
        ' Create a CultureInfo object with proper locale information.
        Dim ci As New System.Globalization.CultureInfo(userInfo.Culture)
        ' Return the time formatted using client's formatting rules.
        Return clientTime.ToString(ci)
    End Function
End Class

' This class defines the information carried with the SOAP header.

Public Class UserInfoHeader
    Inherits SoapHeader

    ' This member contains the culture name of the user.
    Public Culture As String = ""
    ' This member contains the time difference from UTC time.
    Public TimeOffset As Single = 0
End Class
```

When you produce the WSDL contract and use it to generate the proxy class, the client definition of the UserInfoHeader class is generated as well, so the client code can create an instance of this class and initialize it as required. Moreover, the proxy class is extended with a field named *headerclass*Value—UserInfoHeaderValue in this example—so the client can assign the UserInfo-Header object to this field:

```
' How to call an XML Web service method that takes a SOAP header

' Create a header.
Dim userInfo As New localhost.UserInfoHeader()
' This is the identifier for the Italian language.
userInfo.Culture = "it-it"
' Italian time is one hour ahead of Greenwich time.
userInfo.TimeOffset = 1

' Create an instance of the proxy class.
Dim service As New localhost.SampleService()
' Assign the header to the special xxxxValue field.
service.UserInfoHeaderValue = userInfo
' Call the XML Web service.
Dim res As String = service.GetClientTime()
```

The SoapHeader attribute makes the header mandatory and the client gets an exception if no header is associated with the proxy object, but you can make the header optional by adding a Required argument set to False. In this case, you must ensure that the code in the XML Web service method works well even if the client doesn't send a header:

```
<WebMethod(), SoapHeader("userInfo", Required:=False)> _
Function GetClientTime() As String
    ' Provide a default userInfo object if the client omitted it.
    If userInfo Is Nothing Then
        userInfo = New UserInfoHeader()
        ' In this case, UTC time is returned to the client.
    End If

    ' ...(The remainder of the method as before)...
    ⋮
End Function
```

One more thing about SOAP headers: Headers are sent to the XML Web service but aren't returned to the client, to save bandwidth. In other words, the header object works as an input-only argument for the XML Web service method. It doesn't have to be so, however, and you have complete control over how headers are sent back and forth. The key to this feature is the Direction argument of the SoapHeader attribute: its default value is In, but you can set it to InOut or Out.

```
<WebMethod(), SoapHeader("userInfo", Required:=False, _
    Direction:=SoapHeaderDirection.InOut)> _
Function GetClientTime() As String
    ' Provide a default userInfo object if the client omitted it.
    If userInfo Is Nothing Then
        ' (This header is returned to the client.)
        userInfo = New UserInfoHeader()
        userInfo.Culture = "EN-US"          ' American English
        userInfo.TimeOffset = -5            ' U.S. eastern time
    End If

    ' ...(The remainder of the method as before)...
    ⋮
End Function
```

I'll illustrate other uses for SOAP headers shortly in the "Custom Authentication" section.

XML Web Service Security

XML Web service security doesn't differ noticeably from standard ASP.NET security, and all the security mechanisms you saw in Chapter 24 are valid with XML Web services. The peculiarities in XML Web service security stem from their noninteractive nature. For example, if you disable anonymous access for an .asmx file from inside IIS, any client request for that .asmx file fails but no dialog is displayed.

Another consequence of the programmatic nature of XML Web services: you can use Forms authentication and redirect all nonauthenticated requests to a given URL (using the LoginURL entry in web.config), but this tactic is of no practical use because the XML Web service client would receive HTML instead of the SOAP message it's expecting. Although this obstacle might be removed if you provided a custom function that manually creates the authentication cookie, in general Forms authentication isn't recommended as a viable authentication method for XML Web services, and I won't cover it in this book.

Windows Authentication

Windows authentication is the simplest authentication method you can use for an XML Web service that can't accept anonymous requests. Whether or not you've protected the .asmx page with Basic, Digest, or Integrated Windows authentication, you can provide your credentials to IIS by assigning a NetworkCredential object to the proxy object's Credential property, as in this code snippet:

```
' Create a System.Net.NetworkCredential object.
Dim nc As New NetworkCredential()
nc.UserName = "username"
nc.Password = "userpwd"
nc.Domain = "domainname"

' Create the proxy object and assign it the user credentials.
Dim service As New localhost.Converter()
service.Credentials = nc
' Make the call.
Dim euros As Decimal = service.DollarToEuro(100)
```

If the .asmx page requires Windows authentication and you pass invalid credentials (or no credentials at all), the client application receives a WebException object whose Message property is

```
The request failed with HTTP status 401: Access Denied.
```

If the client application has a user interface, you might catch this exception, bring up a dialog box, and ask the user to enter her name and password to submit in a second attempt.

Everything I said in Chapter 24 about the various Windows authentication methods holds true for XML Web services. For example, when Basic authentication is used, the username and password are sent in clear text (in Base64-encoded format), and you should use Integrated Windows security if possible.

Custom Authentication

As happens with regular ASP.NET applications, Windows authentication has a major drawback: often you don't want to create one Windows account for each user of your XML Web service. In this section, I show how you can leverage SOAP headers to implement a custom authentication mechanism.

The idea is simple: each call from the client application must include a SOAP header that contains username and password. All the XML Web service methods that require authentication—for example, methods that require some form of subscription—invoke a central function, named ValidateUser, which checks the credentials in the header and throws an exception if the credentials aren't valid or the subscription has expired. Here's the source code of an XML Web service class that contains such a method:

```
Public Class SampleService
    Inherits System.Web.Services.WebService

    Public accountInfo As AccountInfoHeader

    <WebMethod(), SoapHeader("accountInfo")> _
    Function ProtectedMethod() As Boolean
```

(continued)

```
        ' Check that credentials are OK; throw exception if not.
        ValidateAccount()
        ' Return a value.
        ' (A real application should do something more useful than this.)
        Return True
    End Function

    ' Validate username and password (private function).
    Private Sub ValidateAccount()
        ' Throw exception if missing header.
        If accountInfo Is Nothing Then
            Throw New SoapException("Missing user info header", _
                SoapException.ClientFaultCode)
        End If

        ' Throw exception if header members aren't set.
        If accountInfo.UserName = "" Or accountInfo.Password = "" Then
            Throw New SoapException("Missing user info", _
                SoapException.ClientFaultCode)
        End If

        ' Throw exception if invalid user.
        If Not CheckUser(accountInfo.UserName, accountInfo.Password) Then
            Throw New SoapException("Insufficient subscription level", _
                SoapException.ClientFaultCode)
        End If

        ' Exit regularly if everything is OK.
    End Sub

    ' Check that user credentials are valid.
    Function CheckUser(ByVal username As String, ByVal password As String) _
        As Boolean
        ' (A real-world application would use a database.)
        If username = "JoeDoe" And password = "jdpwd" Then
            Return True
        ElseIf username = "AnnSmith" And password = "aspwd" Then
            Return True
        Else
            ' Unknown user or invalid credentials
            Return False
        End If
    End Function
End Class

' This is the SOAP Header class.

Public Class AccountInfoHeader
```

```
    Inherits SoapHeader

    Public UserName As String
    Public Password As String
End Class
```

The client-side code is similar to the code you saw in the "SOAP Headers" section earlier in this chapter:

```
Private Sub CallProtectedMethod()
    ' Prepare the SOAP header with account information.
    Dim accountInfo As New localhost.AccountInfoHeader()
    accountInfo.UserName = "JoeDoe"
    accountInfo.Password = "jdpwd"

    ' Pass account information to the proxy class.
    Dim service As New localhost.SampleService()
    service.AccountInfoHeaderValue = accountInfo
    ' Call the protected XML Web service method.
    Dim res As Boolean = service.ProtectedMethod()
End Sub
```

The beauty of this approach is that you can easily expand the ValidateUser procedure in the XML Web service class to implement sophisticated authorization policies. For example, the procedure can use reflection techniques to retrieve the name of the method that called it—that is, the XML Web service method invoked by the client—and ensure that users have a subscription level that allows them to make the call. Here's an implementation of this concept:

```
' Validate username and password. (Private procedure)
Private Sub ValidateAccount()
    ' Throw exception if missing header.
    If accountInfo Is Nothing Then
        Throw New SoapException("Missing user info header", _
            SoapException.ClientFaultCode)
    End If

    ' Throw exception if header members aren't set.
    If accountInfo.UserName = "" Or accountInfo.Password = "" Then
        Throw New SoapException("Missing user info", _
            SoapException.ClientFaultCode)
    End If

    ' Retrieve the subscription level of this user.
    Dim thisUserSubscriptionLevel As Integer = GetUserSubscriptionLevel _
        (accountInfo.UserName, accountInfo.Password)
    ' Exit if credentials are invalid.
    If thisUserSubscriptionLevel < 0 Then
```

(continued)

```
            Throw New SoapException("Unknown user", _
                SoapException.ClientFaultCode)
        End If

        ' Retrieve the name of the method that called this procedure.
        Dim st As New System.Diagnostics.StackTrace(False)
        ' GetFrame(0) describes the running procedure,
        ' GetFrame(1) describes the calling procedure.
        Dim sf As System.Diagnostics.StackFrame = st.GetFrame(1)
        Dim mb As System.Reflection.MethodBase = sf.GetMethod

        ' Retrieve the required subscription level for the calling method.
        Dim requiredSubscriptionLevel As Integer
        Select Case mb.Name
            Case "ProtectedMethod"
                requiredSubscriptionLevel = 1
            Case "AnotherProtectedMethod"
                requiredSubscriptionLevel = 2
        End Select

        ' Throw exception if subscription level isn't sufficient.
        If thisUserSubscriptionLevel < requiredSubscriptionLevel Then
            Throw New SoapException("Insufficient subscription level", _
                SoapException.ClientFaultCode)
        End If

        ' Exit regularly if everything is OK.
    End Sub

    ' Get user subscription level, or -1 if credentials are invalid.
    Function GetUserSubscriptionLevel(ByVal username As String, _
        ByVal password As String) As Integer
        ' (A real application would use a database instead.)
        If username = "JoeDoe" And password = "jdpwd" Then
            Return 1
        ElseIf username = "AnnSmith" And password = "aspwd" Then
            Return 2
        Else
            ' Unknown user or invalid credentials
            Return -1
        End If
    End Function
```

Now you have a centralized place in which you can control all access to your XML Web service, so you can change your subscription and charge policy without editing the code in any other XML Web service method.

You can improve this mechanism even more by creating a SOAP extension that reads the SOAP header and does the authentication and authorization before the execution flow ever reaches the method, as I explain in the following section.

SOAP Extensions

The XML Web service architecture can be completely redefined by the programmer, if necessary, by means of SOAP extensions. A SOAP extension is a software module that can execute custom code before the SOAP message reaches the XML Web service method. More precisely, there are four points at which a SOAP extension has a chance of executing custom code. They correspond to the four possible stages of a SOAP message. (See the right portion of Figure 26-13.)

- **BeforeDeserialize** The SOAP message has been received from the client, is still in XML format, and hasn't been deserialized into an in-memory object yet.
- **AfterDeserialize** The SOAP message has been serialized into an object and the actual XML Web service method is about to be called.
- **BeforeSerialize** The XML Web service method has completed its execution and the result object is about to be serialized into XML.
- **AfterSerialize** The result object has been serialized into a SOAP message and the XML text is about to be sent to the client.

Interestingly, a SOAP message leaving a client—that is, the proxy object on the client—undergoes the same four stages, but they occur in a different order. (See the left half of Figure 26-13.)

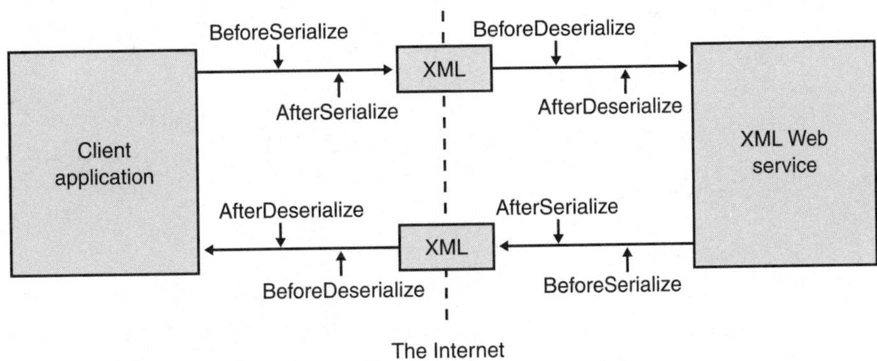

Figure 26-13. The four stages a SOAP message undergoes on the server and on the client.

A SOAP extension can read the XML data being sent from the client to the server and back and can modify it if necessary. So, for example, you might save the XML for logging or debugging reasons or encrypt return values to avoid eavesdropping and tampering—even though this task would require a SOAP extension running on the client that decrypts the result.

From the perspective of a developer, a SOAP extension is just a class that inherits from the System.Web.Services.Protocols.SoapExtension abstract class and overrides a few of its methods. However, before you can see how to build this class, you should learn about how you can associate a SOAP extension with an XML Web service. You can choose from two methods for doing so:

- Adding an entry to the configuration file. (In which case the SOAP extension is invoked for all the methods associated with a WebMethod attribute.)
- Defining a custom attribute and using it to flag only the methods for which you want to activate the SOAP extension. This method is more flexible because you can pass one or more arguments to the custom attribute's constructor and make these arguments available to the SOAP extension class. (This mechanism might be used, for example, to associate a fee with each XML Web service method.)

Let's see how to implement these two activation methods.

Activating a SOAP Extension from a Configuration File

You can install a SOAP extension by adding an <add> tag in the <soapExtensionTypes> block in web.config:

```
<configuration>
 <system.web>
   <webServices>
     <soapExtensionTypes>
      <add type="Logger.LoggerExtension, logger"
           Priority="1" Group="0" />
     <soapExtensionTypes>
    <webServices>
 <system.web>
<configuration>
```

where type is the name of the SOAP extension class, Group is the SOAP extension group (can be 0 or 1), and Priority is the priority inside the group (0 being the highest priority). A SOAP extension can belong to one of three groups:

- **Group 0** SOAP extensions in this group have the highest priority and can process the message before extensions belonging to the other two groups.

- **Medium group** These are the SOAP extensions activated through custom attributes applied to methods in the XML Web service class. (I explain how to activate these extensions in the next section.)
- **Group 1** SOAP extensions in this group have the lowest priority and process the message after extensions that belong to the first two groups.

Activating a SOAP extension by editing the web.config class is the best solution when the extension must be applied to all the methods in the XML Web service and when no argument must be passed to the extension. For example, you might use this technique to activate a SOAP extension that traces all incoming requests or that encrypts the result from all XML Web service methods.

Activating a SOAP Extension with a Custom Attribute

The second and more flexible method for activating a SOAP extension is by means of a custom attribute used to flag the methods in the XML Web service for which the SOAP extension must be used. This technique lets you apply the extension to just a subset of all the existing methods and allows you to define arguments that are passed to the SOAP extension, on a method-by-method basis.

In the following sections, I'll show you how to implement a SOAP extension that monitors access to any XML Web service method marked with a special SoapCustomAuthenticationAttribute. The constructor for this attribute takes an integer that defines the minimum subscription level required for a client to invoke the method that has been flagged with the attribute. (This is the SOAP extension version of the authentication and authorization method described in the "Custom Authentication" section earlier in this chapter.) For example, a method in SampleService.asmx that can be called only by clients whose subscription level is 2 or higher would look like this:

```
<WebMethod(), SoapCustomAuthentication(2), SoapHeader("accountInfo")> _
Function YetAnotherProtectedMethod() As Boolean
    ⋮
End Function
```

The SoapCustomAuthenticationAttribute class must inherit from the SoapExtensionAttribute abstract class. All classes that derive from this abstract class must override its Priority and ExtensionType properties. The latter property is especially important in that it returns the System.Type object that defines the SOAP extension class (named SoapExtensionAuthentication in this example). In the example that follows, the attribute class exposes also an additional property, RequiredSubscriptionLevel, which defines the minimum subscription level that's necessary to invoke the method to which this attribute is applied.

The minimum subscription level is the only argument you must pass to the attribute's constructor:

```
' The custom attribute you must use to flag methods that require
' a given subscription level.

<AttributeUsage(AttributeTargets.Method)> _
Public Class SoapCustomAuthenticationAttribute
    Inherits SoapExtensionAttribute

    ' The attribute constructor
    Sub New(ByVal requiredSubscriptionLevel As Integer)
        Me.RequiredSubscriptionLevel = requiredSubscriptionLevel
    End Sub

    ' You must override the Priority property.

    Dim m_Priority As Integer

    Public Overrides Property Priority() As Integer
        Get
            Return m_Priority
        End Get
        Set(ByVal Value As Integer)
            m_Priority = Value
        End Set
    End Property

    ' The ExtensionType property returns the type of the SoapExtension class.

    Public Overrides ReadOnly Property ExtensionType() As System.Type
        Get
            Return GetType(SoapCustomAuthentication)
        End Get
    End Property

    ' RequiredSubscriptionLevel is a custom property for this attribute.

    Dim m_RequiredSubscriptionLevel As Integer

    Property RequiredSubscriptionLevel() As Integer
        Get
            Return m_RequiredSubscriptionLevel
        End Get
        Set(ByVal Value As Integer)
            m_RequiredSubscriptionLevel = Value
        End Set
    End Property
End Class
```

The SOAP Extension Class

The actual SOAP extension is contained in a class that inherits from the System.Web.Services.Protocols.SoapExtension abstract class and overrides a few of its members. Because the structure of this class is complex, I'll show and comment its listing one method at a time, in the order in which these methods are called by the ASP.NET infrastructure.

The GetInitializer method is called only once during the life of the SOAP extension. There are two overloaded versions for this method, depending on whether the extension is activated by means of an entry in the configuration file or by means of a custom attribute in the XML Web service class. In the former instance, the method receives a System.Type object corresponding to the type of the XML Web service class. (This argument is necessary because a SOAP extension can serve multiple XML Web service classes.) In the latter instance, the GetInitializer method receives a reference to the custom attribute and a MethodInfo object that describes the method to which the attribute has been applied.

In both cases, the GetInitializer method is expected to return an Object value. This value is then passed as an argument to the Initialize method. This double-initialization approach makes the developer's job a bit more complicated but it improves performance. In our specific example, the GetInitializer method returns the RequiredSubscriptionLevel property of the custom attribute or the value 1 if the SOAP extension has been activated by means of an entry in the configuration file:

```
' The Soap extension class

Class SoapCustomAuthentication
    Inherits SoapExtension

    ' This overload of the GetInitializer method is called if the SOAP
    ' extension is installed in web.config; it receives the Type of the
    ' WebService class.

    Public Overloads Overrides Function GetInitializer( _
        ByVal serviceType As System.Type) As Object
        ' In this case, we just return 1, the lowest subscription level
        ' required to access methods in the XML Web service.
        If serviceType Is GetType(SampleService) Then
            Return 1
        End If
    End Function

    ' This overload of the GetInitializer method is called if the SOAP
    ' extension is installed because a method was flagged with a
```

(continued)

```
    ' SoapExtensionAttribute; it receives the attribute in the 2nd argument.

    Public Overloads Overrides Function GetInitializer( _
        ByVal methodInfo As LogicalMethodInfo, _
        ByVal attribute As SoapExtensionAttribute) As Object
        ' Get a strongly typed reference to the attribute.
        Dim scaAttr As SoapCustomAuthenticationAttribute = _
            DirectCast(attribute, SoapCustomAuthenticationAttribute)
        ' Return its RequiredSubscriptionLevel property.
        Return scaAttr.RequiredSubscriptionLevel
    End Function

    ' ...(Other methods of this class are described later)...
    ⋮
End Class
```

Unlike the GetInitializer method—which is called only once in the SOAP extension's lifetime—the Initialize method is called every time ASP.NET receives a request that must be passed to the SOAP extension. The Initialize method receives an Object argument equal to the return value of the GetInitializer method. In our example, this value is the minimum subscription level necessary to access the XML Web service method being invoked. Typically, the code in the Initialize method saves this value in a private variable to make it accessible from other methods in the class:

```
' The Initialize method is called with the RequiredSubscriptionLevel
' integer in its argument.

Dim RequiredSubscriptionLevel As Integer

Public Overrides Sub Initialize(ByVal initializer As Object)
    ' Save the required subscription level for later.
    RequiredSubscriptionLevel = CInt(initializer)
End Sub
```

The third overridden method is ChainStream, which receives the stream used to move the XML text from the client to the XML Web service and back. It can be the original stream used by ASP.NET to read and output data, or it can be a stream created by a SOAP extension of lower priority. The ChainStream method is called before each processing stage the SOAP message goes through. Because the purpose of most SOAP extensions is to read and possibly modify the XML being transmitted from and to the client, you must create a new stream, save both the original and the new stream in a pair of local variables, and return the stream just created:

```
Dim oldStream As Stream
Dim newStream As Stream
```

```
' The ChainStream is called when the SoapExtension class is instantiated.

Public Overrides Function ChainStream(ByVal stream As Stream) As Stream
    ' Save the old stream.
    oldStream = stream
    ' Create a new stream and return it.
    newStream = New MemoryStream()
    Return newStream
End Function
```

The last overridden method that ASP.NET calls into your SOAP extension is also the most important of the group because it's where the real action is. The ProcessMessage method is called once for each possible state the message can be in, and you can tell what these states are by means of the Stage property of the SoapMessage object passed as an argument:

```
' This method is called multiple times for each message.
Public Overrides Sub ProcessMessage(ByVal message As SoapMessage)
    Select Case message.Stage
        Case SoapMessageStage.BeforeDeserialize
            ' Copy from old stream to new stream.
            CopyStream(oldStream, newStream)
            newStream.Position = 0

        Case SoapMessageStage.AfterDeserialize
            ' The message is deserialized, so we can read message headers.
            If EvalSubscriptionLevel(message) < RequiredSubscriptionLevel Then
                ' Throw an exception if subscription level isn't adequate.
                Throw New SoapException("Insufficient subscription level", _
                    SoapException.ClientFaultCode)
            End If
        Case SoapMessageStage.BeforeSerialize
        Case SoapMessageStage.AfterSerialize
            ' Copy from new to old stream.
            newStream.Position = 0
            CopyStream(newStream, oldStream)
    End Select
End Sub

' This is a helper routine that moves data from one stream to another.

Private Sub CopyStream(ByVal source As Stream, ByVal dest As Stream)
    Dim sr As New StreamReader(source)
    Dim sw As New StreamWriter(dest)
    sw.WriteLine(sr.ReadToEnd)
    sw.Flush()
End Sub
```

The EvalSubscriptionLevel is a private function that analyzes all the headers of the SoapMessage object and looks for an AccountInfoHeader object. If such a header is found, the function can determine whether the client's username and password are valid and returns the client's subscription level:

```
Private Function EvalSubscriptionLevel(ByVal message As SoapMessage) _
    As Integer
    ' Check whether there is a header of type AccountInfoHeader.
    Dim header As SoapHeader
    For Each header In message.Headers
        If TypeOf header Is AccountInfoHeader Then
            ' Cast to the propert type.
            Dim accountInfo As AccountInfoHeader = _
                DirectCast(header, AccountInfoHeader)
            ' Check user credentials and return subscription level.
            Return GetUserSubscriptionLevel(accountInfo.UserName, _
                accountInfo.Password)
        End If
    Next

    ' If we get here, credentials were missing or invalid.
    Return -1
End Function
```

(I omitted the source code of the GetUserSubscriptionLevel class because it is the same as the one illustrated in the "Custom Authentication" section earlier in this chapter.) Here's the client-side code that invokes a method protected with a SoapCustomAuthentication attribute:

```
' Prepare account information in the header.
Dim accountInfo As New localhost.AccountInfoHeader()
accountInfo.UserName = "JoeDoe"
accountInfo.Password = "jdpwd"
' Associate account info with the proxy object.
Dim service As New localhost.SampleService()
service.AccountInfoHeaderValue = accountInfo

Try
    ' This call succeeds only if user JoeDoe has a subscription
    ' level of 2 or higher.
    Dim res As Boolean = service.YetAnotherProtectedMethod()
Catch ex As Exception
    MsgBox(ex.Message, MsgBoxStyle.Critical)
End Try
```

The .NET SDK documentation contains the description and the code of a SOAP extension class that saves all the incoming and outgoing XML text into a file. Besides being a good example of what you can do with a SOAP extension, it makes for a great diagnostic tool that can be a real lifesaver when things don't work as expected. In spite of their different purposes, you'll see that the structure of the SDK sample is basically the same as the SOAP extension I've described in these pages.

Client-Side SOAP Extensions

So far, I've described what are called server-side SOAP extensions, which are by far the most common types of SOAP extensions. However, you can also implement client-side SOAP extensions. For example, a client-side SOAP extension might be necessary to decrypt the XML sent by an XML Web service and encrypted by a server-side SOAP extension. You can activate a client-side SOAP extension via custom attributes, exactly as you do for server-side extensions, except the custom attribute is applied to the methods in the proxy class.

A client-side SOAP extension goes through the same four stages that server-side extensions do, but their order is different: BeforeSerialize and AfterSerialize when the SOAP message is being sent to the XML Web service; BeforeDeserialize and AfterDeserialize when the result XML is being received from the XML Web service. (See Figure 26-13.)

Oh well, I know that at this point I should show you an example of a client-side SOAP extension, but I am afraid I have to stop here—or it will be just too difficult to bind this huge volume together.

Front
Top
Left
Back

Index

Send feedback about this index to *mspindex@microsoft.com.*

Symbols and Numbers

A

B

C

D

E

F

G

I

M

N

P

T

U

V

W

X

Z

Francesco Balena

Francesco Balena began his software studies in the late 1970s and had to fight for a while against huge IBM mainframes and tons of punched cards while he waited for the PC to be invented. From those good old days—when the word *megabyte* made little sense and *gigabyte* was pure blasphemy—he has retained the taste for writing the most efficient and resource-aware code possible.

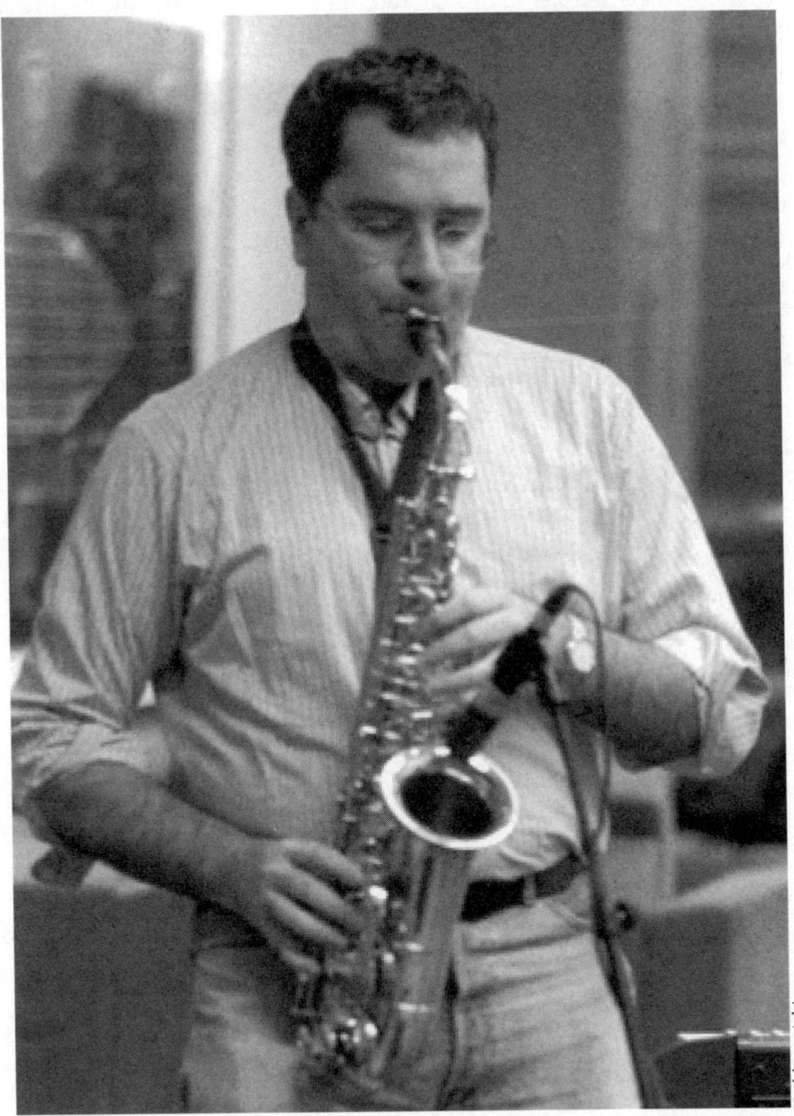

Kathleen Atkins

In more recent years, Francesco became a contributing editor and member of the Technical Advisory board of *Visual Studio Magazine* (formerly *Visual Basic Programmer's Journal*), for which he writes feature articles and columns. He's the author of *Programming Microsoft Visual Basic 6* (Microsoft Press, 2000) and coauthor of *Applied Microsoft .NET Framework Programming in Microsoft Visual Basic .NET* (with Jeffrey Richter, Microsoft Press, slated for mid-2002). Francesco teaches the Visual Basic .NET courses for Wintellect (*www.wintellect.com*) in the United States and Europe and is a regular speaker at developer conferences such as VBITS, SQL2TheMax, WinDev, and WinSummit. He is the founder of the popular VB-2-The-Max site (*www.vb2themax.com*), where you can find hundreds of articles, tips, routines, and updates of this book as they occur.

Francesco is the lead author of VBMaximizer, an add-in for Visual Basic 6 that has won an award from readers of *Visual Studio Magazine;* he is currently working on VSMaximizer for Visual Studio .NET. He has been appointed Microsoft's MSDN Regional Director for Italy and is cofounder of Code Architects, an Italian company that specializes exclusively in .NET programming, training, and consulting.

Francesco lives in Bari, Italy, with his wife Adriana and his son Andrea, but spends a lot of his time abroad. In his previous life, he had a lot of good times playing his alto sax with big bands and jazz combos until he found that computer programming can be just as fun and doesn't require that he be awake and blowing until 4 A.M. each and every night. Only later he realized that—to write code and meet deadlines—he couldn't go to sleep before 4 A.M. anyway, but it was too late to change his mind. He has recently joined the Band On The Runtime and plays with musicians of the caliber of David Chappell, Don Box, and Ted Pattison.

Combination Square

A **combination square** can check both inside and outside angles; it usually includes a small bubble level for quickly checking level and plumb positions as well. Its cast-steel head slides along the flat blade and can be clamped on the blade with the nut. One face of the head is at a 90° right angle to the nut, and the other is at a 45° angle—ideal for marking that angle for mitering. You can use the combination square as a square, a level, a protractor, a depth gauge, or a marking gauge, or for other purposes. You can even remove the head and use the blade as an accurate straightedge.

At Microsoft Press, we use tools to illustrate our books for software developers and IT professionals. Tools are an elegant symbol of human inventiveness and a powerful metaphor for how people can extend their capabilities, precision, and reach. From basic calipers and pliers to digital micrometers and lasers, our stylized illustrations of tools give each book a visual identity and each book series a personality. With tools and knowledge, there are no limits to creativity and innovation. Our tag line says it all: *The tools you need to put technology to work.*

The manuscript for this book was prepared and galleyed using Microsoft Word. Pages were composed by Microsoft Press using Adobe FrameMaker+SGML for Windows, with text in Garamond and display type in Helvetica Condensed. Composed pages were delivered to the printer as electronic prepress files.

Cover Designer:	Methodologie, Inc.
Interior Graphic Designer:	James D. Kramer
Principal Desktop Publisher:	Gina Cassill
Electronic Artist:	Michael Kloepfer
Principal Copy Editor:	Shawn Peck
Indexer:	Lynn Armstrong

Keep your copy of *Programming Microsoft Visual Basic .NET* up-to-date

Visit *www.vb2themax.com* to read any updates, errata, or additions to this book, including brand-new chapters. Or subscribe to our newsletter to receive a new Visual Basic .NET tip each week right in your mailbox.

Learn More About the Microsoft .NET Framework

Browse our huge collection of tips, ready-to-use code routines, utilities, original articles, and unabridged chapters from dozens of Visual Basic and .NET books. We also host a searchable list of the best articles that have appeared in all major developer magazines since 1996 and an index of the most useful Microsoft Knowledge Base articles.

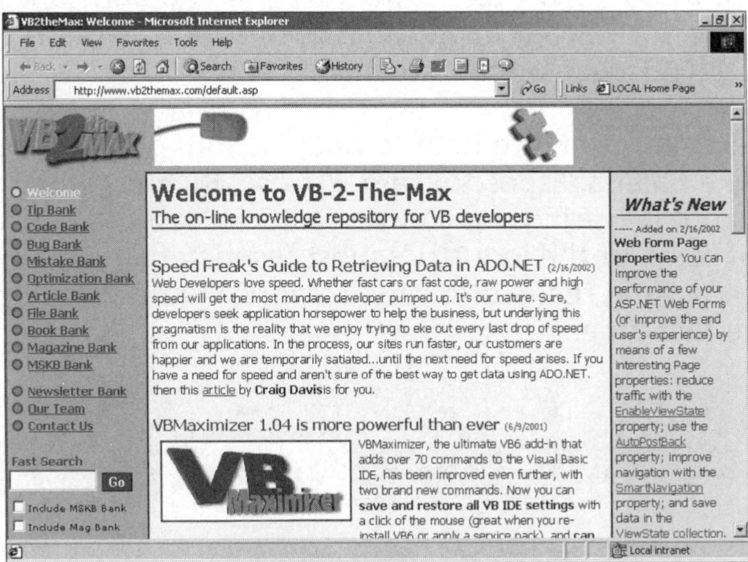

Wintellect
Raise Your Windows IQ®

Proof of Purchase

Use this page as proof of purchase if participating in a promotion or rebate offer on this title. Proof of purchase must be used in conjunction with other proof(s) of payment such as your dated sales receipt—see offer details.

Programming Microsoft® Visual Basic® .NET (Core Reference)
0-7356-1375-3

CUSTOMER NAME

Microsoft Press, PO Box 97017, Redmond, WA 98073-9830

MICROSOFT LICENSE AGREEMENT

Book Companion CD

IMPORTANT—READ CAREFULLY: This Microsoft End-User License Agreement ("EULA") is a legal agreement between you (either an individual or an entity) and Microsoft Corporation for the Microsoft product identified above, which includes computer software and may include associated media, printed materials, and "online" or electronic documentation ("SOFTWARE PRODUCT"). Any component included within the SOFTWARE PRODUCT that is accompanied by a separate End-User License Agreement shall be governed by such agreement and not the terms set forth below. By installing, copying, or otherwise using the SOFTWARE PRODUCT, you agree to be bound by the terms of this EULA. If you do not agree to the terms of this EULA, you are not authorized to install, copy, or otherwise use the SOFTWARE PRODUCT; you may, however, return the SOFTWARE PRODUCT, along with all printed materials and other items that form a part of the Microsoft product that includes the SOFTWARE PRODUCT, to the place you obtained them for a full refund.

SOFTWARE PRODUCT LICENSE

The SOFTWARE PRODUCT is protected by United States copyright laws and international copyright treaties, as well as other intellectual property laws and treaties. The SOFTWARE PRODUCT is licensed, not sold.

1. **GRANT OF LICENSE.** This EULA grants you the following rights:
   a. **Software Product.** You may install and use one copy of the SOFTWARE PRODUCT on a single computer. The primary user of the computer on which the SOFTWARE PRODUCT is installed may make a second copy for his or her exclusive use on a portable computer.
   b. **Storage/Network Use.** You may also store or install a copy of the SOFTWARE PRODUCT on a storage device, such as a network server, used only to install or run the SOFTWARE PRODUCT on your other computers over an internal network; however, you must acquire and dedicate a license for each separate computer on which the SOFTWARE PRODUCT is installed or run from the storage device. A license for the SOFTWARE PRODUCT may not be shared or used concurrently on different computers.
   c. **License Pak.** If you have acquired this EULA in a Microsoft License Pak, you may make the number of additional copies of the computer software portion of the SOFTWARE PRODUCT authorized on the printed copy of this EULA, and you may use each copy in the manner specified above. You are also entitled to make a corresponding number of secondary copies for portable computer use as specified above.
   d. **Sample Code.** Solely with respect to portions, if any, of the SOFTWARE PRODUCT that are identified within the SOFTWARE PRODUCT as sample code (the "SAMPLE CODE"):
      i. **Use and Modification.** Microsoft grants you the right to use and modify the source code version of the SAMPLE CODE, *provided* you comply with subsection (d)(iii) below. You may not distribute the SAMPLE CODE, or any modified version of the SAMPLE CODE, in source code form.
      ii. **Redistributable Files.** Provided you comply with subsection (d)(iii) below, Microsoft grants you a nonexclusive, royalty-free right to reproduce and distribute the object code version of the SAMPLE CODE and of any modified SAMPLE CODE, other than SAMPLE CODE, or any modified version thereof, designated as not redistributable in the Readme file that forms a part of the SOFTWARE PRODUCT (the "Non-Redistributable Sample Code"). All SAMPLE CODE other than the Non-Redistributable Sample Code is collectively referred to as the "REDISTRIBUTABLES."
      iii. **Redistribution Requirements.** If you redistribute the REDISTRIBUTABLES, you agree to: (i) distribute the REDISTRIBUTABLES in object code form only in conjunction with and as a part of your software application product; (ii) not use Microsoft's name, logo, or trademarks to market your software application product; (iii) include a valid copyright notice on your software application product; (iv) indemnify, hold harmless, and defend Microsoft from and against any claims or lawsuits, including attorney's fees, that arise or result from the use or distribution of your software application product; and (v) not permit further distribution of the REDISTRIBUTABLES by your end user. Contact Microsoft for the applicable royalties due and other licensing terms for all other uses and/or distribution of the REDISTRIBUTABLES.

2. **DESCRIPTION OF OTHER RIGHTS AND LIMITATIONS.**
   - **Limitations on Reverse Engineering, Decompilation, and Disassembly.** You may not reverse engineer, decompile, or disassemble the SOFTWARE PRODUCT, except and only to the extent that such activity is expressly permitted by applicable law notwithstanding this limitation.
   - **Separation of Components.** The SOFTWARE PRODUCT is licensed as a single product. Its component parts may not be separated for use on more than one computer.
   - **Rental.** You may not rent, lease, or lend the SOFTWARE PRODUCT.
   - **Support Services.** Microsoft may, but is not obligated to, provide you with support services related to the SOFTWARE PRODUCT ("Support Services"). Use of Support Services is governed by the Microsoft policies and programs described in the

user manual, in "online" documentation, and/or in other Microsoft-provided materials. Any supplemental software code provided to you as part of the Support Services shall be considered part of the SOFTWARE PRODUCT and subject to the terms and conditions of this EULA. With respect to technical information you provide to Microsoft as part of the Support Services, Microsoft may use such information for its business purposes, including for product support and development. Microsoft will not utilize such technical information in a form that personally identifies you.

- **Software Transfer.** You may permanently transfer all of your rights under this EULA, provided you retain no copies, you transfer all of the SOFTWARE PRODUCT (including all component parts, the media and printed materials, any upgrades, this EULA, and, if applicable, the Certificate of Authenticity), **and** the recipient agrees to the terms of this EULA.
- **Termination.** Without prejudice to any other rights, Microsoft may terminate this EULA if you fail to comply with the terms and conditions of this EULA. In such event, you must destroy all copies of the SOFTWARE PRODUCT and all of its component parts.

3. **COPYRIGHT.** All title and copyrights in and to the SOFTWARE PRODUCT (including but not limited to any images, photographs, animations, video, audio, music, text, SAMPLE CODE, REDISTRIBUTABLES, and "applets" incorporated into the SOFTWARE PRODUCT) and any copies of the SOFTWARE PRODUCT are owned by Microsoft or its suppliers. The SOFTWARE PRODUCT is protected by copyright laws and international treaty provisions. Therefore, you must treat the SOFTWARE PRODUCT like any other copyrighted material **except** that you may install the SOFTWARE PRODUCT on a single computer provided you keep the original solely for backup or archival purposes. You may not copy the printed materials accompanying the SOFTWARE PRODUCT.

4. **U.S. GOVERNMENT RESTRICTED RIGHTS.** The SOFTWARE PRODUCT and documentation are provided with RESTRICTED RIGHTS. Use, duplication, or disclosure by the Government is subject to restrictions as set forth in subparagraph (c)(1)(ii) of the Rights in Technical Data and Computer Software clause at DFARS 252.227-7013 or subparagraphs (c)(1) and (2) of the Commercial Computer Software—Restricted Rights at 48 CFR 52.227-19, as applicable. Manufacturer is Microsoft Corporation/One Microsoft Way/Redmond, WA 98052-6399.

5. **EXPORT RESTRICTIONS.** You agree that you will not export or re-export the SOFTWARE PRODUCT, any part thereof, or any process or service that is the direct product of the SOFTWARE PRODUCT (the foregoing collectively referred to as the "Restricted Components"), to any country, person, entity, or end user subject to U.S. export restrictions. You specifically agree not to export or re-export any of the Restricted Components (i) to any country to which the U.S. has embargoed or restricted the export of goods or services, which currently include, but are not necessarily limited to, Cuba, Iran, Iraq, Libya, North Korea, Sudan, and Syria, or to any national of any such country, wherever located, who intends to transmit or transport the Restricted Components back to such country; (ii) to any end user who you know or have reason to know will utilize the Restricted Components in the design, development, or production of nuclear, chemical, or biological weapons; or (iii) to any end user who has been prohibited from participating in U.S. export transactions by any federal agency of the U.S. government. You warrant and represent that neither the BXA nor any other U.S. federal agency has suspended, revoked, or denied your export privileges.

DISCLAIMER OF WARRANTY

NO WARRANTIES OR CONDITIONS. MICROSOFT EXPRESSLY DISCLAIMS ANY WARRANTY OR CONDITION FOR THE SOFTWARE PRODUCT. THE SOFTWARE PRODUCT AND ANY RELATED DOCUMENTATION ARE PROVIDED "AS IS" WITHOUT WARRANTY OR CONDITION OF ANY KIND, EITHER EXPRESS OR IMPLIED, INCLUDING, WITHOUT LIMITATION, THE IMPLIED WARRANTIES OF MERCHANTABILITY, FITNESS FOR A PARTICULAR PURPOSE, OR NONINFRINGEMENT. THE ENTIRE RISK ARISING OUT OF USE OR PERFORMANCE OF THE SOFTWARE PRODUCT REMAINS WITH YOU.

LIMITATION OF LIABILITY. TO THE MAXIMUM EXTENT PERMITTED BY APPLICABLE LAW, IN NO EVENT SHALL MICROSOFT OR ITS SUPPLIERS BE LIABLE FOR ANY SPECIAL, INCIDENTAL, INDIRECT, OR CONSEQUENTIAL DAMAGES WHATSOEVER (INCLUDING, WITHOUT LIMITATION, DAMAGES FOR LOSS OF BUSINESS PROFITS, BUSINESS INTERRUPTION, LOSS OF BUSINESS INFORMATION, OR ANY OTHER PECUNIARY LOSS) ARISING OUT OF THE USE OF OR INABILITY TO USE THE SOFTWARE PRODUCT OR THE PROVISION OF OR FAILURE TO PROVIDE SUPPORT SERVICES, EVEN IF MICROSOFT HAS BEEN ADVISED OF THE POSSIBILITY OF SUCH DAMAGES. IN ANY CASE, MICROSOFT'S ENTIRE LIABILITY UNDER ANY PROVISION OF THIS EULA SHALL BE LIMITED TO THE GREATER OF THE AMOUNT ACTUALLY PAID BY YOU FOR THE SOFTWARE PRODUCT OR US$5.00; PROVIDED, HOWEVER, IF YOU HAVE ENTERED INTO A MICROSOFT SUPPORT SERVICES AGREEMENT, MICROSOFT'S ENTIRE LIABILITY REGARDING SUPPORT SERVICES SHALL BE GOVERNED BY THE TERMS OF THAT AGREEMENT. BECAUSE SOME STATES AND JURISDICTIONS DO NOT ALLOW THE EXCLUSION OR LIMITATION OF LIABILITY, THE ABOVE LIMITATION MAY NOT APPLY TO YOU.

MISCELLANEOUS

This EULA is governed by the laws of the State of Washington USA, except and only to the extent that applicable law mandates governing law of a different jurisdiction.

Should you have any questions concerning this EULA, or if you desire to contact Microsoft for any reason, please contact the Microsoft subsidiary serving your country, or write: Microsoft Sales Information Center/One Microsoft Way/Redmond, WA 98052-6399.